Use and Abuse
of
America's Natural Resources

Use and Abuse
of
America's Natural Resources

Advisory Editor

STUART BRUCHEY
Allan Nevins Professor of American
Economic History, Columbia University

Associate Editor

ELEANOR BRUCHEY

A TREATISE

ON THE

AMERICAN LAW RELATING TO MINES AND MINERAL LANDS

WITHIN THE

PUBLIC LAND STATES AND TERRITORIES

AND

GOVERNING THE ACQUISITION AND ENJOYMENT OF MINING RIGHTS IN LANDS OF THE PUBLIC DOMAIN

BY

CURTIS H. LINDLEY

VOLUME I

ARNO PRESS

A NEW YORK TIMES COMPANY

New York • 1972

Reprint Edition 1972 by Arno Press Inc.

Use and Abuse of America's Natural Resources
ISBN for complete set: 0-405-04500-X
See last pages of this volume for titles.

Manufactured in the United States of America

———————————

Library of Congress Cataloging in Publication Data

Lindley, Curtis Holbrook, 1850-1920.
    A treatise on the American law relating to mines
and mineral lands within the public land states and
territories and governing the acquisition and enjoyment
of mining rights in lands of the public domain.

    (Use and abuse of America's natural resources)
    Reprint of the 2d ed., 1903.
    1. Mining law--United States. 2. United
States--Public lands. I. Title. II. Series.
KF1819.L5 1972   343'.73'02   72-2853
ISBN 0-405-04517-4

A TREATISE

ON THE

AMERICAN LAW RELATING TO MINES AND MINERAL LANDS

WITHIN THE

PUBLIC LAND STATES AND TERRITORIES

AND

GOVERNING THE ACQUISITION AND ENJOYMENT OF MINING RIGHTS IN LANDS OF THE PUBLIC DOMAIN

BY

CURTIS H. LINDLEY

OF THE SAN FRANCISCO BAR

SECOND EDITION

IN TWO VOLUMES

VOLUME I

———

"I hold every man a debtor to his profession; from the which, as men of course do seek to receive countenance and profit, so ought they of duty to endeavor themselves, by way of amends, to be a help and ornament thereto."
Bacon's Tracts.

———

"Et opus desperatum, quasi per medium profundum euntes, cœlesti favore jam adimplevimus."
—From Dedication of Justinian's Institutes.

———

SAN FRANCISCO
BANCROFT-WHITNEY COMPANY
LAW PUBLISHERS AND LAW BOOKSELLERS
1903

PREFACE TO SECOND EDITION.

A SECOND EDITION of this treatise seems opportune. The original edition was not stereotyped and has been out of print for three years. Since the work first appeared, some questions of large importance have been passed upon by the courts, requiring in some instances modification, in others elaboration of the text. The publishers report a constant demand for the work. These considerations have induced the author to present this edition, in the hope that it will measurably, at least, meet the desires of the profession at whose hands the former one was accorded so gracious a reception.

The work has been entirely revised, and in some of its parts rewritten. The original section numbers have not been changed. The new adjudications have been assimilated to the old sections, and where new subjects have been incorporated, supplemental ones have been appropriately grafted into the treatise without disturbing the general plan of arrangement or the logical sequence of the sections. Wherever the subject under consideration would seem to justify or require it, additional diagrams and illustrations have been utilized. In the citation of cases in the notes to the text the official report is given, followed by a reference to the American Reports, American Decisions, or American State Reports, if the case cited appears in any of this series. Also, the report of the case in the National Reporter System. In the table of cases will be found a reference to all standard reports where the case reappears.

The author desires to publicly express his obligations to those whose assistance have enabled him to present the work in its present form,—to Mr. Ross E. Browne, M. E., for his collaboration and illustrations on the subjects of definitions of mining terms employed in the acts of Congress, and identity and continuity of veins involved in the exercise of the extralateral right; to Mr. Myron A. Folsom, of the Spokane bar; Messrs. Henry M. Hoyt, B. L. Quayle, and C. S. Chandler, of the San Francisco bar, all of whom are entitled to the author's grateful acknowledgment for their patient and intelligent assistance in many of the laborious details involved in the preparation and publication of the treatise. The author is also indebted to many members of the bar in the mining states and territories for valuable suggestions and criticisms, to each of whom he returns his sincere thanks. In submitting this edition to the profession the author also desires to express his sense of obligation to the publishers for their uniform kindness and consideration, and for their painstaking effort to present the treatise in a form commensurate with the importance and dignity of the subject.

CURTIS H. LINDLEY.

San Francisco, May, 1903.

PREFACE TO FIRST EDITION.

THE United States cannot be said to possess a National Mining Code, in the sense that the term is used and understood among the older nations of the earth.

The system of rules which sanctions and regulates the acquisition and enjoyment of mining rights, and defines the conditions under which title may be obtained to mineral lands within the public domain of the United States is composed of several elements, most of which find expression in positive legislative enactment. Others, while depending for their existence and application upon the sanction of the General Government, either express or implied, are in a measure controlled by local environment, and are evidenced by the expressed will of local assemblages embodied in written regulations, or rest in unwritten customs peculiar to the vicinage.

American mining law may therefore be said to be found expressed—

(1) *In the legislation of Congress;*

(2) *In the legislation of the various states and territories supplementing Congressional action, and in harmony therewith;*

(3) *In local rules and customs or regulations established in different localities not repugnant to Federal legislation, or that of the state or territory wherein they are operative.*

This system, as thus constituted, is deemed national only in a restricted sense. As a rule of property, it has no application or force in many of the states of the Union.

Generally speaking, its operation is limited geographically to the area acquired by the General Government by cession from the original states, or by treaty with or purchase from foreign powers subsequent to the organization of the General Government, or perhaps, more logically stated, its operation is co-extensive with the area of the public domain, the primary ownership and right of disposal of which resides in the General Government.

It does not seek to regulate or control mines or mining, within lands held in private ownership, except such only as are acquired directly from the Government under the mining laws, and then only forming a muniment of the locator's or purchaser's title, and measuring his rights.

It does not require the payment of either tribute or royalty as a condition upon which the public mineral lands may be explored or worked.

It treats the Government simply as a private proprietor holding the paramount title to its public domain, with right of disposal, upon such terms and conditions, and subject to such limitations, as the law-making power may prescribe.

The National Government acquired no rights of property within the present boundaries of the thirteen original states; nor in the states of Vermont, Kentucky, Maine, or West Virginia, which were severally carved out of territory originally forming a part of some one of the original states; nor in Texas, as by the terms of its admission into the Union the state retained all the vacant and unappropriated public lands lying within its limits, for the purpose of liquidating its debt contracted while it was an independent republic.

The entire area of Tennessee was originally public domain; but the United States donated the same to the state, after deducting the lands necessary to fill the obligations in the deed of cession of North Carolina.

In Arkansas, Illinois, Missouri, Iowa, Michigan, Minnesota, and Wisconsin, lands of the Government containing the baser metals (lead and copper) were ordered sold under special laws, prior to the discovery of gold in California.

By acts of Congress, passed at different times, Alabama, Michigan, Wisconsin, Minnesota, Missouri, and Kansas, were excepted from the operation of the general mining laws.

The system is inoperative in Oklahoma, as by Congressional law all lands within that territory are declared to be agricultural.

With the exception, perhaps, of lands containing deposits of coal, and some of the baser metallic substances, the system is practically confined in its operation to those states and territories lying wholly or in part west of the one hundredth meridian, embracing the states of California, Colorado, Oregon, Washington, Nevada, Idaho, Montana, North Dakota, South Dakota, Wyoming, and Utah, the territories of Arizona and New Mexico, and the district of Alaska. These comprise the precious-metal-bearing states and territories of the "Public Domain."

As thus defined and limited, "American Mining Law" is the subject of this treatise.

While in the treatment of the subject, and in the discussion of the origin and growth of the system, as we understand it, we shall at times encounter the earmarks of an older civilization and find lodged in what we might term a primitive custom, the experience of ages; yet wherever its rules depart from the doctrine of the common law, the system, as such, is of recent birth and modern development. It is an evolution from primitive and peculiar conditions, a crystallization of usages which do not appeal to antiquity for either their force or wisdom.

It is the principal design of this work to treat of this system as it is at present constituted. But as it is in itself an evolution out of antecedent and somewhat complex conditions, some space will be devoted to a consideration of an historical nature concerning the policy of the Government in dealing with its mineral lands prior to the enactment of general laws affecting them, and to trace the growth of the system through its various stages of development.

As an appropriate introduction to a treatise of this nature, the author has inserted a chapter epitomizing the different systems of mining jurisprudence in force at different periods in the countries from which the United States acquired its public domain. We may reasonably expect to find in the growth and development of our own system the influence of those laws. It has also been deemed advisable to insert a brief review of the systems adopted in the states of the Union wherein the Federal Government acquired no property, and where the regulation of the mining industry falls exclusively within the jurisdiction of state legislation.

This comparative review of the mining laws, foreign and state, will at least be of historical interest, if it should serve no other or higher purpose.

As state and territorial legislation supplementing the acts of Congress is permitted, if not in fact contemplated, by the federal laws, careful consideration will be given to these local statutes and the decisions of courts in construing them. The value of a decision as a precedent often depends on local conditions. The legitimate scope of this permissive local legislation is a fruitful subject of controversy.

The existing legislation of each state and territory supplementing the federal laws, together with references to legislation on cognate subjects, will be found in the appendix, with citations under each section indicating where the subject-matter has been discussed and generally treated in the text.

The appendix also contains the various acts of Congress upon the subject of mineral lands, and the regulations of the land department, with back references to the text; also such forms as in the author's judgment might be serviceable to the profession.

In citing authorities the author has adopted the rule of citing the case from the original report only; but in the table of cases will be found the date of the decision, and a citation to every standard report, including the "National Reporter" system, wherein the case appears.

Realizing the importance of a comprehensive and exhaustive index, the author has himself undertaken the work of its preparation.

While the treatise is in the main devoted to a consideration of the federal mining system, to meet the general expectation of the profession we deem it advisable to devote some space to cognate subjects, including rights and liabilities arising out of the conduct of mining ventures, mining partnerships, cotenancy, and obligations flowing from contractual relations.

The necessity for a comprehensive treatise on American mining law is conceded. The literature on this branch of jurisprudence is limited. Most of the works which have been presented to the profession, while possessing great merit, have not attempted a systematic or philosophical treatment of the subject.

The preparation of a work which will fulfill the requirements of the profession and prove measurably satisfactory, is a matter of great moment, involving much time and patient labor.

While not anticipating that the result of his efforts will fully meet the wants of the profession, the author expresses a hope that it will be found of value to those who are interested in the study of the many intricate questions arising out of the mining laws.

When in the preparation of the text he has been instructed or guided by the original work of others, it has been the aim of the author to give due credit in the appropriate place. Yet he has derived so much benefit and assistance in so many ways from various authors and writers upon mining subjects, that he deems it a duty as well as a pleasure to here specifically express his acknowledgments.

Professor Rossiter W. Raymond, lawyer, scholar, and scientist of national renown, has contributed in a marked degree to the literature on mining subjects. His extended experience in the field of practical mining, his connection with much of the important mining litigation in the west, his thorough knowledge of the ever-varying geological conditions, to which are to be applied the unyielding terms of Congressional laws, have made him pre-eminent in the field of mining literature. His reports as Commissioner of Mining Statistics abound with fruitful suggestions, and contributed in no small degree to the adoption of the act of 1872. His monograph, "Relations of " Governments to Mining" (in "Mineral Resources West of " the Rocky Mountains," 1869); his article on "Mines," (appearing in Lalor's "Cyclopedia of Political Science"); his numerous papers read before the American Institute of Mining Engineers, notably, "Law of the Apex," "Lode Loca- " tions," "End Lines and Side Lines," "The Eureka-Rich- " mond Case"; and his occasional contributions to the " Engineering and Mining Journal," have afforded the author great and valuable aid.

Professor Raymond's immediate predecessor in the work of collecting Mining Statistics, Mr. J. Ross Browne, rendered valuable service to the mining industry, and his reports to the government contain much that is valuable and important, giving as they do the early history of mining in the west, and the customs, rules and regulations of miners, which formed the basis of our first mining statutes.

The author has also derived great assistance from previous works on the subject, notably "Mining Claims and Water " Rights," by Hon. Gregory Yale, the pioneer work on the subject of American mining law; "Mining Rights in the " Western States and Territories," by Hon. R. S. Morrison, of the Colorado Bar; Weeks on "Mineral Lands," Copp's " U. S. Mineral Lands," and Wade's "American Mining " Laws."

As the closing chapters of the work were being printed, the " Mineral Law Digest," of Messrs. Clark, Heltman, and Consaul, a conscientious and valuable contribution to mining literature, made its appearance.

The author is under special obligations to the Hon. Wm. H. DeWitt, late judge of the supreme court of Montana, Edwin Van Cise, Esq., of Deadwood, South Dakota, Hon. Jacob Fillius, and Harvey Riddell, Esq., of the Colorado bar, for many valuable and timely suggestions.

The numerous diagrams illustrating the important subjects of "Dip" "Strike," and the "Extralateral Right," are the handiwork of Mr. J. W. D. Jensen, of San Francisco, to whom all credit is due. These figures, except those used for hypothetical purposes, were all reduced by scale from officially authenticated maps and surveys.

With these grateful acknowledgments, the author submits his work to a critical but ever-indulgent profession.

CURTIS H. LINDLEY.

San Francisco, 1897.

TABLE OF CONTENTS.

TITLE I. COMPARATIVE MINING JURISPRUDENCE.

II. HISTORICAL REVIEW OF THE FEDERAL POLICY AND LEGISLATION CONCERNING MINERAL LANDS.

III. LANDS SUBJECT TO APPROPRIATION UNDER THE MINING LAWS, AND THE PERSONS WHO MAY ACQUIRE RIGHTS THEREIN.

IV. STATE LEGISLATION AND LOCAL DISTRICT REGULATIONS SUPPLEMENTING THE CONGRESSIONAL MINING LAWS.

V. OF THE ACQUISITION OF TITLE TO PUBLIC MINERAL LANDS BY LOCATION, AND PRIVILEGES INCIDENT THERETO.

VI. THE TITLE ACQUIRED AND RIGHTS CONFERRED BY LOCATION.

VII. OF THE PROCEEDINGS TO OBTAIN UNITED STATES PATENT AND THE TITLE CONVEYED BY THAT INSTRUMENT.

VIII. RIGHTS AND OBLIGATIONS ARISING OUT OF OWNERSHIP IN COMMON OF MINES AND JOINT PARTICIPATION IN MINING VENTURES.

IX. RIGHTS AND OBLIGATIONS OF PARTIES ENGAGED IN WORKING MINES.

X. MINES AND MINING CLAIMS AS SUBJECTS OF CONTRACT BETWEEN INDIVIDUALS.

XI. ACTIONS CONCERNING MINING CLAIMS OTHER THAN SUITS UPON ADVERSE CLAIMS—AUXILIARY REMEDIES.

XIA. THE MINING INDUSTRY AND LAWS OF INSULAR POSSESSIONS OF THE UNITED STATES.

APPENDIX—MISCELLANEOUS.

XII. FEDERAL STATUTES RELATING TO MINES, TOGETHER WITH LAND DEPARTMENT REGULATIONS.

XIII. STATE AND TERRITORIAL LEGISLATION ON THE SUBJECT OF MINES.

XIV. FORMS AND PRECEDENTS.

TITLE I.

COMPARATIVE MINING JURISPRUDENCE.

CHAPTER I. MINING LAWS OF FOREIGN COUNTRIES.
  II. LOCAL STATE SYSTEMS.

CHAPTER I. MINING LAWS OF FOREIGN COUNTRIES.

§ 1. Introductory.
§ 2. Property in mines under the common law.
§ 3. Royal mines.
§ 4. Local customs.
§ 5. Tin mines of Cornwall.
§ 6. Tin mines of Devonshire.
§ 7. Coal, iron, and other mines in the Forest of Dean.
§ 8. Lead mines of Derbyshire.
§ 9. Severance of title.
§ 10. Existing English laws.
§ 11. Mines under the civil law.
§ 12. Mining laws of France:—*Mines—Minières—Carrières.*
§ 13. Mining laws of Mexico:—Nature and conditions of mining con-
        cessions—Right of discoverer; *pertenencia*—Right to mine,
        how acquired—Denouncement of abandoned mines—Right to
        denounce mines in private property—Rights of one not a dis-
        coverer—Placers—Foreign and religious orders—Extent of
        pertenencia; surface limits—Marking boundaries; rights in
        depth—Rights to all veins found within boundaries of *perte-
        nencias*—Forfeiture for failure to work—Royalties.

CHAPTER II. LOCAL STATE SYSTEMS.

§ 18. Classification of states.
§ 19. First group.
§ 20. Second group.
§ 21. Third group.
§ 22. Limit of state control after patent.

TITLE II.

HISTORICAL REVIEW OF THE FEDERAL POLICY AND LEG-ISLATION CONCERNING MINERAL LANDS.

CHAPTER I. INTRODUCTORY—PERIODS OF NATIONAL HISTORY.
    II. FIRST PERIOD: FROM THE FOUNDATION OF THE GOVERN-
          MENT TO THE DISCOVERY OF GOLD IN CALIFORNIA.
   III. SECOND PERIOD: FROM THE DISCOVERY OF GOLD IN CALI-
          FORNIA UNTIL THE PASSAGE OF THE LODE LAW OF 1866.

IV. THIRD PERIOD: FROM THE PASSAGE OF THE LODE LAW OF
1866 TO THE ENACTMENT OF THE GENERAL LAW OF
MAY 10, 1872.

V. FOURTH PERIOD: FROM THE ENACTMENT OF THE LAW OF
MAY 10, 1872, TO THE PRESENT TIME.

VI. THE FEDERAL SYSTEM.

CHAPTER I. INTRODUCTORY.

§ 25. Introductory—Periods of National History.

CHAPTER II. FIRST PERIOD: FROM THE FOUNDATION OF
THE GOVERNMENT TO THE DISCOVERY OF GOLD IN
CALIFORNIA.

§ 28. Original nucleus of national domain.
§ 29. Mineral resources of the territory ceded by the states.
§ 30. First congressional action on the subject of mineral lands.
§ 31. Reservation in crown grants to the colonies.
§ 32. No development of copper mines until 1845.
§ 33. The Louisiana purchase and legislation concerning lead mines.
§ 34. Message of President Polk.
§ 35. Sales of land containing lead and copper under special laws.
§ 36. Reservation in pre-emption laws.

CHAPTER III. SECOND PERIOD: FROM THE DISCOVERY
OF GOLD IN CALIFORNIA UNTIL THE PASSAGE OF THE
LODE LAW OF 1866.

§ 40. Discovery of gold in California and the Mexican cession.
§ 41. Origin of local customs.
§ 42. Scope of local regulations.
§ 43. Dips, spurs, and angles of lode claims.
§ 44. Legislative and judicial recognition by the state.
§ 45. Federal recognition.
§ 46. Local rules as forming part of present system of mining law.
§ 47. Federal legislation during the second period.
§ 48. Executive recommendations to congress.
§ 49. Coal land laws—Mining claims in Nevada—Sutro tunnel act.

CHAPTER IV. THIRD PERIOD: FROM THE PASSAGE OF
THE LODE LAW OF 1866 TO THE ENACTMENT OF THE
GENERAL LAW OF MAY 10, 1872.

§ 53. The act of July 26, 1866.
§ 54. Essential features of the act.

§ 55. Declaration of governmental policy.
§ 56. Recognition of local customs and possessory rights acquired thereunder.
§ 57. Title to lode claims.
§ 58. Relationship of surface to the lode.
§ 59. Construction of the act by the land department.
§ 60. Construction by the courts.
§ 61. Local rules and customs after the passage of the act.
§ 62. The act of July 9, 1870.
§ 63. Local rules and customs after the passage of the act.
§ 64. Accession to the national domain during the third period.

Chapter V. Fourth Period: From the Enactment of the Law of May 10, 1872, to the Present Time.

§ 68. The act of May 10, 1872.
§ 69. Declaration of governmental policy.
§ 70. Changes made by the act—Division of the subject.
§ 71. Changes made with regard to lode claims.
§ 72. Changes made with regard to other claims.
§ 73. New provisions affecting both classes of claims.
§ 74. Tunnels and millsites.
§ 75. Legislation subsequent to the act of 1872.
§ 76. Local rules and customs since the passage of the act.
§77. Accession to the national domain during the fourth period.

Chapter VI. The Federal System.

§ 80. Conclusions deduced from preceding chapters.
§ 81. Outline of the federal system—Scope of the treatise.

TITLE III.

LANDS SUBJECT TO APPROPRIATION UNDER THE MINING LAWS, AND THE PERSONS WHO MAY ACQUIRE RIGHTS THEREIN.

Chapter I. "Mineral Lands" and Kindred Terms Defined.
    II. The Public Surveys and the Return of the Surveyor-General.
    III. Status of Land as to Title and Possession.
    IV. Of the Persons who may Acquire Rights to Public Mineral Lands.

Chapter I. "Mineral Lands" and Kindred Terms Defined.

§ 85. Necessity for definition of terms.
§ 86. Terms of reservation employed in various acts.
§ 87. "Mine" and "mineral" indefinite terms.
§ 88. English denotation—"Mine" and "mineral" in their primary sense.
§ 89. Enlarged meaning of "mine."
§ 90. "Mineral" as defined by the English and Scotch authorities.
§ 91. English rules of interpretation.
§ 92. Substances classified as mineral under the English decisions.
§ 93. American cases defining "mine" and "mineral."
§ 94. "Mineral lands" as defined by the American tribunals.
§ 95. Interpretation of terms by the land department.
§ 96. American rules of statutory interpretation.
§ 97. Substances held to be mineral by the land department.
§ 98. Rules for determining mineral character of land.

Chapter II. The Public Surveys and the Return of the Surveyor-General.

§ 102. No general classification of lands as to their character.
§ 103. Geological surveys.
§ 104. General system of land surveys.
§ 105. What constitutes the surveyor-general's return.
§ 106. *Prima facie* character of land established by the return.
§ 107. Character of land, when and how established.
§ 108. Jurisdiction of courts to determine character of land when question is pending in land department.

Chapter III. Status of Land as to Title and Possession.

Article I. Introductory.
II. Mexican Grants.
III. Grants to the States and Territories for Educational and Internal Improvement Purposes.
IV. Railroad Grants.
V. Townsites.
VI. Indian Reservations.
VII. Military Reservations.
VIII. National Park and Forest Reservations—Reservations for Reservoir Sites.

IX. HOMESTEAD AND OTHER AGRICULTURAL CLAIMS.
X. OCCUPANCY WITHOUT COLOR OF TITLE.

ARTICLE I. INTRODUCTORY.

§ 112. Only public lands subject to appropriation under the mining laws.

ARTICLE II. MEXICAN GRANTS.

§ 113. Introductory.
§ 114. Ownership of mines under Mexican law.
§ 115. Nature of title conveyed to the United States by the treaty.
§ 116. Obligation of the United States to protect rights accrued prior to the cession.
§ 117. Adjustment of claims to Mexican grants in California.
§ 118. Adjustment of claims under Mexican grants in other states and territories.
§ 119. Claims to mines asserted under the Mexican mining ordinances.
§ 120. Status of grants considered with reference to condition of title.
§ 121. Grants *sub judice.*
§ 122. Different classes of grants.
§ 123. Grants of the first and third classes.
§ 124. Grants of the second class—commonly called ''floats.''
§ 125. Grants confirmed under the California act.
§ 126. Grants confirmed by direct action of congress.
§ 127. Grants which have been finally confirmed under the act of March 3, 1891, situated in Colorado, Wyoming, Utah, Nevada, New Mexico, or Arizona.
§ 128. Conclusions.

ARTICLE III. GRANTS TO THE STATES AND TERRITORIES FOR EDUCATIONAL AND INTERNAL IMPROVEMENT PURPOSES.

§ 132. Grant of sixteenth and thirty-sixth sections.
§ 133. Indemnity grant in lieu of sixteenth and thirty-sixth sections lost to the states.
§ 134. Other grants for schools and internal improvements.
§ 135. Conflicts between mineral claimants and purchasers from the states.
§ 136. Mineral lands exempted from the operation of grants to the states.
§ 137. Restrictions upon the definition of ''mineral lands'', when considered with reference to school land grants.
§ 138. Petroleum lands.
§ 139. Lands chiefly valuable for building-stone.
§ 140. In construing the term ''mineral lands'' as applied to administration of school land grants, the time to which the inquiry is addressed is the date when the asserted right to a particular

tract accrued, and not the date upon which the law was passed authorizing the grant.

§ 141. Test of mineral character applied to school land grants.

§ 142. When grants to the sixteenth and thirty-sixth sections take effect.

§ 143. Selections by the state in lieu of sixteenth and thirty-sixth sections, and under general grants.

§ 144. Effect of surveyor-general's return as to character of land within sixteenth and thirty-sixth sections, or lands sought to be selected in lieu thereof, or under floating grants.

§ 144a. Conclusiveness of state patents as to character of land.

§ 145. Conclusions.

ARTICLE IV. RAILROAD GRANTS.

§ 149. Area of grants in aid of railroads, and congressional legislation donating lands for such purposes.

§ 150. Types of land grants in aid of the construction of railroads, selected for the purpose of discussion.

§ 151. Character of the grants.

§ 152. Reservation of mineral lands from the operation of railroad grants.

§ 153. Grants of rights of way.

§ 154. Grants of particular sections as construed by the courts.

§ 155. Construction of railroad grants by the land department.

§ 156. Distinctions between grants of sixteenth and thirty-sixth sections to states, and grants of particular sections to railroads.

§ 157. Indemnity lands.

§ 158. Restrictions upon the definition of "mineral lands," when considered with reference to railroad grants.

§ 159. Test of mineral character of land applied to railroad grants.

§ 160. Classification of railroad lands under special laws in Idaho and Montana.

§ 161. Effect of patents issued to railroad companies.

§ 162. Conclusions.

ARTICLE V. TOWNSITES.

§ 166. Laws regulating the entry of townsites.

§ 167. Rules of interpretation applied to townsite laws.

§ 168. Occupancy of public mineral lands for purposes of trade or business.

§ 169. Rights of mining locator upon unoccupied lands within unpatented townsite limits.

§ 170. Prior occupancy of public mineral lands within unpatented townsites for purposes of trade, as affecting the appropriation of such lands under the mining laws—The rule prior to the passage of the act of March 3, 1891.

Lindley on M.—ii

§ 171. Correlative rights of mining and townsite claimants recognized by the land department prior to the act of March 3, 1891.

§ 172. Section sixteen of the act of March 3, 1891, is limited in its application to incorporated towns and cities.

§ 173. The object and intent of section sixteen of the act of March 3, 1891.

§ 174. The act of March 3, 1891, not retroactive.

§ 175. Effect of patents issued for lands within townsites.

§ 175a. Difficulty in the application of principles suggested.

§ 176. What constitutes a mine or valid mining claim within the meaning of section twenty-three hundred and ninety-two of the Revised Statutes.

§ 177. In what manner may a townsite patent be assailed by the owner of a mine or mining claim.

§ 178. Ownership of minerals under streets in townsites.

ARTICLE VI. INDIAN RESERVATIONS.

§ 181. Nature of Indian title.

§ 182. Manner of creating and abolishing Indian reservations.

§ 183. Lands within Indian reservations are not open to settlement or purchase under the public land laws.

§ 184. Status of mining claims located within limits of an Indian reservation prior to the extinguishment of the Indian title.

§ 185. Effect of creating an Indian reservation embracing prior valid and subsisting mining claims.

§ 186. Conclusions.

ARTICLE VII. MILITARY RESERVATIONS.

§ 190. Manner of creating and abolishing military reservations.

§ 191. Status of mining claims located within the limits of a subsisting military reservation.

§ 192. Effect of creating a military reservation embracing prior valid and subsisting mining claims.

ARTICLE VIII. NATIONAL PARK AND FOREST RESERVA-
TIONS—RESERVATIONS FOR RESERVOIR SITES.

§ 196. Manner of creating national park reservations, and purposes for which they are created.

§ 197. Manner of creating forest reservations, and purposes for which they are created.

§ 198. Status of mining claims within forest reservations.

§ 199. Forest lien selections under the act of June 4, 1897.

§ 200. Reservoir sites.

ARTICLE IX. HOMESTEAD AND OTHER AGRICULTURAL CLAIMS.

§ 202. Introductory.
§ 203. Classification of laws providing for the disposal of the public lands.
§ 204. Manner of acquiring homestead claims.
§ 205. Nature of inceptive right acquired by homestead claimant.
§ 206. Location of mining claims within homestead entries.
§ 207. Proceedings to determine the character of the land.
§ 208. When decision of land department becomes final.
§ 209. The reservation of ''known mines'' in the pre-emption laws.
§ 210. Timber and stone lands.
§ 211. Scrip.
§ 212. Desert lands.

ARTICLE X. OCCUPANCY WITHOUT COLOR OF TITLE.

§ 216. Naked occupancy of the public mineral lands confers no title— Rights of such occupant.
§ 217. Rights upon the public domain cannot be initiated by forcible entry upon the actual possession of another.
§ 218. Appropriation of public mineral lands by peaceable entry in good faith upon the possession of a mere occupant without color of title.
§ 219. Conclusions.

CHAPTER IV. OF THE PERSONS WHO MAY ACQUIRE RIGHTS TO PUBLIC MINERAL LANDS.

ARTICLE I. CITIZENS.
    II. ALIENS.
    III. GENERAL PROPERTY RIGHTS OF ALIENS IN THE STATES.
    IV. GENERAL PROPERTY RIGHTS OF ALIENS IN THE TERRITORIES.

ARTICLE I. CITIZENS.

§ 223. Only citizens, or those who have declared their intention to become such, may locate mining claims.
§ 224. Who are citizens.
§ 225. Minors.
§ 226. Domestic corporations.
§ 227. Citizenship, how proved.

ARTICLE II. ALIENS.

§ 231. Acquisition of title to unpatented mining claims by aliens.
§ 232. The effect of naturalization of an alien upon a location made by him at a time when he occupied the status of an alien.

§ 233. What is the legal status of a title to a mining claim located and held by an alien who has not declared his intention to become a citizen?

§ 234. Conclusions.

ARTICLE III. GENERAL PROPERTY RIGHTS OF ALIENS IN THE STATES.

§ 237. After patent, property becomes subject to rules prescribed by the state.

§ 238. Constitutional and statutory regulations of the precious-metal-bearing states on the subject of alien proprietorship.

ARTICLE IV. GENERAL PROPERTY RIGHTS OF ALIENS IN THE TERRITORIES.

§ 242. Power of congress over the territories.

§ 243. The alien acts of March 3, 1887, and of March 2, 1897, and the territorial limit of their operation.

TITLE IV.

STATE LEGISLATION AND LOCAL DISTRICT REGULATIONS SUPPLEMENTING THE CONGRESSIONAL MINING LAWS.

CHAPTER I. STATE LEGISLATION SUPPLEMENTAL TO THE CONGRESSIONAL MINING LAWS.

II. LOCAL DISTRICT REGULATIONS.

CHAPTER I. STATE LEGISLATION SUPPLEMENTAL TO THE CONGRESSIONAL MINING LAWS.

§ 248. Introductory.

§ 249. Limits within which state may legislate.

§ 250. Scope of existing state and territorial legislation—Subjects concerning which states and territories may unquestionably legislate.

§ 251. Subjects upon which states have enacted laws, the validity of which is open to question.

§ 252. Drainage, easements, and rights of way for mining purposes.

§ 253. Provisions of state constitutions on the subject of eminent domain.

§ 254. Mining as a "public use."

§ 255. Rights of way for pipe-lines for the conveyance of oil and natural gas.

§ 256. Lateral and other railroads for transportation of mine products.

§ 257. Physical and industrial conditions as affecting the rule of "public "utility."

§ 258. The rule in Nevada, Arizona, Montana, and Georgia.

§ 259. Arizona.

§ 259a. Montana.

§ 260. Georgia.

§ 261. The rule in Pennsylvania, West Virginia, California, and Oregon.

§ 262. West Virginia.

§ 263. California.

§ 263a. Oregon.

§ 264. Conclusions.

Chapter II. Local District Regulations.

§ 268. Introductory.

§ 269. Manner of organizing districts.

§ 270. Permissive scope of local regulations.

§ 271. Acquiescence and observance, not mere adoption, the test.

§ 272. Regulations, how proved—Their existence a question of fact for the jury; their construction a question of law for the court.

§ 273. Regulations concerning records of mining claims.

§ 274. Penalty for noncompliance with district rules.

§ 275. Local rules and regulations before the land department.

TITLE V.

OF THE ACQUISITION OF TITLE TO PUBLIC MINERAL LANDS BY LOCATION, AND PRIVILEGES INCIDENT THERETO.

Chapter I. Introductory—Definitions.

II. Lode Claims, or Deposits "in Place."

III. Placers and Other Forms of Deposit not "in Place."

IV. Tunnel Claims.

V. Coal Lands.

VI. Salines.

VII. Millsites.

VIII. Easements.

Chapter I. Introductory—Definitions.

Article I. Introductory.

II. "Lode," "Vein," "Ledge."

III. "Rock in Place."

IV. "Top," or "Apex."

V. "Strike,"—"Dip," or "Downward Course."

ARTICLE I. INTRODUCTORY.

§ 280. Introductory.
§ 281. Division of the subject.
§ 282. Difficulties of accurate definition.

ARTICLE II. "LODE," "VEIN," "LEDGE."

§ 286. English and Scotch definitions.
§ 287. As defined by the lexicographers.
§ 288. As defined by the geologists.
§ 289. Elements to be considered in the judicial application of definitions—Rules of interpretation.
§ 290. The terms "lode," "vein," "ledge," legal equivalents.
§ 290a. Definition and illustrations formulated by Mr. Ross E. Browne.
§ 291. Classification of cases, in which the terms "lode" and "vein" are to be construed.
§ 292. Judicial definitions, and their application—The Eureka case.
§ 293. The Leadville cases.
§ 294. Other definitions given by state and federal courts.

ARTICLE III. "ROCK IN PLACE."

§ 298. Classification of lands containing valuable deposits.
§ 299. Use of term "in place" in the mining laws.
§ 300. The blanket deposits of Leadville.
§ 301. Judicial interpretation of the term "rock in place."

ARTICLE IV. "TOP," OR "APEX."

§ 305. The "top," or "apex," of a vein, as a controlling factor in lode locations.
§ 306. The term "top," or "apex," not found in the miner's vocabulary—Definitions of the lexicographers.
§ 307. Definitions given in response to circulars issued by the public land commission.
§ 308. Definition by Dr. Raymond.
§ 309. The ideal lode and its apex.
§ 310. Illustrations of a departure from the ideal lode—The case of Duggan v. Davey.
§ 311. The Leadville cases. Iron-Silver Mining Co. v. Cheesman—Stevens & Leiter v. Williams—Iron-Silver Mining Co. v. Murphy.
§ 312. Hypothetical illustrations based upon the mode of occurrence of the Leadville and similar deposits.

§ 312a. Theoretical apex where the true apex is within prior patented agricultural claims, the vein passing on its downward course into public land.

§ 313. The existence and *situs* of the "top," or "apex," a question of fact.

ARTICLE V. "STRIKE," "DIP," OR "DOWNWARD COURSE."

§ 317. Terms "strike" and "dip" not found in the Revised Statutes— Popular use of the terms.

§ 318. "Strike" and "dip" as judicially defined.

§ 319. "Downward course."

CHAPTER II. LODE CLAIMS, OR DEPOSITS "IN PLACE."

ARTICLE I. INTRODUCTORY.

II. THE LOCATION AND ITS REQUIREMENTS.

III. THE DISCOVERY.

IV. THE DISCOVERY SHAFT AND ITS EQUIVALENT.

V. THE PRELIMINARY NOTICE AND ITS POSTING.

VI. THE SURFACE COVERED BY THE LOCATION—ITS FORM AND RELATIONSHIP TO THE LOCATED LODE.

VII. THE MARKING OF THE LOCATION ON THE SURFACE.

VIII. THE LOCATION CERTIFICATE AND ITS CONTENTS.

IX. THE RECORD.

X. CHANGE OF BOUNDARIES AND AMENDED OR ADDITIONAL LOCATION CERTIFICATES.

XI. RELOCATION OF FORFEITED OR ABANDONED CLAIMS.

XII. LODES WITHIN PLACERS.

ARTICLE I. INTRODUCTORY.

§ 322. Introductory.

§ 323. The metallic or nonmetallic character of deposits occurring in veins as affecting the right of appropriation under the laws applicable to lodes.

ARTICLE II. THE LOCATION AND ITS REQUIREMENTS.

§ 327. "Location" and "mining claim" defined.

§ 328. Acts necessary to be performed to constitute a valid lode location under the Revised Statutes in the absence of supplemental state legislation and local district rules.

§ 329. The requisites of a valid lode location under the Revised Statutes where supplemental state legislation exists.

§ 330. Order in which acts are performed immaterial—Time, when non-essential.

§ 331. Locations made by agents.

ARTICLE III. THE DISCOVERY.

§ 335. Discovery the source of the miner's title.
§ 336. What constitutes a valid discovery.
§ 337. Where such discovery must be made.
§ 338. The effect of the loss of discovery upon the remainder of the location.
§ 339. Extent of locator's rights after discovery and prior to completion of location.

ARTICLE IV. THE DISCOVERY SHAFT AND ITS EQUIVALENT.

§ 343. State legislation requiring development work as prerequisite to completion of location.
§ 344. Object of requirement as to development work.
§ 345. Relationship of the discovery to the discovery shaft.
§ 346. Extent of development work.

ARTICLE V. THE PRELIMINARY NOTICE AND ITS POSTING.

§ 350. Local customs as to preliminary notice, and its posting prior to enactment of federal laws—Not required by congressional law.
§ 351. State legislation requiring the posting of notices—States grouped.
§ 352. First group.
§ 353. Second group.
§ 354. Third group.
§ 355. Liberal rules of construction applied to notices.
§ 356. Place and manner of posting.

ARTICLE VI. THE SURFACE COVERED BY THE LOCATION.— ITS FORM AND RELATIONSHIP TO THE LOCATED LODE.

§ 360. The ideal location.
§ 361. Surface area, length, and width of lode claims.
§ 362. Location covering excessive area.
§ 363. Surface conflicts with prior unpatented locations.
§ 363a. Surface conflicts with prior patented mining claims, millsites, and agricultural lands.
§ 364. Surface must include apex—Location on the dip.
§ 365. The end lines.
§ 366. The side lines.
§ 367. Side-end lines.

ARTICLE VII. THE MARKING OF THE LOCATION ON THE SURFACE.

§ 371. Necessity for, and object of, marking.
§ 372. Time allowed for marking.
§ 373. What is sufficient marking under the federal law.
§ 374. State statutes defining character of marking.
§ 375. Perpetuation of monuments.

ARTICLE VIII. THE LOCATION CERTIFICATE AND ITS CONTENTS.

§ 379. The location certificate—Its purpose.
§ 380. State legislation as to contents of location certificate.
§ 381. Rules of construction applied.
§ 382. Variation between calls in certificate and monuments on the ground.
§ 383. "Natural objects" and "permanent monuments."
§ 384. Effect of failure to comply with the law as to contents of certificate.
§ 385. Verification of certificates.

ARTICLE IX. THE RECORD.

§ 389. Time and place of record.
§ 390. Effect of failure to record within the time limited.
§ 391. Proof of record.
§ 392. The record as evidence.

ARTICLE X. CHANGE OF BOUNDARIES AND AMENDED OR ADDITIONAL LOCATION CERTIFICATES.

§ 396. Circumstances justifying change of boundaries.
§ 397. Privilege of changing boundaries exists in the absence of intervening rights, independent of state legislation.
§ 398. Objects and functions of amended certificates.

ARTICLE XI. RELOCATION OF FORFEITED OR ABANDONED CLAIMS.

§ 402. Circumstances under which relocation may be made.
§ 403. New discovery not essential as basis of relocation.
§ 404. Relocation admits the validity of the original.
§ 405. Relocation by original locators.
§ 406. Relocation by one of several original locators in hostility to the others.
§ 407. Relocation by agent or others occupying contractual or fiduciary relations with original locator.

§ 408. Manner of perfecting relocations—Statutory regulations.
§ 409. Right of second locator to improvements made by the first.

ARTICLE XII. LODES WITHIN PLACERS.

§ 413. Right to appropriate lodes within placers.
§ 414. Manner of locating lodes within placers.
§ 415. Width of lode locations within placers.

CHAPTER III. PLACERS AND OTHER FORMS OF DEPOSIT NOT "IN PLACE."

ARTICLE I. CHARACTER OF DEPOSITS SUBJECT TO APPROPRIATION UNDER LAWS APPLICABLE TO PLACERS.

     II. THE LOCATION AND ITS REQUIREMENTS.

     III. THE DISCOVERY.

     IV. STATE LEGISLATION AS TO POSTING NOTICES AND PRELIMINARY DEVELOPMENT WORK.

      V. THE SURFACE COVERED BY THE LOCATION—ITS FORM AND EXTENT.

     VI. THE MARKING OF THE LOCATION ON THE GROUND.

     VII. THE LOCATION CERTIFICATE AND ITS RECORD.

     VIII. CONCLUSION.

ARTICLE I. CHARACTER OF DEPOSITS SUBJECT TO APPROPRIATION UNDER LAWS APPLICABLE TO PLACERS.

§ 419. The general rule.
§ 420. Specific substances classified as subject to entry under the placer laws.
§ 421. Building stone and stone of special commercial value.
§ 422. Petroleum.
§ 423. Natural gas.
§ 424. Brick clay.
§ 425. Phosphatic deposits.
§ 426. Tailings.
§ 427. Subterranean gravel deposits in ancient river beds.
§ 428. Beds of streams.
§ 429. Lands under tide-waters.

ARTICLE II. THE LOCATION AND ITS REQUIREMENTS.

§ 432. Acts necessary to be performed to constitute a valid placer location under the Revised Statutes, in the absence of supplemental state legislation and local district rules.
§ 433. Requisites of a valid placer location where supplemental state legislation exists.

ARTICLE III. THE DISCOVERY.

§ 437. Rules governing discovery the same as in lode locations.
§ 438. Unit of placer locations—Discovery in each twenty-acre tract.

ARTICLE IV. STATE LEGISLATION AS TO POSTING NOTICES AND PRELIMINARY DEVELOPMENT WORK.

§ 442. State statutes requiring posting of notices on placers.
§ 443. Preliminary development work required by state laws upon placer locations.

ARTICLE V. THE SURFACE COVERED BY THE LOCATION— ITS FORM AND EXTENT.

§ 447. Form and extent of placer locations prior to Revised Statutes.
§ 448. Form and extent under Revised Statutes.
§ 448a. Limitation as to size and form of claims under District rules.
§ 448b. Surface conflicts with prior locations.
§ 449. Placer locations by corporations.
§ 450. Locations by several persons in the interest of one—Number of locations by an individual.

ARTICLE VI. THE MARKING OF THE LOCATION ON THE GROUND.

§ 454. Rule as to marking boundaries of placer claims in absence of state legislation.
§ 455. State legislation as to marking boundaries of placer claims.

ARTICLE VII. THE LOCATION CERTIFICATE AND ITS RECORD.

§ 459. State legislation concerning location certificates and their record.

ARTICLE VIII. CONCLUSION.

§ 463. General principles announced in previous chapter on lode locations apply with equal force to placers.

CHAPTER IV. TUNNEL CLAIMS.

ARTICLE I. INTRODUCTORY.
    II. MANNER OF PERFECTING TUNNEL LOCATIONS.
    III. RIGHTS ACCRUING TO THE TUNNEL PROPRIETOR BY VIRTUE OF HIS TUNNEL LOCATION.

ARTICLE I. INTRODUCTORY.

§ 467. Tunnel locations prior to the enactment of federal laws.
§ 468. The provisions of the federal law.

ARTICLE II. MANNER OF PERFECTING TUNNEL LOCATION.

§ 472. Acts to be performed in acquiring tunnel rights.
§ 473. ''Line'' of tunnel defined.
§ 474. ''Face'' of tunnel defined.
§ 475. The marking of the tunnel location on the ground.

ARTICLE III. RIGHTS ACCRUING TO THE TUNNEL PROPRI-
          ETOR BY VIRTUE OF HIS TUNNEL LOCATION.

§ 479. Important questions suggested by the tunnel law.
§ 480. Rule of interpretation applied.
§ 481. Length upon the discovered lode awarded to the tunnel discoverer.
§ 482. Necessity for appropriation of discovered lode by surface loca-
       tion.
§ 483. To what extent does the inception of a tunnel right and its per-
       petuation by prosecuting work with reasonable diligence operate
       as a withdrawal of the surface from exploration by others?
§ 484. The Colorado rule.
§ 485. The Montana rule.
§ 486. The Idaho rule.
§ 487. Judge Hallett's views.
§ 488. The doctrine announced by the circuit court of appeals, eighth
       circuit.
§ 489. Tunnel locations before the supreme court of the United States.
§ 490. Opinions of the land department.
§ 490a. Rights of junior tunnel locator as against senior mining claims
       on the line of the tunnel.
§ 491. Inquiries suggested in the light of rules thus far enunciated by
       the supreme court of the United States as to the extent of the
       rights of a tunnel locator on a vein discovered in the tunnel.

CHAPTER V. COAL LANDS.

ARTICLE I. INTRODUCTORY.
    II. MANNER OF ACQUIRING TITLE TO COAL LANDS.

ARTICLE I. INTRODUCTORY.

§ 495. Classification of coal as a mineral—History of legislation—
       Characteristics of the system.
§ 496. Rules for determining character of land.
§ 497. Geographical scope of the coal land laws.

ARTICLE II. MANNER OF ACQUIRING TITLE TO COAL LANDS.

§ 501. Who may enter coal lands.
§ 502. Different classes of entries.

§ 503. Private entry under Revised Statutes, section twenty-three hundred and forty-seven.

§ 504. Preferential right of purchase under Revised Statutes, section twenty-three hundred and forty-eight.

§ 505. The declaratory statement.

§ 506. Assignability of inchoate rights.

§ 507. The purchase price.

§ 508. The final entry.

§ 509. Conclusions.

Chapter VI. Salines.

§ 513. Governmental policy with reference to salines.

§ 514. The act of January 12, 1877—Territorial limit of its operation.

§ 514a. The Act of January 31, 1901.

§ 515. What embraced within the term "salines."

Chapter VII. Millsites.

§ 519. The law relating to millsites.

§ 520. Different classes of millsites.

§ 521. Right to millsite—How initiated.

§ 522. Location of millsite with reference to lode.

§ 523. Nature of use required in case of location by lode proprietor.

§ 524. Millsites used for quartz mill or reduction works disconnected with lode ownership.

§ 525. Location of junior lode claims conflicting with senior millsites.

Chapter VIII. Easements.

§ 529. Scope of the chapter.

§ 530. Rights of way for ditches and canals—Highways.

§ 531. Location subject only to pre-existing easements.

TITLE VI.

THE TITLE ACQUIRED AND RIGHTS CONFERRED BY LOCATION.

Chapter I. The Character of the Tenure.

II. The Nature and Extent of Property Rights Conferred by Lode Locations.

III. The Extralateral Right.

IV. The Nature and Extent of Property Rights Conferred by Placer Locations.

V. Perpetuation of the Estate by Annual Development and Improvement.

VI. Forfeiture of the Estate, and Its Prevention by Resumption of Work.

Chapter I. The Character of the Tenure.

§ 535. Nature of the estate as defined by the early decisions.
§ 536. Origin of the doctrine.
§ 537. Actual and constructive possession under miners' rules.
§ 538. Federal recognition of the doctrine.
§ 539. Nature of the estate as defined by the courts since the enactment of general mining laws.
§ 540. Nature of the estate compared with copyholds at common law.
§ 541. Nature of the estate compared with the *dominium utile* of the civil law.
§ 542. Nature of the estate compared with inchoate pre-emption and homestead claims.
§ 543. Dower within the states.
§ 544. Dower within the territories.

Chapter II. The Nature and Extent of Property Rights Conferred by Lode Locations.

Article I. Introductory—Intralimital Rights.
       II. Cross Lodes.

ARTICLE I. INTRODUCTORY—INTRALIMITAL RIGHTS.

§ 548. General observations.
§ 549. Classification of rights with reference to boundaries.
§ 550. Extent of the grant as defined by the statute.
§ 551. The right to the surface, and presumptions flowing therefrom.
§ 552. Intralimital rights not affected by the form of surface location.
§ 553. Pursuit of the vein on its course beyond bounding planes of the location not permitted.

ARTICLE II. CROSS LODES.

§ 557. Section twenty-three hundred and thirty-six of the Revised Statutes and its interpretation.
§ 558. The Colorado rule.
§ 559. Cross lodes before the supreme court of Montana.
§ 560. The Arizona-California rule.
§ 561. The views of the supreme court of the United States.

CHAPTER III. THE EXTRALATERAL RIGHT.

ARTICLE I. INTRODUCTORY.

II. EXTRALATERAL RIGHTS ON THE ORIGINAL LODE UNDER PATENTS ISSUED PRIOR TO MAY 10, 1872.

III. EXTRALATERAL RIGHTS FLOWING FROM LOCATIONS MADE UNDER THE ACT OF MAY 10, 1872, AND THE REVISED STATUTES.

IV. CONSTRUCTION OF PATENTS APPLIED FOR PRIOR, BUT ISSUED SUBSEQUENT, TO THE ACT OF 1872.

V. LEGAL OBSTACLES INTERRUPTING THE EXTRALATERAL RIGHT.

VI. CONVEYANCES AFFECTING THE EXTRALATERAL RIGHT.

ARTICLE I. INTRODUCTORY.

§ 564. Introductory.
§ 565. Origin and use of the term "extralateral."
§ 566. The "dip right" under local rules.
§ 567. The right to pursue the vein in depth, prior to patent, under the act of July 26, 1866.
§ 568. Nature of estate in the vein, created by grant of the dip or extralateral right.

ARTICLE II. EXTRALATERAL RIGHTS ON THE ORIGINAL LODE UNDER PATENTS ISSUED PRIOR TO MAY 10, 1872.

§ 572. The right to patent under the act of 1866, and its restriction to one lode.
§ 573. The function of the diagram and the surface lines described in the patent as controlling rights on the patented lode.
§ 574. Rights of patentee under the act of 1866, where the end lines converge in the direction of the dip.
§ 575. Rights of patentee under the act of 1866, where the end lines diverge in the direction of the dip.
§ 576. Under the act of 1866, parallelism of end lines not required— Doctrine of the Eureka case.
§ 577. The Argonaut-Kennedy case.

ARTICLE III. EXTRALATERAL RIGHTS FLOWING FROM LOCATIONS MADE UNDER THE ACT OF MAY 10, 1872, AND THE REVISED STATUTES.

§ 581. Introductory.
§ 582. Parallelism of end lines a condition precedent to the exercise of the extralateral right.
§ 583. "Broad lodes"—Apex bisected by side line common to two locations.

§ 584. Vein entering and departing through the same side line.

§ 585. The extralateral right applied to the ideal lode.

§ 586. Vein crossing two parallel side lines—The Flagstaff case.

§ 587. Same—The Argentine-Terrible case.

§ 588. Same—The King-Amy case.

§ 589. Deductions from side-end line cases—Extralateral right in such cases defined by vertical planes drawn through the side-end lines produced.

§ 590. Vein crossing two opposite non-parallel side lines.

§ 591. Vein crossing one end line and a side line.

§ 591a. Vein crossing one end line, passing out of a side line, then returning and ultimately passing out of either the other side or end line.

§ 592. Vein with apex wholly within the location, but crossing none of its boundaries, or entering at one end line and not reaching any other boundary.

§ 593. Extralateral right as to veins other than the one upon which the location is based.

§ 594. Other illustrations of the applications of the principles discussed.

§ 595. Extralateral rights on other lodes conferred by the act of 1872 on owners of claims previously located where the end lines are not parallel.

§ 596. Extralateral right where the apex is found in surface conflict between junior and senior lode locations—Practical application of the Del Monte case.

§ 597. Extralateral right where the apex is found in surface conflict between junior lode locations and prior placer or agricultural patents.

§ 598. Conclusions.

ARTICLE IV. CONSTRUCTION OF PATENTS APPLIED FOR PRIOR, BUT ISSUED SUBSEQUENT, TO THE ACT OF 1872.

§ 604. Patents applied for under the act of 1866, but issued after May 10, 1872, to be construed as if issued under the prior law.

ARTICLE V. LEGAL OBSTACLES INTERRUPTING THE EXTRA-LATERAL RIGHT.

§ 608. Classes of impediments interrupting the right of lateral pursuit.

§ 609. Prior appropriation by a regular valid location of a segment of the same vein without conflict as to surface area.

§ 610. Qualification of the doctrine that the extent of the extralateral right of different locators on the same vein is to be determined by priority of location.

§ 611. The encountering of a vertical plane drawn through a surface boundary of a prior grant, which grant did not in terms or inferentially reserve the right of underground invasion—Senior mining locations not of this class..

§ 612. Same—Prior agricultural grants.

§ 613. Same—Other classes of grants.

§ 614. Union of veins on the dip.

§ 615. Identity and continuity of veins involved in the exercise of the extralateral right.

ARTICLE VI. CONVEYANCES AFFECTING THE EXTRALATERAL RIGHT.

§ 616. Introductory.

§ 617. Conveyance of the location containing the apex of the vein conveys the extralateral right.

§ 618. Extent of extralateral right passing by conveyance of part of the location.

§ 618a. Effect on extralateral right where the owner of the location conveys the adjoining ground into which the vein penetrates on its downward course.

CHAPTER IV. THE NATURE AND EXTENT OF PROPERTY RIGHTS CONFERRED BY PLACER LOCATIONS.

§ 619. Rights conferred by placer locations as compared with lode locations.

CHAPTER V. PERPETUATION OF THE ESTATE BY ANNUAL DEVELOPMENT AND IMPROVEMENT.

§ 623. Annual labor under local rules—Provisions of the federal law.

§ 624. Requirement as to annual labor imperative in order to protect the claim from relocation.

§ 625. Annual labor upon placer claims.

§ 626. Supplemental state legislation.

§ 627. Division of the subject.

§ 628. "Claim" defined.

§ 629. Work done within the limits of a single location.

§ 630. Work done within the limits of a group of claims in furtherance of a common system of development.

§ 631. Work done outside of the boundaries of a claim or group of claims.

§ 632. Period within which work must be done—Can preliminary work required by state laws as an act of location be credited on the first year's work?

§ 633. By whom labor must be performed.

§ 634. Circumstances under which performance of annual labor is excused.

§ 635. Value of labor and improvements—How estimated.

§ 636. Proof of annual labor under state laws.

§ 637. Obligation to perform labor annually ceases with the final entry at the land office.

§ 638. Millsites.

CHAPTER VI. FORFEITURE OF THE ESTATE, AND ITS PREVENTION BY RESUMPTION OF WORK.

ARTICLE I. ABANDONMENT AND FORFEITURE.

II. RESUMPTION OF WORK.

ARTICLE I. ABANDONMENT AND FORFEITURE.

§ 642. Circumstances under which the locator's estate is terminated.

§ 643. Distinction between abandonment and forfeiture.

§ 644. Acts constituting abandonment—Evidence establishing or negativing it.

§ 645. Forfeiture.

§ 646. Forfeiture to co-owners.

ARTICLE II. RESUMPTION OF WORK.

§ 651. Resumption of work prevents forfeiture.

§ 652. What constitutes a valid resumption of work.

§ 653. When right to resume work must be exercised.

§ 654. Conclusions.

TITLE VII.

OF THE PROCEEDINGS TO OBTAIN UNITED STATES PATENT AND THE TITLE CONVEYED BY THAT INSTRUMENT.

CHAPTER I. THE LAND DEPARTMENT AND ITS FUNCTIONS.

II. THE SURVEY FOR PATENT.

III. THE APPLICATION FOR PATENT AND PROCEEDINGS THEREON.

IV. THE ADVERSE CLAIM.

V. ACTIONS TO DETERMINE ADVERSE CLAIMS, AND THE EFFECT OF JUDGMENT THEREON.

VI. THE CERTIFICATE OF PURCHASE AND TITLE CONVEYED THEREBY.

VII. THE PATENT.

Chapter I. The Land Department and Its Functions.

§ 658. Introductory.

§ 659. The land department—How constituted.

§ 660. Registers and receivers—Their appointment, powers, and duties.

§ 661. The surveyors-general and their deputies.

§ 662. Commissioner of the general land office—Appointment, powers, and duties.

§ 663. Secretary of the interior.

§ 664. Jurisdiction of the land department.

§ 665. The effect of the decisions of the land department upon questions of fact.

§ 666. Decisions of the land department upon questions of law and mixed questions of law and fact.

Chapter II. The Survey for Patent.

§ 670. Application for survey.

§ 671. The survey of lode claims.

§ 672. The survey of placer claims—Descriptive report.

§ 673. The surveyor-general's certificate as to expenditures.

Chapter III. The Application for Patent, and Proceedings Thereon.

Article I. Lode Claims.

II. Placer Claims—Lodes within Placers.

III. Millsites.

Article I. Lode Claims.

§ 677. Posting of the notice and copy of the plat on the claim.

§ 678. The initiatory proceedings in the land office.

§ 679. Land embraced within the claim must be clear on the tract books.

§ 680. The application for patent—Its contents.

§ 681. Application by one of several co-owners—Corporations.

§ 682. Verification of application and other proofs.

§ 683. Proof of posting of notice and plat on the claim.

§ 684. Proof of citizenship.

§ 685. Designation of newspaper—Agreement of publisher.

§ 686. Proof of annual labor.

§687. The abstract of title—Certified copies of location notices.

§ 688. Proof of title by possession, without location under section twenty-three hundred and thirty-two of the Revised Statutes.

§ 689. Proof of mineral character of the land.

§ 690. Publication of notice and proof thereof.

§ 691. The posting of the notice in the register's office and proof thereof.

§ 692. Proof that the plat and notice of application for patent remained posted on the claim during the period of publication.

§ 693. Statement of fees and charges.

§ 694. Application to purchase.

§ 695. Résumé.

§ 696. Applications for patent once instituted must be prosecuted with reasonable diligence—Relocations pending patent proceedings.

§ 697. Effect of dismissal of patent application.

ARTICLE II. PLACER CLAIMS—LODES WITHIN PLACERS.

§ 699. Proceedings to obtain patent to lode claims generally applicable to placers.

§ 700. Description of placer claims upon surveyed lands.

§ 701. Proof of the five hundred dollars expenditure.

§ 702. Proof of mineral character of the land.

§ 703. Proof that no known lodes exist within limits of placer claim.

§ 704. Lodes within placers—How applied for.

ARTICLE III. MILLSITES.

§ 708. Manner of acquiring patents to millsites.

Chapter IV. The Adverse Claim.

Article I. Introductory.

II. What is and What is Not the Subject of an Adverse Claim.

III. How, When, and Where Adverse Claim Must be Asserted.

ARTICLE I. INTRODUCTORY.

§ 712. Distinction between adverse claim and protest.

§ 713. Patent proceedings are essentially *in rem*—Adverse claims must be presented.

ARTICLE II. WHAT IS AND WHAT IS NOT THE SUBJECT OF AN ADVERSE CLAIM.

§ 717. Character of land—Agricultural claimants.

§ 718. Prior patentees and prior patent applicants.

§ 719. Mortgagees—Lienholders—Owners of equitable interests.

§ 720. Lode claimant *v.* placer applicant.

§ 721. Placer claimant *v.* lode applicant.

§ 722. Mineral claimant *v.* townsite applicant.

§ 723. Townsite claimant *v.* mineral applicant.

§ 724. Millsite claimant *v.* Mineral applicant.

§ 725. Tunnel proprietor *v.* lode applicant.

§ 726. Owners of lodes located prior to May 10, 1872.

§ 727. Cross lodes.

§ 728. Co-owners.

§ 729. Easements.

§ 730. Underground conflicts.

§ 731. Parties relocating after period of publication.

ARTICLE III. HOW, WHEN, AND WHERE ADVERSE CLAIM
MUST BE ASSERTED.

§ 734. Adverse claim—How asserted—Contents of the claim—Amendments.

§ 735. Survey of the adverse claim.

§ 736. Verification of the claim.

§ 737. Sufficiency of adverse claims to be determined by land department.

§ 738. When adverse claim must be filed—Time how computed.

§ 739. Where adverse claim must be filed.

§ 740. But one adverse claim need be filed.

§ 741. Filing of adverse claim suspends the powers of the land department.

§ 742. Effect of failure to file an adverse claim.

CHAPTER V. ACTIONS TO DETERMINE ADVERSE CLAIMS,
AND THE EFFECT OF JUDGMENT THEREON.

ARTICLE I. INTRODUCTORY—TRIBUNALS HAVING JURISDICTION.

II. CHARACTER OF THE ACTION—PLEADINGS AND PRACTICE—
FUNCTIONS OF THE LAND DEPARTMENT PENDING THE
ACTION.

III. THE JUDGMENT AND ITS EFFECT.

ARTICLE I. INTRODUCTORY—TRIBUNALS HAVING JURIS-
DICTION.

§ 746. Introductory—What courts are courts of competent jurisdiction.

§ 747. The federal courts.

§ 748. The state courts.

ARTICLE II. CHARACTER OF THE ACTION—PLEADINGS AND
PRACTICE—FUNCTIONS OF THE LAND DEPARTMENT
PENDING THE ACTION.

§ 754. Character of the action—At law or in equity—Pleadings.

§ 755. General rules of pleading.

§ 756. Time within which action must be commenced.
§ 757. Action when deemed commenced.
§ 758. Parties to the action.
§ 759. Functions of the land department, pending the action.

ARTICLE III. THE JUDGMENT AND ITS EFFECT.

§ 763. Form of judgment.
§ 764. When judgment becomes available in the land office.
§ 765. Effect of the judgment.
§ 766. Adverse claim—How waived.

CHAPTER VI. THE CERTIFICATE OF PURCHASE AND
TITLE CONVEYED THEREBY.

§ 770. Issuance of the certificate.
§ 771. The title conveyed by the certificate of purchase.
§ 772. Power of the land department to suspend or cancel the certificate.
§ 773. The certificate of purchase as evidence—Collateral attack.

CHAPTER VII. THE PATENT.

§ 7⁻7. General rules as to conclusiveness of patents.
§ 778. Conclusiveness of patent as to form and extent of surface boundaries.
§ 779. Character of the land established by the patent.
§ 780. What is conveyed by a lode patent.
§ 781. What is conveyed by a placer patent—Reservation of lodes "known to exist."
§ 782. Exceptions in junior patents of conflicting area held under senior title.
§ 783. Title conveyed by patent relates to inception of right—When evidence admissible to prove date of location.
§ 784. Patent—How vacated—Within what time suit must be brought.

TITLE VIII.

RIGHTS AND OBLIGATIONS ARISING OUT OF OWNERSHIP IN
COMMON OF MINES AND JOINT PARTICIPATION IN MIN-
ING VENTURES.

CHAPTER I. TENANTS IN COMMON.
II. MINING PARTNERSHIPS.

CHAPTER I. TENANTS IN COMMON.

§ 788. Cotenancy—How created—General rules governing tenants in common applicable to ownership in common of mines.

§ 789. Right of each cotenant to occupy and use the common property.

§ 789a. Occupying cotenant not liable at common law to account, in absence of exclusion of cotenant—Judicial and statutory modifications.

§ 790. Remedy of excluded cotenant—Accounting between tenants in common.

§ 791. Leases, licenses, and conveyances executed by one of several cotenants.

§ 792. Partition of mining property.

CHAPTER II. MINING PARTNERSHIPS.

§ 796. Nature of relationship.

§ 797. Mining partnership—How created.

§ 798. Special instances wherein mining partnerships held to be created.

§ 799. Special instances where mining partnerships held not to be created.

§ 800. Rights and obligations of mining partners *inter sese*.

§ 801. Authority of the members—Liability of copartnership to third parties.

§ 802. Partnership property.

§ 803. Dissolution.

TITLE IX.

RIGHTS AND OBLIGATIONS OF PARTIES ENGAGED IN WORKING MINES.

CHAPTER I. DRAINAGE OF MINES—RELATIVE RIGHTS AND DUTIES OF MINERS OPERATING AT DIFFERENT LEVELS, WITH RESPECT TO WATER.

II. MUTUAL RIGHTS AND DUTIES WHERE TITLE TO MINERALS IS SEVERED FROM THAT OF THE SURFACE.

III. LATERAL OR ADJACENT SUPPORT.

IV. DEPOSIT OF MINING DEBRIS IN RUNNING STREAMS AND ON LANDS OF OTHERS—PRIVATE NUISANCES.

V. GOVERNMENTAL SUPERVISION OF HYDRAULIC MINING IN CALIFORNIA—THE CALIFORNIA DEBRIS COMMISSION—ITS JURISDICTION AND POWERS.

CHAPTER I. DRAINAGE OF MINES—RELATIVE RIGHTS AND DUTIES OF MINERS OPERATING AT DIFFERENT LEVELS, WITH RESPECT TO WATER.

§ 806. Introductory—Statutory regulations on the subject of mine drainage.

§ 807. The law of natural flow.

§ 808. Foreign water—Flooding.

Chapter II. Mutual Rights and Duties where Title to Minerals is Severed from That of the Surface.

ARTICLE I. GENERAL PRINCIPLES — RIGHTS AND DUTIES OF MINE OWNERS—USE OF SURFACE.

    II. VERTICAL OR SUBJACENT SUPPORT.

    III. RIGHTS AND DUTIES OF SURFACE PROPRIETOR—OWNERSHIP OF SEPARATE STRATA.

ARTICLE I. GENERAL PRINCIPLES—RIGHTS AND DUTIES OF MINE OWNERS—USE OF SURFACE.

§ 812. Application of the doctrine of the common law on the subject of severance—Severance under the federal laws—General principles.

§ 813. To what extent owner of minerals may use surface.

§ 814. Manner of conducting mining operations.

ARTICLE II. VERTICAL OR SUBJACENT SUPPORT.

§ 818. Right of surface support reserved by implication in grant of minerals—Nature of the right.

§ 819. Right of surface support an absolute one—Negligence not involved.

§ 820. Right limited to support of soil in its natural state—Buildings.

§ 821. Waiver or release of the right of surface support.

§ 822. Statutory regulations on subject of subjacent support.

§ 823. Remedies for surface subsidence—Statute of limitations.

ARTICLE III. RIGHTS AND DUTIES OF SURFACE PROPRIETOR—OWNERSHIP OF SEPARATE STRATA.

§ 826. Responsibility of surface owner for injuries to miners' rights.

§ 827. Right of access to lower strata—Reciprocal servitudes as between owners of different strata.

Chapter III. Lateral or Adjacent Support.

§ 831. Introductory.

§ 832. General principles—Negligence as an element.

§ 833. Right limited to support of soil in its natural state.

§ 834. The right of lateral support as applied to mines worked by hydraulic process.

CHAPTER IV. DEPOSIT OF MINING DEBRIS IN RUNNING STREAMS AND ON LAND OF OTHERS—PRIVATE NUISANCES.

§ 838. The use of water in the conduct of mining operations.
§ 839. Pollution of streams—The English rule—Tin streaming in Cornwall.
§ 840. The American rule as declared in states not accepting the Pacific Coast doctrine as to right of appropriation and use of water.
§ 841. The rule in the mining states and territories where the right of appropriation is recognized.
§ 842. The remedy by injunction to prevent pollution of water and deposit of tailings.
§ 843. The deposit of tailings and refuse on the lands of others.
§ 844. Measure of damages for unlawfully depositing debris on another's land.

CHAPTER V. GOVERNMENTAL SUPERVISION OF HYDRAULIC MINING IN CALIFORNIA—THE CALIFORNIA DEBRIS COMMISSION—ITS JURISDICTION AND POWERS.

§ 848. Causes leading up to the passage by congress of the act creating the California debris commission.
§ 849. Hydraulic mining not a nuisance per se—Principles established by the debris cases.
§ 850. Essential features of the congressional act creating the California debris commission and regulating hydraulic mining in the state of California.
§ 851. Necessity for definition of term "hydraulic mining."
§ 852. What constitutes "hydraulic mining," or "mining by the hydraulic process," within the meaning of the act.
§ 853. Judicial interpretation of the act—Its constitutionality.

TITLE X.
MINES AND MINING CLAIMS AS SUBJECTS OF CONTRACT BETWEEN INDIVIDUALS.

CHAPTER I. MISCELLANEOUS CONTRACTS RELATING TO MINING VENTURES AND THEIR DISTINGUISHING FEATURES.

§ 857. Introductory.
§ 858. "Grub stake" and prospecting contracts.
§ 859. Options, working bonds, or executory contracts of sale.

§ 859a. Contracts disposing of mining rights.
§ 859b. Sales of mineral in place.
§ 860. Licenses and their distinguishing attributes.
§ 861. What constitutes a lease.
§ 862. Doctrines peculiar to oil and gas leases.

TITLE XI.

ACTIONS CONCERNING MINING CLAIMS OTHER THAN SUITS UPON ADVERSE CLAIMS—AUXILIARY REMEDIES.

CHAPTER I. TRESPASS—MEASURE OF DAMAGES.
    II. AUXILIARY REMEDIES.

CHAPTER I. TRESPASS—MEASURE OF DAMAGES.

§ 865. Introductory.
§ 866. Burden of proof in cases of underground trespasses.
§ 867. When the statute of limitations commences to run against underground trespasses.
§ 868. Measure of damages.

CHAPTER II. AUXILIARY REMEDIES.

§ 872. Injunction.
§ 873. Inspection and survey.

TITLE XIA.

THE MINING INDUSTRY AND LAWS OF INSULAR POSSESSIONS OF THE UNITED STATES.

CHAPTER I. INSULAR POSSESSIONS OF THE UNITED STATES.

§ 876. Introductory.
§ 877. Hawaii.
§ 878. Porto Rico.
§ 879. Philippine Islands.

APPENDIX—MISCELLANEOUS.

TITLE XII.

FEDERAL STATUTES RELATING TO MINES, TOGETHER WITH LAND DEPARTMENT REGULATIONS.

I. LODE AND WATER LAW OF JULY 26, 1866.

II. PLACER LAW OF JULY 9, 1870.

III. GENERAL MINING ACT OF MAY 10, 1872.

IV. TITLE XXXII, CHAPTER 6, OF UNITED STATES REVISED STATUTES EMBODYING EXISTING LAWS RELATING TO MINERAL LANDS.

V. MINING LEGISLATION FOR THE PHILIPPINE ISLANDS.

VI. LAND DEPARTMENT REGULATIONS UPON THE SUBJECT OF MINERAL LANDS OTHER THAN COAL.

VII. COAL LAND LAW WITH REGULATIONS THEREUNDER.

VIII. INSTRUCTIONS RELATING TO SELECTION OF LANDS BY RAILROADS AND STATES.

IX. PETROLEUM LAW OF FEBRUARY 11, 1897, AND CIRCULAR OF INSTRUCTIONS RELATING THERETO.

X. ALIEN ACT OF MARCH 2, 1897.

XI. LEGISLATION AND REGULATIONS ON THE SUBJECT OF MINING CLAIMS WITHIN FOREST RESERVATIONS.

XII. LEGISLATION CONCERNING THE CUTTING OF TIMBER ON PUBLIC MINERAL LANDS.

TITLE XIII.

STATE AND TERRITORIAL LEGISLATION ON THE SUBJECT OF MINES.

DISTRICT OF ALASKA—(PP. 1779-1791).

I. Federal laws and regulations concerning mines in Alaska.—p. 1779.

    A. Mining statutes relating to Alaska.—p. 1781.

    B. Land department regulations concerning mining in Alaska.—p. 1787.

ARIZONA—(PP. 1792-1801).

I. Act of 1901, relating to the location, development, and forfeiture of mining claims.—p. 1792.

II. Reference to miscellaneous legislation on mining subjects.—p. 1800.

ARKANSAS—(PP. 1802-1805).

I. Act of March 18, 1899, to provide for the better preservation of mining records.—p. 1802.

II. Act of May 23, 1901, to fix the statute of limitations relating to mining claims, and for other purposes.—p. 1803.

III. Reference to miscellaneous legislation on mining subjects.—p. 1805.

CALIFORNIA—(PP. 1806-1823).

I. Act of 1891 relating to performance and proof of labor.—p. 1807.

II. Provisions on subject of recording.—p. 1809.

III. Regulating the sale of mineral lands belonging to the state.—p. 1810.

IV. Congressional act regulating hydraulic mining in California.—p. 1811.

V. Reference to miscellaneous legislation on mining subjects.—p. 1822.

COLORADO—(PP. 1824-1839).

I. Legislation relating to lode claims.—p. 1824.

II. Legislation relating to placer claims.—p. 1831.

III. Legislation relating to tunnels and tunnel claims.—p. 1834.

IV. Reference to miscellaneous legislation on mining subjects.—p. 1836.

IDAHO—(PP. 1840-1852).

I. Persons who may locate and hold mining claims.—p. 1840.

II. Provisions relating to lode claims.—p. 1840.

III. Provisions relating to placer claims.—p. 1844.

IV. Provisions affecting both lode and placer claims.—p. 1845.

V. Reference to miscellaneous legislation on mining subjects.—p. 1850.

MONTANA—(PP. 1853-1861).

I. Laws relating to the location and development of mining claims.—p. 1853.

II. Reference to miscellaneous legislation on mining subjects.—p. 1858.

NEVADA—(PP. 1862-1878).

I. Act of 1897, regulating the location and development of lode, placer, tunnel, and millsite claims.—p. 1862.

II. Act regulating the disposition of certain state mineral lands.—
    p. 1874.
III. Reference to miscellaneous legislation on mining subjects.—p.
    1875.

NEW MEXICO—(PP. 1879-1886).

I. Laws relating to the location, relocation, and development of
    mines.—p. 1879.
II. Reference to miscellaneous legislation on mining subjects.—p.
    1883.

NORTH DAKOTA—(PP. 1886-1892).

I. Legislation relating to the acquisition of title to lode claims.—
    p. 1886.
II. Reference to miscellaneous legislation on mining subjects.—p.
    1891.

OREGON—(PP. 1893-1897).

I. Laws relating to the location and recording of mining claims.—
    p. 1893.
    A. Mining act of October 14, 1898.—p. 1893.
    B. Other provisions.—p. 1896.
II. Reference to miscellaneous legislation on mining subjects.—p.
    1897.

SOUTH DAKOTA—(PP. 1898-1906).

    A. Mining laws enacted by the legislature of South Dakota.—
        p. 1898.
    B. Mining laws of Dakota Territory adopted by South
        Dakota.—p. 1898.
I. Relating to the size, location, and development of mining claims.
    p. 1899.
II. Reference to miscellaneous legislation on mining subjects.—p.
    1904.

UTAH—(PP. 1907-1916).

I. Act of 1899, providing the manner in which lode and placer
    claims may be located and recorded.—p. 1907.
II. Reference to miscellaneous legislation on mining subjects.—p.
    1914.

WASHINGTON—(PP. 1917-1927).

I. Laws relating to location of mining claims and defining locator's
    rights and duties.—p. 1917.

A. Laws antedating the act of 1899.—p. 1917.

B. Act of 1899, providing for the manner of locating and holding lode and placer mining claims.—p. 1920.

II. Reference to miscellaneous legislation on mining subjects.—p. 1925.

WYOMING—(PP. 1928-1938).

I. Laws relating to the location of lode claims and the extent of locator's rights therein.—p. 1928.

II. Laws relating to the location and annual development of placer claims.—p. 1933.

III. Reference to miscellaneous legislation on mining subjects.—p. 1936.

TITLE XIV.

FORMS AND PRECEDENTS—(PP. 1939-1986).

TABLE OF CASES.

Names of Cases.	When De-cided.	Where Reported.	Sections Where Cited in this Work.
Abbey v. Wheeler.....	1895	85 Hun, 226, 32 N. Y. Supp. 1069	790.
Abbott v. Smith.......	1893	3 Colo. App. 264, 32 Pac. 843	801, 858.
Abercrombie, In re....	1887	6 L. D. 393............	209, 784.
Acers v. Snyder.......	1899	8 Okl. 659, 58 Pac. 780.	665, 777.
Acme Cement and Plac-er Co..............	1901	31 L. D. 125..........	184.
Adams v. Briggs Iron Co........	1851	7 Cush. 361............	791.
Adams v. Crawford....	1897	116 Cal. 495, 48 Pac. 488	339, 350, 351, 754.
Adam v. Norris.......	1897	103 U. S. 591, 4 L. Ed. 26	125.
Adams v. Quijada.....	1897	25 L. D. 24............	629, 781.
Adams v. Simmons....	1892	16 L. D. 181...........	521.
Adjutant - General v. Welsh Granite Co...	1887	35 W. R. 617..........	92.
Adolph Peterson, In re	1887	6 L. D. 371, 15 C. L. O. 14	501.
Ah Hee v. Crippen....	1861	19 Cal. 492, 10 Morr. 367	125.
Ahrns v. Chartier Val-ley Gas Co..........	1898	188 Pa. St. 249, 41 Atl. 739	862.
Ah Yew v. Choate.....	1864	24 Cal. 562, 1 Morr. 492.	94, 161, 207.
Aiken v. Ferry........	1879	6 Saw. 79, Fed. Cas. No. 112	542.
Ajax G. M. Co. v. Cal-houn G. M. Co......	1898	1 Leg. Adv. 426.......	490a, 558.
Albert Johnson, In re..	1880	7 Copp's L. O. 35.......	366.
Aldritt v. Northern Pac. R. R. Co...........	1897	25 L. D. 349..........	95, 96, 97, 98, 137, 139, 158, 159, 419, 420, 424.
Alexander v. Kimbro..	1873	49 Miss. 529, 537.......	802.
Alexander v. Sherman.	1887	(Ariz.), 16 Pac. 45, 15 Morr. 638	407, 719.
Alford v. Barnum.....	1873	45 Cal. 482, 10 Morr. 422.	94.
Alford v. Dewin.......	1865	1 Nev. 207............	634.
Alice Edith Lode......	1888	6 L. D. 711, 15 C. L. O. 51	631.
Alice Lode Mining Claim	1901	30 L. D. 481..........	218, 312a, **338,** 363a, 677.
Alice M. Co..........	1898	27 L. D. 661..........	413, 720, 721.

Names of Cases.	When Decided.	Where Reported.	Sections Where Cited in this Work.
Alice Placer Mine, *In re*	1886	4 L. D. 314, 12 C. L. O. 274	717, 765.
Alleghany Oil Co. *v.* Bradford Oil Co.....	1881	21 Hun, 26, 86 N. Y. 638	862.
Alleman *v.* Hawley....	1888	117 Ind. 532, 20 N. E. 441	790.
Allen, *In re*..........	1889	8 L. D. 140..........	501.
Allen *v.* Dunlap.......	1893	24 Or. 229, 33 Pac. 675.	273, 350, 872.
Allen *v.* Pedro........	1902	136 Cal. 1, 68 Pac. 99..	108, 143.
Alta Millsite	1889	8 L. D. 195............	521, 638, 681, 708.
Alta Millsite	1889	9 L. D. 48............	638.
Alta M. and S. Co. *v.* Benson M. and S. Co.	1888	(Ariz.), 16 Pac. 565...	637, 868.
Altoona Q. M. Co. *v.* Integral Q. M. Co.....	1896	114 Cal. 100, 45 Pac. 1047	233, 629, 643, 688, 748, 754, 755.
Amador-Medean G. M. Co. *v.* South Spring Hill	1888	13 Saw. 523, 36 Fed. 668	125, 208, 531, 612, 771.
Amador Queen M. Co. *v.* Dewitt	1887	73 Cal. 482, 15 Pac. 74.	263, 531.
American Cons M. and M. Co. *v.* De Witt....	1898	26 L. D. 580..........	337, 742.
American Flag Lode, *In re*	1887	6 L. D. 320...........	690, 738.
American Hill Quartz Mine	1879	3 Sickle's Min. Dec. 377, 385, 6 Copp's L. O. 1.	542, 637, 771.
American Ins. Co. *v.* Canter	1828	1 Pet. 511, 542, 7 L. Ed. 242	242.
American Mortgage Co. *v.* Hopper	1891	48 Fed. 47............	772.
American Mortgage Co. *v.* Hopper	1893	56 Fed. 67............	772.
American Mortgage Co. *v.* Hopper	1894	64 Fed. 553...........	772.
Ammons *v.* South Penn. Oil Co..............	1900	47 W. Va. 610, 35 S. E. 1004	862.
Anaconda Copper M. Co. *v.* Butte etc. Co......	1896	17 Mont. 519, 43 Pac. 924	789, 790, 797, 872.
Anaconda Copper M. Co. *v.* Heinze	1902	(Mont.), 69 Pac. 909..	872.
Anchor *v.* Howe.......	1892	50 Fed. 366	735.
Anderson, *In re*.......	1898	26 L. D. 575..........	670.
Anderson *v.* Black.....	1886	70 Cal. 226, 11 Pac. 700.	373.
Anderson *v.* Byam.....	1889	8 L. D. 388............	651.

Names of Cases.	When De-cided.	Where Reported.	Sections Where Cited in this Work.
Anderson *v.* Northern Pac. R. R. Co......	1888	7 L. D. 163..........	772.
Anderson *v.* Simpson..	1866	21 Iowa, 399, 9 Morr. 262	860.
Andrews Bros.*v.* Youngstown Coke Co......	1898	86 Fed. 585	282.
Andromeda Lode	1891	13 L. D. 146	338, 363, 671, 673.
Angier *v.* Agnew......	1881	98 Pa. St. 587, 42 Am. Rep. 624	789, 789a.
Angus *v.* Craven.......	1901	132 Cal. 691, 64 Pac. 1091	754.
Antediluvian Lode	1889	8 L. D. 602...........	172, 338.
Antelope Lode	1875	2 Copp's L. O. 2, 5.....	758, 765.
Anthony *v.* Jillson.....	1890	83 Cal. 296, 2ɔ Pac. 419, 16 Morr. 26	233, 273, 432, 454, 624, 754, 755.
Antoine Co. *v.* Ridge Co.	1863	23 Cal. 219, 10 Morr. 97.	270, 868.
Apex Trans. Co. *v.* Garbade	1898	32 Or. 582, 52 Pac. 573, 54 Pac. 367, 882.....	263a.
Apple Blossom Placer *v.* Cora Lee Lode......	1892	14 L. D. 641..........	765.
Apple Blossom Placer *v.* Cora Lee Lode......	1895	21 L. D. 438...........	670.
Archuleta, *In re*.......	1889	15 Copp's L. O. 256....	496.
Arden L. Smith.......	1900	31 L. D. 184..........	199.
Argentine M. Co. *v.* Benedict	1898	18 Utah, 183, 55 Pac. 559	363, 407.
Argentine M. Co. *v.* Terrible M. Co.........	1887	122 U. S. 478, 481, 7 Sup. Ct. Rep. 1356, 30 L. Ed. 1140	345, 364, 367, 553, 587, 609.
Argillite Ornamental Stone Co......	1900	29 L. D. 585..........	80, 428, 671.
Argonaut Cons. M. Co. *v.* Turner	1897	23 Colo. 400, 58 Am. St. Rep. 245, 48 Pac. 685.	558, 591, 615.
Argonaut M. Co. *v.* Kennedy M. Co.........	1900	131 Cal. 15, 82 Am. St. Rep. 317, 63 Pac. 148.	319, 365, 574, 576, 577, 582, 595, 604.
Arimond *v.* Green Bay Co......	1872	31 Wis. 316	843.
Armory *v.* Delamirie...	1722	1 Strange, 504, 10 Morr. 62	868.
Armstrong *v.* Caldwell.	1866	53 Pa. St. 284........	812.
Armstrong *v.* Lake Champlain Granite Co.	1895	147 N. Y. 495, 49 Am. St. Rep. 683, 42 N. E. 186	93, 421.

Names of Cases.	When De-cided.	Where Reported.	Sections Where Cited in this Work.
Armstrong v. Larimer Co. Ditch Co........	1891	1 Colo. App. 49, 27 Pac. 235	838.
Armstrong v. Lower...	1882	6 Colo. 393, 395, 15 Morr. 631	294, 322, 337, 345, 403, 408, 615, 755.
Armstrong v. Lower...	1882	6 Colo. 581, 15 Morr. 458.	218, 615, 688.
Arnold, In re.........	1884	2 L. D. 758...........	685.
Arnold v. Stevens......	1839	24 Pick. 106, 35 Am. Dec. 305, 1 Morr. 176.	175, 812.
Arthur v. Earle.......	1895	21 L. D. 92...........	208, 496.
Ashenfelter v. Williams	1896	7 Colo. App. 332, 43 Pac. 664	798.
Ashley v. Port Huron..	1877	35 Mich. 296, 24 Am. Rep. 552	843.
Aspen v. Seddon......	1875	10 L. R. Ch. App. Cases, 394	821.
Aspen Cons. M. Co. v. Williams	1898	27 L. D. 1............	106, 207, 208, 772.
Aspen Cons. M. Co. v. Williams	1896	23 L. D. 34...........	208.
Aspen Cons. M. Co. v. Rucker	1896	28 Fed. 220..........	535, 792.
Aspen Mountain Tunnel Lode No. 1.........	1898	26 L. D. 81...........	679, 759.
Astiazaran v. Santa Rita L. and M. Co........	1893	148 U. S. 80, 30 Sup. Ct. Rep. 457, 37 L. Ed. 376	108, 116.
Astley Coal Co. v. Tyl-desley Coal Co......	1899	68 L. J. Q. B. 252, 80 L. T. 116..........	867.
Atchison v. Peterson...	1872	1 Mont. 561	841, 843.
Atchison v. Peterson...	1874	20 Wall. 507, 22 L. Ed. 214, 1 Morr. 583.....	838, 841.
Atherton v. Fowler....	1878	96 U. S. 513, 24 L. Ed. 732	217, 218.
Atkins v. Hendree.....	1867	1 Idaho, 95, 2 Morr. 328.	58, 362, 413, 557, 572, 632.
Atkinson v. Hewitt.....	1881	51 Wis. 281, 8 N. W. 211	789a.
Attorney-General v. Coun-cil Birmingham	1858	4 Kay, 528............	807.
Attorney-General v. Myl-chreest	1879	4 App. Cas. 294.......	90, 92.
Attorney-General v. Tom-line	1877	L. R. 5 Ch. D. 750.....	92.
Attorney - General v. Welsh Granite Co....	1887	35 W. R. 617..........	90.
Attwood v. Fricot......	1860	17 Cal. 38, 16 Am. Dec. 651, 2 Morr. 328.....	216, 391, 537, 868.
Auerbach, In re.......	1899	29 L. D. 208..........	331, 398.

Names of Cases.	When De-cided.	Where Reported.	Sections Where Cited in this Work.
Aurora Hill Cons. M. Co. *v.* 85 M. Co.....	1887	12 Law. 355, 34 Fed. 515, 15 Morr. 581...	208, 363, 637, 771, 773, 868.
Aurora Lode *v.* Bulger Hill Placer	1896	23 L. D. 95...........	413, 415, 619, 707, 721, 765.
Austin, Newton F., *In re*	1894	18 L. D. 4.............	200.
Austin *v.* Barrett......	1876	44 Iowa, 488..........	788, 790.
Austin *v.* Huntsville C. etc. Co......	1880	72 Mo. 535, 37 Am. Rep. 446, 9 Morr. 115....	868.
Axion M. Co. *v.* White.	1897	10 S. D. 198, 72 N. W. 462	630, 643, 645.
Aye *v.* Philadelphia Co.	1899	193 Pa. St. 451, 74 Am. St. Rep. 696, 44 Atl. 555	862.
Ayres *v.* Daly........	1877	3 Copp's L. O. 196.....	680.
Baca Float No. 3......	1891	13 L. D. 624..........	126.
Baca Float No. 3......	1899	29 L. D. 44...........	126.
Baca Float No. 3......	1901	30 L. D. 497..........	116, 124, 322.
Back *v.* Sierra Nev. Cons. M. Co.........	1888	2 Idaho, 386, 17 Pac. 83.	473, 486, 725.
Backhouse *v.* Bonomi..	1861	9 H. L. Cases, 503, 13 Morr. 677	820, 823.
Bagnall *v.* L. and N. W. Ry. Co..............	1862	7 Hurl. & N. 423, 1 Hurl. & C. 544, 5 Morr. 366	826.
Bahuaud *v.* Bize......	1901	105 Fed. 485	237, 238.
Bailey and Grand View etc Co., *In re*.......	1885	3 L. D. 386..........	677.
Baird *v.* Williamson....	1863	15 Com. B. Rep. N. S. 376, 4 Morr. 368.....	807, 808.
Baker *v.* Jamison......	1893	54 Minn. 17, 55 N. W. 750	143.
Baker *v.* Wheeler......	1832	8 Wend. 505, 24 Am. Dec. 66	868.
Bakersfield Fuel Co. *v.* Saalburg	1902	31 L. D. 312	199.
Baldwin *v.* Starks......	1883	107 U. S. 463, 2 Sup. Ct. Rep. 473, 27 L. Ed. 526	175, 207, 666.
Ballou *v.* Wood.......	1851	8 Cush. 48............	789a.
Baltzell, *In re*........	1899	29 L. D. 333..........	661.
Bankier Distilling Co. *v.* Young	1892	19 R. 1083, 20 R. H. L. 76	841.
Bank of Hartford *v.* Waterman	1857	26 Conn. 324..........	823.

Names of Cases.	When De-cided.	Where Reported.	Sections Where Cited in this Work.
Bannon v. Mitchell....	1880	6 Ill. App. 17, 2 Morr. 108	807.
Barclay v. Commonwealth	1855	25 Pa. St. 503, 64 Am. Dec. 715	840.
Barclay v. Howell's Lessee	1832	6 Pet. 498, 8 L. Ed. 477.	178.
Barclay v. State of California	1888	6 L. D. 699...........	772.
Barden v. Northern Pac. R. R. Co........	1894	154 U. S. 288, 14 Sup. Ct. Rep. 1030, 38 L. Ed. 992	80, 86, 96, 106, 107, 154, 156, 161, 175, 207, 665.
Bardon v. Northern Pac. R. R. Co........	1892	145 U. S. 535, 538, 12 Sup. Ct. Rep. 856, 36 L. Ed. 806..........	80, 112, 181, 322.
Barklage v. Russell....	1900	29 L. D. 401..........	624, 632, 645, 673, 686, 688, 696, 731, 742.
Barnard v. Ashley....	1856	10 How. 43, 15 L. Ed. 285	448, 660, 662.
Barnard v. Shirley....	1893	135 Ind. 547, 41 Am. St. Rep. 454, 34 N. E. 600, 24 L. R. A. 568	840.
Barnard v. Shirley....	1893	(Ind.), 35 N. E. 117, 24 L. R. A. 575......	840.
Barnard v. Shirley....	1897	151 Ind. 160, 47 N. E. 671, 41 L. R. A. 737.	840.
Barnes v. Sabron......	1856	10 Nev. 217, 4 Morr. 673	530, 838.
Barney v. Winona etc. R. R. Co...........	1886	117 U. S. 228, 6 Sup. Ct. Rep. 654, 29 L. Ed. 858	157.
Barnhart v. Campbell..	1872	50 Mo. 597	791.
Barnum v. Landon.....	1856	25 Conn. 137, 14 Morr. 250	789a, 791.
Bartlett v. Prescott....	1860	41 N. H. 493..........	860.
Barton Coal Co. v. Cox.	1873	39 Md. 1, 17 Am. Rep. 545, 10 Morr. 157....	868.
Basey v. Gallagher.....	1874	20 Wall. 670, 22 L. Ed. 452, 1 Morr. 683.....	838, 841.
Bash v. Cascade M. Co.	1902	(Wash.), 69 Pac. 402..	771, 773.
Basin M. and C. Co. v. White	1899	22 Mont. 147, 55 Pac. 1049	644, 671.
Batavia Mfg. Co. v. Newton Wagon Co...	1878	91 Ill. 230.............	840.
Bateman v. Carroll....	1897	24 L. D. 144..........	210.

Names of Cases.	When De-cided.	Where Reported.	Sections Where Cited in this Work.
Battlements Mesa Forest Reserve	1893	16 L. D. 190..........	197.
Baxter Mt. G. M. Co. v. Patterson	1884	3 N. Mex. 179, 3 Pac. 741	383.
Bay State S. M. Co. v. Brown	1884	10 Saw. 243, 21 Fed. 167	227, 755.
Bazemore v. Davis....	1875	55 Ga. 504............	790.
Beals v. Cone.........	1900	27 Colo. 473, 83 Am. St. Rep. 92, 62 Pac. 948.	250, 289, 290a, 293, 294, 330, 335, 343, 344, 345, 374, 405, 624, 643, 645, 686, 697, 772.
Beals v. Cone.........	1903	(U. S.), 23 Sup. Ct. Rep. 275	712, 746.
Beard v. Federy.......	1866	3 Wall 478, 18 L. Ed. 88	125.
Bear River and Auburn Water Co. v. New York M. Co.........	1857	8 Cal. 327, 68 Am. Dec. 325, 4 Morr. 526....	841.
Beatty and Clements...·	1875	2 Copp's L. O. 82.....	759.
Beatty v. Gregory.....	1864	17 Iowa, 109, 85 Am. Dec. 546, 9 Morr. 234.	860.
Beaudette v. N. P. R. R. Co..............	1899	29 L. D. 248..........	95, 97, 139, 158, 421.
Beck v. O'Connor.....	1898	21 Mont. 109, 53 Pac. 94	406, 646.
Becker, In re..........	1878	Copp's L. O. 51.......	708.
Becker v. Central City Townsite	1875	2 Copp's L. O. 98.....	171, 723, 724.
Becker v. Pugh........	1886	9 Colo. 589, 13 Pac. 906, 15 Morr. 304........	398, 755, 763.
Becker v. Pugh........	1892	17 Colo. 243, 29 Pac. 173	271, 755.
Becker v. Sears.......	1883	1 L. D. 575...........	690.
Bedel v. St. Paul M. and M. Co...............	1898	29 L. D. 254..........	107, 157, 159, 162.
Beecher v. Wetherby...	1877	95 U. S. 517, 24 L. Ed. 440	142, 181, 183.
Behrens v. McKenzie..	1867	23 Iowa, 333, 92 Am. Dec. 428	872.
Beik v. Nickerson.....	1900	29 L. D. 662..........	366, 591, 615, 677, 730.
Belcher Cons. G. M. Co. v. Deferrari	1882	62 Cal. 160	274, 408, 645, 651, 652.
Belden v. Hebbard.....	1900	103 Fed. 532..........	382.
Belk v. Meagher.......	1878	3 Mont. 65, 1 Morr. 522.	218, 219, 322, 363, 409, 632, 651, 652.

Names of Cases.	When De-cided.	Where Reported.	Sections Where Cited in this Work.
Belk v. Meagher.......	1881	104 U. S. 279, 26 L. Ed. 739, 1 Morr. 510....	169, 184, 192, 218, 249, 250, 322, 328, 329, 363, 371, 390, 402, 404, 409, 413, 539, 632, 642, 651, 652, 688.
Belknap v. Belknap....	1889	77 Iowa, 71, 41 N. W. 568	789a.
Bell v. Bed Rock H. and M. Co.	1868	36 Cal. 214, 1 Morr. 45.	274, 643, 644.
Bell v. Brown.........	1863	22 Cal. 671, 5 Morr. 540.	643.
Bell v. Hearne........	1857	19 How. 252, 15 L. Ed. 614	662.
Bell v. Love..........	1883	10 Q. B. D. 547........	820.
Bell v. Skillicorn......	1891	6 N. Mex. 399, 28 Pac. 768	551, 615, 866.
Bell v. Wilson.........	1865	2 Drew & S. 395, L. R. 1 Ch. App. 303......	92.
Bellows v. Champion...	1877	4 Copp's L. O. 17......	209.
Benavides v. Hunt.....	1891	79 Tex. 383, 15 S. W. 396	812.
Bennett's Placer, In re.	1884	3 L. D. 116, 11 Copp's L. O. 213...........	97, 139, 210.
Bennett v. Griffiths....	1861	30 L. J. Q. B. 98, 8 Morr. 21	873.
Bennett v. Harkrader..	1895	158 U. S. 441, 15 Sup. Ct. Rep. 863, 39 L. Ed. 1046	381, 415, 718, 721, 754.
Bennett v. Whitehouse.	1860	28 Beav. 119, 8 Morr. 17.	873.
Benson M. and S. Co. v. Alta etc. Co........	1892	145 U. S. 428, 12 Sup. Ct. Rep. 877, 36 L. Ed. 762	208, 542, 637, 771, 773, 868.
Bequette v. Patterson..	1894	104 Cal. 284, 37 Pac. 917	530.
Benton v. Johncox....	1897	17 Wash. 277, 61 Am. St. Rep. 912, 49 Pac. 495, 39 L. R. A. 107..	838.
Berg v. Koegel........	1895	16 Mont. 266, 40 Pac. 605	251.
Bernal v. Hovious.....	1861	17 Cal. 542, 79 Am. Dec. 147	861.
Berry v. Central Pac. R. R. Co.	1892	15 L. D. 463..........	106.
Berry v. Woodburn....	1895	107 Cal. 504, 40 Pac. 802	799, 858.
Bettman v. Harness...	1896	42 W. Va. 433, 26 S. E. 271, 36 L. R. A. 566..	790, 862.
Bewick v. Muir........	1890	83 Cal. 368, 23 Pac. 389.	327.
Biddle Boggs v. Merced M. Co.	1859	14 Cal. 279, 10 Morr. 517	112, 125.

Names of Cases.	When De- cided.	Where Reported.	Sections Where Cited in this Work.
Bigelow *v.* Finch......	1851	11 Barb. 498	540.
Bigelow *v.* Finch......	1853	17 Barb. 394	540.
Billings *v.* Aspen M. Co.	1892	51 Fed. 338, 341......	233, 234.
Billings *v.* Hanver.....	1884	65 Cal. 593, 4 Pac. 639.	238.
Billings *v.* Smelting Co.	1892	52 Fed. 250..........	233, 234.
Bimetallic Lode	1892	15 L. D. 309..........	363, 363a, 366, 615, 671.
Bisbing, Mary E.......	1891	13 L. D. 45...........	200.
Bishop *v.* Baisley......	1895	28 Or. 119, 41 Pac. 936.	629, 643, 652, 872.
Bissell *v.* Foss........	1885	114 U. S. 252, 5 Sup. Ct. Rep. 851, 29 L. Ed. 126	791, 796, 800.
Black *v.* Elkhorn M. Co.	1891	47 Fed. 600...........	543.
Black *v.* Elkhorn M. Co.	1892	49 Fed. 549...........	205, 535, 539, 542.
Black *v.* Elkhorn M. Co.	1892	52 Fed. 859...........	540, 542, 543.
Black *v.* Elkhorn M. Co.	1896	163 U. S. 445, 16 Sup. Ct. Rep. 1101, 41 L. Ed. 21	80, 539, 543, 642, 646, 861.
Blackburn *v.* Portland etc. Co.	1900	175 U. S. 571, 20 Sup. Ct. Rep. 222, 44 L. Ed. 276	746, 747.
Blackmore *v.* Reilly....	1888	(Ariz.), 17 Pac. 72....	170, 177.
Black Queen Loue *v.* Excelsior No. 1 Lode	1896	22 L. D. 343	759.
Blair *v.* Boswell......	1900	37 Or. 168, 61 Pac. 341.	843.
Blake *v.* Butte S. M. Co.	1872	2 Utah, 54, 9 Morr. 503.	560, 567, 726.
Blake *v.* Thorne.......	1888	(Ariz.), 16 Pac. 270...	407.
Blake *v.* Toll..........	1900	29 L. D. 413	739.
Blakesley *v.* Wheeldon.	1841	1 Hare, 176, 8 Morr. 8.	873.
Blakley *v.* Marshall....	1896	174 Pa. St. 425, 34 Atl. 564	789, 859b, 861.
Block *v.* Standard D. and D. Co...........	1899	95 Fed. 978..........	226.
Bluebird M. Co. *v.* Largey	1892	49 Fed. 289..........	294, 313.
Bluebird M. Co. *v.* Murray	1890	9 Mont. 468, 23 Pac. 1022	866, 873.
Blythe, Estate of......	1893	99 Cal. 472, 34 Pac. 108.	764.
Blythe *v.* Hinckley.....	1900	180 U. S. 333, 21 Sup. Ct. Rep. 390, 45 L. Ed. 557	237, 238.
Blythe *v.* Hinckley.....	1898	173 U. S. 501, 19 Sup. Ct. Rep. 497, 43 L. Ed. 783	237, 238.
Bodie Tunnel etc. Co. *v.* Bechtel Cons. M. Co.	1881	1 L. D. 584...........	490, 725, 738, 742.
Boggs *v.* Merced M. Co.	1859	14 Cal. 279, 10 Morr. 517	112, 125.
Bohanon *v.* Howe......	1888	2 Idaho, 417, 17 Pac. 583	233.
Bond *v.* Lockwood.....	1864	33 Ill. 212	789a.

Names of Cases.	When De- cided.	Where Reported.	Sections Where Cited in this Work.
Bond v. State of California	1901	31 L. D. 34	142, 144.
Bonesell v. McNider...	1891	13 L. D. 286	690, 738.
Bonner v. Meikle	1897	82 Fed. 697	170, 216, 336, 366, 589, 723.
Book v. Justice M. Co..	1893	58 Fed. 106	274, 282, 289, 294, 331, 336, 350, 355, 371, 373, 375, 381, 382, 383, 615, 629, 631, 633, 636, 645.
Boston Franklinite Co. v. Condit	1869	19 N. J. Eq. 394, 14 Morr. 301	791, 792.
Boston etc. Co. v. Montana etc. Co.	1898	89 Fed. 529	618.
Botiller v. Dominguez..	1889	130 U. S. 238, 9 Sup. Ct. Rep. 525, 32 L. Ed. 926	117, 123.
Boucher v. Mulverhill..	1871	1 Mont. 306, 12 Morr. 350	796, 858.
Boulder and Buffalo M. Co.	1888	7 L. D. 54, 15 C. L. O. 147	142, 144, 144a.
Bourquin, In re	1898	27 L. D. 280	95, 142, 781.
Bowers v. Keesecker....	1862	14 Iowa, 301	541, 542.
Boyd v. Blankman	1865	29 Cal. 19, 87 Am. Dec. 146	867.
Boyd v. Desrozier	1898	20 Mont. 444, 52 Pac. 53.	872.
Boyd v. Nebraska	1892	143 U. S. 180, 12 Sup. Ct. Rep. 375, 36 L. 103	227, 684.
Boyle v. Wolfe	1898	27 L. D. 572	542.
Bracken v. Rushville...	1866	27 Ind. 346, 3 Morr. 273.	860.
Bradley v. Dells Lumber Co.	1900	105 Wis. 245, 81 N. W. 394	175, 664, 773.
Brady v. Brady	1900	31 Misc. Rep. 411, 65 N. Y. Supp. 621	93, 421.
Brady v. Husby	1893	21 Nev. 453, 33 Pac. 801.	227, 355, 381, 383.
Brady's Mortgagee v. Harris	1899	29 L. D. 89	177, 673, 766.
Brady's Mortgage v. Harris	1900	29 L. D. 426	86, 173, 177, 209.
Bramlett v. Flick	1899	23 Mont. 95, 57 Pac. 869.	328, 339, 355, 381, 382, 383, 389, 390, 539.
Branagan v. Dulaney..	1885	8 Colo. 408, 8 Pac. 669.	558.
Branagan v. Dulaney..	1884	2 L. D. 744, 11 C. L. O. 67	337, 742, 765.
Brandt v. Wheaton....	1877	52 Cal. 430, 1 Morr. 45.	216, 233.
Bray v. Ragsdale	1873	54 Mo. 170	542.
Brennan v. Hume	1889	10 L. D. 160	505.
Bretell v. Swift	1893	16 L. D. 178	685.
Bretell v. Swift	1893	17 L. D. 558	685.

Names of Cases.	When Decided.	Where Reported.	Sections Where Cited in this Work.
Brewster v. Shoemaker.	1900	28 Colo. 176, 63 Pac. 309.	330, 335, 337, 345, 346, 482.
Bright v. Elkhorn M. Co.	1889	9 L. D. 503, 507	692.
Broad Ax Lode	1896	22 L. D. 244	677.
Broder v. Natoma Water Co.	1879	101 U. S. 274, 25 L. Ed. 790, 5 Morr. 33	45, 56, 306, 530, 567, 838.
Brodie G. Red. Co	1899	29 L. 143	524.
Brooks v. Bruyn	1864	35 Ill. 392	536.
Brooks v. Kunkle	1900	24 Ind. App. 624, 57 N. E. 260	862.
Brown, In re	1898	27 L. D. 582	661.
Brown's Trust	1862	11 W. R. 19	92.
Brown v. Bond	1890	11 L. D. 150	737.
Brown v. Bryan	1896	(Idaho), 51 Pac. 995.	800.
Brown v. Campbell	1893	100 Cal. 635, 647, 38 Am. St. Rep. 314, 35 Pac. 433	764.
Brown v. Corey	1862	43 Pa. St. 495, 5 Morr. 368	256.
Brown v. County Commissioners	1853	21 Pa. St. 37	558.
Brown v. Covillaud	1856	6 Cal. 566, 572	859.
Brown v. Hitchcock	1899	173 U. S. 473, 19 Sup. Ct. Rep. 485, 43 L. Ed. 772	664, 772.
Brown v. Levan	1896	(Idaho), 46 Pac. 661	379, 381, 383, 384.
Brown v. Massey	1842	3 Humph. 470	542.
Brown v. Northern Pac. R. R. Co	1901	31 L. D. 29	97, 495.
Brown v. Robins	1859	4 H. & N. 186	820.
Brown v. Spilman	1894	155 U. S. 665, 15 Sup. Ct. Rep. 245, 39 L. Ed. 304	859b.
Brown v. United States.	1885	113 U. S. 568, 5 Sup. Ct. Rep. 648, 28 L. Ed. 1079	96, 419, 666.
Brown v. Vandergrift	1875	80 Pa. St. 147	423.
Brownfield v. Bier	1895	15 Mont. 403, 39 Pac. 461	294, 336, 781.
Brundy v. Mayfield	1895	15 Mont. 201, 38 Pac. 1067	251, 406, 646, 728.
Brunswick v. Winters' Heirs	1885	3 N. Mex. 241, 5 Pac. 706	790.
Bryan v. McCaig	1887	10 Colo. 309, 15 Pac. 413.	343, 629.
Buchanan v. Cole	1894	57 Mo. App. 11	861.
Buckley v. Fox	1902	(Idaho), 67 Pac. 659.	227, 231, 233, 754.
Buena Vista County v. Iowa Falls etc. Co	1884	112 U. S. 165, 5 Sup. Ct. Rep. 84, 28 L. Ed. 680.	663.

Names of Cases.	When De-cided.	Where Reported.	Sections Where Cited in this Work.
Buffalo Zinc etc. Co. v. Crump	1902	(Ark.), 69 S. W. 572, 576	293, 383, 643, 644, 645, 651, 688. 721.
Buhne v. Chism	1874	48 Cal. 467	143.
Bullard v. Flanagan	1890	11 L. D. 515	504.
Bulli Coal M. Co. v. Osborne	1899	App. Cas. 1899, p. 351.	867.
Bullion B. and C. M. Co. v. Eureka Hill M. Co.	1886	5 Utah, 3, 11 Pac. 515, 15 Morr. 449	294, 364, 583.
Bullion M. Co. v. Crœsus etc. Co	1866	2 Nev. 168, 178, 90 Am. Dec. 526, 5 Morr. 254.	612, 616.
Bullock v. Rouse	1889	81 Cal. 590, 22 Pac. 919.	448.
Bunker Hill Co. v. Pascoe	1901	(Utah), 66 Pac. 574	407.
Bunker Hill etc. M. Co. v. Empire etc. Co.	1901	106 Fed. 471, 472	218, 363, 364, 583.
Bunker Hill etc. Co. v. Empire State etc. Co.	1900	108 Fed. 189	596, 783.
Bunker Hill etc. Co. v. Empire State etc. Co.	1901	109 Fed. 538	175, 218, 312a, 319, 363, 363a, 367, 582, 596, 713, 727, 742, 783.
Bunker Hill etc. Co. v. Empire State etc. Co.	1902	186 U. S. 482, 22 Sup. Ct. Rep. 941, 46 L. Ed. 1260	583.
Burfenning v. Chicago-St. Paul Ry.	1896	163 U. S. 321, 16 Sup. Ct. Rep. 1018, 41 L. Ed. 175	143, 779.
Burgan v. Lyell	1851	2 Mich. 102, 55 Am. Dec. 53, 11 Morr. 287	801.
Burgess, In re	1897	24 L. D. 11	507.
Burgess v. Gray	1853	16 How. 48, 14 L. Ed. 839	216.
Burke v. Bunker Hill etc. Co.	1891	46 Fed. 644	746.
Burke v. McDonald	1887	2 Idaho, 310, 13 Pac. 351	294.
Burke v. McDonald	1890	2 Idaho, 646, 33 Pac. 49	335, 336, 362, 372, 754, 755, 763.
Burke v. McDonald	1892	2 Idaho, 1022, 29 Pac. 98	336.
Burns v. Clark	1901	133 Cal. 634, 85 Am. St. Rep. 233, 66 Pac. 12	216.
Burnside v. O'Connor	1899	29 L. D. 301	741.
Burrell, In re	1899	29 L. D. 328	501.
Burton, In re	1899	29 L. D. 235	523, 725, 741, 759.

Names of Cases.	When De-cided.	Where Reported.	Sections Where Cited in this Work.
Busby v. Holthaus.....	1870	46 Mo. 161............	833.
Busch v. Donohue......	1875	31 Mich. 482	542.
Bush v. Sullivan.......	1851	3 G. Greene, 344, 54 Am. Dec. 506	860.
Buskirk v. King.......	1896	72 Fed. 22	872.
Butler v. Hinckley.....	1892	17 Colo. 523, 527, 30 Pac. 250	799.
Butte & Boston M. Co.	1895	21 L. D. 125..........	177, 413, 720, 784.
Butte City Smokehouse Lode Cases	1887	6 Mont. 397, 12 Pac. 858.	169, 170, 171, 177, 604, 609, 722, 783.
Butte City Townsite...	1876	3 Copp's L. O. 114, 131	171.
Butte etc. Cons. M. Co. v. Montana O. P. Co.	1900	24 Mont. 125, 60 Pac. 1039	790.
Butte etc. Cons. M. Co. v. Montana O. P. Co.	1901	63 Pac. 825	790.
Butte etc. M. Co. v. Société Anonyme des Mines	1899	23 Mont. 177, 75 Am. St. Rep. 505, 58 Pac. 111, 113	364, 614, 615, 618.
Butte etc. M. Co. v. Sloan	1895	16 Mont. 97, 40 Pac. 217.	126, 161.
Butte etc. Ry. Co. v. Montana U. Ry. Co..	1898	16 Mont. 504, 50 Am. St. Rep. 508, 41 Pac. 232, 31 L. R. A. 298......	253, 259a.
Butte Hardware Co. v. Frank	1901	25 Mont. 344, 65 Pac. 1.	535, 642, 719, 789a.
Buttz v. Northern Pac. R. R. Co...........	1886	119 U. S. 55, 7 Sup. Ct. Rep. 100, 30 L. Ed. 330	181, 183.
Buxton v. Traver......	1889	130 U. S. 232, 9 Sup. Ct. Rep. 509, 32 L. 920.	170, 216.
Bybee v. Hawkett.....	1882	12 Fed. 649, 11 Morr. 594	798.
Byrne v. Slauson......	1895	20 L. D. 43	677.
Byrnes v. Douglass....	1897	83 Fed. 45	258.
Cabathuler, John......	1892	15 L. D. 418..........	200.
Caha v. United States..	1894	152 U. S. 211, 14 Sup. Ct. Rep. 513, 38 L. Ed. 415	472, 662.
Cahill v. Eastman.....	1872	18 Minn. 324, 10 Am. Rep. 184	808.
Cahn v. Barnes........	1881	5 Fed. 326............	662.
Cain v. Addenda M. Co.	1897	24 L. D. 18..........	755.
Cain v. Addenda M. Co.	1899	29 L. D. 62..........	632, 679, 696, 712, 731, 742, 755.
Caldwell v. Bush......	1896	6 Wyo. 342, 45 Pac. 488.	207, 208, 637, 772.

Names of Cases.	When De-cided.	Where Reported.	Sections Where Cited in this Work.
Caldwell v. Copeland...	1860	37 Pa. St. 427, 78 Am. Dec. 436, 1 Morr. 189.	812.
Caldwell v. Fulton.....	1858	31 Pa. St. 475, 72 Am. Dec. 760, 3 Morr. 238.	175, 812, 860.
Caldwell v. Gold Bar M. Co.	1897	24 L. D. 258..........	204, 208.
Caledonia G. M. Co. v. Noonan	1882	3 Dak. 189, 14 N. W. 426	184.
Caledonia M. Co. v. Rowen	1883	2 L. D. 714..........	106.
Caledonian R. R. Co. v. Sprot	1856	2 Jurist N. S. 623, 2 Macq. H. L. Cas. 449.	833.
Caley v. Coggswell.....	1899	12 Colo. App. 394, 55 Pac. 939	797, 799.
Calhoun G. M. Co. v. Ajax G. M. Co.......	1899	27 Colo. 1, 59 Pac. 607, 612, 83 Am. St. Rep. 17, 50 L. R. A. 209..	58, 59, 71, 252, 363, 419, 481, 490a, 550, 558, 615, 666, 780, 783, 866.
Calhoun G. M. Co. v. Ajax G. M. Co.......	1901	182 U. S. 499, 21 Sup. Ct. Rep. 885, 45 L. Ed. 1200	69, 71, 252, 363, 481, 490a, 550, 558, 561, 780, 783.
California and Oregon R. R. Co..........	1893	16 L. D. 262.........	156.
California Oil etc. Co. v. Miller	1899	96 Fed. 12	746, 754.
California Redwood Co. v. Litle	1897	79 Fed. 854	772.
Calvert v. Aldrich.....	1868	99 Mass. 74, 96 Am. Dec. 693	790.
Cameron, In re........	1886	4 L. D. 515	687.
Cameron, In re........	1890	10 L. D. 195.........	502.
Cameron Lode	1891	13 L. D. 369.........	173, 177.
Cameron v. United States	1892	148 U. S. 301, 13 Sup. Ct. Rep. 595, 37 L. Ed. 459	112, 123, 322.
Campbell v. Bear River etc. Co.............	1868	35 Cal. 679, 10 Morr. 656	808.
Campbell v. Ellet......	1897	167 U. S. 116, 17 Sup. Ct. Rep. 765, 42 L. Ed. 101	69, 482, 491, 550, 725.
Campbell v. Rankin....	1897	99 U. S. 261, 25 L. Ed. 435, 12 Morr. 257...	216, 272.

Names of Cases.	When Decided.	Where Reported.	Sections Where Cited in this Work.
Campbell v. Wade.....	1889	132 U. S. 34, 10 Sup. Ct. Rep. 9, 33 L. Ed. 240	205, 216, 542.
Camp Bowie Reservation	1879	7 Copp's L. O. 4.......	192.
Cape May etc. Co. v. Wallace	1898	27 L. D. 676..........	413, 415, 720, 742.
Capner v. Flemington M. Co.	1836	3 N. J. Eq. 467.......	789.
Capricorn Placer, In re.	1890	10 L. D. 641..........	684.
Carli v. Union Depot R. R. Co.	1884	32 Minn. 101, 20 N. W. 89	844.
Carlin v. Chappel......	1882	101 Pa. St. 348, 47 Am. Rep. 722	819.
Carls Hildt	1899	28 L. D. 194	200.
Carlyon v. Lovering....	1857	1 Hurl. & N. 784, 26 L. J. Exch. 251, 14 Morr. 397	839, 843.
Carney v. Arizona G. M. Co.	1884	65 Cal. 40, 2 Pac. 734..	625.
Carothers v. Philadelphia Co.....	1888	118 Pa. St. 468, 12 Atl. 314	255.
Carr v. Fife...........	1895	156 U. S. 494, 15 Sup. Ct. Rep. 427, 39 L. Ed. 508	665.
Carr v. Quigley........	1893	149 U. S. 652, 13 Sup. Ct. Rep. 961, 37 L. Ed. 885	124, 183.
Carrasco v. State......	1885	67 Cal. 385, 7 Pac. 766.	238.
Carroll v. Safford......	1845	3 How. 441, 11 L. Ed. 440	208, 542.
Carrie S. G. M. Co.....	1899	29 L. D. 287..........	365, 763.
Carson v. Geutner.....	1898	33 Or. 512, 52 Pac. 506, 43 L. R. A. 130......	838.
Carson v. Hayes.......	1901	39 Or. 97, 65 Pac. 814.	843.
Carson City etc. Co. v. Fitzgerald	1848	4 Morr. Min. Rep. 380, Fed. Cas. No. 8158..	615.
Carson City etc. M. Co. v. North Star M. Co..	1896	73 Fed. 597..........	318, 365, 567, 574, 576, 592, 604, 666, 671, 778.
Carson City etc. M. Co. v. North Star M. Co..	1898	83 Fed. 658	44, 58, 365, 567, 604, 671, 778, 866.
Carter v. Bacigalupi...	1890	83 Cal. 187, 23 Pac. 261.	273, 350, 351, 355, 381, 383.
Carter v. Page........	1844	4 Ired. 424..........	860.
Carter v. Thompson....	1894	65 Fed. 329	107, 126, 161, 175.
Casey v. Northern Pac. R. R. Co.............	1892	15 L. D. 439..........	95.

Names of Cases.	When Decided.	Where Reported.	Sections Where Cited in this Work.
Casey v. Thieviege.....	1897	19 Mont. 341, 61 Am. St. Rep. 511, 48 Pac. 394	781.
Cash Lode	1874	1 Copp's L. O. 97.....	227, 232.
Cassell v. Crothers	1899	193 Pa. St. 359, 44 Atl. 446	862.
Castello v. Bonnie.....	1896	23 L. D. 162..........	772.
Castillero v. United States	1863	2 Black, 17, 17 L. Ed. Ed. 360	17, 114, 119, 125.
Castle v. Womble......	1894	19 L. D. 455..........	95, 336.
Castner, In re.........	1893	17 L. D. 565...........	671.
Castro v. Barry.......	1889	79 Cal. 443, 21 Pac. 946.	754.
Castro v. Hendricks....	1859	23 How. 438, 16 L. Ed. 576	123.
Catholic Bishop etc. v. Gibbon	1895	158 U. S. 155, 15 Sup. Ct. Rep. 779, 39 L. Ed. 931	665.
Catlin Coal Co. v. Lloyd	1898	176 Ill. 275, 52 N. E. 144	812.
Catron v. Lewisohn....	1896	23 L. D. 20...........	759.
Catron v. Old.........	1897	23 Colo. 455, 48 Am. St. Rep. 256, 48 Pac. 687.	584, 593, 594, 615.
Cavanah, In re........	1880	8 Copp's L. O. 5.......	671.
Cecil v. Clark.........	1900	47 W. Va. 402, 81 Am. St. Rep. 802, 35 S. E. 11	789a, 792.
Cedar Canyon Cons. M. Co. v. Yarwood......	1902	(Wash.), 67 Pac. 749..	330, 335, 788.
Central City Townsite..	1877	2 Copp's L. O. 150....	171.
Central Pac. R. R. Co. v. Mammoth Blue Gravel	1874	1 Copp's L. O. 134....	155.
Central Pac. R. R. Co. v. Valentine	1890	11 L. D. 238, 246.....	155.
Chadwick v. Tatem....	1890	9 Mont. 354, 23 Pac. 729	543.
Chaffee, J. B., In re...	1872	Copp's U. S. Min. Dec. 144	473.
Challiss v. Atchison Union Depot	1891	45 Kan. 398, 25 Pac. 894	178.
Chamberlain v. Bell....	1857	7 Cal. 292, 68 Am. Dec. 260	392.
Chambers v. Harrington	1884	111 U. S. 350, 4 Sup. Ct. Rep. 428, 28 L. Ed. 452	45, 56, 192, 306, 539, 542, 624, 630, 631, 754.
Chambers v. Jones.....	1895	17 Mont. 156, 42 Pac. 758	170, 175, 177, 777.
Chambers v. Pitts......	1876	3 Copp's L. O. 162....	737.
Champion M. Co., In re	1886	4 L. D. 362...........	670.

Names of Cases.	When De- cided.	Where Reported.	Sections Where Cited in this Work.
Champion M. Co. *v.* Consolidated Wyoming M. Co........	1888	75 Cal. 78, 16 Pac. 513. 16 Morr. 145.......	583, 614, 730, 742, 777, 783.
Chandler *v.* State of California	1896	(Not reported)	138, 422.
Chapman *v.* Quinn.....	1880	56 Cal. 266...........	472, 662.
Chapman *v.* Toy Long..	1876	4 Saw. 28, Fed. Cas. No. 2610, 1 Morr. 497.	218, 233, 329, 542, 872.
Chappell *v.* Waterworth	1894	155 U. S. 102, 15 Sup. Ct. Rep. 34, 39 L. Ed. 35	747.
Charles *v.* Eshleman...	1879	5 Colo. 107, 2 Morr. 65.	790, 791, 796, 801.
Charles *v.* Rankin......	1856	22 Mo. 566, 66 Am. Dec. 642	833.
Chartiers Block Coal Co. *v.* Mellon	1893	152 Pa. St. 286, 295, 34 Am. St. Rep. 645, 25 Atl. 597	596, 812, 827.
Chase *v.* Savage.......	1866	2 Nev. 9, 9 Morr. 476..	790.
Cheeney *v.* Nebraska etc. Co.	1890	41 Fed. 740.........	868.
Cheesman *v.* Hart......	1890	42 Fed. 98, 12 Morr.263.	381, 551, 615, 866.
Cheesman *v.* Shreve....	1889	37 Fed. 36, 16 Morr. 79.	551, 615, 866, 872.
Cheesman *v.* Shreeve...	1889	40 Fed. 787	282, 290, 290a, 293, 294, 337, 343, 392, 398, 615, 866, 868.
Cheney *v.* Ricks.......	1900	187 Ill. 171, 58 N. E. 234	789a.
Cherokee Nation *v.* Georgia	1831	5 Peters, 1, 8 L. Ed. 25.	181.
Chessman's Placer	1883	2 L. D. 774...........	629, 631.
Chicago *v.* Huenerbein..	1877	85 Ill. 544, 28 Am. Dec. 626	844.
Chicago and Alton R. R. Co. *v.* Brandau......	1899	81 Mo. App. 1........	823.
Chicago etc. R. R. Co. *v.* Whitton	1871	13 Wall. 270, 20 L. Ed. 571	226.
Chicago Q. M. Co. *v.* Oliver	1888	75 Cal. 194, 7 Am. St. Rep. 143, 16 Pac. 780.	161.
Chief Moses Indian Reservation	1882	9 Copp's L. O. 189....	185.
Childers *v.* Neely......	1899	47 W. Va. 70, 81 Am. St. Rep. 777, 34 S. E. 828	796, 797, 800, 803.
Childs *v.* Kansas City R. R. Co.	1891	(Mo.), 17 S. W. 954...	790.
Chollar Potosi etc. Co. *v.* Julia etc. Co........	1873	Copp's Min. Lands, 93; Copp's Min. Dec. 101.	730.
Chormicle *v.* Hiller....	1898	26 L. D. 9............	208, 210.

Names of Cases.	When De-cided.	Where Reported.	Sections Where Cited in this Work.
Chouteau v. Eckhart....	1844	2 How. 344, 11 L. Ed. 343	116.
Chung Kee v. Davidson	1894	102 Cal. 188, 36 Pac.519.	799.
Church of Holy Communion v. Paterson Extension Co........	1901	66 N. J. L. 218, 49 Atl. 1030	823.
Churchill v. Anderson..	1878	53 Cal. 212	143.
City of Leadville v. Colorado M. Co.........	1901	(Colo.), 67 Pac. 289...	178.
City of Leadville v. St. Louis etc. Co........	1902	(Colo.), 67 Pac. 1126...	178.
City of South Bend v. Paxon	1879	67 Ind. 228...........	844.
City of Valparaiso v. Hagen	1899	153 Ind. 337, 74 Am. St. Rep. 305, 54 N. E. 1062	840.
City Rock and Utah v. Pitts	1874	1 Copp's L. O. 146....	227, 684, 734, 737.
Clark v. American Flag G. M. Co...........	1879	7 Copp's L. O. 5......	632.
Clark v. Ervin........	1893	16 L. D. 122..........	139, 210, 421.
Clark v. Ervin........	1893	17 L. D. 550..........	210.
Clark v. Fitzgerald.....	1898	171 U. S. 92, 18 Sup. Ct. Rep. 941, 43 L. Ed. 87.	364, 584, 591.
Clark's Pocket Quartz Mine	1898	27 L. D. 351..........	227, 631, 671, 684.
Clark v. Vermont and C. R. R. Co...........	1855	28 Vt. 103	813.
Clary v. Hazlitt.......	1885	67 Cal. 286, 7 Pac. 701.	125, 413.
Clearwater Shortline Ry. Co. v. San Garde	1900	(Idaho), 61 Pac. 137..	380, 381, 384.
Cleary v. Skiffich......	1901	28 Colo. 362, 65 Pac. 59.	94, 95, 98, 207, 363, 521, 524, 525, 688.
Clegg v. Dearden......	1848	12 Q. B. 576, 8 Morr. 88.	807.
Cleghorn v. Bird.......	1886	4 L. D. 478...........	207.
Cleveland v. Eureka No. 1 etc. M. Co........	1901	31 L. D. 69...........	624, 632, 686, 696, 731, 742.
Clifton Iron Co. v. Dye.	1888	87 Ala. 468, 6 South. 192	842.
Clipper M. Co., In re..	1896	22 L. D. 527..........	697, 721, 759.
Clipper M. Co. v. Eli M. Co.	1902	(Colo.), 68 Pac. 289...	413, 697, 722, 781.
Clute v. Carr.........	1866	20 Wis. 531, 91 Am. Dec. 442	860.
Coal Creek M. etc. Co. v. Moses	1885	15 Lea, 300, 54 Am. Rep. 415, 15 Morr. 544...	868.
Cobb, In re...........	1902	31 L. D. 220..........	199.
Cobb v. Fisher........	1876	121 Mass. 160........	860.
Coffee v. Emigh.......	1890	15 Colo. 184, 25 Pac. 83, 10 L. R. A. 125.....	553.

Names of Cases.	When De-cided.	Where Reported.	Sections Where Cited in this Work.
Coffin, *In re*	1902	31 L. D. 252	197.
Coffin v. Left Hand Ditch Co.	1882	6 Colo. 443	838.
Coffin v. Loper	1875	25 N. J. Eq. 443	789a.
Cole v. Markley	1883	2 L. D. 847	106, 513, 515.
Coleman, *In re*	1874	1 Copp's L. O. 34	631.
Coleman's Appeal	1869	62 Pa. St. 252, 14 Morr. 221	789a, 792.
Coleman v. Chadwick	1875	80 Pa. St. 81, 21 Am. Rep. 93	814, 818.
Coleman v. Coleman	1852	19 Pa. St. 100, 57 Am. Dec. 641, 11 Morr. 183.	535, 792.
Coleman v. Curtis	1892	12 Mont. 301, 30 Pac. 266	635, 636.
Coleman v. Homestake M. Co.	1900	30 L. D. 364	406, 728, 755.
Coleman v. McKenzie	1899	28 L. D. 348	204, 208, 216, 644.
Coleman v. McKenzie	1899	29 L. D. 359	204, 208, 216, 405, 542, 645, 689, 697.
Colgan v. Forest Oil Co.	1899	194 Pa. St. 234, 75 Am. St. Rep. 695, 45 Atl. 119	862.
Collins v. Bartlett	1872	44 Cal. 371	409.
Collins v. Bubb	1896	73 Fed. 735	184.
Coleman v. Clements	1863	23 Cal. 245, 5 Morr. 247.	272, 643, 645.
Colomokas Gold M. Co.	1899	28 L. D. 172	200.
Colorado Cent. C. M. Co. v. Turck	1892	50 Fed. 888	364, 367, 610, 611.
Colorado Cent. C. M. Co. v. Turck	1893	54 Fed. 267	364, 367.
Colorado Cent. C. M. Co. v. Turck	1895	70 Fed. 294	868.
Colorado Coal and Iron Co. v. United States.	1887	123 U. S. 307, 8 Sup. Ct. Rep. 131, 31 L. Ed. 182	94, 127, 142, 176, 209, 496, 784.
Colorado E. Ry Co. v. Union Pac. Ry. Co.	1890	41 Fed. 293	256.
Colton, *In re*	1890	10 L. D. 422	507.
Columbus Hocking Coal etc. Co. v. Tucker	1891	48 Ohio St. 41, 29 Am. St. Rep. 528, 26 N. E. 630	840, 843.
Colvin v. Johnson	1848	2 Barb. 206	540.
Colvin v. McCune	1874	39 Iowa, 502, 1 Morr. Min. Rep. 223	688.
Comitis v. Parkerson	1893	56 Fed. 556	224.
Commissioners of Kings County v. Alexander.	1886	5 L. D. 126	496.
Conant, *In re*	1900	29 L. D. 637	507.
Conant v. Smith	1826	1 Aikens (Vt.), 67, 15 Am. Dec. 669, 11 Morr. 199	792.

Names of Cases.	When De-cided.	Where Reported.	Sections Where Cited in this Work.
Condon v. Mammoth M. Co........	1892	15 L. D. 330..........	685.
Cone v. Jackson.......	1899	12 Colo. App. 461, 55 Pac. 940	759.
Cone v. Roxana G. M. and T. Co..........	1899	2 Legal Adv. 350 (C. C. Dist Colo.).......	80, 249, 252, 263, 322, 490a.
Congdŏn v. Olds.......	1896	18 Mont. 487, 46 Pac. 261	796, 801.
Conger v. Weaver.....	1856	6 Cal. 548, 65 Am. Dec. 528	539.
Connell, In re.........	1900	29 L. D. 574..........	365.
Conlin v. Kelly........	1891	12 L. D. 1...........	97, 139, 158, 210, 421.
Conner v. Terry.......	1892	15 L. D. 310..........	501.
Connole v. Boston etc. S. M. Co...........	1898	20 Mont. 523, 52 Pac. 263	790.
Consolidated Channel Co. v. C. P. R. R. Co.	1876	51 Cal. 269, 5 Morr. 438	263.
Consolidated Coal Co. v. Peers	1894	150 Ill. 344, 37 N. E. 937	861.
Consolidated M. Co., In re	1890	11 L. D. 250..........	363.
Consolidated Repub. M. Co. v. Lebanon M. Co.	1886	9 Colo. 343, 12 Pac. 212, 15 Morr. 490........	623.
Consolidated Wyoming G. M. Co. v. Champion M. Co..............	1894	63 Fed. 540..........	294, 318, 365, 551, 567, 574, 576, 584, 591, 593, 604, 614, 615, 773, 780, 866.
Continental Divide M. Co. v. Bliley........	1896	23 Colo. 160, 46 Pac. 633	800.
Continental G. and S. M. Co..............	1890	10 L. D. 534..........	632.
Contra Costa R. R. Co. v. Moss	1863	23 Cal. 323..........	256.
Contreras v. Merck....	1900	131 Cal. 211, 63 Pac. 336	643, 754.
Conway, In re.........	1899	29 L. D. 388..........	763, 765.
Conway v. Hart.......	1900	129 Cal. 480, 62 Pac. 44.	273, 405, 408.
Cook v. McCord.......	1899	9 Okl. 200, 60 Pac. 497.	665.
Cook v. Stearns.......	1814	11 Mass. 534..........	860.
Cooke v. Blakely......	1897	6 Kan. App. 707, 50 Pac. 981	665.
Cooper v. Roberts.....	1855	18 How. 173, 15 L. Ed. 338	127, 136, 142.

Names of Cases.	When Decided.	Where Reported.	Sections Where Cited in this Work.
Coosaw M. Co. v. South Carolina	1892	144 U. S. 550, 12 Sup. Ct. Rep. 689, 36 L. Ed. 537	428.
Cope v. Braden	1901	(Okl.), 67 Pac. 475...	108.
Copper Glance Lode...	1900	29 L. D. 542	629, 630, 631, 671, 673.
Copper Globe M. Co. v. Allman	1901	(Utah), 64 Pac. 1019.	249, 329, 330, 335, 336.
Copper King Ltd. v. Wabash M. Co	1902	114 Fed. 991	872.
Cornelius v. Kessel....	1888	128 U. S. 456, 9 Sup. Ct. Rep. 122, 32 L. Ed. 482	208, 662, 771, 772.
Corning Tunnel Co. v. Pell	1878	4 Colo. 507, 14 Morr. 612	473, 484, 725.
Corning Tunnel Co. v. Pell	1876	3 Copp's L. O. 130....	473, 490.
Cornwall v. Culver.....	1860	16 Cal. 429	123.
Correction Lode	1892	15 L. D. 67	363.
Cosgriff v. Dewey	1900	164 N. Y. 1, 79 Am. St. Rep. 620, 58 N. E. 1.	789a.
Cosmopolitan M. Co. v. Foote	1900	101 Fed. 518	364, 367, 589, 594.
Cosmos Exploration Co. v. Gray Eagle Oil Co	1900 / 1901	104 Fed. 20 / 112 Fed. 4	86, 106, 108, 142, 143, 161, 199, 207, 208, 209, 216, 217, 336, 437, 472, 772, 779.
Coster v. Tide Water Co.	1866	18 N. J. Eq. 54, 63....	254.
Couch v. Welsh	1901	(Utah), 66 Pac. 600...	861.
County of Kern v. Lee	1900	129 Cal. 361, 61 Pac. 1124	273, 389.
County of Sutter v. Johnson	1902	(Cal.)	853.
County of Yuba v. Cloke	1889	79 Cal. 239, 21 Pac. 740.	849.
Court, In re	1900	29 L. D. 638	197.
Courtnay v. Turner....	1877	12 Nev. 345	233.
Cowell v. Lammers....	1884	10 Saw. 246, 21 Fed. 200	106, 107, 126, 127, 142, 156, 161, 207, 217.
Cowles v. Huff	1897	24 L. D. 81	772.
Cox, In re	1902	31 L. D. 193	322.
Cox v. Glue	1848	5 C. B. 549	9,
Cox v. Mathews	1872	1 Vent. 237	833.
Cox v. McGarrahan....	1870	9 Wall. 298, 19 L. Ed. 579	207.
Craig v. Leitensdorfer.	1887	123 U. S. 189, 8 Sup. Ct. Rep. 85, 31 L. Ed. 114.	660.
Craig v. Radford	1818	3 Wheat. 594, 4 L. Ed. 467	232.
Craig v. Thompson....	1887	10 Colo. 517, 526, 16 Pac. 24	330, 346, 390, 398.

Names of Cases.	When Decided.	Where Reported.	Sections Where Cited in this Work.
Cram, George A., *In re*	1892	14 L. D. 514..........	200.
Crane *v.* Winsor.......	1877	2 Utah, 248, 11 Morr. 69.	841.
Crane's Gulch Placer M. Co. *v.* Scherrer...	1901	134 Cal. 350, 86 Am. St. Rep. 279, 66 Pac. 487.	72, 208, 604, 637, 771.
Cravens *v.* Moore......	1875	61 Mo. 178..........	542.
Craw *v.* Wilson........	1895	22 Nev. 385, 40 Pac. 1076	797.
Crawford *v.* Ritchey...	1897	43 W. Va.‑ 252, 27 S. E. 220	862.
Credo M. and S. Co. *v.* Highland etc. Co....	1899	95 Fed. 911..........	362, 373, 383, 396.
Crest *v.* Jack.........	1834	3 Watts, 238, 27 Am. Dec. 353	790.
Creswell M. Co. *v.* Johnson	1889	8 L. D. 440, 15 C. L. O. 24	94.
Cripple Creek etc. Co. *v.* Mt. Rosa etc. Co....	1898	26 L. D. 622..........	413, 720, 781.
Crocker *v.* Donovan....	1892	1 Okl. 165, 30 Pac. 374.	205.
Crœsus M. and M. Co. *v.* Colorado L. and M. Co.	1894	19 Fed. 78...........	232, 233, 373, 374.
Cronin *v.* Bear Creek M. Co.....	1893	32 Pac. (Idaho) 204...	754.
Crossman *v.* Pendery...	1881	8 Fed. 693, 2 McCrary, 139, 4 Morr. 431.....	216, 218, 335, 339.
Crow Indian Reservation	1879	Copp's Min. Lands, 236.	184.
Crowder, *In re*........	1900	30 L. D. 92...........	198, 495.
Crown Point M. Co. *v.* Buck	1899	97 Fed. 462..........	218, 337, 338, 363, 373, 448b, 550.
Crown Point G. M. Co. *v.* Crismon	1901	39 Or. 364, 65 Pac. 87..	330, 372, 373, 645, 651, 654.
Crumbie *v.* Wallsend Local Board	1891	L. R. 1 Q. B. 503......	823.
Crutsinger *v.* Catron...	1848	10 Humph. 24........	542.
Cullacott *v.* Cash G. S. M. Co...........	1884	8 Colo. 179, 6 Pac. 211, 15 Morr. 392........	382.
Cullen *v.* Rich........	1741	Bull N. C. 102, 2 Strange, 1142	9.
Cunningham, *In re*....	1883	10 Copp's L. O. 206...	728.
Currans *v.* Williams' Heirs	1895	20 L. D. 109..........	542.
Currency M. Co. *v.* Bentley	1897	10 Colo. App. 271, 50 Pac. 920	763, 765.
Currie *v.* State of California	1895	21 L. D. 134..........	197.
Curtis *v.* La Grande Water Co......	1890	20 Or. 34, 23 Pac. 808, 25 Pac. 378, 10 L. R. A. 484	838.

Names of Cases.	When De- cided.	Where Reported.	Sections Where Cited in this Work.
Cutting v. Reininghaus.	1888	7 L. D. 265	94.
Cyprus Millsite, In re.	1888	6 L. D. 706	524, 708.
Dahl v. Montana C. Co.	1889	132 U. S. 264, 10 Sup. Ct. Rep. 97, 33 L. Ed. 325	107, 226.
Dahl v. Raunheim	1889	132 U. S. 260, 10 Sup. Ct. Rep. 74, 33 L. Ed. 324, 16 Morr. 214...	107, 126, 161, 177, 413, 539, 720, 742, 773.
Dakota Cent R. R. Co. v. Downey	1899	8 L. D. 115	153.
Dall v. Confidence S. M. Co.	1868	3 Nev. 531, 93 Am. Dec. 419, 11 Morr. 214...	535, 792.
Dand v. Kingscote	1840	6 M. and W. 174	813.
Darger v. Le Sieur	1892	8 Utah, 160, 30 Pac. 363	379.
Darger v. Le Sieur	1893	9 Utah, 192, 33 Pac. 701	379.
Dargin v. Koch	1895	20 L. D. 384	208.
Dark v. Johnson	1867	55 Pa. St. 164, 93 Am. Dec. 732, 9 Morr. 283.	860.
Darley Main Colliery Co. v. Mitchell	1886	L. R. 11 App. Cas. 127.	823.
Dartt, In re	1879	5 Copp's L. O. 178....	142.
Darvill v. Roper	1855	3 Drewry, 294, 10 Morr. 406	88.
Daugherty v. Marcuse.	1859	3 Head, 323	542.
David Foot Lode	1898	26 L. D. 196	637.
Davidson v. Bordeaux	1895	15 Mont. 245, 28 Pac. 1075	336, 636.
Davidson v. Calkins...	1899	92 Fed. 230	535, 539, 754, 773.
Davidson v. Eliza G. M. Co.	1899	28 L. D. 224	690.
Davidson v. Eliza G. M. Co.	1899	29 L. D. 550	677, 690, 738.
Davidson v. Thompson.	1871	22 N. J. Eq. 83	789a.
Davis, In re	1900	30 L. D. 220	128.
Davis v. Butler	1856	6 Cal. 510, 1 Morr. 7..	643.
Davis v. Getchell	1862	50 Me. 60, 79 Am. Dec. 636	840.
Davis v. Weibbold....	1891	139 U. S. 507, 11 Sup. Ct. Rep. 628, 35 L. Ed. 238	80, 86, 94, 127, 142, 170, 171, 175, 176, 177, 207, 216, 336, 438, 609 777.
Dayton G. and S. M. Co. v. Seawell	1876	11 Nev. 394, 5 Morr. 424	269, 264.
Dean v. Thwaite	1855	21 Beav. 621, 1 Morr. 77.	867.

Names of Cases.	When Decided.	Where Reported.	Sections Where Cited in this Work.
Dearden, *In re*	1890	11 L. D. 351	501.
De Camp *v.* Hibernia R. R. Co	1885	47 N. J. L. 43, 47	256.
Dech's Appeal	1868	57 Pa. St. 467	790.
Decker *v.* Howell	1872	42 Cal. 636, 11 Morr. 492	799, 801.
Deeney *v.* Mineral Creek M. Co	1902	(N. Mex.), 67 Pac. 724.	339, 353, 355, 379, 384, 754, 759.
Deffeback *v.* Hawke	1885	115 U. S. 392, 401, 6 Sup. Ct. Rep. 95, 29 L. Ed. 423	47, 62, 86, 94, 125, 142, 168, 169, 170, 171, 176, 208, 209, 216, 336, 409, 637, 771, 783.
De Garcia *v.* Eaton	1896	22 L. D. 16	757.
De Haro *v.* United States	1867	5 Wall. 599, 18 L. Ed. 861	860.
De la Croix *v.* Chamberlain	1827	12 Wheat. 599, 6 L. Ed. 741	116.
De Lamar's Nevada G. M. Co. *v.* Nesbitt	1900	177 U. S. 523, 20 Sup. Ct. Rep. 715, 44 L. Ed. 872	746.
Delaney, *In re*	1893	17 L. D. 120	97, 210, 421.
Delaware and Hudson Canal Co. *v.* Hughes.	1897	183 Pa. St. 66, 63 Am. St. Rep. 743, 38 Atl. 568, 38 L. R. A. 826.	812.
Delaware and Hudson Canal Co. *v.* Lee	1849	22 N. J. L. 243	823.
Delaware and Hudson Canal Co. *v.* Wright	1848	21 N. J. L. 469	823.
Delaware etc. R. R. Co. *v.* Sanderson	1885	109 Pa. St. 583, 58 Am. Rep. 743, 1 Atl. 394	812, 861.
Dellapiazza *v.* Foley	1896	112 Cal. 380, 44 Pac. 727	801.
Del Monte M. Co. *v.* Last Chance M. Co	1897	171 U. S. 55, 18 Sup. Ct. Rep. 895, 43 L. Ed. 72	1, 2, 4, 9, 13, 45, 53, 56, 58, 59, 60, 71, 218, 312a, 327, 350, 363, 364, 365, 366, 367, 538, 550, 568, 572, 573, 574, 576, 581, 582, 583, 584, 586, 587, 589, 591, 592, 595, 596, 610, 611, 628, 780.

Names of Cases.	When De-cided.	Where Reported.	Sections Where Cited in this Work.
Del Monte M. etc. Co. v. New York and Last Chance M. Co.......	1895	66 Fed. 212...........	583, 591, 592, 596.
De Long v. Hill.......	1882	9 Copp's L. O. 1114...	677.
De Merle v. Matthews.	1864	26 Cal. 455...........	233.
Deno v. Griffin........	1889	20 Nev. 249, 20 Pac. 308.	208, 604, 609, 637, 737, 759, 771, 773, 783.
De Moon v. Morrison..	1890	83 Cal. 163, 23 Pac. 374, 16 Morr. 33	630, 631.
Denys v. Shuchburgh..	1840	4 Y & C. Eq. Ex. 42...	790, 867.
Depuy v. Williams.....	1864	26 Cal. 310, 5 Morr. 251.	274, 623.
Derry v. Ross.........	1881	5 Colo. 295, 1 Morr. 1..	643, 862.
Desloge v. Pearce......	1866	38 Mo. 588, 9 Morr. 247.	860.
Des Moines v. Hall....	1868	24 Iowa, 234.........	178.
Detlor v. Holland......	1898	57 Ohio St. 492, 49 N. E. 690, 40 L. R. A. 266	93, 97, 138, 422, 862.
Devereux v. Hunter....	1890	11 L. D. 214.........	679.
Dewey, In re..........	1882	9 Copp's L. O. 51......	97, 138, 422.
Dibble v. Castle Chief G. M. Co...........	1897	9 S. Dak. 618, 70 N. W. 1055	643, 645.
Dickinson v. Capen....	1892	14 L. D. 426.........	496.
Dieckman v. Good Re-turn M. Co..........	1887	14 Copp's L. O. 237..	735.
Diller v. Hawley.......	1897	81 Fed. 651, 653......	665, 772.
Dilling v. Murray.....	1855	6 Ind. 324, 63 Am. Dec. 385	840.
Dillingham v. Fisher...	1856	5 Wis. 475	542.
Dillon v. Bayliss.......	1891	11 Mont. 171, 27 Pac. 725	227, 379, 383.
Dimick v. Shaw.......	1899	94 Fed. 266	872.
Discovery Placer v. Mur-ray	1897	25 L. D. 460.........	718, 720, 781.
Dixon v. Caledonian and Glasgow Ry. Co.....	1880	L. R. 5 App. C. 820....	92.
Dixon v. White........	1883	10 L. R. App. Cases, 833.	827.
Dobb's Placer	1883	1 L. D. 567...........	106.
Dodge, In re..........	1897	6 Copp's L. O. 122....	671.
Dodge v. Davis........	1892	85 Iowa, 77, 52 N. W. 2.	790.
Dodge v. Marden......	1879	7 Or. 456, 1 Morr. 63..	643, 644.
Doe v. Robertson......	1826	11 Wheat. 332, 6 L. Ed. 488	233.
Doe v. Sanger.........	1890	83 Cal. 203, 23 Pac. 363.	364, 365, 396, 574, 582, 671.
Doe v. Tyler M. Co....	1887	73 Cal. 21, 14 Pac. 375.	373.
Doe v. Waterloo M. Co.	1890	43 Fed. 219...........	754.
Doe v. Waterloo M. Co.	1893	54 Fed. Rep. 935.......	1, 69, 290, 337, 365, 396, 413, 551, 552, 582, 612. 617, 618a, 671, 866.
Doe v. Waterloo M. Co.	1893	55 Fed. 11............	339, 372, 379.

Names of Cases.	When De-cided.	Where Reported.	Sections Where Cited in this Work.
Doe *v.* Waterloo M. Co.	1895	70 Fed. 455	226, 272, 339, 355, 372, 373, 419, 643.
Doe *v.* Wood..........	1819	2 B. & Ald. 182........	860.
Doherty *v.* Morris.....	1888	11 Colo. 12, 16 Pac. 911.	406, 729.
Doherty *v.* Morris.....	1891	17 Colo. 105, 28 Pac. 85.	629, 631.
Dolles *v.* Hamberg Cons. M. Co............	1896	23 L. D. 267..........	630, 633.
Doloret *v.* Rothschild..	1824	1 Sim. & Sut. 590, 598..	859.
Donahue *v.* Meister....	1891	88 Cal. 121, 22 Am. St. Rep. 283, 25 Pac. 1096	271, 356, 371, 754.
Donovan *v.* Cons. Coal Co.	1900	187 Ill. 28, 79 Am. St. Rep. 206, 58 N. E. 290	868.
Doolan *v.* Carr........	1887	125 U. S. 618, 8 Sup. Ct. Rep. 1228, 31 L. Ed. 844	123.
Doon *v.* Tesh..........	1901	131 Cal. 406, 63 Pac. 764	759, 764.
Doran *v.* Central Pac. R. R. Co...........	1864	24 Cal. 246............	21, 153, 536.
Dorsey *v.* Newcomer...	1898	121 Cal. 213, 53 Pac. 557	802.
Dougherty *v.* Chestnut..	1887	86 Tenn. 1, 5 S. W. 444.	868.
Dougherty *v.* Creary...	1866	30 Cal. 291, 89 Am. Dec. 116, 1 Morr. 35.....	426, 790, 797, 801.
Dower *v.* Richards.....	1887	73 Cal. 477, 480, 15 Pac. 105	415, 531.
Dower *v.* Richards.....	1894	151 U. S. 658, 14 Sup. Ct. Rep. 452, 38 L. Ed. 305	142, 176, 336.
Downey *v.* Rogers.....	1883	2 L. D. 707..........	138, 422, 756.
Downs, *In re*..........	1888	7 L. D. 71, 15 C. L. O. 147	94, 631.
Drake *v.* Earhart......	1890	2 Idaho, 716, 23 Pac. 541	838, 841.
Drake *v.* Lady Ensly Coal etc. Co........	1893	102 Ala. 501, 48 Am. St. Rep. 77, 14 South. 749, 24 L. R. A. 64..	840.
Draper *v.* Wills........	1897	25 L. D. 550...........	672, 673, 677, 738. 772.
Drew *v.* Comisky......	1896	22 L. D. 174..........	772.
Dreyfus *v.* Badger.....	1895	108 Cal. 58, 41 Pac. 279.	107, 161.
Driscoll *v.* Dunwoody..	1888	7 Mont. 394, 16 Pac. 726	866.
Drown *v.* Smith.......	1862	52 Me. 141...........	789a.
Drummond *v.* Long....	1887	9 Colo. 538, 13 Pac. 543.	371, 379.
Dubuque *v.* Maloney...	1859	9 Iowa, 450...........	178.
Duchess of Cleveland *v.* Meyrick	1867	16 W. R. 104, 37 L. J. Ch. 125	92.

Names of Cases.	When De-cided.	Where Reported.	Sections Where Cited in this Work.
Ducie v. Ford	1888	8 Mont. 233, 19 Pac. 414.	233, 754.
Duffield v. Michaels....	1900	102 Fed. 820	862.
Dufrene v. Mace's Heirs	1900	30 L. D. 216..........	208.
Dugdale v. Robertson..	1857	3 Kay & J. 795, 13 Morr. 662	818.
Duggan v. Davey......	1886	4 Dak. 110, 26 N. W. 887	282, 309, 310, 317, 318, 551, 866, 873.
Dughi v. Harkins......	1883	2 Land Dec. 721......	94, 95, 106, 207, 438, 496.
Duke of Buccleuch v. Cowan	1876	2 App. Cases, 344......	839.
Dunluce Placer Mine..	1888	6 L. D. 761..........	424.
Duncan v. Fulton......	1900	(Colo. App.), 61 Pac. 244	380, 381, 383, 397, 398.
Dunderberg v. Old.....	1897	79 Fed. 588..........	60.
Dunham v. Kirkpatrick	1882	101 Pa. St. 36, 47 Am. Rep. 696	93, 138, 422.
Dunlap v. Pattison....	1895	(Idaho), 42 Pac. 504..	251, 331, 385.
Du Prat v. James......	1884	65 Cal. 555, 4 Pac. 562, 15 Morr. 341........	218, 373, 405, 624, 629, 645.
Durango etc. Co., In re	1894	18 L. D. 382..........	501.
Durango Land etc. Co. v. Evans	1897	80 Fed. 425..........	666, 772.
Durant v. Comegys....	1891	2 Idaho, 936, 28 Pac. 425	859.
Durant M. Co. v. Percy Cons. M. Co........	1899	93 Fed. 166..........	868.
Durgan v. Redding....	1900	103 Fed. 914.........	724, 754.
Durrant v. Corbin.....	1899	94 Fed. 382..........	450.
Durrell v. Abbott.....	1896	6 Wyo. 265, 44 Pac. 647	754.
Duryea v. Boucher.....	1885	67 Cal. 141, 7 Pac. 421.	381.
Duryea v. Burt.......	1865	28 Cal. 569, 11 Morr. 395	797, 800, 801, 802.
Dutch Flat W. Co. v. Mooney	1859	12 Cal. 534, 6 Morr. 303.	268, 270, 272.
Duxie Lode	1898	27 L. D. 88..........	338.
Eads v. Retherford....	1887	114 Ind. 273, 5 Am. St. Rep. 611, 16 N. E. 587.	646.
Eagle Salt Works.....	1877	Copp's Min. Lands, 336, 5 C. L. O. 4....	97, 513.
Earl of Rosse v. Wainman	1845	14 M. & W. 859, 10 Morr. Min. Rep. 398.	92, 93.
Early v. Friend.......	1860	16 Gratt. 21, 78 Am. Dec. 649, 14 Morr. 271.	790.

lxxiv TABLE OF CASES.

Names of Cases.	When Decided.	Where Reported.	Sections Where Cited in this Work.
East Jersey Iron Co. *v.* Wright	1880	32 N. J. Eq. 248, 9 Morr. 332	860.
East Lake Land Co. *v.* Brown	1894	155 U. S. 488, 15 Sup. Ct. Rep. 357, 39 L. Ed. 233	747.
Eaton *v.* Norris.......	1901	131 Cal. 561, 63 Pac. 856	373.
Eberle *v.* Carmichael...	1895	8 N. Mex. 169, 42 Pac. 95	249, 630, 631, 858.
Eccles Commrs. *v.* N. E. Ry. Co..............	1877	L. R. 4 Ch. D. 845, 12 Morr. 609	868.
Eclipse G. and S. M. Co. *v.* Spring	1881	59 Cal. 304...........	58, 350, 560, 567, 604, 726.
Eclipse Millsite	1896	22 L. D. 496........	523, 708.
Edgewood R. R. Co.'s Appeal	1875	79 Pa. St. 257, 5 Morr. 406	256, 261.
Edsall *v.* Merrill......	1883	37 N. J. Eq. 114, 117..	789a.
Edwards *v.* Allouez M. Co......	1878	38 Mich. 46, 31 Am. Rep. 301, 7 Morr. 577.	843.
Edwards *v.* McClurg...	1883	39 Ohio St. 41.......	859b.
Ege *v.* Kille..........	1877	84 Pa. St. 333, 10 Morr. 212	868.
Eilers *v.* Boatman.....	1884	3 Utah, 159, 2 Pac. 66, 15 Morr. 462	218, 367, 373, 865.
Eilers *v.* Boatman.....	1884	111 U. S. 356, 4 Sup. Ct. Rep. 432, 28 L. Ed. 454, 15 Morr. 471...	373, 383.
Eiseman, *In re*........	1890	10 L. D. 539..........	501.
Elda etc. M. Co.......	1899	29 L. D. 279..........	95, 106, 205, 207, 392, 679.
Elda M. etc. Co. *v.* Mayflower G. M. Co.....	1898	26 L. D. 573.........	415, 720.
Elder *v.* Horseshoe M. Co........ ....'	1897	9 S. D. 636, 70 N. W. 1060, 62 Am. St. Rep. 895	646.
Elder *v.* Horseshoe M. Co......	1901	(S. Dak), 87 N. W. 586.	646.
Elder *v.* Lykens Valley Coal Co............	1893	157 Pa. St. 490, 37 Am. St. Rep. 742, 27 Atl. 545	840.
Electro Magnetic M. and D. Co. *v.* Van Auken.	1887	9 Colo. 204, 11 Pac. 80.	346.
Eley's Appeal	1883	103 Pa. St. 300.......	861.
Elk *v.* Wilkins........	1884	112 U. S. 94, 5 Sup. Ct. Rep. 41, 28 L. Ed. 643.	224.

Names of Cases.	When Decided.	Where Reported.	Sections Where Cited in this Work.
Elk Fork etc. Gas Co. v. Jennings	1898	84 Fed. 839	862.
Ellet v. Campbell	1893	18 Colo. 510, 33 Pac. 521	481, 482, 484, 725.
Ellinghouse v. Taylor	1897	19 Mont. 462, 48 Pac. 757	253, 259a.
Elliott v. Figg	1881	59 Cal. 117	542.
Elliott v. Fitchburg R. R. Co	1852	10 Cush. 191, 57 Am. Dec. 85	840.
Elliott v. Whitmore	1892	8 Utah, 253, 30 Pac. 984.	838.
Ellison, In re	1899	29 L. D. 250	677.
Elwell v. Burnside	1865	44 Barb. 447	789a.
Emblen, In re	1895	161 U. S. 52, 16 Sup. Ct. Rep. 487, 40 L. Ed. 613	664.
Emblen v. Lincoln Land Co	1899	94 Fed. 710	663.
Emblen v. Lincoln Land Co	1900	102 Fed. 559	663.
Emblen v. Lincoln Land Co	1902	184 U. S. 660, 22 Sup. Ct. Rep. 523, 46 L. Ed. 736	664.
Emerson v. McWhirter	1901	133 Cal. 510, 65 Pac. 1036	274, 629, 643, 645, 651, 652.
Emery Co. v. Lucas	1873	112 Mass. 424	859a, 859b.
Emily Lode	1887	6 L. D. 220, 14 C. L. O. 209	629, 631.
Emperor Wilhelm Lode	1887	5 L. D. 685	677.
Empey, In re	1883	10 Copp's L. O. 102	362, 671.
Empire G. M. Co. v. Bonanza G. M. Co	1885	67 Cal. 406, 7 Pac. 810.	868.
Empire M. and M. Co. v. Tombstone etc Co	1900	100 Fed. 910	360, 586, 589.
Empire etc. Co. v. Bunker Hill etc. Co	1902	114 Fed. 417	218, 319, 363, 363a, 364, 365, 583, 596, 615, 727, 742, 783.
Engineer etc. Co	1884	8 L. D. 361	363.
English v. Johnson	1890	17 Cal. 108, 76 Am. Dec. 574, 12 Morr. 202	216, 272, 274, 537, 631.
Enterprise M. Co. v. Rico-Aspen Cons. M. Co	1895	66 Fed. 200	473, 481, 488, 491, 558, 725.
Enterprise M. Co. v. Rico-Aspen M. Co	1897	167 U. S. 108, 17 Sup. Ct. Rep. 762, 42 L. Ed. 96	481, 489, 725.
Equator M. and S. Co	1875	2 Copp's L. O. 114	718, 738.
Erhardt v. Boaro	1881	8 Fed. 692, 4 Morr. 432.	339, 634.

Names of Cases.	When De-cided.	Where Reported.	Sections Where Cited in this Work.
Erhardt v. Boaro	1885	113 U. S. 527, 5 Sup. Ct. Rep. 560, 28 L. Ed. 1113, 15 Morr. 472	250, 268, 335, 336, 339, 343, 344, 345, 355, 356, 362, 372, 373, 379, 405, 542, 634, 872.
Erie Lode v. Cameron Lode	1890	10 L. D. 655	685.
Errington v. Met. Ry. Co.	1882	L. R. 19 Ch. D. 559, 571	92.
Erwin v. Perigo	1899	93 Fed. 608	328, 330, 335, 337, 338, 742.
Esler v. Townsite of Cooke	1885	4 L. D. 212	171.
Esmond v. Chew	1860	15 Cal. 137, 5 Morr. 175.	841, 843.
Esperance M. Co	1884	10 Copp's L. O. 338	448.
Ester v. Townsite of Cooke	1885	4 L. D. 212	723.
Etling v. Potter	1893	17 L. D. 424	106, 335.
Eureka and Try Again Lodes	1899	29 L. D. 158	184.
Eureka Cons. M. Co. v. Richmond M. Co	1877	4 Saw. 302, Fed. Cas. No. 4548, 9 Morr. Min. Rep. 578	43, 58, 282, 286, 350, 364, 365, 567, 573, 576, 604, 609, 617, 742, 783.
Eureka M. Co. v. Jenny Lind M. Co	1873	Copp's Min. Dec. 169, 170	690.
Eureka M. Co. v. Pioneer Cons. M. Co	1881	8 Copp's L. O. 106	730.
Evans v. Consumer's Gas etc. Co	1891	(Ind.), 29 N. E. 398, 31 L. R. A. 673	862.
Evans v. Randall	1876	3 Copp's L. O. 2	765.
Fail v. Goodtitle	1826	Breese (Ill.), 201	773.
Fairbank v. United States	1901	181 U. S. 283, 21 Sup. Ct. Rep. 648, 45 L. Ed. 862	419, 666.
Fairbanks v. Woodhouse	1856	6 Cal. 434, 12 Morr. 86.	272.
Fairchild v. Fairchild	1887	(Pa.), 12 Atl. 74	861.
Fairfax v. Hunter	1813	7 Cranch, 603, 3 L. Ed. 453	232, 233.
Fallbrook Irrigation District v. Bradley	1896	164 U. S. 112, 17 Sup. Ct. Rep. 56, 41 L. Ed. 369	254, 257.

Names of Cases.	When De-cided.	Where Reported.	Sections Where Cited in this Work.
Farmington G. M. Co. v. Rhymney etc. Co..	1899	20 Utah, 363, 77 Am. St. Rep. 913, 58 Pac. 832	355, 381, 373, 383, 392.
Farnum v. Platt.......	1829	8 Pick. (Mass.), 338, 19 Am. Dec. 330, 8 Morr. 330	813.
Farr, In re...........	1897	24 L. D. 1.............	124.
Farrand v. Marshall...	1855	21 Barb. 409..........	832.
Farrand v. Gleason....	1884	56 Vt. 633............	790.
Faulds v. Yates.......	1870	57 Ill. 416, 11 Am. Rep. 24, 3 Morr. 551......	802.
Faxon v. Barnard.....	1880	4 Fed. 702, 9 Morr. 515.	218, 322, 330, 379, 390.
Felger v. Coward......	1868	35 Cal. 652..........	270, 642.
Fenn v. Holme........	1858	21 How. 481, 483, 16 L. Ed. 198..........	773.
Ferguson v. Belvoir Mill Co.............	1892	14 L. D. 43..........	632.
Ferguson v. Hanson...	1895	21 L. D. 336..........	677.
Ferguson v. Neville....	1882	61 Cal. 356..........	233.
Ferrell v. Hoge.......	1894	18 L. D. 81...........	438.
Ferrell v. Hoge.......	1894	19 L. D. 568..........	438.
Ferrell v. Hoge.......	1898	27 L. D. 129..........	438.
Ferrell v. Hoge.......	1899	29 L. D. 12...........	95, 438, 442.
Ferris v. Coover......	1858	10 Cal. 589..........	123, 642.
Ferris v. Montgomery etc. Co......	1891	94 Ala. 557, 33 Am. St. Rep. 146, 10 South. 607	789a.
Field v. Beaumont.....	1818	1 Swanst. 204, 7 Morr. 257	790.
Field v. Grey.........	1881	(Ariz.), 25 Pac. 793...	339.
Figg v. Handley......	1877	52 Cal. 295..........	208, 637.
Filmore v. Reithman...	1881	6 Colo. 120..........	792.
Findlay v. Smith......	1818	6 Munf. 134, 8 Am. Dec. 733, 13 Morr. 182....	789.
Finn v. Hoyt..........	1892	52 Fed. 83	161.
Finney v. Berger......	1875	50 Cal. 248	142.
Firmstone v. Wheeley..	1844	2 Dowling & L. (Q. B.), 203, 12 Morr. 76.....	807.
First Nat. Bank v. Bis-sell	1880	4 Fed. 694, 2 McCrary, 73	791, 800.
First Nat. Bk. etc. v. G. V. B. M. Co........	1898	89 Fed. 449..........	790, 797.
Fishbourne v. Hamilton	1890	L. R. 25 Q. R. 483.....	92.
Fisher v. Seymour.....	1897	23 Colo. 542, 49 Pac. 30.	322, 335, 397, 398, 407.
Fissure M. Co. v. Old Susan M. Co........	1901	22 Utah, 438, 63 Pac. 587	381, 383, 631.

Names of Cases.	When De-cided.	Where Reported.	Sections Where Cited in this Work.
Fitten, *In re*..........	1900	29 L. D. 451, 453......	428.
Fitzgerald *v.* Clark....	1895	17 Mont. 100, 52 Am. St. Rep. 665, 42 Pac. 273, 30 L. R. A. 803.	584, 591, 868.
Fitzpatrick *v.* Montgom-ery	1897	20 Mont. 181, 63 Am. St. Rep. 622, 50 Pac. 416	841, 843.
Flavin *v.* Mattingly...	1888	8 Mont. 242, 19 Pac. 384	381, 383.
Flagstaff Case	1871	Copp's Min. Dec. 61...	59.
Flagstaff S. M. Co. *v.* Tarbet	1879	98 U. S. 463, 25 L. Ed. 253, 9 Morr. 607.....	13, 60, 318, 364, 365, 367, 586, 591, 610.
Flaherty *v.* Gwinn....	....	1 Dak. 509, 12 Morr. 605	268, 270, 272, 274.
Fleetwood Lode	1891	12 L. D. 604.........	142, 144, 144a.
Fleming *v.* Daly.......	1899	12 Colo. App. 439, 55 Pac. 946	345, 346.
Fletcher *v.* Peck......	1810	6 Cranch, 87, 147, 3 L. Ed. 87	181.
Fletcher *v.* Smith.....	1877	2 L. R. App. Cases, 781, 7 L. R. Exch. 305, 5 Morr. 78	808.
Fletcher *v.* Rylands....	1866	1 L. R. Ex. 265........	808.
Fletcher *v.* Rylands....	1877	3 L. R. H. L. 330.....	808.
Flick *v.* Gold Hill M. Co........	1889	8 Mont. 298, 20 Pac. 807	227, 392.
Florida Central and Penn. Ry. Co........	1898	26 L. D. 600..........	97, 136, 152, 158, 425.
Florida Cent. etc. R. R. Co. *v.* Bell.........	1900	176 U. S. 321, 20 Sup. Ct. Rep. 399, 44 L. Ed. 486.............	747.
Floyd *v.* Montgomery..	1898	26 L. D. 122..........	629, 630, 661, 673, 772.
Foley *v.* Wyeth.......	1861	2 Allen, 131, 132, 79 Am. Dec. 771.......	832.
Folsom, *In re*.........	1890	16 Copp's L. O. 279...	630.
Foote, *In re*..........	1883	2 L. D. 773..........	670.
Foote *v.* National M. Co.	1876	2 Mont. 402, 9 Morr. 605	294, 309, 346.
Forbes *v.* Gracey......	1877	94 U. S. 762, 24 L. Ed. 313, 14 Morr. 183...	535, 538, 539, 642.
Ford *v.* Knapp........	1884	31 Hun, 522..........	790.
Forsyth *v.* Wells......	1861	41 Pa. St. 291, 80 Am. 617, 14 Morr. 493....	868.
Forsythe *v.* Weingart..	1898	27 L. D. 680..........	97, 139, 158, 210, 420, 421.

Names of Cases.	When Decided.	Where Reported.	Sections Where Cited in this Work.
Fort Maginnis.........	1881	1 L. D. 552, 8 Copp's Land O. 137.........	191.
Foster, In re..........	1883	2 L. D. 730, 10 C. L. O. 341	507.
Foster v. Elk Fork Oil etc. Co..............	1898	90 Fed. 178, 32 C. C. A. 560	802.
Four Twenty M. and M. Co. v. Bullion M. Co.	1866	2 Copp's L. O. 5.......	755.
Four Twenty M. and M. Co. v. Bullion M. Co.	1874	9 Nev. 240, 1 Morr. 114.	748, 754.
Four Twenty M. and M. Co. v. Bullion M. Co.	1876	3 Saw. 634, Fed. Cas. No. 4989, 11 Morr. 608	688, 754, 792.
Fox v. Mutual etc. Co..	1901	31 L. D. 59...........	644.
France v. Connor......	1896	161 U. S. 65, 16 Sup. Ct. Rep. 497, 40 L. Ed. 619	544.
France v. Connor.....	1891	3 Wyo. 445, 27 Pac. 569	544.
Franchi, In re........	1884	3 L. D. 229...........	136.
Frank G. and S. M. Co. v. Larimer	1881	8 Fed. 724, 1 Morr. 150.	746.
Franklin Coal Co. v. McMillan	1878	49 Md. 549, 33 Am. Rep. 280, 10 Morr. 224...	868.
Franklin M. Co. v. O'Brien	1896	22 Colo. 129, 55 Am. St. Rep. 118, 43 Pac. 1016.	788.
Francoeur v. Newhouse.	1889	40 Fed. 618...........	154, 160.
Francoeur v. Newhouse.	1890	43 Fed. 238...........	154.
Frasher v. O'Connor...	1885	115 U. S. 102, 5 Sup. Ct. Rep. 1141, 29 L. Ed. 311	143.
Freeman, In re........	1879	7 Copp's L. O. 4......	522.
Frees v. State of Colorado	1896	22 L. D. 510..........	496.
Freezer v. Sweeney....	1889	8 Mont. 508, 21 Pac. 20.	96, 97, 210, 273. 421, 454.
Fremont v. Flower....	1861	17 Cal. 199, 79 Am. Dec. 123, 12 Morr. 418...	80, 114, 115, 125, 126, 609.
Fremont v. United States	1855	17 How. 442, 15 L. Ed. 248	125.
French v. Brewer......	1861	3 Wall. Jr. 346, Fed. Cas. No. 5096, 11 Morr. 108	175.
French v. Fyan.......	1876	93 U. S. 169, 23 L. Ed. 812	161.
French v. Lancaster...	1880	2 Dak. 346, 47 N. W. 395	184.
Frisbie v. Whitney....	1870	9 Wall. 187, 19 L. Ed. 668	192, 205, 216, 542.

Names of Cases.	When De-cided.	Where Reported.	Sections Where Cited in this Work.
Frisholm v. Fitzgerald.	1898	25 Colo. 290, 53 Pac. 1109	397, 398.
Frost v. Spitley	1887	121 U. S. 552, 7 Sup. Ct. Rep. 1129, 30 L. Ed. 1010	754.
Fuhr v. Dean	1857	26 Mo. 116, 69 Am. Dec. 484, 6 Morr. 216	860.
Fuller v. Harris	1887	29 Fed. 814	273.
Fuller v. Swan River etc. Co	1888	12 Colo. 12, 14, 19 Pac. 836, 16 Morr. 252	843.
Fulmer's Appeal	1889	128 Pa. St. 24, 15 Am. St. Rep. 662, 18 Atl. 493	789a.
Funk v. Haldeman	1866	53 Pa. St. 229, 7 Morr. 203	93, 859a, 860.
Funk v. Sterrett	1881	59 Cal. 613	373, 754, 755.
Gaffney v. Turner	1900	29 L. D. 470	624, 632, 686, 772.
Gage v. Gunther	1902	136 Cal. 338, 68 Pac. 710	664, 666.
Gaines v. Thompson	1869	7 Wall. 347, 19 L. Ed. 62	207.
Gale v. Best	1889	78 Cal. 235, 12 Am. St. Rep. 44, 20 Pac. 550.	107, 126, 161.
Galey v. Kellerman	1889	123 Pa. St. 491, 16 Atl. 474	862.
Galt v. Galloway	1830	4 Pet. 332, 7 L. Ed. 876.	783.
Gamer v. Glenn	1889	8 Mont. 371, 20 Pac. 654.	381, 383.
Ganssen v. Morton	1830	10 B. & C. 731	860.
Gardner v. Bonestell	1891	180 U. S. 362, 21 Sup. Ct. Rep. 399, 45 L. Ed. 574	665.
Garfield M. and M. Co. v. Hammer	1889	6 Mont. 53, 8 Pac. 153.	227, 249, 329, 371, 379, 643.
Garland v. Towne	1874	55 N. H. 57, 20 Am. Rep. 164	808.
Garrard v. Silver Peak Mines	1897	82 Fed. 578	97, 112, 136, 143, 161, 175, 199, 382, 513, 778, 779.
Garrard v. Silver Peak Mines	1899	94 Fed. 983	97, 136, 143, 161, 513, 778, 779.
Garthe v. Hart	1887	73 Cal. 541, 15 Pac. 93, 15 Morr. 492	218, 270, 322, 363, 642.
Gary v. Todd	1894	18 L. D. 59, S. C. 19 L. D. 414	97, 425.
Gates v. Salmon	1868	35 Cal. 588, 95 Am. Dec. 139	791.

Names of Cases.	When De-cided.	Where Reported.	Sections Where Cited in this Work.
Gatewood v. McLaughlin	1863	23 Cal. 178, 13 Morr. 387	270.
Gaved v. Martyn	1865	19 C. B. N. S. 732	839.
Geissler, In re	1898	27 L. D. 515	513, 514.
Gelcich v. Moriarity	1878	53 Cal. 217, 9 Morr. 498.	373.
General v. Tomline	1877	L. R. 5 Ch. D. 750	90.
Genet v. Delaware etc. Co	1893	136 N. Y. 593, 23 N. E. 1078, 19 L. R. A. 127.	861.
Gentry, Josiah, In re	1882	9 Copp's L. O. 5	158.
George, In re	1875	2 Copp's L. O. 114	521.
Gerhauser, In re	1888	7 L. D. 390	672.
Germania Fire Ins. Co. v. Francis	1870	78 U. S. 210	226.
Germania Ins. Co. v. Hayden	1895	21 Colo. 127, 40 Pac. 453	208.
Germania Iron Co. v. James	1897	82 Fed. 807	772.
Germania Iron Co. v. James	1898	89 Fed. 811	204, 472, 658, 659, 660, 664, 666.
Germania Iron Co. v. United States	1897	165 U. S. 379, 17 Sup. Ct. Rep. 337, 41 L. Ed. 754	772, 784.
Gesner v. Cairns	1853	2 Allen (N. B.), 595	97, 860.
Gesner v. Gas Co	1853	1 James N. S. 72	97.
Gibbs v. Guild	1882	9 Q. B. Div. 67	867.
Gibson, In re	1895	21 L. D. 327	139, 141.
Gibson v. Chouteau	1872	13 Wall. 92, 20 L. D. 534	80, 175, 216, 249.
Gibson v. Puchta	1867	33 Cal. 310, 12 Morr. 227	537.
Gibson v. Tyson	1836	5 Watts, 35, 13 Morr. 72.	93.
Gill v. Weston	1885	110 Pa. St. 313, 1 Atl. 921	93, 97, 138, 422.
Gillan v. Hutchinson	1860	16 Cal. 154, 2 Morr. 317.	218, 537.
Gillett v. Gaffney	1877	3 Colo. 351	792.
Gillett v. Treganza	1858	6 Wis. 343	860.
Gillis v. Downey	1898	85 Fed. 483	539, 632, 696, 731, 754, 773.
Gillis v. Downey	1899	29 L. D. 83	673, 712.
Gilmore v. Driscoll	1877	122 Mass. 199, 23 Am. Rep. 312, 14 Morr. 37.	832, 833.
Gilpin v. Sierra Nevada Cons. M. Co	1890	2 Idaho, 662, 675, 23 Pac. 547, 1014	310, 312, 318, 872.
Gilpin County M. Co. v. Drake	1886	8 Colo. 586, 589, 9 Pac. 787	371, 379, 383.
Girard v. Carson	1896	22 Colo. 345, 44 Pac. 508	337, 338, 742, 755.

Names of Cases.	When Decided.	Where Reported.	Sections Where Cited in this Work.
Gird v. California Oil Co.	1894	60 Fed. 531, 532......	97, 138, 218, 271, 273, 350, 355, 356, 371, 373, 422, 450, 629, 630, 631, 755.
Giroux v. Scheurman...	1896	23 L. D. 546..........	739.
Glacier Mt. S. M. Co. v. Willis	1888	127 U. S. 471, 8 Sup. Ct. Rep. 1214, 32 L. Ed. 173	45, 272, 362, 481, 489.
Glasgow v. Chartiers Gas Co.............	1892	152 Pa. St. 48, 25 Atl. 232	862.
Glasgow and S. W. Ry. Co. v. Bain.........	1893	21 R. 134.............	92.
Glass v. Basin M. and C. Co...............	1899	22 Mont. 151, 55 Pac. 1047	252, 253.
Gleeson v. Martin White M. Co..............	1878	13 Nev. 442, 9 Morr. 529	71, 81, 271, 272, 312, 329, 339, 350, 355, 371, 372, 373, 379, 383, 396.
Godfrey v. Beardsley..	1841	2 McLean, 412, Fed. Case No. 5497	181.
Golden and Cord Mining Claims	1901	31 L. D. 187..........	630, 646, 728.
Gold Blossom Q. M., In re	1882	2 L. D. 767............	637, 742.
Golden Canal Co. v. Bright	1884	8 Colo. 144, 6 Pac. 142..	838.
Golden etc. M. Claims..	1901	31 L. D. 178..........	646.
Golden Fleece G and S. M. Co. v. Cable Cons. Co.	1877	12 Nev. 312, 1 Morr. 120	45, 58, 227, 233, 234, 271, 272, 273, 339, 372, 373, 379, 392, 576, 646, 748, 754, 755.
Golden Link M. L. and B. Co.	1899	29 L. D. 384..........	337, 568.
Golden Reward M. Co. v. Buxton M. Co.....	1897	79 Fed. 868..........	362, 582, 671, 713, 742, 778.
Golden Reward M. Co. v. Buxton M. Co.....	1899	97 Fed. 413..........	868.
Golden Sun M. Co......	1888	6 L. D. 808, 15 C. L. O. 85	671.
Golden Terra M. Co. v. Smith	1881	2 Dak. 374, 462, 11 N. W. 98	184.

Names of Cases.	When Decided.	Where Reported.	Sections Where Cited in this Work.
Golden Terra M. Co. v. Mahler	1879	(Dak.) 4 Morr. Min. Rep. 390	184, 294, 330, 335, 336, 337.
Gold Hill etc. M. Co., In re	1889	16 Copp's L. O. 110	681, 684.
Gold Hill Q. M. Co. v. Ish	1873	5 Or. 104, 11 Morr. 635	106, 161, 192, 209, 539, 542.
Goldsmith v. Tunbridge Wells Impt. Co	1866	L. R. 1 Ch. App. 354	842.
Gold Sovereign M. and T. Co. v. Stratton	1898	89 Fed. 1016	192, 322.
Gold Springs etc. Mill-site	1891	13 L. D. 175	523.
Goldstein v. Townsite of Juneau	1896	23 L. D. 417	172.
Goller v. Fett	1866	30 Cal. 481, 11 Morr. 171	270, 642, 868.
Gonu v. Russell	1879	3 Mont. 358	371, 373, 408, 651.
Gonzales v. French	1896	164 U. S. 338, 17 Sup. Ct. Rep. 102, 41 L. ed. 458	192.
Good Return M. Co, In re	1885	4 L. D. 221	630, 673, 686.
Goodtitle v. Kibbe	1850	9 How. 471, 13 L. Ed. 220	428.
Goodwin v. McCabe	1888	75 Cal. 584, 588, 17 Pac. 705	218.
Goold v. Gt. West Coal Co.	1865	2 De G. J. & S. 600	813.
Gore v. McBrayer	1861	18 Cal. 582, 1 Morr. 645	270, 271, 331, 398, 858.
Gorlinski, In re	1895	20 L. D. 283	661.
Gorman Mining Co. v. Alexander	1892	2 S. Dak. 557, 51, N. W. W. 346	233.
Gotshall v. Langdon	1901	16 Pa. Supr. Ct. Rep. 158	867.
Governeur Heirs v. Robertson	1826	11 Wheat 332, 6 L. Ed. 488	232.
Gowan v. Christie	1873	5 Moak, 114, 8 Morr. 688	
Gowdy v. Connell	1898	27 L. D. 56	677.
Gowdy v. Connell	1899	28 L. D. 240	677.
Gowdy v. Kismet M. Co.	1896	22 L. D. 624	677, 742.
Gowdy v. Kismet G. M. Co.	1897	24 L. D. 191	661, 677.
Gowdy v. Kismet M. Co.	1897	25 L. D. 216	677, 712.
Graham v. Pierce	1869	19 Gratt, 28, 100 Am. Dec. 658, 14 Morr. 308	790.
Grampian Lode	1882	1 L. D. 544	646, 728.
Grand Dipper Lode	1883	10 Copp's L. O. 240	671.

Names of Cases.	When Decided.	Where Reported.	Sections Where Cited in this Work.
Grant v. Oliver........	1891	91 Cal. 158, 27 Pac. 596, 598	124, 207.
Grassy Gulch Placer...	1900	30 L. D. 191..........	700.
Gray v. Todd.........	1894	19 L. D. 475...........	425.
Gray v. Truby........	1882	6 Colo. 278............	346.
Gray's Harbor Co. v. Drumm	1901	23 Wash. 706, 63 Pac. 530	665.
Great Eastern M. Co. v. Esmeralla M. Co....	1883	2 L. D. 704, 10 C. L. O. 192	679.
Greater Gold Belt M. Co.	1899	28 L. D. 398..........	763.
Great Falls Mfg. Co. v. Fernald	1867	47 N. H. 444..........	257.
Great Western Lode Claim	1887	5 L. D. 510, 14 C. L. O. 27	738.
Green v. Covillaud.....	1858	10 Cal. 317, 324, 70 Am. Dec. 725............	859.
Green v. Gilbert.......	1880	60 N. H. 144..........	840.
Greenwall v. Low Beech-burn Coal Co........	1897	L. R. 2 E. B. 165.....	781.
Gregory v. Pershbaker..	1887	73 Cal. 109, 14 Pac. 401	273, 290, 301, 330, 372, 373, 427, 437.
Gregory Lode	1898	26 L. D. 144..........	173, 177, 413,
Griffin v. American G. M. Co.	1902	114 Fed. 887..........	781.
Griffin v. Fellows......	1873	32 R. F. Smith, 114, 8 Morr. Min. Rep. 657	93.
Grisar v. McDowell....	1868	6 Wall. 381, 18 L. Ed. 863	190.
Groeck v. Southern Pac. R. R. Co...........	1900	102 Fed. 32...........	157.
Grogan v. Knight......	1865	27 Cal. 516............	448.
Gropper v. King.......	1882	4 Mont. 367...........	271.
Gross v. Hughes.......	1900	29 L. D. 465..........	677, 690, 712, 738.
Ground Hog Lode v. Parole etc. Lodes....	1889	8 L. D. 430..........	738.
Grubb v. Bayard......	1851	2 Wall Jr. 81, Fed. Case No. 5849, 9 Morr. 199	860.
Grunsfeld, In re.......	1890	10 L. D. 508..........	505.
Guest v. East Dean....	1872	L. R. 7, E. B. 377......	9.
Guffy v. Hukill........	1890	34 W. Va. 49, 26 Am. St. Rep. 901, 11 S. E. 754, 8 L. R. A. 759.......	862.
Guillet v. Durango Land etc. Co.............	1898	26 L. D. 413..........	506.
Guillory v. Buller......	1897	24 L. D. 209..........	772.
Gulf C. and S. F. Ry. Co. v. Clark........	1900	101 Fed. 678..........	208, 771.
Gumbert v. Kilgore....	1886	(Pa.), 6 Cent. Rep. 406.	820.
Gunnison Crystal M. Co. In re................	1884	2 L. D. 722, 11 C. L. O. 70	679.

Names of Cases.	When De-cided.	Where Reported.	Sections Where Cited in this Work.
G. V. B. M. Co. v. First Nat. Bank	1899	95 Fed. 35	790, 796, 797.
Gwillim v. Donnellan	1885	115 U. S. 45, 5 Sup. Ct. Rep. 1110, 29 L. Ed. 348, 15 Morr. 482	169, 192, 322, 328, 337, 338, 413, 539, 642, 741, 742, 755, 763, 765.
Hagland, In re	1882	1 L. D. 591, 593, 11 C. L. O. 102	338, 738.
Hahn v. United States.	1883	107 U. S. 402, 2 Sup. Ct. Rep. 494, 27 L. Ed. 527	419.
Haight v. Lucia	1874	36 Wis. 355, 361	872.
Haldeman v. Bruckhart.	1863	45 Pa. St. 514, 84 Am. Dec. 511, 5 Morr. 108	814.
Hale, In re	1880	7 Copp's L. O. 115	250, 632.
Hale, In re	1899	28 L. D. 524	673.
Hale & Norcross M. Co. v. Storey County	1865	1 Nev. 82, 83, 14 Morr. 155	535.
Hale's Placer, In re	1885	3 L. D. 536, 11 C. L. O. 67	629, 631.
Hall v. Arnott	1889	80 Cal. 348, 22 Pac. 200	397, 398.
Hall v. Duke of Norfolk	1900	L. R. 2 Ch. D 493	823.
Hall v. Equator M. etc. Co.	1879	Morr. Min. Rights, p. 282, Fed. Case No. 5931, Carpenter's Min. Code (3 ed.), p. 65	364, 553, 558.
Hall v. Hale	1885	8 Colo. 351, 8 Pac. 580.	623, 632.
Hall v. Kearny	1893	18 Colo. 505, 33 Pac. 373	630, 631.
Hall v. Litchfield	1876	Copp's Min. Lands, 333	97, 513, 514.
Hall v. Litchfield	1876	2 Copp's L. O. 179	97, 514.
Hall v. Street	1884	3 L. D. 40, 40 C. L. O. 146	718.
Hallack v. Traber	1896	23 Colo. 14, 46 Pac. 110.	398.
Hallett and Hamburg Lodes	1898	27 L. D. 104	363, 671, 677, 685.
Hallowell, In re	1884	2 L. D. 735	505.
Halsey v. Hewitt	1878	5 Copp's L. O. 162	759.
Hamburg M. Co. v. Stephenson	1883	17 Nev. 449, 30 Pac. 1088	520.
Hamer v. Knowles	1861	6 H. & N. 454	820.
Hamilton v. Anderson	1894	19 L. D. 168	207, 496.
Hamilton v. Delhi M. Co.	1897	118 Cal. 148, 50 Pac. 378	327.
Hamilton v. Graham	1871	L. R. 2 Sc. & D. 166	9.
Hamilton v. Huson	1898	21 Mont. 9, 53 Pac. 101	218.

Names of Cases.	When De-cided.	Where Reported.	Sections Where Cited in this Work.
Hamilton *v.* Southern Nev. etc. Co.........	1887	13 Saw. 113, 33 Fed. 562, 15 Morr. 314...	208, 688, 713, 719, 742, 771, 773.
Hammer *v.* Garfield M. & M. Co.............	1889	130 U. S. 291, 9 Sup. Ct. Rep. 548, 32 L. Ed. 964, 16 Morr. 125....	227, 251, 273, 274, 373, 379, 383, 636, 645, 754.
Hand G. M. Co. *v.* Parker	1877	59 Ga. 419, 424.......	260.
Hans Oleson	1854	28 L. D. 25, 31........	322.
Hanson *v.* Fletcher.....	1894	10 Utah, 266, 37 Pac. 480	362, 383.
Hanson *v.* Gardner....	1802	7 Vesey Jr., 305, 308..	790.
Hardenbergh *v.* Bacon..	1867	33 Cal. 356, 381, 1 Morr. 352	270, 642.
Hardin *v.* Jordan......	1891	140 U. S. 371, 11 Sup. Ct. Rep. 808, 838, 35 L. Ed. 428..........	175.
Hardt *v.* Liberty Hill Cons. etc. W. Co.....	1886	11 Saw. 611, 27 Fed. 788	843, 848.
Hargrave *v.* Cook......	1895	108 Cal. 72, 41 Pac. 18, 30 L. R. A. 390......	838.
Hargrove *v.* Robertson.	1892	15 L. D. 499..........	521.
Harkness *v.* Burton....	1874	39 Iowa, 101, 9 Morr. 318	644, 860.
Harkness *v.* Underhill..	1861	1 Black, 316, 17 L. Ed. 208	208, 662.
Harkrader *v.* Carroll...	1896	76 Fed. 474..........	643, 777.
Harkrader *v.* Goldstein.	1901	31 L. D. 87..........	95, 106, 142, 172, 176, 207, 208, 392, 664, 723.
Harlan *v.* Lehigh Coal Co.	1860	35 Pa. St. 287, 8 Morr. 496	861.
Harley *v.* State........	1867	40 Ala. 689..........	232.
Harnish *v.* Wallace....	1891	13 L. D. 108..........	209, 496.
Harper, *In re.*.........	1893	16 L. D. 110..........	139.
Harrel, *In re.*.........	1900	29 L. D. 553...........	199.
Harriet M. Co. *v.* Phœnix M. Co..........	1882	9 Copp's L. O. 165.....	719, 757.
Harrigan *v.* Lynch.....	1898	21 Mont. 36, 52 Pac. 642	790.
Harrington *v.* Chambers	1881	3 Utah, 94, 1 Pac. 362.	294, 336, 345, 631.
Harrington *v.* Wilson..	1898	10 S. D. 606, 74 N. W. 1055	665.
Harris, *In re*..........	1899	28 L. D. 90..........	497.
Harris *v.* Barnhart....	1893	97 Cal. 546, 32 Pac. 589.	764.
Harris *v.* Elliott......	1836	10 Pet. 25	178.
Harris *v.* Equator M. etc. Co.	1881	3 McCrary, 14, 8 Fed. 863, 12 Morr. 178....	539, 688.

Names of Cases.	When De-cided.	Where Reported.	Sections Where Cited in this Work.
Harris v. Gillingham...	1832	6 N. H. 11, 23 Am. Dec. 701	860.
Harris v. Hillegass.....	1880	54 Cal. 463.............	858.
Harris v. Kellogg......	1897	117 Cal. 484, 49 Pac. 708	328, 539, 636, 643, 754, 755.
Harris v. Lloyd........	1891	11 Mont. 390, 28 Am. St. Rep. 475, 28 Pac. 736	791, 796, 800.
Harris v. Ohio Oil Co...	1897	57 Ohio St. 629, 50 N. E. 1129	862.
Harris v. Ryding......	1839	5 Mees & W. 60, 556...	818, 819.
Hart v. Mayor........	1832	3 Paige, 214...........	790.
Hartford v. Miller.....	1874	41 Conn. 112, 3 Morr. 353	791.
Hartman v. Smith.....	1877	7 Mont. 19, 14 Pac. 648	520, 521, 523.
Hartman v. Warren....	1896	22 C. C. A. 30, note....	175, 664, 666, 772. 773, 775, 784.
Hartman v. Warren....	1896	76 Fed. 157, 160.......	322.
Hartney v. Gosling.....	1902	(Wyo.), 68 Pac. 1118..	796, 797, 799, 801.
Hartwell v. Camman...	1854	10 N. J. Eq. 128, 64 Am. Dec. 448, 3 Morr. Min. Rep. 229......	93, 175, 812, 859b.
Harvey v. Ryan.......	1872	42 Cal. 626, 4 Morr. 490	250, 271, 272, 391.
Haskins v. Curran.....	1895	(Idaho), 43 Pac. 559..	798.
Hastings etc. R. R. Co. v. Whiting.........	1889	132 U. S. 357, 10 Sup. Ct. Rep. 112, 33 L. Ed. 363	205, 208, 419, 666.
Hatfield v. Wallace....	1841	7 Mo. 112............	542.
Hauck v. Tide Water Pipe Line Co. Ld....	1893	153 Pa. St. 366, 34 Am. St. Rep. 710, 26 Atl. 644, 20 L. R. A. 642	840.
Hawes, In re..........	1886	5 L. D. 224..........	501.
Hawke v. Deffeback....	1885	4 Dak. 21, 22 N. W. 480	170.
Hawkeye Placer v. Gray Eagle Placer........	1892	15 L. D. 45, 47.......	737.
Hawkins v. Spokane Hydraulic M. Co.......	1893	2 Idaho, 970, 28 Pac. 433	790, 800.
Hawkins v. Spokane Hydraulic M. Co......	1893	(Idaho), 33 Pac. 40....	790.
Hawley v. Diller.......	1900	178 U. S. 476, 20 Sup. Ct. Rep. 986, 44 L. Ed. 1157............	208, 210, 419, 662, 666, 677, 772.
Hawley v. Clowes.....	1816	2 Johns. Ch. 122.......	789a, 790.
Hawley Cons. M. Co. v. Memmon M. Co.....	1876	Sickle's Min. Dec. 235, 2 C. L. O. 178.......	736.
Haws v. Victoria Copper Co.	1895	160 U. S. 303, 16 Sup. Ct. Rep. 282, 40 L. Ed. 436	273, 350, 407.
Haydel v. Dufresne....	1895	17 How. 23, 15 L. Ed. 115......	660.

Names of Cases.	When De-cided.	Where Reported.	Sections Where Cited in this Work.
Hayden v. Jamison....	1893	16 L. D. 537..........	139.
Hayden v. Jamison....	1898	26 L. D. 373..........	96, 97, 210, 421.
Hayden v. Jamison....	1897	24 L. D. 403..........	210, 421.
Hayes v. Lavagnino....	1898	17 Utah, 185, 53 Pac. 1029, 1033..........	289, 290, 294, 335, 336, 403.
Hayes v. Waldron.....	1863	44 N. H. 580, 84 Am. Dec. 105..........	840, 842.
Haynes, In re........	1880	7 Copp's L. O. 130....	632.
Haynes v. Briscoe....	1891	(Colo.), 67 Pac. 156....	643, 646.
Hays v. Parker........	1883	2 Wash. Ty. 198, 202, 3 Pac. 901..........	108.
Hays v. Richardson....	1829	1 Gill & J. 366........	860.
Hays v. Risher........	1858	32 Pa. St. 169, 176.....	256.
Hays v. Steiger.......	1888	76 Cal. 555, 18 Pac. 670	207, 208, 663, 666.
Hazen v. Essex Co.....	1853	12 Cush. 475..........	257.
Heard v. James.......	1873	49 Miss. 236..........	868.
Hecla Cons. M. Co....	1891	12 L. D. 75..........	520, 780.
Heinze v. Boston and Montana etc. Co.....	1898	20 Mont. 528, 52 Pac. 273	872.
Heinze v. Kleinschmidt.	1901	25 Mont. 89, 63 Pac. 927	790.
Helm v. Chapman.....	1885	66 Cal. 291, 5 Pac. 352.	327.
Helmich, In re........	1895	20 L. D. 163..........	661.
Henderson v. Eason....	1851	17 Q. B. 701, 21 L. J. Q. B. 82..........	789a, 790.
Hendricks v. Spring Valley etc. Co......	1881	58 Cal. 190, 41 Am. Rep. 257............	834.
Hendy v. Compton.....	1889	9 L. D. 106..........	143.
Henshaw v. Bissel.....	1874	18 Wall. 255, 21 L. Ed. 835	125.
Henshaw v. Clark......	1859	14 Cal. 461, 14 Morr. 434	843, 872.
Herbian v. Warren....	1894	2 Okl. 4, 35 Pac. 575...	108.
Hermocilla v. Hubbell..	1891	89 Cal. 8, 26 Pac. 611..	133, 142, 144a.
Herron v. Eagle M. Co.	1900	37 Or. 155, 61 Pac. 417	539.
Hess v. Bolinger.......	1874	48 Cal. 349..........	207.
Hess v. Winder.......	1866	30 Cal. 349, 12 Morr. 217 ....!.....	216, 537.
Hess v. Winder........	1867	34 Cal. 270..........	872.
Hestres v. Brennan....	1875	50 Cal. 211..........	208, 663.
Hewitt v. Schultz.....	1900	180 U. S. 139, 21 Sup. Ct. Rep. 309, 45 L. Ed. 463	419, 666.
Hext v. Gill..........	1872	L. R. 7 Ch. App. 699...	90, 92.
Heydenfeldt v. Daney G. and S. M. Co.....	1875	10 Nev. 290, 13 Morr. 204	136.
Heydenfeldt v. Daney Gold M. Co.........	1876	93 U. S. 634..........	136, 142, 480, 783.
Hibberd v. Slack......	1898	84 Fed. 571..........	133, 142, 185, 199.

Names of Cases.	When De- cided.	Where Reported.	Sections Where Cited in this Work.
Hickey's Appeal......	1884	3 L. D. 83, 10 C. L. O. 164	171.
Hicks v. Bell..........	1853	3 Cal. 219.............	21.
Hicks v. Michael......	1860	15 Cal. 107, 116.......	872.
Hidden Treasure etc. Co.	1889	16 Copp's L. O. 110....	682.
Hidden Treasure Lode.	1899	29 L. D. 156..........	338, 673.
Hidden Treasure Lode.	1899	29 L. D. 315..........	338, 673.
Hidee Gold M. Co., In re	1901	30 L. D. 420..........	218, 312a, 338. 363, 363a.
Higgins v. Armstrong..	1886	9 Colo. 38, 10 Pac. 232..	797, 801.
Higgins v. Houghton..	1864	25 Cal. 252, 13 Morr. 195	136, 142.
Higgins v. John G. M. Co.	1897	14 Copp's L. O. 238....	632.
Highland Marie and Marcella Lodes......	1901	31 L. D. 37............	631.
Higueras v. United States	1866	5 Wall. 827, 18 L. Ed. 469......	122.
Hihn v. Peck..........	1861	18 Cal. 640............	789.
Hill v. Cutting........	1874	113 Mass. 107.........	860.
Hill v. King..........	1857	8 Cal. 337, 4 Morr. 533.	841.
Hill v. Smith.........	1865	27 Cal. 476, 4 Morr. 597	841, 843.
Hilton v. Lord Granville	1844	5 Q. B. 701...........	819, 820.
Hilton v. Whitehead...	1860	12 Q. B. 734..........	820.
Hirbour v. Reeding....	1877	3 Mont. 13, 11 Morr. 514	331, 797, 858.
Hirschler v. McKen- dricks	1895	16 Mont. 211, 40 Pac. 290	652.
Hobart v. Ford........	1870	15 Morr. 236, 6 Nev. 77.	530, 550.
Hobart v. Murray.....	1893	54 Mo. App. 249......	861.
Hobbs v. Amador etc. Canal Co..........	1884	66 Cal. 161, 4 Pac. 1147	843.
Hodgson v. Fowler.....	1897	24 Colo. 278, 50 Pac. 1034	798.
Hoffman v. Beecher....	1892	12 Mont. 489, 31 Pac. 92	382, 735, 737.
Hoffman v. Tuolumne County Water Co....	1858	10 Cal. 413..........	808.
Hoffman v. Venard....	1892	14 L. D. 45............	677.
Hogden, In re........	1874	1 Copp's L. O. 135.....	136.
Hoggin, J. B., In re...	1884	2 L. D. 755............	520.
Holbrooke v. Harring- ton	1894	(Cal.), 36 Pac. 365....	406, 646.
Holden v. Joy.........	1872	17 Wall. 211, 21 L. Ed. 523	181.
Hole v. Thomas.......	1802	7 Vesey Jr. 589........	790.
Holladay Coal Co. v. Kirker	1899	20 Utah, 192, 57 Pac. 882....	504.
Hollond v. Mt. Auburn etc. Co.............	1878	53 Cal. 149, 9 Morr. 497	373, 408.
Holmes Placer	1898	26 L. D. 650..........	448.
Holmes Placer	1899	29 L. D 368...........	448, 672.

Names of Cases.	When De- cided.	Where Reported.	Sections Where Cited in this Work.
Holmes v. Self	1881	79 Ky. 297, 299	802.
Holter v. Northern P. R. R. Co.	1901	30 L. D. 442	106, 160.
Homestake Mining Co.'s Case	1900	29 L. D. 689	312, 364, 366, 696.
Honaker v. Martin	1891	11 Mont. 91, 27 Pac. 397	629, 629, 651, 652.
Hoofnagle v. Anderson.	1822	7 Wheat. 212, 5 L. Ed. 437	175.
Hooper, In re	1881	8 Copp's L. O. 120, 1 L. D. 561	95, 138, 158.
Hooper v. Ferguson	1883	2 L. D. 712	106, 205, 679.
Hooper v. Scheimer	1860	23 How. 235, 16 L. Ed. 452	175, 773.
Hope's Appeal	1886	(Pa.), 3 Atl. 23	861.
Hope M. Co., In re	1878	5 Copp's L. O. 116	366.
Hope M. Co. v. Brown	1888	7 Mont. 550, 19 Pac. 218	473, 481, 485, 725.
Hope M. Co. v. Brown	1891	11 Mont. 370, 28 Pac. 732	473, 485, 725.
Hopkins v. Noyes	1883	4 Mont. 550, 2 Pac. 280, 15 Morr. 287	218, 270, 642.
Horner v. Watson	1875	79 Pa. St. 242, 21 Am. Rep. 55, 14 Morr. 1	808, 818.
Hornsby v. United States	1869	10 Wall. 224, 19 L. Ed. 900	122.
Horsky v. Moran	1898	21 Mont. 345, 53 Pac. 1064	173, 177, 208, 209.
Horswell v. Ruiz	1885	67 Cal. 111, 7 Pac. 197, 15 Morr. 488	218, 219, 329, 365, 582.
Horton v. New Pass G. and S. M. Co	1891	21 Nev. 184, 27 Pac. 376	799.
Hosmer v. Wallace	1874	47 Cal. 461	208, 637, 660, 662, 772.
Hosmer v. Wallace	1878	97 U. S. 575, 24 L. Ed. 1130	217.
Hot Springs Cases v. United States	1875	92 U. S. 698, 23 L. Ed. 690	183.
Hough v. Hunt	1902	(Cal.), 70 Pac. 1059	629.
Houswirth v. Butcher.	1882	4 Mont. 299, 1 Pac. 714	330, 335, 362, 373.
Houtz v. Gishorn	1874	1 Utah, 173, 2 Morr. 340	539.
Howell v. McCoy	1832	3 Rawle, 256	840.
Howell v. Slauson	1890	83 Cal. 539, 23 Pac. 692	143, 362.
Howeth v. Sullenger	1896	113 Cal. 547, 45 Pac. 841	373, 671.
Hoyt v. Smith	1854	23 Conn. 177, 60 Am. Dec. 632, 12 Morr. 306	858.
Hoyt v. Smith	1858	27 Conn. 63, 12 Morr. 315	858.
Hudepohl v. Liberty Hill etc. Co	1889	80 Cal. 553, 22 Pac. 339	861.
Huff v. McDonald	1857	22 Ga. 131, 68 Am. Dec. 487, 14 Morr. 262	790.

Names of Cases.	When Decided.	Where Reported.	Sections Where Cited in this Work.
Huff v. McCauley	1866	53 Pa. St. 206, 91 Am. Dec. 203, 9 Morr. 268	860.
Huggins v. Daley	1900	99 Fed. 606	862.
Hughes v. Devlin	1863	23 Cal. 502, 12 Morr. 241	535, 536, 792.
Hughes v. Dunlap	1891	91 Cal. 385, 390, 27 Pac. 642	872.
Hughes v. Ochsner	1898	26 L. D. 540	272, 629, 673.
Hughes v. Ochsner	1898	27 L. D. 396	624, 629, 631, 632, 686, 712, 765, 772.
Hugunin v. McCunniff.	1874	2 Colo. 367	865.
Hulings v. Ward Townsite	1899	29 L. D. 21	173, 175, 177, 722.
Humbird v. Avery	1901	110 Fed. 465	108.
Humphries v. Brogdon.	1850	12 Q. B. 739	812, 818, 819, 820.
Hunt v. Eureka Gulch M. Co.	1890	14 Colo. 451, 24 Pac. 550	713, 738, 742.
Hunt v. Patchin	1888	35 Fed. 816, 13 Sawy. 304	405, 728.
Hunt v. Peake	1860	1 Johnson (Eng.), 705	820.
Hunt v. Steese	1888	75 Cal. 620, 17 Pac. 920	142, 161, 872.
Hunter, In re	1878	Copp's Min. Lands, 231, 5 Copp's L. O. 130	473, 482, 490.
Hunter v. Gibbons	1856	1 Hurl. & N. 459	867.
Huntley v. Russell	1849	13 Q. B. 572	789.
Hurd v. Tomkins	1892	17 Colo. 394, 30 Pac. 247	797.
Hurricane Lode, In re.	1897	Sickles' Min. Dec. 243	679.
Hurt v. Hollingsworth..	1879	100 U. S. 100, 25 L. Ed. 569	872.
Hussey Lode	1886	5 L. D. 93	646, 728.
Hustler and New Year Lode Claims	1900	29 L. D. 668	363.
Hutchings, In re	1877	4 Copp's L. O. 142	501.
Hutchins v. Low (Yosemite Valley Case)..	1873	15 Wall. 77, 21 L. Ed. 82	192, 205, 216. 542.
Hyde, In re	1899	28 L. D. 284	199.
Hyman v. Wheeler	1886	29 Fed. 347, 15 Morr. 519	290a, 293, 294, 615.
Iams v. Carnegie Nat. Gas. Co	1899	194 Pa. St. 72, 45 Atl. 54	862.
Iba v. Central Association	1895	5 Wyo. 355, 42 Pac. 20	748, 754.
Illinois and St. L. Ry. etc. Co. v. Ogle	1879	92 Ill. 353, 25 Am. Rep. 327	868.
Illinois S. M. Co. v. Raff	1893	7 N. Mex. 336, 34 Pac. 544.	293, 294, 313.

Names of Cases.	When Decided.	Where Reported.	Sections Where Cited in this Work.
Ilsley *v.* Wilson.......	1896	42 W. Va. 757, 26 S. E. 551, 555............	868.
Imperial Refining Co.'s Appeal	1892	149 Pa. St. 142, 24 Atl. 161....	862.
Independence Lode....	1889	9 L. D. 571...........	338, 738.
International etc. Co. *v.* Anderson	1891	82 Tex. 516, 27 Am. St. Rep. 902, 17 S. W. 1039	644.
Interstate L. Co. *v.* Maxwell L. G. Co.......	1891	139 U. S. 569, 11 Sup. Ct. Rep. 656, 35 L. Ed. 278	116.
Iola Lode Case.......	1882	1 L. D. 539, 9 C. L. O. 164......	759.
Iowa M. Co. *v.* Bonanza M. Co.	1875	6 Copp's L. O. 75.....	759.
Iron S. M. Co. *v.* Campbell	1892	17 Colo. 267, 29 Pac. 513	175, 305, 322, 366, 551, 615, 777, 780, 866.
Iron S. M. Co. *v.* Campbell	1890	135 U. S. 286, 10 Sup. Ct. Rep. 765, 34 L. Ed. 155...........	175, 177, 336, 665, 717, 718, 723, 781.
Iron S. M. Co. *v.* Cheesman	1881	8 Fed. 297, 9 Morr. 552	290, 293, 311.
Iron S. M. Co. *v.* Cheesman	1886	116 U. S. 529, 6 Sup. Ct. Rep. 481, 29 L. Ed. 712....	290a, 292, 293, 294, 301, 311, 336, 615, 866.
Iron S. M. Co. *v.* Elgin M. Co.	1886	118 U. S. 196, 6 Sup. Ct. Rep. 1177, 30 L. Ed. 98, 15 Morr. 641	58, 318, 356, 364, 365, 552, 567, 576, 582, 593, 594, 866.
Iron S. M. Co. *v.* Mike and Starr etc. Co....	1892	143 U. S. 394, 12 Sup. Ct. Rep. 543, 36 L. Ed. 201............	176, 177, 292, 293, 336, 366, 413, 720, 781, 866.
Iron S. M. Co. *v.* Mike etc. M. Co.	1888	6 L. D. 533, 15 C. L. O. 14	721.
Iron S. M. Co. *v.* Murphy	1880	2 McCrary, 121, 3 Fed. 368, 1 Morr. Min. Rep. 548	311, 364.

Names of Cases.	When Decided.	Where Reported.	Sections Where Cited in this Work.
Iron S. M. Co. v. Reynolds	1888	124 U. S. 374, 8 Sup. Ct. Rep. 598, 31 L. Ed. 466	413, 415, 720, 781.
Irvine v. Marshall	1857	20 How. 558, 561	249.
Irwin v. Covode	1854	24 Pa. St. 162, 15 Morr. 120	789.
Irvine v. Tarbat	1894	105 Cal. 237, 38 Pac. 896	161.
Irwin v. Phillips	1855	5 Cal. 140, 63 Am. Dec. 113, 15 Morr. 178	530, 841.
Ivanhoe M. Co. v. Keystone Cons. M. Co.	1880	102 U. S. 167, 26 L. Ed. 126, 13 Morr. 214	47, 55, 136, 142, 144a, 152.
Jackson v. Babcock	1809	4 Johns. 418	860.
Jackson v. Dines	1889	13 Colo. 90, 21 Pac. 918	233, 754.
Jackson v. Feather River W. Co.	1859	14 Cal. 19, 5 Morr. 594	270.
Jackson v. Green	1831	7 Wend. 333	224, 232.
Jackson v. Harsen	1827	7 Cow. 323, 17 Am. Dec. 517	861.
Jackson v. McMurray	1878	4 Colo. 76, 12 Morr. 164	773.
Jackson v. Roby	1883	109 U. S. 440, 3 Sup. Ct. Rep. 301, 27 L. Ed. 990	45, 268, 624, 625, 629, 630, 631, 754, 755.
Jacob v. Day	1896	111 Cal. 571, 44 Pac. 243	530, 841, 843.
Jacob v. Lorenz	1893	98 Cal. 332, 33 Pac. 119	530, 609, 783.
Jacobs, Elias	1880	7 Copp's L. O. 83	158.
Jacobs, In re	1895	21 L. D. 379	661.
Jacobs v. Allard	1869	42 Vt. 303, 1 Am. Rep. 331	840.
Jacobs v. Seward	1872	5 L. R. H. L. 464, 475, 478	790.
Jacobson v. Bunker Hill etc. Co.	1891	2 Idaho, 863, 29 Pac. 396	544.
James v. Germania Iron Co.	1901	107 Fed. 596	211, 322, 478, 659, 660, 664, 665, 666.
Jamestown and Northern Ry. Co. v. Jones.	1900	177 U. S. 125, 20 Sup. Ct. Rep. 568, 44 L. Ed. 698	153.
Jamie Lee Lode v. Little Forepaugh Lode	1890	11 L. D. 391	759.
Jamieson v. North British Ry. Co.	1868	6 Scot L. Rep. 188	92.
Jantzen v. Arizona Copper Co.	1889	(Ariz.), 20 Pac. 93	227, 392, 763.
Jefferson M. Co. v. Pennsylvania M. Co.	1874	1 Copp's L. O. 66	690.

Names of Cases.	When Decided.	Where Reported.	Sections Where Cited in this Work.
Jeffords v. Hine.......	1886	(Ariz.), 11 Pac. 352, 15 Morr. 575..........	738.
Jeffries v. Williams....	1850	5 Exch. 792, 20 L. J. Ex. 14	820.
Jegon v. Vivian.......	1871	L. R. 6 Ch. App. 742, 8 Morr. 628..........	807.
Jenkins v. Jenkins....	1886	(N. J.), 5 Atl. 134.....	646.
Jennings v. Ricard....	1887	10 Colo. 395, 15 Pac. 677, 15 Morr. 624....	800, 858.
Jennison v. Kirk......	1879	98 U. S. 453, 25 L. Ed. 240, 4 Morr. 504.....	44, 47, 54, 56, 96, 306, 530, 567, 623, 838, 843.
Jenny Lind M. Co., In re	1873	Sickle's Min. Dec. 223,	735, 736, 739.
Jerome v. Ross........	1823	7 Johns. Ch. 334......	843.
Job v. Potton.........	1875	L. R. 20 Eq. 84, 93, 14 Morr. Rep. 329......	789, 790.
Johns v. March........	1892	15 L. D. 196..........	95, 106.
Johnson, In re........	1880	7 Copp's L. O. 35..:....	366.
Johnson v. Buell.......	1879	4 Colo. 557, 9 Morr. 502	60.
Johnson v. California Lustral Co.	1899	127 Cal. 283, 59 Pac. 595	93.
Johnson v. Drew......	1898	171 U. S. 93, 18 Sup. Ct. Rep. 800, 43 L. Ed. 88	143.
Johnson v. Harrington.	1892	5 Wash. 93, 31 Pac. 316	210.
Johnson v. Johnson....	1835	2 Hill Eq. (S. C.) 277, 29 Am. Dec. 72......	790.
Johnson v. Leonard....	1889	1 Wash. 564, 20 Pac. 591	501.
Johnson v. McLaughlin.	1884	1 Ariz. 493, 4 Pac. 130	274.
Johnson v. Munday....'	1900	104 Fed. 594..........	754.
Johnson v. Parks	1858	10 Cal. 447, 4 Morr. 316	43, 58, 339, 350.
Johnson v. Towsley....	1871	13 Wall. 72, 20 L. Ed. 485	161, 175, 177, 207, 660, 665, 772.
Johnson v. Young.....	1893	18 Colo. 625, 34 Pac. 173	274, 363, 398, 636, 643, 645.
Johnson etc. Lessees v. McIntosh	1823	8 Wheat. 543, 5 L. Ed. 681	181.
Johnston v. Gas Co.....	1886	5 Cent. Rep. 564.......	255.
Johnston v. Harrington.	1892	5 Wash. 93, 31 Pac. 316	421.
Johnston v. Morris....	1896	72 Fed. 890..........	106, 144, 612.
Johnstown I. Co. v. Cambria I. Co.	1858	32 Pa. St. 241, 72 Am. Dec. 783, 9 Morr. 226	175.
Jones v. Adams.......	1885	19 Nev. 78, 3 Am. St. Rep. 788, 6 Pac. 442..	838.
Jones v. Clark........	1871	42 Cal. 180, 11 Morr. 473	796, 800, 801, 803.
Jones v. Driver.......	1892	15 L. D. 514..........	208, 496.
Jones v. Jackson......	1858	9 Cal. 238, 14 Morr. 72.	426, 843.

Names of Cases.	When De-cided.	Where Reported.	Sections Where Cited in this Work.
Jones v. Meyers.......	1891	2 Idaho, 794, 35 Am. St. Rep. 259, 26 Pac. 215	772.
Jones v. Prospect Mt. T. Co.	1892	21 Nev. 339, 31 Pac. 642	301, 551, 615, 688, 866.
Jones v. Robertson.....	1886	116 Ill. 543, 56 Am. Rep. 786, 6 N. E. 890, 15 Morr. 703	808.
Jones v. Wagner......	1870	66 Pa. St. 429, 5 Am. Rep. 385, 13 Morr. 690	818, 821.
Jordan v. Duke........	1894	(Ariz.), 36 Pac. 896...	329.
Jordan v. Duke.......	1898	(Ariz.), 53 Pac. 197...	363, 651, 652, 754. 765.
Jordan v. Idaho Aluminum etc. Co.	1895	20 L. D. 500.......:...	424.
Jordan v. Schuerman...	1898	(Ariz.), 53 Pac. 579....	754.
Jourdan v. Barrett....	1846	4 How. 169, 11 L. Ed. 924	216.
Judge v. Braswell.....	1877	13 Bush (Ky.) 69, 26 Am. Rep. 185, 11 Morr. 508	801.
Julia etc. M. Co.......	1872	Copp's Min. Dec. 96..	730.
Junkans v. Bergin.....	1885	67 Cal. 267, 7 Pac. 684	841.
Jupiter M. Co. v. Bodie M. Co.	1881	7 Saw. 96, 11 Fed. 666, 4 Morr. 411.........	250, 271, 272, 273, 274, 294, 330, 335, 335, 336, 361, 362, 373, 375, 379, 383, 403, 631, 633, 651.
Justice M. Co. v. Barclay	1897	82 Fed. 554..........	407, 408, 615, 629, 630, 631, 643, 644, 645, 651.
Justice M. Co. v. Lee...	1895	21 Colo. 260, 52 Am. St. Rep. 216, 40 Pac. 444.	175, 231, 777.
Justin v. Adams......	1898	87 Fed. 377............	217.
Kahn v. Central Smelting Co.	1881	102 U. S. 641, 26 L. Ed. 266, 11 Morr. 540....	796, 800, 803.
Kahn v. Old Telegraph Co.	1877	2 Utah, 174, 11 Morr. 645	175, 604, 609, 777, 783, 796.
Kaler v. Campbell.....	1886	13 Or. 596, 11 Pac. 301.	838.
Kane v. Cook..........	1857	8 Cal. 449.............	867.
Kane v. Vanderburgh..	1814	1 John's Ch. 11 Note..	790.
Kannaugh v. Quartette M. Co.............	1891	16 Colo. 341, 27 Pac. 245	604, 713, 742.
Kansas City etc. Co. v. Clay	1892	(Ariz.), 29 Pac. 9......	175, 779.
Kansas Pac. R. R. Co. v. Atchison etc. R. R. Co.	1884	112 U. S. 414, 5 Sup. Ct. Rep. 208, 28 L. Ed. 794	157.

Names of Cases.	When Decided.	Where Reported.	Sections Where Cited in this Work.
Kansas Pac. Ry. Co. v. Dunmeyer	1885	113 U. S. 629, 5 Sup. Ct. Rep. 566, 28 L. Ed. 1123	154, 322.
Katherine Davis, In re.	1900	30 L. D. 220	124.
Kaweath Colony	1891	12 L. D. 326	210.
Keeler v. Green	1870	21 N. J. Eq. 27, 12 Morr. 465	860.
Keeler v. Trueman	1890	15 Colo. 143, 25 Pac. 311	233, 539, 754.
Kelly v. Taylor	1863	23 Cal. 14, 5 Morr. 598.	383.
Kemp v. Starr	1878	5 Copp's L. O. 130	171.
Kempton Mine	1875	1 Copp's L. O. 178	232.
Kendall v. Hall	1891	12 L. D. 419	502.
Kendall v. San Juan S. M. Co.	1892	144 U. S. 658, 12 Sup. Ct. Rep. 779, 36 L. Ed. 330	184, 329.
Kendall v. San Juan S. M. Co.	1886	9 Colo. 349, 12 Pac. 198	183, 184, 755.
Kenna v. Dillon	1872	Copp's Min. Dec. 93	207.
Kennedy, In re	1883	10 Copp's L. O. 150	338.
Kern County v. Lee	1900	129 Cal. 361, 61 Pac. 1124	250, 273, 389.
Kern Oil Co. v. Clarke	1901	30 L. D. 550	199, 208, 216.
Kern Oil Co. v. Clarke.	1902	31 L. D. 288	143, 199, 208, 660.
Kern Oil Co. v. Clotfelter	1901	30 L. D. 583	97, 199.
Kerr v. Carlton	1883	10 Copp's L. O. 255	501, 506.
Kerr v. Utah-Wyoming Imp. Co.	1883	2 L. D. 727, 10 C. L. O. 255	501.
Keystone Case	1872	Copp's Min. Dec. 105, 109, 125	136, 142.
Keystone Lode v. State of Nevada	1892	15 L. D. 259	136.
Kibling, In re	1888	7 L. D. 327	772.
Kidder v. Rixford	1844	16 Vt. 169, 42 Am. Dec. 504	790.
Kimball, In re	1876	3 Copp's L. O. 50	501.
Kimberly v. Arms	1889	129 U. S. 512, 9 Sup. Ct. Rep. 355, 32 L. Ed. 764	800.
King v. Amy and Silversmith Cons. M. Co.	1890	9 Mont. 543, 24 Pac. 200, 16 Morr. 38	364, 588, 591.
King v. Amy and Silversmith M. Co.	1894	152 U. S. 222, 14 Sup. Ct. Rep. 510, 38 L. Ed. 419	335, 336, 365, 366, 367, 588, 591, 593.
King v. Bradford	1901	31 L. D. 108	92, 97, 424.
King v. Campbell	1898	85 Fed. 814	872.
King v. Edwards	1870	1 Mont. 235, 4 Morr. 480	44, 45, 270, 271, 272, 274, 566, 623.

Names of Cases.	When Decided.	Where Reported.	Sections Where Cited in this Work.
King v. McAndrews....	1900	104 Fed. 430..........	184.
King v. McAndrews....	1901	111 Fed. 860..........	175, 181, 183, 184, 659, 664, 665, 666, 777.
King v. Mullins.......	1897	171 U. S. 420, 18 Sup. Ct. Rep. 925, 43 L. Ed. 214	251.
King v. Randlett.......	1867	33 Cal. 318, 5 Morr. 605	270.
King v. Thomas........	1887	6 Mont. 409, 12 Pac. 865	161, 177.
Kingsley v. Hillside Coal etc. Co........	1892	144 Pa. St. 613, 23 Atl. 250	861.
Kings Co. Commrs. v. Alexander	1886	5 L. D. 126...........	95, 496.
Kinkaid, In re........	1886	5 L. D. 25............	630.
Kinney v. Consolidated Virginia M. Co......	1877	4 Saw. 382, 452, Fed. Case No. 7827.......	270, 688.
Kinney v. Fleming.....	1899	(Ariz.), 56 Pac. 723....	322, 363, 381, 382, 383, 392, 643, 644.
Kinney v. Van Bokern.	1900	29 L. D. 460..........	734, 735.
Kinsler v. Clarke......	1837	2 Hill Ch. (S. C.) 618..	872.
Kirby v. Lewis........	1889	39 Fed. 66............	106.
Kirk v. Bartholomew...	1892	2 Idaho, 1087, 29 Pac. 40	838.
Kirk v. Clark..........	1893	17 L. D. 190..........	631.
Kirk v. Meldrum.......	1901	28 Colo. 453, 65 Pac. 633	216, 218, 272, 337, 448, 763.
Kirwan v. Murphy.....	1897	83 Fed. 275...........	777.
Kjellman v. Rogers....	1901	109 Fed. 1061.........	233.
Klauber v. Higgins....	1897	117 Cal. 451, 49 Pac. 466	107, 126, 161, 282, 779.
Kleppner v. Lemon....	1900	197 Pa. St. 430, 47 Atl. 353	862.
Klopenstine v. Hays...	1899	20 Utah, 45, 57 Pac. 712	408, 631, 651.
Knight, In re..........	1900	30 L. D. 227..........	448, 448b.
Knight v. Indiana C. and I. Co...........	1874	47 Ind. 105, 47 Am. Rep. 692	175, 812.
Knight v. U. S. Land Assn.....	1891	142 U. S. 161, 12 Sup. Ct. Rep. 258, 35 L. Ed. 974	116, 208, 662, 663, 772.
Knowles v. Harris.....	1858	5 R. I. 402, 73 Am. Dec. 77	789a.
Knowlton v. Moore.....	1900	178 U. S. 41, 20 Sup. Ct. Rep. 747, 44 L. Ed. 969	666.
Koehler v. Barin......	1885	25 Fed. 161...........	660.
Koen v. Bartlett.......	1895	41 W. Va. 559, 56 Am. St. Rep. 884, 23 S. E. 664, 31 L. R. A. 128.	789, 859b.

Names of Cases.	When De-cided.	Where Reported.	Sections Where Cited in this Work.
Kohlsaat v. Murphy...	1878	96 U. S. 153, 24 L. Ed. 844	480.
Kohnyo and Fortuna Lodes	1899	28 L. D. 451	741, 772.
Krall v. United States..	1897	79 Fed. 241	192.
Kramer v. Settle	1873	1 Idaho, 485, 9 Morr. 561	331, 625, 631.
Krogstadt, Ole O., In re	1886	4 L. D. 564	232.
Lacey v. Woodward....	1891	5 N. Mex. 583, 25 Pac. 785	651.
Lakin v. Dolly	1891	53 Fed. 333	362, 366, 589, 604.
Lakin v. Roberts	1891	54 Fed. 461	362, 604.
Lakin v. Sierra Buttes M. Co	1885	11 Saw. 231, 241, 25 Fed. 337	405, 643, 651.
Lalande v. McDonald..	1887	2 Idaho, 283, 13 Pac. 347	329.
Lalley, In re	1883	10 Copp's L. O. 55	497.
Lamar v. Hale	1884	79 Va. 147	796.
Lamb v. Davenport....	1873	18 Wall. 307, 21 L. Ed. 759	542.
Lamb v. Walker	1878	L. R. 3 Q. B. 389	823.
Landregan v. Peppin...	1892	94 Cal. 465, 21 Pac. 774	754.
Lane, In re	1890	135 U. S. 443, 447, 10 Sup. Ct. Rep. 760, 43 L. Ed. 219	243.
Laney, Thomas J., In re	1889	9 L. D. 93	94, 338.
Langford v. Butler....	1895	20 L. D. 351	159.
Langdon v. Sherwood...	1887	124 U. S. 74, 8 Sup. Ct. Rep. 429, 31 L. Ed. 344	773.
Largent, In re	1891	13 L. D. 397	507.
Largey v. Bartlett	1896	18 Mont. 265, 44 Pac. 962	407.
Larned v. Jenkins	1902	113 Fed. 634	58, 60, 175.
Larkin v. Upton	1892	144 U. S. 19, 23, 12 Sup. Ct. Rep. 614, 36 L. Ed. 533	309, 337, 364.
Last Chance M. Co. v. Tyler M. Co	1894	61 Fed. 557	319, 364, 365, 396, 582, 591, 604, 609, 772, 783.
Last Chance M. Co. v. Tyler M. Co	1894	157 U. S. 683, 15 Sup. Ct. Rep. 733, 39 L. Ed. 859	319, 364, 591, 609, 759, 783.
Law v. State of Utah..	1900	29 L. D. 622	132, 142.
Lawrence v. Potter....	1900	22 Wash. 32, 60 Pac. 147	660, 663, 665, 666.
Lawrence v. Robinson..	1879	4 Colo. 567, 12 Morr. 387	797, 803, 858.
Lawson v. Kirchner....	1901	50 W. Va. 331, 40 S. E. 344	862.

Names of Cases.	When De-cided.	Where Reported.	Sections Where Cited in this Work.
Laycock v. Parker.....	1899	103 Wis. 161, 79 N. W. 327	833.
Leach v. Day..........	1865	27 Cal. 643............	872.
Leach v. Potter........	1896	24 L. D. 573..........	95, 204, 208.
Lead City Townsite v. Little Nell Lode.....	1893	17 L. D. 291..........	784.
Leadville M. Co. v. Fitzgerald	1879	4 Morr. Min. Rep. 381, Fed. Case No. 8158, 4 Morr. 381.....	293, 300, 301, 364, 551, 615, 866.
Leaming v. McKenna..	1902	31 L. D. 318..........	199.
Leavenworth L. and G. R. Co. v. United States	1875	92 U. S. 733, 23 L. Ed. 634	96, 181, 183, 191.
Lebanon M. Co. v. Cons. Rep. M. Co..........	1882	6 Colo. 371...........	218, 322, 688.
Ledger Lode	1893	16 L. D. 101..........	738.
Ledoux v. Black.......	1856	18 How. 473, 15 L. Ed. 457	123.
Ledoux v. Forester.....	189.3	94 Fed 600..........	335, 362, 371, 373, 373.
Lee v. Johnson........	1885	116 U. S. 48, 6 Sup. Ct. Rep. 249, 29 L. Ed. 570	175, 207, 663, 665, 666, 784.
Lee v. Justice M. Co....	1892	2 Colo. App. 112, 29 Pac. 1020	231.
Lee v. Stahl..........	1886	9 Colo. 208, 11 Pac. 77.	558, 560, 614, 727, 742.
Lee v. Stahl..........	1889	13 Colo. 174, 22 Pac. 436, 16 Morr. 152...	558, 560, 614, 727, 742.
Lee Doon v. Tesh..... .	1885	68 Cal. 43, 6 Pac. 97, 8 Pac. 621	233, 754.
Lee Sing Far v. United States	1899	94 Fed. 834..........	224.
Leet v. John Dare M. Co.	1870	6 Nev. 218, 4 Morr. 487	272.
Leffingwell, In re.......	1900	30 L. D. 139..........	661.
Leggatt v. Stewart.....	1883	5 Mont. 107, 2 Pac. 320, 15 Morr. 358........	362, 373.
Leigh v. Dickenson....	1883	12 Q. B. D. 194........	790.
Lellie Lode Mine Claim.	1901	31 L. D. 21...........	71, 780.
Le Neve Millsite......	1889	9 L. D. 460...........	524, 708.
Lenfers v. Henke......	1874	73 Ill. 405, 24 Am. Rep. 263, 5 Morr. 67......	535, 792.
Lenning, In re.......	1886	5 L. D. 190, 3 C. L. O. 197	521, 523, 524, 708.
Lentz v. Carnegie......	1891	145 Pa. St. 612, 27 Am. St. Rep. 717, 23 Atl. 219	840.

Names of Cases.	When Decided.	Where Reported.	Sections Where Cited in this Work.
Le Roy v. Wright......	1864	4 Saw. 530, 535, Fed. Case No. 8273.......	872.
Levaroni v. Miller.....	1867	34 Cal. 231, 91 Am. Dec. 692, 12 Morr. 232....	843.
Lewey v. Fricke Coke Co.	1895	166 Pa. St. 536, 45 Am. St. Rep. 684, 31 Atl. 261, 28 L. R. A. 283..	823, 867, 868.
Lewis v. Burns........	1895	106 Cal. 381, 39 Pac. 778	644.
Lewis v. Marsh........	1849	8 Hare, 97............	873.
Lezeart v. Dunker.....	1885	4 L. D. 96............	503.
Lillibridge v. Lacka-wanna Coal Co.......	1891	143 Pa. St. 293, 24 Am. St. Rep. 544, 22 Atl. 1035, 13 L. R. A. 627	568, 596, 812, 827.
Lillie Lode M. Claim...	1901	31 L. D. 21...........	60.
Lincoln v. Rodgers.....	1870	1 Mont. 217, 224, 14 Morr. 79	843.
Lincoln Lucky etc. Co. v. Hendry	1897	9 N. Mex. 149, 50 Pac. 330	615, 866.
Lincoln Placer	1888	7 L. D. 81, 15 C. L. O. 81	396, 432, 438, 671, 672.
Lindsay v. Omaha......	1890	30 Neb. 512, 46 N. W. 627, 27 Am. St. Rep. 415	178.
Linksweiler v. Schneider	1899	95 Fed. 203...........	746.
Lipscomb v. Nichols...	1882	6 Colo. 290...........	501.
Litchfield v. The Regis-ter	1870	9 Wall. 575, 19 L. Ed. 681	207.
Litchfield v. Register and Receiver	1868	1 Woolw. 299, Fed. Cas. No. 8388	660.
Little v. Bradbury.....	1903	(Not reported)	739.
Little Annie No. 5 Lode	1901	30 L. D. 488..........	679, 696, 741.
Little Emily M. Co. v. Couch	1896	U. S. C. C. (Idaho), un-reported	233.
Little Gunnel M. Co. v. Kimber	1878	1 Morr. Min. Rep. 536, Fed. Cas. No. 8402, 15 Fed. Cas. 629....	405, 408, 633, 643, 645, 651.
Little Giant Lode, In re	1869	22 L. D. 629..........	759.
Little Giant Lode, In re	1899	29 L. D. 194..........	755.
Little Josephine M. Co. v. Fullerton	1893	58 Fed. 521...........	614.
Little Nell Lode, In re.	1893	16 L. D. 104..........	784.
Little Pete Lode.......	1885	4 L. D. 17............	673.
Little Pittsburg Cons. Co. v. Amie M. Co....	1883	17 Fed. 57............	337, 338.

Names of Cases.	When De-cided.	Where Reported.	Sections Where Cited in this Work.
Little Pittsburg Co. *v.* Little Chief etc. Co..	1888	11 Colo. 223, 7 Am. St. Rep. 226, 17 Pac. 760, 15 Morr. 655........	868.
Live Yankee Co. *v.* Oregon Co.	1857	7 Cal. 41, 12 Morr. 94.	383.
Livingston *v.* Livingston	1822	6 Johns Ch. 497, 10 Am. Dec. 353, 10 Morr. 696.	790.
Livingston *v.* Moingona Coal Co.......	1878	49 Iowa, 369, 31 Am. Rep. 150, 10 Morr. 696	819.
Livingston *v.* Rawyards Coal Co............	1880	L. R. 5 App. Cas. 25, 10 Morr. 291........	868.
Lockhart *v.* Johnson....	1901	181 U. S. 516, 21 Sup. Ct. Rep. 665, 45 L. Ed. 979	80, 114, 116, 124, 322, 331, 343, 344, 345, 390, 405, 728.
Lockhart *v.* Leeds......	1900	(N. Mex.), 63 Pac. 51.	124, 390.
Lockhart *v.* Rollins.....	1889	2 Idaho, 503, 21 Pac. 413, 16 Morr. 16.....	270, 407, 629, 635.
Lockhart *v.* Wills......	1897	9 N. Mex. 263, 50 Pac. 318	634, 644.
Lockhart *v.* Wills......	1898	9 N. Mex. 344, 54 Pac. 336	124, 329, 330, 390, 405, 634.
Lock Lode	1887	6 L. D. 105, 14 C. L. O. 151	661.
Lockwood *v.* Lunsford..	1874	56 Mo. 68, 7 Morr. 532.	860.
Lockwood Co. *v.* Lawrence	1885	77 Me. 297, 52 Am. Rep. 763	840.
Logan, *In re.*.........	1900	29 L. D. 395.........	80, 112, 322, 429.
Logan *v.* Driscoll......	1861	19 Cal. 623, 81 Am. Dec. 90, 6 Morr. 172.....	530, 843.
Lohman *v.* Helmer.....	1900	104 Fed. 178..........	233, 234, 238, 535.
Lone Dane Lode......	1890	10 L. D. 53...........	338.
Lone Jack Min. Co. *v.* Megginson	1897	82 Fed. 89...........	232, 233.
Long, *In re.*..........	8881	9 Copp's L. O. 188.....	522.
Long John Lode Claim.	1900	30 L. D. 298.........	679.
Lonsdale *v.* Curwen....	1799	3 Bligh, 168, 7 Morr. 693	873.
Look Tin Sing, *In re...*	1884	21 Fed. 905...........	224.
Loosemore *v.* Tiverton and North Devon Ry. Co.	1882	L. R. 22 Ch. D. 25.....	90, 92.
Lord *v.* Carbon Iron Mfg. Co....	1884	38 N. J. Eq. 452, 15 Morr. 695	807.
Lorenz *v.* Jacobs.......	1883	63 Cal. 73.............	259a, 263.
Lorenz *v.* Waldron.....	1892	96 Cal. 243, 31 Pac. 54.	530.

Names of Cases.	When De-cided.	Where Reported.	Sections Where Cited in this Work.
Los Angeles Farming etc. Co. v. Thompson.	1897	117 Cal. 594, 49 Pac. 714	778.
Losee v. Buchanan.....	1873	51 N. Y. 476, 10 Am. Rep. 623	808, 832.
Louise M. Co..........	1896	22 L. D. 663..........	432, 438, 631.
Louisville Lode	1882	1 L. D. 548...........	677.
Low v. Holmes........	1864	17. N. J. Eq. 148.......	789a.
Lowe v. Alexander.....	1860	15 Cal. 297	792.
Ludlam, In re.........	1893	17 L. D. 22...........	503.
Ludlam v. Ludlam.....	1863	26 N. Y. 356, 84 Am. Dec. 193	224.
Ludlow v. Hudson R. R. Co.	1872	6 Lans. (N. Y.), 128..	823.
Lunsford v. La Motte Lead Co........	1873	54 Mo. 426, 9 Morr. 308.	860.
Lusk v. Larned Mercantile R. E. Co........	1898	7 Kan. App. 581, 52 Pac. 455	662, 772.
Lux v. Haggin........	1886	69 Cal. 255, 10 Pac. 674.	80, 838, 841.
Lynch v. Versailles Fuel Gas Co........	1895	165 Pa. St. 518, 30 Atl. 984	862.
Lyon, In re...........	1895	20 L. D. 556...........	502.
Lyons v. State.........	1885	67 Cal. 380, 7 Pac. 763.	238.
Lyman v. Schwartz....	1899	13 Colo. App. 318, 57 Pac. 735	798, 801.
Lytle v. Arkansas......	1850	9 How. 314, 13 L. Ed. 153	660.
Mabel Lode...........	1898	26 L. D. 675..........	363, 522.
Mackall v. Goodsell...	1897	24 L. D. 553..........	204, 208.
Mackie, In re.........	1886	5 L. D. 199...........	327, 670, 671.
Maffet v. Quine.......	1899	93 Fed. 347...........	530.
Magalia G. M. Co. v. Ferguson	1884	3 L. D. 234...........	207.
Magalia G. M. Co. v. Ferguson	1887	6 L. D. 218, 14 C. L. O. 21	94, 207.
Magistrates of Glasgow v. Farie	1888	L. R. 13 App. Cas. 657, 683	88, 90, 92.
Magruder, In re.......	1881	1 L. D. 526...........	772.
Magruder v. Oregon & Calif. R. R. R. Co...	1899	28 L. D. 174..........	95, 106, 273, 328, 379, 392.
Maguire v. Tyler......	1862	1 Black, 195, 17 L. Ed. 135	663.
Mahon v. Barnett.....	1898	(Tex.), 45 S. W. 24...	789a.
Mahoney v. Van Winkle	1863	21 Cal. 552...........	123.
Maier, In re..........	1900	29 L. D. 400..........	201.
Majors v. Rinda.......	1897	24 L. D. 277..........	204, 208.

Names of Cases.	When De-cided.	Where Reported.	Sections Where Cited in this Work.
Malaby *v.* Rice........	1900	15 Colo. App. 364, 62 Pac. 228	646, 728.
Mallett *v.* Uncle Sam M. Co..............	1865	1 Nev. 188, 90 Am. Dec. 484, 1 Morr. 17......	271, 274, 537, 642, 643, 644, 790.
Malone *v.* Big Flat G. M. Co........	1888	76 Cal. 578, 18 Pac. 772.	327.
Maloney *v.* King......	1901	25 Mont. 188, 64 Pac. 351	551, 615, 866.
Mamer *v.* Lussem.....	1872	65 Ill. 484............	833.
Manhattan M. Co. *v.* San Joan M. Co....	1883	2 L. D. 698..........	742.
Manley *v.* Tow........	1901	110 Fed. 241..........	665, 666.
Mann *v.* Budlong......	1900	129 Cal. 577, 62 Pac. 120	629, 631.
Mann *v.* Tacoma Land Co......	1894	153 U. S. 273, 14 Sup. Ct. Rep. 820, 38 L. Ed. 714	80, 112, 322.
Mann *v.* Wilson.......	1860	23 How. 457, 16 L. Ed. 584	181.
Manners Construction Co. *v.* Rees..........	1902	31 L. D. 408.........	205, 206.
Manning *v.* San Jacinto Tin Co........	1882	7 Saw. 419, 9 Fed. 726.	125, 126, 142, 161.
Manning *v.* Strehlow...	1888	11 Colo 451, 18 Pac. 625.	754, 755, 763.
Manser Lode Claim....	1898	27 L. D. 326..........	132, 143.
Mantle *v.* Noyes......	1888	5 Mont. 274, 5 Pac. 856.	720.
Manuel *v.* Wulff......	1894	152 U. S. 505, 14 Sup. Ct. Rep. 651, 38 L. Ed. 532	232, 233, 539, 642, 643.
Manville *v.* Parks.....	1883	7 Colo. 128, 134, 2 Pac. 212	797, 798, 801.
Marble Co. *v.* Ripley...	1870	10 Wall. 339, 19 L. Ed. 955	175.
Marburg Lode Mining Claim	1900	30 L. D. 202.........	624, 632, 637, 645, 686, 696, 731.
Marquart *v.* Bradford..	1872	43 Cal. 526, 5 Morr. 528.	644.
Marquez *v.* Frisbie....	1879	101 U. S. 473, 25 L. Ed. 800	108, 175, 207, 662, 666.
Mars M. Co. *v.* Oro Fino M. Co..............	1895	7 S. D. 605, 65 N. W. 19.	754, 757.
Marsh *v.* Brooks.......	1850	8 How. 223, 12 L. Ed. 1056	181.
Marsh *v.* Holley.......	1875	42 Conn. 453, 14 Morr. 687	791.
Marshall *v.* Forest Oil Co........	1901	193 Pa. St. 83, 47 Atl. 927	862.

Names of Cases.	When De-cided.	Where Reported.	Sections Where Cited in this Work.
Marshall *v.* Harney Peak Tin M. Co.........	1890	1 S. D. 350, 47 N. W. 290	339, 345, 356, 372, 643.
Marshall *v.* Wellwood..	1876	38 N. J. L. 339, 20 Am. Rep. 394	808.
Marshall S. M. Co. *v.* Kirtley	1889	12 Colo. 410, 21 Pac. 492	742, 754.
Marvin *v.* Brewster....	1874	55 N. Y. 538, 14 Am. Rep. 322, 13 Morr. 40.	812, 813, 818, 827.
Mary Darling Placer, *In re*	1901	31 L. D. 64..........	448b.
Maryland Ry. *v.* Robinson	1889	L. R. 15 App. C. 19....	92.
Massot *v.* Moses.......	1871	3 S. C. 168, 16 Am. Rep 697, 8 Morr. 607.....	812, 860.
Masterson, *In re*.......	1888	7 L. D. 172, 15 C. L. O. 133	502.
Masterson, *In re*......	1888	7 L. D. 577..........	502.
Matoa G. M. Co. *v.* Chicago-Cripple Creek G. M. Co..........	1899	78 Min. and Scientific Press, p. 374........	322, 490, 550, 868.
Mattingly *v.* Lewisohn.	1888	8 Mont. 259, 19 Pac. 310.	754.
Mattingly *v.* Lewisohn.	1893	13 Mont. 508, 35 Pac. 111	635, 643.
Mauser Lode Claim....	1898	27 L. D. 326..........	108, 717, 755.
Mawson *v.* Fletcher....	1870	L. R. 6 Ch. App. C. 91..	92.
Maxwell, *In re*........	1899	29 L. D. 76..........	661.
Maxwell *v.* Brierly....	1883	10 Copp's L. O. 50.....	138, 139, 158, 210, 421.
Maxwell Land Grant Case	1887	121 U. S. 325, 381, 7 Sup. Ct. Rep. 1015, 30 L. Ed. 949..........	784.
Maye *v.* Yappen	1863	23 Cal. 306, 10 Morr. 101	868.
Mayflower G. M. Co....	1899	29 L. D. 7............	670, 673.
Maylett *v.* Brennan....	1894	20 Colo. 242, 38 Pac. 75.	858.
Mayor of Baltimore *v.* Appold	1875	42 Md. 442..........	840.
Mayor of New York *v.* Baily	1845	2 Denio, 433, 441......	808.
McBurney *v.* Berry....	1885	5 Mont. 300, 5 Pac. 867	251.
McCallum *v.* Germantown W. Co.........	1867	54 Pa. St. 40, 93 Am. Dec. 656	840.
McCandless' Appeal ...	1871	70 Pa. St. 210.........	256.
McCann *v.* McMillan...	1900	129 Cal. 350, 62 Pac. 31	273, 323, 355, 383, 405, 432, 643, 644.
McCarthy, *In re*.......	1892	14 L. D. 105..........	671.

Names of Cases.	When Decided.	Where Reported.	Sections Where Cited in this Work.
McCarthy v. Speed....	1898	11 S. D. 362, 77 N. W. 590, 50 L. R. A. 184.	233, 328, 405, 406, 413, 539, 643, 644, 645, 646, 754, 788.
McCarthy v. Speed....	1901	12 S. Dak. 7, 80 N. W. 135	406, 728.
McCharles v. Roberts..	1895	20 L. D. 564..........	208.
McClintock v. Dana....	1884	106 Pa. St. 386.......	861.
McCloud v. Central Pac. R. R. Co...........	1899	29 L. D. 27..........	144, 156, 159.
McConaghy, In re. ...	1899	29 L. D. 226..........	679, 718.
McConnell, In re.. ...	1894	18 L. D. 414..........	501.
McCord v. Oakland etc. Co..........	1883	64 Cal. 134, 141, 49 Am. Rep. 686, 27 Pac. 863	789, 789a.
McCormick v. Baldwin.	1894	104 Cal. 227, 37 Pac. 903	630, 652.
McCormick v. Hayes...	1895	159 U. S. 332, 16 Sup. Ct. Rep. 37, 40 L. Ed. 171	143, 144a.
McCormick v. Night Hawk etc. Co.......	1899	29 L. D. 373..........	637, 679, 771.
McCormick v. Sutton...	1893	97 Cal. 373, 32 Pac. 444	127, 142, 170, 175.
McCormick v. Varnes..	1879	2 Utah, 355, 9 Morr. 505	60, 271, 364, 586.
McCowan v. Maclay....	1895	16 Mont. 234, 40 Pac. 602	251, 688.
McCreery v. Haskell...	1886	119 U. S. 327, 7 Sup. Ct. Rep. 176, 30 L. Ed. 408	143.
McCully v. Clarke.....	1861	40 Pa. St. 399, 406, 80 Am. Dec. 584........	832.
McDaniel v. Bell......	1889	9 L. D. 15...........	504.
McDonald v. Montana Wood Co..........	1894	14 Mont. 88, 43 Am. St. Rep. 616, 35 Pac. 668	432, 438, 454, 628.
McEvoy v. Hyman.....	1885	25 Fed. 539, 596, 15 Morr. 300, 397......	330, 375, 382, 398, 759.
McEvoy v. Megginson..	1899	29 L. D. 164	232, 233, 686.
McFadden v. Mountain View etc. Co........	1898	87 Fed. 154..........	184, 666.
McFadden v. Mountain View M. and M. Co..	1899	97 Fed. 670..........	80, 81, 183, 184, 322, 419, 666, 746.
McFadden v. Mountain View etc. Co........	1898	26 L. D. 530..........	735.
McFadden v. Mountain View etc. Co........	1898	27 L. D. 358.........	734, 735.
McFeters v. Pierson...	1890	15 Colo. 201, 22 Am. St. Rep. 388, 24 Pac. 1076	192, 233, 322, 327, 539, 754.
McGarrahan v. New Idria M. Co........	1885	3 L. D. 422, 11 C. L. O. 370	738.
McGarrity v. Byington.	1859	12 Cal. 427, 2 Morr. 311	274, 631.

Names of Cases.	When De-cided.	Where Reported.	Sections Where Cited in this Work.
McGillicuddy v. Tompkins	1892	14 L. D. 633	501.
McGinnis v. Egbert	1884	8 Colo. 41, 5 Pac. 652, 15 Morr. 329	75, 330, 398, 623, 632, 636, 651, 754, 755, 763.
McGlenn v. Weinbroeer	1892	15 L. D. 370	97, 139, 210, 421.
McGowan v. Alps Cons. M. Co	1896	23 L. D. 113	697, 772.
McGuire v. Grant	1856	25 N. J. L. 356, 67 Am. Dec. 49	833.
McGuire v. Pensacola City Co	1901	105 Fed. 677	754.
McIntosh v. Perkins	1893	13 Mont. 143, 32 Pac. 653	798.
McKay v. McDougal	1897	19 Mont. 488, 48 Pac. 988	754.
McKay v. McDougall	1901	25 Mont. 258, 87 Am. St. Rep. 395, 64 Pac. 669	408, 623, 643, 652.
McKay v. Wait	1868	51 Barb. 225	789a.
McKean v. Buell	1878	Copp's Min. Lands, 343	97.
McKee v. Colwell	1898	7 Pa. Super. Ct. Rep. 607	862.
McKeon v. Bisbee	1858	9 Cal. 137, 70 Am. Dec. 642, 2 Morr. 309	535, 792.
McKiernan v. Hesse	1877	51 Cal. 594	409.
McKinley v. Wheeler	1889	130 U. S. 630, 9 Sup. Ct. Rep. 638, 22 L. Ed. 1048, 16 Morr. 65	226, 449.
McKinley Creek M. Co. v. Alaska United M. Co	1902	183 U. S. 563, 22 Sup. Ct. Rep. 84, 46 L. Ed. 331	227, 231, 233, 234, 373, 383, 454, 539, 642.
McKinstry v. Clark	1882	4 Mont. 370, 1 Pac. 759	329, 337.
McLane v. Bovee	1874	35 Wis. 27	542.
McLaughlin v. Del Re	1886	71 Cal. 230, 16 Pac. 881	841.
McLaughlin v. Menotti	1891	89 Cal. 354, 26 Pac. 880	154.
McLaughlin v. Powell	1875	50 Cal. 64, 19 Am. Rep. 647, 10 Morr. 424	161.
McLaughlin v. Thompson	1892	2 Colo. App. 135, 29 Pac. 816	335.
McLaughlin v. United States	1882	107 U. S. 526, 2 Sup. Ct. Rep. 802, 27 L. Ed. 806	94, 161, 784.
McMaster's Appeal	1883	2 L. D. 706, 707	737.
McMillan, John	1888	7 L. D. 181	501.
McNeil v. Pace	1884	3 L. D. 267, 11 C. L. O. 307	630, 632.

Names of Cases.	When De-cided.	Where Reported.	Sections Where Cited in this Work.
McQuiddy v. State of California	1899	29 L. D. 181	95, 97, 98, 106, 138, 143, 392, 419, 420.
McRose v. Bottyer	1889	81 Cal. 122, 22 Pac. 393	530.
McShane v. Kenkle	1896	18 Mont. 208, 56 Am. St. Rep. 578, 44 Pac. 979, 33 L. R. A. 851	336, 643.
McWilliams v. Green River Coal Assn	1896	23 L. D. 127	496.
Meaderville etc. Co. v. Raunheim	1900	29 L. D. 465	413, 717.
Meagher v. Reid	1890	14 Colo. 335, 23 Pac. 681	796, 797.
Medley v. Robertson	1880	55 Cal. 397	142, 448.
Meeks, In re	1900	29 L. D. 456	184.
Mégarrigle, In re	1882	9 Copp's L. O. 113	323, 515.
Melder v. White	1899	28 L. D. 412	153.
Melton v. Lambard	1876	51 Cal. 258, 14 Morr. 695	642.
Mendota Club v. Anderson	1899	101 Wis. 479, 78 N. W. 185	107, 161, 175, 207, 779.
Merced M. Co. v. Fre-Mont	1857	7 Cal. 317, 68 Am. Dec. 262, 7 Morr. 313	539, 872.
Mercur v. State Line etc. Co	1895	171 Pa. St. 12, 32 Atl. 1126	791.
Merrell, In re	1877	5 Copp's L. O. 5	632.
Merrill v. Dixon	1880	15 Nev. 401	94.
Merritt v. Cameron	1892	137 U. S. 542, 11 Sup. Ct. Rep. 174, 34 L. Ed. 772	666.
Merritt v. Judd	1859	14 Cal. 60, 6 Morr. 62	409, 535, 792.
Mesick v. Sunderland	1856	6 Cal. 298	392, 646.
Metcalf v. Prescott	1891	10 Mont. 283, 25 Pac. 1037, 16 Morr. 137	251, 381, 383.
Meydenbaur v. Stevens	1897	78 Fed. 787	64, 218, 272, 273, 294, 301, 322, 350, 373, 379, 381, 382, 383, 392.
Meyer v. Hyman	1888	7 L. D. 83, 15 C. L. O. 147	759.
Meyerdorf v. Frohner	1879	3 Mont. 282, 5 Morr. 559	161, 233, 409.
Meylette v. Brennan	1894	20 Colo. 242, 38 Pac. 75	858.
Michael v. Mills	1896	22 Colo. 439, 45 Pac. 429	337, 754.
Michie v. Gothberg	1901	30 L. D. 407	210, 336.
Michigan Lumber Co. v. Rust	1897	168 U. S. 589, 18 Sup. Ct. Rep. 218, 42 L. Ed. 591	208, 664, 772.
Michle v. Douglass	1888	75 Iowa, 78, 39 N. W. 198	818.
Michlethwait v. Winter	1851	6 Exch. 644	92.
Middleton v. Low	1866	30 Cal. 596	448.

Names of Cases.	When Decided.	Where Reported.	Sections Where Cited in this Work.
Midland Ry. Co. v. Checkley	1867	L. R. 4 Ex. C. 19	90, 92.
Midland Ry. Co. v. Haunchwood etc. Co.	1882	L. R. 20 Ch. D. 552....	88, 89, 90, 92.
Migeon v. Montana Central Ry	1896	77 Fed. 249	289, 291, 294, 336, 781.
Miller v. Butterfield	1889	79 Cal. 62, 21 Pac. 543.	858.
Miller v. Girard	1893	3 Colo. App. 278, 33 Pac. 68	338.
Miller v. Grunsky	1901	(Cal.), 66 Pac. 858....	778.
Miller v. Taylor	1881	6 Colo. 41, 9 Morr. 547	373.
Miller Placer	1900	30 L. D. 225	448.
Mills v. Fletcher	1893	100 Cal. 142, 34 Pac. 637	632, 634.
Mills v. Hart	1898	24 Colo. 505, 52 Am. St. Rep. 241, 52 Pac. 680.	728, 788.
Milton v. Lamb	1896	22 L. D. 339	673.
Mimbres M. Co., In re.	1889	8 L. D. 457	690, 691.
Miner, Abraham L., In re	1889	9 L. D. 408	142.
Miner v. Mariott	1884	2 L. D. 709, 10 C. L. O. 339	738.
Mint Lode and Millsite	1891	12 L. D. 624	524.
Minter v. Crommelin	1856	18 How. 87, 15 L. Ed. 279	181.
Mississippi v. Johnson.	1867	4 Wall. 498, 18 L. Ed. 437	660.
Mississippi etc. Broom Co. v. Patterson	1879	98 U. S. 403, 25 L. Ed. 206	252.
Missouri etc. R. Co. v. Kansas Pac. R. R. Co.	1878	97 U. S. 491, 24 L. Ed. 1095	154.
Missouri etc. Ry. v. Roberts	1894	152 U. S. 114, 14 Sup. Ct. Rep. 496, 38 L. Ed. 377	153, 183.
Missouri etc. Ry Co. v. United States	1876	92 U. S. 760, 23 L. Ed. 645	183.
Missouri Pac. Ry. Co. v. Nebraska	1896	164 U. S. 403, 17 Sup. Ct. Rep. 130, 41 L. Ed. 489	254.
Mitchell, In re	1884	2 L. D. 752	335.
Mitchell v. Brovo	1898	27 L. D. 40	337.
Mitchell v. Brown	1884	3 L. D. 65, 11 C. L. O. 214	207, 496, 502.
Mitchell v. Cline	1890	84 Cal. 409, 24 Pac. 164	450, 792.
Mitchell v. Darley Main Colliery Co	1884	L. R. 14 Q. B. 125	823.
Mitchell v. Rome	1873	49 Ga. 19, 15 Am. Rep. 669	833.

Names of Cases.	When Decided.	Where Reported.	Sections Where Cited in this Work.
Moffat v. United States	1884	112 U. S. 24, 5 Sup. Ct. Rep. 10 28 L. Ed. 623	784.
Monarch of the North Mining Claim	1881	8 Copp's L. O. 104.....	365.
Mongram v. N. P. R. R. Co........	1894	18 L. D. 105.........	521.
Monitor Lode	1894	18 L. D. 358..........	646, 728.
Monk, In re..........	1897	16 Utah, 100, 50 Pac. 810	268, 270, 273.
Monmouth Canal Co. v. Hartford	1834	1 C. R. M. & R. 614, 634	813.
Mono Fraction Lode Claim	1901	31 L. D. 122..........	363a, 671.
Mono M. Co. v. Magnolia etc. Co..........	1875	2 Copp's L. O. 68.....	398, 728, 766.
Monroe Lode	1885	4 L. D. 273, 12 C. L. O. 264	171, 766.
Montague v. Dobbs...	1882	9 Copp's L. O. 165....	97, 323, 420.
Montana Cent. R. R. Co.	1897	25 L. D. 250..........	153.
Montana Cent. Ry. Co. v. Migeon	1895	68 Fed. 811..........	175, 336, 777, 781.
Montana Co. Limited v. Clark	1890	42 Fed. 626, 16 Morr. 80	365, 551, 582, 666, 866.
Montana M. Co. Ltd. v. St. Louis etc. Co.....	1894	102 Fed. 430.........	594, 616, 618, 618a, 865.
Montana M. Co. v. St. Louis etc. Co........	1898	20 Mont. 394, 51 Pac. 824	618.
Montana M. Co. v. St. Louis M. etc. Co.....	1894	152 U. S. 160, 14 Sup. Ct. Rep. 506, 38 L. Ed. 398	873.
Montana M. Co. v. St. Louis M. and M. Co..	1902	186 U. S. 24, 22 Sup. Ct. Rep. 744, 46 L. Ed. 1039	584.
Montana Ore Purchasing Co. v. Boston etc. S. M. Co..............	1897	20 Mont. 336, 51 Pac. 159	60, 71, 780.
Montana Ore Purchasing Co. v. Boston and Montana etc. Co.....	1899	22 Mont. 159, 56 Pac. 120	872.
Montana Ore Purchasing Co. v. Boston etc. Co.	1902	(Mont.), 70 Pac. 1114	612, 617, 618, 618a.
Mont Blanc Cons. G. M. Co. v. Debour....	1882	61 Cal. 364, 15 Morr. 286	758.
Moody v. McDonald...	1854	4 Cal. 297, 2 Morr. 187.	818.
Mooney, John, In re...	1876	3 Copp's L. O. 68......	227.

Names of Cases.	When Decided.	Where Reported.	Sections Where Cited in this Work.
Moore, *In re*	1883	11 Copp's L. O. 326....	521.
Moore *v.* Besse........	1872	43 Cal. 511............	542.
Moore *v.* Hamerstag...	1895	109 Cal. 122, 41 Pac. 805	270, 273, 331, 398, 642.
Moore *v.* Miller.......	1848	8 Pa. St. 272........	861.
Moore *v.* Robbins......	1878	96 U. S. 530, 24 L. Ed. 848	161, 175, 207, 665, 666, 765, 777, 784.
Moore *v.* Smaw.......	1861	17 Cal. 199, 79 Am. Dec. 123, 12 Morr. 418....	21, 125.
Moore *v.* Thompson....	1873	69 N. C. 120, 1 Morr. Min. Rep. 221.......	688.
Morager, *In re*........	....	10 Copp's L. O. 54.....	97.
Moran *v.* Horsky......	1900	178 U. S. 205, 20 Sup. Ct. Rep. 856, 44 L. Ed. 1038	177.
More *v.* Massini.......	1867	32 Cal. 590, 596, 7 Morr. 455	872.
More *v.* Steinbach.....	1888	127 U. S. 70, 8 Sup. Ct. Rep. 1067, 32 L. Ed. 51	125.
Morenhaut *v.* Wilson...	1877	52 Cal. 263, 1 Morr. 53.	329, 373, 643, 644.
Morgan *v.* Antlers Park Regent etc. Co......	1899	29 L. D. 114..........	679, 718.
Morgan *v.* Morgan.....	1871	23 La. Ann. 502.......	790.
Morgan *v.* Tillottson..	1887	73 Cal. 520, 15 Pac. 88.	624, 625.
Morganstern *v.* Thrift.	1885	66 Cal. 577, 6 Pac. 689.	800.
Morgenson *v.* Middlesex M. etc. Co..........	1888	11 Colo. 176, 17 Pac. 513	558.
Moritz *v.* Lavelle......	1888	77 Cal. 10, 11 Am. St. Rep. 299, 18 Pac. 803, 16 Morr. 236........	233, 331, 754, 797, 858.
Mormon Church *v.* United States	1890	136 U. S. 1, 10 Sup. Ct. Rep. 792, 34 L. Ed. 478	242, 243.
Morrill *v.* Margaret M. Co............	1890	11 L. D. 563..........	515.
Morrill *v.* Northern Pac. R. R. Co...........	1901	30 L. D. 475..........	95, 97, 98, 139, 158, 421.
Morrison *v.* Lincoln M. Co.............	1879	6 Copp's L. O. 105, Sickle's Min. Dec. 208	738.
Morrison *v.* Marker....	1899	93 Fed. 692..........	754.
Morrison *v.* Regan.....	1902	(Idaho), 67 Pac. 955...	331, 374, 379, 380, 381, 383, 384, 397, 398.
Morrow *v.* Whitney....	1877	95 U. S. 551, 24 L. Ed. 456	216.
Morse *v.* De Ardo.....	1895	107 Cal. 622, 40 Pac. 1018	327.

Names of Cases.	When De-cided.	Where Reported.	Sections Where Cited in this Work.
Morton v. Solambo M. Co......	1864	26 Cal. 527, 4 Morr. 463	44, 331, 398.
Morton v. State of Ne-braska	1874	21 Wall. 660, 22 L. Ed. 639, 12 Morr. 541....	36, 47, 97, 513, 609.
Moss v. Dowman......	1898	88 Fed. 181...........	666.
Moss v. Dowman......	1900	176 U. S. 413, 20 Sup. Ct. Rep. 429, 44 L. Ed. 526	665, 666.
Mott v. Reyes.........	1873	45 Cal. 379..........	123.
Mountain Maid Lode...	1886	5 L. D. 28............	784.
Mower v. Fletcher.....	1886	116 U. S. 380, 6 Sup. Ct. Rep. 409, 29 L. Ed. 593	143.
Mowrer v. State.......	1886	107 Ind. 539, 5 N. E. 561	872.
Moxon v. Wilkinson...	1876	2 Mont. 421, 12 Morr. 602	62, 392, 419.
Moyle v. Bullene.......	1896	7 Colo. App. 308, 44 Pac. 69, 71	177, 337, 398.
Mt. Diablo etc. Co. v. Callison	1879	5 Saw. 439, Fed. Case No. 9886, 9 Morr. 616	274, 290, 327, 373, 381, 630, 631, 645.
Mt. Joy Lode, In re...	1870	Copp's Min. Dec. 27...	59, 730.
Mt. Rosa M. M. and L. Co. v. Palmer....	1899	26 Colo. 56, 77 Am. St. Rep. 245, 56 Pac. 176, 50 L. R. A. 289.....	322, 413, 415, 435, 439, 450.
Muldrick v. Brown....	1900	37 Or. 185, 61 Pac. 428.	336, 872.
Mullan v. United States	1886	118 U. S. 271, 6 Sup. Ct. Rep. 1041, 30 L. Ed. 170	136, 140, 143, 157, 161, 495, 784.
Muller v. Dows........	1877	94 U. S. 444, 24 L. Ed. 207	226.
Mullins v. Butte Hard-ware Co...........	1901	25 Mont. 525, 65 Pac. 1004, 1007	550.
Mumford v. Whitney...	1836	15 Wend. 380, 30 Am. Dec. 60	860.
Mundy v. Rutland.....	1882	23 Ch. Div. 81, 96......	827.
Murchie v. Black......	1865	19 C. B. N. S. 190......	833.
Murdock v. Stickney...	1851	8 Cush. 113..........	257.
Murley v. Ennis.......	1874	2 Colo. 300, 12 Morr. 360	331, 339, 372, 797, 858.
Murphy v. Sanford....	1890	11 L. D. 123..........	772.
Murray v. Allred......	1897	100 Tenn. 100, 66 Am. St. Rep. 740, 43 S. W. 355, 39 L. R. A. 249	90, 93, 97, 138, 422, 423, 812.

Names of Cases.	When Decided.	Where Reported.	Sections Where Cited in this Work.
Murray v. City of Butte	1887	7 Mont. 61, 14 Pac. 656	530.
Murray v. Montana Lumber Mfg. Co....	1901	25 Mont. 14, 63 Pac. 719	718, 719.
Murray v. Polglase....	1896	17 Mont. 455, 43 Pac. 505	208, 637, 772.
Murray v. Polglase....	1899	23 Mont. 401, 59 Pac. 439	637, 754, 758, 772, 773.
Murray Hill etc. M. Co. v. Havenor	1901	24 Utah 73, 66 Pac. 762	636, 754, 763, 771.
Muskett v. Hill.......	1839	3 Bing. N. C. 694......	860, 861.
Mutual M. etc. Co. v. Currency Co....	1898	27 L. D. 191..........	712, 713, 742, 759.
Myers v. Spooner......	1880	55 Cal. 257, 9 Morr. 519	643, 644.
Naftger v. Gregg......	1893	99 Cal. 83, 88, 37 Am. St. Rep. 23, 33 Pac. 757	764.
Nancy Ann Caste......	1884	3 L. D. 169...........	209.
National Bank v. County of Yankton......	1879	101 U. S. 129, 25 L. Ed. 1046	242.
National Bank v. Matthews	1878	98 U. S. 621, 25 L. Ed. 188	226.
National Mining etc. Co..	1879	7 Copp's L. O. 179....	522.
Natoma W. etc. Co. v. Clark	1860	14 Cal. 554...........	872.
Natoma W. etc. Co. v. Hancock	1894	101 Cal. 42, 68, 31 Poc. 112, 35 Pac. 334.....	872.
Navajo Indian Reservation	1901	30 L. D. 515.........	185.
Neal v. Clark........	1878	95 U. S. 704, 24 L. Ed. 586	480.
Negus, In re..........	1890	11 L. D. 32...........	501, 504, 784.
Neill, In re...........	1897	24 L. D. 393..........	661.
Neilson v. Champagne M. etc. Co..........	1900	29 L. D. 491..........	405, 624, 635, 645, 673, 677, 686, 771.
Neilson v. Champagne M. etc. Co..........	1901	111 Fed. 655..........	771, 773.
Neilson v. Champagne M. etc. Co..........	1902	119 Fed. 123..........	731.
Nelson v. Miller......	....	(Pa.), 1 Leg. Rec. 187..	819.
Nelson v. O'Neal......	1871	1 Mont. 284, 4 Morr. 275	843.
Nerce Valle, In re.....	1875	2 Copp's L. O. 178....	211.
Nesbitt v. De Lamar's Nevada etc. Co......	1898	24 Nev. 273, 77 Am. St. Rep. 807, 52 Pac. 609	633, 634, 681, 713, 742, 754, 758.

Names of Cases.	When De-cided.	Where Reported.	Sections Where Cited in this Work.
Nettie Lode v. Texas Lode	1892	14 L. D. 180	738, 756.
Nevada Lode	1893	16 L. D. 532	742.
Nevada Sierra Oil Co. v. Home Oil Co	1899	98 Fed. 673	94, 95, 207, 216, 217, 218, 329, 330, 335, 336, 403, 437.
Nevada Sierra Oil Co. v. Miller	1899	97 Fed. 681	746.
Newhill v. Thurston	1884	65 Cal. 419, 4 Pac. 409	339, 372.
New Cent. C. Co. v. George's Creek C. Co.	1872	37 Md. 537, 559	256.
New Dunderberg M. Co. v. Old	1897	79 Fed. 598	175, 367, 553, 604, 664, 727.
New Dunderberg M. Co. v. Old	1899	97 Fed. 150	868.
Newhall v. Sanger	1875	92 U. S. 761, 23 L. Ed. 769	80, 112, 123, 124, 322.
Newman v. Barnes	1896	23 L. D. 257	765.
Newman v. Driefurst	1886	9 Colo. 228, 11 Pac. 98.	790.
Newman v. Duane	1891	89 Cal. 597, 27 Pac. 66.	754.
New Mexico v. United States Trust Co	1898	172 U. S. 171, 19 Sup. Ct. Rep. 128, 43 L. Ed. 407	153.
New York etc. Establishment v. Fitch	1830	1 Paige, 97, 99	790.
New York Lode and Millsite	1887	5 L. D. 513, 14 C. L. O. 52	677.
New York Hill Co. v. Rocky Bar Co	1886	6 L. D. 318, 15 C. L. O. 3	730.
Nichol, In re	1889	15 Copp's L. O. 255	501.
Nicholas v. Abercrombie	1887	6 L. D. 393	94.
Nicholas v. Becker	1890	11 L. D. 8	630, 755.
Nicholas v. Marsland	1876	L. R. 10 Exch. 255, 2 Exch. Div. 1	808.
Nil Desperandum Placer	1890	10 L. D. 198	677.
Nisbit v. Nash	1878	52 Cal. 540, 11 Morr. 531	796, 800.
Niven v. State of California	1887	6 L. D. 439	142.
Noble v. Union River Logging R. R. Co	1893	147 U. S. 165, 13 Sup. Ct. Rep. 271, 37 L. Ed. 123	663.
Noble v. Sylvester	1869	42 Vt. 146, 150, 12 Morr. 62	644.
Nolan v. Lovelock	1870	1 Mont. 224, 9 Morr. 360	797, 801.
Nome Transp. Co., In re	1900	29 L. D. 447	80, 112, 322.

Names of Cases.	When De- cided.	Where Reported.	Sections Where Cited in this Work.
Noonan *v.* Caledonian G. M. Co............	1883	10 Copp's L. O. 167....	764.
Noonan *v.* Caledonia G. M. Co......	1887	121 U. S. 393, 7 Sup. Ct. Rep. 911, 30 L. Ed. 1061	184.
Noonan *v.* Pardee......	1901	200 Pa. St. 474, 485, 86 Am. St. Rep. 722, 50 Atl. 255	823.
Norager, *In re*........	1881	10 Copp's L. O. 54....	136.
Norman *v.* Phœnix Zinc M. and S. Co........	1899	28 L. D. 361..........	20, 35.
Norris *v.* Gould.......	1884	15 W. N. C. 187.......	789a.
North American Exp. Co. *v.* Adams........	1900	104 Fed. 404........	644.
North Bloomfield etc. Co. *v.* United States.	1898	88 Fed. 664, 673.......	849.
Northern Pacific R. R. Co.	1891	13 L. D. 691..........	155.
Northern Pac. R. R. Co. *v.* Allen	1898	27 L. D. 286..........	154, 781.
Northern Pac. R. R. Co. *v.* Barden	1891	46 Fed. 592..........	154.
Northern Pac. R. R. Co. *v.* Cannon	1893	54 Fed. 252..........	144, 154, 156, **159**.
Northern Pac. R. R. Co. *v.* Champion Cons. Co.	1891	14 L. D. 699..........	155.
Northern Pac. R. R. Co. *v.* Colburn	1896	164 U. S. 383, 17 Sup. Ct. Rep. 98, 41 L. Ed. 479	216.
Northern Pac. R. R. Co. *v.* Marshall	1893	17 L. D. 545..........	106, 155, 335.
Northern Pac. R. R. Co. *v.* Murray	1898	87 Fed. 648..........	153.
Northern Pac. R. R. Co. *v.* Paine	1887	119 U. S. 561, 7 Sup. Ct. Rep. 323, 30 L. Ed. 513	872.
Northern Pac. R. R. Co. *v.* Sanders	1892	49 Fed. 129..........	152, 154, 327.
Northern Pac. R. R. Co. *v.* Sanders	1897	166 U. S. 620, 17 Sup. Ct. Rep. 671, 41 L. Ed. 1139	44, 56, 152, **154**, 306.
Northern Pac. Ry. Co. *v.* Smith	1898	171 U. S. 260, 18 Sup. Ct. Rep. 794, 43 L. Ed. 157	216.
Northern Pac. R. R. Co. *v.* Soderberg	1898	86 Fed. 49..........	107, 159, 161, 207, 779, 872.

Names of Cases.	When Decided.	Where Reported.	Sections Where Cited in this Work.
Northern Pac. R. R. Co. v. Soderberg	1900	99 Fed. 506...........	96, 97, 98, 137, 139, 158, 159, 162, 323, 421.
Northern Pac. R. R. Co. v. Soderberg	1900	104 Fed. 425..........	96, 97, 98, 137, 139, 158, 323, 421.
Northern Pac. R. R. Co. v. Wright	1893	54 Fed. 67.............	154.
Northmore v. Simmons.	1899	97 Fed. 386..........	250, 343, 344, 626, 632.
North Noonday M. Co. v. Orient M. Co......	1880	6 Sawy. 299, 1 Fed. 522, 9 Morr. 529	218, 226, 232, 233, 250, 271, 272, 273, 294, 330, 335, 345, 361, 362, 373, 383, 651.
North Noonday M. Co. v. Orient M. Co......	1880	6 Saw. 503, 11 Fed. 125, 9 Morr. 524.........	227.
North Star Lode......	1899	28 L. D. 41, 44........	415, 718, 720, 755, 781.
North Star M. Co. v. C. P. R. R. Co.......	1891	12 L. D. 608..........	155.
Northwestern Ohio Nat. Gas Co. v. Tiffin.....	1898	59 Ohio St. 420, 54 N. E. 77	862.
Norton v. Evans......	1897	82 Fed. 804..........	205.
Noteware v. Sterns....	1871	1 Mont. 311, 4 Morr. 650	531.
Noyes v. Black........	1883	4 Mont. 527, 2 Pac. 769	218, 329.
Noyes v. Mantle......	1888	127 U. S. 348, 8 Sup. Ct. Rep. 1132, 52 L. Ed. 168, 15 Morr. 611....	169, 176, 413, 415, 539, 720, 781.
Oaksmith v. Johnston..	1876	92 U. S. 343, 23 L. Ed. 682	216.
Obert v. Obert........	1846	5 N. J. Eq. 397........	790.
O'Connor v. Gertgens..	1902	85 Minn. 481, 89 N. W. 866	663, 665, 666.
O'Donnell v. Glenn....	1888	8 Mont. 248, 19 Pac. 302	251, 336, 346, 383.
Oettel v. Dufur........	1896	22 L. D. 77...........	772.
Offerman v. Starr......	1846	2 Pa. St. 394, 44 Am. Dec. 211, 10 Morr. 614	861.
O'Gorman v. Mayfield..	1894	19 L. D. 522..........	505.
Ohio R. R. Co. v. Wheeler	1862	1 Black, 286, 17 L. Ed. 130	226.
O'Keife v. Cunningham	1858	9 Cal. 589, 9 Morr. 451.	843.
Oklahoma Territory v. Brooks	1900	29 L. D. 533..........	513, 514.
Oldtown v. Bangor.....	1870	58 Me. 353...........	224.

Names of Cases.	When De-cided.	Where Reported.	Sections Where Cited in this Work.
Olive Land & Dev. Co. v. Olmstead	1900	103 Fed. 568	106, 142, 143, 199, 207, 216, 330, 335, 336, 422, 437, 717, 771, 772.
Oliver v. Lassing	1899	57 Neb. 352, 77 N. W. 802	406, 646.
Omaha and Grant S. Co. v. Tabor	1889	13 Colo. 41, 16 Am. St. Rep. 185, 21 Pac. 925, 16 Morr. 184, 5 L. R. A. 236	791, 868.
Omaha G. M. Co.	1876	3 Copp's L. O. 36	739.
Omar v. Soper	1888	11 Colo. 380, 7 Am. St. Rep. 246, 18 Pac. 443, 15 Morr. 496	330, 339, 345, 356, 397, 558, 642.
Ontario Nat. Gas. Co. v. Gosfield	1891	18 Ont. App. 626	423.
Ontario S. M. Co.	1886	13 Copp's L. O. 159	521.
Oolagah Coal Co. v. McCaleb	1895	68 Fed. 86	872.
Opie v. Auburn G. M. etc. Co.	1899	29 L. D. 230	677, 686, 690, 738, 765, 772.
Orchard v. Alexander	1895	157 U. S. 372, 15 Sup. Ct. Rep. 635, 39 L. Ed. 737	208, 472, 662, 772.
Oreamuno v. Uncle Sam M. Co.	1865	1 Nev. 179	274.
Oreamuno v. Uncle Sam M. Co.	1865	1 Nev. 215, 1 Morr. 32.	274, 643, 644.
Oregon and C. R. R. Co. v. United States	1901	109 Fed. 514	157.
O'Reilly v. Campbell	1886	116 U. S. 418, 6 Sup. Ct. Rep. 421, 29 L. Ed. 669	233, 373, 684.
Original Min. Co. v. Winthrop Min. Co.	1882	60 Cal. 631	250, 632.
Oscamp v. Crystal River M. Co.	1883	58 Fed. 293	363, 558, 651.
Osterman v. Baldwin	1867	6 Wall. 122, 18 L. Ed. 730	232.
Otaheite G. and S. M. Co. v. Dean	1900	102 Fed. 929	841.
Ouimette v. O'Connor	1896	22 L. D. 538	504.
Oury v. Goodwin	1891	(Ariz.), 26 Pac. 376	257, 259.
Ovens v. Stephens	1882	2 L. D. 699, 9 C. L. O. 190	738, 759.
Overman v. Dardenelles M. Co.	1873	Copp's Min. Dec. 181	737.
Overman S. M. Co. v. Corcoran	1880	15 Nev. 147, 1 Morr. 691	258, 615.
Owers v. Killoran	1899	29 L. D. 160	718.

Names of Cases.	When Decided.	Where Reported.	Sections Where Cited in this Work.
Pacific Coast Marble Co. v. Northern Pac. R. R. Co.	1897	25 L. D. 233..........	95, 96, 97, 98, 137, 139, 158, 323, 419, 420, 421, 425.
Pacific M. & M. Co. v. Spargo	1883	8 Saw. 647, 16 Fed. 348, 16 Morr. 75..	107, 127, 207, 208, 612.
Pacific Slope Lode.....	1891	12 L. D. 686..........	173, 174, 177.
Pacific Slope Lode v. Butte Townsite	1897	25 L. D. 518..........	173, 177, 413.
Packer v. Bird.........	1891	137 U. S. 661, 11 Sup. Ct. Rep. 212, 34 L. Ed. 819	428.
Packer v. Heaton......	1858	9 Cal. 569, 4 Morr. 447.	629, 631.
Page, In re...........	1883	1 L. D. 614..........	523.
Page v. Summers......	1886	70 Cal. 121, 12 Pac. 120, 15 Morr. 617........	407, 800.
Pagosa Springs, In re..	1882	1 L. D. 562..........	515.
Palmer v. Fleshees.....	1663	1 Sid. 167...........	833.
Panton v. Holland.....	1819	17 Johns, 92, 8 Am. Dec. 369	832.
Papina v. Alderson....	1883	10 Copp's L. O. 52.....	171, 723.
Parcher v. Gillen......	1898	26 L. D. 34..........	772.
Pardee v. Murray......	1882	4 Mont. 234, 2 Pac. 16, 15 Morr. 515........	559, 865.
Park Coal Co. v. O'Donnell	1875	7 Leg. Gaz. (Pa.), 149.	814.
Parker v. Duff........	1874	47 Cal. 554..........	144a, 660, 664.
Parker v. Furlong.....	1900	37 Or. 248, 62 Pac. 490.	842, 872.
Parley's Park S. M. Co. v. Kerr	1889	130 U. S. 256, 9 Sup. Ct. Rep. 511, 32 L. Ed. 906	161, 207, 275, 604.
Parrott Silver & Copper Co. v. Heinze.......	1901	25 Mont. 139, 87 Am. St. Rep. 386, 64 Pac. 326.	69, 337, 364, 551, 589, 591, 615, 866.
Parsons v. Venzke.....	1896	164 U. S. 89, 17 Sup. Ct. Rep. 27, 41 L. Ed. 360.	637, 771, 772.
Partridge v. McKinney.	1858	10 Cal. 181, 1 Morr. 185.	644.
Partridge v. Scott.....	1838	3 M. & W. 220, 13 Morr. 640	833.
Patchen v. Keeley.....	1887	19 Nev. 404, 14 Pac. 347.	335, 868.
Patrick v. Weston.....	1895	22 Colo. 45, 43 Pac. 446.	796.
Patterson v. Hitchcock.	1877	3 Colo. 533, 544, 5 Morr. 542	58, 339, 350, 372, 553.
Patterson v. Keystone M. Co...............	1866	23 Cal. 575, 30 Cal. 360, 13 Morr. 169	270, 800.
Patterson v. Tarbell....	1894	26 Or. 29, 37 Pac. 76..	339, 371, 372.
Patterson Quartz Mine.	1876	4 Copp's L. O. 3.......	521.

Names of Cases.	When De-cided.	Where Reported.	Sections Where Cited in this Work.
Paul v. Cragnas.......	1900	25 Nev. 293, 59 Pac. 857, 60 Pac. 983, 47 L. R. A. 540........	791, 792, 860, 861.
Paul Jones Lode......	1899	28 L. D. 120..........	338.
Paul Jones Lode.......	1902	31 L. D. 359..........	338, 363a, 522.
Payne, In re..........	1888	15 Copp's L. O. 97.....	690.
Peabody Gold Mining v. Gold Hill etc. Co....	1899	97 Fed. 657...........	778.
Peabody Gold Mining Co. v. Gold Hill etc. Co.	1901	106 Fed. 241.........	782, 784.
Peabody Gold Mining Co. v. Gold Hill M. Co.	1901	111 Fed. 817.........	161, 175, 207, 604, 671, 778, 784.
Peacock Millsite......	1898	27 L. D. 373.........	677, 708.
Pearsall and Freeman, In re..............	1887	6 L. D. 227, 14 C. L. O. 210	448.
Peavey, In re..........	1902	31 L. D. 186..........	199.
Pecard v. Camens.....	1885	4 L. D. 152, 156.......	677.
Peck, In re...........	1883	10 Copp's L. O. 119....	728.
Peirano v. Pendola....	1890	10 L. D. 536.........	95, 207.
Pelican and Dives M. Co. v. Snodgrass.....	1886	9 Colo. 339, 12 Pac. 206.	330, 408.
Pelican Lode.........	1872	Copp's Min. Dec. 126...	756.
Penn. v. Oldhauber....	1900	24 Mont. 287, 61 Pac. 649	250, 268, 270, 635.
Pennington v. Coxe....	1804	2 Cranch, 33, 2 L. D. 199.	480.
Pennoyer v. McConnaughy	1891	140 U. S. 1, 11 Sup. Ct. Rep. 699, 35 L. Ed. 363	666.
Pennoyer v. Neff......	1877	95 U. S. 714, 24 L. Ed. 565	251.
Pennsylvania Coal Co. v. Sanderson	1880	94 Pa. St. 302, 39 Am. Rep. 785, 11 Morr. 79.	840.
Pennsylvania Coal Co. v. Sanderson	1886	113 Pa. St. 126, 57 Am. Rep. 445, 6 Atl. 453..	840.
Pennsylvania Cons. Min. Co. v. Grass Valley Exp. Co.	1902	117 Fed. 509.........	615.
Pennsylvania M. and Imp. Co. v. Everett and M. C. Ry. Co...	1902	(Wash.), 69 Pac. 628...	153.
Pennybecker v. McDougal	1874	48 Cal. 163...........	409.
People v. De France..	1902	(Colo.), 68 Pac. 267...	873.
People v. District Court	1887	11 Colo. 147, 17 Pac. 298	252, 256, 263, 531.
People v. District Court	1894	19 Colo. 343, 35 Pac. 731.	713.
People v. District Court	1900	27 Colo. 465, 62 Pac. 206.	790.
People v. Folsom.....	1855	5 Cal. 373.............	233.

Names of Cases.	When De-cided.	Where Reported.	Sections Where Cited in this Work.
People v. Gold Run Ditch M. Co........	1884	66 Cal. 138, 56 Am. Rep. 80, 4 Pac. 1150......	843, 848, 849.
People v. Morrill	1864	26 Cal. 360............	872.
People v. Parks	1881	58 Cal. 624..........	806.
People v. Pittsburg R. R. Co.	1879	53 Cal. 694, 12 Morr. 518.	256.
People v. Shearer	1866	30 Cal. 645..........	535.
People v. Taylor	1865	1 Nev. 88.............	535.
Pequignot v. City of Detroit	1883	16 Fed. 211..........	224.
Peralta v. United States	1866	3 Wall. 434, 18 L. Ed. 221	116.
Perego v. Dodge	1896	163 U. S. 160, 16 Sup. Ct. Rep. 971, 41 L. Ed. 113	754, 763, 765,
Pereira v. Jacks	1892	15 L. D. 273..........	142.
Perigo v. Erwin	1898	85 Fed. 904..........	273, 328, 330, 335, 338, 350, 373.
Perkins v. Hendrix	1885	23 Fed. 418..........	872.
Perkins v. Peterson....	1892	2 Colo. App. 242, 29 Pac. 1135	798.
Perrott v. Connick.....	1891	13 L. D. 598..........	772.
Peru Lode and Millsite	1890	10 L. D. 196..........	523.
Peters v. United States	1893	2 Okl. 116, 23 Pac. 1031.	660.
Peterson, Adolph, In re.	1887	6 L. D. 371, 15 C. L. O. 14	501.
Petit v. Buffalo etc. M. Co.......	1889	9 L. D. 563..........	742.
Peyton v. Mayor etc. of London	1829	9 Barn & Cress. 725...	833.
Pfister v. Dascey.......	1884	65 Cal. 403, 4 Pac. 393.	872.
Pharis v. Muldoon.....	1888	75 Cal. 284, 17 Pac. 70, 15 Morr. 348........	339, 372, 373, 408, 651, 652.
Phelps v. Church of Our Lady	1902	115 Fed. 882.........	93, 421.
Phifer v. Heaton......	1898	27 L. D. 57..........	95, 96, 97, 98, 158, 419, 420.
Philadelphia M. Claim v. Pride of the West.	1876	3 Copp's L. O. 82......	396, 582, 671.
Philadelphia M. Co. v. Finley	1884	10 Copp's L. O. 340....	735.
Phillpotts v. Blasdell..	1872	8 Nev. 62, 4 Morr. 341.	294.
Phillips v. Homfray....	1871	6 L. R. C. Ch. App. 770, 14 Morr. 677........	807.
Phillips v. Moore......	1879	100 U. S. 208, 212, 25 L. Ed. 603..........	233.
Phillips v. Watson.....	1884	63 Iowa, 28, 18 N. W. 659	256.
Phœnix M. etc. Co. v. Scott	1898	20 Wash. 48, 54 Pac. 777	535, 539, 543, 544, 719.

Names of Cases.	When De-cided.	Where Reported.	Sections Where Cited in this Work.
Phœnix Water Co. v. Fletcher	1863	23 Cal. 482, 15 Morr. 185	841.
Pico v. Columbet	1859	12 Cal. 414, 73 Am. Dec. 550	789a.
Pike's Peak Lode	1890	10 L. D. 200	415.
Pike's Peak Lode	1892	14 L. D. 47	177, 413.
Pinney v. Berry	1875	61 Mo. 359, 367	844.
Piru Oil Co	1893	16 L. D. 117	138, 422.
Pixley v. Clark	1866	35 N. Y. 520, 91 Am. Dec. 72	808.
Platt v. Union Pac. R. R. Co	1878	99 U. S. 48, 25 L. Ed. 424	480, 612.
Platt Bros. & Co. v. Waterbury	1900	72 Conn. 531, 77 Am. St. Rep. 335, 45 Atl. 154, 48 L. R. A. 692	840.
Plevna Lode	1890	11 L. D. 236	363.
Plummer v. Hillside Coal Co	1900	104 Fed. 208	812, 861.
Plummer v. Hillside Coal etc. Co	1894	160 Pa. St. 483, 28 Atl. 853	812, 862.
Plymouth Lode	1891	12 L. D. 513	173, 174, 177.
Poire v. Wells	1882	6 Colo. 406	161, 175, 177.
Pollard's Lessee v. Hagan	1845	3 How. 212, 11 L. Ed. 565	80, 115, 428.
Pollard's Heirs v. Kibbe	1850	9 How. 471, 13 L. Ed. 220	428.
Pollard v. Shively	1880	5 Colo. 309, 2 Morr. 229.	371, 375, 379, 382, 642.
Poplar Creek Cons. Quartz Mine	1893	16 L. D. 1, 2	337.
Poppe v. Athearn	1872	42 Cal. 607	472, 662.
Port v. Tuston	1763	2 Wils. 172	9.
Portland G. M. Co. v. Uinta Tunnel etc. Co.	1898	1 Leg. Adv. 494	490a.
Porter v. Landrum	1902	31 L. D. 352	679.
Post v. Fleming	1900	(N. Mex.), 62 Pac. 1087.	790.
Postal Tel. Cable Co. v. Alabama	1894	155 U. S. 482, 15 Sup. Ct. Rep. 192, 39 L. Ed. 231	747.
Potter v. Mercer	1879	53 Cal. 667	860.
Potter v. Randolph	1899	126 Cal. 458, 58 Pac. 905	107, 108, 161, 207.
Potter v. United States.	1883	107 U. S. 126, 1 Sup. Ct. Rep. 524, 27 L. Ed. 330	660.
Poujade v. Ryan	1893	21 Nev. 449, 33 Pac. 659.	272, 273, 355, 379.
Powell v. Ferguson	1896	23 L. D. 173	717.

Names of Cases.	When De-cided.	Where Reported.	Sections Where Cited in this Work.
Power v. Sla..........	1900	24 Mont. 243, 61 Pac. 468	631, 643, 645.
Powers v. Leith.......	1879	53 Cal. 711............	207.
Pralus v. Jefferson etc. Co.............	1868	34 Cal. 558, 12 Morr. 473.	537.
Pralus v. Pacific G. and S. M. Co...........	1868	35 Cal. 30, 12 Morr. 478.	273, 363.
Pratt v. Avery........	1880	7 L. D. 554, 15 C. L. O. 244	677.
Prendergast v. Turton.	1841	1 Young & C. Ch. 110..	859.
Prentice v. Geiger.....	1878	74 N. Y. 341..........	840.
Prentice v. Janssen....	1880	79 N. Y. 478..........	646.
Prentiss Case	1836	7 Ohio, 129, part 2....	791.
Preston v. Hunter.....	1895	67 Fed. 996...........	251, 330, 390.
Price v. McIntosh.....	1903	(Unreported), C. C. A..	448a.
Priddy v. Griffith......	1894	150 Ill. 560, 41 Am. St. Rep. 397, 37 N. E. 999.	789.
Pride of the West Mine	1877	4 Copp's L. O. 34.....	756.
Prince v. Lamb........	1900	128 Cal. 120, 60 Pac. 689.	797, 799, 858.
Prince of Wales Lode..	1875	2 Copp's L. O. 2......	355, 381, 383, 692.
Princeton M. Co. v. First Nat. Bank	1888	7 Mont. 530, 19 Pac. 210.	226.
Pringle v. Vesta Coal Co.............	1896	172 Pa. St. 438, 33 Atl. 690	818.
Protector Lode	1891	12 L. D. 662..........	173, 174, 177.
Proud v. Bates........	1865	34 L. J. Ch. 406.......	818, 819.
Providence Gold M. Co. v. Burke	1899	(Ariz.), 57 Pac. 641....	227, 233, 274, 381, 382, 392, 404, 636, 645, 684, 754, 765.
Providence G. M. Co. v. Marks	1900	(Ariz.), 60 Pac. 938....	759.
Pumpelly v. Green Bay Co.........	1871	13 Wall. 166, 20 L. Ed. 557	843.
Purdum v. Laddin.....	1899	23 Mont. 387, 59 Pac. 153	249, 250, 274, 329, 343, 344, 352, 355, 373, 379, 381, 384, 443.
Putnam v. Wise.......	1841	1 Hill, 234, 37 Am. Dec. 309, and note	861.
Queen v. The Earl of Northumberland	1568	Plowd. 310	127.
Quigley v. State of California	1897	24 L. D. 507.........	141.
Quigley v. Gillett......	1894	101 Cal. 462, 35 Pac. 1040	274, 636, 643, 645, 737, 748.
Quinby v. Boyd.......	1884	8 Colo. 194, 6 Pac. 462..	363, 383, 635.

Names of Cases.	When De-cided.	Where Reported.	Sections Where Cited in this Work.
Quinby *v.* Conlan	1882	104 U. S. 420, 26 L. Ed. 800	175, 207, 217, 218, 665.
Quincy *v.* Jones	1875	76 Ill. 231, 20 Am. Rep. 243	833.
Quinn *v.* Chapman	1884	111 U. S. 445, 4 Sup. Ct. Rep. 508, 28 L. Ed. 476	123.
Quinn *v.* Kenyon	1869	38 Cal. 499	542.
Rablin's Placer	1884	2 L. D. 764, 10 C. L. O. 338	428, 448.
Racouillat *v.* Sansevain	1867	32 Cal. 376	233.
Rader *v.* Allen	1895	27 Or. 344, 41 Pac. 154.	773.
Railroad Co. *v.* Hussey.	1894	61 Fed. 231	159.
Ralston *v.* Plowman	1875	1 Idaho 595, 5 Morr. 160	272, 843.
Ramage, *In re*	1875	2 Copp's L. O. 114	718.
Ramus *v.* Humphreys..	1901	(Cal.), 65 Pac. 875	216.
Randall *v.* Meredith	1889	(Tex.), 11 S. W. 170	798, 801.
Randall *v.* Meredith	1890	76 Tex. 669, 13 S. W. 576	801.
Randolph, *In re*	1896	23 L. D. 322	210, 421.
Rankin, *In re*	1888	7 L. D. 411, 15 C. L. O. 208	170.
Rankin's Appeal	1888	(Pa.), 16 Atl. 82, 2 L. R. A. 429	813.
Rattlesnake Jack Placer	1883	10 Copp's L. O. 87	184.
Raunheim *v.* Dahl	1886	6 Mont. 167, 9 Pac. 892	720, 742.
Ray *v.* Western Pennsylvania Nat. Gas. Co.	1891	138 Pa. St. 576, 21 Am. St. Rep. 922, 20 Atl. 1065, 12 L. R. A. 290.	862.
Raymond *v.* Johnson	1897	17 Wash. 232, 61 Am. St. Rep. 809, 49 Pac. 492	858.
Raynolds *v.* Hanna	1893	55 Fed. 783	861.
Rea *v.* Stephenson	1892	15 L. D. 37	208.
Reagan *v.* McKibben..	1898	11 S. Dak. 270, 76 N. W. 943	270, 331, 398, 642, 788, 858.
Rebel Lode	1891	12 L. D. 683	413.
Rebellion M. Co., *In re*.	1881	1 L. D. 542	679.
Red Mountain Cons. M. Co. *v.* Essler	1896	18 Mont. 174, 44 Pac. 523	790.
Red River Roller Mills *v.* Wright	1883	30 Minn. 249, 44 Am. Rep. 194, 15 N. W. 167	840.
Reed, *In re*	1888	6 L. D. 563	772.
Reed *v.* Hoyt	1882	1 L. D. 603	737.
Reed *v.* Nelson	1900	29 L. D. 615	496, 504, 506.
Reed *v.* Reed	1863	16 N. J. Eq. 248	789.

Names of Cases.	When Decided.	Where Reported.	Sections Where Cited in this Work.
Reid v. Lavallee.......	1898	26 L. D. 100..........	208.
Reins v. Montana Copper Co..............	1900	29 L. D. 461..........	632, 637, 696.
Reins v. Murray.......	1896	22 L. D. 409..........	432, 437, 454.
Reins v. Raunheim.....	1899	28 L. D. 526..........	330, 335, 438, 717.
Remmington v. Baudit.	1886	6 Mont. 138, 9 Pac. 819.	629, 631.
Reno Smelting etc. Works v. Stevenson..	1889	20 Nev. 269, 19 Am. St. Rep. 364, 21 Pac. 317, 4 L. R. A. 60........	838.
Renshaw v. Switzer....	1887	6 Mont. 464, 13 Pac. 127, 15 Morr. 345........	624, 643.
Republican M. Co. v. Tyler M. Co.........	1897	79 Fed. 733..........	591, 609.
Rex v. Pagham Commissioners of Sewers.	1828	8 B. & C. 355........	807.
Reynolds v. Iron S. M. Co.........	1886	116 U. S. 687, 6 Sup. Ct. Rep. 601, 29 L. 774, 15 Morr. 591...	293, 413, 414, 415, 419, 720, 781, 866.
Reynolds v. Pascoe....	1901	(Utah), 66 Pac. 1064...	337, 363.
Rhea v. Hughes.......	1840	1 Ala. 219, 34 Am. Dec. 772	542.
Rhodes v. Otis........	1859	33 Ala. 578, 73 Am. Dec. 439	860.
Rhodes v. Treas........	1895	21 L. D. 502..........	106, 432, 438,
Riborado v. Quang Pang Co.	1885	2 Idaho, 131, 6 Pac. 125	272.
Rich v. Johnson.......	1740	2 Str. 1142............	9.
Rich v. Maples........	1867	33 Cal. 102...........	123.
Richards v. Dower.....	1883	64 Cal. 62, 28 Pac. 113..	872.
Richards v. Dower.....	1889	81 Cal. 44, 22 Pac. 304.	127, 142, 176, 209.
Richards v. Jenkins....	1868	18 Law Times (N. S.) 438	818.
Richards v. Wolfling....	1893	98 Cal. 195, 32 Pac. 971.	338.
Richardson v. McNulty.	1864	24 Cal. 339, 1 Morr. 11..	642, 643.
Richart v. Scott.......	1838	7 Watts, 460, 32 Am. Dec. 779	833.
Richmond v. Test......	1897	18 Ind. App. 482, 48 N. E. 610	840.
Richmond M. Co. v. Eureka M. Co.......	1881	103 U. S. 839, 26 L. Ed. 557, 9 Morr. 634.....	365, 576, 616, 617, 618.
Richmond M. Co. v. Rose	1882	114 U. S. 576, 5 Sup. Ct. Rep. 1055, 29 L. Ed. 273	362, 583, 737, 740, 741, 742, 759, 766.
Richter v. State of Utah	1898	27 L. D. 95..........	97, 106, 143, 144, 207, 425, 689.
Rico-Aspen Cons. M. Co. v. Enterprise M. Co..	1892	53 Fed. 321..........	481, 482, 487.

Names of Cases.	When De-cided.	Where Reported.	Sections Where Cited in this Work.
Rico Townsite	1882	1 L. D. 556, 9 C. L. O. 90	171, 520, 521, 723.
Rico Reduction Works v. Musgrave	1890	14 Colo. 79, 23 Pac. 458	790.
Riddle v. Brown.......	1852	20 Ala. 412, 56 Am. Dec. 202, 9 Morr. 219.....	175, 860.
Rigby v. Bennett......	1882	21 Ch. D. 559, 40 L. T. 47	833.
Riley v. Heisch........	1861	18 Cal. 198............	123.
Risch v. Wiseman.....	1900	36 Or. 484, 78 Am. St. Rep. 783, 59 Pac. 1111	218, 688.
Risdon v. Davenport...	1894	4 S. D. 555, 57 N. W. 482	662, 772.
Riste v. Morton.......	1897	20 Mont. 139, 49 Pac. 656	383, 646.
River Wear Commission-ers v. Adamson......	1878	26 W. R. 217.........	808.
Roach v. Gray.........	1860	16 Cal. 383, 4 Morr. 450	270.
Robb v. Carnegie etc. Co....	1891	145 Pa. St. 324, 27 Am. St. Rep. 694, 22 Atl. 649, 14 L. R. A. 329..	840.
Robert v. Bettman.....	1898	45 W. Va. 143, 30 S. E. 95	862.
Robert Lalley, In re...	1883	10 Copp's L. O. 55.....	497.
Roberts v. Eberhardt...	1853	Kay 148, 11 Morr. 301..	790.
Roberts v. Gebhart.....	1894	104 Cal. 67, 37 Pac. 782.	143.
Roberts v. Jepson......	1885	4 L. D. 60.............	106, 138, 207, 422.
Roberts v. Wilson.....	1876	1 Utah, 292, 4 Morr. 498	272, 391, 537.
Robertson v. Jones.....	1874	71 Ill. 405, 10 Morr. 190	868.
Robertson v. Smith....	1871	1 Mont. 410, 7 Morr. 196	531.
Robertson v. Youghiog-heny R. Coal Co.....	1896	172 Pa. St. 566, 33 Atl. 706	821.
Robinette v. Preston's Heirs	1843	2 Rob. (Va.) 278......	791.
Robinson v. Black Dia-mond Coal Co........	1881	57 Cal. 412, 40 Am. Rep. 118, 14 Morr. 93.....	843.
Robinson v. Forrest....	1865	29 Cal. 318............	448.
Robinson v. Grace.....	1872	27 L. T. 648..........	833.
Robinson v. Imperial S. M. Co....	1869	5 Nev. 44, 10 Morr. 370.	634.
Robinson v. Mayger...	1882	9 Copp's L. O. 5, 1 L. D. 538	734, 759.
Rocky Mountain C. & I. Co.....	1873	1 Copp's L. O. 1.......	158, 495.
Rockwell v. Graham...	1886	9 Colo. 36, 10 Pac. 284, 15 Morr. 299	530, 729.
Rogers v. Brenton.....	1847	10 Q. B. 25..........	839.
Rogers v. Clemans.....	1881	26 Kan. 522..........	542.
Rogers v. Cooney......	1872	7 Nev. 215, 14 Morr. 85	373, 426.
Rogers v. Taylor.......	1857	1 H. & N. 706.........	813.
Rogers v. Taylor......	1858	2 Hurl & N. 828........	820.

Names of Cases.	When Decided.	Where Reported.	Sections Where Cited in this Work.
Rogers, Samuel E., *In re*	1885	4 L. D. 284...........	138, 422.
Rogers etc. Works *v.* American Emigrant Co.	1896	164 U. S. 559, 17 Sup. Ct. Rep. 188, 41 L. Ed. 552	143.
Rolfe, H. C., *In re*.....	1875	2 Copp's L. O. 66......	158.
Romance Lode Mining Claim	1901	31 L. D. 51...........	772.
Rood *v.* Wallace.......	1899	109 Iowa, 5, 79 N. W. 449	107, 161, 207, 779.
Rooney *v.* Bourke's Heirs	1898	27 L. D. 596...........	542.
Rose *v.* Dineen........	1898	26 L. D. 107...........	505.
Rose *v.* Nevada etc. Wood & Lumber Co..	1887	73 Cal. 385, 15 Pac. 19..	472.
Rose *v.* Richmond M. Co....	1882	17 Nev. 25, 27 Pac. 1105	362, 583, 737, 740.
Rose Lode Claim......	1896	22 L. D. 83...........	226, 396, 671.
Rosenthal *v.* Ives......	1887	2 Idaho, 244, 12 Pac. 904, 15 Morr. 324........	233, 268, 448a, 754, 755, 763.
Roseville Alta M. C. *v.* Iowa G. M. Co.......	1890	15 Colo. 29, 22 Am. St. Rep. 373, 24 Pac. 920, 16 Morr. 93.........	409, 535.
Rough *v.* Simmons.....	1884	65 Cal. 227, 3 Pac. 804, 15 Morr. 298........	754.
Rowbotham *v.* Wilson..	1857	8 El. & Bl. 142........	9.
Rowbotham *v.* Wilson..	1860	8 H. L. Cases 348.....	812, 821, 827.
Rowe *v.* Portsmouth....	1876	56 N. H. 291, 22 Am. Rep. 464	843.
Rowena Lode	1888	7 L. D. 477...........	677.
Roxanna G. M. Co. *v.* Cone	1899	100 Fed. 168...........	614, 866.
Royal K. Placer.......	1891	13 L. D. 86...........	95.
Royston *v.* Miller......	1896	76 Fed. 50............	406, 629, 630, 631.
Ruabon Brick & Terra Cotta Co. *v.* Great Western Ry. Co......	1893	L. R. 1 Ch. 427........	92.
Rucker *v.* Kinsley.....	1892	14 L. D. 113..........	496.
Ruckgaber *v.* Moore....	1900	104 Fed. 947..........	224.
Rush *v.* French.......	1874	1 Ariz. 99, 25 Pac. 816..	271, 274, 331, 644.
Rush *v.* Valentine......	1882	12 Neb. 513, 11 N. W. 746	660.
Russell *v.* Chumasero...	1882	4 Mont. 309, 1 Pac. 713.	373, 379, 383.
Russel *v.* Hoyt........	1882	4 Mont. 412, 2 Pac. 25..	218.
Russell *v.* Brosseau....	1884	65 Cal. 605, 4 Pac. 643.	218, 405, 645.
Russell *v.* Merchants' Bank	1891	47 Min. 286, 28 Am. St. Rep. 368, 50 N. W. 228	789.
Russell *v.* Wilson Creek Cons. M. Co.........	1900	30 L. D. 321..........	409, 631, 673.

Names of Cases.	When De-cided.	Where Reported.	Sections Where Cited in this Work.
Russell Lode	1877	5 Copp's L. O. 18......	671.
Rutter v. Shoshone M. Co.	1896	75 Fed. 37............	746, 754.
Ryan v. Granite Hill etc. Co.	1899	29 L. D. 22............	717.
Ryan v. Granite Hill M. & M. Co..........	1900	29 L. D. 522..........	170, 413, 717, 723.
Ryckman v. Gillis......	1874	57 N. Y. 68, 15 Am. Rep. 464	812.
Salisbury v. Lane......	1900	(Idaho), 63 Pac. 383...	327.
Salt Bluff Placer......	1888	7 L. D. 549...........	97, 513, 514.
San Bernardino County v. Davidson	1896	112 Cal. 503, 44 Pac. 659	273, 389.
Sanders v. Noble......	1899	22 Mont. 110, 55 Pac. 1037	250, 328, 335, 336, 339, 343, 355, 356, 371, 372, 374, 380, 381, 397.
Sanderson v. Pennsylvania Coal Co.......	1878	86 Pa. St. 401, 27 Am. Rep. 711, 11 Morr. 60.	840.
Sanderson v. Pennsylvania Coal Co.......	1883	102 Pa. St. 370.......	840.
Sanderson v. Scranton City	1884	105 Pa. St. 469........	812.
Sands v. Cruikshank...	1901	(S. D.), 87 N. W. 589..	335, 337.
Sanford, In re........	1874	1 Copp's L. O. 98......	684.
San Francisco M. Co...	1900	29 L. D. 397..........	784.
San Pedro etc. Co. v. United States	1892	146 U. S. 120, 13 Sup. Ct. Rep. 94, 36 L. Ed. 911	126.
Santa Clara M. Assn. v. Quicksilver M. Co....	1882	8 Saw. 330, 17 Fed. 657	797.
Santa Fe Pacific R. R. Co.	1898	27 L. D. 322..........	153.
Santa Fe Pacific Ry....	1899	29 L. D. 36...........	153.
Saratoga Lode v. Bulldozer Lode	1879	Sickle's Min. Dec. 252..	730.
Satisfaction Extension Millsite	1892	14 L. D. 173..........	523.
Satterfield v. Rowan...	1889	83 Ga. 187, 9 S. E. 677.	840.
Saturday Lode Claim..	1900	29 L. D. 627..........	223, 684.
Saunders v. La Purisima G. M. Co.....	1899	125 Cal. 159, 57 Pac. 656	142, 144a, 779.
Saunders v. Mackey...	1885	5 Mont. 527, 6 Pac. 361	405, 406, 646.
Savage v. Boynton.....	1891	12 L. D. 612..........	95, 207.
Savage v. Worsham...	1892	104 Fed. 18...........	108, 207.
Sayer v. Hoosac etc. M. Co.	1879	6 Copp's L. O. 73......	739.

Names of Cases.	When Decided.	Where Reported.	Sections Where Cited in this Work.
Sayers v. Hoskinson...	1885	110 Pa. St. 473, 1 Atl. 308	789.
Schoolfield v. Houle...	1889	13 Colo. 394, 22 Pac. 781	542.
Schrimpf v. Northern Pac. R. R. Co.	1899	29 L. D. 327	95, 97, 98, 139, 158, 420, 421.
Schulenberg v. Harriman	1875	21 Wall. 44, 22 L. Ed. 551	154, 251.
Schultz v. Allyn	1897	(Ariz.), 48 Pac. 960...	754.
Schultz v. Keeler	1887	2 Idaho 305, 13 Pac. 481	331.
Schwab v. Bean	1898	86 Fed. 41, 1 Leg. Adv. 489	428.
Schwerdtle v. Placer Co.	1895	108 Cal. 591, 41 Pac. 448	530.
Scotia M. Co	1899	29 L. D. 308	696.
Scott v. Clark	1853	1 Ohio St. 382, 12 Morr. 276	858.
Scott v. Lockey Inv. Co.	1893	60 Fed. 34	161, 779.
Scott v. Maloney	1896	22 L. D. 274	737.
Scott v. Sheldon	1892	15 L. D. 361	496.
Scranton v. Phillips...	1880	94 Pa. St. 15, 14 Morr. 48	812, 821.
Scudder v. Trenton Del Falls Co	1832	1 N. J. Eq. 694, 23 Am. Dec. 756	257.
Seager v. McCabe	1892	92 Mich. 186, 52 N. W. 299, 16 L. R. A. 247....	789a.
Seamen v. Vawdrey....	1810	13 Morr. Min. Rep. 62, 16 Ves. Jr. 390	9, 644.
Searle Placer	1890	11 L. D. 441	208.
Sears, In re	1881	8 Copp's L. O. 152	688.
Sears v. Sellew	1870	28 Iowa, 501	790.
Sears v. Taylor	1877	4 Colo. 38, 5 Morr. 318.	792.
Settenbre v. Putnam...	1866	30 Cal. 490, 11 Morr. 425	797, 798, 800.
Settle v. Winters	1886	2 Idaho, 199, 10 Pac. 216	859.
Seymour v. Fisher....	1891	16 Colo. 188, 27 Pac. 240	192, 218, 322, 397, 398, 539, 660, 742, 755.
Seymour v. Wood	1892	4 Copp's L. O. 2	755, 756.
Shafer v. Constans....	1879	3 Mont. 369, 1 Morr. 147	192, 542, 724.
Shafer's Appeal	1884	106 Pa. St. 49	802.
Shafto v. Johnson	1863	8 B. and S. 252	871.
Shanklin v. McNamara.	1891	87 Cal. 371, 26 Pac. 345	123, 207, 664.
Shanks v. Dupont	1840	3 Pet. 242, 7 L. Ed. 666	224.
Shaw v. Kellogg	1898	170 U. S. 312, 18 Sup. Ct. Rep. 632, 42 L. Ed. 1050	107, 126, 779.
Sheldon v. Sherman...	1870	42 N. Y. 484, 1 Am. Rep. 569	808.

Names of Cases.	When De-cided.	Where Reported.	Sections Where Cited in this Work.
Shenandoah M .and M. Co. v. Morgan	1895	106 Cal. 409, 39 Pac. 802	143.
Shepard v. Murphy	1899	26 Colo. 350, 58 Pac. 588	390.
Shepherd v. Bird	1893	17 L. D. 82	421, 97, 158.
Shepherd v. McCalmont Oil Co	1885	38 Hun, (N. Y.) 37	862.
Shepley v. Cowan	1876	91 U. S. 330, 23 L. Ed. 424	175, 192, 207, 665.
Sherlock v. Leighton	1901	9 Wyo. 297, 63 Pac. 580	231, 233, 234, 373, 629, 630, 631, 643.
Sherman v. Buick	1893	45 Cal. 656	142.
Shields v. Simington	1898	27 L. D. 369	713, 759.
Shively v. Bowlby	1894	152 U. S. 1, 14 Sup. Ct. Rep. 548, 38 L. Ed. 331	80, 112, 429.
Shiver v. United States	1895	159 U. S. 491, 16 Sup. Ct. Rep. 54, 40 L. Ed. 231	205, 208.
Sholl v. German C. Co.	1887	118 Ill. 427, 59 Am. Rep. 379, 10 N. E. 199	256.
Shonbar Lode	1883	1 L. D. 551	415.
Shonbar Lode	1885	3 L. D. 388	415.
Shoo Fly and Magnolia Lode v. Gisborn	1874	1 Copp's L. O. 135, 138.	719.
Shoshone M. Co. v. Rutter	1898	87 Fed. 801	294, 335, 336, 396, 437, 746, 754.
Shoshone M. Co. v. Rutter	1900	177 U. S. 505, 20 Sup. Ct. Rep. 726, 44 L. Ed. 864	746, 747.
Shreeve v. Copper Belle M. Co	1891	11 Mont. 309, 28 Pac. 315	294, 336.
Shrewsbury, Inhab-itants of, v. Smith	1853	12 Cush. 177	808.
Shrimpf v. N. P. R. R. Co.	1899	29 L. D. 327	97.
Sierra Grande M. Co. v. Crawford	1890	11 L. D. 338	521, 523.
Silsby v. Trotter	1878	29 N. J. Eq. 228, 3 Morr. 137	860.
Silva v. Rankin	1887	80 Ga. 79, 4 S. E. 756.	812.
Silver Bow M. and M. Co. v. Clark	1885	5 Mont. 378, 5 Pac. 570	47, 125, 169, 170, 177, 539, 604, 609, 722, 783.
Silver City G. and S. M. Co. v. Lowry	1899	19 Utah, 344, 57 Pac. 11	338.
Silver Jennie Lode	1888	7 L. D. 6	337.
Silver King M. Co	1895	20 L. D. 116	226.

Names of Cases.	When Decided.	Where Reported.	Sections Where Cited in this Work.
Silver M. Co. v. Fall..	1870	6 Nev. 454, 5 Morr. 283	866.
Silver Peak Mines v. Hanchett	1899	93 Fed. 76............	872.
Silver Peak Mines v. Valcalda	1897	79 Fed. 886...........	522.
Silver Queen Lode....	1893	16 L. D. 186..........	338.
Silver Star Millsite....	1897	25 L. D. 165..........	523, 677.
Simmons, W. A.......	1883	7 L. D. 283, 15 C. L. O. 158	172.
Sims v. Garden M. etc. Co.	1902	(Unreported)	591a.
Sims v. Smith	1857	7 Cal. 148, 68 Am. Dec. 233, 13 Morr. 161...	841.
Single v. Schneider ...	1869	24 Wis. 299..........	868.
Sioux City etc. R. R. Co. v. Chicago etc. R. R. Co.	1886	117 U. S. 406, 6 Sup. Ct. Rep. 790, 29 L. Ed. 928	157.
Sioux City etc. Co. v. Griffey	1892	143 U. S. 32, 12 Sup. Ct. Rep. 362, 36 L. 64..	154.
Sissons v. Sommers ...	1899	24 Nev. 379, 77 Am. St. Rep. 815, 55 Pac. 829	249, 250, 274, 343, 344, 384, 626.
Skillman v. Lachman..	1863	23 Cal. 199, 83 Am. Dec. 96, 11 Morr. 381....	796, 797, 801.
Slade v. Sullivan	1860	17 Cal. 103, 7 Morr. 519	843.
Slater v. Haas	1891	15 Colo. 574, 22 Am. St. Rep. 440, 25 Pac. 1089	796, 803.
Slaughterhouse Cases..	1873	16 Wall. 36, 21 L. Ed. 394	224.
Slavonian M. Co. v. Vacavich	1881	7 Saw. 217, 7 Fed. 331, 1 Morr. 541........	75, 623, 632, 634.
Slidell v. Grandjean...	1883	111 U. S. 412, 4 Sup. Ct. Rep. 475, 28 L. Ed. 321	96.
Small v. Lutz.........	1902	(Or.), 67 Pac. 421.....	779.
Smart v. Morton......	1855	5 Ellis and Bl. (40 Eng. Eq.), 30, 13 Morr. 655	821.
Smith, Arden L.......	1901	31 L. D. 184..........	199.
Smith, G. D...........	1886	13 Copp's L. O. 28.....	155.
Smith, In re.........	1889	16 Copp's L. O. 112....	501.
Smith v. Buckley......	1892	15 L. D. 321..........	496.
Smith v. Cooley......	1884	65 Cal. 46, 48, 2 Pac. 880	792.
Smith v. Darby.......	1872	7 L. R. Q. B. 716......	821.
Smith v. Denniff......	1900	24 Mont. 20, 22, 81 Am. St. Rep. 408, 60 Pac. 398, 50 L. R. A. 737.	253.
Smith v. Doe.........	1860	15 Cal. 101, 5 Morr. 218	218, 537.
Smith v. Ewing.......	1885	11 Saw. 56, 23 Fed. 741	772.
Smith v. Hill.........	1891	89 Cal. 122, 26 Pac. 644	127, 142, 175, 176.

Names of Cases.	When Decided.	Where Reported.	Sections Where Cited in this Work.
Smith v. Hawkins.....	1895	110 Cal. 125, 42 Pac. 453	530.
Smith v. Jones........	1900	21 Utah, 270, 60 Pac. 1104, 1106	9, 596.
Smith v. Kenrick......	1849	7 Com. B. 515, 18 L. J. N. S. C. P. 172, 6 Morr. 142	807.
Smith v. Moore.......	1861	26 Ill. 392............	558.
Smith v. Newell......	1898	86 Fed. 56............	273, 335, 373, 375, 379, 381, 382, 383, 392.
Smith v. North American M. Co..........	1865	1 Nev. 357, 13 Morr. 579	272.
Smith v. Northern Pac. R. R. Co...........	1893	58 Fed. 513...........	153, 154.
Smith v. Seattle......	1898	18 Wash. 484, 63 Am. St. Rep. 910, 51 Pac. 1057	823.
Smith v. Townsend....	1893	148 U. S. 490, 13 Sup. Ct. Rep. 634, 37 L. Ed. 533	612.
Smith v. United States	1898	170 U. S. 372, 18 Sup. Ct. Rep. 626, 42 L. Ed. 1074	660.
Smith Brothers In re..	1879	7 Copp's L. O. 4.......	688.
Smokehouse Lode Cases	1886	4 L. D. 555, 13 C. L. O. 36	723.
Smokehouse Lode Cases	1887	6 Mont. 397, 12 Pac. 858	125.
Smuggler M. Co. v. Trueworthy Lode Claim	1894	19 L. D. 356..........	730.
Smyth v. New Orleans Canal and Bank Co.	1899	93 Fed. 899...........	175.
Snodgrass v. South Penn. Oil Co........	1900	47 W. Va. 509, 35 S. E. 820	862.
Snowflake Lode	1885	4 L. D. 30............	742.
Snyder v. Burnham....	1882	77 Mo. 52, 15 Morr. 562.	797.
Snyder v. Sickles......	1878	98 U. S. 203, 25 L. Ed. 97	663.
Snyder v. Waller......	1897	25 L. D. 7............	717.
Souter v. Maguire....	1889	78 Cal. 543, 21 Pac. 183	273, 322, 363, 373, 754.
South Comstock G. and S. M. Co.	1875	2 Copp's L. O. 146.....	173.
South Dakota v. Vermont Stone Co......	1893	16 L. D. 263..........	97, 139.
South Dakota M. Co. v. McDonald	1900	30 L. D. 357..........	97.
South End M. Co. v. Twiney	1894	22 Nev. 19, 35 Pac. 89.	622.
Southern Cross M. Co. v. Europa M. Co....	1880	15 Nev. 383, 9 Morr. 513	273, 336, 355, 373, 383.

Names of Cases.	When Decided.	Where Reported.	Sections Where Cited in this Work.
Southern Pac. R. R. Co. v. Allen G. M. Co...	1891	13 L. D. 165..........	157.
Southern Pac. R. R. Co. v. Goodrich	1893	57 Fed. 879..........	754.
Southern Pac. R. R. Co. v. Griffin	1895	20 L. D. 485..........	156, 438, 432.
Southern Pac. R. R. Co. v. Whitaker	1895	109 Cal. 268, 41 Pac. 1083	154.
Southmayd v. Southmayd	1881	4 Mont. 100, 5 Pac. 518	798.
South Penn. Oil Co. v. Edgell	1900	48 W. Va. 348, 86 Am. St. Rep. 43, 37 S. E. 596	862.
South Penn. Oil Co. v. Stone	1900	(Tenn.), 57 S. W. 374..	862.
South Spring Hill etc. Co. v. Amador Medean G. M. Co.	1892	145 U. S. 300, 12 Sup. Ct. Rep. 921, 36 L. Ed. 712	612.
South Star Lode......	1893	17 L. D. 280..........	177, 413.
South Star Lode......	1895	20 L. D. 204..........	177, 413, 720.
Southwestern M. Co...	1892	14 L. D. 597..........	513, 514, 515.
Southwestern M. Co. v. Gettysburg	1885	4 L. D. 271, 12 C .L. O. 253	742.
South Yuba Water Co. v. Rosa.............	1889	80 Cal. 333, 22 Pac. 222	838.
Spalding v. Chandler..	1896	160 U. S. 394, 16 Sup. Ct. Rep. 394, 40 L. Ed. 469	183.
Sparks v. Pierce......	1885	115 U. S. 408, 6 Sup. Ct. Rep. 102, 29 L. Ed. 428	216, 233, 409.
Sparrow v. Strong....	1865	3 Wall. 97, 18 L. Ed. 49, 2 Morr. 320.........	45, 56.
Speake v. Hamilton...	1890	21 Or. 3, 26 Pac. 855..	838.
Spear v. Cutter.......	1849	5 Barb. 486..........	790.
Spencer v. Winselman.	1871	42 Cal. 479, 2 Morr. 334	535, 792.
Spratt v. Edwards.....	1892	15 L. D. 290..........	208.
Spur Lode	1885	4 L. D. 160...........	338.
Standard Quicksilver M. Co. v. Habeshaw....	1901	132 Cal. 115, 64 Pac. 113	107, 207, 209, 779.
Standart, In re.......	1896	25 L. D. 262..........	671.
Stanley v. Mineral Union	1900	(Nev.), 63 Pac. 59, 60..	144a.
Staples v. Wheeler....	1854	38 Me. 372...........	858.
Stark v. Barrett......	1860	15 Cal. 370..........	791.
Stark v. Starrs.......	1868	6 Wall. 402..........	609, 771.
Starr, In re..........	1883	2 L. D. 759..........	723, 784.

Names of Cases.	When De-cided.	Where Reported.	Sections Where Cited in this Work.
State *v.* Adams.......	1876	45 Iowa, 99, 24 Am. Rep. 760	224.
State *v.* Black River Phosphate Co.	1893	32 Fla. 82 13 South. 640, 21 L. R. A. 189......	428.
State *v.* Central Pac. R. R. Co.	1890	21 Nev. 94, 25 Pac. 442.	448.
State *v.* District Court	1900	25 Mont. 572, 65 Pac. 1020	218, 312a, 363a, 596, 615, 780, 866, 873.
State *v.* Hudson Land Co.	1898	19 Wash. 85, 52 Pac. 574	238.
State *v.* Indiana etc. Co.	1889	2 Interstate Com. Rep. 758	423.
State *v.* Kennard......	1899	56 Neb. 254, 76 N. W. 545	181.
State *v.* Kennard......	1899	57 Neb. 711, 78 N. W. 282	181.
State *v.* McGraw......	1882	12 Fed. 449...........	784.
State *v.* Morrison.....	1898	18 Wash. 664, 52 Pac. 228	238.
State *v.* Pacific Guano Co.	1884	22 S. C. 50............	868.
State *v.* Parker.......	1884	61 Tex. 265...........	513.
State *v.* Parsons......	1878	40 N. J. L. 1, 5.......	282.
State *v.* Smith........	1886	70 Cal. 153, 12 Pac. 121	238.
State of California, *In re*	1895	20 L. D. 327..........	197.
State of California, *In re*	1896	22 L. D. 294, S. C. 22 L. D. 402...........	144.
State of California, *In re*	1896	23 L. D. 423..........	106, 144.
State of California, *In re*	1899	28 L. D. 57...........	133, 144, 199.
State of California, *In re*	1902	31 L. D. 335..........	133, 142.
State of California *v.* Boddy	1889	9 L. D. 636...........	143.
State of California *v.* Moore	1896	12 Cal. 56, 14 Morr. 110	535.
State of California *v.* Roley	1877	4 Copp's L. O. 18.....	136, 142.
State of California *v.* Wright	1897	24 L. D. 54..........	142.
State of Colorado, *In re*	1887	6 L. D. 412...........	142.
State of Colorado, *In re*	1890	10 L. D. 222..........	514.
State of Louisiana, *In re*	1900	30 L. D. 276..........	80, 322.

Names of Cases.	When De-cided.	Where Reported.	Sections Where Cited in this Work.
State of Montana v. Buley	1885	23 L. D. 116	496.
State of Oregon v. Jones	1897	24 L. D. 116	514.
State of Utah	1899	29 L. D. 69	97, 139, 142.
State of Utah v. Allen.	1898	27 L. D. 53	136, 142.
State of Washington v. McBride	1894	18 L. D. 199	106, 142.
State of Washington v. McBride	1897	25 L. D. 169	437, 438.
Steel v. Gold Lead M. Co.	1883	18 Nev. 80, 1 Pac. 448, 15 Morr. 293	643, 718.
Steel v. St. Louis Smelting Co.	1882	106 U. S. 447, 1 Sup. Ct. Rep. 389, 27 L. Ed. 226	126, 161, 168, 169, 170, 175, 207, 662, 777, 784.
Steele, In re	1884	3 L. D. 115	685.
Steelsmith v. Gartlan..	1898	45 W. Va. 27, 29 S. E. 978, 44 L. R. A. 107.	862.
Stemwinder M. Co. v. Emma etc. M. Co....	1889	2 Idaho, 421, 21 Pac. 1040	362.
Stemwinder M. Co. v. Emma etc. M. Co....	1892	149 U. S. 787, 13 Sup. Ct. Rep. 1052, 37 L. Ed. 941	362.
Stenger v. Edwards....	1873	70 Ill. 631, 9 Morr. 368.	790.
Stephens v. Cherokee Nation	1899	174 U. S. 445, 19 Sup. Ct. Rep. 722, 43 L. Ed. 1041	181.
Stephens v. Wood	1901	39 Or. 441, 65 Pac. 602.	362.
Stephenson v. Wilson..	1875	87 Wis. 482, 13 Morr. Min. Rep. 408	688.
Sterling Iron and Zinc Co. v. Sparks Mfg. Co.	1897	(N. J.), 38 Atl. 426...	840.
Stevens v. Gill	1879	1 Morr. Min. Rep. 576, 580, Fed. Cas. No. 13,398	301, 312, 866.
Stevens v. McKibbin..	1895	68 Fed. 406	799.
Stevens v. Murphey....	1879	4 Morr. Min. Rep. 380, Fed. Cas. No. 8,158..	301.
Stevens v. Thompson..	1845	17 N. H. 103	790.
Stevens etc. v. Williams	1879	1 McCrary, 480, 488, Fed. Cas. No. 13,413, 1 Morr. 566	293, 294, 298, 301, 364, 366, 615.
Stevens v. Williams....	1879	1 Morr. Min. Rep. 557, Fed. Cas. No. 13,414	293, 301, 311, 364, 367, 615.

Names of Cases.	When De-cided.	Where Reported.	Sections Where Cited in this Work.
Stevenson v. Wallace..	1876	27 Gratt. 77..........	833.
Steves v. Carson......	1890	42 Fed. 821, 16 Morr. 12.	756.
Stewart's Appeal	1867	56 Pa. St. 413........	256.
Stewart, In re........	1874	1 Copp's L. O. 34.....	323.
Stewart v. Chadwick...	1859	8 Iowa, 463, 12 Morr. 236	175.
Stewart v. McHarry...	1895	159 U. S. 643, 16 Sup. Ct. Rep. 117, 40 L. Ed. 290	665.
Stewart v. Rees......	1895	21 L. D. 446..........	688.
Stewart v. Rees.......	1897	25 L. D. 447..........	363.
Stimson v. Clarke.....	1891	45 Fed. 760..........	772.
Stinchfield v. Gillis....	1892	96 Cal. 33, 30 Pac. 839.	294, 335, 614, 618.
Stinchfield v. Gillis....	1895	107 Cal. 84, 40 Pac. 98.	614, 618.
Stinchfield v. Pierce...	1894	19 L. D. 12...........	208.
Stockbridge Iron Co. v. Cone Iron Works....	1869	102 Mass. 80, 6 Morr. 317	873.
Stone v. Bumpus......	1873	46 Cal. 218, 4 Morr. 278.	530, 631, 841.
Stone v. Geyser G. M. Co.	1877	52 Cal. 315, 1 Morr. 59.	643, 644.
Stone v. United States.	1865	2 Wall. 525, 17 L. Ed. 765	175, 190.
Stork v. Heron Placer.	1888	7 L. D. 359...........	631.
Stoughton's Appeal ...	1878	88 Pa. St. 198........	138, 422, 859b.
Stoughton v. Leigh....	1808	1 Taunt. 402.........	9.
Stout v. Curry.......	1887	110 Ind. 514, 11 N. E. 487	789a.
St. Clair v. Cash Gold M. Co.	1896	9 Colo. App. 235, 47 Pac. 466	868.
St. Helen's Smelting Co. v. Tipping......	1865	11 House of Lords Cas. 642	840.
St. John v. Kidd......	1864	26 Cal. 264, 4 Morr. 454.	274, 623, 643.
St. Joseph and Denver City R. R. Co. v. Baldwin	1881	103 U. S. 426, 26 L. Ed. 578	153, 154.
St. Lawrence M. Co. v. Albion Cons. M. Co.	1885	4 L. D. 117...........	766.
St. Louis v. Wiggins Ferry Co.	1871	11 Wall. 423, 20 L. Ed. 192	226.
St. Louis etc. M. Co. v. Montana M. Co......	1893	58 Fed. 129..........	872.
St. Louis M. etc. Co. v. Montana M. Co......	1900	102 Fed. 430..........	584.
St. Louis etc. M. Co. v. Montana M. Co......	1900	104 Fed. 664..........	364, 583, 584, 594, 618.

Names of Cases.	When De-cided.	Where Reported.	Sections Where Cited in this Work.
St. Louis etc. M. Co. v. Montana Limited ...	1902	113 Fed. 900..........	490a, 531, 551, 568. 615, 866.
St. Louis etc. M. Co. v. Montana Co.	1890	9 Mont. 228, 23 Pac. 510.	873.
St. Louis etc. M. Co. v. Montana M. Co. Limited	1898	171 U. S. 650, 19 Sup. Ct. Rep. 61, 43 L. Ed. 320	539, 542, 618.
St. Louis Smelting Co. v. Kemp	1879	Fed. Cas. No. 12,239A.	63, 72, 447.
St. Louis Smelting Co. v. Kemp		104 U. S. 636, 26 L. Ed. 875, 11 Morr. 673....	45, 56, 62, 126, 161, 175, 177, 207, 327, 447, 449, 604, 625, 629, 630, 631, 665, 670, 671, 778, 783, 787.
St. Paul and Pac. R. R. Co. v. N. P. R. R. Co.	1891	139 U. S. 1-5, 11 Sup. Ct. Rep. 389, 35 L. Ed. 77	154.
St. Paul M. and M. Co. v. Maloney	1897	24 L. D. 460..........	153.
Strang v. Ryan	1873	46 Cal. 33, 1 Morr. 48..	270.
Stranger Lode	1899	28 L. D. 321..........	337, 363, 742, 763, 766.
Strasburger v. Beecher.	1890	44 Fed. 209..........	274, 746.
Strasberger v. Beecher.	1897	20 Mont. 143, 49 Pac. 740	631, 636, 645.
Stratton v. Gold Sovereign etc. Co........	1898	1 Leg. Adv. 350.......	169, 192, 322, 490a, 539.
Strauder v. West Virginia	1879	100 U. S. 303, 25 L. Ed. 664	224.
Strepey v. Stark......	1884	7 Colo. 614, 5 Pac. 111.	227, 329, 330, 345, 371, 390, 392, 398.
Strettell v. Ballou.....	1881	3 McCrary, 46, 9 Fed. 256, 11 Morr. 220....	535, 792.
Strickley v. Hill.......	1900	22 Utah, 257, 83 Am. St. Rep. 786, 62 Pac. 893	227, 233.
Strother v. Lucas......	1838	12 Peters, 410, 9 L. Ed. 1137	116.
Stuart v. Adams.......	1891	89 Cal. 367, 26 Pac. 970	797, 799, 801, 853, 861.
Sturr v. Beck	1890	133 U. S. 541, 10 Sup. Ct. Rep. 350, 33 L. Ed. 761	838.

Names of Cases.	When De-cided.	Where Reported.	Sections Where Cited in this Work.
Suburban G. M. Co. v. Gibberd	1900	29 L. D. 558	677.
Sucia Islands	1896	23 L. D. 329	191.
Suffern v. Butler	1868	19 N. J. Eq. 202	861.
Suffolk Gold M. etc. Co. v. San Miguel Cons. M. Co	1897	9 Colo. App. 407, 48 Pac. 828	841.
Sullivan v. Hense	1874	2 Colo. 424, 9 Morr. 487.	271, 272.
Sullivan v. Iron S. M. Co.	1892	143 U. S. 431, 12 Sup. Ct. Rep. 555, 36 L. Ed. 214	413, 781.
Sullivan v. Zeiner	1893	98 Cal. 346, 33 Pac. 209.	833.
Sulphur Springs Quick-silver Mine	1896	22 L. D. 715	677, 690.
Sunnyside Coal etc. Co. v. Reitz	1896	14 Ind. App. 478, 43 N. E. 46	868.
Sussenback v. First Nat. Bk.	1889	5 Dak. 477, 41 N. W. 662	406, 646, 728.
Sutter County v. John-son	1902	(Cal.)	853.
Swaim v. Craven	1891	12 L. D. 294	759.
Swank v. State of Cal-ifornia	1898	27 L. D. 411	139, 143.
Sweeney v. Northern Pac. R. R.	1895	20 L. D. 394	106, 630.
Sweeney v. Wilson	1890	10 L. D. 157	632.
Sweet v. Webber	1884	7 Colo. 443, 4 Pac. 752.	218, 250, 329, 371, 432, 454, 625, 626.
Swift Co. v. United States	1882	105 U. S. 691, 26 L. Ed. 1108	666.
Swigert v. Walker	1892	49 Kan. 100, 30 Pac. 162	662, 772.
Table Mountain T. Co. v. Stranahan	1862	20 Cal. 199, 9 Morr. 457.	270, 272, 537, 642.
Table Mountain T. Co. v. Stranahan	1866	31 Cal. 387	270.
Tabor v. Dexter	1878	9 Morr. Min. Rep 614, Fed. Cas. No. 13,723.	301.
Tabor v. Sullivan	1888	12 Colo. 136, 20 Pac. 437	646, 728.
Tacoma Land Co. v. Northern Pac. R. R. Co.	1898	26 L. D. 503	226.
Tait v. Hull	1886	71 Cal. 149, 12 Pac. 391.	644.
Talbot v. King	1886	6 Mont. 76, 9 Pac. 434.	170, 171, 177, 539, 604, 609, 632, 723, 783.

Names of Cases.	When Decided.	Where Reported.	Sections Where Cited in this Work.
Talmadge v. St. John..	1900	129 Cal. 430, 62 Pac. 79.	381, 383.
Tam v. Story.........	1895	21 L. D. 440.........	336, 633.
Tameling v. U. S. Freehold Co.............	1877	93 U. S. 644, 23 L. Ed. 998	116.
Tangerman v. Aurora Hill M. Co..........	1889	9 L. D. 538..........	692.
Tanner v. O'Neill.....	1892	14 L. D. 317..........	143.
Tarpey v. Madsen.....	1900	178 U. S. 215, 20 Sup. Ct. Rep. 849, 44 L. Ed. 1042	216.
Tartar v. Spring Valley M. Co..........	1855	5 Cal. 396, 14 Morr. 371.	838.
Taylor, In re........	1882	9 Copp's L. O. 92......	361, 765.
Taylor v. Baldwin.....	1850	10 Barb. 582..........	790.
Taylor v. Benham.....	1850	5 How. 233, 12 L. Ed. 130	233.
Taylor v. Castle.......	1871	42 Cal. 367, 11 Morr. 484	796, 801, 803.
Taylor v. Longworth...	1840	14 Pet. 172, 174, 10 L. Ed. 405	859.
Taylor v. Middleton...	1885	67 Cal. 656, 8 Pac. 594, 15 Morr. 284........	373, 644.
Taylor v. Parenteau...	1897	23 Colo. 368, 48 Pac. 505	345, 362, 366, 374, 589, 631.
Teller, In re..........	1898	26 L. D. 484..........	331, 398.
Teller v. United States	1902	113 Fed. 273..........	80, 112, 169, 322, 550, 771.
Temescal Oil etc. Co. v. Salcido	1902	137 Cal. 211, 69 Pac. 1010	373, 375, 398, 454, 644, 654.
Tenderfoot Lode	1900	30 L. D. 200..........	673, 690.
Tennessee v. Union and Planters' Bank	1894	152 U. S. 452, 14 Sup. Ct. Rep. 654, 38 L. Ed. 511	747.
Tennessee Coal etc. Co. v. Hamilton	1893	100 Ala. 252, 46 Am. St. Rep. 48, 14 South. 167.	840.
Tennessee Lode	1888	7 L. D. 392...........	677.
Terrible M. Co. v. Argentine M. Co.......	1883	5 McCrary, 639, 89 Fed. 583	343, 345, 553, 587.
Territory v. Lee.......	1874	2 Mont. 124, 6 Morr. 248	233.
Territory v. Mackey...	1888	8 Mont. 168, 19 Pac. 395	336.
Territory of New Mexico, In re..........	1900	29 L. D. 399..........	133.
Territory of New Mexico, In re..........	1902	31 L. D. 389..........	513.

Names of Cases.	When De- cided.	Where Reported.	Sections Where Cited in this Work.
Terry v. McGerle	1864	24 Cal. 610, 85 Am. Dec. 84	448.
Tevis, In re	1900	29 L. D. 575	199.
Texas Pac. Ry. Co. v. Cody	1897	166 U. S. 606, 17 Sup. Ct. Rep. 703, 41 L. Ed. 1132	747.
Thallmann v. Thomas	1900	102 Fed. 925	375, 382, 779.
Thallmann v. Thomas	1901	111 Fed. 277	112, 217, 218.
Thomas v. Allentown M. Co	1877	28 N. J. Eq. 77	873.
Thomas v. Chisholm	1889	13 Colo. 105, 21 Pac. 1019, 16 Morr. 122	226, 763.
Thomas v. Elling	1897	25 L. D. 495	406, 646, 728, 755.
Thomas v. Elling	1898	26 L. D. 220	406, 646, 721, 728, 755.
Thomas v. Hunt	1896	134 Mo. 392, 35 S. W. 581, 32 L. R. A. 857.	178.
Thomas v. Hurst	1896	73 Fed. 372	796.
Thomas v. Oakley	1811	18 Vesey Jr. 184, 7 Morr. 254	790.
Thomas Pressed Brick Co. v. Herter	1894	60 Ill. App. 58	868.
Thompson v. Jacobs	1883	3 Utah, 246, 2 Pac. 714.	623.
Thompson v. McElarney	1876	82 Pa. St. 174	860.
Thompson v. Noble	1870	3 Pittsb. 201	93, 97, 138, 422.
Thompson v. Spray	1887	72 Cal. 528, 14 Pac. 182.	225, 227, 233, 273, 330, 331, 362, 397, 398, 754.
Thor Mine	1877	5 Copp's L. O. 51	671.
Thornburgh v. Savage M. Co	1867	Fed. Cas. No. 13,986, 7 Morr. Min. Rep. 667	873.
Thornton v. Mahoney	1864	24 Cal. 569	123.
Thurber v. Martin	1854	2 Gray, 394, 61 Am. Dec. 468	840.
Thurston v. Dickinson	1846	2 Rich. Eq. 317, 46 Am. Dec. 56	790.
Thurston v. Hancock	1815	12 Mass. 220, 7 Am. Dec. 57	833.
Tibbitts v. Ah Tong	1882	4 Mont. 536, 2 Pac. 761.	233.
Tiernan v. Salt Lake M. Co	1874	1 Copp's L. O. 25	738.
Tilden v. Intervenor M. Co	1882	1 L. D. 572, 9 C. L. O. 93	691, 737, 738.
Tilley v. Noyers	1862	43 Pa. St. 404, 4 Morr. 320	861.
Timm v. Bear	1871	29 Wis. 254	840.
Tinkham v. McGaffrey	1891	13 L. D. 517	207.
Tioga Cons. M. Co	1881	8 Copp's L. O. 88	725.
Tipping v. Eckersley	1855	2 K. & J. 264	841.
Tipping v. Robbins	1888	71 Wis. 507, 37 N. W. 427	791.

Names of Cases.	When Decided.	Where Reported.	Sections Where Cited in this Work.
Tipton G. M. Co	1900	29 L. D. 718	396, 670, 671.
Titamore v. S. P. R. R. Co	1890	10 L. D. 463	232.
Titcomb v. Kirk	1876	51 Cal. 288, 5 Morr. 10.	56.
Todd v. Cochell	1860	17 Cal. 97, 10 Morr. 655.	808.
Tomay v. Stewart	1882	1 L. D. 570	685.
Tombstone M. and M. Co. v. Wayup M. Co.	1883	1 Ariz. 426, 25 Pac. 794.	367.
Tombstone Townsite Cases	1887	(Ariz.), 15 Pac. 26	170, 176, 177, 397, 398.
Topsey Mine, In re	1880	7 Copp's L. O. 20	682.
Tornanses v. Melsing	1901	109 Fed. 710	233.
Town of Aldridge v. Craig	1897	25 L. D. 505	208.
Townsite of Butte	1876	3 Copp's L. O. 114, 3 Copp's L. O. 130	171, 173.
Townsite of Central City	1875	(Colo.), 2 Copp's L. O. 150	171.
Townsite of Coalville	1877	4 Copp's L. O. 46	97.
Townsite of Deadwood	1880	8 Copp's L. O. 18	171.
Townsite of Deadwood v. Mineral Claimants.	1880	8 Copp's L. O. 153	171, 184.
Townsite of Eureka Springs v. Conant	1881	8 Copp's L. O. 3	171.
Townsite of Silver Cliff	1879	6 Copp's L. O. 152, Copp's Land Dec. 161.	142.
Travis Placer M. Co. v. Mills	1899	94 Fed. 909	840, 841.
Treadway v. Sharon	1871	7 Nev. 37	409.
Tredinnick v. Red Cloud M. Co	1887	72 Cal. 78, 13 Pac. 152.	327.
Trevaskis v. Peard	1896	111 Cal. 599, 44 Pac. 246.	634, 643, 644.
Trickey Placer Claim	1888	7 L. D. 52, 15 C. L. O. 147	631.
Tripp v. Dunphy	1899	28 L. D. 14, 16	629.
Trotter v. Maclean	1879	L. R. 13 Ch. D. 574	868.
Tryon, In re	1900	29 L. D. 475	784.
Trout v. McDonald	1876	83 Pa. St. 144, 9 Morr. 32	814.
Trulock v. Taylor	1870	26 Ark. 54	542.
Trustees v. Haven	1850	11 Ill. 554	178.
Tuck v. Downing	1875	76 Ill. 71, 7 Morr. 83	797.
Tucker v. Florida Ry. and N. Co	1894	19 L. D. 414	97, 158, 425.
Tucker v. Linger	1883	L. R. 8 App. C. 508	92.
Tucker v. Masser	1885	113 U. S. 203, 5 Sup. Ct. Rep. 420, 28 L. Ed. 379	778.
Tulare Oil and M. Co. v. Southern Pac. R. R. Co	1899	29 L. D. 269	95, 97, 98, 106, 158,

Names of Cases.	When De-cided.	Where Reported.	Sections Where Cited in this Work.
Tumacacori and Calabazas Grant	1893	16 L. D. 408, 423......	207, 336, 437, 438. 124.
Tunstall v. Christian..	1885	80 Cal. 1, 56 Am. Rep. 581	833.
Tuolumne C. M. Co. v. Maier	1901	134 Cal. 583, 66 Pac. 863	330, 335, 337.
Turner v. Lang........	1870	1 Copp's L. O. 51......	171.
Turner v. Reynolds....	1854	23 Pa. St. 199........	813.
Turner v. Sawyer......	1893	150 U. S. 578, 14 Sup. Ct. Rep. 192, 37 L. Ed. 37	251, 406, 646, 728.
Two Sisters Lode and Millsite	1888	7 L. D. 557...........	521, 523, 524, 525, 708.
Twort v. Twort.......	1809	16 Vesey Jr. 128.......	790.
Tyler M. Co. v. Last Chance M. Co.......	1895	71 Fed. 848..........	319, 364, 365.
Tyler M. Co. v. Last Chance M. Co.......	1898	90 Fed. 15, 21........	568, 617, 618a.
Tyler M. Co. v. Sweeney	1893	54 Fed. 284..........	319, 364, 365, 367, 396, 582, 591, 592, 593, 609.
Tyler M. Co. v. Sweeney	1897	79 Fed. 277, 280.......	319, 589, 591.
Uhlig v. Garrison......	1878	2 Dak. 71, 2 N. W. 253.	183, 184.
Union Coal Co........	1893	17 L. D. 351..........	501.
Union M. etc. Co. v. Daugberg	1897	81 Fed. 73............	838.
Union M. and M. Co. v. Leitch	1901	24 Wash. 585, 85 Am. St. Rep. 961, 64 Pac. 829.	339, 372.
Union Cons. S. M. Co. v. Taylor	1879	100 U. S. 39, 25 L. Ed. 541, 5 Morr. 323.....	270, 642.
Union Oil Co., Ex parte	1896	23 L. D. 222..........	97, 138, 158, 422, 432, 438.
Union Oil Co., Ex parte	1897	25 L. D. 351..........	97, 135, 158, 422, 438.
Union Petroleum Co. v. Bliven P. Co........	1872	72 Pa. St. 173.........	859a.
Union Pac. Ry Co.....	1897	25 L. D. 540..........	153.
Union Pac. Ry. Co.....	1899	29 L. D. 261..........	197.
Unita Tunnel etc. Co. v. Creede and Cripple Creek etc. Co.......	1902	119 Fed. 164..........	725, 783.
United States v. Alger.	1894	152 U. S. 384, 14 Sup. Ct. Rep. 635, 38 L. Ed. 488	666.
United States v. American Lumber Co......	1898	85 Fed. 827..........	757.

Names of Cases.	When De- cided.	Where Reported.	Sections Where Cited in this Work.
United States v. Beebe	1887	127 U. S. 338, 8 Sup. Ct. Rep. 1083, 32 L. Ed. 121	784.
United States v. Benja- min	1884	10 Saw. 264, 21 Fed. 285	210.
United States v. Black- burn	1897	(Ariz.), 48 Pac. 904...	209.
United States v. Bre- ward	1842	16 Peters, 147, 10 L. Ed. 916	106.
United States v. Budd.	1891	144 U. S. 167, 12 Sup. Ct. Rep. 575, 36 L. Ed. 384	107, 161, 207, 779.
United States v. Buffalo etc. Gas Fuel Co.....	1899	172 U. S. 339, 19 Sup. Ct. Rep. 200, 43 L. Ed. 469	423.
United States v. Car- penter	1883	111 U. S. 347, 4 Sup. Ct. Rep. 435, 28 L. Ed. 451	183, 184.
United States v. Castil- lero	1862	2 Black. 17, 17 L. Ed. 360	80, 114, 371.
United States v. Cen- tral Pac. R. R. Co...	1898	84 Fed. 218..........	161, 784.
United States v. Cen- tral Pac. R. R. Co..	1899	93 Fed. 871..........	94, 161, 438.
United States v. Cook..	1874	19 Wall. 591, 22 L. Ed. 210	181.
United States v. Cop- per Queen etc. Co....	1900	(Ariz.), 60 Pac. 885...	98.
United States v. Cruik- shank	1876	92 U. S. 542, 23 L. Ed. 588	224.
United States v. Culver	1892	52 Fed. 81............	161, 784.
United States v. Curtner	1889	38 Fed. 1............	124.
United States v. Fossatt	1858	21 How. 446, 16 L. Ed. 185	123.
United States v. Graham	1884	110 U. S. 219, 3 Sup. Ct. Rep. 582, 28 L. Ed. 126	666.
United States v. Gratiot	1840	1 McLean, 454, Fed. Cas. No. 15,249	80.
United States v. Gratiot	1840	14 Peters, 526, 10 L. Ed. 573	47, 80.
United States v. Han- cock	1890	133 U. S. 193, 10 Sup. Ct. Rep. 264, 33 L. Ed. 601	784.
United States v. Hanson	1842	16 Peters, 196, 10 L. Ed. 935	106.

Names of Cases.	When Decided.	Where Reported.	Sections Where Cited in this Work.
United States v. Holmes	1900	105 Fed. 41	170, 216.
United States v. Iron S. M. Co	1885	24 Fed. 568	629, 631.
United States v. Iron S. M. Co	1888	128 U. S. 673, 9 Sup. Ct. Rep. 195, 32 L. Ed. 571	94, 175, 176, 290, 293, 336, 413, 583, 673, 777, 781, 784.
United States v. Johnston	1888	124 U. S. 236, 8 Sup. Ct. Rep. 446, 31 L. Ed. 389	666.
United States v. King.	1897	83 Fed. 188	673.
United States v. King.	1889	9 Mont. 75, 22 Pac. 498.	336.
United States v. Mackintosh	1898	85 Fed. 333	107, 161, 207, 472, 779.
United States v. Marshall S. M. Co	1889	129 U. S. 579, 9 Sup. Ct. Rep. 343, 32 L. Ed. 734, 16 Morr. 205	660, 784.
United States v. Maxwell L. G. Co	1887	121 U. S. 325, 7 Sup. Ct. Rep. 1015, 30 L. Ed. 949	125.
United States v. McLaughlin	1888	127 U. S. 428, 8 Sup. Ct. Rep. 1177, 32 L. Ed. 213	122, 123, 124, 183.
United States v. Miller	1892	14 L. D. 617	772.
United States v. Minor.	1885	114 U. S. 233, 5 Sup. Ct. Rep. 236, 29 L. Ed. 110	175, 207, 784.
United States v. Missouri K. and T. R. R. Co	1891	141 U. S. 358, 12 Sup. Ct. Rep. 13, 35 L. Ed. 35	157, 784.
United States v. Moore.	1877	95 U. S. 760, 24 L. Ed. 588	96, 419, 666.
United States v. Moreno	1863	1 Wall. 400, 17 L. Ed. 633	116.
United States v. Mullan	1882	7 Saw. 466, 470, 10 Fed. 785	136, 140, 143, 157, 161, 495, 784.
United States v. North Bloomfield G. M. Co.	1892	53 Fed. 625	843, 848.
United States v. North Bloomfield M. Co	1897	81 Fed. 243	849, 852, 853.
United States v. North Bloomfield G. M. Co	1898	88 Fed. 664	852, 853.
United States v. Northern Pac. Ry Co	1899	95 Fed. 864	175, 539, 660, 666,

Names of Cases.	When De-cided.	Where Reported.	Sections Where Cited in this Work.
United States *v.* Northern Pac. R. R. Co....	1900	103 Fed. 389.........	777, 784. 154.
United States *v.* Omdahl	1897	25 L. D. 157.........	20, 75.
United States *v.* Oregon and Cal. R. R. Co....	1900	176 U. S. 28, 20 Sup. Ct. Rep. 261, 44 L. Ed. 358	153, 154.
United States *v.* Reed..	1886	12 Saw. 99, 28 Fed. 482.	94, 161, 207, 209.
United States *v.* Rumsey	1896	22 L. D. 101...........	784.
United States *v.* San Jacinto Tin Co......	1887	125 U. S. 273, 8 Sup. Ct. Rep. 850, 31 L. Ed. 747	784.
United States *v.* San Pedro etc. Co.......	1888	4 N. Mex. 225, 17 Pac. 337	114, 125, 126.
United States *v.* Schurz	1880	102 U. S. 378, 26 L. Ed. 167	662.
United States *v.* Smith	1882	8 Saw. 101, 11 Fed. 487.	210.
United States *v.* Southern Pac. R. R. Co....	1892	146 U. S. 570, 13 Sup. Ct. Rep. 152, 36 L. Ed. 1091	154.
United States *v.* Southern Pac. R. R.......	1902	184 U. S. 49, 22 Sup. Ct. Rep. 285, 46 L. Ed. 425	419, 666.
United States *v.* Steenerson	1892	50 Fed. 504...........	208, 772.
United States *v.* Stone.	1864	2 Wall. 525, 17 L. Ed. 765	664.
United States *v.* Tanner	1893	147 U. S. 661, 13 Sup. Ct. Rep. 436, 37 L. Ed. 321	666.
United States *v.* Throckmorton	1878	98 U. S. 61, 25 L. Ed. 93	784.
United States *v.* Trinidad Coal etc. Co....	1890	137 U. S. 160, 11 Sup. Ct. Rep. 57, 34 L. Ed. 640	501, 784.
United States *v.* Tygh Valley Land Co.....	1896	76 Fed. 693...........	112, 197, 322.
United States *v.* Union Pac. R. R...........	1875	91 U. S. 72, 23 L. Ed. 224	612.
United States *v.* Van Winkle ....:....	1902	113 Fed. 903..........	103.
United States *v.* White.	1883	17 Fed. 561...........	784.
United States *v.* Winona and S. P. R. R. Co...	1895	67 Fed. 948...........	157, 161, 175, 207, 609, 659.
United States *v.* Wong Kim Art	1898	169 U. S. 649, 18 Sup. Ct. Rep. 456, 42 L. Ed. 890	224, 238.

Names of Cases.	When De-cided.	Where Reported.	Sections Where Cited in this Work.
United States Freehold etc. Co. v. Gallegos..	1897	89 Fed. 769, C. C. Colo. 1 Leg. Adv. 412......	872.
Upton v. Larkin.......	1885	5 Mont. 600, 6 Pac. 66.	329, 330, 337, 345.
Upton v. Larkin.......	1888	7 Mont. 449, 17 Pac. 728	328, 335, 337, 371. 381, 383.
Utah M. and M. Co. v. Dickert etc. Co......	1889	6 Utah, 183, 21 Pac. 1002, 5 L. R. A. 259.	407, 634.
Utah Salt Lands......	1886	13 Copp's L. O. 53.....	513, 514.
Valcalda v. Silver Peak Mines	1898	86 Fed. 90............	522, 523, 537, 643, 644.
Valentine v. Valentine.	1891	47 Fed. 597...........	154, 155, 160.
Valley City Salt Co. v. Brown	1874	7 W. Va. 191, 5 Morr. 397	262, 264.
Valley Lode	1896	22 L. D. 317..........	781.
Van Brocklin v. State of Tennessee	1886	117 U. S. 151, 6 Sup. Ct. Rep. 670, 29 L. Ed. 845	249.
Van Buren v. McKinley	1901	(Idaho), 66 Pac. 936..	251, 385.
Vance v. Burbank.....	1880	101 U. S. 514, 25 L. Ed. 929	175, 207.
Vance v. Kohlberg.....	1875	50 Cal. 346..........	208, 772.
Vandoren v. Plested...	1893	16 L. D. 508..........	97, 139, 210, 421.
Van Ormer v. Harley..	1897	102 Iowa, 150, 71 N. W. 241	789a.
Van Reynegan v. Bolton	1877	95 U. S. 33-36, 24 L. Ed. 351	123.
Vansickle v. Haines....	1872	7 Nev. 249............	838.
Vantongeren v. Heffer-nan	1888	5 Dak. 180, 226, 38 N. W. 52.............	208, 772.
Van Valkenburg v. Huff	1865	1 Nev. 115, 149, 9 Morr. 468	331.
Van Wagenen v. Car-penter	1900	27 Colo. 444, 61 Pac. 698	398, 406, 407, 728.
Van Wyck v. Knevals..	1882	106 U. S. 360, 1 Sup. Ct. Rep. 336, 27 L. Ed. 201	154.
Van Zandt v. Argentine M. Co..............	1881	8 Fed. 725, 2 McCrary, 159, 4 Morr. 441....	336, 343, 345, 364.
Vanzandt v. Mining Co.	1880	48 Fed. 770..........	872.
Ventura Oil Co. v. Fretts	1893	152 Pa. St. 451, 25 Atl. 732	862.

Names of Cases.	When Decided.	Where Reported.	Sections Where Cited in this Work.
Vervalen v. Older.....	1849	8 N. J. Eq. 98, 10 Morr. 540	789.
Victor M. Co. v. Morning Star M. Co......	1892	50 Mo. App. 525......	832, 834.
Victor No. 3 Lode.....	1899	28 L. D. 436.........	765.
Vietti v. Nesbitt......	1895	22 Nev. 390, 41 Pac. 151	799.
Vizina Cons. M. Co....	1882	9 Copp's L. O. 92.....	171.
Virginia Lode	1888	7 L. D. 459...........	142.
Volcano Lode M. Claim, The	1901	30 L. D. 482.........	338.
Vollmer's Appeal	1868	61 Pa. St. 118........	860.
Waddell's Appeal	1877	84 Pa. St. 90.........	261.
Wagstaff v. Collins....	1899	97 Fed. 3.............	205, 208, 542.
Wakeman v. Norton...	1897	24 Colo. 192, 49 Pac 283	592, 615, 866.
Walker v. Collins......	1897	167 U. S. 57, 17 Sup. Ct. Rep. 738, 42 L. Ed. 76.	747.
Walker v. Fletcher....	1804	3 Bligh, 172, 8 Morr. 1.	873.
Walker v. Southern Pac. R. R. Co...........	1897	24 L. D. 172.........	95, 106, 157, 216, 336.
Walker v. Taylor......	1896	23 L. D. 110.........	504.
Wallace, In re........	1882	1 L. D. 582, 8 C. L. O. 188	735.
Waller v. Hughes.....	1886	(Ariz.), 11 Pac. 122...	327.
Walrath v. Champion M. Co.....	1894	63 Fed. 552.........	58, 60, 350, 365, 567, 568, 576, 593, 610.
Walrath v. Champion M. Co.......	1896	72 Fed. 978..........	60, 584, 593, 610.
Walrath v. Champion M. Co........	1898	171 U. S. 293, 18 Sup. Ct. Rep. 909, 43 L. Ed. 170	60, 365, 572, 584, 589, 593, 594, 610.
Walsh v. Erwin.......	1902	115 Fed. 531..........	355, 371, 373, 375, 688.
Walton v. Batten......	1892	14 L. D. 54..........	95, 106, 207.
Wandering Boy, In re.	1875	2 Copp's L. O. 2......	227, 684.
Wardell v. Watson....	1887	93 Mo. 107, 5 S. W. 605.	813.
War Eagle Mine......	1873	Copp's Min. Dec. 195..	737.
Waring v. Crow.......	1858	11 Cal. 367, 5 Morr. 204	270, 643, 644, 800.
Warner Valley Stock Co. v. Smith........	1896	165 U. S. 28, 17 Sup. Ct. Rep. 225, 41 L. Ed. 621	772.
Warnock v. De Witt...	1895	11 Utah, 324, 40 Pac. 205, Morr. Mining Rights, 103	373, 405.
Warren v. State of Colorado	1892	14 L. D. 681..........	95, 142.

Names of Cases.	When De-cided.	Where Reported.	Sections Where Cited in this Work.
Warren *v.* Van Brunt..	1874	19 Wall. 646, 22 L. Ed. 219	175, 207.
Warren Millsite *v.* Copper Prince	1882	1 L. D. 555, 9 C. L. O. 71	724, 742.
Washington Market Co. *v.* Hoffman	1879	101 U. S. 112, 25 L. Ed. 782	480.
Waterhouse *v.* Scott...	1891	13 L. D. 718..........	738.
Waterloo M. Co. *v.* Doe	1893	56 Fed. 685..........	335, 336, 778.
Waterloo M. Co. *v.* Doe	1897	82 Fed. 45...........	175, 305, 568, 582, 591a, 615, 666, 778, 872.
Waterloo M. Co. *v.* Doe	1893	17 L. D. 111.........	742.
Waterman *v.* Banks....	1892	144 U. S. 394, 12 Sup. Ct. Rep. 646, 36 L. Ed. 479	859.
Waterman *v.* Buck....	1885	58 Vt. 519...........	840.
Waters *v.* Stevenson...	1878	13 Nev. 157, 29 Am. Rep 293	868.
Watervale *v.* Leach...	1893	(Ariz.), 33 Pac. 418...	364, 367, 560, 727.
Watkins *v.* Garner.....	1891	13 L. D. 414.........	504.
Watson *v.* King.......	1815	4 Campb. 272........	860.
Watson *v.* Mayberry...	1897	15 Utah, 265, 49 Pac. 479	337.
Warnock *v.* De Witt...	1895	6 Watts, 362, 8 Morr. 333	861.
Watts *v.* Keller.......	1893	56 Fed. 1............	859.
Watts *v.* White.......	1859	13 Cal. 321, 13 Morr. 11.	535, 792.
Wax, *In re*..........	1900	29 L. D. 592..........	677.
Weaver *v.* Fairchild...	1875	50 Cal. 360..........	662.
Wedekind *v.* Bell......	1902	(Nev.), 69 Pac. 612...	597.
Wedekind *v.* Craig....	1880	56 Cal. 642...........	136.
Weese *v.* Barker......	1884	7 Colo. 178, 2 Pac. 919.	218.
Weill *v.* Lucerne M. Co.	1876	11 Nev. 200, 3 Morr. 372.	398, 642.
Weise, A. V., *In re*....	1875	2 Copp's L. O. 130.....	211.
Welch *v.* Garrett......	1897	(Idaho), 51 Pac. 405..	530, 531.
Welland *v.* Huber.....	1873	8 Nev. 203, 13 Morr. 363	331.
Welland *v.* Williams...	1892	21 Nev. 230, 29 Pac. 403	790.
Wells *v.* Davis........	1900	22 Utah, 322, 62 Pac. 3.	355, 381.
Wenner *v.* McNulty....	1887	7 Mont. 30, 14 Pac. 643.	251.
Wentz's Appeal	1884	106 Pa. St. 301........	861.
West *v.* Weyer........	1888	46 Ohio St. 66, 15 Am. St. Rep. 552, 18 N. E. 537..............	789a.
West Chester R. R. Co. *v.* McElwee	1871	67 Pa. St. 311.........	832.
Western Pacific R. R. Co. *v.* Tevis........	1871	41 Cal. 489..........	153.
Western Pacific R. R. Co. *v.* United States.	1883	108 U. S. 510, 2 Sup. Ct. Rep. 802, 27 L. Ed. 806	161, 784.

Names of Cases.	When Decided.	Where Reported.	Sections Where Cited in this Work.
Western Pennsylvania Gas Co. *v.* George...	1894	161 Pa. St. 47, 28 Atl. 1004	862.
West Granite Mt. M. Co. *v.* Granite Mt. M. Co.........	1888	7 Mont. 356, 17 Pac. 547.	373.
West Hickory M. Assn. *v.* Reed	1875	80 Pa. St. 38..........	802.
Westmoreland etc. Gas Co. *v.* De Witt......	1889	130 Pa. St. 235, 18 Atl. 724, 5 L. R. A. 731..	93, 423, 812.
West Virginia Trans. Co. *v.* Volcanic C. Co.	1872	5 W. Va. 382, 5 Morr. 389	255.
Wettengill *v.* Gormley..	1894	160 Pa. St. 559, 40 Am. St. Rep. 733, 28 Atl. 934	862.
Weymouth *v.* R. R. Co.	1863	17 Wis. 550, 84 Am. Dec. 763	868.
Whaley *v.* Braucker...	1864	10 L. T. N. S. 155, 8 Morr. 29	873.
Wheatley *v.* Baugh....	1855	25 Pa. St. 528, 64 Am. Dec. 721	814.
Wheatley's Heirs *v.* Calhoun	1841	12 Leigh, 264, 272, 37 Am. Dec. 654	802.
Wheeler *v.* Smith......	1896	23 L. D. 395..........	323, 738.
Wheeler *v.* Smith......	1893	5 Wash. 704, 32 Pac. 784	96, 97, 142, 210, 323, 421.
Wheeler *v.* West......	1886	71 Cal. 126, 11 Pac. 871.	860.
Wheeling *v.* Phillips...	1899	1ʋ Pa. Super. Ct. 634..	862.
White *v.* Lee.........	1889	78 Cal. 593, 12 Am. St. Rep. 115, 21 Pac. 363	373, 432, 454.
White *v.* Sayre........	1825	2 Ohio. 110..........	791.
White Cloud etc. Co..	1896	22 L. D. 252..........	631, 675.
White Oaks Imp Co...	1886	13 Copp's L. O. 159....	505.
Whithead *v.* Shattuck..	1891	138 U. S. 146, 11 Sup. Ct. Rep. 276, 34 L. Ed. 873	754.
Whitman *v.* Haltenhoff	1894	19 L. D. 245..........	742, 766.
Whitney *v.* Spratt....	1901	25 Wash. 62, 87 Am. St. Rep. 738, 64 Pac. 919.	472, 662, 772.
Wight *v.* Dubois......	1884	21 Fed. 693..........	713, 742.
Wight *v.* Tabor	1884	2 L. D. 738, 2 L. D. 743, 10 C. L. O. 392......	250, 397, 742.
Wilcox *v.* Jackson *ex. rel* McConnell	1839	13 Pet. 498, 10 L. Ed. 264	80, 190, 197, 237, 249, 322, 660, 665.
Wildey *v.* Bonny......	1853	26 Miss. 35...........	540.
Wilhelm *v.* Silvester...	1894	101 Cal. 358, 35 Pac. 997	557, 560.

Names of Cases.	When Decided.	Where Reported.	Sections Where Cited in this Work.
Wilkinson v. Northern Pac. R. R. Co.......	1885	5 Mont. 538, 6 Pac. 349.	153.
Willamette Valley and Cascade M. W. R. R. Co................	1899	29 L. D. 344.........	157.
Willeford v. Bell......	1897	(Cal.), 49 Pac. 6......	339, 350, 371, 373.
Willey v. Hunter......	1884	57 Vt. 479.............	844.
Williams, In re........	1890	11 L. D. 321..........	496.
Williams, In re........	1893	17 L. D. 282..........	691.
Williams, In re........	1895	20 L. D. 458..........	337.
Williams v. Bagnall...	1866	12 Jurist & N. S. 987, 13 Morr. 686........	821.
Williams v. Gibson....	1887	84 Ala. 228, 5 Am. St. Rep. 368, 4 South. 350, 16 Morr. 253........	812, 813, 814, 818, 821.
Williams v. Groncott..	1863	4 B. & Sm. 149........	814.
Williams v. Hay......	1888	120 Pa. St. 485, 6 Am. St. Rep. 719, 14 Atl. 379	818, 819, 821.
Williams v. Pomeroy...	1882	37 Ohio St. 583, 6 Morr. 195	867.
Williams v. Santa Clara Min. Assn.	1884	66 Cal. 193, 5 Pac. 85..	327.
Williamson v. Jones...	1894	39 W. Va. 231, 19 S. E. 436, 25 L. R. A. 222.	93, 97, 138, 299, 422.
Williamson v. Jones...	1897	43 W. Va. 562, 64 Am. St. Rep. 891, 27 S. E. 411, 38 L. R. A. 694.	789a.
Wills v. Blain........	1889	4 N. Mex. 378, 20 Pac. 798	404, 539.
Willson v. Cleveland...	1866	30 Cal. 192............	644.
Wilms v. Jess........	1880	94 Ill. 464, 34 Am. Rep. 242, 14 Morr. 56....	818, 819, 820.
Wilson v. Cleveland....	1866	30 Cal. 192............	643.
Wilson v. Davis.......	1897	25 L. D. 514..........	208.
Wilson v. Fine........	1889	14 Saw. 224, 40 Fed. 52.	772.
Wilson v. Henry......	1874	35 Wis. 241, 1 Morr. Min. Rep. 152.......	688.
Wilson v. Triumph Consol. M. Co.........	1899	19 Utah, 66, 75, Am. St. Rep. 718, 56 Pac. 300	216, 218, 226, 233, 234, 255, 381, 383.
Wilson v. Waddell.....	1876	2 L. R. Appeal Cases, 95, 14 Morr. 25.........	808.
Wilson v. Youst.......	1897	43 W. Va. 826, 28 S. E. 781	861.
Wilson Creek Cons. M. Co. v. Independence etc. Co.	1900	1 Colo. Dec. Supp. 1, 3 Leg. Adv. No. 13, p. 1.	720, 781.

Names of Cases.	When De-cided.	Where Reported.	Sections Where Cited in this Work.
Wilson Creek Cons. M. Co. v. Montgomery..	1896	23 L. D. 476..........	781.
Wiltsee v. King of Arizona M. and M. Co..	1900	(Ariz.), 60 Pac. 896...	339, 353, 374, 380, 381.
Winans v. Beidler	1898	6 Okl. 603, 52 Pac. 405.	409.
Winchester v. Craig....	1876	33 Mich. 205..........	868.
Winn v. Abeles.......	1886	35 Kan. 85, 57 Am. Rep. 138, 10 Pac. 443.....	833.
Winscott v. Northern Pac. R. R. Co.	1893	17 L. D. 274..........	106, 155, 156.
Winship v. Pitts......	1832	3 Paige, 259..........	790.
Winter Lode	1896	22 L. D. 362..........	337.
Winters v. Bliss.......	1892	14 L. D. 59...........	95, 207.
Wirth v. Branson.....	1878	98 U. S. 118, 25 L. Ed. 86	771.
Wisconsin Cent. R. R. Co. v. Forsythe......	1895	159 U. S. 48, 15 Sup. Ct. Rep. 1020, 40 L. Ed. 71	124, 666.
Wisconsin Cent. R. R. Co. v. Price County..	1890	133 U. S. 496, 10 Sup. Ct. Rep. 341, 33 L. Ed. 687	143, 157, 199, 208.
Wisconsin Mfg. Co. v. Cooper	1883	10 Copp's L. O. 69....	671.
Wise v. Nixon........	1896	76 Fed. 3.............	746.
Wiseman v. Eastman..	1899	21 Wash. 163, 57 Pac. 398	665, 666.
Witherspoon v. Duncan.	1866	4 Wall. 210, 18 L. Ed. 339	208, 542, 771.
Wittenbrock v. Wheadon	1900	128 Cal. 150, 79 Am. St. Rep. 32, 60 Pac. 664..	542.
Wolenberg, In re......	1900	29 L. D. 302, 304.....	624, 632, 645, 686, 696, 701, 742, 755.
Wolf v. St. Louis Water Co.........	1858	10 Cal. 541, 10 Morr. 636	808.
Wolfley v. Lebanon....	1878	4 Colo. 112...........	58, 60, 125, 268, 350, 364, 553, 586, 604, 713.
Wolsey v. Chapman....	1880	101 U. S. 755, 25 L. Ed. 915	197.
Wolverton v. Nichols...	1886	119 U. S. 485, 7 Sup. Ct. Rep. 289, 30 L. Ed. 474, 15 Morr. 309....	754, 755.
Wood, In re..........	1876	3 Copp's L. O. 69......	232.
Wood v. Aspen M. etc. Co.........	1888	36 Fed. 25............	227.
Wood v. Hyde	1874	1 Copp's L. O. 66......	756.
Wood v. Leadbetter....	1845	13 Mees & W. 838.....	860.
Wood v. Morewood.....	1841	3 Q. B. 440, 10 Morr. 77	868.
Wood v. Sutcliffe......	1851	2 Sim. N. S. 163, 16 Jur. 75, 8 Eng. Law & Eq. 217, 221......	843.

Names of Cases.	When Decided.	Where Reported.	Sections Where Cited in this Work.
Woodenware Co. v. United States	1882	106 U. S. 432, 1 Sup. Ct. Rep. 398, 27 L. Ed. 230	868.
Woodland Oil Co. v. Crawford	1896	55 Ohio St. 161, 44 N. E. 1093, 34 L. R. A. 62	862.
Woodruff v. North Bloomfield G. M. Co.	1883	8 Saw. 628, 18 Fed. 774.	252, 270, 531.
Woodruff v. North Bloomfield G. M. Co.	1884	9 Saw. 441, 18 Fed. 753.	252, 270, 531, 843, 848, 852, 853.
Woods v. Holden	1898	26 L. D. 198	312a, 366, 619, 730, 758.
Woods v. Holden	1898	27 L. D. 375	312a.
Woodside v. Ciceroni	1899	93 Fed. 1	859a.
Woodward v. Worcester	1876	121 Mass. 245	843.
Woody v. Barnard	1901	69 Ark. 579, 65 S. W. 100	635.
Woolley v. Schrader	1886	116 Ill. 29, 4 N. E. 658.	789a.
Worcester v. State of Georgia	1832	6 Peters, 515, 8 L. Ed. 483	181.
Wormouth v. Gardner.	1899	125 Cal. 316, 58 Pac. 20.	665.
Wright v. Killian	1901	132 Cal. 56, 64 Pac. 98.	405, 635.
Wright v. Roseberry	1887	121 U. S. 488, 7 Sup. Ct. Rep. 985, 30 L. Ed. 1039	175.
Wright v. Sioux Cons. M. Co.	1899	29 L. D. 154	381, 671, 677.
Wright v. Taber	1884	2 L. D. 738	335.
Wulff v. Manuel	1890	9 Mont. 279, 23 Pac. 723	232, 233, 643.
Wyatt v. Harrison	1832	3 Barn & Adol. 871	833.
Wynn v. Garland	1857	19 Ark. 23, 68 Am. Dec. 190	860.
Wyoming Cons. M. Co. v. Champion M. Co.	1894	63 Fed. 540	294.
Yandes v. Wright	1879	66 Ind. 319, 32 Am. Rep. 109, 14 Morr. 32	818 819.
Yankee Lode	1900	30 L. D. 289	400, 673.
Yarwood v. Johnson	1902	(Wash.), 70 Pac. 123	407.
Yellow Aster M. etc. Co. v. Winchell	1899	95 Fed. 213	755.
Yoakum, In re	1874	1 Copp's L. O. 3	140.
York v. Davidson	1901	39 Or. 81, 65 Pac. 819.	843.
York Railway Co. v. Winans	1854	17 How. 31, 15 L. Ed. 27	773.
Yosemite Valley Case	1872	15 Wall. 77, 21 L. Ed. 82	192, 205, 216, 542.
Young v. Forest Oil Co.	1899	194 Pa. St. 243, 45 Atl. 119	862.

Names of Cases.	When Decided.	Where Reported.	Sections Where Cited in this Work.
Young v. Goldsteen....	1899	97 Fed. 303..........	170, 172, 723.
Young v. Hanson......	1895	95 Iowa, 717, 64 N. W. 654	772.
Yreka M. Co. v. Knight	1901	133 Cal. 544, 65 Pac. 1091	375, 630.
Zeckendorf v. Hutchinson	1871	1 N. Mex. 476, 9 Morr. 483	630.
Zephyr Lode Mining Claim	1901	30 L. D. 510..........	631, 671, 673.
Zollars and H. C. M. Co. v. Evans	1880	2 McCrary, 39, 5 Fed. 172	345.
Zumwalt, In re........	1895	20 L. D. 32............	197.

AMERICAN LAW RELATING TO MINES AND MINERAL LANDS.

TITLE I.

COMPARATIVE MINING JURISPRUDENCE.

CHAPTER
I. MINING LAWS OF FOREIGN COUNTRIES.
II. LOCAL STATE SYSTEMS.

CHAPTER I.

MINING LAWS OF FOREIGN COUNTRIES.

§ 1. Introductory.

§ 2. Property in mines under the common law.

§ 3. Royal mines.

§ 4. Local customs.

§ 5. Tin mines of Cornwall.

§ 6. Tin mines of Devonshire.

§ 7. Coal, iron, and other mines in the Forest of Dean.

§ 8. Lead mines of Derbyshire.

§ 9. Severance of title.

§ 10. Existing English laws.

§ 11. Mines under the civil law.

§ 12. Mining laws of France: — *Mines—Minières—Carrières.*

§ 13. Mining laws of Mexico: — Nature and condition of mining concessions—Right of discoverer; *pertenencias*—Right to mine, how acquired—Denouncement of abandoned mines — Right to denounce mines in private property— Rights of one not a discoverer —Placers—Foreigners and religious orders—Extent of *pertenencias;* surface limits — Marking boundaries; rights in depth — Right to all veins found within boundaries of *pertenencias*—Forfeiture for failure to work—Royalties.

§ 1. Introductory.—To the student of the system of mining laws in force in the United States, a comparative review of the mining jurisprudence of the different countries of the world is not of controlling importance. The evolution and development of the American system have their parallels in the history of older nations; other countries have recognized and established by written codes the customs of mining communities, and it is by no means difficult to discover in some of the details of our own system the earmarks of ancient mining regulations: yet in construing our laws and applying them to existing conditions we will receive but little material aid from the experience or legal literature of other countries. While this is true, we must consider that the common law of England was to a certain extent grafted into our legal system when we separated from the mother country, and was, and still is, the rule of action in the absence of legislation,[1] and that, at least in the earlier history of our government, English precedents were of controlling force. In this light, not only the English common law, but the rules governing the subject of mines in Great Britain, are worthy of at least passing comment.

When we also consider that, approximately, all of our public mineral domain within the states and territories subject to the general federal mining laws was originally acquired by treaty or purchase from France and Mexico, wherein the civil law was the basis of jurisprudence, and that at the time of cession both of these nations had well-established and defined codes of mining law, it is apparent that a brief presentation of the laws of these ceding nations will not be out of place. We may confidently expect to find in the growth and development of our own system the influence of these laws. These considerations justify the author in presenting such a brief outline of the mining jurisprudence of these several countries as will enable us to note the theories of government upon which the laws are based, their salient features, and to observe to what extent, if any, they have left their impress upon the American law of mines.

§ 2. Property in mines under the common law.— As a general rule, under the common law, minerals were the property of the owner of the land, the property in

---

[1] Del Monte M. Co. v. Last Chance M. Co., 171 U. S. 55, 60, 18 Sup. Ct. Rep. 895; Doe v. Waterloo M. Co., 54 Fed. Rep. 935, 938.

the surface carrying with it the ownership of everything
beneath and above it.[1]

Therefore, the ownership of the surface was the best
prima facie title to the ownership also of the mines.[2]

This *prima facie* ownership continued until rebutted,
by showing either—

(1) That the land contained " royal mines "; or—

(2) That it was subject to some particular custom
that defeated the *prima facie* ownership, as in the case
of the tin mines of Cornwall and Devon and the lead
mines of Derbyshire; or—

(3) That the ownership of the mines and minerals
had become in fact, from divers causes, several and distinct from the ownership of the soil and surface.[3]

§ 3. **Royal mines.** — By the term "royal mines"
was meant mines of gold and silver. These belonged
exclusively to the crown, by prerogative, although in
lands of subjects. In this respect, the rule was the same
as under the civil law. It was at one time contended
that mines or mineral deposits containing the baser
metals in combination with either gold or silver were
royal mines. This contention, however, was set at rest
by statutes enacted during the reign·of William and
Mary,[4] wherein it was declared that no mine should be
deemed royal by reason of its containing tin, copper,
iron, or lead in association with gold or silver. Thus,
those mines only came to be classed as royal in which
were found the precious metals in the pure state. There

[1] 2 Blackstone's Comm., p. 18; Arundel on Mines, p. 3; Del Monte M.
Co. *v.* Last Chance M. Co., 171 U. S. 55, 60, 18 Sup. Ct. Rep. 895.

[2] Bainbridge on Mines, 5th ed., p. 109; MacSwinney on Mines, p. 27;
Rogers on Mines, p. 247; Del Monte M. Co. *v.* Last Chance M. Co., 171
U. S. 55, 60, 18 Sup. Ct. Rep. 895.

[3] Bainbridge on Mines, 4th ed., p. 27.

[4] 1 William and Mary, c. 30; 5 William and Mary, c. 6.

is no authentic record of any such ever having been known to exist in England, unless we accept the traditional accounts of the Roman invasion as establishing their existence.

In certain reigns the crown claimed a right to mines of alum and saltpeter; but the asserted prerogative was rarely exercised, and then only in an arbitrary way.[1]

Mines and minerals of all descriptions underlying the beds of navigable streams belonged to the crown.

As to mines under the sea or its shores, generally speaking, the rule of proprietorship of the soil obtained. The crown owned the sea-bottom adjoining the coasts of the United Kingdom and that part of the seashore from low-water mark to the line of the neap tides. Mines underneath the seashore belonged *prima facie* to the littoral owner or to the crown, as the superjacent soil belonged to the one or the other.[2]

The right of the crown to royal mines, as a branch of the royal prerogative, is said to have had its origin in the king's right of coinage.[3] But, as Mr. Bainbridge observes, it is more probable that the royal right arose in Roman times, and was transmitted to successive sovereigns. As regards imperial mining rights, in mines of gold and silver, there is no difference between the Roman or civil law and the English mining laws.

A mine royal was not an incident inseparable from the crown, but might be severed from it by apt and precise words. But a grant by the crown of lands would not pass gold or silver mines, unless they were expressly named, and this applied to a grant of lands in the colonies.[4]

---

[1] Bainbridge on Mines, 4th ed., p. 133.

[2] MacSwinney on Mines, pp. 30-31; Bainbridge on Mines, 4th ed., p. 171; Rogers on Mines, p. 178.

[3] Bainbridge on Mines, 4th ed., p. 120.

[4] MacSwinney on Mines, p. 40.

Briefly stated, the regalian right to mines, as recognized in England, was confined to those of the precious metals—gold and silver. The baser substances belonged to the owner of the soil, except in certain localities where immemorial custom had modified the rule.

§ 4. **Local customs.**—In certain parts of England and Wales so-called "local customs" were recognized which modified the general rule of the common law.[1] In these excepted localities the ownership of the baser mineral substances continued in the crown, subject to certain so-called customary rights in the subject, which customary rights have been from time to time recognized and defined by statute.[2]

These excepted districts were the Forest of Dean (including the hundred of St. Briavels), in the county of Gloucester, certain parts of Derbyshire, Cornwall, and Devon, and other places of minor importance.

These customs undoubtedly had their origin during the Roman occupation; but they were recognized and established by acts of parliament upon the theory that they existed by virtue of some antecedent grant or concession made by the crown. These customs are of more than passing interest, not only on account of the antiquity of their origin, but because they afforded to the early miners of California, in many particulars, valuable precedents to guide them in framing their primitive local rules. A brief consideration of them will not be out of place.

§ 5. **The tin mines of Cornwall.**—The right of working tin mines was conferred upon all "free tinners," upon the render of a certain proportion of the minerals

---

[1] Del Monte M. Co. *v.* Last Chance M. Co., 171 U. S. 55, 60, 18 Sup. Ct. Rep. 895.

[2] Bainbridge on Mines, 4th ed., p. 113.

raised to the owner or lord of the soil. This proportion was called "dish," or "toll," tin, and was usually one fifteenth of the product. Any tinner was allowed to "bound" any unappropriated waste lands, or inclosed lands which had formerly been waste lands, subject to the custom. He "bounded" the same by delivery of toll tin to the lord of the soil. A tin bound generally consisted of about an acre of land, the four corners of which were marked by turfs or stones at each corner. A side bound of triangular form was also allowed.[1]

The bounder was required to proclaim his bounds at the next ensuing stannary courts, announcing the limits of his bounds and the names of his co-adventurers, if any. This proclamation was repeated at the two ensuing stannary courts; and if no opposition appeared, a writ of possession issued from the court commanding the bailiff to put him in possession. Possession was then delivered, and the tinner became entitled to search for and extract ore.

Bounds were required to be annually renewed, by re-marking the corners. The tinner failing to renew his bounds within the year might, however, be restored to his estate by renewing them at any time before others should enter and bound.[2]

Tin bounds might be sold or demised, were frequently farmed out for a render called "farm tin," and were liable to the payment of debts and legacies. The estate was in the nature of a chattel real, and passed to the executor.[3]

If the owners of bounds left them unworked for a year, other tinners might enter and work them, if they gave the owners notice of their desire to work, and the owners did not within two months resume operations.

[1] Bainbridge on Mines, 4th ed., p. 149.
[2] MacSwinney on Mines, p. 431.
[3] *Id.*, p. 432.

A bounder was not compelled to prosecute his work continuously with absolute strictness. He was allowed a reasonable time for consideration, preparation, and selection of places; but he should not cease to pursue in good faith his original object. If he did, the owner of the soil might resume his exclusive rights.[1]

Stannary courts were local tribunals, existing from time immemorial, and recognized by royal charters. They were courts of record, with both common-law and equity jurisdiction, wherein controversies concerning miners or their property rights were adjusted.

§ 6. **Tin mines in Devonshire.** — Tin-bounding in Devonshire was governed generally by customs similar to those of Cornwall. The estate, however, of the bounder was that of fee simple, and descended to the heir at law.[2]

§ 7. **Coal, iron, and other mines in the Forest of Dean and the hundred of St. Briavels.** — The "free miners" within the hundred of St. Briavels (which embraces the Forest of Dean) were entitled by immemorial custom to have granted to them "gales" of the mines of coal and iron and leases of the quarries of stone within the lands of the crown, and within inclosed lands under certain restrictions. By the term "free miner" was meant all male persons born and abiding within the hundred, of the age of twenty-one and upwards, who had worked a year and a day in the mines within the hundred.

All free miners were required to register with the gaveler of the forest or his deputy, the gaveler being the representative of the crown.

A "gale" was the name given to the holding of mines

---

[1] MacSwinney on Mines, p. 432.   [2] *Id.*, p. 438.

of coal or iron and quarries of stone, the free miner acquiring a gale being styled the "galee," and the rentals paid were called "galeage."[1]

A gale was acquired by written application in writing to the gaveler, setting forth the situation of the proposed gale and the name of the vein proposed to be worked. After obtaining the approval of the commissioner of the woods, the gaveler set out the metes and bounds, and a grant thereof was made and entered in the gaveler's book, and subsequently enrolled in the office of land revenue.

The estate thus granted to a galee was in the nature of an estate in fee simple, and descended to the heir.[2]

The galee was obliged to work in a fair, orderly, and workmanlike manner, and not to desist from working for five years at any one time after the vein in question had been gained.[3]

Gales might be assigned and disposed of by deed or will. Transfers were required to be entered within three months in the books of the gaveler, and unregistered transfers were void. Non-payment of galeage and failure to comply with the rules subject to which gales were held worked a forfeiture.

§ 8. The lead mines of Derbyshire. — The customs recognized and established in certain portions of Derbyshire were confined to lead mines. Under these regulations, any subject of the realm might enter and search for ore in all lands and places within the district, excepting churches, burial-grounds, dwelling-houses, and highways. The first discoverer of a vein was entitled to have assigned to him two "meers" of ground. If the vein was a "rake" vein,—that is, one having an inclination from the horizontal,—the meer was from

---

[1] MacSwinney on Mines, p. 482. [2] Id., p. 483. [3] Id., p. 489.

twenty-seven to thirty-two yards, measured along the vein. If the vein, or stratum, was bedded, or flat, the meer was fourteen square yards, or thereabouts. The meers were measured and set out by the "barmaster," an official who acted as an agent of the crown or its lessees, and also looked after the interest of the miner and enforced the customs of the manor.

The miner was entitled to so much surface land in connection with his vein as was thought necessary by the barmaster and two of the grand jury, for the purpose of laying rubbish, dressing ore, buddling, etc. This was called the "quarter-cord," as originally in the "Low Peak" it consisted of a quarter of a meer in breadth.

Whether this was to be measured from the middle of the vein or the walls, was a mooted question.

Before any ground was set apart, however, ore was required to be raised and the meer freed. "Freeing "the meer" was accomplished by delivering to the crown or its lessee the first "dish" of ore.

This dish, called the "freeing dish," was provided by the barmaster, and was of sufficient size to contain fifteen pints of water.

In like manner, each successive meer allotted on the vein must have been "freed." This ceremony was equivalent to the livery of seisin, and without it title did not pass.

The "duties," or royalties, exacted from the miner were called "lot and cope." "Lot" was usually one thirteenth part of all the ore raised, payable to the crown or its lessees.[1] "Cope" was fourpence for every load of ore, a load consisting of nine dishes.

It was always necessary that the mine should continue to be fairly worked. Originally, if it was capable

---

[1] These duties were usually farmed out.

of being worked, and was suffered to remain idle for several weeks, the barmaster was required to "nick "the spindle" once a week—the spindle being a stake fixed in the ground, marking the boundaries of the meer, and the nick was a notch. An examination of the spindle disclosed the number of notches, and the mine became forfeited a few weeks after the third "nicking," unless the warning was heeded and work resumed. This ceremony was equivalent to an entry after breach of condition, by which the lord or lessor was restored to his former estate. Under the regulations now in force, forfeiture is worked by notice to resume given by the barmaster. If resumption does not take place within three weeks, the claim is forfeited, and may be assigned by the barmaster to any person willing to work it.

The right of possession and enjoyment was guaranteed so long as the regulations were complied with.

Once freed, and kept in lawful possession, the mine was declared to be an estate of inheritance liable to dower and capable of absolute disposition.[1]

While we do not find anything in the authorities expressly defining the extent to which the miner might follow his "rake vein" in depth, it is quite manifest that the vein was the principal thing acquired, and that the surface ground allotted by the barmaster was a mere incident, and that the miner might pursue his vein on its downward course, even under excepted lands, provided no injury resulted to the surface. The working might be suspended or regulated by the steward and grand jury.[2]

§ 9. **Severance of title.**—Under the English law, rights of property in the surface and in the underlying

---

[1] Bainbridge on Mines, 4th ed., p. 141.
[2] MacSwinney on Mines, p. 509.

mines might be shown to be in different owners. Nothing was more common than to sell or demise a piece of land excepting the mines.[1] In like manner, the different strata of the subsoil might be shown to be the subject of different rights.[2] And there might be also in one mine different minerals which were the property of different persons.[3]

Thus, one person might be entitled to the iron, and another to the limestone. One seam or stratum of coal, if in the same lands, might belong to a third person, and another distinct seam to a fourth owner.[4]

When the surface and underlying mines or the different strata of the subsoil were differently owned, they were separate tenements, with all the incidents of separate ownership[5]—a distinct possession and distinct inheritance;[6] and the mines of each stratum might be held in fee simple,[7] or fee tail,[8] or otherwise, as in the case of surface property.[9]

§ 10. **Existing English laws.** — The legislation in England on the subject of mines, except as to the particular districts heretofore noted, is limited, generally

[1] Del Monte M. Co. v. Last Chance M. Co., 171 U. S. 55, 60; 18 Sup. Ct. Rep. 895; Smith v. Jones, 21 Utah 270; 60 Pac. 1104, 1106.

[2] MacSwinney on Mines, p. 27; Cox v. Glue, 5 C. B. 549; Arundel on Mines, p. 5; Bainbridge on Mines, 4th ed., p. 28.

[3] Arundel on Mines, p. 5.

[4] Bainbridge on Mines, 4th ed., p. 28.

[5] MacSwinney on Mines, p. 27, (citing Rombotham v. Wilson, 8 E. & B. 142; Hamilton v. Graham, L. R., 2 Sc. & D. 166; Seaman v. Vaudray, 16 Ves. 392; Guest v. East Dean, L. R., 7 Q. B. 377).

[6] Bainbridge on Mines, 4th ed., p. 28; Cullen v. Rich, Bull N. P. 102; 2 Str. 1142, *sub nom.* Rich v. Johnson.

[7] Stoughton v. Leigh, 1 Taunt. 402.

[8] Port v. Tuston, 2 Wils. 172.

[9] MacSwinney on Mines, p. 27.

A discussion of the law in the United States on the subject of severance of title will be found in a later portion of this treatise (§§ 812-814).

speaking, to acts providing for official inspection and regulations concerning manner of working. England has no general mining laws. Legal questions governing the ownership of mines and minerals have been determined upon the general principles of the common law, except in the localities where ancient customs have been recognized and established by acts of parliament. As we have seen, under the common law, generally speaking, the owner of the soil is the owner of the minerals. The owner of the minerals may deal with them as he pleases, subject only to the general rule governing all classes of property, that he shall injure no one else.

§ 11. **Mines under the civil law.**—Under the Roman law, the ownership proper of all lands was vested in the state. This was the *dominium strictum*. The individual subject could acquire the possessory ownership, with the right to extract minerals, upon the payment of royalties. This was the *dominium utile*.

Under a decree of the Emperor Gratian (A. D. 367-383), the right to the crown in mines of gold and silver was exclusive; that is, the *dominium strictum* and *dominium utile* were united in the state. As to other mines, the crown had a right to receive a proportion of the produce, which proportion, or the measure thereof, was called the *canon metallicus*.

This decree of the Emperor Gratian was embodied in an imperial constitution, which was recognized and adopted by subsequent emperors, and thus became the expression of the measure of Roman imperial rights in mines.[1]

Gamboa, in his commentaries on the mining ordinances of Spain, thus states the rule of the civil law:—

----

[1] Bainbridge on Mines, 4th ed., p. 116.

"By the civil law, all veins and mineral deposits of
" gold or silver ore, or of precious stones, belonged,
" if in·public ground, to the sovereign, and were part
" of his patrimony; but if in private property, they
" belonged to the owner of the land, subject to the con-
" dition, that if worked by the owner, he was bound
" to render a tenth part of the produce to the prince
" as a right attaching to his crown; and if worked by
" any other person, by consent of the owner, the former
" was liable to the payment of two tenths, one to the
" prince and one to the owner.

"Subsequently, it became an established custom in
" most kingdoms, and was declared by the particular
" laws and statutes of each, that all veins of the pre-
" cious metals, and the produce of such veins, should
" vest in the crown, and be held to be a part of the
" patrimony of the king or sovereign prince."[1]

Mr. Arundel Rogers thus states his conclusions from
the various authorities consulted:—

"Under the civil law, in its purest times, gold, silver,
" and other precious metals usually belonged to the
" state, whilst all other minerals, mines, and quarries
" belonged to the owner of the soil, subject in some
" cases to a partial, and in others to a more general,
" control of the *fiscus* (treasury)."

This feature of the civil law underlies most of the
continental systems, as well as those of the Spanish-
American republics. It is the regalian doctrine, which
also prevails as to royal mines (gold and silver), under
the common law of England.[2]

The equitable estate, the *dominium utile,* which was
vested in the subject, was permanent in its character,
and has been defined as an ownership which the possessor could describe and claim as such against all the
world, save and except his lord the emperor.

---

[1] Commentaries of Gamboa—Heathfield Trans., vol. i, p. 15.
[2] Bainbridge on Mines, 4th ed., p. 117.

This estate was analogous to the tenancy by copy-hold under the English common law, the tenant being seised thereof as against all the world, saving and excepting only his lord.[1]

It also bears a striking resemblance to the tenure by which a mining claimant holds a perfected but unpatented mining location upon the public mineral lands of the United States.

The theory of the civil law is thus clearly stated by Mr. Halleck:—

"All continental publicists who have written upon
" the subject lay down the fundamental rule, that
" mines, from their very nature, are not a dependence
" of the ownership of the soil; that they ought not to
" become private property in the same sense as the
" soil is private property; but that they should be held
" and worked with the understanding, that they are
" by nature public property, and that they are to be
" used and regulated in such a way as to conduce most
" to the general interest of society."[2]

§ 12. **Mining laws of France.**— From the earliest times, the French law placed all mines, whether in public or in private lands, at the disposition of the nation, and made the working of them subject to its consent and to the surveillance of the government.[3]

The French law divided the subject of mining into three classes—*mines, minières,* and *carrières.*

Mines, properly speaking, were those wherein the substances were obtained from underground workings, the extraction of which required extensive development and elaborate machinery. In the language of De Fooz,—

"Mines of this kind constitute a part of the domain of
" the state: they are to be ranked as the property of

---

[1] Bainbridge on Mines, p. 200.
[2] Introduction to De Fooz on the Law of Mines, p. x, § 2.
[3] *Id.,* p. xv, § 8.

" society, and should be confided to the sovereign au-
" thority; and this authority should have a general
" control over their extraction.   In this consists the
" system of the regalian rights of mines." [1]

Taking the act of April 21, 1810, as the basis of the
French law, as it existed during the period presently
under consideration, we give the following outline of
its general features:—

Mines.—Those were considered as mines which were
known to contain, in veins, beds, or strata, gold, silver,
platinum, quicksilver, lead, iron (in veins or beds),
copper, tin, zinc, bismuth, arsenic, manganese, antimony, molybdenite, plumbago, or other metallic substances; sulphur, coal, fossilized wood, bituminous
substances, alum, or sulphates.   To this category, by
law of June 17, 1840, salt springs and salt mines were
added.

Mines could only be worked in virtue of an act of
concession, which vested the property in the *conces-
sionaire,* with power to dispose of and transmit the
same like other property, except that they could not be
sold in lots or divided without the consent of the government, given in the same form as the concession.
Royalties were payable to the owners of the surface
and to the government.   No one could make searches
for the discovery of mines in land which did not belong
to him, unless with the consent of the proprietor of the
surface, or with the authorization of the government,
subject to a previous indemnity to the proprietor and
after he shall have been heard.   The proprietor might
make searches without previous formality; but he was
required to obtain a concession before he could establish a mine-working.   From the moment a mine was
conceded, even to the proprietor of the surface, this

[1] Halleck's De Fooz on the Law of Mines, p. 10.

property was distinguished from that of the surface, and was thereafter considered as a new property. Concessions were obtained by petition, addressed to the prefect, who registered it, and posted notice thereof for a period of four months. Proclamations were required to be made at certain places and times at least once a month during the continuation of the postings. Investigations were required to be made by the prefect of the department on the opinion of the engineer of mines, the results being transmitted to the minister of the interior. In the absence of opposition, concessions were granted by an imperial decree, deliberated upon in council of state. The act of concession determined the extent, which was to be bounded by fixed points taken on the surface of the soil, and by passing vertical planes from the surface into the interior of the earth to an indefinite depth. The engineers of mines exercised, under the orders of the minister of the interior and the prefects, a surveillance of police, for the preservation of edifices and the security of the soil. Royalties were payable to the government proportional to the yield, in addition to a fixed tax, called "ground "tax." Forfeiture of the privilege granted by the concession resulted from a failure to comply with its terms, or from suspension of the works, if by such suspension the wants of consumers were affected, or if the suspension had not been authorized by the mining authorities.

Minières included the iron ores called alluvial, pyritous earths suitable for being converted into sulphate of iron, aluminous earths and peats, and such substances as could be worked by open pits or temporary subterranean works. The ownership of *minières* was in the surface proprietor; but they could not be worked by subterranean works except by permission. When worked by open workings, a declaration was required to be made to the prefect of the department. No royalties were paid to the government.

Carrieres (quarries) included slates, building-stones, marble, limestones, chalks, clays, and all varieties of earthy or stony substances, including pyritous earths, regarded as fertilizers, all worked in open cut or with subterranean galleries.

Workings of *carrières* in open cut were made without permission, under the simple surveillance of the police. When the working was carried on by means of subterranean galleries, it was subject to surveillance as in the case of mines. No royalties were paid to the government.

§ 13. **Mining laws of Mexico.** —We have no immediate concern with the present mining laws of Mexico. The existing code of that republic is a substantial departure from the old order of things, and furnishes the best example of a liberal and progressive system of mining laws of any which has heretofore been adopted in any country.[1] But we are dealing with matters of history, and are called upon to consider the state of the Mexican law of mines at the time of the discovery of gold in California and the acquisition by our government of the territory ceded by the treaty of Guadalupe Hidalgo.

Upon the establishment of the independence of Mexico (1821), it adopted, in reference to mining, the laws existing previous to its separation from Spain, with such modifications only as were rendered necessary

[1] For an interesting and accurate synopsis of the existing mining laws of Mexico the reader is referred to a monograph of Mr. Richard E. Chism, M. E., contributed at the Mexican meeting of the American Institute of Mining Engineers, November, 1901. It is published as a part of the transactions of that society.

by the alteration from a monarchical to a republican
form of government.[1]

Questions concerning mines and mining rights in
the republic depended, in a great measure, during the
period which engages our present attention, upon the
provisions of the Spanish ordinance of the 23d of May,
1783; and, in fact, until a comparatively recent period,
these ordinances were still in force, and constituted
the principal Mexican code on that subject.[2]

The following is an epitome of such parts of these
ordinances as are germane to the present inquiry:—

Nature and conditions of mining concessions.—Mines
were declared to be the property of the royal crown.
Without being separated from the royal patrimony,
they were granted to subjects in property and possession in such manner that they might sell, exchange, pass
by will, or in any other manner dispose of all their
property in them upon the terms on which they themselves possessed it, and to persons legally capable of
acquiring it.   This grant was made upon two conditions: First, that the grantees should pay certain pro-
portions of the metal obtained to the royal treasury;
second, that they should carry on their operations in
the mines subject to the provisions of these ordinances,
on failure of which at any time the mines of persons so
making default should be considered as forfeited, and
might be granted to any person who should denounce
them.

Rights of discoverer—Pertenencia.—The discoverers
of new mineral districts were permitted to acquire three
pertenencias, or claims, on the principal vein, a *pertenencia* being two hundred *varas,* or yards, along the

---

[1] Rockwell's Spanish and Mexican Law, p. 21.
[2] Castillero v. United States, 2 Black, 371.

course of the vein.[1] The discoverer of a new vein in
a district known and worked in other parts was entitled
to two *pertenencias,* either contiguous or separated.

Right to mine, how acquired.—The organization of
district tribunals was provided for, called deputations
of miners, to whom, within ten days after discovery,
the discoverer should present a written statement.
This statement was required to contain the discoverer's
name and those of his associates, his place of birth, residence, and occupation, together with the most particular
and distinguishing features of the tract, mountain, or
vein discovered, all of which were noted in the registry
of the deputation. Notices of this statement, its object
and contents, were required to be fixed to the doors of
the church, the government houses, and other public
buildings of the town, for the sake of general noto-
riety. Within ninety days thereafter, the discoverer
was required to make in the vein or veins so registered
an opening a yard and one half wide and ten yards in
depth, that one of the deputies, with an expert and two
witnesses, might inspect it and determine the course
and direction of the vein, its size, its dip, or inclination
from the horizon, and the principal species of mineral
found therein.

The report of the deputy was added to the registry,
together with the act of possession, which must be given
to the discoverer, measuring off his *pertenencias,* and
requiring him to mark their boundaries. A copy of
the entries in the register constituted his "titulo de
"posesion," or evidence of his possessory right.

If during the period of ninety days any adverse

[1] The term "claim" is here used as the equivalent of the Spanish
word *pertenencia* (literally, a portion), without regard to the technical
definition of the word given by some of the American courts in later
years.

claimant appeared and claimed the property, as being a prior discoverer, a brief judicial hearing was granted, and judgment given in favor of him who best proved his claim. If a question arose as to who had been the first discoverer of a vein, he was considered as such who first found metal therein, even though others might have made an opening previously; and in case of further doubt, priority of registration established a priority of right.

Denouncement of abandoned mines.—Restorers of ancient mines which had been abandoned enjoyed the same privileges as discoverers. In case of such abandoned mines, the party desiring to acquire them was called upon to present to the deputation a statement similar to that required of a discoverer, showing, in addition, the name of the last possessor and those of the neighboring miners, all of whom should be lawfully summoned. If no one appeared within ten days, the denouncements were required to be publicly declared on the three following Sundays. This meeting with no opposition, the denouncer was required within sixty days to clear and reinstate the abandoned workings to some considerable depth, or at least ten yards perpendicular and within the bed of the vein, in order that it might be inspected and the facts ascertained as required in case of original discoveries. These things being done, the *pertenencias* were measured, boundaries marked, and possession given as in other cases.

Right to denounce mines in private property.—Any one might discover or denounce a vein, not only on common land, but also on the property of any individual, provided he paid for the overlying surface and compensated the owner of the soil for the damage caused by exploration, the amount of such damage to be fixed by arbitration, in case of disagreement between the parties.

Rights of one not a discoverer.—One not a discoverer was prohibited from denouncing two contiguous mines upon one and the same vein; but there was no limit to the number he might acquire by purchase, gift, inheritance, or just title.

Placers.—Placers and other deposits in beds of gold and silver, precious stones, copper, lead, tin, quicksilver,[1] antimony, zinc, bismuth, rock salt, or fossils, perfect or mixed metals, bitumen, mineral tar, asphaltum, etc., might also be registered and denounced.

Foreigners and religious orders.—Foreigners were originally prohibited from working the mines; but by decree (October 27, 1823) they were permitted to supply miners with capital and hold shares (*acciones*) in the enterprise, and later (March 16, 1842), foreigners resident in the republic might acquire ownership of mines. Religious orders of both sexes were prohibited from acquiring mines, "as being contrary to the sanc- " tity and exercise of their profession."

Extent of pertenencia—Surface limits—Rights in depth.—With reference to surface ground in connection with the vein, and the extent to which the vein might be worked, it would seem that prior to promulgation of the "new ordinances" it was "one of the great- " est and most frequent causes of litigation and " dissension among the miners." To avoid this, it was decreed that the lateral extent of a *pertenencia* on a vein was to be regulated according to the inclination of the vein. To illustrate: A *pertenencia* was two hundred yards along the vein. The miner was to have

---

[1] As to quicksilver, it was originally provided that the government should have the preferential right of working the mines, indemnifying the discoverer in some equitable way; or the discoverer might work them, but was required to deliver the product to the agents of the royal treasury, and receive therefor a stipulated price. These provisions, however, became obsolete and inoperative in Mexico.

a parallelogram two hundred yards long by one hundred yards wide, the lateral measurement to be at right angles to the former. The inspection of the preliminary work by the deputy and expert was supposed to determine the position of the vein in the earth. If it was perpendicular, the one hundred yards was to be measured on either side of the vein, or divided on both sides, as the miner might prefer. If the vein was not perpendicular,—as it never was,—the miner was allowed lateral measurement proportionally to the inclination of the vein, the maximum being two hundred yards on the square, on the declivity, or "pitch," of the vein. So that a *pertenencia* on a vein might equal, but could never exceed, "the square of two hundred level yards." Ordinarily, the miner was limited to vertical planes drawn through his surface boundaries,[1] and was therefore compelled to stop the pursuit of his vein upon reaching his bounding plane, unless the ground outside was unclaimed (*terreno virgen*), in which case he was called upon to denounce the adjoining ground.

As to placers and other kindred deposits, the size of the *pertenencias* was regulated by the district deputations of mines, attention being paid to the extent and richness of the place and to the number of applicants for the same, with preference to the discoverers.

Marking boundaries.—The *pertenencias* having been regulated by the deputation, the miner was required to mark his boundaries by permanent stakes or landmarks such as should be secure and easy to be distinguished, and to enter into an obligation to keep and observe them forever, without being able to change them, though he may allege that his vein has varied in course or direction; "but he must content himself with the lot Provi-

[1] Del Monte M. Co. *v.* Last Chance M. Co., 171 U. S. 55, 61, 18 Sup. Ct. Rep. 895; Flagstaff S. M. Co. *v.* Tarbet, 98 U. S. 463, 468.

"dence has decreed him, and enjoy it without
"disturbing his neighbors." If he had no neighbors, he
might alter his boundaries, with the consent and under
the authority of the deputation.

*Right to all veins found within boundaries of perte-
nencia.*—The mine owner was entitled to possess not
only the principal vein in the *pertenencia* denounced
by him, but likewise all those which in any form or
manner whatever are to be found in his property; so
that if a vein takes its rise in one property, and, passing
on, is found in another, each proprietor was entitled
to enjoy the part of it which passes through his particular limits, and no one was entitled to claim entire
possession of a vein from having its source in his portion, or on any other pretense whatever.

Forfeiture for failure to work.—With reference to
working the mine, stringent regulations were established, compelling the mine owner to work at least four
paid workmen in "some exterior or interior work of
"real utility" for eight months during each year,
counting from the day of his coming into possession.

Royalties.—A certain percentage of the product of
mines was payable to the government, the amount of
which varied at different periods.

§ 14. **Authorities consulted.**—In the preparation of
the foregoing chapter, the author has availed himself
of the painstaking labor of jurists and writers on the
subject of foreign mining laws, whose works should
be specially mentioned. That due credit may be given
and to the end that those desiring to pursue the study
of comparative mining jurisprudence beyond what we
consider the legitimate scope of this treatise may be
invited into broader fields of investigation, we take
pleasure in here enumerating the various authors whose
works we have been so fortunate as to possess.

The monographs of Dr. Rossiter W. Raymond, at

present secretary of the American institute of mining engineers, scientist, scholar, and lawyer, one of the ablest living contributors not only to the literature of mining jurisprudence, but to mining subjects generally, have been freely consulted. Such of the productions of his pen as deal directly with the subject of foreign mining laws are, his treatise on "Relations of "Governments to Mining," forming part II of his first report as commissioner of mining statistics,[1] and his contribution to Lalor's "Cyclopædia of Political "Science," under the title of "*Mines.*"[2]

General H. W. Halleck's introduction to "De Fooz "on the Law of Mines,"[3] and Hon. Gregory Yale's "Mining Claims and Water Rights,"[4] contain valuable contributions on the subject of foreign mining systems, and have been freely consulted.

Arundel Rogers, Esq., in his work on the "Law of "Mines, Minerals, and Quarries,"[5] devotes considerable space to a discussion of foreign systems, including a chronological review of legislation on mining subjects in the United States.

From the standpoint of practical utility, the work of Oswald Walmesley, Esq., barrister at law of Lincoln's Inn, "Guide to the Mining Laws of the World,"[6] is commended.

Mr. Walmesley has gathered and grouped together a vast amount of valuable authentic information. While written principally as a guide to persons seeking mining investments in foreign countries, it is the work of a trained lawyer, and valuable to the professional student of comparative mining jurisprudence.

Other authorities which have been consulted on this subject will be found in the notes.

---

[1] Mineral Resources, 1869, pp. 173-256.
[2] 1883, vol. ii, pp. 844-854.
[3] San Francisco, 1860.
[4] San Francisco, 1867.
[5] London, 1876.
[6] London, 1894.

CHAPTER II.

LOCAL STATE SYSTEMS.

§ 18. Classification of states.
§ 19. First group.
§ 20. Second group.

§ 21. Third group.
§ 22. Limit of state control after patent.

§ 18. Classification of states. — Many of the states of the union have enacted laws governing the mining industry. These states may be grouped into three classes: —

(1) Those states wherein the federal government acquired no public mineral land, and for that reason were not included in the scope of federal mining legislation;

(2) Those states which are public land states, but are exempted from the operation of the congressional mining laws (with the exception of those relating to the disposal of saline lands), either for the reason that the mineral lands therein were sold under special laws prior to the enactment of general laws on the subject of mining, or because congress has by later laws in terms excluded them from the operation of these general laws;

(3) Those public land states and territories wherein the federal system is in full force, and wherein supplemental state and territorial legislation is authorized by the expressed terms of the federal laws.

§ 19. First group. — In states falling within the first group, such as the thirteen original states, and those carved out of the territory claimed by them, it is quite manifest that no federal legislation touching mining tenures is possible, and that such regulations as are found must be sought in the laws of the several states. The individual states comprised within this group, being the paramount proprietors of their mineral lands, could alone prescribe the terms upon which mining rights could be acquired thereon. To this class the states of Tennessee and Texas may be added.

In most of these states there is no distinction between the methods of acquiring mineral lands and lands that do not fall within this designation. Some of them, particularly those where coal mining is carried on extensively, have elaborate systems in the nature of police regulations, prescribing the manner in which mines shall be worked, providing for their official inspection, proper ventilation, means of escape in case of accident, and provisions looking to the protection of the miners. Pennsylvania,[1] Kentucky,[2] West Virginia,[3] Tennessee,[4] New York,[5] New Jersey,[6] North Carolina,[7] and

---

[1] Brightley's Purdon's Digest, 1894, vol. ii, pp. 1340 to 1386. And see Laws of 1897, pp. 157, 279, 287, 475; 1899, pp. 66, 68, 180; 1901, pp. 342, 535-545.

In the act to establish the department of forestry is a provision empowering the commissioners to execute leases for the mining of "any "valuable minerals" in the forest reservation. Laws of 1901, p. 12.

For an article on "Mine legislation and inspection in the anthracite "coal regions of Pennsylvania," see Mining and Scientific Press, July 23, 1898, vol. lxxvii, p. 84.

[2] Laws of 1891-1892, p. 54; 1894, p. 55; Gen. Stats. of 1887, p. 267; Id., p. 1130.

[3] Laws of 1897, ch. 59, p. 117; 1893, ch. 22, p. 336; 1891, ch. 15, p. 22; 1891, ch. 35, p. 60; 1891, ch. 82, p. 209; 1889-1890, p. 161; Code of 1899, p. 1047; Laws of 1901, ch. 106, p. 224.

[4] Laws of 1887, ch. 206, p. 336; Code of 1884, pp. 75, 327 et seq.; Laws of 1891, p. 203; Acts of 1901, ch. 37, p. 51; ch. 172, p. 306.

[5] Gen. Laws (1900), vol. 3, ch. 32, art. ix, §§ 120-129, pp. 2630-2633.

[6] Laws of 1894, p. 66; Gen. Stats. (1895), p. 1904.

[7] Laws of 1897, ch. 251, p. 423. See, also, as to rights of lessees in certain cases, Code (1883), § 1763.

Maine,[1] have more or less elaborate codes, confined, however, in the main to regulating the manner of working the mines. No mining legislation of a general character is found in Delaware, Georgia, Connecticut, Massachusetts, Rhode Island, Vermont, Virginia,[2] New Hampshire, or Maryland.[3]

Some of the states, such as Massachusetts,[4] Kentucky,[5] Tennessee,[6] Georgia,[7] and North Carolina,[8] regard the industry of mining as in the nature of a public use, and permit private property to be condemned for purposes of rights of way and drainage.

South Carolina has enacted some special legislation affecting phosphatic deposits in navigable waters, marshes, and creeks belonging to the state, and providing for a system by which licenses may be granted to extract them upon payment of royalties to the state;[9] but no distinction is made between the method of acquiring mineral lands and other lands, or in the tenures by which they are held.

The legislature of Tennessee in 1845 passed an act

---

[1] Rev. Stats. Supp. of 1895, p. 294; Laws of 1893, p. 348. See, also, ten years' exemption of mines from taxation; Rev. Stats. (1883), p. 128, § 6.

[2] Virginia has a statute authorizing owners of land adjoining coal mines to enter the coal mines at intervals to determine encroachments. Code (1887), §§ 2570-2572. See, also, as to liens of laborers, id. 2485, as amended, Supp. 1890.

[3] Maryland has an act concerning mining companies, their organization and powers, and regulating the building and operation of railroads by such companies. Pub. Gen. Laws of 1888, pp. 289, 291, 343-346. Also, an act requiring mining companies to pay their employees semi-monthly. Laws of 1896, p. 212.

[4] Pub. Stats. of 1882, ch. 189, §§ 19 to 28.

[5] Gen. Stats. (1887), pp. 1130-1131.

[6] Code of 1884, § 1854, p. 328.

[7] Code (1895), §§ 650-657; Amended Laws of 1897, p. 21. See, also, concerning mining interests in leases of land, Code (1895), § 3114.

[8] Code (1883), §§ 3292-3301.

[9] Rev. Stats. South Carolina, §§ 1893-1894, vol. i, pp. 36-38.

providing that the discoverer of any mines or minerals on vacant unappropriated land north and east of the congressional reservation line shall have a preference of entry on such land for a period of six months, making it unlawful for others to enter during that period, and providing that an entry made thereafter by others is unlawful and void unless preceded by a thirty days' written notice to the discoverer of an intention to make such entry.[1] With this exception, the law governing the acquisition of title to mineral land seems to be the same as that to other land. Of all the states found within the first group, New York[2] and Texas[3] are the only ones having anything like a general mining code.

New York.—New York has from the earliest period of its history asserted its ownership of mines of the precious metals by virtue of its sovereignty. A history of the legislation in this state would serve no useful purpose in this treatise. Briefly stated, the existing laws contain the following declaration as to the state's ownership.

The following mines are the property of the people of the state in their right of sovereignty:—

(1) All mines of gold and silver discovered or hereafter to be discovered;

(2) All mines of other metals discovered upon lands owned by persons not being citizens of the United States;

(3) All mines of other metals discovered upon lands owned by a citizen of the United States, the ore of which on an average shall contain less than two equal third

---

[1] Stats. of 1845, ch. 38; Whitney's Land Laws, p. 335.

[2] Gen. Laws (1900), vol. i, p. 667; Laws of 1894, vol. i, ch. 317, p. 589 et seq.; *Id.*, vol. ii, ch. 745, p. 1852.

[3] Sayle's Civ. Stats. Supp., 1888-1893, tit. 64b, art. 3361b, p. 612.

parts in value of copper, tin, iron, and lead, or any of
these metals;

(4) All mines and all minerals and fossils discovered,
or hereafter to be discovered, upon lands belonging to
the state.[1]

It is not our purpose to either analyze or criticise
this law,[2] but simply to outline it. As will be observed,
its fundamental theory bears a striking analogy to
that of the civil law. Citizens of the state discovering
mineral upon lands in the state are required to give
notice of the discovery to the secretary of state, who
is required to register the notice, and is allowed a fee
of one dollar therefor.[3] The simple filing of this
notice inaugurates the right to work, and to secure
the sole benefit of the products of the mine upon
payment into the state treasury of a royalty of
two per centum of their market value. There are no
statutory provisions fixing the area or extent of the
property which may be worked under this notice; nor
is there any direction as to marking of boundaries. The
discoverer, his executors, administrators, and assigns,
are exempted from paying any royalty for the term of
twenty-one years, and after the end of that period he or
his heirs or assigns are to have the sole benefit of all
products therefrom on the payment of a royalty of one
per centum on their market values.

Mining corporations are authorized under certain
conditions and restrictions, if the written consent of the
owner cannot be obtained, to condemn so much of the

---

[1] Laws of 1894, vol. i, ch. 317, p. 589; General Laws (1900), vol. i,
p. 667; as amended, Laws of 1901, vol. ii, p. 1104.

[2] For review of the New York mining laws, see Dr. Raymond's monographs—Trans. Am. Inst. M. E., vol. xvi, p. 770, and vol. xxiv, p. 712;
Eng. and Min. Journal, vol. lviii, p. 560.

[3] Laws of 1899, vol. i, p. 361; Gen. Laws (1900), p. 554.

land in or upon which mines are situated as are necessary to operate the same. A similar right is given to
the discoverer, his executors, administrators, or assigns,
upon depositing money or securities with the county
treasurer as security for the payment of any damages
that may be awarded to the owner under the condemnation law. The county clerks are required to record
copies of the location notice when presented by the locator and certified by the secretary of state, and it is
provided that priority of locations shall be determined
by the priority of the record with the county clerk of
the notice thereof.

Texas.—Texas has a general mining law,[1] which in
the main follows the congressional laws, with the exception that no extralateral right is conferred, and
the miner is not granted anything beyond vertical
planes drawn through his surface boundaries. Patents
are issued if applied for within five years, the price
being twenty-five dollars per acre for lode claims, and
ten dollars per acre for placer claims. Prior to patent,
one hundred dollars must be expended on each claim
annually, and fifty dollars per claim per annum must
be paid to the state treasurer, the amount of such payments to be credited upon the purchase price when
patent is obtained. The state after patent exacts no
royalty, and does not concern itself with the manner
of working the mines. After title passes from the state,
the tenure by which mining property is held is the
same as other property.

§ 20. **Second group.**— Public lands of the United
States which were subject to the legislative control of
the federal congress were included within the present

---

[1] Sayles's Civ. Stats. Supp., tit. 64b, art. 3361b, p. 612. Texas has also
a law concerning the casing and operation of oil wells. Sayles and
Willison's Stats. Supp. (1900), tit. 75½, p. 139.

boundaries of the following states and territories: Alabama, Alaska (district), Arizona, Arkansas, California, Colorado, Florida, Idaho, Illinois, Indian territory, Indiana, Iowa, Kansas, Louisiana, Michigan, Minnesota, Mississippi, Missouri, Montana, Nebraska, Nevada, New Mexico, North Dakota, Ohio, Oklahoma, Oregon, South Dakota, Utah, Washington, Wisconsin, and Wyoming. To these may be added Hawaii,[1] Porto Rico,[2] and the Philippine islands.[3]

By acts of congress passed at different times the following were excepted from the operation of the federal mining laws: Alabama,[4] Kansas,[5] Michigan, Minnesota,[6] Missouri,[7] and Wisconsin.[8]

These laws were never in practical operation in either Illinois, Indiana, Iowa, or Ohio, owing to the fact that most of the public domain embraced therein had been

[1] None of the public land laws of the United States have been extended to Hawaii, the former laws of the republic being continued in force. There is no local legislation on the subject of mineral lands, and it is extremely doubtful if the islands contain any deposits which might render mining legislation necessary or expedient.

[2] By act of congress July 1, 1902, (Stats., 1st Sess. 57th Cong., p. 731,) all public lands passing to the United States by treaty have been ceded to the government of Porto Rico, to be held and disposed of for the use and benefit of the people of the island. There is as yet no mining legislation passed by the territorial legislature, nor are we advised as to the necessity for any such legislation.

[3] By act of congress, July 1, 1902, (Stats. 1st Sess. 57th Cong., p. 691,) a complete mining code for these islands was passed. It is framed on the lines of the general federal mining law, with the exception that there is no extralateral right arising out of lode locations. A discussion of this act will be found in a later portion of this treatise, and the act itself is printed in full in the appendix.

[4] 22 Stats. at Large, p. 487; Commissioners' letter to district land officers, 1 L. D. 655.

[5] Stats. at Large, p. 52.

[6] 17 Stats. at Large, p. 465; United States v. Omdahl, 25 L. D. 157.

[7] 19 Stats. at Large, p. 52.

[8] 17 Stats. at Large, p. 465; United States v. Omdahl, 25 L. D. 157.

disposed of prior to the enactment of the general mining laws. In Illinois, Iowa, Arkansas, Missouri, Michigan, Minnesota, and Wisconsin lands of the government containing lead, and, in Michigan and Wisconsin, copper and other valuable ores, were ordered sold under special laws prior to the discovery of gold in California.[1] It would seem that the federal mining laws are still operative in lands of the public domain in Arkansas as to minerals other than lead. It is so treated by the land department,[2] and that state has enacted legislation supplemental to the federal laws concerning the acquisition of title to public mineral lands.[3]

These laws are also in force in Florida, Mississippi, and Louisiana.[4]

The federal mining laws, so far as they relate to the acquisition of title to saline lands, are operative in all the states and continental territories wherein the public domain remains to any extent undisposed of. By act of congress the states above enumerated, which were exempted from the operation of the federal mining laws, were again brought under the operation of such laws so far as deposits of salt, salt springs, and saline lands are concerned.[5]

By act of congress all lands in Oklahoma were declared to be agricultural,[6] but by the act of June 6, 1900, congress extended the mining laws over the lands in the territory of Oklahoma ceded to the United States

---

[1] See, post, § 35.

[2] Norman v. Phoenix Zinc M. and S. Co., 28 L. D. 361.

[3] See appendix.

[4] Comr. G. L. O., 31 L. D. 131.

[5] Act of June 31, 1901, (31 Stats. at Large, p. 745); Circular instructions, 31 L. D. 130, 131. As to laws governing public saline lands, see, post, §§ 513-515.

[6] 26 Stats. at Large, p. 1026.

by the Comanche, Kiowa, and Apache tribes of Indians.[1]

The following states, therefore, fall within the second class enumerated in section eighteen: Alabama, Illinois, Indiana, Iowa, Kansas, Michigan, Minnesota, Missouri, Ohio, and Wisconsin.

The extent of the power of these states over the mining industry on lands of the public domain other than saline lands is limited to regulating the manner in which mines may be worked with regard to the safety of the miners; that is to say, police regulations such as are found in Pennsylvania.[2]

This power has been exercised in Alabama,[3] Illinois,[4] Indiana,[5] Iowa,[6] Kansas,[7] Michigan,[8] Mis-

---

[1] 31 Stats. at Large, pp. 672, 680. And see the instructions of Secretary Hitchcock to the commissioner of the general land office, Dec. 6, 1901, (31 L. D. 154), as to the limitations to be placed upon the operative force of this statute.

[2] Brightley's Purdon's Digest of 1894, vol. ii, p. 1340 et seq.

[3] Civil Code (1896), §§ 2899-2936; Acts of 1896-1897, pp. 1099-1112; General Acts of 1898-1899, p. 86.

[4] Starr & Curtiss's Revision, 1885, p. 1618 et seq.; Starr & Curtiss's Sup. of 1885, ch. 92, p. 872; Laws of 1895, p. 252 et seq.; Amended Laws of 1899, p. 300; Rev. Stats (1899), ch. 93, p. 1156; Laws of 1901, p. 247.

[5] Horner's Annot. Stats. (1896), §§ 5458-5480y; Burns's Annot. Stats. (1894), § 7429-7483; Acts of 1897, pp. 127, 269; Acts of 1899, pp. 246, 382; Acts of 1901, pp. 170, 548, 571.

[6] Acts of 1894, p. 95; Acts of 1890, p. 71; Revision of 1888, § 2449 et seq.; Code (1897), §§ 2478-2502; Id., §§ 1967-1974, 2031; Laws of 1898, ch. 59, p. 38; Laws of 1900, chs. 79-82, pp. 61-62.

[7] Gen. Stats. of 1889, vol. i, § 3835 et seq.; Laws of 1893, p. 270; Gen. Stats. of 1897, pp. 813-827; Laws of 1899, p. 331; Laws of 1901, p. 475.

[8] Howell's Annot. Stats. (Supp. of 1890), p. 3205, §§ 2887 d 2-2287 d 9; Pub. Acts of 1897, p. 140; Id., 1899, p. 93. Michigan has, also, numerous provisions concerning the organization and powers of mining and smelting corporations and associations (Howell's Annot. Stats. (1882), §§ 3984-4121); and a provision for the inspection of coal mines by adjoining owners to determine as to encroachments (Id., §§ 4122-4126).

souri,[1] and Ohio,[2] where codes more or less elaborate are found.

The legislature of Michigan, by an act approved April 28, 1846,[3] adopted a mining code for that state, the validity of which may be open to question, so far as it attempts to deal with minerals on the public domain, particularly when it is remembered that the federal mining laws applied to public lands in Michigan prior to February 17, 1873.[4] The act seems to be an assertion of the regalian theory, based upon the idea that the states have succeeded to the rights of the king in respect to the minerals found within their boundaries. The main provisions of the act, briefly stated, are as follows:—

The property in the following mines is vested in the people of the state of Michigan in their right of sovereignty,—

(1) All mines of gold and silver or either of them within the territorial limits of the state;

(2) All mines of other metals or minerals connected with or containing gold in any proportion.

This right of the people to mines and minerals shall not be enforced against any citizen of the state who has or may hereafter acquire the ownership in fee of the land containing such mines or minerals by a *bona fide* purchase from either the general or state government. The act shall not affect the lessees of the United States government, when the lands leased by them shall be proved to belong to the state.

[1] Rev. Stats. of 1889, vol. ii, § 7034 et seq.; Laws of 1895, p. 225; Rev. Stats. of 1899, vol. ii, § 8766 et seq.; Laws of 1901, pp. 211-215.

[2] Bate's Annot. Stats. of 1897, §§ 290-306a, 4374-4379, 4379-1 to 4379-6, 6871; Laws of 1898, pp. 33, 163, 164, 237; Laws of 1900, p. 180.

[3] Howell's Annot. Stats. (1882), §§ 5475-5479.

[4] See, *post*, § 249.

State mineral lands are reserved from sale until further direction of the legislature. A specific tax of four per cent is imposed upon all ores and products of all mines within the state (to be in lieu of all state taxes), " whether the lands containing them have been sold " to *bona fide* purchasers of the general government or " not," but the tax on the product of iron mines is limited to two per cent. Annual statements of the yield of the mines are required, and the state is authorized to seize the ore or products when the tax is not paid on legal demand being made therefor.

By a subsequent act,[1] the state mineral lands reserved from sale are authorized to be leased upon certain conditions. And, later, provision is made for the sale of the mineral lands in the Upper Peninsula.[2]

Minnesota still carries upon her books a statute entitled: "An act to regulate mining upon the public " lands of the United States within the state of Minne- " sota,"[3] adopted in 1867, which contains provisions substantially similar to the supplemental legislation of the states wherein the federal mining law is in full operation. This statute provides for the organization of mining districts, requires locations to be made in person by the claimant, limits the length and width of claims, authorizes the discoverer of a mine to make an additional location thereon, requires measurement of claims, posting and recording of location notices, development work, defines acts of forfeiture and abandonment, prescribes a penalty for defacing notices, defines "mineral claim," etc. At the time of the adoption of this act it undoubtedly had all the force possessed by any of the mining legislation of the public

---

[1] May 18, 1846; Howell's Annot. Stats. (1882), §§ 5480-5490.

[2] June 22, 1863; *Id.*, §§ 5355-5358.

[3] Gen. Stats. (1894), §§ 4063-4075.

mining states, but when congress, on February 17, 1873,[1] declared that the federal mining laws should no longer apply to Minnesota, it virtually closed the public domain in that state so far as exploration for minerals and the acquisition of title thereto under the federal mining laws is concerned, and the supplemental legislation of Minnesota, having nothing upon which to operate, became practically a dead letter, except so far as concerns rights which had their inception prior to February 17, 1873. As heretofore noted, the federal mining laws on the subject of saline lands are now operative in this state.

Minnesota has several other statutes relating to state mineral lands to which, of course, the above remarks have no application. These consist of provisions,—

(1) For the leasing of state lands containing iron ore in blocks of not more than one hundred and sixty acres each, on payment to the state of twenty-five dollars down and one hundred dollars per year for five years, and twenty-five cents per ton on all ore mined thereafter, but on at least five thousand tons per year;[2]

(2) For leasing of mineral lands belonging to persons under guardianship;[3]

(3) Prescribing a method by which an owner or owners of at least one-half of any lands containing minerals which belong to a plurality of owners may have mines thereon legally opened and operated;[4]

(4) Concerning organization and powers of companies for mining and smelting ores and manufacturing metals;[5]

---

[1] 17 Stats. at Large, p. 465.

[2] Gen. Stats. (1894), §§ 4076-4084; Laws of 1895, p. 227; 1897, pp. 578, 582.

[3] Laws of 1899, p. 147.

[4] Gen. Stats. (1894), §§ 5830-5838.

[5] Id., §§ 2827-2837; Laws of 1897, p. 360.

(5) For geological survey of the state;[1]

(6) Concerning mine laborer's lien;[2]

(7) Making unmined minerals real estate for purposes of taxation;[3]

(8) Requiring reservation in the state of "all the " iron, coal, copper, gold, or other valuable mineral" in deeds of state lands, and authorizing disposition thereof by leasing on the same terms as other mineral lands.[4]

Wisconsin has certain mining statutes that are worthy of notice. These, in brief, are as follows:—

(1) Providing rules to govern in mining contracts and leases in the absence of contract to the contrary,— viz., (a) A license or lease to a miner is not revocable after valuable discovery, unless forfeited by the miner's negligence; (b) The discoverer of a crevice or range containing ores or minerals is entitled thereto, subject to payment of rent to his landlord; but cannot recover the value of ores from a person digging on his range in good faith and known to be mining thereon, until he shall have given such person notice of his claim; (c) Usages and customs may be proved in explanation of mining contracts to the same extent as usage may be proved in other branches of business;[5]

(2) Providing that in case of conflicting claims to a crevice or range bearing ores or minerals the court may continue the action for the purpose of allowing parties to prove up their mines; and may in the mean time appoint a receiver to take charge of the mine;[6]

(3) Providing for forfeiture of his lease by a lessee who conceals or disposes of ore or mineral for purposes of defrauding his lessor of rent;[7]

[1] Gen. Stats. (1894); §§ 3928-3957.
[2] Laws of 1897, p. 617.
[3] Laws of 1899, p. 268.
[4] Laws of 1901, p. 108.
[5] San. & B. Stats. (1898), § 1647.
[6] Id., § 1648.
[7] Id., § 1649.

(4) Authorizing the condemnation by a miner of the right to conduct water across the land of another, and prescribing the procedure therefor; [1]

(5) Requiring smelters and purchasers of ores and minerals to keep a record thereof in a book to be kept open for inspection by all persons, at all reasonable times, and prescribing penalty for failure so to do; [2]

(6) Regulating employment of children in mines; [3]

(7) Providing for condemnation by a miner of right of way for ditch or drain from mine across land of another, and prescribing the procedure therefor; [4]

(8) Imposing a penalty for digging and carrying away ore from land of another or of the state; [5]

This is the extent of the mining legislation of any importance found in the states of this group.

§ 21. Third group.—This group includes what may be generally called the precious-metal-bearing states and territories, and will be fully considered when dealing generally with the federal system, as by that system supplemental state and territorial legislation is permissive. This local legislation, where found, is essentially a part of the national law, as administered in the respective local jurisdictions. These state and territorial laws, to a large extent, supplant the local rules and customs, and in some of the states and territories are quite elaborate, embodying so many elements that they demand individual treatment in another portion of this work, after we shall have laid the foundation therefor.

It may be of historical interest to note that it was at one time held in California that the mines belonged to

---

[1] San. & B. Stats. (1898), §§ 1650-1654.
[2] *Id.*, §§ 1656-1657.
[3] *Id.*, § 1728a.
[4] *Id.*, §§ 1379-1 to 1379-10
[5] *Id.*, §§ 4441-4442.

the state, in virtue of her sovereignty, and that the state alone could authorize them to be worked. The doctrine was asserted that the several states of the union, in virtue of their respective sovereignties, were entitled to the *jura regalia* which pertained to the king at common law.[1]

In support of this view, the rules followed in the states of New York and Pennsylvania were cited. Of course, in those two states the national government owned no lands. The primary ownership was in the states, and not in the general government. Therefore, the states were at liberty to determine for themselves the policy to be pursued with reference to their own property.

This early California doctrine was subsequently repudiated.[2]

The legislature of Michigan in its early legislation upon this subject asserted the same regalian doctrine as first announced by the California courts, and such legislation still remains upon the Michigan statute-books.[3]

§ 22. **Limit of state control after patent.** — It may not be out of place to here remark that the government of the United States does not concern itself with mining lands or the mining industry after it parts with the title. This title vests in the patentee absolutely, to the extent of the property granted. No royalties are reserved; nor is any governmental supervision (except, perhaps, in the isolated case of hydraulic mines in certain parts of California) attempted. Upon the issuance of the deed of the government, the mineral land becomes

---

[1] Hicks *v.* Bell, 3 Cal. 219.

[2] Moore *v.* Smaw, 17 Cal. 199, 217, 79 Am. Dec. 123; Doran *v.* C. P. R. R., 24 Cal. 245.

[3] See, *ante,* § 20.

private property, subject to the same rules as other property in the state with reference to the transfer, devolution by descent, and all other incidents of private ownership prescribed by the laws of the state. The federal law remains, of course, a muniment of title; but beyond that it possesses no potential force. Its purpose has been accomplished, and, like a private vendor, the government loses all dominion over the thing granted. The state may not increase, diminish, nor impair the rights conveyed by a federal patent, but may, of course, and frequently does, exercise its police power and regulate the manner of working the mines, in the same manner that it might regulate any other industry. Briefly stated, property in mines, once vested absolutely in the individual, becomes subject to the same rules of law as other real property within the state.

TITLE II.

————

HISTORICAL REVIEW OF THE FEDERAL POLICY AND LEGISLATION CONCERNING MINERAL LANDS.

————

CHAPTER

I. INTRODUCTORY—PERIODS OF NATIONAL HISTORY.

II. FIRST PERIOD: FROM THE FOUNDATION OF THE GOVERNMENT TO THE DISCOVERY OF GOLD IN CALIFORNIA.

III. SECOND PERIOD: FROM THE DISCOVERY OF GOLD IN CALIFORNIA UNTIL THE PASSAGE OF THE LODE LAW OF 1866.

IV. THIRD PERIOD: FROM THE PASSAGE OF THE LODE LAW OF 1866 TO THE ENACTMENT OF THE GENERAL LAW OF MAY 10, 1872.

V. FOURTH PERIOD: FROM THE ENACTMENT OF THE LAW OF 1872 TO THE PRESENT TIME.

VI. THE FEDERAL SYSTEM.

CHAPTER I.

INTRODUCTORY.

§ 25. Introductory—Periods of national history.

§ 25. Introductory — Periods of national history.—

Positive law is the result of social evolution. Its development keeps pace with the intellectual and industrial progress of a nation. The history of a nation's laws is the history of the economic forces of which they are but the resultants, or, as aptly stated by a distinguished writer, "Each nation has evolved its existing " economy as the outcome of its history, character, " environment, institutions, and general progress."

A brief historical review of the growth of our nation, its policy and legislation on the subject of mineral lands, and the discovery and development of its mineral resources, will materially aid us in arriving at a proper interpretation of the existing system of laws governing the acquisition and enjoyment of property rights and privileges on the public mineral domain of the United States.

This branch of national history logically divides itself into four distinct periods, marked either by the occurrence of important events or emphasized by a distinctive change of national policy. These periods may be defined as follows:—

First—From the foundation of the government to the discovery of gold in California;

Second—From the discovery of gold in California until the passage of the lode law of 1866;

Third—From the passage of the lode law of 1866 to the enactment of the general law of May 10, 1872;

Fourth—From the enactment of the general law of May 10, 1872, to the present time.

CHAPTER II.

FIRST PERIOD: FROM THE FOUNDATION OF THE GOVERN-
MENT TO THE DISCOVERY OF GOLD IN CALIFORNIA.

§ 28. Original nucleus of national domain.

§ 29. Mineral resources of the territory ceded by the states.

§ 30. First congressional action on the subject of mineral lands.

§ 31. Reservation in crown grants to the colonies.

§ 32. No development of copper mines until 1845.

§ 33. The Louisiana purchase and legislation concerning lead mines.

§ 34. Message of President Polk.

§ 35. Sales of land containing lead and copper under special laws.

§ 36. Reservation in pre-emption laws.

§ 28. **Original nucleus of the national domain.**—
The national government acquired no rights of property within the present boundaries of the thirteen
original states, nor in the states of Vermont, Kentucky,
Maine, or West Virginia, which were severally carved
out of territory originally forming a part of some of
the original states.

The first acquisition of national domain which became subject to the disposal of congress was by cessions
of territory claimed by seven of the original states.
These cessions, commencing with that by the state of
New York (March 1, 1781), and ending with that of
Georgia (April 24, 1802), brought within the jurisdiction and control of the federal government all that portion of the present area of the United States now

Lindley on M.—4

comprising the states of Tennessee, Illinois, Indiana, Ohio, Michigan, Wisconsin, those portions of Alabama and Mississippi lying north of the thirty-first parallel, and that portion of Minnesota lying east of the Mississippi river.[1] This area, with the exception of Tennessee (in which the public lands were practically absorbed by the claims of North Carolina, the surplus being subsequently ceded to the state),[2] constituted the original nucleus of our national domain.[3]

§ 29. **Mineral resources of the territory ceded by the states.** —In this period of our national history but little was known of the mineral resources of the country, and economic minerals were but little known or used.[4]

Gold had been found in moderate quantities in use among the Indian tribes of the present southern states, and the Spaniards, under the leadership of De Soto, were supposed to have discovered gold in North and South Carolina and Georgia; but the existence of this royal metal in any considerable quantity was purely legendary.[5]

Copper was known to exist in the Lake Superior region. The Jesuit priests had made extensive explorations on the upper peninsula, and had given glowing accounts of the abundance of copper there found. Other explorers confirmed these discoveries, and brought back legends of gold and precious stones.[6]

[1] Public Domain, pp. 65-88.
[2] *Id.*, p. 83.
[3] Florida was ceded to us in 1821 by Spain (Public Domain, 116), but until a very recent period was not known to contain any substances commercially classed as mineral. Its phosphate and other mineral deposits on public lands are subject to the general mining laws of congress.
[4] Public Domain, p. 306.
[5] Century of Mining—Trans. Am. Inst. M. E., vol. v, p. 166.
[6] *Id.*, p. 169.

In 1771, when this region had passed from the dominion of France, a company was organized in London, the Duke of Gloucester being one of the incorporators, to mine copper on the Ontonagon river. What little metal was obtained was shipped to England; but nothing resulted from the venture.[1]

The definitive treaty of peace between Great Britain and the United States, concluded at Paris, September 3, 1783, practically settled our northern boundary, although this was a subject of controversy for several years afterwards. When the lake region became subject to the unquestioned jurisdiction of the United States, the territory was in the occupancy of the Indians, and no settlements were attempted in that section until a much later period.

This was practically the extent of public information upon the subject at the time congress passed its first ordinance on the subject of mineral lands.

§ 30. **First congressional action on the subject of mineral lands.**—The first legislative declaration of congress with reference to mineral lands is found in the ordinance of May 20, 1785, entitled "An ordinance for " ascertaining the mode of disposing of lands in the " western territory."

Under this ordinance surveyors were to be appointed from each state, to act under the direction of the geographer. The territory was to be divided into townships six miles square, and these townships subdivided into sections one mile square (six hundred and forty acres). Meridian and base lines were to be established, and the rectangular system of surveys, which has ever since been in general use, was adopted.

In making these surveys, the surveyors were required

---

[1] Trans. Am. Inst. M. E., vol. xix, p. 679.

to note all mines, salt licks, and mill seats that should come to their knowledge.

Reservations were made of four sections in each township for the use of the United States, one section (the sixteenth) for the maintenance of schools in that township, and a certain proportion, equal to one seventh of all the lands surveyed, was to be distributed to the late continental army.

There was also reserved, to be sold or otherwise disposed of as congress should thereafter direct, one third of all gold, silver, lead, and copper mines.

The unreserved sections or lots were to be allotted to the several states, according to their *pro rata*, and the lands thus allotted were to be sold at public vendue by the commissioners of the loan offices of the several states, by whom deeds were to be given. Each of these deeds was to contain a clause, "excepting therefrom " and reserving one third part of all gold, silver, lead, " and copper mines within the same." [1]

Considering the then state of public information as to the mineral resources of the newly acquired national domain, it is manifest that the reservations in the ordinance were not based upon any economic reasons. The impression undoubtedly existed, as it had from the period of the earliest discoveries and explorations in America, that the newly acquired territory was rich in precious and economic metals, and that some day they might prove a source of national revenue. But it is apparent that the policy of thus reserving a portion of this class of lands was but an adaptation of the system pursued by the mother country in dealing with her colonies, and following the example set by the crown, to whose rights the American confederation had succeeded.

[1] Journals of Congress, vol. x, p. 118.

§ **31.   Reservation in crown grants to the colonies.**— In almost all of the crown grants to the colonies, clauses were inserted reserving to the sovereign a certain fixed proportion of the royal metals discovered.

The charter of North Carolina (1584), granted to Sir Walter Raleigh by Elizabeth, contained the following reservation:—

"Reserving always to us, our heirs and successors, " for all services, duties, and demands the fifth part of " all the ore of gold and silver that from time to time, " and at all times after such discovery, subduing, and " possessing, shall be there gotten and obtained."[1]

This form of reservation is found, with few exceptions, in all of the succeeding grants,—viz., the three charters of Virginia (1606, 1609, 1611),[2] the first of which also reserved one fifteenth of all copper; Massachusetts bay (1629);[3] the grant of New Hampshire by the president and council of New England to Captain John Mason (1629—confirmed 1635);[4] the charter of Maryland to Lord Baltimore (1632), upon whom was imposed the additional burden of rendering annually two Indian arrows;[5] the grant of the province of Maine to Sir Ferdinando Gorges (1639);[6] Rhode Island and Providence plantations (1643);[7] Connecticut (1632);[8] the charter of Carolina, granted by Charles the Second to the Earl of Clarendon, Duke of Albermarle, and others (1663, 1665), reserved a royalty of one fourth of the royal metals and the annual payment of twenty marks.[9]

---

[1] Charters and Constitutions, part ii, p. 1380.
[2] *Id.*, part ii, pp. 1890, 1898, 1904.
[3] *Id.*, part i, p. 932.
[4] *Id.*, part ii, pp. 1271, 1274.
[5] *Id.*, part i, p. 812.
[6] *Id.*, part i, p. 776.
[7] *Id.*, part ii, p. 1602.
[8] *Id.*, part i, p. 257.
[9] *Id.*, part ii, p. 1383.

The grant of the province of Maine by Charles the Second to James Duke of York (1664), was an exception.[1] In this grant, "our dearest brother" covenanted and promised to yield and render to his sovereign annually forty beaver skins when they shall be demanded, and in return received a grant of all the mines and minerals.

William Penn was required to yield and pay "two " beaver skins, to be delivered at our castle of Windsor " on the first day in January of every year,"[2] in addition to the one fifth part of all gold and silver ores.

It was but natural that the United States in its first dealings with its public lands should follow these precedents and provide for similar reservations. It was the force of precedent rather than considerations of public and economic policy that suggested those provisions of the ordinance reserving a part of the mineral lands for the use of the government.

§ 32. No development of copper mines until 1845.— By resolution of April 16, 1800, congress authorized the president to employ an agent to collect information relative to copper mines on the south side of Lake Superior, and "to ascertain whether the Indian title to " such lands as might be required for the use of the " United States, in case they should deem it expedient " to work the said mines, be yet subsisting, and, if so, " on what terms the same can be extinguished."[3] It is a matter of history that the Indian title was not extinguished until the treaty with the Chippewas in 1837,[4] and it was not until 1845 that systematic mining in the copper regions was commenced. In 1845, the

[1] Charters and Constitutions, part i, p. 784.
[2] Id., part ii, p. 1510.
[3] 2 Stats. at Large, p. 87.
[4] 7 Stats. at Large, p. 536.

total production of copper in the United States was estimated at one hundred tons.[1] The total production from 1776 to 1851 is estimated at six thousand tons.[2] It is needless to remark that the government never deemed it expedient to embark in mining enterprises on its own account in any portion of its public domain.

§ 33. The Louisiana purchase and legislation concerning lead mines.—In 1803, the territory acquired by purchase from France,[3] commonly called "the Louis- " iana purchase," added over a million square miles to the national domain, embracing parts of Alabama and Mississippi, the states of Louisiana, Arkansas, Missouri, Iowa, Kansas (except a portion in the southwest corner), Nebraska, all of Colorado east of the Rocky mountains and north of the Arkansas river; North and South Dakotas; the greater part of Montana; a part of Wyoming; and the Indian territory.[4]

Lead mining was begun in what is now the state of Missouri as early as 1720, while that section of country belonged to France, and under the patent granted to Law's famous Mississippi colony. Mine La Motte was one of the earliest discoveries (1702), and has been in operation at intervals ever since.[5] In 1788, Dubuque

[1] Mineral Industry, vol. i, p. 108.

[2] Trans. Am. Inst. M. E., vol. xi, p. 8.

[3] See Treaty, 8 Stats. at Large, p. 200.

[4] As to whether Oregon, Washington, and Idaho were included in this cession has been the subject of considerable argumentative discussion. The current of authority, however, excludes these states from the Louisiana purchase. The area covered by them was acquired either through the discovery of the Columbia river by Captain Gray (1792), the exploration by the Lewis and Clarke expedition (1805), the grant from Spain which ceded the Floridas (1819), or the Astoria settlement (1811),—or practically the United States derived title through all these sources.

[5] Century of Mining—Trans. Am. Inst. M. E., vol. v, p. 170.

obtained from the Indians the grant under which he mined.[1]

The total production of lead in Missouri from 1720 to 1803 is estimated at sixteen thousand and ninety-five tons.[2] From 1776 to 1824, it is estimated at four thousand four hundred and thirty-two tons.[3]

On March 3, 1807, congress passed a law wherein it was provided:—

"That the several lead mines in the Indiana territory " . . . . shall be reserved for the future disposal of " the United States; and any grant which may here- " after be made for a tract of land containing a lead " mine which had been discovered previous to the pur- " chase of such tract from the United States shall be " considered fraudulent and null, and the president of " the United States shall be and is hereby authorized to " lease any lead mine which has been or may hereafter " be discovered in the Indiana territory for a term not " exceeding five years."[4]

This legislation inaugurated the policy of the United States of leasing mineral lands.[5] These leases were given under the supervision of the war department. Where given, they covered tracts, at first three miles, afterwards one mile, square, and bound the lessees to work the mines with due diligence and return to the United States six per cent of all the ores raised.[6]

Hon. Abram S. Hewitt[7] gives the following interesting summary of the practical operation of this law and the policy inaugurated by it:—

" No leases were issued under the law until 1822, and " but a small quantity of lead was raised previous to

---

[1] Century of Mining—Trans. Am. Inst. M. E., p. 170.

[2] Mineral Industry, vol. ii, p. 387.

[3] Trans. Am. Inst. M. E., vol. v, p. 194.

[4] 2 Stats. at Large, p. 488, § 5.

[5] Public Domain, p. 307.

[6] Century of Mining—Trans. Am. Inst. M. E., vol. v, p. 180.

[7] In an address before the Am. Institute of Mining Engineers.

"1826, from which time the production began to in-
"crease rapidly."

" 'For a few years the rents were paid with tolerable
"'regularity, but after 1834, in consequence of the im-
"'mense number of illegal entries of mineral land at
"'the Wisconsin land office, the smelters and miners
"'refused to make any further payments, and the gov-
"'ernment was entirely unable to collect them. After
"'much trouble and expense, it was, in 1847, finally
"'concluded that the only way was to sell the mineral
"'land and do away with all reserves of lead or any
"'other metal, since they had only been a source of
"'embarrassment to the department.'[1]

"Meanwhile, by a forced construction (afterward de-
"clared invalid) of the same act, hundreds of leases
"were granted to speculators in the Lake Superior
"copper region, which was from 1843 to 1846 the scene
"of wild and baseless excitement. The bubble burst
"during the latter year; the issue of permits and leases
"was suspended as illegal, and the act of 1847, author-
"izing the sale of the mineral lands and a geological
"survey of the district, laid the foundation of a more
"substantial prosperity."[2]

§ 34. **Message of President Polk.**— President Polk,
in his first message to congress (December 2, 1845)
made the following special mention of these lands and
the system of leasing them authorized by the act of
March 3, 1807:—

"The present system of managing the mineral lands
"of the United States is believed to be radically defect-
"ive. More than a million acres of the public lands,
"supposed to contain lead and other minerals, have
"been reserved from sale, and numerous leases upon
"them have been granted to individuals upon a stipu-
"lated rent. The system of granting leases has proved
"to be not only unprofitable to the government, but

---

[1] Quoting from Professor Whitney's work on the Metallic Wealth of
the United States.
[2] Century of Mining—Trans. Am. Inst. M. E., vol. v, p. 180.

" unsatisfactory to the citizens who have gone upon the
" lands, and must, if continued, lay the foundation of
" much future difficulty between the government and
" the lessees. According to the official records, the
" amount of rents received by the government for the
" years 1841, 1842, 1843, and 1844, was $6,354.74, while
" the expenses of the system during the same period, in-
" cluding salaries of the superintendents, agents, clerks,
" and incidental expenses, were $26,111.11, the income
" being less than one fourth of the expense. To this
" pecuniary loss may be added the injury sustained
" by the public in consequence of the destruction of
" timber, and the careless and wasteful manner of work-
" ing the mines. The system has given rise to much
" litigation between the United States and individual
" citizens, producing irritation and excitement in the
" mineral region, and involving the government in
" heavy additional expenditures. It is believed that
" similar losses and embarrassments will continue to
" occur while the present system of leasing these lands
" remains unchanged. These lands are now under the
" superintendence and care of the war department, with
" the ordinary duties of which they have no proper or
" natural connection. I recommend the repeal of the
" present system, and that these lands be placed under
" the superintendence and management of the general
" land office as other public lands, and be brought into
" market and sold upon such terms as congress in their
" wisdom may prescribe, reserving to the government
" an equitable percentage of the gross amount of min-
" eral product, and that the pre-emption principle be
" extended to resident miners, and settlers upon them,
" at the minimum price which may be established by
" congress."

§ 35. **Sales of land containing lead and copper under
special laws.** —The first sale of mineral lands was that
of the reserved lead mines and contiguous lands in the
state of Missouri, under the act of March 3, 1829.[1]

---

[1] 4 Stats at Large, p. 364.

They were to be exposed for sale as other public lands, at two dollars and fifty cents per acre; but lead and other mineral lands on the public domain, elsewhere than in Missouri, were still reserved from sale.

The act of July 11, 1846,[1] ordered the reserved lead mines and contiguous lands in Illinois, Arkansas,[2] and the territories of Wisconsin and Iowa, to be sold as other public lands, after six months' public notice, following the Missouri act of 1829, with the addition of the provision that the lands should be offered and held subject to private entry before pre-emptions were allowed. The register and receiver were to take proof as to character of lands, whether mineral (*i. e.* containing lead) or agricultural.

The act of March 1, 1847,[3] opened for sale lands in the Lake Superior land district, state of Michigan, containing copper, lead, or other valuable ores, after geological examination and survey, and provided that there should be public advertisement for six months, and then public sale at not less than five dollars per acre, those not disposed of at public auction to be subject to private sale at five dollars per acre. This act also transferred the management and control of " the mineral lands " from the war department to the treasury department.

The act of March 3, 1847,[4] authorized the sale of lands in Chippewa district, in Wisconsin, containing copper, lead, and other valuable ores. The language of the act follows closely that of March 1, 1847, (*supra*).

It will be thus observed that from the period of 1785 to the discovery of gold in California, in 1848, the legis-

---

[1] 9 Stats. at Large, p. 37.

[2] But as to lands containing other minerals the general mining laws are in force. Norman *v.* Phoenix Zinc M. and S. Co., 28 L. D. 361. And see legislation of the state of Arkansas, appendix.

[3] 9 Stats. at Large, p. 146.

[4] *Id.,* p. 179, § 10.

lation of the congress of the United States as to survey, lease, and sale of mineral lands had been for lead, copper, and other base metals, and applied to the territory in the region of the great lakes, in the now states of Michigan, Wisconsin, Minnesota, Iowa, and Illinois, and the present state of Missouri. Under these various laws the copper, lead, and iron lands of the above mentioned regions were sold.[1]

§ 36. **Reservation in pre-emption laws.**—During this period numerous laws were passed granting pre-emption rights to settlers upon the public lands. These laws, as a general rule, excepted from their operation lands previously reserved from sale by former acts; but no specific reservation of mineral lands, or lands containing mines, was incorporated into any of them until the pre-emption act of September 4, 1841, was passed. This act[2] contained the provision that "no " lands on which are situated any known salines or " mines shall be liable to entry under and by virtue of " the provisions of this act." It also embodied the limitation that its terms should not extend to lands reserved for salines, "or other purposes."

At the time of the passage of this act, the only mines that could have been in contemplation of congress were those of lead and other base metals in the region of the Mississippi valley and the copper mines in the regions of the great lakes.

As to salines, until a very recent period[3] the policy of the government since the acquisition of the northwest territory, and the inauguration of our land system to

---

[1] Public Domain, p. 319.

[2] 5 Stats. at Large, p. 453.

[3] By act of congress passed January 31, 1901, (31 Stats. at Large, p. 745,) public saline lands are classified as mineral, and are sold and disposed of under the general mining laws.

reserve salt springs from sale, has been uniform,[1] with the exception of the act of March 3, 1829,[2] passed on the same day with the act exposing for sale the lead lands of Missouri,[3] which authorized the sale, in the same manner as other public lands, of "the reserved salt " springs and contiguous lands in the state of Missouri, " belonging to the United States, and unclaimed by " individuals."

[1] See Morton v. State of Nebraska, 88 U. S. 660, wherein legislation as to salines is reviewed. The court, however, seems to have overlooked the act of March 3, 1829.

[2] 4 Stats. at Large, p. 364.

[3] See, ante, § 35.

CHAPTER III.

SECOND PERIOD: FROM THE DISCOVERY OF GOLD IN CALI-
FORNIA UNTIL THE PASSAGE OF THE LODE LAW
OF 1866.

§ 40. Discovery of gold in California and the Mexican
cession.

§ 41. Origin of local customs.

§ 42. Scope of local regulations.

§ 43. Dips, spurs, and angles of
lode claims.

§ 44. Legislative and judicial recognition by the state.

§ 45. Federal recognition.

§ 46. Local rules as forming part
of present system of min-
ing law.

§ 47. Federal legislation during
the second period.

§ 48. Executive recommendations
to congress.

§ 49. Coal land laws — Mining
claims in Nevada—Sutro
tunnel act.

§ 40. **Discovery of gold in California and the Mexican cession.**—Commodore Sloat raised the American flag at Monterey, July 7, 1846. Marshall discovered gold at Coloma in January, 1848. The treaty of Guadalupe Hidalgo was concluded February 2, exchanged May 30, and proclaimed July 4, 1848. This treaty added to the national domain an area of more than half a million square miles, embracing the states of California, Nevada, Utah, the territories of Arizona (except the Gadsden purchase of 1853) and New Mexico west of the Rio Grande and north of the Gadsden purchase, and the state of Colorado west of the Rocky mountains, and the southwestern part of Wyoming.[1]

[1] The Gadsden purchase added to the public domain 45,532 square miles, and formed part of the present territories of Arizona and New Mexico.

The discovery of gold and reports of its extensive distribution throughout the foothill regions of the Sierra Nevadas brought to the shores of the Pacific a tide of immigration from all parts of the world. All nationalities, creeds, and colors were soon represented and swarmed into the mineral regions of the golden state, which thenceforward became a beehive of gold-seekers, with their attendant camp-followers.

§ 41. **Origin of local customs.**—No system of laws had been devised to govern the newly acquired territory. By virtue of the treaty, the title to the lands containing the newly discovered wealth was vested in the federal government.

Until March 3, 1849, no attempt was made by congress to extend the operation of any of the federal laws over California, and on this date the revenue laws only were so extended.[1]

Until the admission of the state into the union, California was governed by the military authorities. Colonel Mason, on February 12, 1848, issued a proclamation as military governor, wherein he attempted to put an end to local uncertainty on this delicate subject of international law, by decreeing that "From and after this "date the Mexican laws and customs now prevailing "in California relative to the denouncement of mines "are hereby abolished."[2]

Whether the power to abolish laws if they had a potential existence was confided to a military commandant or not, the force of the proclamation was recognized for the time, and the mining population found itself under the necessity of formulating rules for the government of the several mining communities, and establish-

---

[1] 9 U. S. Stats. at Large, p. 400; Yale on Mining Claims, p. 16.
[2] Yale on Mining Claims, p. 17.

ing such regulations controlling the occupation and enjoyment of mining privileges as the exigencies of the case demanded and as the disorganized condition of society required. Of course, these pioneer miners were all trespassers. They had no warrant or license from the paramount proprietor. Colonel Mason, who, in connection with Lieutenant W. T. Sherman, visited the scenes of the earliest mining operations, thus pictures the situation:—

"The entire gold district, with very few exceptions " of grants made some years ago, by the Mexican au- " thorities, is on land belonging to the United States. " It was a matter of serious reflection with me how I " could secure to the government certain rents or fees " for the privilege of procuring this gold; but upon " considering the large extent of country, the character " of the people engaged, and the small scattered force " at my command, I resolved not to interfere, but per- " mit all to work freely."[1]

Thus left to "work freely," some show of order was brought out of chaos by the voluntary adoption of local rules or general acquiescence in customs whose antiquity dated from the discovery of the "diggings."

Thus originated a system which, in the course of time, extended throughout the mining regions of the west as new discoveries were made, and subsequently came to be recognized as having the force of established law.

Naturally, these regulations varied in the different districts as local conditions varied.

§ 42. **Scope of local regulations.**—Some of the primitive codes were quite comprehensive in their scope, and undertook to legislate generally on the subject of civil rights and remedies, crimes and punishments, as well

[1] Public Domain, p. 314.

as providing rules for the possession and enjoyment of mining claims. For example, those adopted at Jacksonville, California, provided for the election of an alcalde, who propounded the law in a court from whose judgment there was no appeal, and wherein the rule of practice was "to conform as nearly as possible to that " of the United States; but the forms of no particular " state shall be required or adopted."

To steal a mule or other animal of "draught or bur- " den," or to enter a tent or dwelling and steal therefrom gold-dust, money, provisions, goods, or other valuables amounting in value to one hundred dollars or over, was considered a felony, and on conviction thereof the culprit should suffer "death by hanging."

Should the theft be of property of less value, the offender was to be "disgraced" by having his head and eyebrows close-shaved, and by being driven out of camp.

The willful and premeditated taking of human life was an offense of the same grade as stealing a mule, death being the penalty.

A sheriff was elected to carry judgments into effect, and, generally, to enforce the decrees of the judge and preserve the peace.

When we consider the conditions under which these rules were framed, we can readily appreciate their virtue. Generally speaking, however, the miner's code confined itself to regulating the mining industry. At first the miner's labor and research were confined to surface deposits, and to the banks, beds, and "bars" of the streams,—that is, to the claims usually called "placers,"—quartz or lode mining not having been inaugurated until a later period.

A detailed review of the rules and customs adopted and in force in the various districts would serve no

useful purpose. A unique collection of them will be
found in the interesting and valuable report made by
Mr. J. Ross Browne while acting as commissioner of
mining statistics.[1]

Mr. Yale, in his work on mining claims and water
rights,[2] also gives a full and accurate synopsis of the
local mining codes.

The main object of the regulations was to fix the
boundaries of the district, the size of the claims, the
manner in which the claims should be marked and recorded, the amount of work which should be done to
hold the claim, and the circumstances under which the
claim was considered abandoned and open to occupation by new claimants.[3]

Of these rules and customs, Mr. Yale thus sums up
his views:—

"Most of the rules and customs constituting the code
" are easily recognized by those familiar with the Mex-
" ican ordinances, the continental mining codes, espe-
" cially the Spanish, and with the regulations of the
" stannary convocations among the tin bounders of
" Devon and Cornwall, in England, and the High Peak
" regulations for the lead mines in the county of Derby.
" These regulations are founded in nature, and are
" based upon equitable principles, comprehensive and
" simple, have a common origin, are matured by prac-
" tice, and provide for both surface and subterranean
" work, in alluvion, or rock *in situ*. In the earlier days
" of placer diggings in California, the large influx of
" miners from the western coast of Mexico, and from
" South America, necessarily dictated the system of
" work to Americans, who were almost entirely inex-
" perienced in this branch of industry. With few ex-
" ceptions from the gold mines of North Carolina and
" Georgia, and from the lead mines of Illinois and Wis-

[1] Mineral Resources, 1867, pp. 235-247.
[2] Mining Claims and Water Rights, p. 73.
[3] J. Ross Browne in Mineral Resources, 1867, p. 226.

" consin, the old Californians had little or no experi-
" ence in mining. The Cornish miners soon spread
" themselves through the state, and added largely, by
" their experience, practical sense, and industrious hab-
" its, in bringing the code into something like system.
" The Spanish-American system which had grown up
" under the practical working of the mining ordinances
" for New Spain, was the foundation of the rules and
" customs adopted. . . . They reflect the matured
" wisdom of the practical miner of past ages, and have
" their foundation, as has been stated, in certain nat-
" ural laws, easily applied to different situations, and
" were propagated in the California mines by those
" who had a practical and traditional knowledge of
" them in their varied form in the countries of their
" origin, and were adopted, and no doubt gradually
" improved and judiciously modified, by the Ameri-
" cans."

Halleck aptly states the main source and underlying
theory of these local regulations:—

"The miners of California have generally adopted,
" as being best suited to their peculiar wants, the main
" principles of the mining laws of Spain and Mexico,
" by which the right of property in mines is made to
" depend upon *discovery* and *development;* that is, *dis-*
" *covery* is made the source of title, and *development,*
" or *working,* the condition of the continuance of that
" title. These two principles constitute the basis of all
" our local laws and regulations respecting mining
" rights." [1]

§ 43. **Dips, spurs, and angles of lode claims.**—
With respect to lode, or "quartz," claims, as they were
then locally termed, in contradistinction to gravel
claims, the miners' rules and customs established a rule
of property at total variance with the Mexican laws.
We refer to the right to work the vein to an indefinite
depth, regardless of the occupation or possession of the

---

[1] Introduction to De Fooz on the Law of Mines, p. vii.

surface underneath which it might penetrate, and to hold in connection with the main vein, without regard to any inclosing surface boundaries, the "dips, spurs, " angles, and variations" of the located vein. Neither the form nor extent of the surface area controlled the rights in the located lode. It did not measure the miners' rights, either to the linear feet upon its course or to follow the dips, angles, and variations of the vein.[1] The lode was the principal thing, and the surface a mere incident.[2]

This departure from the rule of vertical planes drawn through surface boundaries may possibly be traced to the customs then in vogue among the lead miners of Derbyshire with reference to *"rake veins."* [3]

We find no trace of such an innovation in any other of the contemporaneous mining systems. Under the early German codes of the sixteenth and seventeenth centuries, what may be called an inclined location (*gestrecktfeld*) was sanctioned, which gave the right to follow the vein to an indefinite depth, and to work within planes parallel to the downward course of the vein, thirty feet from the hanging-wall and thirty feet from the foot-wall of the vein, forming a parallelopipedon.[4] But this system had become obsolete long before the discovery of gold in California.[5]

This feature of the miners' rules and customs as adopted in California was embodied in the first mining legislation of congress,[6] and was the basis of what is

---

[1] Eureka Case, 4 Saw. 302-323, Fed. Cas., No. 4548.

[2] Johnson *v.* Parks, 10 Cal. 447.

[3] See, *ante,* § 8.

[4] Dr. R. W. Raymond—Mineral Resources, 1869, p. 195.

[5] Klosterman, in his treatise on the Prussian mining laws (Berlin, 1870), says that the abolition of inclined locations was brought about principally by the "interminable lawsuits inherent in the system."

[6] Act of July 26, 1866.

now termed the extralateral right under the existing system.

A further discussion of this subject will be reserved for a succeeding chapter, where it will be dealt with in connection with the present laws.

§ 44. **Legislative and judicial recognition by the state.** — California was admitted as a state of the union, September 9, 1850. The act of admission contained no reference to mineral lands, and the new state came into existence with the local systems in full force and operation in the mining districts.

The legislature of the state in 1851 gave recognition to the existing conditions and the controlling force of the local system by inserting a provision in the civil practice act to the effect that the "customs, usages, or " regulations, when not in conflict with the constitution " and laws of the state, shall govern the decision of " the action."

As to the effect of this legislative declaration, and generally with reference to the attitude of the state and federal government, upon the subject of mineral lands in California, during this interesting period, the supreme court of California, speaking through Chief Justice Sanderson, thus announced its views : —

"The six hundred and twenty-first section of the " practice act provides that 'In actions respecting min- " 'ing claims proof shall be admitted of the customs, " 'usages, or regulations established and in force at " 'the bar or diggings embracing such claims; and " 'such customs, usages, or regulations, when not in " 'conflict with the constitution and laws of this state, " 'shall govern the decision of the action.'

"At the time the foregoing became a part of the law " of the land, there had sprung up throughout the min- " ing regions of the state local customs and usages by " which persons engaged in mining pursuits were

" governed in the acquisition, use, forfeiture, or loss
" of mining ground (we do not here use the word *for-*
" *feiture* in its common-law sense, but in its mining-
" law sense, as used and understood by the miners, who
" are the framers of our mining codes). These customs
" differed in different localities, and varied to a greater
" or less extent, according to the character of the mines.
" They prescribed the acts by which the right to mine
" a particular piece of ground could be secured and
" its use and enjoyment continued and preserved, and
" by what non-action on the part of the appropriator
" such right should become forfeited or lost, and the
" ground become, as at first, *publici juris* and open to
" the appropriation of the next-comer. They were few,
" plain, and simple, and well understood by those with
" whom they originated. They were well adapted to
" secure the end designed to be accomplished, and were
" adequate to the judicial determination of all contro-
" versies touching mining rights. And it was a wise
" policy on the part of the legislature, not only not to
" supplant them by legislative enactments, but, on
" the contrary, to give them the additional weight
" of a legislative sanction. These usages and cus-
" toms were the fruit of the times, and demanded
" by the necessities of communities who, though
" living under the common law, could find therein
" no clear and well-defined rules for their guid-
" ance applicable to the new conditions by which they
" were surrounded, but were forced to depend upon
" remote analogies of doubtful application and unsatis-
" factory results. Having received the sanction of the
" legislature, they have become as much a part of the
" law of the land as the common law itself, which was
" not adopted in a more solemn form. And it is to be
" regretted that the wisdom of the legislature in thus
" leaving mining controversies to the arbitrament of
" mining laws has not always been seconded by the
" courts and the legal profession, who seem to have
" been too long tied down to the treadmill of the com-
" mon law to readily escape its thraldom while engaged
" in the solution of a mining controversy. These cus-

" toms and usages have, in progress of time, become
" more general and uniform, and in their leading fea-
" tures are now the same throughout the mining regions
" of the state; and, however it may have been hereto-
" fore, there is no reason why judges or lawyers should
" wander with counsel for the appellant in this case
" back to the time when Abraham dug his well, or ex-
" plore with them the law of agency or the statute of
" frauds, in order to solve a simple question affecting
" a mining right; for a more convenient and equally
" legal solution can be found nearer home in the 'cus-
" 'toms and usages of the bar or diggings embracing
" 'the claim' to which such right is asserted or de-
" nied."[1]

Mr. Justice Field, who was the author of the provision of the California civil practice act referred to in the
decision above quoted, and who was recognized as the
"end of the law" on mining subjects, in speaking for
the supreme court of the United States, thus presents
his views upon that branch of the law, as to which he
was so peculiarly fitted to speak:—

"The discovery of gold in California was followed,
" as is well known, by an immense immigration into
" the state, which increased its population within three
" or four years from a few thousand to several hundred
" thousand. The lands in which the precious metals
" were found belonged to the United States, and were
" unsurveyed and not open by law to occupation and
" settlement. Little was known of them further than
" that they were situated in the Sierra Nevada moun-
" tains. Into these mountains the emigrants in vast
" numbers penetrated, occupying the ravines, gulches,
" and canyons, and probing the earth in all directions
" for the precious metals. Wherever they went they
" carried with them that love of order and system and
" of fair dealing which are the prominent characteris-
" tics of our people. In every district which they
" occupied they framed certain rules for their govern-

---

[1] Morton *v.* Solambo M. Co., 26 Cal. 527.

" ment, by which the extent of ground they could sever-
" ally hold for mining was designated, their possessory
" right to such ground secured and enforced, and con-
" tests between them either avoided or determined.
" These rules bore a marked similarity, varying in the
" several districts only according to the extent and
" character of the mines; distinct provision being made
" for different kinds of mining, such as placer mining,
" quartz mining, and mining in drifts or tunnels. *They*
" *all recognized discovery,* followed by appropriation,
" as the foundation of the possessor's title, and develop-
" ment by working as the condition of its retention.
" And they were so framed as to secure to all comers
" within practicable limits absolute equality of right
" and privilege in working the mines. Nothing but
" such equality would have been tolerated by the
" miners, who were emphatically the law-makers, as
" respects mining upon the public lands in the state.
" The first appropriator was everywhere held to have,
" within certain well-defined limits, a better right than
" others to the claims taken up; and in all controversies,
" except as against the government, he was regarded
" as the original owner, from whom title was to be
" traced. . . . These regulations and customs were
" appealed to in controversies in the state courts, and
" received their sanction; and properties to the value
" of many millions rested upon them. For eighteen
" years, from 1848 to 1866, the regulations and customs
" of miners, as enforced and molded by the courts and
" sanctioned by the legislation of the state, constituted
" the law governing property in mines and in water
" on the public mineral lands." [1]

This exposition of the law governing mining rights,
as it existed in the early history of the mining industry
in the west, leaves nothing to be added by the author.
The decision stands as a forensic classic. Judge Field
was a part of the history of which he wrote. He served

---

[1] Jennison *v.* Kirk, 98 U. S. 453; cited in N. P. R. R. *v.* Sanders, 166
U. S. 620, 17 Sup. Ct. Rep. 671.

as an alcalde during the chaotic period antedating the admission of California as a state. He served his state in its first legislatures, and was the author of many of its early laws. As chief justice of its supreme court, his was the task to solve the great and overshadowing questions which arose over land titles in a new state coming into the union under peculiar and novel conditions, and he carried to the supreme bench of the United States not only the practical knowledge acquired by personal contact with the mining communities, but a trained judicial mind.

These local systems are said to have constituted the American common law of mines,[1] and their binding force has been recognized from the beginning by the legislation of the states and by a uniform line of decisions in the state and territorial courts.[2]

§ 45. **Federal recognition.** — The federal judiciary followed the rules thus adopted.[3] Congress has always recognized their binding force.[4]

The land department of the government and the supreme court of the United States have uniformly acted upon the rule that all mineral locations were to be governed by the local regulations and customs in force at the time of the location, when such location was made prior to the passage of any mineral law made by congress.[5]

[1] King v. Edwards, 1 Mont. 235.

[2] Carson City G. M. Co. v. North Star M. Co., 83 Fed. 658, 667.

[3] Sparrow v. Strong, 3 Wall. 97; Del Monte M. Co. v. Last Chance M. Co., 171 U. S. 55, 62, 18 Sup. Ct. Rep. 895.

[4] St. Louis Smelting Co. v. Kemp, 104 U. S. 636; Chambers v. Harrington, 111 U. S. 350, 4 Sup. Ct. Rep. 428; Golden Fleece v. Cable Cons., 12 Nev. 313; King v. Edwards, 1 Mont. 235.

[5] Glacier Mt. S. M. Co. v. Willis, 127 U. S. 471, 8 Sup. Ct. Rep. 1214; Broder v. Natoma Water Co., 101 U. S. 274; Jackson v. Roby, 109 U. S. 440, 3 Sup. Ct. Rep. 301; Chambers v. Harrington, 111 U. S. 350, 4 Sup. Ct. Rep. 428.

§ **46. Local rules as forming part of present system of mining law.**—To a limited extent, local regulations have still a place in our legal system. They are permitted to have controlling force in certain directions and under certain restrictions; but they are gradually becoming superseded by statutory enactments in the various states and territories, which, of course, are but another form of expressing local rules. In many parts of the mining regions the right to supplement congressional laws by the adoption of local codes is not exercised. In other places we still find the right asserted. In this aspect district laws and regulations, as well as state and territorial enactments, form an integral part of the present system, and will be dealt with in their appropriate place. The purpose of this chapter has been largely historical, and enough has been said to show the origin, development, scope, and legal *status* of local rules to enable us to award them their proper place in the evolution of the existing system.

§ **47. Federal legislation during the second period.** —On March 3, 1849, congress passed an act creating the department of the interior,[1] and thereupon the supervision of mineral lands was transferred to the general land office in that department.

The act of September 26, 1850,[2] ordered the mineral lands in the Lake Superior district in Michigan to be offered at public sale, in the same manner, at the minimum, and with the same rights of pre-emption, as other public lands, but not to interfere with leased rights.[3]

This is the extent of affirmative action by congress during the second period touching its mineral lands,

---

[1] 9 Stats. at Large, p. 395.   [3] Public Domain, p. 308.
[2] *Id.*, p. 472.

with the exception of the act providing for a district and circuit court for the district of Nevada, approved February 27, 1865.[1]

Section nine of this act provided:—

"That no possessory action between individuals in
" any of the courts for the recovery of a mining title
" or for damages to any such title shall be affected by
" the fact that the paramount title to the land on which
" such mines lie is in the United States, but each case
" shall be adjudged by the law of possession."

The same provision is perpetuated in the Revised Statutes.[2] This act was the first formal recognition by congress of the possessory rights of mineral occupants of the public lands.

In all general laws granting the right of pre-emption to settlers upon public land, mineral lands were reserved from their operation. The act of September 4, 1841, excepts from its operation all lands on which are situated any "known salines or mines." Whenever, upon the admission of a new state into the union, the provisions of this general pre-emption law were extended to it, this reservation was emphasized, if not enlarged. Thus, by the act of congress passed March 3, 1853, it was provided that all the public lands in the state of California, whether surveyed or unsurveyed, *excepting mineral lands,* should be subjected to the provisions of the act of 1841; and it was further provided that no person should obtain the benefits of the act by a settlement or location on *mineral lands.*

In grants to the several states, and in aid of the construction of railroads, similar reservations were made. The language of the reservation is not always precisely

---

[1] 13 Stats. at Large, p. 440.   [2] Rev. Stats., § 910.

the same, but there is no departure from the established policy, that mineral lands were uniformly reserved for the use of the United States, or to be disposed of by such special laws as congress might see fit to enact.

In another portion of this treatise the extent and operation of the several excepting clauses contained in the different classes of grants will be considered. Sufficient historical data has here been given justifying the conclusion reached by the courts in announcing the doctrine that, prior to 1866, it had been the settled policy of the government in disposing of the public lands to reserve the mines and mineral lands for the use of the United States. Prior to that date, the uniform reservation of mineral lands from survey, from sale, from pre-emption, and from all grants, whether for railroads, public buildings, or other purposes, fixed and settled the policy of the government in relation to such lands.[1]

§ 48. **Executive recommendations to congress.**— Colonel Mason, in August, 1848, had made a graphic and interesting report to the war department, announcing officially the discovery of gold, giving a glowing account of the extent and richness of the deposits. He recommended the establishment of a mint at San Francisco, the survey of the districts into small parcels, and their sale at public auction to the highest bidder.

On December 2, 1849, President Fillmore, in his annual message to congress, referred to the subject in the following terms:—

"I also beg leave to call your attention to the pro-
" priety of extending at an early day our system of land

---

[1] Silver Bow M. and M. Co. v. Clarke, 5 Mont. 378, 410; Ivanhoe M. Co. v. Keystone Cons. M. Co., 102 U. S. 167; U. S. v. Gratiot, 14 Peters, 526; Morton v. State of Nebraska, 21 Wall. 660; Jennison v. Kirk, 98 U. S. 453, 458; Deffeback v. Hawke, 115 U. S. 392, 401, 6 Sup. Ct. Rep. 95.

" laws, with such modifications as may be necessary,
" over the state of California and the territories of Utah
" and New Mexico. The mineral lands of California
" will, of course, form an exception to any general
" system which may be adopted. Various methods of
" disposing of them have been suggested. I was at
" first inclined to favor the system of leasing, as it
" seemed to promise the largest revenue to the govern-
" ment, and to afford the best security against monopo-
" lies; but further reflection and our experience in
" leasing the lead mines and selling lands upon credit,
" have brought my mind to the conclusion that there
" would be great difficulty in collecting the rents, and
" that the relation of debtor and creditor between the
" citizens and the government would be attended with
" many mischievous consequences. I therefore recom-
" mend that instead of retaining the mineral lands
" under the permanent control of the government, they
" be divided into small parcels and sold, under such
" restrictions as to quantity and time as will insure the
" best price and guard most effectually against combi-
" nations of capitalists to obtain monopolies."

On the day following, Hon. Thomas Ewing, then
secretary of the interior, laid before congress an elaborate report concerning the discovery of gold in California, wherein he called attention to the fact that no
existing law gave the executive power to deal with the
mines or protect them from intrusion, and some legal
provision was necessary for their protection and disposition. He recommended a transfer by sale or lease,
reserving a part of the gold collected as seigniorage.

Nothing, however, came of these recommendations.
Senator Fremont, on September 24, 1850, introduced
a bill in the United States senate "to make temporary
" provision for the working and discovery of gold
" mines and placers in California, and preserving order
" in the mines," and contemplated a system of licenses

to be granted upon payment of a nominal monthly rental. This bill passed the senate, but not the house.[1]

§ 49. Coal land laws — Mining claims in Nevada — Sutro tunnel act.

There were several minor attempts made to pass a general mining law applicable to the gold regions, but they met with no success. While all admitted something should be done, sentiment was divided on questions of policy.

Laws were passed regulating the sale and disposal of coal lands; one on July 1, 1864,[2] and one on March 3, 1865;[3] and two laws, special and local in their nature —viz., the act of May 5, 1866,[4] concerning the boundaries of the state of Nevada, wherein it was provided that "all possessory rights acquired by citizens of the " United States to mining claims discovered, located, " and originally recorded, in compliance with the rules " and regulations adopted by miners in the Pah Rana- " gat and other mining districts in the territory incor- " porated by the provisions of this act into the state " of Nevada, shall remain as valid, subsisting mining " claims; but nothing herein contained shall be so con- " strued as granting a title in fee to any mineral lands " held by possessory titles in the mining states and

---

[1] Yale on Mining Claims and Water Rights, pp. 340-349.

[2] 13 Stats. at Large, p. 343.

[3] *Id.*, p. 529. These two acts provided for the disposal of coal lands and the sale of town property upon the public domain. The act of March 3, 1865, § 2, contains the following proviso, with reference to the sale of town lots: "*Provided, further,* That where mineral veins are possessed, "which possession is recognized by local authority, and to the extent so "possessed and recognized, the title to town lots to be acquired shall be "subject to such possession and the recognized use thereof. *Provided,* "however, that nothing herein shall be construed as to recognize any "color of title in possessors for mining purposes as against the govern- "ment of the United States."

[4] 14 Stats. at Large, p. 43.

" territories." The second was the Sutro tunnel act, approved July 25, 1866,[1] which granted the right of way and other privileges to Adolph Sutro and his assigns to aid in the construction of a draining and exploring tunnel to the Comstock lode in the state of Nevada. This act conferred upon Sutro the right of pre-emption as to lodes within two thousand feet on each side of the tunnel, cut or discovered by the tunnel, excepting the Comstock lode and other lodes in the actual possession of others. The act also recognized the mining rules and regulations prescribed by the legislature of Nevada.[2] On the day following, congress passed the law generally known as the "lode and water " law of 1866," to which we will now devote our attention.

[1] 14 Stats. at Large, p. 242.
[2] Yale on Mining Claims and Water Rights, pp. 351-352.

CHAPTER IV.

THIRD PERIOD: FROM THE PASSAGE OF THE LODE LAW
OF 1866 TO THE ENACTMENT OF THE GENERAL LAW
OF MAY 10, 1872.

§ 53. The act of July 26, 1866.

§ 54. Essential features of the act.

§ 55. Declaration of governmental policy.

§ 56. Recognition of local customs and possessory rights acquired thereunder.

§ 57. Title to lode claims.

§ 58. Relationship of surface to the lode.

§ 59. Construction of the act by the land department.

§ 60. Construction by the courts.

§ 61. Local rules and customs after the passage of the act.

§ 62. The act of July 9, 1870.

§ 63. Local rules and customs after the passage of the act.

§ 64. Accession to the national domain during the third period.

§ 53. The act of July 26, 1866.— This act was entitled "An act granting the right of way to ditch and "canal owners through the public lands, and for other "purposes." The title gives no clue to the scope of the act. As a matter of fact, the title belonged to another act which had passed the house, and for which the mining act was substituted in the senate, without any attempt to change the title, and in this form passed both houses.[1]

It was the first general law passed under which title might be acquired to any of the public mineral lands within what are known as the precious-metal-bearing

[1] Yale on Mining Claims and Water Rights, p. 12.

states and territories.[1] While most of the provisions
of this act have been repealed and superseded by subsequent legislation, it remains a muniment of title to
many mining properties, rights to which attached prior
to its repeal. To this extent it is still operative.[2]

§ 54. **Essential features of the act.**—No one has ever
claimed that this act was a model piece of legislation. It
is faulty and crude in the extreme, and the embarrassments surrounding its proper interpretation are still
encountered in the courts, where property rights arising
under it come in conflict with those acquired under the
later laws. Yet the mining communities accepted it as
being a step in the right direction. Mr. Yale says
of it:—

"As the initial act of the legislation which must neces-
"sarily follow, it is more commendable as an acknowl-
"edgment of the justice and necessity which dictated it,
"and its expediency as a means to the advancement of
"the material interests of the state and nation, than for
"the perfection of its provisions or their exact adapta-
"tion to the accomplishment of the object intended. We
"must not, however, find fault with the law on account
"of its imperfections or the introduction of objectionable
"features in the mode to be followed in acquiring a title
"under it. These imperfections can be remedied, the
"rights of the parties amplified in many particulars, and
"the system so changed as to work with more facility
"than now anticipated."[3]

It is certainly due to Senators Stewart and Conness,
the authors of the bill, to explain that at the time of its
passage it was extremely difficult to secure the consideration of any measure touching the subject of mineral

---

[1] Del Monte M. Co. *v.* Last Chance M. Co., 171 U. S. 55, 62, 18 Sup.
Ct. Rep. 895.

[2] The full text of the act will be found in the appendix.

[3] Yale on Mining Claims and Water Rights, pp. 9-10.

lands. Eastern sentiment was divided on questions of governmental policy, and the delegations from the western states were not harmonious. If future experience has shown defects to exist in the law, the authors and friends of the measure are entitled to the gratitude of those engaged in the mining industry for the establishment of at least three important and beneficent principles:—

First—That all the mineral lands of the public domain should be free and open to exploration and occupation.

Second—That rights which had been acquired in these lands under a system of local rules, with the apparent acquiescence and sanction of the government, should be recognized and confirmed; [1]

Third—That titles to at least certain classes of mineral deposits or lands containing them might be ultimately obtained.

§ 55. **Declaration of governmental policy.**—By the first of these provisions, the government, for the first time in its history, inaugurated a fixed and definite legislative policy with reference to its mineral lands. It forever abandoned the idea of exacting royalties on the products of the mines,[2] and gave free license to all its citizens, and those who had declared their intention to become such, to search for the precious and economic minerals in the public domain, and, when found, gave the assurance of at least some measure of security in possession and right of enjoyment. What had theretofore been technically a trespass became thenceforward a licensed privilege, untrammeled by governmental surveillance or the exaction of burdensome conditions. Such conditions as were imposed were no more onerous than

---

[1] Jennison *v.* Kirk, 98 U. S., 453, 458; Blake *v.* Butte S. M. Co., 101 U. S. 274.

[2] Ivanhoe M. Co. *v.* Keystone Cons. M. Co., 102 U. S. 167, 173.

those which the miners had imposed upon themselves by
their local systems. That such a declaration of governmental policy stimulated and encouraged the development of the mining industry in the west, is a matter of
public history.

§ 56. Recognition of local customs and possessory rights acquired thereunder.

—As was observed in the
preceding chapter, the federal government had practically acquiesced from the beginning in the system of
local rules established in the various mining districts.
That is to say, no overt act was done by the government
to overthrow or repudiate the system. No attempt was
made to interfere with mining upon the public domain.
The process by which these primitive systems came to
be recognized, first by the states, and then by the national
government, was natural. When mineral discoveries
were made in other territories and states, the system
inaugurated in California was adopted to govern and
regulate the new mining districts.[1]

Local legislatures and local courts followed the precedent set in California, by enacting and upholding laws
confirming the right in the newly discovered mineral
districts to established rules governing the mining industry. As the supreme court of the United States said,
before the act of 1866 was passed:—

"We cannot shut our eyes to the public history which
"informs us that under the legislation (state and terri-
"torial), not only without interference by the national
"government, but under its implied sanction, vast min-
"ing interests have grown up, employing many millions
"of capital and contributing largely to the prosperity
"and improvement of the whole country." [2]

---

[1] St. Louis Smelting Co. *v.* Kemp, 104 U. S. 636, 650.

[2] Sparrow *v.* Strong, 3 Wall. 97, 104. See, also, Del Monte M. Co. *v.*
Last Chance M. Co., 171 U. S. 55, 18 Sup. Ct. Rep. 895.

The unqualified legislative recognition of these local systems was a simple act of justice. Any other course would have involved a practical confiscation of property acquired and developed by the tacit consent of the government. That this act was such unqualified recognition has been abundantly established by the highest judicial authority.[1]

§ 57. **Title to lode claims.** —It may seem strange that the first mining law under which title to mining property could be absolutely acquired was limited in its operation in this direction to lode, or vein, claims. All mineral lands, whatever the forms in which the deposits therein occurred, were thrown open to exploration; but only lode claims could be patented. We are at a loss to understand the reason for this, unless it is accounted for by the state of the industry at the time the act was passed. Placer mining, which had occupied the attention exclusively of the early miners of California, was on the decline, and the quartz, or lode, mining was in the ascendency. The auriferous quartz veins of California were being developed to an important extent. Nevada, with its great Comstock lode, was attracting the attention of the civilized world. Much expensive litigation had arisen there,[2] and the necessity for some law giving a degree of certainty to mining titles was urgent. In addition to this, important quartz veins of great value had been discovered in other portions of Nevada, and in Colorado,

[1] Jennison v. Kirk, 98 U. S. 453, 459; Broder v. Natoma Water Co., 101 U. S. 274; Chambers v. Harrington, 111 U. S. 350, 352, 4 Sup. Ct. Rep. 428; N. P. R. R. Co. v. Sanders, 166 U. S. 620, 17 Sup. Ct. Rep. 671; Titcomb v. Kirk, 51 Cal. 288.

[2] The surveyor-general for the state of Nevada, in his report for 1865, expressed the belief that one fifth of the output of the Comstock, estimated up to that date by Mr. J. Ross Browne at forty-five millions of dollars, was spent in litigation. (Mineral Resources of the West, 1867, p. 32.)

Idaho, Montana, and other of the precious-metal-bearing states and territories. All these facts considered, it is safe to assume that the lode-mining industry was the one which was uppermost in the public mind, and which was most in need of national statutory regulation. At all events, until the passage of the placer law of 1870, no ultimate title to any mineral lands could be acquired, except to a "vein, or lode, of quartz or other' rock in "place, bearing gold, silver, cinnabar, or copper."

The method of obtaining this title provided for in the act was simple; but the nature of the thing granted, the relationship of the surface and its boundaries to the lode, the extent of the dip or extralateral right, and some of the terms used in the act were, and still are, matters of serious contention and controversy.

The historical importance of the act of July 26, 1866, consists in the establishment of the three important principles enumerated in section fifty-four.

§ 58. **Relationship of surface to the lode.**—Under local rules, as well as under the act of 1866, the lode was the principal thing, and the surface was in reality an incident.[1] The manifest' purpose of section two of the act of 1866 was a conveyance of the vein, and not the conveyance of a certain area of land in which was the vein.[2] Nowhere in the act of 1866 was there any express limitation as to the amount of land to be conveyed. Obviously, the statute contemplated the patenting of a certain number of feet of the particular vein claimed by the locator, no matter how irregular its course. No pro-

---

[1] Johnson v. Parks, 10 Cal. 447; Patterson v. Hitchcock, 3 Colo. 533, 544; Wolfley v. Lebanon, 4 Colo. 112; Walrath v. Champion M. Co., 63 Fed. 552.

[2] Del Monte M. Co. v. Last Chance M. Co., 171 U. S. 55, 63, 18 Sup. Ct. Rep. 895; Calhoun G. M. Co. v. Ajax G. M. Co., 59 Pac. 607, 612, 27 Colo. 1, 83 Am. St. Rep. 17.

vision was made as to the surface area, leaving the land department in each particular case to grant so much of the surface "as was fixed by local rules" or was, in the absence of such rules, in its judgment necessary for the convenient working of the mine.[1]

While in some districts the precise quantity of surface allowed in connection with a lode was fixed by local rules, in many others no fixed quantity was mentioned. The lode only was located, the claims being staked, if at all, at the ends only. The notice of location usually called for so many feet on the vein, and a misdescription as to its course did not vitiate the location. The locator had a right prior to patent to follow it wherever it ran.[2]

Neither the form nor extent of the surface area claimed controlled the rights on the located lode. It did not measure the miner's rights either to the linear feet upon its course or to follow the dips, angles, and variations of the vein.[3]

The local rules fixed no bounding planes across the course of the vein, and end lines were not in terms provided for, although they were, according to the decision in the Eureka case, implied. But there was no implication that they should be parallel.[4]

Under the local rules, there was no question raised as to any side lines, for there were none provided for.[5]

A locator could hold but one lode, or vein,[6] even if his

---

[1] Del Monte M. Co. v. Last Chance M. Co., 171 U. S. 55, 63, 18 Sup. Ct. Rep. 895.

[2] Johnson v. Parks, 10 Cal. 447; Larned v. Jenkins, 113 Fed. 634.

[3] Eureka Case, 4 Saw. 302, 323, Fed. Cas., No. 4548; Golden Fleece G. and S. M. Co. v. Cable Cons. Co., 12 Nev. 312, 328.

[4] Eureka Case, 4 Saw. 302, 319, Fed. Cas., No. 4548; Iron S. M. Co. v. Elgin, 118 U. S. 196, 208, 6 Sup. Ct. Rep. 1177.

[5] Carson City G. M. Co. v. North Star M. Co., 83 Fed. 658, 666.

[6] Eureka Case, 4 Saw. 302, 323, Fed. Cas., No. 4548; Eclipse G. and S. M. Co. v. Spring, 59 Cal. 304; Walrath v. Champion M. Co., 63 Fed. 552; Calhoun G. M. Co. v. Ajax G. M. Co., 59 Pac. 607, 612, 27 Colo. 1, 83 Am. St. Rep. 1.

claim had fixed surface boundaries. But the fact that two ledges existed within the bounds was required to be first established before the subsequent claimant had any lawful right to invade the surface boundaries of the senior locator.[1]

In all patents issued under the act, a recital was inserted restricting the grant to the one vein, or lode, described therein, and providing that any other vein, or lode, discovered within the surface ground described should be excepted and excluded from the operation of the grant.

§ 59. **Construction of the act by the land department.** —Shortly after the passage of the act the commissioner of the general land office issued "circular "instructions" for the guidance of the registers, receivers, and surveyors-general in carrying the law into effect.[2] These instructions provided for the establishment of end lines at right angles to the ascertained or apparent general course of the vein, and permitted the applicant to apply for patent to a vein without any inclosing surface, the estimated quantity of superficial area in such cases being equal to a horizontal plane, bounded by the given end lines and the walls on the sides of the vein. As was said by the commissioner of the general land office, an applicant for a patent under this act might include surface ground lying on either or both sides of the vein as part of his claim, or he might apply for a patent for the vein alone. His rights upon the vein and in working it were precisely the same, whatever might be the form of his surface ground, or whether he had any or none.[3]

---

[1] Atkins v. Hendree, 1 Idaho 107.

[2] January 14, 1867—Copp's Min. Dec., p. 239.

[3] Mt. Joy Lode—Copp's Min. Dec., p. 27.

"As might be expected, the patents issued under this
"statute described surface areas very different and
"sometimes irregular in form. Often they were like a
"broom, there being around the discovery shaft an
"amount of ground deemed large enough for the con-
"venient working of the mine, and a narrow strip
"extending therefrom as the handle of the broom. This
"strip might be straight or in a curved or irregular
"line, following, as was supposed, the course of the vein.
"Sometimes the surface claimed and patented was a
"tract of considerable size, so claimed with a view of
"including the apex of the vein, in whatever direction
"subsequent explorations might show it to run. And,
"again, where there were local rules giving to the dis-
"coverer of a mine possessory rights in a certain area of
"surface, the patent followed those rules, and conveyed
"a similar area." [1]

As to the effect of such patent, when issued, the
department took the view that the patentee was fully
invested with the title to his lode for the linear extent
specified in the grant, whatever course the vein might
be found to pursue underground; [2] and that he might
follow the particular lode named in the patent to the
number of feet expressed in the grant, although the
ledge in its course should leave the surface ground
described in the patent. [3] In other words, the department
inclined to the opinion that the right of a lode claimant
to pursue the vein to the extent of the number of linear
feet claimed, whatever might be its course, was the same
after patent as before.

Under this construction of the law, patents were issued
in several instances describing a small area of surface,
upon which the improvements were erected, within

[1] Del Monte M. Co. v. Last Chance M. Co., 171 U. S. 55, 64, 18 Sup. Ct.
Rep. 895; and see Calhoun G. M. Co. v. Ajax G. M. Co., 59 Pac. 607, 612,
27 Colo. 1, 83 Am. St. Rep. 17.

[2] Flagstaff Case—Copp's Min. Dec., p. 61.

[3] Commissioner's letter—Copp's Min. Dec., pp. 154, 201.

which surface a few hundred linear feet of the lode only was included, the remainder of the feet claimed being indicated by a line extending beyond the defined surface area in the direction and to the extent claimed.[1] An example of a patent issued under this interpretation is found in the case of the famous Idaho mine in Grass Valley, California. We present for illustrative purposes a copy of the plat accompanying this patent (Figure 1):—

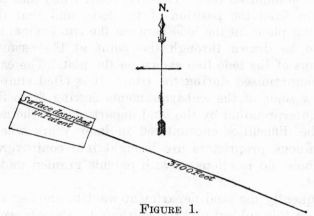

N.

Surface described in Patent

3100 Feet

FIGURE 1.

This patent described the surface ground shown on the plat, and granted ''the said mineral claim, or lot of ''land, above described, with the right to follow said ''vein, or lode, to the distance of thirty-one hundred ''linear feet, with its dips, angles, and variations, ''although it may enter the land adjoining.'' Just what was in fact granted by the patent to a line might be the cause for serious controversy, even if the line correctly followed the outcrop of the vein. But subsequent development proved that this outcrop, or top, was considerably north of the patented line. Litigation arose between

[1] Del Monte M. Co. v. Last Chance M. Co., 171 U. S. 55, 64, 18 Sup. Ct. Rep. 895; Calhoun G. M. Co. v. Ajax G. M. Co., 59 Pac. 607, 612.

the Idaho and the Maryland, adjoining on the east, as to where the right of the Idaho on the vein terminated and that of the Maryland began, and as to what was the bounding plane on the dip between the two companies. Under the interpretation followed by the land department, it would seem that the Idaho company could follow the vein in whatever direction it ran, after leaving the surface boundaries, to the extent of the thirty-one hundred feet. The trial court ruled that the diagram fixed the position of the lode, and that the bounding plane on the lode between the two companies was to be drawn through the point at the eastern terminus of the lode line shown on the plat. The case was compromised during the trial. It is cited simply to show some of the embarrassments flowing from the early interpretation by the land department of the act, and the difficulties encountered in later years where coterminous proprietors are brought into controversy with these old locations or with patents granted under this act.

Frequently the land department went to another extreme on this subject of surface ground. Patents were issued covering a few hundred feet of a lode, embraced within irregular surface boundaries which covered an area of several hundred acres.

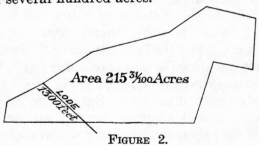

Area 215 3½⁄₁₀₀ Acres

LODE 1300 feet

FIGURE 2.

Figure 2 presents an illustration of this. It is taken from a patent issued by the department, based upon a claim to the lode, originating under the act of 1866, upon proceedings completed and entry made prior to the passage of the act of May 10, 1872.

So long as the act of 1866 was in force, which granted but the one lode, the legal controversies likely to arise over a proper construction of such a patent were not particularly serious. But when we consider that the act of 1872 purports to grant to the holder of such a patent all other lodes which have their tops, or apices, within the patented surface area, it will be seen that many complications might arise as to end-line planes and dip rights between coterminous proprietors. All of this, however, will be reserved for future discussion. Our object has been simply to illustrate the rules of interpretation which prevailed in the land department.

§ 60. **Construction by the courts.**—The courts of last resort have uniformly overruled the interpretation of this act adopted by the land department, and have established the rule that surface lines, both side and end, were contemplated by the act of 1866, and that when a patent was once obtained the patentee was not permitted to follow the vein on its course beyond the surface boundaries.[1]

The Flagstaff lode claim, in reference to which, on application for patent, the land department announced its interpretation [2] that the patentee might follow the lode to the linear extent claimed, whatever might be its course, came before the courts after the patent was issued, in two cases, one of which reached the supreme court of the United States. As the Flagstaff case is a

---

[1] McCormick v. Varnes, 2 Utah 355; Flagstaff M. Co. v. Tarbet, 98 U. S. 463; Del Monte M. and M. Co. v. Last Chance M. Co., 171 U. S. 55; Montana Ore Purchasing Co. v. Boston and M. C. C. and S. M. Co., 20 Mont. 336, 51 Pac. 159; Lillie Lode M. Claim, 31 L. D. 21.

[2] Copp's Min. Dec., p. 61.

noted one, and has served as a precedent in a number of controversies, we herewith present a diagram (Figure 3)[1] illustrating the several controversies.

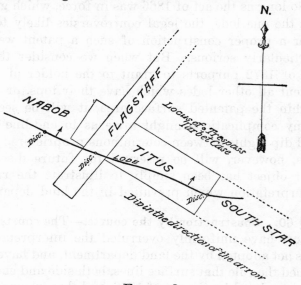

FIGURE 3.

The Flagstaff patent granted a superficies one hundred feet wide by twenty-six hundred feet long, with the right to follow the vein to the extent of twenty-six hundred feet. It appeared that the lode crossed the side lines, as indicated on the diagram. Two controversies arose; one with the Nabob, on the west, and the other with the Titus, on the east. In each case the Flagstaff company contended that they had a right to the lode for the length thereof claimed, though it ran in a different direction from that in which it was supposed to run when the location was made.

[1] This diagram, so far as it relates to the case of Flagstaff M. Co. v. Tarbet, is taken from a certified copy of the map used at the trial. The Nabob claim is designated thereon from the description given in McCormick v. Varnes, 2 Utah, 355.

The supreme court of Utah passed upon both cases, the Nabob case alone being reported, so far as that court was concerned.[1] It held in that case that the Flagstaff patented ground did not cover or embrace any part of the vein on its course, or strike, outside of and beyond the side lines.

The Titus case was decided on parallel lines, and was appealed to the supreme court of the United States,[2] where the ruling was affirmed, and the doctrine firmly established that the right to the lode only extended to so much of the lode as is found within the surface boundaries.[3] If the patentee located crosswise of the lode, and his claim was only one hundred feet wide, that one hundred feet is all he had a right to.[4]

Prior to this decision of the supreme court of the United States, the supreme court of Colorado had announced the same doctrine. as the supreme court of Utah,[5] but without referring to the Utah cases. It is more than probable that the two courts reached the same conclusions without either having knowledge of the action of the other.

The doctrine of the Flagstaff case has been applied frequently to cases of somewhat similar character,[6] and was fully discussed approvingly by the supreme court of the United States in two interesting cases.[7]

[1] McCormick v. Varnes, 2 Utah, 355.

[2] Flagstaff M. Co. v. Tarbet, 98 U. S. 463.

[3] See Del Monte M. Co. v. Last Chance M. Co., 171 U. S. 55, 18 Sup. Ct. Rep. 285; Montana Ore Purchasing Co. v. Boston and M. Co., 20 Mont. 336, 51 Pac. 159.

[4] See, also, Del Monte M. Co. v. Last Chance M. Co., 171 U. S. 55, 18 Sup. Ct. Rep. 895; Walrath v. Champion M. Co., 171 U. S. 293, 18 Sup. Ct. Rep. 909.

[5] Wolfley v. Lebanon, 4 Colo. 112; Johnson v. Buell, 4 Colo. 557.

[6] Walrath v. Champion M. Co., 63 Fed. 552; S. C. (C. C. A), 72 Fed. 978; Dunderberg v. Old, 79 Fed. 588; Larned v. Jenkins, 113 Fed. 634.

[7] Del Monte M. Co. v. Last Chance M. Co., 171 U. S. 55, 18 Sup. Ct. Rep. 895; Walrath v. Champion M. Co., 171 U. S. 293, 305, 18 Sup. Ct. Rep. 909.

It will be thus seen that until a locator defined his claim for purposes of patent, under the act of 1866, he could follow the lode in any direction it might take to the length claimed; but after patent he was confined to the lines of his survey. As was said by the circuit court of appeals for the eighth circuit:—

"A discoverer of a vein cannot be permitted to locate "his claim, present his diagram, and obtain a grant for "the lode and the land he claims, and then disregard "the limitations of the grant and follow the lode without "his location wherever it happens to lead." [1]

As to the extent of the dip or extralateral right under locations held and patents issued under the act of 1866, we reserve the discussion for a succeeding chapter. To a considerable extent this act and the titles issued under it are brought into connection, and are at least partly blended with the later, or present, legislative system and the titles held thereunder.

§ 61. Local rules and customs after the passage of the act.—It will be observed that the act left to local regulation all the details of location, limiting, however, the linear extent of an individual location to two hundred feet, with an additional claim to the discoverer, and providing that not more than three thousand feet should be taken in any one claim by any association of persons. The law also granted to the locators the right to follow the vein to any depth, with all its dips, angles, and variations. This was the rule in most mining districts before the passage of the act, although in certain localities lode claims were required to be "square," with no right to follow the vein on the dip beyond vertical planes drawn through the surface boundaries. As the act did not apply to placers, this class of claims continued to be

---

[1] Larned v. Jenkins, 113 Fed. 634, 636. See, also, Del Monte M. and M. Co. v. Last Chance M. Co., 171 U. S. 55, 64, 18 Sup. Ct. Rep. 895.

entirely governed by local rules until the passage of the
placer law of July 9, 1870. Lode claims continued to be
so governed within the limitation as to length of claim
and the extent which might be held by location on a given
lode by any association.

§ 62. **The act of July 9, 1870.** —This is commonly
known as the placer law, in contradistinction to the lode
law of 1866, and was amendatory of and supplemental
to that law. It provided, in terms, that claims usually
called "placers," including all forms of deposit, excepting veins of quartz or other rock in place, should be
subject to entry and patent under like circumstances and
conditions and upon similar proceedings as were provided for vein or lode claims, with the exception that
a survey was not necessary where the proposed entry
conformed to legal subdivisions. It fixed the price for
such lands at two dollars and fifty cents per acre, and
authorized their subdivision into ten-acre tracts. It
limited the extent of a placer location, whether by an
individual or an association of persons, to one hundred
and sixty acres. Hitherto no limitation had been
imposed as to the area which might be included in a
location.[1] It also provided, that where a person or
association of persons shall have held and worked their
claims for a period equal to the time prescribed by the
statute of limitations for mining claims of the state or
territory where the same may be situated, evidence of
possession and working of the claims for such period
should be sufficient, in the absence of adverse claims,
to entitle the applicant to a patent.[2] In other words,
possession and working for the statutory period, with-

[1] St. Louis Smelting Co. v. Kemp, 104 U. S. 636.
[2] The land department construed this provision to apply to lode claims
as well as placers. Circ. Inst.—Copp's Min. Dec., p. 253.

out location, ripened into an equitable title against the government itself.

As we have heretofore observed, placer claims were first patentable under this act.[1]

The historical importance of the act (the full text of which will be found in the appendix). lies in the extension of the right to patent to placers and other forms of deposit not included within the lode law of 1866.

§ 63. **Local rules and customs after the passage of the act.**—Under the placer law, placer locations were still to conform to local rules as to the extent of the claims, subject to the limitation that no more than one hundred and sixty acres could be located by an individual or an association of persons. In this respect individuals and associations seem to have been placed upon the same footing; that is, either might take up one hundred and sixty acres.[2]

With this limitation, and the requirement that placer locations upon surveyed land should conform to the public surveys, the manner of locating, working, and conditions under which forfeiture arose were left to local regulation. The act remained in force less than two years, when it was superseded by the general mining act of May 10, 1872, which preserved its essential features.

§ 64. **Accession to the national domain during the third period.**—The purchase of Alaska from Russia, in March, 1867, was the only accession to the public domain within this period. It was not until 1884 however, that the laws relating to mining claims and rights incident thereto became operative in this district.

---

[1] Deffeback v. Hawke, 115 U. S. 392, 6 Sup. Ct. Rep. 95; Moxon v. Wilkinson, 2 Mont. 421.

[2] St. Louis Smelting Co. v. Kemp, Fed. Cas., No. 12,239A.

The act providing for a civil government for Alaska [1]
made such laws applicable, subject to regulations to be
prescribed by the secretary of the interior,[2] and also
provided that parties who had previously located mines
or mineral privileges therein should not be disturbed,
but should be allowed to perfect their claims. Prior to
the passage of this act patents for mining claims in
Alaska could not be obtained.[3]

[1] May 17, 1884—23 Stats. at Large, p. 24.
[2] 4 Land Decisions, p. 128; Meydenbaur v. Stevens, 78 Fed. 787, 789.
[3] Commissioner's letter—Copp's Min. Dec., p. 215.

CHAPTER V.

FOURTH PERIOD: FROM THE ENACTMENT OF THE LAW OF MAY 10, 1872, TO THE PRESENT TIME.

§ 68. The act of May 10, 1872.

§ 69. Declaration of government-al policy.

§ 70. Changes made by the act—Division of the subject.

§ 71. Changes made with regard to lode claims.

§ 72. Changes made with regard to other claims.

§ 73. New provisions affecting both classes of claims.

§ 74. Tunnel and millsites.

§ 75. Legislation subsequent to the act of 1872.

§ 76. Local rules and customs since the passage of the act.

§ 77. Accession to the national domain during the fourth period.

§ 68. **The act of May 10, 1872.**—On May 10, 1872, congress passed a law entitled "An act to promote the "development of the mining resources of the United "States," which reaffirmed the policy of the government as to the exploration, development, and purchase of its mineral lands by its citizens, or those who had declared their intentions to become such, yet, particularly with respect to lode claims, it made a radical departure. This act is practically embodied in the Revised Statutes of the United States, and, to all intents and purposes, constitutes the present system. It is printed in full in the appendix, where will also be found the various sections of the revision embodying its terms. It is not our purpose here to deal with it analytically. The entire treatise will practically be devoted to a discussion and exposition of it. It is our present purpose

to simply outline its salient features, draw attention
to the changes in the law made by the act, and give it
its proper place in the history of mining legislation.

§ 69. **Declaration of governmental policy.**—With
reference to the declaration of governmental policy, it
embodies the spirit of the preceding enactments, making
such changes in expression as were necessitated by
substituting one enactment, embracing all classes of
mineral lands, for two practically separate ones, dealing
with two distinct classes.

The act of 1866 declared that the mineral lands of
the public domain should thenceforward be free and
open to exploration and occupation by all citizens and
those who had declared their intention to become such,
and granted the privilege to the claimants of a vein, or
lode, of obtaining title to the *mine*. The act of 1870
extended like privileges to the owners of placer and
other forms of deposit. The act of May 10, 1872,
declares that all *mineral deposits* in land belonging to
the United States are hereby open to exploration and
purchase, and the *lands in which they are found to
occupation and purchase*.[1] The language in italics, particularly the last sentence, "the lands in which they are
" found," seems to foreshadow the intent of the act in
its radical departure from the method theretofore in
vogue of locating lode claims. As a declaration of
policy, however, we can see no essential difference in
the spirit of the old and that of the new. The latter
was, to all intents and purposes, a reaffirmance of the
former. Let us briefly examine and discuss the changes
made by the act in other respects, bearing in mind that

[1] Campbell *v.* Ellet, 167 U. S. 116, 17 Sup. Ct. Rep. 765; Calhoun G.
M. Co. *v.* Ajax G. M. Co., 182 U. S. 499, 508, 21 Sup. Ct. Rep. 885; Doe *v.*
Waterloo M. Co., 54 Fed. 935, 937; Parrot S. and C. Co. *v.* Heinze,
64 Pac. 326, 329, 25 Mont. 139.

it is not our present intention to critically discuss the latter law in all its aspects. We simply wish to invite attention to the principal modifications of the old system, and enumerate the salient features of the new.

§ 70. Changes made by the act — Division of the subject. — We can best deal with the subject by distributing it into three distinct heads : —

(1) Changes made with regard to lode claims;

(2) Changes made with regard to other claims;

(3) New provisions affecting both classes of claims.

We will discuss these in the order enumerated.

§ 71. Changes made with regard to lode claims.— The act of 1866 left the manner of locating these claims to local regulation, limiting the linear extent of each individual claim to two hundred feet, except in case of the discoverer, and to a maximum of three thousand feet to an association of persons.

We have seen that under the local rules locations were made of the *vein* and a given number of linear feet on the course was claimed; also, that prior to patent the locator could follow that vein, wheresoever it might run, to the extent claimed. His surface ground was for the convenient working of his lode, and its extent was regulated entirely by local custom. His right to the vein in length or depth was not dependent upon the form or extent of the surface ground. When he applied for and received a patent, he received title to but one lode, and could only follow that on its course to the extent which it was included within his surface lines. While end lines were implied, his right to pursue the vein in depth was not based upon their substantial parallelism.

The new law changed all this. As was said by Judge Beatty, "Disagreeable as the awakening may be, it is

" time we are opening our eyes to the fact that a new
" system has been introduced."[1]

Under the act of 1872 the miner locates a surface
which must be so defined as to include the top, or apex,
of his lode. Failing in this, he obtains nothing. If he
mistakes the course of his vein, it is his loss. He can
only hold the vein on its course to the extent that the
top, or apex, thereof is found within his boundaries.[2]
He may thus acquire a superficies fifteen hundred feet
in length by six hundred feet in width, if local regulations do not restrict these measurements.

In other words, under the old law he located the *lode*.
Under the new, he must locate a piece of land containing the top, or apex, of the lode. While the vein is still
the principal thing, in that it is for the sake of the vein
that the location is made, the location must be of a
piece of land including the top, or apex, of the vein.
If he makes such a location, containing the top, or apex,
of his discovered lode, he will be entitled to all other
lodes having their tops, or apices, within their surface
boundaries.[3] His end lines must be parallel and crosswise of the vein; otherwise, he cannot pursue his lode
or lodes on their downward course beyond vertical
planes drawn through his surface side lines, (and
perhaps, these side lines produced, as in such case the
side lines perform the functions of end lines). The
law in terms does not so state; but this is the interpretation reached by the courts.[4]

The foregoing states the essential differences in

---

[1] Gleeson *v.* Martin White M. Co., 13 Nev. 442, 459.

[2] Del Monte M. and M. Co. *v.* Last Chance M. Co., 171 U. S. 55, 84;
18 Sup. Ct. Rep. 895; Montana Ore Purchasing Co. *v.* Boston and M. C. C.
and S. M. Co., 20 Mont. 336, 51 Pac. 159; Lellie Lode Mine Claim,
31 L. D. 21.

[3] Del Monte M. and M. Co. *v.* Last Chance M. Co., 171 U. S. 55, 88,
18 Sup. Ct. Rep. 895; Calhoun G. M. Co. *v.* Ajax G. M. Co., 27 Colo. 1,
83 Am. St. Rep. 17, 59 Pac. 607; *Id.*, 182 U. S. 499, 508, 21 Sup. Ct.
Rep. 885.

[4] See, *post*, § 586.

theory between the two acts. By this act of 1872 there was also granted to the owners of "one lode" patents, or locations, all lodes other than the one originally located, with the right to follow them in depth.

It may also be observed that the act of 1866 applied to claims upon lodes, or veins, of quartz, or other rock in place, bearing gold, silver, cinnabar, or copper. With reference to claims located prior thereto, the act of 1872 added to the list of metallic substances named lead, tin, and "other valuable deposits."

The act also contained rules for the determination of controversies between claimants of cross lodes and those uniting on the dip, and other minor details, all of which will be considered at the proper time.

§ 72. **Changes made with regard to other claims.**— No radical changes in the method of acquiring title to placers and other forms of deposit not in place were made by the act; but the quantity of ground which might be acquired by an individual was limited to twenty acres. The act is silent as to the quantity which might be taken by an association of persons. Judge Hallett was of the opinion that the one-hundred-and-sixty-acre limitation in this respect contained in the act of 1870 remained unrepealed.[1] Be that as it may, the Revised Statutes re-enacted this provision of the act of 1870.[2]

Provisions were also made for obtaining titles to lodes known to exist within placers, and reserving such lodes from the operation of the placer patents, where they were not claimed by the placer applicant, a subject upon which the act of 1870 was silent.[3]

---

[1] St. Louis Smelting Co. v. Kemp, Fed. Cas., No. 12,239A.

[2] Rev. Stats., § 2330.

[3] Where entry and payment has been made under the act of 1870, the decision of the land department is conclusive that the land was placer, and that there were no "known lodes." Crane's Gulch Placer M. Co. v. Scherrer, 134 Cal. 350, 86 Am. St. Rep. 279, 66 Pac. 487.

§ **73. New provisions affecting both classes of claims.**
—The act of 1872 went beyond the preceding legislation in many details. It fixed the amount of annual work to be performed in order to maintain the integrity of locations made both before and after the passage of the act. It provided for the marking of the boundaries of claims, prescribed the contents of records where local rules required record, and the conditions under which forfeiture might be worked. The proceedings to obtain patent and the method of asserting and determining adverse claims were much more elaborate than in the preceding act, as well as much more satisfactory.

§ **74. Tunnels and millsites.**—The act also provided a method of acquiring title to non-mineral land for the purpose of a millsite, either in connection with a located lode or where used by the owner of a mill or reduction works. It also incorporated a provision with reference to tunnels as a means of discovering blind lodes and securing certain rights on the discovered lodes to the locator and projector of the tunnel. These subjects will be fully discussed in their appropriate place.

§ **75. Legislation subsequent to the act of 1872.**— Several amendments were made to the original act and some supplemental legislation of a minor character is to be noted before closing this historical review. A brief enumeration of these acts is all that will be here required.

The act of February 18, 1873,[1] excepted Michigan, Wisconsin, and Minnnesota from the operation of the general mining laws. Mineral lands in these states, with the exception of salines,[2] are subject to entry under agricultural land laws.[3]

---

[1] 17 Stats. at Large, p. 465; C. M. L. 23.
[2] See, *post*, §§ 513-515.
[3] United States *v.* Omdahl, 25 L. D. 157.

The acts of March 1, 1873,[1] and June 6, 1874,[2] extended the time for the performance of annual labor on claims located prior to the act of 1872; and the act of January 22, 1880,[3] fixed a uniform time for the performance of labor upon all claims located subsequent to the act of 1872.[4]

The act of March 3, 1873,[5] excepted Missouri and Kansas, and that of March 3, 1883,[6] exempted Alabama, from the operation of the general mining acts. The act of January 12, 1877,[7] in relation to salines; the act of June 3, 1878,[8] in relation to timber cutting, and an act passed on the same day,[9] commonly known as "the " stone and timber act," and the amendment to the latter act, passed August 4, 1892; [10] the act of February 11, 1897, specifically authorizing the location of petroleum lands under the placer mining laws; [11] the act passed in 1900, providing a code for Alaska, and providing a method for acquiring beach claims; [12] the act of January 31, 1901, extending the mining laws to saline lands; [13] and the act of 1902 relating to the Philippine islands, and outlining a system for locating and patenting mining claims therein,[14] are the only other enactments during the period that are worthy of note.

[1] 17 Stats. at Large, p. 483; C. M. L. 23.
[2] 18 Stats. at Large, p. 61; C. M. L. 23.
[3] 21 Stats. at Large, p. 61; C. M. L. 24.
[4] McGinnis v. Egbert, 8 Colo. 41, 5 Pac. 652; Slavonian M. Co. v. Dacavich, 7 Saw. 217, 7 Fed. Rep. 331.
[5] 19 Stats. at Large, p. 52.
[6] 1 Land Decisions, p. 656.
[7] 19 Stats. at Large, p. 221.
[8] 20 Stats. at Large, p. 88.
[9] Id., p. 89.
[10] Sup. R. S., vol. ii, p. 65.
[11] See, post, § 422.
[12] 31 U. S. Stats., pp. 321, 329.
[13] See, post, §§ 513, 515.
[14] Stats. 1st Sess. 57th Cong., p. 691.

Some of these acts have performed a temporary purpose; others, to some extent, form a part of the existing system, and, as such, will be again referred to in treating of the different subjects to which they relate.

With reference to the Revised Statutes, approved June 22, 1874, it may be said that in the main they were a mere revision and consolidation of the general laws existing and in force on December 1, 1873. The existing system of mining law, with the exception of a few acts passed since December 1, 1873, is found codified or consolidated into the Revised Statutes. In treating of this system in the future we will simply refer to the sections of the Revised Statutes, unless the subject under discussion necessitates a reference to the original act.

§ 76. **Local rules and customs since the passage of the act.**—Subject to the limitations enumerated in the act, the miners of each mining district may make regulations not in conflict with the laws of the United States or with the laws of the state or territory in which the district is situated, governing the location, manner of recording, and amount of work necessary to hold possession. While this privilege is thus granted, it is not universally exercised. Generally, in California the district organizations are things of the past; and we believe it is the case in other states and territories. The mining laws themselves are, under ordinary conditions, sufficient for all practical purposes. Yet we do encounter districts which still possess a potential existence. Therefore, local rules must be dealt with as a part of the existing system, though much limited in their scope.

They have performed their part in the scheme of evolution, and have, for the most part, disappeared, to be replaced by higher forms of legislation.

As to the state and territorial legislation, the tendency in later years has been in the direction of individual mining codes, more or less comprehensive. While the existing federal laws largely dispense with the necessity for local regulation and circumscribe the field within which states may legitimately act, yet we find individual codes in some instances re-enacting many of the provisions of the federal laws and supplementing them with numerous provisions, some of which are subject to the criticism of being in conflict with the paramount law. The force and effect of this class of legislation will receive due attention when the subjects to which they relate are under discussion.

What is here said with reference to the tendency to abandon the system of local rules has its exception in the district of Alaska. That district has no legislature. This fact, taken with the unique manner of occurrence of some of the auriferous deposits there discovered, has resulted in the framing of local codes, which are in some instances quite elaborate. Some of the provisions are of doubtful value, and, as might be expected, some are repugnant to the federal laws. In another portion of this treatise we shall endeavor to point out the legitimate scope of such regulations and the limits within which the miners are permitted by the congressional laws to legislate.

§ 77   **Accession to the national domain during the fourth period.** —By treaty of cession entered into between the United States and the republic of Hawaii, adopted by joint resolution of congress July 7, 1898, all lands within the Hawaiian islands covered by the treaty which were the property of the republic, as distinguished from lands held in private ownership, passed to the United States, and became subject to the disposal of congress the same as other public lands. As yet the public land laws of the United States have not been extended to the new territory of Hawaii, and, pending further action by congress, the laws of the republic existing at the time of the treaty of cession regulating the sale and disposal of the public lands are continued in force. None of these last-named laws provide for the sale or other disposition of lands classified as mineral. It is extremely doubtful if there exists within any of these islands any deposits of commercial value which fall within the definition of mineral lands, as these terms are construed by the courts of the United States.

By the treaty of Paris terminating the Spanish-American war, there was ceded to the United States by Spain the island of Porto Rico. By this cession all lands in that and other islands of the West Indies (excepting Cuba) which theretofore belonged to the crown of Spain passed to the United States. By act of congress, July 1, 1902,[1] all such lands were ceded by the United States to the territory of Porto Rico for the use and benefit of the people of that island. As to what, if any, may be the mineral resources of Porto Rico, no accurate data is obtainable. The sale and disposal of all public lands within Porto Rico is intrusted entirely to the territorial government. None of the federal land laws are there in operation, and as yet the island government has enacted no laws either classifying its lands or providing for their sale or other disposal.

By the same treaty last above referred to the United States acquired from Spain the Philippine archipelago, the treaty passing to the first-named power ''all build-'' ings, wharves, barracks, forts, structures, public high-'' ways, and other immovable property which, in con-

---

[1] Stats. 1st Sess. 57th Congress, p. 731.

" formity with the law, belong to the public domain,
" and as such belong to the crown of Spain."

It was not until July 1, 1902, that any action was
taken by congress to provide a system of mining laws
for these islands, although the need for early legislation
on the subject was generally felt and urged upon the
attention of congress.[1] On that date there was approved
an act temporarily providing for the administration
of the affairs of civil government in the Philippine
islands,[2] which contained a code of laws governing the
disposal of public lands valuable for minerals much
like the federal laws on the subject in force in the mining states. The notable difference is, that the Philippine
code denies to the mineral claimant the right "to mine
" outside the boundary lines of his claim continued
" vertically downward,"—*i. e.* the right of extralateral
pursuit of the vein.

The full text of the law in its application to public
mineral lands in these islands is printed in the appendix.

[1] Report of Chief of Mining Bureau, Appendix K, Taft Commission
Report, part II, p. 354.
[2] Stats. 1st Sess. 57th Congress, p. 691.

CHAPTER VI.

THE FEDERAL SYSTEM.

§ 80. Conclusions deduced from preceding chapters.

§ 81. Outline of the federal system —Scope of the treatise.

§ 80. Conclusions deduced from preceding chapters.

—In the preceding chapters we have given a short synopsis of such foreign mining laws as might reasonably be supposed to have exerted an influence on our system. We have also traced the origin and gradual development of the body of substantive law which now governs the acquisition and enjoyment of mining rights upon the public domain of the United States, and have endeavored to show the relationship which the several states have occupied in the past, and now occupy, with reference to public mineral lands within their respective boundaries. From the general review, we are permitted to deduce the following general conclusions:—

Mines in the United States are not ranked as the property of society, the working of which is to be confided to the federal government. Mining with us is not a "public utility." It is simply a private industry, to be fostered and encouraged as all other economic industries are fostered and encouraged; but the exploitation and development of mines are no more governmental functions than is the cultivation of the soil or the business of manufacturing. The United States is the paramount proprietor of the public mineral lands, holding them not as an attribute of sovereignty, but as property acquired by cession and purchase. As such paramount proprietor, it has the same right of dominion and power of alienation as is incident to absolute ownership in individuals.[1] By the term "public lands," we mean such as are subject to sale or other disposal under general laws. Land to which any claims or rights of others have attached does not fall within the designation of "public land."[2]

"Public lands belonging to the United States for " whose sale or other disposition congress has made " provision by its general laws, are to be regarded as " legally open for entry and sale under such laws, " unless some particular lands have been withdrawn " from sale by congressional authority, either express " or implied."[3]

Whenever a tract of land has once been legally appropriated for any purpose, from that moment it becomes severed from the mass of public lands.[4]

While in the various treaties of cession and purchase through which territory was acquired and added to the national domain the federal government recognized and obligated itself to protect the rights and equities of grantees of the ceding nation or state, and by virtue of its federated system of government held certain property in trust for future states,[5] the great mass of the

[1] Lux v. Haggin, 69 Cal. 255, 10 Pac. 674.

[2] Newhall v. Sanger, 92 U. S. 761; Bardon v. Northern Pac. R. R. Co., 145 U. S. 535, 538, 12 Sup. Ct. Rep. 856; Mann v. Tacoma Land Co., 153 U. S. 273, 284, 14 Sup. Ct. Rep. 820; McFadden v. Mountain View M. and M. Co., 97 Fed. 670, 679; State of Louisiana, 30 L. D. 276, and cases cited.

[3] Lockhart v. Johnson, 181 U. S. 516, 520, 21 Sup. Ct. Rep. 665.

[4] Wilcox v. McConnell, 13 Peters, 498; Teller v. United States, 113 Fed. 273.

[5] Tide lands—Shively v. Bowlby, 152 U. S. 1, 14 Sup. Ct. Rep. 548; In re Logan, 29 L. D. 395; Nome Transp. Co., 29 L. D. 447; Lands under navigable waters—Pollard's Lessee v. Hagan, 3 How. 212; Argillite Ornamental Stone Co., 29 L. D. 585.

acquired territory falls within the designation of "pub-
" lic lands," and passed to the United States untrammeled by either the tradition, laws, or policy of the
ceding power, or by compact with the new states.[1]

As such absolute owner, the government might, at
its pleasure, withhold its lands from occupation or purchase, lease them for limited periods,[2] donate them to
states for educational or other purposes, and to individuals or corporations to aid in the construction of railways and other internal improvements, sell or otherwise
dispose of them absolutely or conditionally, and prescribe the terms and conditions under which private
individuals might acquire permanent ownership, or the
right of temporary enjoyment.[3]

"With respect to the public domain the constitution
" vests in congress the power of disposition and of
" making all needful rules and regulations. That power
" is subject to no limitations; congress has the absolute
" right to prescribe the terms, the conditions, and the
" mode of transferring this property, or any part of
" it, to designate the persons to whom the transfer shall
" be made. No state legislation can interfere with this
" right or embarrass its existence." [4]

On the other hand, congress has no power to legislate
after the government has conveyed its title.[5]

The regalian doctrine of ownership in the crown of
the royal metals, wheresoever found, based upon the
theory that these metals were a prerogative of the crown,
which prevailed in England, France, Spain, and Mexico, was never recognized in this country. A grant or

[1] Pollard's Lessee v. Hagan, 3 How. 212.
[2] United States v. Gratiot, 1 McLean, 454, Fed. Cas., No. 15,249; S. C.,
14 Peters, 526.
[3] Black v. Elkhorn M. Co., 163 U. S. 445, 16 Sup. Ct. Rep. 1101.
[4] Gibson v. Chouteau, 13 Wall. 92, 99.
[5] Cone v. Roxana G. M. and T. Co., 2 Legal Adv. 350 (C. C. Dist. Colo.
1899).

conveyance by the United States carries all minerals, unless reserved expressly or by implication in the law or instrument purporting to pass the title.[1]

In countries from which the United States acquired its properties the contrary doctrine prevailed, and minerals did not pass to the grantee unless specially named in the instrument.[2]

§ 81. Outline of the federal system — Scope of the treatise.—It follows as a corollary from what has been heretofore stated, that the system of rules which sanctions and regulates the acquisition and enjoyment of mining rights, and defines the conditions under which title may be obtained to mineral lands within the public domain of the United States, is composed of several elements, most of which find expression in positive legislative enactment. Others, while depending for their existence and force upon the sanction of the general government, either express or implied, are, in a measure, controlled by local environment, and are evidenced by the expressed will of local assemblages, embodied in written regulations, or rest in unwritten customs peculiar to the vicinage.

American mining law may therefore be said to be found expressed:—

(1) In the legislation of congress;

(2) In the legislation of the various states and territories supplementing congressional legislation and in harmony therewith;

(3) In local rules and customs, or regulations estab-

---

[1] Fremont v. Flower, 17 Cal. 199, 79 Am. Dec. 123; Barden v. N. P. R. R., 154 U. S. 288, 14 Sup. Ct. Rep. 1030; Davis v. Weibbold, 139 U. S. 507, 11 Sup. Ct. Rep. 628.

[2] Fremont v. Flower, 17 Cal. 199, 79 Am. Dec. 123; United States v. Castillero, 2 Black, 1; Halleck's Introduction to De Fooz on the Law of Mines, § 7.

lished in different localities, not in conflict with federal legislation or that of the state or territory wherein they are operative.

This system does not seek to regulate or control mines or mining within lands held in private ownership, except such only as are acquired directly from the government under the mining laws, and then only forming a muniment of the locator's or purchaser's title. It does not require the payment of tribute or royalty as a condition upon which the public mineral lands may be explored or worked. As heretofore observed, it treats the government simply as a proprietor holding the paramount title to its public domain, with right of disposal upon such terms and conditions, and subject to such limitations, as the law-making power may prescribe. With the exception, perhaps, of saline lands and lands containing deposits of coal and some of the baser substances, the system is practically confined in its operation to those states and territories lying wholly or in part west of the hundredth meridian, embracing the states of California, Colorado, Oregon, Washington, Nevada, Idaho, Montana, North Dakota, South Dakota, Wyoming, Utah, the territories of Arizona, New Mexico, and the district of Alaska.[1] These comprise the precious-metal-bearing states and territories of the public domain. This system, as thus defined and limited, is the subject of this treatise.

[1] As to saline lands, the act of congress of January 31, 1901, placed them in the category of mineral lands, and authorized their entry and purchase under the laws relating to placers. This act applies to all public land states wherein there are unoccupied lands of the United States containing salt springs or deposits of salt in any form (Circ. Inst., 31 L. D. 131). The general mining laws are also in force in Florida, Mississippi, Louisiana, and Arkansas; but from a practical standpoint their operation in these states is not very extensive. By act

This system is by no means symmetrical or perfect. It is one of the most difficult branches of the law to even logically arrange for the purpose of treatment, and the embarrassments surrounding its philosophical exposition are almost insurmountable. It has received attention in a fragmentary way at the hands of eminent writers, who are most logical and instructive when discoursing upon its imperfections and apparent absurdities. The courts are not harmonious with regard to rules of interpretation. No one tribunal has exclusive jurisdiction to determine questions arising under it. Its proper interpretation does not always involve federal questions, conferring upon the federal courts jurisdiction. It has thus come to pass that the courts of last resort in several of the states and territories, in construing the same law, have reached diametrically opposite conclusions; and in many of its most important features we have conflicting theories enumerated by different courts of equal dignity and equal ability, until we are almost constrained to say that "chaos has come " again."

It is not our purpose to condemn the system, but to

of congress all lands in Oklahoma were originally declared to be agricultural (26 Stats. at Large, p. 1026). On March 3, 1901, (31 Stats. at Large, p. 680,) congress extended the mining laws over the lands within the territory of Oklahoma ceded to the United States by the Comanche, Kiowa, and Apache Indians (Instructions, 31 L. D. 154). Porto Rico, the Hawaiian Islands, and the Philippines contain public lands of the United States, but the land laws have not been extended over them as yet (Op. Atty.-Gen., 29 L. D. 32; McFadden v. Mountain View M. Co., 97 Fed. 670). In Hawaii the land laws existing during the republic are continued in force (Act of April 30, 1900; Instructions, 30 L. D. 195). Congress has ceded to the territory of Porto Rico all the public lands for the use and benefit of the people of that island (Stats. 1st Sess. 57th Cong., p. 731). Congress has recently enacted a comprehensive mining code for the Philippine islands, a full discussion of which will be found in another portion of this treatise.

endeavor to deal with it fairly as we find it. In the language of Judge Beatty,—

"Nobody can pretend that it is perfect; but to our
" minds it is a great improvement on the system which
" it displaced. We are willing to admit that cases may
" arise to which it will be difficult to apply the law; but
" this only proves that such cases escaped the foresight
" of congress, or that, although they foresaw the possi-
" bility of such cases occurring, they considered that
" possibility so remote as not to afford a reason for
" departing from the simplicity of the plan they chose
" to adopt. So far the wisdom of the congressional
" plan has been sufficiently vindicated by experience."[1]

[1] Gleeson v. Martin White M. Co., 13 Nev. 442.

TITLE III.

LANDS SUBJECT TO APPROPRIATION UNDER THE MINING LAWS, AND THE PERSONS WHO MAY ACQUIRE RIGHTS THEREIN.

CHAPTER

I. "MINERAL LANDS" AND KINDRED TERMS DEFINED.

II. THE PUBLIC SURVEYS AND THE RETURN OF THE SURVEYOR-GENERAL.

III. STATUS OF LAND AS TO TITLE AND POSSESSION.

IV. OF THE PERSONS WHO MAY ACQUIRE RIGHTS IN PUBLIC MINERAL LANDS.

CHAPTER I.

"MINERAL LANDS" AND KINDRED TERMS DEFINED.

§ 85. Necessity for definition of terms.

§ 86. Terms of reservation employed in various acts.

§ 87. "Mine" and "mineral" indefinite terms.

§ 88. English denotation—"Mine" and "mineral" in their primary sense.

§ 89. Enlarged meaning of "mine."

§ 90. "Mineral" as defined by the English and Scotch authorities.

§ 91. English rules of interpretation.

§ 92. Substances classified as mineral under the English decisions.

§ 93. American cases defining "mine" and "mineral."

§ 94. "Mineral lands" as defined by the American tribunals.

§ 95. Interpretation of terms by the land department.

§ 96. American rules of statutory interpretation.

§ 97. Substances held to be mineral by the land department.

§ 98. Rules for determining mineral character of land.

§ 85. **Necessity for definition of terms.** — It becomes necessary for us to determine precisely what character of lands fall within the purview of the mining laws, and to define, at least with reasonable certainty, what may be the subject of appropriation under them. To say that these laws apply to mineral lands only, and that mineral lands alone can be occupied and enjoyed under them, states the fact broadly. But what are *mineral lands ?* What is the test of the character of a given tract, when its mineral quality is asserted by a claimant under the mining laws, and that assertion is denied by an agricultural claimant to the same tract? To enable us to intelligently answer these questions, we are called upon to consider the phrases employed in the various acts of congress, and sift them down to a generic or comprehensive term, from which we may proceed to evolve a definition as accurate as the nature of the subject will permit.

§ 86.   **Terms of reservation employed in various acts.** —As we have already observed,[1] in the earlier legislation of congress, establishing a system for the pre-emption and settlement of the public domain, as well as in most of the legislative grants to the states for universities and schools, for the construction of public buildings, and in aid of railroads and other works of internal improvement, mineral lands were uniformly reserved from the operation of the law, and were excepted from the grant. The terms employed in specifying what was reserved are not altogether uniform. A few examples will illustrate this.

The pre-emption act of 1841 (section ten) provided that no lands on which are situated any *known* salines or mines should be liable to entry under and by virtue of the provisions of the act.[2]

The act of September 27, 1850, creating the office of surveyor-general of Oregon, and providing for surveys, and making donations to settlers, directs "that no min-" eral lands, nor lands reserved for salines, shall be "liable to any claim under and by virtue of the pro-" visions of this act."

---

[1] See, *ante*, § 47.

[2] "Congress on March 3, 1891, by an act entitled 'An act to repeal "'the timber culture laws and for other purposes' (26 Stats., p. 1095), "repealed the pre-emption law, and thereby also eliminated from the "homestead law the words 'known salines or mines,' which were in the "latter by adoption (Rev. Stats., § 2289). But congress left in force "the provisions of section 2302 of the Revised Statutes, by which it is "declared, among other things, that 'no mineral lands shall be liable to "'entry and settlement under the provisions of the homestead laws.'" (Cosmos Exploration Co. *v.* Gray Eagle Oil Co., 104 Fed. 40, 46.)

The act of March 3, 1853, for the survey of public lands in California, the granting of pre-emption rights therein, and for other purposes, directs that none other than township lines shall be surveyed where the lands are mineral or are deemed unfit for cultivation, excluding in express terms "mineral lands" from the operation of the pre-emption act of 1841, and further interdicting any person from obtaining the benefit of the act by a settlement or location on "mineral lands." [1]

By the fourth section of the act of July 22, 1854, to establish the offices of surveyors-general of New Mexico, Kansas, and Nebraska, to grant donations to actual settlers therein, and for other purposes, it is directed that none of the provisions of the act shall extend to "mineral lands," salines, etc.

The act of July 4, 1866, giving authority for varying surveys from the rectangular system in Nevada, reserves from sale in all cases "lands valuable for mines " of gold, silver, quicksilver, or copper."

The acts of July 1, 1862,[2] and July 2, 1864,[3] commonly known as the "Pacific railroad acts," reserve "mineral " lands," excepting coal and iron, from the designation.

Illustrations might be multiplied indefinitely, but the foregoing are sufficient for our present purpose.

No legislative interpretation or definition of the term " mineral lands," which were so reserved and excepted, was ever attempted. This was left for judicial or departmental construction.

As during the early periods of our legislative history the ownership of these reserved lands remained in the government, and were withheld from private ownership, conflicts of asserted title rarely, if ever, arose, and opportunity for judicial interpretation was not afforded.

---

[1] Public Domain, p. 311.
[2] 12 Stats. at Large, p. 489.
[3] 13 Stats. at Large, p. 356.

When a change in the policy of the government took place, and that which had theretofore been uniformly reserved became subject to sale and appropriation as "mineral land," "lands valuable for mines," " lands containing valuable mineral deposits," "lands " claimed for valuable deposits," and other designations, *ejusdem generis,* the necessity arose for a rule of interpretation sufficiently comprehensive to embrace the terms when used either as words of exception in a grant or act of congress, or as defining the subject of a grant under the mining laws.

While the land department, in passing upon the character of land sought to be entered as mineral under these laws, in the absence of protest or controversy as to its character, might be satisfied with a much less degree of proof than would be required to bring the same tract within the excepting clause of a prior grant, logically the term "mineral lands," and its equivalent terms, wherever used in the acts or grants of congress, either as words of reservation or in the mining laws authorizing their appropriation, has the same limit and breadth of signification. What had been reserved by one series of legislative enactments, and in the different legislative grants, is identically that the appropriation of which is encouraged and sanctioned by another series of laws.

The term "known mines," as used in the pre-emption act of 1841, and in the homestead law, which was in the latter by adoption,[1] is not the precise equivalent of the term "mineral lands," as used in the mining laws, and should undoubtedly receive a more limited interpretation. As was said by Judge Ross:—

"The words 'mineral lands' are certainly more gen- " eral and much broader than the words 'lands in which " 'are situated any known salines or mines,' formerly

---

[1] Rev. Stats., § 2289.

" existing in the pre-emption and homestead laws. The
" wide distinction between them is clearly pointed out
" in Bardon v. Northern Pacific Railroad Company, 154
" U. S. 288; Davis (admr.) v. Wiebbold, 139 U. S. 507;
" Deffeback v. Hawke, 115 U. S. 392."[1]

This discussion of this particular term may therefore
remain in abeyance until we enter upon the subject of
pre-emption claims in conflict with asserted mining
rights.

Eliminating, therefore, from present consideration
"known mines," as the words are used in the act above
referred to, we are called upon to consider the following
terms and phrases:—

(1) "Mineral lands," as used in statutes reserving
them from sale, or other disposal, and in section one of
the act of July 26, 1866;

(2) "All forms of deposit," in section twelve of the
act of July 9, 1870, and section twenty-three hundred
and twenty-nine of the Revised Statutes;

(3) "Lands containing valuable mineral deposits,"
in section one of the act of 1872, and section twenty-
three hundred and nineteen, Revised Statutes;

(4) "Land claimed for valuable deposits," in section
six, act of 1872, and section twenty-three hundred and
twenty-five, Revised Statutes;

(5) "Lands valuable for minerals," in section twenty-three hundred and eighteen, Revised Statutes;

(6) "Lands valuable for mines," as used in the act
of July 4, 1866, giving authority for varying surveys
in Nevada.

While the supreme court of the United States [2] seems
to intimate that the expression "lands containing valu-
" able mineral deposits," used for the first time in

---

[1] Cosmos Exploration Co. v. Gray Eagle Oil Co., 104 Fed. 20, 46.
[2] Deffeback v. Hawke, 115 U. S. 392, 6 Sup. Ct. Rep. 95.

the act of 1872, and re-enacted in the Revised Statutes, is of broader import than the term "mineral lands" used in the previous acts, a careful study and analysis of all cases decided by that court, as well as all courts in the mining regions, fail to disclose any material distinction in the meaning of the two terms. "Mineral "lands" are lands that contain "valuable mineral de-"posits," and *vice versa*. The same may be said of the other terms.

From a well-considered examination of all the authorities on this subject, there is no room for any conclusion other than that the expressions "mineral lands," "all "forms of deposits," "lands containing valuable min-"eral deposits," "valuable deposits," "lands valuable "for minerals," "lands valuable for mines," are, generally speaking, legal equivalents, and may be, and frequently are, used interchangeably.[1]

In this view our preliminary inquiry may be addressed to a consideration of the terms "mines" and "minerals."

§ 87. "Mine" and "mineral" indefinite terms.—
Mr. Ross Stewart, in the opening chapter of his valuable work on mines, quarries, and minerals in Scotland,[2] says:—

"The terms 'mine' and 'mineral' are not definite "terms: they are susceptible of limitation according to "the intention with which they are used; and in con-"struing them regard must be had not only to the deed "or statute in which they occur, but also to the relative "position of the parties interested and the substance "of the transaction or arrangement which the deed or "statute embodies. Consequently, in themselves, these "terms are incapable of a definition which would be "universally applicable." [3]

[1] See Brady's Mortgagee v. Harris, 29 L. D. 426, and cases cited.
[2] Edinburgh, 1894.
[3] Stewart on Mines, p. 1.

§ 88. **English denotation — "Mine" and "mineral"
in their primary sense.**—An examination of the English
authorities shows what may be appropriately termed
an evolution of denotation, beginning in the earlier
history of English jurisprudence with the primary or
etymological significance of the words, and gradually
enlarging their meanings until their original derivation
and early judicial application became all but obsolete.
In this primary sense, a "mine" denoted an underground excavation made for the purpose of getting minerals;[1] and, as a corollary, minerals primarily were
the substances obtained through underground excavations.

The word "mine" was used in contradistinction to
"quarry," and "minerals" meant substances of a mineral character which could only be worked by means of
mines, as distinguished from *quarries.*[2] In other words,
regard was there had entirely to the *mode* in which the
substance was obtained, and not to its chemical or
geological character.[3]

William's law dictionary [4] defines "minerals" to be
" anything that grows in mines and contains metals,"
and "mines" is defined as "quarries or places where-
" out anything is dug; this term is likewise applied
" to hidden treasure dug out of the earth." These
same definitions recur in Tomlin's law dictionary.[5]

Lord Halsbury says:—

"I should think that there could be no doubt that the
" word 'minerals' in old times meant the substances

[1] Midland Ry. Co. *v.* Haunchwood B. & T. Co. (1882), L. R. 20 Ch.
D. 552.
[2] Darvill *v.* Roper, 3 Drewry, 294.
[3] Bainbridge on Mines, 4th ed., p. 5.
[4] London, 1816.
[5] London, 1835.

" got out by mining; and I think 'mining' in old times
" meant subterranean excavation." [1]

§ 89. **Enlarged meaning of "mine."**—These primary
significations were soon enlarged, so that in time the
word "mine" was construed to mean, also, the place
where minerals were found, and soon came to be used
as an equivalent of "vein," "seam," "lode," or to
denote an aggregation of veins, and, under certain circumstances, to include quarries and minerals obtained
by open workings. [2]

§ 90. **"Mineral" as defined by the English and
Scotch authorities.**—In reference to the term "mineral,"
we quote the following from Bainbridge:—

"A mineral has been defined, in the narrow sense of
" the word, to be a fossil, or what is dug out of the earth,
" and which is predominantly metalliferous in char-
" acter. The term may, however, in the most enlarged
" sense, be described as comprising all the substances
" which now form, or which once formed, part of the
" solid body of the earth, both external and internal,
" and which are now destitute of and incapable of sup-
" porting animal or vegetable life. In this view, it will
" embrace as well the bare granite of the high moun-
" tains as the deepest hidden diamonds and metallic
" ores." [3]

Mr. Stewart says:—

"Both scientifically and popularly the term 'mineral'
" has been applied to substances whose chemical and
" physical properties are sufficiently uniform to admit
" of identification and classification, whether they exist
" in a mine or upon the surface of the ground." [4]

---

[1] Magistrates of Glasgow v. Farie, L. R. 13 App. Cas. 657.

[2] Midland Ry. Co. v. Haunchwood B. & T. Co. (1882), L. R. 20 Ch.
D. 558; Stewart on Mines, p. 2.

[3] Bainbridge on Mines, 4th ed., p. 1. See, also, Stewart on Mines, p. 9.

[4] Stewart on Mines, p. 9.

A few illustrations from comparatively recent authorities will enable us to understand the modern signification given to the term "mineral" by the English courts.

In Midland Railway *v.* Checkley,[1] Lord Romilly, master of the rolls, said:—

"Stone is, in my opinion, a mineral, and, in fact,
" everything except the mere surface which is used
" for agricultural purposes. Anything beyond that
" which is useful for any purpose whatever, whether
" it is gravel, marble, fire-clay, or the like, comes within
" the word 'mineral,' when there is a reservation of
" the mines and minerals from a grant of land."

In Midland Railway Co. *v.* Haunchwood B. & T. Co.,[2] Mr. Justice Kay expressed the view that "minerals" meant, primarily, all substances (other than the agricultural surface of the ground) "which may be got for
" manufacturing or mercantile purposes, whether from
" a mine, as the word would seem to signify, or such as
" stone or clay, which are gotten by open working."

In the leading case of Hext *v.* Gill,[3] the house of lords announced the rule that a reservation of "min
" erals" includes every substance which can be obtained from underneath the surface of the earth for the purpose of profit, unless there is something in the context or in the nature of the transaction to induce the court to give it a more limited meaning.[4]

In Attorney-General *v.* Welsh Granite Co.,[5] Lord Esher, master of the rolls, said:—

"The many cases which have been cited go to estab
" lish the definition, especially Attorney-General *v.*

---

[1] (1867), L. R. 4 Eq. C. 19.
[2] (1882), L. R. 20 Ch. D. 552.
[3] (1872), L. R. 7 Ch. App. 699.
[4] This doctrine was approved and followed in a later case (Attorney-General *v.* Tomline (1877), L. R. 5 Ch. D. 750).
[5] (1887), 35 W. R. 617.

" Mylchreest,[1] and Hext *v.* Gill, where Mellish, L. J.,
" states the result of authorities. It is evident from
" these cases that 'minerals' means substances which
" can be got from beneath the surface, not by mining
" only, but also by quarrying, for the purpose of
" profit."

In Magistrates of Glasgow *v.* Farie, before the house
of lords, involving the interpretation of a reservation
in an act of parliament authorizing the construction of
water-works,[2] wherein it was provided that the under-
takers of the project "shall not be entitled to any mines
" of coal, ironstone, slate, or other minerals under any
" land purchased by them," Lord Herschell thus announced his view:—

"I think the reservation must be taken to extend to
" all bodies of mineral substances lying together in
" seams, beds, or strata, as are commonly worked for
" profit." [3]

In Loosemore *v.* Tiverton and North Devon Ry. Co.,[4]
Mr. Justice Fry, following Hext *v.* Gill, says:—

"There being no such restrictive context in the pres-
" ent case, the inquiry is whether the clay which was
" got out was clay which could be worked for a profit."

Lord Halsbury, in the Farie case (*supra*), criticises
the doctrine of Hext *v.* Gill. He says:—

"In the first place, it introduces as one element the
" circumstances that the substance can be got at a
" profit. It is obvious that if that is an essential part
" of the definition, the question whether a particular
" substance is or is not a mineral may depend on the
" state of the market; and it may be that a mineral one
" year is not a mineral the next."

[1] (1879), 4 App. C. 294.
[2] Waterworks Clauses Act (1847), 10 & 11 Vict. c. 17.
[3] L. R. 13 App. C. 685.
[4] (1882), L. R. 22 Ch. D. 25.

Lord Herschell, in the same case, thus expresses his views:—

"In its widest significance the word 'mineral' proba-
" bly means every organic substance forming a part of
" the crust of the earth other than the layer of soil which
" sustains vegetable life. In some of the reported cases
" it seems to be laid down or assumed that to be a
" mineral a thing must be of commercial value or work-
" able at a profit. Be that as it may, it has been laid
" down that the word 'minerals,' when used in a legal
" document, or in any act of parliament, must be under-
" stood in its widest signification, unless there be some-
" thing in the context, or in the nature of the case, to
" control its meaning."[1]

Of course, the element of profitable working is in no sense a part of the definition of the word in its primary or etymological sense.

While these criticisms of Lord Herschell are plausible when the primary or etymological signification of the word is considered, yet the doctrine of Hext *v.* Gill and the later cases following it may be fairly said to present a reasonable definition in the light of the progressiveness of the age and advancement in the natural sciences, with which the courts seem to have kept pace.

This element of commercial value, which to a large extent controls the acquisition of mining titles in the United States, is by no means new. The German codes contained a limitation prohibiting the prospector from claiming mineral or ore which did not offer the basis for practical and *lucrative* mining or metallurgical operations. Under the French and Belgian systems, before a mining concession could be obtained, it was necessary "to ascertain whether the land contains a " layer which is susceptible of a profitable working."[2]

---

[1] Magistrates of Glasgow *v.* Farie (1888), L. R. 13 App. C. 689-690.

[2] Halleck's De Fooz on the Law of Mines, p. 110.

In Sweet's dictionary of English law,[1] we find the following definition:—

"In the most general sense of the term, minerals are " those parts of the earth which are capable of being " got from underneath the surface for the purpose of " profit."[2]

§ 91. **English rule of interpretation.** — Mr. Stewart enunciates certain rules as being sanctioned by current authority in England and Scotland, governing the construction of the term "mineral." These are as follows:—

"*First*—The word 'mineral,' when used in a legal " document or in an act of parliament, must be under- " stood in its widest signification, unless there be some- " thing in the context or nature of the case to control " its meaning.

"*Second*—The meaning of the word 'mineral,' " though not easily restricted, yields to the context " when the relative positions of the parties interested, " their intention, or the substance of the transaction so " indicates.

"*Third*—In doubtful cases, the custom of the district, " or such usages without which a deed or statute would " be inconsistent, may limit the word 'minerals.'

"*Fourth*—Where the terms 'mines' and 'minerals' " are both used in the same deed or statute, the word " 'minerals' is not on that account to suffer limitation " of its meaning."[3]

In treating of the rules governing the interpretation of American statutory law, we will have occasion to recur to the foregoing.

[1] London, 1882.
[2] This definition was also adopted in Rapalje and Lawrence's law dictionary, published in America the following year. Many of the English cases are cited in Murray v. Allard, 100 Tenn. 100, 66 Am. St. Rep. 740, 43 S. W. 355.
[3] Stewart on Mines, pp. 10-13.

§ 92. **Substances classified as "mineral" under the English decisions.**—Before leaving the subject of the English law and decisions, it is not out of place to enumerate some of the substances which have been adjudicated to be within the term "mineral."

It is hardly necessary to mention gold, silver, the common metals, or coal, as they fall within the earlier definition of the term, and were usually obtained through underground excavations. In addition to these, the following substances have been successively held to be minerals:—

Beds of stone, obtained either by mining or quarrying; [1]

Stone, obtained by quarrying; [2]

Stone, for road-making and paving; [3]

Freestone (sandstone); [4]

[1] Earl of Rosse *v.* Wainman (1845), 14 M. & W. 859; S. C., 10 Morr. Min. Rep. 398—construing act of parliament (55 Geo. III, c. 18—inclosure act) reserving to the lords "all mines and minerals."

[2] Micklethwait *v.* Winter, 6 Exch. 644.

[3] Midland Railway *v.* Checkley (1867), L. R. 4 Eq. C. 19.

Reservation in canal act (1796) of the mines and minerals within and under the lands through which the canal was to be made. In this case the master of the rolls said that every species of stone, whether marble, limestone, or ironstone, came within the category of "minerals."

In Bell *v.* Wilson (*post*), the vice-chancellor said that in strictness the term "mineral" comprises chalk, slate, and all kinds of stone, whether freestone, sandstone, or granite.

In Adjutant-General *v.* Welsh Granite Co. (1887), 35 W. R. 617—construing inclosure act (1812), similar to that considered in Rosse *v.* Wainman (*supra*),—it was held that the term "mineral" included granite.

[4] Bell *v.* Wilson (1865), 2 Drew. & S. 395; S. C. on appeal, L. R. 1 Ch. App. 303—construing an exception in a lease of "mines and seams of "coal and other mines, metals, or minerals, as well opened as not "opened."

Jamieson *v.* North British Ry. Co., 6 Scot. L. Rep. 188—construing Scotch railway clauses act, which is identical with English act.

Glasgow and S. W. Ry. Co. *v.* Bain (1893), 21 R. 134; Mawson *v.* Fletcher (1870), L. R. 6 Ch. App. C. 91, 94.

Limestone; [1]

Flint stones, turned up with the plow by the tenant in the course of husbandry; [2]

Slate; [3]

Clay; [4]

Brick clay; [5]

[1] Fishbourne v. Hamilton (1890), L. R. 25 Ir. 483; Md. Ry. v. Robinson (1889), L. R. 15 App. C. 19; Brown's Trust, 11 W. R. 19; Glasgow and S. W. Ry. Co. v. Bain (1893), 21 R. 134; Mawson v. Fletcher (1870), L. R. 6 Ch. App. C. 91; Dixon v. Caledonian and Glasgow Ry. Co., L. R. 5 App. C. 820.

[2] Tucker v. Linger (1883), L. R. 8 App. C. 508—construing reservation in lease of "mines and minerals, quarries of stone, brickearth, and "gravel pits." But tenant held to be entitled to them by virtue of local custom.

[3] Duchess of Cleveland v. Meyrick, 16 W. R. 104; 37 L. J. Ch. 125.

[4] Ruabon Brick and Terra Cotta Co. v. Great Western Ry. Co. (1893), L. R. 1 Ch. 427. Within the meaning of the "railway clauses act."

Errington v. Met. Ry. Co. (1882), L. R. 19 Ch. D. 559, 571. Within the meaning of the "railway clauses act."

Attorney-General v. Mylchreest (1879), 4 App. C. 294.

Lord Herschell, in Magistrates of Glasgow v. Farie (1888), L. R. 13 App. C. 683.

[5] Midland Ry. Co. v. Haunchwood B. and T. Co. (1882), L. R. 20 Ch. D. 552. (For comment on this case by the United States land department, see King v. Bradford, 31 L. D. 108.)

In this case a controversy arose under acts of parliament known as the "railway clauses acts." These acts, among other things, prescribe the methods by which railway companies may obtain, by what is termed "compulsory purchase," land for their road-beds, stations, and other necessary adjuncts. Similar acts are in force in both England and Scotland, and appear to be a substitute for the condemnation proceedings used in this country. The following extracts from one of these acts will serve to show the context under consideration in this case, as well as in a number of others which may be referred to:—

"And, with respect to mines lying under or near the railway, be it "enacted:—

"SEC. 77. The company shall not be entitled to any mines of coal, "ironstone, slate, or other minerals under any land purchased by them, "except only such parts thereof as shall be dug or carried away, or used "in the construction of the works, unless the same shall have been "expressly purchased; and all such mines shall be deemed excepted out

China clay (kaolin—sometimes called porcelain, or
 fire-clay) ; [1]

Coprolites (phosphatic nodules). [2]

The foregoing illustrations will serve to demonstrate
the evolution of denotation referred to in a preceding
paragraph, and give a fair outline of the meaning given
to the terms "mines" and "minerals" by the courts of
last resort in England and Scotland. Considering the
scope of this treatise, a more critical review of the English authorities would serve no useful purpose.

§ 93. The American cases defining "mine" and "mineral."

—In America, until a comparatively recent
period, controversies over the construction of the terms
"mines" and "minerals" have been limited to cases
arising, as in many of the English cases, out of the use
of these terms in conveyances, leases, and the like, where
the context, or the peculiar situation of the parties, or

"of the conveyance of such lands, unless they shall have been expressly
"named therein and conveyed thereby."

Subsequent sections provide that the owner of the minerals desiring
to work within forty yards of the railway or under the same must give
the company notice. Thereupon the company may exercise the option
of purchasing the minerals, the value thereof to be ascertained by
appraisement. If the company does not give notice within thirty days
of the exercise of that option, the owner of the minerals may work under
the railway.

[1] Exception in grant of freehold in copyhold tenement, by Duke of
Cornwall (1799), reserving "all mines and minerals within and under
"the premises, with full and free liberty of ingress, egress, and regress,
"to dig, search for, and to take, use, and work, for the said excepted
"mines and minerals." Hext v. Gill (1872), L. R. 7 Ch. App. 699.

Working for china clay in this case was by stripping the soil from
the bed and turning a stream of water over the clay, similar to the tin
"streaming" practiced in some portions of Cornwall, and to the hydraulic process in vogue in this country.

Loosemore v. Tiverton and N. Devon Ry. Co. (1882), L. R. 22 Ch. D.
25—construing section 77, "railway clauses act" of 1845.

[2] Attorney-General v. Tomline (1877), L. R. 5 Ch. Div. 750.

the subject of the litigation, to some extent at least, controlled. A brief review of some of these authorities will be of interest.

In Gibson v. Tyson,[1] the supreme court of Pennsylvania had under consideration a grant reserving to the grantee "all minerals or magnesia of any kind." This was held to include chromate of iron; but the court intimated that had it not been for the parol evidence concerning the supposed character of the land, and the situation of the parties at the time the instrument was executed, it would have excluded the substance afterwards found and designated as chromate of iron, because it was non-metallic, and the "great mass of " mankind do not consider anything mineral that is not " metallic."

In Hartwell v. Camman,[2] the New Jersey court of chancery, in construing the terms of a conveyance granting "all mines, minerals, opened or to be opened," thus states its views:—

"By the use of the terms 'mines' and 'minerals,' it " is clear that the grantor did not intend to include " everything embraced in the mineral kingdom, as dis- " tinguished from what belongs to the animal and vege- " table kingdom. If he did, he parted with the soil " itself. . . . Nor can I see any more propriety in " confining the meaning of the terms used to any one " of the subordinate divisions into which the mineral " kingdom has been subdivided by chemists, either " earthy, metallic, saline, or bituminous. . . . I do " not think the term should be confined to the metals, " or metallic ores. I cannot doubt if a stratum of salt, " or even a bed of coal, had been found, they would " have passed under the grant."

The court holds that "paint-stone" falls within the term "minerals," as the substance was valuable for its

---

[1] 5 Watts, 35.
[2] 10 N. J. Eq. 128, 64 Am. Dec. 448, 3 Morr. Min. Rep. 229.

mineral properties, could be converted into a merchantable article adapted to the mechanical and ornamental arts, and was embraced in the definition given by men of science.[1]

In Funk v. Haldeman,[2] the supreme court of Pennsylvania treated petroleum oil as a mineral, saying that " until our scientific knowledge on the subject is in- " creased, that is the light in which the courts will be " likely to regard this valuable production of the " earth."

Under a statute of Pennsylvania, passed April 25, 1850, it was provided that suit in the county where the lands were situated might be brought by a tenant in common of "minerals." Under this act the court of common pleas of Erie county [3] held that petroleum was a mineral, and the fact that it was unknown as a product from land at the time the act was passed did not prevent its application.

In Griffin v. Fellows,[4] a question arose as to the construction of an instrument, executed in 1796, leasing a tract of public land, "together with the mines or " minerals of whatever description." There were no opened mines or quarries on the premises at the date of the lease. Mining of coal was first commenced by the tenant in 1810, and quarrying stone in 1855. It was held by the supreme court of Pennsylvania, adopting the views of the trial court, that "the term 'min- " 'erals' embraces everything not of the mere surface, " which is used for agricultural purposes; the granite " of the mountains, as well as metallic ores and fossils, " are comprehended within it,"[5] and consequently that,

---

[1] See also Johnson v. California Lustral Co., 127 Cal. 283, 59 Pac. 595.
[2] (1866), 53 Pa. St. 229.
[3] Thompson v. Noble (1870), 3 Pittsb. 201.
[4] (1873), 32 P. F. Smith, 114; 8 Morr. Min. Rep. 657.
[5] Citing the English case of Earl of Rosse v. Wainman, 14 M. & W. 859.

" by the terms of the lease, the lessee and his assigns
" have the right to mine coal and quarry stone."

In Dunham *v.* Kirkpatrick,[1] in construing a deed
containing a reservation of ".all minerals," the supreme
court of Pennsylvania held that while it was true that
petroleum was a mineral, yet in popular estimation it
was not so regarded; and following the rule of construction invoked in Gibson *v.* Tyson, the court concluded,
that in contemplation of the parties to the instrument
petroleum was not within the reservation.

The same court, however, in a more recent case,[2]
seems to have ignored the doctrine of Dunham *v.* Kirkpatrick.

The legislature of Pennsylvania had passed an act
providing, among other things, for the mortgaging of
a "leasehold of any colliery, *mining land,* manufactur-
" ing, or other premises." In passing upon the act,
the court held that petroleum was a mineral substance
obtained from the earth by a process of mining, and
lands from which it is obtained may, with propriety,
be called mining lands. Therefore, the act applied to
and authorized a mortgage of a leasehold of oil land,
although the act was passed *before petroleum was discovered,* substantially following the doctrine announced
in Thompson *v.* Noble (*supra*).

The same court, in a still later case,[3] holds that natural gas is a mineral, although it possesses peculiar
attributes, which require the application of precedents
arising out of ordinary mineral rights with much more
careful consideration, and terms it a mineral *feræ
naturæ.*

In Murray *v.* Allard,[4] the supreme court of Tennes-

---

[1] (1882), 101 Pa. St. 36, 47 Am. St. Rep. 696.
[2] Gill *v.* Weston (1885), 110 Pa. St. 316.
[3] Westmoreland & Cambria Nat. Gas Co. *v.* De Witt, 130 Pa. St. 235.
[4] 100 Tenn. 100, 66 Am. St. Rep. 740, 43 S. W. 355.

see, in a case involving the question as to whether petroleum was a mineral within the meaning of a reservation in a conveyance of "mines, minerals, and " metals," reviewed the English and American cases defining minerals and held that petroleum was a mineral and within the reservation, denying the force of Dunham v. Kirkpatrick (*supra*).

The supreme court of Ohio holds that petroleum is not included within the terms of a conveyance which grants in perpetuity the right of "mining and remov-" ing such coal, or other minerals." The court followed Dunham v. Kirkpatrick, and while admitting that the words "other minerals," or "other valuable minerals," taken in their broadest sense, would include petroleum oil, held that the parties did not intend to include oil in the word "minerals." [1]

In West Virginia it has been held that petroleum is a mineral.[2]

A recent case, decided by the New York court of appeals,[3] involved the construction of two deeds executed by the owner of a tract of land. The first deed conveyed all the "mineral ores" in the tract, "reserving " all other rights and interests in said lands, save said " mineral ores and the right to raise and remove the " same." By the second deed, which made no reference to the first, there was conveyed to the same grantees all the mineral *and* ores on the same tract, with the right to mine and remove the same; also, the right to sink shafts, and sufficient surface to erect suitable buildings necessary and usual in mining and raising ores; also, the right of ingress and egress for mining purposes, and to make exploration for minerals and ores.

---

[1] Detlor v. Holland, 57 Ohio St. 492, 49 N. E. 690, 692.

[2] Williamson v. Jones, 39 W. Va. 231, 19 S. E. 436, 441.

[3] Armstrong v. Lake Champlain Granite Co., 147 N. Y. 495, 49 Am. St. Rep. 683, 42 N. E. 186.

The plaintiff was the owner of whatever passed by these two conveyances. The defendant was the owner of what remained of the tract. The controversy arose over the right of the defendant to quarry granite on the tract. The granite was discovered on the premises after the first two deeds were executed, but prior to the acquisition of title by defendant. The court, after reviewing several of the English cases hereinbefore cited and the New Jersey case of Hartwell v. Camman (*supra*), reached the conclusion that the term "mineral ores" used in the first deed did not include granite; that the words "minerals and ores" used in the second deed, standing alone, would include granite; that it would be an unwarrantable limitation to exclude from the operation of the grant beds of coal or other non-metallic mineral deposits of commercial value, or to confine it to such minerals as were known or supposed to be on the premises at the time.[1] But the court held that the context of the second deed conveying the "mineral and ores" limited the grant to such minerals as could be obtained by underground workings; and as granite is not so obtained, it did not pass under the conveyance.

The court also held that the meaning of the words "minerals and ores" in a deed could not be limited or explained by declaration of the parties thereto as to what was intended to be covered by the deed, reformation thereof not being sought.

Marble in place is a mineral, and is included within a reservation of "all minerals." [2]

The foregoing line of authorities serves to illustrate the views of the various courts of the United States in dealing with the terms "mines" and "minerals" in

---

[1] Followed in Brady v. Brady, 65 N. Y. Supp. 621. See, also, Phelps v. Church of Our Lady, 115 Fed. 852, 854.

[2] Brady v. Brady, 65 N. Y. Supp. 621; Phelps v. Church of Our Lady, 115 Fed. 882.

cases having no connection with the various acts of congress which we are called upon to construe. In interpreting these acts it cannot be demonstrated that either the English or American cases have been an appreciable factor, or have been either cited or relied upon as precedents; yet it is manifest that they have exerted some influence, and that we shall observe their earmarks as we progress.

§ 94. "Mineral lands," as defined by the American tribunals. —In a preceding section [1] it has been assumed that the term "mineral lands" is sufficiently comprehensive to embrace the various kindred designations found in the various acts of congress, and that these various terms may be, and frequently are, used interchangeably. Upon this assumption, let us consider what is meant by the term "mineral lands" and its legal equivalents.

On this subject there has been great uniformity of decision by those courts of the states and of the United States which have had the most frequent occasion to consider the subject, and by the land department.[2]

The supreme court of California as early as 1864 gave its views upon the question in a well-considered case,[3] the earmarks of which may be plainly observed in many, if not all, the subsequent decisions bearing upon the subject. It thus presented its views:—

"It is not easy in all cases to determine whether any "given piece of land should be classed as mineral land "or otherwise. The question may depend upon many "circumstances: such as whether it is located in those "regions generally recognized as mineral lands or in "a locality ordinarily regarded as agricultural in its

[1] See, *ante*, § 86.
[2] Davis *v.* Weibbold, 139 U. S. 507, 11 Sup. Ct. Rep. 628.
[3] Ah Yew *v.* Choate, 24 Cal. 562.

" character. Lands may contain the precious metals,
" but not in sufficient quantities to justify working
" them as mines or make the locality generally valuable
" for mining purposes, while they are well adapted to
" agricultural pursuits; or they may be poorly adapted
" to agricultural or grazing pursuits, but rich in min-
" erals, and there may be every gradation between the
" two extremes. There is, however, no certain, well-
" defined, obvious boundary between the mineral lands
" and those that cannot be classed in that category.
" Perhaps the true criterion would be to consider
" whether, upon the whole, the lands appear to be bet-
" ter adapted to mining or other purposes. However
" that may be, in order to determine the question, it
" would, at all events, be necessary to know the condi-
" tion and circumstances of the land itself, and of the
" immediate locality in which it is situated. It is the
" duty of the officers of the government having the mat-
" ter in charge, before making a grant, to ascertain
" these facts and to determine the problem whether the
" lands are mineral or not."

In a later case,[1] construing the mineral reservation in
the Pacific railroad acts, the same court determined as
follows:—

"The mere fact that portions of the land contained
" particles of gold or veins of gold-bearing quartz rock
" would not necessarily impress it with the character
" of mineral land, within the meaning of the acts re-
" ferred to. It must, at least, be shown that the land
" contains metals [2] in quantities sufficient to render it
" available and valuable for mining purposes. Any
" narrower construction would operate to reserve from
" the uses of agriculture large tracts of land which are
" practically useless for any other purpose, and we can-
" not think this was the intention of congress."

[1] Alford v. Barnum, 45 Cal. 482.

[2] The use of the term "metals" in this connection is of no controlling
importance. It was undoubtedly used without any design to restrict the
meaning of the word "mineral" to metallic substances.

This case was cited approvingly by the supreme court of the United States, and the general rule of interpretation thus enunciated:—

"The exceptions of minerals from pre-emption and
" settlement, and from grants to states for universities
" and schools, for the construction of public buildings,
" and in aid of railroads and other works of internal
" improvement, are not held to exclude all lands in
" which minerals may be found, but only those where
" the mineral is in sufficient quantity to add to their
" richness, and to justify expenditure for its extraction,
" and known to be so at the date of the grant. There
" are vast tracts of country in the mining states which
" contain precious metals in small quantities, but not
" to a sufficient extent to justify the expense of their
" exploitation. It is not to such lands that the term
" 'mineral,' in the sense of this statute, is applicable." [1]

The mere fact that the land contains "copper, gold " and silver-bearing quartz" does not impress it with the character of mineral land within the meaning of the act of congress excluding mineral lands from the grant to the Central Pacific railroad. Only lands valuable for mining purposes are reserved from sale.[2]

In United States v. Reed,[3] before the circuit court for the district of Oregon, a bill was filed by the United States to set aside a patent issued upon a homestead entry, on the ground that the land was mineral, and not agricultural, and was at the date of entry more valuable for mining than for agricultural purposes, and was so to the knowledge of the patentee. Judge Deady, in disposing of the question, said:—

"The nature and extent of the deposit of precious " metals which will make a tract of land mineral, or

[1] Davis v. Weibbold, 139 U. S. 507, 11 Sup. Ct. Rep. 628; United States v. Central Pac. R. R. Co., 93 Fed. 871, 873.

[2] Merrill v. Dixon, 15 Nev. 401; United States v. Central Pac. R. R. Co., 93 Fed. 871, 873.

[3] 12 Saw. 99-104, 28 Fed. 482.

" constitute a mine thereon within the meaning of the
" statute, has not been judicially determined. Atten-
" tion is called to the question in McLaughlin v. United
" States, 107 U. S. 526,[1] but no opinion is expressed.
" The land department appears to have adopted a rule
" that if the land is worth more for agriculture than
" mining, it is not mineral land, although it may con-
" tain some measure of gold or silver, and the bill in
" this case is drawn on that theory of the law. In my
" judgment, that is the only practical rule of decision
" that can be applied to the subject. Nor can account
" be taken in the application of this rule of profits that
" would or might result from mining under other and
" more favorable conditions and circumstances than
" those which actually exist, or may be produced or
" expected in the ordinary course of such pursuit or
" adventure on the land in question."

In Dughi v. Harkins,[2] which was before the interior
department in November, 1883, there was a contest
between mineral and agricultural claimants, the land
having been returned as agricultural by the surveyor-
general. In disposing of it, Secretary Teller, in a communication to the commissioner of the general land
office, said:—

"The burden of proof is therefore upon the mineral
" claimant, and he must show, not that neighboring or
" adjoining lands are mineral in character, or that that
" in dispute may hereafter, by possibility, develop min-
" erals in such quantity as .will establish its mineral
" rather than its agricultural character, but that as a
" present fact it is mineral in character; and this must
" appear from actual production of mineral, and not
" from any theory that it may produce it; in other
" words, it is fact, and not theory, which must control
" your office in deciding upon the character of this class
" of land. Nor is it sufficient that the mineral claimant
" shows that the land is of little agricultural value. He
" must show affirmatively, in order to establish his

---

[1] 2 Sup. Ct. Rep. 802.   [2] 2 Land Decisions, p. 721.

" claim, that the mineral value of the land is greater " than its agricultural value." [1]

Rulings to the same effect upon applications for mineral patents are found in decisions of the department for many years. They are, that such applications should not be granted unless the existence of mineral in such quantities as would justify expenditure in the effort to obtain it is established as a present fact. If mineral patents will not be issued unless the mineral exist in sufficient quantity to render the land more valuable for mining than for other purposes, which can only be known by developments or exploration, it should follow that the land may be patented for other purposes, if that fact does not appear.[2]

The leading case of Davis v. Weibbold (*supra*) reviews these rulings, and so clearly affirms their doctrine that nothing more is required than to freely quote this case. Says the court:—

"It would seem from this uniform construction of " that department of the government specially intrusted " with supervision of proceedings required for the " alienation of the public lands, including those that " embrace minerals, and also of the courts of the mining " states, federal and state, whose attention has been " called to the subject, that the exception of mineral " lands from grant in the acts of congress should be " considered to apply only to such lands as were at the " time of the grant known to be so valuable for their " minerals as to justify expenditure for their extrac-" tion. The grant or patent, where issued, would thus " be held to carry with it the determination of the proper " authorities that the land patented was not subject to

---

[1] Quoted in Davis v. Weibbold, 139 U. S. 507, 11 Sup. Ct. Rep. 628; and in United States v. Central· Pac. R. R. Co., 93 Fed. 871, 874.

[2] Magalia G. M. Co. v. Ferguson, 6 L. D. 218; Nicholas Abercrombie, *Id.* 393; John Downs, 7 L. D. 71; Cutting v. Reininghaus, *Id.* 265; Creswell M. Co. v. Johnson, 8 L. D. 440; Thomas J. Laney, 9 L. D. 83.

" the exception stated. There has been no direct adjudi-
" cation on this point by this court, but this conclusion
" is a legitimate inference from several of its decisions.
" It was implied in the opinion in Deffeback v. Hawke,
" 115 U. S. 392,[1] and in the cases of Colorado C. & I.
" Co. v. United States, 123 U. S. 307;[2] United States v.
" Iron S. M. Co., 128 U. S. 673." [3]

§ 95. Interpretation of terms by the land department.— As in all contests between agricultural and mineral claimants prior to final entry, in all applications to
enter lands under the mining laws, and in administering
the various grants to railroads, as to lands remaining
unpatented, the land department is the sole judge of the
character of the land and the final arbiter upon this subject, it is deemed important to supplement the foregoing
selection of authorities by presenting the rulings of that
department on the subject: They enter somewhat more
into detail, and will furnish a reliable guide to those who
may have occasion to deal with that special tribunal
upon the subject of mineral lands.

Commissioner Drummond [4] thus enunciates the rule
which has since governed the land department:—

" In the sense in which the term ' mineral ' was used
" by congress, it seems difficult to find a definition that
" will embrace what mineralogists agree should be
" included. . . . From a careful examination of the
" matter, the conclusion I reach as to what constitutes a

[1] 6 Sup. Ct. Rep. 95.
[2] 8 Sup. Ct. Rep. 131.
[3] 9 Sup. Ct. Rep. 195.
To the same effect see Nevada Sierra Oil Co. v. Home Oil Co., 98 Fed.
673; Cleary v. Skiffich (Colo.), 65 Pac. 59.
[4] Circ. of Instructions, July 15, 1873. This circular is referred to and
accepted, as stating the correct rule, in Pacific Coast Marble Co. v.
N. P. R. R., 25 L. D. 233, 238. To the same effect, see Aldritt v.
N. P. R. R., 25 L. D. 349; Phifer v. Heaton, 27 L. D. 57; Schrimpf v.
N. P. R. R. Co., 29 L. D. 327; Morrill v. N. P. R. R., 30 L. D. 475;
Beaudette v. N. P. R. R. Co., 29 L. D. 248.

" valuable mineral deposit is this: That whatever is
" recognized as a mineral by the standard authorities
" on the subject, where the same is found in quantities
" and quality to render the land sought to be patented
" more valuable on this account than for the purpose
" of agriculture, should be treated by the office as com-
" ing within the purview of the mining act of May 10,
" 1872.[1]

" The only safe rule for the department to follow is
" that already laid down and adhered to in many cases—
" that the coal or mineral character of the land must be
" determined by the actual production from mining on
" the tract in dispute, or by satisfactory evidence that
" mineral (coal) exists on the land in question in suf-
" ficient quantities to make the same more valuable for
" mining than for agriculture. . . .

" It has been repeatedly held by this department that
" the proof of the mineral character of the land must
" be specific, and show actual production of mineral
" therefrom; that it is not enough to show that land in
" the neighborhood, or adjoining lands, are mineral in
" character, or that the lands in question may hereafter
" be found to be mineral. (Kings County v. Alexander,
" 5 L. D. 126; and Dughi v. Harkins, 2 L. D. 721.) The
" proof must show satisfactorily the mineral (coal)
" character, and not be based upon a theory.[2]

" It is contended that the mining statutes provide
" that in an *ex parte* case, 'land containing gold *in any*
" ' *quantity* is mineral land, and that they contemplate
" ' inquiry into the value of the deposit only when the
" ' application of the mineral locator conflicts with that
" ' of some other locator or claimant.' . . .

" It must be apparent that, for the purpose of issuing
" patent, there is lodged somewhere the authority and
" duty to ascertain whether a claim contains 'valuable
" ' deposits,' for no other land can be so acquired. It is
" equally clear that for the same purpose such authority
" is vested in this department, charged, as it is, with the
" determination of the facts prior to the issuance of

---

[1] Copp's Min. Dec., p. 317; W. H. Hooper, 1 L. D. 561.
[2] Savage v. Boynton, 12 L. D. 612.

Lindley on M.—10

" patent. Should the question of the character of the
" land be properly presented at any time before patent,
" it would manifestly be the duty of the department to
" ascertain whether or not the land contains 'valuable
" ' deposits,' in an *ex parte* case or a contest. The fact
" that a claim is contested would not change the char-
" acter of the land to be taken under this law. In any
" event, it must contain 'valuable deposits.'[1]

" The proof of the mineral character of the land must
" be specific, and based upon the actual production of
" mineral; that it is not enough to show that neighboring
" or adjoining lands are mineral in character, and that
" the lands in controversy may hereafter develop min-
" erals to such an extent as to show its mineral character,
" but it must appear from actual production of mineral,
" and not from a theory that the lands may hereafter
" produce it."[2]

The present existence of mineral in such quantity as
to render the land more valuable for mining than agriculture must be shown, to defeat an agricultural entry.[3]

" It is not necessary that, to meet the requirements,
" there should be upon the land a mine in working order,
" from which gold is being actually produced. It is
" sufficient if it be shown by satisfactory proof that
" mineral exists in paying quantities, and such proof
" will usually be based on mining operations or explora-
" tions. In the present case it has not been shown that
" any mining has been carried on on this land. The
" evidence consists of the testimony of persons, most of
" them claiming to be expert miners, who went upon this
" land and panned out small quantities of earth. The
" preponderance thereof shows that the land bears gold,
" and taking the testimony of the witnesses for the min-
" eral claimants alone, it sustains the conclusion that
" it is there in paying quantities."[4]

[1] Royal K. Placer, 13 L. D. 86.

[2] Warren *v.* State of Colorado, 14 L. D. 681.

[3] Winters *v.* Bliss, 14 L. D. 59; Walton *v.* Batten, *Id.* 54; Peirano *v.* Pendola, 10 L. D. 536.

[4] Johns *v.* March, 15 L. D. 196.

" When the development, and its results, display such
" promise that the prudent, reasonable man would be
" justified in expending money and labor in legitimate
" mining operations, untainted by an appearance of
" speculation, the land must be held mineral within the
" meaning of that term as used in the granting act.
" (Pacific railroad acts.) If it was held otherwise, the
" mining industry, so far as it pertained to odd sections
" within the grant, would be paralyzed. The rule is
" that paying mines are only shown to exist after years
" of labor and much money expended in the develop-
" ment. Prospectors do not find riches on the surface.
" Profit is not received from the grass-roots down. They
" must have an opportunity given them to open the
" mine as their means permit." [1]

" After careful consideration of the subject, it is my
" opinion that where minerals have been found, and
" the evidence is of such a character that a person of
" ordinary prudence would be justified in the further
" expenditure of his labor and means, with a reasonable
" prospect of success, in developing a valuable mine, the
" requirements of the statute have been met. To hold
" otherwise would tend to make of little avail, if not
" entirely nugatory, that provision of the law whereby
" ' all valuable mineral deposits in lands belonging to
" ' the United States . . . are . . . declared to be free
" ' and open to exploration and purchase.' For if as
" soon as minerals are shown to exist, and at any time
" during exploration, before the returns become remu-
" nerative, the lands are to be subject to other disposi-
" tion, few would be willing to risk time and capital in
" the attempt to bring to light and make available the
" mineral wealth which lies concealed in the bowels of
" the earth, as congress obviously must have intended
" the explorers should have proper opportunity to do." [2]

" The invitation is to explore and purchase 'all valu-
" ' able mineral deposits' in the public lands and to

[1] Casey v. N. P. R. R., 15 L. D. 439.

[2] Castle v. Womble, 19 L. D. 455; Walker v. S. P. R. R. Co., 24 L. D.
172; Leach v. Potter, 24 L. D. 573; Magruder v. Oregon & Calif. R. R.
Co., 28 L. D. 174; McQuiddy v. State of California, 29 L. D. 181.

" occupy and purchase the lands in which they may be
" found. Broader or more comprehensive language
" could hardly have been used. Wherever mineral
" deposits are found in the public lands, they are
" declared to be free and open to exploration and pur-
" chase, with only one qualification—they must be *val-*
" *uable* mineral deposits." [1]

Mere indications of mineral do not prove that the
lands contain permanent valuable deposits.[2] Nor does
the fact that a mining location has been made indicate
that the land is valuable for mineral.[3] A tract cannot
be assumed to be mineral because it is situated in
a mineral belt and is adjacent to numerous mining
claims.[4]

In determining what constitutes mineral land within
the meaning of the acts of congress, we have treated the
subject generally, without regard to the form in which
the mineral deposits occur—*i. e.* whether " in place," as
in quartz veins, or not "in place," as in case of auriferous gravels, clays, and other substances usually
encountered in horizontal beds or isolated deposits.
What constitutes a vein or lode, or whether a given
character of deposit may be located and acquired as
" in place," or not " in place," will be discussed under
appropriate heads in other portions of this work. The
rulings cited and definitions quoted apply equally to all
forms of deposits, with perhaps this suggestion: In
lode locations non-mineral surface ground is embraced
therein for the convenient working of the lode. But in
places it is contemplated that the entire area should fall

[1] Pacific Coast Marble Co. *v.* Northern Pac. R. R. Co., 25 L. D. 233, 243.

[2] Tulare Oil and M. Co. *v.* Southern Pac. R. R. Co., 29 L. D. 269, 272.
See, also, Nevada Sierra Oil Co. *v.* Home Oil Co., 98 Fed. 673.

[3] Harkrader *v.* Goldstein, 31 L. D. 87; In re Bourquin, 27 L. D. 280.

[4] Elda Mining Company, 29 L. D. 279. See, also, Cleary *v.* Skiffich
(Colo.), 65 Pac. 59.

within the designation of mineral—not necessarily homogeneous throughout, but all mineral.[1]

§ 96. American rules of statutory interpretation.—

In addition to the ordinary canons of statutory interpretation, there are certain recognized rules applicable to the acts of congress which are within the scope of this treatise. These may be briefly enumerated as follows:—

(1) The mining laws are to be read in the light of matters of public history, relating to the mineral lands of the United States;[2]

(2) Where a statute operates as a grant of public property to an individual, or the relinquishment of a public interest, that construction should be adopted which will support the claim of the government rather than that of the individual;[3]

(3) In the case of a doubtful or ambiguous law, the contemporaneous construction of those who have been called upon to carry it into effect is entitled to great respect, and ought not to be overruled without cogent reasons.[4]

We might add a fourth rule, deducible from the foregoing and from the current of American authority and decisions of the land department, and that is, that the word "mineral," as used in these various acts, should

---

[1] See Ferrell v. Hoge, 29 L. D. 12.

[2] Jennison Exr. v. Kirk, 98 U. S. 453.

[3] Slidell v. Grandjean, 111 U. S. 412, 4 Sup. Ct. Rep. 475; Leavenworth L. and G. R. Co. v. United States, 92 U. S. 733; Barden v. N. P. R. R. Co., 154 U. S. 228, 14 Sup. Ct. Rep. 1030.

[4] United States v. Moore, 95 U. S. 760; Brown v. United States, 113 U. S. 568, 5 Sup. Ct. Rep. 638; Barden v. N. P. R. R. Co., 154 U. S. 228, 14 Sup. Ct. Rep. 1030; Northern Pac. R. R. Co. v. Soderberg, 104 Fed. 425; Pacific Coast Marble Co. v. N. P. R. R. Co., 25 L. D. 233; Aldritt v. N. P. R. R. Co., Id. 349; Phifer v. Heaton, 27 L. D. 57; Hayden v. Jamison, 26 L. D. 373; Beaudette v. N. P. R. R. Co., 29 L. D. 327.

be understood in its widest signification. [1] We do
not conceive that there is anything in the context of
the several acts, or in their nature, to restrict its meaning. This is practically the English rule announced by
Mr. Ross Stewart, which has heretofore been referred
to, and which is amply supported by the highest English authority.[2]

Judge Hanford, United States district judge for the
district of Washington, thus clearly states the rule:—

" In its common and ordinary signification the word
" 'mineral' is not a synonym for 'metal,' but is a com-
" prehensive term including every description of stone
" and rock deposits, whether containing metallic sub-
" stances or entirely non-metalic." [3]

This rule is in conflict with the decision of the supreme
court of the state of Washington in the case of
Wheeler v. Smith,[4] wherein that court seeks to limit the
meaning of the term "mineral," as used in the congressional mining laws, to *metallic* substances. In so
doing the courts treats the rulings of the land department as possessing no force or virtue, and refuses
to adopt the reasoning and conclusions reached in a
parallel case by the supreme court of Montana,[5] a court
noted for its experience and ability in dealing specially
with mining questions and controversies arising out of
the mining laws. This decision of the supreme court of
Washington also conflicts with a number of carefully
considered cases, which will be noted when we come
to enumerate the various substances which have been
held to be within the reasonable definition of the term
"mineral." [6]

---

[1] Northern Pac. R. R. Co. v. Soderberg, 99 Fed. 506, 104 Fed. 425.
[2] See, *ante*, § 91.
[3] Northern Pac. R. R. Co. v. Soderberg, 99 Fed. 506, 507, S. C. on
appeal, 104 Fed. 425.
[4] 5 Wash. 704, 32 Pac. 784.
[5] Freezer v. Sweeney, 8 Mont. 508, 21 Pac. 20.
[6] The Washington case is commented on in Pacific Coast Marble Co. v.
Northern Pac. R. R. Co., 25 L. D. 233, 241.

§ 97. **Substances held to be mineral by the land department.**—Lands containing the following substances have been held by the land department to fall within the designation of mineral lands, and as such to be subject to entry under the mining laws:—

Asphaltum;[1]
Petroleum and the mineral hydrocarbons; [2]
Borax;[3]
Nitrate and carbonate of soda, sulphur, and alum; [4]
Kaolin, or china clay; [5]
Mica;[6]
Umber;[7]
Gypsum;[8]
Limestone;[9]
Marble;[10]
Diamonds; [11]

[1] Copp's Min. Lands, p. 50; Tulare Oil and M. Co. v. S. P. R. R. Co., 29 L. D. 269. See, also, Gesner v. Gas Co., 1 James, N. S. 72; Gesner v. Cairns, 2 Allen, N. B. 595.

[2] Union Oil Co. (on review), 25 L. D. 351 (reversing S. C., 23 L. D. 222); Copp's Min. Lands, p..160; 1 Copp's L. O., p. 179; A. A. Dewey, 9 Copp's L. O., p. 51; McQuiddy v. State of California, 29 L. D. 181; Kern Oil Co. v. Clotfeter, 30 L. D. 583. See, also, act of congress, 29 Stats. at Large, p. 526; Murray v. Allard, 100 Tenn. 100, 66 Am. St. Rep. 740, 43 S. W. 355; Williamson v. Jones, 39 W. Va. 231, 19 S. E. 441; Thompson v. Noble, 3 Pittsb. 201; Gill v. Weston, 110 Pa. St. 313; Gird v. California Oil Co., 60 Fed. 531; and see Detlor v. Holland, 59 Ohio St. 492, 49 N. E. 690.

[3] Copp's Min. Lands, pp. 50, 100, 2 L. D. 707.

[4] *Id.*

[5] *Id.*, pp. 121, 176; 1 Land Dec. 578; Aldritt v. Northern Pac. R. R. Co., 25 L. D. 349.

[6] Copp's Min. Lands, p. 182.

[7] *Id.*, p. 161.

[8] *Id.*, p. 309; Phifer v. Heaton, 27 L. D. 57; McQuiddy v. California, 29 L. D. 181.

[9] Morrill v. Northern Pac. R. R. Co., 30 L. D. 475; 10 Copp's L. O., p. 50; 12 L. D. 1; Shepherd v. Bird, 17 L. D. 82; Copp's Min. Lands, pp. 176, 309. See, also, Freezer v. Sweeney, 8 Mont. 508, 21 Pac. 20; *contra,* Wheeler v. Smith, 5 Wash. 704, 32 Pac. 784.

[10] Copp's Min. Lands, p. 176; Pacific Coast Marble Co. v. Northern Pac. R. R. Co., 25 L. D. 233; Forsythe v. Weingart, 27 L. D. 680; Shrimpf v. N. P. R. R. Co., 29 L. D. 327.

[11] Copp's Min. Lands, p. 88.

Clay; [1]   Slate for roofing pur-
Phosphates; [2]   poses; [5]
Building stone, and stone of   Cement (gypsum); [6]
  special commercial value; [3]   Guano; [7]
Coal; [4]

By an act approved January 31, 1901,[8] congress declared that lands chiefly valuable for deposits of salt should be subject to location under the placer mining laws, with the proviso that the same person should not locate or enter more than one claim. At one time prior to the passage of this act the land department had ruled that salt lands were mineral and within the reservation

---

[1] Montague v. Dobbs, 9 Copp's L. O., p. 165; Aldritt·v. N. P. R. R. Co., 25 L. D. 349; but not brick clay (King v. Bradford, 31 L. D. 108).

[2] Gary v. Todd, 18 L. D. 59; but see S. C. (on review), 19 L. D. 414; Pacific Coast Marble Co. v. N. P. R. R. Co., 25 L. D. 233 (overruling Tucker v. Florida Ry. and N. Co., 19 L. D. 414); Florida Cent. and Penn. Ry. Co., 26 L. D. 600.

[3] Conlin v. Kelly, 12 L. D. 1 (overruling In re Bennet, 3 L. D. 116); McGlenn v. Weinbroeer, 15 L. D. 370; Vandoren v. Plested, 16 L. D. 508; Re Delaney, 17 L. D. 120; Hayden v. Jamison, 26 L. D. 373; Forsythe v. Weingart, 27 L. D. 680; Northern Pac. R. R. Co. v. Soderberg, 99 Fed. 506, 104 Fed. 425; Beaudette v. N. P. R. R. Co., 29 L. D. 248. But see South Dakota v. Vermont S. Co., 16 L. D. 263; State of Utah, 29 L. D. 69. The passage of the act of 1892 (27 Stats. at Large, p. 348) removes all future controversy on the subject, and permits those lands to be entered as mineral.

[4] McKean v. Buell, Copp's Min. Lands, p. 343; Townsite of Coalville, 4 Copp's L. O., p. 46; In re Norager, 10 Copp's L. O., p. 54; Brown v. N. P. R. R. Co., 31 L. D. 29. Coal, however, is disposed of under special laws, and will be separately considered under another portion of this treatise.

[5] Schrimpf v. N. P. R. R. Co., 29 L. D. 327; Copp's Min. Lands, p. 143.

[6] Phifer v. Heaton, 27 L. D. 57.

[7] Richter v. Utah, 27 L. D. 57. Congress has enacted special laws regulating the discovery of guano islands in the high seas (Rev. Stats. U. S., §§ 5570-5578; 20 Stats. at Large, p. 30; 23 Stats. at Large, p. 11).

[8] 31 Stats. at Large, p. 745.

contained in the railroad grants and state grants,[1] and permitted them to be acquired under the mining laws;[2] but later the department held that such lands were not subject to disposal, except at public auction or private sale, under the act of January 12, 1877.[3]

Land chiefly valuable because of a cavern therein, and containing crystalline deposits marketable as curiosities, is not patentable under the mining laws.[4]

Other than the decisions and rulings of the land department, we encounter a limited number of cases involving specific substances. This is easily accounted for. The land department is the tribunal specially charged with the determination of the character of lands falling within the purview of the laws considered in this treatise. This question being one of fact, the determination by the department culminating in the issuance of a patent is conclusive, and not open to collateral attack. Such controversies, therefore, rarely find their way into the courts. In a succeeding chapter, treating of placers and other deposits, will be found cited the few cases which we have been able to discover upon the subject.

§ 98. **Rules for determining mineral character of lan** .—While it is difficult to formulate a definition sufficiently comprehensive in itself to cover all possible exigencies, we think that a conservative application of the rules governing statutory construction, heretofore enumerated in connection with the adjudicated cases

[1] Eagle Salt Works, Copp's Min. Lands, p. 336; Hall *v.* Litchfield, *Id.*, p. 333. See, also, Garrard *v.* Silver Peak Mines, 82 Fed. 578, 587, S. C. 94 Fed. 983; Morton *v.* Nebraska, 21 Wall. 660; Circular, 31 L. D. 130.

[2] Copp's Min. Lands, p. 333.

[3] 19 Stats. at Large, p. 221; Salt Bluff Placer, 7 L. D. 549; Hall *v.* Litchfield, Copp's Min. Lands, p. 333.

[4] South Dakota M. Co. *v.* McDonald, 30 L. D. 357.

and rulings of the land department, permits us to deduce the following:—

The mineral character of the land is established when it is shown to have upon or within it such a substance as—

(*a*) Is recognized as mineral, according to its chemical composition, by the standard authorities on the subject; or—

(*b*) Is classified as a mineral product in trade or commerce; or—

(*c*) Such a substance (other than the mere surface which may be used for agricultural purposes) as possesses economic value for use in trade, manufacture, the sciences, or in the mechanical or ornamental arts;—

And it is demonstrated that such substance exists therein or thereon in such quantities as render the land more valuable for the purpose of removing and marketing the substance than for any other purpose, and the removing and marketing of which will yield a profit; or, it is established that such substance exists in the lands in such quantities as would justify a prudent man in expending labor and capital in the effort to obtain it.[1]

---

[1] The land department thus states its conclusions: "Whatever is "recognized as mineral by the standard authorities on the subject, "whether of metallic or other substances, when the same is found in the "public lands in quantity and quality to render the land more valuable "on account thereof than for agricultural purposes, should be treated as "coming within the purview of the mining laws." Pacific Coast Marble Co. *v.* Northern Pac. R. R. Co., 25 L. D. 233, 244. See, also, Aldritt *v.* Northern Pac. R. R. Co., 25 L. D. 349; Phifer *v.* Heaton, 27 L. D. 57; McQuiddy *v.* State of California, 29 L. D. 181; Tulare Oil and M. Co. *v.* S. P. R. R. Co., *Id.* 269; Schrimpf *v.* Northern Pac. R. R. Co., *Id.* 327; Morrill *v.* Northern Pac. R. R. Co., 30 L. D. 475; Northern Pac. R. R. Co. *v.* Soderberg, 99 Fed. 506; S. C. on appeal, 104 Fed. 425; United States *v.* Copper Queen etc. Co. (Ariz.), 60 Pac. 885; Cleary *v.* Skiffich (Colo.), 65 Pac. 59.

CHAPTER II.

THE PUBLIC SURVEYS AND THE RETURN OF THE SURVEYOR-GENERAL.

§ 102. No general classification of lands as to their character.

§ 103. Geological surveys.

§ 104. General system of land surveys.

§ 105. What constitutes the surveyor-general's return.

§ 106. *Prima facie* character of land established by the return.

§ 107. Character of land, when and how established.

§ 108. Jurisdiction of courts to determine character of land when the question is pending in the land department.

§ **102. No general classification of lands as to their character.**—No general systematic classification of the public lands, according to their mineral or non-mineral character, for the purpose of sale or other disposal, has ever been attempted.

Geological examination and survey of lands in the Lake Superior district, and in the Chippewa land district, in Wisconsin, were provided for by acts of congress, passed in 1847.[1]

These acts conferred authority on the president to sell at public auction such land as contained copper, lead, or other valuable ores, at the minimum price of five dollars per acre. And such examination and survey were for the purpose of establishing the character of the lands in these regions, for the express purpose of sale as mineral lands.

[1] March 1, 1847, 9 Stats. at Large, p. 146; March 3, 1847, *Id.*, p. 179.

But three years later (September 26, 1850), this policy was abandoned, and this class of lands in these districts was directed to be sold in the same manner, at the minimum price, and with the same rights of pre-emption as other public lands.[1]

§ 103. Geological surveys.

— Since then extensive geological surveys have been and are now being made in various parts of the United States; but although these surveys are conducted under the supervision of the department of the interior, and are of great economic as well as scientific value, the results obtained perform no function in the public land system, are not noted in the tract-books in the different land offices, and are not necessarily considered in determining the mineral or non-mineral character of the land embraced within the limits of the geological survey.[2]

§ 104. General system of land surveys.

—It is a matter of common knowledge that the public lands are ordinarily surveyed into rectangular tracts, bounded by lines conforming to the cardinal points. These surveys are made under the immediate supervision of the United States surveyors-general in their respective surveying districts. The actual surveys in the field are conducted by deputies appointed by the surveyors-general, or by parties to whom contracts are let for such surveys, under the direction of the surveyors-general, to whom all reports are primarily made.

---

[1] 9 Stats. at Large, p. 472.

[2] In United States v. Van Winkle, 113 Fed. 903, the circuit court of appeals, ninth circuit, in a suit brought by the government to recover for timber cut on public land, the defense being that it was cut from "mineral land," held that there was no error harmful to the United States in admitting a map of the geological survey for the purpose of showing the general nature of the land, its elevation and surroundings, the map not purporting to classify the land as mineral or otherwise.

In prosecuting work in the field, the parties conducting the field-work are charged with the duty of noting at
the end of their notes of survey coal banks or beds, peat
or turf grounds, minerals, and ores, with particular
description of the same as to quality and extent, and all
"diggings" therefor; also, salt springs and licks, together with a general description of the township in the
aggregate, as respects the face of the country, its soil
and geological features, timber, minerals, water, and
the like.[1]

§ 105. **What constitutes the surveyor - general's
return.** —The original field-notes and accompanying
data, with a topographical sketch of the country surveyed, are returned to the surveyor-general, who ex-
amines them, and, if found correct, approves them,
whereupon the draughtsman protracts the same on township plats in triplicate. After approving the plats, the
surveyor-general files the original in his office, the duplicate is sent to the local land office, to enable the register
and receiver to dispose of the lands embraced in the
several townships, and the triplicate is transmitted to
the commissioner of the general land office. These approved field-notes, taken in connection with the township plats protracted in the office, constitute what is
known as the surveyor-general's return.

§ 106. **Prima facie character of land established by
the return.** —The lands embraced in the survey are
treated *prima facie* as being of the character shown by
this return, and are said thenceforward to be borne on
the official records as agricultural, timber, or mineral
land, according to the facts developed by the return.
The books of the land office are presumed to correctly

---

[1] Instructions to surveyors-general, Public Domain, p. 575 et seq.

show the character and condition of the land.[1] If lands are noted on the plat as mineral, they are *prima facie* mineral lands, and no entry thereof will be permitted, except under the mining laws, until the presumption arising from the return is overcome by satisfactory proofs.[2]

A return by the surveyor that sixteenth and thirty-sixth sections granted to the states for school purposes are mineral, and the approval of his field-notes and plats, and the filing thereof in the general land office, are a sufficient determination that the lands are mineral to authorize a selection of indemnity school lands by the state.[3]

If the lands are not returned as mineral, the presumption obtains that they are agricultural in character,[4] and therefore cannot be entered under the mining laws until the return is contradicted. At all inquiries held for the purpose of investigating the character of surveyed lands, this return has been said to rank as a deposition.[5]

It is unnecessary to say that this return is open to contradiction.[6] It concludes no one.[7] The return may be overcome by showing a discovery of sufficient mineral

---

[1] Olive Land and D. Co. *v.* Olmstead, 103 Fed. 568, 574.

[2] Gold Hill Q. M. Co. *v.* Ish, 5 Or. 104; Cowell *v.* Lammers, 10 Saw. 246, 21 Fed. 200; Johnston *v.* Morris, 72 Fed. 890; Dobbs' Placer, 1 L. D. 567; Dughi *v.* Harkins, 2 L. D. 721; Cole *v.* Markley, *Id.* 847; Hooper *v.* Ferguson, *Id.* 712; Roberts *v.* Jepson, 4 L. D. 60; Cosmos Co. *v.* Gray Eagle Co., 104 Fed. 20, 48; Richter *v.* State of Utah, 27 L. D. 95.

[3] Johnston v. Morris, 72 Fed. 890; *In re* State of California, 23 L. D. 423.

[4] Bedel *v.* St. Paul M. and M. Co., 29 L. D. 254.

[5] Kirby *v.* Lewis, 39 Fed. 66; United States *v.* Breward, 16 Peters, 147; United States *v.* Hanson, *Id.* 196. The return of the commission appointed under the act of February 26, 1895, (see, *post,* § 160,) is given by the land department the same legal effect as the surveyor-general's return. Circular, 25 L. D. 446.

[6] Caledonia M. Co. *v.* Rowen, 2 L. D. 714.

[7] Winscott *v.* N. P. R. R. Co., 17 L. D. 274.

to make the land more valuable for mining than for agriculture.[1]

Indications of mineral do not demonstrate that there is a valuable deposit.[2] A mere location certificate is not in itself evidence of the mineral character of the land, and will not be sufficient to overcome the return.[3] But when a legal mineral location has been made (which, of course, must be based upon a sufficient discovery), the slight presumption in favor of the return is overcome, and the burden of proof shifts to the party attacking the mineral claim.[4] The allowance of a mineral entry of a tract, as a matter of course, overcomes a return as agricultural.[5]

While the rule which treats the surveyor-general's return as establishing *prima facie* the character of the land is a convenient one in controversies arising between individuals over an asserted right to enter public lands, as determining upon whom rests the burden of proof, it has been productive of iniquitous results in administering the colossal land grants to railroad companies; and we are justified in asserting that its force as a universal rule has been materially weakened by the recent decisions of both the land department and the courts of last resort. The return constitutes but a small element of consideration when the question of the character

---

[1] Magruder *v.* Oregon and Cal. R. R. Co., 28 L. D. 174, overruling Sweeney *v.* N. P. R. R. Co., 20 L. D. 394; Walker *v.* S. P. R. R. Co., 24 L. D. 172, and other cases.

[2] Tulare Oil and M. Co. v. S. P. R. R. Co., 29 L. D. 269.

[3] Etling *v.* Potter, 17 L. D. 424; Berry *v.* C. P. R. R. Co., 15 L. D. 463; Magruder *v.* Oregon and Cal. R. R. Co., 28 L. D. 174; McQuiddy *v.* State of California, 29 L. D. 181; Elda Mining Co., *Id.* 279; Holton *v.* N. P. R. R. Co., 30 L. D. 442; Harkrader *v.* Goldstein, 31 L. D. 87.

[4] State of Washington *v.* McBride, 18 L. D. 199; N. P. R. R. *v.* Marshall, 17 L. D. 545; Rhodes *v.* Treas, 21 L. D. 502; Walker *v.* S. P. R. R., 24 L. D. 172.

[5] Johns *v.* Marsh, 15 L. D. 196; Walton *v.* Batten, 14 L. D. 54.

of the land is in issue.[1] It is chiefly important as determining upon whom rests the burden of proof.[2]

When it is considered that sections of one mile square are the smallest tracts the outboundaries of which the law requires to be actually surveyed; that the minor subdivisions are not surveyed in the field, but are defined by law, and protracted in the surveyor-general's office on the township plats, the lines being imaginary;[3] that surveyors, as a rule, are neither practical miners nor geologists; that they are compensated not for the volume of information furnished as to the character of the lands, but for the number of linear miles surveyed in the field; that their investigation as to the character of the land is wholly superficial,—it would seem that but little weight should be given to these returns. If the surveyor, in subdividing a township into sections, encounters a mine in active operation, we may find some mention of that fact in his field-notes; but usually he does not go beyond this. A fair illustration of the unreliability of these returns in this respect may be found in almost all the mineral districts over which the public surveys have been extended. We note the following caustic criticism of the land department itself on this subject. In an official communication (March 11, 1872) from Mr. Drummond, commissioner of the general land office, to Mr. Delano, secretary of the interior, the commissioner says:—

"To illustrate the unreliability of the surveyors' re-
" turns as to the character of these lands, and the abso-
" lute necessity for the rule which, with your advice
" and consent, I have adopted, it may be proper to refer
" in this connection to some of the applications for

---

[1] Aspen Cons. M. Co. v. Williams, 27 L. D. 1.

[2] Magruder v. Oregon and Cal. R. R. Co., 28 L. D. 174; Tulare Oil Co. v. S. P. R. R. Co., 29 L. D. 269.

[3] Public Domain, p. 184.

" patents for mines in California, the lands embracing
" which were returned on the official township plats as
" agricultural in character, the existence of mines there-
" in not becoming known to this office until after the
" receipt of such applications for mining title."

(Here follows a list of thirty-five mines.)

"The foregoing claims are all within the Sacramento
"district, and many more could be enumerated were
" it necessary to illustrate the want of reliability of the
" surveyor's returns as to the character of these lands.
" . . . But with the kind of returns furnished it is
" totally impossible to determine whether any given
" tract in the mineral district is properly agricultural
" land within the meaning of the law or not, or whether
" this office could, with a due regard for the execution
" of the law, proceed to patent such as agricultural
" land without further investigation."[1]

And in an earlier communication the same commissioner uses the following apt language:—

"I am impressed with the conviction that it is neither
" in harmony with the spirit or intent of the laws of
" congress, nor with the true public policy, to sanction
" the indiscriminate absorption of the lands in what
" has heretofore been known as the reserved mineral
" belt in the public domain under laws only applicable
" to lands clearly non-mineral, simply because the dep-
" uty surveyors failed to return the same as mineral
" in character. This view is strengthened by the fact
" that very many, in fact the majority, of the applica-
" tions for mineral patents, are found, upon consulting
" our official township plats, to be within subdivisions
" not reported as mineral in character."[2]

In a circular letter issued in December, 1871, to the
registers and receivers of land offices in the mining
regions of California, instructing them to withhold from

---

[1] Copp's Min. Dec., p. 308.   [2] *Id.*, p. 297.

agricultural entry a large number of townships, the same commissioner thus expresses his views:—

"Experience having shown that this office can not " with any degree of safety judge of the character of " these lands, whether mineral or agricultural, from " the data furnished by such returns, and there being " no authority of law for the employment of a compe- " tent geologist to investigate the matter, the head of " the department has, in consideration of the public " interests and to prevent the indiscriminate absorption " of the mineral lands of the public domain through " the instrumentality of insufficient returns, found it " imperatively necessary to adopt the course herein " announced, both for the protection of those who have " already expended time, capital, and labor in opening " and developing these mines, and those of the citizens " of the United States who may hereafter desire to " exercise their legal right to do so." [1]

In the light of these conceded facts, it is a marvel that either the land department or the courts ever announced the doctrine that such returns were *prima facie* evidence of anything save their own inherent weakness and insufficiency for this purpose.

The question as to the effect of these returns was before the supreme court of the United States in a case,[2] in which Justice Field, delivering the opinion of the court, said:—

"Some weight is sought to be given by counsel of the " plaintiff to the allegation that the lands in controversy " are included in the section which was surveyed in " 1868, and a plat thereof filed by the surveyor in the " local land office in September of that year, from which " it is asserted that the character of the land was ascer- " tained and determined, and reported to be agricul- " tural, and not mineral. But the conclusive answer to

[1] Copp's Min. Dec., p. 302.
[2] Barden v. N. P. R. R. Co., 154 U. S. 288, 14 Sup. Ct. Rep. 1030.

" such alleged determination and report is that the
" matters to which they relate were not left to the sur-
" veyor-general. Neither he nor any of his subordi-
" nates was authorized to determine finally the character
" of any lands granted, or make any binding report
" thereon.

"Information of the character of all lands surveyed
" is required of surveying officers, so far as knowledge
" respecting them is obtained in the course of their
" duties, but they are not clothed with authority to es-
" pecially examine as to these matters outside of their
" other duties, or to determine them, nor does their
" report have any binding force. It is simply an addi-
" tion made to the general information obtained from
" different sources on the subject."[1]

§ 107. **Character of land, when and how established.**
—The character of a given tract of land is always a
question of fact, to be determined, generally speaking,
by the land department, on hearings ordered for that
purpose, or at the time patent is applied for, and the
decision of the department, culminating in the issuance
of a patent, is final.[2]

The precise point of time when the character of a
given tract of land is to be determined will depend some-

---

[1] See, also, Winscott v. Northern Pac. R. R. Co., 17 L. D. 274, 276;
Aspen Cons. M. Co. v. Williams, 27 L. D. 1, 21.

[2] Pac. M. and M. Co. v. Spargo, 8 Saw. 647, 16 Fed. 348; Cowell v.
Lammers, 10 Saw. 255, 21 Fed. 200; Barden v. N. P. R. R. Co., 154 U. S.
288, 14 Sup. Ct. Rep. 1030; Gale v. Best, 78 Cal. 235, 12 Am. St. Rep.
44, 20 Pac. 550; Dahl v. Mont. C. Co., 132 U. S. 264, 10 Sup. Ct. Rep. 97;
Dahl v. Raunheim, 132 U. S. 260, 10 Sup. Ct. Rep. 74; Carter v. Thomp-
son, 65 Fed. 329; Klauber v. Higgins, 117 Cal. 541, 49 Pac. 466; United
States v. Budd, 144 U. S. 167, 12 Sup. Ct. Rep. 575; United States v.
Mackintosh, 85 Fed. 333, 336; Shaw v. Kellogg, 170 U. S. 312, 18 Sup.
Ct. Rep. 632; Northern Pac. R. R. Co. v. Soderberg, 86 Fed. 49; Mendota
Club v. Anderson, 101 Wis. 479, 78 N. W. 185; Rood v. Wallace, 109
Iowa 5, 79 N. W. 449; Potter v. Randolph, 126 Cal. 458, 58 Pac. 905;
Standard Quicksilver M. Co. v. Habeshaw, 132 Cal. 115, 64 Pac. 113;
Dreyfus v. Badger, 108 Cal. 58, 41 Pac. 279.

what upon the nature of the right asserted, and the date to which it is supposed to relate. This subject will be fully discussed under appropriate heads, when considering the various congressional grants out of which mineral lands are reserved, and the various methods of acquiring public lands other than mineral, and in the chapter treating of the land department and its functions.

§ 108. Jurisdiction of courts to determine character of land when the question is pending in land department.—It will not be doubted that, while the title to land remains in the United States, and controversies arise between occupants or possessors over the right of possession, neither party having invoked the jurisdiction of the land department for the purpose of acquiring the ultimate title, the courts have power to determine the rights of the respective parties based upon the law of possession,[1] and incidentally to pass upon the question of the character of the land, should such question be necessarily involved.[2]

But that the courts have no jurisdiction to determine questions of fact with reference to the public lands while the claims of the respective parties are pending before the land department, is axiomatic.[3] With the orderly exercise of the functions of that department in administering the public land laws the courts cannot interfere.[4] When, therefore, the jurisdiction of the land department is once set in motion, and that tribunal is engaged in the

---

[1] Marquez v. Frisbie, 101 U. S. 473, 475.

[2] Potter v. Randolph, 126 Cal. 458, 58 Pac. 905.

[3] Marquez v. Frisbie, 101 U. S. 473, 475; Astiazaran v. Santa Rita Land and M. Co., 148 U. S. 80, 30 Sup. Ct. Rep. 457; Hays v. Parker, 2 Wash. Ter. 198, 202, 3 Pac. 901; Humbird v. Avery, 110 Fed. 465, 471; Savage v. Worsham, 104 Fed. 18; Herbien v. Warren, 2 Okl. 4, 35 Pac. 575; Allen v. Pedro, 136 Cal. 1, 68 Pac. 99.

[4] See, *post*, §§ 664, 665.

investigation which necessarily involves a determination of the character of the land, the courts are precluded from trying or determining this question.

As to whether the pendency of proceedings before the land department deprives the courts of all jurisdiction in cases involving this issue or simply suspends their functions to await the ultimate judgment of the department, does not clearly appear from the adjudicated cases. This suggests a refinement which may be the subject of metaphysical discussion, but is not of large practical importance. The views of the courts may be briefly stated.

Judge Ross said, in Cosmos Exploration Co. *v.* Gray Eagle Oil Co.:—[1]

"The demurrers to the present bills raise the questions of jurisdiction and the sufficiency of the bills themselves. The bills expressly allege that upon the making of the selections under which the complainants claim, and the publishing of the notice required by the local rules and regulations of the land department, the defendants to the bills initiated in the land office contests by written protests against such selections, on the ground that the lands selected were mineral lands, and not therefore subject to selection under the act of June 4, 1897, and that those contests are still pending in the land department. Those averments in the bills, in my opinion, state the complainants out of court; for no court can lawfully anticipate what the decision of the land department may be in respect to the contests, nor direct in advance what its decision should be, even in matters of law, much less in respect to matters of fact, such as is that relating to the character of any particular piece of land." [2]

The circuit court of appeals affirmed the decision of Judge Ross, and said, among other things:—

[1] 104 Fed. 20, 40.
[2] See, also, Savage *v.* Worsham, 104 Fed. 18.

"We are of the opinion that the federal courts are
" without jurisdiction to entertain a suit to determine
" the respective rights of the parties to any land to
" which the title remains in the government of the
" United States in regard to which, as shown by the
" averments in the present bill, a contest between the
" parties is pending in the land department of the
" government." [1]

The supreme court of California,[2] while conceding
that a court should not attempt to determine questions
of fact pending before, and when they are within the
exclusive jurisdiction of, the land department, held that
a court has jurisdiction of an action which involves
such a controversy, but has no power to decide that
question, and should suspend proceedings until the land
department has determined it. The suit was brought
by a homestead claimant to quiet title to lands a portion
of which were claimed by defendant under mining locations. The defendant alleged that a contest was pending
in the land department to determine the character of the
land. Before the trial took place, the department decided
the case in favor of the homestead claimant, and the
court proceeded to judgment in his favor. On appeal,
defendant contended that the action should have been
dismissed because it was commenced at a time when the
controversy was pending in the land office. The supreme
court said, among other things:—

"The court certainly had jurisdiction of the cause.
" The real contention was that it could not determine the
" issues raised by the pleadings, because they involved a
" question which it could not try, and for the determi-
" nation of which a special tribunal had been created.
" If that were so a dismissal would have been the proper
" course. But was it so? . . . The land department of
" the United States is not a special tribunal organized

[1] 112 Fed. 46.
[2] Potter v. Randolph, 126 Cal. 458, 58 Pac. 905.

" to determine who is the owner of land. The depart-
" ment is the medium through which parties may
" acquire the title of the United States. . . . It deter-
" mines the existence or non-existence of alleged facts,
" to enable it to select the person who is entitled to pur-
" chase. . . . The court very properly, then, delayed the
" trial until the question as to the character of the land
" was determined by the land department, which alone
" had the power to decide that controversy. The court
" had jurisdiction of the action, but could not try that
" particular controversy, which was involved in the
" action. Being a suit to quiet title, and not to recover
" possession, there was no special reason for antici-
" pating the action of the department."

The court then intimates that if the suit had been
one to recover possession, it would have had power to
try such questions so far as necessary to determine the
right of possession, but that its decision would not trench
upon or conclude the land department.[1]

It was further held that the decision of the land
department as to the character of the land was properly
admitted as evidence, and was conclusive upon the question.

The issuance of a patent is not necessary before
courts can take jurisdiction. When the proceeding is
terminated in the land department by action which is a
finality, that of itself is sufficient to enable the courts
to act.[2]

---

[1] Upon this point see Marquez v. Frisbie, 101 U. S. 473, 475; Humbird v.
Avery, 110 Fed. 465, 472. See, also, Manser Lode, 27 L. D. 326.

[2] Cope v. Braden, (Okl.), 67 Pac. 474.

CHAPTER III.

STATUS OF LAND AS TO TITLE AND POSSESSION.

ARTICLE I. INTRODUCTORY.

II. MEXICAN GRANTS.

III. GRANTS TO STATES FOR EDUCATIONAL AND INTERNAL IMPROVEMENT PURPOSES.

IV. RAILROAD GRANTS.

V. TOWNSITES.

VI. INDIAN RESERVATIONS.

VII. MILITARY RESERVATIONS.

VIII. NATIONAL PARK AND FOREST RESERVATIONS.

IX. HOMESTEAD AND OTHER AGRICULTURAL CLAIMS.

X. OCCUPANCY WITHOUT COLOR OF TITLE.

ARTICLE I. INTRODUCTORY.

§ 112. Only public lands subject to appropriation under the mining laws.

§ 112. **Only public lands subject to appropriation under the mining laws.** — The mineral character of a given tract of land having been ascertained as a present fact, according to the rules enunciated in a preceding chapter, it becomes necessary to determine the *status* of the land as to title and possession before any legal right of appropriation under the mining laws can be asserted and maintained by the mineral claimant. Only public mineral lands can be entered under the mining laws. Land to which any claim or right of others has legally attached does not fall within the definition of "public land."[1]

While under the system in vogue on the continent of Europe, in Mexico, and the South American republics, mining privileges may be acquired in lands of private proprietors under certain restrictions and governmental regulations, no such right exists in any of the states and territories of the United States wherein the federal mining laws are operative. Lands held in private ownership in such states and territories cannot be invaded.[2] The land sought to be entered upon as mineral land must be free, open, public land, and not legally reserved, appropriated, dedicated to any other use or purpose, or otherwise legally disposed of. As to whether a given tract of land sought to be entered as mineral is free and open to acquisition under the mining laws, is sometimes a difficult question to solve. To enable us to intelligently deal with this subject, it will be necessary to examine the various methods by which the government parts with its title to its lands, its obligation under treaties of cession, the nature and extent of grants previously made, and the reservations of certain parts of its territory made for public purposes, pursuant to special laws.

[1] See, *ante,* § 80; *post,* § 322; Newhall *v.* Sanger, 92 U. S. 761; Bardon *v.* N. P. R. R. Co., 145 U. S. 535, 538, 12 Sup. Ct. Rep. 856; Mann *v.* Tacoma Land Co., 153 U. S. 273, 284, 14 Sup. Ct. Rep. 820; Teller *v.* United States, 113 Fed. 273; Cameron *v.* United States, 148 U. S. 301, 13 Sup. Ct. Rep. 595; United States *v.* Tygh Valley Land Co., 76 Fed. 693; Shively *v.* Bowlby, 152 U. S. 1, 14 Sup. Ct. Rep. 548; *In re* Logan, 29 L. D. 395; Nome Transp. Co., *Id.* 447; Thallman *v.* Thomas, 111 Fed. 279; Garrard *v.* Silver Peak Mines, 82 Fed. 578.

[2] Biddle Boggs *v.* Merced M. Co., 14 Cal. 376.

Article II. Mexican Grants.

§ 113. Introductory.
§ 114. Ownership of mines under Mexican law.
§ 115. Nature of title conveyed to the United States by the treaty.
§ 116. Obligation of the United States to protect rights accrued prior to the cession.
§ 117. Adjustment of claims under Mexican grants in California.
§ 118. Adjustment of claims under Mexican grants in other states and territories.
§ 119. Claims to mines asserted under the Mexican mining ordinances.
§ 120. *Status* of grants considered with reference to condition of title.
§ 121. Grants *sub judice*.
§ 122. Different classes of grants.
§ 123. Grants of the first and third classes.
§ 124. Grants of the second class, — commonly called "floats."
§ 125. Grants confirmed under the California act.
§ 126. Grants confirmed by direct action of congress.
§ 127. Grants which have been finally confirmed under the act of March 3, 1891, situated in Colorado, Wyoming, Utah, Nevada, New Mexico, or Arizona.
§ 128. Conclusions.

§ **113. Introductory.**—For a period commencing with the cession by Mexico under the treaty of Guadalupe Hidalgo, and ending with the dissolution of the court of private land claims, originally established by act of congress, March 3, 1891, to investigate and determine the validity and extent of Mexican grants in Arizona, New Mexico, Colorado, Wyoming, Utah, and Nevada,[1] the relationship of Mexican grants to the great body of the public domain has been the subject of congressional legislation and judicial inquiry, presenting many interesting and complicated ques-

---

[1] The existence of this court has been prolonged from time to time, June 30, 1903, being the date now fixed for its dissolution. Stats. 1st Sess. 57th Cong., p. 170.

tions. At the present time, with the possible exception of isolated grants which were not required to be presented for confirmation to the court above named,— *i. e.* grants which were *perfect* prior to the treaty,—it is presumed that all rights and claims of every nature to lands arising out of Mexican grants have been finally adjudicated, their limits ascertained, and the line of demarcation between grant and public lands clearly defined. The subject, if deserving of a place in a discussion of the American law of mines, is of historical interest only. Nevertheless, the recent acquisition by the United States of the Philippines, Porto Rico, and Hawaii, accompanied by treaty stipulations regarding the recognition and protection of pre-existing rights and equities in lands previously granted by the ceding nations, renders it expedient to give the subject of Mexican grants, their mode of administration, their relationship to the great body of the public lands, and the operation of the mining laws in respect thereto, some prominence.

With a comprehensive mining code recently enacted by congress governing the acquisition of possessory rights in the public mineral lands of the Philippine islands, many questions analagous to those which have arisen in the continental area of the public domain, respecting grants from foreign nations, will undoubtedly be made the subject of judicial inquiry. These considerations we think justify the treatment of the subject within reasonable limitations.

§ 114. **Ownership of mines under Mexican law.**— Under the laws in force in Mexico at the date of the treaty of Guadalupe Hidalgo, mines, whether in public or private property, belonged to the supreme government.[1]

---

[1] Castillero *v.* United States, 2 Black, 17.

No interest in the minerals of gold and silver passed
by a grant from the government of the land in which
they were contained, without express words designating
them. Such grant only passed an interest in the soil
distinct from that of the minerals.[1]

The interest in minerals was conveyed through the
operation of the mining ordinances, or by proceedings
upon denouncement, when a mine, once discovered and
registered, had been abandoned and forfeited.[2]

Mining rights under the Mexican laws were held upon
conditions not affecting the title to the land as derived
under the ordinary conveyances; and such rights might
be acquired and held by others besides the owner of the
land under the ordinary grants, and were terminable
when, by their use, the minerals contained in the soil
were wholly removed.[3]

In other words, there was a severance of the title to
the minerals from the title to the land. The minerals,
particularly gold, silver, and quicksilver, were *jura
regalia,* and were considered to belong to the supreme
government in virtue of its sovereignty.

This was substantially the law of the ceding country
at the date of the ratification and exchange of the treaty.

§ 115. **Nature of title conveyed to the United
States by the treaty.**—By the treaty of cession, all of
the property theretofore belonging to Mexico within
the limits defined by the compact between the two nations
passed to the United States.[4]

[1] Fremont *v.* Flower, 17 Cal. 199, 79 Am. Dec. 123; Lockhart *v.* Johnson, 181 U. S. 516, 524, 21 Sup. Ct. Rep. 665.

[2] Fremont *v.* Flower, 17 Cal. 199, 79 Am. Dec. 123; United States *v.* San Pedro etc. Co., 4 N. Mex. 225, 17 Pac. 407; United States *v.* Castillero, 2 Black, 17.

[3] Castillero *v.* United States, 2 Black, 17.

[4] Fremont *v.* Flower, 17 Cal. 199, 79 Am. Dec. 123.

The government of the United States was based upon different theories from that of the ceding country. By the operation of the treaty, none of the Mexican theories of government were grafted upon the American system. The ownership conferred by the cession was not an incident of sovereignty, and the United States hold the minerals and the lands in which they are found just as they hold any other public property which they acquired from Mexico.[1]

No foreign government could, by treaty or otherwise, impart to the United States any of its sovereign prerogatives; nor have the United States the capacity to receive or power to exercise them. Every nation acquiring territory by treaty or otherwise must hold it subject to the constitution and laws of its own government, and not according to those of the government ceding it.[2]

§ 116. **Obligation of the United States to protect rights which accrued prior to the cession.** —It is a matter of political history that within the territory ceded, particularly within the area now comprising the states of California and Colorado and the territories of New Mexico and Arizona, and to a limited extent, perhaps, in other states, rights were asserted to a large number of tracts of land by title derived from the ceding nation. These tracts varied in area from comparatively few acres to immense bodies of land, in some instances embracing principalities within their claimed boundaries. Most of these claimed grants were either grants for colonization or for the purposes of stock-raising and agriculture. A very few were for mines claimed to have been acquired under the mining ordinances. Most of them were inchoate—that is to say, something remained

[1] Fremont v. Flower, 17 Cal. 199, 79 Am. Dec. 123.
[2] Pollard v. Hagan, 3 How. 212.

to be done to either perfect and establish the title or to fix the boundaries. Many were spurious and fraudulent. As to all these asserted rights, the treaty of Guadalupe Hidalgo imposed upon the government of the United States the obligation to protect titles acquired under Mexican rule.[1] This obligation was imposed upon our government by international law independent of treaty stipulation.[2]

These rights were consecrated by the law of nations.[3] A right of any validity before the cession was equally valid afterwards.[4] The duty of providing the mode of securing these rights and of fulfilling the obligations imposed upon the United States belonged to the political department of the government. Congress might either itself discharge that duty or delegate it to the judicial department.[5] In the larger sense, however, all the lands ceded were "public lands" until congress placed them in a state of reservation to abide the investigation into the nature and extent of the title asserted by parties claiming under grants from the ceding nation.[6]

§ 117. **Adjustment of claims under Mexican grants in California.**—With reference to Mexican grants in California, congress provided for the appointment of a board of land commissioners,[7] to whom all persons claiming lands by virtue of any right or title derived

---

[1] Peralta v. United States, 3 Wall. 434; Knight v. U. S. Land Assn., 142 U. S. 161, 12 Sup. Ct. Rep. 258.

[2] Strother v. Lucas, 12 Peters, 410.

[3] United States v. Moreno, 1 Wall. 400; 1 Wharton's Internat. Dig., § 4.

[4] United States v. Moreno, 1 Wall. 400; Interstate L. Co. v. Maxwell L. G. Co., 139 U. S. 569, 11 Sup. Ct. Rep. 656.

[5] Astiazaran v. Santa Rita L. & M. Co., 148 U. S. 80, 13 Sup. Ct. Rep. 457; De la Croix v. Chamberlain, 12 Wheat. 599; Chouteau v. Eckhart, 2 How. 344; Tameling v. U. S. Freehold Co., 93 U. S. 644.

[6] Lockhardt v. Johnson, 181 U. S. 516, 21 Sup. Ct. Rep., 665. See Baca Float No. 3, 30 L. D. 497.

[7] Act of March 3, 1851, 9 Stats. at Large, p. 631.

from the Spanish or Mexican government were required to present their claims. The action of the commissioners was subject to review by the United States district court, and the right to appeal to the supreme court of the United States was given. Under this act most of the Mexican land grants in California were adjudicated, and patents issued for such as were ultimately confirmed. A similar method had been pursued with reference to grants claimed in the territory ceded by Spain and France.[1]

The government of the United States, when it came to consider this statute, was not without large experience in a somewhat similar class of cases arising under the treaties for the purchase of Florida from Spain and the territory of Louisiana from France. In the latter case, particularly, a very much larger number of claims by private individuals existed to the soil acquired by the treaty, some of whom resided on the lands which they claimed, while others did not, and the titles asserted were as diverse in their nature as those arising under the cession from Mexico.[2]

§ 118. **Adjustment of claims under Mexican grants in other states and territories.** —As to claimed Mexican grants situated within the territory of New Mexico, congress, on July 22, 1854, passed an act[3] providing, among other things, that the surveyor-general for that territory should examine into and report to the interior department upon the *status* of private land claims within his jurisdiction. The provisions of •this act were extended to Colorado by the act of February 28, 1861,[4] and to Arizona by the act of February 24, 1863.[5]

---

[1] Public Domain, p. 375.
[2] Botiller *v.* Dominguez, 130 U. S. 238, 9 Sup. Ct. Rep. 525.
[3] 10 Stats. at Large, p. 308.
[4] 12 Stats. at Large, p. 172.
[5] *Id.,* p. 664.

Some of the grants so reported upon under these acts were presented to congress, and were confirmed. But by far the greater proportion awaited the passage of some general law providing a uniform method of adjustment. Such a law was passed March 3, 1891.[1]

This act created a court of private land claims, consisting of a chief justice and four associate justices, to which tribunal all persons claiming lands within the limits of the territory derived by the United States from the republic of Mexico, and now embraced within the territories of New Mexico and Arizona, and the states of Nevada, Colorado, Wyoming, and Utah, were called upon to submit their claims.[2] The object for which this court was created has in the main been accomplished. Its existence has been prolonged from time to time, June 30, 1903, being now fixed as the date of its formal dissolution.[3] A large number of claimed grants were submitted to it. It confirmed some, and rejected others. The act creating this tribunal may be said to have been drawn on lines parallel to the one passed for California, but, in one respect at least, it made a radical innovation. The California act made no mention of or reference to mineral lands distinctively. The law now under consideration contains the following provision:—

"No allowance or confirmation of any claim shall
" confer any right or title to any gold, or silver, or
" quicksilver mines, or minerals of the same, unless the
" grant claimed effected the donation or sale of such
" mines or minerals to the grantee, or unless the grantee
" has become otherwise entitled thereto in law or equity;
" but all such mines and minerals shall remain the prop-
" erty of the United States, with the right of working

---

[1] 26 Stats. at Large, p. 854.

[2] The California act required all classes of claimed grants to be presented, whether perfect or inchoate. The act of 1891 leaves it optional with the owner of a perfect grant to present it or not, as he sees fit.

[3] Act of April 28, 1902, Stats. 1st Sess 57th Cong., p. 170.

" the same, which fact shall be stated in all patents
" issued under this act. But no such mine shall be
" worked on any property confirmed by this act without
" the consent of the owner of such property, until spe-
" cially authorized thereto by an act of congress here-
" after passed."

Whatever may be the proper interpretation to be
placed upon this proviso on final analysis, it might seem
from a casual reading to foreshadow a radical departure
from the previous policy of the government. All reservations heretofore made or authorized by congress, with
the exception of "known mines," in the pre-emption
act of 1841, and "veins," or "lodes," in the townsite act
of 1865, have been of the *lands* containing mineral, not
the mineral within the lands. The effect of these new
provisions and the construction of the patents to be
issued under them will be duly considered at the proper
time.

§ 119. **Claims to mines asserted under the Mexican
mining ordinances.** —It may be conceded on the thresh-
old that where a valid claim to a mine or a mining
right existed prior to the cession within the territory
ceded, such right was to be respected, and should have
been determined in the same manner as claims to other
land were determined.[1] We are not aware of any such
claim ever having been thus far successfully established.

But few were ever asserted in California; and, of
course, the time for such assertion has long since elapsed.
Only two strictly mining titles were presented for confirmation to the court of private land claims created
under the act of March 3, 1891. Both of these were
rejected upon the ground that the officer of the
former government purporting to make the grant had

---

[1] Castillero *v.* United States, 2 Black, 17.

no authority to make it. Therefore, we have no further concern with this class of claims. We are to deal only with rights asserted to lands claimed either under the colonization laws of Mexico or for agricultural, pastoral, and kindred purposes.

§ 120. **Status of grants considered with reference to condition of title.** —The *status* of lands embraced within claimed Mexican grants pending the investigation and determination of title and defining boundaries depended to some extent upon the nature of the grant,—that is, whether it was perfect or inchoate, had definitely fixed boundaries, or was simply a float,—and also to a greater degree upon the policy of congress expressed from time to time in its legislation on the subject. This will be made manifest as we proceed with the discussion. So far as the inquiry is pertinent to the questions considered in this treatise, Mexican grants may be considered in four different aspects:—

(1) Grants *sub judice*—that is to say, awaiting final confirmation and determination of boundaries;

(2) Grants confirmed finally by action of the judicial tribunals under the California act, and the boundaries fixed;

(3) Grants confirmed by direct action of congress;

(4) Grants which have been confirmed under the act of March 3, 1891, situated in Colorado, Wyoming, Utah, Nevada, New Mexico, or Arizona.

Let us consider these in the order named.

§ 121. **Grants sub judice.** —With respect to all classes of Mexican grants, it may be said that they were *sub judice* until the title had been established and the boundaries finally defined by the tribunals charged with these functions, or the right finally declared invalid and without foundation, or until the period fixed by the various acts requiring presentation to the respective tribunals passed without such presentation having been made.[1]

§ 122. Different classes of grants. —Mexican grants were of three kinds:—

(1) Grants by specific boundaries, where the donee is entitled to the entire tract;

(2) Grants of quantity, as of one or more leagues within a larger tract, described by what are called outside boundaries, where the donee is entitled to the quantity specified and no more;

(3) Grants of a place or rancho by name, where the donee is entitled to the whole tract, according to the boundaries given, or, if not given, according to the extent as shown by previous possession.[2]

§ 123. Grants of the first and third classes. —With respect to lands containing mines or mineral deposits within the claimed exterior boundaries of any grant falling within the first and third classes in California, or in New Mexico, Utah, Arizona, Wyoming, and Nevada, prior to the act of March 3, 1891, it may be stated generally that no right to any such lands could be acquired under the general mining laws so long as the grant remained *sub judice.* Such lands were not "public lands" within the meaning of that term as used

---

[1] Under the California act all classes of grants, whether perfect or imperfect, were required to be presented. Under the act of March 3, 1891, the owners of *perfect* grants may present their claims or not, as they see fit.

[2] United States *v.* McLaughlin, 127 U. S. 428, 8 Sup. Ct. Rep. 1177; Higueras *v.* United States, 5 Wall. 827; Hornsby *v.* United States, 10 Wall. 224.

in the acts of congress respecting the disposition of the public domain.[1]

And it is immaterial whether the claim was *lawfully* made or not. As was said by the supreme court of the United States,—

"Claims, whether grounded upon an inchoate or per-
" fected title, were to be ascertained and adequately
" protected. This duty, enjoined by a sense of natural
" justice and by treaty obligations, could only be
" discharged by prohibiting intrusion upon the claimed
" lands until an opportunity was afforded the parties
" in interest for a judicial hearing and determination.
" It was to be expected that unfounded and fraudulent
" claims would be presented for confirmation. There
" was, in the opinion of congress, no mode of separating
" them from those which were valid without investiga-
" tion by a competent tribunal; and our legislation was
" so shaped that no title could be initiated under the
" laws of the United States to lands covered by a
" Spanish or Mexican claim, until it was barred by lapse
" of time or rejected."[2]

The theory by which grants of the two classes under consideration were while *sub judice* withheld from appropriation under the general land laws of congress is thus stated by the same tribunal:—

"The right to make the segregation rested exclusively
" with the government, and could only be exercised by
" its officers. Until they acted and effected the segre-
" gation, the confirmees were interested in preserving
" the entire tract from waste and injury and in improv-
" ing it; for until then they could not know what part
" might be assigned to them. Until then no third
" person could interfere with their right to the posses-
" sion of the whole. No third person could be permitted
" to determine in advance of such segregation that any

[1] Cameron *v.* United States, 148 U. S. 301, 13 Sup. Ct. Rep. 595; Doolan *v.* Carr, 125 U. S. 618, 8 Sup. Ct. Rep. 1228.

[2] Newhall *v.* Sanger, 92 U. S. 761, 764.

"particular locality would fall within the surplus,
"and thereby justify his intrusion upon it and its
"detention from them. . . . If the law were otherwise
"than as stated, the confirmees would find their posses-
"sions limited, first in one direction, and then in
"another, each intruder asserting that the parcel
"occupied by him fell within the surplus, until in the
"end they would be excluded from the entire tract."[1]

This was the doctrine early announced by the supreme
court of the state of California, and maintained through
a long line of decisions.[2]

It has been said that the primary object of the act of
March 3, 1851, to ascertain and settle the private land
claims in the state of California, was to distinguish the
vacant public lands from those that were private property.[3]

Until a confirmation of a grant, no valid title as
against the United States is vested to any specific land.
Nor does a confirmation locate the claim and sever the
land from the public domain without a survey.[4]

Until such confirmation and final survey, lands within
the claimed limits were reserved from the operation of
the general land laws, and no title to any portion could
be obtained under the pre-emption or other laws.

When the limits have been definitely fixed, the surplus
for the first time becomes open to settlement and purchase.[5]

A like result follows in cases where the grant is finally

[1] Van Reynegan v. Bolton, 95 U. S. 33-36 (citing Cornwall v. Culver, 16
Cal. 429; Mahoney v. Van Winkle, 21 Cal. 552; Riley v. Heisch, 18
Cal. 198).

[2] Ferris v. Coover, 10 Cal. 589; Mahoney v. Van Winkle, 21 Cal. 552;
Thornton v. Mahoney, 24 Cal. 569; Rich v. Maples, 33 Cal. 102; Mott v.
Reyes, 45 Cal. 379; Shanklin v. McNamara, 87 Cal. 371, 26 Pac. 345.

[3] Castro v. Hendricks, 23 How. 438.

[4] Ledoux v. Black, 18 How. 473.

[5] United States v. McLaughlin, 127 U. S. 428, 8 Sup. Ct. Rep. 1177;
Quinn v. Chapman, 111 U. S. 445, 4 Sup. Ct. Rep. 508.

rejected, or where the claimant fails to present his claim within the time specified in the act.[1]

§ 124. **Grants of the second class, commonly called "floats."**—Do the foregoing rules apply to cases falling within the second class of grants, commonly called "floats"?—for example, a grant of ten square leagues within claimed exterior boundaries of one hundred square leagues. This was the case of the Mariposa grant in California, claimed by and ultimately confirmed to General John C. Fremont.

The decisions heretofore quoted and the rules enunciated applied to conditions antedating the enactment of general mining laws. Prior to July 26, 1866, no mineral lands, even on the unquestioned public domain, could be acquired in absolute private ownership. The various acts passed from 1851 to 1891 regulating the settlement of private land claims made no mention of minerals or mineral lands.

The California act, by legislative intendment, as we have heretofore shown, reserved these claimed lands from pre-emption and homestead settlement.

The acts conferring authority upon surveyors-general in the territories to examine and report upon Mexican grants contained a provision to the effect that "until " final action of congress on such claims, all lands cov- " ered thereby shall be reserved from sale or other dis- " position by the government." [2]

Would these inhibitions imply that lands lying within the claimed exterior boundaries of a float were not open

[1] Botiller v. Dominguez, 130 U. S. 238, 9 Sup. Ct. Rep. 525; United States v. Fossat, 21 How. 446.

[2] As will be hereafter noted, the act of March 3, 1891, repealed the clause as to claimed grants in Arizona, New Mexico, Utah, Nevada, and Wyoming. The *status* of those grants after that date were somewhat different. The rule here stated is, we think, the correct one as to all Mexican grants prior to March 3, 1891.

to exploration and purchase, as lands containing gold and silver? Confessedly, titles to these minerals could not have been obtained under the Mexican government by proceedings other than under the mining ordinances; and it can be plausibly asserted that the United States was under no legal or equitable obligation to confer upon these grantees something more than they could have acquired had there been no change in the paramount proprietorship.

And yet we fail to see anything in the adjudicated cases which would not reserve the entire claimed tract from occupation and purchase under the mining laws until such time as the boundaries are finally fixed and the surplus becomes public domain.

The supreme court of the United States thus distinguishes this class of grants:—

"It is in the option of the government, not of the " grantee, to locate the quantity granted; and, of course, " a grant by the government of any part of the territory " contained within the outside limits of the grant only " reduces by so much the area within which the original " grantee's proper quantity may be located. If the gov- " ernment has the right to say where it shall be located, " it certainly has the right to say where it shall not be " located; and if it sells land to a third person at a place " within the general territory of the original grant, it " is equivalent to saying that the quantity due to the " original grantee is not to be located there. In other " words, if the territory comprehended in the outside " limits and bounds of a Mexican grant contains eighty " leagues, and the quantity granted is only ten leagues, " the government may dispose of seventy leagues with- " out doing any wrong to the original grantee." [1]

The case was that of a railroad grant evidenced by patent for a section of land within a float. Suit was brought to vacate the patent on the ground that the land

[1] United States v. McLaughlin, 127 U. S. 428, 8 Sup. Ct. Rep. 1177.

patented was at the time of the patent embraced within the exterior boundaries of a claimed Mexican grant, then *sub judice,* and that therefore the patent was void, relying upon the case of Newhall *v.* Sanger,[1] which involved precisely the same grant, although, as presented for the consideration of the supreme court in that case, it appeared to be a grant by specific boundaries, and not a float.

The case of United States *v.* McLaughlin established the doctrine that the government might, by *direct congressional grant,* dispose of lands within a float so long as sufficient remained to satisfy the call of the grant for quantity. This rule was subsequently reannounced, and followed in later cases.[2]

But, as we understand the McLaughlin case, the court did not intend to infer that any such lands were subject to appropriation *under general laws.* In fact, the court says:—

"It may be that the land office might properly sus-
" pend ordinary operations in the disposal of lands
" within the territory indicated; and in that sense they
" might not be considered as public lands."

We think a review of the authorities justifies the conclusion that floats were not exceptions to the general doctrine that Mexican grants while *sub judice* were to the extent of their claimed exterior boundaries, as defined in the *expediente,* withdrawn from exploration and purchase under the general mining laws; and this is true wheresoever within the ceded territory these grants were found prior to the passage of the act of March 3, 1891. Under this act a different policy was inaugurated. It

---

[1] 92 U. S. 761.

[2] Carr *v.* Quigley, 149 U. S. 652, 13 Sup. Ct. Rep. 961; Wis. Cent. R. R. Co. *v.* Forsythe, 159 U. S. 48, 15 Sup. Ct. Rep. 1020; United States *v.* Gurtner, 38 Fed. 1; Grant *v.* Oliver, 91 Cal. 158, 27 Pac. 596, 598.

repealed the provisions of the act of July 22, 1854, which placed all lands within this class of claimed grants in a state of reservation. By this repeal, lands which were *in fact* public lands belonging to the United States, although within the claimed limits of a Mexican grant, became open to entry and sale under the laws of the United States.[1]

This may be illustrated. A mining location could not have been made within the claimed limits of a Mexican grant prior to March 3, 1891, so long as such grant was *sub judice*. Since that date such a location could be made; and if it is ultimately determined that the asserted claim to the grant was mineral, or did not embrace within its limits as finally confirmed the *locus* of the mining claim, the mining location would be valid. In other words, a prospector might locate a mining claim within the limits of a claimed grant which was *sub judice*, taking his chances that the grant would either not be confirmed or would not embrace his location.[2]

§ 125. **Grants confirmed under the California act.**— As to grants confirmed finally, with boundaries fixed by action of the judicial tribunals, under the California act, such grants occupy the *status* of patented lands, and will be so considered. A right to a patent is equivalent to a patent issued.

The question as to whether mines of the precious

[1] Lockhardt *v.* Johnson, 181 U. S. 516, 521, 21 Sup. Ct. Rep. 665; Lockhart *v.* Wills, 9 N. Mex. 344, 54 Pac. 336; Lockhart *v.* Leeds, 63 Pac. 48.

[2] Lockhardt *v.* Johnson, 181 U. S. 516, 525. Previous to this decision the land department held that all such lands remained in a state of reservation until the grant was finally disposed of, and that no rights under the public land laws could be acquired within the claimed limits of a grant so long as it remained *sub judice*. Tumacacori and Calabazas Grant, 16 L. D. 408, 423; *In re* Farr, 24 L. D. 1; Baca Float No. 3, 30 L. D. 497; *In re* Katherine Davis, *Id.* 220.

metals passed by confirmation to a grantee of a Mexican grant has never been in terms judicially determined by the supreme court of the United States.

In the case of the Mariposa grant,[1] General Fremont's right to confirmation was assailed upon the ground that the grant embraced mines of gold or silver. The supreme court of the United States confirmed the grant, holding that the only question before it was the validity of the title; that, under the mining laws of Spain and Mexico, the discovery of a mine did not destroy the title of the individual to the land granted; that whether there were any mines on the grant in question, and, if there were, what were the rights of sovereignty in them, were questions which must be decided in another form of proceeding, and were not subjected to the jurisdiction of the commissioners or the court by the act of 1851. But in the later case of the New Almaden quicksilver mine,[2] a direct application for confirmation of a mining title was made; and the same court, while denying the validity of the asserted right, held that rights to mines acquired from Spain and Mexico prior to the cession were interests in land, and as such were subject to the jurisdiction of the commissioners. The Fremont case was not mentioned by the court, although in the court below (Judge Hoffman), sustaining the jurisdiction, held that the rule announced by him was not in conflict with the Fremont case, the only question there being the validity of the grant.

After the patent was issued to Fremont, the question arose in the California courts as to whether the minerals of gold and silver discovered within the grant passed to the confirmee under the patent, and the supreme court of that state thus announced its conclusions:—

[1] Fremont v. United States, 17 How. 442, 476.
[2] Castillero v. United States, 2 Black, 17.

"The United States occupy, with reference to their
" real property within the limits of the state, only the
" position of a private proprietor, with the exception
" of exemption from state taxation, and their patent of
" such property is subject to the same general rules of
" construction which apply to conveyances of individ-
" uals. From the operation of conveyances of this
" nature—that is, of individuals,—the minerals of gold
" and silver are not reserved, unless by express terms.
" They pass with the transfer of the soil in which they
" are contained. And the same is true of the operation
" of the patent, the instrument of transfer of the govern-
" mental proprietor, the United States; no interest in
" the minerals remains in them without a similar reser-
" vation.

"The United States have uniformly regarded the
" patent as transferring all interests which they could
" possess in the soil, and everything imbedded in or
" connected therewith. Wherever they have claimed
" mines, it has been as part of the *lands* in which they
" were contained; and whenever they have reserved the
" minerals from sale or other disposition, it has only
" been by reserving the lands themselves. It has never
" been the policy of the United States to possess inter-
" ests in land in connection with individuals."[1]

This doctrine seems logical. We are not aware of its
ever having been seriously questioned. It was commented on and distinguished by the supreme court of
New Mexico in a case involving a patent issued under
a special act of congress, confirming a grant,[2] to be
hereafter discussed; but we do not think its force has
been destroyed or weakened.

Unquestionably, the United States might have said
to these claimants: "The title asserted by you as the

---

[1] Fremont *v.* Flower, 17 Cal. 199, 79 Am. Dec. 123; Moore *v.* Smaw,
Id. See, also, Ah Hee *v.* Crippen, 19 Cal. 492; Biddle Boggs *v.* Merced
M. Co., 14 Cal. 279; Manning *v.* San Jacinto Tin Co., 7 Saw. 419, 9
Fed. 726.

[2] United States *v.* San Pedro etc. Co., 4 N. Mex. 225, 17 Pac. 337.

" grantee of the Mexican government did not convey
" to you the right to the minerals of gold, silver, or
" quicksilver which are within your claimed grant. It
" is not our purpose to convey to you lands containing
" these metals; and before any title is bestowed upon
" you by this government, you must demonstrate that
" the lands are non-mineral in character. If mineral
" lands are found within your boundaries, they must
" be segregated out, as in the case of pre-emption, home-
" stead, and other classes of grant, and you will be
" given a title to the remainder."

Or it might have gone farther and offered a title
reserving all minerals, as it is claimed was attempted
in the later act applicable to Colorado, New Mexico,
Arizona, Utah, Nevada, and Wyoming. But the government imposed no such conditions as to grants in California. Its patent passed everything it had acquired
from the Mexican government, and the United States
ceased to have any further concern with the land or its
constituent elements.

A patent issued upon a confirmed Mexican grant
passes whatever interest the United States may have
had in the premises.[1] It operates, in consequence, as
an absolute bar to all claims under the United States
having their origin subsequent to the petition for confirmation. It is, in effect, a declaration that the rightful
ownership never had been in the United States, but at
the time of the cession it had passed to the claimant or
those under whom he claimed.[2]

If the grantee received more than he could have acquired from the Mexican government, it is not a matter

---

[1] Beard v. Federy, 3 Wall. 478, Adam v. Norris, 103 U. S. 591; More v.
Steinbach, 127 U. S. 70, 8 Sup. Ct. Rep. 1067; Henshaw v. Bissel, 18
Wall. 255.

[2] Adam v. Norris, 103 U. S. 591, and cases therein cited.

concerning which outsiders may lawfully complain. The United States might confirm and patent a Mexican grant for a much larger quantity of land than it was possible to be obtained under the Mexican law.[1]

Why did it not possess the same power with reference to the minerals? Possessing that power, it exercised it by issuing a patent containing no reservation. As a matter of fact, the California act did not authorize the insertion of a reservation; and if a patent issued under that law contained such, it would have been to that extent void, as being unauthorized.[2]

§ 126. **Grants confirmed by direct action of congress.** —We are aware of no principle of law which permits us to draw distinctions beween the legal effect of a patent issued under an act of congress, directly confirming a grant, and one issued as a result of an investigation by tribunals created by congress for that purpose. We should not have divided the question, and placed direct congressional confirmation in a separate category, were we not confronted by a very able and thoughtful opinion promulgated by the supreme court of New Mexico,[3] wherein that court announces the doctrine that an act of congress confirming to a claimant his title to a tract of land granted to him by the Mexican government under the colonization laws of Mexico and Spain, and a patent issued in accordance therewith, conveys no title to the mineral lands included in such grant.

The record in this case is very voluminous, and the

[1] United States v. Maxwell L. G. Co., 121 U. S. 325, 7 Sup. Ct. Rep. 1015.

[2] Deffeback v. Hawke, 115 U. S. 392, 6 Sup. Ct. Rep. 95; Amador-Medean G. M. Co. v. S. Spring Hill, 13 Saw. 523, 36 Fed. 668; Smoke-house Lode Cases, 6 Mont. 397, 12 Pac. 858; Clary v. Hazlitt, 67 Cal. 286, 7 Pac. 701; Silver Bow M. and M. Co. v. Clark, 5 Mont. 378, 5 Pac. 570; Wolfley v. Lebanon M. Co., 4 Colo. 112.

[3] United States v. San Pedro and Cañon del Agua Co., 4 N. M. 225, 17 Pac. 337.

opinion of the court lengthy. An epitome of the facts,
the issues raised, and conclusions reached by the court
are essential to a proper consideration of the force and
value of the decision as a precedent. The confirmatory
act in question is very short, and for convenience' sake
we quote it:—

"Be it enacted, . . . That the grant to José Sera-
" fin Ramirez, of the Cañon del Agua, as approved by
" the surveyor-general of New Mexico, January 20,
" 1860, and designated as number seventy in the tran-
" script of private land claims in New Mexico, trans-
" mitted to congress by the secretary of the interior,
" January 11, 1861, is hereby confirmed; *provided,* that
" this confirmation shall only be construed as a relin-
" quishment on the part of the United States, and shall
" not affect the adverse rights of any persons whom-
" soever." [1]

A patent was issued pursuant to this confirmation,
describing the grant by metes and bounds, as shown in
the field-notes of the approved survey, containing no
reserving or excepting clauses other than the one provided for in the act.

The grant, as patented, included within its exterior
boundaries rich and valuable mines of gold, silver, iron,
copper, and lead, some of which were worked prior to
the treaty of cession by Mexican citizens. Others were
thereafter discovered, occupied, and developed by American citizens, it being generally understood that they
were situated upon the public domain, and not upon
private property.

Suit was brought by the government to vacate and
annul the patent, on the ground that the claimant had,
by a fraudulent conspiracy with the surveyor-general,
his clerk, the deputy surveyor, and other persons,
secured a survey of said claimed grant which included

[1] (June 12, 1866), 14 U. S. Stats. at Large, p. 588.

land not conveyed nor intended to be conveyed by the Mexican government; that this fraudulent survey, upon which the patent was based, embraced the mines, whereas a proper construction of the terms of the grant, as presented for confirmation, would have excluded them.

There was an abundance of evidence to substantiate the fraudulent character of the survey, and to sustain the ruling of the supreme court of New Mexico setting aside and annulling the patent.

But a supplemental bill had been filed in the trial court without objection which raised another legal issue. It was therein alleged as follows:—

"That said defendant is now, and has been, in pos-
" session of large portions of said tract of land men-
" tioned and described in said original bill of complaint
" as being the property of the United States, and by
" said fraudulent survey now included and embraced
" within the boundaries mentioned and described in the
" patent of the United States, as set forth in said bill
" of complaint; and that said defendant is now in pos-
" session of many mines, leads, lodes, and veins of
" mineral-bearing quartz or rock belonging to the
" United States, and situated upon said tract of land,
" the property of the United States. The said mines,
" leads, lodes, and veins are very rich and valuable for
" gold, silver, copper, and other ores. That said de-
" fendant claims said land, with its mines, leads, lodes,
" and veins of mineral-bearing rock and mineral de-
" posits, by and under said patent of the United States."

This was followed by a prayer for an injunction prohibiting the defendant from mining or appropriating the ores.

Upon this issue, although the supreme court of New Mexico had determined that the patent, having been fraudulently obtained, was null and void, and therefore conveyed nothing, felt constrained to go farther, and enunciate the doctrine that, even if valid, the patent did not convey the minerals, and granted an injunction.

If the conclusion of the court was correct, and it undoubtedly was, that a proper survey made under the grant would exclude the mines, it was quite evident that the United States had a right to prevent the claimant from wasting the substance of its property by extracting and removing the metal-bearing ores, and an injunction was very properly sought, evidently upon this theory. It was quite unnecessary, in order to support the judgment awarding the injunction, to hold that the minerals did not pass by the patent. Therefore, all that the court said with reference to minerals not passing by the patent, which they had declared to be void, and to have passed nothing, was *obiter,* and wholly unnecessary.

The reasoning of the court on this branch of the case rests upon the assumption that as the claimant under the grant could not have obtained from the Mexican government the right to the minerals, therefore he could not *demand* them from the United States. But this is not the question at issue. The question is, What did the patent, assuming it to have been valid, convey?

In speaking of the California cases of Moore *v.* Smaw and Fremont *v.* Flower, heretofore cited, the court says that a careful study of these cases will prove that there were circumstances in the grant confirmation indicating an intent not disclosed in the Cañon del Agua case. A thorough knowledge of the Mariposa grant, its history, and the various judicial controversies arising out of it between the mineral claimants and the grantees under the Mexican government, enables us to assert that there are no differences in essential characteristics between the two grants. Neither asserted title under the mining ordinances. One was for colonization purposes, and the

other for pastoral. The patent in one case was issued
on a confirmation made by special act of congress, and
in the other on a confirmation made by tribunals especially created by congress for that purpose.

The Cañon del Agua case was appealed to the supreme
court of the United States, where the judgment of the
supreme court of New Mexico was affirmed;[1] but the
question as to whether the patent, if valid, carried the
right to the mines was neither discussed nor decided.

With all due deference to the supreme court of New
Mexico, we think we are justified in the conclusion that
its decision in the Cañon del Agua case does not militate
against the doctrine of the California cases, nor weaken
the force of the line of decisions on the subject of patents
to confirmed Mexican grants reviewed in the preceding
paragraphs.

The decision in Fremont v. Flower was written by
Judge Field. It has always stood unquestioned. As
was said by Dr. Raymond in a recent monograph,—

"That a United States patent for land passes to the
" patentee (in the absence of explicit reservations au-
" thorized by law) all the interest of the United States,
" whatever it may be, in everything connected with the
" soil, or forming any portion of its bed, or fixed to its
" surface,—in short, everything embraced within the
" term 'land,'—was declared long ago in the cases aris-
" ing out of the Mexican land grants in California.
" (See Fremont v. Flower, 17 Cal. 199, 79 Am. Dec. 123,
" and other cases.) The very acute and sound decisions
" of the supreme court of California in these cases (the
" chief credit for which is due to Stephen J. Field, now
" on the bench of the United States supreme court)
" may be said to have placed upon indestructible foun-
" dations the public land system of the United States,
" the corner-stone of which is the completeness and in-
" vulnerability of the title of the patentee. It is worthy

[1] 146 U. S. 120, 13 Sup. Ct. Rep. 94.

" of notice, that in these cases the land in question had
" been granted by the Mexican government, with reser-
" vation of the precious metals, the deposits of which
" that government has always claimed to own, and the
" ownership of which therefore passed, under treaty,
" unimpaired by the agricultural grants, to the United
" States. Nevertheless, it was held that, in confirming
" the Mexican grants and issuing its patents for the
" territory, the United States actually conveyed to the
" patentees rights which they had never obtained from
" Mexico, on the broad principle that the unqualified
" grant of a patent for 'land' *gives all.* In other words,
" though the United States might have reserved the
" mineral right, it could only have done so in explicit
" terms, failing which, all its interests passed with its
" patent. The wisdom of this timely decision is univer-
" sally admitted. Unquestionably it saved us from an
" intolerable chaos and confusion." [1]

Before leaving this subject, it may be well to invite
attention to another class of grants made by congress,
in satisfaction of rights asserted, having their origin
under the Mexican rule. In several instances, in recognition of equities, congress has authorized claimants to
select certain lands in lieu of those originally claimed.
This authorization is generally accompanied with a
restrictive clause prohibiting the selection of mineral
lands. Under these conditions, the land department ad-
ministers the grant, and necessarily in doing so passes
upon the character of the land,[2] as of the date of selection.[3] The duty devolves upon the claimant to establish
the non-mineral character of the lands selected.[4]

---

[1] "The Force of the United States Mineral Land Patent," Mineral
Industry, vol. iv, p. 781.

[2] Or, as in some cases, the duty of determining the character of the
land is lodged with the surveyor-general, who acts under the supervisory
control of the secretary of the interior. Shaw *v.* Kellogg, 170 U. S. 312,
18 Sup. Ct. Rep. 632.

[3] Baca Float No. 3, 29 L. D. 44, 52.

[4] *Id.,* 13 L. D. 624.

Should any lands be included within the selection which are determined to be mineral in character, as that term is defined and understood by the land department and the courts, a segregation would be required as to such lands, and patent would issue for the remainder. Such patent when issued would be conclusive that the land was non-mineral, and it could not be thereafter collaterally assailed.[1]

§ 127. **Grants which have been finally confirmed under the act of March 3, 1891, situated in Colorado, Wyoming, Utah, Nevada, New Mexico, or Arizona.**— What is the true intent and meaning of the proviso contained in the act of March 3, 1891?—

" No allowance or confirmation of any claim shall " confer any right or title to any gold or silver or " quicksilver mines, or minerals of the same, unless the " grant claimed effected the donation or sale of such " mines or minerals to the grantee, or unless the grantee " has become otherwise entitled thereto in law or " equity; but all such mines and minerals shall remain " the property of the United States, with the right of " working the same, which fact shall be stated in all " patents issued under this act. But no such mines shall " be worked on any property confirmed by this act with- " out the consent of the owner of such property, until " specially authorized thereto by an act of congress " hereafter passed."

The inquiry presents some difficulty. Its proper solution involves the consideration of a number of elements.

---

[1] Carter v. Thompson, 65 Fed. 329; Dahl v. Raunheim, 132 U. S. 260, 10 Sup. Ct. Rep. 74; Steel v. Smelting Co., 106 U. S. 447, 1 Sup. Ct. Rep. 387; Cowell v. Lammers, 10 Saw. 247, 21 Fed. 200; Manning v. San Jacinto Tin Co., 7 Saw. 419, 9 Fed. 726; St. Louis Smelting Co. v. Kemp, 104 U. S. 636; Butte & B. M. Co. v. Sloan, 16 Mont. 97, 40 Pac. 217; Gale v. Best, 78 Cal. 235, 12 Am. St. Rep. 44, 20 Pac. 550; Klauber v. Higgins, 117 Cal. 451, 49 Pac. 466. As to conclusiveness of patent as to character of land, see, *post*, § 779.

That the individual proprietor of the soil may grant a tract of land, reserving the mines, opened or unopened, or the minerals or any specific mineral which may be found therein, whether known to exist or otherwise, is elementary.[1]

The government of the United States in this respect is clothed with the same privileges as individual proprietors. If the reservation is effectual for any purpose other than to safeguard and protect equitable rights in mines which at the time the grant was confirmed had been discovered and were being worked by parties other than the grant claimants, the legislation is so opposed to the antecedent policy of the government, so inconsistent with all its legislation during the last half-century at least, and so thoroughly inconsistent with the land system which prevails in other portions of the public land states and territories, that we hardly know how to deal with it. These provisions of the law looking to the reservation of the minerals of gold, silver, and quicksilver fairly bristle with legal interrogation-marks.

What are mines of gold and silver?

In the great case of mines (the Queen v. the Earl of Northumberland), it was held that mines of the baser metals, such as copper and lead, which contained gold or silver, were royal mines, and were reserved to the crown; and it required acts of parliament in the reign of William and Mary to change this rule.

To what extent may the government utilize this privilege, and enjoy the reserved estate? Certainly it can not extend the operation of the general mining laws over the patented grants. The act does not sanction the carving out of any defined quantity of surface area to be used in connection with mining operations. If we

[1] See, *ante*, § 9, and cases cited.

are left to the rule applicable in cases of individuals, it could occupy only so much of the surface as was necessary in the usual and reasonable course of working; [1] and this would necessarily vary in each particular instance, dependent upon the character of the ore and its mode of occurrence. Neither the government nor its licensees could condemn rights of way or surface ground for mining purposes under the law of eminent domain; for mining is not a governmental function, nor is it a public use. Besides, the right of eminent domain is a right of municipal sovereignty, to be exercised in accordance with the rules prescribed by the individual states. It is true that the act contains the saving grace which inhibits any one without the consent of the owner of the grant from working the mines "until specially author-" ized thereto by act of congress, to be hereafter "passed," thus preventing a general invasion by enterprising explorers of the possession of the grant-owner, and giving congress an opportunity to readjust its legislation in this behalf, to harmonize with the established policy of the government.

We do not see why a preliminary investigation as to the character of the land embraced within a claimed grant should not have been authorized, and the mineral lands segregated, as in the case of railroad grants, homestead entries, and donations to states for educational purposes. If it is objected that a surface examination might not disclose the mineral possibilities, the answer is, that such is often the case with other classes of titles on the public domain. A discovery of mineral upon lands after they have been patented under the homestead, townsite, railroad, school, or other grants, would not defeat the patent or enable the government, or any

---

[1] MacSwinney on Mines, p. 282; Stewart on Mines, p. 33.

one else, to abridge the right of the patentee to the land granted, or sanction an intrusion upon his possession.[1]

We cannot see the propriety of adopting one policy with reference to by far the greater portion of the public domain, and another one, based on different theories, applicable to the remainder. While it may not be fairly within the author's privilege to speculate as to what troubles may arise, or what difficulties may be encountered in executing the act in question, we are very much inclined to believe that the proviso will be a serious annoyance to both the government and the grant-owner, without any compensating features.

At the first session of the fifty-seventh congress a bill framed for the purpose of giving effect to the proviso was introduced in the house of representatives, the first section of which is as follows:—

"*Be it enacted by the senate and house of representa-* " *tives of the United States of America in congress* " *assembled,* That hereafter all gold, silver, and quick- " silver deposits, or mines, or minerals of the same, on " lands embraced within any land claim confirmed by " the decree of the court of private land claims, or as to " which a suit for confirmation shall be pending in any " court having jurisdiction thereof, are hereby declared " to be free and open to exploration and purchase, under " the mining laws of the United States, the local mining " laws and regulations, and such regulations in addition " thereto and consistent therewith as may be prescribed " by the secretary of the interior from time to time, by " citizens of the United States and those who have " declared their intention to become so."

[1] Cowell *v.* Lammers, 10 Saw. 246, 21 Fed. 200; Colo. C. and I. Co. *v.* United States, 123 U. S. 307, 8 Sup. Ct. Rep. 131; Pac. Coast M. and M. Co. *v.* Spargo, 8 Saw. 645, 16 Fed. 348; Richards *v.* Dower, 81 Cal. 44, 22 Pac. 304; Cooper *v.* Roberts, 18 How. 173; Davis *v.* Weibbold, 139 U. S. 507, 11 Sup. Ct. Rep. 628; McCormick *v.* Sutton, 97 Cal. 373, 32 Pac. 444; Smith *v.* Hill, 89 Cal. 122, 26 Pac. 644.

Upon reference to the committee on mines and mining, that committee requested the views of the secretary of the interior upon the measure, a customary courtesy when legislation affecting the public domain is under consideration by the national legislature. The views of Secretary Hitchcock in response to the request, formulated with the aid of the assistant attorney-general of the department, are herewith appended. They are to be commended for their persuasive logic.

" After careful consideration of the subject, the " department is of opinion that only mines of gold, " silver, or quicksilver, or minerals of the same, known " to exist within a confirmed private land claim at the " date of its confirmation, and not the property of the " grantee by the terms of the confirmed grant, or other-" wise, in law or in equity, were by said act declared to " remain the property of the United States, the work-" ing of which mines, after confirmation of the grant, " and without the owner's consent, was to be provided " for by future legislation. This construction appears " to be a reasonable one, and one which it seems to the " department will effectuate the purposes of the act.

" Considerations of equity and justice, as well as the " stability of titles based upon decrees of confirmation " rendered by the court of private land claims, and " patents issued in pursuance thereof, require that there " shall be a time with respect to which such titles must " be considered as settled. This could not be so if the " view should obtain that all lands in claims confirmed " by the court and patented by the government, are " nevertheless to be free and open to exploration for " gold, silver, and quicksilver deposits, or mines or " minerals of the same, under the mining laws of the " United States, as the bill in question proposes to " declare. It is not believed that such was the intention " of congress in the enactment of the above-quoted pro-" vision of the act of March 3, 1891.

" This view is strengthened by the declaration in the " act that no *such mine* shall be *worked* on any con-

" firmed claim without the consent of the owner thereof,
" until specially authorized by a future act of congress.
" What congress had in mind evidently was the reserva-
" tion and future *working of mines* of gold, silver, or
" quicksilver, existing within the limits of a confirmed
" claim at the time of confirmation. The act deals with
" gold, silver, and quicksilver *mines,* and minerals of
" the *same;* that is, minerals of the *mines.* To properly
" come within the designation of *mines,* the existence of
" the minerals referred to must have been known at
" the date of the decree of confirmation.

" It is not in terms declared that no allowance or con-
" firmation of any claim shall confer any right or title
" to minerals of gold, silver, or quicksilver not known
" to exist in the land at the time of confirmation of the
" claim, and which may be discovered after confirmation
" and patent. To so construe the act would tend to dis-
" turb and render uncertain all titles issued upon
" decrees of confirmation made by the court of private
" land claims. It cannot be considered that congress
" contemplated a result so unreasonable and so mani-
" festly out of harmony with all previous legislation
" relating to the disposal of the public lands, in the
" absence of language plainly and unmistakably ex-
" pressive of such intention. There is nothing in the
" statute which requires or would warrant such a
" construction.

" The future legislation contemplated by the act
" relates only to the working of *'mines or minerals of*
" *'the same,'*—that is, to develop claims and the miner-
" als therein—mines and minerals,—which had been
" discovered at the time of confirmation, and not to
" minerals which were then wholly unknown and which
" may be found many years after the confirmation and
" after the issuance of patent by the government. Legis-
" lation making provision for the working of all mines
" of gold, silver, or quicksilver, which were known at
" the date of the confirmation of any claim to exist
" within its limits, and which were not conveyed to the
" grantee by the terms of the grant, and to which he
" has not become otherwise entitled, in law or in equity,

" would, in the judgment of the department, be appro-
" priate legislation.

" Many private land claims have been finally adjudi-
" cated and patented under the act of March 3, 1891.
" To hold that the titles thus granted by the government
" are liable to be in whole or in part subverted and
" rendered nugatory by future discoveries in the patent-
" ed lands of valuable deposits of gold, silver, or quick-
" silver, as would have to be done to support the bill
" under consideration, would be in direct contravention
" of what has come to be regarded as settled law, sup-
" ported by a long line of judicial and departmental
" decisions, that when a person once establishes his
" right to a patent from the government for a portion
" of the public domain, he thereby acquires a vested
" interest in the land to which title is sought; and if
" the land is not then known to contain valuable deposits
" of minerals, no discoveries of minerals thereafter
" made therein, either before or after the actual issuance
" of patent, will in any manner affect his right to a
" patent for the land or his right to and exclusive owner-
" ship of all such subsequently discovered minerals. It
" is not believed that by the act of March 3, 1891, con-
" gress intended to make so grave a departure from
" long-established principles and precedents governing
" the disposal of the public lands.

" For these reasons I cannot approve the proposed
" bill."

§ 128. **Conclusions.** —From the foregoing exposition
of the law, we are authorized to deduce the following
conclusions:—

(1) No right can be acquired under the general mining laws to any mineral lands lying within the claimed
boundaries of any Mexican grant, so long as the grant
remains *sub judice.* The only exception to this rule is
the case of grants in New Mexico, Arizona, Colorado,
Utah, Nevada, and Wyoming, when, since March 3, 1891,
locations may be made within the exterior limits of
claimed grants which are *sub judice,* the determination

of the ultimate validity of such locations to abide the final action of the court of private land claims, as pointed out in section one hundred and twenty-four.

(2) Lands lying within the exterior boundaries of a claimed grant are restored to the public domain, and become open to exploration and purchase under the mining laws, either (*a*) when the grant is finally rejected, or (*b*) where the claimant fails to present his claim for confirmation within the time fixed by law.[1]

(3) In case of floats, the surplus remaining after satisfaction of the grant becomes public domain when the action of the tribunals fixing the boundaries becomes final.

(4) Final confirmation of a grant, and the patent issued pursuant thereto, convey to the grantee all the minerals, with the possible exception of grants falling within the jurisdiction of the court of private land claims created by the act of March 3, 1891. As to the latter class of grants, no definite rule may be dogmatically stated. But the construction of the act in question by the secretary of the interior, as heretofore outlined, is of persuasive force. Under the present state of the law, none of this last class of confirmed grants can be invaded for the purposes of mineral exploration, nor can any rights be initiated within their boundaries, under the general mining laws. A locator on such lands would be a naked trespasser, and could be ejected by the owner of the grant.

---

[1] The final judgment rejecting the grant restores the land to the public domain without any action on the part of the land department. *In re* Davis, 30 L. D. 220.

ARTICLE III. GRANTS TO THE STATES AND TERRITORIES
FOR EDUCATIONAL AND INTERNAL IMPROVEMENT
PURPOSES.

§ 132. Grant of sixteenth and thirty-sixth sections.

§ 133. Indemnity grant in lieu of sixteenth and thirty-sixth sections lost to the states.

§ 134. Other grants for schools and internal improvements.

§ 135. Conflicts between mineral claimants and purchasers from the states.

§ 136. Mineral lands excepted from the operation of grants to the states.

§ 137. Restrictions upon the definition of "mineral lands," when considered with reference to school land grants.

§ 138. Petroleum lands.

§ 139. Lands chiefly valuable for building-stone.

§ 140. In construing the term "mineral lands," as applied to administration of school land grants, the time to which the inquiry is addressed is the date when the asserted right to a particular tract accrued, and not the date upon which the law was passed authorizing the grant.

§ 141. Test of mineral character applied to school land grants.

§ 142. When grants of the sixteenth and thirty-sixth sections take effect.

§ 143. Selections by the state in lieu of sixteenth and thirty-sixth sections, and under general grants.

§ 144. Effect of surveyor-general's return as to character of land within sixteenth and thirty-sixth sections, or lands sought to be selected in lieu thereof, or under floating grants.

§ 144a. Conclusiveness of state patents as to character of land.

§ 145. Conclusions.

§ 132. **Grant of sixteenth and thirty-sixth sections.**
—The ordinance of May 20, 1785, "for ascertaining the
" mode of disposing of the lands in the western terri-
" tory," contained the following provision:—

"There shall be reserved the lot number sixteen of
" every township for the maintenance of public schools
" within said township."

This was an endowment of six hundred and forty acres of land in each township, equivalent to one thirty-sixth of the entire public domain.[1]

This reservation was thereafter specially provided for in the organization of each new state up to the time of the formation of Oregon territory. In the act creating this territory,[2] an additional grant of the thirty-sixth section in each township was provided for, for the use of the future state, and ever since that date every new state, upon its admission to the union, has received a donation of at least the sixteenth and thirty-sixth sections, or twelve hundred and eighty acres, in each township. Under the act of July 16, 1894, Utah was granted sections two, sixteen, thirty-two, and thirty-six in each township.[3] In 1880 congress granted to Nevada two million acres for common-school purposes in lieu of the sixteenth and thirty-sixth sections.[4] Reservations of sixteenth and thirty-sixth sections have likewise been made in all the territories, to be granted and confirmed to such new states as may be carved out of them,[5] and in one instance at least congress has granted the sixteenth and thirty-sixth sections to a territory (New Mexico), the grant taking immediate effect, without waiting for its admission as a state.[6]

§ 133. Indemnity grant in lieu of sixteenth and thirty-sixth sections lost to the states.—Upon extending the surveys over the public lands in the various states, it was discovered that in many instances a sixteenth or thirty-sixth section, and sometimes both, in numerous

[1] Public Domain, p. 224.
[2] August 14, 1848, 9 Stats. at Large, p. 323.
[3] 28 Stats. at Large, pp. 107, 109; Law v. State of Utah, 29 L. D. 622.
[4] 21 Stats. at Large, p. 288; Manser Lode, 27 L. D. 327.
[5] Public Domain, p. 226.
[6] Act of June 21, 1898, (30 Stats. at Large, 484); Instructions, 29 L. D. 364, 27 L. D. 281, 31 L. D. 261.

townships were lost to the state; that is, by reason of a prior legal occupancy or settlement, or an antecedent grant, appropriation, or reservation, it was impossible for the grant as to these sections to take effect. In such cases the sections were said not to be *in place*. To remedy this, and compensate the state for the loss thus occurring, congress enacted laws granting indemnity; that is, the state was authorized to select other unoccupied and unreserved public lands within its boundaries *in lieu* of the sixteenth or thirty-sixth sections so lost to the state. States may also select non-mineral lands to compensate for the failure of the grant of these sections by reason of the ascertained mineral character of the land.[1]

In addition to this, the government has in recent years inaugurated a policy of placing large areas under a state of reservation, and there have been created a great many forest reserves which embrace surveyed lands, including many sixteenth and thirty-sixth sections, title to which had, prior to the establishment of the reserves, become vested in the state. It has been held by the land department that the state had a right to waive its title to such lands, and select others in lieu thereof.[2]

On June 4, 1897,[3] congress passed an act enabling parties who had theretofore acquired title from the government to land included within the limits of these reserves to exchange them for other lands beyond such

---

[1] Act of Feb. 28, 1891, (26 Stats. at Large, 796,) amending Rev. Stats., § 2275; State of California, 31 L. D. 335.

[2] Under the provisions of section 2275 of the Revised Statutes, as amended by the act of February 28, 1891, (26 Stats. at Large, 796). State of California (on review), 28 L. D. 57; Territory of New Mexico, 29 L. D. 399. The circuit court for the ninth circuit, southern district of California, does not agree with the land department as to its interpretation of the law. Hibberd v. Slack, 84 Fed. 571.

[3] 30 Stats. at Large, 11, 36.

limits. This act the land department construes as
authorizing the states, or purchasers from them, to
exchange such lands for others,[1] although this construction is questioned by at least one of the federal courts.[2]

Our present purpose is not to critically analyze these
various laws but to define and classify the different
character of grants to states, and explain the manner of
administering them in connection with the public mineral land laws, which are unquestionably, to some extent
at least, *in pari materia.*

§ 134. Other grants for schools and internal improve-
ments.

— In addition to the grant of sixteenth and thirty-
sixth sections, and lands in lieu thereof, where they are
lost to the state, congress has from time to time made
other grants to the several states, not of any designated
sections or townships, but of a given quantity of land,
to be selected from the body of the public domain.

On September 4, 1841,[3] congress granted to each of
the public land states then admitted, and to each new
state to be thereafter admitted, five hundred thousand
acres of public lands for internal improvements, to be
selected from the body of the public lands within the
respective states. This is commonly called "the five-
" hundred-thousand-acre grant."

A grant was also made to each of the public land
states of two townships, or forty-six thousand and
eighty acres, for university purposes, the grant to be
satisfied by selection of unoccupied and unappropriated
public lands within the respective states.

A further grant was made to the various states of
the union, to those containing no public lands as well

---

[1] Circ. Instructions, 28 L. D. 328.
[2] Hibberd v. Slack, 84 Fed. 571, 581, 582.
[3] 5 Stats. at Large, p. 453.

as to those which were essentially public land states.[1] This grant, commonly called "the agricultural college " grant," was of thirty thousand acres for each senator and representative to which the state was entitled under the apportionment of 1860.[2] In the public land states the grant was to be satisfied by selection of public lands within their respective boundaries. To the states wherein there was no public land, scrip was issued, commonly known as "agricultural college scrip." This scrip could be located anywhere on the unreserved and unappropriated public domain in any state, and could be used in the payment of pre-emption or commuted homestead entries. It was sold to speculators and individuals, who subsequently utilized it by locating it on lands subject to private entry.

Congress also made other donations of a similar character, but we have here given a sufficient outline of grants to states to enable us to discuss their operation and effect with reference to mineral lands on the public domain.

§ 135. Conflicts between mineral claimants and purchasers from the states.—In administering grants of such extensive character, it is quite natural that conflicts should arise between the miner and the purchaser of state lands, particularly in the mineral regions of the west. These controversies found their way into the courts and the land department, and, as a result, certain principles of law have been announced which may be best presented by first considering the character of the lands which could pass by the grant, and at what time the respective grants take effect and become operative as to particular tracts.

[1] July 2, 1862, 12 Stats. at Large, p. 503.
[2] Public Domain, p. 229.

§ 136. Mineral lands exempted from the operation of grants to the states.—Some of the grants to the states in terms reserved mineral lands from their operation. This was the case with the agricultural college grant, which contained the reservation "that no mineral lands " shall be selected or purchased under the provisions " of this act." And the grant of seventy-two sections to the state of California for seminary purposes [1] contained a similar clause. Kindred exceptions were inserted in all the more recent grants; but in some of the earlier ones, notably those donating sixteenth and thirty-sixth sections, and the five-hundred-thousand-acre grant, the law was silent as to mineral lands. But, as we have already seen, the uniform policy of the government prior to the enactment of the general mining laws was to reserve mineral lands from sale, pre-emption, and all classes of grants.[2] Of course, since the passage of the mining laws, title to mineral lands can be obtained only under these laws.

In California, the supreme court of that state early announced the doctrine in reference to the grant of sixteenth and thirty-sixth sections, that, as there was no statement in the act of any condition, exception, reservation, or limitation, mineral lands were not withdrawn from the operation of the act, but passed to the state.[3] But this case was subsequently overruled.[4]

The supreme court of Nevada, in construing a similar grant to that state, held that mineral lands within sections sixteen or thirty-six did not pass; but the decision was based upon an estoppel upon the part of the state by reason of the passage by congress of an act concern-

---

[1] 10 Stats. at Large, p. 244.

[2] See, *ante*, § 47, and cases there cited.

[3] Higgins *v.* Houghton, 25 Cal. 252. See, also, Wedekind *v.* Craig, 56 Cal. 642.

[4] Hermocilla *v.* Hubbell, 89 Cal. 8, 26 Pac. 611.

ing certain lands granted to the state, which act provided
that in all cases lands valuable for mines of gold, silver,
quicksilver, or copper should be reserved from sale.[1]
The legislature of the state accepted the grants subject
to this clause.[2] And the court very properly held that
by reason of this acceptance the state was estopped from
asserting title to mineral lands found within the sixteenth and thirty-sixth sections.[3]

The land department, in recent years at least, by a
uniform line of decisions, has held that mineral lands
did not pass to the state under the school grants.[4]

The supreme court of the United States had this question under consideration in reference to the grant of
sixteenth and thirty-sixth sections to the state of Michigan, in Cooper v. Roberts,[5] where it was held that mineral lands passed by the grant, even as against a license
from the government to search for and extract lead
and other ores. The grant in question became operative
at a period prior to the discovery of gold in California,
and at a time when the policy of leasing lead mines by
the government was in force.[6]

But at a later period the question was again brought
before the supreme court of the United States in the
case of the Ivanhoe M. Co. v. Keystone M. Co.,[7] and the

---

[1] 14 Stats. at Large, p. 85, § 5.

[2] Nev. Stats. (1867), p. 57; Comp. Laws Nevada, vol. ii, §§ 3835, 3836,
3837.

[3] Heydenfeldt v. Daney G. and S. M. Co., 10 Nev. 290; S. C. on writ
of error, 93 U. S. 634.

[4] In re Hogden et al., 1 Copp's L. O. 135; Copp's Min. Dec., p. 30; The
Keystone Case, Id., 105, 109, 125; In re Le Franchi, 3 L. D. 229;
Keystone Lode v. State of Nevada, 15 L. D. 259; State of California v.
Poley, 4 Copp's L. O. 18; In re Chas. Norager, 10 Copp's L. O. 54; State
of Utah v. Allen, 27 L. D. 53, 55; Florida Central etc. R. R. Co., 26 L. D.
600.

[5] 18 How. 173.

[6] See, ante, § 33.

[7] 102 U. S. 167.

doctrine was finally established that congress in making these grants to the states did not intend to depart from the uniform policy theretofore adopted in reserving mineral lands from sale, and that mineral lands found within a sixteenth or thirty-sixth section, known to be such at the time the grant took effect, did not pass to the state.

It may be observed that in the Ivanhoe-Keystone case no mention is made of the Michigan case.

The rule having been thus announced, it follows as a corollary that no lands can be selected or located in satisfaction of *any* of the grants to the states which at the time of the proposed selection are known to be mineral lands.[1]

§ 137. **Restrictions upon the definition of "mineral "lands," when considered with reference to school land grants.**—In a preceding chapter, we have endeavored to establish a general definition of the term "mineral " lands," as that term is used in the various mining acts of congress; and we have also attempted to formulate definite rules of statutory construction to be applied to such acts and these terms when found therein.[2]

Thus, we have heretofore said [3] that the word "min- " eral," as used in these various acts, should be understood in its widest signification, and that all substances which are classified as a mineral product in trade or commerce, or possess economic value for use in trade, manufacture, the sciences, or the arts, fall within the designation of the term "mineral." That this is true

[1] United States *v.* Mullan, 7 Saw. 466, 470, 10 Fed. 785, S. C. on appeal, 118 U. S. 271, 6 Sup. Ct. Rep. 1041; Garrard *v.* Silver Peak Mines, 82 Fed. 578, 587, S. C. on appeal, 94 Fed. 983.

[2] Tit. III, ch. i, §§ 85-96.

[3] See, *ante,* § 96.

as a general rule, we have no doubt.[1] We are firmly convinced that it should be accepted as a universal rule in dealing with the public lands. But when we are confronted with the administration of the school land grants, railroad grants, and other grants of a like character, we find that the land department at certain periods of its history has been disposed to discriminate in some instances between those substances which are obviously mineral and those which, owing to the advancement in science and the industrial arts, become classified commercially or scientifically as mineral products.

§ 138. Petroleum lands.—This disposition on the part of the land department to restrict the definition of the term "mineral lands" was exhibited by Secretary Smith in the case of petroleum lands. He first held that petroleum was not a mineral within the meaning of the mining laws.[2]

He subsequently, and in harmony with his conception of the law as thus expressed, ruled that lands containing petroleum in sufficient quantities to render them more valuable for that purpose than for any other were not mineral lands, and were subject to selection by the states in lieu of lost sixteenth and thirty-sixth sections.[3]

In support of his first ruling, from which the second logically followed, he cited the Pennsylvania case of Dunham v. Kirkpatrick,[4] to the effect that a reservation of "mineral" in a deed does not include petroleum, although it is admitted petroleum is technically a mineral.

---

[1] See Northern Pac. R. R. Co. v. Soderberg, 99 Fed. 506, 104 Fed. 425; Pacific Coast Marble Co. v. Northern Pac. R. R. Co., 25 L. D. 233; Aldritt v. Northern Pac. R. R. Co., 25 L. D. 349.

[2] Ex parte Union Oil Co., 23 L. D. 222.

[3] Chandler v. State of California, Oct. 27, 1896, (not reported).

[4] 101 Pa. St. 36, 47 Am. Rep. 696.

This decision is in conflict with prior cases decided in Pennsylvania,[1] and has been practically overruled or its doctrine ignored by the same court in a later case.[2]

Secretary Smith's views were in direct conflict with a decision by Judge Ross in the case of Good v. California Oil Co.,[3] where it was said:—

" The premises in controversy are oil-bearing lands
" the government title to which, under existing laws,
" can alone be acquired pursuant to the provisions of
" the mining laws relating to placer claims."

They were also contrary to the prior rulings of the land department.[4]

Acting Secretary Ryan, however, overruled the decision of Secretary Smith, and in the course of his opinion thus stated the result of his examination of the records of the land department on the subject of petroleum lands:—

" From an examination of the records of your office
" [commissioner of the general land office] which I have
" caused to be made, it is ascertained that ever since the
" circular of July 13, 1873, until the date of the decision
" complained of, the practice of allowing entry and
" patent for lands chiefly valuable for their deposits of
" petroleum under the law and regulations relating to
" placer claims has been continued and uniform. Under

---

[1] Stoughton's Appeal, 88 Pa. St. 198; Thompson v. Noble, 3 Pittsb. 201. See, also, 10 Morr. Min. Rep., p. 421.

[2] Gill v. Weston, 110 Pa. St. 313, 1 Atl. 921. The doctrine of Dunham v. Kirkpatrick (supra) has been followed by the supreme court of Ohio (Detlor v. Holland, 57 Ohio St. 492, 49 N. E. 690), but repudiated in Tennessee (Murray v. Allard, 100 Tenn. 100, 66 Am. St. Rep. 740, 43 S. W. 355) and West Virginia (Williamson v. Jones, 39 W. Va. 231, 19 S. E. 441).

[3] 60 Fed. 531, 532.

[4] Copp's Min. Lands, p. 61; Sickles's Min. Laws, p. 491; In re Hooper, 1 L. D. 560; Maxwell v. Brierly, 10 Copp's L. O. 50; Roberts v. Jepson, 4 L. D. 60; Piru Oil Co., 16 L. D. 117; In re Dewey, 9 Copp's L. O. 51; Downey v. Rogers, 2 L. D. 707; Samuel E. Rogers, 4 L. D. 284.

" the practice a large number of patents have been
" issued and very large and valuable property interests
" acquired." [1]

Subsequently it was specifically held by the department that land chiefly valuable for its petroleum deposits could not be selected by the states in satisfaction of their floating grants.[2]

Shortly after the announcement of the ruling of Secretary Smith above referred to, congress passed an act providing in terms that lands valuable for petroleum may be acquired under the placer mining laws.[3] This was but the adoption by the national legislature of the construction (uniform, except for the sporadic case above cited) theretofore placed upon the mining laws by the tribunal charged with their administration.[4]

It follows that land chiefly valuable for its deposits of petroleum never could, nor can it now, be selected by the states in satisfaction of any of their grants.

§ 139. **Lands chiefly valuable for building-stone.**— Prior to the passage by congress of the act of August 4, 1892, specifically placing lands chiefly valuable for their deposits of building-stone in the category of mineral lands subject to entry under the placer mining laws, the land department had frequently held that such lands were mineral in character and subject to such appropriation,[5] although there were rulings to the contrary.[6]

---

[1] Union Oil Co. (on review), 25 L. D. 351, 354.

[2] McQuiddy v. State of California, 29 L. D. 181.

[3] Feb. 11, 1897, 29 Stats. at Large, p. 526.

[4] See, *post*, § 422.

[5] Bennett's Placer, 3 L. D. 116; McGlenn v. Weinbroeer, 15 L. D. 370; Van Doren v. Plested, 16 L. D. 508; Forsythe v. Weingart, 27 L. D. 680; Maxwell v. Brierly, 10 Copp's L. O. 50.

[6] Conlin v. Kelly, 12 L. D. 1; Hayden v. Jamison, 16 L. D. 537; Clark v. Erwin, *Id*. 122.

In the case of Pacific Coast Marble Co. *v.* Northern Pacific R. R. Co.,[1] a careful and analytical review of the prior decisions of the department on this subject was made by Secretary Bliss, from which it clearly appears that the weight of departmental authority is decidedly in favor of the broad interpretation of the term "mineral " lands," and placing lands chiefly valuable for their deposits of building-stone within the purview of the mining laws. So far as the federal courts have expressed themselves on the subject, the departmental construction has been commended and followed.[2]

That building-stone lands are to be classified as mineral lands, and as such are reserved from grants made to railroad companies, is well settled by the rulings of both the land department[3] and the courts.[4]

A similar rule should be applied in the administration of land grants to the states, unless there is something in the language of the act of August 4, 1892, which inhibits such application. This act contains the following provision:—

" That any person authorized to enter lands under " the mining laws of the United States may enter lands " that are chiefly valuable for building-stone under the " provisions of the law in relation to placer mining " claims; *provided,* that lands *reserved* for the benefit " of public schools or donated to any state shall not be " subject to entry under this act."[5]

---

[1] 25 L. D. 233.

[2] Northern Pac. Ry. Co. *v.* Soderberg, 99 Fed. 506, S. C. on appeal, 104 Fed. 425.

[3] Pacific Coast Marble Co. *v.* Northern Pac. R. R. Co., 25 L. D. 233; Aldritt *v.* Northern Pac. R. R. Co., *Id.* 349; Beaudette *v.* Northern Pac. R. R. Co., 29 L. D. 248; Schrimpf *v.* Northern Pac. R. R. Co., *Id.* 327; Morrill *v.* Northern Pac. R. R. Co., 30 L. D. 475.

[4] Northern Pac. ·Ry. Co. *v.* Soderberg, 99 Fed. 506, S. C. on appeal, 104 Fed. 425.

[5] 27 Stats. at Large, p. 348.

The only lands specifically *reserved* in the legislative grants to the states are the sixteenth and thirty-sixth sections. These acquire precision by the approval of the survey, and title thereupon vests in the state without further action by the land department, if the state has been admitted at the time of the survey, or upon its admission if it occupied the *status* of a territory at the time of the grant.

As to these lands, it would seem that the proviso of the act above quoted applies, and building-stone lands within sixteenth and thirty-sixth sections would pass to the state. The land department has so determined.[1]

It has also been held that a mining location made upon building-stone lands prior to the passage of the act at a time when such locations were recognized, which location had passed to entry in the land office prior to a grant to the state, took precedence over the grant to the state.[2]

The land department has also decided, in effect, that the terms of reservation embodied in the act of August 4, 1892, included the floating and indemnity grants to the state, and that building-stone lands can be selected by the state in satisfaction of their floating grants.[3] This seems to us illogical. By the terms of the grants falling within this category there are no reservations of any particular tracts. No part of the public domain is placed in a state of reservation or withdrawn from location and entry under the mining laws to await the selection by the state of its quota of lands under floating or indemnity grants. These grants are donations of unidentified acres to be selected from the non-mineral public domain. Such

---

[1] *In re* Hooper, 16 L. D. 110; South Dakota *v.* Vermont Stone Co., *Id.* 263, (although, as to this last case, see *In re* Gibson, 21 L. D. 327).

[2] *In re* Gibson, 21 L. D. 327.

[3] State of Utah, 29 L. D. 69.

grants do not acquire precision until after the selection and its approval.[1]

It would seem that as building-stone lands fall by legislative definition as well as by departmental ruling within the term "mineral lands," and are subject to location under the mining laws, it should follow that the states cannot select lands of this character in satisfaction of its floating grants, no specific lands being reserved or donated under such grants. The proviso under discussion is not so clear in its terms as to enable us to dogmatically assert that building-stone lands may not be selected by the state in satisfaction of this class of grants; but to reach the contrary conclusion requires, in our judgment, the application of extremely liberal rules of interpretation and a reading between the lines, which is not always a safe method to adopt in construing statutes. In the absence of this proviso, the rule applicable to selection of lands under indemnity railroad grants would apply, as the two classes of laws in this regard are in all respects similar.[2]

§ 140. **In construing the term "mineral lands," as applied to administration of school land grants, the time to which the inquiry is addressed is the date when the asserted right to a particular tract accrued, and not the date upon which the law was passed authorizing the grant.**—We have digressed for the moment to discuss a question which might be more appropriately presented when dealing with the character of lands subject to appropriation under the so-called placer laws; but it seems necessary for us here to present the matter as introductory to the main subject presently under consideration.

---

[1] See, *post*, § 143.
[2] Swank *v.* State of California, 27 L. D. 411.

There is nothing in the context of the school land-grant laws where the reservation of "mineral lands" appears which restricts the meaning of the term. If a restricted meaning is to be applied, it must be by reason of the relative position of the parties or the substance of the transaction.[1]

In considering this relative position of the parties, and the substance of the transaction, to what point of time must we direct our attention in dealing with school land grants and rights asserted under them? To the date of the passage of the act making the grant or authorizing the selection, or the time when the state or its grantees become first entitled to assert a claim to a particular tract of land?

Fortunately, this question has been satisfactorily settled for us; so that lengthy discussion will be avoided.

Prior to the passage of the coal land act of July 1, 1864,[2] the land department did not regard or treat coal lands or coal mines as mineral lands, within the meaning of the prior acts of congress.[3] This act provided:—

"That when any tracts embracing coal-beds or coal-
" fields constituting portions of the public domain, and
" which, as mines, are excluded from the pre-emption
" act of 1841, and which, under past legislation, are not
" liable to ordinary entry, it shall and may be lawful
" for the president to cause such tracts in suitable legal
" subdivisions to be offered at public sale to the highest
" bidder."

Assuming that the above ruling of the land department was correct, prior to the passage of that act coal lands might be selected under previously enacted school land-grant laws.

[1] Stewart on Mines, pp 10-13. See, ante, § 91.
[2] 13 Stats. at Large, p. 343.
[3] In re Yoakum, 1 Copp's L. O. 3.

In 1868, one Mullan applied to the state surveyor-general of California to purchase a half-section of land selected by the state under the act of March 3, 1853, in lieu of the corresponding half of a sixteenth section theretofore lost to the state. His application was favorably considered, and in due process of time the secretary of the interior listed the land to the state, and Mullan or his grantee received a state patent. At the time Mullan instituted the proceedings culminating in the listing and issuance of the state patent the land was notoriously coal land, and was being actually worked for its coal deposits by the Black Diamond coal company. These facts were brought to the attention of the government, and suit was instituted in its behalf to vacate the listing. The case was tried before the late Judge Sawyer, in the circuit court of the United States (ninth circuit),[1] who held that whatever might have been originally the proper construction of the word "mines," as used in the pre-emption act of 1841, the act of July 1, 1864, gave a legislative construction to the term which thenceforth attached to all known "coal-beds or coal-fields" *in which no interest had before become vested,* and withdrew such coal lands from the operation of all other acts of congress; that thereafter known coal lands were not subject to selection by the state as lieu lands; and that the state has no indefeasible rights to select such lieu lands from any particular class of lands.

The supreme court of the United States affirmed this decision,[2] thus summing up its views:—

"At the time the selection was actually made, there-"fore, it cannot be doubted that the land was mineral "land, both in law and in fact, within the meaning of "the act under which the state, and those who purchased

---

[1] United States v. Mullan, 7 Saw. 466, 10 Fed. 785.
[2] Mullan v. United States, 118 U. S. 271, 6 Sup. Ct. Rep. 1041.

" from the state, undertook to acquire title, and we agree
" with the circuit court in the opinion that the *rights*
" *of the parties are to be determined by the law as it*
" *stood then.*"

The enactment of the general mining laws by congress
incorporated into the land system a new element,
announced new principles and a new policy, in the light
of which all pre-existing land-grant laws to the extent
that they remain unsatisfied are to be administered.
All land-grant acts passed subsequent to the enactment
of the mining laws operative in any of the precious-
metal-bearing states or territories, contain the usual
clauses of reservation as to mineral lands.

§ 141. **Test of mineral character applied to school
land grants.**—As conclusions logically flowing from
what has been heretofore said, the question as to whether
a given tract of land is mineral, and its selection under
school land-grant laws for that reason inhibited, or is
non-mineral, and subject to selection, is one to be determined according to the state of the law as it exists at the
time the right to select is asserted.

If the mineral character of such tract is established
according to the rules announced in section ninety-
eight, then it cannot pass under the grants to states for
educational purposes.[1] This rule is subject to the qualification discussed in a previous section,[2] that since the
act of 1892 lands containing deposits of building-stone
probably vest in the state under its grants of particular
sections, and possibly may be selected under its indemnity or floating grants.

It is, of course, conceded that after a right has once
vested to a tract of land which, at the time it became

---

[1] If a discovery of mineral has been made on each twenty acres of a
placer location, the whole location is excepted from school indemnity
selection. Quigley *v.* State of California, 24 L. D. 507.

[2] See, *ante,* § 139.

segregated from the body of the public domain and passed to states or individuals, was non-mineral, according to the state of the law and the facts then existing, no subsequent change in commercial conditions nor advancement in the industrial arts can affect those rights.[1] But tracts still open to selection are, in turn, to be governed by the new condition of things, and controlled by such enlarged definitions as may be then applied by the current of judicial or departmental authority. This rule injures no one. It is consistent with the progressiveness of the age and the spirit of our laws.

§ 142. **When grants of the sixteenth and thirty-sixth sections take effect.**—Until the survey of the township and the designation of the specific sections, the right of the state rests in compact, binding, it is true, the public faith, and dependent for execution upon the political authorities. Courts of justice have no authority to mark out and define the land which shall be the subject of the grant. But when the political authorities have performed this duty, the compact has an object upon which it can attach; and if there is no legal impediment, the title then vests absolutely in the state,[2] by virtue of the survey. The government does not certify or patent sixteenth or thirty-sixth sections to the states.[3]

While the grant of these sections is one *in præsenti*, it is, before the lands are surveyed, essentially a float, a grant of a quantity of lands equal in amount to twelve hundred and eighty acres in each township.

[1] *In re* Gibson, 21 L. D. 327.
[2] Cooper *v.* Roberts, 18 How. 173; Hibberd *v.* Slack, 84 Fed. 571, 574. See, also, Beecher *v.* Wetherby, 95 U. S. 517; State of Utah, 29 L. D. 418; Sherman *v.* Buick, 45 Cal. 656; Higgins *v.* Houghton, 25 Cal. 252; Finney *v.* Berger, 50 Cal. 248; Medley *v.* Robertson, 55 Cal. 397, 399.
[3] 31 L. D. 212.

Until the *status* of the lands is fixed by a survey, and they are capable of identification, congress reserves absolute power over them, compensating the state for such loss as might accrue to it to the extent that legal impediments prevent the title from passing.[1]

Until the survey is finally approved, the state has no title which it can convey to a purchaser.[2]

Therefore, in determining whether or not the lands embraced within these sections are mineral lands, and exempted from the operation of the grant, the inquiry is addressed to their known character at the time of the final approval of the survey. If at the time of such approval they are known to be mineral, within the meaning of that term as heretofore defined,[3] title does not pass to the state,[4] but remains in the general government and subject to its disposal under the mining laws.[5]

---

[1] Heydenfeldt *v.* Daney G. M. Co., 93 U. S. 634.

Under act of February 28, 1891, (26 Stats. at Large, p. 796,) states are awarded indemnity by reason of losses accruing to them on account of mineral character of sixteenth and thirty-sixth sections. And under a recent ruling, where these sections fall within the grants to states of swamp and overflowed lands, the states may select other lands in lieu thereof. State of California, 31 L. D. 335, construing same act.

[2] Finney *v.* Berger, 50 Cal. 248; Medley *v.* Robertson, 55 Cal. 397; State of California *v.* Wright, 24 L. D. 54; Niven *v.* State of California, 6 L. D. 439.

[3] See, *ante,* §§ 93-98. The existence of a placer location within a school section, or the pendency of an application for a placer patent at the date when the grant of school lands became effective, will not operate to except such lands from the grant to the state, if said lands were not in fact mineral in character. George M. Bourquin, 27 L. D. 289. See, also, Harkrader *v.* Goldstein, 31 L. D. 87.

[4] Ivanhoe M. Co. *v.* Keystone Cons. M. Co., 102 U. S. 167; Heydenfeldt *v.* Daney, 93 U. S. 634; Hermocilla *v.* Hubbell, 89 Cal. 5, 26 Pac. 611; Pereira *v.* Jacks, 15 L. D. 273. But see Saunders *v.* La Purisima G. M. Co., 125 Cal. 159, 57 Pac. 656, and the discussion in section 144a, *post,* as to the conclusiveness of a state patent upon the character of the land.

[5] Hermocilla *v.* Hubbell, 89 Cal. 5, 26 Pac. 611; Olive Land and Dev. Co. *v.* Olmstead, 103 Fed. 568, 576; Cosmos Exploration Co. *v.* Gray Eagle Oil Co., 104 Fed. 20; S. C. on appeal, 112 Fed. 4.

If they were not known to be mineral at the date of the approval of the survey, they pass to the state, and discovery of minerals on such lands subsequent to such approval does not defeat the title of the state.[1]

As was said by the supreme court of the United States,[2] a change in the conditions occurring subsequently to the taking effect of the grant, whereby new discoveries are made, or by means whereof it may become profitable to work the mineral deposits, cannot affect the title, as it passed at the time of the grant. This is a general rule, applicable to all classes of grants.[3]

It is also true that if at the time the grant would have taken effect, in the absence of legal impediments, the land was known to be mineral in character, the subsequent exhaustion of the mineral and its abandonment for mining purposes would not operate to vest title in the state.[4]

When a state seeks to select indemnity lands in lieu of others which it claims are mineral in character at the time of the survey, unless it be shown that such lands were actually lost to the state, a hearing should be had to determine the character of such lands.[5]

---

[1] Wheeler v. Smith, 5 Wash. 704, 32 Pac. 784; Townsite of Silver Cliff, 6 Copp's L. O. 152; Keystone Case, Copp's Min. Dec., pp. 105, 109, 125; State of California v. Poley, 4 Copp's L. O. 18; In re J. Dartt, 5 Copp's L. O. 178; In re State of Colorado, 6 L. D. 412; Virginia Lode, 7 L. D. 459; In re Abraham L. Miner, 9 L. D. 408; Pereira v. Jacks, 15 L. D. 273.

[2] Colo. C. and I. Co. v. United States, 123 U. S. 307, 8 Sup. Ct. Rep. 131.

[3] Deffeback v. Hawke, 115 U. S. 404, 6 Sup. Ct. Rep. 95; Davis v. Weibbold, 139 U. S. 507; Hunt v. Steese, 75 Cal. 620, 17 Pac. 920; Cowell v. Lammers, 10 Saw. 247, 21 Fed. 200; Manning v. San Jacinto Tin Co., 7 Saw. 419, 9 Fed. 726; Richards v. Dower, 81 Cal. 51, 22 Pac. 304, S. C. on writ of error, 151 U. S. 658, 14 Sup. Ct. Rep. 452; McCormick v. Sutton, 97 Cal. 373, 32 Pac. 444; Smith v. Hill, 89 Cal. 122, 26 Pac. 644.

[4] Hermocilla v. Hubbell, 89 Cal. 5, 26 Pac. 611.

[5] Bond v. State of California, 31 L. D. 34.

What we have heretofore said as to the time when grants to sixteenth and thirty-sixth sections take effect applies to surveys made subsequent to the admission of the state into the union. Where lands have been surveyed prior to the admission of the state, the grant takes effect as of the date of admission; and in such cases the inquiry as to the character of the land is directed to that point of time.[1]

Where grants are made of specific sections to the territories, as in the case of New Mexico,[2] title vests as of the date of the survey, as in the case of grants made to states after their admission.

We reserve for future discussion [3] the effect of a state patent as an adjudication of the character of the land.

§ 143. Selections by the state in lieu of sixteenth and thirty-sixth sections, and under general grants. —It follows as a corollary from what has heretofore been said that the states cannot select lands of known mineral character in satisfaction of any of their land grants,[4] with the possible exception of lands containing deposits of building-stone, as explained in a previous section.[5]

The point of time when the character of a given tract sought to be selected by the state in satisfaction of any of its floating grants is to be determined is the time

[1] Townsite of Silver Cliff, 6 Copp's L. O. 152; Boulder & Buffalo M. Co., 7 L. D. 54; Fleetwood Lode, 12 L. D. 604; Warren v. State of Colorado, 14 L. D. 681; State of Washington v. McBride, 18 L. D. 199; State of Utah v. Allen, 27 L. D. 53; Law v. State of Utah, 29 L. D. 623.

[2] 30 Stats. at Large, 484; 27 L. D. 281; 29 L. D. 364; 31 L. D. 261.

[3] See, *post*, § 144a.

[4] United States v. Mullan, 7 Saw. 470, 10 Fed. 785; Mullan v. United States, 118 U. S. 271, 6 Sup. Ct. Rep. 1041; Garrard v. Silver Peak Mines, 82 Fed. 578, 587, S. C. on appeal, 94 Fed. 983; Richter v. State of Utah, 27 L. D. 95; Manser Lode Claim, *Id.* 326; McQuiddy v. State of California, 29 L. D. 181.

[5] See, *ante*, § 139.

when the selection is made,[1] and a selection is not made until it has been approved by the land department.[2]

The act of August 4, 1854, carried forward in the revised statutes as section two thousand four hundred and forty-nine, provides as follows:—

"Where lands have been or shall hereafter be granted
" by any law of congress to any one of the several states
" and territories, and where such law does not convey
" the fee-simple title of the lands or require patents
" to be issued therefor, the lists of such lands which
" have been or may hereafter be certified by the com-
" missioner of the general land office under the seal of
" his office, either as originals or copies of the originals
" or records, shall be regarded as conveying the fee
" simple of all the lands embraced in such lists that are
" of the character contemplated by such act of congress,
" and intended to be granted thereby; but where lands
" embraced in such lists are not of the character
" embraced by such acts of congress, and are not
" intended to be granted thereby, the lists, so far as
" these lands are concerned, shall be perfectly null and
" void, and no right, title, claim, or interest shall be
" conveyed thereby."[3]

It has been frequently held that a certified list issued under and pursuant to this statute is of the same effect as a patent.[4]

[1] Olive Land and Development Co. v. Olmstead, 103 Fed. 568, 576. See, also, McCreery v. Haskell, 119 U. S. 327, 331, 7 Sup. Ct. Rep. 176; Howell v. Slauson, 83 Cal. 539, 23 Pac. 692; Shenandoah M. and M. Co. v. Morgan, 106 Cal. 409, 39 Pac. 802.

[2] Wisconsin Central R. R. Co. v. Price County, 133 U. S. 496, 511-514, 10 Sup. Ct. Rep. 341; Cosmos Exploration Co. v. Gray Eagle Oil Co., 104 Fed. 20, 43, S. C. on appeal, 112 Fed. 4; Swank v. State of California, 27 L. D. 411; McQuiddy v. State of California, 29 L. D. 181; Kern Oil Co. v. Clarke, on review, 31 L. D. 288.

[3] 10 Stats. at Large, p. 346; Rev. Stats., § 2449.

[4] Frasher v. O'Connor, 115 U. S. 102, 5 Sup. Ct. Rep. 1141; Mower v. Fletcher, 116 U. S. 380, 6 Sup. Ct. Rep. 409; McCreery v. Haskell, 119 U. S. 327, 7 Sup. Ct. Rep. 176; Garrard v. Silver Peak Mines, 94 Fed. 983, 984; Howell v. Slauson, 83 Cal. 539, 23 Pac. 692; Shenandoah M. and M. Co. v. Morgan, 106 Cal. 409, 39 Pac. 802.

It operates upon the selection as of the day when made and reported to the local land office, or cuts off, as would a patent in such cases, all subsequent claimants.[1]

A patent once issued is conclusive evidence that the land is of the character purporting to be conveyed by it.

As was said by the supreme court of the United States, speaking through Mr. Justice Brewer,—

" It has undoubtedly been affirmed over and over " again that in the administration of the public land " system of the United States questions of fact are for " the consideration and judgment of the land depart- " ment. Whether, for instance, a certain tract is swamp " land or not, saline land or not, mineral land or not, " presents a question of fact not resting on record, de- " pendent on oral testimony; and it cannot be doubted " that the decision of the land department one way or " the other in reference to these questions is conclusive " and not open to re-litigation in the courts, except in " those cases of fraud, etc., which permit any determi- " nation to be re-examined."[2]

In another case it was said, upon the authority of for- mer adjudications as well as upon principle, that parol evidence is inadmissible to show in opposition to the concurrent action of federal and state officers having authority in the premises, that the lands listed and certi- fied were, as a matter of fact, at the time of the selection and its approval of such character that their selection was inhibited by the legislation creating the grant.[3]

In the case of Garrard v. Silver Peak Mines,[4] a doc-

---

[1] McCreery v. Haskell, 119 U. S. 327, 331, 7 Sup. Ct. Rep. 176; Howell v. Slauson, 83 Cal. 546, 23 Pac. 694.

[2] Burfenning v. Chicago, St. Paul Ry., 163 U. S. 321, 323, 16 Sup. Ct. Rep. 1018. See, also, post, § 779, and cases there cited.

[3] McCormick v. Hayes, 159 U. S. 332, 348, 16 Sup. Ct. Rep. 37. See, also, Rogers Locomotive Works v. American Emigrant Co., 164 U. S. 559, 17 Sup. Ct. Rep. 188; Johnson v. Drew, 171 U. S. 93, 18 Sup. Ct. Rep. 800.

[4] 82 Fed. 578.

trine was announced which as a matter of first impression would seem to place a radical limitation on this rule. The facts of the case, so far as they are essential to the present discussion, were briefly as follows:—

The predecessors in title of the Silver Peak Mines had, long prior to any selection by the state of the lands in controversy, located, under state possessory laws passed prior to the enactment of any mining law by congress, a tract of land and millsite containing one hundred and sixty acres, and had also erected thereon extensive and valuable improvements. There also had been prior to said time located on said premises a lode mining claim called the "Manser mining claim." Subsequently the state of Nevada made application to select certain lands embracing a portion of the millsite and mining claim. This selection was duly approved, and the land listed or certified to the state. Garrard acquired the title from the state through mesne conveyances, with full knowledge of the true character of the lands and the adverse occupancy of the Silver Peak Mines. He brought ejectment to recover possession. The defense relied upon the facts above outlined as to the known mineral character of the tract and its adverse occupancy at the time of the selection; and one of the important questions discussed in the case was as to whether the state patent, predicated upon the approved selection and certification by the land department, could be collaterally assailed by parol evidence establishing the known antecedent mineral character of the land. On this branch of the case Judge Hawley said:—

"The state authorities were to select the land granted " from any unappropriated non-mineral public land. " They were not invested with the duty of passing upon " the question of fact as to whether or not each particu- " lar section of land was non-mineral or unappro- " priated; nor was this duty imposed upon the

" commissioner of the general land office when he
" certified to the selection, or upon the secretary of the
" interior when he approved the same, to the same
" extent as in cases of applications made by individuals
" or corporations for patent to agricultural or mineral
" lands, where specific proofs are required, and the
" land department is clothed with the power to hear
" and determine all questions as to the character of the
" land, the right of the applicant to apply for and
" receive the same, and the sufficiency of the proofs to
" show a compliance with the law entitling the appli-
" cant to a patent. All of these acts upon the part of
" the officers were subject to the reservations specified
" in the act itself."

This doctrine was upheld by the circuit court of appeals.[1] The land department adopted this construction of the law and issued its patent to the Silver Peak Mines for the Manser mining claim, and this without any independent investigation on its part as to the antecedent history or character of the land,[2] although it had frequently held that after it has approved and certified lands to states the title to the lands so certified passes to the state as completely as though patent had issued, and precludes the exercise of further departmental jurisdiction over the land until such certification is vacated by judicial proceedings.[3]

In the Garrard case a court of equity would undoubtedly have erected a trust in favor of the mineral claimant upon the state title, or the government might have successfully prosecuted an action to vacate the listing. But if the case it to be accepted as authority to the effect that after approval of the selection and certification to the state, which is in effect a conveyance of the title, the

---

[1] 94 Fed. 983.
[2] Manser Lode Claim, 27 L. D. 326.
[3] State of California v. Boddy, 9 L. D. 636; Hendy v. Compton, *Id.* 106; Tanner v. O'Neill, 14 L. D. 317.

land department still retains jurisdiction to review its action, investigate the character of the land, and, if found to be mineral, vacate the listing and issue a mineral patent, the reconciliation of the doctrine so announced with the long line of decisions enunciated by the supreme court of the United States heretofore cited is not without embarrassment. The suggestion found in the court's opinion above quoted, that the duty imposed upon the commissioner of the general land office to investigate the character of land is to be performed with a greater degree of diligence and circumspection in the case of individuals and corporations than in the case of state selections, does not, in our judgment, strengthen the ultimate conclusion.

Be this as it may, until the selection is finally approved by the officers of the government charged with this duty, and the land is certified or listed to the state, the state has no title which it can convey to the purchaser.[1]

Without such approval, neither the state nor its grantee can question any further disposition which the United States may make of the land embraced in the attempted selection.[2]

§ 144. **Effect of surveyor-general's return as to character of land within sixteenth and thirty-sixth sections, or lands sought to be selected in lieu thereof, or under floating grants.**—We have already had occasion to comment on the general unreliability of that class of returns of surveyors-general [3] from

---

[1] Churchill v. Anderson, 53 Cal. 212; Buhne v. Chism, 48 Cal. 467; Wisconsin Cent. R. R. Co. v. Price County, 133 U. S. 496, 10 Sup. Ct. Rep. 341; Allen v. Pedro, 136 Cal. 1, 68 Pac. 99; Baker v. Jamison, 54 Minn. 17, 55 N. W. 750.

[2] Roberts v. Gebhart, 104 Cal. 67, 37 Pac. 782.

[3] See, ante, § 106. Also, Instructions, 31 L. D. 212.

which an inference or presumption is said to arise that the lands are non-mineral in character. Where the lands, however, are returned as mineral, it suggests direct knowledge brought to the attention of the surveyor of the notorious mineral character of the land. And in such cases, perhaps, more weight should be given to the returns. Be that as it may, where a given sixteenth or thirty-sixth section is returned as mineral by the surveyor, and his field-notes and plat are filed in the general land office, this is a sufficient determination that the lands are mineral to authorize the state to select indemnity lands in lieu thereof.[1]

But if the lands are returned as agricultural lands, or if the character of the lands is not sufficiently shown by the survey, the state should not be permitted to select indemnity lands until it has been determined that the lands which it claims to have lost by reason of their mineral character were in fact of that character at the date of the approval of the survey.[2]

Of course, the state having selected lieu lands in such a case, it would be estopped from ever after claiming that the surveyor-general's return upon which it based its right to select lieu land was false. The selection when made would operate as a waiver of its right to the land relinquished.[3] A like estoppel should rest upon the government. It should not be permitted to assert that the lands relinquished are not mineral in character, as it is only by reason of this character that the government retains dominion and control over the lands.

Where, however, no application is made to select land in lieu of sixteenth and thirty-sixth sections, returned

[1] Johnson v. Morris, 72 Fed. 890; *In re* State of California, 23 L. D. 423. But see Instructions, 31 L. D. 212.
[2] Bond v. State of California, 31 L. D. 34. See Instructions, *Id.* 212.
[3] *In re* State of California, 28 L. D. 57.

as mineral, the state has a right to be heard upon the question of the character of the land, in whatever tribunal the question is raised.[1] If a mining location is made upon such a section, and application is made for a mineral patent, the state is a necessary party to the investigation touching the character of the land and the time when it became known as such.[2]

It cannot be deprived of this right by any proceeding to which it is not a party, or of which it has had no legal notice.

In the case of applications for mineral patents for lands within railroad land-grant limits, the publication and posting of the patent application has been held to operate as such notice.[3]

The publication, however, of a notice of a hearing ordered by the land department to determine the character of the land is not sufficient. The railroad company, through its officers, should be personally served.[4]

A similar rule should undoubtedly be applied where the claims of the mineral locator conflict with asserted rights under grants to states which rights are still in any sense subject to administration, or over which the land department retains jurisdiction sufficient to enable it to pass upon the character of the land.

As sixteenth and thirty-sixth sections pass to the state in the absence of legal impediment, by the survey *ex propria vigore*, or by the admission of the state after survey, there is no preliminary adjudication,[5] actual or presumed, by the land department as to the character of the land. There is no antecedent judgment, as there is in pre-emption or homestead cases, which is final and

[1] Richter *v.* State of Utah, 27 L. D. 95.
[2] Boulder & Buffalo M. Co., 7 L. D. 54; Fleetwood Lode, 12 L. D. 604.
[3] Northern Pac. R. R. *v.* Cannon, 54 Fed. 252.
[4] McCloud *v.* Central Pac. R. R. Co., 29 L. D. 27.
[5] See, *post*, § 144a.

conclusive upon collateral attack. The return of the surveyor-general is in no sense such an adjudication. It follows that the question may be raised at any time by any one in privity with the government of the United States. The holder of a valid subsisting mining location is in such privity.

We reserve for discussion in the next section the effect of a state patent as evidence of the character of the land.

With reference to the state selecting lieu lands, or lands in satisfaction of its floating grants, it is not precluded from applying for lands returned as mineral. It has a right to contest this return, and establish upon hearings ordered for that purpose the non-mineral character of the land, the same as any other applicant to purchase or make private entry of public lands.

But before such selection can be preliminarily accepted, the state must "prove the mineral off," upon notice given of a hearing for that purpose.[1]

§ 144a. **Conclusiveness of state patents as to character of land.**—It does not necessarily follow that the state must, under its laws regulating the sale of its lands acquired from the general government, by its conveyance vest in the grantee the same title and right acquired by it. As the paramount proprietor of its granted lands, it may pass such laws and prescribe such rules and regulations governing the administration of its grants as the legislature may deem expedient, and the state's vendee takes title subject to such laws.[2]

Land which at the time of survey, in the case of sixteenth and thirty-sixth sections, or at the time of listing and certification, in the case of lieu or floating grants,

---

[1] Regulations of the Department, pars. 100-105, appendix; State of California, 22 L. D. 294; S. C. (on review), *Id.* 402; Commissioner's Letter, Copp's Min. Dec., p. 40; Richter *v.* State of Utah, 27 L. D. 95.

[2] Stanley *v.* Mineral Union (Nev.), 63 Pac. 59, 60.

may, so far as its known character is concerned, be non-mineral. Exploitation after the state has acquired its title may develop its mineral character. The legislature of the state may impress upon its conveyance to grantees limitations and reservations in the light of which all state patents must be construed.[1]

It is impossible to state any general rule as to the operative force of such instruments, as legislation in this regard may not be, and in fact is not, the same in all the states. In the absence of any legislation imposing limitations upon the title so conveyed, it may be assumed where the general government has approved and certified to the state, lands in satisfaction of its indemnity or floating grants, that such certification, followed by a state patent, would make the title in the vendee impervious to collateral attack.[2]

In the case of sixteenth and thirty-sixth sections, we have heretofore observed [3] that there is no preliminary investigation by the land department as to the character of the land. Neither the law nor regulations of the department prescribe any procedure for a determination of the question as a condition precedent to the vesting of title in the state. As there is neither certification nor patent for these sections emanating from the general government, there is nothing upon which to base a conclusive presumption that the lands at the date of the survey were of any particular character.

For many years it has been the custom in California, and perhaps elsewhere, for the state land officers, prior to disposing of the lands within sixteenth and thirty-sixth sections, to obtain from the register of the local United States land office a certificate showing the *status*

[1] Stanley *v.* Mineral Union (Nev.), 63 Pac. 59, 60.
[2] McCormick *v.* Hayes, 159 U. S. 332, 348, 16 Sup. Ct. Rep. 37.
[3] See, *ante*, § 144.

of these sections as disclosed in the tract-books,[1]—that is, as to whether it appears from such books that there are pre-emption or homestead filings covering these sections, or other facts which might impair the title of the state. If there appear on these books no notations showing the existence of any impediments, the register has, at the request of the state, so certified, and noted the fact of certification in the tract-books. There is absolutely no authority for this so-called "certificate." The action of the register is not supplemented by any action on the part of the commissioner or secretary of the interior. The certificate does not purport to deal with the character of the land, the only evidence as to that fact being the United States surveyor-general's return, which, as heretofore pointed out, is not entitled to serious weight. Registers of the land office have no powers except such as are defined in the acts of congress and in departmental regulations made in pursuance of law,[2] and the power to give such certificates is not given either expressly or by implication in either the acts of congress or departmental regulations.

The attention of the secretary of the interior has (we think for the first time) been recently called to this practice of issuing certificates from the register's office, through a report made to the commissioner of the general land office by one of the registers, which report was as follows:—

"I find noted upon the tract-books these words (with " regard to a certain section 16) 'Certified to the state " 'per J. W. Garden, register, Oct. 8, 1885.' Our tract- " books are filled with notations of this kind or similar " notations to sections sixteen and thirty-six, and I pre- " sume that it was the practice of former registers, as it " is now, to certify to the state, upon inquiry by the state

---

[1] See, *post*, § 660.

[2] Parker *v.* Duff, 47 Cal. 554. See, *post*, § 660.

" surveyor-general, the *status* of the lands in sections
" sixteen and thirty-six as shown by the records."

With reference to this procedure, the secretary
says:—

"It is apparent by this statement of the register that
" neither his predecessors nor he has comprehended the
" nature of their duties respecting these school sections.
" No such notations as is here indicated should have
" been issued. The character of school sections in Cali-
" fornia as to whether mineral or non-mineral is not to
" be wholly determined by the surveyor-general's re-
" turn, nor indeed is his return considered as a very
" high or persuasive evidence of the character of the
" lands when it is once drawn in question. . . . It is
" also possible that lands in a school section might be
" excepted from a grant to a state because of other
" things than their mineral character, which would not
" necessarily be shown upon the records of the local
" office.

"While it is competent and proper for the local
" officers, in response to legitimate inquiries, to give
" such information as is shown by the records of their
" office,—as, for instance, whether a given section six-
" teen has been returned as mineral or non-mineral, or
" whether any portion thereof is or is not included in a
" homestead or other entry,—it is not competent or
" proper that these officers should also undertake to
" state in a manner which may be erroneously accepted
" as a certification or authorized statement that the sec-
" tion has or has not passed to the state."[1]

The supreme court of California seems to have treated
this class of certificates issued by the register as possessing the same legal effect as a certification by the
commissioner of the general land office approving lieu
or indemnity selections or selections in satisfaction of
floating grants, and has said that such certification fol-

[1] Instructions, 31 L. D. 212.

lowed by the issuance of a state patent renders the title so evidenced immune from collateral attack.[1]

A previous decision by the same court sanctioned a collateral attack on a state patent by a mineral claimant, and upheld the title to the mining claim upon the findings of the trial court, that at the date of the survey the land was known to be mineral.[2]

It is manifest that either the court in its last expression has given to the register's certificate unwarranted legal value or the secretary of the interior has without legal justification inhibited the practice of issuing such certificates. With all possible deference to the supreme court of California, the logic of the situation would seem to be with the secretary of the interior. A state patent cannot transmit a title which the state did not receive. If the lands are known to be mineral at the date of the survey, the title does not pass to the state.[3]

One occupying the *status* of a *bona fide* mining locator at the date of survey, not being in privity with the state, could under the later decision of the supreme court of California be deprived of his "day in court" by the issuance of a state patent. We do not think the question of the known character of the land within a sixteenth or thirty-sixth section, is foreclosed by the issuance of such patent. The question may be investigated at any time, either by the courts, in the absence of a contest pending before the land department, or by that tribunal, at the instigation of an applicant for a mineral patent, due notice of such application being given to the state or its grantee.[4]

---

[1] Saunders *v.* La Purisima G. M. Co., 125 Cal. 159, 57 Pac. 656.
[2] Hermocilla *v.* Hubbell, 89 Cal. 5, 26 Pac. 611.
[3] Ivanhoe M. Co. *v.* Keystone M. Co., 102 U. S. 167.
[4] Fleetwood Lode, 12 L. D. 604; Boulder and Buffalo M. Co., 7 L. D. 54.

§ 145. **Conclusions.**—From the foregoing exposition of the law, we deduce the following conclusions:—

(1) That lands embraced within sixteenth or thirty-sixth sections, known to be mineral in character at the date of the final approval of the survey, do not pass to the state, but remain a part of the public mineral domain, subject to exploration and purchase, the same as other public mineral lands.

(2) The state may not select as lieu lands, or lands in satisfaction of its floating grants, any tract whose mineral character is known or established prior to the final approval of the selection and listing to the state.

(3) The approval by the commissioner of the land office of a selection by a state of lands under an indemnity or other floating grant is in the absence of fraud a conclusive adjudication of the character of such lands. Such approval and certification have the effect of a patent.

(4) Where sixteenth and thirty-sixth sections are returned by the surveyor as mineral, and the state accepts this return and selects other lands in lieu thereof, both the state and general government are estopped from threafter asserting that the lands are non-mineral.

(5) Where such sections are returned as mineral, and the state does not accept the return as establishing the character of the land, it has a right to its "day in court" for the purpose of impeaching the return. Where it desires to select lands, either in lieu of sixteenth and thirty-sixth sections or under its floating grants, which lands are returned by the surveyor-general as mineral, it has a right to "prove the mineral off," and, if successful, to have other lands listed to it.

(6) Whether or not a given tract is of a known mineral character at the time the grant or selection would

take effect, in the absence of legal impediments, must be determined by the facts as they exist at that time, and the then state of the law, as recognized by the current of judicial authority.

ARTICLE IV. RAILROAD GRANTS.

§ 149. Area of grants in aid of railroads, and congressional legislation donating lands for such purposes.

§ 150. Types of land grants in aid of the construction of railroads, selected for the purpose of discussion.

§ 151. Character of the grants.

§ 152. Reservation of mineral lands from the operation of railroad grants.

§ 153. Grants of rights of way.

§ 154. Grants of particular sections as construed by the courts.

§ 155. Construction of railroad grants by the land department.

§ 156. Distinctions between grants of sixteenth and thirty-sixth sections to states and grants of particular sections to railroads.

§ 157. Indemnity lands.

§ 158. Restrictions upon the definition of "mineral lands," when considered with reference to railroad grants.

§ 159. Test of mineral character of land applied to railroad grants.

§ 160. Classification of railroad lands under special laws in Idaho and Montana.

§ 161. Effect of patents issued to railroad companies.

§ 162. Conclusions.

§ 149. Area of grants in aid of railroads, and congressional legislation donating lands for such purposes. —From the year 1850 to June 30, 1880, congress granted to states, territories, and railroad corporations, in aid of the construction of railways, upwards of one hundred and fifty million acres of the public domain. Of these, more than one hundred million acres were within the precious-metal-bearing states and territories.[1]

[1] Public Domain, pp. 273-287.

Prior to 1862, grants of this character were generally made to states as trustees and agents of transfer for the benefit of companies projecting the railways; but with the passage of the Pacific railroad act, July 1, 1862,[1] was inaugurated a complete change in the system of land bounties to aid in the construction of railroads. The grants were thenceforward direct to the corporation.[2] As to grants made prior to 1862, we have no particular concern. Most, if not all, of the roads extending into the mineral regions of the west received their donations either under the Pacific railroad acts of 1862 and 1864 or under acts subsequently passed.

It is not within the purview of this treatise to deal with railroad grants in any respect other than as the operation of such grants within the precious-metal-bearing states and territories requires us to analyze the general character of the grants, and to determine the nature and extent of the things granted, the time when such grants take effect as to particular tracts, and such collateral questions as may be incidentally necessary to elucidate or explain the reasons for the rules established by the courts and the land department in administering the various grants.

For this purpose it will not be necessary to enumerate or discuss all the acts of congress granting lands in aid of the construction of railroads, but it will be sufficient for us to take as a basis certain pronounced types. So far as the scope of this treatise is concerned, these types represent features common to all grants. While there may be limitations in some of the later acts which do not appear in the selected types, and perhaps larger privileges and immunities are conferred by some than by others, yet in so far as the administration of the grants within the mineral regions and their application

---

[1] 12 Stats. at Large, p. 489.   [2] Public Domain, p. 267.

and effect with reference to mineral lands are concerned, we do not understand that there is any opportunity for differentiation.

§ 150.   **Types of land grants in aid of the construction of railroads, selected for the purpose of discussion.** —We select for the purpose of discussion the following acts and resolutions of congress:—

(1) An act to aid in the construction of a railroad and telegraph line from the Missouri river to the Pacific ocean, and to secure to the government the use of the same for postal, military, and other purposes (approved July 1, 1862),[1] and the act amendatory thereof (approved July 2, 1864) ;[2]

(2) An act granting lands in aid of the construction of a railroad and telegraph line from Lake Superior to Puget Sound on the Pacific coast by the northern route (approved July 2, 1864) ;[3]

(3) Joint resolution reserving mineral lands from the operation of all acts passed at the first session of the thirty-eighth congress granting lands or extending the time of former grants.[4]

A consideration of the grants provided for by these acts, taken in connection with the joint resolution of congress, will enable us to present the subject under discussion fairly, to note the adjudicated cases, and from them formulate what we understand to be the rules to be applied in construing and administering grants of this character according to the existing state of the law.

§ 151.   **Character of the grants.** —The act of July 1, 1862, granted to the corporations therein named, commonly called the "Pacific railroad companies," rights

---

[1] 12 Stats. at Large, p. 489. [3] *Id.*, p. 365.
[2] 13 Stats. at Large, p. 356. [4] *Id.*, p. 567.

of way over the public lands to the extent of two hundred feet in width on each side of the road, together with all necessary grounds for stations, buildings, workshops, and depots, machine-shops, turn-tables, switches, side-tracks, and water-stations. In addition, there was also granted every alternate section of public land not sold, reserved, or otherwise disposed of, designated by odd numbers, to the amount of five alternate sections per mile on each side of the respective roads, on the line thereof, and within the limits of ten miles on each side of said roads.

The amendatory act of July 2, 1864, enlarged this grant from five to ten alternate sections, and the lateral limits from ten to twenty miles. Neither of these acts contained any provision authorizing the selection of indemnity lands in lieu of odd-numbered sections, which might be subsequently ascertained to be lost to the companies by reason of their prior sale, reservation, or other disposition.

The act of July 2, 1864, incorporating the Northern Pacific railroad company, made a like grant to that company of rights of way and lands for necessary depot and other purposes. In the territories through which the projected roads might pass a land grant was given of every alternate odd-numbered section to the amount of twenty alternate sections per mile, and in the states ten alternate sections per mile.

There were also granted indemnity lands for odd-numbered sections which might be ascertained to be lost to the company, by reason either of their mineral character or their prior sale, reservation, or disposal, such indemnity lands to be selected within certain limits specified in the act.

We therefore have to deal with practically three classes of grants:—

(1) Grants of rights of way and lands for depots, side-tracks, and kindred purposes;

(2) Grants of particular sections within certain defined limits, generally called "primary," or "place," limits;

(3) A right to select lands in lieu of and as indemnity for losses accruing to the respective companies by reason of the odd-numbered sections having been previously sold, reserved, or otherwise disposed of, this right of selection to be exercised within certain defined limits, generally called "indemnity limits."

We will presently consider these different classes of grants and their attributes.

§ 152. **Reservation of mineral lands from the operation of railroad grants.**—At the time the Pacific railroad land-grant acts were passed there was no congressional law authorizing the acquisition of title to mineral lands. They were passed during what we have denominated, in a previous chapter,[1] as the second period of our national history, during which rights and privileges upon the public mineral lands were regulated by local rules and customs, with the passive acquiescence of the government. As was said by the circuit court of appeals (ninth circuit), in dealing with mining locations within the limits of railroad grants, claims to mineral lands could be lawfully initiated by discovery, possession, and development, according to the customs of miners and local regulations at and previous to the date of the railroad grant (1864).[2]

When these railroad acts became laws, the policy of the government of reserving the mines and mineral

---

[1] Tit. II, ch. iii, §§ 40-49.

[2] N. P. R. R. Co. *v.* Sanders, 49 Fed. 129, 134, S. C. on writ of error, 166 U. S. 620, 17 Sup. Ct. Rep. 671.

lands for the use of the United States was fixed; and if there had been no special clauses of reservation in the acts, the courts would have been forced to the conclusion that such lands were reserved by implication from the donations to railroads, following the doctrine announced with reference to grants of sixteenth and thirty-sixth sections to the states for school purposes.[1]

This doctrine of implied reservation has been applied by the land department to a grant of lands in Florida to aid in the construction of a railroad.[2]

However, in framing the later railroad acts, congress deemed it prudent to leave no room for dispute or discussion on this score, and inserted in each one of the acts clauses of reservation. The act of July 1, 1862,[3] contained the proviso "that all mineral lands shall be " excepted from the operation of this act." The amendatory act of July 2, 1864, provided that "any lands " granted by this act or the act to which this is an " amendment . . . shall not include . . . mineral " lands, . . . or any lands returned and denominated " as mineral lands." It also provided "that the term " 'mineral land,' wherever the same occurs in this act " and the act to which this is an amendment, shall not " be construed to include coal and iron land." The act of July 2, 1864, incorporating the Northern Pacific railroad company, contained reservations and limitations of similar import.[4]

At the second session of the same congress (thirty-eighth) which passed the act amendatory of the original Pacific railroad act and the Northern Pacific act, a joint resolution was adopted by the senate and house of representatives which provided,—

[1] Ivanhoe M. Co. v. Keystone M. Co., 102 U. S. 167. See, ante, § 136.
[2] Florida Cent. and Peninsular R. R. Co., 26 L. D. 600.
[3] 12 Stats. at Large, p. 492, § 3.
[4] 13 Stats. at Large, p. 367, § 3.

"That no act passed at the first session of the thirty-
" eighth congress granting lands to states or corpora-
" tions to aid in the construction of roads or for other
" purposes . . . shall be so construed as to embrace
" mineral lands, which in all cases shall be and are
" reserved exclusively to the United States, unless other-
" wise specially provided in the act making the grant."[1]

The mining act of July 26, 1866, followed.

The circuit court of appeals for the ninth circuit has
held that these reservations in railroad grants were
made in contemplation of future legislation as well as
the existing laws.[2]

In the light of this legislation, it is difficult to understand how any serious controversy could arise over the
administration of these land grants in the mineral regions. But such conflicts did arise, generally between
purchasers of the railroad title and mineral claimants,
and the battle was fiercely waged in all the tribunals,
both state and federal. These controversies involved a
discussion as to the character of the grants and the
time when they took effect as to particular tracts. We
have observed that there are found in this class of legislation grants of three different kinds: (1) the grant of
the right of way and for side-tracks, stations, and kindred purposes; (2) grants of particular sections; (3)
indemnity lands. We will consider each class with
reference to the mineral reservations found in the several acts.

§ 153. **Grants of right of way.**—The grants of rights
of way found in the various railroad acts contain no
reservations or exceptions. They are present, absolute
grants, subject to no conditions, except those necessarily
implied, such as that the road shall be constructed and

---

[1] 13 Stats. at Large, p. 567.
[2] N. P. R. R. Co. v. Sanders, 49 Fed. 129.

used for the purposes designated. They are in effect grants of the fee.[1] All persons acquiring any portion of the public lands, after the passage of such acts, take the same subject to the right of way conferred by them for the proposed road.[2]

The grants are floats until the line of the road is " definitely fixed" by filing the map of definite location. When so filed, and approved by the secretary of the interior, title vests to the lands within the limits of the right of way, as fixed by the act, as of the date of the passage of the act.[3]

The line of the road may also be "definitely fixed" by the actual construction of the road without having previously filed the map or profile,[4] and such actual construction precludes location of mining claims within the right of way limits.[5]

The reservation of "mineral lands" found in these acts does not apply to the lands embraced within the right of way limits. This right of way extends to and covers all public lands, whether mineral or not.[6]

If at the time the right of way attaches mineral lands over which the road is to pass are unoccupied, a subse-

[1] Missouri, Kansas and Texas Ry. *v.* Roberts, 152 U. S. 114, 14 Sup. Ct. Rep. 496; New Mexico *v.* United States Trust Co., 172 U. S. 171, 19 Sup. Ct. Rep. 128; Melder *v.* White, 28 L. D. 412.

[2] St. Joseph and Denver City R. R. Co. *v.* Baldwin, 103 U. S. 426; Montana Cent. R. R. Co., 25 L. D. 250.

[3] St. Joseph and Denver City R. R. Co. *v.* Baldwin, 103 U. S. 426; Smith *v.* N. P. R. R. Co., 58 Fed. 513; W. P. R. R. Co. *v.* Tevis, 41 Cal. 489; Northern Pac. R. R. Co. *v.* Murray, 87 Fed. 648; United States *v.* Oregon and Cal. R. R. Co., 176 U. S. 28, 20 Sup. Ct. Rep. 261.

[4] Jamestown and Northern Ry. Co. *v.* Jones, 177 U. S. 125, 20 Sup. Ct. Rep. 568.

[5] Pennsylvania M. and Imp. Co. *v.* Everett and M. C. Ry. Co. (Wash.), 69 Pac. 628.

[6] Doran *v.* C. P. R. R. Co., 24 Cal. 246; Wilkinson *v.* N. P. R. R. Co., 5 Mont. 538, 548, 6 Pac. 349; Pennsylvania M. and Imp. Co. *v.* Everett and M. C. Ry. Co. (Wash.), 69 Pac. 628.

quent location thereof, followed by a patent to the locators, is inferior to the right of way to the company, and must yield to the superior legal title, without resort to a court of equity to set the patent aside.

As was said by the supreme court of Montana,—

"The mineral lands excluded from the operation of
" this act are evidently not those covered by the right of
" way. . . . And it would be destructive of the rights
" of the railroad company if mining claims could at
" any time be located and worked upon the track and
" land covered by the right of way. . . . The operations
" of mining and the business of railroads cannot be
" conducted at the same time upon the same ground;
" and a reservation of such a character would beget
" a conflict of rights and a confusion of interests not in
" contemplation of intelligent legislative action."[1]

The limits of the grant of the right of way once fixed by the filing and approval of the map of definite location, or by the actual construction of the road in the absence of such filing and approval, cannot thereafter be changed to the detriment of any other party.[2]

It will be remembered that these decisions are under acts passed prior to the mining act of July 26, 1866. We do not concede that a right of way granted to a railroad company subsequent to the passage of that act would take precedence over a prior valid subsisting mining location. As we understand the law, since the passage of the mining acts the location of a valid mining claim operates to withdraw the land embraced within it from the public domain. It is a grant from the government. A railroad corporation claiming a right of way under a subsequent grant by congress could not cross the located mining claim (provided the same is

[1] Wilkinson v. N. P. R. R. Co., 5 Mont. 538, 548, 6 Pac. 349.
[2] Smith v. N. P. R. R. Co., 58 Fed. 513, and cases cited; Northern Pac. R. R. Co. v. Murray, 87 Fed. 648.

upon *mineral* land) without condemning the land and
paying the miner compensation.[1] In this respect, as we
will hereafter endeavor to show, mining claims differ
from inchoate homestead and pre-emption claims.[2] As
to lands for depot, side-track, and other kindred purposes, no controversies are likely to arise. For the
most part, these adjuncts are necessarily within the
right of way limits, if in fact the laws do not contemplate they should be. If other lands necessary to be
used for these collateral purposes may be selected outside of the right of way limits, then their selection would
necessarily be under the supervision of the land department, and rights thereto would not attach until final
approval of the selection.[3]

§ 154. **Grants of particular sections, as construed
by the courts.** —The grants of the alternate sections are
said to be of lands "in place," and the limits within
which they are granted are called "primary" or
"place" limits, contradistinguished from "indemnity"
limits in cases of grants which provide for indemnity
or lieu selections, as well as for lands "in place."

Grants of particular sections or of lands "in place"
do not acquire precision until the lands are surveyed
and the line of the road is definitely fixed. Until such
time the grant is said to be a float. Such grants are,
however, grants *in præsenti.* They attach to particular
tracts as soon after the filing of the map of definite
location of the road as these tracts become identified
by survey; and when so identified, title vests in the company, in the absence of legal impediments, by relation

[1] Montana Cent. Ry. Co., 25 L. D. 250.
[2] St. Paul M. and M. Co. *v.* Maloney, 24 L. D. 460; Dakota Cent. R. R.
Co. v. Downey, 8 L. D. 115; Santa Fe Pacific Ry., 29 L. D. 36.
[3] See Union Pac. Ry., 25 L. D. 540; Santa Fe Pacific R. R. Co., 27 L.
D., 322; 29 L. D. 36; Opinion attorney-general, 28 L. D. 130.

as of the date of the passage of the act. This is too well
settled to require argument. The authorities in support
of it are numerous and uniform.[1]

While this is true as to such lands as are within the
purview of the grant, it is not to be inferred that the
mineral or non-mineral character of the land is to be
determined as of the date of either the survey or filing
the map of definite location.

This question came before the circuit court of the
United States for the ninth circuit, northern district of
California, upon the demurrer to the complaint in the
case of Francœur v. Newhouse,[2] wherein the late Judge
Sawyer announced the rule that the exception of mineral lands from the grant to the Pacific railroads only
extended to lands *known* to be mineral and apparently
mineral at the time *when the grant attached;* and a discovery of a gold mine in the lands after the title has
vested in the company by full performance of the conditions did not defeat the title of the railroad company,
although at the time of the discovery no patent had
been issued to the railroad.

Subsequently, at the trial of this cause, the same
judge charged the jury to the same effect; that the
words "mineral land," as used in the act of congress,
meant land known to be mineral at the time the grant

---

[1] United States v. Oregon and Cal. R. R. Co., 176 U. S. 28, 20 Sup. Ct.
Rep. 261; Van Wyck v. Knevals, 106 U. S. 360, 1 Sup. Ct. Rep. 336; Kan.
P. Ry. Co. v. Dunmeyer, 113 U. S. 629, 5 Sup. Ct. Rep. 566; St. Paul and
Pacific R. R. Co. v. N. P. R. R. Co., 139 U. S. 1-5, 11 Sup. Ct. Rep. 389;
Sioux City and I. F. T. L. and L. Co. v. Griffey, 143 U. S. 32, 12 Sup.
Ct. Rep. 362; Smith v. N. P. R. R. Co., 58 Fed. 513; United States v.
S. P. R. R. Co., 146 U. S. 570, 13 Sup. Ct. Rep. 152; Schulenberg v.
Harriman, 21 Wall. 44, 60; Missouri, K. and T. R. Co. v. Kansas Pac.
R. R. Co., 97 U. S. 491; St. Joseph and Denver City R. R. Co. v. Baldwin,
103 U. S. 426; N. P. R. R. Co. v. Wright, 54 Fed. 67; United States v.
Northern Pac. R. R. Co., 103 Fed. 389; S. P. R. R. Co. v. Whitaker, 109
Cal. 268, 41 Pac. 1083; McLaughlin v. Menotti, 89 Cal. 354, 26 Pac. 880.
[2] 40 Fed. 618.

took effect and attached to the specific land in question, or lands which there was satisfactory reason to believe were such at said time; that only such land as was known to be mineral, or which there was satisfactory reason to believe was mineral, at the time the grant attached to the land is excepted from the grant.[1] The doctrine thus announced was maintained or accepted in several later cases in the same circuit.[2]

The case of Northern Pacific Railroad *v.* Barden,[3] arose in the same circuit in the district of Montana, the hearing being had before Judges Sawyer and Knowles. Judge Sawyer reiterated his views as expressed in the Francœur-Newhouse case; but Judge Knowles dissented, holding that the mineral character of the land might be established at any time prior to the issuance of the patent to the railroad company, and when so established such land was not within the purview of the grant, and the title thereto never vested in the company.

This case went to the supreme court of the United States on writ of error,[4] and that tribunal settled the controversy. The grant there under consideration was to the Northern Pacific railroad, under the act of July 2, 1864, heretofore referred to. It appeared that the line of the road opposite and past the lands in controversy became definitely fixed on July 6, 1882, by filing with the commissioner of the general land office the required plat. The quartz-mining claims were on an odd-numbered section of the railroad grant, within the "place" or "primary" limits, and were discovered in 1888. Prior to such discovery, the railroad company

---

[1] Francœur *v.* Newhouse, 43 Fed. 238.

[2] Valentine *v.* Valentine, 47 Fed. 597; N. P. R. R. Co. *v.* Barden, 46 Fed. 592; N. P. R. R. Co. *v.* Sanders, 49 Fed. 129; N. P. R. R. Co. *v.* Cannon, 54 Fed. 252.

[3] 46 Fed. 592.

[4] Barden *v.* N. P. R. R. Co., 154 U. S. 288, 14 Sup. Ct. Rep. 1030.

had applied to the government to have the section in question certified to it under its grant, and such application had been approved by the commissioner of the general land office; but no action had been taken thereon by the secretary of the interior. The land in question had been returned by the surveyor-general as agricultural land.

Upon this state of facts the supreme court of the United States enunciated the following rules of law:—

(1) The Northern Pacific railroad company cannot recover under the grant to it by the act of congress of July 2, 1864, mineral lands from persons in possession thereof who have made locations, although the mineral character of the land was not discovered until the year 1888, no patent having been issued to said company therefor;·

(2) It was the intention of congress to exclude from the grant of lands to the Northern Pacific railroad company actual mineral lands, whether known or unknown, and not merely such as were at the time known to be mineral;

(3) The reservation in the grant of mineral lands was intended to keep them under government control for the public good, in the development of the mineral resources of the country, and for the benefit and protection of the miner and explorer, instead of compelling him to litigate or capitulate with a stupendous corporation and ultimately succumb to such terms, subject to such conditions, and amenable to such servitudes as it might see proper to impose;

(4) The government has exhibited its beneficence in reference to its mineral lands, as it has in the disposition of its agricultural lands, where the claims and rights of the settlers are fully protected. The privilege of exploring for mineral lands was in full force at the

time of the location of the definite line of the road, and
was a right reserved and excepted out of the grant at
that time.

This is the law of the land; and in the light of these
rules all grants to railroads are to be construed and
administered. A discovery of mineral on lands falling
within the primary or place limits of any railroad
grant, at any time prior to the issuance of the patent,
if it be demonstrated that such lands are in fact mineral, within the meaning of that term as defined by the
current of judicial authority, establishes the fact that
the lands are not within the grant, and title thereto
never vested in the railroad company. But non-mineral
land is not excepted from the grant by reason of a
" claim" thereto under the mining laws, unless it is
one which has been asserted before the local land office,
and is pending of record there at the time the line of
road is definitely fixed.[1]

It will be observed that the grant in question in the
Barden case was one which in addition to the grant of
alternate sections also granted indemnity to the Northern Pacific railroad, in lieu of such lands as might be
lost to it by reason of their mineral character. In the
decision of the court this fact is noted. But we do not
apprehend that this element was of controlling force.
The same principles of law as applied to grants which
contain indemnity provisions apply with equal force to
grants which do not contain them, such as the original
Pacific railroad act of July 1, 1862. In the former class
of grants, congress has simply declared that the grant
as to quantity should not suffer diminution. In the
latter, congress has simply granted the lands to the
railroad company to the extent that they are of the class

---

[1] Northern Pac. R. R. Co. v. Allen, 27 L. D. 286; Northern Pac. R. R.
Co. v. Sanders, 166 U. S. 620, 17 Sup. Ct. Rep. 671.

which is properly patentable under the act. To the extent that the lands within the limits are within the reservation clauses, then, and to that extent, the grant as to quantity is diminished.

§ 155. Construction of railroad grants by the land department.—The rule announced by the supreme court of the United States in the Barden case was always followed by the land department in administering railroad grants. This fact is so stated in the decision in that case, and the ruling announced by Secretary Noble in C. P. R. R. v. Valentine [1] is thus quoted at length:—

"The very fact, if it be true, that the office of the " patent is to define and identify the land granted, and " to evidence the title which vested by the act, neces- " sarily implies that there exists jurisdiction in some " tribunal to ascertain and determine what lands were " subject to the grant and capable of passing there- " under. Now, this jurisdiction is in the land depart- " ment, and it continues, as we have seen, until the lands " have been either patented or certified to or for the " use of the railroad company. By reason of this juris- " diction, it has been the practice of that department " for many years past to refuse to issue patents to rail- " road companies for lands found to be mineral in " character at any time before the date of the patent. " Moreover, I am informed by the officers in charge of " the mineral division of the land department that ever " since the year 1867 (the date when that division was " organized) it has been the uniform practice to allow " and maintain mineral locations within the geograph- " ical limits of railroad grants, based upon discoveries " made at any time before patent, or certification where " patent is not required. This practice having been " uniformly followed and generally accepted for so " long a time, there should be, in my judgment, the " clearest evidence of error, as well as the strongest " reasons of policy and justice, controlling before a

[1] 11 Land Decisions, 238, 246.

" departure from it should be sanctioned. It has, in " effect, become a rule of property." [1]

§ 156. Distinctions between grants of sixteenth and thirty-sixth sections to states and grants of particular sections to railroads.—Grants to railroads of particular sections bear a striking resemblance to the grants to the states of sixteenth and thirty-sixth sections for school purposes. Both are grants *in præsenti*. But in cases of school grants no patents issue to the state. The state has nothing to do or perform as a condition precedent to the taking effect of the grant. Nor is any action of the land department invoked preliminarily as to determination of the character of the land.[2] It has the power, when called upon at the instigation of either party, to make the investigation; but it is not an exclusive power, and nothing in ordinary cases ever issues to the state which is evidence of any judgment of the land department upon the question of the character of the land. In cases of railroad grants the company is required to comply with a number of conditions before it can assert its right to a patent. The land department retains exclusive jurisdiction over these railroad lands until patent issues, for the purpose of determining whether

---

[1] This case involved the same property in controversy in Valentine *v.* Valentine (47 Fed. 597). The author was counsel for the mineral claimant in both proceedings. Before the land department the inquiry was limited to the *present* character of the land. In the circuit court, under the previous ruling in that circuit, in Francœur *v.* Newhouse (40 Fed. 618), the inquiry was addressed to the date of the passage of the railroad act and the filing of the map of definite location. The ruling of the secretary in the case before the land department has been quoted approvingly and followed in later cases. North Star M. Co. *v.* C. P. R. R. Co., 12 L. D. 608; N. P. R. R. Co., 13 L. D. 691; Winscott *v.* N. P. R. R. Co., 17 L. D. 274; N. P. R. R. Co. *v.* Marshall, *Id.*, 545; N. P. R. R. Co. *v.* Champion Cons., 14 L. D. 699. See, also, the earlier cases of C. P. R. R. Co., *v.* Mammoth Blue Gravel, 1 Copp's L. O. 134; G. D. Smith, 13 Copp's L. O. 28.

[2] See, *ante*, 144a.

or not the conditions have been complied with, and necessarily to adjudicate upon the patentability of the lands under the particular act in question. The late Judge Sawyer thus forcibly stated the rule:—

"Under the statute [Pacific railroad act] it is as
" clearly the duty of the officers authorized to issue
" patents to the railroad companies, to ascertain whether
" the lands patented are embraced in the congressional
" grant, and patentable, or are mineral lands, and not
" patentable, as it is in the case of pre-emption, home-
" stead, or other entry and sale of public lands to ascer-
" tain the facts authorizing the issue of the patent. . . .
" There must be some point of time when the character
" of the land must be finally determined; and, for the
" interest of all concerned, there can be no better point
" to determine this question than at the time of issuing
" the patent."[1]

The supreme court of the United States thus announced the rule in the Barden-N. P. R. R. case,[2] heretofore discussed, after quoting the ruling of the land department in the case of C. P. R. R. v. Valentine:—

"The fact remains that under the law the duty of
" determining the character of the lands granted by
" congress and stating it in instruments transferring
" the title of the government to the grantees reposes in
" officers of the land department. Until such patent
" is issued, defining the character of the land granted
" and showing that it is non-mineral, it will not comply
" with the act of congress in which the grant before
" us was made.
"The grant, even when all the acts required of the
" grantees are perfomed, only passes a title to non-
" mineral lands; but a patent issued in proper form
" upon a judgment rendered after a due examination
" of the subject by the officers of the land department

---

[1] Cowell v. Lammers, 10 Saw. 255, 257, 21 Fed. 200. See, also, N. P. R. R. Co. v. Cannon, 54 Fed. 252.
[2] 154 U. S. 330, 14 Sup. Ct. Rep. 1030.

" charged with its preparation and issue that the lands
" were non-mineral, would, unless set aside and annulled
" by direct proceedings, estop the government from con-
" tending to the contrary."

As in case of sixteenth or thirty-sixth sections there
is no "instrument transferring the title issued by the
" department, no patent in proper form upon a judg-
" ment rendered after due examination of the subject
" by the officers of the land department," the question
remains to be litigated whenever and wherever it may
arise.

As we have heretofore seen, when dealing with school
grants, the surveyor-general's return concludes no one.[1]
Neither does it, for that matter, in the case of railroad
grants.[2]

The foregoing illustrates the distinctions to be made
between the two classes of grants. We think it nothing
more than right that where a given tract of land has
been applied for by a railroad company, and its selection thereof is of record, that the company should be
notified in some way of an adverse application.[3] The
published notice of application for a mineral patent required by section twenty-three hundred and twenty-
five has been held to be sufficient by the United States
circuit court of appeals for the ninth circuit.[4]

But the mere publication of a notice of a hearing
ordered by the land officers to determine the character of
the land disconnected with the patent proceeding is not
sufficient. In such cases the railroad company is entitled
to personal notice.[5]

[1] See, ante, §§ 144, 144a.
[2] Barden v. N. P. R. R. Co., 154 U. S. 288, 14 Sup. Ct. Rep. 1030; Winscott v. N. P. R. R. Co., 17 L. D. 274; Cal. and Ore. R. R. Co., 16 L. D.
262. See, also, ante, § 106.
[3] S. P. R. R. Co. v. Griffin, 20 L. D. 485.
[4] N. P. R. R. Co. v. Cannon, 54 Fed. 252.
[5] McCloud v. Central Pac. R. R. Co., 29 L. D. 27.

§ 157. **Indemnity lands.**—Ordinarily, it will not appear at the time the line of the road is definitely fixed how many acres of land or what lands are excepted from the grant of land "in place," by reason of their mineral character, prior sales, or reservations. Until this is ascertained the grant is a float, extending over the indemnity limits defined by the act. When any deficiency of the lands in place is determined, the right to select lands in lieu thereof arises, and selection may then be made from any of the lands of the United States within the indemnity limits of the grant; and when such selection is made and approved, the grant for the first time attaches to any specific lands within those limits.[1]

The rules applicable to selection by the states of lands in lieu of sixteenth and thirty-sixth sections are alike applicable to the selection of indemnity lands under acts of congress granting aid to railroads. These rules will be found stated in a preceding section.[2]

As mineral lands cannot inure to the railroad companies within the primary or place limits of their respective grants, it follows, as a matter of course, that mineral lands within the indemnity limits cannot be selected in lieu of lands lost to the companies within the place limits.[3]

[1] United States *v.* Winona and St. P. R. R. Co., 67 Fed. 948, 967; Kansas Pac. R. R. Co. *v.* Atchison, T. and S. F. R. R. Co., 112 U. S. 414, 5 Sup. Ct. Rep. 208; Barney *v.* Winona and St. P. R. R. Co., 117 U. S. 228, 6 Sup. Ct. Rep. 654; Sioux City and St. P. R. R. Co. *v.* Chicago, M. and St. P. R. R. Co., 117 U. S. 406, 6 Sup. Ct. Rep. 790; Wisconsin Cent. R. R. Co. *v.* Price County, 133 U. S. 496, 10 Sup. Ct. Rep. 341; United States *v.* Missouri, K. and T. R. R. Co., 141 U. S. 358, 12 Sup. Ct. Rep. 13; Oregon and C. R. R. Co. *v.* United States; and see Willamette Valley and Cascade M. W. R. R. Co., 29 L. D. 344.

[2] See, *ante*, § 143.

[3] United States *v.* Mullan, 7 Saw. 470, 10 Fed. 785; Mullan *v.* United States, 118 U. S. 271, 6 Sup. Ct. Rep. 1040; S. P. R. R. Co. *v.* Allen G. M. Co., 13 L. D. 165.

Until the selection is finally approved [1] and certified to the railroad company, the land department retains jurisdiction for the purpose of investigating the character of the land. If it is found to be mineral, it remains a part of the public domain, and subject to exploration and purchase under the mining laws.[2]

An interesting difference in phraseology between that usually employed in railroad grants and that found in an act passed August 5, 1892, granting certain indemnity lands to the St. Paul, Minneapolis, and Manitoba Railway, should be noted. By the latter act, the company was permitted to select an equal quantity of non-mineral public lands *so classified as non-mineral* at the time of actual government survey, which has been or shall hereafter be made.[3] The land department has held under that act that the failure to designate lands upon the field-notes and plat as mineral is to classify them as non-mineral, rendering them subject to the grant.[4]

§ 158. **Restrictions upon the definition of "mineral "lands," when considered with reference to railroad grants.**—In most of the acts granting lands in aid of the construction of railroads, it is expressly stated that coal and iron are not to be classified as mineral within the meaning of that term as employed in the reservation clauses. Where such legislative declaration is found, of course, lands containing coal and iron will pass to the railroad company under the grants of particular sec-

---

[1] An act of July 27, 1866, granting lands to the Southern Pacific Railroad Company, and providing that lands shall be selected under the direction of the secretary of the interior, does not require that the selection shall be approved by the secretary. Groeck *v.* Southern Pac. R. R. Co., 102 Fed. 32.

[2] Walker *v.* Southern Pac. R. R. Co., 24 L. D. 172.

[3] 27 Stats. at Large. p. 390.

[4] Bedal *v.* St. Paul, Minneapolis and Manitoba Ry. Co., 29 L. D. 254.

tions;[1] and where the right of indemnity selection is
given, lands containing coal and iron within the indemnity limits may be selected by the railroad company
with the same effect as if they were agricultural in character. It follows, as a matter of course, that if the
granting act is silent upon the subject of these two
commodities, lands containing them do not pass, nor
can they be selected as indemnity lands.

In the administration of the railroad grants there
was at one time the same disposition upon the part of
the land department to restrict the meaning of the term
" mineral," as used in the reservation clauses of these
grants, which prevailed in dealing with grants to states.
What we have heretofore said with reference to this
rule of construction when considering the latter class
of grants applies with equal force to railroad grants.[2]

More recent decisions of the department have, however, given a liberal interpretation to the term "min-
" eral."[3]

Let us review the action of the land department in
dealing with this subject as applied to railroad grants.

As early as 1875 the department held that lands more
valuable for the deposits of limestone than for agriculture might be patented under the mining laws. This
ruling has been followed in later cases.[4]

---

[1] Rocky Mountain C. and I. Co., 1 Copp's L. O. 1.

[2] See, *ante*, §§ 137-141.

[3] Pacific Coast Marble Co. *v.* Northern Pac. R. R. Co., 25 L. D. 233;
Aldritt *v.* N. P. R. R. Co., *Id.* 349; Union Oil Co. (on review), *Id.* 351;
Florida and Penin. R. R. Co., 26 L. D. 600; Phifer *v.* Heaton, 27 L. D.
57; Forsythe *v.* Weingart, *Id.* 680; Beaudette *v.* N. P. R. R. Co., 29 L.
D. 248; Tulare Oil and M. Co. *v.* S. P. R. R. Co., *Id.* 269; Schrimpf *v.*
N. P. R. R. Co., *Id.* 327; Morrill *v.* N. P. R. R. Co., 30 L. D. 475.

[4] *In re* H. C. Rolfe, 2 Copp's L. O. 66; *In re* W. H. Hooper, 8 Copp's
L. O. 120; *In re* Josiah Gentry, 9 Copp's L. O. 5; Maxwell *v.* Brierly, 10
Copp's L. O. 50; Conlin *v.* Kelly, 12 L. D. 1; Shepherd *v.* Bird, 17 L. D.
82; Morrill *v.* N. P. R. R. Co., 30 L. D. 475.

In the case of Elias Jacob,[1] Commissioner Williamson made a contrary ruling; but this decision was overruled by the secretary in the Hooper case.[2] We thus have established, by a uniform series of decisions, a departmental rule of construction, that lands valuable for deposits of lime are mineral in character, and may be entered under the mining laws.

In 1873, the department issued a circular[3] for the guidance of surveyors-general and registers and receivers, wherein it classified borax, carbonate and nitrate of soda, sulphur, alum, and asphalt as minerals, and open to entry under the mining laws. We are not aware that this classification has ever been questioned. Secretary Hoke Smith announced the rule that in administering railroad grants the word "mineral," as used in the reservation clauses, is to be understood to apply only to the more valuable metals, such as gold, silver, cinnabar, and copper.[4]

His argument proceeded upon the theory that at the time of the *passage of the act* wherein mineral lands were reserved, either expressly or by implication, the substances in controversy (phosphates and petroleum) were not minerals in contemplation of congress, and therefore passed to the railroad; that congress at that time only had in contemplation the more valuable metals.

The vice of the distinguished secretary's reasoning is found in his assumption that after the passage of the railroad acts, and before title vests under them, congress has no power to change its policy or enlarge

[1] 7 Copp's L. O. 83.
[2] 8 Copp's L. O. 120.
[3] Copp's Min. Dec., p. 316.
[4] Tucker *et al. v.* Florida Ry. and Nav. Co., 19 L. D. 414 (subsequently overruled: Pacific Coast Marble Co. *v.* N. P. R. R. Co., 25 L. D. 233); Union Oil Co., 23 L. D. 222 (reversed on review: 25 L. D. 351).

the scope of its legislation with respect to mineral lands. That this view is erroneous, we think we have fully demonstrated in the preceding article on the subject of grants to states for educational purposes.

His decision was overruled by his successor, and the liberal rule now prevails.[1]

Secretary Smith's ruling would have enabled railroad companies in the future to obtain title under the unadministered grants to a large class of valuable deposits, such as limestone, alum, soda, asphalt, marble, borax, sulphur, etc., which, by legislative and judicial construction, are within the purview of the mining laws.

Recently the following substances have been held to be mineral within the meaning of the reservation in the railroad grants: Granite,[2] asphaltum,[3] marble and slate,[4] limestone,[5] phosphates generally,[6] and sandstone.[7]

In the instructions issued to the commissioners appointed under the act providing for the classification of mineral lands within railroad grants in Idaho and Montana, the secretary was not unmindful of the injunction contained in that act, "That all said lands shall be " classified as mineral which, by reason of valuable " mineral deposits, are open to exploration, occupation, " and purchase under the provisions of the United " States mining laws."[8] Is this not a legislative decla-

---

[1] Pacific Coast Marble Co. v. N. P. R. R. Co., 25 L. D. 233; Union Oil Co. (on review), Id. 351.

[2] Northern Pac. R. R. Co. v. Soderberg, 99 Fed. 506, S. C. on appeal, 104 Fed. 425.

[3] Tulare Oil Co. v. S. P. R. R. Co., 29 L. D. 269.

[4] Schrimpf v. Northern Pac. R. R. Co., Id. 327.

[5] Morrill v. Northern Pac. R. R. Co., 30 L. D. 475.

[6] Florida Cent. and Penin R. R. Co., 26 L. D. 600.

[7] Beaudette v. N. P. R. R., 29 L. D. 248.

[8] 20 Land Decisions, 351. See Beaudette v. Northern Pac. R. R. Co., 29 L. D. 248; Schrimpf v. Northern Pac. R. R. Co., Id. 327; Morrill v. Northern Pac. R. R. Co., 30 L. D. 475; Northern Pac. R. R. Co. v. Soderberg, 99 Fed. 506, 104 Fed. 425.

ration that no lands which are subject to entry under those laws shall be patented to a railroad company? We think it is, although we are of the opinion that this was the law prior to the passage of this act.[1]

§ 159. Test of mineral character of land applied to railroad grants. —We think we are amply justified in here reiterating the doctrine applied by us to the administration of school land grants.

The question whether a given tract of land within the primary or place limits of a railroad grant is mineral, and therefore excepted out of the grant, is to be determined according to the state of the law and the facts as they exist at the time the railroad company applies for its patent. If the mineral character is then established according to the rules announced in section ninety-eight, it does not pass under the grant.[2]

Where a mining location is made within the primary limits of a railroad grant upon lands returned as agricultural and listed under the grant, and hearing is ordered at the instigation of the mineral claimant, the railroad company is entitled to personal notice of the hearing,—posting and publication not being sufficient.[3]

Where, however, a mineral claimant applies for a patent and proceeds with the posting and publication required by section twenty-three hundred and twenty-five of the Revised Statutes,—the proceeding being characterized as one essentially *in rem*,[4]—such posting and publication are sufficient.[5]

[1] Pacific Coast Marble Co. *v.* Northern Pac. R. R. Co., 25 L. D. 233; Aldritt *v.* Northern Pac. R. R. Co., *Id.* 349; Morrill *v.* Northern Pac. R. R. Co., 30 L. D. 475.

[2] *Id.*

[3] McCloud *v.* Central Pac. R. R. Co., 29 L. D. 27.

[4] See, *post*, § 713.

[5] Northern Pac. R. R. Co. *v.* Cannon, 54 Fed. 252.

With respect to indemnity selections, the state of the law and the facts as they exist at the time of the selection are alone to be considered, unless the act itself provides a different time.[1] If the lands sought to be selected fall within the rules announced in section ninety-eight of this treatise, they cannot be selected by the railroad company.

These rules apply to all railroad grants to the extent that they remain unadministered. As we shall hereafter see, a patent issued to such companies is conclusive evidence that the lands are non-mineral. Consequently, changed conditions arising after the issuance of patents or final approval of selections cannot affect the title.

While courts do not attempt to determine the mineral character of lands [2] falling within the limits of a railroad grant in advance of the decision of the land department upon the subject, they will protect the land from irreparable injury or destruction in a suit by a railroad company prior to such decision by the department.[3]

§ 160. **Classification of railroad lands under special laws in Idaho and Montana.**—To facilitate the administration of the land grants to the Northern Pacific railroad, and to provide for a more expeditious method of determining the character of lands within the primary and indemnity limits of this grant in the states of Idaho and Montana, congress, on February 26, 1895, passed an act, entitled ''An act to provide for the examination '' and classification of certain mineral lands in the states '' of Montana and Idaho.''[4]

This is the act referred to in section one hundred and

---

[1] Bedal v. St. Paul, M. and M. Ry. Co., 29 L. D. 254.

[2] See, *ante*, § 108.

[3] Northern Pac. R. R. Co. v. Soderberg, 86 Fed. 49, S. C. 99 Fed. 506; Railroad Co. v. Hussey, 61 Fed. 231.

[4] 28 Stats. at Large, p. 683.

fifty-eight of this treatise. It establishes an auxiliary board, consisting of three commissioners for each state, appointed by the president, whose duties are to make examinations in their respective districts, take testimony of witnesses, and generally to investigate the mineral or non-mineral character of the lands within the railroad limits in their respective jurisdictions.

The act makes provision for determining protests and controversies relative to the character of lands, the results of all such investigations to be reported through the customary channels to the land department. The action of this board only becomes final upon the approval of its reports by the secretary of the interior.

It is unnecessary here to detail the particulars of the act. The functions of the board are largely those of referees or "roving commissioners" under the equity practice; and in this aspect it is a mere adjunct of the land department. A mineral return by the commissioners would not prevent the commissioner of the general land office from making such disposition of the land as is proper upon a subsequent showing as to its character, but the classification should be considered as of the same effect as the returns of mineral lands made by the government surveyor.[1]

The act does not contemplate the classification of even sections, and the character of these sections is only considered when the mineral or non-mineral character of the odd sections cannot be otherwise satisfactorily ascertained.[2] The secretary of the interior, shortly after the passage of the act, issued elaborate instructions, prescribing the duties of the commissioners, under which they are now acting.[3]

The act, however, possesses some general features of

---

[1] Circ. Inst., 25 L. D. 446.   [3] 20 Land Decisions, p. 351.
[2] *Id.*, 26 L. D. 684.

more than passing interest. In addition to the definition of the term "mineral lands," referred to in the preceding section, it provides that in determining the character of the lands the commissioners may take into consideration certain conditions which, according to the previous rulings of the department and the courts, have not been considered as elements of controlling weight.

Thus, where mining locations have been made or patents issued for mining ground in any section of land, this shall be taken as *prima facie* evidence that the forty-acre subdivision within which it is located is mineral land.[1] It is further provided that the examination and classification of lands shall be made without reference or regard to any previous examination, report, or classification; that the commissioners shall take into consideration the mineral discovered or developed on or adjacent to such land, and the geological formation of all lands to be examined and classified, or the lands *adjacent* thereto, and the *reasonable probabilities* of such land containing valuable mineral deposits because of its formation, location, or character.

These provisions seem wise and beneficent. As the railroad company has no vested right to any particular class of lands, the rules established by the act can work no legal hardship. What is lost to the company in the place limits may be compensated by selections within the indemnity limits. Nor do we think, taking a common-sense view of the situation, that any cause of complaint could be urged by any land-grant road to which similar laws might be made applicable, even where there are no provisions for indemnity selections. Judge Sawyer[2] and Judge Hawley[3] have both held that lands

[1] Holter *v.* Northern Pac. R. R. Co., 30 L. D. 442.
[2] Francœur *v.* Newhouse, 40 Fed. 618.
[3] Valentine *v.* Valentine, 47 Fed. 597.

reasonably supposed to be mineral do not pass to the railroad companies; and the mineral character of a given tract may be reasonably inferred from geological conditions and local environment. It is to be hoped that the experiment will prove beneficial, and that like provisions may be made for the adjustment of all railroad land grants within the mineral regions.

§ 161. **Effect of patents issued to railroad companies.**—The supreme court of California has held in several cases that in an action at law a patent issued to a railroad company can be attacked by showing that the lands in controversy are mineral lands.[1]

These decisions were based upon the construction of patents which contained the reservation of "all mineral " lands, *should any be found to exist.*" Judge Sawyer, in the case of Cowell *v.* Lammers,[2] has conclusively shown that this exception is void, not being authorized by law. However, in later cases the supreme court of California has recognized the rule that when a law of congress provides for the disposal of certain public lands, upon the ascertainment of certain facts, the officers of the land department have jurisdiction to inquire into and determine those facts, and the patent issued thereon is a conclusive declaration that the facts have been found in favor of the patentee, and that this rule applies to the determination of the particular character of the land which is the subject of the patent.[3]

The federal courts, whose views, in the end, on a

---

[1] McLaughlin *v.* Powell, 50 Cal. 64, 19 Am. Rep. 647; Chicago Q. M. Co. *v.* Oliver, 75 Cal. 194, 7 Am. St. Rep. 143, 16 Pac. 780; Hunt *v.* Steese, 75 Cal. 620, 17 Pac. 920.

[2] 10 Saw. 246, 21 Fed. 200.

[3] Gale *v.* Best, 78 Cal. 235, 12 Am. St. Rep. 44, 20 Pac. 550; Irvine *v.* Tarbatt, 105 Cal. 237, 38 Pac. 896; Dreyfus *v.* Badger, 108 Cal. 65, 41 Pac. 279; Klauber *v.* Higgins, 117 Cal. 451, 49 Pac. 466.

question like this must prevail,[1] have from the beginning unhesitatingly announced the rule that the land department has jurisdiction to determine the character of lands, and its determination, culminating in the issuance of a patent, is conclusive. Such patent is not open to collateral attack.[2]

If mineral lands have been patented under railroad or homestead laws, and were known to be mineral prior to final entry and certification, such patents may be vacated by the United States.[3]

In a suit by the United States to vacate a patent issued under a railroad grant on the ground that the land was mineral, the burden rests on the complainant to over-

---

[1] Gale v. Best, 78 Cal. 240, 12 Am. St. Rep. 44, 20 Pac. 550.

[2] Barden v. N. P. R. R. Co., 154 U. S. 288, 14 Sup. Ct. Rep. 1030; French v. Fyan, 93 U. S. 169; Johnston v. Towsley, 13 Wall. 72; Moore v. Robbins, 96 U. S. 530; St. Louis Smelting Co. v. Kemp, 104 U. S. 636; Steel v. Smelting Co., 106 U. S. 447, 1 Sup. Ct. Rep. 389; Dahl v. Raunheim, 132 U. S. 260, 10 Sup. Ct. Rep. 74; Parley's Park S. M. Co. v. Kerr, 130 U. S. 256, 9 Sup. Ct. Rep. 511; United States v. Winona and St. P. R. R. Co., 67 Fed. 948; Carter v. Thompson, 65 Fed. 329; Scott v. Lockey Inv. Co., 60 Fed. 34; United States v. Mackintosh, 85 Fed. 333, 336; Northern Pac. R. R. Co. v. Soderberg, 86 Fed. 49; Mendota Club v. Anderson, 101 Wis. 479, 78 N. W. 185; Rood v. Wallace, 109 Iowa, 5, 79 N. W. 449; United States v. Budd, 144 U. S. 167, 12 Sup. Ct. Rep. 575; Peabody G. M. Co. v. Gold Hill M. Co., 111 Fed. 817. See Garrard v. Silver Peak Mines, 82 Fed. 578, 94 Fed. 983; Cosmos Exploration Co. v. Gray Eagle Oil Co., 104 Fed. 20, 112 Fed. 4; Potter v. Randolph, 126 Cal. 458, 58 Pac. 905. See, also, King v. Thomas, 6 Mont. 409, 12 Pac. 865; Manning v. San Jacinto Tin Co., 7 Saw. 419, 9 Fed. 726; Butte and B. M. Co. v. Sloane, 16 Mont. 97, 40 Pac. 217; Ah Yew v. Choate, 24 Cal. 562 (state patent); Poire v. Wells, 6 Colo. 406; Meyerdorf v. Frohner, 3 Mont. 282.

[3] W. P. R. R. Co. v. United States, 108 U. S. 510, 2 Sup. Ct. Rep. 802; McLaughlin v. United States, 107 U. S. 528, 2 Sup. Ct. Rep. 802; Mullan v. United States, 118 U. S. 271, 6 Sup. Ct. Rep. 1041; United States v. Mullan, 7 Saw. 466, 10 Fed. 785; United States v. Reed, 12 Saw. 99, 28 Fed. 482; United States v. Culver, 52 Fed. 81; Finn v. Hoyt, Id. 83; United States v. Central Pac. R. R. Co., 84 Fed. 218, 93 Fed. 871; Cosmos Exploration Co. v. Gray Eagle Oil Co., 104 Fed. 20, 39; Gold Hill Q. M. Co. v. Ish, 5 Or. 104.

come the presumption in favor of the patent by satisfactory proof, not only that the land was known mineral
land at the time the patent was issued, but that it is
chiefly valuable for mineral purposes. Evidence that
gold placer mining had formerly been carried on in a
stream on the tract, but that it had been abandoned as
worked out prior to the date of the patent, and neither
at that time nor since had there been any mines on the
land producing mineral and capable of being worked at
a profit, is insufficient, as is also evidence of the mineral
character of adjoining land.[1]

Authorities might be multiplied indefinitely. Sufficient space has been devoted to this subject at this juncture. We shall have occasion to recur to it again when
considering the force and effect of federal patents generally, in a later portion of the work.

§ 162. **Conclusions.**—We are authorized to deduce
the following general conclusions from the foregoing
exposition of the law:—

(1) That lands embraced within the primary or
place limits of a railroad grant, whose mineral character is known or established at any time prior to the
issuance of a patent, are not patentable to the railroad
company, and are excepted out of the grant.

(2) Lands mineral in character within the indemnity
limits of any railroad grant, where indemnity selections
are authorized by the act, can not be selected in lieu of
lands lost to the company within the place limits.

(3) Whether a given tract within either the primary
or indemnity limits is mineral or not must be determined
according to the state of the law and facts as they exist
at the time patent is applied for or application to select
is made, unless the act under which the grant is claimed

---

[1] United States v. Central Pac. R. R. Co., 93 Fed. 871.

specifies a different period (as for example, the date of survey).[1] Until patent is issued or selections are finally approved, the land department retains jurisdiction to pass upon the character of the land; and its judgment, culminating in the issuance of a patent or final approval of a selection, is conclusive, and not open to collateral attack.

(4) The term "mineral land," as used in the reservation clauses of railroad grants, includes all valuable deposits, metallic and non-metallic, which are or may be subject to entry under the mining laws, except coal and iron, where these substances are excepted out of the mineral reservation.[2]

(5) Mineral lands within either the primary or indemnity limits of railroad grants, prior to patent or certification, belong to the public domain, and are open to exploration and purchase under the mining laws, the same as any other public mineral lands.

Article V. Townsites.

§ 166. Laws regulating the entry of townsites.

§ 167. Rules of interpretation applied to townsite laws.

§ 168. Occupancy of public mineral lands for purposes of trade or business.

§ 169. Rights of mining locator upon unoccupied lands within unpatented townsite limits.

§ 170. Prior occupancy of public mineral lands within unpatented townsites for purposes of trade, as affecting the appropriation of such lands under the mining laws — The rule prior to the passage of the act of March 3, 1891.

§ 171. Correlative rights of mining and townsite claimants recognized by the land department prior to the act of March 3, 1891.

§ 172. Section sixteen of the act of March 3, 1891, is limited in its application to incorporated towns and cities.

[1] Bedal v. St. Paul, M. and M. Ry. Co., 29 L. D. 254.
[2] Northern Pac. Ry. Co. v. Soderberg, 99 Fed. 506.

§ 173. The object and intent of section sixteen of the act of March 3, 1891.

§ 174. The act of March 3, 1891, not retroactive.

§ 175. Effect of patents issued for lands within townsites.

§ 175a. Difficulty in the application of principles suggested.

§ 176. What constitutes a mine or valid mining claim within the meaning of section twenty - three hundred and ninety-two of the Revised Statutes.

§ 177. In what manner may a townsite patent be assailed by the owner of a mine or mining claim.

§ 178. Ownership of minerals under streets in townsites.

§ 166. **Laws regulating the entry of townsites.**—The laws of the United States providing for the reservation and sale of townsites on the public lands are found in title thirty-two, chapter eight, of the Revised Statutes, sections twenty-three hundred and eighty to twenty-three hundred and ninety, supplemented by section sixteen of the act of March 3, 1891, entitled "An act to " repeal timber-culture laws, and for other purposes." [1]

These laws provide three methods of acquiring title to town property on the public domain:—

(1) Where the president of the United States has directed the reservation provided for by section twenty-three hundred and eighty of the Revised Statutes;

(2) In cases where towns have already been established, or parties desire to found a town under the provisions of section twenty-three hundred and eighty-two;

(3) Under section twenty-three hundred and eighty-seven, by the terms of which the entry of land settled and occupied as a townsite may be made by the corporate authorities if the town be incorporated, or, if unincorporated, by the county judge, for the use and benefit of the several occupants.

We have no particular concern with townsites falling

[1] 26 Stats. at Large, p. 1095.

within sections twenty-three hundred and eighty or twenty-three hundred and eighty-two.

Section twenty-three hundred and eighty-seven is but a restatement or codification of the law as it existed at the time of the revision.[1]

It is under this section and the acts from which it was framed that most of the flourishing towns of the west have applied for and received patents, and it is the only one of the three methods of acquiring title to town property on the public lands which requires particular consideration at our hands,[2] although the principles of law discussed apply to all classes of townsites, by whatsoever method they are sought to be acquired.

Section twenty-three hundred and eighty-seven of the Revised Statutes is as follows:—

"Whenever any portion of the public lands have been "or may be settled upon and occupied as a townsite, not "subject to entry under the agricultural pre-emption "laws, it is lawful, in case such town be incorporated, "for the corporate authorities thereof, and if not incor- "porated, for the judge of the county court for the "county in which such town is situated, to enter at the "proper land office, and at the minimum price, the land "so settled and occupied, in trust for the several use "and benefit of the occupants thereof, according to their "respective interests; the execution of which trust, as "to the disposal of the lots in such town, and the pro- "ceeds of the sales thereof, to be conducted under such "regulations as may be prescribed by the legislative "authority of the state or territory in which the same "may be situated."

The townsite acts and the chapter of the Revised Statutes into which their provisions are incorporated contain certain restrictions and limitations upon the subject

---

[1] Act of March 2, 1867, 14 Stats. at Large, p. 541; Act of June 8, 1868, 15 Stats. at Large, p. 67.

[2] Public Domain, pp. 298, 299.

of mineral lands, which are necessary to be considered
for the purpose of obtaining a proper understanding of
the adjudicated cases, and to enable us to draw correct
conclusions as to the rules of interpretation to be
applied. These réstrictions and limitations are as follows:—

Section twenty-three hundred and eighty-six of the
Revised Statutes provides that,—

. . . "where mineral veins are possessed, which posses-
" sion is recognized by local authority, and to the extent
" so possessed and recognized, the title to town lots to be
" acquired shall be subject to such recognized posses-
" sion and the necessary use thereof; but nothing con-
" tained in this section shall be so construed as to
" recognize any color of title in the possessors for min-
" ing purposes as against the United States."

This is but a re-enactment of the proviso contained in
the act of March 3, 1865,[1] and, of course, its original
enactment antedates all legislation of congress, granting
in express terms the right to explore and acquire by
location any class of public mineral lands. Considering
the state of the law on the subject of this class of lands
at the time of the revision of the federal statutes (December, 1873), it would seem that this section, framed to
apply to conditions which no longer existed, was superfluous, and might with all propriety have been omitted.
Since the original act was passed, congress, by its legislation, has given to valid mining locations the *status* of
legal estates. As the law now stands, no possession of
public mineral lands can be lawfully recognized by local
authority which possession is not acquired and held
under the sanction of the general mining laws. So far
as an intelligent interpretation of the townsite laws is
sought, under existing conditions, section twenty-three

[1] 13 Stats. at Large, p. 530.

hundred and eighty-six performs but little, if any, function beyond that of an historical landmark or a link in the chain of evolution.

The act of March 2, 1867, entitled "An act for the "relief of the inhabitants of cities and towns upon "public lands," contained the following provision:—

"No title shall be acquired under the foregoing pro-"visions of this chapter to any mine of gold, silver, "cinnabar, or copper." [1]

At the time this act was passed, the first mining act of July 26, 1866, was in full force, which declared that the mineral lands of the public domain should thereafter be free and open to exploration and occupation, and provided for the acquisition of title to veins, or lodes, of quartz or other rock in place bearing gold, silver, cinnabar, and copper. It is obvious that the townsite act of 1867 was framed in the light of the first mining act. The act of June 8, 1868, added to the above quoted provisions of the act of March 2, 1867, the following clause:—

. . . "or to any valid mining claim or possession held "under existing laws." [2]

The foregoing provisions of the two acts were united and incorporated into the Revised Statutes, and are embodied in section twenty-three hundred and ninety-two of the chapter relating to townsites, which now reads as follows:—

"SEC. 2392. No title shall be acquired under the "foregoing provisions of this chapter to any mine of "gold, silver, cinnabar, or copper, or to any valid min-"ing claim or possession held under existing laws."

It may be noted that the mining act of May 10, 1872, which was in force when the Revised Statutes went into

[1] 14 Stats. at Large, p. 541.
[2] 15 Stats. at Large, p. 67.

effect, covered claims for lands bearing gold, silver, cinnabar, *lead, tin,* copper, *or other valuable deposits,* the words in italics not appearing in either the act of 1866 or the townsite laws.

As thus outlined, these laws stood, and were construed and interpreted by the highest courts in the land, and a fair understanding of their provisions was about being reached, when congress, by a provision inserted in the "Act to repeal the timber-culture laws, and for other " purposes," passed March 3, 1891, (principally *for other purposes,*)[1] injected some new elements into the townsite laws which thus far have not received the attention of the courts. The provisions referred to are found in section sixteen of the act in question, and are as follows:—

"SEC. 16. That townsite entries may be made by
" incorporated towns and cities on the mineral lands of
" the United States, but no title shall be acquired by
" such towns or cities to any vein of gold, silver, cin-
" nabar, copper, or lead, or to any valid mining claim or
" possession held under existing law. When mineral
" veins are possessed within the limits of an incorpo-
" rated town or city, and such possession is recognized
" by local authority or by the laws of the United States,
" the title to town lots shall be subject to such recog-
" nized possession and the necessary use thereof; and
" when entry has been made or patent issued for such
" townsites to such incorporated town or city, the pos-
" sessor of such mineral vein may enter and receive
" patent for such mineral vein and the surface ground
" appertaining thereto; *provided,* that no entry shall be
" made by such mineral vein claimant for surface
" ground where the owner or occupier of the surface
" ground shall have had possession of the same before
" the inception of the title of the mineral vein ap-
" plicant."

[1] 26 Stats. at Large, p. 1095.

To what extent this act is an innovation upon the system theretofore existing, and how far the rules of law theretofore established by the current of judicial authority are strengthened, weakened, or have become obsolete, will be noted as we proceed.

It appears, however, that the act is limited in its application to incorporated cities or towns, and its provisions do not apply to cases of townsite entries made by the county judge or the judicial officer performing his functions for the use and benefit of the occupants, or entries made by trustees appointed by the secretary of the interior. In enumerating the minerals, the act adds *lead* to the category, as found in section twenty-three hundred and ninety-two of the Revised Statutes.

§ 167. **Rules of interpretation applied to townsite laws.**—It is not to be inferred from the caption to this section that in construing the townsite laws we are authorized or required to invoke any rules of interpretation peculiar to this branch of the public land laws. We are called upon simply to apply general rules, and note the instances where special application of these rules to the laws under consideration has been made by the courts.

The townsite laws, as they now exist, consist simply of a chronological arrangement of past legislation, an aggregation of fragments, a sort of "crazy quilt," in the sense that they lack harmonious blending. This may be said truthfully of the general body of the mining laws. The rules adopted for the interpretation of the one apply with equal force to the other.

We have endeavored to formulate these rules in a preceding section.[1] We may supplement these with another rule specially applicable; *i. e.* the townsite laws

---

[1] See, *ante*, § 96.

are to be read and construed in connection with all the
existing legislation of congress regulating the sale and
disposal of the public lands—that is, these laws are to
be considered with all other laws which are essentially
in pari materia.

§ 168. **Occupancy of public mineral lands for purposes of trade or business.**—Important mineral discoveries in new quarters, however remote from civilized
centers, are invariably followed by a large influx of
population. The advance-guard sets its stakes upon the
most convenient spot, erects tents, or constructs primitive habitations, which form the nucleus of the future
town. As was said by Judge Field, speaking for the
supreme court of the United States,—

"Some of the most valuable mines in the country are
" within the limits of incorporated cities which have
" grown up on what was, on its first settlement, part of
" the public domain; and many of such mines were
" located and patented after a regular municipal gov-
" ernment had been established. Such is the case with
" some of the famous mines of Virginia City, in Nevada.
" Indeed, the discovery of a rich mine in any quarter
" is usually followed by a large settlement in its immedi-
" ate neighborhood, and the consequent organization of
" some form of local government for the protection of
" its members. Exploration in the vicinity for other
" mines is pushed in such case by new-comers with
" vigor, and is often rewarded with the discovery of
" valuable claims." [1]

That conflicts should arise between mineral claimants
and occupants of lands for purposes of business and
trade in the newly discovered mineral regions is but
natural. Frequently these controversies are of an
aggravated nature, and resort to force is a matter of

[1] Steel *v.* St. Louis Smelting Co., 106 U. S. 447, 449, 1 Sup. Ct. Rep.
389; Deffeback v. Hawke, 115 U. S. 392, 406, 6 Sup. Ct. Rep. 95.

common occurrence, particularly so before the organization of any form of local government. But eventually the more important ones find their way into the courts, whose decisions have resulted in establishing certain definite rules of law, governing the respective rights of the miner and the merchant within the limits of the settlement. These limits are not always well defined. Until application is made to enter and purchase the townsite, the exact area which may properly be considered as within the site of the future town may be limited by the extent of actual occupancy. In some instances, some enterprising individual surveys a tract of land into lots and blocks, streets and alleys, thus giving a semblance to a claim within the exterior limits of the survey. When such town is incorporated, the territorial limits over which municipal jurisdiction is asserted are, of course, defined by the act of incorporation. When application is made to enter the townsite by the town authorities, if incorporated, or by the county judge, if unincorporated, the area which may be thus entered will depend upon the number of inhabitants, the maximum area allowed being twenty-five hundred and sixty acres.[1]

It frequently happens that a large portion of this area, as finally entered and patented, is unoccupied, and remains so indefinitely. We are called upon to determine the respective rights of the two classes of claimants within the asserted limits of the townsite, both before and after patents are issued to one or the other.

§ 169. **Rights of mining locator upon unoccupied lands within unpatented townsite limits.**—It is hardly necessary to state that the owner of a valid and subsisting mining location which had its inception at a time

---

[1] Rev. Stats., § 2389.

prior to any occupancy within the surface limits of his claim, for purposes of trade or business, cannot be deprived of any of his rights flowing from such location by settlement thereon of later arrivals desiring to engage in commercial traffic or to assist in the founding of a city. The land embraced within the mining location is just as much withdrawn from the public domain as the fee is by a valid grant from the United States under authority.[1] Such location is a grant from the government.[2]

There is no room for a further grant; for the government would have nothing to convey.[3]

That the mining location is within the claimed or actual limits of the unpatented townsite is therefore of no moment. As was said by the supreme court of the United States,—

"To such claims, though within the limits of what " may be termed the site of the settlement or new town, " the miner acquires as good a right as though his dis- " covery was in a wilderness."[4]

§ 170. **Prior occupancy of public mineral lands within unpatented townsites for purposes of trade, as affecting the appropriation of such lands under the mining laws—The rule prior to the passage of the act of March 3, 1891.**—In discussing the effect of a prior occupancy of public mineral lands for townsite purposes, upon the right of subsequent appropriation under

[1] Silver Bow M. and M. Co. v. Clark, 5 Mont. 406, 5 Pac. 570.

[2] Butte City Smokehouse Lode Cases, 6 Mont. 397, 12 Pac. 858; Belk v. Meagher, 104 U. S. 284; Gwillim v. Donnellan, 115 U. S. 45, 49, 5 Sup. Ct. Rep. 1110. See, also, Noyes v. Mantle, 127 U. S. 348, 8 Sup. Ct. Rep. 1132; Teller v. United States, 113 Fed. 273; Stratton v. Gold Sovereign M. and T. Co., 1 Leg. Adv. 350. See, post, § 322.

[3] Silver Bow M. and M. Co. v. Clark, 5 Mont. 406, 5 Pac. 570.

[4] Steel v. St. Louis Smelting Co., 106 U. S. 447, 449, 1 Sup. Ct. Rep. 389; Deffeback v. Hawke, 115 U. S. 392, 6 Sup. Ct. Rep. 95.

the mining laws, it is our purpose to first arrive at a
correct understanding, if it be possible, of the state
of the law as it existed prior to the passage of the act
of March 3, 1891. This will enable us to consider "the
"old law, the mischief, and the remedy" in logical order.

In a subsequent article,[1] we have endeavored to state
the law, generally, with reference to the right of mere
occupants of public lands without color of title, as
against one seeking to appropriate such lands under the
mining laws. Much that is there said will apply to the
subject presently under consideration, and need not be
here repeated. We deem it sufficient for our present
purpose to deal with those cases wherein the courts have
had under consideration controversies between mining
claimants and prior occupants for the purposes of trade
or business—*i. e.* under the townsite laws.

In reviewing the decisions of the supreme court of
the United States upon this and kindred subjects, we
meet with apparent contradictions, rendering it difficult to reach satisfactory conclusions. Language employed in one decision, construed literally, cannot be
harmonized with expressions found in another. One
case does not necessarily overrule the other, as the ultimate results reached are consistent; but an analysis of
the reasoning employed and the terms used in reference
to the question now being considered have a tendency
to raise different inferences in different cases.

In none of the reported cases, other than those decided
by the land department, do we find the question presented between the two classes of claimants unaided by
presumptions flowing from a patent.

In all such cases coming under our observation an
attempt has been made to collaterally assail a federal
patent, issued to either the townsite or the mineral

---

[1] See, *post,* art. x, §§ 216-219.

claimant. In some instances both classes of claimants
possessed patents. In all of these cases the operative
force of the patent as a judgment, and its conclusiveness against collateral attack, have rendered the
consideration of conditions existing prior to its issuance to a large extent unnecessary. With these preliminary suggestions, we proceed to examine the
decisions.

The supreme court of the United States has made use
of the following language:—

"Land embraced within a townsite on the public
" domain, when *unoccupied,* is not exempt from location
" and sale for mining purposes. Its exemption is only
" from settlement and sale under the pre-emption laws
" of the United States. . . . The acts of congress relat-
" ing to townsites recognize the possession of mining
" claims within their limits, and forbid the acquisition
" of any mine of gold, silver, cinnabar, or copper within
" them under proceedings by which title to other lands
" there situated are secured, thus leaving the mineral
" deposits within the townsites open to exploration, and
" the land in which they are found to occupation and
" purchase in the same manner as such deposits are
" elsewhere explored and possessed and the lands con-
" taining them are acquired. Whenever, therefore,
" mines are found in lands belonging to the United
" States, whether within or without townsites, they may
" be claimed and worked, provided existing *rights of*
" *others from prior occupation* are not interfered
" with." [1]

The italics employed in the excerpt are ours. Literally construed, it would appear that the supreme court
had in mind all classes of occupancy of the public lands,
thus giving sanction to the rule that occupancy for trade
or business purposes on lands confessedly mineral prevents their appropriation under the mining laws,

[1] Steel *v.* St. Louis Smelting Co., 106 U. S. 447, 449, 1 Sup. Ct. Rep. 389.

although such appropriation might be effected without force or violence.[1]

In the case of Davis v. Weibbold, the same court, referring to its language used in Steel v. Smelting Company, says:—

"It was in reference to mines in *unoccupied* public
" lands in unpatented townsites that the language was
" used; and to them, and to mines in public lands in
" patented townsites outside of the limits of the patent,
" it is only applicable."[2]

This seems to strengthen the inference that prior occupancy for townsite purposes, although upon land confessedly mineral, withdraws it from appropriation under the mining laws.

In the same case, the court, referring to the case of Deffeback v. Hawke,[3] thus states its views:—

"In Deffeback v. Hawke, the mining patentee's rights
" antedated those of the occupants under the townsite
" law, and wherever such is the case his rights will be
" enforced against the pretensions of the townsite
" holder; but where the latter has acquired his rights
" in advance of the discovery of any mines, and the
" initiation of proceedings for the acquisition of their
" title or possession, his rights will be deemed superior
" to those of the mining claimant."[4]

When we consider the circumstances surrounding the Deffeback-Hawke case (hereafter more fully discussed), where there were two patents issued,—one to the mining claimant, and one to the townsite, the former by relation to the certificate of purchase being the senior,—

---

[1] The land department, however, cites this case as authority for the rule that the occupancy of land by townsite settlers is no bar to its entry under the mining laws, provided the land is mineral, and belongs to the United States. *In re* Rankin, 7 L. D. 411.

[2] 139 U. S. 507, 529, 11 Sup. Ct. Rep. 628.

[3] 115 U. S. 392, 6 Sup. Ct. Rep. 95.

[4] 139 U. S. 526, 11 Sup. Ct. Rep. 628.

and the admitted facts that the land was occupied for townsite purposes prior to the inception of the mineral right, we must conclude that the supreme court in speaking of the *rights* of a townsite claimant referred to *rights under the townsite patent.* Otherwise, the statement that the "mining patentee's rights antedated those of the "occupants" would be in direct conflict with the facts which were admitted for the purpose of the decision.

In Steel *v.* Smelting Company, an action of ejectment, the townsite claimants endeavored to assail a patent issued to a mineral claimant upon the ground that the land embraced in such patent was, prior to the initiation of the mining right, occupied and improved for townsite purposes. It was held that the patent could not be thus collaterally assailed.[1]

Davis *v.* Weibbold was a case involving a tract of land in the townsite of Butte, Montana, for which a patent had been issued in 1877. There was no suggestion that at the time the townsite was patented the land was known to be mineral, or that there were any valuable mineral lands within the townsite. The mineral claimant asserted rights under a mineral patent issued in 1880, based upon a discovery and appropriation made years after the issuance of a patent to the townsite. It was held that the discovery of minerals after the issuance of the townsite patent could not affect the holder of the townsite title.[2]

The case of Hawke *v.* Deffeback [3] was an action of ejectment. It involved a placer claim within the limits of the townsite of Deadwood, Dakota. The land become subject to the operation of the public land laws, February 28, 1877, by the extinguishment of the Indian title,

[1] 106 U. S. 447, 1 Sup. Ct. Rep. 389.
[2] 139 U. S. 507, 11 Sup. Ct. Rep. 628.
[3] 4 Dak. 21, 22 N. W. 480.

by treaty with the Sioux Indians. The precise date of the location of the mining claim does not appear. The application for patent therefor was filed on November 10, 1877, the entry and payment were made on January 31, 1878, and patent issued on January 31, 1882. No protest or adverse claim was filed. In July, 1878, the town of Deadwood being unincorporated, the probate judge entered at the local land office the townsite, paid the government price therefor, and received duplicate receipt, in trust for the use and benefit of the occupants.

The defendant, Deffeback, was the owner of a lot within the townsite. His contention was that upon the extinguishment of the Indian title the tract in question was, with other lands, laid out into lots, blocks, streets, and alleys, for municipal purposes and for trade; that the land in controversy was one of the lots originally laid out and occupied for townsite purposes, and had always been thus occupied by defendant and his grantor, with the buildings and improvements thereon, for the purposes of business and trade, and not for agriculture; that the placer mining claim was not located or claimed by plaintiff or any other person until after the selection and settlement upon, and appropriation of, that and adjacent lands for townsite purposes.

The mineral character of the land was not disputed. The foregoing facts were deemed admitted for the purpose of the decision. They were set up as an equitable defense, and a decree was asked by the owner of the town lot adjudging that the holder of the placer patent was a trustee for the benefit of the prior townsite occupant.

The supreme court of Dakota, in an able opinion, sustained a demurrer interposed to the equitable defense, and, the defendant failing to amend, judgment was entered for the mining patentee.

The case was appealed to the supreme court of the
United States, from whose opinion we select the following extracts:—

"It is plain, from this brief statement of the legisla-
" tion of congress, that no title from the United States
" to land known at the time of the sale to be valuable
" for its minerals of gold, silver, cinnabar, or copper
" can be obtained under the pre-emption or homestead
" laws, or the townsite laws, or in any other way than
" as prescribed by the laws specially authorizing the
" sale of such lands, except in the state of Michigan
" (and other states). . . . In the present case there is
" no dispute as to the mineral character of the land
" claimed by plaintiff. It is upon the alleged prior
" occupation of it for trade and business, the same being
" within the settlement or townsite of Deadwood, that
" defendant relies, as giving him a better right to the
" property. But the title to the land being in the United
" States, its occupation for trade or business did not
" and could not initiate any right to it, the same being
" mineral land, nor delay proceedings for the acquisi-
" tion of the title under the laws providing for the sale
" of lands of that character." [1]

In a later portion of the decision, when dealing with
the effects of a townsite patent within the limits of which
are found land that was known to be mineral at the date
of the townsite patent, and also lands that were not so
known, the supreme court supplements the foregoing
with the following:—

"Whilst we hold that a title to known valuable mineral
" land can not be acquired under the townsite laws, and
" therefore could not be acquired to the land in contro-
" versy under the entry of the townsite of Deadwood by
" the probate judge of the county in which that town is
" situated, we do not wish to be understood as express-
" ing any opinion against the validity of the entry, so
" far as it affected property other than mineral lands,

---

[1] Deffeback v. Hawke, 115 U. S. 392, 405, 6 Sup. Ct. Rep. 95.

" if there were any such at the time of entry. . . . It
" would seem, therefore, that the entry of a townsite,
" even though within its limits mineral lands are found,
" would be as important to the occupants of other lands
" as if no mineral lands existed. Nor do we see any
" injury resulting therefrom, nor any departure from
" the policy of the government, the entry and the patent
" being inoperative as to all lands known at the time to
" be valuable for their minerals or discovered *to be such*
" *before their occupation or improvement for residences*
" *or business under the townsite title.*" [1]

The language last quoted has led some of the trial
courts into the error of ruling that mines discovered
within *patented* townsites before the occupation of a lot
for business or residence purposes could be held as
against the grantee from the townsite, although not discovered until after patent to the townsite had issued.[2]

The question as to whether a mining location could be
legally made on mineral lands in possession of a prior
occupant for business purposes within the limits of an
unpatented townsite *was* raised in the Deffeback-Hawke
case, and while the issuance of a patent to the mineral
claimant, without any adverse claim or protest on the
part of the townsite claimant, and prior to the entry of
the townsite, was a conclusive determination that the
lands were mineral and rightfully patented to the mineral claimant, the decision of the supreme court of the
United States does hold, as that court has uniformly
held, that mineral lands could only be appropriated
under the mining laws, and that no title to such lands
could be initiated by mere occupancy under the townsite laws. The time when the character of the land
within a claimed townsite is to be determined is when
application to enter is made. This is the rule as to all

---

[1] Deffeback *v.* Hawke, 115 U. S. 407, 6 Sup. Ct. Rep. 95.
[2] McCormick v. Sutton, 97 Cal. 375, 32 Pac. 444.

classes of grants, such as grants to states of other than
sixteenth or thirty-sixth sections,[1] grants to railroads
within both place and indemnity limits,[2] and entries
under the pre-emption and homestead laws.[3] If the lands
are mineral, the fact of their mere occupancy for purposes of trade or business is of no moment. Such occupancy is not color of title as against the government or
those in privity with it, and a mining locator is in such
privity.

The case of Sparks v. Pierce was considered by the
supreme court of the United States at the same time as
Deffeback v. Hawke, and involved the same controversies, with the exception that no application to enter the
townsite (Central City, Dakota) had been made. The
case presented was that of occupants of the public lands
without title resisting the enforcement of the patent of
the United States, on the ground of occupation antedating the acquisition of any mining right or claim of
right.

The court held that—

"Mere occupancy of the public lands and improve-
" ments thereon give no vested right therein as against
" the United States, and consequently not against any
" purchaser from them."[4]

When the application for the mineral patent in this
case was before the land department, the commissioner
of the general land office held that, although it was sufficiently established that the land was occupied for townsite purposes prior to the initiation of rights under the

[1] See, ante, §§ 140, 143.
[2] See, ante, §§ 156, 157.
[3] See, post, § 207.
[4] 115 U. S. 408, 413, 6 Sup. Ct. Rep. 95; United States v. Holmes, 105
Fed. 41; Cosmos Exploration Co., v. Gray Eagle Oil Co., 112 Fed. 4;
Buxton v. Traver, 130 U. S. 232, 9 Sup. Ct. Rep. 509. But see Bonner v.
Meikle, 82 Fed. 697, and Young v. Goldsteen, 97 Fed. 303.

mining claim, yet, as the lands were in fact mineral, the
occupants had no right to it. Patent was issued to the
mineral claimant in accordance with this ruling, without any reservation. The townsite claimants endeavored
to erect a trust upon the mineral patent, on the ground
that the commissioner erred as a matter of law in issuing the mineral patent without reserving their asserted
rights as occupants. Concerning this plea, the supreme
court held that "to entitle a party to relief against a
" patent of the government, he must show a better right
" to the land than the patentee, such as in law should
" have been respected by the land department, and,
" being respected, would have given him the patent."

There can be no doubt that the case clearly indicates
that priority of occupation of mineral lands for townsite purposes establishes no claim which the government
is called upon to recognize, as against a subsequent
appropriation under the mining laws.

In the case of Bonner v. Meikle,[1] Judge Hawley, sitting as circuit judge, announced the view that occupants
of town lots in a town situated upon unsurveyed public
lands of the United States have rights which will prevail
over those of a mineral claimant, unless the latter can
show that at the time the townsite claimants acquired or
purchased the lots, the land was known to contain mineral of such extent and value as to justify expenditures
for the purpose of extracting it. He held that the fact
that the townsite claimants had taken no steps to obtain
title would not affect the rule. It was further pointed
out that the mineral claimant had acquired no title from
the United States, and therefore was in no better position than the townsite claimant.

The action arose out of an application for a patent
for a mining claim. The lot-owners filed an adverse

[1] 82 Fed. 697.

claim in the land office under section twenty-three hundred and twenty-six of the Revised Statutes, and later instituted the suit in support of it.

The character of the land at the time the lot-owners took possession, seems to have been the sole fact sought to be inquired into and adjudicated. This being true, it is difficult to perceive how the court could entertain jurisdiction of the cause. The filing of the application for the mining patent set the jurisdiction of the land department in motion. The commencement of the suit only suspended its jurisdiction to enable the court to pass upon such questions as the law contemplates should be litigated in the courts. The question of the character of the land under such circumstances is one which the courts cannot pass upon.[1]

A claimant asserting only rights of occupancy of non-mineral land under the townsite laws cannot maintain an adverse suit under section twenty-three hundred and twenty-six of the Revised Statutes.[2]

Be this as it may, we find some difficulty in reconciling the ruling of Judge Hawley with the previous decisions of the supreme court of the United States heretofore cited.

Considering the facts involved in the several cases which we have heretofore reviewed, and construing the townsite laws in connection with the general mining laws and other enactments *in pari materia,* we feel that we are justified in the conclusion that the supreme court of the United States never intended to establish the rule that prior occupancy of the public mineral lands for trade or business purposes operated to withdraw such lands prior to the issuance of a townsite patent from appropriation under the mining laws, provided always that such appropriation was effected by peaceable

---

[1] See, *ante,* § 108.

[2] Ryan *v.* Granite Hill M. and D. Co., 29 L. D. 522. See, *post,* § 723.

methods, and without resort to force or violence. The
expressions found in the cases noted leading to a contrary inference were not intended to be of controlling
weight. There may be some room for doubt as to the
correctness of the conclusions reached by us; but we are
forced to accept one of the two constructions. We have
adopted that which to us seems to be in consonance with
the general theories of the public land laws, according
to the tenor of all the decisions promulgated by the court
of last resort. We can conceive of no middle ground.
If prior occupants for townsite purposes were to be considered as being entitled to equities as against the subsequent mining locators, there would have been no
necessity for the legislation found in section sixteen of
the act of March 3, 1891. The conclusions here reached
are in harmony with the views of the supreme court of
Montana[1] and the supreme court of Arizona.[2]

**§ 171. Correlative rights of mining and townsite
claimants recognized by the land department prior to
the act of March 3, 1891.**—In passing upon applications
for patents to mineral lands within the claimed limits
of townsites, the land department has until within a
comparatively recent period proceeded upon the theory
that there were correlative or reciprocal rights existing
between townsite occupants and mineral claimants
which were to be regarded and properly provided for
when patents were issued.

General Burdett, when commissioner of the general
land office, thus expressed his views:—

"The townsite laws clearly contemplate that towns
" will exist in mining localities; by clear implication,

---

[1] Talbot v. King, 6 Mont. 76, 9 Pac. 434; Silver Bow M. and M. Co. v.
Clark, 5 Mont. 406, 5 Pac. 570; Butte City Smokehouse Lode Cases, 6
Mont. 397, 12 Pac. 858; Chambers v. Jones, 17 Mont. 156, 42 Pac. 758.

[2] Tombstone Townsite Cases, 15 Pac. 26; Blackmore v. Reilly, 17
Pac. 72.

" townsite entries are to be permitted on mineral lands.
" This is indicated by the clause excepting title to mines
" from the title acquired by the town. It is inevitable
" that where the surface is suitable, it will, in a mining
" vicinity, be populated, and attain the character of a
" town or city. Where any branch of business flour-
" ishes there capital and population will concentrate.
" The various trades and callings will center there.
" Hotels will be a necessity. Dwellings will be built,
" and permanent homes established; all the various
" interests which constitute valuable property rights as
" connected with the soil will be created. And this is
" not necessarily antagonistic to the miners. The pro-
" tection of municipal government is in the miner's
" interest, as it is in the interest of any other class of
" business men." [1]

The secretary of the interior had previously held that persons in possession of the surface of a lode claim were adverse claimants within the meaning of the mining law of 1866, and were entitled to be heard in the local courts before patent was issued.[2]

Out of this and similar rulings, originated the practice of inserting reservation clauses in mineral patents to lode claims of the following character:—

"Excepting and excluding from said patent all town-
" site property rights upon the surface, and all houses,
" buildings, lots, blocks, streets, alleys, or other munici-
" pal improvements on the surface of said mining claim
" not belonging to the grantees, and all rights necessary
" or proper to the occupation, possession, and enjoy-
" ment of the same."

Such reservations, however, were not inserted, it seems, where the discovery and location of the mining claim antedated the town settlement.[3]

---

[1] Townsite of Central City, Colo., 2 Copp's L. O. 150.
[2] Becker v. Central City Townsite, Id. 98. See, also, Papina v. Alderson, 10 Copp's L. O. 52.
[3] Monroe Lode, 4 L. D. 273.

In townsite patents, in addition to the limiting clause sanctioned by section twenty-three hundred and ninety-two of the Revised Statutes the following proviso, or its equivalent, was inserted.

"That the grant hereby made is held and declared to " be subject to all the conditions and restrictions con- " tained in section twenty-three hundred and eighty- " six of the Revised Statutes of the United States, so " far as the same are applicable thereto." [1]

A different rule prevailed with reference to placer patents, for the reason that in this class of mining claims the surface of the ground is absolutely necessary to the successful working of the mine; therefore, it could not be included in a townsite entry or patent, nor could any surface rights therein be reserved, under any circumstances, to the townsite occupant. [2]

But the courts have uniformly held these reservations void. The officers of the land department are merely agents of the government, and have no authority to insert in a patent any other terms than those of conveyance, with recitals showing compliance with the conditions which the law prescribes. Could they insert clauses in patents of their own description, they could limit or enlarge without warrant of law. [3]

In accordance with this action by the courts, the land

[1] Turner v. Lang, 1 Copp's L. O. 51; Central City Townsite, 2 Copp's L. O. 150; Butte City Townsite, 3 Copp's L. O. 114, 131; Hickey's Appeal, 3 L. D. 83; Commissioners' Letter, Copp's Min. Dec., p. 207; Townsite of Eureka Springs v. Conant, 8 Copp's L. O. 3; Papina v. Alderson, 10 Copp's L. O. 52; Rico Townsite, 1 L. D. 556; Vizina Cons. M. Co., 9 Copp's L. O. 92; Esler v. Townsite of Cooke, 4 L. D. 212.

[2] Townsite of Butte, 3 Copp's L. O. 114; Townsite of Deadwood, 8 Copp's L. O. 18, 153; Commissioners' Letter, Copp's Min. Dec., p. 156; Kemp v. Starr, 5 Copp's L. O. 130.

[3] Davis v. Weibbold, 139 U. S. 507, 11 Sup. Ct. Rep. 628; Deffeback v. Hawke, 115 U. S. 392, 6 Sup. Ct. Rep. 95; Talbot v. King, 6 Mont. 76, 9 Pac. 434; Butte City Smokehouse Lode Cases, 6 Mont. 397, 12 Pac. 858.

department considers it to be fully established as a principle of law that the government could not (at least prior to March 3, 1891) by its patent "partition lands "horizontally," and the practice of inserting these correlative reservations ceased.[1]

§ 172. Section sixteen of the act of March 3, 1891, is limited in its application to incorporated towns and cities.—We have in a previous section [2] quoted the provisions of the act of March 3, 1891, so far as it supplements the prior existing townsite laws. It is manifest that this supplemental legislation was intended to apply only to cases of *incorporated* towns, the territorial limits of which are subject to an organized form of municipal government. As to towns and settlements upon the public mineral domain for townsite purposes which are unincorporated, including those which must be entered and patented to the county judge, or the judicial officer performing his functions, as well as all other classes of townsites, the townsite laws, as heretofore understood and explained by the courts, as shown in the preceding sections, remain in force, and are unaffected by the act of March 3, 1891. We are not aware that any judicial interpretation of this act has yet been made. We reason simply from the language of the text and the application of the familiar rule, *Expressio unius est exclusio alterius*. The land department has not, to our knowledge, issued any circular instructions giving its views upon the act in question; nor do we find that the act has been referred to by the department in any of its decisions, except in a case involving the townsite of Juneau, in the district of Alaska.

---

[1] W. A. Simmons *et al.*, 7 L. D. 283; Antediluvian Lode and Millsite, 8 L. D. 602; Secretary's Letter, 5 L. D. 256.

[2] See, *ante*, § 166.

The act providing a civil government for Alaska, passed May 17, 1884,[1] provided for a government for this district, and made it a land district of the United States, over which was extended only the mineral laws of the United States. The general laws of Oregon, then in force, were declared to be the law of the district. The act also preserved the *status quo* as to use and occupancy for other than mining purposes until congress should act, and declared that nothing in the act should be construed to put in force in said district the general land laws of the United States.

By section eleven of the act of March 3, 1891, (section sixteen of which we are now considering,) the provisions of section twenty-three hundred and eighty-seven of the Revised Statutes (the townsite law) were made applicable to Alaska, with the proviso that the entry of the townsites should be made by a trustee or trustees designated by the secretary of the interior, for the use and benefit of the occupants.

The trustee appointed by the secretary made application to enter the townsite of Juneau, against which a protest was filed by a mineral claimant, and the question involved was the mineral or non-mineral character of the land.

Upon the first hearing the burden of proof was placed upon the townsite claimants; the finding was, that the land was mineral, and the secretary directed that the townsite entry should be canceled as to the land covered by the mineral location. He considered as a factor section sixteen of the act of March 3, 1891.[2] Subsequently the department vacated this decision, reinstated the entry, and announced the rule that in order to except mineral land from the operation of a townsite or other entry made in pursuance of law, the land must

---

[1] 23 Stats. at Large, p. 24.
[2] Goldstein v. Townsite of Juneau, 23 L. D. 417.

be known at the time of the entry to contain minerals
of such character and value as to justify expenditures
for the purpose of extracting them.[1] In the later decision no reference is made to the act of March 3, 1891.
The general mining laws having been put in force by the
act of 1884,[2] the townsite provisions, subsequently made
applicable by section eleven of the act of 1891, are necessarily to be construed in the light of the mining laws
theretofore in force. It follows that the rules of construction, as applied by the courts to the system thus
extended to Alaska, have the same controlling force
there as elsewhere. The act seems to be clear and un-
ambiguous in this respect.[3]

§ 173. The object and intent of section sixteen of
the act of March 3, 1891.—We think that an analysis
of this act, when considered with reference to the state
of the law as it existed at the time of its enactment,
viewed in connection with those statutes *in pari materia*
remaining in force, justifies us in deducing the following as the true object and intent of the law:—

(1) The old law inhibited the acquisition of title to
mineral lands under townsite laws, whether located as
such under the mining laws at the time of the proposed
townsite entry or not. The land department at the time
application was made to enter under the townsite was
called upon to investigate the character of the land. If
its mineral character was established, patent could not
issue, although it might be unoccupied or unclaimed by
any one under the mining laws. The new law permits
mineral lands within incorporated towns, if so unoccu-

---

[1] Harkrader *v.* Goldstein, 31 L. D. 87.

[2] The act of June 6, 1900, making further provision for a civil government for Alaska, re-enacts this provision, subject to certain limitations
not necessary to here note. (See appendix.)

[3] See Young *v.* Goldsteen, 97 Fed. 303.

pied and unclaimed, to be entered under the townsite law. It would therefore seem that, as to future entries applied for by this class of towns, the character of the land, if unoccupied and unclaimed under the mining laws, is not a fact necessarily to be passed upon by the department. If mineral, the fact of the existence or non-existence of such occupancy or claim must necessarily be adjudicated prior to the issuance of a patent. The probable force of such a patent and its unassailable character on collateral attack will be considered in a subsequent section. This much may be here said, however. The issuance of such patent to an incorporated city or town is no longer a conclusive determination that the land was non-mineral in character, as the department has now, under a certain state of facts, the power to issue townsite patents for mineral lands. It may be that such patent would be conclusive evidence of the patentability of such lands under the townsite laws.

(2) The provisions of section twenty-three hundred and ninety-two of the Revised Statutes, that—

. . . "no title shall be acquired under the foregoing
" provisions of this chapter to any mine of gold, silver,
" cinnabar, or copper, or to any valid mining claim or
" possession under existing laws,"

and of section twenty-three hundred and eighty-six, that—

. . . "where mineral veins are possessed, which pos-
" session is recognized by local authority, and to the
" extent so possessed and recognized the title to town
" lots to be acquired shall be subject to such recognized
" possession and the necessary use thereof,"

are re-enacted. To this last provision, which, as we have heretofore shown,[1] was passed prior to the enactment of the lode law of July 26, 1866, is added the following:—

---

[1] See, *ante,* § 166.

. . . "and when entry has been made or patent issued
" for such townsites to such incorporated town or city,
" the possessor of such mineral vein may enter and
" receive patent for such mineral vein, and the surface
" ground appertaining thereto."[1]

The purpose of this supplemental clause is evidently
to relieve the land department from embarrassments
caused by their previous construction of the prior existing law. That department had held that with the issuance of a townsite patent their jurisdiction as to all land
embraced therein terminated, and that, although the law
as well as the patent contained the proviso that no title
should be thereby acquired to any mine of gold, silver,
cinnabar, or copper, or to any valid mining claim or
possession held under existing laws, and although it
may be sufficiently established that at the date of the
issuance of the patent there existed within the limits of
the townsite as patented such a mine or claim as was
clearly within the proviso, yet it had no power to issue
a patent to such claim; that the only remedy was by a
proceeding in equity, brought by the United States to
annul the townsite patent.[2]

At one time a contrary rule obtained,[3] and in 1897 the
department again announced the rule that it had power
to issue a patent for mineral veins expressly excepted
from a townsite patent previously issued. The decisions
in Pacific Slope Lode and Cameron Lode *(supra)* were
overruled.[4] While the department in the cases last cited

[1] 26 Stats. at Large, p. 1095, § 16.

[2] Pacific Slope Lode, 12 L. D. 686; Cameron Lode, 13 L. D. 369;
Protector Lode, 12 L. D. 662; Plymouth Lode, *Id.*, 513. And see Horsky
v. Moran (Mont), 53 Pac. 1064.

[3] South Comstock G. and S. M. Co., 2 Copp's L. O. 146; Townsite of
Butte, 3 Copp's L. O. 114; *Id.*, 130.

[4] Pacific Slope Lode *v.* Butte Townsite, 25 L. D. 518. Followed in
Gregory Lode, 26 L. D. 144; Brady's Mortgagee *v.* Harris (on review),
29 L. D. 426.

did not base its conclusions upon the act of 1891, in a later case its decision was directly referable to that act.[1]

The correctness of this interpretation by the land department of its reserved powers in this regard depends upon the effect to be given a townsite patent, a question which is discussed in succeeding sections.[2]

(3) As to placers, if they are unclaimed under the mining laws, they may be patented by an incorporated city or town. Patents may issue on valid placer locations within such limits, independently of prior occupation, for purposes of trade or business; but only one patent may issue, as no correlative rights between townsite and mineral claimants are possible.

(4) Where the right to a lode claim within the limits of an incorporated town or city originates after settlement within the surface boundaries for townsite purposes, the prior townsite occupant is entitled to be protected in his surface rights, if they are not on the vein or lode; and it is probable that the extent and boundaries of such surface occupation will be required to be shown through adverse proceedings. Heretofore such adverse proceedings were not sanctioned, as nothing could inure to the townsite claimant by virtue of such proceedings. He could obtain no patent, and the law made no provision for the severance of any portion of the surface for his benefit.[3]

The provisions of the law of March 3, 1891, in this

[1] Hulings v. Ward Townsite, 29 L. D. 21.

[2] See, *post*, §§ 175, 177.

[3] We are aware that there are several cases arising under the law as it existed prior to March 3, 1891, which, in discussing mining patents within townsites, seem to lay some stress upon the failure of the townsite claimant to adverse the mineral applicant. But, as we understand the cases, such ruling was not necessary for the purpose of the case under consideration. We shall discuss this question further when dealing with the subject of adverse claims. See *post*, § § 722, 723.

behalf will require either a segregation of such surface
at the time lode patents are issued or the insertion of
reservation clauses, protecting prior surface occupants,
and defining the extent of such occupancy. The act
undoubtedly gives sanction to a practice as to lode
claims within townsites which has heretofore been declared by the courts to be improper.

The department has announced the rule that under
this act a townsite entry should not be permitted to
include lands theretofore patented under the mining
law.[1]

Except as herein stated, we do not understand
that the townsite laws, as they existed prior to March 3,
1891, have been modified.

§ 174. **The act of March 3, 1891, not retroactive.**—
There is nothing in the terms of the act making it
retrospective in its operation. The language clearly
indicates that it was intended to apply only to entries
made after its passage. This is the view taken by the
land department, and it is manifestly correct.[2]

§ 175. **Effect of patents issued for lands within townsites.**—It is difficult to intelligently discuss the force
and effect of patents for any particular class of lands
without involving the consideration of the general principles of law applicable to all land patents issued by the
government. We appreciate the fact that at some place
in this treatise the full consideration of such general
principles will be a necessity; but we doubt the propriety
of doing so every time we are called upon to deal with
patents to an individual class. When we shall have
passed that portion of the work dealing with the method

---

[1] Hulings v. Ward Townsite, 29 L. D. 21.

[2] Plymouth Lode, 12 L. D. 513; Protector Lode, *Id.* 662; Pacific Slope
Lode, *Id.* 686.

of initiating and perfecting title to mineral lands, and have outlined the proceedings culminating in the issuance of the patent, we hope to present the subject fully. For the present, we are considering the question of patents for lands issued within townsites, a somewhat limited, though by no means unimportant, class. In doing so it will be sufficient to simply epitomize what we understand to be the underlying principles controlling the courts in determining the operative force and effect of a federal patent.

We understand the general rules to be as follows:—

(1) A patent for land is the highest evidence of title, and is conclusive against the government and all claiming under junior patents or titles, until set aside or annulled;[1]

(2) The land department is a tribunal appointed by congress to decide certain questions relating to the public lands, and its decision upon matters of fact cognizable by it, in the absence of fraud or imposition, is conclusive everywhere else.[2] When a patent is attacked

---

[1] Stone v. United States, 2 Wall. 525; Hooper v. Scheimer, 23 How. 235; Johnson v. Towsley, 13 Wall. 72; Gibson v. Chouteau, Id. 92; Warren v. Van Brunt, 19 Wall. 646; St. Louis Smelting Co. v. Kemp, 104 U. S. 636; Hoofnagle v. Anderson, 7 Wheat. 212.

[2] Lee v. Johnson, 116 U. S. 48, 6 Sup. Ct. Rep. 249; Johnson v. Towsley, 13 Wall. 72; Warren v. Van Brunt, 19 Wall. 646; Shepley v. Cowan, 91 U. S. 330; Moore v. Robbins, 96 U. S. 530; Marquez v. Frisbie, 101 U. S. 473; Vance v. Burbank, Id. 514; Quinby v. Conlan, 104 U. S. 420; St. Louis Smelting Co. v. Kemp, Id. 636; Steel v. St. Louis Smelting Co., 106 U. S. 447, 1 Sup. Ct. Rep. 389; Baldwin v. Starks, 107 U. S. 463, 2 Sup. Ct. Rep. 473; United States v. Minor, 114 U. S. 233, 5 Sup. Ct. Rep. 236; Davis v. Weibbold, 139 U. S. 507, 11 Sup. Ct. Rep. 628; Barden v. N. P. R. R., 154 U. S. 288, 14 Sup. Ct. Rep. 1030; Waterloo M. Co. v. Doe, 82 Fed. 45, 51; New Dunderberg M. Co. v. Old, 79 Fed. 598; Mendota Club v. Anderson, 101 Wis. 479, 78 N. W. 185; United States v. Northern Pac. Ry., 95 Fed. 864; Bunker Hill and Sullivan M. and C. Co. v. Empire State-Idaho Co., 109 Fed. 538; Peabody Gold M. Co. v. Gold Hill M. Co., 111 Fed. 817; King v. McAndrews, Id. 860.

two questions are presented, Did the department have power to issue the patent and to determine the questions which conditioned its issue? and, Was the judgment induced by fraud, mistake of fact, or error in law?[1]

(3) The government having issued a patent, cannot by the authority of its own officers invalidate that patent by the issuing of a second one for the same property;[2]

(4) A patent may be collaterally impeached in any action, and its operation as a conveyance defeated, by showing that the department had no jurisdiction to dispose of the lands; that is, that the law did not provide for selling them, or that they had been reserved from sale or dedicated to special purposes, or had been previously transferred to others.[3] The test of jurisdiction is whether or not the tribunal has power to enter upon the inquiry, not whether its conclusion in the course of it is right or wrong.[4]

Applying these principles to the class of patents under consideration, we are justified in deducing the following:—

(A) A mining patent issued prior to the final entry of a townsite is conclusive evidence that all antecedent steps necessary to its issue have been properly and legally taken,[5] and necessarily inhibits the issuance of

---

[1] United States v. Northern Pac. Ry. Co., 95 Fed. 864.

[2] Iron S. M. Co. v. Campbell, 135 U. S. 286, 10 Sup. Ct. Rep. 765; Davis v. Weibbold, 139 U. S. 507, 11 Sup. Ct. Rep. 628.

[3] Wright v. Roseberry, 121 U. S. 488, 7 Sup. Ct. Rep. 985; Davis v. Weibbold, 139 U. S. 507, 11 Sup. Ct. Rep. 628; Hardin v. Jordan, 140 U. S. 371, 11 Sup. Ct. Rep. 808, 838; United States v. Winona and St. P. R. R. Co., 67 Fed. 948; Garrard v. Silver Peak Mines, 82 Fed. 578, 583; Smyth v. New Orleans Canal and Bank Co., 93 Fed. 899. And see Kansas City M. and M. Co. v. Clay (Ariz.), 29 Pac. 9.

[4] New Dunderberg M. Co. v. Old, 79 Fed. 598; Bradley v. Dells Lumber Co., 105 Wis. 245, 81 N. W. 394; King v. McAndrews, 111 Fed. 860; note to Hartman v. Warren, 22 C. C. A. 30.

[5] Davis v. Weibbold, 139 U. S. 507, 11 Sup. Ct. Rep. 628; Iron S. M. Co. v. Campbell, 17 Colo. 267, 29 Pac. 513; Kahn v. Old Tel. Co., 2 Utah

a subsequent patent to the townsite claimants covering the same property.[1] In cases of incorporated cities and towns, under the present state of the law granting certain surface privileges to prior occupants of the surface of lode claims, we think the law gives this prior occupant the *status* of an adverse claimant, and that, to protect his rights to the surface, he must file his adverse claim and pursue his remedy in the courts. Failing in this, the patent issued will be a conclusive adjudication that no such prior occupancy existed. We might go a step farther, and assert that a general reservation in a patent of surface rights would not protect the prior occupant or enable him to collaterally assail the mineral patent. The fact and extent of his occupancy should be definitely determined when the mineral patent is issued, and the boundaries and extent inserted in a special reserving clause. This would enable the government to subsequently patent the surface under a townsite application, and the two patents, when taken together, would clearly show jurisdiction in the land department to issue both. The thing reserved by one would be granted by the other.[2]

That the government, as the paramount proprietor, can create such a severance of title, cannot be denied. It was of frequent occurrence under the common law.[3] And the right of a private owner to separate the ownership of the minerals from that of the overlying surface has always been recognized in America.[4]

174; Chambers *v.* Jones, 17 Mont. 156, 42 Pac. 758; Poire *v.* Wells, 6 Colo. 406; Justice M. Co. *v.* Lee, 21 Colo. 260, 52 Am. St. Rep. 216, 40 Pac. 444; United States *v.* Iron S. M. Co., 128 U. S. 673, 9 Sup. Ct. Rep. 195; Mont. Cent. Ry. Co. *v.* Migeon, 68 Fed. 811.

[1] Hulings *v.* Ward Townsite, 29 L. D. 21.
[2] Iron S. M. Co. *v.* Campbell, 135 U. S. 286-292, 10 Sup. Ct. Rep. 765.
[3] See, *ante*, § 9; *post*, §§ 812-814.
[4] Hartwell *v.* Camman, 2 Stockt. Ch. 128, 64 Am. Dec. 448; Stewart *v.* Chadwick, 8 Iowa, 463; Caldwell *v.* Fulton, 31 Pa. St. 475, 72 Am. Dec.

The surface proprietor, as an incident to his grant, would, of course, be entitled to the right of subjacent support; and the mineral patentee would be compelled to so conduct mining operations underneath the surface as not to interfere with the full enjoyment of the surface and the buildings and improvements thereon.[1] This subject is more fully treated in a subsequent chapter of this work.[2]

(b) When a townsite patent is issued, it is in law such a declaration of the patentability of the land under the townsite laws that no subsequent discovery of minerals can deprive the townsite owner of his property. The patent to the townsite effectually withdraws the land from the body of the public domain, and it is no longer subject to exploration and purchase under the mining laws, based upon discoveries subsequent to the townsite patent.[3]

(c) In the case of patents to incorporated cities or towns issued under the act of March 3, 1891, the patent is no longer conclusive evidence of the fact that the lands are non-mineral, as the department is no longer called upon to determine the character of the land, unless it be to segregate the known veins, or lodes, and determine upon proper proceedings in that behalf the fact of the existence of such veins, or lodes, or of valid subsisting mining claims, and segregating them from

760; Arnold v. Stevens, 24 Pick. 106, 35 Am. Dec. 305; Johnstown I. Co. v. Cambria I. Co., 32 Pa. St. 241, 72 Am. Dec. 783; Knight v. Indiana C. and I. Co., 47 Ind. 105, 110, 47 Am. Rep. 692; Marble Co. v. Ripley, 10 Wall. 393; Riddle v. Brown, 20 Ala. 412, 56 Am. Dec. 202; French v. Brewer, 3 Wall. Jr. 346, Fed. Cas. No. 5096.

[1] 6 Lawson's Rights and Remedies, § 2787, p. 4544, and cases there cited.

[2] See, post, § § 818, 823.

[3] Davis v. Weibbold, 139 U. S. 507, 11 Sup. Ct. Rep. 628; McCormick v. Sutton, 97 Cal. 373, 32 Pac. 444; Smith v. Hill, 89 Cal. 122, 26 Pac. 644; Carter v. Thompson, 65 Fed. 329; Larned v. Jenkins, 113 Fed. 634.

the other lands subject to entry under the townsite, that patents may issue ultimately to the mineral claimant, as contemplated in the act. We doubt the propriety of inserting general clauses of reservation. The two patents when issued should show that the property granted by the junior patent is identically that which is reserved out of the senior patent. A reservation of a specific boundary, laid down so as to be identified in the first patent, needs no judicial action to determine what it is that is reserved.[1]

§ 175a. Difficulty in the application of principles suggested.—The foregoing principles, except so far as we have dealt with the effect of patents issued for townsite lands within the limits of incorporated cities or towns—as to which there are no adjudications—are well settled. Some difficulty is encountered in applying these principles to cases involving the operation of so much of the statute as inhibits the acquisition of title under the townsite laws to mines of gold, silver, and cinnabar, or to valid mining claims or possessions under existing laws. The crucial questions presented for consideration may be thus stated: (1) What constitutes a mine or valid mining claim the title to which cannot be acquired under the townsite laws? (2) On whom devolves the duty of determining the existence of such mine or mining claim —the land department prior to the issuance of a townsite patent, or the courts after its issuance? Or, in other words, can a townsite patent, valid on its face and purporting to convey all the lands within defined boundaries, be assailed by mineral claimants asserting title to mines or claims within the townsite limits originating prior to the townsite entry? We shall discuss the questions in the order stated.

[1] Iron S. M. Co. v. Campbell, 135 U. S. 286, 292, 10 Sup. Ct. Rep. 765.

§ 176. **What constitutes a mine or valid mining claim within the meaning of section twenty-three hundred and ninety-two of the Revised Statutes.**—Section twenty-three hundred and ninety-two of the Revised Statutes provides that no title can be acquired under the townsite laws to any mine of gold, silver, cinnabar, or copper, or to any valid mining claim or possession under existing laws.

What is meant by the term "mine," as used in this section?

We have heretofore had occasion to discuss the meaning of the word "mine" in its etymological sense, and have shown that the word is not a definite term, but is susceptible of limitation, according to the intention with which it is used. We have also traced what we have called the evolution of denotation, showing the gradual extension of the meaning, from an underground excavation made for the purpose of getting minerals, to its use as an equivalent for "vein," "seam," or "lode."[1]

A valid mining claim can only be based upon a discovery within the limits of the claim, and the existence of mineral in such quantities as to render the land more valuable for mining than for any other purpose, or as will justify a prudent man in the expenditure of time and money in its exploitation and development.[2]

The existence of a mere location is not of itself evidence of the mineral character of the land.[3]

The character of the land being thus established, its proper location, marking of boundaries, and compliance with the local laws, if any such exist, is necessary to perfect a valid mining claim.

In order to exempt such veins, lodes, or claims from

---

[1] See, *ante*, §§ 88, 89.
[2] See, *ante*, §§ 98, 106; *post*, §§ 207, 392.
[3] Harkrader *v.* Goldstein, 31 L. D. 87.

the operation of the townsite laws, they must at the time of its issuance be *known* to be valuable for their minerals. To use the language of the supreme court of the United States:—

" We say 'land *known* at the time of the sale to be " ' *valuable* for its minerals,' as there are vast tracts of " public land in which minerals of different kinds are " found, but not in such quantity as to justify expend- " itures in the effort to extract them. . . . We also say " lands *known* at the time of their sale to be thus valu- " able, in order to avoid any possible conclusion against " the validity of titles which may be issued for other " kinds of land in which years afterwards rich deposits " of mineral may be discovered." [1]

"It is established by former decisions of this court " that under the acts of congress which govern this case, " in order to except mines or mineral lands from the " operation of a townsite patent, it is not sufficient that " the lands do in fact contain minerals, or even valuable " minerals, when the townsite patents take effect, but " that they must at that time be known to contain min- " erals to such extent and value as to justify expendi- " tures for the purpose of extracting them; and if the " lands are not known at that time to be so valuable for " mining purposes, the fact that they have once been " valuable or are afterwards discovered to be still valu- " able for such purposes does not defeat or impair the " title of persons claiming under the townsite patent." [2]

The case from which the last quotation is made was taken to the supreme court of the United States on writ of error to the supreme court of California.

It appears from the facts in this case that the defend- ant, Dower, claimed that the portion of the lot which was in his possession was not granted by the patent,

[1] Deffeback v. Hawke, 115 U. S. 392, 404, 6 Sup. Ct. Rep. 95.
[2] Dower v. Richards, 151 U. S. 658, 663, 14 Sup. Ct. Rep. 452, (citing Deffeback v. Hawke, 115 U. S. 392, 6 Sup. Ct. Rep. 95; Davis v. Weib- bold, 139 U. S. 507, 11 Sup. Ct. Rep. 628). Quoted in Harkrader v. Goldstein, 31 L. D. 87, 95.

being reserved or excepted out of its operation, by
reason of the fact that it contained a gold-bearing quartz
vein, the existence of which was known at and before the
date of the patent. The defendant did not claim under
a location made prior to the patent to the townsite, but
his asserted rights accrued under a location made subsequent to the issuance of such patent. It appeared that
at one time during the history of the town, but prior to
the patent, the lode in question was successfully and
profitably worked, but that it had been abandoned, and
work thereon had ceased for a number of years before
the defendant's location. Upon this state of facts the
supreme court of the state of California thus announced
its views:—

" Assuming, then, that at the date of the issuance of
" the townsite patent that part of the Wagner ledge
" embraced in these lots was regarded as worked out
" and as of no further value for mining purposes, we
" find that the predecessors of plaintiffs purchased the
" lots from the patentee, went into possession of them,
" fenced them, divided them into different inclosures,
" built valuable houses and outhouses upon them,
" planted them with fruit-trees, filled up the old min-
" ing excavations, and, in short, devoted them to the
" purposes of a home.

" After fifteen years, and more, during which there
" was a complete cessation of mining on the lode, the
" defendants entered upon the possession of the plain-
" tiffs, made a location of the ledge, claiming three
" hundred feet of surface on each side of the croppings,
" —a strip of six hundred feet in width across plain-
" tiffs' lots,—and proceeded to dig up their garden and
" orchard, demolish their fences, and undermine their
" houses.

" All this the defendants justify upon the ground that
" the ledge and adjacent surface which they have
" located was reserved by the United States out of the
" land patented to the townsite trustee. It remains to

" consider whether they are correct in their construc-
" tion of the law upon this point. . . .

" The question, then, is reduced to this: What was a
" mine of gold within the meaning of the act of 1867?
" Without the aid of any judicial or legislative con-
" struction, we should say, without hesitation, that one
" essential requisite of a gold mine would be a natural
" deposit of rock or earth containing a sufficient quan-
" tity of gold to admit of profitable working. If lands
" are known to contain precious metals, but in quan-
" tities so small as not to justify the attempt to extract
" them, they are not properly called mineral lands; and
" even if they might be mined at a very small profit,
" but are clearly of more value for agriculture than for
" mining, they are agricultural rather than mineral
" lands." [1]

In a later case a similar rule was declared by the same
court:—

" The term ' mine of gold, silver, cinnabar, or
" 'copper,' as used in the exception found in the act, and
" in the reservation of the patent, means a paying mine
" known to exist at the time of the grant to the county
" judge, or one which there was good reason to believe
" then existed." [2]

The supreme court of the United States announced
similar doctrines in reference to " known mines," as
that term was used in the pre-emption act of 1841,[3] and
with reference to lodes within patented placers known
to exist at the time of the application for patent, and
which are unclaimed by the applicant.[4]

Following the construction given to placer patents

---

[1] Richards v. Dower, 81 Cal. 44, 49, 22 Pac. 304.

[2] Smith v. Hill, 89 Cal. 122, 125, 26 Pac. 644.

[3] Colo. C. and I. Co. v. United States, 123 U. S. 307, 328, 8 Sup. Ct. 131.

[4] United States v. Iron S. M. Co., 128 U. S. 673-683, 9 Sup. Ct. Rep. 195; Iron S. M. Co. v. Mike & Starr Co., 143 U. S. 394-404, 12 Sup. Ct. Rep. 543.

Lindley on M.—20

reserving lodes known to exist prior to the filing of the placer application and not claimed by the applicant, it would seem that where a location of a vein or lode of mineral or other deposits has, prior to the issuance of a townsite patent, been made under the law, and its boundaries have been specifically marked on the surface so as to be readily traced, and notice of the location has been recorded in the usual books of record, that vein is such a " mine" as is, under the terms of the law, reserved from the operation of the townsite patent, although personal knowledge of its existence may not be possessed by the applicant for patent. The information which the law requires the locator to give to the public must be deemed sufficient to acquaint the placer applicant with the existence of the vein or lode.[1]

If it were a valid perfected lode claim, it would be embraced within the last clause of section twenty-three hundred and ninety-two of the Revised Statutes, and there is no necessity to resort to the rule in the case of lodes within placers for analogy.

But where there is no location embracing it, if we accept the analogies of lodes within placers, the vein, or lode, or "mine," if falling within the designation as heretofore defined, is just as much excepted from the operation of the townsite patent as if it were a located lode.

If it is such a known vein, it may be located at any time. This is the rule applied by the supreme court of the United States in the case of known lodes within patented placers.[2]

As to the valid mining claim which is reserved from the operation of the townsite patent, it must necessarily

[1] Noyes v. Mantle, 127 U. S. 348, 8 Sup. Ct. Rep. 1132.
[2] Iron S. M. Co. v. Mike & Starr etc. Co., 143 U. S. 394, 12 Sup. Ct. Rep. 543.

have been located with all the formalities required by
law, and be subsisting at the time the townsite patent
takes effect. If the location were fatally defective
at that time, an amended location, made subsequent to
the issuance of the townsite patent, would not relate back
to the original invalid location.

A case of this character was considered by the
supreme court of Arizona, which court thus states its
views:—

"A location of a mining claim, to fix the title as
"against after-acquired rights by entry and patent,
"should be sufficiently clear to designate the ground
"claimed, and should be marked on the ground by
"monuments, showing the extent of possession. If the
"location on its face be uncertain, the uncertainty could
"be aided by evidence of the possession, or of monu-
"ments; but a location notice, on its face uncertain and
"without evidence of what land was occupied, cannot
"be evidence for any purpose. An amendment, after-
"wards made, describing different land or making cer-
"tain what was uncertain, cannot revert back to the
"original defective location. The entry of the town-
"site intervening after the first location and before the
"amendment, must be prior in right, as it is prior in
"time." [1]

§ 177. In what manner may a townsite patent be
assailed by the owner of a mine or mining claim.—
Where a mine or valid mining claim exists within the
patented townsite at the time the patent is issued,—or,
to be more exact, at the time final entry thereof is made,
and certificate of purchase is issued,—does the title to
such mine or claim pass to the townsite patentee, or may
the mineral claimant defend against the patent by showing the prior existence of said mine or claim, on the
theory that title to such mine or claim is reserved by the
law under which the patent issued?

[1] Tombstone Townsite Cases, (Ariz.), 15 Pac. 26.

Upon this question there is much confusion of thought observable in the judicial decisions, and the rule may be said to be involved in doubt. A review of these decisions is necessary to a proper understanding of the situation.

It was said by the supreme court of Montana, in the Smokehouse Lode cases, —

" An exception in a townsite patent, excluding from
" its operation all mines, mining claims, and possessions
" held under existing laws, is an exception required by
" the law, and is made by the law itself, and is conclu-
" sive upon the question that the government did not,
" and did not intend, by such townsite patent to convey
" any valid mine or mining claim or possession held
" under existing laws; and it is therefore impossible,
" under a patent to a townsite, to acquire any interest
" in any valid mine or mining claim, or in the surface
" thereof. . . . A valid location of a quartz-lode min-
" ing claim on the public mineral lands of the United
" States is a grant from the government to the locator
" thereof, and carries with it the right, by a compliance
" with the law, of obtaining a full and complete title
" to all the lands included within the boundaries of the
" claim, which by the location are withdrawn from sale
" or pre-emption; and the patent, when issued, relates
" back to the location, and is not a distinct grant, but
" the consummation of the grant which had its incep-
" tion in the location of the claim." [1]

The same court, in a previous case, thus states its views: —

" If, then, the location of a mining claim has the effect
" of a grant by the United States to the locator of the
" right to the present and exclusive possession of the
" ground located, it follows that there could not be a
" like grant of the same property to any other person.
" There would be no room for a further grant; for the
" government would have nothing further to convey.

[1] Butte City Smokehouse Lode Cases, 6 Mont. 397, 401, 12 Pac. 858.

" After such a grant, which also carries with it the right
" to purchase the absolute title, the land described
" within the grant ceases to be public land, and the pre-
" emption laws, and laws providing for the sale and
" purchase of the public domain, have no application to
" it or effect upon it. It is just as much withdrawn from
" the public domain as the fee is by a valid grant from
" the United States under authority, or the possession
" by a valid and subsisting homestead or pre-emption
" entry. It is already sold, and becomes private prop-
" erty, which may be disposed of at the will of the
" owner. And so land thus sold and disposed of is not
" affected one way or another by the subsequent acts of
" congress providing for the entry of townsites upon
" the public lands. The application and entry for town-
" sites is only authorized on the public lands; and after
" the lands have been granted and sold, as in the case of
" a valid mining location and claim, the entry of a town-
" site does not affect such claim, though situate within
" the boundaries of the townsite. The reason is that the
" mining claim and ground has already been granted
" and sold, and has thereby ceased to be a portion of
" the public lands, for which only the townsite entry
" could be made; and, for a further reason, the townsite
" act expressly provides that no title shall be acquired
" under the provisions of said act to any mine of gold,
" silver, cinnabar, or copper, or to any valid mining
" claim or possession under existing laws. If no title
" can be acquired to a mining claim or possession by
" virtue of the townsite act, then the defendants herein,
" who claim by virtue of a subsequent townsite entry
" and patent, cannot disturb the exclusive possession of
" the plaintiff, who claims by virtue of a prior valid
" location and patent of the mining claim in question."[1]

To the same purport is the case of Talbot v. King,
decided by the same court.[2]

These Montana cases were not appealed to the supreme court of the United States, but were referred to

[1] Silver Bow M. and M. Co. v. Clark, 5 Mont. 378, 415, 5 Pac. 570.
[2] 6 Mont. 76, 9 Pac. 434.

by that tribunal in the case of Davis v. Weibbold;[1] and the language then used would seem to imply a sanction of the doctrine announced by the supreme court of Montana.[2]

The force of this rule was recognized by the court of appeals of Colorado, although the question there raised in this respect was merely collateral to the main issue. This court, speaking through Presiding Judge Reed, says:—

" The first contention of appellant is, that the court
" erred in refusing to allow the plaintiff to prove that
" the discovery of the ' Lady B ' was within the
" patented limits of the town of Blackhawk. All the
" evidence shows that the existence of a mineral-bear-
" ing vein at the place the discoveries were made was
" known long previous to the application for a receipt
" of the title by the town. That under the statute was
" sufficient. The town took no title." [3]

This rule is necessarily based upon the theory that the land department had no jurisdiction to convey to the townsite that which had already been withdrawn from the public domain by appropriation under the mining laws. The results reached seem illogical. With the exception of the case of incorporated cities and towns, townsite entries can not be permitted upon mineral lands. The patent when issued is entitled to the presumption that the lands are non-mineral. As the supreme court of the United States has said, the presumption in favor of the validity of a patent is so potential and efficacious that it has been frequently held by the supreme court of the United States that if under any

---

[1] 139 U. S. 530, 11 Sup. Ct. Rep. 628.

[2] King v. Thomas, 6 Mont. 409, 12 Pac. 865. See, also, decision of Judge De Witt in Chambers v. Jones, 17 Mont. 156, 42 Pac. 758; Tombstone Townsite Cases, (Ariz.), 15 Pac. 26; Blackmore v. Reilly, (Ariz.), 17 Pac. 72.

[3] Moyle v. Bullene, 7 Colo. App. 308, 44 Pac. 69, 71.

circumstances in the case the patent might have been rightfully issued, it will be presumed on collateral attack that such circumstances existed.[1]

If there existed at the time of the townsite entry a mine or valid mining claim within the limits of the town, it necessarily follows that some of the lands, at least, were mineral, and the patent was to such extent wrongfully issued. If it is necessary to determine the fact of the existence or non-existence of mineral in paying quantities within the limits of a townsite before patent could issue, why is the patent not a judgment that it is non-mineral,—therefore, that no mine or valid mining claim exists? This question was presented and the conclusion was reached by the trial court in Horsky v. Moran,[2] that a patent issued under such circumstances was not open to collateral attack. A majority of the members of the appellate court concurred in this view, though the decision was based upon another question. The case was taken to the supreme court of the United States, but that court, after discussing the question, held that it had no jurisdiction, because of the existence of a non-federal question broad enough to sustain the judgment.[3]

The question seems to us uncomfortably close.

The difficulties of the situation were appreciated by the supreme court of the United States in a case involving a claimed known lode within a prior placer patent to which the placer applicant asserted no right at the time of filing his application, a junior patent to the lode claimant having been issued. The supreme court thus announced its views:—

[1] St. Louis Smelting Co. v. Kemp, 104 U. S. 636, 646. See, also, dissenting opinion in Iron S. M. Co. v. Mike & Starr etc. Co., 143 U. S. 394, 407, 12 Sup. Ct. Rep. 543.

[2] 21 Mont. 345, 53 Pac. 1064.

[3] Moran v. Horsky, 178 U. S. 205, 20 Sup. Ct. Rep. 856.

" We are not ignorant of the many decisions by which
" it has been held that the rulings of the land officers in
" regard to the facts on which patents for lands are
" issued are decisive in actions at law, and that such
" patents can only be impeached in regard to those facts
" by a suit in chancery, brought to set the grant aside.
" But these are cases in which no prior patent had been
" issued for the same land, and where the party con-
" testing the patent had no evidence of a superior legal
" title, but was compelled to rely on the equity growing
" out of frauds and mistakes in issuing the patent to his
" opponent.

" Where each party has a patent from the govern-
" ment, and the question is as to the superiority of the
" title under those patents, if this depends upon ex-
" trinsic facts not shown by the patents themselves, we
" think it is competent in any judicial proceeding where
" this question of superiority of title arises to establish
" it by proof of these facts. We do not believe that the
" government of the United States, having issued a
" patent, can, by the authority of its own officers, invali-
" date that patent by the issuance of a second one for
" the same ground." [1]

From the doctrine as announced by the majority court
in this case, the chief justice and Justice Brewer dissented. Justice Brewer, speaking for the minority of
the court, said:—

" From Johnson v. Towsley (13 Wall. 72) to the pres-
" ent time, the uniform ruling of this court has been
" that questions of fact passed upon by the land depart-
" ment are conclusively determined, and that only ques-
" tions of law can be brought into court. The right to
" this patent depends solely upon these two questions of
" fact, which were considered by the land office when
" the original patent was issued. I think that its deter-
" mination was conclusive."

In a later case before the same tribunal,[2] the lode

---

[1] Iron S. M. Co. v. Campbell, 135 U. S. 286, 292, 10 Sup. Ct. Rep. 765.

[2] Iron S. M. Co. v. Mike & Starr etc. Co., 143 U. S. 394, 407, 12 Sup. Ct.
Rep. 543.

claimant had no patent, but rested his case upon a location made after the final entry of the placer claim, but upon a lode which, it was claimed, was known to exist at the time of the application for the placer patent, and which was not included in the application. The right to establish these facts by extrinsic evidence, and thus to limit the operation of the placer patent, was upheld by the majority of the court. The minority of the court, speaking through Justice Field, thus presented its views:—

" I am unable to agree with my associates in the disposal of this case. The decision and the opinion upon which it is founded will do much, in my judgment, to weaken the security of patents of the United States for mineral lands, and leave them open to attack and overthrow upon mere surmises, notions, and loose gossip of the neighborhood, which ought not to interfere with any rights of property resting upon the solemn record of the government."

In Dahl v. Raunheim,[1] Judge Field, speaking for the entire court, in a case of the same class, says:—

" That it was *placer* ground is conclusively established in this controversy against the defendant by the fact no adverse claim was asserted by him to the plaintiff's application for patent of the premises as such ground. That question is not now open to litigation by private parties seeking to avoid the effect of plaintiff's proceedings."

In Moran v. Horsky,[2] Justice Brewer said:—

" Now, as we have heretofore noticed, the patent in the case before us for the townsite purported to convey the entire tract. On the face of the instrument there was nothing to suggest any exception. While it may be conceded under the authorities which are referred to, that, in an action at law by a claimant under that patent, the existence of a mining claim at

[1] 132 U. S. 260, 263, 10 Sup. Ct. Rep. 74.
[2] 178 U. S. 205, 211, 20 Sup. Ct. Rep. 856.

" the time of its issue might be shown and be a valid
" defense to a recovery of so much of the ground as was
" included within the mining claim, and in that view it
" may perhaps be not inaptly said that the patent was
" to that extent void. But be this as it may, whenever
" the invalidity of a patent does not appear upon the
" face of the instrument, or by matters of which the
" courts will take judicial notice, and the land is appar-
" ently within the jurisdiction of the land department
" as ordinary public land of the United States, then it
" would seem to be technically more accurate to say that
" the patent was voidable, not void."

In perfecting mining locations the government is not
an actor. It assures to the explorer the right to his mining location, but it does not surrender the right to determine for itself the qualifications of the locator, the fact
of his discovery, his compliance with the law, and the
character of the land. A judgment by a court of competent jurisdiction in proceedings brought upon adverse
claims does not conclude the government as to these
matters. There is no notice brought to the attention of
the government of the existence of mining locations or
known lodes prior to the application for patent. The
only record made is with an officer who has no connection
with the land department, and who owes no responsibility to the government. And yet a townsite patent
issued by the government may be assailed in an action
between individuals, and its operation defeated by showing facts the existence of which the government neither
actually nor constructively could have any knowledge,
unless it was a part of its duty to ascertain them when
the townsite patent was applied for; and if it was a part
of its duty, the patent should be conclusive evidence that
that duty was performed. To say that a perfected mining claim is a grant from the government, is true in one
sense; but it does not follow that in establishing the
existence of such a grant the government has no voice.

It is not a grant in the sense that the government has absolutely parted with its title. It does not seem right, where only one patent is issued, and where the government has not attempted to issue a second one covering any portion of the premises described in the first, that the operative effect of the prior patent should be limited by judgments in actions to which the government is in no sense a party. It would seem that the remedy in such cases should be by action instituted by the government to vacate the patent, after notice of the facts brought to its attention.[1]

The land department at one time took the position that its jurisdiction was exhausted by the issuance of a prior patent to a townsite, and until that was set aside it was not authorized to issue a junior mineral patent within the limits of the townsite.[2]

The department subsequently abandoned this doctrine, overruled the cases which established it, and now holds that it may issue ·a patent to a mineral claimant after having issued a townsite patent.[3]

If the lode or mining claim is by operation of law reserved out of the patent, it certainly follows that the department may subsequently issue a patent for the thing so reserved. This is the rule now followed by the department with reference to lodes known to exist within patented placers.[4]

[1] See Horsky v. Moran, 21 Mont. 345, 53 Pac. 1064, S. C., 178 U. S. 205, 20 Sup. Ct. Rep. 856; Hulings v. Ward Townsite, 29 L. D. 21.

[2] See, ante, § 173; Pacific Slope Lode, 12 L. D. 686; Cameron Lode, 13 L. D. 369; Protector Lode, 12 L. D. 662; Plymouth Lode, Id., 513.

[3] Pacific Slope Lode v. Butte Townsite, 25 L. D. 518; Gregory Lode, 26 L. D. 144; Hulings v. Ward Townsite, 29 L. D. 21; Brady's Mortgagee v. Harris, Id. 89; S. C. on review, Id. 426.

[4] South Star Lode, 20 L. D. 204 (on review); Butte and Boston M. Co., 21 L. D. 125, reversing Pike's Peak Lode, 14 L. D. 47, and commissioners' decision, South Star Lode, 17 L. D. 280; post, § 413.

See Pacific Slope Lode v. Butte Townsite, 25 L. D. 518, where the analogy is recognized.

Of course, the propriety of this departmental practice depends on the correct determination of the question as to the conclusiveness of the townsite patent. Logically, we think the mineral claimant's remedy in this class of cases is in equity to erect a trust on the townsite patent; or, perhaps, an application to the land department to institute a suit to vacate the patent *pro tanto*.

§ 178. **Ownership of minerals under streets in townsites.**—It cannot be doubted that a patent issued by the government under the townsite laws vests in the grantee the complete title to all the land described, regardless of the fact that some of the land may have become dedicated to a public use by the laying out of streets and highways. If it is subsequently ascertained that minerals underlie these portions of the tract which are subject to the public easement, it cannot be said that the title to these minerals remains in the United States. This ownership must primarily vest in the immediate grantee from the government,—*i. e.* either in the municipality, if the town be incorporated, or in the county or superior judge in trust for the inhabitants. Whether the title to the minerals underlying the streets and alleys remains in the municipality, or judge as trustee, as the case may be, or passes to the abutting lot-owners, will depend entirely upon the laws of the particular state wherein the townsite is situated.

The federal townsite laws contemplate that each state or territory shall appropriately provide by legislation for the disposal of the lots within the tract embraced within the townsite.[1] In determining the nature and character of the title conveyed by the trust patentee, and the boundaries of the several tracts conveyed, resort must in each instance be had to this supplemental state or territorial legislation. Without attempting any critical analysis of this class of legislation, we apprehend

[1] Rev. Stats., § 2387.

that whether the lot-owners take by virtue of their conveyance to the middle of the street, or their rights are to be determined by the abutting line of the street, will depend largely upon whether or not the common law or its statutory re-enactment is in force in that particular state, or the rules of the common law have been abrogated by legislative action.

At common law the public has a mere easement in highways to use them for passage to and fro and for other purely public purposes appropriate to their nature as such. The fee of the soil and mineral therein belongs to the abutting owners, whose titles, presumptively at least, extend to the middle of the highway.[1]

This presumption may, of course, be overcome where it clearly appears from the instrument of conveyance that the parties intended that the side line of the street should form the boundary.

We are not here concerned, however, with the interpretation of conveyances, but deal with the subject from the standpoint of general law.

In some states the common law is operative by general legislative adoption. In others the common-law rule on the particular subject under discussion has received express legislative sanction. This is the case in California.[2] In still others the common law has been so modified as to provide that a dedication of streets and alleys shall vest a fee simple in the municipality or the public.[3] This seems to be the rule in Colorado.[4]

---

[1] Barclay v. Howell's Lessee, 6 Pet. 498, 513; Harris v. Elliott, 10 Pet. 25, 55; Dubuque v. Maloney, 9 Iowa, 450.

[2] Cal. Civ. Code, § 831.

[3] Des Moines v. Hall, 24 Iowa, 234; Trustees v. Haven, 11 Ill. 554; Chaliss v. Atchison Union Depot, 45 Kan. 398, 25 Pac. 894; Lindsay v. Omaha, 30 Neb. 512, 46 N. W. 627, 27 Am. St. Rep. 415. Compare Thomas v. Hunt, 134 Mo. 392, 35 S. W. 581.

[4] Mills' Annot. Stats. 1891, § 4360; City of Leadville v. Coronado M. Co. (Colo.), 67 Pac. 289; City of Leadville v. St. Louis S. and R. Co. (Colo.), Id. 1126.

Article VI.   Indian Reservations.

§ 181. Nature of Indian title.

§ 182. Manner of creating and
        abolishing Indian reser-
        vations.

§ 183. Lands within Indian reser-
        vations are not open to
        settlement or purchase
        under the public land
        laws.

§ 184. *Status* of mining claims lo-
        cated within limits of an
        Indian reservation prior
        to the extinguishment of
        the Indian title.

§ 185. Effect of creating an Indi-
        an reservation embracing
        prior valid and subsist-
        ing mining claims.

§ 186. Conclusions.

§ 181. **Nature of Indian title.**—The scope of this treatise neither calls for nor permits elaborate discussion of the legal or ethical relationship existing between the government of the United States and the "wards of "the nation," as the Indian tribes within our borders are popularly styled. The government legislates upon the conduct of strangers or citizens within the limits of their reservations, and for many years innumerable treaties formed with them acknowledged them to be independent people.[1]

But by the act of congress passed March 3, 1871,[2] it was declared that no Indian nation or tribe within the territory of the United States should thereafter be recognized as an independent nation, tribe, or power with whom the United States might contract by treaty.[3]

It was determined in the early history of our country that the absolute, ultimate title to lands in the possession of the Indians was acquired by the discoverers of the country, subject only to the Indian title of occupancy,

[1] Fletcher *v.* Peck, 6 Cranch, 87, 147.

[2] 16 Stats. at Large, p. 566.

[3] Public Domain, p. 244; Stephens *v.* Cherokee Nation, 174 U. S. 445, 483, 19 Sup. Ct. Rep. 722.

and that the discoverers possessed the exclusive right of acquiring this title; or, in other words, the exclusive right of pre-emption. As was said by Chief Justice Marshall,—

" It has never been contended that the Indian title " amounted to nothing. Their right of possession has " never been questioned. The claim of the government " extends to the complete ultimate title, charged with " this right of possession, and to the exclusive power of " acquiring that right." [1]

Indians have a right to the lands they occupy until that right is extinguished by voluntary cession to the government.[2]

The courts have said of the interest of the Indians:—

" For all practical purposes they owned it; as the " actual right of possession, the only thing they deemed " of value, was secured to them by treaty until they " should elect to surrender it to the United States." [3]

But they do not hold a fee in the land of their original occupation, but only a usufruct, the fee being in the United States, if within the public land states or territories, or in some of the several states, if the national government acquired no lands therein.[4]

Lands conveyed by the government to an Indian nation in lieu of original territory surrendered by them

[1] Johnson & Graham's Lessees v. McIntosh, 8 Wheat. 543, 603.

[2] Cherokee Nation v. Georgia, 5 Peters, 1; Godfrey v. Beardsley, 2 McLean, 412, Fed. Cas. No. 5497; Holden & Warner v. Joy, 17 Wall. 211.

[3] Leavenworth L. and G. R. Co. v. United States, 92 U. S. 743; Bardon v. Northern Pac. R. R. Co., 145 U. S. 535, 543, 12 Sup. Ct. Rep. 856; King v. McAndrews, 111 Fed. 860, 870.

[4] United States v. Cook, 19 Wall. 591; Marsh v. Brooks, 8 How. 223; Mann v. Wilson, 23 How. 457; Minter v. Crommelin, 18 How. 87; Beecher v. Wetherby, 95 U. S. 517; Worcester v. State of Georgia, 6 Peters, 515; United States v. Cook, 19 Wall. 591; State v. Kennard (on rehearing), 57 Neb. 711, 78 N. W. 282; S. C., 56 Neb. 254, 76 N. W. 545. And see Buttz v. Railroad Co., 119 U. S. 55, 7 Sup. Ct. Rep. 100; and Leavenworth L. and G. R. Co. v. United States, 92 U. S. 753.

under treaties, for the purpose of inducing a change of habitat, are alike subject to the preferred right of the government to extinguish or acquire the Indian title.

§ 182. **Manner of creating and abolishing Indian reservations.**—Mr. Donaldson thus explains the manner of creating and abolishing Indian reservations:—

" The method of making an Indian reservation is by " an executive order withdrawing certain lands from " sale or entry and setting them apart for the use and " occupancy of the Indians, such reservation previously " having been selected by officers acting under the direc- " tion of the commissioner of Indian affairs or that of " the secretary of the interior, and recommended by the " secretary of the interior to the president. The exec- " utive order is sent to the office of Indian affairs, and " copy thereof is furnished by that office to the general " land office, upon receipt of which the reservation is " noted upon the land-office records, and local land " officers are furnished with a copy of the order, and " are directed to protect the reservation from inter- " ference.

" When such reservation is no longer required, and " the president is so informed by the secretary of the " interior, an executive order is issued restoring the " lands to the public domain, and the order being " received by the commissioner of Indian affairs, a copy " thereof is furnished to the general land office, where " it is noted, and information is communicated to the " United States land officers, after which the lands are " disposed of as other public lands." [1]

Indian reservations existing by virtue of treaty stipulations are usually abolished, and the Indian title extinguished, by compact between chiefs of the tribes and agents of the government, the agreement being subject to approval by congress and the president.[2]

[1] Public Domain, p. 243.　　　[2] *Id.*, p. 244.

§ 183. **Lands within Indian reservations are not opon to settlement or purchase under the public land laws.**— It has been the policy of the government from the beginning to prohibit the settlement of lands in the occupation of the Indians.[1]

As was said by the supreme court of the United States,—

  " That lands dedicated to the use of the Indians
  " should upon every principle of natural right be care-
  " fully guarded by the government and saved from a
  " possible grant, is a proposition which will command
  " universal assent."[2]

While the government may dispose of the fee of the land, it remains burdened with the right of occupancy in the Indians.[3] This right of occupancy can not be interfered with nor determined, except by the United States. No private individual can invade it, and the manner, time, and conditions of its extinguishment are matters solely for the consideration of the government, and are open to contestation in the judicial tribunals.[4] Where land is reserved for the use of an Indian tribe by treaty, the treaty is notice that the land will be retained for the use of the Indians, and this purpose cannot be defeated by the action of any officers of the land department.[5] The lands embraced therein are no longer public lands.[6]

---

[1] Hot Springs Cases, Rector & Hale v. United States, 92 U. S. 698.

[2] Leavenworth L. and G. R. Co. v. United States, 92 U. S. 733; Missouri, K. and T. Ry. Co. v. United States, *Id.* 760.

[3] Beecher v. Wetherby, 95 U. S. 517; Buttz v. N. P. R. R., 119 U. S. 55, 7 Sup. Ct. Rep. 100.

[4] *Id.*

[5] United States v. Carpenter, 111 U. S. 347, 4 Sup. Ct. Rep. 435.

[6] Missouri, K. and T. Ry. Co. v. Roberts, 152 U. S. 114, 14 Sup. Ct. Rep. 114; Spalding v. Chandler, 160 U. S. 394, 405, 16 Sup. Ct. Rep. 394; King v. McAndrews, 111 Fed. 860, 870; McFadden v. Mountain View M. and M. Co., 97 Fed. 670.

The nature of this use requires the absolute reservation and withdrawal of every foot of land within the defined limits, and no portion of it is disposable to settlers or to purchasers so as to enable them to invade the Indian occupancy. In this respect Indian reservations differ from that class of Mexican grants called "floats," within the exterior boundaries of which the government may grant lands to others than the claimants, so long as sufficient land remains to satisfy the grant.[1]

In most of the compacts entered into between the government and Indian tribes, the United States has agreed that only such persons as were specified in the treaty should ever be permitted to pass over, settle upon, or reside in the territory so set apart for the use of the Indians. The treaty with the Sioux Indians, proclaimed February 24, 1869, embracing within its limits the famous Black Hills, in Dakota, and with the confederated band of Ute Indians, in Colorado, contained these stipulations.[2]

But in the absence of such specific stipulations, the policy of the government has been to preserve the reservation from invasion by those seeking to establish settlement within the boundaries.

§ 184. **Status of mining claims located within limits of an Indian reservation prior to the extinguishment of the Indian title.**—It logically follows from the nature and object of a reservation of land for the use and occupancy of the Indians that no rights can be lawfully initiated to mineral lands within the limits of such reservation. It would be a violation of public faith to permit

[1] United States v. McLaughlin, 127 U. S. 428, 8 Sup. Ct. Rep. 1177; Carr v. Quigley, 149 U. S. 652, 13 Sup. Ct. Rep. 961. See, *ante,* § 124.

[2] Uhlig v. Garrison, 2 Dak. 71-95, 2 N. W. 253; Kendall v. San Juan S. M. Co., 9 Colo. 349, 12 Pac. 198.

these lands, so long as the Indian title remains unextinguished, to be invaded with a view to their exploration and appropriation for mining purposes. Such invasion, although peaceful in its inception, would invariably end in conflicts. The government could not lend its sanction to such intrusion without being charged with a violation of its solemn obligations.[1]

The supreme court of Colorado, in a case which involved a mining claim within the limits of what was at the time of its discovery and location the Ute Indian reservation in that state, clearly announced the rule:—

" The effect of the treaty was to withdraw the whole
" of the land embraced within the reservation from
" private entry or appropriation, and during its exist-
" ence the government could not have authorized the
" plaintiffs to enter upon the ground in controversy for
" the purpose of discovering and locating a mining
" claim. On the contrary, the government stood pledged
" to prevent its citizens from entering upon the reserva-
" tion for any such purposes. The right to locate
" mineral lands of the United States is declared to be
" a privilege granted by congress. No such grant
" including the premises in controversy existed at the
" time of the plaintiff's location. It is also held that a
" location to be effective must be good at the time it
" was made, and that it can not be good when made if
" there is then an outstanding grant of the exclusive
" right of possession to another. The possession of the
" plaintiffs at the time of their location of the Bear lode
" was tortious. Such being the character of their pos-
" session, and assuming to locate a claim, not only *with-*
" *out legal* authority, but in violation of law, the
" attempted location was a nullity. It was just as if it
" has never been made." [2]

---

[1] See the interesting account of the settlement of Deadwood and the Black Hills region, in 8 Copp's L. O. 153.

[2] Kendall v. San Juan S. M. Co., 9 Colo. 349, 357, 12 Pac. 198, (citing United States v. Carpenter, 111 U. S. 347, 4 Sup. Ct. Rep. 435; Belk v. Meagher, 104 U. S. 279).

The supreme court of the United States affirmed the rule thus announced. Said that court:—

" The effect of the treaty was to exclude all intrusion
" for mining or other private pursuits upon the terri-
" tory thus reserved for the Indians. It prohibited any
" entry of the kind upon the premises, and no interest
" could be claimed or enforced in disregard of this pro-
" vision. Not until the withdrawal of the land from this
" reservation of the treaty by a new convention with
" the Indians, and one which would throw the lands
" open, could a mining location therein be initiated by
" the plaintiffs. The location of the Bear lode, having
" been made whilst the treaty was in force, was inoper-
" ative to confer any rights upon the plaintiffs." [1]

The supreme court of Dakota set its seal of condemnation upon the attempted assertion of rights to occupy lands within the Black Hills region prior to the extinguishment of the title of the Sioux Indians;[2] and with reference to attempted mining locations it established the rule that a party can not acquire a mining claim by acts performed within an Indian reservation. But it was also held that a party in possession on the day the Indian title became extinguished, with the requisite discovery, with surface boundaries marked and notice posted, could adopt these antecedent steps, and manifest their adoption by then recording his notice of location in the proper office, and by so doing and performing the amount of labor and making improvements could date his rights from that day;[3] and this doctrine also met with the approval of the supreme court of the United States.[4]

[1] Kendall v. San Juan S. M. Co., 144 U. S. 658, 663, 12 Sup. Ct. Rep. 779. Followed in McFadden v. Mountain View M. and M. Co., 97 Fed. 670.

[2] Uhlig v. Garrison, 2 Dak. 71, 95.

[3] Caledonia G. M. Co. v. Noonan, 3 Dak. 189, 14 N. W. 426.

[4] Noonan v. Caledonia G. M. Co., 121 U. S. 393, 7 Sup. Ct. Rep. 911.

The general rule with reference to mining claims within Indian reservations was first announced by the supreme court of Dakota in the case of French *v.* Lancaster;[1] but no written opinion was filed. In this case it seems that both parties litigant, being rival mineral claimants *in pari delictu,* stipulated to waive all objections that might have been raised to evidence of acts of location and appropriation performed prior to the extinguishment of the Indian title. The trial court acted upon the stipulation, and determined the case regardless of the existence of the reservation.[2]

The appellate court, however, held that public policy required that notice should be taken of the facts, and held the attempted locations invalid.

The general doctrine announced in this case was followed by the same court in a later case.[3]

The land department has uniformly adhered to the doctrine that the occupancy and location of a mining claim within an Indian reservation prior to the extinguishment of the Indian title is an open violation of solemn treaty obligations, and without even a shadow of right.[4]

In the case of the Colville reservation in Washington, created by an executive order, the circuit court of appeals for the ninth circuit held that an act of congress providing for the restoration of the lands included within the reservation did not operate of itself, in advance of a proclamation by the president, to give a

---

[1] 2 Dak. 346, 47 N. W. 395.

[2] See Golden Terra M. Co. *v.* Mahler, 4 Morr. Min. Rep. 390, 405.

[3] Golden Terra M. Co. v. Smith, 2 Dak. 374, 462, 11 N. W. 97.

[4] Townsite of Deadwood *v.* Mineral Claimants, 8 Copp's L. O. 153; Rattlesnake Jack Placer, 10 Copp's L. O. 87; Crow Indian Reservation, Copp's Min. Lands, p. 236; Circ. Instructions, 3 L. D. 371, 6 L. D. 341; *In re* Meeks, 29 L. D. 456. And see King *v.* McAndrews, 111 Fed. 860, reversing 104 Fed. 430; Acme Cement and Placer Co., 31 L. D. 125.

right to locate mining claims therein.[1] Judge Hanford, sitting in the circuit, had reached an opposite conclusion.[2] Subsequently, by act of congress, the mineral land laws were expressly extended to the north half of this reservation.[3]

Manifestly, the precise time when the Indian title becomes effectually extinguished, and the reserved lands become open to entry and occupation for any purpose, depends upon the facts of each particular case.[4]

The land department has held, that under an act passed June 6, 1900,[5] extending the mining laws over the Fort Hall reservation in Idaho, and providing that lands allotted to Indians should be subject to exploration for mining purposes, after an allotment had been made to an Indian the land embraced therein could not be explored for minerals and was not subject to exploration; but prior to such allotment mineral location might be made.[6] This ruling seems to us to be correct and in accordance with the spirit of the act.[7]

§ 185. Effect of creating an Indian reservation embracing prior valid and subsisting mining claims.— The land department, following the opinion of the attorney-general with reference to military reserva-

---

[1] McFadden v. Mountain View M. and M. Co., 97 Fed. 670.

[2] McFadden v. Mountain View, 87 Fed. 154; Collins v. Bubb, 73 Fed. 735.

[3] 29 Stats. at Large, p. 9.

[4] See McFadden v. Mountain View M. and M. Co., 97 Fed. 670. Congress has passed several special acts opening lands within Indian reservations to occupation, location, and purchase, under the provisions of the mineral laws only, with a preference right of purchase to those who had located prior to the opening of the reservation—for example, the Blackfeet, Fort Belknap, (Eureka, and Try Again Lodes, 29 L. D. 158,) and San Carlos reservations. (1st Sess. 54th Cong.)

[5] 31 Stats. at Large, pp. 672, 680.

[6] Acme Cement and Plaster Co., 31 L. D. 125.

[7] See, to same effect, instructions, Id. 154.

tions,[1] has held that mining claims valid and subsisting cannot be included within an Indian reservation set apart after the location of such claims so as to deprive the locator of his previously acquired rights. Where an Indian reservation has been made including such claim, the locators may show by proper proof, that their claims were valid and subsisting at the date of such reservation.[2]

Considering the dignity accorded to a mining title perfected and acquired at a time when the lands were a part of the public domain, we think the ruling in harmony with the spirit and intent of the mining laws. Such locators have the right to go upon or across the reservation for the purpose of maintaining their right to their claims and to develop them. If their claims are abandoned or become subject to relocation, they do not lapse into the reservation, but may be relocated, and the relocator is entitled to the same privileges as are accorded to the original locator.[3]

§ 186. Conclusions.—We announce the following as our conclusions from the foregoing exposition of the law:—

No right to appropriate a mining claim within the limits of an Indian reservation can be initiated so long as the Indian title remains unextinguished. Acts which in the absence of such reservation might be valid may be adopted upon the extinguishment of the Indian title, if such adoption is manifested by perfection of the location and the performance of the required work or making improvements. Otherwise, the claim may be located

---

[1] See, *post*, § 192.

[2] Chief Moses Indian Reservation, 9 Copp's L. O. 189; Navajo Indian Reservation, 30 L. D. 515. See, for an analogous case, Hibberd v. Slack, 84 Fed. 571.

[3] Navajo Indian Reservation, 30 L. D. 515.

by the first-comer, regardless of the acts done by others while the land was withdrawn from the public domain. A mining claim valid and subsisting at the time an Indian reservation is created is not affected by such reservation, nor are the rights of the prior locator impaired, so long as he perpetuates his estate by the performance of the requisite annual labor; and upon the abandonment or forfeiture of the claim, it does not become subject to the reservation; the estate of the original locator may be restored by resumption of work, or the claim may in default of this be relocated.

Article VII. Military Reservations.

§ 190. Manner of creating and abolishing military reservations.

§ 191. *Status* of mining claims located within the limits of a subsisting military reservation.

§ 192. Effect of creating a military reservation embracing prior valid and subsisting mining claims.

§ 190. **Manner of creating and abolishing military reservations.**—The method of creating military reservations is thus outlined by Mr. Donaldson:—

" The commanding officer of a military department " recommends the establishment of a reservation, with " certain boundaries; the secretary of war refers the " papers to the interior department, to know whether " any objection exists to the declaration of the reserve " by the president. If no objection is known to the " general land office, and it is so reported, the reservation " tion is declared by the president, upon application of " the secretary of war for that purpose, and the papers " are sent to the general land office, through the secretary " tary of the interior, for annotation upon the proper " records. If upon surveyed land, the United States " land officers are at once instructed to withhold the

" same from disposal, and respect the reservation. If
" upon unsurveyed land, the United States surveyor-
" general is furnished with a full description of the
" tract, and is instructed to close the lines of public
" surveys upon the outboundaries of the reserve; the
" United States land officers are also instructed not to
" receive any filing of any kind for the reserved
" lands." [1]

The authority of the president, acting through the
secretary of war and his officers, to have posts and forts
established, with a proper quantity of ground appropriated for military purposes, is unquestioned.[2]

This authority has been held to extend to Hawaii,
where a military reservation may be carved out of the
public lands.[3]

Such reservation is vacated, or "reduced," by executive proclamation.

Whenever in the opinion of the president of the
United States the lands, or any portion of them, included
within the limits of any military reservation have
become useless for military purposes, he causes the
same, or so much thereof as he shall designate, to be
placed under the control of the secretary of the interior
for disposition under the general laws relating to the
public lands, and causes to be filed with the secretary
of the interior a notice thereof.[4]

The lands thus restored are not always opened immediately for entry and settlement for agricultural purposes. Congress usually provides for their sale or
extends the privilege of settlement upon them under the
homestead laws. But with reference to mineral lands,

[1] Public Domain, p. 249.

[2] Wilcox v. Jackson, 13 Peters, 498; Stone v. United States, 2 Wall.
525; Grisar v. McDowell, 6 Wall. 381.

[3] Opinion Atty.-Gen., 29 L. D. 32.

[4] Act of July 5, 1884, 23 Stats. at Large, p. 103. See, also, Act of Aug.
23, 1894, 28 Stats. at Large, p. 491; Act of Feb. 15, 1895, Id., p. 664.

the act of July 5, 1884,[1] in terms provides that whenever any lands containing valuable mineral deposits shall be vacated by the reduction or abandonment of any military reservation under the provisions of the act, the same shall be disposed of exclusively under the mineral land laws of the United States.

§ 191. Status of mining claims located within the limits of a subsisting military reservation.—Every tract set apart for some special use is reserved to the government, to enable it to enforce that use; and there is no difference in this respect, whether it be appropriated for Indian occupancy or for other purposes. There is an equal obligation resting on the government to see that neither class of reservation is diverted from the uses to which it was assigned.[2]

Much that has been said in the preceding articles with reference to Indian reservations applies with equal force to military reservations. In an opinion given by Attorney-General McVeagh to the secretary of war, that officer was advised that mineral lands might be included in reservations for military purposes, and they are not subject to appropriation by mineral claimants while such reservation exists.[3] And this is the rule recognized by the land department.[4]

The law is too well settled to require discussion that no right exists under any of the public land laws to invade the limits of a subsisting reservation for the purpose of initiating a title to the lands therein.

The creation of the reservation is a withdrawal of the lands from the operation of the public land laws; and

---

[1] 23 Stats. at Large, p. 103.
[2] Leavenworth L. and G. R. Co. *v.* United States, 92 U. S. 733.
[3] Fort Maginnis, 1 L. D. 552.
[4] Sucia Islands, 23 L. D. 329.

so long as such reservation remains in force, no entry thereon can be lawfully made under the mining or other public land laws.

§ 192. Effect of creating a military reservation embracing prior valid and subsisting mining claims.—Mr. Armstrong, while acting commissioner of the general land office, held that the subsequent enlargement of a military reservation, so as to include within its limits previously located mining claims, prevented the locator from perpetuating his title by performance of annual work, his only remedy being to relocate the claim upon the restoration of the reservation to the public domain.[1]

But in the opinion given by Attorney-General Mc-Veagh at the request of the secretary of war, referred to in the preceding section, a contrary rule is stated. Mr. McVeagh thus expresses his views:—

" It seems to me that where such rights have attached " to mineral lands in favor of the locator of a mining " claim, the land during the continuance of the claim " (*i. e.* so long as it is maintained in accordance with " law) becomes by force of the mining laws appro-" priated to a specific purpose—namely, the develop-" ment and working of the mine located; and unless " congress otherwise provides, it can not, while that " right exists, notwithstanding the title thereto remains " in the government, be set apart for public uses." [2]

Ever since the promulgation of this opinion the land department has accepted the rule as stated by the attorney-general, and has applied it to the Yosemite national park,[3] and to reservoir sites.[4] This is the

---

[1] Camp Bowie Reservation, 7 Copp's L. O. 4.
[2] 1 Land Decisions, 552, 554; 8 Copp's L. O. 137.
[3] 25 L. D. 50.
[4] 15 L. D. 418.

accepted doctrine of that department with reference to previously located mining claims within Indian reservations.[1]

The rule is different with reference to inchoate preemption claims. As to such classes of claims, the government does not enter into any contract with the settler or incur any obligation that the land occupied by him shall ever be put up for sale. Whatever may be the possessory rights of such occupant as against other claimants under the ordinary land laws, such rights cannot avail against the power of congress to make whatsoever disposition of such lands as it pleases at any time prior to the final entry and purchase.[2]

As was said by the supreme court of the United States,—

" Mere settlement upon the public lands with the
" intention to obtain title under the pre-emption laws
" does not create in the settler such a vested interest as
" deprives congress of the power to dispose of the prop-
" erty." [3]

But a mining claim perfected under the law is property, in the highest sense of that term. It has the effect of a grant by the government of the right of present and exclusive possession of the lands located[4] against every one, including the United States itself.[5]

A patent issued to the locator adds but little to the

---

[1] See, *ante*, § 185.

[2] Frisbie *v.* Whitney, 9 Wall. 187; Hutchins *v.* Low (Yosemite Valley Case), 15 Wall. 77.

[3] Shepley *v.* Cowan, 91 U. S. 330, 338; Gonzales *v.* French, 164 U. S. 338, 17 Sup. Ct. Rep. 102.

[4] Belk *v.* Meagher, 104 U. S. 279, 284; Gwillim *v.* Donnellan, 115 U. S. 45, 5 Sup. Ct. Rep. 1110; Stratton *v.* Gold Sovereign M. and T. Co., 1 Leg. Adv. 350, (appeal dismissed on stipulation, 89 Fed. 1016). See, *post*, § 322.

[5] McFeters *v.* Pierson, 15 Colo. 201, 15 Pac. 1076; Gold Hill Q. M. Co. *v.* Ish, 5 Or. 104; Seymour *v.* Fisher, 16 Colo. 188, 27 Pac. 240.

security of his title.[1] Mineral lands of the government are always for sale.[2]

One locating them does so upon the express invitation of the government, and under a compact by which he is seceured the absolute and exclusive right of enjoyment of his properly discovered and located claim, so long as he complies with the law. While the right of the government undoubtedly exists to extinguish an imperfect and incomplete pre-emption claim, we cannot admit that a similar right exists with reference to perfected mining claims. The nature of the estate held by a pre-emptor and that owned by a locator of a valid and subsisting mining claim is essentially different.

If the rule is correctly stated, it follows necessarily that a locator holding a valid mining claim, subsisting at the time the reservation for military purposes is created, has a right to perpetuate his estate and enjoy his property by operating and developing it, and should be entitled to the right of ingress and egress at all reasonable times over the reservation, as well as to all other privileges reasonably necessary or incident to the full and fair enjoyment of the property granted to him by the government. These privileges include the right to appropriate water for mining purposes, notwithstanding ing the fact that a military reservation had been previously created below the point of diversion. Of course, only such water as had not been appropriated for the use of the reservation could be appropriated by the mineral claimant.[3]

The conclusions reached in reference to Indian reservations, announced in section one hundred and eighty-six, are equally applicable to military reservations.

[1] Chambers v. Harrington, 111 U. S. 350, 4 Sup. Ct. Rep. 428; Shafer v. Constans, 3 Mont. 369.

[2] Rev. Stats., § 2319.

[3] Krall v. United States, 79 Fed. 241.

ARTICLE VIII. NATIONAL PARK AND FOREST RESERVATIONS—RESERVATIONS FOR RESERVOIR SITES.

§ 196. Manner of creating national park reservations, and purposes for which they are created.

§ 197. Manner of creating forest reservations, and purposes for which they are created.

§ 198. *Status* of mining claims within forest reservations.

§ 199. Forest lieu selections under act of June 4, 1897.

§ 200. Reservoir sites.

§ 196. **Manner of creating national park reservations, and purposes for which they are created.**—The most renowned of all national parks is the "Yellowstone," embracing within its limits thirty-five hundred and seventy-five square miles, or two million two hundred and eighty-eight thousand acres, the largest reservation of its kind in the world.[1] It was dedicated and set apart as a public park and pleasure-ground for the benefit and enjoyment of the people, by a special act of congress, passed March 1, 1872.[2]

All lands within its limits were by the terms of the act withdrawn from settlement, occupancy, or sale under the laws of the United States, and the secretary of the interior was authorized to make regulations for the government of the park, which provide, among other things, for the preservation from injury or spoliation of all timber, mineral deposits, natural curiosities, or wonders within the park, and their retention in their natural condition.[3]

The act further declares that all persons who should

---

[1] Public Domain, p. 1294.

[2] Rev. Stats., §§ 2474, 2475.

[3] For regulations governing the park, see Public Domain, p. 1296.

locate, settle upon, or occupy the same, or any part thereof, except for certain prescribed purposes, under permission of the secretary of the interior, shall be considered as trespassers.

Several other reservations were subsequently created, for similar purposes, the acts of dedication being drawn upon lines parallel to the Yellowstone act. The acts of September 25, 1890,[1] and of October 1, 1890, reserving lands in the vicinity of the Yosemite valley in California,[2] are of this class. Mining rights which were in existence at the time of the creation of the latter reservation are protected, together with the right of ingress and egress.[3] In the absence of an express provision to the contrary, the effect of these reservations is the same as in the case of Indian and military reservations,—that is, to absolutely withdraw the lands from settlement, entry, occupation, and purchase,—and the rules of law applicable to the latter classes of reservations apply with equal force to national parks. It is unnecessary to here repeat these rules. The case of Mount Rainier national park in Washington, created in 1899,[4] is an exception to the rule. The act creating the park expressly provides (§ 5) :—

" That the mineral land laws of the United States are " hereby extended to the lands lying within the said " reserve and said park."

The department has ruled that by this section the mineral lands within the reservation are subject to *bona fide* exploration, development, and purchase; but no one shall be permitted to despoil or injure the mineral deposits, natural curiosities, or wonders under the guise of prospecting or developing minerals.[5] As these parks

[1] 26 Stats. at Large, p. 478.
[2] *Id.*, p. 650.
[3] Opinion, 25 L. D. 48.
[4] 30 Stats. at Large, p. 993.
[5] Opinion, 28 L. D. 492.

are dedicated by act of congress, it will probably require a congressional act to restore them to the public domain.

§ 197. **Manner of creating forest reservations, and purposes for which they are created.**—We do not encounter forest reservations as a distinctive class until within a comparatively recent period. By an act of congress, passed March 3, 1891,[1] the president of the United States was authorized to set apart and reserve from time to time in any state or territory having public land bearing forests any part of the public lands, wholly or in part covered with timber or undergrowth, whether of commercial value or not, as public reservations, the establishment of such reservations and their limits to be declared by executive proclamation.

Under this law, numerous forest reservations have been declared, notably those adjoining the Yellowstone park,[2] and in the several states and territories, as tabulated on the opposite page.

The original object of these reservations was to reserve public lands in mountainous and other regions which are covered with timber or undergrowth, at the head-waters of rivers, and along the banks of streams, creeks, and ravines, where such timber or undergrowth is the means provided by nature to absorb and check the mountain torrents and to prevent the sudden and rapid melting of the winter snows and the resultant inundation of the valleys below.[3]

By act of congress passed in 1897, the purpose was declared to be "to improve and protect the forests with- " in the reservations, or for the purpose of securing

[1] 26 Stats. at Large, p. 1103, § 24.

[2] *Id.*, p. 1565; 27 Stats. at Large, p. 989.

[3] See instructions relating to timber reservations, May 15, 1891, 12 L. D. 499.

FOREST RESERVES.

STATE OR TERRITORY.	NAME.	DATE OF PROCLAMATION.	REFERENCE.
Alaska........	Afognak Island.......	Dec. 24, 1892	27 Stats. at Large, p. 1052
"	Alexander Archipelago..	1902	
Arizona.......	Black Mesa...........	Aug. 17, 1898	30 Stats. at Large, p. 1782
"	Grand Cañon.........	Feb. 20, 1893	27 Stats. at Large, p. 1064
"	Prescott.............	Oct. 21, 1899	{ 30 Stats. at Large, p. 1771 / 31 Stats. at Large, p. 1956
"	San Francisco Mts.....	Aug. 17, 1898	30 Stats. at Large, p. 1780
California.....	Lake Tahoe..........	Apr. 13, 1899	31 Stats. at Large, p. 1953
"	Pine Mt. and Zaca Lake..	June 29, 1898	{ 30 Stats. at Large, pp. 1767, 1776
"	San Bernardino.......	Feb. 25, 1893	27 Stats. at Large, p. 1068
"	San Gabriel.........	Dec. 20, 1892	27 Stats. at Large, p. 1049
"	San Jacinto..........	Feb. 22, 1897	29 Stats. at Large, p. 893
"	Santa Ynez...........	Oct. 2, 1899	31 Stats. at Large, p. 1954
"	Sierra...............	Feb. 14, 1893	27 Stats. at Large, p. 1059
"	Stanislaus...........	Feb. 22, 1897	29 Stats. at Large, p. 898
"	Trabuco Cañon.......	Feb. 25, 1893	27 Stats. at Large, p. 1066
Colorado......	Battlement Mesa......	Dec. 24, 1892	27 Stats. at Large, p. 1053
"	Pike's Peak..........	Feb. 11, 1892	27 Stats. at Large, p. 1006
"	Plum Creek..........	June 23, 1892	27 Stats. at Large, p. 1029
"	South Platte.........	Dec. 9, 1892	27 Stats. at Large, p. 1044
"	White River..........	Oct. 16, 1891	27 Stats. at Large, p. 993
Montana......	Bitter Root..........	Feb. 22, 1897	29 Stats. at Large, p. 899
"	Flathead.............	Feb. 22, 1897	29 Stats. at Large, p. 911
"	Gallatin.............	Feb. 10, 1899	30 Stats. at Large, p. 1788
"	Lewis & Clarke........	Feb. 22, 1897	29 Stats. at Large, p. 907
New Mexico....	Gila................	Mar. 2, 1897	
"	Pecos River	May 27, 1898	{ 27 Stats. at Large, p. 998 / 30 Stats. at Large, p. 1773
Oregon.......	Ashland.............	Sep. 28, 1893	28 Stats. at Large, p. 1243
"	Bull Run............	June 17, 1892	27 Stats. at Large, p. 1027
"	Cascade.............	Sep. 28, 1893	28 Stats. at Large, p. 1240
South Dakota..	Black Hills..........	Sep. 19, 1898	{ 29 Stats. at Large, p. 902 / 30 Stats. at Large, p. 1783
Utah.........	Fish Lake...........	Feb. 10, 1899	30 Stats. at Large, p. 1787
"	Uintah..............	Feb. 22, 1897	29 Stats. at Large, p. 895
Washington....	Mount Rainier*........	Feb. 22, 1897	29 Stats. at Large, p. 896
"	Olympic.............	Apr. 7, 1900	{ 29 Stats. at Large, p. 901 / (Reduced, 31 Id., p. 1962)
"	Priest River..........	Feb. 22, 1897	29 Stats. at Large, p. 903
"	Washington..........	Feb. 22, 1897	29 Stats. at Large, p. 904
Wyoming......	Big Horn.............	Feb. 22, 1897	{ 29 Stats. at Large, p. 909 / 31 Stats. at Large, p. 1977
"	Crow Creek..........	Oct. 10, 1900	31 Stats. at Large, p. 1981
"	Teton...............	Feb. 22, 1897	29 Stats. at Large, p. 906
"	Yellowstone..........	Mar. 30, 1891	27 Stats. at Large, p. 989

*Superseding "Pacific Forest Reserve." The congressional act of March 2, 1899, (30 Stats. at Large, p. 993,) establishing the Mount Rainier National Park, took out of this reservation land covered by the park.

This list is not intended to be exhaustive. New reservations are being constantly created by executive order.

" favorable conditions of waterflows, and to furnish a
" continuous supply of timber for the use and necessi-
" ties of citizens of the United States." [1]

The data upon which these reservations are proclaimed are supplied by reports of special agents of the
general land office, and upon these reports the commissioner of the general land office or secretary of the
interior orders the lands embraced in the report temporarily withdrawn from the operation of the public
land laws pending the formal proclamation by the president. This action of the department officers in ordering
these withdrawals is deemed in law the act of the president.[2]

An order of withdrawal takes effect on the day of its
date, not on the date notice is received at the local office.[3]

As was said by Judge Bellinger, sitting as circuit
judge for the district of Oregon,[4] the reservation of these
lands is an appropriation to a special public use, and is
therefore a disposal of them, so far as the public domain
is concerned.

Reservations of this class may be restored to the
public domain by executive proclamation, or may be
reduced or changed, without special authority of
congress.[5]

Congress itself suspended certain of the proclamations for a limited time.[6]

---

[1] 30 Stats. at Large, p. 35.

[2] Wolsey v. Chapman, 101 U. S. 755, 769; Wilcox v. Jackson, 13 Peters,
498; In re State of California, 20 L. D. 327; Battlement Mesa Forest
Reserve, 16 L. D. 190; Union Pac. Ry. Co., 29 L. D. 261; In re Court,
Id. 638.

[3] In re Zumwalt, 20 L. D. 32; Currie v. State of California, 21 L. D.
134; In re Coffin, 31 L. D. 252.

[4] United States v. Tygh Valley L. and S. Co., 76 Fed. 693.

[5] Opinion of Asst. Atty.-Gen. Shields, 14 L. D. 209; 30 Stats. at Large,
p. 34, 36.

[6] 30 Stats. at Large, p. 34.

§ 198. **Status of mining claims within forest reservations.**—In the case of forest reservations the proclamations themselves provide specially for preserving the
status of mining claims valid and subsisting at the date
of the withdrawal. In a monograph published in the
transactions of the American institute of mining engineers, Mr. Pinchot, of the bureau of forestry, points out
that it was not the intention of the government in creating forest reserves to antagonize the mining industry.
The object was to protect the timber from destructive
fires and other waste, in order that it might be used in
such legitimate industries as mining and agriculture.[1]

All the proclamations creating forest reservations,
with one or two exceptions, contain the following
clauses:—

" Excepting from the force and effect of this procla-
" mation all lands which may have been prior to the date
" hereof embraced in any legal entry, or covered by any
" lawful filing, duly of record in the proper United
" States land office, or upon which any valid settlement
" has been made pursuant to law, and the statutory
" period within which to make entry or filing of rec-
" ord has not expired; and all mining claims duly
" located and held according to the laws of the United
" States and rules and regulations not in conflict there-
" with.

" *Provided,* that this exception shall not continue to
" apply to any particular tract of land, unless the entry-
" man, settler, or claimant continues to comply with the
" law under which the entry, filing, settlement, or loca-
" tion was made."

In some instances congress has passed special acts
opening forest reservations for the location of mining
claims. An act of this character was passed at the first
session of the fifty-fourth congress (February 26, 1896),[2]

[1] 28 Trans. Am. Inst. M. E., p. 339.
[2] 29 Stats. at Large, p. 11.

which provides that the Pike's Peak, Plum Creek, and South Platte forest reservations, in Colorado,—

" shall be open to the location of mining claims therein
" for gold, silver, and cinnabar, and that title to such
" mining claims may be acquired in the same manner
" as it may be acquired to mining claims upon the other
" mineral lands of the United States for such purposes;
" *provided,* that all locations of mining claims hereto-
" fore made in good faith within said reservation, and
" which have been held and worked in the same manner
" as mining claims are held and worked under existing
" law upon the public domain, are validated by this
" act."

And, by a subsequent section, the right to cut timber from such claim for actual mining purposes was authorized.[1]

Mineral claimants within forest reserves are permitted to use water thereupon.[2] They may also take timber and stone from the general reserve for use on the claim when the supply on the claim itself proves inadequate,[3] but the privilege does not extend to corporations.[4]

In the sundry civil appropriation bill passed June 4, 1897, congress declared with reference to forest reservations:—

" It is not the purpose or intent of these provisions,
" or of the act providing for such reservations, to
" authorize the inclusion therein of lands more valuable
" for the mineral therein, or for agricultural purposes,
" than for forest purposes." [5]

And in the same act it is provided:—

[1] See, for similar act relating to the Mount Rainier reserve, 30 Stats. at Large, p. 993.
[2] 30 Stats. at Large, p. 36.
[3] 21 L. D. 593; 31 L. D. 173.
[4] 31 L. D. 173.
[5] 30 Stats. at Large, p. 35.

" Nor shall anything herein prohibit any person from
" entering upon such forest reservations for all proper
" and lawful purposes, including that of prospect-
"ing, locating, and developing the mineral resources
" thereof; *provided,* that such persons comply with the
" rules and regulations covering such forest reserva-
" tions " [1]

The act provides for the restoration to the public
domain of tracts more valuable for mining or agricultural purposes, and then proceeds:—

" And any mineral lands in any forest reservation
" which have been or may be shown to be such and
" subject to entry under the existing mining laws of the
" United States and the rules and regulations applying
" thereto, shall continue to be subject to such location
" and entry, notwithstanding any provisions herein
" contained." [2]

Under these statutes it is now held by the land department that all forest reserves are open to the location of
mining claims.[3] There can be no doubt of the meaning
of congress upon this subject. Lands within forest
reserves are subject to the operation of the mining laws.[4]

§ 199. **Forest lieu selections under the act of June
4, 1897.**—The sundry civil expense act of June 4, 1897,[5]

[1] 30 Stats. at Large, p. 36.
[2] *Id.,* p. 37.
[3] Regulations of April 4, 1900, 30 L. D. 28.
[4] Coal is a mineral within the meaning of these acts. *In re* Crowder,
30 L. D. 92.

By an act of congress, passed May 14, 1896, the secretary of the
interior is empowered to permit the use of a right of way to the extent
of twenty-five feet, with the use of necessary ground, not exceeding forty
acres, within forest reservations, for the purpose of generating, manufacturing, and distributing electric power. See, also, act of May 11,
1898, which further extends the powers of the secretary of the interior
in this direction (30 Stats. at Large, p. 404). He is, moreover, authorized to lease portions of forest reserve for certain purposes (act of Feb.
28, 1899, 30 Stats. at Large, p. 908).

[5] 30 Stats., pp. 11, 34-36.

contained various provisions relating to forest reservations, one of which is as follows:—

" That in cases in which a tract covered by an unper-
" fected *bona fide* claim or by a patent is included within'
" the limits of a public forest reservation, the settler or
" owner thereof may, if he desires to do so, relinquish
" the tract to the government, and may select in lieu
" thereof a tract of *vacant land open to settlement,* not
" exceeding in area the tract covered by his claim or
" patent; and no charge shall be made in such cases for
" making the entry of record or issuing the patent to
" cover the tract selected; *provided further,* that in cases
" of unperfected claims the requirements of the law
" respecting settlement, residence, improvements, and so
" forth, are complied with on the new claims, credit
" being allowed for the time spent on the relinquished
" claims."

By a subsequent act,[1] it was provided that the selections should be confined to " *vacant, surveyed, non-*
" *mineral public lands which are subject to homestead*
" *entry*" with the proviso that the act should not affect
the rights of those who, previous to October 1, 1900,
should have relinquished their claims and made application for specific tracts in lieu thereof.

The purpose of the foregoing act, as stated by the land
department, was to relieve the situation in which the
settlers were placed by the creation of the reserves, and
to promote the objects for which the reservations were
established. Settlers and other claimants, by the establishment of the reserves, were placed in a state of greater
or less isolation from market, business centers, churches,
schools, and social advantages. The objects of the government being to improve and protect the forests, it
would be greatly assisted in accomplishing that object
by securing exclusive control of the lands within the

[1] 31 Stats. at Large, pp. 588, 614.

reservation; and at the same time the settlers would be benefited by an opportunity to exchange their claims for those less isolated. The act in question contains an offer by the government to exchange any of its lands that are vacant and open to settlement for a like quantity of lands within a forest reservation for which a patent has been issued, or to which an unperfected *bona fide* claim has been acquired.[1] The person desiring to select lieu lands under this act is confined to vacant lands open to settlement. They must not be occupied lands or lands reserved from settlement because of their mineral character.[2]

The land department has held that in case of forest lieu selections, lands must be shown by the selector to be non-mineral in character at the time the selection is approved.[3]

" Nor can selections be lawfully accepted until there
" is a showing that the selected land is vacant and not
" known to be valuable for minerals. No other lands
" are subject to selection, and no selection can be
" regarded as complete until these essential conditions
" are made to appear." [4]

" For the purpose of such determination resort must
" generally be had to outside evidence. This evidence
" must be furnished by the selector. It is his duty to
" show, in so far as physical conditions are concerned,
" that the land to which he seeks title is of the class and
" character subject to selection. He can not entitle him-
" self to a patent until he has made such showing. Until
" then his selection is not complete. Until then he has
" not complied with the terms and conditions necessary
" to the acquisition of a patent, and can not be regarded

[1] Kern Oil Co. *v.* Clarke, ·30 L. D. 550, 555.
[2] *Id.*
[3] *Id.,* S. C. on review, 31 L. D. 288.
[4] *Id.;* Leaming *v.* McKenna, 31 L. D. 318; Kern Oil Co. *v.* Clotfelter, 30 L. D. 583.

" as having acquired any vested interest in the selected " land." [1]

Whatever may have been the rule prior to October, 1900, subsequent to that time only such lands might be selected as were subject to homestead entry. [2]

If the land sought to be selected is occupied by others who have performed all the acts of location of a mining claim, excepting discovery, and who are diligently prosecuting work with a view to discovering mineral, the lands are not vacant or subject to selection. [3]

The act permitting the exchange of lands situated within forest reserves did not contemplate the relinquishment of a mineral claim as a basis for lieu selection. [4]

The department at one time ruled that unsurveyed as well as surveyed lands might be selected in lieu of those relinquished. [5]

But by the later statute, congress provided that surveyed lands only were subject to selection. [6]

Scrip may not be issued in lieu of lands patented within the reservation. [7]

[1] Kern Oil Co. *v.* Clarke (on review), 31 L. D. 288; Bakersfield Fuel and Oil Co. *v.* Saalburg, *Id.* 312; *In re* Cobb, *Id.* 220; Cosmos Exploration Co. *v.* Gray Eagle Oil Co., 112 Fed. 4, 104 Fed. 20. See Garrard *v.* Silver Peak Mines, 82 Fed. 578; Wisconsin Cent. R. R. Co. *v.* Price, 133 U. S. 496, 10 Sup. Ct. Rep. 341; Olive Land and D. Co. *v.* Olmstead, 103 Fed. 568; *In re* Harrel, 29 L. D. 553.

[2] 31 Stats. at Large, p. 614.

[3] Kern Oil Co. *v.* Clarke (on review), 31 L. D. 288; Cosmos Exploration Co. *v.* Gray Eagle Oil Co., 112 Fed. 4.

[4] Instructions, 28 L. D. 328; 31 Stats. at Large, pp. 558, 614. See, *ante,* § 143.

[5] *In re* Hyde, 28 L. D. 284.

[6] 31 Stats. at Large, pp. 588, 614. See Arden L. Smith, 31 L. D. 184; *In re* Peavey, *Id.* 186.

[7] Opinion, 28 L. D. 472. As to the right of the state to exchange sixteenth and thirty-sixth sections within the limits of forest reserves for other lands, see Hibberd *v.* Slack, 84 Fed. 571; State of California, 28 L. D. 57; Circ., *Id.,* p. 195; *In re* Hyde, *Id.* 284.

One who desires to select lieu lands is required to tender with his relinquishment of land formerly held a formal application to make the selection.[1]

The selected land must be of the same area as that relinquished.[2]

§ 200. **Reservoir sites.**—In addition to the reservations of public lands heretofore discussed, two other classes should be noted. Congress has provided for the selection of certain lands by the government for reservoir sites for irrigation purposes, and has provided for the location of reservoir sites by individuals and corporations engaged in the business of raising live-stock.

An act approved October 2, 1888,[3] provided that the director of the geological survey, under the supervision of the secretary of the interior, should investigate the extent to which the arid regions of the United States could be redeemed by irrigation, and select sites for reservoirs and other hydraulic works necessary for the storage and utilization of water for irrigation and the prevention of floods and overflows. The act contained the following reservation:—

"And all the lands which may hereafter be designated " or selected by such United States surveys for sites for " reservoirs, ditches, or canals for irrigation purposes, " and all the lands made susceptible of irrigation by " such reservoirs, ditches, or canals, are from this time " henceforth hereby reserved from sale as the property " of the United States, and shall not be subject after " the passage of this act to entry, settlement, or occu- " pation, until further provided by law."

So much of the foregoing act as provided for the withdrawal of the public lands from entry, occupation,

---

[1] *In re* Tiers, 29 L. D. 575.   [3] 25 Stats. at Large, p. 526.
[2] Circ. Inst., 29 L. D. 578, 580.

and settlement was repealed by the act of August 30, 1890,[1] which provided that settlement and entries might be made upon said lands " in the same manner as if " said law [*i. e.* the law of 1888] had not been enacted," adding, however, " Except that reservoir sites here- " tofore located or selected shall remain segregated " and reserved from entry or settlement as provided " by said act, unless otherwise provided by law, and " reservoir sites hereafter located or selected on public " lands shall in like manner be reserved from the date of " location or selection thereof."

The seventeenth section of the act of March 3, 1891,[2] provided that reservoir sites theretofore selected and thereafter to be selected should contain only so much land as might be necessary for the maintenance of reservoirs, excluding, so far as possible, lands occupied by actual settlers at the date of selection.

Under these acts reservoirs were selected by the government. The land department held that under the act of 1888 a selection of a reservoir site took effect as of the date of the act, and that rights of settlers which accrued subsequent thereto would be invalidated by the selection of the reservoir site.[3]

Rights of settlers which accrued after the selection and prior to the act of August 30, 1890, are not protected.[4]

Mineral or other entries made under such circumstances may be suspended by the department to await the determination of the authorities in the matter of the actual location of the reservoir; and if it appears that

---

[1] 26 Stats. at Large, p. 391.

[2] *Id.*, p. 1095.

[3] Attorney-general's opinion, 11 L. D. 220; Mary E. Bisbing, 13 L. D. 45; Newton Austin, 18 L. D. 4.

[4] George A. Cram, 14 L. D. 514.

the lands are not necessary for that purpose, the entries may be completed.[1]

The act of October 2, 1888, did not except mineral lands from selection as reservoir sites.[2] But a mineral location made subsequent to the act of August 30, 1890, (which repealed parts of the prior act,) and prior to the selection of a reservoir site, operated to defeat the selection in so far as the land selected was in conflict with the mineral location.[3]

But even, under the act of 1890, if a reservoir site has been selected prior to the location of a mining claim, the mineral claimant acquires no rights.[4]

The secretary of the interior has authority to release from a reservation portions of the land selected for a reservoir site. He has exercised this authority in favor of a homestead claimant.[5]

In addition to the provisions for the selection of reservoir sites by the government for irrigation purposes heretofore outlined, congress has provided for the location and purchase by individuals of public lands for reservoir sites.[6] The legislation upon this subject was enacted for the benefit of persons and corporations engaged in raising live-stock. Any person or corporation desiring to secure the benefit of the laws upon the subject must file a declaratory statement in the district land office. After the approval of a map showing the location of the reservoir, the land shown to be necessary for the proper use thereof is reserved from other disposition so long as the same is maintained and water

---

[1] Newton Austin, 18 L. D. 4; Colomokas Gold M. Co., 28 L. D. 172; Mary E. Bisbing, 13 L. D. 45.

[2] *Id.*

[3] John Gabathuler, 15 L. D. 418.

[4] Colomokas Gold M. Co., 28 L. D. 172.

[5] Carls Hildt, *Id.* 194.

[6] Act of January 13, 1897, 29 Stats. at Large, p. 484.

kept therein. The secretary of the interior is given power to administer the act, and has prescribed certain regulations governing the subject.[1] An exhaustive discussion of this legislation would not come within the legitimate scope of this work. It is sufficient to say that by the express provisions of the act authorizing the location of such reservoir sites by individuals, mineral lands are excepted from selection.[2]

ARTICLE IX. HOMESTEAD AND OTHER AGRICULTURAL CLAIMS.

§ 202. Introductory.

§ 203. Classification of laws providing for the disposal of the public lands.

§ 204. Manner of acquiring homestead claims.

§ 205. Nature of inceptive right acquired by homestead claimant.

§ 206. Location of mining claims within homestead entries.

§ 207. Proceedings to determine the character of the land.

§ 208. When decision of land department becomes final.

§ 209. The reservation of ''known mines'' in the pre-emption laws.

§ 210. Timber and stone lands.

§ 211. Scrip.

§ 212. Desert lands.

§ 202. Introductory.—We have no particular concern with the manner of acquiring title to lands of the public domain, other than those falling within the purview of the mining laws, except in so far as the administration of the public land system requires the adjustment of controversies between mineral claimants and those asserting privileges under the homestead and other laws applicable to public lands which are non-mineral in character. Incidentally, we are called upon to investigate the general scope of the latter class of laws, the character of lands to which they relate, the rules govern-

[1] 27 L. D. 200; 28 L. D. 552; In re Maier, 29 L. D. 400.
[2] 29 Stats. at Large, p. 484.

ing the determination of conflicts arising between mineral and other claimants, and the point of time in the proceedings seeking the transmission of title when these controversies are to be finally determined.

§ 203. **Classification of laws providing for the disposal of the public lands.**—The existing laws providing for the disposal of the public domain may be thus classified:—

(1) Those regulating the acquisition and enjoyment of rights upon public mineral lands, including in this designation laws applicable to coal and salines;

(2) The townsite laws;

(3) The homestead laws;

(4) Laws regulating the sale of lands chiefly valuable for timber or stone;

(5) Laws applicable to desert lands;

(6) The appropriation of lands by " covering" with bounty land warrants, agricultural college, private land, and other classes of "scrip," or lieu selections under special laws.

The pre-emption laws which, in one form or another, existed from an early period of our history until March 3, 1891, were repealed on that date,[1] and no longer form a part of our public land system, except so far as may be necessary to preserve and perfect rights accruing prior to the passage of the repealing act.

The timber-culture laws, originally enacted March 3, 1873,[2] a substitute for which was passed June 14, 1878,[3] were abrogated by section one of the same act, which effected the repeal of the pre-emption laws.

As to sales at public auction, they are no longer per-

[1] 26 Stats. at Large, p. 1093.   [3] 20 Stats. at Large, p. 113.
[2] 17 Stats. at Large, p. 605.

mitted,[1] except in cases of abandoned military or other reservations, isolated and disconnected fractional tracts authorized to be sold by section twenty-four hundred and fifty-five of the Revised Statutes, and other lands under special acts having local application.

Since March 2, 1889, with the exception of lands in the state of Missouri and in other specified localities, no sales or locations at private entry are allowed.[2]

As to the townsite laws, we have in a preceding article[3] fully discussed their provisions, and it is unnecessary to further consider them.

For the purposes announced in the introduction to this article, we need devote our attention only to those branches of the public land system which deal with homesteads, timber and stone lands, desert lands, and scrip locations. For certain illustrative purposes, we may also include in the category deserving consideration the repealed pre-emption laws.[4]

§ 204.   Manner of acquiring homestead claims.—The homestead laws secure to the head of a family, of lawful age, who is a citizen of the United States, or who has declared his intention to become such, the right to settle upon, enter, and acquire title to not exceeding one hundred and sixty acres of unappropriated non-mineral public lands, by establishing and maintaining residence thereon, and improving and cultivating the land for the continuous period of five years.[5]

---

[1] Act of March 3, 1891, §§ 9, 10; 26 Stats. at Large, p. 1099.

[2] 25 Stats. at Large, p. 854.

[3] See, ante, art. v, §§ 166-177.

[4] Act of May 18, 1898, abolishes the distinction previously obtaining between offered and unoffered lands. All are to be treated hereafter as unoffered (Missouri excepted). 30 Stats. at Large. p. 418.

[5] Rev. Stats., § 2289, as amended by act of March 3, 1891, § 5; 26 Stats. at Large, p. 1093. See, also, act of May 17, 1900, 31 Stats. at Large, p. 179.

To obtain an inceptive right to a homestead, the applicant files with the register of the local land office an
application, stating his qualifications, and describing the
land he desires to enter. If it appears from the tract-
books that the land is of the character subject to entry
under the law, and is clear,—that is, unappropriated,—
the applicant is permitted to make entry of the land;[1]
the receiver of the land office issues a receipt for the
fees paid for filing the application, a record is made in
the local office, and the fact reported to the general land
office. If the lands are returned as mineral, and borne
on the tract-books as such, the homestead claimant will
not be permitted to initiate his right until a hearing is
had for the purpose of determining the character of the
land. To use the common expression, the mineral must
be " proved off," before any right to the land can be
inaugurated under the agricultural land laws. If there
has been one hearing and an adjudication that the land
is mineral, it is improper to allow a homestead application to be filed until a hearing has been had as to conditions arising subsequent to the former adjudication.[2]
The prior adjudication is conclusive, and the department will not order another hearing as to the conditions
existing prior to first adjudication.[3] If, upon a hearing,
land is adjudged to be agricultural, the burden is upon
a mineral claimant thereafter asserting the mineral character to prove that fact.[4] Whatever may be the effect
of the surveyor-general's return as evidence in litigated
cases involving the character of the land,[5] the land

---

[1] As to practice in this regard see Germania Iron Co. v. James, 89
Fed. 811.

[2] Coleman v. McKenzie, 28 L. D. 348; S. C. on review, 29 L. D. 359;
Caldwell v. Gold Bar M. Co., 24 L. D. 258.

[3] Mackall v. Goodsell, 24 L. D. 553; Leach v. Potter, Id. 573.

[4] Majors v. Rinda, Id. 277.

[5] See, ante, §§ 105, 106, 107.

officers in administering the land laws accept such
return as controlling their action in the first instance.

§ 205.   **Nature of inceptive right acquired by homestead claimant.**—It would seem that the estate acquired
by a homestead claimant who has filed his application
and received his preliminary receipt from the receiver
of the land office is similar to that acquired by filing a
declaratory statement under the pre-emption laws.[1]   By
the pre-emption laws the United States did not enter
into any contract with the settler, or incur any obligation that the land occupied by him should ever be offered
for sale.   They simply declared that, in case their lands
were thrown open for sale, the privilege to purchase
should be first given to parties who had settled upon
and improved them.[2]

Public land covered by a pre-emption filing, as to
which there has been no payment made or final certificate issued, may be appropriated by congress to public
purposes, or otherwise disposed of, without infringing
any legal right held by the pre-emptioner.   A similar
rule is applied to inchoate homesteads.[3]

The supreme court of the United States has defined
the estate of a homestead claimant in the following
language:—

   " The right which is given to a person or corporation
" by a reservation of public lands in his favor is in-
" tended to protect him against the actions of third
" parties, as to whom his right to the same may be
" absolute.   But, as to the government, his right is only

---

[1] Shiver v. United States, 159 U. S. 491, 495, 16 Sup. Ct. Rep. 54;
Norton v. Evans, 82 Fed. 804, 807.

[2] Frisbie v. Whitney, 9 Wall. 187; Hutchins v. Low (Yosemite Valley
Case), 15 Wall. 77; Campbell v. Wade, 132 U. S. 34, 10 Sup. Ct. Rep. 9;
Black v. Elkhorn M. Co., 49 Fed. 549.

[3] Wagstaff v. Collins, 97 Fed. 3; Norton v. Evans, 82 Fed. 804;
Manners Construction Co. v. Rees, 31 L. D. 408.

" conditional and inchoate. . . . From this résumé of
" the homestead act it is evident, first, that the land
" entered continues to be the property of the United
" States for five years following the entry, and until a
" patent is issued; second, that such property is subject
" to divestiture upon proof of the continued residence
" of the settler upon the land for five years; third, that
" meantime such settler has the right to treat the land
" as his own, so far, and so far only, as is necessary to
" carry out the purposes of the act."[1]

Innumerable filings under the pre-emption laws have
been accepted for the same tract by the land office; but
from the moment a homestead entry is accepted and
the preliminary receipt issued no further applications
or filings for the tract are permitted, so long as the
entry remains uncanceled.

Although the land may be in fact mineral in character,
and a mining claim be located thereon, no application to
patent such mining claim will be received by the land
officers until a hearing is had to determine the character of the land.[2]

If the land be found at such hearing to be mineral in
character, a cancellation *pro tanto* of the homestead
entry will be ordered, and the mineral lands will be
segregated, whereupon the mineral applicant may proceed to patent. The extent of the segregation will necessarily depend upon the circumstances of each particular
case.

The filing of the preliminary homestead declaratory

---

[1] Shiver *v.* United States, 159 U. S. 491, 496, 497, 16 Sup. Ct. Rep. 54;
Hastings etc. R. R. Co. *v.* Whitney, 132 U. S. 357, 364, 10 Sup. Ct. Rep.
112; Frisbie *v.* Whitney, 9 Wall. 187; The Yosemite Valley Case, 15
Wall. 77; Norton *v.* Evans, 82 Fed. 804, 807; Wagstaff *v.* Collins, 97
Fed. 3; Crocker *v.* Donovan, 1 Okl. 165, 30 Pac. 374. But see opinion
of attorney-general, 2 Copp's Pub. Land Laws, p. 1198.

[2] Hooper *v.* Ferguson, 2 L. D. 712; Elda M. and M. Co., 29 L. D. 279.

statement, accompanied by non-mineral affidavits, establishes *prima facie* the agricultural character of the land.[1]

§ 206. Location of mining claims within homestead entries.—It would seem that when a given tract of land is lawfully covered by a homestead declaratory statement, and the claimant enters into possession, the land being *prima facie* non-mineral, the right of the homestead claimant against every one save the government immediately attaches. If a patent is subsequently issued, the title would relate back to the first act in the series of acts,—to wit, settlement, or the filing of the declaratory statement. It might also be plausibly asserted that in investigations which are subsequently instituted for the purpose of determining the character of the land, the time to which inquiry in this behalf should be directed would be the date of the inception of the rights of the homestead claimant. But this is not the rule followed by the land department. That tribunal proceeds upon the principle that a preliminary homestead filing and entry will not interdict mining locations within the land filed upon; that by such filing and entry the homestead claimant acquires no vested rights to the land, and if it is mineral in character it is subject to location and purchase under the mining laws.[2]

This ruling is deducible from a consideration of the nature of the inceptive right acquired by a homestead claimant outlined in the preceding section. But there is another important principle which is also to be recognized. No rights under the public land laws can be initiated through a trespass.[3] We do not think the law would sanction an invasion of a homestead claimant's

---

[1] Elda M. and M. Co., 29 L. D. 279.
[2] Manners Construction Co. *v.* Rees, 31 L. D. 408.
[3] See, *post*, § 218.

inclosure for the purpose of prospecting for minerals.
If the existence of minerals within the limits of an inchoate homestead become known, a mineral claimant
might enter peaceably, without force and in good faith,
for the purpose of perfecting a mining location, and thus
acquire a *status* which would enable him to initiate a
contest as to the character of the land, and if it were
shown to be mineral, secure a cancellation of the homestead claims *pro tanto*.[1]

**§ 207. Proceedings to determine the character of
the land.**—As heretofore indicated,[2] a mineral claimant
may take the initiative in securing an investigation as to the character of the land covered by
a homestead filing for the purpose of clearing the
records and enabling him to proceed to his patent.
Should this not be done, the determination of the quality
and character of the land necessarily arises at the time
the homestead claimant presents his application to make
final proof for the purpose of obtaining his patent. The
practice governing these proceedings is controlled by
the regulations prescribed by the secretary of the interior, and will be found in the appendix to this treatise.
Provisions are made for citing the interested parties to
appear before the local land officers, where testimony
may be adduced in support of their respective contentions. In these proceedings the return of the surveyor-
general is *prima facie* evidence of the character of the
land, and the burden of proof rests upon him who seeks
to contradict the return.[3] The mineral character of

---

[1] As to the protection afforded one who has secured a homestead receipt
or patent, see, *post*, § § 208, 779.

[2] See, *ante*, § 205.

[3] See, *ante*, § 106, and notes; Richter *v.* State of Utah, 27 L. D. 95;
Tulare Oil and M. Co. *v.* S. P. R. R. Co., 29 L. D. 269; Olive Land and
D. Co. *v.* Olmstead, 103 Fed. 568.

the land must be established as a present fact,[1] or where entry has been made and certificate of purchase issued the time to which the inquiry is to be addressed is the date of the entry.[2]

The question is really one of comparative value. Is the tract more valuable as a present fact for the mineral which it contains than for agricultural purposes? [3]

We have heretofore endeavored to formulate such rules for the determination of this question as seem to fall within the sanction of the law as determined by the courts and the land department. These rules will be found stated in a previous chapter,[4] and further repetition is unnecessary. The land sought to be subjected to the operation of the mining laws must be mineral in fact, and not in theory. Mere indications are insufficient.[5] Proximity to other mining claims does not establish the land as mineral;[6] neither does the fact that the land has been located as a mining claim establish such fact.[7] A tract of land containing mineral products in quantities sufficient to justify a prudent man in the

[1] Hamilton v. Anderson, 19 L. D. 168; Magalia G. M. Co. v. Ferguson, 6 L. D. 218; Dughi v. Harkins, 2 L. D. 721; Cleghorn v. Bird, 4 L. D. 478; Roberts v. Jepson, Id. 60. See ante, §§ 94, 98.

[2] Aspen M. Co. v. Williams, 27 L. D. 1; Olive Land and D. Co. v. Olmstead, 103 Fed. 568.

[3] Davis v. Weibbold, 139 U. S. 507, 11 Sup. Ct. Rep. 628; United States v. Reed, 28 Fed. 482; Ah Yew v. Choate, 24 Cal. 562; Mitchell v. Brown, 3 L. D. 65; Magalia G. M. Co. v. Ferguson, Id., 234; Peirano v. Pendola, 10 L. D. 536; Tinkham v. McCaffrey, 13 L. D. 517; Winters v. Bliss, 14 L. D. 59; Savage v. Boynton, 12 L. D. 612; Walton v. Batten, 14 L. D. 54.

[4] Tit. III, ch. i, §§ 94-98.

[5] Nevada Sierra Oil Co. v. Home Oil Co., 98 Fed. 673, 676; Cleary v. Skiffich, (Colo.), 65 Pac. 59; Tulare Oil and M. Co. v. S. P. R. R. Co., 29 L. D. 269; Olive Land and D. Co. v. Olmstead, 103 Fed. 568.

[6] Elda Mining and Milling Co., 29 L. D. 279.

[7] Harkrader v. Goldstein, 31 L. D. 87. See, ante, §§ 106, 107.

expenditure of time and money in extracting or developing it, is mineral in fact;[1] but the law cannot be subverted
to gratify a mere whim. One claiming land as a mining
location must establish, as against a prior location of
another class, that the ground so claimed is valuable to
operate as a mine, and unless this does appear as a fact
he will not be permitted to take it from another who has
previously located it in good faith for a different purpose.[2] While the mining interests are entitled to and
must receive protection against the encroachments of
persons who, under the guise of agricultural claimants,
seek to secure title to large tracts of mining land, the
rights of *bona fide* homestead claimants to lands clearly
agricultural in character are also entitled to the same
protection against adverse combinations of miners.[3]

The question of the character of land is always one
of fact; and the decisions of the land department upon
questions of fact in cases clearly within its jurisdiction
are conclusive.[4]

[1] See, *ante*, § 98.
[2] Cleary *v*. Skiffich, (Colo.), 65 Pac. 59, 60.
[3] Kenna *v*. Dillon, Copp's Min. Dec., p. 93.
[4] Parley's Park *v*. Kerr, 130 U. S. 256, 9 Sup. Ct. Rep. 511; Pac. M.
and M. Co. *v*. Spargo, 8 Saw. 645, 16 Fed. 348; Cowell *v*. Lammers, 10
Saw. 248, 257, 21 Fed. 200; Barden *v*. N. P. R. R. Co., 154 U. S. 288,
14 Sup. Ct. Rep. 1030; United States *v*. Winona and St. P. R. R. Co.,
67 Fed. 948; Lee *v*. Johnson, 116 U. S. 48, 6 Sup. Ct. Rep. 249; Johnson
v. Towsley, 13 Wall. 72; Warren *v*. Van Brunt, 19 Wall. 646; Shepley *v*.
Cowan, 91 U. S. 330; Moore *v*. Robbins, 96 U. S. 530; Marquez
v. Frisbie, 101 U. S. 473; Vance *v*. Burbank, *Id*. 514; Quinby *v*. Conlan,
104 U. S. 420; St. Louis Smelting Co. *v*. Kemp, *Id*. 636; Steele *v*. St.
Louis Smelting Co., 106 U. S. 447, 1 Sup. Ct. Rep. 389; Baldwin *v*.
Stark, 107 U. S. 463, 2 Sup. Ct. Rep. 473; United States *v*. Minor, 114
U. S. 233, 5 Sup. Ct. Rep. 836; Grant *v*. Oliver, 91 Cal. 158, 27 Pac. 596,
861; Shanklin *v*. McNamara, 87 Cal. 371, 26 Pac. 345; Powers *v*. Leith,
53 Cal. 711; Hays *v*. Steiger, 76 Cal. 555, 18 Pac. 670; Hess *v*. Bolinger,
48 Cal. 349; Caldwell *v*. Bush, 6 Wyo. 342, 45 Pac. 488; United States *v*.
Budd, 144 U. S. 167, 12 Sup. Ct. Rep. 575; United States *v*. Mackintosh,
85 Fed. 333; Northern Pac. R. R. Co. *v*. Soderberg, 85 Fed. 49; Mendota

The courts will not interfere with the officers of the government while in the discharge of their duties in disposing of the public lands.[1]

§ 208. When decision of land department becomes final.

—Before final certificate issues, a homestead entry is open to attack on the ground that the land embraced therein is mineral in character, without regard to the date of the alleged discovery.[2]

The submission of final homestead proof will not preclude a hearing as to the subsequent discovery of mineral upon the land involved where final certificate is not issued and the general land office requires new proof to be made.[3]

Any intermediate determination of the character of the land which does not result, and which is not intended to result, in its final disposal to one claimant or the other, does not preclude subsequent investigation on the part of the department as to the character of such land, inasmuch as the department retains jurisdiction to consider and determine the character of the land claimed until deprived thereof by the issuance of the patent.[4]

A decision of the department in such intermediate proceedings, holding a tract to be non-mineral, is con-

Club v. Anderson, 101 Wis. 479, 78 N. W. 185; Rood v. Wallace, 109 Iowa, 5, 79 N. W. 449; Potter v. Randolph, 126 Cal. 458, 58 Pac. 905; Standard Quicksilver Co. v. Habishaw, 132 Cal. 115, 64 Pac. 113; Peabody Gold M. Co. v. Gold Hill M. Co., 111 Fed. 817.

[1] For discussion of this subject see, ante, § 108; Litchfield v. The Register, 9 Wall. 575; Gaines v. Thompson, 7 Wall. 347; Cox v. McGarrahan, 9 Wall. 298; Savage v. Worsham, 104 Fed. 18; Cosmos Exploration Co. v. Gray Eagle Oil Co., Id. 20, S. C. on appeal, 112 Fed. 4. See, also, Potter v. Randolph, 126 Cal. 458, 58 Pac. 905.

[2] Jones v. Driver, 15 L. D. 514. Note the difference in case of forest lieu selections (Kern Oil Co. v. Clarke, 30 L. D. 550, S. C. on review, 31 L. D. 288.)

[3] Spratt v. Edwards, 15 L. D. 290.

[4] Searle Placer, 11 L. D. 441.

clusive up to the period covered by the hearing; but such decision will not preclude a further consideration, based on subsequent exploration.[1]

When the land has once been adjudged to be mineral, if subsequent development prior to patent demonstrates that the mineral then found has disappeared, or that it is worthless and unprofitable to work as a mining claim, and abandoned as such, it is not in any sense a readjudication of the former issues.[2] But the effect of the prior adjudication could not be overcome by the mere allegation that the land contained no valuable mineral; nor could the mineral claimant be called upon to sustain the mineral character of the land upon a mere repetition of the allegation made by the original agricultural claimant, that it is not mineral land.[3] A failure of the mineral claimant to perform his annual labor after a decision in his favor establishing the mineral character of the land will not inure to the benefit of the agricultural claimant.[4]

Lands duly and properly entered for a homestead under the homestead laws are, and continue to be, from the time of entry and pending proceedings before the land department, lands of the United States until patent is issued.[5]

The patent, when issued, is the judgment of a tribunal charged under the law with investigating the facts, and

[1] Stinchfield v. Pierce, 19 L. D. 12; McCharles v. Roberts, 20 L. D. 564; Dargin v. Koch, Id., 384; Caldwell v. Gold Bar M. Co., 24 L. D. 258; Mackall v. Goodsell, Id. 553; Leach v. Potter, Id. 573; Town of Aldridge v. Craig, 25 L. D. 505; Wilson v. Davis, Id. 514; Coleman v. McKenzie, 28 L. D. 348; Majors v. Linda, 24 L. D. 277.

[2] Dargin v. Koch, 20 L. D. 384.

[3] Coleman v. McKenzie, 28 L. D. 348, 353.

[4] Id., (2d review), 29 L. D. 359.

[5] Shiver v. United States, 159 U. S. 491, 16 Sup. Ct. Rep. 54; Wagstaff v. Collins, 97 Fed. 3.

thereafter the character of the land is no longer open to contestation.[1]

The final certificate issued by the receiver of a United States land office after the submission of final proof and payment of the purchase price, where such is required, has been repeatedly held to be the equivalent of a patent.

The holder of such certificate is vested with the complete equitable title; and after its issuance the government holds the dry legal title for the benefit of such holder.[2]

Such certificate having been once issued upon a perfected final agricultural entry, no subsequent discovery of mineral can defeat the title of the holder.[3]

A hearing will not be ordered to determine the character of land to which a certificate has been issued to a homestead claimant, unless the protestant alleges that the land was known to be valuable for minerals at the date of the issuance of final certificate.[4]

While such certificate, so long as it remains uncanceled, possesses the force of the patent, yet the power of supervision by the commissioner of the general land

[1] See, *post*, § 779.

[2] Witherspoon v. Duncan, 4 Wall. 210; Carroll v. Safford, 3 How. 441; Wisconsin R. R. Co. v. Price Co., 133 U. S. 496, 10 Sup. Ct. Rep. 341; Cornelius v. Kessel, 128 U. S. 456, 9 Sup. Ct. Rep. 122; Deffeback v. Hawke, 115 U. S. 392, 8 Sup. Ct. Rep. 95; Benson M. and S. Co. v. Alta M. and S. Co., 145 U. S. 428, 12 Sup. Ct. Rep. 877; Hamilton v. Southern Nev. G. and S. M. Co., 13 Saw. 113, 33 Fed. 562; Amador Medean Co. v. S. Spring Hill Co., 8 Saw. 523, 36 Fed. 668; Aurora Hill Cons. M. Co. v. 85 M. Co., 12 Saw. 355, 34 Fed. 515; Pac. Coast M. and M. Co. v. Spargo, 8 Saw. 645, 16 Fed. 348; Deno v. Griffin, 20 Nev. 249, 20 Pac. 308; Gulf C. and S. F. Ry. Co. v. Clark, 101 Fed. 678; Crane's Gulch M. Co. v. Scherer, 184 Cal. 350, 86 Am. St. Rep. 279, 66 Pac. 487; Horsky v. Moran, 21 Mont. 345, 53 Pac. 1064.

[3] Pac. Coast M. and M. Co. v. Spargo, 8 Saw. 645, 16 Fed. 348; Arthur v. Earle, 21 L. D. 92; Rea v. Stephenson, 15 L. D. 37; Dufrene v. Mace's Heirs, 30 L. D. 216; Reid v. Lavelle, 26 L. D. 100. See, also, Cosmos Exploration Co. v. Gray Eagle Oil Co., 104 Fed. 20, 44; S. C. on appeal, 112 Fed. 4, 11; Harkrader v. Goldstein, 31 L. D. 87; Chormicle v. Hiller, 26 L. D. 9; Aspen Min. Co. v. Williams, 27 L. D. 1.

[4] Dufrene v. Mace's Heirs, 30 L. D. 216.

office over the acts of the register and receiver of the local land office in the disposition of the public lands undoubtedly authorizes him, in proper cases, to correct and annul entries of land allowed by them. The exercise of such power is necessary to the administration of the land department.[1]

If the proceedings before the register and receiver are defective, or the proofs insufficient or fraudulent, or the jurisdictional facts wanting, the certificate may afterwards be canceled by the commissioner or secretary of the interior; or the entry may be suspended, a hearing ordered, and the party notified to show, by supplemental proof, a full compliance with the law, and on failure to do so, the entry may then be canceled.[2]

An agricultural entry covering land that is mineral in character, with the knowledge of prior mineral locations thereon, and of the fact that the land was at such time regarded by many in the vicinity as valuable for the mineral therein, must be canceled, as having been allowed for "known" mineral land.[3]

When such certificate is suspended, it cannot be used as evidence so long as the suspension continues.[4] Its cancellation, of course, deprives it of all force.[5]

[1] Harkness v. Underhill, 1 Black, 316; Knight v. U. S. Land Assn., 142 U. S. 161, 12 Sup. Ct. Rep. 258; Cornelius v. Kessel, 128 U. S. 456, 461, 9 Sup. Ct. Rep. 122; Ger. Ins. Co. v. Hayden, 21 Colo. 127, 40 Pac. 453; Orchard v. Alexander, 157 U. S. 372, 383, 15 Sup. Ct. Rep. 635; Michigan Lumber Co. v. Rust, 168 U. S. 589, 593, 18 Sup. Ct. Rep. 218; Hawley v. Diller, 178 U. S. 476, 20 Sup. Ct. Rep. 986.

[2] Hastings etc. R. R. Co. v. Whitney, 132 U. S. 357, 364, 10 Sup. Ct. Rep. 112; Caldwell v. Bush, 6 Wyo. 342, 45 Pac. 488; Hosmer v. Wallace, 47 Cal. 461; Hays v. Steiger, 76 Cal. 555, 18 Pac. 670; Michigan Lumber Co. v. Rust, 168 U. S. 589, 593, 15 Sup. Ct. Rep. 635; Hawley v. Diller, 178 U. S. 476, 20 Sup. Ct. Rep. 986. See, post, § 772.

[3] Aspen Cons. M. Co. v. Williams, 23 L. D. 34.

[4] Figg v. Handley, 52 Cal. 295; Vance v. Kohlberg, 50 Cal. 346; Vantongeren v. Heffernan, 5 Dak. 180, 226, 38 N. W. 52; Hestres v. Brennan, 50 Cal. 211; United States v. Steenerson, 50 Fed. 504.

[5] Murray v. Polglase, 17 Mont. 455, 43 Pac. 505.

This power of supervision and correction, however, is not an unlimited or arbitrary power. It can be exerted only when the entry was made upon false testimony or without authority of law. It cannot be exercised so as to deprive any person of land lawfully entered.[1]

Generally speaking, and for all practical purposes, the issuance of the final certificate to an agricultural entryman closes the case, and no collateral attack on the certificate so issued is allowed.

The land embraced in such final entry is absolutely withdrawn from the public domain, and is no longer subject to exploration or purchase under the mining laws, although it may subsequently appear that the lands are essentially mineral. Where a contest is pending, as a rule the certificate does not issue until final disposal is made, on appeal to the commissioner, and from him to the secretary, if such appeals be taken. Under ordinary circumstances, the supervision of the general land office at Washington is confined to an examination of the record as made in the local offices, for the purpose of ascertaining whether the facts presented justify the conclusions reached, the requisite jurisdictional facts appearing.

§ 209. The reservation of "known mines" in the preemption laws.—We have heretofore said [2] that the term " known mines," as used in the pre-emption act of 1841, and incorporated into the homestead laws by adoption under the provisions of section twenty-two hundred and eighty-nine of the Revised Statutes,[3] is not the precise equivalent of the term " mineral lands," as used in the mining laws, and should undoubtedly receive a more

---

[1] Cornelius v. Kessel, 128 U. S. 456, 461, 9 Sup. Ct. Rep. 122; Michigan Lumber Co. v. Rust, 168 U. S. 589, 18 Sup. Ct. Rep. 208.

[2] See, ante, § 86.

[3] Cosmos Exploration Co. v. Gray Eagle Oil Co., 104 Fed. 20, 46.

limited interpretation. It will be borne in mind that when this pre-emption act was passed the only mines of which the government had any knowledge were those containing copper, in the region of the great lakes, and those containing lead, in the Mississippi valley.[1]

The privilege of pre-emption during that period could be exercised only as to surveyed lands, and the public surveys had not been extended west of the Mississippi river. The government had at that time inaugurated a policy of leasing lead mines, and it is probable that the framers of these earlier laws had particular reference to those which came within the category of opened mines. In construing the term "known mines," as used in this law, which was subsequently re-enacted in later acts, and incorporated into the homestead law by adoption,[2] the supreme court of the United States announced its opinion that, so far as the decision of that court had gone, no lands had been held to be "known mines," unless at the time the rights of the purchaser accrued there was upon the ground an actual and opened mine which had been worked or was capable of being worked.[3]

Said that court, after reviewing the case of Deffeback v. Hawke:—[4]

"If upon the premises at that time there were not "actual 'known mines' capable of being profitably "worked for their product, so as to make the land more "valuable for mining than for agriculture, a title to "them acquired under the pre-emption act can not be "successfully assailed."[5]

[1] See, ante, § 36.

[2] Cosmos Exploration Co. v. Gray Eagle Oil Co., 104 Fed. 20, 46.

[3] Colo. C. and I. Co. v. United States, 123 U. S. 307, 327, 8 Sup. Ct. Rep. 121; Standard Quicksilver M. Co. v. Habishaw, 132 Cal. 115, 64 Pac. 113.

[4] 115 U. S. 392, 6 Sup. Ct. Rep. 95.

[5] Colo. C. and I. Co. v. United States, 123 U. S. 307, 328, 8 Sup. Ct. Rep. 121. See, also, Richards v. Dower, 81 Cal. 44, 22 Pac. 304; United

We think we are justified in our view, that " known
" mines " and " mineral lands " are not legal equivalents. As was said by Judge Ross, the words "min-
" eral lands" are certainly more general and much
broader than the words, " lands on which are situated
" any known salines or mines." [1] At all events, the pre-
emption laws have been repealed, and the term " known
" mines " has been eliminated from the homestead
laws.[2] The nearest approach to an equivalent still
remaining in the public land laws is the word " mine,"
as used in the townsite laws,[3] which laws have been
fully discussed in a previous article.[4]

§ 210.   Timber and stone lands.—The act of June 3,
1878,[5] commonly called the "Stone and timber act,"
was originally confined in its operations to California,
Oregon, Nevada, and Washington;[6] but by an amendatory act, passed August 4, 1892, its provisions were
extended to all the public land states.[7]

Under this act lands chiefly valuable for timber or
stone, unfit for cultivation, and consequently not subject
to disposal under the homestead laws, may be entered.
The quantity is limited to one hundred and sixty acres
to any one person.

States v. Reed, 28 Fed. 482; Gold Hill Q. M. Co. v. Ish, 5 Or. 104; *In re*
Abercrombie, 6 L. D. 393; Bellows v. Champion, 4 Copp's L. O. 17;
Nancy Ann Caste, 3 L. D. 169; Harnish v. Wallace, 13 L. D. 108; United
States v. Blackburn, (Ariz.), 48 Pac. 904.

[1] Cosmos Exploration Co. v. Gray Eagle Oil Co., 104 Fed. 20, 46. But
see Brady v. Harris, 29 L. D. 426.

[2] Cosmos Exploration Co. v. Gray Eagle Oil Co., 104 Fed. 20, 46.

[3] Rev. Stats., § 2392.

[4] See, *ante*, art. v, § 176. For comparison of various classes of patents,
see Horsky v. Moran, 21 Mont. 345, 53 Pac. 1064.

[5] 20 Stats. at Large, p. 89.

[6] United States v. Smith, 8 Saw. 101, 11 Fed. 487; United States v.
Benjamin, 10 Saw. 264, 21 Fed. 285.

[7] 27 Stats. at Large, p. 348.

An application to purchase under this act must be supported by evidence that the tract contains no mining or other improvements, except for ditch or canal purposes (when any such exist), nor any valuable deposit of gold, silver, cinnabar, copper, or coal. If the tract embraces a mining location based upon a discovery of a lode, and the showing is such as would justify a prudent man in spending his money in developing the same, the mining location may be segregated, and the balance of the land passed to entry under the stone and timber act.[1]

Provisions are made for the determination of the character of the lands prior to the issuance of patents, and for the issuance of final certificates of entry upon payment.

The lands embraced within an application to purchase under this act are not withdrawn from the mass of the public domain until such final certificate is issued,[2] and until that time are subject to exploration and purchase under the mining laws, if they are, in fact, mineral in character.[3]

The same principles of law in this respect apply to timber and stone entries as to inchoate homestead entries, discussed in preceding sections. The judgment of the department, culminating in the issuance of the final receipt or certificate, is final and conclusive as to the character of the land, and no subsequent discovery of mineral can affect the title of the purchaser.[4] This is a universal rule governing all classes of entries on the public domain.

With particular reference to lands chiefly valuable for

---

[1] Michie v. Gothberg, 30 L. D. 407.
[2] See Hawley v. Diller, 178 U. S. 476, 20 Sup. Ct. Rep. 986.
[3] Kaweah Colony, 12 L. D. 326.
[4] Chormicle v. Hiller, 26 L. D. 9.

building-stone, the department had held at different times that prior to passage of the stone and timber act such lands might be entered under the placer mining laws,[1] which practice was sustained by some of the courts,[2] and denied by others.[3]

The passage of the act of August 4, 1892,[4] however, restored this class of lands to the category of mineral lands, and henceforward they are subject to entry under the so-called placer mining laws. Such lands are mineral within the meaning of the railroad grants;[5] but are not reserved from grants to the state of sixteenth and thirty-sixth sections.[6] In the opinion of the land department, this last act did not withdraw such lands from entry under the stone and timber act,[7] thus holding that stone lands may be entered either as placers or under the stone and timber act, at the option of the claimant.[8] Lands must be unoccupied to be subject to entry under this act.[9]

§ 211. Scrip.—There are innumerable classes of so-called land scrip—such as agricultural college, Porterfield, Valentine, Sioux half-breed, supreme court, and others in infinite variety, issued under special laws of

---

[1] Bennett's Placer, 3 L. D. 116; McGlenn v. Weinbroeer, 15 L. D. 370; Vandoren v. Plested, 16 L. D. 508; Maxwell v. Brierly, 10 Copp's L. O. 50; Hayden v. Jamison, 26 L. D. 373, (reversing S. C., 24 L. D. 403). Contra: In re Delaney, 17 L. D. 120; Clark v. Ervin, Id., 550; Id., 16 L. D. 122; Conlin v. Kelly, 12 L. D. 1; In re Simon Randolph, 23 L. D. 322. See, ante, § 139.

[2] Freezer v. Sweeney, 8 Mont. 508, 21 Pac. 20; Johnson v. Harrington, 5 Wash. 93, 31 Pac. 316.

[3] Wheeler v. Smith, 5 Wash. 704, 32 Pac. 784.

[4] 27 Stats. at Large. p. 348.

[5] See, ante, §§ 158-159.

[6] See, ante, § 139.

[7] See Circ., 15 L. D. 360; 23 L. D. 322.

[8] Forsythe v. Weingart, 27 L. D. 680.

[9] Bateman v. Carroll, 24 L. D. 144.

congress, enabling the holder to " cover" unappropriated public lands, surrendering such scrip in payment for the lands sought to be entered. The term
" scrip" is frequently used in connection with forest
lieu lands, but no scrip is in fact issued in lieu of land
contained in forest reserves.[1] The subject of forest
lieu selections has already been discussed.[2] Mineral
lands cannot be so selected or covered with any class of
scrip.[3]

Selections of land for the purpose of utilizing scrip
are, of course, under the supervision of the land department, whose jurisdiction over the land is retained until
the selection is finally approved, a certificate to that
effect issued, and the scrip surrendered. As in case of
other entries, the land department passes upon the character of the land applied for. A scrip entry, whether
void or valid, segregates the land from the public domain and appropriates it to private use, so that
no legal entry of it can be made by any one so long as
such scrip entry remains uncanceled on the tract-books.[4]
But this does not necessarily inhibit a mining location
from being made on the land if such land was in fact at
the time of the scrip entry mineral in character, if such
location is made peaceably and in good faith. Upon
cancellation of the entry and clearing the tract-books
the mineral claimant could proceed to patent. The mining location would give the locator the *status* of a claimant such as would enable him to apply for a cancellation
of the scrip entry.

[1] Opinion Attorney-General, 28 L. D. 472.
[2] See, *ante*, § 200.
[3] *In re* A. V. Weise, 2 Copp's L. O. 130; *In re* Nerce Valle, *Id.* 178;
Commissioner's Letter, 3 Copp's L. O. 83.
[4] James *v.* Germania Iron Co., 107 Fed. 596.

§ 212. **Desert lands.**—By the act of March 3, 1877,[1] supplemented by the act of March 3, 1891,[2] provision is made for the reclamation of desert lands, and the transmission of the title in quantities not exceeding six hundred and forty acres. Mineral lands cannot be acquired under this act. Desert land claimants will rarely come in conflict with mining claimants. Of course, beds of gypsum, borax, nitrate, and carbonate of soda are found in the desert regions, but their mineral character is generally so obvious that no controversy is likely to arise. It would be much cheaper and more expeditious for a claimant to enter these classes of lands under the placer laws than to attempt to acquire title under the onerous provisions of the desert land laws. Should such conflicts arise, they would be governed by the same general rules of law applicable to other classes of entries discussed in the preceding sections of this article.

ARTICLE X.   OCCUPANCY WITHOUT COLOR OF TITLE.

§ 216. Naked occupancy of the public mineral lands confers no title—Rights of such occupant.

§ 217. Rights upon the public domain cannot be initiated by forcible entry upon the actual possession of another.

§ 218. Appropriation of public mineral lands by peaceable entry in good faith upon the possession of a mere occupant without color of title.

§ 219. Conclusions.

§ 216. **Naked occupancy of the public mineral lands confers no title—Rights of such occupant.**—Title to mineral lands of the public domain can be initiated and acquired only under the mining laws.[3] As was said by the supreme court of the United States,—

---

[1] 19 Stats. at Large, p. 377; 26 Stats. at Large, p. 1095.
[2] 26 Stats. at Large, p. 1095.
[3] Burns v. Clark, 133 Cal. 634, 85 Am. St. Rep. 233, 66 Pac. 12.

" No title from the United States to land known at
" the time of sale to be valuable for its minerals of gold,
" silver, cinnabar, or copper can be obtained under the
" pre-emption, homestead, or townsite laws, or in any
" other way than as prescribed by the laws specially
" authorizing the sale of such lands."[1]

There can be no strictly lawful possession of such
lands, unless that possession is referable to the mining
laws.

" There can be no color of title in an occupant who
" does not hold under any instrument, proceeding, or
" law purporting to transfer to him the title, or to give
" to him the right of possession. And there can be no
" such thing as good faith in an adverse holding, where
" the party knows that he has no title, and that under
" the law, which he is presumed to know, he can acquire
" none by his occupation."[2]

As heretofore shown,[3] it is a general rule that mere
occupancy of the public lands and placing improvements
thereon give no vested right therein as against the
United States, or one connecting himself with the government, by compliance with the law.[4]

---

[1] Deffeback v. Hawke, 115 U. S. 392, 404, 6 Sup. Ct. Rep. 95; Davis v.
Weibbold, 139 U. S. 507, 11 Sup. Ct. Rep. 628; Walker v. Southern Pac.
R. R. Co., 24 L. D. 172; Coleman v. McKenzie, 28 L. D. 348, 352, S. C.
on review, 29 L. D. 359.

[2] Deffeback v. Hawke, 115 U. S. 392, 404, 6 Sup. Ct. Rep. 95.

[3] See, ante, § 170.

[4] Sparks v. Pierce, 115 U. S. 408, 6 Sup. Ct. Rep. 102; Frisbie v. Whitney, 9 Wall. 187; Hutchins v. Low, 15 Wall. 77; Campbell v. Wade, 132
U. S. 34, 10 Sup. Ct. Rep. 9; Jourdan v. Barrett, 4 How. 169; Burgess v.
Gray, 16 How. 48; Gibson v. Chouteau, 13 Wall. 92; Oaksmith v. Johnston, 92 U. S. 343; Morrow v. Whitney, 95 U. S. 551; Buxton v. Travers,
130 U. S. 232, 9 Sup. Ct. Rep. 509; Northern Pac. R. R. Co. v. Colburn,
164 U. S. 383, 17 Sup. Ct. Rep. 98; Northern Pac. Ry. Co. v. Smith, 171
U. S. 260, 18 Sup. Ct. Rep. 794; Olive Land and D. Co. v. Olmstead
103 Fed. 568; Cosmos Exploration Co. v. Gray Eagle Oil Co., 104 Fed.
20, 46, S. C. on appeal, 112 Fed. 4; United States v. Holmes, 105 Fed. 41.
Judge Hawley held that a prior occupant of public land for business

While this is true, the occupant has certain rights based upon the fact of actual possession, which, from motives of public policy, are accorded to him.

As was said by the supreme court of California,—

" As against a mere trespasser, one in possession of a
" portion of the public land will be presumed to be the
" owner, notwithstanding the circumstance that the
" court has judicial notice that he is not the owner, but
" that the government is. This rule has been main-
" tained from motives of public policy, and to secure
" the quiet enjoyment of possessions which are intru-
" sions upon the United States alone." [1]

This is nothing more than a reiteration of the familiar rule, that, as against a mere intruder, or one claiming no higher or better right than the occupant, possession is *prima facie* evidence of title.[2]

But this is all that can be claimed. As against one connecting himself with the government, this occupancy must yield to the higher right.[3]

In Crossman *v.* Pendery,[4] Justice Miller said:—

" A prospector on the public mineral domain may
" protect himself in the possession of his *pedis posses-*
" *sionis* while he is searching for mineral. His posses-
" sion so held is good as a possessory title against all the

purposes could not be deprived of the same by a mineral claimant, unless the land was known to be mineral before the townsite claimant acquired or purchased his lot. (Bonner *v.* Meikle, 82 Fed. 697. See, also, Tarpey *v.* Madsen, 178 U. S. 215, 220, 20 Sup. Ct. Rep. 849.)

[1] Brandt *v.* Wheaton, 52 Cal. 430; Wilson *v.* Triumph Consol. M. Co. 19 Utah, 66, 75 Am. St. Rep. 718, 56 Pac. 300; Ramus *v.* Humphreys (Cal.), 65 Pac. 875.

[2] Campbell *v.* Rankin, 99 U. S. 261; Atwood *v.* Fricot, 17 Cal. 38, 16 Am. Dec. 567; English *v.* Johnson, 17 Cal. 108, 76 Am. Dec. 574; Hess *v.* Winder, 30 Cal. 349; Tarpey *v.* Madsen, 178 U. S. 215, 220, 20 Sup. Ct. Rep. 849; Kirk *v.* Meldrum (Colo.), 65 Pac. 633.

[3] Wilson *v.* Triumph Consol. M. Co., 19 Utah 66, 75 Am. St. Rep. 718, 56 Pac. 300.

[4] 8 Fed. 693.

" world, except the government of the United States.
" But if he stands by and allows others to enter upon his
" claim and first discover mineral in rock in place, the
" law gives such first discoverer a title to the mineral so
" first discovered, against which the mere possession of
" the surface cannot prevail."

In the case of Cosmos Exploration Co. *v.* Gray Eagle
Oil Co.,[1] the court held that lands which were actually
occupied and which were being explored for mineral
were not subject to selection in lieu of lands surrendered
under the forest reserve act of June 4, 1897. That act
permitted only such lands to be selected as were vacant
and open to settlement. The court recognizes the general rule that a mere occupant acquires no right against
one who is authorized to acquire the government title,
but in this case held that the forest lieu claimant was not
authorized to acquire the government title to occupied
land.[2]

§ 217. **Rights upon the public domain can not be
initiated by forcible entry upon the actual possession
of another.**—To what extent actual possession of any
portion of the public mineral lands prevents their valid
appropriation under the mining laws depends upon the
facts and circumstances of each particular case. There
are certain recognized principles, however, which are
necessarily involved in all such cases, the application of
which will, generally speaking, result in their proper
solution.

It is a doctrine well established that no rights upon
the public domain can be initiated by a forcible entry
upon the possession of another. A forcible and tortious
invasion of such possession confers no privilege upon
the invader, and cannot be made the basis of a posses-

---

[1] 112 Fed. 4.

[2] See, also, Kern Oil Co. *v.* Clarke, 30 L. D. 550.

sory title. A rightful seisin cannot flow from a wrongful disseisin.[1]

It has been distinctly held in cases arising under the former pre-emption laws that no right of possession could be established by settlement and improvement upon a tract of land conceded to be public where the pre-emption claimant forcibly intruded upon the actual possession of another who, having no other valid title than possession, had already settled upon, inclosed, and improved the tract; that such an intrusion was but a naked and unlawful trespass, and could not initiate a right of pre-emption.[2]

In conformity with this rule, it was wisely said by the late Judge Sawyer, in the ninth circuit, district of California, that the laws no more authorize a trespass upon the actual possession and occupation of another claiming a pre-emption right, for the purpose of locating and acquiring the title to a piece of mineral land, than to initiate an ordinary pre-emption right to a tract of agricultural land; that the law does not encourage or permit for any purpose unlawful intrusions and trespasses upon the actual occupation and possession of another. To permit a right to accrue or confer authority to thus initiate a title to the public land, would be to encourage strife, breaches of the peace, and violence of such character as to greatly disturb the public tranquillity.[3]

§ 218 **Appropriation of public mineral lands by peaceable entry in good faith upon the possession of a mere occupant without color of title.**—Conceding that

---

[1] Nevada Sierra Oil Co., v. Home Oil Co., 98 Fed. 673; Cosmos Exploration Co. v. Gray Eagle Oil Co., 104 Fed. 40, 46; S. C. on appeal, 112 Fed. 4; Thallmann v. Thomas, 111 Fed. 277.

[2] Atherton v. Fowler, 96 U. S. 513; Quinby v. Conlan, 104 U. S. 421; Hosmer v. Wallace, 97 U. S. 575; Justin v. Adams, 87 Fed. 377.

[3] Cowell v. Lammers, 10 Saw. 246, 21 Fed. 200; Nevada Sierra Oil Co. v. Home Oil Co., 98 Fed. 673; Thallmann v. Thomas, 111 Fed. 277.

the law is correctly stated in the three preceding sections, it is not to be understood that a mere occupant of the public mineral lands can by virtue of such occupancy prevent, under all circumstances, their appropriation for mining purposes. The law interdicts entries effected with force and violence for any purpose. But a mere intruder upon the public lands, a mere occupant, whose possession is not referable to some law or right conferred by virtue of an instrument giving color of title, can not by reason of such occupancy prevent a peaceable entry in good faith by one seeking to avail himself of the privilege vouchsafed by the mining laws.

The doctrine that by mere entry and possession a right may be acquired to the exclusive enjoyment of any given quantity of the public mineral lands, was condemned by the supreme court of California in its earliest decisions. If such doctrine could be maintained, said that court, —

" It would be fraught with the most pernicious and " disastrous consequences. The appropriation of these " lands in large tracts for agricultural and grazing pur- " poses, and the concentration of the mining interest in " the hands of a few persons, to the exclusion of the " mass of the people of the state, are some of the evils, " which would necessarily result from such a doc- " trine." [1]

There is no grant from the government under the acts of congress regulating the disposal of mineral lands, unless there is a location according to law and the local rules and regulations. Such a location is a condition precedent to the grant. If a party enters into possession, marks his boundaries, and performs his work for the period equal to the statute of limitations, such possession may ripen into a title equivalent to a location.[2]

---

[1] Smith v. Doe, 15 Cal. 101, 105; Gillan v. Hutchinson, 16 Cal. 154.
[2] See, post, § 688; Risch v. Wiseman (Or.), 59 Pac. 1111.

But mere possession for a shorter period, not based upon a valid location, would not prevent a valid location under the law.[1] This doctrine is clearly established by the supreme court of the United States in Belk v. Meagher,[2] affirming the decision of the supreme court of Montana. In that case Belk undertook to locate a mining claim. His entry was peaceable, and he did all that was necessary to perfect his rights, if the premises had been at the time open for that purpose. But at the time of such attempted appropriation the ground was covered by a prior, and, as the court found, a valid, subsisting location.   Subsequently this prior subsisting location lapsed, and thereafter Meagher relocated the claim, his entry for that purpose being made peaceably and without force. Belk brought ejectment, and being unsuccessful in the territorial courts, took the case on writ of error to the supreme court of the United States.

It having been established that when Belk made his relocation, in December, 1876, the claim of the original locators was still subsisting and valid, and remained so until January 1, 1877, the supreme court considered three propositions of law as necessarily arising in the case:—

(1) Whether Belk's relocation was valid as against everybody but the original locators, his entry being peaceable and without force;

(2) Whether, if Belk's relocation was invalid when made, it became effectual in law on the 1st of January, 1877, when the original claims lapsed;

(3) Whether, even if the relocation of Belk was invalid, Meagher could, after the 1st of January, 1877, make a relocation which would give him, as against Belk,

---

[1] Belk v. Meagher, 3 Mont. 65, 80.
[2] 104 U. S. 279, 284.

an exclusive right to the possession and enjoyment of the property, the entry for that purpose being made peaceably and without force.

All three propositions were resolved against Belk, the court holding that he had made no such location as prevented the lands from being in law vacant, and that others had the right to enter for the purpose of taking them up, if it could be done peaceably and without force. His possession might have been such as would have enabled him to bring an action of trespass against one who entered without any color of right, but it was not enough to prevent an entry made peaceably and in good faith for the purpose of securing a right under the acts of congress to the exclusive possession and enjoyment of the property.

This doctrine was held not to be in conflict with the rule announced by the same court in Atherton *v.* Fowler,[1] cited in a preceding section, wherein it was determined that a right of pre-emption could not be established by a *forcible* intrusion upon the possession of one who had already settled upon, improved, and inclosed the property.

The controlling force of the doctrine of Belk *v.* Meagher has been abundantly recognized by the courts since its promulgation.[2]

"Any other rule would make the wrongful occupation " of public land by a trespasser superior in right to a " lawful entry of it under the acts of congress by a " competent locator."[3]

---

[1] 96 U. S. 513.

[2] Noyes *v.* Black, 4 Mont. 527, 2 Pac. 769; Hopkins *v.* Noyes, 4 Mont. 550, 2 Pac. 280; Sweet *v.* Weber, 7 Colo. 443, 4 Pac. 752; Horswell *v.* Ruiz, 67 Cal. 111, 7 Pac. 197; Russell *v.* Hoyt, 4 Mont. 412, 2 Pac. 25; Du Prat *v.* James, 65 Cal. 555, 4 Pac. 562; Russell *v.* Brosseau, 65 Cal. 605, 4 Pac. 643; Garthe *v.* Hart, 73 Cal. 541, 15 Pac. 93; Nevada Sierra Oil Co. *v.* Home Oil Co., 98 Fed. 673; Thallmann *v.* Thomas, 111 Fed. 277.

[3] Thallmann *v.* Thomas, 111 Fed. 277.

A similar doctrine had been previously announced by Judge Deady, United States district judge, in Oregon,[1] where a location of mining ground in the possession of Chinese was upheld, on the theory that this class of aliens could acquire no rights by location, purchase, or occupancy upon the mineral lands of the public domain.

As was said by the supreme court of Montana,—

" Possession within a mining district, to be protected " or to give vitality to a title, must be in pursuance of " the law and the local rules and regulations. Posses- " sion, in order to be available, must be properly sup- " ported. . . . The mere naked possession of a mining " claim upon the public lands is not sufficient to hold " such claim against a subsequent location made in pur- " suance of the law, and kept alive by a compliance " therewith." [2]

The right of possession comes only from a valid location.[3]

The circuit court of appeals for the eighth circuit said:—

" Every competent locator has the right to initiate a " lawful claim to unappropriated public land by a " peaceable adverse entry upon it while it is in the pos- " session of those who have no superior right to acquire " the title or to hold the possession. . . . Any other " rule would make the wrongful occupation of the pub- " lic land by a trespasser superior in right to a lawful " entry of it under the acts of congress by a compe- " tent locator." [4]

Possession is good as against mere intruders;[5] but it is not good as against one who has complied with the

---

[1] Chapman v. Toy Long, 4 Saw. 28, Fed. Cas. No. 2610.

[2] Hopkins v. Noyes, 4 Mont. 550, 556, 2 Pac. 280.

[3] Russel v. Hoyt, 4 Mont. 412, 2 Pac. 25; Belk v. Meagher, 104 U. S. 284; Hamilton v. Huson, 21 Mont. 9, 53 Pac. 101.

[4] Thallmann v. Thomas, 111 Fed. 277, 279.

[5] Meydenbauer v. Stevens, 78 Fed. 787; Wilson v. Triumph Consol. M. Co., 19 Utah 66, 75 Am. St. Rep. 718, 56 Pac. 300.

mining laws.[1] A prospector may protect himself in his *pedis possessio,* while searching for mineral.[2]

Several cases appear in the reports which might be construed to be not entirely in harmony with the rule announced in the foregoing cases.[3] Some of them recognize the doctrine as to all ground not covered by the *pedis possessio.* Others do not mention the element of force as entitled to controlling weight in determining the question. In most of these cases the statement of facts upon which the decisions are based is very meager, and we are therefore unable to say to what extent, if at all, any of them repudiate the doctrine of Belk v. Meagher. Be that as it may, it cannot be denied that if there is any conflict between the decisions here referred to and the doctrine announced by the supreme court of the United States, they must, to the extent of such conflict, be disregarded.

While mere occupation without color of title is insufficient to prevent a competent locator from entering upon the land in a peaceable manner, for the purpose of making a location, no such entry may be made where title to the land has been secured or a valid location of the same has been made.[4] This rule is subject to the qualification that the lines of a junior lode location may

---

[1] Garthe v. Hart, 73 Cal. 541, 543, 15 Pac. 93; Cosmos Exploration Co. v. Gray Eagle Oil Co., 112 Fed. 4, 14.

[2] Crossman v. Pendery, 8 Fed. 693; Cosmos Exploration Co. v. Gray Eagle Oil Co., 112 Fed. 4.

[3] Eilers v. Boatman, 3 Utah, 159, 2 Pac. 63; Armstrong v. Lower, 6 Colo. 581; Weese v. Barker, 7 Colo. 178, 2 Pac. 919; Lebanon M. Co. v. Con. Rep. M. Co., 6 Colo. 380; Faxon v. Barnard, 4 Fed. 702; North Noonday v. Orient, 6 Saw. 507, 11 Fed. 125; Gird v. California Oil Co., 60 Fed. 531, 541; Quinby v. Conlan, 104 Fed. 420, 423; Goodwin v. McCabe, 75 Cal. 584, 588, 17 Pac. 705; Crossman v. Pendery, 8 Fed. 643; Cosmos Exploration Co. v. Gray Eagle Oil Co., 112 Fed. 4, 18. And see Kirk v. Meldrum (Colo.), 65 Pac. 633.

[4] Thallmann v. Thomas, 111 Fed. 277; Seymour v. Fisher, 16 Colo. 188, 27 Pac. 240; Belk v. Meagher, 104 U. S. 279.

be laid upon a valid senior location for the purposes of securing underground or extralateral rights not in conflict with any rights of the senior location;[1] and the land department has held that the lines of the junior claim may be so laid, though the senior claim has been *patented;*[2] but the supreme court of Montana doubts that this is the law.[3] The land department has also permitted the lines of a location to be laid upon prior patented agricultural land.[4] This subject will be fully discussed in another portion of this work.[5]

§ **219. Conclusions.**—We are justified in deducing the following general rules upon the subject under discussion:—

(1) Actual possession of a tract of public mineral land is valid as against a mere intruder, or one having no higher or better right than the prior occupant;

(2) No mining right or title can be initiated by a violent or forcible invasion of another's actual occupancy;

(3) If a party goes upon the mineral lands of the United States and either establishes a settlement or works thereon without complying with the requirements of the mining laws, and relies exclusively upon his possession or work, a second party who locates peaceably a mining claim covering any portion of the same ground, and in all respects complies with the requirements of the

[1] Del Monte Min. Co. *v.* Last Chance Min. Co., 171 U. S. 55, 83; Crown Point Min. Co. *v.* Buck, 97 Fed. 462; Empire State-Idaho M. and D. Co. *v.* Bunker Hill and Sullivan M. and C. Co., 109 Fed. 538; Empire State etc. Co. *v.* Bunker Hill etc. Co., 106 Fed. 471; Hidee Gold M. Co., 30 L. D. 420.

[2] Hidee Gold Min. Co., 30 L. D. 420. See, also, Empire State etc. Co. *v.* Bunker Hill etc. Co., 106 Fed. 471, S. C. (on appeal), 114 Fed. 417.

[3] State *v.* District Court (Mont.), 65 Pac. 1020.

[4] Alice Lode Claim, 30 L. D. 481.

[5] See, *post,* §§ 363, 365.

mining laws, is entitled to the possession of such mineral ground to the extent of his location as against the prior occupant, who is, from the time said second party has perfected his location and complied with the law, a trespasser.[1]

The peaceable adverse entry by the locator, coupled with the perfection of his location, operates in law as an ouster of the prior occupant.[2]

The lines of a junior lode location may be laid across a senior lode location for the purpose of defining the extralateral rights of the junior location; and the lines may be so laid across any unpatented public land, and perhaps across patented land, if done openly and peaceably.

In some of the states laws are enacted protecting the right of a discoverer upon the public mineral lands for a limited period of time, to enable him to perfect his location. Where no such local statutes are in force, according to the current of authority, by the policy of the law a reasonable time is allowed to such discoverer to complete his appropriation. During such periods the possession or occupation of the discoverer will be protected as against subsequent locators. This subject will be fully considered in another portion of this treatise, and the application of the doctrines above enunciated to such cases will there be fully explained.[3]

---

[1] This is substantially the charge to the jury upheld in Horswell *v.* Ruiz, 67 Cal. 111, 7 Pac. 197.

[2] Belk *v.* Meagher, 3 Mont. 65, 80.

[3] See, *post,* § 339.

CHAPTER IV.

OF THE PERSONS WHO MAY ACQUIRE RIGHTS TO PUBLIC MINERAL LANDS.

ARTICLE I. CITIZENS.
    II. ALIENS.
    III. GENERAL PROPERTY RIGHTS OF ALIENS IN THE STATES.
    IV. GENERAL PROPERTY RIGHTS OF ALIENS IN THE TERRITORIES.

ARTICLE I. CITIZENS.

§ 223. Only citizens, or those who have declared their intention to become such, may locate mining claims.

§ 224. Who are citizens.

§ 225. Minors.

§ 226. Domestic corporations.

§ 227. Citizenship, how proved.

§ 223. **Only citizens, or those who have declared their intention to become such, may locate mining claims.**—As the paramount proprietor of its public domain, the United States has not only the right to regulate the terms and conditions under which it may be disposed of, but it is also its privilege to designate the persons who may be the recipients of its bounty, and prescribe the qualifications of those who may acquire and enjoy permanent estates on its lands. In the exercise of this privilege, it has ordained that,—

" All valuable mineral deposits in lands belonging to
" the United States, both surveyed and unsurveyed, are
" hereby declared to be free and open to exploration and
" purchase, and the lands in which they are found to

" occupation and purchase, by citizens of the United
" States, and those who have declared their intention to
" become such, under regulations prescribed by law,
" and according to the local customs or rules of miners
" in the several mining districts, so far as the same are
" applicable and not inconsistent with the laws of the
" United States." [1]

Therefore, to lawfully locate and hold a mining claim,
the locator must either be a citizen of the United States
or he must have declared his intention to become such
in the manner provided by the naturalization laws of
congress.[2] To entitle an alien who has declared his intention of becoming a citizen of the United States to these
privileges, it must appear that such intention is a *bona
fide* existing one at the time of purchase.[3] Enlistment in
the army is a declaration of an intention to become a
citizen.[4] As to who may attack a location made by an
alien, and how it may be attacked, will be fully considered in a succeeding section. We here state simply the
abstract rule of law.

§ 224. **Who are citizens.**—It is hardly within the
legitimate scope of this treatise to exhaustively discuss
the law of citizenship. But as introductory to the pres-

---

[1] Rev. Stats., § 2319. Officers and employees in the United States land
office are prohibited from becoming interested in the purchase of any
public lands. Rev. Stats. § 452.

[2] By statute (30 Stats. at Large, p. 409), in Alaska a native-born
citizen of the dominion of Canada may enjoy the same mining rights
which are accorded citizens of the United States in British Columbia
and the Northwest territory; but no greater rights may be accorded to
such a Canadian citizen than are accorded to an American. This
statute has been declared to be inoperative at present because Americans
are not given any mining rights in Canada except the right to lease
mines, and our system does not contemplate the leasing of mines. 27
L. D. 267.

[3] Saturday Lode Claim, 29 L. D. 627.

[4] Strickley *v.* Hill (Utah), 62 Pac. 893.

entation of the law governing the qualifications of locators of mining claims, and the effect of alienage upon the validity of titles during the various stages of transmission from the government, as the primary source, to the ultimate grantee, we are justified in presenting in general outline the laws of congress upon the subject, and the decisions of the courts construing them in cases arising under the mining laws.

The fourteenth amendment to the constitution of the United States provides that,—

"All persons born or naturalized in the United " States, and subject to the jurisdiction thereof, are " citizens of the United States and of the state wherein " they reside."

The clause "subject to the jurisdiction of the United " States" means completely subject to the political jurisdiction of the United States,—owing direct and immediate allegiance.[1]

They may be citizens of the United States without being citizens of any particular state.[2]

Neither age nor sex is involved in the definition of the word "citizen." It therefore includes men, women, and children,[3] and, for certain purposes, as we shall have occasion to observe later on, corporations organized under the laws of the several states.[4]

Citizenship is either—

(1) By birth; or

(2) By naturalization.

Citizens by birth are those born within the United

---

[1] Elk *v.* Wilkins, 112 U. S. 94, 5 Sup. Ct. Rep. 41; Slaughterhouse Cases, 16 Wall. 36; Strauder *v.* West Virginia, 100 U. S. 303.

[2] Slaughterhouse Cases, 16 Wall 36; United States *v.* Cruikshank, 92 U. S. 542.

[3] 1 Bouvier's Law Dict., "*Citizen.*"

[4] See, *post,* § 226.

States, or in a foreign country, if at the time of their birth their fathers were citizens.[1]

There are certain exceptions to this rule of natural citizenship.

Children born in the United States of ambassadors and diplomatic representatives, whose residence, by a fiction of law, is regarded as a part of their own country, are not citizens.[2]

Indians born members of any of the Indian tribes within the United States which still hold their tribal relations are not citizens. They are not citizens, even if they have separated themselves from their tribe and reside among white citizens of a state, but have not been naturalized, or taxed, or recognized as citizens by the United States, or by any of the states.[3]

To become citizens, they must comply with some treaty providing for their naturalization or some statute authorizing individuals of special tribes to assume citizenship by due process of law.[4]

The fact that the parents of a child (Chinese) born in the United States are prohibited from becoming citizens does not militate against the citizenship of the child. Such child is a citizen.[5]

Generally speaking, citizenship by birth is the rule. Ordinarily, a married woman partakes of the husband's nationality,[6] although marriage with an alien produces no dissolution of the native allegiance of the wife,[7] unless

---

[1] Rev. Stats., § 1993; Ludlam v. Ludlam, 26 N. Y. 356, 84 Am. Dec. 193; Oldtown v. Bangor, 58 Me. 353; State v. Adams, 45 Iowa, 99, 24 Am. Rep. 760.

[2] In re Look Tin Sing, 21 Fed. 905.

[3] Elk v. Wilkins, 112 U. S. 94, 5 Sup. Ct. Rep. 41.

[4] 3 Am. and Eng. Ency. of Law, (1st ed.), p. 245, note 1.

[5] United States v. Wong Kim Ark, 169 U. S. 649, 18 Sup. Ct. Rep. 456; Lee Sing Far v. United States, 94 Fed. 834; In re Look Tin Sing, 21 Fed. 905.

[6] Wharton on Conflict of Laws, § 11.

[7] Shanks v. Dupont, 3 Peters, 242.

there be a withdrawal by her from her native country, or equivalent act expressive of her election to renounce her former citizenship as a consequence of her marriage.[1]

The law recognizes the right of expatriation; but instances of it among Americans are so rare that the subject deserves no attention here.

One not a citizen may become such by complying with the provisions of the federal naturalization laws.[2]

Naturalization gives the alien all the rights of a natural-born citizen. He thereby becomes capable of receiving property by descent and of transmitting it in the same way, whereas, as an alien, he might not so receive it.[3]

Ordinarily, naturalization is not complete until the lapse of a probationary period after a preliminary declaration of intention to become a citizen. During this period, between the taking out of "first" and "second" papers, the declarant is not considered as a citizen to the extent that he may either exercise the elective franchise or hold office. He is entitled to no privileges other than those specially vouchsafed to him by the law. In the location of mining claims he is endowed with the full rights of a citizen, to the same extent as if his naturalization were completed by taking the final oath and the issuance to him of his final papers. Therefore, for all purposes within the purview of this treatise, we shall treat an alien who has declared his intention to become a citizen as if he were fully naturalized; and when we employ the word "naturalization," it is to be understood as designating the act which con-

---

[1] Ruckgaber v. Moore, 104 Fed. 947; Comititis v. Parkerson, 56 Fed. 556. But see Pequignot v. City of Detroit, 16 Fed. 211.

[2] Rev. Stats., §§ 2165-2174.

[3] Jackson, ex dem. Doran v. Green, 7 Wend. 333.

fers upon the alien the right to enjoy, in common with
citizens, the privilege of locating and purchasing mining
claims upon the public domain.

§ 225. **Minors.**—Minors born in the United States are
citizens, and may locate mining claims. There is no
requirement in the general mining laws that the citizen
shall be of any particular age. To say that minors are
not qualified locators is to say that they are not citizens.
The conclusion is strengthened by the circumstance that
in some instances the statutes expressly require that the
citizen shall be of a particular age before he may acquire
certain classes of public lands. Thus, in reference to
coal lands, the provision is, that every person above the
age of twenty-one years who is a citizen of the United
States may enter such lands.[1] A similar provision exists
as to homesteads under the federal laws.[2] The expression of a requirement as to age in some instances, and
the omission of it in others, is significant.[3] It is quite
true that minors may not transmit title during infancy
with the same freedom as adults. During this minority
they are incapacitated from entering into binding contracts, except for necessaries, and, generally speaking,
may act only through guardians, under the supervision
of the courts. But this circumstance does not prevent
them from acquiring property. As was said by the supreme court of California,—

"Nor is there any reason in the nature of things why
" a minor may not make a valid location. . . . It may
" be added that, so far as we know, it is the practice in
" many mining communities for minors to locate
" claims."[4]

[1] Rev. Stats., § 2347.
[2] *Id.*, § 2289.
[3] Thompson *v.* Spray, 72 Cal. 528, 14 Pac. 182.
[4] *Id.*

Lindley on M.—25

The fact that this is the recognized practice in many mining communities is, perhaps, not of controlling weight; but it carries with it the suggestion that a contrary rule would disturb many titles acquired in good faith, and that such rule should not be invoked without the most substantial and cogent reasons.

§ 226. **Domestic corporations.**—By domestic corporations, we mean those created or organized under the laws of the several states of the union, using the term in contradistinction to foreign corporations, or those who owe their existence to the laws of foreign countries. The latter class will receive attention when we deal with the subject of aliens. A corporation is a citizen of the state which created it.[1]

A corporation created and existing under the laws of a state is to be deemed a citizen within the meaning of the statute regulating the right to acquire public mineral lands,[2] and as such is competent to purchase and hold a mining claim.[3]

The supreme court of the United States has held that a corporation created under the laws of the states of the union, *all of whose members are citizens* of the United States, is competent to locate, or join in the location, of a mining claim upon the public lands of the United States in like manner as individual citizens.[4]

The italics in the above quotation are ours. Judge

---

[1] St. Louis v. Wiggin's Ferry Co., 11 Wall. 423; Chicago and N. W. R. R. v. Whitton, 13 Wall. 270; Muller v. Dows, 94 U. S. 444; Germania Fire Ins. Co. v. Francis, 78 U. S. 210; Block v. Standard D. and D. Co., 95 Fed. 978; Wilson v. Triumph Cons. M. Co., 19 Utah, 66, 75 Am. St. Rep. 718, 56 Pac. 300.

[2] Rev. Stats., § 2319.

[3] North Noonday M. Co. v. Orient M. Co., 6 Saw. 299, 316, 1 Fed. 522. See, also, Tacoma Land Co. v. Northern Pac. R. R. Co., 26 L. D. 503.

[4] McKinley v. Wheeler, 130 U. S. 630, 9 Sup. Ct. Rep. 638, followed in Dahl v. Montana C. Co., 132 U. S. 264, 10 Sup. Ct. Rep. 97; Thomas v. Chisholm, 13 Colo. 105, 21 Pac. 1019.

Knowles, speaking for the circuit court of appeals in the ninth circuit, is of the opinion that the inference to be drawn from this decision, although not so stated, is that only corporations whose stockholders are citizens can locate mining claims.[1] We do not think that the supreme court intended to lay particular stress upon the word "*all.*" If it did, it went entirely beyond the exigencies of the case under consideration. There was nothing in the facts requiring such a ruling. It is probable that the expression was used unadvisedly, and not with the intention of establishing a fixed rule that a corporation organized under the laws of a state can not lawfully acquire or hold unpatented mining claims if one of its stockholders is an alien. In the territories, under the alien act of March 3, 1887,[2] aliens were prohibited from acquiring real estate; yet domestic corporations might freely acquire such lands, and aliens were permitted to own and hold twenty per cent of the stock of such domestic corporations. The act was subsequently superseded by an act which contained no provision with reference to corporations.[3] Is it to be presumed in the states wherein the laws make no discrimination between aliens and citizens, with regard to the acquisition and enjoyment of landed estates, that the government should insist that none of the stock of a domestic corporation holding or locating an unpatented mining claim shall be held by an alien, under penalty of being refused a title by patent, if sought, or of suffering escheat after patent, should the government see fit to enforce it? Judge Knowles, in the case above referred to,[4] gives a logical solution of the question. Where a corporation is created by the laws of a state, the

[1] Doe v. Waterloo M. Co., 70 Fed. 455.
[2] 24 Stats. at Large, p. 477.
[3] 29 Stats. at Large, p. 618.
[4] Doe v. Waterloo M. Co., 70 Fed. 455.

legal presumption is, that its members are citizens of the same state.[1]

A suit may be brought in the federal courts by or against a corporation; but in such case it is regarded as a suit brought by or against the stockholders of a corporation, and for the purposes of jurisdiction it is *conclusively presumed* that *all* the stockholders are citizens of the state which by its laws created the corporation.[2]

In the language of Judge Knowles,—

"Congress was familiar with this rule, and, it seems " probable, intended to establish a similar rule under " the mineral land act of 1872."

This view is strengthened by a consideration of the section of the Revised Statutes regulating the proof of citizenship in proceedings under the mining laws.

"Proof of citizenship under this chapter may consist, " in the case of an individual, of his own affidavit " thereof; in the case of an association of persons unin- " corporated, of the affidavit of their authorized agent, " made on his own knowledge or upon information and " belief; and in the case of a corporation organized " under the laws of the United States, or of any state " or territory thereof, by the filing of their charter or " certificate of incorporation."[3]

Under this section, the land department holds that a properly authenticated certificate of incorporation filed by a corporation that is applying for a mineral patent is sufficient proof of citizenship.[4]

It is not within the power of the land department to determine whether such corporation is authorized under its charter to acquire patent for mineral lands.[5]

---

[1] Ohio R. R. Co. *v.* Wheeler, 1 Black, 286.

[2] Muller *v.* Dows, 94 U. S. 444.

[3] Rev. Stats., § 2321.

[4] Rose Lode Claim, 22 L. D. 83; Silver King M. Co., 20 L. D. 116; Gen. Min. Circ., par. 76. (See appendix.)

[5] Rose Lode Claim, 22 L. D. 83.

Where a corporation is incompetent by its charter to take a title to real estate, a conveyance to it is not void, but only voidable, and the sovereign (*i. e.* the state to which it owes its existence) alone can object. It is valid until assailed in a direct proceeding for that purpose.[1]

The supreme court of Montana has held that the fact that an alien owns stock in a corporation which has acquired title to mining claims does not disturb the title of the corporation to such claims.[2]

If it be true that all of the stockholders of a domestic corporation seeking to locate public mineral lands must be citizens, as may be inferred from the ruling of the supreme court of the United States, then a properly authenticated certificate of such corporation is conclusive evidence of such citizenship.[3]

We think we are justified in deducing the rule that within the states domestic corporations may locate and hold mining claims, and that an inquiry as to the citizenship of stockholders is not permitted, for the simple reason that such citizenship is conclusively presumed. As to the *status* of such corporations in the territories, we will have occasion to investigate it in a subsequent section.

The supreme court of the United States has suggested the question as to the extent of ground which may be located by a corporation; that is, whether it will be treated as one person, and is entitled to locate only to the extent permitted to a single individual, or otherwise.[4]

We do not consider that, in the case of lode claims, the situation presents any embarrassment, as no one

---

[1] National Bank *v.* Matthews, 98 U. S. 621, 628.

[2] Princeton M. Co. *v.* First Nat. Bank, 7 Mont. 530, 19 Pac. 210.

[3] Doe *v.* Waterloo M. Co., 70 Fed. 455; Ohio R. R. *v.* Wheeler, 1 Black, 286; Muller *v.* Dows, 94 U. S. 444.

[4] McKinley *v.* Wheeler, 130 U. S. 630, 9 Sup. Ct. Rep. 638.

person or association of persons can locate by one location in excess of the statutory limit of fifteen hundred by six hundred feet of surface. As to placers, it might be considered as an association of persons, which it is in one sense, and so be entitled to locate as such one hundred and sixty acres, if it had eight stockholders, and they usually have many more. We think, however, that the safer rule is to consider the corporation as a single individual and entitled to locate but twenty acres of placer ground. The "association" referred to in the statute is evidently a number of individual locators, uniting for the purpose of making a joint location, and not an incorporated company.

§ 227. **Citizenship, how proved.**—Citizenship may be proved like any other fact.[1] It is a question for the jury.[2]

In proceedings before the land department, and in actions brought in the local courts under the sanction of the Revised Statutes,[3] to determine the right of possession, the judgment in such actions being advisory to the land department, the law provides that proof of citizenship may consist, in the case of an individual, of his own affidavit thereof; in the case of an association of persons unincorporated, by the affidavit of their authorized agent, made on his own knowledge, or upon information and belief; and in the case of a corporation organized under the laws of the United States, or of any state or territory thereof, by the filing of a certified copy of their charter or certificate of incorporation.[4] However, proof

---

[1] Thompson v. Spray, 72 Cal. 528, 14 Pac. 182; Strickley v. Hill, 22 Utah, 257, 83 Am. St. Rep. 786, 62 Pac. 893.

[2] Golden Fleece M. Co. v. Cable Cons., 12 Nev. 313.

[3] Rev. Stats., § 2326.

[4] Id., § 2321; North Noonday M. Co. v. Orient M. Co., 6 Saw. 503, 11 Fed. 125; Clark's Pocket Quartz Mine, 27 L. D. 351.

by affidavit is not the only method of establishing citizenship.[1] It may be established by any other competent legal evidence. In fact, in the case of naturalized citizens, some of the courts have insisted that exemplifications of the record of naturalization should be produced,[2] or its loss accounted for, and the foundation laid for the introduction of secondary evidence. This is not the rule in the land department, however, which is governed entirely by the provisions of the Revised Statutes.[3] Neither is it the rule sanctioned by all the courts.[4]

In all actions between individuals disconnected with proceedings to obtain title under the federal mining laws, if we admit that the question of citizenship may in any such action be properly the subject of inquiry,—a proposition we are not prepared to concede,[5]—the rules of evidence prescribed by the several states would control. In such cases, we do not understand that an *ex parte* affidavit would be admissible. The opposing party could not be deprived of the right to cross-examine the witness by whose oath the fact of citizenship is sought to be proved.

It may be here noted, although we shall have occasion to again refer to the subject, that in proceedings before the land department upon applications for patents under the mining laws, proof of citizenship is not required of

---

[1] Thompson v. Spray, 72 Cal. 528, 14 Pac. 182; Boyd v. Nebraska, 143 U. S. 180, 12 Sup. Ct. Rep. 375; Providence Gold M. Co. v. Burke (Ariz.), 57 Pac. 641; Strickley v. Hill, 22 Utah, 257, 83 Am. St. Rep. 786, 62 Pac. 893.

[2] Wood v. Aspen M. Co., 36 Fed. 25.

[3] *In re* John Mooney, 3 Copp's L. O. 68; Circ. Instructions, Aug. 2, 1876, *Id.* 68; Mining Regulations, July 26, 1901, par. 68. (See appendix.)

[4] Strickley v. Hill, 22 Utah, 257, 83 Am. St. Rep. 786, 62 Pac. 893.

[5] Buckley v. Fox (Idaho), 67 Pac. 659; McKinley Creek M. Co. v. Alaska United M. Co., 183 U. S. 563, 22 Sup. Ct. Rep. 84.

the original locators or intermediate owners, but of the applicant for patent or adverse claimants only.[1]

It has been said that a presumption of citizenship arises from the fact of residence.

The supreme court of Arizona has held that—

"It will be presumed that a man being a resident of " the United States, and who has made a mining loca- " tion, was a citizen of the United States, . . . where " it appears that he recorded at or near the time a loca- " tion notice reciting these facts. Such evidence will " make out a *prima facie* title."[2]

This was on the assumption that a location notice, when recorded, is, by reason of the law authorizing or requiring the record, *prima facie* evidence of the facts therein recited, following the rule approved in Colorado[3] and elsewhere.[4]

In the opinion of Judge Sawyer, in the class of proceedings provided for by the Revised Statutes,[5] no presumptions of fact should be indulged, but each party must establish his right by evidence.[6] These presumptions, if properly considered to any extent, are, of course, disputable.

After patent or certificate of purchase has once issued, however, the citizenship of the patentee is conclusively presumed. This presumption arises from the accepted rule that the qualifications of an applicant for patent are necessarily involved in the inquiry made by the land

[1] Cash Lode, 1 Copp's L. O. 97; City Rock and Utah *v.* Pitts, *Id.* 146; Wandering Boy, 2 Copp's L. O. 2.

[2] Jantzen *v.* Arizona C. Co. (Ariz.), 20 Pac. 93, 94.

[3] Strepey *v.* Stark, 7 Colo. 614, 5 Pac. 111.

[4] Flick *v.* Gold Hill M. Co., 8 Mont. 298, 20 Pac. 807; Dillon *v.* Bayliss, 11 Mont. 171, 27 Pac. 725; Brady *v.* Husby, 21 Nev. 453, 33 Pac. 801; Garfield M. and M. Co. *v.* Hammer, 6 Mont. 53, 8 Pac. 153; Hammer *v.* Garfield M. and M. Co., 130 U. S. 291, 9 Sup. Ct. Rep. 548; Wood *v.* Aspen, 36 Fed. 25.

[5] Rev. Stats., § 2326.

[6] Bay State S. M. Co. *v.* Brown, 10 Saw. 243, 21 Fed. 167.

department, and the patent, when issued, is a conclusive adjudication that the patentee possessed the *status* of a citizen.[1]

As between individuals, the question of the alienage of a locator or claimant of a mining claim can only arise in the proceedings brought before the land department upon application for patent, or in actions brought under section twenty-three hundred and twenty-six of the Revised Statutes. In all other classes of cases it is not open to question. We have attempted to demonstrate this in a succeeding section.[2]

ARTICLE II. ALIENS.

§ 231. Acquisition of title to unpatented mining claims by aliens.

§ 232. The effect of naturalization of an alien upon a location made by him at a time when he occupied the *status* of an alien.

§ 233. What is the legal *status* of a title to a mining claim located and held by an alien who has not declared his intention to become a citizen?

§ 234. Conclusions.

§ 231. **Acquisition of title to unpatented mining claims by aliens.**—As we have already seen, aliens who have not declared their intention to become citizens can not lawfully locate mining claims upon the public mineral domain. But it frequently occurs that such aliens do so locate such claims and transmit the title so acquired apparently the same as if this disqualification did not exist; and there are innumerable examples of aliens purchasing from citizen locators, and in turn transmit-

---

[1] Justice M. Co. v. Lee, 21 Colo. 260, 52 Am. St. Rep. 216, 40 Pac. 444, (overruling the decision of the court of appeals in the same case); Lee v. Justice M. Co., 2 Colo. App. 112, 29 Pac. 1020.

[2] See, § 233. See, also, Buckley v. Fox (Idaho), 67 Pac. 659; Sherlock v. Leighton (Wyo.), 63 Pac. 580; McKinley Creek M. Co. v. Alaska United M. Co., 183 U. S. 563, 22 Sup. Ct. Rep. 84.

ting the title so acquired to others. These facts suggest the following inquiries:—

(1) What is the *status* of the title to a mining claim located and held by an alien?

(2) What estate may such alien transmit to another?

(3) What is the effect of subsequent naturalization upon a location made at a time when the locator occupied the *status* of an alien?

(4) What is the *status* of the title to a mining claim located and held jointly by an alien and a citizen?

In discussing these questions and others incidentally arising out of them, we shall encounter but little difficulty in arriving at the true state of the law. Although in the decisions of the courts of last resort heretofore rendered in the several states we find differences of opinion, diversity of views, and inharmonious conclusions, the supreme court of the United States, the final arbiter of these problems, has comprehensively dealt with the situation and cleared the atmosphere.

This follows necessarily from the fact that the courts of each state act independently of the courts of other states. While all are called upon to construe the same laws in controversies between individuals arising out of rights asserted in public mineral lands, and to a limited degree in their several jurisdictions are auxiliary to the land department in administering these laws, yet no one state is bound by the rules announced by another. Results are reached on independent lines of reasoning. A rule of interpretation announced in one state is directly negatived in another; in still another, the rule is accepted in a modified form. Such questions are essentially federal in their nature, and the doctrine once definitely announced by the supreme court of the United States practically dispenses with the necessity of analyzing or attempting to harmonize the views theretofore announced by the state courts. The attitude of the state courts in the past, however, as well as of some of the subordinate federal tribunals, touching these questions is of sufficient interest to justify comment, and in this light they will be discussed in the succeeding sections.

§ 232. **The effect of naturalization of an alien upon a location made by him at a time when he occupied the status of an alien.**—Let us first consider what effect the act of naturalization has upon the estate, if any, acquired by an alien by virtue of a discovery and location of public mineral lands, in all respects valid, except as affected by the alienage of the locator. Let us examine the adjudicated cases on this and analogous subjects, commencing with the rulings of the land department. We note the decisions of the executive department, arranged in chronological order:—

"Naturalization has a retroactive effect, so as to be " deemed a waiver of all liability to forfeiture and a " confirmation of the alien's former title." [1]

"A foreigner may make a mining location and dispose " of it, providing he becomes a citizen before disposing " of the mine." [2]

"Naturalization has a retroactive effect, so as to be " deemed a waiver of all liability to forfeiture and a " confirmation of his former title." [3]

An alien having made a homestead entry, and subsequently filed his intention to become a citizen, it is held that, in the absence of an adverse claim, the alienage at the time of entry will not defeat the right of purchase.[4]

An alien can acquire no right to public land before filing a declaration of intention to become a citizen, and

[1] Cash Lode, 1 Copp's L. O. 97.
[2] Kempton Mine, *Id.*, 178.
[3] *In re* Wm. S. Wood, 3 Copp's L. O. 69.
[4] Ole Krogstad, 4 L. D. 564.

his subsequent qualification will not relate back so as to defeat an intervening right.[1]

A mining location made by an alien is not void but voidable, and a subsequent declaration to become a citizen made by the locator prior to the inception of any adverse right relates back to the date of the location and validates the same.[2]

In the case of Wulff v. Manuel,[3] Judge De Witt, speaking for the supreme court of Montana, in an able opinion, took the extreme view that an alien could not take title by *purchase* from a citizen locator, and therefore the subsequent naturalization (during a trial involving the alien's right to a patent in a suit upon an adverse claim) could not retroact in favor of such alien. We shall have occasion to refer particularly to this case and the reasoning of the distinguished judge when dealing with the nature of the title acquired and held by an *alien locator*. Undoubtedly, entertaining these views in the case of a purchase by an alien from a citizen locator, the supreme court of Montana would have announced in the hypothetical case under consideration that naturalization could not retroact in favor of an alien locator.

The supreme court of New York has held that naturalization gives the alien all the rights of a natural-born citizen; he thereby becomes capable of receiving property by descent, and of transmitting it in the same way. It also has a retroactive operation, and lands purchased by an alien who is afterwards naturalized may be held by him and transmitted by him in the same manner as lands acquired after naturalization.[4]

[1] Titamore v. S. P. R. R., 10 L. D. 463. This was the case of a pre-emption filing within railroad indemnity limits.

[2] McEvoy v. Megginson, 29 L. D. 164.

[3] 9 Mont. 279, 23 Pac. 723.

[4] Jackson, *ex dem.* Doran v. Green, 7 Wend. 333.

The same rule is recognized in Alabama.[1]

Judge Hallett announced his views that, in the absence of any intervening rights, upon declaring his intention to become a citizen of the United States, an alien locator may have the advantage of work previously done and of a record previously made by him in locating a mining claim on the public mineral lands.[2]

And the late Judge Sawyer held that if a locator, even though not a citizen, performed all the acts necessary to make a valid location, and did the work necessary to keep his claim good, had he been a citizen, until he conveys to a citizen, such citizen grantee, taking possession and control, keeping up the monuments and markings, and performing the necessary conditions to keep the claim good, acquires a good and valid right to the claim as against those asserting rights subsequent to such conveyance.[3]

The supreme court of the United States has frequently held that if an alien holding under a purchase becomes a citizen before "office found," that the act of naturalization retroacts to the original acquirement of title, and perfects the title in the alien.[4]

In accordance with this doctrine, that tribunal has held, reversing the supreme court of Montana, that in the case of a purchase by an alien from a qualified locator, the subsequent naturalization retroacted in his favor, removed the infirmity, and entitled him to a patent.[5] The case in which this rule was established involved the right to a patent, the action being instituted under sec-

---

[1] Harvey v. State, 40 Ala. 689.

[2] Crœsus M. and M. Co. v. Colo. L. and M. Co., 19 Fed. 78.

[3] North Noonday M. Co. v. Orient M. Co., 6 Saw. 299, 315, 1 Fed. 522.

[4] Wulff v. Manuel, 9 Mont. 279, 23 Pac. 723, (citing Osterman v. Baldwin, 6 Wall. 122; Craig v. Radford, 3 Wheat. 594; Fairfax v. Hunter, 7 Cranch, 607; Governeur v. Robertson, 11 Wheat. 332). See, also, Long Jack Min. Co. v. Megginson, 82 Fed. 89.

[5] Manuel v. Wulff, 152 U. S. 505, 14 Sup. Ct. Rep. 651.

tion twenty-three hundred and twenty-six of the Revised Statutes, in which form of action citizenship of the applicant for patent was necessarily involved.

§ 233. What is the legal status of a title to a mining claim located and held by an alien who has not declared his intention to become a citizen?—In the hands of a citizen locator, the estate acquired by a perfected valid location is property in the highest sense of the term; it may be conveyed, mortgaged, taxed, sold on execution, is descendible to heirs, and may be the subject of devise. It is an estate acquired by purchase. Washburn, in his treatise on real property, says:—

" In one thing all writers agree, and that is, in con-
" sidering that there are two modes only, regarded as
" classes, of acquiring title to land,—namely, *descent*
" and *purchase,*—purchase including every mode of ac-
" quisition known to the law, except that by which an
" heir on the death of an ancestor becomes substituted
" in his place as owner by the act of the law." [1]

" Purchase," said Lord Coke, "includes every other
" method of coming to an estate but merely that by an
" inheritance, wherein the title is vested in a person,
" not by his own act or agreement, but by single opera-
" tion of law." [2]

Purchase denotes any means of acquiring an estate out of the common course of inheritance.[3]

" Certainly," said the supreme court of Montana,
" no one would contend that when a person locates min-
" ing ground he acquires a right to the same by descent.
" He must acquire it, then, by purchase." [4]

But the same court held in a case where an alien purchaser from a citizen locator was endeavoring to obtain a patent (having been naturalized during the trial and

[1] 3 Washburn on Real Property, 4.
[2] Co. Litt. 18, cited in 2 Black. Com. 241; 2 Bouvier's Law Dict. 403.
[3] 2 Black. Com. 242.
[4] Meyendorf *v.* Frohner, 3 Mont. 282, 320.

prior to judgment), that the parallel of the alien heir claiming by descent and the alien miner claiming under the mining laws was complete as to the principle under consideration, and that such alien was not entitled to hold the estate purchased. In fact, he took nothing.[1] This doctrine, however, was denied by the supreme court of the United States.[2]

An estate cast by descent upon one having inheritable blood might certainly be conveyed by purchase to an alien, who might hold until office found. Why should not the estate acquired by an alien from a citizen locator by purchase be subject to the same rule?

Nothing is better settled under the common law than that an alien could take by purchase and hold until deprived of his estate by action of the sovereign, in proceedings called "inquest of office."[3]

Said the supreme court of the United States:—

" By the common law an alien cannot acquire real
" property by operation of law, but may take it by act
" of the grantor and hold it until office found; that is,
" until the fact of alienage is authoritatively established
" by a public officer, upon an inquest held at the instance
" of the government. The proceedings which contain
" the finding of the fact upon the inquest of the officer is
" technically designated in the books of law as 'office
" 'found.' It removes the fact upon which the law
" divests the estate and transfers it to the government
" from the region of uncertainty, and makes it a matter
" of record. It was devised, according to the old law-
" writers, as an authentic means to give the king his
" right by solemn matter of record, without which he,
" in general, could neither take nor part with anything;
" for it was deemed a part of the liberties of England,

[1] Wulff v. Manuel, 9 Mont. 279, 23 Pac. 723.

[2] Manuel v. Wulff, 152 U. S. 505, 14 Sup. Ct. Rep. 651.

[3] Taylor v. Benham, 5 How. 233; Fairfax v. Hunter, 7 Cranch, 603, 618; 2 Kent's Com. 54; 1 Washburn on Real Property, 49; People v. Folsom, 5 Cal. 373; Territory v. Lee, 2 Mont. 124, 129; Racouillat v. Sansevain, 32 Cal. 376; De Merle v. Matthews, 26 Cal. 455.

" and greatly for the safety of the subject, that the king
" may not enter upon or seize any man's possession
" upon bare surmises without the intervention of a
" jury. By the civil law some proceeding equivalent
" in its substantive features was also essential to take
" the fact of alienage from being a matter of mere sur-
" mise and conjecture and to make it a matter of record.
" Such a proceeding was usually had before the local
" magistrate or council, and might be taken at the in-
" stance of the government or upon the denouncement
" of a private citizen." [1]

Said the same court, in a previous case, speaking
through Justice Johnson :—

" That an alien can take by deed and can hold until
" office found, must now be regarded as a positive rule
" of law, so well established that the reason of the rule
" is little more than a subject for the antiquary. It, no
" doubt, owes its present authority, if not its origin, to
" a regard to the peace of society and a desire to protect
" the individual from arbitrary aggression. . . . But
" there is one reason assigned by a very judicious com-
" piler which for its good sense and applicability to the
" nature of our government makes it proper to intro-
" duce it here. I copy it from Bacon. 'Every person,'
" says he, 'is supposed a natural-born subject that is
" 'resident in the kingdom and that owes a local alle-
" 'giance to the king till the contrary be found by office.'
" This reason, it will be perceived, applies with double
" force to the resident who has acquired of the sovereign
" himself, whether by purchase or by favor, a grant of
" freehold." [2]

If the government can, by direct conveyance to an
alien, vest in him a title to the absolute fee without doing
a vain thing, why may not an alien acquire a more limited estate, subject to an inquiry as to his qualifications,
when he seeks a conveyance of the ultimate fee?

In Governeur's Heirs v. Robertson,[3] from which we

---

[1] Phillips v. Moore, 100 U. S. 208, 212.
[2] Doe, ex dem. Governeur's Heirs v. Robertson, 11 Wheat. 332.
[3] 11 Wheat. 332, 355.

have heretofore quoted, the grant in question was by the commonwealth of Virginia to Brantz, an alien, his title being assailed by a subsequent grantee from the same commonwealth. The question argued and intended to be exclusively presented was whether a patent for land to an alien was not an absolute nullity. It was there said that the king is a competent grantor in all cases in which an individual may grant, and any person *in esse* and not *civiliter mortuus* is a competent grantee, *femes covert,* infants, aliens, persons attainted of treason or felony, and many others are expressly enumerated as competent grantees.

In cases of alien locators, the objection suggests itself that the government does not *grant;* there is no act done or performed by it prior to the issuance of a patent. The alien accepts an invitation which was not extended to him, but was exclusively confined to others, and attempts by his own act to create the relationship of grantor and grantee.

The reply to this is: A citizen obtains the grant by his own act; that is, by complying with the provisions of the law laid down by the paramount proprietor. The lands are the property.of the government. It alone has the power to object and inquire into the qualifications of the locator. " With a regard to the peace of society and " a desire to protect the individual from arbitrary ag- " gression," the government reserves to itself the right to inquire into these qualifications. For this purpose, at least, the presumption indulged by Bacon, quoted by the supreme court of the United States (*supra*), " that every person is supposed a natural-born subject " that is resident in the kingdom and that owes alle- " giance to the king, till the contrary be found by office," as well as those mentioned in a preceding section,[1] may

---

[1] See, *ante,* § 227.

be invoked for the purpose of preserving the estate from invasion, "upon base surmises without the intervention " of a jury."

It has been authoritatively determined by the supreme court of the United States, that the estate created by a perfected mining location and transferred to an alien is not analogous to an estate created by descent; in other words, that it is not an estate created by operation of law.[1]

It has been definitely determined that a mining locator takes his estate in the claim located by purchase.[2]

We think we are justified in asserting that the following principles have been established by the weight of authority:—

(1) That a location made by an alien, if otherwise valid, creates in him an estate which can be divested only at the instigation of the government in a proceeding to which it is either directly or indirectly a party;[3]

(2) That such estate when vested in a citizen is as complete as if originally acquired by him by location, and no one, not even the government, can assail his title.

While the supreme court of the United States was extremely guarded in its decision in Manuel v. Wulff (*supra*), and avoided any intimation that a transfer from an alien locator to an alien would be considered as vesting any estate, yet its use of the term "qualified " locator" was simply a statement of the fact in that particular case, as there was no controversy over the qualification of the locator. He was an admitted citizen. It was not necessary, nor did the court propose, inferentially or otherwise, to rule upon a state of facts not

---

[1] Manuel v. Wulff, 152 U. S. 505, 14 Sup. Ct. Rep. 651.

[2] McKinley M. Co. v. Alaska United M. Co., 183 U. S. 563, 571, 22 Sup. Ct. Rep. 84.

[3] *Id.*

before it. In a later case, however, the supreme court
distinctly held that "the meaning of the case of Manuel
" v. Wulff is, that the location by an alien and all the
" rights following from such location are voidable, not
" void, and are free from attack by any one except the
" government." [1]

The circuit court of appeals of the eighth circuit had
previously held, in a case where an alien was one of the
locators, that mining rights acquired by such alien by
his location constitute no exception to the general rule
that the right to defeat a title on the ground of alienage
is reserved to the government alone.[2]

This rule has been adhered to by several courts,[3] and,
as heretofore observed, has been finally settled by the
supreme court of the United States.

A contrary rule was at one time asserted by the supreme court of Montana, that court holding that a possessory title of mineral land, founded on a valid location,
and held by compliance with local mining laws, may be
transferred from one to another, so long as it does not
pass into the hands of one incapable of acquiring complete title, in which latter case the grant reverts to the
government, and the land becomes subject to relocation.[4]

In a case where alien Chinese were in possession of
public mineral lands in Oregon,[5] Judge Deady issued an

---

[1] McKinley M. Co. v. Alaska United M. Co., 183 U. S. 563, 572, 22 Sup.
Ct. Rep. 84.

[2] Billings v. Aspen M. Co., 51 Fed. 338, 341; S. C. on rehearing, 52
Fed. 250.

[3] Wilson v. Triumph Cons. M. Co., 19 Utah, 66, 75 Am. St. Rep. 718,
56 Pac. 300; Lone Jack M. Co. v. Megginson, 82 Fed. 89 (C. C. A., 9th
Ct.); Tornanses v. Melsing, 109 Fed. 710 (C. C. A., 9th Ct.); Kjellman
v. Rogers, 109 Fed. 1061; Little Emily M. Co. v. Couch (U. S. C. C.,
Idaho, unreported). See, also, Crœsus Min., M. and S. Co. v. Colorado
Land and M. Co., 19 Fed. 78.

[4] Tibbitts v. Ah Tong, 4 Mont. 536.

[5] Chapman v. Toy Long, 4 Saw. 28, Fed. Cas., No. 2610. But see Lohman v. Helmer, 104 Fed. 178.

injunction, at the suit of citizens who had located such
lands while in the occupancy of the Chinese; but it does
not appear from the report of the case that the Chinese
claimed to be in possession under any location made by
them or others through whom they entered. In addition,
some stress was laid upon the inhibition of the constitution of that state, that " No Chinaman not a resident of
" the state at the adoption of this constitution shall ever
" hold any real estate or mining claim, or work any min-
" ing claim therein."

In California, the question is incidentally discussed
in several cases, brought under the provisions of section
twenty-three hundred and twenty-six of the Revised
Statutes, to determine a right to a patent. We quote
from the opinion of that court:—

" It would seem to follow that as the right to posses-
" sion and the right to a patent are made to depend upon
" citizenship, the complaint which forms the basis upon
" which these rights are supported should show the
" plaintiffs to possess those qualifications without which
" the judgment they seek and the consequences to flow
" from that judgment cannot be reached. Where a right
" is conferred upon a particular class of persons, or by
" reason of possessing some special qualification or
" *status*, he who claims such a right must show himself
" to belong to the class designated or to possess the
" qualification prescribed or the *status* mentioned as the
" basis of the right."

When we come to analyze the decisions of other tribunals in the quest of apt analogies, we find much conflict
of opinion. As a matter of historical interest we will
review them.

Judge Sawyer, in the ninth circuit court, held that if
a citizen and an alien jointly locate a claim, not exceeding the amount of ground allowed by law to one locator,
such location is valid as to the citizen, and a conveyance

from both of such locators to a citizen gives a valid title.[1]

The same rule has been announced in Arizona and Utah.[2]

The supreme court of Nevada has intimated that a mining claim located by an alien might be relocated and held by a citizen.[3]

The same court also announced that an alien should be protected in the possession of the public lands the same as a citizen;[4] but, in the light of its other rulings, there is but little doubt that it entertained the view that a location made by an alien was not protected from a peaceful entry by a citizen for the purpose of relocating, and that such relocation would connect the relocator with the government title. The same rule was announced by the supreme court of Utah, though that court admitted the rule that the government alone could raise the question of non-citizenship.[5]

That an alien may purchase an unpatented mining claim, and has full and complete right to convey the same, his estate being valid against every person but the government, has been determined in several of the states.[6]

It has also been determined that in the absence of an inhibition in the state laws, an alien may succeed to the title to a mining claim by descent and may maintain any

---

[1] North Noonday M. Co. v. Orient M. Co., 6 Saw. 299, 1 Fed. 522.

[2] Providence G. M. Co. v. Burke (Ariz.), 57 Pac. 641; Strickley v. Hill, 22 Utah, 257, 83 Am. St. Rep. 786, 62 Pac. 893.

[3] Golden Fleece G. and S. M. Co. v. Cable Cons., 12 Nev. 313. See, also, McEvoy v. Megginson, 29 L. D. 164.

[4] Courtnay v. Turner, 12 Nev. 345.

[5] Wilson v. Triumph Cons. M. Co., 19 Utah, 66, 75 Am. St. Rep. 718, 56 Pac. 300, citing Sparks v. Pierce, 115 U. S. 408, 6 Sup. Ct. Rep. 102; Brandt v. Wheaton, 52 Cal. 430.

[6] Ferguson v. Neville, 61 Cal. 356; Gorman Mining Co. v. Alexander, 2 S. Dak. 557, 51 N. W. 346; Territory v. Lee, 2 Mont. 124; Strickley v. Hill, 22 Utah, 257, 83 Am. St. Rep. 786, 62 Pac. 893.

action to protect it which is not connected with the patent proceeding.[1]

The court in the Nevada case (*supra*) was careful to add:—

"We must not be understood as holding that in all "actions in relation to mining claims it is necessary for "plaintiffs to aver citizenship. We are discussing the "requirements of a complaint in the special case pro- "vided by the act of congress to determine the right of "possession of a mining claim under the laws of con- "gress, in which the successful party becomes entitled "on the judgment-roll to apply for patent—a case in "which the parties must connect themselves with the "title of the government, and show compliance with the "acts of congress, and our conclusions are limited to "such action."[2]

The action provided for by section twenty-three hundred and twenty-six of the Revised Statutes is undoubtedly equivalent in its legal effect to "inquest of office." Each party is called upon to establish his qualifications to receive patent, and the question of citizenship is a material one. In this class of actions, the courts have generally insisted that citizenship of the litigating parties must be alleged, and, of course, proved.[3]

In ordinary actions, some courts have held that this is not necessary.[4] Others hold that in all classes of actions

---

[1] Lohmann v. Helmer, 104 Fed. 178.

[2] Lee Doon v. Tesh, on rehearing in bank, 68 Cal. 43, 8 Pac. 621. For opinion rendered by department, see 6 Pac. 97.

[3] Jackson v. Dines, 13 Colo. 90, 21 Pac. 918; McFeters v. Pierson, 15 Colo. 201, 22 Am. St. Rep. 388, 24 Pac. 1076; Lee Doon v. Tesh, 68 Cal. 43, 8 Pac. 621; Keeler v. Trueman, 15 Colo. 143, 25 Pac. 311; Rosenthal v. Ives, 2 Idaho, 244, 12 Pac. 904; Strickley v. Hill, 22 Utah, 257, 83 Am. St. Rep. 786, 62 Pac. 893; Lohman v. Helmer, 104 Fed. 179. But see Sherlock v. Leighton (Wyo.), 63 Pac. 580, 934; and McKinley Min. Co. v. Alaska United M. Co., 183 U. S. 563, 22 Sup. Ct. Rep. 84.

[4] McFeters v. Pierson, 15 Colo. 201, 22 Am. St. Rep. 388, 24 Pac. 1076; Lee Doon v. Tesh, 68 Cal. 43, 8 Pac. 621; Thompson v. Spray, 72 Cal. 528, 14 Pac. 182; Moritz v. Lavelle, 77 Cal. 10, 11 Am. St. Rep. 229, 18 Pac. 803; Lohmann v. Helmer, 104 Fed. 179; Buckley v. Fox (Idaho),

such citizenship must be averred.[1] Still others dispense with the necessity of alleging, but insist upon its being proved.[2]

The supreme court of the United States has decided that an objection to the alienage of a locator cannot be taken for the first time in the appellate court.[3] As this was a suit upon an adverse claim, citizenship should have been alleged in the pleadings.

Judge Sawyer decided that the citizenship of a locator through whom a party litigant claimed must be shown in an action of trespass;[4] and this rule was followed by the supreme court of the state of California.[5]

The rule, however, as established by the supreme court of the United States, destroys the value of these state and federal decisions as precedents, and removes the question from the domain of academic discussion.[6]

§ 234. **Conclusions.**—The following conclusions are clearly deducible from the current of judicial authority:—

(1) An alien may locate or purchase a mining claim, and until "inquest of office" may hold and dispose of the same in like manner as a citizen;[7]

67 Pac. 659; Sherlock v. Leighton (Wyo.), 63 Pac. 580; McKinley M. Co. v. Alaska United M. Co., 183 U. S. 563, 22 Sup. Ct. Rep. 84; McCarthy v. Speed, 11 S. Dak. 362, 77 N. W. 590.

[1] Bohanon v. Howe, 2 Idaho, 417, 17 Pac. 583, (but see Buckley v. Fox (Idaho), 67 Pac. 659); Ducie v. Ford, 8 Mont. 233, 19 Pac. 414.

[2] Altoona Q. M. Co. v. Integral Q. M. Co., 114 Cal. 100, 45 Pac. 1047.

[3] O'Reilly v. Campbell, 116 U. S. 418, 6 Sup. Ct. Rep. 421. See, also, Sherlock v. Leighton (Wyo.), 63 Pac. 934; Jackson v. Dines, 13 Colo. 90, 21 Pac. 918.

[4] North Noonday M. Co. v. Orient M. Co., 6 Saw. 299, 1 Fed. 522.

[5] Anthony v. Jillson, 83 Cal. 296, 23 Pac. 419; Altoona Q. M. Co. v. Integral Q. M. Co., 114 Cal. 100, 45 Pac. 1047.

[6] 183 U. S. 563, 572, 22 Sup. Ct. Rep. 84.

[7] McKinley M. Co. v. Alaska United M. Co., 183 U. S. 563, 22 Sup. Ct. Rep. 84; Wilson v. Triumph Cons. M. Co., 19 Utah, 66, 75 Am. St. Rep. 718, 56 Pac. 300.

(2) Proceedings to obtain patents are in the nature of "inquest of office," and in such proceedings citizenship is a necessary and material fact to be alleged and proved;

(3) In all other classes of actions between individuals with which the government has no concern citizenship is not a fact in issue; it need be neither alleged nor proved;

(4) Naturalization of an alien at any time subsequent to either location or purchase is retroactive and enables him to proceed to patent. The antecedent bar to patent by reason of his alienage is removed.

(5) An alien may take title by descent to an unpatented mining claim in the absence of a state law inhibiting it. He may hold such title until "office found." [1]

These conclusions are not altogether palatable, but we consider that they are forced upon us by the logic of the law.

There is one limitation upon these conclusions which was tentatively suggested by the author and has been discussed by the courts,[2] and that is this: A qualified locator may relocate a claim in the possession of an alien who has not declared his intention to become a citizen, if such relocation may be made without force or violence and prior to the naturalization of the alien, as the alien might be deemed a mere occupant without color of title, and the rules announced in the article on "occupancy" might apply.[3]

The theory advanced in support of the speculative suggestion was, that the relocator would then be in a

---

[1] Lohmann v. Helmer, 104 Fed. 178.

[2] Wilson v. Triumph Cons. M. Co., 19 Utah, 66, 75 Am. St. Rep. 718, 56 Pac. 300; Golden Fleece G. and S. M. Co. v. Cable Cons. Co., 12 Nev. 313; Sherlock v. Leighton (Wyo.), 63 Pac. 580, 934.

[3] See, ante, §§ 216-218.

position to contest the alien's right to a patent; that he would have the *status* of an adverse claimant, without which he would have no standing in court; and the alienage of the original locator would not avail the subsequent citizen locator so as to permit the court to award the claim to him for that reason; but the latter would be enabled through the patent proceedings, which are the equivalents of "inquests of office," to have alienage established, and thus clear the records. This same result could be accomplished by filing a protest in the land office. We have reached the conclusion, however, that this "suggestion" cannot be logically supported or plausibly maintained.

We think that the decision by the supreme court of the United States in McKinley M. Co. *v.* Alaska United M. Co.,[1] to the effect that a location by an alien is free from attack except by the government, establishes the law that no rights may be initiated by a citizen through a relocation of the ground appropriated by an alien, until the latter's title has been determined by the government. Prior to that time the ground would not be open to location or relocation. One attempting to relocate the ground could not connect himself with the government title, and would acquire no rights whatever. If he should institute an adverse suit based upon such pretended relocation he might assist the government in preventing the alien from securing a patent, but such a result would not validate his pretended location.[2]

[1] 183 U. S. 563, 22 Sup. Ct. Rep. 84.
[2] See Billings *v.* Smelting Co., 52 Fed. 250; Sherlock *v.* Leighton (Wyo.), 63 Pac. 580, 934.

ARTICLE III. GENERAL PROPERTY RIGHTS OF ALIENS IN
THE STATES.

§ 237. After patent, property becomes subject to rules
prescribed by the state.

§ 238. Constitutional and statutory regulations of the
precious - metal - bearing
states on the subject of
alien proprietorship.

§ 237. **After patent, property becomes subject to
rules prescribed by the state.**—The rights of aliens to
acquire, hold, and transmit real property in the states,
after the title to such property has passed out of the
general government, are regulated exclusively, in the
absence of treaty stipulations, by the constitution and
laws of the several states.[1]

The mining laws contain the express provision that
nothing in them shall be construed to prevent the alienation of title conveyed by a patent to any person whatever.[2]

As we have heretofore observed,[3] property in mines,
once vested absolutely in the individual, becomes subject to the same rules of law as other real property within the state. The federal law remains a muniment of
title, but beyond this it possesses no potential force.
Its purpose has been accomplished, and, like a private
vendor, the government loses all dominion over the
thing granted. To determine, therefore, what disabili-
ties, if any, are imposed upon aliens as to property in
the states, held in absolute private ownership after the
government has absolutely parted with its title, the constitution and laws of the several states must be consulted.

[1] Blythe *v.* Hinckley, 172 U. S. 501, 19 Sup. Ct. Rep. 497; Wilcox *v.*
McConnell, 13 Pet. 498; Bahaud *v.* Bize, 105 Fed. 485.

[2] Rev. Stats., § 2326.

[3] See, *ante,* § 22.

§ 238. Constitutional and statutory regulations of the precious-metal-bearing states on the subject of alien proprietorship.—The tendency in almost all the precious-metal-bearing states, and those within the purview of this treatise, has been in the line of a liberal policy on the subject of alien ownership. A treaty made by the United States is the supreme law of the land,[1] and where a treaty has been made removing the disability of aliens to hold property any state legislation would be inoperative.[2] But, in the absence of a treaty, the subject is within the exclusive power of a state.[3] For the purpose of convenient reference, we note the present *status* of aliens in the several states.

California.—Aliens, either resident or non-resident, may take, hold, and dispose of property, real or personal.[4] A non-resident foreigner may take by succession, but must claim the estate within five years from the death of the decedent to whom he claims succession.[5]

Colorado.—All aliens may acquire, inherit, possess, enjoy, and dispose of real property as native-born citizens.[6] But similar rights over personal property seem to be limited to resident aliens.

Idaho.—The civil code of this state has the following provision:—

" Any person, whether citizen or alien (except as " hereinafter provided), natural or artificial, may take;

---

[1] Const. of U. S., art. vi.

[2] Bahaud *v.* Bize, 105 Fed. 485.

[3] Blythe *v.* Hinckley, 178 U. S. 501, 19 Sup. Ct. Rep. 497.

[4] Civ. Code, § 671; Const. (1879), art. i, § 17; Estate of Billings, 65 Cal. 593, 4 Pac. 639; Lyons *v.* State, 67 Cal. 380, 7 Pac. 763; Carrasco *v.* State, Id. 385, 7 Pac. 766; State *v.* Smith, 70 Cal. 153, 12 Pac. 121.

[5] Civ. Code, §§ 672, 1404.

[6] Const., art. ii, § 27; Mills' Annot. Stats. 1891, ch. iii, § 99, p 421. See, also, as to descent, *Id.*, § 1529, p. 1021.

" hold, and dispose of mining claims and mining prop-
" erty, real or personal, tunnel rights, millsites, quartz-
" mills and reduction works, used or necessary or proper
" for the reduction of ores, and water rights used for
" mining or milling purposes, and any other lands or
" property necessary for the working of mines or the
" reduction of the products thereof; *provided,* that
" Chinese, or persons of Mongolian descent not born
" in the United States, are not permitted to acquire
" title to land or any real property under the provisions
" of this title." [1]

But aliens are prohibited from acquiring other kinds
of real property.[2]

Montana.—Aliens and denizens have the same right
as citizens to acquire, purchase, possess, enjoy, convey
and transmit, and inherit mines and mining property,
and milling, reduction, concentrating, and other works,
and real property necessary for or connected with the
business of mining and treating ores and minerals.[3]

Resident aliens may take generally by succession the
same as citizens, but a non-resident foreigner only if he
appears and claims the succession within five years
after the death of his decedent.[4]

Nebraska.—No distinction is made between resident
aliens and citizens, in reference to the possession, enjoyment, or descent of property.[5] But non-resident aliens
and corporations not incorporated under the laws of the
state are prohibited from acquiring title to or taking
or holding any lands or real estate by descent, devise,
purchase, or otherwise. This provision is inoperative
as against citizens of France, by reason of a treaty.[6]
Exception is made in favor of a widow and heirs of
aliens who acquired lands prior to the adoption of the

[1] Civil Code, § 2555.   [4] Civil Code, § 1867.
[2] *Id.,* § 2355.   [5] Const., art. i, § 25.
[3] Const., art. iii, § 25.   [6] Bahaud *v.* Bize, 105 Fed. 485.

constitution. These may hold by devise or descent for a period of ten years; but within that period they must be sold to a *bona fide* purchaser, or suffer escheat.[1]

Nevada.—Any non-resident alien, person or corporation, except subjects of the Chinese empire, may take, hold, and enjoy any real property, or any interest in lands, tenements, or hereditaments within the state of Nevada, as fully, freely, and upon the same terms and conditions as any resident, citizen, person, or domestic corporation.[2]

North Dakota.—Any person, whether citizen or alien, may take, hold, and dispose of property, real or personal, within this state.[3]   And aliens may take by succession as well as citizens.[4]

Oregon.—" No Chinaman, not a resident of the state " at the adoption of this constitution, shall ever hold any " real estate or mining claim, or work any mining claim " therein." [5]
White resident foreigners shall enjoy the same rights in respect to the possession, enjoyment, and descent of property as native-born. citizens.[6]
Aliens may acquire and hold lands or interest therein, by purchase, devise, or descent, the same as if they were native-born citizens. Foreign corporations not prohibited by the constitution from carrying on business in the state may acquire, hold, use, and dispose of all real estate necessary or convenient to carry into effect the objects of its organization, and also any interest in real

---

[1] Comp. Stats. Neb. 1893, ch. lxxiii, § 70.
[2] Cutting's Comp. Laws of Nevada, § 2725.
[3] Rev. Code 1899, § 3277, p. 834.
[4] *Id.*, p. 890.
[5] Const., art. xv, § 8. See United States *v.* Wong Kim Ark, 169 U. S. 649, 18 Sup. Ct. Rep. 456.
[6] Const., art. i, § 31.

estate, by mortgage or otherwise, as security for moneys due or loans made by such corporation.[1]

An alien woman is entitled to dower in the property of the estate of her deceased husband.[2]

An alien may take title to an *unpatented* mining claim by descent in this state.[3]

South Dakota.—The constitution of this state provides that—

" No distinction shall ever be made by law between " resident aliens and citizens in reference to the posses- " sion, enjoyment, or descent of property."[4]

Legislation as to non-resident aliens is permissive, but there is no statute on the subject. Hence non-resident aliens occupy the *status* of citizens or resident aliens, with reference to the acquisition and enjoyment of property.

Utah.—There is nothing in its recently adopted constitution or its laws discriminating between citizens and aliens on the question of property rights. Aliens may take in all cases by succession as well as citizens.[5]

Washington.—It is provided by the laws of this state that—

" The ownership of lands by aliens other than those " who in good faith have declared their intention to " become citizens of the United States is prohibited in " this state, except where acquired by inheritance, under " mortgage, or in good faith in the ordinary course of " justice in the collection of debts; and all conveyances " of land hereafter made to any alien, directly or in " trust for such alien, shall be void; provided, that the

---

[1] Hill's Annot. Stats. 1892, § 2988.
[2] *Id.*, § 2974.
[3] *Lohman v. Helmer*, 104 Fed. 178.
[4] Const., art. vi, § 14.
[5] Rev. Stats. 1898, § 2847.

" provisions of this section shall not apply to lands con-
" taining valuable deposits of minerals, metals, iron,
" coal, or fire-clay, and the necessary land for mills and
" machinery to be used in the development thereof and
" the manufacture of the products therefrom. Every
" corporation the majority of the capital stock of which
" is owned by aliens shall be considered an alien for the
" purposes of this prohibition."[1]

Wyoming.—There is no distinction between resident
aliens and citizens with reference to property rights.[2]

ARTICLE IV.   GENERAL PROPERTY RIGHTS OF ALIENS IN THE TERRITORIES.

§ 242. Power of congress over the   § 243. The alien acts of March 3,
        territories.   1887, and March 2, 1897,
                                              and the territorial limit
                                              of their operation.

§ 242.   **Power of congress over the territories.**—The
power of congress over the territories of the United
States is general and plenary, arising from and incidental to the right to acquire the territory itself, and
from the power given by the constitution to make all
needful rules and regulations respecting the territory
or other property belonging to the United States.[3]
As was said by Chief Justice Marshall,—

" Perhaps the power of governing a territory belong-
" ing to the United States, which has not by becoming
" a state acquired the means of self-government, may
" result necessarily from the facts that it is not within
" the jurisdiction of any particular state, and is within

---

[1] Const., art ii, § 33; State *v.* Morrison, 18 Wash. 664, 52 Pac. 228;
State *v.* Hudson Land Co., 19 Wash. 85, 52 Pac. 574.   See, also, Ballinger's Annot. Codes and Stats. 1897, § 4548.

[2] Const., art. i, § 29.

[3] Justice Bradley, in Mormon Church *v.* United States, 136 U. S. 1, 42,
10 Sup. Ct. Rep. 792.

" the power and jurisdiction of the United States. The
" right to govern may be the inevitable consequence of
" the right to acquire territory. Whichever may be the
" source whence the power is derived, the possession of
" it is unquestioned." [1]

And by Chief Justice Waite,—

" Congress may not only abrogate laws of the territo-
" rial legislatures, but it may itself legislate directly
" for the local government. It may make a void act of
" the territorial legislature valid, and a valid act void.
" In other words, it has full and complete legislative
" authority over the people of the territories and all the
" departments of the territorial governments. It may
" do for the territories what the people under the consti-
" tution of the United States may do for the states." [2]

These propositions are elementary and self-evident.[3]

§ 243.   The alien acts of March 3, 1887, and of March
2, 1897, and the territorial limit of their operation.—
Congress having this unquestioned power to establish
rules of property in the territories, on March 3, 1887,
passed an act entitled "An act to restrict the ownership
" of real estate in the territories to American citi-
" zens," [4] the first two sections of which are as follows:—

" SEC. 1.   That it shall be unlawful for any person or
" persons not citizens of the United States, or who have
" not lawfully declared their intention to become such
" citizens, or for any corporation not created by or
" under the laws of the United States or of some state
" or territory of the United States, to hereafter acquire,
" hold, or own real estate so hereafter acquired, or any
" interest therein, in any of the territiories of the United
" States, or in the District of Columbia, except such as
" may be acquired by inheritance or in good faith in the

[1] American Ins. Co. v. Canter, 1 Peters, 511, 542.
[2] National Bank v. County of Yankton, 101 U. S. 129, 133.
[3] Mormon Church v. United States, 136 U. S. 1, 43, 10 Sup. Ct. Rep. 792.
[4] 24 Stats. at Large, p. 476.

" ordinary course of justice in the collection of debts
" heretofore created; *provided,* that the prohibition of
" this section shall not apply to cases in which the right
" to hold or dispose of lands in the United States is
" secured by existing treaties to the citizens or subjects
" of foreign countries, which rights, so far as they may
" exist. by force of any such treaty, shall continue to
" exist so long as such treaties are in force, and no
" longer.

" SEC. 2. That no corporation or association more
" than twenty per centum of the stock of which is or
" may be owned by any person or persons, corporation
" or corporations, association or associations, not citi-
" zens of the United States, shall hereafter acquire, or
" hold, or own any real estate hereafter acquired in any
" of the territories of the United States or of the District
" of Columbia."

By section four the attorney-general is directed to
enforce the forfeitures provided for by the act, by bill
in equity or other proper process.

Whatever legislation theretofore existed in any of the
territories upon the subject of alienage, it became inoperative and ineffectual, and thenceforward had no
potential existence. Since the passage of this act, all
of the then organized territories except New Mexico
and Arizona have been admitted into the union. Unquestionably, the alien act of 1887 remained in force in
these territories until the act of 1897 was passed.

The act of March 3, 1887, was amended by an act
approved March 2, 1897,[1] (except in so far as it applied
to the District of Columbia). The latter act remodels
the original act, and while providing that, except in
certain cases, no alien or person who had not declared
his intention to become a citizen of the United States
should acquire title to or own any land in any of the
territories of the United States, contained the following
clauses:—

[1] 29 Stats., p. 618.

" This act shall not be construed to prevent any per-
" sons not citizens of the United States from acquiring
" or holding lots or parcels of land in any incorporated
" or platted city, town, or village, or in any mine or
" mining claim in any of the territories of the United
" States." [1]

" This act shall not in any manner be construed . . .
" to authorize aliens to acquire title from the United
" States to any public lands in the United States, or to
" in any manner affect or change the laws regulating
" the disposal of the public lands of the United
" States." [2]

This, in our judgment, makes the last clause of section twenty-three hundred and twenty-six of the Revised Statutes—" Nothing herein contained shall be construed " to prevent the alienation of a title conveyed by a patent " to any person whatever"—operative in the territories as well as in the states.[3]

The rights of aliens which have been secured by treaty are protected, as well as the rights acquired by aliens prior to the original act, and the rights of *bona fide* resident aliens. No reference whatever is made in the act of 1897 to corporations. The provisions contained in the act of 1887 having been omitted, corporations organized under the laws of any state or territory may purchase lands in the territories regardless of the citizenship of the stockholders.[4] A full copy of the act of 1897 will be found in the appendix.

Did the act of 1887 apply to Alaska?

The act prohibited persons not citizens or who have not lawfully declared their intention to become such, and corporations not created by or under the laws of some state or territory of the United States, from hereafter

---

[1] Act of March 2, 1897, § 3.
[2] *Id.*, § 7.
[3] See Opinion of Attorney-General, 28 L. D. 178.
[4] *Id.*

acquiring, holding, or owning real estate so hereafter acquired, or any interest therein, in any of *the territories of the United States or in the District of Columbia.*

Was Alaska a territory at the time this act was passed, within the meaning of the law? Popularly, it has never been so considered. By the act of July 27, 1868,[1] it was created a customs district, and called the *District of Alaska.* It has been referred to in some of the legislation of congress as an *unorganized territory.*[2] By the act passed March 17, 1884, entitled "An act providing a " civil government for Alaska,"[3] it was created a civil, judicial, and land district, and throughout the entire act it is referred to and denominated as a *district.* This act does not clothe the "district" with legislative functions. It establishes a temporary seat of government at Sitka, and authorizes the appointment of a governor, district judge, and minor officers. The general laws of the state of Oregon in force at the date of the passage of the act are declared to be the law in said district, so far as the same may be applicable and not in conflict with the provisions of the act or the laws of the United States. It is expressly provided that nothing contained in the act should put in force in said district the general land laws of the United States. But the laws relating to mining claims and rights incident thereto were declared thenceforward to be in force in said district. These laws, as we have heretofore observed,[4] embody a provision that nothing therein contained should be construed to prevent the alienation of a title conveyed by a patent for a mining claim to any person whatever.[5]

This was the political *status* of Alaska when the alien act was passed in 1887, and is substantially its *status* at the present time. The acts of 1899 and 1900 providing

---

[1] 15 Stats. at Large, p. 240.
[2] Rev. Stats., ch. iii, p. 342.
[3] 23 Stats. at Large, p. 24.

[4] See, *ante,* § 237.
[5] Rev. Stats., § 2326.

for the punishment of crime in Alaska, and providing for the civil government thereof, refer to Alaska as " district."[1] Was it included within the designation " territories" mentioned in the alien act of 1887? We are of opinion that it was not. We think we are materially aided in this view by a decision of the supreme court of the United States with reference to that portion of Indian territory now known as Oklahoma, prior to its organization into a territory. The decision referred to was based upon the following state of facts:—

On February 9, 1889, congress passed an act[2] providing:—

" That every person who shall carnally and unlaw-
" fully know any female under the age of sixteen years,
" or who shall be accessory to such carnal and unlawful
" knowledge before the fact in the District of Columbia
" or other place, *except the territories*, over which the
" United States has exclusive jurisdiction, . . . shall
" be guilty of a felony."

The accused was charged with having committed the offense within that part of Indian territory commonly known as Oklahoma. He was tried and convicted, and applied to the supreme court of the United States for a writ of *habeas corpus*, his counsel contending that Oklahoma was a *territory* within the exception of the act of congress, and that the trial court was without jurisdiction. The supreme court, in denying the writ, thus expressed its views:—

" We think the words 'except the territories' have
" reference exclusively to that system of organized gov-
" ernment long existing within the United States by
" which certain regions of the country have been erected
" into civil governments. These governments have an
" executive, a legislative, and a judicial system. They
" have the powers which all these departments of gov-

[1] 30 Stats. at Large, p. 1253; 31 Stats. at Large, p. 321.
[2] 25 Stats. at Large, p. 658.

" ernment have exercised, which are conferred upon
" them by act of congress, and their legislative acts are
" subject to the disapproval of the congress of the
" United States. . . . It is this class of governments,
" long known by the name of territories, that the act of
" congress excepts from the operations of this statute.
" . . . Oklahoma was not of this class of territories.
" It had no legislative body. It had no government.
" It had no established or organized system of govern-
" ment for the control of the people within its limits,
" as the territories of the United States have, and al-
" ways have had. We are therefore of opinion that the
" objection taken on this point by the counsel for the
" prisoner is unsound." [1]

Suppose the crime in question had been committed
in Alaska. Is there any reason for holding that a valid
conviction could not have been had for lack of jurisdiction?

It seems to us that the inference is logically deducible
that the alien act of 1887 under consideration was not
applicable to Alaska, and that after patent the patentee
might transfer his title to "any person whatever."
The act of 1897,[2] which superseded the former act, does
not prohibit the acquisition by aliens of patented mining
ground in the territories, and therefore need not be discussed in this connection. This act, of course, applies
to unpatented mining claims only. Unpatented mining
claims in the territories may be acquired only by the
persons authorized to acquire them in the states.[3] In
1898, congress accorded native-born citizens of the dominion of Canada the same mining rights and privileges
in the district of Alaska accorded to citizens of the
United States in British Columbia and the Northwest
territory, with the proviso that such Canadian citizens

---

[1] *In re* Lane, 135 U. S. 443, 447, 10 Sup. Ct. Rep. 760.
[2] 29 Stats., p. 618.
[3] Opinion, 28 L. D. 178.

should not enjoy greater privileges in Alaska than were enjoyed by American citizens.[1] The land department has held this act to be inoperative, because no rights, except to lease from the government, are accorded to citizens of the United States in British Columbia or the Northwest territory, and as our system does not contemplate leases by the government, to accord to citizens of Canada the right to lease mining claims would be to accord them rights which are not given to our citizens.

For all practical purposes, the rule that a location by an alien is voidable at the instance of the United States government is in force everywhere within the United States.[2]

As to Oklahoma, it became an organized territory by act of congress, passed subsequent to the enactment of the alien law of 1887.[3]

It might well be doubted if the law of 1887 became operative upon the formal creation of the territory, *ex propria vigore*. The language of the first section might be construed to include only such territories as were then organized. The legislature of Oklahoma has legislated only upon the right of aliens to take by succession.

In New Mexico there does not seem to have been any legislation prior to the passage of the alien act of congress above referred to.

In Arizona, at the time that act was passed, a territorial law was in existence which provided that any alien might acquire by purchase or operation of law, and possess, hold, own, and dispose of any mines or minerals within the territory.[4]

The passage of the alien act of 1887, however, super-

---

[1] 30 Stats. at Large, p. 409.
[2] See, *ante*, §§ 231, 234.
[3] May 2, 1890, 26 Stats. at Large, p. 81.
[4] Laws 1885, p. 40.

seded this; and in the revision of the laws of Arizona the former territorial act was omitted.

In these two last-named territories the congressional act was, of course, in full force until the act of 1897 was passed. As heretofore noted, the latter act superseded the act of 1887, and contained no prohibition against aliens acquiring *patented* mines or mining claims in the territories.[1]

[1] 28 L. D. 178.

TITLE IV.

STATE LEGISLATION AND LOCAL DISTRICT REGULATIONS SUPPLEMENTING THE CONGRESSIONAL MINING LAWS.

CHAPTER
I. STATE LEGISLATION SUPPLEMENTAL TO THE CONGRESSIONAL MINING LAWS.

II. LOCAL DISTRICT REGULATIONS.

CHAPTER I.

STATE LEGISLATION SUPPLEMENTAL TO THE CONGRES-
SIONAL MINING LAWS.

§ 248. Introductory.

§ 249. Limits within which state may legislate.

§ 250. Scope of existing state and territorial legislation — Subjects concerning which states and territories may unquestionably legislate.

§ 251. Subjects upon which states have enacted laws the validity of which is open to question.

§ 252. Drainage, easements, and rights of way for mining purposes.

§ 253. Provisions of state constitions on the subject of eminent domain.

§ 254. Mining as a "public use."

§ 255. Rights of way for pipelines for the conveyance of oil and natural gas.

§ 256. Lateral and other railroads for transportation of mine products.

§ 257. Physical and industrial conditions as affecting the rule of "public utility."

§ 258. The rule in Nevada, Arizona, Montana, and Georgia.

§ 259. Arizona.

§ 259a. Montana.

§ 260. Georgia.

§ 261. The rule in Pennsylvania, West Virginia, California, and Oregon.

§ 262. West Virginia.

§ 263. California.

§ 263a. Oregon.

§ 264. Conclusions.

§ 248. Introductory. — As preliminary to the analysis and general exposition of the law regulating the manner in which mining rights in the public mineral lands may be held, enjoyed, and perpetuated, it is appropriate that we define with reasonable certainty the limit and extent of legislative power conceded to the several states and territories by the express or implied sanction of the general government. We have heretofore shown that the federal system of mining law is composed of three elements:—

(1) The legislation of congress;

(2) The legislation of the various states and territories supplementing congressional legislation, and in harmony therewith;

(3) Local rules and customs, or regulations established in different localities, not in conflict with federal legislation or that of the state or territory wherein they are operative.[1]

We have traced the evolution of this system through the different periods of our national history, from the embryotic stage, which had its genesis in the local rules and customs of the mining camps of the west, to the development of higher forms of law. While in this progressive development the primitive forms have not altogether disappeared, they have been relegated from the position of controlling importance to that of mere subordinate and subsidiary functions. It is entirely unnecessary to here retrace the steps by which the present results were obtained. In the early chapters of this treatise,[2] we have endeavored to present such an historical review as will suffice for all practical purposes and enable the student to acquaint himself with the process of crystallization which has given us as a resultant the existing unique system. We are immediately concerned with the present practical operation of this system, and shall now consider the general nature and scope of state and territorial legislation supplemental to the congressional mining laws, a minor subsidiary element in the system, but in its particular sphere important.

§ 249. Limits within which state may legislate.—
When it is recognized that the government simply occupies the *status* of a landed proprietor, holding the paramount title to its public domain, with the sole right of

---

[1] See, *ante*, § 81.   [2] See, *ante*, title II, chs. i-vi, §§ 28-81.

disposal upon such terms and conditions and subject to such limitations as it may from time to time prescribe,[1] and that the congressional mining laws are but a statement of such terms, conditions, and limitations, it follows necessarily that neither individuals nor states have the power to control, modify, or nullify any of such terms, conditions, or limitations.

If, by compliance with congressional law, an estate in public lands is granted, the state may not destroy or impair it.[2] If no such estate in such lands is created by or under the authority of federal law, the state has no power to create or transfer it.[3] After an estate is once granted, and a right of property becomes vested, it is subject to the general laws of the state the same as any other property,[4] and congress has thereafter no power to affect the property by legislation;[5] but we now speak only of the terms, conditions, and limitations under which estates, either equitable or legal, are carved out of the public lands by the act of the paramount proprietor.

If the state may prescribe any additional or supplemental rules, increasing the burdens or diminishing the benefits granted by the federal laws in lands of the public domain, it is simply because the government, as owner of the property, sanctions, expressly or by implication, the exercise of such powers.

At one period of the national history, the states as-

---

[1] See, *ante,* §§ 80, 81.

[2] The exercise of the right of eminent domain, which involves the payment of compensation, is an exception to this rule. See, *post,* § 253 et seq.

[3] Gibson *v.* Chouteau, 13 Wall. 92, 99; Irvine *v.* Marshall, 20 How. 558, 561; Van Brocklin *v.* State of Tennessee, 117 U. S. 151, 168, 6 Sup. Ct. Rep. 670.

[4] Wilcox *v.* McConnel, 13 Pet. 498, 516. And see cases cited in Rose's Notes on U. S. Reports, vol. 3, p. 867.

[5] Cone *v.* Roxana G. M. and Tun. Co. (U. S. Cir. Ct., Colo.), 2 Leg. Adv. 350, 352.

sumed the right to confer possessory rights in the public
lands upon its citizens. The national government acquiesced in the assumed power for a number of years.
It might have repudiated this intervention by the state,
and dispossessed the occupants; but having failed to do
so, certain possessory privileges were acquired, to the
extent and under such circumstances that the government became, morally and in good conscience, bound to
recognize them.[1]

This it did gracefully. But this was before the government, by legislative enactment, adopted any general
laws expressly providing for the sale or disposal of its
mineral lands in the precious-metal-bearing states. The
legislative era succeeded the period of passive recognition, and with the passage of laws providing for the
method of vesting legal or equitable estates in the public
lands, the right of the states to legislate in this direction
was no longer recognized, except to the extent that such
power was conceded by the congressional laws.

State statutes in reference to mining rights upon the
public domain must therefore be construed in subordi-
nation to the laws of congress, as they are more in the
nature of regulations under these laws than independent
legislation.[2]

State and territorial legislation, therefore, must be
entirely consistent with the federal laws, otherwise it
is of no effect. The right to supplement federal legislation conceded to the state may not be arbitrarily exercised; nor has the state the privilege of imposing
conditions so onerous as to be repugnant to the liberal
spirit of the congressional laws. On the other hand,
the state may not by its legislation dispense with the
performance of the conditions imposed by the national

[1] See, *ante,* § 56.
[2] Eberle v. Carmichael, 8 N. Mex. 169, 42 Pac. 95, 98.

law, nor relieve the locator from the obligation of performing in good faith those acts which are declared by it to be essential to the maintenance and perpetuation of the estate acquired by location. Within these limits, the state may legislate.[1] Beyond them the state should not be permitted to go.[2] And when the state has enacted such legislation its provisions must be complied with before any valid right to a mining claim can be perfected.[3]

§ 250. **Scope of existing state and territorial legislation—Subjects concerning which states and territories may unquestionably legislate.**—Many of the states and territories have enacted codes, more or less comprehensive, supplementing congressional laws, while others have but few provisions. In the appendix will be found the legislation of this character now in force in each state and territory.

That a correct understanding of the general scope of the existing state and territorial legislation may be gleaned, we enumerate the subjects covered by such laws, indicating which states and territories have legislated upon such subjects, first considering those concerning which such legislation is unquestionably proper, within reasonable limits.

(1) *Length of lode claims.*—

Colorado,[4]   North Dakota,[5]

---

[1] Sissons *v.* Sommers, 24 Nev. 379, 388, 77 Am. St. Rep. 815, 55 Pac. 899.

[2] *Id.*

[3] Belk *v.* Meager, 104 U. S. 279, 284; Garfield M. and M. Co. *v.* Hammer, 6 Mont. 53, 59, 8 Pac. 153; Purdum *v.* Laddin, 23 Mont. 387, 389, 59 Pac. 153; Copper Globe Min. Co. *v.* Allman (Utah), 64 Pac. 1019.

[4] Same as federal law; limit, fifteen hundred feet. Mills' Annot. Stats., § 3148.

[5] Same as federal law; limit, fifteen hundred feet. Rev. Pol. Code, 1895, § 1426; *Id.*, 1899, § 1426.

South Dakota,[1]   Washington,[3]
Utah,[2]   Wyoming,[4]

While it is evident that under the congressional act
the states and territories may limit the number of linear
feet on a lode, or vein, which may be embraced within a
single location to less than fifteen hundred feet, no state
or territory has attempted any such restriction. Those
states which have legislated at all upon the subject,
simply repeat the general language of section twenty-
three hundred and twenty of the revised statutes. Of
course, this does not add any force to the federal enactment; nor does it detract from it. It is altogether harm-
less. Throughout the mining regions the unit of a lode
location as to length is fifteen hundred feet.

(2) *Width of lode claims.*—

Colorado,[5]   North Dakota,[7]
Idaho,[6]

[1] Same as federal law. Pol. Code Dak. 1887, § 1997. Adopted by act
of legislature—Laws of 1890, ch. cv, § 1, p. 254; Grantham's Annot.
Stats. (1899), § 2656.

[2] Same as federal law; limit, fifteen hundred feet. Laws of 1899, p.
26, § 1.

[3] Same as federal law. Hill's Annot. Stats. (Wash.), § 2211; Ballinger's Annot. Codes and Stats. of Washington, § 3152.

[4] Not to exceed fifteen hundred feet. Local rules may not limit to less
than that length. Laws of 1888, p. 87, § 13; Rev. Stats. of Wyoming
(1899), § 2544.

[5] In Gilpin, Clear Creek, Boulder, and Summit counties, seventy-five
feet on each side of the center of the vein; in all other counties, one hundred and fifty feet on each side of the center of the vein or crevice, unless
enlarged or diminished by vote of electors of a county at a general election. Mills' Annot. Stats., § 3149.

[6] May extend to three hundred feet on each side of the center of the
vein. Rev. Stats., § 3100; as amended, Laws of 1895, p. 25, § 1; Civil
Code (1901), § 2556.

[7] One hundred and fifty feet on each side of the center of vein, unless
enlarged to not more than three hundred feet or diminished by majority
of votes cast at a general election in a county. Rev. Pol. Code, 1895,
§ 1427; *Id.* 1899, § 1427.

South Dakota,[1]   Washington,[3]
Utah,[2]   Wyoming.[4]

There can be no doubt about the power of state legislatures to limit the width of lode claims to any reasonable number of feet on each side of the center of the vein less than three hundred, and in the absence of any action in that behalf by the state, the local district organizations may regulate the subject.[5]

As to the provision of the statutes in Colorado and North Dakota[6] authorizing the counties to determine upon a greater width than that fixed by the state law, by a majority of the legal votes cast at a general election, Mr. Morrison, in his "Mining Rights,"[7] says that he knows of no instance where any such attempt has been made by any of the counties to avail themselves of the privilege. He also doubts the constitutionality of the law. It is suggested that if such action should be taken, and the result accepted and acted upon, it might have the force of a local regulation which does not acquire valid-

[1] Three hundred feet on each side of the center of the vein, unless diminished to not less than twenty-five feet by a county at a general election. Pol. Code Dak. 1887, § 1998. Adopted by South Dakota— Laws of 1890, ch. cv, § 1, p. 254; as amended, Laws of 1899, p. 148; Grantham's Annot. Stats. (1899), § 2657.

[2] Same as federal statute. Comp. Laws of 1888, vol. ii, p. 138, § 2790; as amended, Laws of 1899, p. 26.

[3] Not more than three hundred feet on each side of the middle of the vein. Local rules may not restrict to less than fifty feet. Hill's Annot. Stats. (Wash.), § 2211; Ballinger's Annot. Codes and Stats. of Washington, § 3152.

[4] Not to exceed three hundred feet. Local rules may not limit to less than one hundred and fifty feet. Laws of 1888, p. 87, § 14; Rev. Stats. of Wyoming (1899), § 2545.

[5] North Noonday M. Co. v. Orient M. Co., 6 Saw. 305, 1 Fed. 522; Jupiter M. Co. v. Bodie M. Co., 7 Saw. 104, 11 Fed. 666.

[6] South Dakota formerly had the same provision, but its law is now changed as above indicated.

[7] Morr. Min. Rights, 8th ed. 20; Id., 10th ed. 22.

Lindley on M.—28

ity by mere adoption, but from customary obedience and acquiescence of the miners.[1]

(3) *Posting notices of location.*—

Arizona,[2]	North Dakota,[8]
Colorado,[3]	South Dakota,[9]
Idaho,[4]	Oregon,[10]
Montana,[5]	Utah,[11]
Nevada,[6]	Washington,[12]
New Mexico,[7]	Wyoming.[13]

(4) *Contents of notices and certificates of location.*—

Arizona,[14]	Idaho,[16]
Colorado,[15]	Montana,[17]

[1] North Noonday M. Co. *v.* Orient M. Co., 6 Saw. 299, 307, 1 Fed. 522; Jupiter M. Co. *v.* Bodie M. Co., 7 Saw. 96, 106, 11 Fed. 666; Harvey *v.* Ryan, 42 Cal. 626. See, *post*, § 271.

[2] Rev. Stats. (1901), § 3232. Placers: *Id.*, § 3242.

[3] Placers: Mills' Annot. Stats., § 3136. Lodes: *Id.*, § 3152.

[4] Lodes: Rev. Stats., § 3101, as amended—Laws of 1895, p. 26, § 2; Civil Code (1901), § 2557. Placers: Laws of 1897, p. 12; Civil Code (1901), § 2563.

[5] Pol. Code, 1895, § 3610. Held reasonable and not in conflict with federal law: Purdum *v.* Laddin, 23 Mont. 387, 389, 59 Pac. 153.

[6] Comp. Laws of 1900, § 208. Placers: *Id.*, § 220.

[7] Comp. Laws of 1884, § 1566; Comp. Laws of 1897, § 2286.

[8] Rev. Pol. Code, 1895, § 1430; *Id.*, 1899, § 1430.

[9] Pol. Code Dak. 1887, § 2001. Adopted by South Dakota—Laws of 1890, ch. cv, § 1, as amended, Laws of 1899, p. 148; Grantham's Annot. Stats. (1899), § 2660.

[10] Stats. 1898, p. 16, as amended—Laws of 1901, p. 140.

[11] Laws of 1899, p. 26, § 2.

[12] Laws of 1899, p. 70, § 2. Placers: *Id.*, p. 71, § 10; as amended, Laws of 1901, p. 292.

[13] Lodes: Laws of 1888, p. 88, § 17; Rev. Stats of Wyoming (1899), § 2548. Placers: Laws of 1888, p. 89, § 22; Rev. Stats. of Wyoming, § 2553, as amended—Laws of 1901, p. 104.

[14] Rev. Stats. (1901), § 3232. Placers: *Id.*, § 3242.

[15] Placers: Mills' Annot. Stats., § 3136. Lodes: *Id.*, §§ 3150, 3151. Must claim but one location: *Id.*, § 3163.

[16] Lodes: Rev. Stats., § 3101, as amended—Laws of 1895, p. 26, § 2; Rev. Stats., § 3102; Civ. Code (1901), § 2557. Must claim but one location: *Id.*, § 2561. Placers: Laws of 1897, p. 12; Civ. Code (1901), § 2563.

[17] Pol. Code, 1895, § 3610, 3612, as amended—Laws of 1901, p. 141,

Nevada,[1]	South Dakota,[5]
New Mexico,[2]	Utah,[6]
North Dakota,[3]	Washington,[7]
Oregon,[4]	Wyoming.[8]

Where state or territorial laws require a location notice, certificate, or declaratory statement to be recorded, the act of congress provides what such record must contain.[9] While states and territories may enlarge these requirements, they may not dispense with any of them.[10]

(5) *Recording notices and certificates of location.—*

Arizona,[11]	California,[13]
Arkansas,[12]	Colorado,[14]

§ 2. Held reasonable and not in conflict with federal laws: **Purdum v.** Laddin, 23 Mont. 387, 389, 59 Pac. 153.

[1] Comp. Laws of 1900, §§ 208, 210, 219, 231. Placers: *Id.*, §§ 220, 221.

[2] Comp. Laws of 1884, § 1566; Comp. Laws of 1897, § 2286.

[3] Rev. Pol. Code, 1895, § 1428; *Id.*, 1899, §§ 1428, 1429, 1430, 1440.

[4] Laws of 1898, p. 16, as amended—Laws of 1901, p. 140.

[5] Pol. Code. Dak., § 1999. Adopted by South Dakota—Laws of 1890, ch. cv, § 1, as amended—Laws of 1899, p. 148; Grantham's Annot. Stats. (1899), § 2658; Comp. Laws of Dak. (1887), § 2001; Grantham's Annot. Stats. (1899), § 2660; as amended—Laws of 1899, p. 148; Comp. Laws of Dak. (1887), § 2000; Grantham's Annot. Stats. (1899), § 2659; Comp. Laws of Dak. (1887), § 2011; Grantham's Annot. Stats. of S. D. (1899), § 2670.

[6] Laws of 1899, p. 26, § 2.

[7] Laws of 1899, pp. 69, 70, §§ 1, 2. Placers: *Id.*, p. 71, § 10, as amended—Laws of 1901, p. 292.

[8] Rev. Stats. of Wyoming (1899), §§ 2539, 2546, 2547, 2548. Placers: *Id.*, § 2553, as amended—Laws of 1901, p. 104.

[9] Rev. Stats., § 2324.

[10] See, *ante*, § 249.

[11] Rev. Stats. 1887, p. 412, § 2349; Rev. Stats. (1901), §§ 3234, 3250. Placers: *Id.*, §§ 3244, 3250.

[12] Acts of 1899, p. 113.

[13] Civ. Code, § 1159; Kern Co. v. Lee, 129 Cal. 361, 61 Pac. 1124.

[14] Placers: Mills' Annot. Stats., § 3136. Lodes: *Id.*, § 3150. Tunnel claims: *Id.*, § 3140.

Idaho,[1]   South Dakota,[6]

Montana,[2]   Oregon,[7]

Nevada,[3]   Utah,[8]

New Mexico,[4]   Washington,[9]

North Dakota,[5]   Wyoming,[10]

(6) *Posting certificate of recorder to the fact that the location certificate is recorded.*

South Dakota,[11]

(7) *Authorizing amended locations and amended location certificates.—*

Arizona,[12]   Montana,[15]

Colorado,[13]   Nevada,[16]

Idaho,[14]   New Mexico,[17]

---

[1] Lodes: Laws of 1895, p. 27, §§ 4, 12; p. 30, § 14; Civ. Code (1901), §§ 2559, 2568. Placers: Laws of 1897, p. 12; Civ. Code (1901), §§ 2563, 2568.

[2] Pol. Code of 1895, §§ 3612 (as amended, Laws of 1901, p. 141, § 2), 3613.

[3] Comp. Laws of Nevada (1900), §§ 210, 232. Placers: *Id.,* § 221. Millsites: *Id.,* § 224. Tunnels: *Id.,* § 228.

[4] Comp. Laws of 1884, § 1566; Comp. Laws of 1897, § 2286.

[5] Rev. Pol. Code of 1895, § 1428; *Id.,* 1899, § 1428.

[6] Pol. Code. Dak. 1887, § 1999. Adopted by South Dakota—Laws of 1890, ch. cv, § 1. Grantham's Annot. Stats. (1899), § 2658, as amended —Laws of 1899, p. 148.

[7] Laws of 1898, p. 17, as amended—Laws of 1901, p. 140.

[8] Laws of 1899, p. 26, §§ 4, 8, 9.

[9] Hill's Annot. Stats. (Wash.), §§ 2214, 2216; Ballinger's Annot. Codes and Stats., §§ 3155, 3157; Laws of 1899, p. 69. Placers: *Id.,* p. 72, § 10, subd. 2, as amended—Laws of 1901, p. 292.

[10] Rev. Stats. of Wyoming (1899), § 2546. Placers: *Id.,* § 2553, as amended—Laws of 1901, p. 1104.

[11] Comp. Laws of Dak. (1887), § 1999; Grantham's Annot. Stats. (1899), § 2658, as amended—Laws of 1899, p. 146.

[12] Rev. Stats. (1901), § 3238.

[13] Mills' Annot. Stats., § 3160.

[14] Laws of 1895, p. 27, § 5; Civil Code (1901), § 2566.

[15] Laws of 1901, p. 56, §§ 1-2.

[16] Comp. Laws (1900), § 213.

[17] Comp. Laws of 1897, § 2301.

North Dakota,[1]　　Washington,[3]
South Dakota,[2]　　Wyoming.[4]

(8) *Marking of boundaries and defining the character.*
of posts and monuments. —

Arizona,[5]　　　　North Dakota,[11]
Colorado,[6]　　　 Oregon,[12]
Idaho,[7]　　　　　South Dakota,[13]
Montana,[8]　　　　Utah,[14]
Nevada,[9]　　　　 Washington,[15]
New Mexico,[10]　　Wyoming.[16]

(9) *Requiring sinking of discovery shaft or its equiv-*
alent prior to completion of location. —

Arizona,[17]　　　　Colorado,[18]

---

[1] Rev. Pol. Code, 1895, § 1437; *Id.*, 1899, § 1437.

[2] Comp. Laws Dak., 1887, § 2008. Adopted by South Dakota—Laws of 1890, ch. cv, § 1; Grantham's Annot. Stats. S. D. (1899), § 2667.

[3] Laws of 1899, p. 70, § 5.

[4] Rev. Stats. 1899, § 2538.

[5] Rev. Stats. (1901), §§ 3234, 3236. Placers: Stats. (1901), §§ 3242, 3243.

[6] Placers: Mills' Annot. Stats., § 3136. Lodes: *Id.*, 3153.

[7] Lodes: Rev. Stats., § 3101, as amended—Laws of 1895, p. 25, et seq.; Laws of 1899, p. 633; Civ. Code (1901), § 2557. Placers: Laws of 1897, p. 12; Civil Code (1901), § 2563.

[8] Pol. Code, 1895, § 3611, as amended—Laws of 1901, p. 140, § 1. Held reasonable and not in conflict with federal laws: Purdum *v.* Laddin, 23 Mont. 387, 389, 59 Pac. 153.

[9] Comp. Laws (1900), § 209. Placers: *Id.*, § 220.

[10] Comp. Laws (1897), § 2286; Laws of 1899, p. 111.

[11] Rev. Pol. Code, 1895, § 1431; *Id.*, 1899, §§ 1430, 1431.

[12] Laws of 1898, p. 16, as amended—Laws of 1901, p. 140.

[13] Comp. Laws Dak. 1887, § 2002. Adopted by South Dakota—Laws of 1890, ch. cv, § 1. Grantham's Annot. Stats. S. D. (1899), § 2661; Comp. Laws Dak. (1887), § 2001; Grantham's Annot. Stats. S. D. (1899), § 2660.

[14] Laws of 1899, p. 26, § 3.

[15] Laws of 1899, p. 70, § 2.

[16] Rev. Stats. of Wyoming, § 2548. Placers: *Id.*, § 2553.

[17] Rev. Stats. (1901), §§ 3234, 3277.

[18] Mills' Annot. Stats., §§ 3152, 3154, 3155.

Idaho,[1]   Oregon,[6]
Montana,[2]   South Dakota,[7]
Nevada,[3]   Washington,[8]
New Mexico,[4]   Wyoming.[9]
North Dakota,[5]

Secretary Teller expressed a doubt whether a state legislature has the right to attach this condition to the appropriation of mineral land,[10] although Commissioner Williamson held that such requirement is not in conflict with the congressional laws.[11]

The state courts have uniformly enforced this class of provisions;[12] and there being no authoritative ruling denying the right to the state to so legislate, these conditions may be assumed to be valid. All the statutes on this subject mentioned above require the sinking of a discovery shaft or its equivalent prior to the completion of location and as a necessary part of the act of location. In the case of Northmore v. Simmons,[13] however,

---

[1] Laws of 1895, p. 27, § 3; Civ. Code (1901), § 2558.

[2] Pol. Code, 1895, § 3611. Held reasonable and not in conflict with federal law: Sanders v. Noble, 22 Mont. 110, 117, 55 Pac. 1037; Purdum v. Laddin, 23 Mont. 387, 388, 59 Pac. 153.

[3] Comp. Laws (1900), § 209; as amended, Stats. 1901, p. 97.

[4] Comp. Laws (1897), § 2298.

[5] Rev. Pol. Code 1895, §§ 1430, 1432, 1433; Id., 1899, §§ 1430, 1432, 1433.

[6] Laws of 1898, p. 17, § 3, as amended—Laws of 1901, p. 141.

[7] Comp. Laws Dak. 1887, §§ 2001, 2003, adopted by South Dakota—Laws of 1890, ch. cv, § 1; Grantham's Annot. Stats. S. D. (1899), §§ 2660, 2662, as amended—Laws of 1899, p. 148.

[8] Laws of 1899, p. 69, §§ 2, 3, p. 71, §§ 8, 9.

[9] Rev. Stats. of Wyoming (1899), §§ 2548, 2550.

[10] Wight v. Tabor, 2 L. D. 738, 742, S. C. on review, Id. 743.

[11] In re Alfred H. Hale, 7 Copp's L. O. 115.

[12] Sisson v. Sommers, 24 Nev. 379, 388, 55 Pac. 829; Sanders v. Noble, 22 Mont. 110, 117, 55 Pac. 1037; Purdum v. Laddin, 23 Mont. 387, 389, 59 Pac. 153; Beals v. Cone, 27 Colo. 473, 499, 83 Am. St. Rep. 92, 62 Pac. 948. And see Erhardt v. Boaro, 113 U. S. 527, 5 Sup. Ct. Rep. 560, and dissenting opinion in Northmore v. Simmons, 97 Fed. 386, 392.

[13] 97 Fed. 386.

the circuit court of appeals for the ninth circuit had under consideration a mining district regulation which required the sinking of a shaft "within ninety days of "location," not as a part of the location, but as a condition to the holding of the claim,—in other words, as a part of the annual labor. The majority of the court held that it was competent for the laws of a state or the local regulations of a district to increase the amount of annual work required to hold a mining claim by the federal law and upheld the validity of the regulation.

(10) *Requiring affidavit of sinking discovery shaft or its equivalent to be attached to and recorded with the notice of location.*

Oregon.[1]

(11) *Fixing time within which location shall be completed after discovery.*—

Arizona,[2]	New Mexico,[7]
Colorado,[3]	North Dakota,[8]
Idaho,[4]	Oregon,[9]
Montana,[5]	South Dakota,[10]
Nevada,[6]	Utah,[11]

[1] Laws of 1898, p. 16, as amended—Laws of 1901, p. 141 §§ 2, 3.

[2] Rev. Stats. (1901), § 3234.

[3] Placers: Mills' Annot. Stats., § 3136. Lodes: *Id.*, § 3155.

[4] Lodes: Laws of 1895, p. 26, et seq., §§ 2, 3, 4; Civ. Code (1901), §§ 2557, 2558, 2559. Placers: Laws of 1897, p. 12; Civ. Code (1901), § 2563.

[5] Pol. Code, 1895, §§ 3611, 3612, as amended—Laws of 1901, pp. 140, 141. Held reasonable and not in conflict with the federal laws: Purdum *v.* Laddin, 23 Mont. 387, 389, 59 Pac. 153.

[6] Comp. Laws (1900), §§ 209, 210. Placers: *Id.*, § 221.

[7] Comp. Laws of 1884, § 1566; Comp. Laws of 1897, §§ 2286, 2298.

[8] Rev. Pol. Code, 1895, § 1428; *Id.*, 1899, §§ 1428, 1433.

[9] Laws of 1898, p. 17, §§ 2, 3, as amended—Laws of 1901, p. 140.

[10] Comp. Laws of Dak., 1887, §§ 1999, 2004, adopted in South Dakota —Laws of 1890, ch. cv, § 1. Grantham's Annot. Stats. S. D. (1899), § 2663.

[11] Laws of 1899, p. 26, § 4.

Washington,[1]   Wyoming.[2]

(12) *Providing for the manner of relocating aban-*
     doned claims.—

Arizona,[3]   North Dakota,[9]
Colorado,[4]   Oregon,[10]
Idaho,[5]   South Dakota,[11]
Montana,[6]   Washington,[12]
Nevada,[7]   Wyoming.[13]
New Mexico,[8]

(13) *Amount of annual work.—*

Arizona,[14]   New Mexico,[18]
Arkansas,[15]   North Dakota,[19]
Colorado,[16]   South Dakota,[20]
Nevada,[17]   Utah,[21]

[1] Laws of 1899, p. 69, § 1. Placers: *Id.*, p. 72, § 10, as amended—
Laws of 1901, p. 292.
[2] Lodes: Rev. Stats. of Wyoming (1899), § 2550. Placers: *Id.*, § 2553.
[3] Rev. Stats. (1901), § 3241.
[4] Mills' Annot. Stats., § 3162.
[5] Laws of 1895, p. 28, § 7; Civ. Code (1901) § 2560.
[6] Pol. Code, 1895, § 3615.
[7] Comp. Laws (1900), § 214.
[8] Comp. Laws (1897), § 2300.
[9] Rev. Pol. Code, § 1439; *Id.*, 1899, § 1439.
[10] Laws of 1898, p. 17, § 4.
[11] Comp. Laws of Dak., 1887, § 2010, adopted by South Dakota—Laws
of 1890, ch. cv, § 1; Grantham's Annot Stats. S. D. (1899), § 2669.
[12] Laws of 1899, p. 71, § 8.
[13] Rev. Stats. of Wyoming (1899), § 2552.
[14] Re-enacts the federal law—Rev. Stats. (1901), § 3239.
[15] Provides that miners of county may regulate the amount. Acts of
1899, p. 113, § 6.
[16] Placers: Mills' Annot. Stats., § 3137. Declared in conflict with federal law: Sweet *v.* Webber, 7 Colo. 443, 450, 4 Pac. 752.
[17] One hundred dollars annually; fixing value of day's labor at four
dollars for eight hours. Comp. Laws (1900), § 216.
[18] Fixing value of day's labor at four dollars for eight hours. Comp.
Laws, 1884, § 1568; *Id.*, (1897), § 2288.
[19] Same as the federal law. Rev. Pol. Code, § 1438; *Id.*, 1899, § 1439.
[20] Same as the federal law. Comp. Laws of Dak., § 2009, adopted by
South Dakota—Laws of 1890, ch. cv, § 1; Grantham's Annot. Stats. S.
D. (1899), § 2668.
[21] Laws of 1899, p. 26, § 6.

Washington,[1]   Wyoming.[2]

No state has a right to decrease the amount of labor which the congressional law requires to be done annually on a mining claim.[3] The law clearly implies that the states and territories, or the district organizations, in the absence of state or territorial legislation, may increase the amount of such labor.[4]

In the case of Northmore v. Simmons (*supra*), a majority of the court held a local regulation of a mining district to be valid which required the sinking of a shaft to a depth of ten feet "within ninety days of location," and provided that "otherwise the claim shall be subject " to relocation." This regulation plainly made the sinking of this shaft a part of the annual work, and not a part of the location. The decision was placed upon the ground that the mining district had power to increase the amount of annual work required by the federal laws, and to shorten the time within which a portion of it is to be done. There is an able dissenting opinion by Judge Ross, who takes the position that congress having expressly provided that the period within which the annual work is required to be done,—"shall commence " on the first day of January succeeding the date of " location,"—a state or mining district has no power to shorten this time. And this, it seems to us, is the true ground. While a state or mining district may increase

---

[1] Same as federal law. Ballinger's Annot Codes and Stats. of Wash., § 3154. Placers: Laws of 1899, p. 72, § 10 (subd. 3), as amended—Laws of 1901, p. 282. See Laws of 1899, p. 73, § 14.

[2] Placers: One hundred dollars per annum on claims consisting of one hundred and sixty acres; on claims of less than one hundred and sixty acres, sixty-two and a half cents per acre. Revised Stats. of Wyoming (1899), §§ 2554, 2560, as amended—Laws of 1901, p. 105.

[3] Penn v. Oldhauber, 24 Mont. 287, 290, 61 Pac. 649; Sweet v. Webber, 7 Colo. 443, 450, 4 Pac. 752.

[4] Rev. Stats., § 2324; Northmore v. Simmons, 97 Fed. 386, 387; Sisson v. Sommers, 24 Nev. 379, 388, 55 Pac. 829.

the amount of labor required to hold the claim, it can only do so when it does not thereby impair an estate granted by congressional laws. When a locator has perfected his location, he is granted under the acts of congress the right to exclusive possession of his claim until the end of the year succeeding that in which the location is made without any further act on his part.[1] Such a local rule as the one in question is an attempt to declare that right forfeited unless certain further acts are done by the locator within ninety days, and is therefore an effort to impair a right or an estate granted by congress in the public lands. In this view we are upheld by the decision of the supreme court of the state of California in the case of Original Co. of the W. & K. *v.* W. M. Co.[2]

The statutory declaration, as in New Mexico, that a day's work of eight hours is of the value of four dollars, and must be so computed in estimating the amount of annual labor performed on a mining claim, is of questionable propriety. Mr. Morrison is of the opinion that such provisions "amount to absolutely " nothing."[3]

The supreme court of Montana, in the case of Penn *v.* Oldhauber,[4] held a local custom of similar purport to be in conflict with section twenty-three hundred and twenty-four of the Revised Statutes, and consequently invalid.

(14) *Posting notice that annual or development work is in progress.*—

Utah.[5]

---

[1] Belk *v.* Meagher, 104 U. S. 279, 285.
[2] 60 Cal. 631.
[3] Morr. Min. Rights, 8th ed., p. 67; *Id.*, 10th ed., p. 86.
[4] 24 Mont. 287, 61 Pac. 649.
[5] Laws of 1899, p. 26, § 5.

(15) *Authorizing the recording of affidavits of performance of annual labor.*—

Arizona,[1]	Nevada,[7]
Arkansas,[2]	New Mexico,[8]
California,[3]	Utah,[9]
Colorado,[4]	Washington,[10]
Idaho,[5]	Wyoming.[11]
Montana,[6]	

(16) *Prescribing manner of organizing mining districts.*—

Wyoming.[12]

(17) *Authorizing survey of claim to be made by deputy mineral surveyor, and when recorded to become a part of the location certificate and become prima facie evidence as to all facts therein contained.*—

Montana,[13]   Nevada.[14]

(18) *Manner of locating tunnel claims and length allowed on discovered lodes.*—

Colorado,[15]   Nevada.[16]

---

[1] Rev. Stats. (1901), § 3240.
[2] Acts of 1901, p. 330, § 2.
[3] Civ. Code, § 1159, as amended in 1891. See, also, Laws of 1891, p. 219.
[4] Mills' Annot. Stats., § 3161; Laws of 1889, p. 261.
[5] Laws of 1895, p. 27, § 6; Laws of 1899, p. 634; Civ. Code (1901), § 2565.
[6] Pol. Code, 1895, § 3614.
[7] Comp. Laws (1900), § 217.
[8] Comp. Laws (1897), § 2315.
[9] Laws of 1899, p. 27, § 6.
[10] Laws of 1899, p. 70, § 6. Placers: *Id.*, p. 72, § 10 (subd. 4), as amended—Laws of 1901, p. 292.
[11] Placers: Rev. Stats. of Wyoming (1899), § 2559, as amended—Laws of 1901, p. 105, § 3.
[12] Rev. Stats. of Wyoming (1899), §§ 2533, 2534.
[13] Pol. Code, 1895, § 3616.
[14] Comp. Laws (1900), § 215.
[15] Mills' Annot. Stats., §§ 3140, 3141; Laws of 1897, pp. 181, 182.
[16] Comp. Laws (1900), §§ 226, 229.

(19) *Manner of locating millsites, and area allowed
          therefor.—*
    Nevada.[1]

While it is manifest that the states and territories may
legislate within a reasonable limit upon the foregoing
subjects, we do not intend that it should be inferred that
all of the legislation hereinbefore noted is absolutely in
harmony with the letter and spirit of the national law.
It is not our purpose at the present time to deal with
individual state and territorial legislation analytically.
When we come to consider the requirements of a valid
location, the conditions required to perfect and perpetuate it, we shall note under each appropriate head the
nature and force of such legislation. We are now presenting generally the subjects upon which, to some
extent, states and territories are permitted to legislate.

§ 251. **Subjects upon which states have enacted
laws the validity of which is open to question.**—It
is extremely difficult to draw the line between what is
proper supplemental state legislation and what is not.
But there are some subjects upon which there has been
state and territorial legislation, which legislation is
either clearly obnoxious to the federal law or open to
criticism as being ineffectual, by reason of its being a
mere reiteration of the provisions of the Revised Statutes. We note the following instances which illustrate
this:—

(1) *Laws giving a locator the right to all lodes which
          have their top, or apex, within the location,
          and defining the extralateral right.—*
    Colorado,[2]   Nevada,[3]

[1] Laws of 1897, p. 103, §§ 15-18; Comp. Laws (1900), §§ 222-225.
[2] Mills' Annot. Stats., § 3156.
[3] Comp. Laws (1900), § 211.

North Dakota,[1]   Washington,[3]
South Dakota,[2]   Wyoming.[4]

(2) *Rights of parties in cases of lodes crossing or uniting.* —

Colorado.[5]

(3) *Rights of locators of two crevices, found to be the same lode.*

Colorado.[6]

(4) *Prohibiting the proprietor of a mining claim from pursuing his vein on its strike beyond vertical planes drawn through surface boundaries.* —

Colorado,[7]   North Dakota,[9]
Nevada,[8]   South Dakota.[10]

These four classes of legislation clearly trench upon the power of congress. These subjects can only be regulated by the federal law, as they attempt to define and limit the character of the estate granted by the government.[11] We do not understand that any of these provisions conflict with the federal law. But their re-enactment by the states gives them no force. If in harmony with the federal law, they are unnecessary; if obnoxious to it, they are void.

[1] Rev. Pol. Code, 1895, § 1434; *Id.*, 1899, § 1434.

[2] Comp. Laws of Dak., 1887, § 2005, adopted by South Dakota—Laws of 1890, ch. cv, § 1; Grantham's Annot. Stats. S. D. (1899), § 2664.

[3] Hill's Annot. Stats. (Wash.), § 2212; Ballinger's Annot. Codes and Stats. of Wash., § 3153.

[4] Laws of 1888, p. 89, § 20; Rev. Stats. of Wyoming (1899), § 2551.

[5] Mills' Annot. Stats., § 3142.

[6] *Id.*, § 3143.

[7] *Id.*, § 3157.

[8] Comp. Laws (1900), § 212.

[9] Rev. Pol. Code, 1895, § 1435; *Id.*, 1899, § 1435.

[10] Comp. Laws of Dak., 1887, § 2006, adopted by South Dakota—Laws of 1890, ch. cv., § 1; Grantham's Annot. Stats. S. D. (1899), § 2665.

[11] See, *ante*, § 249.

(5) Verification of location certificates by oath.—

Idaho,[1]   Montana.[2]

In Wenner v. McNulty, the supreme court of Montana expressed its doubt of the right of the then territory to impose the additional burden upon the locator of verifying the notice of location by oath, and stated that this rule trenched very closely upon the federal law.[3] The law had been previously enforced in a case in which its validity was apparently not questioned.[4] But in O'Donnell v. Glenn,[5] the court squarely upheld the law. In a still later case, Judge De Witt, speaking for the court, conceived that there were doubts about the validity of the rule, but declined to overrule O'Donnell v. Glenn and sustained the doctrine of that case.[6] This ruling has been followed in cases since decided by that court.[7] It was raised in the federal courts, but was not passed upon.[8]

The Idaho statute was held to be valid by the supreme court of that state in Van Buren v. McKinley.[9]

(6) Providing methods for forfeiting estate of delinquent co-owner.—

Arizona,[10]   California,[11]

[1] Rev. Stats., § 3104, as amended—Laws of 1895, p. 29, § 13; Civ. Code (1901), § 2564.

[2] Declaratory statement on oath. Pol. Code, 1895, § 3612, as amended —Laws of 1901, p. 141.

[3] 7 Mont. 30, 37, 14 Pac. 643.

[4] McBurney v. Berry, 5 Mont. 300, 5 Pac. 867.

[5] 8 Mont. 248, 252, 19 Pac. 302.

[6] Metcalf v. Prescott, 10 Mont. 283, 293, 25 Pac. 1037.

[7] McCowan v. Maclay, 16 Mont. 235, 40 Pac. 290; Berg v. Koegel, 16 Mont. 266, 40 Pac. 605.

[8] Preston v. Hunter, 67 Fed. 996, 999.

[9] Idaho (1901), 66 Pac. 936, 938. See, also, Dunlap v. Pattison (Idaho), 42 Pac. 504.

[10] Laws of 1891, p. 140; Rev. Stats. (1901), §§ 3245-3249.

[11] Stats. 1891, ch. clv, p. 219.

Colorado,[1]   Nevada.[2]

The act of congress on this subject [3] is perhaps open
to the criticism that it attempts to deprive a person of
property without due process of law. Ordinarily, forfeitures may only be adjudged by courts of competent
jurisdiction, after a full investigation as to the facts.[4]
It might be held that the act contemplates, after the
failure on the part of the co-owner to comply with the
forfeiture notice, the institution of a judicial action for
the purpose of adjudging a forfeiture.[5] In any event,
as was said by Judge De Witt, speaking for the supreme
court of Montana, the statute must be strictly construed.[6]

If compliance with the provisions of the act of congress is insufficient to divest the title of the co-owner, we
do not see how the state may supplement it by laws
which do not contemplate the institution of judicial
proceedings. If the federal law is sufficient, there
is no necessity for state legislation. We do not
think that this subject is within the legitimate scope
of state or territorial legislation. A state might
create a lien in favor of the co-owner who pays more
than his proportion of the annual expenditures, and
authorize proceedings to foreclose that lien; but to
sanction a forfeiture through the method of *ex parte*
proceedings is repugnant to the spirit of the law. It
may be accomplished under the federal law. But we
deny the right of the state to legislate, except within the
lines herein suggested.

[1] Mills' Annot. Stats., § 3137.

[2] Laws of 1897, p. 103, § 11; Comp. Laws of Nevada (1900), § 218.

[3] Rev. Stats., § 2324.

[4] Schulenberg *v.* Harriman, 21 Wall. 44; Hammer *v.* Garfield M. and M.
Co., 13Q U. S. 291, 9 Sup. Ct. Rep. 548; King *v.* Mullen, 171 U. S. 420,
18 Sup. Ct. Rep. 925; Pennoyer *v.* Neff, 95 U. S. 714, 733.

[5] Brundy *v.* Mayfield, 15 Mont. 201, 208, 38 Pac. 1067.

[6] *Id.*, 15 Mont. 201, 206, 38 Pac. 1067. See, also, **Turner** *v.* Sawyer, 150
U. S. 578, 585, 14 Sup. Ct. Rep. 192; *post,* § 646.

(7) *Specifying the character of deposits which may be located under the placer laws.—*

Montana.[1]

While all the substances named in the Montana act fall within the definition of the term "mineral," as we understand it,[2] making legislation of this character unnecessary, yet the state has no right by its legislature to construe federal laws. A provision like the foregoing would be eminently proper in a congressional law, and if enlarged and adopted by congress, it would have the effect of removing the ambiguities and uncertainties now existing. But we cannot understand how it is within the power of a state to dictate to the national government what substances it shall dispose of under its mineral laws.

§ 252. **Drainage, easements, and rights of way for mining purposes.**—By section twenty-three hundred and thirty-eight of the Revised Statutes, it is enacted, that—

"As a condition of sale, in the absence of necessary " legislation by congress, the local legislation of any " state or territory may provide rules for working " mines, involving easements, drainage, and other neces- " sary means to their complete development, and those " conditions shall be fully expressed in the patent."

Arizona,[3] Colorado,[4] and Wyoming[5] have enacted laws providing for and regulating drainage of mines; and in the following territories and states we find local legislation prescribing methods of obtaining easements

---

[1] Gold or other deposit of minerals, including building-stone, limestone, marble, clay, sand, and other mineral substances having a commercial value. Pol. Code, 1895, § 3610.

[2] *Ante*, § 98.

[3] Rev. Stats., 1887, §§ 2352-2357; *Id.* (1901), §§ 3252-3257.

[4] Mills' Annot. Stats., §§ 3172-3180.

[5] Rev. Stats. of Wyoming (1899), § 2535.

and rights of way for mining purposes and providing for condemnation proceedings:—

Arizona,[1]	New Mexico,[7]
California,[2]	North Dakota,[8]
Colorado,[3]	South Dakota,[9]
Idaho,[4]	Utah,[10]
Montana,[5]	Washington,[11]
Nevada,[6]	Wyoming.[12]

This class of legislation, in the states at least, is not, strictly speaking, supplemental to the federal law. It is more in the nature of independent legislation, the validity and operative force of which is to be determined from a consideration of the limitation upon legislative action prescribed by the organic laws of the respective states.

In the case of The People *ex rel.* Aspen M. and S. Co. *v.* District Court, considered by the supreme court of Colo-

[1] Laws of 1881, p. 167; Rev. Stats. (1887), p. 314; *Id.* (1901), § 2445, subd. 5.

[2] Code Civ. Proc., as amended, 1895, § 1238.

[3] Mills' Annot. Stats., § 3158.

[4] Acts 1877, 1881; Rev. Stats., 1887, §§ 3130-3142; Civ. Code (1901), §§ 2572-2574. As to mining tunnels: *Id.*, §§ 3575-3578.

[5] Pol. Code, 1895, §§ 3630-3640; Code Civ. Proc., § 2211; Laws of 1899, p. 125 (subds. 4 and 5). And see Glass *v.* Basin M. and C. Co., 22 Mont. 151, 55 Pac. 1047.

[6] Comp. Laws, § 120; Stats. 1887, pp. 102, 103, § 1; Comp. Laws (1900), § 281.

[7] Comp. Laws (1897), §§ 2328-2336.

[8] Comp. Laws of Dak., 1887, §§ 2016-2028; Rev. Codes N. D., 1899, § 5956 (subds. 4 and 5).

[9] Comp. Laws of Dak. (1887), §§ 2016-2028; Grantham's Annot. Stats. S. D. (1899), §§ 2674-2686.

[10] Laws of 1896, p. 316; Rev. Stats., § 3588, as amended—Laws of 1901, p. 19.

[11] Laws of 1897, p. 95; Ballinger's Annot. Codes and Stats., § 4282; Laws of 1899, p. 261.

[12] Laws of 1888, p. 84, § 5; Rev. Stats. of Wyoming (1899), §§ 2536, 3059; Rev. Stats. (1887), § 525.

rado,[1] it was urged that section twenty-three hundred and thirty-eight of the Revised Statutes imposed upon mineral lands acquired under the mining laws conditions which could not be ignored by the states; that they amounted practically to a burden charged upon the land and a limitation of the estate conveyed. Therefore, that these provisions were above and beyond state legislation upon the subject of eminent domain; that the state could not by its constitution abridge or curtail the privileges sanctioned by the law of congress; and that the doctrine of public "utility" in no way controlled this class of easements.

The contention, however, was not sustained. The supreme court of Colorado was of the opinion that, so far as the territories were concerned, congress might authorize the organization of a local government, with authority to enact laws, or it might legislate directly for the government of the territory. But upon the admission of a territory into the union as a sovereign state, the right of local self-government passes to the state.[2] The power of legislation thereafter resides in the people of the state, and is absolute and uncontrolled save as to the enumerated powers reserved to the national government by the federal constitution and the restraints upon state legislation imposed by that instrument. Other limitations upon the powers of the legislative department of a state are to be found in the state constitution. One of the powers of state sovereignty which may be exercised in the regulation and control of private property is termed the right of eminent domain. The exercise of this power within the states by the federal government extends only to appropriations by the United States for sites for post-offices, court-houses,

---

[1] 11 Colo. 147, 17 Pac. 298.
[2] See, also, Woodruff v. North Bloomfield G. M. Co., 18 Fed. 774, 775.

forts, arsenals, light-houses, custom-houses, and other
public uses.

"The foregoing principles," said the supreme court
of Colorado, "declaratory of the sovereign powers
" pertaining to the federal and state governments re-
" spectively, do not sustain the broad proposition of
" counsel that congress may ignore state constitutions
" and authorize local legislatures, regardless of state
" constitutions, to pass laws providing rules for the
" working of mines and involving easements upon min-
" eral lands. It is the solemn duty of the courts of a
" state to enforce the state constitution as the paramount
" law, whenever an act of the state legislature is found
" to be clearly in conflict therewith. Assuming that the
" state constitution is a valid instrument, the authority
" of congress to authorize the state legislature to pass
" laws upon any subject in conflict therewith cannot
" be admitted. But congress has not assumed to exer-
" cise such a power. The rules and easements intended
" to be authorized by the fifth section of the congres-
" sional act of July 26, 1866,[1] were evidently such as
" should be enacted in accordance with the fundamental
" law of the state or territory. Considered with refer-
" ence to the territories, the section is unobjectionable
" in any view of the question, since, as we have seen, the
" power of congress to govern them is absolute. . . .
" As applicable to state governments, the provision may
" be regarded as authorizing them to supplement the
" act of congress with necessary and proper rules and
" requirements, to be observed by citizens who have
" availed or might avail themselves of the privilege
" given to explore, occupy, and mine the mineral lands
" of the public domain with a view to acquiring title
" thereto. In so far as the provisions of the act may
" be regarded as conferring power upon the state legis-
" lature, to regulate the manner of using and operating
" mining claims, with a view to the protection of the
" rights of the several claimants, and to render avail-
" able their respective locations, by imposing restraints
" on the mode of operating and using them, including

---

[1] Now embodied in § 2338, Rev. Stats.

" necessary easements over the same, it would seem
" from the authorities cited that the states already
" possessed this power. Being comparatively a new
" question, however, at the date of the passage of the
" congressional act, this and the other permissive
" clauses were properly and wisely inserted. The opin-
" ion of Mr. Justice Field, in Jennison v. Kirk, (98
" U. S. 453-460), upon other portions of this act, shows
" that the intention of congress by the insertion of pro-
" visions of this character was not to grant easements
" upon mining claims, but to sanction such as might be
" regularly granted by the local authorities, and in
" order that they might be perpetuated as property
" rights after the title had passed from the government.
" This precaution prevents any controversy in the
" future as to the power of either territory or state to
" impose easements on these lands while they belong to
" the United States.

"From these principles and considerations, we arrive
" at the conclusion, that, unless a state statute imposing
" an easement upon mining claims is in accord with the
" state constitution, it can not be enforced by our
" courts." [1]

The case under consideration arose out of an attempt
to condemn a right of way for a tramway across the
lands of another, to enable the Aspen mining and smelting company to transport ores from its mines to the
sampling works in the town of Aspen, under a statute
which provided that all mining claims now located, or
which may be hereafter located, shall be subject to the
right of way for any tramway, whether now in use or
which may hereafter be laid across any such location, to
be condemned as in case of land taken for public highways when the consent of the owner can be obtained.[2]

The constitution of the state limited the power of the
legislative department to the taking of private property

---

[1] People ex. rel. Aspen M. and S. Co. v. District Court, 11 Colo. 147,
17 Pac. 298.

[2] Gen. Stats. Colo., 1887, § 2407; Mills' Annot. Stats., § 3158.

for public use, and for the following *private* uses: "For "private ways of necessity and for reservoirs, drains, "flumes, or ditches for agricultural, mining, milling, "domestic, or sanitary purposes."[1]

The court held that as tramways were not within the sanction of the constitution, the act of the legislature in question was void.

The rule announced in this case was approved and followed by Judge Hallet, sitting as United States circuit judge in the district of Colorado, in the recent case of Cone *v.* The Roxanna G. M. and T. Co.[2]

In the case of Calhoun G. M. Co. *v.* Ajax G. M. Co.[3] it was held that since section twenty-three hundred and thirty-eight of the Revised Statutes provides only for easements for the development of mines, no rights thereunder could be acquired under a statute of Colorado giving a right of way for tunnels located for the purpose of discovery.

From a consideration of these cases, the doctrine of which is in harmony with the views announced by Judge Cooley, the most eminent of all writers on constitutional law,[4] it cannot be doubted that the validity of the laws of the several states purporting to provide for securing easements and rights of way over the lands of others, for purposes connected with the industry of mining, must be determined regardless of the federal laws, and in the light of the respective state constitutions. The exercise by the state of its sovereign right of eminent domain cannot be interfered with by the United States.[5]

[1] Const., art. ii, §§ 14, 15.
[2] 2 Legal Adv. 350, 352.
[3] 27 Colo. 1, 26, 83 Am. St. Rep. 17, 59 Pac. 607, on appeal, 182 U. S. 499, 509, 21 Sup. Ct. Rep. 885.
[4] Cooley's Const. Limit., 6th ed., 645.
[5] Mississippi and Rum River Boom Co. *v.* Patterson, 98 U. S. 403.

§ **253. Provisions of state constitutions on the subject of eminent domain.**—As preliminary to a discussion of the general features of state legislation on this subject, we think it not inappropriate to present an epitome of the constitutional provisions of the several states where laws of this class have been enacted, so far as such provisions are germane.

California.—

" Private property shall not be taken or damaged for public " use without just compensation having been first made to, " or paid into court for, the owner, and no right of way shall " be appropriated to the use of any corporation other than " municipal until full compensation therefor be first made in " money or ascertained or paid into court for the owner, " irrespective of any benefit for any improvement proposed " by such corporation, which compensation shall be ascer- " tained by a jury, unless a jury be waived, as in other civil " cases in a court of record, as shall be prescribed by law." [1]

" The exercise of the right of eminent domain shall never " be so abridged or construed as to prevent the legislature " from taking the property and franchises of incorporated " companies and subjecting them to public use, the same as " the property of individuals." [2]

" The use of all water now appropriated, or that may here- " after be appropriated, for sale, rental, or distribution, is " hereby declared to be a public use, and subject to the regu- " lation and control of the state, in the manner to be pre- " scribed by law." [3]

Colorado.—

" That private property shall not be taken for private use " unless by consent of the owner, except for private ways of " necessity, and except for reservoirs, drains, flumes, or " ditches on or across the land of others, for agricultural, " mining, milling, domestic, or sanitary purposes." [4]

[1] Const. Cal., art. i, § 14.　　　[3] *Id.*, art. xiv, § 1.
[2] *Id.*, art. xii, §8.　　　[4] Const. Colo., art. ii, § 14.

" That private property shall not be taken or damaged,
" for public or private use, without just compensation. Such
" compensation shall be ascertained by a board of commis-
" sioners, of not less than three freeholders, or by a jury
" when required by the owner of the property, in such manner
" as may be prescribed by law, and until the same shall be
" paid to the owner, or into court for the owner, the property
" shall not be needlessly disturbed, or the proprietary rights
" of the owner therein divested; and whenever an attempt is
" made to take private property for a use alleged to be public,
" the question whether the contemplated use be really public
" shall be a judicial question, and determined as such without
" regard to any legislative assertion that the use is public." [1]

Idaho.—

" The necessary use of lands for the construction of reser-
" voirs or storage basins, for the purpose of irrigation, or for
" rights of way for the construction of canals, ditches, flumes,
" or pipes, to convey water to the place of use, for any useful,
" beneficial, or necessary purpose, or for drainage; or for the
" drainage of mines or the working thereof, by means of
" roads, railroads, tramways, cuts, tunnels, shafts, hoisting
" works, dumps, or other necessary means to their complete
" development, or any other use necessary to the complete
" development of the material resources of the state, or the
" preservation of the health of its inhabitants, is hereby
" declared to be a public use, and subject to the regulation
" and control of the state.

" Private property may be taken for public use, but not
" until a just compensation, to be ascertained in a manner
" prescribed by law, shall be paid therefor." [2]

Montana.—

" Private property shall not be taken or damaged for pub-
" lic use without just compensation having been first made
" to, or paid into the court for, the owner." [3]

[1] Const. Colo., art. ii, § 15.   [3] Const. Mont., art. iii, § 14.
[2] Const. Idaho, art. i, § 14.

" The use of all water now appropriated, or that may here-
" after be appropriated, for sale, rental, distribution, or other
" beneficial use, and the right of way over the lands of others,
" for all ditches, drains, flumes, canals, and aqueducts neces-
" sarily used in connection therewith, as well as the sites for
" reservoirs necessary for collecting and storing the same,
" shall be held to be a public use. Private roads may be
" opened in the manner to be prescribed by law; but in every
" case the necessity of the road, and the amount of all dam-
" age to be sustained by the opening thereof, shall be first
" determined by a jury, and such amount, together with the
" expenses of the proceeding, shall be paid by the person to be
" benefited." [1]

Under this clause the supreme court of Montana held
" the use of water for the purpose of irrigating a par-
" ticular tract of agricultural land, or working a par-
" ticular mine," to be a public use.[2]

Nevada.—

. . . " Nor shall private property be taken for public use
" without just compensation having been first taken or se-
" cured, except in cases of war, riot, fire, or great public
" peril, in which case compensation shall be afterward
" made." [3]

North Dakota.—

" Private property shall not be taken or damaged for public
" use without just compensation having been first made to,
" or paid into court for, the owner, and no right of way shall
" be appropriated to the use of any corporation other than
" municipal, until full compensation therefor be first made in
" money, or ascertained and paid into court for the owner,

---

[1] Const. Mont., art. iii, § 15.
[2] Ellinghouse v. Taylor, 19 Mont. 462, 464, 48 Pac. 757; Smith v.
Denniff, 24 Mont. 20, 22, 81 Am. St. Rep. 408, 60 Pac. 398. And see
Butte, A. and P. Ry. Co. v. Montana U. Ry. Co., 16 Mont. 504, 50 Am.
St. Rep. 508, 41 Pac. 232; Glass v. Basin M. and C. Co., 22 Mont. 151,
55 Pac. 1047.
[3] Const. Nev., art. i, § 8.

" irrespective of any benefit from any improvement proposed
" by such corporation, which compensation shall be ascer-
" tained by a jury, unless a jury be waived." [1]

South Dakota.—

" Private property shall not be taken for public use, or
" damaged, without just compensation, as determined by a
" jury, which shall be paid as soon as it can be ascertained,
" and before possession is taken. No benefit which may accrue
" to the owner as a result of an improvement made by any
" private corporation shall be considered in fixing the com-
" pensation for property taken or damaged. The fee of land
" taken for railroad tracks or other highways shall remain in
" such owners, subject to the use for which it is taken." [2]

Utah.—

" Private property shall not be taken or damaged for a
" public use without just compensation." [3]

Washington.—

" Private property shall not be taken for private use,
" except for private ways of necessity, and for drains, flumes,
" or ditches on or across the lands of others for agricultural,
" domestic, or sanitary purposes. No private property shall
" be taken or damaged for public or private use without just
" compensation having been first made, or paid into court
" for the owner, and no right of way shall be appropriated to
" the use of any corporation other than municipal until full
" compensation therefor be first made in money, or ascer-
" tained and paid into court by the owner, irrespective of any
" benefit from any improvement proposed by such corporation,
" which compensation shall be ascertained by a jury, unless a
" jury be waived, as in other civil cases in courts of record, in
" the manner prescribed by law. Whenever an attempt is
" made to take private property for a use alleged to be public,
" the question whether the contemplated use be really public

---

[1] Const. N. Dak., art. i, § 14.　　[3] Const. Utah, art. i, § 22.
[2] Const. S. Dak., art. vi, § 13.

" shall be a judicial question, and determined as such, without
" regard to any legislative assertion that the use is public." [1]

Wyoming.—

" Private property shall not be taken for private use un-
" less by consent of the owner, except for private ways of
" necessity, and for reservoirs, drains, flumes, or ditches on
" or across the lands of others, for agricultural, mining, mill-
" ing, domestic, or sanitary purposes, nor in any case without
" due compensation." [2]

" Private property shall not be taken or damaged for pub-
" lic or private use without just compensation." [3]

It will thus be seen that private property may be subjected to burdens for certain specified purposes that
may generally be classified as private, in Colorado,
Idaho, Montana,[4] Washington, and Wyoming. In these
states, it would seem that, within the limitations prescribed by the respective constitutions, the local legislatures may act, although some of the uses are not
essentially public. The legislation in the remaining
states,—*i. e.* California, Nevada, North Dakota, and
South Dakota,—and in the other states, for purposes not
within the specified limitations, must necessarily be confined to such uses as are essentially public in their
nature.

§ 254. **Mining as a "public use."**—An exhaustive
discussion of the law of eminent domain is hardly within
the scope of this treatise, but it is necessary to deal with
it to some extent.

The organic law of a state may not properly provide
for the condemnation of private property for private

---

[1] Const. Wash., art. i, § 16.

[2] Const. Wyo., art. i, § 32.

[3] *Id.*, art. i, § 33.

[4] Ellinghouse *v.* Taylor, 19 Mont. 462, 48 Pac. 757; Smith *v.* Denniff,
24 Mont. 20, 81 Am. St. Rep. 408, 60 Pac. 398; Glass *v.* Basin M. and
C. Co., 22 Mont. 151, 55 Pac. 1047.

use. The use must be public. Otherwise, the property is taken without due process of law.[1] But what is a public use depends largely upon the facts and circumstances surrounding the particular subject-matter of the use. The people of a state and the members of its legislature are more familiar with the facts and circumstances surrounding a particular subject-matter within the state than a stranger to the state can be. Consequently constitutional declarations, acts of legislature, and decisions of the courts of a state as to what is and what is not a public use within the state, while not conclusive, are entitled to great respect in the federal courts.[2]

Mr. Lewis, in his work on the "Law of Eminent " Domain," states that, apart from constitutional considerations, it is not essential in order to constitute an act of eminent domain that the use for which property is taken should be of a public nature. It is sufficient that the use of the particular property is necessary to enable individual proprietors to cultivate and improve their land to the best advantage, or to develop certain natural and exceptional resources incident thereto, such as a water privilege or a mine. In such cases, the public welfare is promoted, though indirectly, by the increased prosperity which necessarily results from developing the natural resources of the country.[3]

This is an exceedingly optimistic view of the rule, not concurred in by other writers, and is contrary to the authorities above cited. It is expressly disapproved by Mr. Randolph.[4]

[1] Fallbrook Irrigation District v. Bradley, 164 U. S. 112, 159, 17 Sup. Ct. Rep. 56; Missouri Pac. Ry. v. Nebraska, 164 U. S. 403, 417, 17 Sup. Ct. Rep. 130.

[2] Fallbrook Irrigation District v. Bradley, 164 U. S. 112, 159, 160, 17 Sup. Ct. Rep. 56.

[3] Lewis on Eminent Domain, § 1.

[4] The Law of Eminent Domain, § 39.

Mr. Mills thus states his conclusions upon the subject of condemnation for private use:—

"The use to which property is condemned must be " public. As between individuals, no necessity, how- " ever great, no exigency, however imminent, no im- " provement, however valuable, no refusal, however " unneighborly, no obstinacy, however unreasonable, no " offers of compensation, however extravagant, can " compel or require a man to part with one inch of his " estate." [1]

Judge Cooley says:—

"It is conceded on all hands that the legislature has " no power, in any case, to take the property of one " individual and pass it over to another, without refer- " ence to some use to which it is to be applied for public " benefit." [2]

Only a few of the state constitutions in terms prohibit the taking of private property for private use. All the courts, however, agree that this can not be done.[3]

As was said by the supreme court of New Jersey,—

"There is no prohibition in the constitution of this " state, or in any of the state constitutions that I know " of, against taking private property for private use. " But the power is nowhere granted to the legislature. " The constitution vests in the senate and general as- " sembly the legislative or law-making power. They " may make laws, the rules prescribed to govern our " civil conduct. They are not sovereign in all things; the " executive and judicial power is not vested in them. " Taking the property of one man and giving it to " another is not making a law or rule of action; it is " not legislation, it is simply robbery." [4]

While this may be true, the rule announced is based upon a taking for a purely private purpose, unaccompanied by any supposed indirect public benefit.

---

[1] Mills on Eminent Domain, § 22.
[2] Cooley's Const. Limit., 6th ed., 651.
[3] Lewis on Eminent Domain, § 157, and cases cited in note.
[4] Coster v. Tide Water Co., 18 N. J. Eq. 54, 63.

As to what constitutes a "public use" is a difficult question. It is impossible for us to supply a definition sufficiently comprehensive to cover all possible cases. Nor is it necessary that we should do so. The question as to whether a given use is or is not public is a judicial one. The legislature can not so determine that the use is public as to make the determination conclusive upon the courts; but the presumption is in favor of the public character of a use declared to be public by the legislature; and unless it is seen at first blush that it is not possible for the use to be public, the courts can not interfere.[1]

§ 255. **Rights of way for pipe-lines for the conveyance of oil and natural gas.**—In the application of these principles to the class of state legislation under consideration, we find that the decisions of the courts are not altogether uniform. The power of eminent domain has been exercised for pipe-lines for the conveyance of oil and natural gas.[2]

The theory in such cases seems to be, that pipe-lines for such purposes are public highways, and their owners common carriers engaged in the transportation of oil or gas.

But, independently of this view, these uses are just as much public in their nature as supplying water to municipalities. Fuel and light are just as essential commodities as water, and their general distribution to

---

[1] Mills on Eminent Domain, § 10; Lewis on Eminent Domain, § 158; Fallbrook Irrigation Dist. v. Bradley, 164 U. S. 112, 159, 160, 17 Sup. Ct. Rep. 56. The rule is different in Colorado and Washington, whose constitutions provide that the question is to be determined without regard to any legislative assertion. Const. Colo., art. ii, § 15; Const. Wash., art. i, § 16.

[2] Randolph on Eminent Domain, § 47; West Va. Trans. Co. v. Volcanic C. Co., 5 W. Va. 382; Johnston v. Gas Co., 5 Cent. Rep. 564; Carothers v. Philadelphia Co., 118 Pa. 468, 12 Atl. 314.

the public for domestic, manufacturing, or industrial purposes is of unquestioned "public utility."

The legislatures of Arizona,[1] California,[2] and Utah,[3] have declared "oil pipe-lines" to be a public use.

§ 256. Lateral and other railroads for transportation of mine products.—The mining interests in certain localities have been deemed sufficiently important to justify statutes enabling a mine-owner to condemn rights of way from his mine to the nearest available thoroughfare, by means of what are termed "lateral " railroads." But the laws authorizing the construction and maintenance of such railroads over the lands of another provide that all persons who may have occasion to do so may utilize them, thus making the use at least *quasi* public.[4]

A railroad company organized under a law making it a common carrier of passengers and freight may, of course, condemn land for its road-bed. And the fact that the road terminates at a mine, and is used for transporting the mined product, does not alter the public character of the use.[5]

But, in respect to the transportation of mine products, it has been held that a mine-owner can not condemn land for a railroad to be used exclusively for the product of his own mine.[6] Such use is a mere private one, to which the law of eminent domain is inapplicable.[7]

[1] Laws of 1899, p. 62; Rev. Stats. (1901), § 2445, subd. 8.

[2] Code Civ. Proc., § 1238, as amended—Laws of 1891, p. 48.

[3] Rev. Stats. (1898), § 3588, as amended—Laws of 1901, p. 19.

[4] Randolph on Eminent Domain, § 47; Hays v. Risher, 32 Pac. St. 169, 176; De Camp v. Hibernia R. R. Co., 47 N. J. L. 43, 47; New Cent. C. Co. v. George's Creek C. Co., 37 Md. 537, 559; Phillips v. Watson, 63 Iowa, 28; Brown v. Corey, 43 Pa. St. 495, 503.

[5] Contra Costa R. R. v. Moss, 23 Cal. 323; Colorado E. Ry. Co. v. Union Pac. Ry. Co., 41 Fed. 293.

[6] Randolph on Eminent Domain, § 47; Stewart's Appeal, 56 Pa. 413; McCandless's Appeal, 70 Pa. 210; Sholl v. German C. Co. 118 Ill. 427. 59 Am. Rep. 379, 10 N. E. 199.

[7] People v. Pittsburg R. R., 53 Cal. 694.

This was the rule announced as to tramways by the supreme court of Colorado, heretofore discussed;[1] also by the supreme court of Pennsylvania,[2] and the supreme court of West Virginia.[3]

§ 257. Physical and industrial conditions as affecting the rule of "public utility."—Mr. Randolph, in his work on eminent domain,[4] says:—

"The magnitude of the interests involved seems to " have been in some cases the determining factor in " upholding the necessity for condemnation.[5]

"This seems to account for the distinction drawn by " Chief Justice Shaw between a single mill and a great " mill power—the latter a public use,[6] and the former " not.[7]

"Whatever merit there is in this particular dis- " tinction, there is doubtless some, albeit an indefinable " force of principle. One might admit the publicity of " lateral railroads and irrigation works in states con- " taining great mineral deposits and vast tracts of arid " land,[8] and deny the necessity of these works in states " where mineral wealth and desert land are so insignifi- " cant as to render the public gain by their development " absurdly disproportionate to the private benefit.

"There is some force in the suggestion that 'what " 'shall be considered a public use may depend some- " 'what on the situation and wants of the community " 'for the time being.' "[9]

---

[1] People ex rel. Aspen M. Co. v. District Court, 11 Colo. 147, 17 Pac. 298.

[2] Edgewood R. R.'s Appeal, 79 Pa. St. 257.

[3] Valley City S. Co. v. Brown, 7 W. Va. 191.

[4] Randolph on Eminent Domain, § 52.

[5] Great Falls Mfg. Co. v. Fernald, 47 N. H. 444.

[6] Hazen v. Essex Co., 12 Cush. 475.

[7] Murdock v. Stickney, 8 Cush. 113.

[8] See Oury v. Goodwin (Ariz.), 26 Pac. 376. This case very ably presents the question as applied to waterways for irrigation purposes, in many of its aspects. The opinion is replete with authorities, and presents the law logically.

[9] Scudder v. Trenton Del. Falls Co., 1 N. J. Eq. 694, 729, 23 Am. Dec. 756.

This view is upheld by the supreme court of the
United States in Fallbrook Irrigation District *v.* Bradley.[1]

§ 258. **The rule in Nevada, Arizona, Montana, and
Georgia.**—In these states certain private enterprises,
such as mining and irrigation, which on account of physical and industrial conditions are of the first importance
to the people of the state, are regarded as public utilities,
and it is held that the power of eminent domain may be
invoked in their aid. The decisions announced by the
courts in each of these states will be separately considered.

The state of Nevada enacted a law which provided
that—

"The production and reduction or ores are of vital
" necessity to the people of this state; are pursuits in
" which all are interested, and from which all derive a
" benefit; so the mining, milling, smelting, or other
" reduction of ores are hereby declared to be for the
" public use, and the right of eminent domain may be
" exercised therefor."[2]

We have already noted the provisions of the Nevada
constitution on this subject.

An action was brought under this statute to condemn
a strip of land to enable the Dayton mining company to
transport over it the wood, lumber, timbers, and other
materials required by it in the conduct of its business of
mining. The district court declined to act upon the
application on the ground that the statute in question
was unconstitutional and void.

A writ of mandate was applied for, to compel the district court to act, upon which application the supreme
court of the state admitted that private property could

[1] 164 U. S. 112, 159, 17 Sup. Ct. Rep. 56.
[2] Stats. 1875, § 111; Comp. Laws (1900), §§ 283-300.

not be taken for private use; that the declaration by the legislature was not conclusive upon the courts, and that the sole question to be determined was whether the use was a public one. Upon this the court, speaking through Chief Justice Hawley, said:—

"The reasons in favor of sustaining the act under
" consideration are certainly as strong as any that have
" been given in support of the mill-dam or flowage
" acts, as well as some of the other objects heretofore
" mentioned. Mining is the greatest of the industrial
" pursuits in this state. All other interests are sub-
" servient to it. Our mountains are almost barren of tim-
" ber, and our valley lands could never be made profit-
" able for agricultural purposes, except for the fact of a
" home market having been created by the mining
" developments in different sections of the state. The
" mining and milling interests give employment to
" many men, and the benefits derived from this busi-
" ness are distributed as much, and sometimes more,
" among the laboring classes than with the owners of
" the mines and mills. The mines are fixed by the laws
" of nature, and are often found in places almost inac-
" cessible. For the purpose of successfully conducting
" and carrying on the business of 'mining, milling,
" 'smelting, or other reduction of ores,' it is necessary
" to erect hoisting-works, to build mills, to construct
" smelting furnaces, to secure ample grounds for dump-
" ing waste rock and earth; and a road to and from the
" mine is always indispensable. The sites necessary for
" these purposes are oftentimes confined to certain fixed
" localities. Now, it so happens, or at least is liable to
" happen, that individuals, by securing a title to the
" barren lands adjacent to the mines, mills, or works,
" have it within their power, by unreasonably refusing
" to part with their lands for a just and fair compensa-
" tion, which capital is always willing to give without
" litigation, to greatly embarrass, if not entirely defeat,
" the business of mining in such localities. In my opin-
" ion, the mineral wealth of this state ought not to be
" left undeveloped for the want of any quantity of land
" actually necessary to enable the owner or owners of

" mines to conduct and carry on the business of mining.
" Nature has denied to this state many of the advan-
" tages which other states possess, but, by way of com-
" pensation to her citizens, has placed at their doors the
" richest and most extensive silver deposits ever yet dis-
" covered. The present prosperity of the state is
" entirely due to the mining developments already
" made, and the entire people of the state are directly
" interested in having the future developments unob-
" structed by the obstinate action of any individual or
" individuals." [1]

A like doctrine was affirmed by the same court in a
later case, where a mine-owner sought to condemn the
land of another for the purpose of sinking a shaft
thereon.[2]

The rule thus established was adhered to by the circuit court of appeals for the ninth circuit, holding that
a mining company may, under the Nevada statute, condemn for use in reaching its mine an old and partially
ruined tunnel in a neighboring claim which is not used
by the owners of that claim, there being nothing in the
record to show any present intention on the part of such
owners to use it for mining purposes.[3]

The decision in the case of Dayton M. Co. v. Seawell,
supra, presents the question of "public use," as applied
to the class of state legislation under consideration, in
the most favorable light for the mining industry. In
its diction it is a classic; in its logic it is persuasive, considering the local conditions existing in that state.

§ 259. **Arizona.**—The supreme court of Arizona, by
a parallel line of reasoning, reached the same conclusions as to the validity of the laws of that territory
authorizing the condemnation of land for the purpose of

---

[1] Dayton M. Co. v. Seawell, 11 Nev. 394, 408.
[2] Overman S. M. Co. v. Corcoran, 15 Nev. 147.
[3] Byrnes v. Douglass, 83 Fed. 45.

a canal or ditch for irrigating purposes. Said that
court:—

"May a state or territory, in view of its natural advan-
" tages and resources and necessities, legislate in such a
" way, exercising the power of eminent domain, that
" these advantages and resources may receive the fullest
" development for the general welfare, the laws being
" general in their operation? This territory is vast in
" extent, and rich in undeveloped natural resources.
" Mountains and deserts are not an inviting prospect
" when viewed by a stranger in transit. But the moun-
" tains abound in the precious metals, gold and silver,
" 'the jewels of sovereignty'; and the deserts may be
" made to 'bloom and blossom as the rose.' The one
" great want is water. With this resource of nature
" made available, the mountains and the deserts may
" be made to yield fabulous wealth, and Arizona become
" the home of a vast, prosperous, and happy people.
" But with water in this territory 'cribbed, cornered,
" 'and confined,' it will continue and remain the mys-
" terious land of arid desert plains, and barren hillsides,
" and bleak mountain peaks. The legislature of the ter-
" ritory, seeing what was apparent to all, adopted at an
" early day a policy—' a general and important public
" 'policy.' That policy was to protect against private
" ownership and monopoly the one thing indispensable
" to the growth, development, and prosperity of the ter-
" ritory,—the element that would serve to uncover the
" gold and silver hidden in the hills and mountains, and
" transform the desert into a garden. . . . The wisdom
" of this policy, under the physical conditions existing
" in the territory, must be apparent to every one."[1]

§ 259a. Montana.—The section of the constitution of
Montana[2] declaring certain uses of water to be public
has been quoted above.[3] The legislature enacted a law
authorizing a proceeding to condemn a right of way over
the lands of another for ditches used for irrigating pur-

[1] Oury v. Goodwin (Ariz.), 26 Pac. 376, 382.　　[3] See, ante, § 253.
[2] Art. iii, § 15.

poses. Under this act a proceeding was commenced by Ellinghouse to condemn a right of way for his irrigating-ditch across the lands of Taylor. The latter contended that the statute was unconstitutional, as authorizing the taking of private property for private uses, and that the constitutional provision restricted the public use of water to the sale, rental, distribution, and *kindred* beneficial uses. The court refused to sustain this contention, saying:—

"We cannot agree with this construction of section " fifteen, article three, of the constitution of Montana. " The phrase 'other beneficial use' clearly included in " the term 'public use' the use of water for the purpose " of irrigating a particular tract of agricultural land or " working a particular mine, as well as the use of water " for irrigating a number of tracts of land or working " a number of mines owned by different persons. In " California, whose constitutional provision on the sub-" ject of the use of water, it is insisted by appellant, is " substantially the same as that of Montana, a much " narrower interpretation of the term 'public use' has " been adhered to than we can agree with. In Lorenz " *v.* Jacobs [1] the supreme court of California held that " 'The right of eminent domain is restricted to the tak-" 'ing of private property for public use. It cannot be " 'exercised in favor of the owners of mining claims, to " 'enable them to obtain water for their own use in work-" 'ing such claims, though the intention may also be to " 'supply water to others for mining and irrigating pur-" 'poses.'

. . . .

"The constitutional provision of California, however, " is not the same as that of Montana on the subject of " the use of water. The former does not contain the " phrase 'other beneficial use.' But even if this phrase " were not included in the Montana provision, we should " not feel disposed to follow the California construction. " It impresses us as narrow and retrogressive. Under

[1] 63 Cal. 73.

" this language in the constitution of each state,—
" namely, 'the appropriation of water for distribution,'
" —we think the courts of either state would be justified
" in declaring the use of water for one or two tracts of
" land or mines a 'public use.'

. . . .

"The public policy of the territory and the state of
" Montana has always been to encourage in every way
" the development of the minerals contained in its
" mountains, and the necessity for adding to its tilled
" acreage is manifest. This state is an arid country,
" and water is essential to the proper tillage of its scat-
" tered agricultural valleys. With all this in view, it was
" expressly declared in our state's constitution that the
" use of water by private individuals for the purpose of
" irrigating their lands should be a public use. The
" statute of 1891 regulating the manner in which rights
" of way for irrigating ditches should be acquired was
" enacted under the constitution in order to carry out
" the intention of its framers and the people who
" adopted it." [1]

A similar doctrine had previously been announced
with reference to a lateral railroad having its terminus
at a mine.[2]

§ 260. Georgia.—The supreme court of Georgia
upheld an act of the state legislature creating a private
corporation and empowering it to condemn lands for the
purpose of enabling it to work its mines for gold or
other valuable minerals by the hydraulic process, thus
stating its reasons:—

"Gold and silver is the constitutional currency of the
" country, and to facilitate the production of gold from
" the mines in which it is imbedded, for the use of the
" public, is for the public good, though done through
" the medium of a corporation or individual enterprise.

[1] Ellinghouse v. Taylor, 19 Mont. 462, 48 Pac. 757.
[2] Butte A. and P. Ry. Co. v. Montana Union Ry. Co., 16 Mont. 504, 50
Am. St. Rep. 508, 41 Pac. 232.

"The increased production of gold from the mines of
"Lumpkin county by the means as provided for in the
"defendant's charter must necessarily be for the public
"good, inasmuch as it will increase for the use of the
"public a safe, sound constitutional circulating me-
"dium, which is of vital importance to the permanent
"welfare and prosperity of the people of the state of
"Georgia, as well as of the people of the United
"States." [1]

We cannot perceive upon what principle, particularly
in states like Georgia, the industry of mining should be
considered of "public utility" any more than the cultivation of the soil and the raising of cotton, sugar-cane,
cereals, or any other product so essential to the use of
mankind. There may be some plausibility for the rule
as announced in Nevada, based, as it is, upon the peculiar conditions existing in that state. But certainly the
reasons given by the supreme court of Georgia are
neither logical nor persuasive.

§ 261. The rule in Pennsylvania, West Virginia, California, and Oregon.—In these states a private enterprise
such as mining is not regarded as a public utility in the
sense of authorizing the exercise of the power of eminent
domain in its behalf. The decisions of the respective
courts on this subject will be considered in order.

An act of the legislature of Pennsylvania[2] provided
for a right of way across or under rivers or other
streams of this commonwealth, for the better and more
convenient mining of anthracite coal. The supreme
court of that state held the act to be unconstitutional and
void, as conferring authority to take private property
for private use.[3]

---

[1] Hand G. M. Co. v. Parker, 59 Ga. 419, 424.
[2] Purd. Dig., § 1967.
[3] Waddell's Appeal, 84 Pa. St. 90.

In the case of Edgewood R. R. Co.'s appeal,[1] the same court refused to permit a condemnation of land for a railroad which was a mere appurtenant to a mine, thus stating its views:—

"The commonwealth transfers to its citizens her " power of eminent domain only when some existing " public need is to be supplied or some present public " advantage is to be gained. She does not confer it with " a view to contingent results, which may or may not " be produced, and may or may not justify the grant, " as a projected speculation may prove successful or " disastrous."

§ 262. **West Virginia.**—In West Virginia an act was passed providing that any person owning land having timber upon it, or containing coal, ore, or other minerals, who desires to obtain a subterranean or surface right of way by railroad or otherwise, under, through, or over land belonging to another, for the purpose of mining for such minerals, or conveying such timber or minerals to market, or for the purpose of draining any coal or mineral lands under, through, or over lands belonging to another, might institute proceedings for the condemnation of such lands for such purposes.[2]

Under this act, the Valley City salt company, owning some thirty acres of coal land, sought to condemn a subterranean right of way through the land of another, for the purpose of extracting and transporting its coal. The supreme court of West Virginia held that the intended use was strictly private in its nature, and that the right of eminent domain could not be exercised for any such purpose.[3]

§ 263. **California.**—The supreme court of California has, in several instances, had under consideration a stat-

---

[1] 79 Pa. St. 257, 269.
[2] Code W. Va., ch. xliii, §§ 44, 45.
[3] Valley City Salt Co. v. Brown, 7 W. Va. 191.

ute of that state which provides that the right of eminent
domain may be exercised in behalf of certain enumerated
public uses, including "tunnels, ditches, flumes, pipes,
" and dumping-places for working mines; also, outlets,
" natural or otherwise, for the flow, deposit, or conduct
" of tailings or refuse matter from the mines." [1]

In the case of the Consolidated Channel Co. *v.* C. P.
R. R. Co.[2] the attempt was made by the plaintiff, as the
owner of a gold mine, to condemn a right of way for the
purpose of constructing a ditch and flume to carry off
the tailings from the mine.

" It is clear," said the court, "that the object sought is
" the appropriation of the private property of the de-
" fendants to the private use of plaintiff. The proposed
" flume is to be constructed solely for the purpose of
" advantageously and profitably washing and mining
" plaintiff's mining ground. It is not even pretended
" that any person other than the plaintiff will derive
" any benefit whatever from the structure when com-
" pleted. No public use can possibly be subserved by
" it. It is a private enterprise, to be conducted solely
" for the personal profit of the plaintiff, and in which
" the community at large have no concern. It is clear
" that this case does not come within the meaning of
" that clause of the constitution which permits the tak-
" ing of private property for a public use. . . . It would
" be difficult to suppose a case more completely within
" the exception stated, and in which the absence of all
" possible public interest in the purposes for which the
" land is sought to be condemned is more clear and
" palpable, than in the case at bar."

In Lorenz *v.* Jacobs,[3] the same court held that the
right of eminent domain could not be exercised in favor
of the owners of mining claims, to enable them to obtain
water for their own use in working such claims, though

[1] Code Civ. Proc., § 1238, (subd. 5). See, also, Laws of 1891, § 2,
p. 221.
[2] 51 Cal. 269.
[3] 63 Cal. 73.

the intention may also be to supply water to others for mining and irrigating purposes.

In the case of Amador Queen M. Co. *v.* Dewitt,[1] the plaintiff undertook to condemn the right of way through defendant's ground, for the purpose of a tunnel to enable plaintiff to extract ore from its mine and transport it to its mill, defendant's land intervening between plaintiff's mine and its mill. The federal statute was invoked, as in the Colorado case of People *ex rel.* Aspen M. and S. Co. *v.* District Court (*supra*). But the court held that the language of the Revised Statutes of the United States contained no reservation of such right in favor of plaintiff,[2] that the mine of defendant was his private property, the use for which it was sought to be condemned was a private use, and the proceeding could not be maintained.

§ 263a. **Oregon.**—The legislature of Oregon enacted a law[3] authorizing any corporation organized for the purpose of transporting timber, lumber, or cordwood to condemn rights of way for railroads, skid roads, tramways, chutes, and flumes which "shall be deemed to be " for the public benefit, . . . and shall afford to all " persons equal facilities in the use thereof for the " purposes to which they are adapted, upon payment or " tender of reasonable compensation for such use." The Apex transportation company sought, under this act, to condemn a right of way over the land of the defendant for a skid road. But the supreme court of Oregon held that the use for which condemnation was sought was private, and, consequently, that the act was unconstitutional.[4]

---

[1] 73 Cal. 482, 15 Pac. 74.

[2] Cited approvingly in Cone *v.* Roxana G. M. Co., U. S. Cir. Ct., Dist. of Colo., 2 Leg. Adv. 350.

[3] Laws of 1895, p. 5.

[4] Apex Trans. Co. *v.* Garbade, 32 Or. 582, 52 Pac. 573, 54 Pac. 367, 882.

§ 264. Conclusions.[1]—While in states and territories surrounded by such physical and industrial conditions as exist in Nevada and Arizona, and probably Montana, judicial discretion may, with some show of reason, be exercised in favor of the rule that mining in the hands of individuals is a "public use," yet such a rule elsewhere is against the logic of the law and the weight of authority.

We may appropriately close this discussion by quoting from the opinions of two distinguished courts as to what constitutes a public use:—

"No question has ever been submitted to the courts "upon which there is a greater variety and conflict of "reasoning and results than that presented as to the "meaning of the words 'public use,' as found in the "different state constitutions regulating the right of "eminent domain. The reasoning is in many of the "cases as unsatisfactory as the results have been uncer- "tain. The beaten path of precedent, to which courts "when in doubt seek refuge, here furnishes no safe "guide to lead us through the long lane of uncertainty "to the open highway of public justice and of right. "The authorities are so diverse and conflicting that, no "matter which road the court may take, it will be sus- "tained, and opposed, by about an equal number of the "decided cases. In this dilemma, the meaning must, "in every case, be determined by the common sense of "each individual judge who has the power of deciding "it." [2]

"What, then, constitutes a public use, as distinguished "from a private use? The most extended research will "not likely result in the discovery of any rule or set of "rules or principles of certain and unusual application "by which this question can be determined in all cases.

---

[1] In the state of New York mining is a "public utility," for the reason that the ownership of the precious metals is in the state by virtue of its sovereignty, and the fundamental theory is analogous to the doctrine of the civil law. See, *ante*, §§ 11, 19.

[2] Dayton G. and S. M. Co. *v.* Seawell, 11 Nev. 394, 400.

" Eminent jurists and distinguished writers upon public
" law do not express concurrent or uniform views upon
" this subject. It is a question, from its very nature, of
" great practical, perhaps of insuperable, difficulty, to
" determine the degree of necessity or the extent of
" public use which justifies the exercise of this extraor-
" dinary power upon the part of a state, by which the
" citizen, without his will, is deprived of his prop-
" erty." [1]

[1] Valley City Salt Co. v. Brown, 7 W. Va. 191, 195.

CHAPTER II.

LOCAL DISTRICT REGULATIONS.

§ 268. Introductory.

§ 269. Manner of organizing districts.

§ 270. Permissive scope of local regulations.

§ 271. Acquiescence and observance, not mere adoption, the test.

§ 272. Regulations, how proved— Their existence a ques-

tion of fact for the jury; their construction a question of law for the court.

§ 273. Regulations concerning records of mining claims.

§ 274. Penalty for non-compliance with district rules.

§ 275. Local rules and regulations before the land department.

§ 268. **Introductory.**—In the beginning the miners made the laws governing the mining industry, unhampered by congressional or state legislation. In their district assemblages they adopted regulations which covered most of the exigencies of the situation, and frequently much more. They amended, altered, and repealed their rules at will, as changed conditions suggested the necessity, propriety, or convenience. Some of these regulations were wise, and others were otherwise. That these early prospectors were pioneers of extreme western civilization in America, and assisted in laying the foundation of great states, is undoubted. For this they deserve, and have received, full meed of praise. But that they originated a system which is deserving of perpetuation for all time is open to serious question. We doubt whether there is any reason at the present time for permitting local district regulations of any character. If congress will not remodel the national

477   INTRODUCTORY.   § 268

mining laws in such a way as to prohibit legislation by
local assemblages, the several states and territories
should so cover the ground as to render mining districts
as law-making factors not only unnecessary—for that
they usually are—but impossible. In a previous chapter,[1] we have traced the origin and noted the general
character of district rules and miners' customs during
the period when they constituted the American common
law of mines. The change in governmental policy
wrought by the act of July 26, 1866, and the
subsequent legislation crystallizing into the existing
system, have circumscribed the limits within which
such rules and customs may have controlling force,
and they now constitute but a small part in the
scheme of mining jurisprudence. When we further
consider that in most of the precious-metal-bearing
states the legislatures have enacted mining codes of
more or less comprehensive nature, leaving but little to
be regulated by district rules, we are forced to recognize
the fact that the tendency is towards the absolute elim-
ination of miners' regulations and customs as elements
controlling mining rights. Nevertheless, in some states
legislation is meager, and the subjects with which district organizations may deal are limited only by the laws
of congress. In all of the states and territories some
vestige of power still resides in these local mining communities. Local rules may still be adopted, if they do
not contravene congressional or state legislation.[2]

It therefore becomes necessary to deal with them to a
limited extent, to consider the field in which they may
legitimately be made operative, the manner of their

[1] Tit. II, ch. iii, §§ 40-46.
[2] Erhardt v. Boaro, 113 U. S. 527, 5 Sup. Ct. Rep. 560; Jackson v. Roby,
109 U. S. 440, 3 Sup. Ct. Rep. 301; Rosenthal v. Ives, 2 Idaho, 244, 12
Pac. 904; Dutch Flat W. Co. v. Mooney, 12 Cal. 534; Flaherty v. Gwinn,
1 Dak. 509; Wolfley v. Lebanon M. Co., 4 Colo. 112; In re Monk, 16
Utah, 100, 50 Pac. 810; Penn v. Oldhauber, 24 Mont. 287, 61 Pac. 649.

adoption, the manner of proving their existence, and the rules of construction to be applied to them.

§ 269. **Manner of organizing districts.**—With the exception of the state of Wyoming,[1] no attempt has ever been made to prescribe the manner of creating mining districts. They generally come into existence without much formality. Any new discovery attracts prospectors. Usually the advance-guard is limited in number; but however few, they are sufficient to organize full-fledged districts, and equip them with "rules and regu-" lations" on short notice. The geographical limits are defined, a recorder is elected, and the district is ready for business. When the first or any subsequent set of rules requires amendment, modification, or abrogation, the miners convene at some appointed place, usually upon notice posted, and thus the legislative machinery is set in motion. As we shall see later, the courts do not closely scrutinize methods by which these rules are adopted. This was the primitive way, and for a time served a useful purpose, simply because the necessities of the case demanded and justified it.

Judge W. H. Beatty gives some very excellent reasons for the total abolition of the system:—

" In districts," said that distinguished jurist, "where " the rules are in writing, where they have been some " time in force, and generally recognized and respected, " the law may be tolerably well settled. But there is " often a question whether the rules have been regularly " adopted or generally recognized by the miners of a " district. There may be two rival codes, each claiming " authority and each supported by numerous adherents; " evidence may be offered of the repeal or alteration of " rules, and this may be rebutted by evidence that the " meeting which undertook to effect the repeal was " irregularly convened or was secretly conducted in

---

[1] Laws of 1888, p. 83; Rev. Stats. (1899), §§ 2533, 2534.

" some out-of-the-way corner, or was controlled by
" unqualified persons; customs of universal acceptance
" may be proved which are at variance with the written
" rules; the boundaries of districts may conflict, and
" within the lines of conflict it may be impossible to
" determine which of two codes of rules is in force;
" there may be an attempt to create a new district within
" the limits of an old one; a district may be deserted for
" a time, and its records lost or destroyed; and then a
" new set of locators may reorganize it and relocate the
" claims. This does not exhaust the list of instances
" within my own knowledge in which it has been a ques-
" tion of fact for a jury to determine what the law was
" in a particular district. Other instances might be
" cited, but I think enough has been said to prove that
" local regulations, being of no use, ought to be
" abolished." [1]

§ 270. **Permissive scope of local regulations.**—As to
the subjects concerning which district organizations may
prescribe rules, or which in any way may be controlled
by local customs in the absence of state legislation,
Judge W. H. Beatty, then chief justice of the supreme
court of Nevada, now chief justice of the supreme court
of California, in his testimony given before the public
land commission,[2] gave it as his opinion that under the
existing laws of congress the miners *may,* in the absence
of state legislation,—

First—Restrict themselves to smaller claims than the
maximum allowed by acts of congress;

Second—Require claims to be more thoroughly
marked than would be absolutely necessary to satisfy the
terms of the statutes;

Third—Require more work than the statutes require;

Fourth—Provide for the election of a recorder and
the recording of claims.

---

[1] Report of Public Land Commission, § 398.   [2] *Id.,* § 397.

This is in consonance with section twenty-three hundred and twenty-four of the Revised Statutes.

As to the first three points, said the judge, it may be safely assumed that no such regulations will be adopted in any district hereafter organized. As to the fourth, under existing legislation, local rules are worse than useless. The monuments on the ground do well and completely what the notice and record do only imperfectly and in part.

But the facts remain that miners may make rules, and that they do organize districts, perhaps as a matter of precedent and habit, and with vague notions as to the legitimate scope within which they may act. Much of the adjudicated law upon this subject is now obsolete, and a critical review of the decisions applicable to the primitive conditions is neither necessary nor justifiable. A few illustrations as to what local districts might *not* do may not be out of place.

It was always exacted that a local rule should be reasonable.[1] A local mining custom or regulation adopted after the location of a claim could not be given in evidence to limit the extent of a claim previously located.[2] But where changes were made in local rules with reference to amount of work to be done to perpetuate rights, or providing methods by which such work was condoned, prior locators were called upon to comply with the new regulations as a condition to the continuance of their rights.[3] A local custom fixing twenty days' work as equivalent to the amount required for annual assessment work was held void.[4]

---

[1] King *v.* Edwards, 1 Mont. 235; Flaherty *v.* Gwinn, 1 Dak. 509; Penn *v.* Oldhauber, 24 Mont. 287, 61 Pac. 649.

[2] Table Mountain T. Co. *v.* Stranahan, 31 Cal. 387; Roach *v.* Gray, 16 Cal. 383.

[3] Strang *v.* Ryan, 46 Cal. 33.

[4] Penn *v.* Oldhauber, 24 Mont. 287, 61 Pac. 649.

Rights held and sanctioned by general laws could not be divested by mere local rules and neighborhood customs.[1] Nor could rules and customs authorize acts amounting to a public nuisance.[2]

Prior to 1860, in California and Nevada, a written instrument was not required to transfer a mining claim. during that period evidence of local customs permitting such transfer by parol, accompanied by delivery of possession, was admissible.[3] But since that date conveyances in writing are necessary throughout the mining regions.[4]

Perfected mining locations are now considered as property in the highest sense of the term, and the rules applicable to other real estate govern their transfer. An agreement not in writing to convey an unpatented mining claim cannot be enforced.[5] One exception to this rule prevails, to-wit: "grub-stake" contracts need not be in writing.[6] Neither a transfer nor its recordation is now subject to regulation by local customs.

Where a state or territory has passed laws on any given subject within the privilege granted by the federal laws, to that extent, at least, the districts are powerless.[7]

[1] Waring v. Crow, 11 Cal. 367, 372; Dutch Flat W. Co. v. Mooney, 12 Cal. 234.

[2] Woodruff v. North Bloomfield M. Co., 9 Saw. 441, 18 Fed. 753.

[3] Jackson v. Feather River W. Co., 14 Cal. 19; Table Mountain T. Co. v. Stranahan, 20 Cal. 199; Gatewood v. McLaughlin, 23 Cal. 178; Patterson v. Keystone M. Co., 23 Cal. 575, 30 Cal. 360; Antoine Co. v. Ridge Co., 23 Cal. 219, 222; Hardenbergh v. Bacon, 33 Cal. 356, 381; Goller v. Fett, 30 Cal. 421; Folger v. Coward, 35 Cal. 652; Gore v. McBrayer, 18 Cal. 582; King v. Randlett, 33 Cal. 318; Kinney v. Con. Virginia M. Co., 4 Saw. 382, 452, Fed. Cas. No. 7827; Union S. M. Co. v. Taylor, 100 U. S. 37; Lockhardt v. Rollins, 2 Idaho, 503, 21 Pac. 413.

[4] Garthe v. Hart, 73 Cal. 541, 15 Pac. 93; Moore v. Hamerstag, 109 Cal. 122, 41 Pac. 805; Hopkins v. Noyes, 4 Mont. 550, 2 Pac. 280.

[5] Reagan v. McKibben, 11 S. Dak. 270, 76 N. W. 943.

[6] See, post, § 858.

[7] In re Monk, 16 Utah, 100, 50 Pac. 810.

Lindley on M.—31

Where a state or territory, by its general law, has only partially exercised its privilege of supplemental legislation, district regulations may, in turn, supplement such legislation within the field not covered by state or territorial laws, if within the sanction of the federal laws.

§ 271. **Acquiescence and observance, not mere adoption, the test.**—As heretofore observed, it is not necessary that any rules or regulations should be adopted. Compliance with the federal law and state legislation, if any, is sufficient.[1] But when adopted, and acquiesced in, if not in conflict with federal or state legislation, they have the force of positive law,[2] and substantial compliance with them is essential to a perfect mining title.[3]

As a rule, courts will not inquire into the regularity of the modes by which miners adopt their local rules, unless fraud or some other like cause be shown. It is enough that they agree upon their laws, and that they are recognized as the rules.[4]

Local regulations do not acquire operative force by mere adoption, but from customary obedience and acquiescence of the miners following the enactment;[5] and they become void whenever they fall into disuse or are generally disregarded.[6]

[1] Golden Fleece M. Co. v. Cable Cons. M. Co., 12 Nev. 312.

[2] Mallett v. Uncle Sam M. Co., 1 Nev. 203, 90 Am. Dec. 484; Gropper v. King, 4 Mont. 367; Rush v. French, 1 Ariz. 99, 25 Pac. 816; Gird v. California Oil Co., 60 Fed. 531, 535; McCormick v. Varnes, 2 Utah, 355.

[3] Gleeson v. Martin White M. Co., 13 Nev. 443; Becker v. Pugh, 17 Colo. 243, 29 Pac. 173; King v. Edwards, 1 Mont. 235; Sullivan v. Hense, 2 Colo. 424; Donahue v. Meister, 88 Cal. 121, 22 Am. St. Rep. 283, 25 Pac. 1096.

[4] Gore v. McBrayer, 18 Cal. 583, 589.

[5] North Noonday M. Co. v. Orient M. Co., 6 Saw. 299, 307, 1 Fed. 522; Jupiter M. Co. v. Bodie Cons. M. Co., 7 Saw. 96, 106, 11 Fed. 666; Harvey v. Ryan, 42 Cal. 626.

[6] North Noonday M. Co. v. Orient M. Co., 6 Saw. 299, 307, 1 Fed. 522; Jupiter M. Co. v. Bodie Cons. M. Co., 7 Saw. 96, 106, 11 Fed. 666.

A custom to be binding ought to be so well known, understood, and recognized in the district that locators should have no reasonable ground for doubt as to what is required.[1]

§ 272. Regulations, how proved—Their existence a question of fact for the jury; their construction a question of law for the court.—Judicial notice cannot be taken of the rules, usages, and customs of a mining district, and they should be proved at the trial, like any other fact, by the best evidence that can be obtained respecting them.[2] If one desires to attack the validity of another's location upon the ground that local rules and regulations were not complied with by the locators, he must show what such rules and regulations were.[3] The record books of the district into which written rules are transcribed are, of course, the best evidence as to such rules, and if lost or destroyed, secondary evidence is admissible.[4] But this record will not prove itself. It must be produced by the proper officer, and its authenticity as such established.[5]

Where copies of district rules are sought to be introduced in evidence, it is necessary that it should appear that they come from the proper repository, and that such custodian was empowered to give certified copies, and that such were copies of the laws prevailing and in force in the district.[6]

All of the written rules making up the body of the local law constitute one entire instrument; and it is

[1] Jupiter M. Co. v. Bodie Cons. M. Co., 7 Saw. 106, 111, 11 Fed. 666.

[2] Sullivan v. Hense, 2 Colo. 424; Meydenbauer v. Stevens, 78 Fed. 787.

[3] Kirk v. Meldrum (Colo), 65 Pac. 633; Dutch Flat Water Co. v. Mooney, 12 Cal. 534. See Glacier etc. M. Co. v. Willis, 127 U. S. 482, 8 Sup. Ct. Rep. 1214; Hughes v. Ochsner, 26 L. D. 540.

[4] Sullivan v. Hense, 2 Colo. 425; Campbell v. Rankin, 99 U. S. 261.

[5] Roberts v. Wilson, 1 Utah, 292.

[6] Harvey v. Ryan, 42 Cal. 626; Roberts v. Wilson, 1 Utah, 292.

necessary to a fair understanding of any one part that the whole should be inspected.[1]

Parol evidence of a mining custom cannot be given when there are written rules or regulations of the mining district in force on the same subject.[2] But if the proof renders it doubtful as to whether or not the written rules are in force, both the written laws and parol evidence of the mining customs may be offered in evidence.[3]

The existence of a custom relating to a subject not covered by the written laws, such as posting a notice on a claim, as an act indicating appropriation, may, of course, be shown.[4]

Rules and regulations once proved to have been adopted and acquiesced in, a presumption arises that they continue in force until something appears showing that they have been repealed or have fallen into disuse, and another practice has been generally adopted and acquiesced in.[5]

The mere violation of a rule by a few persons only would not abrogate it, if still generally observed. The disregard and disuse must become so extensive as to show that in practice it has become generally disused.[6] Such fact may be proved by a series of circumstances and conditions in the district.[7]

The existence of mining customs may be proved, however recent the date or short the duration of their estab-

[1] English v. Johnson, 17 Cal. 108, 119, 76 Am. Dec. 574; Roberts v. Wilson, 1 Utah, 292.

[2] Ralston v. Plowman, 1 Idaho, 595.

[3] Colman v. Clements, 23 Cal. 245.

[4] Harvey v. Ryan, 42 Cal. 626.

[5] North Noonday M. Co. v. Orient M. Co., 6 Saw. 299, 308, 1 Fed. 522; Jupiter M. Co. v. Bodie Cons. M. Co., 7 Saw. 96, 107, 11 Fed. 666; Riborado v. Quang Pang Co., 2 Idaho, 131, 6 Pac. 125.

[6] North Noonday M. Co. v. Orient M. Co., 6 Saw. 299, 308, 1 Fed. 522.

[7] Jupiter M. Co. v. Bodie Cons. M. Co., 7 Saw. 96, 112, 11 Fed. 666; Flaherty v. Gwinn, 1 Dak. 509.

lishment. The common-law doctrine as to customs in such cases does not govern.[1]

Whether a given rule or custom is in force at any given time, is a question of fact to be determined by the jury.[2] But the court must construe the rule;[3] and it shall be so construed as to harmonize with the entire body of the mining law,[4] including all other rules in force in the district.[5]

There is no distinction between the effect of a "custom" or usage, the proof of which must rest in parol, and a "regulation," which may be adopted at a miners' meeting, and embodied in a written local law.[6]

Some of the courts have held that a discoverer has a reasonable time to perfect his location after discovery, in the absence of a state statute or local rule fixing the time.[7] In such cases, it is said, the court may consider evidence of a general custom upon this subject prevalent in different sections of the mining regions as to what constitutes a reasonable time, following the principle announced in early days as to what was a reasonable extent of ground embraced in a mining location, in the absence of any local rule fixing it.[8]

[1] Smith v. North American M. Co., 1 Nev. 357, 359.

[2] North Noonday M. Co. v. Orient M. Co., 6 Saw. 299, 307, 1 Fed. 522; Jupiter M. Co. v. Bodie Cons. M. Co., 7 Saw. 96, 112, 11 Fed. 666; King v. Edwards, 1 Mont. 235; Poujade v. Ryan, 21 Nev. 449, 33 Pac. 659; Golden Fleece v. Cable Cons. M. Co., 12 Nev. 312; Sullivan v. Hense, 2 Colo. 424; Harvey v. Ryan, 42 Cal. 626.

[3] Fairbanks v. Woodhouse, 6 Cal. 434; Ralston v. Plowman, 1 Idaho, 595.

[4] Leet v. John Dare M. Co., 6 Nev. 218.

[5] English v. Johnson, 17 Cal. 108, 119, 76 Am. Dec. 574; Roberts v. Wilson, 1 Utah, 292.

[6] Harvey v. Ryan, 42 Cal. 626, 628; North Noonday M. Co. v. Orient M. Co., 6 Saw. 299, 307, 1 Fed. 522; Jupiter M. Co. v. Bodie Cons. M. Co., 7 Saw. 96, 106, 11 Fed. 666; Doe v. Waterloo M. Co., 70 Fed. 455, 459; Flaherty v. Gwinn, 1 Dak. 509.

[7] Doe v. Waterloo M. Co., 70 Fed. 455; Gleeson v. Martin White M. Co., 13 Nev. 443; Golden Fleece M. Co. v. Cable Cons. M. Co., 12 Nev. 312, 329.

[8] Table Mountain T. Co. v. Stranhan, 20 Cal. 199.

§ 273. **Regulations concerning records of mining claims.**—The mining laws of congress do not require any notice or certificate of location to be recorded. In the absence of some state or territorial law, or local rule or custom, providing for such record, it is unnecessary,[1] and proof of recording, without some regulation or custom requiring it, is irrelevant and inadmissible.[2]

If a notice is required, by either state law or local rules, to be recorded, it must contain all the requisites prescribed by section twenty-three hundred and twenty-four of the Revised Statutes.[3]

In some states district recorders have been required to turn over their records to the county recorder. Such legislation is valid.[4]

The popular understanding of the requirements of the mining law is, that notices of location should be recorded somewhere. This has led to an almost universal custom, in states where there are at present no

[1] Haws v. Victoria Copper Co., 160 U. S. 303, 16 Sup. Ct. Rep. 282; North Noonday M. Co. v. Orient M. Co., 6 Saw. 299, 311, 1 Fed. 522; Jupiter M. Co. v. Bodie Cons. M. Co., 7 Saw. 96, 111, 114, 11 Fed. 666; Southern Cross M. Co. v. Europa M. Co., 15 Nev. 383; Anthony v. Jillson, 83 Cal. 296, 23 Pac. 419; Gregory v. Pershbaker, 73 Cal. 109, 14 Pac. 401; Thompson v. Spray, 72 Cal. 528, 14 Pac. 182; Souter v. Maguire, 78 Cal. 543, 21 Pac. 183; Freezer v. Sweeney, 8 Mont. 508, 21 Pac. 20; Carter v. Bacigalupi, 83 Cal. 187, 23 Pac. 261; Fuller v. Harris, 29 Fed. 814; Allen v. Dunlap, 24 Or. 229, 33 Pac. 675; Gird v. California Oil Co., 60 Fed. 531; Moore v. Hamerstag, 109 Cal. 122, 41 Pac. 805; Meydenbauer v. Stevens, 78 Fed. 787, 792; Smith v. Newell, 86 Fed. 56; Perigo v. Erwin, 85 Fed. 904; Magruder v. Oregon and California R. R. Co., 28 L. D. 174; Kern County v. Lee, 129 Cal. 361, 61 Pac. 1124; Conway v. Hart, 129 Cal. 480, 62 Pac. 44.

[2] Golden Fleece M. Co. v. Cable Cons. M. Co., 12 Nev. 312.

[3] Hammer v. Garfield M. and M. Co., 130 U. S. 291, 9 Sup. Ct. Rep. 548; Gleason v. Martin White M. Co., 13 Nev. 443; North Noonday M. Co. v. Orient M. Co., 6 Saw. 299, 312, 1 Fed. 522; Jupiter M. Co. v. Bodie Cons. M. Co., 7 Saw. 96, 112, 11 Fed. 666; Poujade v. Ryan, 21 Nev. 449, 33 Pac. 659; Meydenbauer v. Stevens, 78 Fed. 787, 792; Smith v. Newell, 86 Fed. 56; Conway v. Hart, 129 Cal. 480, 62 Pac. 44.

[4] In re Monk, 16 Utah, 100, 50 Pac. 810.

laws or regulations on the subject, of recording all such notices in the county recorder's office of the several counties. Where provisions for recording are found only in local rules, the county recorder may not be required to so record. If he does, his act is not that of a county recorder elected by the people, but as a person selected by the miners to do an act not provided for by the recording laws of the state.[1] The county recorder's books, showing records of such claims in any considerable number, are competent evidence, as tending to establish such custom and its general observance.[2] But such custom, to be binding, ought to be so well known, understood, and recognized in the district, that locators should have no reasonable ground for doubt as to what was required as to the place of record.[3] When such a custom has been generally followed and acquiesced in, it gives the record validity and entitles it, or certified copies of it, to be introduced in evidence; but a failure to record would not work a forfeiture of the claim, or make it subject to relocation, unless the custom or rule so provided. This is the view adopted by the supreme courts of California and Arizona, and by Judge Sawyer; but the opposite conclusion has been reached by the courts of Montana and Nevada.[4]

Where such custom has become recognized and generally observed, the records of the county recorder, besides tending to establish a regulation sanctioning the recording of mining claims, also furnish evidence of a persuasive character, tending to show in many instances that local written regulations at one time formally adopted, and never formally repealed, have fallen into disuse. Instances of this character are found in several

---

[1] San Bernardino County v. Davidson, 112 Cal. 503, 44 Pac. 659. See the later case of County of Kern v. Lee, 129 Cal. 361, 61 Pac. 1124.

[2] Pralus v. Pacific G. and S. M. Co., 35 Cal. 30.

[3] Jupiter M. Co. v. Bodie Cons. M. Co., 7 Saw. 96, 111, 11 Fed. 666.

[4] See, *post*, § 274.

of the mining counties of California, and undoubtedly elsewhere. Prior to the passage of the act of May 10, 1872, written regulations adopted at a miners' meeting limited the width of lode claims to one hundred feet on each side of the lode, and provided for recording with a district recorder. After the passage of this act, it seems that, almost uniformly, location notices were recorded with the county recorder; and from such records it appeared that the new locations invariably claimed the statutory limit of three hundred feet on each side of the center of the vein. There can be no doubt that these records should be considered as competent evidence tending to establish the fact that the local rules had become obsolete, and were no longer of controlling force. A discussion of the method of proving local rules and customs concerning the location and recording of claims will be found in a preceding section.[1]

§ 274. **Penalty for non-compliance with district rules.** —While it has been frequently said that a forfeiture may be worked for failure to comply with local rules,[2] the supreme court of California at an early date announced the doctrine that—

"The failure to comply with any one of the mining " rules and regulations of the camp is not a forfeiture of " title. It would be enough to hold the forfeiture as a " result of the non-compliance with such of them as " make a non-compliance a cause of forfeiture." [3]

This doctrine was acquiesced in, in a later case, decided by the same court,[4] and reaffirmed at a still later date by the same tribunal, in the following terms:—

---

[1] See, *ante*, § 272. See, also, McCann *v.* McMillan, 129 Cal. 350, 62 Pac. 31.

[2] Mallett *v.* Uncle Sam M. Co., 1 Nev. 203; Oreamuno *v.* Uncle Sam M. Co., 1 Nev. 179; St. John *v.* Kidd, 26 Cal. 264; Depuy *v.* Williams, 26 Cal. 310; Purdum *v.* Laddin, 23 Mont. 387, 59 Pac. 153.

[3] McGarrity *v.* Byington, 12 Cal. 427.

[4] English *v.* Johnson, 17 Cal. 108, 117, 76 Am. Dec. 574.

" The objection taken to this instruction is, that it
" directs the jury to find for the defendants, if they find
" from the evidence that the plaintiff had failed to com-
" ply with certain regulations, without accompanying
" the same with a further charge as to whether these
" rules and regulations declared a forfeiture as the
" result of such non-compliance. The failure of a party
" to comply with a mining rule or regulation can not
" work a forfeiture, unless the rule itself so provides.
" There may be rules and regulations which do not pro-
" vide that a failure to comply with their provisions
" shall work a forfeiture. If so, a failure will not work
" a forfeiture; hence, in charging the jury upon a ques-
" tion of forfeiture, the charge should be narrowed to
" such rules as expressly provide that a non-compliance
" with their provisions shall be cause of forfeiture." [1]

This is now the settled rule in California.[2]

The rule announced by the California court was
accepted by the supreme court of Arizona,[3] and by the
late Judge Sawyer, circuit judge of the ninth circuit.[4]

The supreme court of Montana, however, while conceding that the decisions in California generally deserve
great weight upon the subject of mining, expresses the
opinion that upon this particular point they are far from
satisfactory, and declines to follow them.[5]

The supreme court of Nevada has also adopted a rule
different from that recognized in California and Arizona. That court has held that failure to comply with
laws or local rules works a forfeiture whether such laws
or rules provide for such forfeiture or not.[6]

---

[1] Bell v. Bed Rock H. and M. Co., 36 Cal. 214.

[2] Emerson v. McWhirter, 133 Cal. 510, 65 Pac. 1036.

[3] Johnson v. McLaughlin, 1 Ariz. 493, 4 Pac. 130, 132; Rush v. French,
1 Ariz. 99, 25 Pac. 816.

[4] Jupiter M. Co. v. Bodie Cons. M. Co., 7 Saw. 96, 117, 11 Fed. 666.
See, also, Flaherty v. Gwinn, 1 Dak. 509, 511.

[5] King v. Edwards, 1 Mont. 235, 241. See Purdum v. Laddin, 23 Mont.
387, 59 Pac. 153.

[6] Mallett v. Uncle Sam G. and S. M. Co., 1 Nev. 188, 90 Am. Dec. 484;
Oreamuno v. Uncle Sam M. Co., 1 Nev. 215; Sissons v. Sommers, 24 Nev.
379, 77 Am. St. Rep. 815, 55 Pac. 829.

The existing mining laws, however, relieve to a large extent the embarrassments which might flow from a conflict of opinion on this subject, particularly with reference to the performance of annual labor and the result of non-compliance with the terms of the law. As to other matters within the scope of local regulation which may be considered of minor importance, we think the California rule, as was said by the supreme court of Arizona, "is a safe and conservative rule of decision, " tending to the permanency and security of mining " titles." [1]

Forfeitures have always been deemed in law odious, and the courts have universally insisted upon their being clearly established before enforcing them.[2]

We shall have occasion to again consider this subject in another portion of this treatise, in connection with the perpetuation of estates acquired by location.

§ 275. **Local rules and regulations before the land department.**—In proceedings to obtain patents under the mining laws, it devolves upon the land department, in the absence of adverse claims, and suits brought to determine them, to decide what rules and regulations are in force in a given district, and its decision upon the subject is final.[3]

As a rule, the land department has followed closely the doctrines announced by the courts in the mining regions, in applying and construing local customs and

---

[1] Johnson v. McLaughlin, 1 Ariz. 493, 4 Pac. 130, 133. To the same effect, see Emerson v. McWhirter, 133 Cal. 510, 65 Pac. 1036.

[2] See, *post*, § 645; Hammer v. Garfield M. and M. Co., 130 U. S. 291, 9 Sup. Ct. Rep. 548; Mt. Diablo M. and M. Co. v. Callison, 5 Saw. 439, Fed. Cas. No. 9886; Belcher Cons. M. Co. v. Deferari, 62 Cal. 160; Quigley v. Gillett, 101 Cal. 462, 35 Pac. 1040; Johnson v. Young, 18 Colo. 625, 34 Pac. 173; Book v. Justice M. Co., 58 Fed. 106; Strasburger v. Beecher, 49 Fed. 740; Providence G. M. Co. v. Burke (Ariz.), 57 Pac. 641; Emerson v. McWhirter, 133 Cal. 510, 65 Pac. 1036.

[3] Parley's Park M. Co. v. Kerr, 130 U. S. 256, 262, 9 Sup. Ct. Rep. 511.

regulations. In suits upon adverse claims, where most of the questions arise, the local courts determine the facts and apply the law, and their judgment is a guide to the land department in the issuance of patents. We do not encounter in the decisions of this department much that is instructive at the present time, as applied to existing conditions.

(1) The legislation of congress; and at

(2) The legislation of the various states and territories, supplementing congressional legislation, and in harmony therewith; and

(3) Local rules and customs, or regulations established in conformity therewith, or not in conflict with the federal legislation or that of the state or territory wherein they are operative.[1]

We have traced the evolution of this system through the different periods of our national history, from the embryotic stage, which had its genesis in the local rules and customs of the mining camps of the west, to the development of higher forms of law. While in this progressive development the primitive forms have not altogether disappeared, they have been relegated from the position of controlling importance to that of mere subordinate and subsidiary functions. It is entirely unnecessary to here retrace the steps by which the present results were obtained. In the early chapters of this treatise,[2] we have endeavored to present such an historical review as will suffice for all practical purposes and enable the student to acquaint himself with the process of crystallization which has given us as a resultant the existing unique system. We are immediately concerned with the present practical operation of this system, and shall now consider the general nature and scope of state and territorial legislation supplemental to the congressional mining laws, a minor subsidiary element in the system, but in its particular sphere important.

§ 249. Limits within which state may legislate.—When it is recognized that the government simply occupies the *status* of a landed proprietor, holding the paramount title to its public domain, with the sole right of

TITLE V.

OF THE ACQUISITION OF TITLE TO PUBLIC MINERAL LANDS BY LOCATION, AND PRIVILEGES INCIDENT THERETO.

CHAPTER
- I. INTRODUCTORY—DEFINITIONS.
- II. LODE CLAIMS OR DEPOSITS "IN PLACE."
- III. PLACERS AND OTHER FORMS OF DEPOSIT NOT "IN "PLACE."
- IV. TUNNEL CLAIMS.
- V. COAL LANDS.
- VI. SALINES.
- VII. MILLSITES.
- VIII. EASEMENTS.

CHAPTER I.

INTRODUCTORY—DEFINITIONS.

ARTICLE I.   INTRODUCTORY.
  II.   "LODE," "VEIN," "LEDGE."
  III.   "ROCK IN PLACE."
  IV.   "TOP," OR "APEX."
  V.   "STRIKE," "DIP," OR "DOWNWARD COURSE."

ARTICLE I. INTRODUCTORY.

§ 280. Introductory.
§ 281. Division of the subject.
§ 282. Difficulties of accurate definition.

§ **280. Introductory.**—In the preceding chapters of this treatise we have endeavored to determine what lands are subject to appropriation under the mining laws, to outline the general nature of the legal system which sanctions such appropriation, and to designate the persons who may or may not under this system acquire, hold, and enjoy rights upon the mineral lands of the public domain. We are now to consider the manner in which such rights may be acquired, and the acts necessary to be done and performed as a condition precedent to such acquisition.

§ **281. Division of the subject.**—Some of the requirements of the law are general in their nature, and apply with equal force to all classes of mineral deposits. Others, by reason of the nature of the thing to be appropriated, or on account of a difference in governmental policy respecting it, are essentially of special application to individual groups. The embarrassments surrounding the arrangement of the subject for the purpose of philosophical, or even methodical, treatment are not to be underestimated. The body of the mining law is complex and incongruous, illogically arranged, and inharmoniously blended. Perhaps the mere form in which the subject is presented is of minor importance, and may be left to the discretion of the author without furnishing justification for serious criticism. At the same time, some orderly method should be adopted by which the practitioner or student may find the state of the law from the author's standpoint, on any given branch, without reading the work from preface to appendix. A comprehensive index may lessen the evil flowing from a want of systematic arrangement, but this cannot wholly supply the necessity for grouping individual classes, and treating them separately, when their nature will permit. We think the object will be fairly accomplished by the division and distribution of the subject into the following heads:—

(1) Lode claims, or the appropriation of deposits " in place";

(2) The appropriation of claims usually called "placers," and other forms of deposit not "in place";

(3) Tunnel claims;

(4) Coal lands;

(5) Salines;

(6) Millsites;

(7) Easements.

§ 282. **Difficulties of accurate definition.**—Before entering upon the formal discussion of the mode of acquiring mining rights upon the public domain, there are certain words and phrases of such frequent occurrence in the mining laws that some attempt at defining them is advisable. In analyzing these various laws and their judicial interpretation by the courts, we encounter numerous terms, few, if any, of which are susceptible of exact definition. By "exact definition" we mean one that contains every attribute which belongs to the thing defined, and excludes all others. Definitions are most often too narrow, but not infrequently too broad.[1] While they are more or less essential, to avoid repetition and the necessity for frequent descriptive explanation of the sense in which such words and phrases are used and of the ideas they are intended to convey, it is not to be expected that absolute exactitude will be obtained. The circumstances surrounding the employment of the terms and the conditions to which they are to be applied are so variable that differentiation will be frequently found necessary. Judge Hawley, one of the most experienced and distinguished judges in the mining states, said, that while there was no conflict in the decisions, yet the result is, that some definitions have been given in some of the states that are not deemed applicable to the conditions and surroundings of mining districts in other states, or other districts in the same state.[2]

The old maxim, that definitions are always dangerous because it is always difficult to prevent their being or becoming inaccurate, finds ample justification when the attempt is made to define the words and phrases of a more or less technical character in the mining statutes. As Judge Field observed in the Eureka case,[3] it is difficult to give any definition of some of the terms as used and understood in the acts of congress which will not be subject to criticism. Many of these terms, said Judge Phillips, are not susceptible of

---

[1] Andrews Bros. v. Youngstown Coke Co., 86 Fed. 585, 588.

[2] Book v. Justice M. Co., 58 Fed. 106.

[3] Eureka Cons. M. Co. v. Richmond M. Co., 4 Saw. 302, 311, Fed. Cas. No. 4548.

Lindley on M.—32

arbitrary definition; nor are they capable of being defined by one set phrase so unvarying as to apply to every case, regardless of the differing conditions of locality and mineral deposit.[1] Even if such a result could be reached, "important questions of law are not "to be determined by a slavish adherence to the letter "of arbitrary definition."[2]

We are admonished not to "yield our minds to the "rigor of verbal definitions," but to "emancipate our- "selves from such bondage and look at the purpose of "the law."[3]

It is our purpose to present such definitions of the terms found in the mining statutes as have been formulated by lexicographers and writers upon geological subjects, together with those approved by the various tribunals charged with the administration and judicial construction of these laws. It is possible that with this aggregation no individual case may arise which will suffer for lack of a suitable definition.

Article II. "Lode," "Vein," "Ledge."

§ 286. English and Scotch definitions.

§ 287. As defined by the lexicographers.

§ 288. As defined by the geologists.

§ 289. Elements to be considered in the judicial application of definitions—Rules of interpretation.

§ 290. The terms "lode," "vein," "ledge" legal equivalents.

§ 290a. Definition and illustrations formulated by Mr. Ross E. Browne.

§ 291. Classification of cases, in which the terms "lode," and "vein" are to be construed.

§ 292. Judicial definitions, and their application — The Eureka case.

§ 293. The Leadville cases.

§ 294. Other definitions given by state and federal courts.

[1] Cheesman v. Shreeve, 40 Fed. 792.

[2] Duggan v. Davey, 4 Dak. 110, 140, 26 N. W. 887.

[3] State ex rel. Van Riper v. Parsons, 40 N. J. L. 1, 5; Klauber v. Higgins, 117 Cal. 451, 49 Pac. 466, 468.

§ 286. **English and Scotch definitions.**—We are indebted to Mr. Archibald Brown for the following:—

"A mineral lode, or vein, is a flattened mass of metal-
" lic or earthy matter, differing materially in its nature
" from the rocks or strata in which it occurs. Its
" breadth varies from a few inches to several feet, and it
" extends in length to a considerable distance, but often
" with great irregularity of course. It is often
" perpendicular, or nearly so, in its position, and
" descends in most cases to an unknown depth. Some-
" times the sides are parallel, and sometimes they recede
" from each other so as to form large accumulations,
" or, as they are called, bellies, of mineral matter; and
" occasionally they approach each other so as almost,
" if not wholly, to cause the vein to disappear. Veins
" also traverse each other, and smaller ones ramify or
" spring out from the larger." [1]

And to Mr. Ross Stewart for the following:—

" 'Vein,' 'seam,' 'lode,' which appear to signify the
" same thing, viz: a layer or stratum of material of a
" different nature from the stratification in which it
" occurs, are equivalent to the term 'mine,' when by it is
" understood an unopened mine." [2]

We do not find the term discussed in Collyer, Arundel, or Rogers. MacSwinney contents himself with definitions given by the lexicographers, without venturing to formulate one of his own.

§ 287. **As defined by the lexicographers.**—

Century Dictionary:—

"LODE. A metalliferous deposit, having more or less
" of a veinlike character; that is, having a certain de-
" gree of regularity, and being confined within walls.
" *Lode,* as used by miners, is nearly synonymous with
" the term *vein,* as employed by geologists. The word
" would not be used for a flat or stratified mass."

---

[1] Bainbridge on Mines, 4th ed., p. 7. This definition is somewhat modified in the later (5th) edition, *q. v.,* p. 6.

[2] Stewart on Mines, p. 3.

"VEIN. An occurrence of ore, usually disseminated
" through a gangue, or veinstone, and having a more or
" less regular development in length, width, and depth.
" A vein and a lode are, in common usage, essentially
" the same thing, the former being rather the scientific,
" the latter the miners', name for it."

"LEDGE. In mining, *ledge* is a common name in the
" Cordilleran region for the lode, or for any outcrop
" supposed to be that of a mineral deposit or vein. It
" is frequently used to designate a quartz vein."

Webster's Dictionary:—

"LODE. A metallic vein; any regular vein or course,
" whether metallic or not."

"LEDGE. A lode; a limited mass of rock, bearing
" valuable mineral."

"VEIN. A narrow mass of rock intersecting other
" rocks, and filling inclined or vertical fissures not cor-
" responding with the stratification; a lode; a dike;—
" often limited, in the language of miners, to a mineral
" vein or lode; that is, to a vein which contains useful
" minerals or ores.

"A fissure, cleft, or cavity, as in the earth or other
" substance."

Standard Dictionary:—

"LODE. A somewhat continuous unstratified metal-
" bearing vein."

"VEIN. The filling of a fissure or fault in a rock, par-
" ticularly if deposited by aqueous solutions. When
" metalliferous, it is called by miners a *lode*. . . . A
" bed or shoot of ore parallel with the bedding."

"LEDGE. A metal-bearing rock-stratum; a quartz
" vein."

Richardson's Dictionary:—

"VEINS. Lineal streaks in mineral."

Encyclopædia Britannica:—

"VEINS. Fissures or cracks in the rocks which are
" filled with materials of quite a different nature from
" the rocks in which the fissures occur."

§ 288. As defined by the geologists.—

Von Cotta:—

"*Veins* are aggregations of mineral matter in fissures
" of rocks. *Lodes* are therefore aggregations of mineral
" matter containing ores in fissures." [1]

Dana:—

"Veins are the fillings of fissures, or of open spaces
" made in any way, exclusive of those called *dikes,*
" which are due to intrusions of melted rock.[2] Where
" ores occur along a vein, it is, in miners' language, a
" *lode.*" [3]

Geike:—

"Into the fissures opened in the earth's crust there
" have been introduced various simple minerals and
" ores, which, solidifying there, have taken the form of
" mineral veins.

" A true mineral vein consists of one or more minerals
" filling up a fissure, which may be vertical, but is us-
" ually more or less inclined, and may vary in width
" from less than an inch up to one hundred and fifty
" feet or more." [4]

Le Conte:—

"All rocks, but especially metamorphic rocks, in
" mountain regions are seamed and scarred in every
" direction, as if broken and again mended, as if
" wounded and again healed. All such seams and scars
" are often called by the general name of *veins*. True
" veins are accumulations, mostly in fissures, of certain
" mineral matters, usually in a purer and more sparry
" form than they exist in the rocks." [5]

Lindgren:—

"A fissure vein may be regarded as a mineral mass,
" tabular in form as a whole, though frequently irregu-

---

[1] Von Cotta's Treatise on Ore Deposits (1859), Prime's translation
(1870), p. 26, referred to in the Eureka case, 4 Saw. 302, Fed. Cas.
No. 4548.

[2] Dana's Manual of Geology, 4th ed. (1895), p. 327.

[3] *Id.*, p. 331.

[4] Geike's Geology (1886), p. 275.

[5] Le Conte's Elements of Geology (1895), p. 234.

" lar in detail, occupying or accompanying a fracture or
" set of fractures in the inclosing rock; this mineral
" mass has been formed later than the country rock and
" the fracture, either through the filling of open spaces
" along the latter, or through chemical alterations of the
" adjoining rock." [1]

§ 289. **Elements to be considered in the judicial
application of definitions—Rules of Interpretation.**—
Dr. Raymond, one of the expert witnesses whose evidence is quoted and referred to in the Eureka case, thus
states his views:—

"The miners made the definition first. As used by
" miners, before being defined by any authority, the
" term 'lode' simply meant that formation by which the
" miner could be led or guided. It is an alteration of
" the verb 'lead,' and whatever the miner could follow,
" expecting to find ore, was his lode. Some formation
" within which he could find ore, and out of which he
" could not expect to find ore, was his lode." [2]

At the time the act of July 26, 1866, was passed, the
first congressional enactment wherein the words "lode"
and "vein" were used, the center of activity in the mining industry was found in the auriferous quartz belt of
California, and the Comstock lode, in Nevada. Up to
that time there is but little doubt that the experience of
the western miner in lode mining was, with rare exceptions, confined to a class of deposits that would readily
fall within the narrowest definition of a "lode"; that
is, "a fissure in the earth's crust filled with mineral mat-
" ter; an aggregation of mineral matter containing ore
" in a fissure."

Dr. Raymond is of the opinion that the term was used
by the miner in a more enlarged sense, because "cinna-

---

[1] Metasomatic Processes in Fissure Veins.—Trans. Am. Inst. M. E., vol.
xxx, pp. 578, 580.

[2] Eureka case, 4 Saw. 302, 311, Fed. Cas. No. 4548.

" bar" was included in the category of minerals specified in the statute, and "cinnabar" occurs not in fissure
veins, but as "impregnations and masses of ore dis-
" tributed through zones of rock." [1]

This same illustration is employed by the supreme
court of Utah as indicating that it was not the intention
of the framers of the acts of congress that purely scientific definitions should be applied in giving them effect.[2]

When it is considered that up to the year 1866 the
quicksilver product of the Pacific slope (and it was not
known to occur elsewhere in the United States) was
confined to three mines, two of which were then claimed
under Mexican grants,—the New Almaden, in Santa
Clara county, California, and the New Idria (Panoche
Grande), in Fresno county, California,—and that active
search for cinnabar deposits was not inaugurated until
1874,[3] popular knowledge on the subject of the mode of
occurrence was not particularly extended.[4]   It is not
likely, therefore, that the inclusion of cinnabar with gold
and silver in the act was based upon any very clear
conception of its mode of occurrence.   However, as we
understand the matter now, the typical cinnabar deposits are in fact fissured, fractured, and mineralized
zones, formed in a way somewhat similar to the more
complex of the gold, silver, copper, and lead-bearing

[1] Monograph in Eureka-Richmond case,—Trans. Am. Inst. M. E., vol.
vi, 382. See, also, Dr. Raymond's testimony, quoted by the court in
the Eureka case, 4 Saw. 302, 311, Fed. Cas. No. 4548.

[2] Hayes v. Lavagnino, 17 Utah, 185, 53 Pac. 1029, 1033.

[3] Becker's Geology of the Quicksilver Deposits of the Pacific Slope,
pp. 10, 11.

[4] The ignorance of many of the early miners of California on geological
subjects is thus quaintly suggested by Mr. J. Ross Browne ("Mineral
"Resources of the West," 1867) : : —

"Many believed that there must be some volcanic source from which
"the gold had been thrown up and scattered over the hills; and they
"thought that if they could only find that place, that they would have
"nothing to do but to shovel up the precious metal and load their mules
"with it."

lodes. They were probably regarded as lodes by the
miner. There may be differences of opinion among
scientists regarding the proper place for these deposits
in a system of classification; but that is a matter of little
moment here. They have become "lodes" in the eye
of the law. Be that as it may, the miner first applied the
terms "lode" and "vein," and they had with him a
definite meaning. Whether it accorded with scientific
theories and abstractions is, at this late day at least, of
no serious moment.

Speaking of the essential differences between the
miner and the scientist on the subject of definitions, Dr.
Foster, in his contribution to the "Quarterly Journal of
" the Geological Society," on the Great Flat lode in
Cornwall, quoted by Dr. Raymond in his monograph on
the Eureka-Richmond case,[1] presents some suggestions
on the subject of the definition of these terms which are
worthy of repetition here:—

"The terms 'lode,' or 'mineral vein,' commonly re-
" garded as synonymous, are usually taken to mean the
" mineral contents of a fissure. I have endeavored to
" show that the Great Flat lode is in the main a band of
" altered rock. Much of the veinstone extracted from
" some of the largest Cornish mines, such as Dolcoath,
" Cook's Kitchen, Tincroft, Carn Brea, and Phœnix, for
" instance, closely resembles the contents of the Great
" Flat lode, and was probably formed in a similar
" manner; indeed, I question very much whether at
" least half the tin ore of the country is not obtained
" from tabular masses of stanniferous altered granite.
" If, then, many of the important lodes of such classic
" ground as Cornwall do not satisfy the common defini-
" tion, one of two things ought to be done; either the
" miner should give up the term 'lode' for these reposi-
" tories, or else the meaning attached to the word by
" geologists should be extended. I need hardly say that
" the first alternative is not likely to be adopted; nor do
" I think it is one to be recommended—for I believe that

[1] Trans. Am. Inst. M. E., vol. vi, pp. 371, 381.

" one and the same fissure traversing killas and granite
" may produce two kinds of lodes. . . . I should pro-
" pose, therefore, that the term 'lode,' or 'mineral vein,'
" should include not only the contents of fissures, but
" also such tabular masses of metalliferous rock as
" those I have been describing. . . . If, however, this
" course should be thought on the whole undesirable,
" the geologist and miner must agree to differ in their
" language, and some of the *lodes* of the latter will have
" to be designated as tabular stockworks by men of
" science."

We do not conceive that from a judicial standpoint it
is a matter of vital importance that the miner and the
scientist should harmonize their differences on the subject of mere definition. The danger lies in accepting the
definitions of either as broadly comprehensive or rigidly
restrictive, and attempting to apply them to conditions
not within the reasonable contemplation of the law, or
in attempting to deprive a locator of the benefit of his
discovery, if the thing discovered can not be forced into
the mold of arbitrary definition, either popular or scientific.

If in the construction of the terms used in the mining
laws there is one evil to be avoided as great as the servile
adherence to arbitrary definition, it is the blind application of a rule announced in one case, where local conditions may justify it, to other cases, where a similar
application of the rule, by reason of modified or totally
different conditions, would produce absurd results.

" Many definitions of veins have been given, varying
" according to the facts under consideration. The term
" is not susceptible of arbitrary definition applicable to
" every case. It must be controlled, in a measure at
" least, by conditions of locality and deposit." [1]

As was said by Judge Hawley, sitting as circuit judge
in the case of Book *v.* Justice M. Co.,—

[1] Beals *v.* Cone, 27 Colo. 473, 83 Am. St. Rep. 92, 62 Pac. 948, 953.

"Various courts have at different times given a defini-
" tion of what constitutes a vein, or lode, within the
" meaning of the act of congress; but the definitions
" that have been given, as a general rule, apply to the
" peculiar character and formation of the ore deposits,
" or vein matter, and of the country rock, in the par-
" ticular district where the claims are located." [1]

And in a later case,—

"The mining laws of the United States were drafted
" for the purpose of protecting the *bona fide* locators of
" mining ground and at the same time to make neces-
" sary provision as to rights of agriculturists and claim-
" ants of townsite lands. The object of each section and
" of the whole policy of the entire statute should not be
" overlooked. The particular character of each case
" necessarily determines the rights of the respective
" parties, and must be kept constantly in view, in order
" to enable the court to arrive at a correct conclusion.
" What is said in one character of cases may or may
" not be applicable in the other. Whatever variance,
" if any, may be found in the views expressed in the
" different decisions touching these questions arises
" from the difference in the facts and a difference in the
" character of the cases and the advanced knowledge
" which experience in the trial of the different kinds of
" cases brings to the court. . . . The definition of a lode
" must always have special reference to the formation
" and peculiar characteristics of the particular dis-
" trict." [2]

As was said by Judge Field, speaking of the act of
July 26, 1866,—

The mining acts "were not drawn by geologists or
" for geologists. They were not framed in the interest
" of science, and consequently with scientific accuracy
" in the use of terms. They were framed for the pro-
" tection of miners in the claims which they had located

[1] 58 Fed. 106, 121.
[2] Migeon v. Montana Cent. Ry., 77 Fed. 249, 254.

" and developed, and should receive such a construc-
" tion as will carry out this purpose."[1]

§ 290. The terms "lode," "vein," "ledge," legal
equivalents.—The act of July 26, 1866, used the term
" vein, or lode." The act of May 10, 1872, added the
word "ledge," and all these terms occur in the Revised
Statutes.

Of the three terms, the word "lode" is the more comprehensive. A lode may, and often does, contain more
than one vein.[2] Instances have been known of a broad
zone, generally recognized as a lode, itself having well-
defined boundaries, but being traversed by mineralized
fissure veins, each possessing such individuality as to
be the subject of location.[3] A lode may or may not be a
fissure vein, but a fissure vein is, in contemplation of
law, a lode.

"Ledge" is more of a local term, at one time in common use in California and some parts of Nevada. It is
mentioned in the act of May 10, 1872, and is incorporated into the Revised Statutes, but it is practically
unrecognized in many mining localities.

Generally speaking, the terms are used interchangeably.[4] As observed by Dr. Raymond, "lode" is an
alteration of the verb "lead." In many localities the
word "lead" is used as synonymous with "lode."
" Lead" is also applied in California to certain subterranean auriferous gravel deposits, which, however,
can be acquired only under the placer laws,[5] according

---

[1] Eureka case, 4 Saw. 302, 311, Fed. Cas. No. 4548. See, also, Hayes v.
Lavagnino, 17 Utah, 185, 53 Pac. 1029, 1033.

[2] United States v. Iron S. M. Co., 128 U. S. 673, 9 Sup. Ct. Rep. 195.

[3] Mt. Diablo M. and M. Co. v. Callison, 5 Saw. 439, Fed. Cas. No. 9886.
See, also, Doe v. Waterloo M. Co., 54 Fed. 935.

[4] Iron S. M. Co. v. Cheesman, 8 Fed. 297, 301; Cheesman v. Shreeve, 40
Fed. 787, 792; Morr. Min. Rights, 8th ed., p. 113; Hayes v. Lavagnino,
17 Utah, 185, 53 Pac. 1029, 1032.

[5] Gregory v. Pershbaker, 73 Cal. 109, 14 Pac. 401.

to the rules established by the land department.[1] The terms "lode" and "vein" are always associated in the existing mining statutes, and are invariably separated by the disjunctive. For all practical purposes, they may be considered as legal equivalents. Unless the authority cited itself makes the distinction heretofore suggested, the definitions hereafter given apply equally to both words.

§ 290a. **Definition and illustrations formulated by Mr. Ross E. Browne.**—A proper conception of the difficulties encountered in framing comprehensive definitions of the terms used in the mining laws requires more or less familiarity and experience with those "brute " beasts of the intellectual domain," the *facts* as they are encountered in the operation and exploitation of mines. A practical knowledge of what we may term structural geology, derived from actual contact involved in the investigation and working of mines, is quite as essential as a familiarity with the law, in order to enable one to present any satisfactory illustration of the nature of the things to which the law is to be applied. Lawyers specializing on the legal phases of mining law necessarily absorb some general information from the mining engineers with whom they are brought in contact. But as a rule this familiarity with structural conditions is to a large degree superficial. The mining engineer and expert with a broad experience, not only in the field of mining operations, but in mining litigation, occupies a unique position, not only as the mentor of counsel, but as an important aid to the court in the ascertainment of the facts to which the law is to be applied. Among the engineers there is no one better qualified to speak from a practical standpoint upon the subject under considera-

[1]Copp's Min. Dec. 78. *Post*, § 427.

tion than Mr. Ross E. Browne, who has had a wide experience in mining and has been connected with some of the most important mining litigation of the west. At the author's request, he has formulated certain definitions and illustrations which we here present.

"Originally the word 'vein' was narrow in its sig-
" nificance, defining a single clearly marked seam or
" fissure-filling in the country rock. The word 'lode'
" was a broader term, applied not only to ore-bearing
" veins in a narrow sense, but to various more compli-
" cated forms of ore-deposit as well.

"Under the influence of the mining acts of congress,
" it has gradually become more and more customary to
" use the two terms synonymously, and to give to the
" word 'vein' the broad definition that would formerly
" have been regarded as more properly applicable to
" the word 'lode.' Still the custom is not rigid, and
" the miner, as a rule, continues to make certain dis-
" tinctions in the use of the terms. For example, when
" his deposit contains separate parallel seams, or sheets,
" of ore, and he regards the whole as a unit, he may call
" it either a 'lode' or a 'vein,' but the separate sheets
" he designates as distinct veins within the limits of
" his lode. He calls the entire mass vein-matter, and
" his conception is, that the word 'vein' refers either
" to the entire mass or to narrow streaks within the
" mass, while the word 'lode' always refers to the entire
" mass.

"In a very general way a lode may be described as a
" mass of mineralized rock in place, the word 'mineral'
" referring only to commercially valuable constituents.
" The form is usually more or less tabular or sheet-like,
" but occasionally too irregular to fit such descrip-
" tion.

"Referring to ores of the more valuable metals, such
" as gold, silver, quicksilver, copper, lead, etc., the
" lodes in which they are found are generally formed
" by fissuring of the country rock and subsequent
" introduction of mineralizing solutions depositing ore-
" bearing material in the fissures and occasionally min-
" eralizing portions of the wall-rocks by processes of

" metamorphism and impregnation, occasionally filling
" pre-existing cavities, such as occur in limestone.

"The lode as it commonly occurs may then be defined
" as the ore-bearing filling of a single fissure or of a
" system of interconnected fissures and pre-existing
" cavities in the country rock, together with occasional
" mineralized masses of the wall-rocks.[1]

"The lode material consists not only of the valuable
" ores, but also of the associate gangue minerals depos-
" ited by the same solutions.

"There are frequently encountered fragmentary or
" detached masses of unaltered country rock, wholly or
" substantially surrounded by lode material,—so-called
" 'horses,'—which are regarded as
" belonging to the lode.

" The lateral boundaries are
" formed either by the walls of the
" fissures or by the more irregular
" limits of mineralization.[2]

" The following diagrams will
" illustrate in vertical cross-section
" the common occurrences.

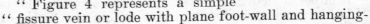

FIGURE 4.

" Figure 4 represents a simple
" fissure vein or lode with plane foot-wall and hanging-
" wall boundaries.

[1] AUTHOR'S NOTE.— The acts of congress are so construed as to include in the category of lodes, veins, and ledges certain deposits which would not fall under the above definition. As, for example, certain tilted beds or sedimentary strata containing ores as original constituents, and not formed by subsequent fissuring and mineralization. The geologist would call these beds, and not lodes, but we understand that the intent of the law is not to make distinctions based upon the genetic principle. It is doubtless true that a very small percentage of the ore deposits of the precious metals occur as tilted beds in place, unassociated with subsequent fissuring and mineralization; but when such are found, they are undoubtedly subject to location as veins or lodes within the meaning of the statutes.

[2] AUTHOR'S NOTE.— The vein must have boundaries, but it is not necessary that they be seen. Their existence may be determined by assay and analysis. Beals v. Cone, 27 Colo. 473, 83 Am. St. Rep. 92, 62 Pac. 948, 953, (citing Cheesman v. Shreeve, 40 Fed. 787, Hyman v. Wheeler, 29 Fed. 347; Iron S. M. Co. v. Cheesman, 116 U. S. 529, 6 Sup. Ct. Rep. 481).

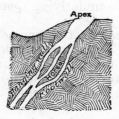

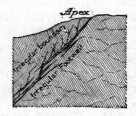

FIGURE 5.   FIGURE 6.

"Figure 5 represents a complex fissure-vein or lode,
" still having comparatively simple boundaries. The
" foot and hanging walls are more or less broken by
" insignificant spurs or offshoots.

"Figure 6 is a complex lode with jagged or complex
" fissure-wall boundaries.

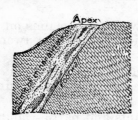

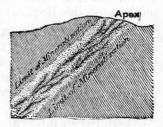

FIGURE 7.   FIGURE 8.

"Figure 7 is a complex lode, consisting of fissure-
" fillings and mineralized wall-rock. The foot-bound-
" ary is a simple fissure-wall, the hanging boundary is
" the somewhat indefinite limit of mineralization.

"Figure 8 is a complex lode with both boundaries
" formed only by the
" irregular limits of
" mineralization.

"Figure 9 is the
" Eureka - Richmond
" belt of fissured and
" partly mineralized
" limestone, adjudged
" to be a lode. The
" boundaries practi-
" cally confining the
" mineralization, are

FIGURE 9.

" the surfaces of contact with the underlying quartzite
" and the overlying shale.

"There are other forms that need not be enumerated
" here. Suffice it to say, that the mineralization of
" rock in place is an essential element in the definition;
" the nature of the material, the form of the deposit, the
" character of the boundaries are widely variant."

§ 291. **Classification of cases in which the terms
"lode" and "vein" are to be construed.**—Judge Hawley, speaking for the circuit court of appeals in the case
of Migeon v. Montana Cent. Ry.,[1] says:—

"There are four classes of cases where the courts have
" been called upon to determine what constitutes a lode
" or vein, within the intent and meaning of different
" sections of the Revised Statutes:—

" (1) Between miners who have located claims on the
" same lode, under the provisions of section twenty-
" three hundred and twenty;

" (2) Between placer and lode claimants, under the
" provisions of section twenty-three hundred and thirty-
" three;

" (3) Between mineral claimants and parties holding
" townsite patents to the same ground;

" (4) Between mineral and agricultural claimants to
" the same land."

To these we may add another:—

(5) Controversies between a lode miner, who has
penetrated into and underneath lands adjoining in the
development of what he has located under the law applicable to lode claims, and the adjoining or neighboring
surface proprietor, whose claim to the underlying mineral deposits rests solely upon presumptions flowing
from surface ownership.

In interpreting these terms the nature of the controversy is an undoubted element to be considered. In

[1] 77 Fed. 249, 254.

some classes of cases a more liberal rule is followed than
would be justified in others. It is useless, in our judgment, to search for a judicial definition which would be
absolutely applicable under every conceivable state of
facts and in all classes of controversies.

§ 292. Judicial definitions and their application—
The Eureka case.—It may be safely asserted that as to
the terms "lode" and "vein," when applied to geological conditions existing in most mining localities,
there is no essential difference between their definition
as given by the scientist and that applied by the practical
miner. But it is when we encounter certain classes of
deposits, and meet with new and unique conditions, the
existence of which was neither known nor contemplated
when the "miners made the definitions," nor when congress enacted the mining laws, that the courts have been
forced to admit that "what constitutes a lode, or vein,
" of mineral matter has been no easy thing to define."[1]

The first reported case in which a judicial definition
of any of these terms was attempted is the case of the
Eureka M. Co. v. Richmond M. Co.,[2] one of the most
famous of the mining cases considered by the
courts. It was tried before three of the most eminent
mining judges,—Field, Sawyer, and Hillyer,—who had
the benefit of the testimony of some of the most distinguished scientists of the period.

It was a case involving rights accruing under the act
of 1866, and the following is the definition formulated:—

"We are of the opinion that the term (lode) as used
" in the acts of congress is applicable to any zone or belt
" of mineralized rock lying within boundaries clearly

---

[1] Iron S. M. Co. v. Cheesman, 116 U. S. 529, 6 Sup. Ct. Rep. 481.
[2] 4 Saw. 302, Fed. Cas. No. 4548; Judge Field, in Iron S. M. Co. v.
Mike & Starr G. and S. M. Co., 143 U. S. 394, 12 Sup. Ct. Rep. 543.

" separating it from the neighboring rock. It includes
" . . . all deposits of mineral matter found through a
" mineralized zone, or belt, coming from the same
" source, impressed with the same forms, and appear-
" ing to have been created by the same processes."

The zone to which this definition was applied was of
dolomitic limestone, a sedimentary deposit, broken,
crushed, and fissured, resting on a foot-wall of quartzite,
and having a hanging-wall of clay shale.[1] The width of
the zone varied from a few inches to four hundred and
fifty feet. Its mean width was about two hundred and
fifty feet. The hanging-wall had a dip of eighty to
eighty-five degrees, while the foot-wall had an average
inclination of forty-five degrees. Throughout this body
of limestone, vugs, chambers, and large caverns were
encountered, in the bottoms of which ore—lead carbon-
ates, carrying gold and silver—was invariably found.
Overlying the hanging-wall was another zone of limestone, which differed from that lying on the quartzite,
being plainly stratified, and contained neither ores nor
caverns.

No one connected with the case contended that this
mineral-bearing zone was the filling of a fissure.[2]

While we are not concerned with the genesis of these
ore deposits, it is a matter of common knowledge that
the inclosing rock (limestone) being soluble and fissured, the caves, vugs, and chambers resulted from the
chemical action of percolating waters, creating the
larger spaces for the subsequent deposit of the ores.

Professor Le Conte, in his "Elements of Geology," [3]
gives a cross-section, exhibiting a homely illustration of

[1] A cross-section of this lode is shown in figure 9, *ante*, § 290a, forming one of Mr. Browne's illustrations.

[2] See monographs of W. S. Keyes and R. W. Raymond, Trans. Am.
Inst. M. E., vol. vi, pp. 344, 393.

[3] 3d ed., p. 76.

the result of the erosive action of the water in rocks of this character, and cites the Mammoth Cave, in Kentucky, Wier's Cave, in Virginia, and Nicojack Cave, in Tennessee, as examples. The Eureka ore-chambers were all presumed to be interconnected by fissures, but the irregularity of distribution was such as to make the continuous tracing of persistent fissure-veins impracticable. Our apology for introducing these elements into the discussion is found in the admonition of the courts, referred to in a preceding section, that in applying a definition we must look to the facts, circumstances, and conditions of structural geology which justified its creation before we can intelligently determine whether it should be applied to other cases.

We do not complain that the law was incorrectly applied in the Eureka case. But there is hardly a mining case of any considerable importance involving the broad lode question in which one side or the other does not attempt to apply the zone theory announced in this case to conditions materially different from those encountered on Ruby Hill.

The Eureka case stands as a judicial classic; but its force as a precedent ought to be limited to cases where the conditions are parallel, or at least analogous.

The passage of the act of May 10, 1872, introduced new terms, and created new complications, which must be considered when dealing with the present state of the law.

§ 293. **The Leadville cases.**[1] — We shall have occasion to analyze the group of cases arising out of the unique geological conditions existing at and in the vicinity of Leadville, Colorado, when we discuss the subject of "apex" in the succeeding article, presenting a cross-section which gives a fair illustration of the mode in

[1] For a full presentation and discussion of these cases, see Dr. Raymond's "Law of the Apex."

which these so-called "veins" occur. As we shall there
fully explain our understanding of these local conditions
to which definitions have been applied, we confine our-
selves presently to quotations from these various cases,
most of which refer to and apply the Eureka case:—

In general, it may be said that a lode, or vein, "is a
" body of mineral, or mineral-bearing rock, within de-
" fined boundaries in the general mass of the moun-
" tain." [1]

"In this definition the elements are the body of min-
" eral or mineral-bearing rock and the boundaries.
" With either of these things established, very slight
" evidence may be accepted as to the existence of the
" other. A body of mineral or mineral-bearing rock
" in the general mass of the mountain, so far as it may
" continue unbroken and without interruption, may be
" regarded as a lode, whatever the boundaries may be.
" In the existence of such body, and to the extent of it,
" boundaries are implied. On the other hand, with
" well-defined boundaries, very slight evidence of ore
" within such boundaries will prove the existence of a
" lode." [2]

"Such boundaries constitute a fissure; and if in such
" fissure ore is found, although at considerable inter-
" vals, and in small quantities, it is called a lode, or
" vein. . . .

"A continuous body of mineral or mineral-bearing
" rock extending through loose, disjointed rocks, is a
" lode as fully and certainly as that which is found in
" more regular formation." [3]

<hr/>

[1] Judge Hallett, in Iron S. M. Co. v. Cheesman, 8 Fed. 299, 301, quoted
by Justice Miller in Stevens & Leiter v. Williams, 1 McCrary, 480, 488,
Fed. Cas. No. 13,413; Buffalo Zinc and Copper Co. v. Crump (Ark.), 69
S. W. 572, 575.

[2] Quoted in Cheesman v. Shreeve, 40 Fed. 787, 795.

[3] Judge Hallett, as quoted and approved in Iron S. M. Co. v. Chees-
man, 116 U. S. 529, 6 Sup. Ct. Rep. 481; United States v. Iron S. M. Co.,
128 U. S. 673, 9 Sup. Ct. Rep. 195. See, also, Hyman v. Wheeler, 29
Fed. 347, 353; Illinois S. M. Co. v. Raff, 7 N. Mex. 336, 34 Pac. 544;
Beals v. Cone, 27 Colo. 473, 83 Am. St. Rep. 92, 62 Pac. 948; Buffalo
Zinc and Copper Co. v. Crump (Ark.), 69 S. W. 572, 575.

"The thinness or thickness of the matter in particular
" places does not affect its being a vein or lode. Nor
" does the fact that it is occasionally found in the gen-
" eral course of the vein or shoot, in pockets deeper
" down in the earth, or higher up, affect its character as
" a vein, lode, or ledge." [1]

"By veins, or lodes, are meant lines or aggregations
" of metal embedded in quartz or other rock in place.
" The terms are found together in the statutes, and
" both are intended to indicate the presence of metal in
" rock. Yet a lode may, and often does, contain more
" than one vein." [2]

"With ore in mass and position in the body of the
" mountain, no other fact is required to prove the exist-
" ence of a lode or the dimensions of the ore. As far as
" it prevails, the ore is a lode; and it is not at all neces-
" sary to decide any question of fissures, contacts, sel-
" vages, slicken-sides, or other marks of distinction, in
" order to establish its character." [3]

"It has sometimes been contended that the lode must
" have a certain position in the earth; that is to say, it
" must be more or less vertical, before this rule which
" is given in the act of congress can be applied; but we
" have heretofore held, and we are still of the opinion,
" that it applies to all lodes which have an inclination
" below the plane of the horizon, whatever it may be." [4]

In Stevens v. Williams [5] is found the following by
Judge Hallett:—

"As to the word 'vein,' or 'lode,' it seems to me that
" these words may embrace any description of deposit
" which is so situated in the general mass of the country,
" whether it is described in any one way or another;
" that is to say, whether, in the language of the geol-

---

[1] Justice Miller, in Stevens v. Williams (second trial), 1 Morr. Min. Rep.
573, Fed. Cas. No. 13,413.

[2] United States v. Iron S. M. Co., 128 U. S. 673, 9 Sup. Ct. Rep. 195.

[3] Hyman v. Wheeler, 29 Fed. 347, 353; Cheesman v. Shreeve, 40 Fed.
795.

[4] Leadville M. Co. v. Fitzgerald, 4 Morr. Min. Rep. 380, Fed. Cas. No.
8158.

[5] 1 Morr. Min. Rep. 557, Fed. Cas. No. 13,414.

" ogist, we say it is a bed, or a segregated vein, or gash
" vein, or true fissure vein, or merely a deposit. . . .
" Whenever a miner finds a valuable mineral deposit
" in the body of the earth (in place) he calls that a lode,
" whatever its form may be, and however it may be
" situated, and whatever its extent in the body of the
" earth."

The same judge, in another case, held that an impregnation to the extent to which it may be traced as a
body of ore is as fully within the broad terms of the act
of congress as any other form of deposit.[1]

While the supreme court of the United States, in the
cases of Iron S. M. Co. *v.* Cheesman,[2] United States *v.*
Iron S. M. Co.,[3] and Reynolds *v.* Iron S. M. Co.,[4] had
accepted the definition of a lode, or vein, announced by
Judge Hallett, thus determining that the blanket deposits of Leadville were in law embraced within the
definition of the terms "lode" and "vein," their position was vigorously assailed in the later case of Iron
S. M. Co. *v.* Mike & Starr G. and S. M. Co.[5] This case
was twice argued, a reargument having been ordered,
and the attention of counsel directed to the question,
among others, as to what constituted a vein, or lode,
within the meaning of sections twenty-three hundred
and twenty and twenty-three hundred and thirty-three of
the Revised Statutes. The action was brought by the
plaintiff in error as the owner of the William Moyer
placer to eject the defendant. The defense was "known
" lode" existing at the time of the application for the
placer patent, called the Goodell lode. The verdict was
for the lode claimant. Plaintiff appealed. The judg-

[1] Hyman *v.* Wheeler, 29 Fed. 347, 353. See, also, Beals *v.* Cone, 27
Colo. 473, 83 Am. St. Rep. 92, 62 Pac. 948.
[2] 116 U. S. 529, 6 Sup. Ct. Rep. 481.
[3] 128 U. S. 673, 9 Sup. Ct. Rep. 195.
[4] 116 U. S. 687, 6 Sup. Ct. Rep. 601.
[5] 143 U. S. 394, 12 Sup. Ct. Rep. 543.

ment was affirmed by the supreme court of the United States, in an opinion from which we quote:—

" There was an earnest inquiry . . . as to whether, in
" view of the disclosures made in this, as in prior cases,
" of the existence of a body of mineral underlying a
" large area of country in the Leadville mining district,
" whose general horizontal direction, together with the
" sedimentary character of the superior rock, indicated
" something more of the nature of a deposit, like a coal-
" bed, than of the vertical and descending fissure vein
" in which silver and gold are ordinarily found, it did
" not become necessary to hold that the only provisions
" of the statute under which title to any portion of this
" body of mineral or the ground in which it is situated
" can be acquired are those with respect to placer
" claims. . . .
"Our conclusions are that the title to portions of this
" horizontal vein or deposit—"blanket vein," as it is
" generally called—may be acquired under the sections
" concerning veins, lodes, etc. The fact that so many
" patents have been obtained under these sections, and
" that so many applications for patent are still pending,
" is a strong reason against a new and contrary ruling.
" That which has been accepted as law, and acted upon,
" by that mining community for such a length of time,
" should not be adjudged wholly a mistake and put en-
" tirely aside because of difficulties in the application of
" some minor provisions to the peculiarities of this vein
" or deposit."

Judges Field, Harlan, and Brown dissented, but not as to the legal conclusions. They were of the opinion that the evidence was insufficient to establish the existence of a "known lode."

The embarrassing results flowing from this decision will be demonstrated when we discuss the question of apex and extralateral rights.

§ 294. **Other definitions given by state and federal courts.**—The supreme court of Montana has given the following definition:—

"In construing this language, regard must be had to
" what in truth a lode, or lead, is, and when so tested the
" problem seems easy of solution and free from doubt.
" A lead, or lode, is not an imaginary line without
" dimensions; it is not a thing without shape or form.
" But before it can legally and rightfully be denomi-
" nated a lead, or lode, it must have length, and width,
" and depth; it must be capable of measurement; it
" must occupy defined space, and be capable of identi-
" fication. Before a quartz claim can be legally located,
" a lead, or lode, containing gold or silver must be dis-
" covered; and before such discovery can be called a
" discovery, at least one well-defined wall,[1] or side, to
" the lode must be found. What, then, is a quartz lode?
" It is a fissure, or seam, in the country rock, filled with
" quartz matter, bearing gold or silver. This fissure
" may be wide or narrow; it varies in width from one
" inch, or even less, to one hundred feet, or much more.
" The sides of a lead are represented and defined by the
" walls of the country rock, and these walls must be
" discovered, and the lead identified thereby, before it
" can be located and held as a lead." [2]

Judge Hawley, sitting as circuit judge in the ninth
circuit, after reviewing most of the adjudicated law
upon the subject, thus expressed his views:—

"This statute was intended to be liberal and broad
" enough to apply to any kind of a lode, or vein, of
" quartz or other rock bearing mineral, in whatever
" kind, character, or formation the mineral might be
" found. It should be so construed as to protect locators
" of mining claims who have discovered rock in place,
" bearing any of the precious metals named therein,
" sufficient to justify the locators in expending their
" time and money in prospecting and developing the
" ground located.[3] It must be borne in mind that the

---

[1] At the time this case was decided a law existed in Montana making
it a prerequisite to a valid location that the workings should disclose at
least one wall,—a limitation on the definition of a vein which we think
repugnant to the spirit and intent of the federal law and not within
the province of state legislation.

[2] Foote v. National M. Co., 2 Mont. 403.

[3] Quoted in Wyoming Cons. M. Co. v. Champion M. Co., 63 Fed. 540, 544.

" veins and lodes are not always of the same character.
" In some mining districts the veins, lodes, and ore
" deposits are so well and clearly defined as to avoid
" any questions being raised. In other localities the
" mineral is found in seams, narrow crevices, cracks,
" or fissures in the earth, the precise extent and char-
" acter of which can not be fully ascertained until
" expensive explorations are made, and the continuity of
" the ore and existence of the rock in place, bearing
" mineral, is established. It never was intended that
" the locator of a mining claim must determine all these
" facts before he would be entitled, under the law, to
" make a valid location. Every vein, or lode, is liable
" to have barren spots and narrow places, as well as
" rich chimneys and pay chutes, or large deposits of
" valuable ore. When the locator finds rock in place
" containing mineral, he has made a discovery within
" the meaning of the statute, whether the rock or earth
" is rich or poor, whether it assays high or low. It is
" the finding of the mineral in the rock in place, as
" distinguished from float rock, that constitutes the dis-
" covery, and warrants the prospector in making a loca-
" tion of a mining claim." [1] . . .

And in a later case, speaking for the circuit court of
appeals,—

"When a locator of a mining claim finds rock in place
" containing mineral in sufficient quantity to justify him
" in expending his time and money in prospecting and
" developing the claim, he has made a discovery within
" the meaning of the statute, whether the rock or earth
" is rich or poor, whether it assays high or low." [2]

In Hyman v. Wheeler,[3] Judge Hallett, after referring
to the decisions in some of the Leadville cases, adds the
following:—

"An impregnation to the extent to which it may be
" traced as a body of ore is as fully within the broad

[1] Book v. Justice M. Co., 58 Fed. 106, 120. Commented on and reaffirmed
in Cons. Wyoming M. Co. v. Champion M. Co., 63 Fed. 540, 544; quoted
approvingly in Shoshone M. Co. v. Rutter, 87 Fed. 801, 807.
[2] Migeon v. Mont. Cent. Ry., 77 Fed. 249, 255.
[3] 29 Fed. 347, 353.

" terms of the act of congress as any other form of
" deposit."

The supreme court of Colorado, speaking through
Justice Gabbert, contributes the following comprehensive statement:—

"Many definitions of veins have been given, varying
" according to the facts under consideration. The term
" is not susceptible of an arbitrary definition applicable
" to every case. It must be controlled, in a measure at
" least, by the conditions of locality and deposit. The
" distinguishing feature between a vein and the forma-
" tion inclosing it may be visible. It must have bound-
" aries, but it is not necessary that they be seen. Their
" existence may be determined by assay and analysis.
" The controlling characteristic of a vein is a continu-
" ous body of mineral-bearing rock in place in the gen-
" eral mass of the surrounding formation. If it possess
" these requisites, and carry mineral in appreciable
" quantities, it is a mineral-bearing vein within the
" meaning of the law, even though its boundaries may
" not have been ascertained." [1]

The supreme court of Utah also furnishes a valuable
and interesting discussion of the subject.[2]

Some of the courts accept the liberal interpretation
suggested by Dr. Raymond in the Eureka case—that a
" lode is whatever a miner could follow and find ore." [3]

Others lean toward the narrow definition—that it is
a seam or fissure in the earth's crust, filled with quartz
or other rock in place, carrying gold, silver, etc.[4]

[1] Beals v. Cone, 27 Colo. 473, 83 Am. St. Rep. 92, 62 Pac. 948, 952,
(citing Cheesman v. Shreeve, 40 Fed. 787; Hyman v. Wheeler, 29 Fed.
347; Iron S. M. Co. v. Cheesman, 116 U. S. 529, 6 Sup. Ct. Rep. 481).

[2] Hayes v. Lavagnino, 17 Utah, 185, 53 Pac. 1029.

[3] Harrington v. Chambers, 3 Utah, 94, 1 Pac. 362, 375; Burke v. Mc-
Donald, 2 Idaho, 310, 13 Pac. 351; Shreve v. Copper Bell M. Co., 11
Mont. 309, 28 Pac. 315; Brownfield v. Bier, 15 Mont. 403, 38 Pac. 1067.

[4] North Noonday M. Co. v. Orient M. Co., 6 Saw. 299, 309, 1 Fed. 522;
Jupiter M. Co. v. Bodie Cons. M. Co., 7 Saw. 96, 107, 11 Fed. 666; Foote
v. National M. Co., 2 Mont. 402; Stinchfield v. Gillis, 96 Cal. 33, 30
Pac. 839.

In a case arising in Nevada, at Treasure Hill, where the formation is limestone, and the conditions were parallel to those existing in the Eureka case, the supreme court of that state held that the term "lode" might be applied to ore deposits in a succession of chambers connected by a seam, varying in width, and more or less barren, and with walls of different character.[1]

All cases seem to agree that neither the size[2] nor the richness of the ore[3] is an element of the definition.[4]

As to whether a given deposit is a vein, or lode, is a question of fact.[5]

ARTICLE III.   "ROCK IN PLACE."

§ 298. Classification of lands containing valuable deposits.

§ 299. Use of term "in place" in the mining laws.

§ 300. The blanket deposits of Leadville.

§ 301. Judicial interpretation of the term "rock in place."

§ 298. Classification of lands containing valuable deposits.

—The laws of the United States prescribing the terms upon which its lands containing valu able deposits, other than coal, shall be sold, used, or

---

[1] Phillpotts v. Blasdell, 8 Nev. 62.

[2] Stinchfield v. Gillis, 96 Cal. 33, 30 Pac. 839; Stevens v. Williams, 1 Morr. Min. Rep. 566, Fed. Cas. No. 13,413; Jupiter M. Co. v. Bodie Cons. M. Co., 7 Saw. 96, 107, 11 Fed. 666; North Noonday M. Co. v. Orient M. Co., 6 Saw. 299, 309, 1 Fed. 522; Meydenbauer v. Stevens, 78 Fed. 787.

[3] Stinchfield v. Gillis, 96 Cal. 33, 30 Pac. 839; Book v. Justice M. Co., 58 Fed. 106; Migeon v. Mont. Cent. Ry., 77 Fed. 249; Shoshone M. Co. v. Rutter, 87 Fed. 801, 807.

[4] Golden Terra M. Co. v. Mahler, 4 Morr. Min. Rep. 390; Armstrong v. Lower, 6 Colo. 393; Jupiter M. Co. v. Bodie Cons. M. Co., 7 Saw. 96, 108, 11 Fed. 666; North Noonday M. Co. v. Orient M. Co., 6 Saw. 299, 309, 1 Fed. 522.

[5] Bluebird M. Co. v. Largey, 49 Fed. 289; Bullion B. and C. M. Co. v. Eureka Hill M. Co., 5 Utah, 3, 11 Pac. 515; Illinois S. M. Co. v. Raff, 7 N. Mex. 336, 34 Pac. 544.

occupied, have divided such lands into two distinct classes:—

(1) Those which contain veins, or lodes, of quartz or of other rock in place; [1]

(2) Those containing placers and other forms of deposit other than those found "in place." [2]

To determine the proper manner of appropriating public lands containing such valuable deposits, it is necessary to first ascertain whether they are found in veins, or lodes, of rock in place, or not. If of rock in place, a method is to be pursued differing from that applicable to other deposits, and the nature and extent of rights conferred by the appropriation of one class differ in some respects from those conferred by the other. It becomes necessary to arrive at an understanding of what is meant by "rock in place."

§ 299. Use of term "in place" in the mining laws.— A vein, or lode, is necessarily "in place." The condition of being "in place" is one of its essential attributes The term "quartz or other rock in place," as used in section twenty-three hundred and twenty of the Revised Statutes, refers to its constituent elements, or the " filling " of veins and lodes. Experience has shown that mineral substances in veins, or lodes, are not always found in quartz. Sometimes the vein material is composed mainly of the same character of rock as the inclosing walls—the occurrence of mineral being in the form of impregnations, penetrating the country rock, or the mineral may be but a replacement of the original rocks. So the statute recognizing that while the material of most veins consists of quartz, yet, as this

[1] Rev. Stats., § 2320.

[2] Id., § 2329. Justice Miller, in Stevens v. Williams, 1 McCrary, 480, 1 Morr. Min. Rep. 566, 572, Fed. Cas. No. 13,413; Gen. Circ. Inst. (July 15, 1873), Copp's Min. Dec. 316, 318.

is not universally true, the alternative, "or other rock
" in place," was introduced. As quartz in a vein is
rock in place, the statute would have been equally as
comprehensive if instead of saying "veins, or lodes, of
" quartz or other rock in place," it had simply said
" veins, or lodes, of rock in place."

The term "rock in place," occurs in all of the mining
legislation of congress. There is nothing cabalistic in
its use. It is simply the *in situ* of the geologist, and as
explained by the commissioner of the general land office
in the mining circulars issued by him, the term has
always received the most liberal construction of which
the language would admit. Every class of claims that
either according to scientific accuracy or popular usage
can be classed and applied for as a vein or lode may be
patented under the law, as a vein or lode of rock in
place.[1]

In this class the commissioner included all lands
wherein the mineral matter is contained in veins or
ledges occupying the original *habitat,* or location, of
the metal or mineral, whether in true or false veins, in
zones, in pockets, or in the several other forms in which
minerals are found in the *original rock.*[2]

Petroleum is said to be "in place" when it occupies
the undisturbed position in the earth between the inclosing rocks, where it was placed by natural processes; and
so with subterranean salt water.[3]

Ordinarily, there should be but little difficulty in
determining whether a given deposit is a vein or lode
of rock in place or not. But circumstances have arisen
which have provoked discussion as to what is meant by
the term "in place," and it has frequently occupied the
attention of the courts.

[1] Commissioner Drummond (July 20, 1871), Copp's Min. Dec. 46.
[2] Copp's Min. Dec. 316, 319, 1 Copp's L. O. 11.
[3] Williamson *v.* Jones, 39 W. Va. 231, 257, 19 S. E. 436.

§ 300. The blanket deposits of Leadville.—The blanket deposits at and in the vicinity of Leadville, Colorado, have given rise to most of the controverted questions on the subject of "lodes," "veins," "in "place," "top," and "apex"; and the burden of solving many of these difficulties in the first instance fell to the lot of Judge Hallett. His decisions have furnished the text for other courts, in other jurisdictions, where analogous conditions have been to a limited extent encountered.

The conditions which created the necessity for a rule of interpretation to be applied to the term "in place" are thus stated by the distinguished judge:—

"Until the discovery of mineral deposits near Lead-
"ville no controversy had arisen in Colorado as to
"whether a lode, or vein, is in place within the meaning
"of the act of congress.

"The mines opened in Clear Creek, Gilpin, Boulder,
"and other counties descend into the earth so directly
"that no question could arise whether they were in-
"closed in the general mass of the country; whatever
"the character of the vein, and whatever its width, it
"was sure to be within the general mass of the moun-
"tain; but the Leadville deposits were found to be of
"a different character. In some of them at least, the
"ore was found on the surface or covered only by the
"superficial mass of slide, débris, detritus, or mov-
"able stuff which is distinguishable from the general
"mass of the mountain, while others were found
"beneath an overlying mass of fixed and immovable
"rock which could be called a wall as well as that which
"was found below them. It then became necessary to
"consider very carefully the meaning of the words 'in
"'place' in the act of congress, in order to determine
"whether these deposits were of the character described
"in that act." [1]

[1] Leadville M. Co. v. Fitzgerald, 4 Morr. Min. Rep. 381, Fed. Cas. No. 8158.

As the character of these deposits is frequently involved in the discussion of numerous phases of the mining law, we think it advisable to give a short account of the nature of their occurrence. Much has been written upon them, and the scientists are by no means harmonious as to the theory of their origin. On the question of structural geology, however, there is but little room for controversy. The records of geological history exposed in the mine workings are read by all alike; and there is a general consensus of opinion as to what is there found. Professor Emmons thus states the result of his investigations:—

"By far the most important of the ores of Leadville
" and vicinity, both in quantity and quality, occur in the
" blue-gray dolomitic limestone, known as blue or ore-
" bearing limestone, and at or near its contact with the
" overlying sheet of white porphyry. They thus con-
" stitute a sort of contact sheet whose upper surface,
" being formed by the base of the porphyry sheet, is
" comparatively regular and well defined, while the
" lower surface is ill-defined and irregular, there being a
" gradual transition from ore into unaltered limestone,
" the former extending to varying depths from the sur-
" face, and even occupying at times the entire thick-
" ness of the blue limestone. This may be regarded as
" the typical form of the Leadville deposits; there are,
" however, variations from it, and also in the character
" of the inclosing rock, which do not necessarily involve
" any difference in origin or mode of formation. As
" variations in form, the ore sometimes occurs in irregu-
" larly shaped bodies, or in transverse sheets, not
" always directly connected with the upper or contact
" surface of the ore-bearing bed or rock. It also occurs
" at or near the contact of sheets of gray or other por-
" phyries with the blue limestone, and less frequently
" in sedimentary beds, both calcareous and silicious,
" and in porphyry bodies, sometimes on or near contact
" surfaces, sometimes along joint or fault planes. . . .
" "The material of which they were composed was not
" a deposit in a pre-existing cavity in the rock, but the

" solutions, which carried them, gradually dissolved out
" the original rock material and left the ore or vein
" material in its place. . . .

"The mineral solutions or ore currents concentrated
" along natural water channels, and followed by prefer-
" ence the bedding planes at a certain geological hori-
" zon; but they also penetrated the adjoining rocks
" through cross-joints and cleavage planes." [1]

A glance at the geological atlas accompanying this
monograph shows that in many portions of this mineral
belt these deposits lie in a position approaching the
horizontal, sometimes forming a basin, at others alternating in anticlinal and synclinal folds, shown in an
emphasized form in figure 22. [2]

In places erosion has carried off the overlying porphyry, leaving the vein material lying between the
bedding of limestone and superficial deposit of slide and
detritus. The continuity of the vein material is frequently interrupted by faults and intrusive dikes as
well as by a broken or "jumbled-up" condition of the
country rock. This is substantially the character of
deposits with which the courts are confronted in the
application of the mining laws.

§ 301. Judicial interpretation of the term "rock in
" place."— In some of Judge Hallett's decisions he
speaks of the *lode* being "in place." Notably in the
case of Stevens *v.* Williams,[3] where that distinguished
jurist uses the following language:—

"As to the meaning of these words 'in place,' they
" seem to indicate the body of the country which has not
" been affected by the action of the elements; which
" may remain in its original state and condition as dis-
" tinguished from the superficial mass which may lie

---

[1] Geology and Mining Industry of Leadville, pp. 375, 378.
[2] See, *post,* § 312, p. 560.
[3] 1 Morr. Min. Rep. 558, 559, 560, Fed. Cas. No. 13,414.

" above it. . . . And when the act speaks of veins or
" lodes *in place*, it means such as lie in fixed position in
" the general mass of country rock or in the general
" mass of the mountain. . . . Now, whenever we find a
" vein, or lode, in this general mass of country rock we
" may be permitted to say that it is *in place*, as dis-
" tinguished from the superficial deposit; and that is
" true, whatever the character of the deposit may be—
" that is to say, as to whether it belongs to one class of
" veins or another; it is *in place* if it is held in the em-
" brace, is inclosed by the general mass—of the
" country."

. . . .

"It is not material as to the character of the vein
" matter whether it is loose and disintegrated or
" whether it is solid material. In these lodes the earth
" that is found in them, the earthy matter which may
" be washed or treated with water or steam, is often
" the most valuable part.

"It was never understood here or elsewhere, so far as
" I know, that such earthy matter was not embraced in
" the location because it was of that character. It is the
" surrounding mass of country rock; it is that which
" incloses the lode, rather than the material of which it
" is composed, which gives it its character. So that,
" even if it be true, as counsel have stated in the course
" of their arguments, that this is mere sand, is a loose
" and friable material, which cannot be called rock, in
" the strict definition of the word—if that be true, it
" does not affect the character of the lode. If it were all
"of that character, it would still be a vein or lode *in
" place* if the wall on each side, the part which holds the
" lode, is fixed and immovable."

And in Stevens *v.* Gill [1] he says:—

"The act of congress speaks of veins or lodes *in place*,
" by which, according to our interpretation, it is re-
" quired that the vein, or lode, shall be in the general
" mass of the mountain. It may not be on the surface or
" covered only by movable parts, called slide, or débris.

[1] 1 Morr. Min. Rep. 576, 580, Fed. Cas. No. 13,398.

Lindley on M.—34

" But if it is in the general mass of the mountain,
" although the inclosing rocks may have sustained frac-
" ture and dislocation in the general movement of the
" country, it is in place." [1]

The judge does not give the exact language of the
statute, which is "veins, or lodes, *of* quartz or other rock
" in place."

Dr. Raymond, in his "Law of the Apex," calls attention to the misquotation. But it seems to us that, taken
in connection with Judge Hallett's other rulings, his
intent is manifest.[2]

In the second trial of the Stevens & Leiter case, Justice Miller charged the jury as follows:—

"By 'rock in place' I do not mean merely hard rock,
" merely quartz rock, but any combination of rock,
" broken up, mixed with mineral and other things, is
" rock in place, within the meaning of the statute.

"I give that instruction [that the mineral must be of
" quartz or other rock], but with the distinct under-
" standing that all this substance between the porphyry
" and limestone that has been explained to you which
" contains mineral—I mean which contains ore—is
" *rock in place.*" [3]

And in Iron S. M. Co. *v.* Cheesman, Judge Hallett
says:—

" Excluding the wash, slide, or debris, on the sur-
" face of the mountain, all things in the mass of the
" mountain are *in place.*"

This was quoted and approved by the supreme court
of the United States.[4]

---

[1] See, also, Leadville M. Co. *v.* Fitzgerald, 4 Morr. Min. Rep. 381,
Fed. Cas. No. 8158; Stevens & Leiter *v.* Murphey, 4 Morr. Min. Rep. 380.

[2] See, also, Judge Hallett's definitions of "vein" and "lode," *ante,*
§ 293.

[3] Stevens & Leiter *v.* Williams, 1 McCrary, 480, 1 Morr. Min. Rep.
566, 569, 571, Fed. Cas. No. 13,413.

[4] Iron S. M. Co. *v.* Cheesman, 116 U. S. 529, 537, 6 Sup. Ct. Rep. 481.
See, also, Jones *v.* Prospect Mt. T. Co., 21 Nev. 339, 31 Pac. 642.

The decisions of Judge Hallett and Justice Miller were quoted with approval in a case decided by the supreme court of Nevada, the facts of which and conclusions drawn from them are thus stated in the opinion of the court:—

" A certain formation which the defendant claimed " to be the ledge had been traced on its inclination " outside the plaintiff's boundaries, and a large amount " of work there done upon it. If this was the ledge, as " the defendant claimed, it tended to show that its apex " was outside those boundaries. According to the wit- " nesses, it consisted of broken limestone, boulders, " low-grade ore, gravel, and sand, which appeared to " have been subjected to the action of water. This was " found at a depth of several hundred feet, and where " there seems to have been no question that it was within " the original and unbroken mass of the mountain. So " far as was shown, the rock on either side was fixed, " solid, and immovable. Mineral matter so situated, no " matter where it was originally formed or deposited, is " in place within the meaning of the law. The manner in " which mineral was deposited in the places where it is " found is at best but little more than a matter of mere " speculation, and to attempt to draw a distinction " based upon the mode, or manner, or time of its deposit " would be utterly impracticable and useless. The " question was long ago settled by the courts." [1]

A mere superficial deposit, although originally in place, the overlying rock having been eroded and replaced by débris, or wash, is not in place.[2]

Auriferous cement gravel beds found in the channels of ancient rivers, lying upon bed-rock and covered with thick deposits of other gravel, the whole frequently capped with a lava of great thickness, would seem to be "in place" within the definitions heretofore given. But

---

[1] Jones v. Prospect Mt. T. Co., 21 Nev. 339, 351, 31 Pac. 642.

[2] Tabor v. Dexter, 9 Morr. Min. Rep. 614, Fed. Cas. No. 13,723. See Judge Delaney's charge to jury in Meydenbauer v. Stevens (Alaska), 78 Fed. 787.

the land department,[1] as well as the courts,[2] treats them as deposits of rock not "in place," and requires them to be located under the laws applicable to placers.

ARTICLE IV. "TOP," OR "APEX."

§ 305. The "top," or "apex" of a vein, as a controlling factor in lode locations.

§ 306. The term "top," or "apex," not found in the miner's vocabulary —Definitions of the lexicographers.

§ 307. Definitions given in response to circulars issued by the public land commission.

§ 308. Definition by Dr. Raymond.

§ 309. The ideal lode and its apex.

§ 310. Illustrations of a departure from the ideal lode—The case of Duggan v. Davey.

§ 311. The Leadville cases.

§ 312. Hypothetical illustrations based upon the mode of occurrence of the Leadville and similar deposits.

§ 312a. Theoretical apex where the true apex is within prior or patented agricultural claims, the vein passing on its downward course into public land.

§ 313. The existence and *situs* of the "top," or "apex," a question of fact.

§ 305. The "top," or "apex," of a vein as a controlling factor in lode locations. —The importance of a correct definition of the terms "top," or "apex," or at least a proper application of their definitions to the varying geological conditions encountered in the administration of the mining laws, cannot be overestimated. The top, or apex, of the vein which is the subject of appropriation, is the prime factor in determining the extent of the rights acquired by a lode location. This is apparent when we consider the following requirements of the law:—

(1) No lode location is valid unless it includes, to some extent at least, within vertical planes drawn through the surface boundaries, the top, or apex, of a

[1] Copp's Min. Dec. 78.
[2] Gregory v. Pershbaker, 73 Cal. 109, 14 Pac. 401.

discovered vein, at least as against a subsequent locator properly inclosing such apex within his surface boundaries.[1]

(2) The right to pursue the vein on its strike ceases at the point where the apex of the vein passes beyond the surface boundaries or vertical planes drawn through them;

(3) The right to pursue the vein on its downward course out of and beyond a vertical plane drawn through the side-line, into and underneath the lands adjoining, when this right exists to any degree, can only be exercised to the extent that the top, or apex, of the located vein is found within the surface boundaries of the location, or within vertical planes drawn through them.[2]

It is not our purpose to here discuss these elements. They will be fully considered under appropriate heads in other portions of this treatise. We enumerate them simply to demonstrate the necessity of an accurate understanding of what is meant by the terms "top," or "apex," and the care with which principles announced in one case are to be applied to another.

In the light of the rules announced in the previous articles, if a given mineral deposit is in place, it is a lode. The law assumes that the lode has a top, or apex, and provides for the acquisition of title by location upon this apex. A lode without an apex is not contemplated and no provision is made for locating it. It can-

[1] It is possible that under some circumstances a location overlying the dip of a vein may be valid to the extent of whatever may be found within the vertical bounding planes. The statement in the text should be read in the light of the discussion found in a subsequent section, (*post*, § 364).

[2] "The grant is as to lodes having their apex in the ground patented. "The fact that a part of the apex might be in the ground granted would "not give any right to that part of the apex which is not therein, "although the apex might be cut by both end-lines of the granted "premises." Waterloo M. Co. *v.* Doe, 82 Fed. 45, 55.

not be located under the placer laws, because these laws
apply only to deposits *not* in place, and before it can be
legally located as a lode, the apex, or top, must be found.
If a location is made on the side or on the dip, whoever
discovers and properly locates the apex will be entitled
to enjoy the full rights accorded to regular valid lode
locations, and the rights of those who have located on
the side edge, or dip, must yield.

The most serious difficulty in defining the apex has
arisen in connection with certain flat, or "blanket,"
deposits, which have been judicially determined to be
lodes within the meaning of the statutes. It is often
quite impracticable to fix upon any exposure of such a
deposit which properly constitutes the apex. It is true
that after a lode patent is issued, the existence of an
apex within the patented ground will be conclusively
presumed,[1] but not necessarily the apex of the vein in
dispute. Nor will it be presumed that any particular
exposure of the vein is that apex. It must still remain
a question of proof.

§ 306. **The terms "top," or "apex," not found in
the miner's vocabulary — Definitions of the lexicographers.** — Prior to the passage of the act of July 26,
1866, the terms "vein" and "lode" formed a part of
the miner's vocabulary. They were incorporated into
local rules, and their signification was fairly understood
throughout the mining regions. The first congressional
law on the subject of mining on the public domain was
but a crystallization of these rules;[2] and it was no more
than natural that when the courts came to construe the
terms which had thus found their way into legislative

---

[1] Iron S. M. Co. *v.* Campbell, 17 Colo. 267, 29 Pac. 513.

[2] Jennison *v.* Kirk, 98 U. S. 453; Broder *v.* Natoma W. Co., 101 U. S.
274; Chambers *v.* Harrington, 111 U. S. 350, 4 Sup. Ct. Rep. 428; N. P.
R. R. *v.* Sanders, 166 U. S. 620, 17 Sup. Ct. Rep. 671. See, *ante*, § 56.

enactments, they should be interpreted according to the understanding of those who first made the definitions and applied them. In addition to this, the terms "vein" and "lode" had a recognized scientific meaning which did not differ from the popular one, except as applied to novel and peculiar conditions.

But neither "top" nor "apex" found a place in the miner's glossary at any period in the history of the mining industry, either in the mining regions of the west or elsewhere; nor had they ever been recognized or applied by scientists for the purpose of designating any part of a vein, lode, or mineral deposit of any kind. Neither miner nor geologist is entitled to the credit for their appearance in the public statutes; nor are they to be held responsible for the perplexities and embarrassments surrounding their proper interpretation. Thus left without custom, precedent, or scientific definition to guide them, the courts were forced to take the statute by its "four corners" and evolve a definition which would, measurably at least, effectuate the object and end of the law. The rule that words employed in a statutory enactment are to be given their ordinary meaning unless a contrary intention appear was not necessarily violated. The courts simply were forced to the conclusion that the ordinary acceptation of the terms was not what congress intended.

Webster defines an apex to be "the top, point, or sum-" mit of anything."

Compilers of dictionaries which have made their appearance since the act under consideration was passed have not been particularly lucid in their definitions. For instance:—

Standard Dictionary:—
"(1) The pointed or angular end, or highest point, " as of a pyramid, spire, or mountain; extreme point; " tip; top.

" (2) The vertex of a plane or solid angle.

" (3) The highest point of a stratum; as a coal
" seam."

Century Dictionary:—

" (1) The tip, point, or summit of anything. In
" *geometry,* the angular point of a cone or conic section.
" The angular point of a triangle opposite the base.

" (2) In *geology,* the top of an anticlinal fold of
" strata. This term, as used in United States Revised
" Statutes, has been the occasion of much litigation. It
" is supposed to mean something nearly equivalent to
" outcrop; but precisely in what it differs from out-
" crop has not been, neither does it seem capable of
" being, distinctly made out."

Evidently the courts even now can receive but little
assistance from the lexicographers.

§ 307. **Definitions given in response to circulars
issued by the public land commission.**—Under an act
of congress passed March 3, 1879, a public land commission was appointed for the purpose of codifying the then
existing laws relating to the survey and disposition of
the public domain, and to make such recommendations
as it might deem wise in relation to the best methods of
disposing of the public lands. This commission consisted of J. A. Williamson, commissioner of the general
land office; Clarence King, director of the geological
survey; A. T. Britton, Thomas Donaldson, and J. W.
Powell. For the purpose of informing themselves generally on conditions existing in the west, the commissioners issued a circular containing a series of questions,
to which answers were received. These circulars were
sent to mining engineers, surveyors, lawyers, judges,
and practical miners. Under the head of "Lode
" Claims," the fourth question was:—

"*What do you understand to be the top, or apex, of a
" vein or lode ?"

We select from the list of answers quoted by Dr. Raymond in his "Law of the Apex":—

"The highest point at which the ore or rock is found "'in place' or between the walls of the vein, and not a "'blow out,' or part of the ledge broken down outside "the walls."

"The croppings, or the exposed surface of the vein, "or lode."

"The highest point at which it approaches or reaches "the natural surface of the ground."

"The highest point of its outcrop in rock in place."

"That point at which the vein enters or emerges from "rock in place."

"The top, or apex, is generally understood to be that "part of the lode that is first discovered. A vertical "lode has its apex at the surface."

"Where the mineral-bearing crevice-matter is first "met, either on the surface, or, as in blind lodes, under-"ground; but wherever it is met, there begins the "apex."

"The croppings, or highest point of the ledge appear-"ing above or discovered beneath the surface."

"The highest point of the center of the ledge."

"The outcrop in the highest geological level, whether "this is accidentally higher or lower than some outcrop "caused by denudation, or slip."

"Where it comes through or to the surface of the rock "in which it is incased, though it may be covered, and "sometimes is, with twenty or thirty feet of loose "earth."

"That portion of the lode along its course which out-"crops to the surface, or, if 'blind,' which comes near-"est to the surface."

"Croppings."

"The line such vein would make in its intersection "with the surface, calculated from its true dip at each "point."

"The uppermost part of the ledge between the two
" walls, although these may be missing."

"In case the vein outcrops at the surface, I would
" call any portion of such outcrop the top, or apex. If
" the vein does not reach the surface, then the highest
" point to which the vein, or lode, can be traced is the
" apex—not necessarily the nearest point to the surface,
" but the absolute highest point."

"The summit, comb, crest, or highest point on the
" ridge of a vein, or lode."

"The upper edge; that part which is first reached or
" passed, in developing a mine."

"The outcrop, or, in case of a blind ledge, that line
" of the vein, or lode, which approaches the surface the
" nearest."

"That portion of the vein that is visible in the
" country rock when the loose dirt or earth has been
" removed. Some veins stand up above the country
" rock like a wall. The top of such veins would be the
" highest part of such wall above the ground or bed-
" rock."

"Its highest point at any given place."

"The outcrop."

"The point at surface where the ore is met with;
" either superficially seen in the croppings, or just
" beneath the surface."

"Either the outcrop or crevice between walls at the
" top of bed-rock."

"The vein at the surface."

"Outcrops generally."

"The width of the vein, or lode, on the surface; but
" the United States mining law means the top, or apex,
" to be the width of the claim, six hundred by fifteen
" hundred feet."

"The outcropping of the vein."

"Where it has been projected through the country
" rock by an acting subterranean agency or force."

Judge Beatty, then chief justice of Nevada, gave the clearest and most comprehensive of all the definitions. It is as follows:—

"The top, or apex, of any part of a vein is found by
" following the line of its dip up to the highest point
" at which vein-matter exists in the fissure. According
" to this definition, the top, or apex, of a vein is the
" highest part of the vein along its entire course. If
" the vein is supposed to be divided into sections
" by vertical planes at right angles to its strike, the
" top, or apex, of each section is the highest part
" of the vein between the planes that bound that sec-
" tion." . . .

"Of course, there are irregular mineral deposits
" departing widely in their characteristics from the
" typical or ideal vein which seems to have been in
" the mind of the framer of the act of 1872. To
" such deposits the foregoing definitions will not
" apply; and, in my opinion, great difficulty will be
" experienced in any attempt to apply the existing law
" to them."[1]

§ 308. Definition by Dr. Raymond.—Dr. Raymond, in his "Law of the Apex," with reference to these terms and their use in the act of May 10, 1872, says:—

"I have reason to believe that they were used instead
" of the word 'outcrop,' in order to cover 'blind lodes,'
" which do not crop out. The conception of an apex,
" which is properly a point, was probably taken from
" the appearance of a blind lode in a cross-section,
" where the walls appear as lines and the upper edge as
" a point. The term may also have been intended to
" cover the imaginary case of an ore deposit which ter-
" minates upwards in a point. We may, however, dis-
" miss from consideration the case of a simple point,
" and safely assume that the apex is the same as a top,
" and is either a line or a surface."

---

[1] Report of Public Land Commission, p. 399; Dr. Raymond on Law of the Apex, p. 28.

The definition crystallized by him and found in his
" Glossary of Mining and Metallurgical Terms,"[1] is,
" the end or edge of a vein nearest the surface."

We think this definition should be qualified to some
extent. Our views will be found in the next section.

§ 309. **The ideal lode and its apex.**— For the purpose
of elementary consideration of the subject, we present
in figure 10, a ver-
tical cross - section,
showing two veins,
or lodes, of the
simplest type, two
steeply inclined fis-
sures filled with
ore-bearing materi-
al, the one outcrop-

FIGURE 10.

ping on the surface, the other terminating on its upward
course before reaching the surface.

These are doubtless the veins which the miner had in
mind when he furnished the descriptions which served
as guides in the enactment of the law. There appears
no room for doubt concerning the meaning of the word
"apex" as used
in the statutes,
when applied to
these veins. It re-
ferred to the upper
terminal edge of the
sheet-like vein, wheth-
er reaching the sur-
face or not.

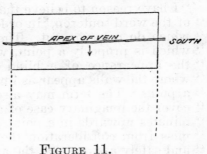

FIGURE 11.

An ideal location
covering one such apex is represented in figure 11, and
the rights flowing from it are unquestioned.

[1] Trans. Am. Inst. M. E., vol. ix, p. 102.

How should this apex be defined? It is evidently a surface, bounded by the walls of the vein. It has both length and breadth, and cannot be described as a point or a line.

The apex of the ideal vein within the location is a surface bounded by the walls of the vein and the end-lines of the location. This surface is, of course, irregular. It may be higher at one place within the boundaries than it is in another; but mere elevation of the upper edge of the vein at different points within the location is of no moment. If the top of the mountain were ground down to a horizontal plane, the vein as exposed would be a plane surface; but, nevertheless, it would be an apex. The fact that the exposed edge of the vein is ragged, or that the surface of the outcrop is higher in one place above a given datum plane than it is in another, makes no difference in the principle.

If this upper edge does not outcrop so as to be visibly traceable on the surface, but is "blind," covered with detritus or a capping of country rock, it is still a surface bounded by the walls of the vein and vertical planes drawn downward through the end-lines. The plane of contact of the upper edge of the vein with the detritus or capping, intersected by the walls of the vein, would be the apex surface. We cannot conceive that an apex of a lode, within the meaning of the act of congress, can be anything but a surface, although we are aware that the supreme court of the United States has said that an apex is often a *line* of great length.[1] But it undoubtedly meant a surface, because in another portion of the same case it speaks of the "apex in its full " width." Mathematically speaking, there is no width to a line. As was said by the supreme court of Montana, a lead, or lode, is not an imaginary line without dimensions; it is not a thing without shape or form.

[1] Larkin v. Upton, 144 U. S. 19, 23, 12 Sup. Ct. Rep. 614.

But before it can legally and rightfully be denominated a lead, or lode, it must have length, and width, and depth; it must be capable of measurement; it must occupy defined space, and be capable of identification.[1] Of course, in speaking of the edge of the vein nearest to the surface, we mean the surface along the course of the vein, the upper edge, and not the lower edge, or side edge. As absolute horizontality does not exist in nature, save in the case of the level of the sea, every vein, lode, or deposit, whatever its form, has either an upper and lower edge, or a top and a bottom, as well as sides. It may be difficult to find them, or to determine their relative position, but they exist, in the nature of things.

To further illustrate, recurring again to figure 10: Suppose that, instead of the mountain being in its normal condition, the south face of the hill was abraded, cut down vertically, as you would cut a cheese, as shown in cross-section on the figure, leaving the edge of the vein from the original outcrop to the bottom of the figure between the hanging- and foot-wall planes, there indicated, exposed to the observer as we see it in the figure. In other respects, the vein preserves its position in the mountain as described. Will it be seriously contended that the exposure of the edge thus described constitutes an apex, because it appears at the surface on the perpendicular face of the hill? It has been so claimed. In the case of Duggan v. Davey, decided by the supreme court of Dakota, a case soon to be considered by us, it was stated by Professor Dickerman, a distinguished expert, in response to an inquiry as to what would be the apex of a vein cropping out at an angle of one degree from the vertical on a perpendicular hillside, and cropping out also at a right angle with that along the level

---

[1] Foote v. National M. Co., 2 Mont. 403.

summit of the hill (which is the case assumed by us
with reference to figure 10), that in his opinion the whole
line of the exposure from the bottom upward to the
original outcrop and clear over the hill, as far as it
extended, would be the apex of the vein. In other
words, one part of the apex surface can be perpendicular, or at right angles to the other.[1] Of course, the court
declined to follow him.

Mr. Ross E. Browne furnishes the following definition and illustration:—

"The vein is limited in extent. It terminates hori-
" zontally, upward, and ultimately downward. Let
" figure 12 represent in isometric projection, the plane

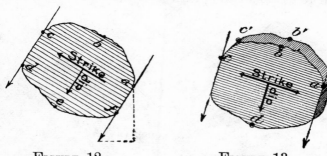

FIGURE 12.   FIGURE 13.

" of an ideal narrow vein, comparable with a sheet of
" paper. The line *a-b-c-d-e-f* represents the terminal
" edge, with tangent dip-lines at *a* and *c*. Then *a-b-c*
" is the top edge or apex, *a-f* and *c-d* are the side edges,
" and *d-e-f* is the bottom edge. From any point of the
" apex *a-b-c* the vein may be followed downward in the
" direction of its true dip. From the bottom edge *d-e-f*
" the vein does not extend further downward. Hence
" the definition which follows: 'The apex is all that
" 'portion of the terminal edge of the vein from which
" 'the vein has extension downward in the direction of
" 'its dip.' But a vein is not generally so thin as a sheet
" of paper; it has a material and widely varying thick-

[1] Duggan *v.* Davey, 4 Dak. 110, 140, 26 N. W. 887.

" ness, and its apex is a surface rather than an edge.
" The above definition may then apply more strictly to
" the lateral boundaries or walls of the vein, and the
" apex of the vein itself may be described as the surface
" included between the apices of its lateral boundaries
" —a-b-c-c'-b'-a', on figure 13.

"The apex may outcrop or it may be blind,—that is,
" not reach up to the surface."

The above definition, which accords with our views,
involves the elements of terminal edge, and downward
course therefrom.

According to it, the horizontal sheet *a* on figure 14
and the anticlinal fold *b* have no apices, while the synclinal fold *c* has two apices.

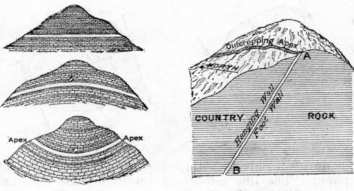

FIGURE 14.   FIGURE 15.

It has sometimes happened, especially with veins of
slight inclination from the horizontal, that in the process
of erosion, the side edge, representing a dip-line, has
been exposed to constitute an outcrop. For example,
assume that the vertical cross-section cut shown on
figure 15 is the result of natural erosion, then the exposure *a-b* would be such an outcrop. It is quite apparent
that such outcrops do not constitute apices.

§ 310. Illustration of a departure from the ideal lode—The case of Duggan v. Davey.—One of the most interesting and instructive of all the adjudicated cases involving the interpretation of the terms "top," or "apex," is Duggan *v.* Davey,[1] decided by the supreme court of Dakota. The decision follows, in the main, the opinion given by the trial court. It is a lucid and masterly presentation of the law, and, as presented, affords us an opportunity to illustrate and explain by diagrams the position of the vein in the earth, its exposure on both top and side, the contention of the respective parties as to what constituted the apex, and the conclusions of the court deduced from the facts. It is one of the few cases which affords a full opportunity of explaining by simple methods the true definition of the term "top," or "apex," as well as the "strike" and "dip," and their relationship one to the other. Entertaining these views as to the importance of the case, we are justified in presenting it fully.

EAST.   WEST.

BARE BUTTE CREEK

FIGURE 16.

Figure 16 is a perspective, showing an edge or outcrop of the vein exposed along the western face of Custer Hill, traversing it in a northerly and southerly direction, and an edge or outcrop traversing the northern slope in an easterly and westerly direction. We take the following description from the opinion of the trial court:—

[1] 4 Dak. 110, 26 N. W. 887.

Lindley on M.—35

The western slope of the hill presents a lateral face from south to north, along the line of the outcrop, of thirteen hundred feet. At its northern extremity it turns to the east, and its northern slope presents a lateral face from west to east of upwards of three thousand feet. Along its base and following it in this turn in the direction indicated is a small stream called Bare Butte creek. These slopes are quite steep, and extend from base to summit about twelve hundred to thirteen hundred feet. The whole country is hilly and broken, and the hill is only one of a series of similar elevations, with which it is more or less directly connected.

Beginning at or near the southern extremity of the western slope of Custer Hill, at a point (marked x on figure 16) half-way up the slope, there is found an outcropping layer or stratum of reddish quartzite, or metamorphic sandstone, of several feet in thickness, overlaid by a body or stratum of limestone or dolomitic shale, of a thickness not definitely ascertained. From this point the croppings may be readily traced in several places by high reef-like ledges, jutting out boldly from the face of the hill along the western face to its northern extremity.

The general bearing of this line of croppings may be stated as N. 11° W., the distance twelve hundred and forty-three feet, and the angle of inclination upward from south to north, approximately, three degrees.

At the northern extremity of the hill this line of outcrop of quartzite, with its overlying limestone or dolomite, turns and extends along the northern slope with a downward inclination, thus gradually nearing the base of the hill until, at a distance of something over twenty-five hundred feet, it disappears beneath the bed of the creek.

The course of the outcrop along the northern slope of the hill is for a distance of nineteen hundred and fifty feet, N. 70° 30′ E., and the angle of declination eight degrees, from west to east.

The "vein" consists of the underlying quartzite, impregnated with iron and silver in various forms, the width of the so-called vein material not being uniform. The richer ore deposits are usually found along the contact with the overlying limestone.

The entire line of outcrop on both slopes of Custer Hill appears to have been appropriated by different locations, but the controversies in the case under consideration arose out of claims located on the northern slope. We present in figure 17 a diagram showing the

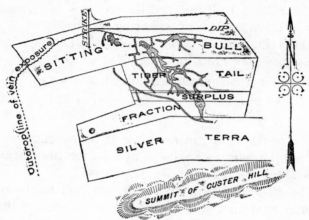

FIGURE 17.

surface boundaries of the claims, the "vein exposure," and the underground workings, in horizontal projection. From this figure it will appear that the Sitting Bull, belonging to the defendants, covers about thirteen hundred and eighty feet of the outcrop on the northern slope of the hill. Its end-lines are parallel, and if this outcrop or vein exposure is the "top," or "apex," of the vein, the location approximates the ideal shown in figure 11.[1]

[1] *Ante*, § 309.

The plaintiffs owned the Silver Terra, some distance south and up the hill from the Sitting Bull. It does not appear upon what vein the Silver Terra location was based. It was not material for the purposes of the case that it should be shown. Both parties had lode patents for their respective claims. The Sitting Bull had, in following the vein southerly into the hill with its underground works, penetrated underneath the surface of the Silver Terra, whereupon the owners of that claim brought an action in equity to enjoin the owners of the Sitting Bull from trespassing within the boundaries of the Silver Terra.

The Sitting Bull justified its presence underneath the Silver Terra surface by asserting ownership of the apex of the vein, and its right to follow it between its end-line planes to an indefinite depth.

The principal question involved was—

"Is the top, or apex, of this vein, or lode, within the " lines of the Sitting Bull location ?"

The court below, in arriving at its conclusions, considered the relative angles of declination in determining which was the top, or apex, of the vein.

The strike and dip, so far as exposed in the underground workings, was testified to as follows: Witnesses for the Sitting Bull claimed the average strike to be N. 18 E. and the dip S. 72 E., seven and one half to eight degrees. Witnesses for the Silver Terra claimed the strike N. 8½ W. and the dip N. 81½ E., seven degrees. The court found the strike to be north and south, and the dip east, at an angle of seven and one half to eight degrees, as shown in figure 17. This dip-line shows that the outcrop in the Sitting Bull location is *substantially* on the side edge of the vein not forming an apex. To be sure, a small part of the outcrop at the westerly end of the location is apex, according to our definition, but this is not the controlling part involved in the case.

As to what constitutes the "top," or "apex," of a vein, the court expressed its view as follows:—

"The definition of the top, or apex, of a vein usually
" given is the end or edge of a vein nearest the sur-
" face; and to this definition the defendants insist we
" must adhere with absolute, literal, and exclusive
" strictness, so that wherever, under any circumstances,
" an edge of a vein can be found at any surface, regard-
" less of all other circumstances, that is to be considered
" as the top, or apex, of the vein. The extent to which
" this view was carried by the defendants—and I must
" confess its logical results were exhibited by Pro-
" fessor Dickerman, their engineer, who, replying to
" an inquiry as to what would be the apex of a vein
" cropping out at an angle of one degree from the
" vertical, on a perpendicular hillside, and crop-
" ping out also at a right angle with that along the
" level summit of the hill, stated that, in his opinion,
" the whole line of that outcrop, from the bottom clear
" over the hill, so far as it extended, would be the apex
" of the vein. Some other witnesses had similar opin-
" ions. The definition given is no doubt correct, under
" most circumstances, but, like many other definitions,
" is found to lack fullness and accuracy in special cases,
" and I do not think important questions of law are to be
" determined by a slavish adherence to this letter of an
" arbitrary definition.

"It is indeed difficult to see how any serious question
" could have arisen as to 'the practical meaning of the
" terms top, or apex, but it seems, in fact, to have
" become somewhat clouded. . . .

" Justice Goddard, a jurist of experience in mining
" law, in his charge to the jury in the case of Iron S.
" M. Co. *v.* Louisville, defines 'top,' or 'apex,' as the
" highest or terminal point of a vein, where it ap-
" proaches nearest the surface of the earth, and where
" it is broken on its edge so as to appear to be the begin-
" ning or end of the vein."

After quoting Judge Beatty's definition given to the public land commission, referred to in a preceding section, the court continues:—

" I am aware that in several adjudged cases 'top,'
" or 'apex,' and 'outcrop' have been treated as synony-
" mous, but never, so far as I am aware, with reference
" to a case presenting the same features as the present.
" The word 'apex' ordinarily designates a point, and so
" considered the apex of a vein is the summit; the high-
" est point in a vein is the ascent along the line of its
" dip, or downward course, and beyond which the vein
" extends no farther; so that it is the end, or, reversely,
" the beginning, of the vein. The word 'top,' while
" including 'apex,' may also include a succession of
" points,—that is, a line,—so that by the top of a vein
" would be meant the line connecting a succession of
" such highest points or apices, thus forming an edge.''

Applying these definitions to the facts of the case
under consideration, the court below held that the Sitting
Bull location did not cover the top, or apex, of the vein.
That the outcrop shown on the northern slope of Custer
Hill was merely an exposure of the edge of the vein on
the line of its dip, just as the exposure of the side edge
of the ideal fissure veins represented in figures 10
and 15.[1]

Judgment passed for the plaintiff. The supreme
court of Dakota adopting the views of the trial court,
affirmed the judgment. It was not in terms decided that
the outcrop on the west slope of the hill was the top, or
apex, of the vein. It was not necessary to do so in order
to defeat the extralateral right claimed by the Sitting
Bull. But if the owner of a location covering the outcrop on the western slope should pursue his vein easterly with his underground works so as to intersect the
workings of the Sitting Bull, showing identity and
continuity, and establishing that the angles of declination disclosed in such workings were the same as in the
case proved, the conclusion is irresistible that the western outcrop would be the true apex of the vein, and this

[1] *Ante,* § 309.

is in consonance with the rule applied to veins of steeper inclination.

The Idaho case of Gilpin *v.* Sierra Nevada Cons. M. Co.,[1] shows a state of facts similar to that appearing in the South Dakota case, and is illustrated on figure 18.

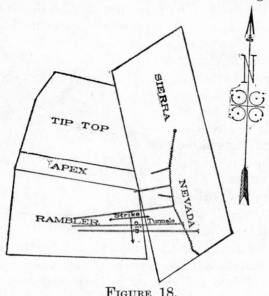

FIGURE 18.

The location of the defendant's claim, the Sierra Nevada, was upon the outcropping side edge of the vein following the dip, the line of exposure or outcrop being shown on figure 18 by the zigzag line within the Sierra Nevada claim. The defendant's works, following the vein on the strike by tunnels driven at right angles to the outcrop, extended underneath the surface of plaintiff's claims, the Apex and the Rambler.

An injunction was sought and denied by the lower court. The supreme court of Idaho reversed the order and directed an injunction principally on the ground that the location of the Sierra Nevada did not cover the

[1] 2 Idaho, 662, 23 Pac. 547, 1014.

apex, and that the showing made did not justify or authorize its presence underneath the plaintiff's surface.[1]

In each of the above cases the failure of the locator of the outcrop to maintain an extralateral right was due to the fact that the outcrop was the side edge and not the apex of the vein. The principle may be illustrated by reference to figure 19, representing a conical hill cut through by an inclined vein, having a northerly and souther-ly strike and an east-erly dip. The top of the hill is removed to expose the plane of the vein. The line *a-b-c-d* is all outcrop, but only the upper portion *d-a-b* is "apex" sub-ject to lode - location.

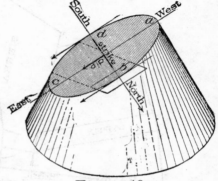

FIGURE 19.

The Sitting Bull location is indicated at *b*. Its end-lines were so placed that the vertical planes passed through them intersected the vein on a downward course; still the extralateral right was denied because the location was not upon the apex. Figure 19, showing the approx-imate location, is to be considered in the light of our observation previously made, that, accurately speaking, the location covered a small part of what we deem to be apex, but the court disregarded this in its findings.

§ 311.   The Leadville cases.—As in almost all other phases of the mining law, the flat deposits of Leadville have produced their full quota of adjudicated law on the subject of "tops" and "apices." As these deposits are legally held to be veins, or lodes, of rock in place, subject

---

[1] For dissenting opinion, see Gilpin *v.* Sierra Nevada Cons. M. Co., 2 Idaho, 675, 23 Pac. 1014.

to mineral location, the law contemplated that they should have apices. We have heretofore given an outline of the formation in which these deposits occur, and the manner of their occurrence.[1]

But in connection with the quotation of some of the definitions of the words "top," or "apex," as applied by the Colorado courts, we think it instructive to present in cross-section, illustrations showing the physical conditions surrounding some of the litigated cases, where these definitions have been announced and applied. A much better understanding of the views of the court in a given case is reached by the aid of diagrams.

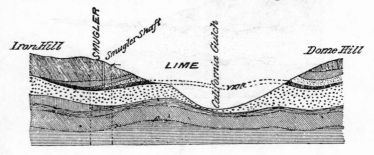

FIGURE 20A.

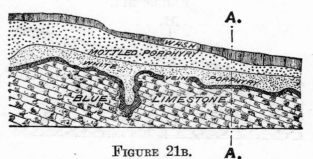

FIGURE 21B.

Iron Silver Mining Co. v. Cheesman.[2] —

Figures 20A and 21B are longitudinal sections on the line of the strike of the vein north and south, the latter

[1] *Ante,* § 300. [2] 8 Fed. 297; 116 U. S. 529, 6 Sup. Ct. Rep. 481.

section being along the joint Lime-Smuggler side-line, along plane B B of figure 20B.

Figures 21A and 20B are cross-sections on the line of the dip, east and west, through the Lime incline, although in figure 20B the incline is not drawn.

Figures 20A and 21A are reduced, with slight modifications, from the atlas sheets of Mr. Emmons accompanying his monograph on "The Geology and Mining "Industry of Leadville."[1]

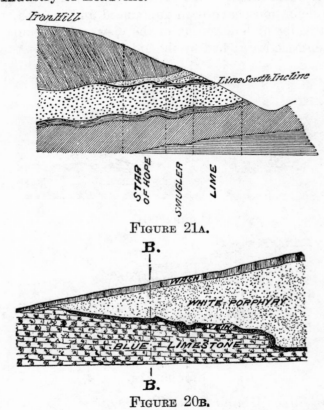

FIGURE 21A.

FIGURE 20B.

Figures 20B and 21B are practically reproductions of the sections prepared by Mr. C. M. Rolker, accompany-

[1] Monograph XII of the U. S. Geological Survey.

ing his "Notes on Leadville Ore Deposits," read before
the American Institute of Mining Engineers.[1]

An inspection of figure 20A indicates that the only
vein exposure is on the slope of the hill facing California
Gulch; this exposure, and the one appearing on the
opposite side in Dome Hill, having resulted from natural erosion. Bearing in mind the description of the
character of the vein and its inclosing rocks, given in a
preceding section, the facts involved in the case were
substantially as follows:—

The Iron Silver Mining Company owned by patent
the Lime claim. Adjoining it on the east was the Smuggler, owned by the defendants. Prior to location, the
defendants sunk a vertical shaft (see figure 20A) to the
depth of forty feet, and at the bottom found a large
body of mineral. After the discovery of the mineral in
the Smuggler claim the owners of the Lime ran inclines (see figure 21A) from the Lime claim into and
upon the Smuggler claim, and connected them with the
Smuggler workings. Thereupon the Iron S. M. Co.
commenced their action against defendants to eject them
from the body of mineral they had discovered and developed within the Smuggler location, claiming that it
was the lode or vein of mineral which had its apex
within the Lime claim. This the Smuggler owners
disputed, claiming that there was no vein or lode within
the Lime ground; that whatever mineral was there was
not in place, but had been removed to that point from
some other locality.

The case was tried three times by jury.[2]

[1] Trans. Am. Inst. M. E., vol. xiv, p. 283.

[2] The first resulted in a verdict for the defendant. Plaintiff demanded
a second trial as a matter of right, a practice at that time permissible
under the laws of Colorado. The second trial resulted in a disagreement;
the third in a verdict and judgment for defendant, which was affirmed
by the Supreme Court of the United States. Iron S. M. Co. v. Cheesman,
116 U. S. 529, 6 Sup. Ct. Rep. 481.

We have already noted the charge of Judge Hallett
in this case, as to what constitutes a lode, or vein, which
was the principal contention between the parties. Upon
the subject of "apex," we quote the following from
Judge Hallett's charge to the jury:—

"A good deal has been said by the witnesses as to
" whether there is a top, or apex, of the vein. That de-
" pends very much as to whether there is any vein, or
" lode, there. If you find that there is a vein, or lode, to
" my mind the evidence is clear enough that the top of
" it is in the Lime location; and if there is none there,
" of course that which does not exist, does not exist in
" any part—it does not exist by its top nor by its bot-
" tom, nor anywhere between the two points." [1]

The jury found that there was no vein, or lode, which
was the customary finding in all cases where the Iron
Silver Mining Company attempted to assert extralateral
rights. This was the unwritten law of Leadville. While
the deposits were veins, or lodes, within the definitions
given by the courts, they were not such, as a matter of
fact, when the question was left to a jury of the neighborhood, if their verdict would uphold the right to pass
on the dip of the vein through and beyond vertical
planes, drawn through the side-lines. [2]

We cite the charge of Judge Hallett for the purpose
of illustrating his views on the subject of "top," or
"apex." This charge, as a whole, was approved by the
supreme court of the United States. [3]

Stevens & Leiter v. Williams. [4] —

This case involved a controversy between the Iron
and Grandview claims, situated upon Iron Hill, where

---

[1] Iron S. M. Co. *v.* Cheesman, 8 Fed. 297, 302.

[2] For an interesting discussion of this, see Dr. Raymond's "Law of the
"Apex."

[3] Iron S. M. Co. *v.* Cheesman, 116 U. S. 529, 535, 6 Sup. Ct. Rep. 481.

[4] First trial, 1 Morr. Min. Rep. 557, Fed. Cas. No. 13,414; second trial,
Id. 566, Fed. Cas. No. 13,413.

the occurrence of the vein and vein exposure were similar to those found in the Lime-Smuggler case. The question of apex in the Iron-Grandview case received full consideration in two trials, at the first of which Judge Hallett presided, and at the second Justice Miller. Although the case was never passed upon by the supreme court of the United States, the charges to the two juries given by the presiding judges are considered to be a full exposition of the law on the subject. We are justified in quoting them fully. Judge Hallett's charge is as follows:—

"We have now to consider the question which was "so much discussed by counsel as to the location with "reference to the top and apex of a vein; and upon that "point it is clear, from an examination of the act, that "it was framed upon the hypothesis that all lodes and "veins occupy a position more or less vertical in the "earth,—that is, that they stand upon their edge in the "body of the mountain,—and these words 'top' and "'apex' refer to the part which comes nearest to the "surface. The words used are 'top,' or 'apex,' as if "the writer was somewhat doubtful as to which word "would best describe or best convey the idea which he "had in his mind. It was with reference to that part "of the lode which comes nearest to the surface that this "description was used; probably the words were not "before known in mining industry; at least, they are "not met with elsewhere, so far as I am informed. "Perhaps, they were not the best that could have been "used to describe the manner in which the lode should "be taken and located. But whether that be true or not, "they are in the act of congress, and there seems to be "little doubt as to their meaning; they are not at all "ambiguous. In some instances, they may perhaps "refer to the *floe* of the lode; that is, a part of the lode "which has been detached from the body of mineral "in the crevice and flowed down on the surface. In "others, where there is no such outcrop, they may mean "that part which stands in the solid rock, although "below a considerable body of the superficial mass,

" which I have attempted to describe to you. We are
" all agreed, however, the courts and counsel, every one,
" that that is the meaning of the words; that they are to
" be taken in some such sense as that, as being the part
" of the lode which comes nearest the surface; and the
" act requires that the location shall be along the line of
" this top, or apex. Supposing the lode to have a some-
" what vertical position in the earth, with this line of
" outcrop, or of appearance on the surface, or nearest
" to the surface, it shall be taken up and occupied by the
" claimant as his location; and he must find where this
" top, or apex, is and make his location with reference
" to that." [1]

On the second trial, Justice Miller charged the jury,
as follows:—

" I think that you will agree with me, as all counsel
" agree, and all the witnesses agree substantially, con-
" ceding that there is a vein, that the top, or the apex,
" of a vein, within the meaning of the act of congress,
" is the highest point of that vein where it approaches
" nearest to the surface of the earth, and where it is
" broken on its edge so as to appear to be the beginning
" or end of the vein. The word 'outcrop' has been used
" in connection with it, and in the true definition of the
" word 'outcrop,' as it concerns a vein, is probably an
" essential part of the definition of its apex, or top; but
" that does not mean the strict use of the word 'out-
" 'crop.' That would not, perhaps, imply the presen-
" tation of the mineral to the naked eye on the surface
" of the earth; but it means that it comes so near to the
" surface of the earth that it is found easily by digging
" for it, or it is the point at which the vein is nearest
" to the surface of the earth; it means the nearest point
" at which it is found towards the surface of the earth.
" And where it ceases to continue in the direction of the
" surface, is the top, or apex, of that vein. It is said in
" this case that the point claimed to be the top, or apex,
" is not such, because at the points where plaintiff shows

[1] Stevens & Leiter v. Williams, 1 Morr. Min. Rep. 557, 561, Fed. Cas.
No. 13,414.

" or attempts to prove an interruption of that vein in its
" ascent toward the surface, and what he calls the begin-
" ning of it, the defendant says that it is only a wave or
" roll in the general shoot of the metal, and that from
" that point it turns over and pursues its course down-
" ward as a part of the same vein in a westerly or south-
" westerly direction. It is proper, I should say to you,
" if the defendant's hypothesis be true, if at that point
" which the plaintiff calls the *highest point, the apex,*
" is merely a swell in the mineral matter, and that it
" turns over and goes on down in a declination to the
" west, that it is not a true apex within the statute. It
" does not mean merely the highest point in a contin-
" uous succession of rolls or waves in the elevation and
" depression of the mineral nearly horizontal." [1]

Iron Silver Mining Company v. Murphy. [2]—
This involved a controversy between the Iron and
Loella claims. Judge Hallett charged the jury as fol-
lows:—

" The top, or apex, is the end, or edge, or terminal
" point of the lode nearest to the surface of the earth.
" It is not required that it shall be on or near or within
" any given distance of the surface. If found at any
" depth, and the locator can define on the surface the
" area which will inclose it, the lode may be held by
" such location."

§ 312. **Hypothetical illustrations, based upon the
mode of occurrence of the Leadville and similar deposits.**—It is not our purpose in this article to deal with
the subject of extralateral rights or treat of the apex, as
affecting those rights. We reserve this important element of the mining law for individual treatment in a
later portion of this work. We are now interested in
determining what is or is not a "top," or "apex." In

---

[1] Stevens & Leiter *v.* Williams, 1 Morr. Min. Rep. 566, 574, Fed. Cas.
No. 13,413.
[2] 1 Morr. Min. Rep. 548.

the course of investigation, however, reference to the
extralateral right is incidentally involved, to the end
that the conclusions reached may be rationally explained
and applied to cases within reasonable probabilities.

We have heretofore considered two classes of deposits: those whose position in the earth approximates
the perpendicular, and those approaching the horizontal.
The geological conditions at Leadville suggest additional complications, by reason of the fact that the
veins do not always occupy the same plane, but are
frequently found in alternating anticlinal and synclinal
folds, which are best expressed by the use of the term
"undulating."

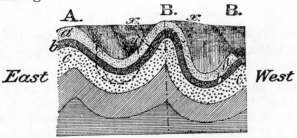

FIGURE 22.

For purposes of illustration, we present in figure 22 a
cross-section. In the figure the stratum d d represents
the overlying white porphyry; b b, the vein material;
c c, the underlying blue limestone. The lines A x and
B B represent the crests of the ridges formed by the
anticlinal folds.

If the overlying porphyry on the crests of the anticlinal folds were removed, leaving the vein material
there exposed, and assuming that in this uncovered position the deposit would still fall within the definition of
a vein or lode,[1] neither A x nor B B would be apices.

---

[1] Judge Hallett inclines to the view that such a deposit would not be
in place. Stevens *v.* Gill, 1 Morr. Min. Rep. 576, 580, Fed. Cas. No.
13,398. *Ante,* § 301.

They are tops, or crests, of the folds, but not apices of the deposit. The exposed surface would be part of the top of the deposit, contradistinguished from the bottom lying on the limestone.

With the vein in position, as shown on figure 22, it might be said that its highest part, or the part approaching nearest to the surface (assuming that there was no surface exposure elsewhere), would be along the crest of the fold. But this would not be the top, or apex, of the *vein*. It would be the top, or apex, of a fold in the vein. If this line were the apex of the vein, a location with side-lines along the crest would give the locator the right to follow the vein in both directions, east and west, "up hill and down dale," indefinitely, so far as the vein preserved its continuity and identity.

The only exposures of the vein in position as shown in figure 22 that can possibly answer to the definitions given by the courts are those indicated by the abrupt terminations at the east and west. As to which of these two exposures would be considered the true apex, is a difficult question, and might have to be determined mathematically, by ascertaining which occupied the higher elevation above a given datum plane.

Eliminating from consideration the inquiry as to which of the two exposures is the higher above a given datum plane, a location on the east or west would cover an apex; and if it covers an apex, the right of extra-lateral pursuit would inure to the locator, to the extent that the identity and continuity of the vein could be established up and down the undulations or folds.

If we can assume that the crest of the anticlinal fold has been eroded, as represented by the dotted line *x x*, we would have then two distinct veins, with their attributes of apices, strike, and dip. But suppose the erosion occurred in the synclinal fold, as illustrated by the dotted line *y y,* leaving two exposures,—would these be apices? They would not be, according to the rule announced in the case of Gilpin *v.* Sierra Nevada Consolidated, heretofore referred to, unless, as suggested by Judge J. H. Beatty in that case, the course upward proved, on subsequent development, to be caused by a mere local fold or dislocation.[1]

It is hardly profitable to pursue this discussion further. Enough has been said to show the absurdity of the law, when applied to geological conditions which were not in contemplation of the law-makers when the laws were enacted. But it is nevertheless the law, if these deposits are "veins, or lodes, of rock in place," and the courts hold that they are.[2]

Geologists have always insisted that this character of deposits should be separately classified. There is no reason why the law-makers should not so classify them, or else abandon the entire element of lateral pursuit, and limit the locator to vertical planes drawn through surface boundaries. In considering the difficulties surrounding the application of the law to conditions similar to those existing at Leadville, we recall the almost prophetic language of Judge W. H. Beatty, then chief justice of Nevada:—

"We are willing to admit that cases may arise to " which it will be difficult to apply the law; but this only " proves that such cases escaped the foresight of con- " gress, or, that although they foresaw the possibility of " such cases occurring, they considered that possibility " so remote as not to afford a reason for departing from " the simplicity of the plan they chose to adopt."[3]

---

[1] *Ante,* § 310.

[2] The views of the land department as to what constitutes a blanket vein and how side-lines are to be constructed when it is desired to locate on top of such deposit may be gleaned from the secretary's opinion in the case of the Homestake Mining Company, 29 L. D. 689.

[3] Gleeson *v.* Martin White M. Co., 13 Nev. 442.

§ **312a. Theoretical apex where the true apex is within prior patented agricultural claims, the vein passing on its downward course into public land.**—Where the true apex of a vein lies within a prior placer or agricultural patent, thus possibly [1] inhibiting a location covering such apex, and the vein on its downward course passes out of and beyond a vertical plane, drawn through the agricultural or placer boundary, into unappropriated public domain, how may that portion of the vein lying outside of and beyond such boundary be appropriated? Is it impossible to acquire it under the mining laws by reason of the fact that the true apex is within patented lands? Will the courts theorize an apex on the line of intersection of the vein on its dip with the vertical plane of the agricultural or placer patented boundary? If it may be located, could such a location confer any extralateral right?

These are questions that cannot under the present state of the law be answered categorically; nor is there enough precedent or authority to enable us to even discuss them other than tentatively. Some of them involve a consideration of extralateral right problems, a subject which must in the main be reserved for future discussion in another part of the work. We must rest content for the time being with a presentation of the views of

---

[1] We say *possibly*, having in mind the doctrine established by the supreme court of the United States in the case of Del Monte M. and M. Co. *v.* Last Chance M. Co., 171 U. S. 55, 18 Sup. Ct. Rep. 895, to the effect that a junior location may be laid upon or across the surface of a valid senior location for the purpose of defining for or securing to such junior location underground or extralateral rights not in conflict with any rights of the senior location. This doctrine has been held by the land department to apply to prior patented lode mining claims (Hidee G. M. Co., 30 L. D. 420, cited by the circuit court of appeals, ninth circuit, in Bunker Hill and Sullivan M. and C. Co., 109 Fed. 538, 542), and to be also applicable in cases of patented agricultural claims (Alice Lode Mining Claim, 30 L. D. 481). The supreme court of Montana, however, expresses grave doubts as to the soundness of these views. State. *v.* District Court, 25 Mont. 504, 517, 65 Pac. 1020, 1025.

the only tribunal which has thus far ventured to any extent upon this delicate and somewhat dangerous ground. This venture, as we shall see, was simply upon the border-line of the subject, and was, we deferentially suggest, not altogether essential to a proper adjustment of the controversies arising in the case under consideration. We refer to the case of Woods v. Holden,[1] the facts of which may be illustrated by reference to figure 23, a plan exhibiting the boundaries of the conflicting lode and placer claim, and figure 24, a vertical cross-section drawn through the line A-B on figure 23, showing the apex in the placer at X and passing out of the vertical placer boundary, at Y.

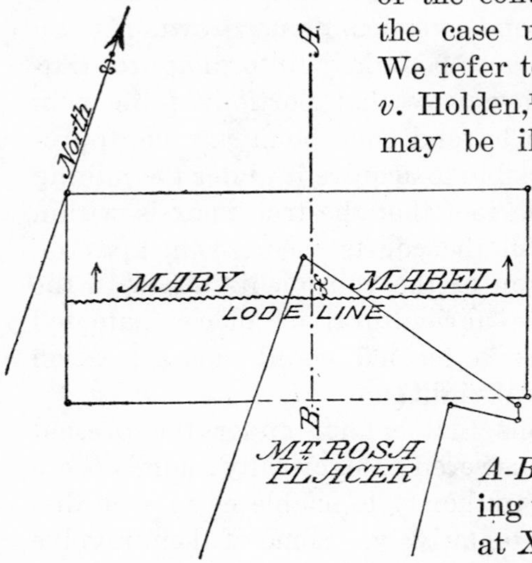

FIGURE 23.

We quote so much of the secretary's opinion as suggests his views upon the subject under discussion:—

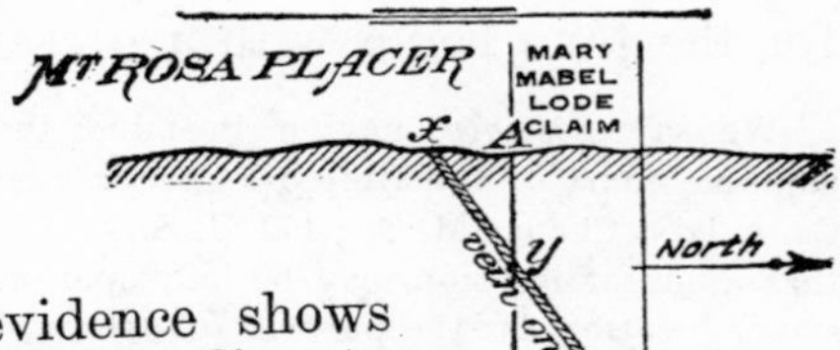

"The undisputed evidence shows "that the Mary Mabel vein dips to "the north, that only the apex and a "small portion of the vein upon its "dip is located within the placer, and "that in dipping to the north the vein "passes into that portion of the Mary

FIGURE 24.

[1] 26 L. D. 198, S. C. on review, 27 L. D. 375.

" Mabel location lying between the northerly side-line
" thereof and the placer. Along its course from west to
" east the vein has an actual existence within the Mary
" Mabel from one end-line to the other, so that the loca-
" tion of that claim does not involve or present a viola-
" tion of the statutory requirement that a lode mining
" claim shall be located 'along the vein.' The vein
" after dipping out of the Mt. Rosa placer, is either
" lawfully included in the Mary Mabel claim, or a valid
" location thereof cannot be made. This latter part of
" this alternative proposition cannot be recognized, be-
" cause it has no support in any statute and is incon-
" sistent with the express provision of section 2319,
" Rev. Stats., which declares:—

" 'All valuable mineral deposits in lands belonging to
" 'the United States, both surveyed and unsurveyed,
" 'are hereby declared to be free and open to explora-
" 'tion and purchase, and the lands in which they are
" 'found to occupation and purchase.'

" There is no claim that the existence of this lode was
" known at the time of the Mt. Rosa placer entry or
" patent, and therefore the portion thereof within the
" placer passed to the placer claimants under the pro-
" visions of section 2333, which reads:—

" . . . 'but where the existence of a vein or lode in
" 'a placer claim is not known, a patent for the placer
" 'claim shall convey all valuable mineral and other
" 'deposits within the boundaries thereof.'

" It has been indisputably settled, and is admitted by
" protestants, that a placer claimant cannot follow a
" vein or lode beyond the surface boundaries of his
" claim extended vertically downward. The portion of
" this vein lying outside of the placer is 'in lands be-
" 'longing to the United States,' and under section 2319
" is 'free and open to exploration and purchase.' While
" the actual apex of the vein is within the placer, the
" United States has dealt with and disposed of the
" placer claim as non-lode ground, and for all purposes
" of disposition by the United States under future ex-
" ploration and discovery any vein or lode in adjacent
" ground stops at the point of its intersection with the

" boundary of the placer. Within the placer it is not
" subject to exploration or purchase, except according
" to the will of the private owner. For the purpose of
" discovery and purchase under the mining laws, the
" legal apex of a vein like the Mary Mabel, dipping out
" of ground disposed of under the placer or non-mineral
" laws, is that portion of the vein within the public lands
" which would constitute its actual apex if the vein had
" no actual existence in the ground so disposed of. Un-
" der this view the apex of the vein extends throughout
" the entire length of the Mary Mabel claim, if that be
" necessary to the valid entry thereof. Protestant's
" contention that the Mary Mabel vein or lode is segre-
" gated and divided into two non-contiguous parts by
" the Mt. Rosa placer, and that the location and entry
" of the easterly part is thereby rendered invalid, cannot
" be sustained."[1]

If we are to accept the assertion contained in the foregoing extract from the opinion, that "For the purpose
" of discovery and purchase under the mining laws, the
" legal apex of a vein like the Mary Mabel, dipping out
" of ground disposed of under the placer or non-mineral
" laws, is that portion of the vein within the public lands
" which would constitute its actual apex if the vein had
" no actual existence in the ground so disposed of," as a
correct exposition of the law, we have to deal with a
new element in the solution of extralateral right problems. There may be no question but that the locator of
the vein, having made an underground discovery outside of the placer boundary, might acquire by location
fifteen hundred feet in length and at least three hundred
feet in width, and be entitled to everything within his

---

[1] This decision of the secretary was rendered prior to the promulgation
of the opinion by the supreme court of the United States in Del Monte
M. and M. Co. v. Last Chance M. Co., 171 U. S. 55, 18 Sup. Ct. Rep. 895.
The application of the doctrine there announced to the case of the Mabel
lode would have rendered the opinion of the secretary on this subject
unnecessary.

vertical planes drawn through his surface boundaries, there being no apex proprietor with extralateral privileges to challenge his rights. But whether or not such locator could himself predicate an extralateral right upon this so-called "legal apex," is a question we cannot see our way clear to answer without further light from an inspired source. We shall have occasion to recur to this again when dealing with the manner of making lode locations, and also in connection with the extralateral right problems.

§ 313. **The existence and situs of the "top," or "apex," a question of fact.**—When we consider that most, if not all, of the definitions of "top," or "apex," found in this article are contained in charges to juries, it is hardly necessary to cite authorities to show that the existence and *situs* of the "top," or "apex," are questions of fact. What constitutes an apex, is a question of law to be determined by the court; but whether a given portion of a lode, or vein, is its "top," or "apex," and what is its course through the ground of contending parties, is a question for the jury.[1]

This accounts for the presence in the literature of the law of so many able and logical statements as to what constitutes a "top," or "apex," and the absence of recorded cases establishing the existence of any such tops, or apices, within the Leadville belt. It would seem that among the muniments of a lode locator's title in this section of the country is the unwritten law of the neighborhood, that no extralateral rights should be permitted.

[1] Illinois S. M. Co. *v.* Raff, 7 N. Mex. 336, 34 Pac. 544; Bluebird M. Co. *v.* Largey, 49 Fed. 289. See, also, cases cited in § 311, *ante*.

ARTICLE V.   "STRIKE," "DIP," OR "DOWNWARD "COURSE."

§ 317. Terms "strike" and "dip" not found in the Revised Statutes—Popular use of the terms.

§ 318. "Strike" and "dip" as judicially defined.

§ 319. "Downward course."

§ 317. **Terms "strike" and "dip" not found in the Revised Statutes—Popular use of the terms.**—The act of July 26, 1866, granted the right to follow the located vein, "with its dips, angles, and variations, to any " depth." The Revised Statutes, in defining the extra-lateral right, use the terms "entire depth" and "course " downward," as a substitute for the terms "dips, "angles, and variations." The term "dip" is the one in common use. "Dip" and "depth" are of the same origin, and, colloquially speaking, "dip" and "course " downward" are synonymous. In a popular sense, " dip " is the "downward course," the direction, or inclination, towards the "depth." [1]

"Strike" does not appear in any of the mining laws. It is a term used to designate the longitudinal or horizontal course of the vein.

§ 318. **"Strike" and "dip" as judicially defined.**— Judge W. H. Beatty, in his testimony before the public land commission, thus defined these terms:—

" The strike, or course, of a vein is determined by a " horizontal line drawn between its extremities at that " depth at which it attains its greatest longitudinal " extent. The dip of a vein, its 'course downward' " (Rev. Stats., § 2322), is at right angles to its strike; " or, in other words, if a vein is cut by a vertical plane " at right angles to its course, the line of section will be " the line of its dip. . . .

[1] Duggan v. Davey, 4 Dak. 110, 141, 26 N. W. 887.

" The strike, or course, of a vein can never be exactly " determined until it has been explored to its greatest " extent; but a comparatively slight development near " the surface will generally show its course with suf- " ficient accuracy for the purposes of a location. The " dip having an exact mathematical relation to the " course of the vein is, of course, undetermined until " the strike is determined; but, practically, the line of " dip is closely approximated by taking the steepest " (the nearest a vertical) line by which a vein can be " followed downward." [1]

The miner in locating his claim, although he is called upon to locate it "along the vein," has but little opportunity to explore the ground and determine prior to location what is its course, or strike. He is compelled to exercise his best judgment from surface indications and such primitive development as the limited time allowed him to perfect his location will permit. A vein does not always outcrop to any considerable distance, so as to present to the miner's observation its longitudinal direction. His location usually precedes any extended exploration, and, in most cases, is made without accurate knowledge of the course or direction of the vein.[2]

Mathematically speaking, the true course (strike) of a vein (underground) is never demonstrated until after extensive investigation and the expenditure of time and money. In a case decided by Judge Hawley, sitting as circuit judge in the ninth circuit,[3] one of the veins in controversy had been located for forty years, and at different times during that period the mine was in active operation. At the trial the course of this vein was a disputed and closely contested question, although there were extensive underground workings.

[1] Report of Public Land Commission, p. 399.

[2] Iron S. M. Co. v. Elgin M. Co., 118 U. S. 196, 204, 6 Sup. Ct. Rep. 1177.

[3] Cons. Wyoming G. M. Co. v. Champion M. Co., 63 Fed. 540, 548.

In addition to this, the lower levels of a mine frequently show a different direction from that which guided the
miner in making his location, and are at variance with
conditions shown in openings nearest to the surface.
This was the case in the famous Flagstaff mine in
Utah,[1] where the croppings showed that the direction,
or course, of the apex of the vein at or near the surface,
was nearly east and west. By following a level beneath
the surface, the strike of the vein ran in a northwesterly
direction, so that if, by a process of natural abrasion,
the mountain had been ground down, the course of the
apex would have been northwest instead of west.

Upon this state of facts the supreme court of the
United States thus expressed its views:—

" We do not mean to say that a vein must necessarily
" crop out upon the surface in order that locations may
" be properly laid upon it. If it lies entirely beneath
" the surface, and the course of its apex can be ascer-
" tained by sinking shafts at different points, such
" shafts may be adopted as indicating the position of the
" vein, and locations may be properly made on the
" surface above it, so as to secure a right to the vein
" beneath. . . . Perhaps the law is not so perfect in
" this regard as it might be; perhaps the true course of
" a vein should correspond with its strike, or the line of
" a level run through it; but this can rarely be ascer-
" tained until considerable work has been done, and
" after claims and locations have become fixed. The
" most practicable rule is to regard the course of the
" vein as that which is indicated by surface outcrop
" or surface explorations and workings. It is on this
" line that claims will naturally be laid, whatever be
" the character of the surface, whether level or in-
" clined."

An interesting and important case involving this question is that of the Carson City Gold and Silver Mining
Company *v.* North Star Mining Company, tried before

[1] Flagstaff S. M. Co. *v.* Tarbet, 98 U. S. 463, 469.

Judge James H. Beatty, United States district judge of
Idaho, sitting as circuit judge. Figure 25 represents the
properties in controversy and the underground workings of the North Star mine in horizontal projection.

The line C D traversing the center of the North Star
surface was the line connecting the collar of the main
working shaft, the mouth of the Larimer incline, the

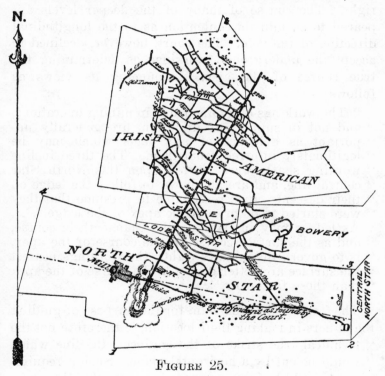

FIGURE 25.

East Star shaft, all sunk on the vein, and a shallow vertical shaft at D. The course of the vein to the west
was interrupted at the point C by the occurrence of a
"crossing," or a zone of fractured country rock, into
which the vein, as far as developed, was not shown to
have penetrated. The vein was located in 1851, and had

been worked by the North Star Company and its predecessors, with casual interruptions, ever since. The
plaintiff in the case, owning the Irish-American ground,
contended that the true course of the vein was south-
easterly from the point C and across the side line *1 2,*
presenting a case, according to its contention, wherein
the North Star Company was denied any extralateral
right. The course of many of the deeper levels appeared to sustain its contention as to the longitudinal
direction of the vein. The court, however, declined to
accept the underground workings as determining the
true course of the apex, announcing its views as
follows:—

" The workings of a mine made in mining operations,
" and not in support of litigation, are generally im-
" portant as evidence of any facts which may be
" legitimately inferred from them. The three incline
" working shafts were started upon this North Star
" central line, and are all shown to follow the ledge on
" their descent. It is reasonable to presume that they
" were started upon or near the apex of the ledge. . . .
" As ledges may in their depths change their course,
" and as the surface course, or the course of the apex,
" is to govern the miner's rights, the workings nearest
" the surface are better guides to the course of the apex
" than those far below." [1]

The "course" of the vein, for the purpose of guiding
the miners in making their location, is therefore not the
" technical true strike of the engineer, the line which
" would be cut by a horizontal plane. Such a require-
" ment would be in many cases impracticable." [2]
The true method of determination is found in the rule
laid down by the supreme court of the United States in
the Flagstaff case, and followed by Judge Beatty in the
North Star case, that the workings nearest the surface

[1] Carson City G. and S. M. Co. *v.* North Star M. Co., 73 Fed. 597, 601.
[2] Duggan *v.* Davey, 4 Dak. 110, 143, 26 N. W. 887.

are better guides to the course of the apex than those far
below.

The "strike" once determined, the ascertainment of
the direction of the "dip" follows as a mathematical
deduction. The true average dip of a vein is always at
right angles to the strike.[1]

Mr. Phillips in his treatise on ore deposits thus
explained this:—

"Where a bed has been tilted from a horizontal posi-
" tion, its maximum inclination towards the horizon is
" called its *dip,* and the amount of this dip may be stated
" in degrees, or by saying that it falls so many feet or
" inches in a given distance. The line at right angles
" to the dip of a bed which is consequently a horizontal
" line is called its *strike,* and is described by its line of
" compass-bearing, either true or magnetic."[2]

§ 319. **Downward course.**—Confusion often arises in
using popular terms which, through loose custom, have
gradually acquired many shades of meaning.

We believe the words "strike" and "dip," in so far
as they concern us here, are the surveyor's terms, and
should be used in the sense in which he applies them,—
i. e. as mathematical terms applied to an inclined plane
to accurately describe its po-
sition. The terms are doubtless so understood by the
intelligent miner.

Let *a-c-d-f* on figure 26 be
an inclined plane; *b-k-i-e,* a
horizontal plane intersecting
the inclined plane in line *b-e;*
h-m-g, a vertical plane at

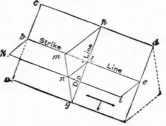

FIGURE 26.

right angles to the inclined plane. Then *b-e* is the
"strike-line" and *h-g* the "dip-line" of the inclined

[1] Gilpin *v.* Sierra Nevada Cons. M. Co., 2 Idaho, 662, 23 Pac. 547.
[2] Phillips' "Ore Deposits," p. 12.

plane. The angle n-l-g is the dip-angle, measuring the *greatest* declination of the plane below the horizon. It is easily shown mathematically that the strike and dip lines form a rectangular intersection.

The "strike" is defined by the bearing of the strike-line, the "dip" by the angle of declination and the bearing of the dip-line; for example, strike "N. 10° W.," dip "45° to S. 80° W."

The walls of veins are never true planes. They are always more or less irregularly curved, constituting " warped" surfaces. The strike and dip of the wall at any point are the strike and dip of an imaginary plane drawn tangent to the wall at the given point. In many veins the strike and dip vary widely, both longitudinally and in depth.

The word "course" is applicable to any line in the vein,—to an apex-line, a strike-line, a dip-line, or any inclined line between strike and dip. The wall of a vein has extent, length, course, in any direction along its surface. Some miners may mean by "course of the " vein" the course of the apex, others the strike of the vein. It is an expression that calls for qualification to fix its meaning definitely.

The "course of the vein" appearing on the surface is plainly the course of its apex, which is generally inclined and undulating and departs more or less materially from the "strike." The miner is required to locate his claim "along the vein," which plainly means along the outcrop or course of the apex. It would be impracticable for him to locate it along the strike, as it usually takes years of underground work to determine the strike through the length of his claim. It is often difficult even to locate properly along the apex, especially where the walls are obscured by surface disintegration or are covered with a capping or a large accumulation of detritus.

It sometimes happens where the dip of the vein is at a small angle from the horizontal, and the surface of the ground is steeply inclined, that the course of the apex departs widely from the strike of the vein developed in the underground working, as illustrated on figure 27. Some veins are curved and warped to an unusual extent, with greatly varying strike and dip, as illustrated on figure 28. The smaller the dip the greater the varia-

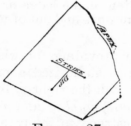 

FIGURE 27.   FIGURE 28.

tions in strike. These facts often lead to disputes concerning identity of the various parts explored,[1] but with the identity once established, the departure of the apex from the strike-line and the variations in strike and dip do not affect the rights attaching to a proper location along the line of the apex.

"Downward course" is a popular term, and might be applied to the dip-course or any course between the strike and dip. "The downward course" might have been construed to mean strictly the dip-line course, but for certain exigencies arising out of the requirements in placing the end-lines of a location, as will be explained later on.

Under the miner's rules and customs which controlled rights on the vein prior to the enactment of any federal mining laws, as well as under the act of July 26, 1866,

---

[1] The subject of identity, or vein-tracing, on both strike and dip will be fully dealt with when considering the subject of extralateral rights. *Post,* § 615.

planes constructed at right angles to the general course
of the vein at the surface and applied at the extreme
points on the vein covered by the location carved out
the underground segment of the vein which the locator
was privileged to enjoy. As was said by Justice Field
in the Eureka case,—

"Lines drawn vertically down through the ledge or
" lode at right angles with a line representing the gen-
" eral course of the ends of claimant's location, will
" carve out, so to speak, a section of the ledge or lode
" within which he is permitted to work and out of which
" he cannot pass."[1]

The act of July 26, 1866, in providing for what is
now called the extralateral right, authorized a patent
" granting such mine, together with the right to follow
" such vein with the *dips, spurs, angles,* and *varia-*
" *tions."* As this act was construed to imply extralateral planes at right angles to the course of the vein
within the location, the word "dips" found in this statute may be taken to mean the true dip of the vein, bearing a mathematical relationship (right angle) to the
strike of the vein, as illustrated on figure 26.

The act of May 10, 1872, however, gave controlling
force to surface lines, through which it was contemplated extralateral bounding-planes were to be drawn.
As we have heretofore observed, none of the words,
" dips, spurs, angles, variations," used in the former
act were retained in the later legislation. The words
" downward course" were substituted, as, under the
new system, end-lines were not required to cross the
apex of the lode at any particular angle.[2]

The rectangular, or true dip, theory was therefore
not applicable.

[1] 4 Saw. 302, 323,—followed in Argonaut M. Co. *v.* Kennedy M. Co.,
131 Cal. 15, 63 Pac. 148.
[2] *Post,* § 365.

The term "downward course," a more flexible term, may therefore have been advisedly used in the new law to apply to a course from a higher to a lower level in the plane of the vein following downward along the intersecting vertical end-line plane, which only in extremely rare instances would be coincident with the true dip-line.

To illustrate: On figure 29 the line A-E is a true dip-

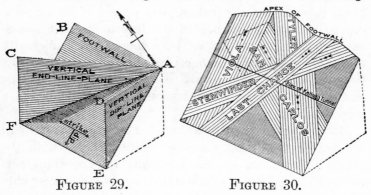

FIGURE 29.   FIGURE 30.

line,—*i. e.* at right angles to the strike. The line A-F is the intersection of the plane of the vein with the vertical end-line plane, which obviously at the surface crosses the lode at an angle less than a right angle. The course along the intersecting plane from A to F is essentially downward, just as much so as that from A to E.

We do not desire at this juncture to anticipate the discussion of the larger problems involved in the grant of the extralateral right, but there is an apt illustration of the application of the term "downward course" to a series of claims on the same vein, known as the Bunker Hill lode in the Cœur d'Alenes, Idaho.

Figure 30 represents, in isometric projection, the Bunker Hill vein upon which were the locations thereon named.

The Viola does not depart far from the true dip-line, but the San Carlos is nearer to the strike-line than to the dip-line.[1] The Stemwinder follows a line between the strike and dip.

While litigation over these properties is still pending in the courts, up to the present writing extralateral rights have been awarded to the respective owners (subject to certain priorities not necessary to enumerate here) between the vertical end-line planes of the respective locations, as delineated on figure 30—not necessarily to the full extent as there shown, but sufficiently to establish the negative doctrine that the right to follow the vein on its "downward course" conferred by the statute does not mean that such course must be on a true dip-line.[2]

Many of the questions here under discussion will necessarily reappear when we come to deal with the manner of making surface locations, the functions performed by end-lines, extralateral rights, and other subjects which are intimately associated with that of definitions. Our present investigation is limited to the subject of definitions.

Further elaboration here is unnecessary, and may be deferred until we reach the domain of practical application.

---

[1] From the facts found by the court, the side-line common to the Viola and San Carlos bisected a broad apex—the Viola covering the foot-wall, and the San Carlos the hanging-wall. For diagram showing these claims, see 114 Fed. 418.

[2] The extralateral rights of the respective claims shown on figure 30 were discussed, and to some extent at least adjudicated in the cases appearing in the reports as indicated: Tyler and Last Chance, 157 U. S. 683, 15 Sup. Ct. Rep. 733; 61 Fed. 557, 71 Fed. 848, 54 Fed. 284, 79 Fed. 277; Viola and San Carlos, 114 Fed. 417; Stemwinder, 109 Fed. 538.

CHAPTER II.

LODE CLAIMS, OR DEPOSITS "IN PLACE."

ARTICLE I. INTRODUCTORY.

II. THE LOCATION AND ITS REQUIREMENTS.

III. THE DISCOVERY.

IV. THE DISCOVERY SHAFT AND ITS EQUIVALENT.

V. THE PRELIMINARY NOTICE AND ITS POSTING.

VI. THE SURFACE COVERED BY THE LOCATION—ITS FORM AND RELATIONSHIP TO THE LOCATED LODE.

VII. THE MARKING OF THE LOCATION ON THE SURFACE.

VIII. THE LOCATION CERTIFICATE AND ITS CONTENTS.

IX. THE RECORD.

X. CHANGE OF BOUNDARIES AND AMENDED OR ADDITIONAL LOCATION CERTIFICATES.

XI. RELOCATION OF FORFEITED OR ABANDONED CLAIMS.

XII. LODES WITHIN PLACERS.

ARTICLE I. INTRODUCTORY.

§ 322. Introductory.

§ 323. The metallic or non-metallic character of deposits occurring in veins as affecting the right of appropriation under the laws applicable to lodes.

§ 322. Introductory.—In the preceding chapters of this work, it has been demonstrated that only the public mineral lands of the United States may be appropriated under the mining laws.[1] By "public lands" is meant such as are subject to sale or disposal under general laws.[2] Land to which any claims or rights of others have attached does not fall within the designation of

---

[1] *Ante*, § 112.

[2] McFadden *v.* Mountain View M. and M. Co., 97 Fed. 670; *In re* Logan, 29 L. D. 395; Nome Transp. Co., *Id.* 447; State of Louisiana, 30 L. D. 276.

" public lands."[1] As was said by the supreme court of
the United States,—

"Public lands belonging to the United States for
" whose sale or other disposition congress has made
" provision by its general laws, are to be regarded as
" legally open for entry and sale under such laws, unless
" some particular lands have been withdrawn from sale
" by congressional authority or by an executive with-
" drawal under such authority, either express or im-
" plied."[2]

We have also attempted to illustrate [3] the nature and
character of the appropriation under laws (other than
those exclusively applicable to the acquisition of mineral
lands) which operate as a segregation of a given tract
from the body of public land, and inhibit its acquisition,
although mineral in character, under the mining laws.
What constitutes such an appropriation of mineral
lands under these last-named laws as will remove them
from the category of "public lands" and inhibit their
acquisition by other mining claimants can be deter-

[1] *Ante*, § 80; Newhall *v.* Sanger, 92 U. S. 761; Bardon *v.* N. P. R.
R., 145 U. S. 535, 12 Sup. Ct. Rep. 856; Mann *v.* Tacoma Land Co., 153
U. S. 273, 14 Sup. Ct. Rep. 820; Wilcox *v.* Jackson, 13 Pet. (U. S.) 498;
Cameron *v.* United States, 148 U. S. 301, 13 Sup. Ct. Rep. 595; United
States *v.* Tygh Valley Land and L. S. Co., 76 Fed. 693; James *v.* Iron
Co., 107 Fed. 597, 603; Hartman *v.* Warren, 76 Fed. 157, 160; Kansas
Pacific Ry. Co. *v.* Dunmeyer, 113 U. S. 629, 5 Sup. Ct. Rep. 566; Teller
v. United States, 113 Fed. 273, 281.

[2] Lockhart *v.* Johnson, 181 U. S. 516, 21 Sup. Ct. Rep. 665. See Baca
Float No. 3, 30 L. D. 497.

In the nomenclature of the public land laws, the word "withdrawal"
is generally used to denote an order issued by the president, secretary
of the interior, commissioner of the general land office, or other proper
officer, whereby public lands are withheld from sale and entry under
the general lands laws, in order that presently or ultimately they may
be applied to some distinctly public use or disposed of in some special
way. Sometimes these orders are not made until there is an immediate necessity therefor, but more frequently the necessity for their being
made is anticipated. Hans Oleson, 28 L. D. 25, 31; *In re* Cox, 31
L. D. 193.

[3] *Ante*, §§ 112-219.

mined only after an analysis of the law regulating the acquisition of title to such lands. After we shall have outlined the methods provided by law for such acquisition, we shall endeavor to explain fully the nature and extent of the title so acquired, the tenure by which it is held, the property rights flowing therefrom, and the conditions under which such rights may be lost or extinguished. The general statement may here be properly made, however, that a perfected, valid appropriation of public mineral lands, under the mining laws, operates as a withdrawal of the tract from the body of the public domain, and so long as such appropriation remains valid and subsisting the land covered thereby is deemed private property.[1]

We are now to consider the manner in which public mineral lands containing veins or lodes of quartz or other rock in place may be lawfully appropriated.

§ 323. **The metallic or non-metallic character of deposits occurring in veins of rock in place as affecting the right of appropriation under the laws applicable to lodes.**—In defining what constitutes "mineral " land" within the meaning of the acts of congress, using that term as the legal equivalent of the various words and phrases of a kindred nature found in the mining laws,[2] we have heretofore treated the subject

---

[1] Gwillim v. Donnellan, 115 U. S. 45, 5 Sup. Ct. Rep. 1110; Belk v. Meagher, 104 U. S. 279, S. C., 3 Mont. 65; McFeters v. Pierson, 15 Colo. 201, 22 Am. St. Rep. 388, 24 Pac. 1076; Iron S. M. Co. v. Campbell, 17 Colo. 267, 29 Pac. 513; Seymour v. Fisher, 16 Colo. 188, 27 Pac. 240; Fisher v. Seymour, 23 Colo. 542, 49 Pac. 30; Garthe v. Hart, 73 Cal. 541, 15 Pac. 93; Souter v. Maguire, 78 Cal. 543, 21 Pac. 183; Armstrong v. Lower, 6 Colo. 393; Lebanon M. Co. v. Cons. Rep. M. Co., 6 Colo. 371; Faxon v. Barnard, 4 Fed. 702; Meydenbauer v. Stevens, 78 Fed. 787; Stratton v. Gold Sovereign M. and T. Co., 1 Leg. Adv. 350, S. C. 89 Fed. 1016; Matoa G. M. Co. v. Chicago Cripple G. M. Co., vol. 178 Min. and Scientific Press, p. 374; Cone v. Roxana G. M. Co. (Colo.), 2 Leg. Adv. 350; Mt. Rosa M. M. and L. Co. v. Palmer, 26 Colo. 56, 77 Am. St. Rep. 245, 56 Pac. 176; Kinney v. Fleming (Ariz.), 56 Pac. 723.

[2] Ante, § 86.

regardless of the form in which the deposits occur—*i. e.* whether "of rock in place," as in quartz veins, or not "in place," as in the case of auriferous gravels and other substances encountered in surface beds.[1]

The conclusions there reached[2] were intended to apply to all classes of deposits, without any attempt at classification as to form of occurrence. We are now called upon to consider a special class of mineral lands, and to determine to what extent, if any, the metallic or non-metallic character of the deposits found in veins of rock in place controls the manner in which lands containing them may be appropriated.

The act of July 26, 1866, provided for the acquisition of title to veins or lodes of quartz or other rock in place bearing gold, silver, cinnabar, or copper. By necessary intendment it excluded all other classes of metallic substances, as well as all which were non-metalliferous. The placer law of July 9, 1870, extended the right of entry and patent "to claims usually called 'placers,' " including all forms of deposit, excepting veins of " quartz or other rock in place."

The act of May 10, 1872, provided in terms for the appropriation of lands containing veins or lodes of quartz or other rock in place bearing gold, silver, cinnabar, *lead, tin,* copper, or other *valuable deposits.*

This is preserved in the Revised Statutes, which also contain the provisions of the placer law of 1870, heretofore referred to. Therefore, under the existing law we find the classification to be as follows:—

(1) Lands containing veins or lodes of quartz or other rock in place bearing gold, silver, cinnabar, lead, tin, copper, or other *valuable deposits;* [3]

(2) Claims usually called "placers," including all forms of deposit, excepting veins of quartz or other rock in place.[4] And in prescribing the method for obtaining

---

[1] *Ante,* § 95.

[2] *Ante,* § 98.

[3] Rev. Stats., § 2320.

[4] *Id.,* § 2329.

patents, both classes seem to have been grouped under the term "valuable deposits."[1]

It may be said that, ordinarily, nothing but metalliferous ores are encountered in veins of rock in place. There are, however, exceptions to this rule. Coal occurs in veins, and in many instances with as pronounced dip and strike as in the auriferous quartz lodes. But lands containing coal are sold under special laws. Marble, borax,[2] onyx, asphaltum, gilsonite, or uintaite (a species of asphaltum), gypsum, talc, graphite, rock phosphates, chalk, marls, oil-stones, mica, asbestos, fluorspar, sulphur, and mineral paint are non-metallic substances, and occur in veins of rock in place. All of these have commercial value, and in many instances yield as much profit in proportion to the cost of exploitation and extraction as the metalliferous veins. When any of

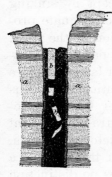

FIGURE 30A.

these substances occur in the form of superficial deposits, lands containing them may be appropriated under the placer laws, as they are not veins of rock in place. But suppose they occupy a vertical or pronounced inclined position in the mass of the mountain. A typical illustration showing the occurrence of non-metallic substances in veins is afforded by the deposits of uintaite, or gilsonite, found in Utah. Figure 30A is a cross-section taken from the monograph of Mr. George H. Eldridge on these deposits.[3] So far as structure is concerned, it exhibits the highest type of a fissure vein, and if the vein-filling or gangue carried metalliferous ores

---

[1] Rev. Stats., § 2325.

[2] See McCann v. McMillan, 129 Cal. 350, 62 Pac. 31.

[3] U. S. Geological Survey, 17 Annual Rep., part 1, p. 932.

it would respond fully to the scientific as well as popular definition of a true fissure vein. In the illustration the vein occupies practically a vertical position which eliminates from discussion the subject of the extralateral right. But a reading of Mr. Eldridge's monograph shows that in many of these deposits the plane of the vein is inclined, rendering the discussion which follows pertinent. How is this class of deposits to be appropriated? If by the placer laws, and if they are on surveyed lands, they must be taken up in some subdivision of the government surveys. If the deposit should exist in the form of an ideal vein, there would be but one exposure upon which a discovery could be based, and nothing overlying the dip beyond the vertical plane drawn through the surface boundary of, for example, a twenty-acre tract, could be located without discovery, and discovery would be impossible except by sinking vertical shafts at great expense, with no adequate protection in the meanwhile in the possession of the tract. We cannot see, since the act of 1872 was passed increasing the number of terms used in the prior law, that there is any foundation to support the contention that veins or lodes must be metalliferous in order to be appropriated under the lode laws. The extralateral right may be of as much value to the proprietor of a mica, rock phosphate, asphaltum, gilsonite, or talc vein as a gold vein. The act itself in terms makes no distinction based upon the chemical composition of the deposit. But it groups the classes according to the *form* in which the valuable deposits occur. In our judgment, there is no more reason for insisting that veins or lodes of mica, graphite, asphaltum, gilsonite, or other non-metallic substance in place should be located as placers than it has to require cinnabar deposits to be located as lodes, independently of the form of their occurrence.[1]

[1] Copp's Min. Dec. 47, 60.

How shall they be appropriated?

The term "deposits" used in section twenty-three hundred and twenty of the Revised Statutes is just as comprehensive as the same term found in section twenty-three hundred and twenty-nine.

The deliberate addition in the statute of the term "valuable deposits" to the enumeration of metallic substances, is of itself evidence of the highest character that the intention of the law-makers was to enlarge the scope of the lode laws, and embrace every character of deposit found in veins of rock in place which fall within the meaning of "mineral" in its broadest sense. If the meaning of the term "valuable deposits" was intended to be restricted to such substances as were metallic in their nature, it is fair to presume that congress would have used the term "valuable metallic or metalliferous " deposits." Gold occurs in veins of rock in place, and when so found the land containing it must be appropriated under the laws applicable to lodes. It is also found in placers, and when so found the land containing it must be appropriated under the laws applicable to placers. Iron ore is found in veins of rock in place. It also occurs in beds and superficial deposits. Where it is found in veins, lands containing it must be appropriated under the lode laws. Where it is not found in veins of rock in place, the proceedings to obtain government title are the same as those prescribed for placers.[1]

Iron is not named in the act of 1872, nor in the corresponding section of the Revised Statutes. Prior to the passage of that act, lands containing it were sold the same as agricultural lands. That act, as interpreted by the land department, was comprehensive enough to include iron ore, and thenceforth lands containing

---

[1] *In re* Stewart, 1 Copp's L. O. 34; Commr.'s Letter, Copp's Min. Dec. 235.

such substances were patented only under the mining laws.[1]

The large number of non-metallic substances mentioned in a previous chapter of this work [2] have been held by the land department to fall within the definition of "mineral" and "deposit," as these terms are used in the mining statutes. True, in the cases wherein this rule was established the substances occurred in the form of superficial deposits. But if it is once determined that they are "mineral" or "valuable deposits," they then become subject to classification for the purpose of appropriation the same as the metallic substances enumerated in the act.

We are not unmindful of the decision of the supreme court of Washington,[3] wherein that court announced that, in its judgment, a mining claim, whether lode or placer, is not established or entitled to be patented under the mineral laws, unless it contains some of the *metals* for which mining works are prosecuted; nor do we overlook the ruling of Secretary Hoke Smith, arising out of the same case, wherein the supreme court of Washington was criticised by the distinguished secretary for invading his jurisdiction; but the conclusions reached by the secretary went further than did the offending state court. The secretary said:—

"It appears to me so plain that congress only contemplated lands that were valuable for the *more precious metals* should be patented as lode claims, that it needs no argument to convince one of the proposition." [4]

This view was subsequently overruled in so far as it purported to limit the definition of "mineral" to metallic substances or the "more precious metals," and the

---

[1] Commr.'s Letter, Copp's Min. Dec. 214.

[2] *Ante,* § 97.

[3] Wheeler *v.* Smith, 5 Wash. 704, 32 Pac. 784.

[4] *Id.,* 23 L. D. 395, 399.

rule adopted that the term "mineral" includes all classes of deposit, whether metallic or non-metallic.[1] But the question here under consideration was neither involved nor discussed in the later departmental rulings.

It is not difficult to account for the dearth of adjudicated cases upon the subject now under consideration, so far as the courts are concerned. Primarily it is peculiarly within the province of the land department to interpret and apply the law to occurrences of this character. A careful search through the official reports of land department decisions, as well as the periodical literature dealing with mining questions, discloses the fact that there are few authentic expressions of opinion by the officials of the land department, and these are not sufficient to justify the assertion that there has been such a contemporaneous and uniform interpretation of the law as would be binding upon the courts. We give such instances as have come under observation.

Commissioner McFarland expressed the opinion that veins of clay or non-metalliferous substances were not subject to location as lodes, but might be entered as placers.[2]

At a time when the department entertained the view that salt deposits were subject to location under the mining laws a ruling was made to the effect that when a deposit of rock salt was found in an inclined position in the mass of the mountain in the form of a ledge it was subject to location under the lode laws.[3]

As to deposits of asphaltum or gilsonite, the occurrence of which in veins is illustrated in figure 30A, we

---

[1] Pacific Coast Marble Co. v. Northern Pacific R. R. Co., 25 L. D. 233. To same effect, Northern Pacific R. R. Co. v. Soderberg, 99 Fed. 506, 104 Fed. 425.

[2] Montague v. Dobbs, 9 Copp's L. O. 165.

[3] *In re* Megarrigle, 9 Copp's L. O. 113; *post,* § 515.

quote the following from the "Mining and Scientific "Press":—[1]

"The commissioner of the United States land office " has ruled that hydrocarbon claims, for example " asphaltum, bitumen, and gilsonite, must be located as " lode claims, not as placers. The ruling was made in a " contest between a senior placer location of a gilsonite " deposit in Rio Blanco county, Colorado, and a junior " lode location of the same ground. The ground of the " ruling was that gilsonite was found in fissures and " was logically a lode deposit."[2]

It is unnecessary for us to here reiterate the conclusions heretofore reached by us[3] as to what is meant by the terms "mineral land" and "valuable deposits," as these terms are used in the mining laws. We think those conclusions were based upon the weight of authority. If they are correct, it follows, in our judgment, that land containing any substance, metallic or non-metallic, which possesses economic value for use in trade, manufacture, the sciences, or in the mechanical or ornamental arts, if such substance exists therein in veins or lodes *of rock in place* in sufficient quantities to render the land more valuable for the purpose of removing and marketing the product than for any other purpose, such land must be appropriated under the laws applicable to lodes.

This may be contrary to the popular notion. But if there is any logic in the law, it seems to us that there is

[1] Vol. 83, p. 118.

[2] The author was confronted with this question with reference to a vein of borax, occurring in San Bernardino county, California. Desiring to fortify his views as expressed in the first edition of the treatise, he asked the commissioner of the general land office for his opinion. It was given tentatively, with the suggestion that it was not to be considered in the light of an official precedent, but rather as an impression. His opinion thus given was as follows: The question whether a vacant tract of public land should be located as a placer or lode mining claim depends upon the geological formation, and not upon the kind of mineral.

[3] *Ante,* § 98.

but one conclusion to be deduced, and that is the one we
have adopted.

Perhaps instances of non-metallic substances occurring in veins of rock in place are rare, and the solution of
the question not of great public importance. But it *is*
a matter of public importance that the mining laws
should be consistently construed, and that arbitrary
interpretation should be avoided.

We are of the opinion that the metallic or non-metallic
character of the contents of veins or lodes of rock in
place is entirely immaterial, if they otherwise fulfill the
requirements announced in section ninety-eight of this
treatise.[1]

ARTICLE II. THE LOCATION AND ITS REQUIREMENTS.

§ 327. "Location" and "mining "claim" defined.

§ 328. Acts necessary to constitute a valid lode location
under the Revised Stat-
utes, in the absence of
supplemental state legis-
lation and local district
rules.

§ 329. The requisites of a valid
lode location where sup-
plemental state legislation
exists.

§ 330. Order in which acts are performed immaterial; time,
when non-essential.

§ 331. Locations made by agents.

§ 327. "Location" and "mining claim" defined.—
"Location" and "mining claim" may not always or
necessarily mean the same thing. The supreme court of
the United States has said that a mining claim is a
parcel of land containing precious metal in its soil or
rock.[2] A location is the act of appropriating such parcel

---

[1] This rule, however, would not apply to rock salt occurring in veins.
See, *post*, § 513.

[2] The use of the term "precious metal" in this connection is manifestly of no controlling importance. The Revised Statutes enumerate a
number of metals which are in no sense "precious," and, as such statutes
are interpreted, they include a great variety of substances which are not
metallic.

according to certain established rules. The "location" in time became among the miners synonymous with the "mining claim" originally appropriated. If the miner has only the ground covered by one location, his "min-" ing claim" and his "location" are identical, and the two designations may be indiscriminately used to denote the same thing. But if by purchase he acquires other adjoining "locations," and adds them to his own, then the term "mining claim" is frequently used colloquially to describe the ground embraced by all the locations.[1]

Judge Hillyer defined a "mining claim" to be that portion of the public mineral lands which the miner for mining purposes takes up and holds in accordance with the mining laws.[2]

As generally or colloquially used, the term "mining " claim" has no reference to the different stages in the acquisition of the government title. It may include all mines contiguous to each other and held under one own-ership, whether patented or unpatented, if acquired under the mining laws.[3]

Where these terms are used in statutes, federal or state, their true meaning is to be determined from a consideration of the entire context, which involves, of course, the general scope and character of the legisla-tion. A few illustrations from the adjudicated cases will serve to demonstrate this.

As was said by the supreme court of the United States,—

"That which is located is called in section twenty-" three hundred and twenty of the Revised Statutes and " elsewhere a 'claim,' or 'mining claim.' Indeed, the

---

[1] St. Louis Smelting Co. v. Kemp, 104 U. S. 636; McFeters v. Pierson, 15 Colo. 201, 22 Am. St. Rep. 388, 24 Pac. 1076. See, also, N. P. R. R. Co. v. Sanders, 49 Fed. 129, 135; *In re* Mackie, 5 L. D. 199.

[2] Mt. Diablo M. and M. Co. v. Callison, 5 Saw. 439, Fed. Cas. No. 9886.

[3] Bewick v. Muir, 83 Cal. 368, 372, 23 Pac. 389.

" words 'claim' and 'location' are used interchange-
" ably." [1]

As used in section twenty-three hundred and twenty-
four of the Revised Statutes, requiring a certain amount
of work to be done annually upon "each claim," and in
section twenty-three hundred and twenty-five, prescribing the amount of labor or improvements required as a
condition precedent to the issuance of a patent, the word
" claim" means "location." [2]

As used in the revenue acts of the different states and
territories, providing for the taxation or exemption from
taxation of property, the term "mining claim" does not
include patented mines. [3]

"Location" is the inception of the miner's title.

A statute of California provides that "every person
" who performs labor upon any 'mining claim' has a
" lien upon the same." [4]

In construing this law, the supreme court of that state
has held that the lien extends to the *whole claim*, [5] but
by such a "claim" was meant a portion of the public
lands to which the right of enjoyment has been asserted
under the mining laws; that a Mexican grant containing
eleven hundred and nine acres, and another three hundred and fourteen acres, upon which mining was conducted, the whole being known as the Guadalupe mine,
was not a "mining claim," and no lien could be filed
thereon. [6]   Nor is a tract of one hundred and sixty acres

[1] Del Monte M. and M. Co. *v.* Last Chance M. Co., 171 U. S. 55, 74,
18 Sup. Ct. Rep. 895.

[2] Opinion of Assistant Attorney-General Van Devanter, 27 L. D. 91.
Post, §§ 628, 673.

[3] Salisbury *v.* Lane (Idaho), 63 Pac. 383; Waller *v.* Hughes (Ariz.),
11 Pac. 122.

[4] Cal. Code Civ. Proc., § 1183.

[5] Helm *v.* Chapman, 66 Cal. 291, 5 Pac. 352.

[6] Williams *v.* Santa Clara Min. Assn., 66 Cal. 193, 5 Pac. 85; U. S. Min.
Dec. 136, 142; Week's Min. Lands, 118.

of land, held under agricultural patent, upon which parties were engaged in mining, such a "claim" as is lienable.[1] But a consolidation of numerous *mining locations,* held and operated under one ownership, the aggregation being designated by a general name, such as the "Red Cloud mine," is a "mining claim," and the whole *claim* is lienable.[2]

While the law prescribes a limitation as to the size of a *location,* there is no limitation to the number of *claims* one person may hold by purchase.[3] A single location is a "claim," as that term is used in the Revised Statutes. But, as we have heretofore seen, "claim" may, colloquially speaking, embrace a number of locations.

§ 328. **Acts necessary to constitute a valid lode location under the Revised Statutes, in the absence of supplemental state legislation and local district rules.** —It is not necessary that any supplemental state legislation or local district regulations should exist. Where they do not exist, a location may be perfected by following the requirements of the federal law. The acts to be performed in the absence of state or district regulations are few and simple. "The intricacies are those found " by the courts of the states and territories wherein " mineral lands are situated arising out of complex " state or territorial legislation supplementing the fed- " eral laws."[4] The requisites of such location are:—

(1) The discovery;

---

[1] Morse v. De Ardo, 107 Cal. 622, 40 Pac. 1018.

[2] Tredinnick v. Red Cloud M. Co., 72 Cal. 78, 84, 13 Pac. 152. See, also, Malone v. Big Flat G. M. Co., 76 Cal. 583, 18 Pac. 772; Hamilton v. Delhi M. Co., 118 Cal. 148, 50 Pac. 378.

[3] St. Louis Smelting Co. v. Kemp, 104 U. S. 636, 648; Malone v. Big Flat G. M. Co., 76 Cal. 578, 583, 18 Pac. 772.

[4] Sanders v. Noble, 22 Mont. 110, 55 Pac. 1037; Upton v. Larkin, 7 Mont. 449, 17 Pac. 728.

(2) The marking of the location on the ground so that its boundaries can be readily traced.[1]

No notice need be posted [2] nor recorded; [3] no particular kind of marking is required so long as the "bound-"aries may be readily traced." The taking and holding of actual possession is wholly unnecessary, and this applies to all classes of locations, wherever made, and whether state legislation or local rules exist or not. Actual possession is no more necessary for the protection of title acquired by a valid mining location than it is for any other grant from the United States.[4] Such a discovery having been made as will satisfy the law,[5] the marking of the location on the ground including the place of his discovery completes the location and clothes the locator with the complete possessory title. No development or discovery work is required. In fact, no labor need be performed nor improvements made until within the year commencing on the first day of January succeeding the date of the location.[6]

§ 329. The requisites of a valid lode location under the Revised Statutes where supplemental state legislation exists. — Most of the precious-metal-bearing states have availed themselves of the privilege of supplement-

[1] Upton v. Larkin, 7 Mont. 449, 17 Pac. 728; Sanders v. Noble, 22 Mont. 110, 55 Pac. 1037; Erwin v. Perigo, 93 Fed. 608.

[2] Post, § 350; Perigo v. Erwin, 85 Fed. 904; Harris v. Kellogg, 117 Cal. 484, 49 Pac. 708; Gwillim v. Donnellan, 115 U. S. 45, 5 Sup. Ct. Rep. 1110; McCarthy v. Speed, 11 S. Dak. 362, 77 N. W. 590; Bramlett v. Flick, 23 Mont. 95, 57 Pac. 869.

[3] Post, §§ 389-392; Perigo v. Erwin, 85 Fed. 904; Magruder v. Oregon and Cal. R. R. Co., 28 L. D. 174.

[4] Belk v. Meagher, 104 U. S. 279, 283; Harris v. Kellogg, 117 Cal. 484, 49 Pac. 708; Gwillim v. Donnellan, 115 U. S. 45, 5 Sup. Ct. Rep. 1110; McCarthy v. Speed, 11 S. Dak. 362, 77 N. W. 590; Bramlett v. Flick, 23 Mont. 95, 57 Pac. 869.

[5] Post, § 336.

[6] Amend. to § 2324 Rev. Stats. Jan. 22, 1880, 21 Stats. at Large, 61.

ing federal legislation, and have adopted systems more or less comprehensive. We have heretofore given an outline of the general scope and character of this legislation,[1] from which it will be readily observed that in some of the states certain requirements exist which are not found in others. A location made with all the formalities required by the federal statute only might be valid in California, but would not be in Colorado. Where state laws or local regulations exist which are not repugnant to the federal statutes, compliance with such supplemental law is requisite to the validity of a location.[2] As state laws form an important element of the federal system in their respective jurisdictions, it is necessary to a satisfactory presentation of the subject under consideration to give them their proper place, distributed under the several appropriate heads. We think the object may be intelligently accomplished by selecting as a type of such state legislation the local code which is the most comprehensive, and note the differences between that code and the existing laws of other states and territories. In this way we shall be enabled to present, under appropriate subdivisions approaching methodical arrangement, the rule in each state or territory touching the subject immediately under consideration, in connection with the treatment of the requirements of the congressional laws. For this purpose we select the state of Colorado, and will divide our subject, for purpose of treatment, on the basis of the Colorado mining laws, noting wherein the requirements of other states are similar or are different.

Under the laws of Colorado the following acts are required to complete a valid lode location:—

---

[1] *Ante*, §§ 248-252.

[2] Purdum *v.* Laddin, 23 Mont. 387, 59 Pac. 153; Belk *v.* Meagher, 104 Fed. 284; Garfield M. Co. *v.* Hammer, 6 Mont. 53, 8 Pac. 153.

(1) The discovery;

(2) The sinking of a discovery shaft of certain prescribed dimensions, or its equivalent;

(3) The posting of a notice;

(4) The marking of surface boundaries in a certain specified manner;

(5) The making of a location certificate;

(6) The recording of such certificate.[1]

A substantial compliance with the requirements of the laws, federal and state, as well as local rules, where they exist and are not repugnant to state or federal legislation, is a condition precedent to the completion of a valid location.[2]

Mere possession without complying with the law confers no rights.[3]

In the nature of things, we cannot deal with local district regulations in detail. We have heretofore outlined our views as to their legitimate scope and the extent to which they may be operative.[4] Where they exist and are in harmony with state and federal legislation they are to be considered and construed in the light

[1] Strepey v. Stark, 7 Colo. 614, 5 Pac. 111.

[2] Belk v. Meagher, 104 U. S. 279, 284; Upton v. Larkin, 5 Mont. 600, 6 Pac. 66; Garfield M. and M. Co. v. Hammer, 6 Mont. 53, 8 Pac. 153; Strepey v. Stark, 7 Colo. 614, 5 Pac. 111; McKinstry v. Clark, 4 Mont. 370, 395, 1 Pac. 759; Noyes v. Black, 4 Mont. 527, 2 Pac. 769; Gleeson v. Martin White M. Co., 13 Nev. 443; Sweet v. Webber, 7 Colo. 443, 4 Pac. 752; Lalande v. McDonald, 2 Idaho, 283, 13 Pac. 347; Lockhart v. Wills, 9 N. Mex. 344, 54 Pac. 336; Kendall v. San Juan M. Co., 144 U. S. 658, 12 Sup. Ct. Rep. 779; Nevada Sierra Oil Co. v. Home Oil Co., 98 Fed. 673; Copper Globe M. Co. v. Allman (Utah), 64 Pac. 1019; Purdum v. Laddin, 23 Mont. 387, 59 Pac. 153.

[3] Ante, §§ 216-219; Horswell v. Ruiz, 67 Cal. 111, 7 Pac. 197; Morenhaut v. Wilson, 52 Cal. 263; Chapman v. Toy Long, 4 Saw. 28, Fed. Cas. No. 2610; Belk v. Meagher, 104 U. S. 279, 284; Jordan v. Duke (Ariz.), 36 Pac. 896.

[4] Ante, §§ 268-275.

of the general principles, which will be enunciated in reference to state legislation in the succeeding articles.

§ 330. **Order in which acts are performed immaterial—Time, when non-essential.**—The order in which the several acts required by law are to be performed is non-essential, in the absence of intervening rights.[1]

The marking of the boundaries may precede the discovery, or the discovery may precede the marking; and if both are completed before the rights of others intervene, the earlier act will inure to the benefit of the locator.[2] But if the boundaries are marked before discovery, the location will date from the time discovery is made.[3]

The supreme court of Colorado has thus expressed the rule:—

"The validity of the location of a mining claim is
" made to depend primarily upon the discovery of a
" vein or lode within its limits. Section 2320, Rev.
" Stats., U. S. Until such discovery, no rights are
" acquired by location. The other requisites which
" must be observed in order to perfect and keep alive a
" valid location are not imperative, except as against the

[1] Golden Terra v. Mahler, 4 Morr. Min. Rep. 390; Thompson v. Spray, 72 Cal. 528, 14 Pac. 182; Gregory v. Pershbaker, 73 Cal. 109, 14 Pac. 401; Perigo v. Erwin, 85 Fed. 904; Erwin v. Perigo, 93 Fed. 608; Jupiter M. Co. v. Bodie Cons. M. Co., 11 Fed. 666, 676; North Noonday M. Co. v. Orient M. Co., 1 Fed. 522, 531.

[2] Erwin v. Perigo, 93 Fed. 608; Cosmos Exploration Co. v. Gray Eagle Oil Co., 112 Fed. 4, 14; Reins v. Raunheim, 28 L. D. 526; Olive Land and D. Co. v. Olmstead, 103 Fed. 568; Beals v. Cone, 27 Colo. 473, 62 Pac. 948; Brewster v. Shoemaker, 28 Colo. 176, 63 Pac. 309; Cedar Canyon Cons. M. Co. v. Yarwood (Wash.), 67 Pac. 749.

[3] Beals v. Cone, 27 Colo. 473, 83 Am. St. Rep. 92, 62 Pac. 948; Brewster v. Shoemaker, 28 Colo. 176, 63 Pac. 309; Tuolumne C. M. Co. v. Maier, 134 Cal. 583, 66 Pac. 863; Erwin v. Perigo, 93 Fed. 608; Cosmos Exploration Co. v. Gray Eagle Oil Co., 112 Fed. 4; Jupiter M. Co. v. Bodie Cons. M. Co., 11 Fed. 666, 676; Reins v. Raunheim, 28 L. D. 526; North Noonday M. Co. v. Orient M. Co., 1 Fed. 522, 531; Nevada Sierra Oil Co. v. Home Oil Co., 98 Fed. 671.

" rights of third persons. If the necessary steps outside
" of discovery are not taken within the time required by
" law, but are complied with before the rights of third
" parties intervene, they relate back to the date of loca-
" tion. But not so with discovery, for it is upon that act
" that the very life of a mineral location depends; and
" from the time of such discovery only would the loca-
" tion be valid, provided, of course, that others had not
" acquired rights therein." [1]

The case of Erwin *v.* Perigo [2] involved a mining
claim on which a discovery was not made until after the
marking of the boundaries. The court said:—

"The marking of the boundaries of the claim may
" precede the discovery, or the discovery may precede
" the marking; and if both are completed before the
" rights of others intervene, the earlier act will inure to
" the benefit of the locator as of the date of the later,
" and a complete possessory title to the premises will
" vest in him as of the later date."

This language is undoubtedly correct as applied to the
facts under discussion by the court. But it may be
questioned whether the statement is correct as applied
to a case where the marking occurs subsequent to the
discovery. In such a case we think, in the absence of a
state statute fixing a definite time, a discoverer of
mineral has a reasonable time within which to mark his
boundaries,[3] and if he complete the marking within a
reasonable time, his title will date from the time of discovery. It has frequently been held that discovery is the
source of a miner's title.[4]

The failure to perform any of the given acts within
the time limited by the laws or local rules may subject
the ground to relocation; but if the requirements are

---

[1] Beals *v.* Cone, 27 Colo. 473, 83 Am. St. Rep. 92, 62 Pac. 498, 952.
[2] 93 Fed. 608.
[3] *Post,* § 339.
[4] *Post,* § 335.

complied with prior to the acquisition of any intervening rights, no one has a right to complain. Of course, the locator delays at his peril; but if the appropriation becomes complete before any one else initiates a right, the antecedent delay is condoned, and the right becomes perfected.[1] But unless completed within the time prescribed the attempted location is of no avail as against intervening rights,[2] assuming, of course, that the subsequent entry for the purpose of location is peaceable and in good faith.[3]

§ 331. Locations made by agents.—There is nothing in the Revised Statutes that prohibits one from initiating a location of a mining claim by an agent.[4] As the title comes from appropriation made in accordance with the law, and as it is not necessary that a party should personally act in taking up a claim, or in doing the acts required to give evidence of the appropriation, or to perfect the appropriation, it would seem, at least in the absence of a local rule or state statute to the contrary, that such acts are valid if done by one for another, or with his assent.[5] A location may be made without the knowledge of the principal, if there is a local rule authorizing it; otherwise, there may be antecedent

[1] McGinnis v. Egbert, 8 Colo. 41, 5 Pac. 652; North Noonday M. Co. v. Orient M. Co., 6 Saw. 299, 314, 1 Fed. 522; Jupiter M. Co. v. Bodie Cons. M. Co., 7 Saw. 96, 115, 11 Fed. 666; Omar v. Soper, 11 Colo. 380, 7 Am. St. Rep. 246, 18 Pac. 443; McErvy v. Hyman, 25 Fed. 596; Preston v. Hunter, 67 Fed. 996, 999; Faxon v. Barnard, 4 Fed. 702; Strepey v. Stark, 7 Colo. 614, 5 Pac. 111; Craig v. Thompson, 10 Colo. 517, 16 Pac. 24; Lockhart v. Willis, 9 N. Mex. 344, 54 Pac. 336; Crown Point G. M. Co. v. Crismon, 39 Or. 364, 65 Pac. 87.

[2] Pelican & Dives M. Co. v. Snodgrass, 9 Colo. 339, 12 Pac. 206; Hauswirth v. Butcher, 4 Mont. 299, 1 Pac. 714; Upton v. Larkin, 5 Mont. 600, 6 Pac. 66; Copper Globe M. Co. v. Allman (Utah), 64 Pac. 1019.

[3] Ante, § 219.

[4] Schultz v. Keeler, 2 Idaho, 305, 13 Pac. 481.

[5] Gore v. McBrayer, 18 Cal. 582, 587.

authority or subsequent ratification.[1] Such authority
need not be in writing.[2]

A party in whose name a mining claim is located is
presumed to have assented to the location,[3] upon the
principle that a party is presumed to assent to a deed
or other act manifestly for his benefit.[4]

One of several co-locators of a mining claim may
cause a notice of a mining claim to be recorded in the
name of himself and others not present, and the location
will be valid.[5]

When a location is made by one in the name of others,
the persons in whose names it is made become vested
with the legal title to the claim.[6] The estate so acquired
cannot be divested by making a second location leaving
out the names of the original locators, so long as the
first location remains valid and subsisting.[7] If, however, they have abandoned or forfeited their rights by
failure to comply with the conditions of the agreement
under which the location was originally made, a relo-

[1] Thompson v. Spray, 72 Cal. 528, 14 Pac. 182; Murley v. Ennis, 2
Colo. 300; Morton v. Solambo C. M. Co., 26 Cal. 527, 534; Hirbour v.
Reeding, 3 Mont. 13; Welland v. Huber, 8 Nev. 203; Moritz v. Lavelle, 77
Cal. 10, 11 Am. St. Rep. 229, 18 Pac. 803; Book v. Justice M. Co., 58
Fed. 106; Reagan v. McKibben, 11 S. Dak. 270, 76 N. W. 943, 945; Mor-
rison v. Regan (Idaho), 67 Pac. 956.

[2] Morrison v. Regan (Idaho), 67 Pac. 956; Reagan v. McKibben, 11
S. Dak. 270, 76 N. W. 943, 946; Moritz v. Lavelle, 77 Cal. 10, 11 Am.
St. Rep. 229, 18 Pac. 103; Book v. Justice M. Co., 58 Fed. 106, 119;
Moore v. Hamerstag, 109 Cal. 122, 41 Pac. 805.

[3] Kramer v. Settle, 1 Idaho, 485; Van Valkenburg v. Huff, 1 Nev. 142,
149; Rush v. French (Ariz.), 25 Pac. 816.

[4] Gore v. McBrayer, 18 Cal. 582, 588.

[5] Kramer v. Settle, 1 Idaho, 485; Dunlap v. Pattison (Idaho), 42 Pac.
504.

[6] Van Valkenburgh v. Huff, 1 Nev. 142, 149; Moore v. Hamerstag, 109
Cal. 122, 41 Pac. 805.

[7] Van Valkenburgh v. Huff, 1 Nev. 115, 149; Thompson v. Spray, 72
Cal. 528, 14 Pac. 182; Gore v. McBrayer, 18 Cal. 582; Morton v. Solambo
C. M. Co., 26 Cal. 533; In re Auerbach, 29 L. D. 208; In re Teller, 26
L. D. 484.

cation may be made by the original co-locator or agent in his own name.[1]

Where the location becomes subject to relocation by reason of the failure of the co-locators to perform the annual labor required by law a different question arises —a subject fully discussed in subsequent sections.[2]

If an agent makes a location on behalf of his principal, but, pursuant to a conspiracy with others, permits the location to lapse, in order that a relocation may be made in his own and others' behalf, the remedy of the principal after such relocation would be an action for breach of contract or to establish and enforce a trust in the claim as relocated against the parties relocating.[3]

ARTICLE III. THE DISCOVERY.

§ 335. Discovery the source of the miner's title.

§ 336. What constitutes a valid discovery.

§ 337. Where such discovery must be made.

§ 338. The effect of the loss of discovery upon the remainder of the location.

§ 339. Extent of locator's rights after discovery and prior to completion of location.

§ 335. Discovery the source of the miner's title.— Discovery in all ages and all countries has been regarded as conferring rights or claims to reward. Gamboa, who represented the general thought of his age on this subject, was of the opinion that the discoverer of mines was even more worthy of reward than the inventor of a useful art. Hence, in the mining laws of all civilized countries the great consideration for granting mines to individuals is *discovery*. "Rewards so bestowed," says Gamboa, "besides being a proper return for the labor

[1] Murley v. Ennis, 2 Colo. 300.
[2] *Post*, §§ 405, 406.
[3] Lockhart v. Johnson, 181 U. S. 516, 529, 21 Sup. Ct. Rep. 665.

" and anxiety of the discoverers, have the further effect
" of stimulating others to search for veins and mines,
" on which the general prosperity of the state de-
" pends." [1]

While in some of the older countries of Europe, as in
France and Belgium, the nature of the reward to the
discoverer was something less than an absolute preference in the right of enjoyment, yet in Spain and
Spanish-America there was guaranteed to him "an
" absolute right of property in the mine which he dis-
" covers if he will take the proper measures to denounce
" it and have it duly registered. No one can have any
" preference over him, and he loses the rights which
" result from his discovery only through his own neglect
" to make it publicly known in the manner in which the
" law directs." [2]

This wise and liberal policy which pervaded the Mexican system at the time of the conquest and the acquisition of California by the United States became the
recognized basis of mining rights and privileges as they
were held and enjoyed under the local rules and regulations established by the miners occupying the public
mineral lands within the newly acquired territory, and
in all subsequent legislation, whether congressional,
state, or territorial, discovery is recognized as the
primary source of title to mining claims.[3]

As was said by Halleck in his introduction to De Fooz
on the "Law of Mines," [4] "*Discovery* is made the source
" of title, and *development,* or working, the condition
" of the continuance of that act."

Whatever may be the rule governing the acquisition
of title to "claims usually called placers, including all

---

[1] Halleck's De Fooz on the Law of Mines, p. xxvi.
[2] *Id.*, p. xxvii.
[3] Erhardt *v.* Boaro, 113 U. S. 527, 5 Sup. Ct. Rep. 560.
[4] San Francisco, 1860.

"forms of deposit, excepting veins of quartz or other "rock in place," of which we treat in a subsequent chapter, there can be no valid appropriation of a lode claim unless there has been an antecedent discovery. "No location of a mining claim shall be made until the "discovery of the vein or lode within the limits of the "claim located."[1]

But this provision of the statute does not require that the locator of the claim must be the original discoverer of the vein or lode. If there has been a discovery by some one other than the locator, and the latter has knowledge of the existence of mineral and adopts the former discovery, he is entitled to make a location.[2]

A location can rest only upon an actual discovery of the vein or lode.[3] Such discovery must precede the location,[4] or be in advance of intervening rights.[5]

[1] Rev. Stats., § 2320.

[2] Hayes v. Lavagnino, 17 Utah, 185, 53 Pac. 1029; Jupiter M. Co. v. Bodie Cons. M. Co., 11 Fed. 666. See Erhardt v. Boaro, 113 U. S. 527, 5 Sup. Ct. Rep. 560; Nevada Sierra Oil Co. v. Home Oil Co., 98 Fed. 673, 678; Copper Globe Cons. M. Co. v. Allman (Utah), 64 Pac. 1019.

[3] King v. Amy & Silversmith M. Co., 152 U. S. 222, 14 Sup. Ct. Rep. 510; Tuolumne Cons. M. Co. v. Maier, 134 Cal. 583, 66 Pac. 863.

[4] Hauswirth v. Butcher, 4 Mont. 299, 1 Pac. 714; Upton v. Larkin, 7 Mont. 449, 17 Pac. 728; North Noonday M. Co. v. Orient M. Co., 6 Saw. 299, 309, 1 Fed. 522; Jupiter M. Co. v. Bodie Cons. M. Co., 7 Saw. 96, 109, 11 Fed. 666; Burke v. McDonald, 2 Idaho, 646, 33 Pac. 49; Stinchfield v. Gillis, 96 Cal. 33, 30 Pac. 839; McLaughlin v. Thompson, 2 Colo. App. 135, 29 Pac. 816; Waterloo M. Co. v. Doe, 56 Fed. 685; Etling v. Potter, 17 L. D. 424; N. P. R. R. Co. v. Marshall, Id. 545; Ledoux v. Forester, 94 Fed. 600; Tuolumne Cons. M. Co. v. Maier, 134 Cal. 583, 66 Pac. 863.

[5] Patchen v. Keeley, 19 Nev. 404, 14 Pac. 347; North Noonday M. Co. v. Orient M. Co., 6 Saw. 299, 309, 1 Fed. 522; Jupiter M. Co. v. Bodie Cons. M. Co., 7 Saw. 96, 109, 11 Fed. 666; Golden Terra M. Co. v. Mahler, 4 Morr. Min. Rep. 390; Wright v. Taber, 2 L. D. 738, 743; In re Mitchell, Id. 752; Beals v. Cone, 27 Colo. 473, 83 Am. St. Rep. 92, 62 Pac. 948; Brewster v. Shoemaker, 28 Colo. 176, 63 Pac. 309; Fisher v. Seymour, 23 Colo. 542, 49 Pac. 30; Perigo v. Erwin, 85 Fed. 904; Erwin v. Perigo, 93 Fed. 608; Reins v. Raunheim, 28 L. D. 526; Nevada Sierra

The proof of recording and marking a claim will not authorize the court to presume a discovery.[1]

If no discovery is made until after the acts of location have been performed, the location will date from the time of discovery.[2]

Priority of discovery gives priority of right against naked location and possession, without discovery.[3]

It has been said that this requirement as to antecedent discovery is made for the benefit of the United States, so that land cannot be acquired under this law until its character is first ascertained to be mineral.[4]

It will be necessary for us to determine:—

(1) What constitutes a valid discovery;

(2) Where such discovery must be made;

(3) The effect of the loss of discovery upon the remainder of the location;

(4) The extent of a locator's rights after discovery and prior to completion of location.

§ 336. **What constitutes a valid discovery.**—In determining what constitutes such a discovery as will satisfy the law and form the basis of a valid mining location, we find, as in the case of the definition of the terms "lode" or "vein," that the tendency of the courts

Oil Co. v. Home Oil Co., 98 Fed. 673; Olive Land and D. Co. v. Olmstead, 103 Fed. 568; Sands v. Cruikshank (S. Dak.), 87 N. W. 589; Cedar Canyon Cons. M. Co. v. Yarwood (Wash.), 67 Pac. 749.

[1] Smith v. Newell, 86 Fed. 56.

[2] *Ante*, § 330; Beals v. Cone, 27 Colo. 473, 83 Am. St. Rep. 92, 62 Pac. 948; Tuolumne M. Co. v. Maier, 134 Cal. 583, 66 Pac. 863; Brewster v. Shoemaker, 28 Colo. 176, 63 Pac. 309; Erwin v. Perigo, 93 Fed. 608; Jupiter M. Co. v. Bodie Cons. M. Co., 11 Fed. 666, 676; North Noonday M. Co. v. Orient M. Co., 1 Fed. 522, 531; Nevada Sierra Oil Co. v. Home Oil Co., 98 Fed. 671.

[3] Crossman v. Pendery, 8 Fed. 693; Beals v. Cone, 27 Colo. 443, 83 Am. St. Rep. 92, 62 Pac. 948.

[4] Upton v. Larkin, 7 Mont. 449, 27 Pac. 728; Shoshone M. Co. v. Rutter, 87 Fed. 801, 808; Sanders v. Noble, 22 Mont. 110, 55 Pac. 1037.

is toward marked liberality of construction where a question arises between two miners who have located claims upon the same lode, or within the same surface boundaries, and toward strict rules of interpretation when the miner asserts rights in property which either *prima facie* belongs to some one else or is claimed under laws other than those providing for the disposition of mineral lands, in which latter case the *relative* value of the tract is a matter directly in issue. The reason for this is obvious. In the case where two miners assert rights based upon separate alleged discoveries on the same vein, neither is hampered with presumptions arising from a prior grant of the tract, to overcome which strict proof is required. In applying a liberal rule to one class of cases and a rigid rule to another, the courts justify their action upon the theory that the object of each section of the Revised Statutes, and the whole policy of the entire law, should not be overlooked.

The particular character of each case must be kept continually in view. "The fact is," said the circuit court of appeals for the ninth circuit, "that there is " a substantial difference in the object and policy " of the law between the cases where the determi- " nation of the question as to what constitutes the dis- " covery of a vein, or lode, between different claimants " of the same lode under section twenty-three hundred " and twenty of the Revised Statutes, on the one hand, " and a 'lode known to exist' within the limits of a " placer claim at the time the application is made for a " patent therefor under section twenty-three hundred " and thirty-three, on the other." [1]

In the first class of cases, it was never intended to "weigh scales" to determine the value of the mineral

---

[1] Migeon *v.* Mont. Cent. Ry., 77 Fed. 249, 255. See, also, Bonner *v.* Meikle, 82 Fed. 697, 703.

found.[1] In the latter class, the rule is different. Slight evidence of the existence of a lode might satisfy the demands of the law upon the question of discovery as the basis of location, when clear and convincing pr̆oof would be required to establish the existence of a "known vein" within a prior townsite or placer patent.

The supreme court of the United States clearly recognizes the distinction between the two classes of cases, by intimating that the land officers might, on a *prima facie* case, decide the right of an applicant to a vein or lode and issue a patent therefor, upon proof less conclusive than would be required where a conflict arises between a prior placer and subsequent lode patent.[2]

Even in the same line of cases, that court at one time approved a liberal definition of a lode "known to " exist" within a placer;[3] and at another insisted upon adhering to strict rules of construction,[4] and ultimately announced its conclusion, that after all it is a question for the jury; that it cannot be said as a matter of law, in advance, how much gold or silver must be found in a vein before it will justify exploitation and properly be called a "known vein."[5]

Judge De Witt, of the supreme court of Montana, in a dissenting opinion filed in the case of Shreve *v.* Copper Bell M. Co.,[6] and speaking for the court in the later case of Brownfield *v.* Bier,[7] reviewed all the adjudicated law upon the subject of what constitutes a "lode," as well as a "discovery," and clearly showed the reasons for the distinctions drawn between the two classes of cases.

---

[1] Bonner *v.* Meikle, 82 Fed. 697, 703; Shoshone M. Co. *v.* Rutter, 87 Fed. 801, 808.

[2] Iron S. M. Co. *v.* Campbell, 135 U. S. 286, 10 Sup. Ct. Rep. 765.

[3] Iron S. M. Co. *v.* Cheesman, 116 U. S. 529, 6 Sup. Ct. Rep. 481.

[4] United States *v.* Iron S. M. Co., 128 U. S. 673, 9 Sup. Ct. Rep. 195.

[5] Iron S. M. Co. *v.* Mike & Starr Co., 143 U. S. 394, 405, 12 Sup. Ct. Rep. 543.

[6] 11 Mont. 309.

[7] 15 Mont. 403.

To hold that, in order to constitute a discovery as the basis of the location, it must be demonstrated that the discovered deposit will, when worked, yield a profit, or that the lands containing it are, in the condition in which they are discovered, more valuable for mining than for any other purpose, would be to defeat the object and policy of the law.

Most, if not all, of the decisions arising out of controversies between lode claimants on the one hand and the owners of prior patented placers on the other, or between the holders of title under patented townsites and parties asserting rights under the mining laws, insist that, to fulfill the designation of known lodes, or veins, which are reserved out of that class of patents, such lodes, or veins, must be clearly ascertained and be of such extent as to render the land more valuable on that account and *justify* their exploitation.[1]

No court has ever held that in order to entitle one to locate a mining claim ore of commercial value, in either quantity or quality, must first be discovered. Such a theory would make most mining locations impossible. "Logically carried out," says Judge Hawley,[2] "it "would prohibit a miner from making any valid loca- "tion until he had fully demonstrated that the vein, or "lode, of quartz or other rock in place bearing gold or "silver which he had discovered, would pay all the "expenses of removing, extracting, crushing, and re- "ducing the ore, and leave a profit to the owner. If this "view should be sustained, it would lead to absurd, "injurious, and unjust results."

---

[1] United States *v.* Iron S. M. Co., 128 U. S. 673, 9 Sup. Ct. Rep. 195; Deffeback *v.* Hawke, 115 U. S. 392, 6 Sup. Ct. Rep. 95; Davis *v.* Weibbold, 139 U. S. 507, 11 Sup. Ct. Rep. 628; Dower *v.* Richards, 151 U. S. 658, 14 Sup. Ct. Rep. 452. *Ante,* § 176.

[2] Book *v.* Justice M. Co., 58 Fed. 106, 124, (followed in Bonner *v.* Meikle, 82 Fed. 697, 703).

It has been frequently said that a valid location may be made whenever the prospector has discovered such indications of mineral that he is willing to spend his time and money in following it, in expectation of finding ore, and such a location may be made of a ledge deep in the ground and appearing at the surface, not in the shape of ore, but in vein matter only.[1]

But Judge Ross, in speaking of petroleum lands, forcefully said:—

"Mere indications, however strong, are not, in my " opinion, sufficient to answer the requirements of the " statute, which requires as one of the essential condi- " tions to the making of a valid location of unappro- " priated public land of the United States under the " mining laws, a discovery of mineral within the limits " of the claim. . . . Indications of the existence of a " thing is not the thing itself."[2]

An *expectation* is something more than a *hope*. A location made in the "hope of finding some ore in it at " some time" is worthless,[3] unless the hope should be realized before some one else makes a discovery. While the courts permit a liberal construction, the liberality must be exercised within reasonable and common-sense limits. Locations are not permitted upon a conjectural or imaginary existence of a vein.[4]

There must be something beyond a mere guess on the part of the miner to authorize him to make a location which will exclude others from the ground, such as the discovery of the presence of the precious metals in it, or

---

[1] Burke *v.* McDonald, 2 Idaho, 1022, 33 Pac. 49; Harrington *v.* Chambers, 3 Utah, 94, 1 Pac. 362; Mont. Cent. Ry. *v.* Migeon, 68 Fed. 811.

[2] Nevada Sierra Oil Co. *v.* Home Oil Co., 98 Fed. 671, 675. To same effect, see Tulare Oil Co. *v.* S. P. R. R. Co., 29 L. D. 269; Olive Land and D. Co. *v.* Olmstead, 103 Fed. 568.

[3] Waterloo M. Co. *v.* Doe, 56 Fed. 685.

[4] King *v.* Amy & Silversmith M. Co., 152 U. S. 222, 227, 14 Sup. Ct. Rep. 510.

in such proximity to it as to justify a reasonable belief in their existence.[1]

Every crevice or seam in the rock, even if filled with vein matter, does not necessarily constitute a vein.[2] But something must be found to distinguish it from the surrounding mass. "While the contents of ore-bearing " veins widely differ," said the supreme court of Idaho, " there is that indescribable peculiarity in the ledge " matter, the matrix of all ledges, by which the experi- " enced miner easily recognizes his vein when discov- " ered." [3]

Judge Hallett was of the opinion that the discovery must be of vein matter *in place* in the form of a vein, or lode.[4]

Discovery of detached pieces of quartz, mere bunches, or "float," is not sufficient.[5]

Neither the size nor richness of the vein is material.[6]

Any *genuine* discovery is sufficient.[7]

While the courts may be unable to define with sufficient accuracy for all purposes what is necessary to constitute a discovery, they may have no difficulty in discriminating between the genuine and the counterfeit, the real and the sham.

The land department, whose function it is to determine in all applications for patent what constitutes a discovery, has uniformly adopted a liberal rule of construction. In the judgment of that tribunal, a mineral

[1] Erhardt *v.* Boaro, 113 U. S. 527, 536, 5 Sup. Ct. Rep. 560; Shoshone M. Co. *v.* Rutter, 87 Fed. 801, 807; Copper Globe M. Co. *v.* Allman (Utah), 64 Pac. 1019.

[2] Burke *v.* McDonald, 2 Idaho, 646, 33 Pac. 49; Mont. Cent. Ry. *v.* Migeon, 68 Fed. 811.

[3] Burke *v.* McDonald, 2 Idaho, 646, 33 Pac. 49.

[4] Van Zandt *v.* Argentine M. Co., 8 Fed. 725, 727.

[5] Jupiter M. Co. *v.* Bodie Cons. M. Co., 7 Saw. 96, 107, 11 Fed. 666; Book *v.* Justice M. Co., 58 Fed. 106.

[6] *Ante*, § 294.

[7] O'Donnell *v.* Glenn, 8 Mont. 248, 252, 19 Pac. 302.

discovery sufficient to warrant the location of a mining claim may be regarded as proven when mineral is found and the evidence shows that a person of ordinary prudence would be justified in a further expenditure of his labor and means with a reasonable prospect of success.[1]

The value of a mineral deposit is a matter into which the government does not inquire as between two mineral claimants. Inquiries of this character are confined to controversies between mineral and agricultural claimants.[2]

There is a material difference between a discoverer being *willing* to spend his time and money in exploiting the ground and being *justified* in doing so. The former is a question to be answered by the miner himself; the latter would present a question for expert testimony and determination by a jury.[3]

But it would seem that the question should not be left to the arbitrary will of the locator. Willingness, unless evidenced by actual exploitation, would be a mere mental state which could not be satisfactorily proved. The facts which are within the observation of the discoverer, and which induce him to locate, should be such as would *justify* a man of ordinary prudence, not necessarily a skilled miner, in the expenditure of his time and money in the development of the property.[4]

In Shoshone M. Co. *v.* Rutter[5] the circuit court of appeals for the ninth circuit said:—

[1] Castle *v.* Womble, 19 L. D. 455, Walker *v.* S. P. R. R. Co., 24 L. D. 172; Michie *v.* Gothberg, 30 L. D. 407.

[2] Tam *v.* Story, 21 L. D. 440.

[3] Burke *v.* McDonald, 2 Idaho, 1022, 29 Pac. 98.

[4] McShane *v.* Kenkle, 18 Mont. 208, 56 Am. St. Rep. 578, 44 Pac. 979; Bonner *v.* Meikle, 82 Fed. 697, 703; Shoshone M. Co. *v.* Rutter, 87 Fed. 801, 808; Sanders *v.* Noble, 22 Mont. 110, 55 Pac. 1037; Muldrick *v.* Brown, 37 Or. 185, 61 Pac. 428; Michie *v.* Gothberg, 30 L. D. 407.

[5] 87 Fed. 801, 807.

"The discovery of seams containing mineral-bearing
"earth and rock, which were discovered before the
"location was made, were similar in their character to
"the seams or veins of mineral matter that had induced
"other miners to locate claims in the same district,
"which, by continued developments thereon, were
"found to be a part of a well-defined lode or vein con-
"taining ore of great value. The discovery made at the
"time of the Kirby location was therefore such as to
"justify a belief as to the existence of such a lode or
"vein within the limits of the ground located." [1]

Judge Hawley's definition seems to answer all practical purposes:—

"When the locator finds rock in place containing
"mineral, he has made a discovery within the meaning
"of the statute, whether the earth or rock is rich or
"poor, whether it assays high or low. It is the finding
"of the mineral in the rock in place, as distinguished
"from float rock, that constitutes the discovery and
"warrants the prospector in making a location of a
"mining claim." [2]

§ 337. **Where such discovery must be made.**—It is
almost unnecessary to repeat what we have heretofore said, that title to a mining claim can only be initiated by discovery upon the unappropriated lands of
the government.[3] No rights are acquired by an entry
within the surface lines of patented lands,[4] or other

---

[1] See, also, Hayes v. Lavagnino, 17 Utah, 185, 53 Pac. 1029.

[2] Book v. Justice M. Co., 58 Fed. 106, 120; Shoshone M. Co. v. Rutter,
87 Fed. 801, 807.

The question of "discovery" will be found discussed to a limited
extent in the following cases, not heretofore cited: Southern Cross M.
Co. v. Europa M. Co., 15 Nev. 383, 385; Territory v. McKey, 8 Mont.
168, 19 Pac. 395; Davidson v. Bordeaux, 15 Mont. 245, 38 Pac. 1075;
Golden Terra M. Co. v. Mahler, 4 Morr. Min. Rep. 390; United States v.
King, 9 Mont. 75, 22 Pac. 498.

[3] Sands v. Cruikshank (S. D.), 87 N. W. 589.

[4] Moyle v. Bullene, 7 Colo. App. 308, 44 Pac. 69; Golden Terra M. Co.
v. Mahler, 4 Morr. Min. Rep. 390; Brewster v. Shoemaker, 28 Colo. 176,
63 Pac. 308; Kirk v. Meldrum, 28 Colo. 453, 65 Pac. 633.

lands which are withdrawn from the body of the public domain.[1]

The discovery must be made within the limits of the location as it is ultimately marked upon the ground.[2]

A location based upon a discovery made within the limits of another existing and valid location is void.[3]

It is, however, essential that the senior locator make timely assertion of his rights by adversing the application of the junior locator, else he is barred from afterwards charging that the claimed discovery of the lode applicant is in fact on land appropriated by his prior location.[4]

If a senior location includes the apex of a vein, and is so located that it has extralateral rights, a junior claimant can predicate no rights upon a discovery made upon the dip of such vein and within the extralateral rights of the senior location. The reason for this rule is, that the extralateral portion of the vein has been withdrawn from the public domain to the same extent as that portion of the vein within the surface boundaries.[5] But if the apex has not been appropriated by a valid location, or if it has been so appropriated as to leave an under-

[1] Michael v. Mills, 22 Colo. 439, 45 Pac. 429; Armstrong v. Lower, 6 Colo. 393. See, ante, § 322; Branagan v. Dulaney, 2 L. D. 744; Winter Lode, 22 L. D. 362.

[2] Gwillim v. Donnellan, 115 U. S. 45, 50, 5 Sup. Ct. Rep. 1110; Larkin v. Upton, 144 U. S. 19, 23, 12 Sup Ct. Rep. 614; Upton v. Larkin, 7 Mont. 449, 17 Pac. 728; Id., 5 Mont. 600, 6 Pac. 66; Cheesman v. Shreeve, 40 Fed. 787; Michael v. Mills, 22 Colo. 439, 45 Pac. 429; Girard v. Carson, 22 Colo. 345, 44 Pac. 508.

[3] Branagan v. Dulaney, 2 L. D. 744; Little Pittsburg Cons. Co. v. Amie M. Co., 17 Fed. 57; In re Williams, 20 L. D. 458; Watson v. Mayberry, 15 Utah, 265, 49 Pac. 479; Erwin v. Perigo, 93 Fed. 608; Crown Point M. Co. v. Buck, 97 Fed. 462, 465; Golden Link M. L. and B. Co., 29 L. D. 384; Tuolumne Cons. M. Co. v. Maier, 134 Cal. 583, 66 Pac. 863; Reynolds v. Pascoe (Utah), 66 Pac. 1064.

[4] American Cons. M. and M. Co. v. De Witt, 26 L. D. 580; Mitchell v. Brovo, 27 L. D. 40; Stranger Lode, 28 L. D. 321.

[5] Golden Link M. L. Co., 29 L. D. 384.

ground segment of the vein unappropriated, a discovery of such unappropriated segment would be sufficient, except as against one subsequently locating a portion of the apex in such a manner as to include the underground segment of the vein within the extralateral. rights of his claim.[1]

We are not to be understood as stating that the locator of such an unappropriated segment of a vein would be entitled to extralateral rights. That question will be discussed in a subsequent chapter.

It is no proof of discovery within the limits of a location that a vein discovered in another location *may* penetrate the ground sought to be located, where there is no outcrop in the latter, and no physical evidence of the existence of the vein.[2]

Any portion of the apex on the course, or strike, of the vein found within the limits of a claim is sufficient discovery to entitle the locator to obtain title.[3]

It has been held that where a vein has been discovered far below the surface, a valid location can be made by marking the boundary on the surface so as to include the place at which the vein, if continued to the surface, would be disclosed,[4] in the absence of some proof that the actual position of the apex is outside of the claim as located, and the location itself would be subject to the extralateral right of a subsequent locator covering the apex if it was subsequently discovered outside of the limits of the prior location.

[1] *Ante,* § 314; *post,* § 364; and see Doe *v.* Waterloo M. Co., 54 Fed. 935; Parrot Silver and Copper Co. *v.* Heinze, 25 Mont. 139, 87 Am. St. Rep. 386, 64 Pac. 326.

[2] Michael *v.* Mills, 22 Colo. 439, 45 Pac. 429; Silver Jennie Lode, 7 L. D. 6.

[3] Larkin *v.* Upton, 144 U. S. 19, 23, 12 Sup. Ct. Rep. 614; Upton *v.* Larkin, 5 Mont. 600, 6 Pac. 66; *Id.,* 7 Mont. 449, 17 Pac. 728; Golden Terra M. Co. *v.* Mahler, 4 Morr. Min. Rep. 390.

[4] Brewster *v.* Shoemaker, 28 Colo. 176, 63 Pac. 309.

A discovery of mineral must be treated as an entirety and as the proper basis of but one location.[1] Therefore, it is not susceptible of subdivision for the purpose of two locations having a common end-line that bisects the discovery shaft.[2]

Yet where a discovery shaft sunk by a junior locator bisects a common boundary between him and a prior appropriator, and a portion of apex is found disclosed within the limits of the junior location, such a discovery is sufficient upon which to base the subsequent location.[3]

§ 338. The effect of the loss of discovery upon the remainder of the location.—As the discovered lode must lie within the limits of the location which is made by reason of it, if the title to the discovery fails, so must the location which rests upon it.

If there is but one point of discovery, and all workings are done at that point, a patent issued to another claimant, covering the place of working, restores the remainder of the ground to the public domain.[4]

Where, however, a new discovery is made and work prosecuted thereon in good faith, loss of the original discovery point by patent to another will not work a loss of

---

[1] Reynolds v. Pascoe (Utah), 66 Pac. 1064.

[2] Poplar Creek Cons. Quartz Mine, 16 L. D. 1, 2. See, also, McKinstry v. Clark, 4 Mont. 370; Morr. Min. Rights, 10th ed. 40.

In a case arising under the laws of New Mexico as they existed in 1871, a locator divided his claim into three parts, and conveyed two of them to other parties. There was but one discovery shaft. The supreme court held that the severance of title as to the two parts conveyed rendered a separate shaft on each part necessary. The case as reported does not state whether or not the discovery shaft had been sunk prior to the conveyance. Zeckendorf v. Hutchison, 1 N. Mex. 476; 9 Morr. Min. Rep. 483.

[3] Larkin v. Upton, 144 U. S. 19, 23, 12 Sup. Ct. Rep. 614.

[4] Gwillim v. Donnellan, 115 U. S. 45, 50, 5 Sup. Ct. Rep. 1110; Miller v. Girard, 3 Colo. App. 278, 33 Pac. 68; Girard v. Carson, 22 Colo. 345, 44 Pac. 508.

the balance of the domain.[1] Nor will a prior location be lost where a junior locator is allowed to obtain, without contest, a patent which includes a portion of the prior claim containing the discovery, under an agreement to reconvey such portion to the prior claimant after patent, provided the acts of the parties are in good faith.[2]

The land department refuses to issue a patent upon an application from which is excepted the land containing the discovery shaft and improvements, where the proof fails to show the discovery or existence of mineral on the claim as applied for.[3]

A lode claim which is intersected by a patented millsite must be confined to that part which contains a discovery shaft and improvements,[4] unless a valid discovery of the same vein can be shown upon the other part.[5]

Such showing will authorize the entry of such remainder, as in such case it is not restored to the public domain.[6] And the applicant may be permitted, after entry at the local land office, and prior to patent, to establish these facts by supplemental proof.[7]

The rule that a patent may not be issued for both parts of a lode claim which is intersected by a millsite does not apply to a lode claim which is intersected by a placer claim.[8] It was formerly held[9] that if a lode

---

[1] Silver City G. and S. M. Co. v. Lowry, 19 Utah, 334, 57 Pac. 11.

[2] Duxie Lode, 27 L. D. 88.

[3] In re J. G. Kennedy, 10 Copp's L. O. 150; Antediluvian Lode, 8 L. D. 602; Independence Lode, 9 L. D. 571; Lone Dane Lode, 10 L. D. 53; In re Thomas J. Laney, 9 L. D. 93; Hidden Treasure Lode, 29 L. D. 156, S. C. on review, Id. 315.

[4] Andromeda Lode, 13 L. D. 146; Mabel Lode, 26 L. D. 675.

[5] Paul Jones Lode, 31 L. D. 359.

[6] In re Hagland, on review, 1 L. D. 593; Paul Jones Lode, 31 L. D. 359; Perigo v. Erwin, 85 Fed. 904; Erwin v. Perigo, 93 Fed. 608.

[7] Spur Lode, 4 L. D. 160.

[8] The Vulcano Lode M. Claim, 30 L. D. 482.

[9] Silver Queen Lode, 16 L. D. 186.

claim is intersected by a prior lode location, both parts of such intersected claim could not be retained. But under the recent decisions of the department we think the opposite conclusion would be reached.[1]

Judge Hallett has ruled, that a locator may sell or otherwise dispose of that portion of his location which covers his discovery and workings without affecting his right to the remainder.[2]

In the case in which this rule was announced the sale was evidently brought about by the pendency of adverse proceedings. The decision was made before that of the supreme court of the United States in Gwillim v. Donnellan, heretofore cited.

The supreme court of Utah has held that where the original discovery of a lode claim has been included within the patent lines of a junior claim, but before the issuance of such patent a discovery is made on that portion of the senior location not included within the junior claim, such senior location is valid.[3]

The supreme court of California has attempted to qualify the rule announced by the supreme court of the United States in Gwillim v. Donnellan, and which has been followed uniformly by the land department, in a case where the discovery and workings were embraced within an agricultural patent, the mining locator subsequently acquiring the agricultural title.[4]

The court evidently strained the law to avoid sanctioning what it deemed an injustice. Work done on the patented agricultural land, if it had a manifest tendency

---

[1] Paul Jones Lode, 31 L. D. 359; Hidee Gold M. Co., 30 L. D. 420; Alice Lode M. Claim, *Id.* 481. See Crown Point G. M. Co. v. Buck, 97 Fed. 462, 465.

[2] Little Pittsburg Cons. M. Co. v. Amie M. Co. 17 Fed. 57.

[3] Silver City G. and S. M. Co. v. Lowry, 19 Utah, 334, 57 Pac. 11. See Paul Jones Lode, 28 L. D. 120, 31 L. D. 359.

[4] Richards v. Wolfling, 98 Cal. 195, 32 Pac. 971.

to develop that part of the location excluded from the
agricultural entry, would be considered in law as the
equivalent of work done within the limits of the claim.
But a discovery, without which no location possesses any
potential force or vitality, once passing by patent to
another, can no more be used as the basis of acquiring title to unpatented lands, although held by the same
owner, than can a discovery in one mining claim be
used as the basis of locating another. Certainly,
no patent could ever be obtained to the remainder
of the mining claim upon the facts shown in the
California case, unless other discoveries were made
within such remainder. It is manifest that the ruling
of Judge Hallett and the decision of the supreme
court of California are opposed to the weight of authority. Loss of discovery results in loss of location, unless
a new discovery is made within the excluded ground
prior to the inception of intervening rights. Such new
discovery will save the remainder from reverting to the
body of the public domain.

§ 339. **Extent of a locator's right after discovery
and prior to completion of location.**—Discovery is but
one step in acquiring title to a mining claim. It must be
followed by location.[1] When a prospector has made
such a discovery as will satisfy the law and form the
basis of the location, he is allowed, in most of the states
and territories, a specified time in which to perform the
remaining acts which are requisite to perfect the location. As to whether, in the absence of such legislation
and district rules, the discoverer has any appreciable
time within which to mark his boundaries and complete
his location is a subject upon which the courts differ.
The supreme court of California holds that while if the

---

[1] Adams v. Crawford, 116 Cal. 495, 48 Pac. 488.

locator be on the ground actually engaged in making the
location, another could not locate over him, yet, in the
absence of local rules authorizing it, no time is allowed
to perfect the location; that until it is actually marked on
the ground the claim is not appropriated so as to prevent its acquisition by a subsequent locator.[1]

This rule was followed by the supreme court of Oregon.[2]

The supreme court of New Mexico holds that under
the laws of that territory such a perfected notice of location as will, when recorded, fulfill the requirements of
the federal statutes must be posted contemporaneously
with discovery.[3]

The circuit court of appeals for the ninth circuit was
called upon to determine the question upon the same evidence and the same state of facts arising in one of the
California cases,[4] and that tribunal declined to accept
the rule announced by the California courts. The court
of appeals held that after a discovery and posting a
notice thereof the locator had a reasonable time in
which to complete the location; what was a reasonable
time would depend upon the facts of each particular
case; that evidence of customs prevalent in other localities on this subject might be received for the purpose of
aiding the court in its determination, and that, under the
circumstances of that case, twenty days was a reasonable
time.[5]

The doctrine announced by the circuit court of appeals is in consonance with the views expressed by the

---

[1] Newbill v. Thurston, 65 Cal. 419, 4 Pac. 409; Pharis v. Muldoon,
75 Cal. 284, 17 Pac. 70.

[2] Patterson v. Tarbell, 26 Or. 29, 37 Pac. 76. See, *post*, § 372.

[3] Deeney v. Mineral Creek M. Co. (N. Mex), 67 Pac. 724.

[4] Newbill v. Thurston, 65 Cal. 419, 4 Pac. 409.

[5] Doe v. Waterloo M. Co., 70 Fed. 455; affirming decision of Judge
Ross, Doe v. Waterloo, 55 Fed. 11.

supreme courts of Nevada,[1] Idaho,[2] Montana,[3] and Washington,[4] and accords with the spirit of the law as interpreted by the supreme courts of Colorado,[5] and South Dakota,[6] and the supreme court of the United States.[7]

To hold that the miner, as soon as he discovers a lode, must immediately stake the territory which he is entitled to claim, in order to protect it from invasion and claims of other persons, would be an unreasonable, if not impossible, requirement.[8]

What is a reasonable time for the completion of the location depends upon the nature of the ground to be located, the means of properly marking, and the ability to properly ascertain the dimensions and course, or strike, of the vein.[9]

As so much depends upon the locator determining the position of his vein in the earth and the course of its apex, and as a failure to make his location and establish his end-lines as the law contemplates is accompanied with such serious results, it would seem that congress never intended to compel the discoverer to immediately proceed at his peril with the marking of his boundaries. The posting of a preliminary notice, though not specially authorized by statute, should be sufficient to protect the discoverer for a reasonable time, at least,

---

[1] Golden Fleece M. Co. v. Cable Cons. M. Co., 12 Nev. 312, 329; Gleeson v. Martin White M. Co., 13 Nev. 442; testimony of Chief Justice Beatty, Rep. Pub. Land Com. 399.

[2] Burke v. McDonald, 2 Idaho, 646, 33 Pac. 49.

[3] Sanders v. Noble, 22 Mont. 110, 55 Pac. 1037, 1045.

[4] Union M. and M. Co. v. Leitch, 24 Wash. 585, 85 Am. St. Rep. 961, 64 Pac. 829.

[5] Murley v. Ennis, 2 Colo. 300; Patterson v. Hitchcock, 3 Colo. 533.

[6] Marshall v. Harney Peak Tin M. Co., 1 S. Dak. 350, 47 N. W. 290.

[7] Erhardt v. Boaro, 113 U. S. 527, 5 Sup. Ct. Rep. 560.

[8] Omar v. Soper, 11 Colo. 380, 7 Am. St. Rep. 243, 18 Pac. 443; Sanders v. Noble, 22 Mont. 110, 55 Pac. 1037, 1045.

[9] Doe v. Waterloo M. Co., 70 Fed. 455, 460.

within which he might determine approximately the all-important facts upon which the value of his property to a great degree depends.[1]

What is a reasonable time is a question of law,[2] and depends upon the circumstances of each case.[3]

In states or localities where the laws or district regulations fix a given time within which certain acts subsequent to the discovery are required to be performed, the posting of a preliminary notice, specifying the name of the lode, date of discovery, and the intention to locate the claim, is equivalent to actual possession.[4]

Whenever preliminary work is required to define and describe the claim located, the first discoverer must be protected in the possession of the claim until sufficient excavations and development can be made to disclose whether a vein or deposit of such richness exists as to justify the work to extract the metal.[5] Otherwise, the whole purpose of allowing the free exploration of the public lands for the precious metals would in such cases be defeated, and force and violence in the struggle for possession, instead of previous discovery, would determine the rights of the claimants.[6]

The effect of this rule is practically to reserve, after the discovery and during the statutory period allowed for perfecting the claim, a surface area circular in form, the radius of which may be the length claimed on the discovered lode, within which area the location may be

---

[1] Union M. and M. Co. *v.* Leitch, 24 Wash. 585, 85 Am. St. Rep. 961, 64 Pac. 828.

[2] Patterson *v.* Hitchcock, 3 Colo. 533, 540.

[3] Union M. and M. Co. *v.* Leitch, 24 Wash. 585, 85 Am. St. Rep. 961; 64 Pac. 828.

[4] Erhardt *v.* Boaro, 8 Fed. 692.

[5] Sanders *v.* Noble, 22 Mont. 110, 55 Pac. 1037, 1045.

[6] Erhardt *v.* Boaro, 113 U. S. 527, 535, 5 Sup. Ct. Rep. 560; Marshall *v.* Harney Peak Tin M. Co., 1 S. Dak. 350, 47 N. W. 290; Omar *v.* Soper, 11 Colo. 380, 7 Am. St. Rep. 243, 18 Pac. 443.

ultimately made. "The locator may use his discovery " as a pivot, and move his lines, at least in the gen- " eral course of his vein given in his notice, so as to " secure the full benefit of his discovery."[1] Such is the manifest intent of the rule. This was the custom under the act of 1866. The miner posted his notice, claiming so many linear feet on the vein; and under the law as then interpreted, prior to fixing the *situs* of his lode, by filing a diagram for patent purposes, he might follow the vein wheresoever it ran to the length claimed.[2]

When he filed his diagram and inclosed his lode within surface boundaries, his right to pursue the vein on its course ceased where it passed out of his surface lines.[3]

Under the existing state of the law, the location must be marked within a certain period of time, whereupon the locator's rights became definitely fixed and confined, except as to the extralateral right, to his marked bound- aries. Until this is done, however, and within the pre- scribed periods, his right to be protected to the extent heretofore stated is well settled.[4]

If, however, he marks his boundaries indicating the extent of the location without waiting for the time allowed him, and other locations are made, guided by the boundaries as marked, he will not be permitted subse- quently to swing his location so as to include the surface of the intervening locations.[5]

If he fails to comply with the law within the statutory period, his rights would thereafter be no greater than the rights of one in possession without discovery. He might protect his *pedis possessio* against forcible intrusion

---

[1] Sanders v. Noble, 22 Mont. 110, 55 Pac. 1037, 1046.

[2] Johnson v. Parks, 10 Cal. 447. See, *ante*, § 58.

[3] *Ante*, § 60.

[4] Sanders v. Noble, 22 Mont. 110, 55 Pac. 1037, 1045; Bramlett v. Flick, 23 Mont. 95, 57 Pac. 869.

[5] Wiltsee v. King of Arizona M. and M. Co. (Ariz.), 60 Pac. 896.

and hold it as against one having no higher right; [1] but he would be a mere occupant without color of title, and his possession must yield to any one possessing the necessary qualifications, who enters peaceably and in good faith for the purpose of perfecting a valid location. [2]

ARTICLE IV. THE DISCOVERY SHAFT AND ITS EQUIVALENT.

§ 343. State legislation requiring development work as prerequisite to completion of location.

§ 344. Object of requirement as to development work.

§ 345. Relationship of the discovery to the discovery shaft.

§ 346. Extent of development work.

§ 343. State legislation requiring development work as prerequisite to completion of location.—Of the precious-metal-bearing states, California and Utah have thus far enacted no laws requiring work of any character to be performed as a prerequisite to the completion of a location; therefore, as to these states this article is inapplicable.

The states and territories hereinafter enumerated, however, have supplemented federal legislation by requiring that certain preliminary development work in the nature of a discovery shaft, or its equivalent, shall be performed as a condition precedent to the completion of a lode location. This legislation has been held to be valid. [3] As these state statutes are frequently important

---

[1] Crossman v. Pendery, 8 Fed. 693; Field v. Grey (Ariz.), 25 Pac. 793. See Cosmos Exploration Co. v. Gray Eagle Oil Co., 112 Fed. 4, 14.

[2] See, ante, "Occupancy without color of title," §§ 216-219; Willeford v. Bell (Cal.), 49 Pac. 6.

[3] Ante, § 250 (15); Northmore v. Simmons, 97 Fed. 386; Sissons v. Sommers, 24 Nev. 379, 77 Am. St. Rep. 815, 55 Pac. 829; Sanders v. Noble, 22 Mont. 110, 55 Pac. 1037, 1039; Purdum v. Laddin, 23 Mont. 387, 59 Pac. 153. And see Erhardt v. Boaro, 113 U. S. 527, 5 Sup. Ct. Rep. 560; Lockhart v. Johnson, 181 U. S. 516, 526, 21 Sup. Ct. Rep. 665. But see Beals v. Cone, 27 Colo. 473, 83 Am. St. Rep. 92, 62 Pac. 948, 958.

factors necessary to be considered in construing and applying decisions of the state courts, we will present an outline of the provisions found in the several states and territories upon this subject, taking the state of Colorado as a basis of comparison.

Colorado.—The laws of Colorado require the filing for record of a location certificate within three months from the date of discovery.[1] Prior to the expiration of this time, and within sixty days from the time of uncovering or disclosing the lode,[2] the discoverer must sink a discovery shaft upon the lode to the depth of at least ten feet from the lowest part of the rim of the shaft at the surface, or deeper if necessary, to show a well-defined crevice.[3] The word "crevice," as here used, clearly means a mineral-bearing vein.[4] The discovery of some other vein within the limits of the claim cannot supply the absence of the one required to be exposed in the discovery shaft.[5]

Any open cut, crosscut, or tunnel which shall cut a lode at the depth of ten feet below the surface, or an adit of at least ten feet in, along the lode from the point where the lode may be in any manner discovered, is equivalent to the discovery shaft.[6]

Arizona.—Within ninety days from the date of discovering the lode and posting notice thereon,[7] a discovery shaft must be sunk within the premises claimed to

---

[1] Mills' Annot. Stats., § 3150.

[2] *Id.*, § 3155.

[3] *Id.*, § 3152.

[4] Bryan v. McCaig, 10 Colo. 309, 15 Pac. 413; Beals v. Cone, 27 Colo. 473, 83 Am. St. Rep. 92, 62 Pac. 946, 958; Van Zandt v. Argentine M. Co., 8 Fed. 725; Terrible M. Co. v. Argentine M. Co., 89 Fed. 583; Cheesman v. Shreeve, 40 Fed. 787.

[5] Beals v. Cone, 27 Colo. 473, 83 Am. St. Rep. 92, 62 Pac. 946, 958.

[6] Mills' Annot. Stats., § 3154.

[7] Laws of 1895, p. 54, § 6.

a depth of at least ten feet from the lowest rim of such shaft at the surface, and deeper if necessary, until there is disclosed in said shaft mineral in place.[1]

Any open cut, adit, or tunnel which shall be made as above provided, as a part of the location, and which shall be equal in amount of work to a shaft ten feet deep and four feet wide by six feet long, and which shall cut a lode or mineral in place at the depth of ten feet from the surface, is equivalent as discovery work to a shaft sunk from the surface.[2]

Idaho.—The locator must complete his location by marking his boundaries within ten days from the date of discovery.[3] Within sixty days from the date of location, the locator must sink a shaft upon the lode to the depth of at least ten feet from the lowest part of the rim of such shaft at the surface, and of not less than sixteen square feet in area. Any excavation which shall cut such vein ten feet from the lowest part of the rim of such shaft, and which shall measure one hundred and sixty cubic feet in extent, shall be considered a compliance with this provision.[4]

Montana.—After discovery, the initial step in the series of acts culminating in a completed location is the posting of a notice.[5] Before the expiration of sixty days from the date of such posting, the locator must sink a discovery shaft to the same depth as required by the laws of Colorado, except that to the words "well-"defined crevice" is added " or valuable deposit." The equivalent of such shaft is the same as in Colorado.[6]

---

[1] Rev. Stats. (1901), § 3234.
[2] *Id.*, § 3237.
[3] Rev. Stats., § 3101, as amended—Laws of 1895, p. 26; as amended—Laws of 1899, p. 633; Civ. Code (1901), § 2557.
[4] Stats. 1895, p. 27, § 3; Civ. Code (1901), § 2558.
[5] Pol. Code, § 3610.
[6] *Id.*, § 3611; as amended—Laws of 1901, p. 140, § 1.

This requirement has been held to be valid and mandatory.[1]

Nevada.—The posting of a notice is required, and before the expiration of ninety days thereafter the locator must sink a discovery shaft to a depth of at least ten feet from the lowest part of the rim of such shaft at the surface, or deeper if necessary, to show by such work a lode deposit of mineral in place. A cut, crosscut, or tunnel which cuts the lode at a depth of ten feet, or an open cut along the ledge or lode equivalent in size to a shaft four feet by six feet by ten feet deep is equivalent to a discovery shaft.[2] This legislation has been held to be valid.[3]

New Mexico.—Within ninety days from the time of taking possession,[4] and prior to recording the notice of location (three months after posting), the locator must sink a discovery shaft upon the claim to the depth of at least ten feet from the lowest part of the rim of such shaft at the surface, or must drive a tunnel, open cut, or adit upon such claim, exposing mineral in place at least ten feet below the surface.[5]

North Dakota.—The locator must record a location certificate within sixty days from the date of discovery,[6] and before filing such certificate for record, must sink a discovery shaft on the claim sufficient to show a well-defined mineral vein or lode.[7] There is also a provision granting the locator sixty days from the time of uncover-

---

[1] Purdum *v.* Laddin, 23 Mont. 387, 59 Pac. 153.

[2] Comp. Laws (1900), § 209; as amended—Stats. 1901, p. 97.

[3] Sissons *v.* Sommers, 24 Nev. 379, 77 Am. St. Rep. 815, 55 Pac. 829.

[4] There is nothing in the statutes of New Mexico fixing the time within which *possession* is to be taken, or defining what constitutes such possession. A notice is required to be posted, and within three months to be recorded. The posting of this notice is probably "taking possession."

[5] Laws of 1889, p. 42; Comp. Laws (1897), § 2298.

[6] Rev. Pol. Code of 1895, § 1428; *Id.* 1899, § 1428.

[7] *Id.* 1895, § 1430; *Id.* 1899, § 1430.

ing or disclosing the lode in which to sink such shaft.[1]
The statute is evidently drawn on the lines of the Colorado law, with this marked distinction: In Colorado
the shaft must be sunk within *three months* from the
date of the discovery, and within sixty days from uncovering or disclosing the lode, suggesting that the locator
might have thirty days after discovery to uncover or
disclose his lode. In North Dakota the time is fixed at
sixty days from date of discovery (*i. e.* before recording
the notice), and sixty days from uncovering or disclosing the lode. To give the statute effect in all its parts,
the uncovering or disclosing the lode must be construed
as meaning the *discovery.* If this be not true, then the
locator might have an indefinite time in which to uncover and disclose his lode.

If a discovery should be made on January 1st, the certificate must be recorded on or before March 2d. If the
lode is not uncovered or disclosed until the 5th of
January, unless the construction we place upon the law
is correct, the locator would have until March 8th to
sink his shaft, rendering nugatory the requirement that
he should perform this development work before the
certificate is recorded. It would therefore seem that the
provision allowing sixty days from the uncovering of the
lode in which to sink the shaft is inoperative unless that
act is understood to mean the *discovery.*

Any open cut, crosscut, or tunnel, at a depth sufficient
to disclose the mineral vein or lode, or an adit of at least
ten feet along the lode from the point where the lode may
be in any manner discovered, is equivalent in North Dakota to a discovery shaft.[2]

Oregon.—The locator is required to post a notice of
discovery, and before the expiration of sixty days from

---

[1] Rev. Pol. Code, 1895, § 1433.
[2] *Id.*, § 1432; *Id.*, 1899, § 1432.

the date of such posting, and before recording the notice of location, must sink a discovery shaft upon the claim located to a depth of at least ten feet from the lowest part of the rim of such shaft at the surface, or deeper if necessary, to show by such work a lode, or vein, of mineral deposit in place. A cut, crosscut, or tunnel which cuts the lode at a depth of ten feet, or an open cut at least six feet deep, four feet wide, and ten feet in length along the lode, from a point where the same may be in any manner discovered, is equivalent to such discovery shaft. It is provided that such work shall not be deemed a part of the assessment work required by the Revised Statutes of the United States. An affidavit showing compliance with the foregoing provisions is required to be made and attached to the notice of location and recorded therewith.[1]

South Dakota.—The laws upon this subject in South Dakota are the same as in North Dakota, with the exception that the discovery shaft must not be less than ten feet in depth on the lower side, and the open cut, to be equivalent to a discovery shaft, is required to be of at least ten feet face.[2]

Washington.—The discoverer is required within ninety days from the date of discovery to record a location notice. Before filing the same for record he must sink a discovery shaft upon the lode to the depth of ten feet from the lowest part of the rim of such shaft at the surface. Any open cut or tunnel having a length of ten feet, which shall cut a lode at the depth of ten feet below the surface, shall hold the lode the same as if a discovery shaft were sunk thereon, and shall be equivalent

---

[1] Laws of 1898, p. 17, as amended—Laws of of 1901, p. 141.

[2] Comp. Laws of Dak. 1887, § 1999; Grantham's Annot. Stats. (1899), § 2658, as amended—Laws of 1899, p. 146; §§ 2659, 2660, as amended—Laws of 1899, p. 148; § 2662, as amended—Laws of 1899, p. 148; § 2663.

thereto.[1] These provisions do not apply to claims lying
west of the summit of the Cascade mountains.

Wyoming.—The locator is required to sink a shaft
upon the discovered lode or fissure to the depth of ten
feet from the lowest rim of the shaft at the surface
within sixty days from the date of discovery.[2]

Any open cut which shall cut the vein ten feet in
length, and with face ten feet in height, or any crosscut
tunnel, or tunnel on the vein, ten feet in length which
shall cut the vein ten feet below the surface, measured
from the bottom of such tunnel, is considered the equivalent of a discovery shaft.[3]

§ 344. **Object of requirement as to development
work.**—The object of this class of legislation is twofold:—

(1) To demonstrate to a reasonable degree of certainty that the deposit sought to be located as a lode is in
fact a vein of quartz or other rock in place;

(2) To compel the discoverer to manifest his intention
to claim the ground in good faith under the mining laws.

The Colorado act, which is the parent of all the others,
was passed in 1874, about the time of the discovery of
the blanket carbonate deposits in the Leadville regions.
In these localities, the vein exposures, such as answered
the popular definition of outcrop, were few, along the
sides of eroded gulches, and the underlying beds were in
the main reached by vertical shafts sunk from the surface through the overlying "slide" and white porphyry
to the contact with the blue limestone, where the ore
bodies, in certain geological horizons, were usually
encountered. In many of these cases there was no real

---

[1] Laws of 1899, p. 69.
[2] Laws of 1888, p. 88, § 17; *Id.*, § 19, as amended—Laws of 1890, p.
180; Laws of 1895, ch. 108, § 2; Rev. Stats. (1899), §§ 2548, 2550.
[3] Laws of 1888, p. 88, § 18; Rev. Stats. (1899), § 2549.

discovery from the surface. The miner's "indications" consisted of the development of work of his neighbors and the generally accepted geological theories.

The vertical depth from the surface to the deposits varied in different localities, so the law required the shaft to be sunk to a sufficient depth to show a well-defined crevice. These local conditions, if they were not the moving cause of the enactment, certainly proved its wisdom.

On the other hand, in the absence of this class of state legislation, alleged discoveries may be made, and after marking boundaries, the locator is allowed a year from the first day of January next succeeding the date of his location within which to do one hundred dollars' worth of work. Until that time elapses, he is not called upon to do anything. In many instances he does no work until compelled to, and about the time the period elapses, he "resumes" work which he never commenced, and each succeeding first day of January finds him again in a state of "resumption." During this period, in a large number of cases which have come under our personal observation, the location is a threat, preventing others who might be willing to develop the ground from acquiring rights. The requirement that some genuine development work should be done as a condition precedent to the perfection of a lode location is wise and beneficial, and the courts uniformly enforce the law—not with rigid strictness, but with fairness and liberality. In our judgment, this class of state legislation was contemplated by congress when it enacted the mining laws. Where such laws have been passed upon by the courts, their validity has been upheld.[1]

---

[1] Sissons v. Sommers, 24 Nev. 379, 77 Am. St. Rep. 815, 55 Pac. 829; Northmore v. Simmons, 97 Fed. 386; Purdum v. Laddin, 23 Mont. 387, 59 Pac. 153. See Erhardt v. Boaro, 113 U. S. 527, 5 Sup. Ct. Rep. 560, and Lockhart v. Johnson, 181 U. S. 516, 526, 21 Sup. Ct. Rep. 665. But see Beals v. Cone, 27 Colo. 473, 83 Am. St. Rep. 92, 62 Pac. 948, 958.

§ 345. **Relationship of the discovery to the discovery shaft.**—As Mr. Morrison in his "Mining Rights" tersely states,[1] "the fact of discovery is a fact of itself, " to be totally disconnected from the idea of discovery " shaft. The discovery shaft is a part of the process of " location subsequent to discovery."[2]

When we speak of the discovery shaft, we mean to include in that term the various equivalents provided for by the several state enactments, as hereinbefore outlined.[3]

As heretofore demonstrated, the discovery must be within the limits of the location as ultimately defined, and upon land that is free and open to exploration.[4] The same rule applies to the discovery shaft.[5] But it is not required that the development work shall be performed at the point where the first discovery is made; neither is it required that the discovery shaft should be equidistant from the end-lines.[6] The locator may make any shaft he may sink his discovery shaft,[7] provided always, that he discloses within it some well-defined crevice or mineral "in place." Such a disclosure in the discovery shaft is necessary, and the mere discovery of some other vein within the limits of the claim cannot supply the absence of the one required to be exposed in the discovery

---

[1] 10th ed., p. 30.

[2] Quoted in Brewster v. Shoemaker, 28 Colo. 176, 63 Pac. 309, 310, 89 Am. St. Rep. —.

[3] Brewster v. Shoemaker, 28 Colo. 176, 63 Pac. 309, 310, 89 Am. St. Rep. —.

[4] *Ante,* § 337.

[5] Armstrong v. Lower, 6 Colo. 393; Upton v. Larkin, 5 Mont. 600, 6 Pac. 66; Morr. Min. Rights, 10th ed., p. 36.

[6] Taylor v. Parenteau, 23 Colo. 368, 48 Pac. 505.

[7] Charge of Judge Hallett in Terrible M. Co. v. Argentine M. Co., as outlined in Argentine M. Co. v. Terrible M. Co., 122 U. S. 478, 481, 7 Sup. Ct. Rep. 1356. This charge is reported in 5 McCrary, 639, 89 Fed. 583.

shaft.[1] In neither of these cases was the court called upon to determine whether the state statute was objectionable on the ground that it conflicted with the requirements of the federal statute. It is possible that it would be held invalid on this account. The first discovery may not always indicate to the miner the appropriate place where economic considerations require his development work to be done.[2] For the purpose of enabling him to determine these facts and select his place, the state laws grant him fixed periods within which to make his selection and complete his location, with the necessary condition attached, that if he fails to disclose his vein at or below the depth required by the local laws, and within the specified period, his ground will become subject to relocation by the next comer.

His original discovery will protect him in his possession during the statutory period,[3] but if he permits that period to elapse, and fails to perform his development work and accomplish the results contemplated by law, his possession must yield to the next comer who succeeds by peaceable methods in initiating a right.[4] As is said by Mr. Morrison, the neglect of the locator to comply with this requirement is equivalent to an abandonment of the inchoate right given by discovery.[5] The discovery has performed its office. The perfected location rests ultimately on the completed development work. This we understand to be the rule announced by Judge Hallett in the Adelaide-Camp Bird case,[6] and we are not

[1] Beals v. Cone, 27 Colo. 473, 83 Am. St. Rep. 92, 62 Pac. 948, 958; Fleming v. Daly, 12 Colo. App. 439, 55 Pac. 946.

[2] Harrrington v. Chambers, 3 Utah, 94, 1 Pac. 362.

[3] Erhardt v. Boaro, 113 U. S. 527, 5 Sup. Ct. Rep. 560; Marshall v. Harney Peak Tin Co., 1 S. Dak. 350, 47 N. W. 290; Omar v. Soper, 11 Colo. 380, 7 Am. St. Rep. 243, 11 Pac. 443.

[4] Lockhart v. Johnson, 181 U. S. 516, 21 Sup. Ct. Rep. 665.

[5] Morr. Min. Rights, 10th ed., p. 30.

[6] Van Zandt v. Argentine M. Co., 8 Fed. 725.

aware of any adjudicated case to the contrary. It is true that the supreme court of Utah[1] and the United States circuit court, ninth circuit, district of California,[2] have announced that it is not necessary that the locator should show the existence of a vein in any particular place, provided it is shown to exist in some portion of the claim; but it must be borne in mind that neither the laws of Utah nor California require the performance of development work as a prerequisite to a perfected location,[3] and in the absence of such local legislation it is not required.

An original discovery may be made in the discovery shaft, even after a location has been perfected, and this will be sufficient in the absence of intervening rights.[4]

§ 346. **Extent of development work.**—In the state of North Dakota the requirements of the law are satisfied when the discovery shaft or opening shows a well-defined mineral vein, or lode, regardless of the vertical distance from the surface at which it is disclosed. The other precious-metal-bearing states [5] require a certain depth in case of the shaft, and length in case of other openings, and this requirement must be fulfilled, although the vein is disclosed before reaching the required distance,[6] thus giving sanction to the view hereinbefore expressed, that the object of requiring development work was twofold.[7]

For example, the discovery shaft must be at least ten feet deep. It must be deeper if, at the required vertical

---

[1] Harrington v. Chambers, 3 Utah, 94, 1 Pac. 362.

[2] North Noonday M. Co. v. Orient M. Co., 6 Saw. 299, 1 Fed. 522.

[3] *Ante*, § 343.

[4] Strepy v. Stark, 7 Colo. 619, 5 Pac. 111; Zollars & H. C. C. M. Co. v. Evans, 2 McCrary, 39, 5 Fed. 172. *Ante*, § 330.

[5] Colorado, Arizona, Idaho, Montana, Nevada, New Mexico, Oregon, South Dakota, Washington, and Wyoming.

[6] Morr. Min. Rights, 10th ed., p. 38.

[7] *Ante*, § 344.

distance from the lowest rim, the vein or crevice be not disclosed. It is hardly profitable to discuss the consequences flowing from a failure to strictly comply with the requirements as to depth if the proper vein exposure is found within the required distance. Prudent miners will not jeopardize valuable rights by failing to comply fully with the law, and courts will readily detect a manifest attempt at evasion.

The requirement as to disclosing the vein, crevice, or deposit in place, which terms are legal equivalents, is unquestionably mandatory. What constitutes such a vein, is to be determined by the rules announced by the courts in the adjudicated cases, which have been fully presented in preceding articles,[1] and need not here be repeated.

A former statute of Montana required the discovery shaft to disclose at least one wall of the vein,[2] but this has since been repealed. It has been decided in Colorado that the requirements of the discovery-shaft laws do not involve the uncovering of the walls. When the shaft is sunk to the necessary depth on the vein, the statutory condition in that respect is fulfilled. When a given formation is determined to be a lode, the walls are a geological necessity. Their existence is as certain as that of the vein.[3]

In construing the provisions of the Colorado statute providing for development by adit, which in mining parlance is an opening on and along the vein used for drainage, the supreme court of Colorado has held that it was the legislative intention to substitute horizontal development in and along the lode for ten feet, in lieu of a discovery shaft of that depth, and that the distance

[1] *Ante*, §§ 286-301.

[2] Foote *v.* National M. Co., 2 Mont. 402; O'Donnell *v.* Glenn, 8 Mont. 248, 19 Pac. 302.

[3] Fleming *v.* Daly, 12 Colo. App. 439, 55 Pac. 946.

below the surface at which the vein appeared in place as the result of this class of development was immaterial.[1]

The same court also determined that an "adit" need not be altogether under cover.[2]

ARTICLE V.   THE PRELIMINARY NOTICE AND ITS POSTING.

§ 350. Local customs as to prelim-
         inary notice, and its post-
         ing prior to enactment of
         federal laws — Not re-
         quired by congressional
         law.

§ 351. State legislation requiring
         the posting of notices —
         States grouped.

§ 352. First group.

§ 353. Second group.

§ 354. Third group.

§ 355. Liberal rules of construc-
         tion applied to notices.

§ 356. Place and manner of post-
         ing.

§ 350. **Local customs as to preliminary notice, and its posting prior to enactment of federal laws—Not required by congressional law.**—During the period when mining privileges upon the public domain were governed exclusively by the local regulations and customs of miners, the first step in the inception of the miner's right, after the discovery, was the posting of a notice at some point on, or in reasonable proximity to, the discovered lode, usually upon a tree, stake, or mound of rocks.[3] The posting of this notice served to manifest the intention of the discoverer to claim the vein to the extent described, and to warn all others seeking new discoveries that there was a prior appropriation of the lode to which the posted notice applied.

Gray v. Truby, 6 Colo. 278; Craig v. Thompson, 10 Colo. 517, 526, 16 Pac. 24; Brewster v. Shoemaker, 28 Colo. 176, 63 Pac. 309, 89 Am. St. Rep. —.

[2] Electro-Magnetic M. and D. Co. v. Van Auken, 9 Colo. 204, 11 Pac. 80; Craig v. Thompson, 10 Colo. 517, 526, 16 Pac. 24.

[3] Yale on Mining Claims and Water Rights, p. 78; J. Ross Browne's Mineral Resources, 1867, pp. 236-242; Gleeson v. Martin White M. Co., 13 Nev. 450.

These notices were of the simplest character, were required to be in no particular form, and were generally prepared by unlettered men. They served the purpose, however, and enabled any one seeking in good faith to locate claims to ascertain the extent and nature of the right asserted on the particular lode by the prior discoverer.

During this period, it will be remembered, as well as during the period immediately preceding the passage of the act of May 10, 1872, the lode was the principal thing sought, and the surface was a mere incident.[1]

The locator could hold but one vein,[2] and while surface boundaries were eventually in some way defined, neither the form nor extent of such surface, prior to filing the diagram for patent, controlled the rights on the located lode.[3]

While the act of 1872 changed all this,[4] and required the marking of surface limits inclosing the located lode, it did not dispense with the necessity of posting the preliminary notice, when such was required by state or district rules, nor destroy its usefulness in the absence of any such regulations. While, in the absence of state legislation or district regulations, the posting of a notice on the claim is not required at any stage of the proceedings culminating in the completion of the location,[5] the

[1] *Ante,* § 58; Johnson v. Parks, 10 Cal. 447; Patterson v. Hitchcock, 3 Colo. 533, 544; Wolffey v. Lebanon M. Co., 4 Colo. 112; Walrath v. Champion M. Co., 63 Fed. 552; Del Monte M. Co. v. Last Chance M. Co., 171 U. S. 55, 18 Sup. Ct. Rep. 895.

[2] Eureka Case, 4 Saw. 302, 323, Fed. Cas. No. 4548; Eclipse G. and S. M. Co. v. Spring, 59 Cal. 304.

[3] *Ante,* § 58.

[4] *Ante,* §§ 70, 71.

[5] Haws v. Victoria C. M. Co., 160 U. S. 303, 16 Sup. Ct. Rep. 282; Gird v. California Oil Co., 60 Fed. 531, 536; Book v. Justice M. Co., 58 Fed. 106, 115; Allen v. Dunlap, 24 Or. 229, 33 Pac. 675; Carter v. Bacigalupi, 83 Cal. 187, 192, 43 Pac. 361; Meydenbauer v. Stevens, 78 Fed. 787; Willeford v. Bell (Cal.), 49 Pac. 6; Perigo v. Erwin, 85 Fed. 904. But see Adams v. Crawford, 116 Cal. 495, 498, 48 Pac. 488.

prospector's first impulse upon discovering a lode is to post his notice. While his failure to so do, where the state law or local custom does not require it, is accompanied with no deprivation of right, yet it may be safely said that the practice of posting a notice of this character is almost universal.

§ 351. **State legislation requiring the posting of notices.—States grouped.**—There is no state statute requiring the posting of any notice whatever in California.

The supreme court of that state, notwithstanding the absence of any state legislation on that subject, has specified the posting of a notice as one of the preliminary requirements to the perfection of a valid location.[1] This expression in the opinion of the court is merely by way of recital. It states what is undoubtedly the customary practice. But if it was intended to go beyond this the decision is opposed to the authorities cited in the preceding section, including one of its own decisions.[2]

For the purpose of disclosing the nature of the legislation on this subject in the other precious-metal-bearing states and territories, we may group them into three classes:—

(1) Those requiring a preliminary notice which has no reference to the recorded certificate of location;

(2) Those wherein the posted notice bears a direct relation to the recorded certificate;

(3) Those requiring two different notices to be posted —one a preliminary, or discovery notice, the other conforming to the certificate which must ultimately be recorded.

---

[1] Adams v. Crawford, 116 Cal. 495, 498, 48 Pac. 488.
[2] Carter v. Bacigalupi, 83 Cal. 187, 192, 43 Pac. 361.

§ 352. First group.—

Colorado requires to be posted at the point of discovery on the surface a plain sign, or notice, containing: (1) the name of the lode; (2) the name of the locator; (3) the date of discovery. This posting must precede the recording of the certificate of location, but otherwise the posted notice is wholly disconnected from the recorded instrument.[1]

Montana.—The Montana law adds to the requirements of the Colorado law: (4) the number of linear feet each way from the point of discovery; (4*a*) the width on each side of the center of the vein; (4*b*) the general course of the vein. Nothing is said as to when the notice shall be posted, but the inference is that it should be done at the time of the discovery.[2]

Nevada.—The requirements in this state are the same as those of Montana.[3]

North Dakota[4] and *South Dakota*[5] add to the Colorado requirements: (4) the number of feet claimed in length on either side of the discovery; (5) number of feet in width on either side of the lode.

Washington.—The contents of the notice required in Washington are the same as those in Colorado.[6]

Wyoming.—The requirements in this state are the same as in Colorado, except that the name of the discov-

[1] Mills' Annot. Stats., § 3152.

[2] Validity upheld: Purdum v. Laddin, 23 Mont. 387, 39 Pac. 153; Rev. Code, 1895, § 3610.

[3] Comp. Laws (1900), § 208.

[4] Rev. Codes, § 1430, subd. 2; *Id.* (1899), § 1430.

[5] Comp. Laws of Dakota, 1887, § 2001, adopted by South Dakota— Laws of 1890-1891, ch. cv, § 1; Grantham's Annot. Stats. S. Dak. (1899), § 2660, as amended--Laws of 1899, p. 148.

[6] Laws of 1899, p. 69.

erer must also appear, suggesting that the locator and discoverer may be different persons.[1]

§ 353.   Second group.—

Arizona requires the posting, at or contiguous to the point of discovery on the surface, of a location notice, which must contain: (1) name of claim; (2) name of locator; (3) date of location; (4) the length and width of the claim in feet, and the distance from the point of discovery to each end of the claim; (5) the general course of the claim; (6) locality of the claim with reference to natural monuments. A copy of the location notice must be recorded.[2]

New Mexico provides for the posting, in some conspicuous place on the location, of a notice in writing, stating: (1) the names of the locators; (2) the intent to locate the claim; (3) a description by reference to some natural object or permanent monument. A copy of this notice as posted must be recorded.[3]

Oregon requires the locator to post on the claim a notice of discovery and location, which shall contain: (1) name of the claim; (2) name of locator; (3) date of the location; (4) number of linear feet claimed along the vein or lode each way from the point of discovery, with the width on each side of the lode or vein; (5) the general course, or strike, of the vein, or lode, as nearly as may be, with reference to some natural object or permanent monument in the vicinity thereof. A copy of the

---

[1] Laws of 1888, p. 88, § 17; Rev. Stats. (1899), § 2548.

[2] Rev. Stats. (1901), § 3232. Statute commented on in Wiltsee *v.* King of Arizona M. and M. Co. (Ariz.), 60 Pac. 896.

[3] Comp. Laws of 1884, p. 754, § 1566; *Id.* (1897), § 2286. The posting of this notice must be practically contemporaneous with the discovery. No appreciable time is allowed. Deeney *v.* Mineral Creek M. Co. (N. Mex.), 67 Pac. 624.

notice so posted, together with an affidavit of sinking of the discovery shaft, must be recorded.[1]

Utah requires posting, at the place of discovery, of a notice of location, which shall contain: (1) the name of the lode or claim; (2) the name of the locator; (3) the date of location; (4) the number of linear feet claimed in length along the course of the vein, each way from the point of discovery, with the width on each side of the center of the vein, and the general course of the vein, or lode, and such a description of the claim located by reference to some natural object or permanent monument, as will identify the claim. A substantial copy of such notice of location must be recorded.[2]

§ 354.   Third group.—

Idaho is the only state in this group. Its laws provide for the posting of two notices:—

(1) At the time of the discovery, when a monument must be erected at the place of discovery, upon which the locator must place his name, the date of discovery, and the distance claimed along the vein each way from such monument;

(2) At the time of marking his boundaries he must post another notice, the requirements of which are much more elaborate, and a substantial copy of which must be recorded.[3]

§ 355.   Liberal rules of construction applied to notices.—

The statutory requirements found in the first group of states, and the first requirement in the third group, are nothing more than the perpetuation of the

---

[1] Laws of 1898, p. 16, §§ 1, 2, as amended—Laws of 1901, p. 140.

[2] Laws of 1899, p. 26, §§ 2, 4.

[3] Laws of 1895, p. 26, amending § 3101, Rev. Stats.; Laws of 1899, p. 336, § 2, as amended—Laws of 1899, p. 633; Civ. Code (1901), § 2557.

system in vogue during the early history of the mining industry of the west. They preserve the simplicity of the primitive system and recognize the fact that miners are unacquainted with legal forms, and usually are out of reach of legal assistance.[1] A sample of these preliminary notices may be found in the reports of any of the mining states. A case involving the following notice, arising under the statute of Colorado, heretofore referred to, reached the supreme court of the United States: "Hawk Lode.—We, the undersigned, claim fif- " teen hundred feet on this mineral-bearing lode, vein, " or deposit,"—dated and signed by the locators. It was contended, and the court below held, that the notice was insufficient because it failed to designate the number of feet on each side of the discovery point. The supreme court of the United States ruled, however, that as the law did not require the linear distances from the discovery monument to be stated, the notice and its posting was a valid appropriation of the lode to the extent of seven hundred and fifty feet on each side of the posted notice.[2] In construing these notices, both the courts and land department have been uniformly liberal. As was said by the supreme court of Utah,—[3]

" When the location was evidently made in good " faith we are not disposed to hold the locator to a " very strict compliance with respect to his location " notice."

As such notices are generally made by unlettered men, it would be productive of a great hardship if prospectors should be held to technical accuracy in their preparation. If they are sufficiently certain to put an honest

---

[1] Carter *v.* Bacigalupi, 83 Cal. 187, 193, 23 Pac. 361.

[2] Erhardt *v.* Boaro, 113 U. S. 527, 5 Sup. Ct. Rep. 560; Bramlett *v.* Flick, 23 Mont. 95, 57 Pac. 869.

[3] Farmington G. M. Co. *v.* Rhymney, 20 Utah, 363, 77 Am. St. Rep. 913, 58 Pac. 832.

inquirer in the way of ascertaining where the lode is, that is sufficient.[1]

When we deal with cases, however, arising under laws similar to those found in Arizona, New Mexico, Oregon, and Utah, and provisions like those of Idaho in reference to the second notice required by that state to be posted, we encounter a different element. Where the posted notice is the basis of the one to be ultimately recorded, the provisions of the federal law are operative, and the posted notice must contain the requirements of that law as to the contents of the record.[2]

"The distinction between the notice of discovery or
" notice of location required to be posted on the claim
" and the certificate or declaratory statement required
" to be filed for record is a substantial one, easily
" understood when the purpose of each is kept in
" mind."[3]

A notice might serve the purpose of a notice of discovery manifesting an intention to locate, and be wholly insufficient as a notice of perfected location which is to be recorded.[4]

In the absence of a state statute or local rule requiring it, the posted notice need not contain any reference to natural objects or permanent monuments, but the recorded notice must contain such description.[5]

[1] Prince of Wales Lode, 2 Copp's L. O. 2; Carter v. Bacigalupi, 83 Cal. 187, 193, 23 Pac. 361; Gird v. California Oil Co., 60 Fed. 531, 544; Book v. Justice M. Co., 58 Fed. 106; Doe v. Waterloo M. Co., 70 Fed. 455; Sanders v. Noble, 22 Mont. 110, 55 Pac. 1037; Wilson v. Triumph Cons. M. Co., 19 Utah, 66, 75 Am. St. Rep. 718, 56 Pac. 300; McCann v. McMillan, 129 Cal. 350, 62 Pac. 31; Wells v. Davis, 22 Utah, 322, 62 Pac. 3; Walsh v. Erwin, 115 Fed. 531.

[2] Deeney v. Mineral Creek M. Co. (N. Mex.), 67 Pac. 724.

[3] Sanders v. Noble, 22 Mont. 110, 55 Pac. 1037, 1046.

[4] Doe v. Waterloo M. Co., 70 Fed. 455, 458; Gleeson v. Martin White M. Co., 13 Nev. 465; Gird v. California Oil Co., 60 Fed. 531, 536.

[5] Brady v. Husby, 21 Nev. 453, 33 Pac. 801; Poujade v. Ryan, 21 Nev. 449, 33 Pac. 659; Southern Cross M. Co. v. Europa M. Co., 15 Nev. 383.

Where a statute or local rule prescribes the form of a notice to be posted, and provides that a copy of such notice shall be recorded, if such notice does not contain the requirement of the federal and state [1] statutes it is an insufficient record. The supreme court of California has said that where district rules provide for the recording of a copy of a posted notice, such record is sufficient; [2] but this must not be understood as sanctioning a rule that the record of a posted notice is sufficient where such posted notice does not contain the facts required by section twenty-three hundred and twenty-four of the Revised Statutes providing for the contents of the record. Neither a local rule nor a state statute can dispense with the plain requirements of the federal law. [3]

§ 356. **Place and manner of posting.**—Most of the state laws requiring notices to be posted fix the point of discovery as the place of posting. Naturally, this will be on the lode, or in such reasonable proximity as will identify it. In California, a local district custom required that a notice of location of a quartz claim should be in writing, "and posted conspicuously in a conspicu-" ous place upon the claim located, at or near the lode " line of said claim."

The supreme court of that state held that such a notice, written on one side of a sheet of paper which was folded with the writing inside and placed upon a mound of rocks three feet high, underneath two flat rocks, with a margin of the paper exposed to view, the rest being obscured by the two stones which covered it, was a conspicuous posting in a conspicuous place, and satisfied the rule. [4]

[1] Purdum v. Laddin, 23 Mont. 387, 59 Pac. 153.
[2] Carter v. Bacigalupi, 83 Cal. 187, 23 Pac. 361.
[3] Post, §§ 389-392.
[4] Donahue v. Meister, 88 Cal. 121, 22 Am. St. Rep. 283, 25 Pac. 1096.

An artificial mound of rocks on the line of a lode is a conspicuous object which would naturally attract the attention of one seeking information as to a former location of a lode, and the slightest examination of the mound would result in the discovery of a written notice.

In another case in the same state, it was held, that a written notice placed in a tin can, and the can placed in a mound of rocks, was sufficient posting.[1]

It is manifest that some precaution should be taken to protect the notice from destruction by exposure to wind and weather.

In the absence of any specific direction in the state statute or district regulation prescribing the manner of posting, any device adopted which would enable one seeking information in good faith to discover the existence of the notice, should be sufficient.[2]   The posting of such a notice after a *bona fide* discovery is an appropriation of the territory specified for the period allowed by local rules or state legislation for the performance of the remaining acts required to complete the location, and the appropriator is entitled during that period to be protected in his possession against all comers.[3]

[1] Gird *v.* California Oil Co., 60 Fed. 531, 544.

[2] *Id.*

[3] *Ante,* § 339; Erhardt *v.* Boaro, 113 U. S. 527, 537, 5 Sup Ct. Rep. 560; Marshall *v.* Harney Peak Tin M. and M. Co., 1 S. Dak. 350, 47 N. W. 290; Omar *v.* Soper, 11 Colo. 380, 387, 7 Am. St. Rep. 246, 18 Pac. 443; Sanders *v.* Noble, 22 Mont. 110, 55 Pac. 1037; Iron Silver M. Co. *v.* Elgin, 118 U. S. 196, 8 Sup. Ct. Rep. 1177.

ARTICLE VI. THE SURFACE COVERED BY THE LOCATION—
ITS FORM AND RELATIONSHIP TO THE LOCATED LODE.

§ 360. The ideal location.

§ 361. Surface area, length, and width of lode claims.

§ 362. Location covering excessive area.

§ 363. Surface conflicts with prior unpatented locations.

§ 363a. Surface conflicts with prior patented mining claims, millsites, and agricultural lands.

§ 364. Surface must include apex. —Location on the dip.

§ 365. The end-lines.

§ 366. The side-lines.

§ 367. Side-end lines.

§ 360. The ideal location.—When we speak of an ideal location, we mean one which not only responds to all the requirements of the law, but one which confers upon its possessor the greatest possible property right, and conforms to the judicial theories of what constitutes the highest type of a perfected location. The ideal is rarely encountered in the practical mining world, but it furnishes a convenient standard with which the every-day location may be compared, enabling us to show to what extent a departure from the ideal diminishes the property rights which are susceptible of acquisition under a location of the highest possible type.

The ideal location must have for its basis an ideal lode, such a one as we have described and illustrated in a preceding section.[1] With this assumed, we should describe the highest type of a location as a rectangular parallelogram, the lines crossing the apex of the lode at right angles to the general course of the vein, termed in law the end-lines, the extremities of which are equidistant from the center of the vein, the side-lines parallel to the course of the vein; that is, equidistant throughout from a line drawn through the center of the apex on its

[1] Ante, § 309.

longitudinal course;[1] such a location as is represented in figure 11.[2] Without intending to enter into a discussion at this time of the extralateral right, we may say that this form of location confers upon the possessor the greatest property rights susceptible of being conveyed under the mining laws applicable to lode claims. It is to this standard that the various forms of locations on the surface which may come under discussion in the future will be compared.

§ 361. **Surface area, length, and width of lode claims.** — Prior to the passage of the act of July 26, 1866, the number and length of claims on a discovered lode, and the extent of surface ground which might be occupied and enjoyed therewith, was, like everything else connected with mining upon the public domain during that period, regulated by district rules or local customs. The act of 1866 fixed the limit of a single claim at two hundred feet in length along the vein, for each locator, except the discoverer, who was entitled to two claims. No person could make more than one location on the same lode, and not more than three thousand feet could be taken by any association of persons.[3]

As to width, this was left entirely to local regulations. When the claimant filed the diagram of his lode on application for patent, he was called upon to extend his claim laterally, so as to conform to the local laws, customs, and rules of miners.[4] In some districts, the width was specified with reference to either the center of the vein or its inclosing walls. In others, the locator was allowed a reasonable quantity of surface. As the lode was the principal thing, and the surface a mere incident, neither

---

[1] Empire M. and M. Co. *v.* Tombstone M. and M. Co., 100 Fed. 910, 913.
[2] *Ante*, § 309.
[3] 14 Stats. at Large, p. 252, § 4.
[4] *Id.*, p. 252, § 2.

the form nor extent of the surface area controlled the rights on the located lode.[1]

The act of May 10, 1872, which is incorporated into the Revised Statutes, changed this rule, giving to the surface boundaries a controlling importance.[2] It fixed the maximum length on the vein at fifteen hundred feet, and a maximum surface width of six hundred feet, three hundred feet on each side of the middle of the vein at the surface.[3]

State or district regulation may limit this width to a minimum of twenty-five feet on each side of the middle of the vein,[4] and we cannot see why the length of a claim may not likewise be limited by state or local rules within the maximum.[5]

Be that as it may, where state statutes deal with the subject at all they follow the lines of the federal law,[6] and no such limitation has ever been attempted by district regulations within our knowledge.

As to width, the maximum allowed by the federal law is the rule, except in a few localities. In Gilpin, Clear Creek, Boulder, and Summit counties, in the state of Colorado, the width is fixed by statute at seventy-five feet on each side of the center of the vein. In all other counties of that state, it is one hundred and fifty feet on each side of the center of the vein,[7] which rule obtains in North Dakota.[8]

These two states also provide that any county at any

[1] *Ante,* § 58.
[2] *Ante,* § 71.
[3] 17 Stats. at Large, p. 91, § 2.
[4] Rev. Stats., § 2320; North Noonday M. Co. *v.* Orient M. Co., 6 Saw. 299, 305, 1 Fed. 522; Jupiter M. Co. *v.* Bodie Cons. M. Co., 7 Saw. 96, 104, 11 Fed. 666; Copp's Min. Dec. 201; *In re* Taylor, 9 Copp's L. O. 52, 92.
[5] Mr. Morrison, in his ''Mining Rights,'' (10th ed., p. 19,) doubts the power of the state to so limit the length, and assigns as a reason that it is a federal limitation.
[6] *Ante,* § 250 (1).
[7] Mills' Annot. Stats., § 3149; Morr. Min. Rights, 10th ed., p. 21.
[8] Rev. Code, 1895, § 1427; *Id.* 1899, § 1427.

general election may determine upon a greater width within the limitations of the federal laws, but Mr. Morrison informs us,[1] that this privilege has never been exercised in Colorado.[2]

With the exceptions above noted, the customary surface area is therefore fifteen hundred by six hundred feet, embracing twenty and two-thirds acres. This may be called the unit of lode locations.

It is entirely immaterial how many or how few locators participate in this class of locations. The size of the "claim," or, more properly, the location, is not governed by the number of persons participating in its appropriation. There is nothing in the law which prevents any one locator or any set of locators from appropriating as many locations on the same lode as they may be able to find independent discoveries upon which to base them,[3] but no *location* may exceed the statutory limit as to length and width.

§ 362.   **Location covering excessive area.**— It frequently happens that the locator marking his surface without the aid of chain or compass includes within his boundaries an area in excess of the statutory limit.

The courts uniformly hold that such a location, where it injures no one at the time it is made, and where it has been made in good faith, is voidable only to the extent of the excess.[4]

---

[1] Morr. Min. Rights, 10th ed., p. 22.

[2] *Ante*, § 250 (2).

[3] Copp's Min. Dec. 207.

The federal laws applicable to the Philippines, however, provide "that no holder shall be entitled to hold in his, its, or their name, or in "the name of any other person, corporation, or association more than "one mineral claim on the same vein or lode." The laws of Oregon (Hill's Annotated Laws, 1892, § 3829) limit the locator to one claim in the same vein. We do not think this is a matter which may be controlled by state legislation. See Appendix.

[4] Rose *v.* Richmond M. Co., 17 Nev. 25, 27 Pac. 1115; Richmond M. Co. *v.* Rose, 114 U. S. 576, 580, 5 Sup. Ct. Rep. 1055; Glacier Mt. S. M. Co. *v.* Willis, 127 U. S. 471, 481, 8 Sup. Ct. Rep. 1214; Hauswirth *v.*

Upon application for patent, the monuments may be moved and the lines drawn in to cast off the excess.[1]

An excessive location cannot be said to be a fraud upon others. It cannot take away rights already acquired by prior appropriation. A location within the statutory limit cannot accomplish this. As to subsequent locators, they can measure the ground from the preliminary discovery notice, which is universally posted at, or in reasonable proximity to, the point of discovery.[2] This notice itself, as a rule, specifies the linear distance claimed from the discovery point, and where it does not, the locator can only claim seven hundred and fifty feet along the vein on each side of his discovery notice.[3]

If the prior locator has too much ground, it is easy to discover it; and all the benefit that a subsequent locator can claim is, that he shall be entitled to maintain his right to the excess.[4]

In a locality where neither state law nor district rules require the posting of a preliminary notice at the discovery point,[5] a case might arise where a location, as

---

Butcher, 4 Mont. 299, 1 Pac. 714; Leggatt v. Stewart, 5 Mont. 107, 109, 2 Pac. 320; Lakin v. Dolly, 53 Fed. 333, S. C. on appeal, 54 Fed. 461; Thompson v. Spray, 72 Cal. 528, 14 Pac. 182; North Noonday M. Co. v. Orient M. Co., 6 Saw. 299, 1 Fed. 522; Jupiter M. Co. v. Bodie Cons. M. Co., 7 Saw. 96, 107, 11 Fed. 666; Atkins v. Hendree, 1 Idaho, 95; Burke v. McDonald, 2 Idaho, 646, 33 Pac. 49; Stemwinder M. Co. v. Emma & L. C. M. Co., 2 Idaho, 421, 21 Pac. 1040, (affirmed on appeal to U. S. Sup. Ct., 149 U. S. 787, 13 Sup. Ct. Rep. 1052, Law. Co-op. ed., book 37, p. 941); Hanson v. Fletcher, 10 Utah, 266, 37 Pac. 480; Howeth v. Sullenger, 113 Cal. 547, 45 Pac. 841; Taylor v. Parenteau, 23 Colo. 368, 48 Pac. 505; Stephens v. Wood, 39 Or. 441, 65 Pac. 602.

[1] *In re* Empey, 10 Copp's L. O. 102; Howeth v. Sullenger, 113 Cal. 547, 45 Pac. 841. See Golden Reward M. Co. v. Buxton M. Co., 79 Fed. 868; Credo M. and S. Co. v. Highland M. and M. Co., 95 Fed. 911, where this rule was applied.

[2] *Ante,* § 350.

[3] Erhardt v. Boaro, 113 U. S. 527, 5 Sup. Ct. Rep. 560.

[4] Atkins v. Hendree, 1 Idaho, 95, 100.

[5] *Ante,* § 350.

marked, includes so large an area as to give rise to the suspicion of bad faith. In such a case, where such preliminary notice is wanting, there would be nothing to guide the subsequent locator, and the excessive location should be held worthless for any purpose.[1] A fifteen-hundred-foot claim cannot be shifted from one end to the other of a two-thousand-foot claim, as circumstances might require, to cover the discovery of a third person within the two-thousand-foot location.[2]

As we have heretofore stated, however, the general, if not universal, rule is to hold this class of location void only as to the excess.

§ 363. **Surface conflicts with prior unpatented locations.**—In the first edition of this treatise the author thus expressed his views on the subject of surface conflicts with prior locations:—

"As a mining location can only be carved out of the "unappropriated public domain, it necessarily follows "that a subsequent locator may not invade the surface "territory of his neighbors and include within his "boundaries any part of a prior valid and subsisting "location. But conflicts of surface area are more than "frequent. Many of them arise from honest mistake, "others from premeditated design. In both instances "the question of priority of appropriation is the con-"trolling element which determines the rights of the "parties. Two locations cannot legally occupy the "same place at the same time. These conflicts some-"times involve a segment of the same vein, on its "strike; at others, they involve the dip-bounding "planes underneath the surface. More frequently, "however, they pertain to mere overlapping surfaces. "The same principles of law apply with equal force "to all classes of cases. Such property rights as are "conferred by a valid prior location, so long as such

[1] Ledoux v. Forester, 94 Fed. 600.
[2] Hauswirth v. Butcher, 4 Mont. 299, 1 Pac. 714; Leggatt v. Stewart, 5 Mont. 107, 109, 2 Pac. 320.

" location remains valid and subsisting, are preserved
" from invasion, and cannot be infringed or impaired
" by subsequent locators.   To the extent, therefore,
" that a subsequent location includes any portion of the
" surface lawfully appropriated and held by another,
" to that extent such location is void.''

The decisions of the courts rendered since the appearance of the first edition, as well as those of the land department, taking its text to some degree at least from the judicial exposition of the law, require a modification of the author's previous views.

It is well settled that a junior locator cannot by invading the limits of a prior grant, and attempting to make a location conflicting with such grant, acquire any rights which might in any way infringe upon those of the previous locator.   However regular in form such a junior location might be, it is of no effect as against rights conferred upon the prior locator so long as the prior location is subsisting.[1]

As was said by the supreme court of the United States in this behalf,—

"A valid location appropriates the surface, and the
" rights given by such location cannot, so long as it
" remains in force, be disturbed by any acts of third
" parties.   Whatever rights on or beneath the surface
" passed to the first locator can in no manner be dimin-
" ished or affected by a subsequent location.''[2]

It does not necessarily follow from this that a junior locator may not lay any of the lines of his lode location over, upon, or across the lines of a senior location for

---

[1] Belk v. Meagher, 3 Mont. 65, S. C. on appeal, 104 U. S. 279; Garthe v. Hart, 73 Cal. 541, 15 Pac. 93; Souter v. Maguire, 78 Cal. 543, 21 Pac. 183; Aurora Hill Cons. M. Co. v. 85 Mining Co., 12 Saw. 355, 34 Fed. 515; Stewart v. Rees, 25 L. D. 447; Argentine M. Co. v. Benedict, 18 Utah, 183, 55 Pac. 559; Kinney v. Fleming (Ariz.), 56 Pac. 729.

[2] Del Monte M. and M. Co. v. Last Chance M. Co., 171 U. S. 55, 79, 18 Sup. Ct. Rep. 895.

the purpose of acquiring rights not in conflict with the claim having priority. It is now well settled that the lines of such junior locator may be so laid as to create a surface conflict with the prior location for the purpose of defining for or securing to such junior location underground or extralateral rights not in conflict with any rights of the senior location.[1]

A simple illustration of this principle will suffice. Figure 31 represents three lode claims, A, B, and D, with priorities in the order named. The underground

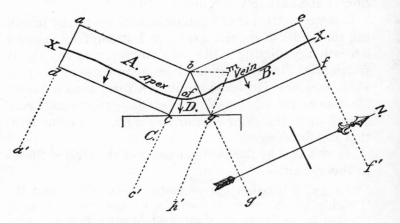

FIGURE 31.

segment of the vein c-c' and g-h' has not been appropriated by either A or B. D has located by the lines describing the parallelogram b-m-g-c, inclosing the triangle b-c-g, which is free unappropriated public land containing the apex of a discovered vein. In doing so, a part of his surface overlaps the claim of B, and the conflict area, b-m-g, contains a part of the apex of the vein.

In making the location in this way, D has deprived B

---

[1] Del Monte M. and M. Co. v. Last Chance M. Co., *supra*.

of nothing. If B should ultimately abandon the location, the conflict area would not fall to D.[1]

D might subsequent to the abandonment of the conflict area by B amend his location and include the overlapping surface,[2] but, without some act on his part manifesting an intention to make a new appropriation or acquire a new right after the abandonment or forfeiture became effectual, this area would not by mere gravity become a part of the junior location,[3] except for the purpose of defining the extralateral right.

The placing by D of the location lines across and upon B's surface is not necessarily a trespass.[4] It may be conceded that such a conflicting junior location may not be made by a forcible entry upon the actual possession of the senior. Perhaps the senior locator might prevent the making of the junior location so far as the placing of the lines over the prior claim was concerned.[5] But an entry upon the surface of the senior claim, openly and peaceably and in good faith, claiming nothing as against the prior claim, gives no cause of complaint to the senior claimant.

"Certainly if the rights of the prior locator are not "infringed upon, who is prejudiced by awarding to the "second locator all the benefits which the statute gives "to the making of a claim?"[6]

The circuit court of appeals for the ninth circuit expresses the following views:—

[1] Belk *v.* Meagher, 104 U. S. 279, 285; Oscamp *v.* Crystal River M. Co., 58 Fed. 293, 295; Jordan *v.* Duke (Ariz.), 53 Pac. 197; Reynolds *v.* Pascoe (Utah), 66 Pac. 1064.

[2] Johnson *v.* Young, 18 Colo. 625, 34 Pac. 173.

[3] Pralus *v.* Pacific G. and S. M. Co., 35 Cal. 30, 36.

[4] Del Monte M. and M. Co. *v.* Last Chance M. Co., 171 U. S. 55, 83, 18 Sup. Ct. Rep. 895; Cleary *v.* Skiffich, 28 Colo. 362, 365, 65 Pac. 59, 60.

[5] Bunker Hill and Sullivan M. and C. Co. *v.* Empire State-Idaho M. and D. Co., 109 Fed. 538, 541.

[6] Del Monte M. and M. Co. *v.* Last Chance M. Co., 171 U. S. 55, 84, 18 Sup. Ct. Rep. 895.

"It is the settled law that for the purpose of acquir-
"ing the extralateral rights conferred by the statute a
"locator may place his lines on a prior mining location
"with the consent of such prior locator, or when it is
"done openly and aboveboard without objection on his
"part, which in reality constitutes consent."[1]

To what limit this doctrine may be applied is a question difficult to determine. Some unique contentions
are made with regard to it which will be considered in
the discussion of the extralateral-right problems.

The land department has elaborated this doctrine to
some extent, and in passing upon patent applications
has recognized the right of a junior locator to cross a
senior location, the patent issuing to the junior proprietor for the tract described, excepting and reserving
the area in conflict with the senior location.

The following figures illustrate the present views of
the department on the subject.

Figure 32 exhibits the Hallett and Hamburg lode
claims for which a patent was applied, and which
were in conflict with the numerous prior locations shown
on the diagram. The patent application excluded the
area in conflict with the locations having priority. A
protest was filed against the issuance of the patent on
the ground, among others, that the end-lines and corners
of the claims applied for were within and upon the
surface of valid prior locations. The secretary dismissed the protests, upholding the validity of the locations in the form shown on the figure, citing the Del
Monte case[2] as authority for his ruling.[3] It requires
more intimate familiarity with the properties delineated
on the diagram than the author possesses to determine

[1] Empire State-Idaho M. and D. Co. v. Bunker Hill and Sullivan M.
and C. Co., 114 Fed. 417, 419.
[2] 171 U. S. 55, 18 Sup. Ct. Rep. 895.
[3] Hallett and Hamburg Lodes, 27 L. D. 104.

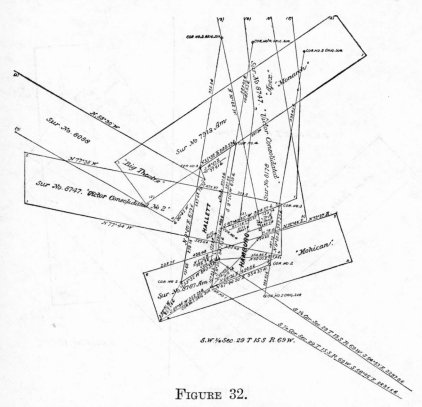

FIGURE 32.

just what passed by the patent to the Hallett and Hamburg claims after deducting the conflicting areas.

Figure 33 presents a later case involving the same method of location. The Hustler and New Year claims, shown on this figure, were contiguous and held in common ownership. A group patent was applied for. Owing to the conflict between the Hustler and Fort Wilcox, the latter being the prior location, the commissioner of the general land office, directed the drawing in of the Hustler end-lines, and making a new end-line, *c-d*. This destroyed the contiguity of the group applied for, and as the applicant accepted for the time being the com-

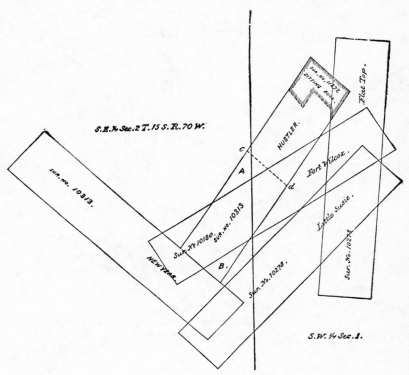

FIGURE 33.

missioner's ruling, he received a patent for the New Year alone. He subsequently repented of his action, and applied to the secretary of the interior for a reinstatement of his entry and requested that patent issue for the Hustler, after deducting conflicts with senior locations. The secretary reversed the action of the commissioner, principally on the ground that the ruling cut the claimant off from two small triangular areas marked A and B on the figure, which were embraced within the original location. Patent was directed to issue in accordance with the claimant's application. The Del Monte case was cited as authority for this decision.[1]

[1] Hustler and New Year Lode Claims, 29 L. D. 668.

In the case of the War Dance lode,[1] a junior location, which ran entirely across a senior location and terminated in another junior but excepted claim, was passed to patent on the strength of the Del Monte case and the decision of the secretary in Hallett and Hamburg lodes (*supra*), as there was a small parcel of free ground outside of the conflicting and excluded area which was within the limits of the original War Dance location. It is manifest from a consideration of the series of decisions handed down by the secretary of the interior on this subject that the rule announced by the supreme court of the United States in the Del Monte case has been applied with extreme liberality, and in several instances at least to conditions which did not fall within either the motive or *rationale* of the judicial decision upon which the later departmental rulings were based. In the light of the later revelation, it would be difficult to conceive of a case of junior conflicts with senior locations which would not receive the sanction of the department. Evidently the simplicity of the rule announced by the author in the first edition of the work, and quoted at the beginning of the section, has given way to one of complexity by a progressive method of interpretation.

Prior to the decision of the Del Monte case, the land department enforced the rule that the rights of the junior locator did not extend beyond an end-line passing through the point where the lode intersected the exterior line of the senior location,[2] and that the surface right as an adjunct to the lode could not extend beyond that point.[3]

If a junior lode location so intersected a prior claim as to divide the later claim into two parts, the claim-

---

[1] 29 L. D. 256.

[2] Engineer M. and D. Co., 8 L. D. 361; Consolidated M. Co., 11 L. D. 250; Correction Lode, 15 L. D. 67; Stranger Lode, 28 L. D. 321.

[3] Pleona Lode, 11 L. D. 236.

ant was either compelled to elect which of the two disconnected parts he would take or the entry was confined to that part containing his discovery.[1]

The Del Monte case did not in terms purport to decide
anything more than that a junior locator might, for the
purpose of defining an extralateral right not secured
by prior location, place his end-lines upon the senior
claim. The land department permits the laying of such
lines entirely across the senior claim, not only for this
purpose, but for the purpose of acquiring surfaces not
covered by the older location. When the patent issues
for this class of claims, it necessarily reserves all property rights pertaining to the senior claim. We do not
conceive that there is any wrong done to any one by
the adoption of this rule. An interpretation of this
kind seems the only possible solution of some of the
difficulties surrounding locations in districts situated
as in Cripple Creek, Colorado, with its intricate network
of veins running in every conceivable direction. In
fact, the "cross-lode" questions arising in this district,
and the difficulty of their solution, have undoubtedly
influenced the later departmental rulings. Such rulings
have received the sanction of the courts,[2] and the practice based thereon may be said to be definitely settled.

§ 363a. **Surface conflicts with prior patented mining claims, millsites, and agricultural lands.** —The rule
having once been sanctioned that junior lode claimants
might lay the lines of their locations upon or across

[1] Andromeda Lode, 13 L. D. 146; Bimetallic Lode, 15 L. D. 309;
Mabel Lode, 26 L. D. 675.

[2] Calhoun G. M. Co. v. Ajax G. M. Co., 27 Colo. 1, 22, 83 Am. St. Rep.
17, 59 Pac. 607, 616, S. C. on appeal, 182 U. S. 499, 21 Sup. Ct. Rep. 885;
Bunker Hill and Sullivan M. and C. Co. v. Empire State-Idaho M. and D.
Co., 109 Fed. 538, 541; Id., 106 Fed. 471, 472, S. C. on writ of error,
sub nom. Empire State-Idaho M. and D. Co. v. Bunker Hill and Sullivan
M. and C. Co., 114 Fed. 417, 419; Crown Point M. Co. v. Buck, 97
Fed. 462.

those of a senior lode location, the extension of the doctrine to patented mining claims, millsites, and agricultural lands was not only accompanied with no serious embarrassment, but such result was natural and logical. A valid unpatented mining location, as against every one save the government, is in effect a grant. The estate enjoyed is in the nature of an estate in fee.[1]

There is no reason which could be urged in support of permitting junior locators to lay the lines of their claims across prior unpatented claims which could not be invoked in behalf of similar doctrine as applied to patented claims of all classes. This is quite forcibly pointed out in the opinion of the secretary of the interior in the case of the Hidee lode,[2] hereafter to be specially noted.

Judge Hallett, in his opinion dismissing the bill in the Del Monte case, (from whose decision an appeal was taken to the circuit court of appeals, which certified the case to the supreme court of the United States,) thus announced his views:—

"I think that the lines of a claim may be located "wholly or partly upon other territory,—that is, terri- "tory which is not open to location,—for the purpose "of determining the extralateral questions. In other "words, the locator, in order to make a valid location, "is bound to locate his lines so as to be of a rectangular "form, and if in so locating them he gets upon the "territory of other claimants, whether at the time of "such location the claims adjacent have or have not "been patented, his lines are well laid with reference "to the territory subject to location; . . . and even if "the lines fell upon other claims which had already "passed to patent, the result would be the same."[3]

---

[1] *Post*, § 539.

[2] 30 L. D. 420.

[3] Not reported. Judge Hallett's opinion did not form a part of the record certified up to the supreme court of the United States by the circuit court of appeals, eighth circuit. The opinion, however, was

The secretary of the interior, in an ably prepared opinion in the Hidee lode case,[1] reached the result concisely and comprehensively stated in the *syllabus* to the case as follows:—

"The location lines of a lode mining claim are used
" only to describe, define, and limit property rights in
" the claim, and may be laid within, upon, or across the
" surface of patented lode claims for the purpose of
" claiming the free and unappropriated ground within
" such lines and the veins apexing in such ground, and
" of defining and securing extralateral underground
" rights upon all such veins where such lines (*a*) are
" established openly and peaceably, (*b*) do not embrace
" any larger area of surface, claimed and unclaimed,
" than the law permits."[2]

A similar rule was subsequently prescribed with regard to placing the lines of a junior lode location over prior patented agricultural land.[3] A contrary doctrine had been previously announced.[4]

Following the same line of reasoning, it was also held that an application for a patent to a lode mining claim may embrace ground lying on opposite sides of an intersecting millsite, with the proviso, however, that the lode or vein upon which the location is based has been discovered in both parts of the lode location which were not in conflict with the millsite.[5]

The courts have approached the question determined in the case of the Hidee lode cautiously, and as yet it cannot be said that there is unquestioned judicial authority for the principle there announced.

before the court of last resort, it having been printed in the brief and argument of appellee (Messrs. Teller, Wolcott, and Vaile), from which the foregoing extract was taken. The secretary of the interior, in his opinion in the Hidee lode, refers to it (30 L. D. 420, 427).

[1] 30 L. D. 420.
[2] Rule reannounced in Mono Fraction Lode Claim, 31 L. D. 122.
[3] Alice Lode Mining Claim, 30 L. D. 481.
[4] Bimetallic Lode, 15 L. D. 309.
[5] Paul Jones Lode, 31 L. D. 359.

The circuit court of appeals for the ninth circuit upon
one occasion, where the precise question was not necessarily involved, stated the rule laid down by the secretary of the interior without comment.[1] In a subsequent
case, where the point was directly raised, but not necessary to be decided, as the ultimate determination was
reached upon grounds not involving the question, the
same court, after announcing the doctrine of the Del
Monte case, said: "And perhaps the same thing may
" be done on patented claims where the lines are estab-
" lished openly and peaceably."[2]

The supreme court of Colorado expressed grave
doubts as to the soundness of the secretary's decision
in the Hidee case. While conceding the force of the
doctrine of the Del Monte case as applied to junior locations overlapping prior unpatented claims, it fails to
find in that case any support for the contention that
the junior locator may have that privilege with reference to a senior patented claim. Said that court:—

"After patent has issued, the legal title to the land
" conveyed by it has passed wholly from the govern-
" ment. The holder of this title is wholly beyond the
" jurisdiction of the land department; and it would
" seem that no one can initiate by trespass upon his
" tract any right whatever, whether it be committed
" ignorantly or not. . . . If the law is as counsel con-
" tend, then a patent does not convey an absolute
" estate, but only a qualified fee, and leaves the land
" still subject to some rights in the government, a doc-
" trine for which there seems to be no warrant in the
" statute. So long as the land is not patented, the legal
" title is still in the government, and it may be argued
" with some force that while held under location merely,
" it is still within the jurisdiction of the land depart-

[1] Bunker Hill and Sullivan M. and C.. Co. v. Empire State-Idaho M.
and D. Co., 109 Fed. 538, 542.

[2] Empire State-Idaho M. and D. Co. v. Bunker Hill and Sullivan M.
and C. Co., 114 Fed. 417, 419.

" ment, and for that reason it is within the province of
" its authority to say that a junior locator may law-
" fully go upon it and mark his boundaries and erect
" his monuments upon its surface in order to initiate
" rights in lands not carried by it." [1]

"We do not understand, however, how the United
" States government may convey any right to lands by
" consent of an adjoining owner under patent which it
" could not convey without such consent." [2]

The case in which the language was used was an
extreme one, wherein the doctrine of the Del Monte case,
as well as the Hidee case, was put to a very severe test.
But as the questions there involved were decided, "con-
" ceding for the purpose of the discussion" that the
rule announced in the Hidee case was a correct exposition of the law, it cannot be said that the decision of the
Colorado court is a precedent which condemns the
Hidee rule where invoked in a proper case.

The application of these rules will confront us when
we come to deal with the law on the subject of extralateral rights, where we shall have occasion to recur to
this subject. The foregoing are all the expressions of
both courts and land department touching these questions which have come under our observation. We have
here been dealing exclusively with the privileges of
junior lode claimants. Some discussion of these principles will be necessary when we reach the subject of
placer claims.

§ 364. Surface must include apex of vein—Location
on the dip.—There can be no question but that the act
of July 26, 1866, contemplated a linear location along
the course of the vein as exposed at the surface, where
there was an outcropping exposure, or along the top or

---

[1] State v. District Court (Colo.), 65 Pac. 1020, 1024.
[2] Id., 1025.

upper edge of the vein nearest to the surface, where there was no outcrop.[1]

The existing laws require that the top, or apex, of the vein, to some extent at least, should be found within the limits of the location, as defined on the surface,[2] at least as a condition precedent to the enjoyment of the extralateral right. We do not feel justified in asserting that a location on the dip of the vein which does not include any part of the apex is under all circumstances void. It might happen that the true apex of a vein is embraced within a prior grant of such a character as to prevent the owner from following the vein on its downward course out of his vertical boundaries, conditions such as are outlined or suggested in a preceding section;[3] or the deposit may be a bedded vein, occupying a horizontal position in the mass of the mountain, without any definable apex,[4] or where the inclination of the vein from the horizontal is so slight as to require extensive development in order to ascertain which is the top and which the side edge or bottom of the vein, as illustrated in the South Dakota and Idaho cases, discussed in section three hundred and ten, and to some degree in the Leadville cases, referred to in section three hundred and eleven. Under such conditions it is quite possible that by a surface location not covering the true apex the locator might acquire the exclusive right to the surface and the underlying vein as against all persons save those who fortuitously covered the true apex in such a way as to confer upon

---

[1] Eureka Case, 4 Saw. 302, Fed. Cas. No. 4548; McCormick v. Varnes, 2 Utah, 355; Wolfley v. Lebanon, 4 Colo. 112.

[2] Flagstaff M. Co. v. Tarbet, 98 U. S. 463, 467; Argentine M. Co. v. Terrible M. Co., 122 U. S. 478, 485, 2 Sup. Ct. Rep. 256; Iron S. M. Co. v. Elgin, 118 U. S. 196, 6 Sup. Ct. Rep. 1177; Doe v. Sanger, 83 Cal. 203, 23 Pac. 363; Watervale v. Leach (Ariz.), 33 Pac. 418; King v. Amy & Silversmith M. Co., 9 Mont. 543, 24 Pac. 200.

[3] *Ante,* § 312a.

[4] See Homestake M. Co., 29 L. D. 689.

them the right to laterally pursue the vein underneath
the surface of the claim overlying the dip. We are now
considering the general rule as announced by the courts,
whose opinions do not necessarily deal with all conceivable exceptions. A discussion of possible exceptions
involves a consideration of extralateral-right problems
which must be reserved for future consideration.

This general rule may be thus concisely stated: A
location cannot be made on the middle of a vein or otherwise than on the top, or apex.[1]

As was said by Judge Hallett in one of the early
Leadville cases,— "It is a part of the statute law of the
" United States that locations shall be upon the top and
" apex of the vein; . . . that being done, gives the
" miner the whole vein,[2] and that the locator must find
" where the top or apex is and make his location with
" reference to that." [3]

It is true, he subsequently charged a jury that a
junior location along the line of the top, or apex, could
not prevail against a senior location on the dip;[4] but this
last ruling is not in accord with the decisions of the
supreme court of the United States, as we shall have
occasion to point out in a subsequent section.[5]

The question of priority is an important and material
inquiry only where there are overlapping surfaces,
or where the contending parties have some portion
of the apex of the same vein and a conflict arises between
them involving extralateral bounding planes under-

[1] Iron S. M. Co. v. Murphy, 2 McCrary, 121, 3 Fed. 368, 1 Morr. Min.
Rep. 548; Stevens v. Williams, 1 Morr. Min. Rep. 557, Fed. Cas. No.
13,414; Leadville M. Co. v. Fitzgerald, 4 Morr. Min. Rep. 380, Fed. Cas.
No. 8158; Larkin v. Upton, 144 U. S. 19, 12 Sup. Ct. Rep. 614; Colorado
Central C. M. Co. v. Turck, 50 Fed. 888, S. C. on rehearing, 54 Fed. 267.

[2] Iron S. M. Co. v. Murphy, 2 McCrary, 121, 3 Fed. 368, 1 Morr. Min.
Rep. 548, 550, 551.

[3] Stevens v. Williams, 1 Morr. Min. Rep. 557, 562, Fed. Cas. No. 13,414.

[4] Van Zandt v. Argentine M. Co., 8 Fed. 725, 728.

[5] Post, § 611.

neath the surface, such as are found in the Del Monte case,[1] in the Tyler-Last Chance litigation,[2] in the Stem-winder-Emma-Last Chance litigation,[3] and other cases to be noted under the topic of extralateral rights.

Any portion of the apex on its course will be sufficient to support the location,[4] but upon the extent and course of this apex within the location depends the extent of rights acquired.[5]

As was said by the supreme court of Montana,—

"On principle the identity of the apex of a vein with
" its spurs and extensions must be the crucial test by
" which are to be fixed the proprietary rights to that
" vein and the mineral therein." [6]

Sometimes it happens that a prior locator fails to include the entire width of the apex of the vein within his boundaries, and that such apex is bisected along its course by a side-line common to two locations. While in such cases some of the courts have held that both locations are valid to the extent of everything within their vertical boundaries, but that neither claim has any extralateral right,[7] others award the extralateral right to the prior location.[8] Still others award an extra-

---

[1] 171 U. S. 55, 18 Sup. Ct. Rep. 895.

[2] 54 Fed. 284; 71 Fed. 848; 61 Fed. 557; 157 U. S. 683, 15 Sup. Ct. Rep. 733.

[3] 114 Fed. 417.

[4] Larkin v. Upton, 144 U. S. 19, 12 Sup. Ct. Rep. 644.

[5] Del Monte M. and M. Co. v. Last Chance M. Co., 171 U. S. 55, 66, 67, 18 Sup. Ct. Rep. 895; Stevens v. Williams, 1 McCrary, 480, 1 Morr. Min. Rep. 566, Fed. Cas. No. 13,413; Cosmopolitan M. Co. v. Foote, 101 Fed. 518, and cases there cited.

[6] Butte and Boston M. Co. v. Société Anonyme des Mines, 23 Mont. 177, 75 Am. St. Rep. 505, 58 Pac. 111, 113.

[7] Hall v. Equator, Carpenter's Mining Code, 3 ed., p. 65; Raymond's "Law of the Apex." The case is not reported elsewhere. See quotations from this case under the Broad lode discussion, *post*, § 583.

[8] Bullion Beck and Champion M. Co. v. Eureka Hill M. Co., 5 Utah, 3, 11 Pac. 515; St. Louis M. and M. Co. v. Montana Limited, 104 Fed. 664; Bunker Hill and Sullivan M. and C. Co. v. Empire State-Idaho M. and D. Co., 106 Fed. 471.

lateral right to both, that of the junior taking effect within the plane of his extended end-lines after they pass beyond the conflict with those of the one having priority.[1] But all courts agree that such a location covering a part of the width of the apex is valid, to some extent at least. They differ only as to the extent of the rights conferred on the respective locators. We shall necessarily elaborate the discussion of the "broad lode" question when dealing with the subject of extralateral rights.[2] Questions of this character are so intimately associated with other problems as to render it impossible to consider them without anticipating, to some degree at least, their application in connection with the subjects with which they are blended.

It has been strenuously urged that a location, in order to enjoy any extralateral privileges, should be so laid on the surface as to cover the true course of the vein on a level,—i. e. the engineer's strike, as explained in a previous section,[3]—regardless of the course of the apex at or near the surface; that the locator must before perfecting his location ascertain the strike, or course, of the vein on a level, and so lay his end-lines that in following the vein in its downward course he would not follow it more along the course than upon the true dip. This contention, however, has thus far received no encouragement from the courts.

It was said by the supreme court of the United States in the Flagstaff case (italics are ours):—

" We do not mean to say that a vein must necessa-
" rily crop out upon the surface in order that locations
" may be properly laid upon it. If it lies entirely
" beneath the surface and the *course* of its *apex* can be
" ascertained by sinking shafts at different points, such

[1] Empire State-Idaho M. and D. Co. *v.* Bunker Hill and Sullivan M. and C. Co., 114 Fed. 417, reversing 106 Fed. 471, *supra.*
[2] *Post*, § 583.
[3] § 319.

" shafts may be adopted as indicating the position and
" course of the vein, and locations may be properly
" made on the surface above it so as to secure a right
" to the vein beneath. But where the vein does crop
" out along the surface, or is so slightly covered by
" foreign matter that the *course* of its *apex* can be ascer-
" tained by ordinary surface exploration, we think that
" the act of congress requires that this course should
" be substantially followed in laying claims and loca-
" tions upon it. Perhaps the law is not so perfect in
" this regard as it might be; perhaps the true course
" of a vein should correspond with its strike or the line
" of a level run through it; but this can rarely be ascer-
" tained until considerable work has been done and
" after claims and locations have become fixed. The
" most practicable rule is to regard the course of the
" vein as that which is indicated by surface outcrop,
" or surface explorations and workings. It is on this
" line that claims will naturally be laid, whatever be
" the character of the surface, whether level or
" inclined." [1]

The contention that surface location lines should be
placed with regard to the course of the vein on a level
rather than the course of the apex was urged before
Judge Beatty in another case,[2] and before the circuit
court of appeals,[3] but it was practically ignored.

That such a contention cannot be reconciled with the
adjudicated cases on the subject may be easily demonstrated by the illustration of a hypothetical case.
Figure 34 represents two locations—A and B. The
outcropping vein is exposed on a steep hillside, so that
the course of the outcropping apex is widely divergent
from that of the true course of the vein on a level,—
i. e. the *strike*-line. This is not an uncommon occurrence. It is plain that the course of the apex, *x-y-z*,

---

[1] Flagstaff *v.* Tarbet, 98 U. S. 463, 469.
[2] Bunker Hill and Sullivan M. and C. Co. *v.* Empire State-Idaho M.
and D. Co., 108 Fed. 189, 195.
[3] *Id.,* on writ of error, 114 Fed. 420.

is the "true course of the vein upon the surface."
Let x represent the point of discovery, and let the strike
be determined by means of a short discovery tunnel,
x-w. The question suggested is, Should the discoverer
on making his location follow the line of strike as in
location A, ignoring the segment of the apex, y-z, or
should he follow the apex as in location B?

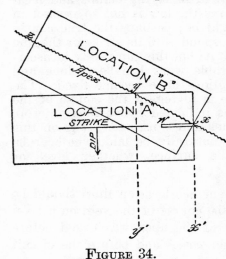

FIGURE 34.

If he selected A, he
would lose all rights
on the vein after it
departed out of the
side-line at y. This
has been conclusively
determined by the
courts.[1]

Sufficient has been
said to demonstrate
that in making loca-
tions on the surface
regard should be had
to the position of the
apex, outcropping or
blind, as it actually

exists in the ground located, if the locator desires to
secure the maximum rights on the vein at and underneath the surface as contemplated by the mining laws.
His rights will suffer diminution in proportion to his
disregard of this requirement.

"Whenever a party has acquired the title to ground
" within whose surface area is the *apex* of a vein with
" a few or many feet along its" (*the apex's*) "course or
" strike, a right to follow the vein on its dip for the
" same length ought to be awarded to him if it can be

[1] Del Monte M. and M. Co. *v.* Last Chance M. Co., 171 U. S. 55, 18 Sup.
Ct. Rep. 895; Clark *v.* Fitzgerald, 171 U. S. 92, 18 Sup. Ct. Rep. 941;
Parrot Silver and Copper Co. *v.* Heinze, 25 Mont. 139, 87 Am. St. Rep.
386, 64 Pac. 326, 328.

" done, and only if it can be done under any fair and
" natural construction of the language of the statute.
" If the surface of the ground was everywhere level
" and veins constantly pursued a straight line, there
" would be little difficulty in legislation to provide for
" all contingencies, but mineral is apt to be found in
" mountainous regions where great irregularity of sur-
" face exists and the course or strike of veins is as
" irregular as the surface, so that many cases may arise
" in which statutory provisions will fail to secure to a
" discoverer of a vein such an amount thereof as equi-
" tably it would seem he ought to receive." [1]

It requires no argument to demonstrate that in the
use of the terms "course" and "strike of the vein,"
appearing in the foregoing quotation, the court had no
reference to the technical engineer's strike of the vein or
to the course of the vein on a level. "Strike," as we
have heretofore explained, is the equivalent to the
course on a level.[2] Where the ground is undulating
there can be no "strike" of an apex. The court in
its opinion referred to the course of the *apex*. This
is not only manifest from the entire context, but is
emphasized in another portion of the opinion,[3] where
the court quotes approvingly from a decision by Judge
Beatty, United States district judge of Idaho, sitting
as circuit judge, as follows (italics are ours) :—

" Upon the fact that *an apex* is within the surface
" lines all his underground rights are based. When,
" then, he owns an *apex*, whether it extends through
" the entire or through but a part of his location, it
" should follow that he owns an equal length of the
" ledge to its utmost depth. These are the important
" rights granted by the law. Take them away and we
" take all from the law that is of value to the miner." [4]

[1] Del Monte M. and M. Co. *v.* Last Chance M. Co., 171 U. S. 55, 66,
18 Sup. Ct. Rep. 895.

[2] *Ante*, § 319.

[3] 171 U. S. 91, 18 Sup. Ct. Rep. 895.

[4] Tyler M. Co. *v.* Last Chance M. Co., 71 Fed. 848, 851.

§ **365.   The end-lines.**—The function of end-lines may be said to be twofold:—

(1) They stop the pursuit of the vein on its strike;

(2) When properly constructed with reference to the located lode, permitting the exercise of the extralateral right, they may be produced indefinitely in their own direction, so that vertical planes drawn downward through them, as so produced, carve out a segment of the vein throughout its entire depth, the ownership of which becomes vested in the locator, provided that the end-line planes as extended do not conflict with the extralateral-right planes of a prior locator.

The location of a mining claim, as made and defined, must control not only the rights of the claimant to the vein or lode within its surface, but also any extralateral rights. The locator must stand upon his own location, and can take only what it will give him under the law. The courts cannot relocate his claim and make new side- or end-lines.[1]

As heretofore observed,[2] the act of 1866 did not in terms mention end-lines, although in the sense that they were necessary to determine the right to pursue the vein on the longitudinal or horizontal course, they were implied.[3] They were not required to be parallel.[4]

Under the act of May 10, 1872, however, their sub-

---

[1] King v. Amy & Silversmith M. Co., 152 U. S. 222, 14 Sup. Ct. Rep. 510; Del Monte M. and M. Co. v. Last Chance M. Co., 171 U. S. 55, 18 Sup. Ct. Rep. 895.

[2] *Ante*, § 58.

[3] Eureka Case, 4 Saw. 302, Fed. Cas. No. 4548.

[4] Iron S. M. Co. v. Elgin M. Co., 118 U. S. 196, 208, 6 Sup. Ct. Rep. 1177; Walrath v. Champion, 63 Fed. 552, 556; Cons. Wyoming v. Champion, 63 Fed. 540, 550; Carson City G. and S. M. Co. v. North Star M. Co., 73 Fed. 597, 599; *Id.*, C. C. A., 83 Fed. 658, 669; Eureka case, 4 Saw. 302, 309, Fed. Cas. No. 4548; Richmond M. Co. v. Eureka M. Co., 103 U. S. 839, 847.

stantial parallelism, or at least their non-divergence in the direction of the dip, is an absolute essential to the right of extralateral pursuit. It has been said that the provisions of this act as to parallelism are merely directory, and that no consequence is attached to a deviation from its direction.[1] But this is undoubtedly an erroneous view.[2]

A location with non-parallel end-lines is not necessarily wholly void. There is liberty of surface form within the statutory limits.[3] If other conditions are complied with, such a location will, subject to the dip rights of others who have properly located on the apex, hold everything within vertical planes drawn through the surface boundaries. The rights conferred, however, by such a location are not so great as in case of one having the end-lines parallel. The consequences of non-parallelism of end-lines will be fully presented in a subsequent chapter, when dealing with the subject of extralateral rights.[4]

While it may be true that the highest type of the ideal or theoretical location may suggest that the end-lines of a location should be at right angles to the true course of the vein, there is nothing in the law which requires it, either expressly or by implication. In fact, locations, as a rule, which, as we have heretofore explained, are required to conform to the surface course of the apex, could rarely be made to also conform to such ideal, without the loss of substantial rights on the vein.[5] While the ideal location may suggest the form shown in

[1] Eureka Case, 4 Saw. 302, 319; Horswell v. Ruiz, 67 Cal. 111.

[2] Iron S. M. Co. v. Elgin M. Co., 118 U. S. 196, 6 Sup. Ct. Rep. 1177; Argonaut M. Co. v. Kennedy M. Co., 131 Cal. 15, 23; 82 Am. St. Rep. 317, 63 Pac. 148.

[3] Walrath v. Champion M. Co., 171 U. S. 293, 312, 18 Sup. Ct. Rep. 909.

[4] *Post*, § 582.

[5] *Ante*, § 364.

figure 35, where the end-lines cross the lode at right
angles to its general course, a location marked on the

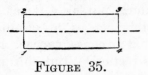

FIGURE 35.

ground with end-lines crossing the apex of the lode at
acute or obtuse angles, as indicated in figures 36 and 37,

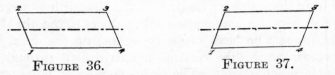

FIGURE 36.   FIGURE 37.

is just as valid and complete, and the extent of property
rights conferred thereby just as great, as in the ideal
location, because the end-lines cross the lode, and are
parallel. The land officers have no right to require that
an end-line shall make a right angle, or any other particular angle, with the general direction of the vein. It is
the locator's privilege to give such direction to his end-
lines as he pleases, so long as they are across the apex
of the vein, are parallel to each other, and the length of
the lode measured between them, on direct line between
the extreme points on the vein within the location, does
not exceed the statutory limit of fifteen hundred feet.[1]

It is a matter of common knowledge that veins are
not of uniform value throughout, but that frequently the
"pay ore" occurs in "shoots," at intervals in the course
of the vein, and that these "shoots" have frequently,
in the language of the miner, a right- or left-hand
"pitch." There is no reason why the locator should
not be permitted to mark his end-lines, observing the
statutory requirement as to parallelism, with regard to

[1] Monarch of the North Mining Claim, 8 Copp's L. O. 104.

the pitch of the ore bodies within the vein, if he is
fortunate enough to detect their existence and direction
during his work of preliminary exploration.

If it be true, and the courts so assert, that the theory
of the law requiring this parallelism is, that the miner
may have only as much of the lode underneath as he has
apex within his surface,[1] then the object is accomplished
by making a location in the form suggested by figures 36
and 37, as well as by that suggested by figure 35. The
subsequent locator is in no sense injured, and will be
compelled to either make his location conform to the
lines of the first discoverer or take the chance of losing
a segment of the vein by underground conflict with the
prior appropriator.[2]

As heretofore observed, however, the failure to construct the end-lines so that they are parallel to each other
does not render the location absolutely void, so long
as it is within the statutory limit. A location in the
form of a horseshoe [3] or an isosceles triangle [4] will, subject to the extralateral right of others who have properly
located the apex, hold whatever may be found within
vertical planes drawn through the surface boundaries.

The requirement as to parallelism of end-lines, as a
condition precedent to the exercise of the extralateral
right, means that they should be parallel throughout, or
at least should not diverge in the direction of the dip.[5]
This requirement of the law is not satisfied by con-

[1] Del Monte M. and M. Co. v. Last Chance M. Co., 171 U. S. 55, 85,
18 Sup. Ct. Rep. 895; Doe v. Sanger, 83 Cal. 203, 213, 23 Pac. 365;
Carson City G. and S. M. Co. v. North Star M. Co., 83 Fed. 658, 669.

[2] Flagstaff M. Co. v. Tarbet, 98 U. S. 463; Eureka Case, 4 Saw. 302,
Fed. Cas. No. 4548.

[3] Iron S. M. Co. v. Elgin M. Co., 118 U. S. 196, 6 Sup. Ct. Rep. 1177.

[4] Montana Co. Limited v. Clark, 42 Fed. 626; Walrath v. Champion
M. Co., 171 U. S. 293, 312, 18 Sup. Ct. Rep. 909.

[5] For full discussion of the subject of converging end-lines and the
extent of the extralateral right which may be enjoyed therewith, see,
post, § 582.

structing broken end-lines. "They must be straight "lines, not broken or curved."[1] A survey for patent

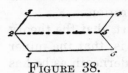

FIGURE 38.

made in the form indicated in figure 38 would be rejected.[2] Where the location as originally marked upon the ground has non-parallel end-lines, it may be rectified at any time, if such rectification does not interfere with intervening rights.[3]

A locator of a mining claim may abandon a portion of his original location without forfeiting any rights he may have to the remainder of the claim.[4]

There is no necessity for the two end-lines being of the same length. If they both cross the lode and are parallel to each other, the fact that one may be six hundred feet long and the other shorter is entirely immaterial.

In previous sections[5] we have fully explained the state of the law regarding the privileges granted to junior locators of placing lines over senior locations, as well as over patented lands, both mining and agricultural. It is unnecessary to repeat what was there said.

The difference between the former rulings of the land department and those now governing that tribunal in the administration of the mining laws may be illustrated by the use of a diagram (figure 39). Formerly A, the junior locator, would have been compelled to draw his end-line at X where the apex of the vein entered the side-line of the senior claim, making a reconstructed end-line, *b-a*. Under the present rulings the

---

[1] Walrath *v.* Champion M. Co., 171 U. S. 293, 311, 18 Sup. Ct. Rep. 909.

[2] Instructions to surveyor-general, 10 Copp's L. O. 86.

[3] Doe *v.* Sanger, 83 Cal. 203, 23 Pac. 365; Doe *v.* Waterloo M. Co., 54 Fed. 935.

[4] Tyler M. Co. *v.* Sweeney, 54 Fed. 284; Last Chance M. Co. *v.* Tyler M. Co., 61 Fed. 557; Tyler M. Co. *v.* Last Chance M. Co., 71 Fed. 848; Carrie S. G. M. Co., 29 L. D. 287; *In re* Connell, *Id.* 574.

[5] §§ 363, 363A.

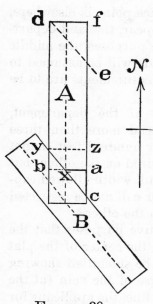

FIGURE 39.

junior may place his end-line entirely within the senior claim, as indicated in the diagram, or he may extend his side-lines entirely across the senior claim, placing the end-line on unappropriated ground; and this may be done whether the senior claim has passed to patent or not. The author, in the first edition of this treatise, contended that the junior locator was compelled, if he desired to secure extralateral rights, to reform his north end-line, *d-f*, so as to parallel the crossed side-line of the senior location, creating the new end-line, *d-e*. As we have heretofore seen, this view of the author failed to receive the sanction of either the department or the courts.

§ 366.   **The side-lines.**—The primary function of the side-lines is, to connect the opposite extremities of the end-lines, and to complete the inclosure of a surface within which is found the apex of the discovered lode. As the width of a location is fixed with reference to the middle of the vein, the law contemplates that this must be ascertained by actual exploration and development, and cannot be assumed to be in an unexplored position.[1]

Where the vein outcrops at the surface, there can be no question as to the point from which the lateral measurement must begin. When the discovery shaft develops the vein at some distance below the surface, and the locator does not determine by any further develop-

[1] *In re* Albert Johnson, 7 Copp's L. O. 35.
Lindley on M.—43

ment that the nearest actual surface point is elsewhere, and the fact does not otherwise appear, the land department has ruled that, for executive purposes, the middle of the vein as disclosed in the shaft will be assumed to be the point from which lateral measurements are to be calculated.[1]

According to the regulations of the department, lateral measurements cannot extend more than three hundred feet on either side. Four hundred feet cannot be taken on one side and two hundred on the other; but if, by reason of prior claims, the full width allowed cannot be taken on one side, the locator will not be restricted to less than three hundred feet on the other.[2]

It must be presumed for executive purposes that the lode proceeds in a straight line in the center of the plat of patent survey, unless evidence be submitted showing a different direction. If the course of the vein (at the surface) diverges from a straight line, the applicant for patent should indicate the direction and adjust his survey accordingly.[3]

The ingenuity of the law officers of the land department has been severely taxed in an effort to determine the position of the "middle of the vein" in the case of bedded or blanket deposits, for the purpose of establishing the side-lines of a claim located thereon. The department was admonished by the supreme court of the United States that this class of deposits fell within the legal definition of a lode, and was subject to location under the lode laws.[4]

The admonition of Judge Hallett to the miner, that

---

[1] Taylor v. Parenteau, 23 Colo. 368, 48 Pac. 505, 507; *In re* Hope M. Co., 5 Copp's L. O. 116; par. 5, Circ. Instructions, July 26, 1901, (see Appendix.

[2] Par. 5, Circ. Instructions, July 26, 1901, (see Appendix),

[3] Bimetallic M. Co., 15 L. D. 309.

[4] Iron S. M. Co. v. Mike & Starr G. and S. M. Co., 143 U. S. 394, 12 Sup. Ct. Rep. 543.

he "must find where this top, or apex, is, and make his " location with reference to that," possesses but little persuasive force, when considered with reference to a horizontal, or blanket, vein, which has no apex. The land department pointed a way out of the dilemma by establishing the following rule : —

" The only reasonable solution of the problem seems " to be to hold that the apex of the lode is coextensive " with the distance between the side-lines of the location, " and that every part or point of such apex within those " limits is as much the middle of the vein within the " intent and meaning of section 2320 of the Revised " Statutes as any other part." [1]

In other words, the entire upper surface of the "blanket" is apex, and the middle of the apex is anywhere one chooses to establish an arbitrary line. While the result reached by the secretary is a rational one, the reasoning is not altogether faultless; but considering the embarrassments surrounding cases of this character, any rational or equitable result should be exempt from adverse criticism. After a patent issues for a claim of this character an apex would be conclusively presumed to exist within the limits of the claim,[2] and the same presumption would be indulged as to the regularity of the form of the surface.[3] The patentee or locator on this class of deposits would hold everything within his vertical boundaries, without serious danger from outside apex proprietors on the same vein.

Side-lines, properly drawn, run on each side of the course of the vein, distant not more than three hundred feet from the middle of such vein;[4] but there is no command that they should be parallel.[5] So long as

---

[1] Homestake M. Co., 29 L. D. 689, 691.

[2] Iron S. M. Co. v. Campbell, 17 Colo. 267, 272, 29 Pac. 513.

[3] *Post*, § 778.

[4] King v. Amy & Silversmith M. Co., 152 U. S. 222, 14 Sup. Ct. Rep. 510.

[5] Del Monte M. and M. Co. v. Last Chance M. Co., 171 U. S. 55, 84, 18 Sup. Ct. Rep. 895; Woods v. Holden, 26 L. D. 198, 206; Stevens v. Williams, 1 Morr. Min. Rep. 566, 1 McCrary, 480, Fed. Cas. No. 13,413.

they keep within the statutory width they may have angles and elbows, as in figure 40, or converge toward each other, as in figure 41, without jeopardizing any rights, so far as the located lode is concerned, if the end-lines are properly constructed with reference to such lode. A locator, whose surface lines are constructed as in figure 41, of course obtains less area than is embraced in the ideal location, but otherwise he

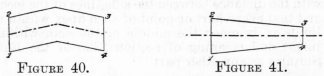

FIGURE 40.   FIGURE 41.

suffers no diminution of rights from those acquired by the ideal. The parallelism or non-parallelism of the side-lines may, however, become an important factor if the locator makes a mistake, as he frequently does, as to the course of his vein, and locates crosswise instead of along the vein.

The validity of a location is not impaired by the later determination that the apex of the vein runs out of a line located as a side-line.[1] The extent of the rights conferred by the location, under such conditions, would necessarily be abridged.

Where a location is of excessive width, the excess should be cast off, so that the middle of the vein will be in the center of the location.[2]

§ 367. **Side-end lines.**—End-lines are not always those which are designated as such by the locator. If the vein does not cross the line called by him an end-line, it is not in law an end-line. In such case it performs the mere function of a side-line. In all cases where a vein crosses a side-line, the side-line performs the function of an end-line, to the extent, at least, that

[1] Beik v. Nickerson, 29 L. D. 662.

[2] Lakin v. Dolly, 53 Fed. 333; Taylor v. Parenteau, 23 Colo. 368, 48 Pac. 505, 507; Bonner v. Meikle, 82 Fed. 697, 705.

it stops the pursuit of the vein on its strike. It is therefore to this extent in law an end-line,[1] whether so intended by the locator or not.[2] We call it a side-end line for
descriptive purposes. Whether the side-end line
performs the function of an end-line for the purpose
of determining the extralateral right, will depend upon
circumstances. If the vein crosses two side-lines, substantially as in the Flagstaff-Tarbet[3] and Argentine-
Terrible[4] cases, where the crossed side-lines are
parallel, there is no reason why the vein may not be
followed on its downward course throughout its entire
depth, between vertical planes drawn downward through
the side-end lines, produced indefinitely in their own
direction, and the courts have so held. If the side-end
lines are not parallel, as those lines are indicated in figure 41, and the dip of the vein is toward their conver-
gence, these lines may be extended in their own direction
until they meet, and the locator may pursue the vein in
depth to the vertical line of junction between the two
planes. If the dip is in the direction of the divergence,
there certainly is no extralateral right. The consideration, however, of this character of cases, together with
those where a vein crosses one end-line and one side-line,
will be deferred until we reach the subject of extralateral rights.

[1] Flagstaff M. Co. v. Tarbet, 98 U. S. 463; Argentine M. Co. v. Terrible M. Co., 122 U. S. 478, 17 Sup. Ct. Rep. 1356; King v. Amy & Silver-
smith M. Co., 152 U. S. 222, 14 Sup. Ct. Rep. 510; Del Monte M. and
M. Co. v. Last Chance M. Co., 171 U. S. 55, 18 Sup. Ct. Rep. 895; Eilers
v. Boatman, 3 Utah, 159, 2 Pac. 66; Stevens v. Williams, 1 Morr. Min.
Rep. 557, Fed. Cas. No. 13,414; Tombstone M. and M. Co. v. Wayup M.
Co., 1 Ariz. 426, 25 Pac. 794; Watervale M. Co. v. Leach (Ariz.), 33
Pac. 418; Colorado Cent. R. R. v. Turck, 50 Fed. 888; *Id.* on rehearing,
54 Fed. 262; Tyler M. Co. v. Sweeney, 54 Fed. 284; New Dunderberg
M. Co. v. Old, 79 Fed. 588, 606; Cosmopolitan M. Co. v. Foote, 101
Fed. 518.

[2] Bunker Hill and Sullivan M. and C. Co. v. Empire State-Idaho M.
and D. Co., 109 Fed. 538, 540.

[3] 98 U. S. 463.

[4] 122 U. S. 478, 7 Sup. Ct. Rep. 1356.

ARTICLE VII. THE MARKING OF THE LOCATION ON THE SURFACE.

§ 371. Necessity for, and object of, marking.

§ 372. Time allowed for marking.

§ 373. What is sufficient marking under the federal law.

§ 374. State statutes defining the character of marking.

§ 375. Perpetuation of monuments.

§ 371. Necessity for, and object of, marking.—The Revised Statutes of the United States [1] contain the mandatory provision, that the "location must be distinctly " marked on the ground so that its boundaries can " be readily traced." There is no escape from this requirement. While it is possible that state statutes or local district regulations may particularize as to the character of the marking, they cannot dispense with the necessity for compliance with the law of congress. While, as we shall hereafter point out, time is allowed within which to establish the boundaries, until this is done the location is not complete.[2] The requirement is an imperative and indispensable condition precedent to a valid location,[3] and is not to be "frittered away by " construction." [4] After the discovery, it is the main act of original location.[5] This was the rule under the Spanish and Mexican law.[6] The object of the law in requiring the location to be marked on the ground is,

---

[1] § 2324.

[2] Belk v. Meagher, 104 U. S. 279; Strepey v. Stark, 7 Colo. 614, 5 Pac. 111; Garfield M. and M. Co. v. Hammer, 6 Mont. 53, 8 Pac. 153; Gilpin County M. Co. v. Drake, 8 Colo. 586, 589, 9 Pac. 787; Sweet v. Webber, 7 Colo. 443, 4 Pac. 752.

[3] Ledoux v. Forester, 94 Fed. 600.

[4] Gleeson v. Martin White M. Co., 13 Nev. 442, 456.

[5] Donahue v. Meister, 88 Cal. 121, 131, 22 Am. St. Rep. 283, 25 Pac. 1096.

[6] United States v. Castillero, 2 Black, 17; Gonu v. Russell, 3 Mont. 358.

to fix the claim, to prevent floating or swinging, so that those who in good faith are looking for unoccupied ground in the vicinity of previous locations may be enabled to ascertain exactly what has been appropriated, in order to make their locations upon the residue.[1] It also operates to determine the right of the claimant as between himself and the general government.[2]

§ 372. **Time allowed for marking.**—Under the United States laws a claim may be marked at any time prior to the acquisition of an intervening right, regardless of the question as to whether the time within which such marking was made was reasonable or not.[3] In the absence of state legislation or district regulation, it has been held, in California, that while a party in actual possession, proceeding with diligence to mark his boundaries, would be protected as against a stranger attempting to relocate, yet, strictly speaking, no time is allowed to the locator to complete his location by marking it on the surface.[4] This view is also adopted by the supreme court of Oregon.[5]

But, as heretofore indicated,[6] the circuit court of appeals for the ninth circuit, upon the same state of facts, presented in one of the Califorina cases,[7] declined

---

[1] Gleeson v. Martin White M. Co., 13 Nev. 442, 462; Patterson v. Tarbell, 26 Or. 29, 37 Pac. 76, 78; Gird v. California Oil Co., 60 Fed. 531, 536; Willeford v. Bell (Cal.), 49 Pac. 6; Upton v. Larkin, 7 Mont. 449, 17 Pac. 728; Sanders v. Noble, 22 Mont. 110, 55 Pac. 1037; Walsh v. Erwin, 115 Fed. 531, 536; Book v. Justice M. Co., 58 Fed. 106, 114.

[2] Pollard v. Shively, 5 Colo. 309, 317. See, also, Drummond v. Long, 9 Colo. 538, 13 Pac. 543.

[3] *Ante,* § 330; Crown Point G. M. Co. v. Crismon, 39 Or. 364, 65 Pac. 87.

[4] Newbill v. Thurston, 65 Cal. 419, 4 Pac. 409; Gregory v. Pershbaker, 73 Cal. 109, 14 Pac. 401; Pharis v. Muldoon, 75 Cal. 284, 17 Pac. 70.

[5] Patterson v. Tarbell, 26 Or. 29, 37 Pac. 76.

[6] *Ante,* § 339.

[7] Newbill v. Thurston, 65 Cal. 419, 4 Pac. 409.

to accept the doctrine of the California courts,[1] but follows the rule announced by the supreme courts of Nevada [2] and Idaho,[3] and the manifest intent of the law as suggested by the supreme court of the United States [4] and by the courts of last resort in Colorado,[5] South Dakota,[6] Washington,[7] and Montana.[8] It is unnecessary to here repeat what we have said on this subject in a preceding section.[9] For the reasons therein suggested, we are of the opinion that the rule, as announced in California and Oregon, is opposed to both the spirit of the law and the weight of authority.

§ 373. **What is sufficient marking under the federal law.**—As noted in the succeeding section, some of the states have enacted laws defining the character of monuments, or marks, to be placed on the ground. In the absence of such state legislation or local regulation, what constitutes a sufficient marking is a question to be determined by the jury, according to the circumstances in each particular case.[10] It naturally depends upon the conformation of the ground. What might be sufficient in the case of a comparatively level or bare surface might not answer the requirements of the law in a moun-

---

[1] Doe v. Waterloo M. Co., 70 Fed. 455, affirming 55 Fed. 11.

[2] Golden Fleece M. Co. v. Cable Cons. M. Co., 12 Nev. 312, 329; Gleeson v. Martin White M. Co., 13 Nev. 442.

[3] Burke v. McDonald, 2 Idaho, 646, 33 Pac. 49.

[4] Erhardt v. Boaro, 113 U. S. 527, 5 Sup. Ct. Rep. 560.

[5] Murley v. Ennis, 2 Colo. 300; Patterson v. Hitchcock, 3 Colo. 533.

[6] Marshall v. Harney Peak Tin M. Co., 1 S. Dak. 350, 47 N. W. 290.

[7] Union M. and M. Co. v. Leitch, 24 Wash. 585, 85 Am. St. Rep. 961, 64 Pac. 829.

[8] Sanders v. Noble, 22 Mont. 110, 55 Pac. 1037, 1045.

[9] *Ante,* § 339.

[10] Taylor v. Middleton, 67 Cal. 656, 8 Pac. 594; Anderson v. Black, 70 Cal. 226, 11 Pac. 700; Du Prat v. James, 65 Cal. 555, 4 Pac. 562; Farmington G. M. Co. v. Rhymney G. and C. Co., 20 Utah, 363, 77 Am. St. Rep. 913, 58 Pac. 832; Eaton v. Norris, 131 Cal. 561, 63 Pac. 856; Russel v. Chumasero, 4 Mont. 309, 1 Pac. 713, (decided before act of 1895), Purdum v. Laddin, 23 Mont. 387, 59 Pac. 153.

tainous region where the hills are precipitous or the surface covered with timber or undergrowth.[1]

" This requirement is not fulfilled by simply setting " a post at or near the place of discovery, and setting " stakes at each of the corners of the claim and at the " center of the end-lines, unless the topography of the " ground is such that a person accustomed to tracing " the lines of mining claims can, after reading the de- " scription of the claim in the posted notice of location, " by a reasonable and *bona fide* effort to do so, find all " of the stakes, and thereby trace all of the lines. Where " the country is broken, and the view from one corner to " another is obstructed by intervening gulches and tim- " ber and brush, it is necessary to blaze the trees along " the lines, or cut away the brush, or set more stakes, at " such distances that they may be seen from one to " another, or dig up the ground in a way to indicate the " lines, so that the boundaries may be readily traced." [2]

In this view of the law, adjudicated cases are not often of controlling weight. They depend for their value as precedents upon the reasoning of the courts and the similarity as to facts existing in the case to which they are sought to be applied.

While the commissioner of the general land office has advised the erection of posts at the corners, and the erection of a signboard at the location point, the law may be satisfied by something less.[3]

We have collated the following examples, wherein the marking in the manner designated was held to satisfy the law:—

In a district where the extent of a claim on each side of the center line is established by local rule, it has been said, that the object of the law is attained by marking this center line; that a man of common intelligence,

---

[1] Book *v.* Justice M. Co., 58 Fed. 106, 113.

[2] Ledoux *v.* Forester, 94 Fed. 600.

[3] Gleeson *v.* Martin White M. Co., 13 Nev. 442, 462.

acquainted with the customs of the country, seeing the discovery monument, the preliminary posted notice, and the stakes marking this center line, would be informed by the rules of the district and the laws of the land that the boundaries of the claim were formed by lines parallel to the center line, at the distance prescribed by local rules, and by end-lines at right angles thereto. With this knowledge, he could easily trace the boundaries and ascertain exactly where he could locate with safety.[1]

Judge Sawyer held that the sinking of a discovery shaft, posting a notice thereon, and placing a monument and post at *one* extremity of the linear measurement, was a compliance with the law.[2]

We think these cases stretch the law to the utmost limit of liberality. It is almost a return to the primitive rules, prevalent when the lode was the principal thing located and the surface a mere incident, when the locator could hold but one vein, and his rights as to that vein were not defined by surface boundaries.[3]

Under the existing law, a grant of the surface is sought, and the rights on the discovered lode, as well as all others whose apices may be found therein, are defined exclusively by the form of the location and the direction of the boundary lines. What the existing law evidently contemplates is physical evidence on the ground of *marks* which will enable one to trace the lines on the surface.[4]

Posted or recorded notices may be an aid in determining the *situs* of monuments,[5] but they cannot be substituted for all markings. They therefore constitute a

---

[1] Gleeson *v.* Martin White M. Co., 13 Nev. 442, 463. See, also, Mt. Diablo M. and M. Co. *v.* Callison, 5 Saw. 439, 449, Fed. Cas. No. 9886.

[2] North Noonday M. Co. *v.* Orient M. Co., 6 Saw. 299, 311, 1 Fed. 522.

[3] *Ante,* § 58.

[4] Willeford *v.* Bell (Cal.), 49 Pac. 6.

[5] McKinley Creek M. Co. *v.* Alaska United M. Co., 183 U. S. 563, 570, 22 Sup. Ct. Rep. 84.

part of the marking, as does every other object placed on the ground for that purpose, if in fact it does aid such result.[1]

In many cases, stakes driven into the ground are the most certain means of identification.[2]

Fencing is not necessary;[3] in fact, where in California the early occupants inclosed their ground with substantial inclosures, it was an open invitation for prospectors to enter, as it indicated a holding for agricultural purposes.

Stakes firmly planted in the ground, marked as corner stakes, with stone mounds placed around them, which stakes and mounds were found by the court to be "prom- " inent and permanent monuments," were held to justify the legal conclusion that the location was distinctly marked on the ground so that the boundaries could be readily traced.[4]

Stakes and stone monuments at each corner of the claim, and at the center of each of the end-lines, are, according to the supreme court of Nevada, as much as has ever been required under the most stringent construction of the law;[5] and yet there are states which require eight posts and monuments, the additional two being placed at the center of the side-lines.

[1] Eaton v. Norris, 131 Cal. 561, 63 Pac. 856; Meydenbauer v. Stevens, 78 Fed. 787, 792; Temescal Oil and D. Co. v. Salcido, 137 Cal. 211, 69 Pac. 1010; Walsh v. Erwin, 115 Fed. 531, 536.

[2] Hammer v. Garfield M. and M. Co., 130 U. S. 291, 299, 9 Sup. Ct. Rep. 548; Eaton v. Norris, 131 Cal. 561, 63 Pac. 856.

[3] Rogers v. Cooney, 7 Nev. 215, 219.

[4] Du Prat v. James, 65 Cal. 555, 4 Pac. 562; Gird v. California Oil Co., 60 Fed. 531, 537; Book v. Justice M. Co., 58 Fed. 106; Credo M. and S. Co. v. Highland M. and M. Co., 95 Fed. 864.

[5] Southern Cross G. and S. M. Co. v. Europa M. Co., 15 Nev. 383. See, also, Souter v. Maguire, 78 Cal. 543, 21 Pac. 183; Book v. Justice M. Co., 58 Fed. 106; Howeth v. Sullenger, 113 Cal. 547, 45 Pac. 841; Meydenbauer v. Stevens, 78 Fed. 787; Smith v. Newell, 86 Fed. 56; Credo M. and S. Co. v. Highland M. and M. Co., 95 Fed. 911; Sherlock v. Leighton, 9 Wyo. 297, 63 Pac. 580.

A location marked by a discovery monument, on which was placed the notice of location, and by a stake at each of three of the corners of the claim, and a monument at the center of each end-line, leaving one corner unmarked, was held to be sufficient to comply with the law.[1]

The omission to mark one end of a claim where the ground was so inaccessible that the surveyor when surveying for patent was compelled to determine the position of the end-line by triangulation, the remainder of the claim being marked by stakes and mounds at the accessible corners, the center of one end-line, a discovery monument and blazed trees on the center line, was held not to be an evasion of the law. Under the circumstances, the marking was sufficient.[2] Posting notices on trees, one at each end of the claim,[3] or posting a notice in the center of the claim without any attempt at marking,[4] has been held to be wholly insufficient. These notices would serve the purpose for which they were originally intended, as notices of intention to locate, but would only preserve the right for a reasonable time to enable the locator to mark his boundaries.

The supreme court of the United States, in the case of McKinley Creek Mining Co. v. Alaska United Mining Co.,[5] has sustained the validity of a placer location where no attempt was made to actually mark the boundaries. All that was done was to post notices on a snag, or stump, in a creek, claiming a certain number of feet running with the creek and three hundred feet on each side of the center of the creek, and referring to

---

[1] Warnock v. De Witt, 11 Utah, 324, 40 Pac. 205; Walsh v. Erwin, 115 Fed. 531.

[2] Eilers v. Boatman, 3 Utah, 159, 2 Pac. 66; affirmed, 111 U. S. 356, 4 Sup. Ct. Rep. 432.

[3] Holland v. Mt. Auburn G. Q. M. Co., 53 Cal. 149, 151.

[4] Gelcich v. Moriarity, 53 Cal. 217; Morenhaut v. Wilson, 52 Cal. 263, 269; Doe v. Waterloo M. Co., 70 Fed. 455.

[5] 183 U. S. 563, 22 Sup. Ct. Rep. 84.

the claim as the east extension of a certain named claim and the west extension of another. Unless some facts or circumstances were represented to the court which cannot be gleaned from the official report of the case, such a location would seem to fall short of the requirement that the claim shall be "distinctly marked " on the ground, so that its boundaries may be readily " traced." [1]

As intimated in a previous section, the marks, stakes, or monuments should be within the statutory limit as to area; [2] yet this rule is to be understood in the light of the doctrine that excessive locations are not wholly void, but are invalid only as to the excess. [3]

In so far as the ground taken is vacant, each location, if properly made in other respects, will be valid. [4]

The right to place marks upon claims previously appropriated has been heretofore discussed. [5]

A failure to comply with the law as to the marking within a reasonable time after discovery, where there is no local rule or state statute fixing the time, or within the time fixed by statute or local rule, renders the ground subject to relocation; [6] but if the ground is marked before conflicting rights accrue, the claim will be valid. [7] In case of a relocation, the right of the relocator is lost if he fails to mark his boundaries prior to the resumption

---

[1] Rev. Stats., §§ 2324, 2329; *post,* § 454.

[2] Leggatt *v.* Stewart, 5 Mont. 107, 109, 2 Pac. 320; Hauswirth *v.* Butcher, 4 Mont. 299, 1 Pac. 714.

[3] *Ante,* § 362; Ledoux *v.* Forester, 94 Fed. 600.

[4] Doe *v.* Tyler, 73 Cal. 21, 14 Pac. 375; West Granite Mt. M. Co. *v.* Granite Mt. M. Co., 7 Mont. 356, 17 Pac. 547; Perigo *v.* Erwin, 85 Fed. 904; Crown Point M. Co. *v.* Buck, 97 Fed. 462.

[5] *Ante,* §§ 363, 363a.

[6] White *v.* Lee, 78 Cal. 593, 12 Am. St. Rep. 115, 21 Pac. 363; Funk *v.* Sterrett, 59 Cal. 613.

[7] *Ante,* §§ 330, 372; Crown Point G. M. Co. *v.* Crismon, 39 Or. 364, 65 Pac. 87.

of work by the former owner,[1] always assuming that the failure to perfect the location is not caused by the fraud or tortious acts of the relocator.[2] Failure to mark the boundaries within the time allowed by law or prescribed by state or local regulation cannot be taken advantage of by a subsequent locator, if the prior locator perfects his location in advance of any intervening rights.[3] A location when perfected relates back to the discovery.[4] Boundaries once established cannot be changed to the detriment of intervening locators.[5] In considering the question as to the sufficiency of marking, the court is not confined to the monuments placed at the corners of the claim at the inception of the location for the purpose of marking it, but may consider also all other objects placed on the ground, either then or subsequently, prior to the subsequent location, either for the purpose of serving as monuments or otherwise.[6]

§ 374. **State statutes defining character of marking.** —There is no legislation upon the subject of marking the location in California. The following statutory requirements are found in the other precious-metal-bearing states and territories:—

Colorado.—Before filing the certificate of location for record (within three months after discovery),[7] the sur-

---

[1] Gonu v. Russell, 3 Mont. 358, 363; Pharis v. Muldoon, 75 Cal. 284, 17 Pac. 70; Holland v. Mt. Auburn G. Q. M. Co., 53 Cal. 149. But see, *post*, § 408.

[2] Erhardt v. Boaro, 113 U. S. 527; Miller v. Taylor, 6 Colo. 41.

[3] North Noonday M. Co. v. Orient M. Co., 6 Saw. 299, 314, 1 Fed. 522; Jupiter M. Co. v. Bodie Cons. M. Co., 7 Saw. 96, 115, 11 Fed. 666. See, *ante*, § 330.

[4] Doe v. Waterloo M. Co., 70 Fed. 455; Gregory v. Pershbaker, 73 Cal. 109, 14 Pac. 401.

[5] O'Reilly v. Campbell, 116 U. S. 418, 6 Sup. Ct. Rep. 421; Golden Fleece M. Co. v. Cable Cons. M. Co., 12 Nev. 312; Crœsus M. and S. Co. v. Colorado L. and M. Co., 19 Fed. 78.

[6] Eaton v. Norris, 131 Cal. 561, 63 Pac. 856.

[7] Mills' Annot. Stats., § 3150.

face boundaries must be marked by six posts, hewed or marked on the side, or sides, in toward the claim, and sunk into the ground, one at each corner, and one at the center of each side-line. If bedrock prevents the sinking of posts, the boundary may be placed on a pile of stones. Where it is impracticable (because of danger in placing or other reason) to put the post at the proper place, it may be placed at the nearest practicable point, suitably marked to designate the proper place.[1] The cutting of a letter in a solid rock will not suffice in lieu of the placing of a post.[2] These provisions cannot be invoked when the setting of the stake at the true corner is merely difficult or inconvenient.[3]

Idaho.—Within ten days from the date of discovery, the discoverer must mark his boundaries by establishing at each corner thereof, and at any angle in the side-lines, a monument of any material or form which will readily give notice, which shall be marked with the name of the claim and the corner, or angle, it represents. If the monument cannot be safely planted at the true angle, or corner, it may be placed as near thereto as practicable, and so marked as to indicate the place of such corner, or angle. If of posts or trees, the monuments must be hewn, and marked upon the side facing discovery, and must be four inches square, or in diameter. All monuments must be four feet high.[4]

Arizona.—Before filing location certificate (ninety days after location),[5] the surface boundaries must be marked by six substantial posts, projecting at least four

---

[1] Mills' Annot. Stats., § 3153.

[2] Taylor *v.* Parenteau, 23 Colo. 368, 48 Pac. 505. See, also, Crœsus M. and M. Co. *v.* Colorado L. and M. Co., 19 Fed. 78.

[3] Beals *v.* Cone, 27 Colo. 473, 83 Am. St. Rep. 92, 62 Pac. 948.

[4] Rev. Stats., § 3101, as amended—Laws of 1895, p. 27, § 2; Laws of 1899, p. 633; Civil Code (1901), § 2557. See Morrison *v.* Regan (Idaho), 67 Pac. 955.

[5] Rev. Stats. 1887, § 2349; *Id.* 1901, § 3234.

feet above the surface of the ground, or by substantial stone monuments, at least three feet high,—to wit, one at each corner of said claim, and one at the center of each end-line thereof.[1]

Montana.—The locator must within thirty days after posting notice of location define the boundaries of his claim, by marking a tree or rock in place, or by setting a post or stone, at each corner, or angle, of the claim. If a post is used, it must be at least four inches square by four feet six inches in length, set one foot in the ground, with a monument of earth or stone at least four feet in diameter by two feet in height around the post. If a stone is used, not a rock in place, it must be at least six inches square and eighteen inches in length, set two thirds of its length in the ground, which trees, stakes, or monuments must be so marked as to designate the corners.[2]

Nevada.—The locator must define the boundaries of his claim by marking a tree or rock in place, or by setting a post or stone one at each corner, and one at the center of each side-line. In other respects the requirements are the same as those in Montana.[3]

New Mexico.—No time is provided within which marking is to be effected. Ninety days are allowed to sink discovery shaft and three months to record copy of notice of location. The inference is plausible that the locator should be allowed to complete his development work before marking his boundaries.[4] In any event, he is allowed a reasonable time. Surface boundaries are to be marked by four substantial posts or monuments,

[1] Rev. Stats. (1901), § 3236. This statute is discussed in Wiltsee *v.* King of Arizona M. and M. Co. (Ariz.), 60 Pac. 896.

[2] Rev. Code of 1895, § 3611, as amended—Laws of 1901, p. 140, § 1. Right to swing claim within time: Sanders *v.* Noble, 22 Mont. 110, 55 Pac. 1037.

[3] Comp. Laws (1900), § 209, as amended—Stats. 1901, p. 97.

[4] *Ante,* § 372.

one at each corner of the claim, thus distinctly marking the claim on the ground, so that its boundaries can be readily traced.[1]

North Dakota.—Before filing the certificate of location for record (sixty days from date of discovery), the boundaries shall be marked by eight substantial posts, hewed, or blazed, on the side facing the claim, and marked with the name of the lode and the corner, end, or side of the claim that they respectively represent, and sunk into the ground as follows: One at the corner, and one at the center of each side-line, and one at each end of the lode; but when it is impracticable, on account of rock or precipitous ground, to sink such posts, they may be placed in a monument of stone.[2]

Oregon.—Within thirty days after posting of the notice of location the boundaries shall be marked by six substantial posts, projecting not less than three feet above the surface of the ground, and not less than four inches square or in diameter, or by substantial mounds of stone or earth and stone, at least two feet in height,— to wit, one such post or mound of rock at each corner and at the center ends of such claims.[3]

South Dakota.—Same as North Dakota.[4]

Utah.—Mining claims must be distinctly marked on the ground, so that the boundaries thereof can be readily traced. No time is fixed within which this should be done. The sinking of a discovery shaft is not required. The locator would therefore be allowed a reasonable time to mark his boundaries.[5]

---

[1] Laws of 1899, p. 111.

[2] Rev. Code of 1895, §§ 1428, 1430, 1431; *Id.*, 1899, §§ 1428, 1430, 1431.

[3] Laws of 1898, p. 16, as amended—Laws of 1901, p. 140.

[4] Comp. Laws of Dak. 1887, § 2002. Adopted by South Dakota—Laws of 1890, ch. cv.; Grantham's Annot. Stats. S. D., § 2661.

[5] Laws of 1899, p. 26, § 3.

Washington.—The locator is required to record a notice of location within ninety days from the date of discovery, and before filing the same for record must mark the surface boundaries of the claim by placing substantial posts or stone monuments, bearing the name of the lode and date of location; one post or monument must appear at each corner of said claim; such posts or monuments must be not less than three feet high. If posts are used, they shall be not less than four inches in diameter and shall be set in the ground in a substantial manner. If the claim is on ground, wholly or partly covered with brush or trees, such brush shall be cut and trees marked, or blazed, to indicate the lines of such claim.[1]

Wyoming.—Substantially the same as Colorado.[2]

While the requirements of these several laws should be fulfilled to a reasonable degree, a substantial compliance, where the good faith of the locator is manifest, would undoubtedly be held sufficient. Such statutes are, as a rule, liberally construed. Slight variations should not be permitted to invalidate a location otherwise valid.[3]

§ 375.   **Perpetuation of monuments.**—Under the rules and customs governing the rights of tin bounders in Cornwall, bounds were required to be renewed annually, in default of which the estate was subject to re-entry by others.[4]

These bounds, however, were marked, and possession delivered after proceedings had in the stannary courts, the writ of possession being executed by the court bailiff.

---

[1] Laws of 1899, p. 69.

[2] Laws of 1888, p. 88, § 17; Rev. Stats. (1899), § 2548.

[3] But see Crœsus M. and M. Co. *v.* Colorado L. and M. Co., 19 Fed. 78; Taylor *v.* Parenteau, 23 Colo. 368, 48 Pac. 505.

[4] *Ante,* § 5.

The "gales" of the free miner, in the coal and iron mines of the Forest of Dean, were set out and marked by the gaveler of the forest;[1] and among the lead miners of Derbyshire, the "meers" were measured by the bar-master, an agent of the crown, in conjunction with two of the grand jury.[2]

In Mexico, the boundaries were marked, after meas-urement, by an agent of the mining deputation, who was usually a skilled engineer, and the miner was called upon to enter into an obligation to "keep and observe " them forever."[3]

These methods of establishing boundaries, succeed-ing, as they did, a formal adjudication as to the right to possession, suggest the propriety of permanency. In the United States, however, we are required to mark our boundaries first, and determine our right to pos-session afterwards. Even when a survey for patent is made, the deputy mineral surveyor is an agent of the claimant, and his acts in no sense bind the government, and, as we shall observe when dealing with patent pro-ceedings, surveys are made, in the first instance, of the ground *claimed,* regardless of overlapping surfaces or interference with prior surveys or locations. Relative rights arising out of these conflicts are frequently not determined until after long litigation. Therefore, there would be but little use in compelling the erection of indestructible monuments for the purpose of marking the extent of the ground *claimed.* Ordinary prudence will suggest to the locator the advisability of preserving his marks. But the law does not require it. Therefore, it has been held that where a mining claim is once suf-ficiently marked on the ground, and all other necessary acts of location are performed, a right vests in the locator, which cannot be divested by the subsequent

[1] *Ante,* § 7.   [2] *Ante,* § 8.   [3] *Ante,* § 13, p 21.

obliteration of the marks or removal of the stakes without the fault of the locator.[1]

Where the evidence shows that the boundaries were originally marked, the fact that the stakes then set could not in later years be found raises no presumption against the validity of the original marking.[2]

The supreme court of Colorado suggests a sensible exception to this rule: Where there is a variation between the calls of the recorded location certificate and the monuments established on the ground, the locator, in order to avail himself of the rule of law which gives controlling effect to the monuments as they were placed on the ground, must keep up his markings. The reason given in support of this is, that as the erroneous record fails to give constructive notice, if the monuments are swept away, no search, no exercise of prudence, diligence, or intelligence, would advise the subsequent locator of the extent and limits of the prior appropriation,[3] and this is one of the principal objects of marking.

The rule that monuments shall control courses and distances is recognized only in cases where the monuments are clearly ascertained. If there be doubt as to monuments, as well as to the course and distance, there can be no reason for saying that monuments shall prevail, rather than the course.[4]

---

[1] Jupiter M. Co. v. Bodie Cons. M. Co., 7 Saw. 96, 110, 11 Fed. 666; Book v. Justice M. Co., 58 Fed. 106, 114; McEvoy v. Hyman, 25 Fed. 596, 598; Smith v. Newell, 86 Fed. 56; Yreka M. Co. v. Knight, 133 Cal. 544, 65 Pac. 1091; Walsh v. Erwin, 115 Fed. 531, 537.

[2] Temescal Oil and D. Co. v. Salcido, 137 Cal. 211, 69 Pac. 1010.

[3] Pollard v. Shively, 5 Colo. 309, 318.

[4] Thallmann v. Thomas, 102 Fed. 925.

ARTICLE VIII. THE LOCATION CERTIFICATE AND ITS
CONTENTS.

§ 379. 'The location certificate —
    Its purpose.

§ 380. State legislation as to con-
    tents of location certifi-
    cate.

§ 381. Rules of construction ap-
    plied.

§ 382. Variation between descrip-
    tive calls in certificate

and monuments on the
ground.

§ 383. "Natural objects" and "per-
    "manent monuments."

§ 384. Effect of failure to comply
    with the law as to con-
    tents of certificate.

§ 385. Verification of certificates.

§ 379. The location certificate — Its purpose. — In
speaking of the "location certificate," we have no reference to the preliminary posted notice of discovery and
intention to locate, discussed in a preceding article,[1]
except in so far as such posted notice forms the basis of
the recorded notice, as it does in Oregon and Utah and
the territories of Arizona and New Mexico.[2] In this
latter class of cases, the posted notice performs the
function of a certificate of location, as it is termed in
most states. This certificate is also equivalent in its
legal effect to the "declaratory statement" provided for
by the laws of Montana.[3]

By the term "certificate of location," we mean the
instrument prepared by the locator after the completion
of the development work and the marking of his location, which certificate is required by the state laws or
local rules to be recorded. This instrument when
recorded is a statutory writing affecting realty, being,
in the states or localities where it is required, the basis
of the miner's "right of exclusive possession" of his
mining location granted by the laws of congress.[4] It is
the first muniment of his paper title, upon the record of

[1] *Ante,* §§ 350-356.

[2] *Ante,* § 353.

[3] *Post,* § 380.

[4] Pollard *v.* Shively, 5 Colo. 309, 312.

which proceedings for patent are based, and as recorded is intended to impart constructive notice to all subsequent locators of the existence of the claim, its precise locality and extent,[1] as the marking of the location on the ground is intended to impart actual notice of these facts. The preliminary posted notice performs a temporary function; the recorded certificate a more permanent one.[2] This recorded certificate, notice, or declaratory statement, by whatever name it may be called, is the genesis of the locator's paper title.

The congressional laws do not in terms require any such certificate, but they provide that where a record of the location is made such record "shall contain the name " or names of the locators, the date of the location, and " such a description of the claim or claims located, by " reference to some natural object or permanent monu- " ment, as will identify the claim." [3] In the absence of a state law or local rule requiring a record to be made, congress has not undertaken to prescribe the nature of the notices which a miner may be compelled by such laws or rules to post, or which he may see fit to post on his own motion. It is only when such notice, or its equivalent, is required to be recorded that the provisions of the federal law become mandatory.[4]

Where state laws or local rules require a record to be made, the recorded instrument must contain at least the elements provided for by the Revised Statutes,[5] and if

---

[1] Magruder v. Oregon and Cal. R. R. Co., 28 L. D. 174.

[2] Sanders v. Noble, 22 Mont. 110, 55 Pac. 1037, 1046.

[3] Rev. Stats., § 2324.

[4] Gleeson v. Martin White M. Co., 13 Nev. 443, 464; Golden Fleece M. Co. v. Cable Cons. M. Co., 12 Nev. 312; Jupiter M. Co. v. Bodie Cons. M. Co., 7 Saw. 96, 112, 11 Fed. 666; Poujade v. Ryan, 21 Nev. 449, 33 Pac. 659; Doe v. Waterloo C. M. Co., 55 Fed. 11; Erhardt v. Boaro, 113 U. S. 527, 5 Sup. Ct. Rep. 560.

[5] Brown v. Levan (Idaho), 46 Pac. 661, (but see Morrison v. Regan (Idaho), 67 Pac. 955); Drummond v. Long, 9 Colo. 538, 13 Pac. 543; Faxon v. Barnard, 4 Fed. 702; Gilpin County M. Co. v. Drake, 8 Colo. 586,

such state laws or local rules prescribe the contents of such recorded notice, it must comply with this additional requirement.[1]

A few of the states provide for a record, but do not prescribe the contents of the notice or certificate to be recorded. In such cases compliance with the federal law is all that is necessary. Most of the states and territories, however, within the purview of this treatise have provided by law for the contents of such instruments. Before proceeding with a discussion of the nature of these certificates it is advisable to present an outline of the state legislation upon the subject.

§ 380. **State legislation as to contents of location certificate.**—

Colorado.—The location certificate must contain: (1) name of the lode; (2) name of locator; (3) date of location; (4) number of feet in length claimed on each side of the center of discovery shaft; (5) the general course of the lode; [2] (6) a description of the claim sufficient to identify it.[3]

Idaho.—The laws of Idaho provide for two notices: one preliminary, to be posted only; the other a final one, to be both posted and recorded.[4] The final notice must contain: (1) name of locator; (2) name of the claim;

9 Pac. 787; Darger v. Le Sieur, 8 Utah, 160, 30 Pac. 363, S. C. on rehearing, 9 Utah, 192, 33 Pac. 701; Dillon v. Bayliss, 11 Mont. 171, 27 Pac. 725; Russell v. Chumasero, 4 Mont. 309, 1 Pac. 713, (this case commented on in Purdum v. Laddin, 23 Mont. 387, 59 Pac. 153); Garfield M. and M. Co. v. Hammer, 6 Mont. 53, 8 Pac. 153; Hammer v. Garfield M. and M. Co., 130 U. S. 291, 9 Sup. Ct. Rep. 548; Poujade v. Ryan, 21 Nev. 449, 33 Pac. 659; Gleeson v. Martin White M. Co., 13 Nev. 443; Smith v. Newell, 86 Fed. 56; Meydenbauer v. Stevens, 78 Fed. 787; Deeney v. Mineral Creek M. Co. (N. Mex.), 67 Pac. 724.

[1] Purdum v. Laddin, 23 Mont. 387, 55 Pac. 153.

[2] Mills' Annot. Stats., § 3150.

[3] *Id.*, § 3151. See Duncan v. Fulton (Colo. App.), 61 Pac. 244.

[4] *Ante*, § 354.

(3) date of discovery; (4) direction and distance claimed along the ledge from the discovery; (5) distance claimed on each side of the middle of the ledge; (6) distance and direction from discovery monument to some natural object by which the claim may be identified; (7) name of mining district, county, and state.[1]

Arizona.—The notice or certificate of location must contain: (1) name of the claim; (2) name of locator; (3) date of location; (4) length and width of the claim in feet, and number of feet claimed on each side of point of discovery to each end of the claim; (5) general course of the claim; (6) the locality of the claim with reference to some natural object or permanent monument as will identify the claim.[2]

Montana.—The instrument which is to be recorded is called the "declaratory statement." It must contain: (1) name of lode or claim; (2) name of locator; (3) date of location, and such a description with reference to natural objects or permanent monuments as will identify the claim; (4) the number of linear feet claimed along the course of the vein each way from point of discovery, with the width on each side of the center of the vein, and the general course of the vein as near as may be; (5) dimensions and location of discovery shaft, cut, or tunnel, or its equivalent, sunk upon the lode. The declaratory statement must be verified by the oath of a locator, or one of the locators, and, in case of a corporation, by a duly authorized officer.[3]

[1] Laws of 1895, p. 25, § 2, as amended—Laws of 1899, p. 633; Civil Code (1901), § 2557. See Morrison *v.* Regan (Idaho), 67 Pac. 955, explaining Clearwater Shortline Ry. *v.* San Garde (Idaho), 61 Pac. 137; Brown *v.* Levan (Idaho), 46 Pac. 661.

[2] Rev. Stats. (1901), § 3232. See Wiltsee *v.* King of Arizona M. and M. Co. (Ariz.), 60 Pac. 896.

[3] Rev. Code of 1895, § 3612, as amended—Laws of 1901, p. 141, § 2.

The statute is mandatory, and a substantial compliance with its provisions is necessary to perfect a valid location.[1]

Nevada.—The contents of this location certificate are the same as those required in Montana, with the addition of (6) location and description of each corner with the markings thereon. The certificate need not be verified.[2]

New Mexico.—A copy of the posted notice is required to be recorded. This must contain: (1) the names of the locators; (2) the intent to locate the claim; (3) a description by reference to some natural object or permanent monument.[3]

North Dakota.—The location certificate must contain: (1) name of lode; (2) name of locator; (3) date of location; (4) number of feet in length claimed on each side of the discovery shaft; (5) number of feet in width claimed on each side of lode; (6) general course of lode as near as may be;[4] (7) such a description as shall identify the claim with reasonable certainty.[5]

Oregon.—The location notice shall contain: (1) name of the lode or claim; (2) name of locator; (3) date of location; (4) number of linear feet claimed along the lode each way from the point of discovery with the width on each side of the lode; (5) the general course or strike of the vein as nearly as may be with

---

[1] Purdum *v.* Laddin, 23 Mont. 387, 59 Pac. 153. See, also, Sanders *v.* Noble, 22 Mont. 110, 55 Pac. 1037.

[2] Comp. Laws (1900), § 210.

[3] Comp. Laws of 1884, § 1566; *Id.* 1897, § 2286; *ante*, § 353. Under this statute posting and discovery must be contemporaneous, no appreciable time being allowed between the discovery and the posting of the statutory notice. Moreover, the notice must be such as, when recorded, will fulfill the requirements of the federal statute.

[4] Rev. Code 1895, § 1428; *Id.* 1899, § 1428.

[5] *Id.* 1895, § 1429.

reference to some natural object or permanent monument in the vicinity thereof.[1]

South Dakota.—The requirements as to certificate of location are the same as in North Dakota.[2]

Utah.—The requirements as to the contents of the location notice are substantially the same as those of Oregon.[3]

Washington.—The location notice is required to contain: (1) name of locator; (2) date of location; (3) number of feet in length claimed on each side of the discovery; (4) the general course of the lode; (5) such a description by reference to natural objects or permanent monuments as will identify the claim.[4]

Wyoming.—The certificate must contain: (1) name of the lode; (2) name of the locator or locators; (3) date of location; (4) length of claim along the vein, measured from center of discovery shaft, and general course of the vein as far as known; (5) amount of surface ground claimed on either side of the center of the discovery shaft or workings; (6) a description of the claim by such designation of natural or fixed objects as will identify the claim beyond question.[5]

§ 381. **Rules of construction applied.**—In the initiation of rights upon public mineral lands, as well as in the various steps taken by the miner to perfect his location, his proceedings are to be regarded with indulgence, and the notices required invariably receive at the hands

[1] Laws of 1898, p. 16, as amended—Laws of 1901, p. 140.

[2] Comp. Laws of 1887, §§ 1999, 2000. Adopted by South Dakota—Laws of 1890, ch. cv, § 1; Grantham's Annot. Stats. S. D. (1899), § 2658, as amended—Laws of 1899, p. 146.

[3] Laws of 1899, p. 26.

[4] Laws of 1899, p. 69, § 1.

[5] Session Laws of 1890-91, ch. xlvi, pp. 179-180, amended—Laws of 1895, ch. cviii, § 1; Rev. Stats. (1899), § 2546.

of the courts a liberal construction.[1] The mining laws
are "to be expounded with as little differentiation as
" may be between former known actual customs of
" miners and the formulated expressions of congress
" based upon those customs in present positive law."[2]

"The courts always construe these notices liberally,
" and if by any intendment the proof can be reconciled
" and made consistent with the statement contained in
" them, the jury will be allowed to say whether or not,
" upon the whole proof, the identification is sufficient."[3]

To hold the locator to absolute technical strictness in
all the minor details, would be practically to defeat the
manifest end and object of the law. The pioneer prospector, as a rule, is neither a lawyer nor a surveyor.
Neither mathematical precision as to measurement nor
technical accuracy of expression in the preparation of
notices is either contemplated or required.[4] The law
being designed for the encouragement and benefit of the
miners should be liberally interpreted,[5] "looking to
" substance, rather than shadow, and should be admin-
" istered on the lines of obvious common sense."[6] Mere
imperfections in the certificate will not render it void.[7]

[1] Carter v. Bacigalupi, 83 Cal. 187, 23 Pac. 361; Farmington G. M. Co.
v. Rhymney G. and C. Co., 20 Utah, 363, 77 Am. St. Rep. 913, 58 Pac.
832; Fissure M. Co. v. Old Susan M. Co., 22 Utah, 438, 63 Pac. 587;
Wiltsee v. King of Arizona M. and M. Co. (Ariz.), 60 Pac. 896; Talmadge v. St. John, 129 Cal. 430, 62 Pac. 79; Morrison v. Regan (Idaho),
67 Pac. 955; Prince of Wales Lode, 2 Copp's L. O. 2, 3.

[2] Sanders v. Noble, 22 Mont. 110, 55 Pac. 1037.

[3] Bramlett v. Flick, 23 Mont. 95, 57 Pac. 869.

[4] Book v. Justice M. Co., 58 Fed. 106, 115; Smith v. Newell, 86 Fed. 56;
Sanders v. Noble, 22 Mont. 110, 55 Pac. 1037, 1047; Wilson v. Triumph
Cons. M. Co. (Utah), 56 Pac. 300; Farmington G. M. Co. v. Rhymney
G. and C. Co., 20 Utah, 363, 58 Pac. 832; Morrison v. Regan (Idaho),
67 Pac. 955.

[5] Meydenbauer v. Stevens, 78 Fed. 787; Sanders v. Noble, 22 Mont. 110,
55 Pac. 1037, 1046; Bramlett v. Flick, 23 Mont. 95, 57 Pac. 869.

[6] Cheesman v. Hart, 42 Fed. 98, 99.

[7] Bennett v. Harkrader, 158 U. S. 441, 443, 15 Sup. Ct. Rep. 863;
Farmington G. M. Co. v. Rhymney G. and C. Co., 20 Utah, 363, 77 Am.
St. Rep. 913, 58 Pac. 832; Wells v. Davis, 22 Utah, 322, 62 Pac. 3.

As was said by the supreme court of Utah,—

"If by any reasonable construction, in view of the
" surrounding circumstances, the language employed in
" the description will impart notice to subsequent loca-
" tors, it is sufficient."[1]

In matters of description, calls that are erroneous will
not destroy the validity of the notice or certificate, if by
excluding them a sufficient description remain to enable
its application to be ascertained.[2]

Thus, where a certificate of a location specified its
situs as being in the wrong county, it being otherwise
valid, and having been recorded in the right county, the
erroneous statement was mere surplusage, and as such
was rejected.[3]

In the absence of a local requirement to that effect,
the certificate need not state either the district, county,
or state in which the location is situated.[4]

And where a state statute requires two notices, one
preliminary, and the other final, if the former contained
the name of the county, and the final one omitted it, but
refers to the preliminary notice, the defect is cured.[5]

The position of the monuments as built upon the
ground may be described in such a way as to direction
as to be confusing. But if the other statutory requirements were complied with the notice would be sufficiently correct to allow its admission in evidence.[6]

[1] Wells v. Davis, 22 Utah, 322, 62 Pac. 3.

[2] Duryea v. Boucher, 67 Cal. 141, 7 Pac. 421; Smith v. Newell, 86 Fed.
56; Bramlett v. Flick, 23 Mont. 95, 57 Pac. 869.

[3] Metcalf v. Prescott, 10 Mont. 283, 25 Pac. 1037. Note the difference
in case of notice of application for patent where this defect would render
such notice void. Wright v. Sioux Cons. M. Co., 29 L. D. 154, S. C.
29 L. D. 289.

[4] Carter v. Bacigalupi, 83 Cal. 187, 23 Pac. 361.

[5] Talmadge v. St. John, 129 Cal. 430, 62 Pac. 79.

[6] Kinney v. Fleming (Ariz.), 56 Pac. 723; Providence G. M. Co. v.
Burke (Ariz.), 57 Pac. 641; Bramlett v. Flick, 23 Mont. 95, 57 Pac. 869.

A mistake in the certificate as to the direction and course, such as "northerly" instead of "northeasterly," the description being aided by monuments on the ground, is of no moment.[1]

The certificate is not required to show the precise boundaries of the claim as marked on the ground, but it is sufficient if it contains directions, which, taken in connection with such boundaries, will enable a person of reasonable intelligence to find the claim and trace the lines.[2]

The object of any notice at all being to guide the subsequent locator and afford him information as to the extent of the claim of the prior locator, whatever does this fairly and reasonably should be held to be a good notice. Great injustice would follow if, years after a miner had located a claim and taken possession, and worked upon it in good faith, his notice of location were to be subject to any very nice criticism.[3]

§ 382. **Variation between calls in certificate and monuments on the ground.**—When it is once conceded that a recorded certificate of location is a statutory in-

---

[1] Book v. Justice M. Co., 58 Fed. 106, 115; Meydenbauer v. Stevens, 78 Fed. 787; Sanders v. Noble, 22 Mont. 110, 55 Pac. 1037, 1046; Bramlett v. Flick, 23 Mont. 95, 55 Pac. 869; Wiltsee v. King of Arizona M. Co. (Ariz.), 60 Pac. 896.

[2] Brady v. Husby, 21 Nev. 153; Duncan v. Fulton (Colo. App.), 61 Pac. 244; Bramlett v. Flick, 23 Mont. 95, 57 Pac. 869; Smith v. Newell, 86 Fed. 56; Kinney v. Fleming (Ariz.), 56 Pac. 723; Providence G. M. Co. v. Burke (Ariz.), 57 Pac. 641; Morrison v. Regan (Idaho), 67 Pac. 955; Gamer v. Glenn, 8 Mont. 371, 20 Pac. 654; Upton v. Larkin, 7 Mont. 449, 17 Pac. 728; Flavin v. Mattingly, 8 Mont. 242, 19 Pac. 384.

The adoption in Montana of a more exacting law (Pol. Code of 1895, § 3612) has rendered the earlier Montana cases inapplicable in that state. Purdum v. Laddin, 23 Mont. 387, 59 Pac. 153. And see Clearwater etc. Ry. Co. v. San Garde (Idaho), 61 Pac. 137; Brown v. Levan (Idaho), 46 Pac. 661, (explained in Morrison v. Regan (Idaho), 67 Pac. 955).

[3] Mt. Diablo M. and M. Co. v. Callison, 5 Saw. 439, Fed. Cas. No. 9886; Talmadge v. St. John, 129 Cal. 430, 62 Pac. 79.

strument affecting real property,[1] it follows that general rules regarding descriptive calls in this class of instruments apply generally to the construction of such certificates. But it has been held that where the position of the monuments as built upon a mining claim are described in such a way as to direction as to be confusing, the notice would nevertheless be sufficiently correct to be admitted in evidence.[2]

Mr. Washburn states the general rule to be, that courses and distances are generally regarded as more or less uncertain, and always give place, in questions of doubt or discrepancy, to monuments and boundaries that are referred to as indicating and identifying the land.[3]

This doctrine has been uniformly applied by the courts to certificates of location of mining claims.[4]

The general rule applicable to patents, deeds, and other instruments of conveyance, that where a monument is referred to in a descriptive call, and it has been obliterated or destroyed, parol evidence may be introduced to show where it was actually located in the field, does not, it seems, apply to certificates of location. As heretofore indicated, in order to invoke the rule that courses and distance yield to monuments, these monuments must be actually existing, and parol evidence is inadmissible to point out where they were originally

---

[1] *Ante*, § 379.

[2] Kinney *v.* Fleming (Ariz.), 58 Pac. 723; Providence G. M. Co. *v.* Burke (Ariz.), 57 Pac. 641; Bramlett *v.* Flick, 23 Mont. 95, 57 Pac. 869.

[3] 3 Washburn on Real Property, 3d ed., p. 348; 2 Devlin on Deeds, § 1029; Garrard *v.* Silver Peak Mines, 82 Fed. 578, 585; Belden *v.* Hebbard, 103 Fed. 532.

[4] Pollard *v.* Shively, 5 Colo. 309, 313; Book *v.* Justice M. Co., 58 Fed. 106, 115; Hoffman *v.* Beecher, 12 Mont. 489, 31 Pac. 92; Cullacott *v.* Cash G. S. M. Co., 8 Colo. 179, 6 Pac. 211; McEvoy *v.* Hyman, 25 Fed. 596, 599; Smith *v.* Newell, 86 Fed. 56; Meydenbauer *v.* Stevens, 78 Fed. 787.

placed.[1] The reason for this rule has been fully explained in a preceding section.[2]

§ 383. "Natural objects" and "permanent monu-"ments."— The words "natural objects" and "per-" manent monuments" are general terms, susceptible of different shades of meaning, depending largely upon their application. What might be regarded as a permanent monument for one purpose, might not be so considered with reference to a different purpose. The same rule applies to natural objects.[3] There is no particular necessity for drawing a distinction between "natural " objects," such as streams, rivers, ponds, highways, trees, and other things, *ejusdem generis,* and "perma-" nent monuments," which may imply an element of artificial construction, it being the manifest intent of the law that any object of a fairly permanent character, whether natural or artificial, may, if sufficiently prominent, serve for the purpose of reference and identification.

As to whether a given notice or certificate of location contains such a description of the claim as located by reference to some natural object or permanent monument as will identify it, is a question of fact to be determined by the jury,[4] and parol evidence is admissible for the purpose of proving that the thing named

[1] Pollard *v.* Shively, 5 Colo. 309, 318; Thallmann *v.* Thomas, 102 Fed. 925.

[2] *Ante,* § 375.

[3] Quinby *v.* Boyd, 8 Colo. 194, 6 Pac. 462.

[4] Eilers *v.* Boatman, 111 U. S. 356, 4 Sup. Ct. Rep. 432; Bramlett *v.* Flick, 23 Mont. 95, 57 Pac. 869; Farmington G. M. Co. *v.* Rhymney G. M. Co., 20 Utah, 363, 77 Am. St. Rep. 913, 58 Pac. 832; Fissure M. Co. *v.* Old Susan M. Co., 22 Utah, 438, 63 Pac. 587; Gamer *v.* Glenn, 8 Mont. 371, 20 Pac. 654; Brady *v.* Husby, 21 Nev. 453, 33 Pac. 801; Flavin *v.* Mattingly, 8 Mont. 242, 19 Pac. 384; Metcalf *v.* Prescott, 10 Mont. 283, 25 Pac. 1037; Russell *v.* Chumasero, 4 Mont. 309, 1 Pac. 713.

in the certificate is, in fact, a natural object or permanent monument.[1] In the absence of evidence for, or against, the sufficiency of the reference in the notice, it will be presumed to be sufficient to identify the claim.[2]

The following cases indicate the views of the courts as to what are natural objects or permanent monuments:—

Prominent posts, or stakes, firmly planted in the ground;[3] stones, if of proper size and properly marked;[4] monuments,[5] prospect holes,[6] and shafts,[7] a depot and cliff of rocks,[8] may be sufficient as permanent monuments within the meaning of the law.[9] The boundary lines of well known claims have uniformly been held to be such.[10] It has been held that if a notice refers to a

---

[1] Carter v. Bacigalupi, 83 Cal. 187, 23 Pac. 361; O'Donnell v. Glenn, 8 Mont. 248, 19 Pac. 302; Flavin v. Mattingly, 8 Mont. 242, 19 Pac. 384; Metcalf v. Prescott, 10 Mont. 283, 25 Pac. 1037; Dillon v. Bayliss, 11 Mont. 171, 27 Pac. 725; Kelly v. Taylor, 23 Cal. 14; Prince of Wales Lode, 2 Copp's L. O. 2, 3.

[2] Brady v. Husby, 21 Nev. 453, 33 Pac. 801; Gleeson v. Martin White M. Co., 13 Nev. 442; Hammer v. Garfield M. and M. Co., 130 U. S. 291, 299, 9 Sup. Ct. Rep. 548; Bramlett v. Flick, 23 Mont. 95, 57 Pac. 869; Buffalo Zinc and Copper Co. v. Crump (Ark.), 69 S. W. 572, 576.

[3] Jupiter M. Co. v. Bodie Cons. M. Co., 7 Saw. 96, 112, 11 Fed. 666; Russell v. Chumasero, 4 Mont. 309, 1 Pac. 713; O'Donnell v. Glenn, 8 Mont. 248, 19 Pac. 302; Hanson v. Fletcher, 10 Utah, 266, 37 Pac. 480; Bramlett v. Flick, 23 Mont. 95, 57 Pac. 869; Credo M. and S. Co. v. Highland M. and M. Co., 95 Fed. 911; Duncan v. Fulton (Colo App.), 61 Pac. 244.

[4] Russell v. Chumasero, 4 Mont. 309, 1 Pac. 713; Gamer v. Glenn, 8 Mont. 371, 20 Pac. 654.

[5] Hansen v. Fletcher, 10 Utah, 266, 37 Pac. 480; Talmadge v. St. John, 129 Cal. 430, 62 Pac. 79; Credo M. Co. v. Highland Co., 95 Fed. 911.

[6] Hansen v. Fletcher, 10 Utah, 266, 37 Pac. 480.

[7] Jupiter M. Co. v. Bodie Cons. M. Co., 7 Saw. 96, 111, 11 Fed. 666; North Noonday M. Co. v. Orient M. Co., 6 Saw. 299, 312, 1 Fed. 522.

[8] Farmington Co. v. Rhymney Co., 20 Utah, 363, 77 Am. St. Rep. 913, 58 Pac. 832.

[9] Meydenbauer v. Stevens, 78 Fed. 787.

[10] Upton v. Larkin, 7 Mont. 449, 17 Pac. 728; Russell v. Chumasero, 4 Mont. 309, 1 Pac. 713; Hammer v. Garfield M. and M. Co., 130 U. S. 291, 9 Sup. Ct. Rep. 548; Metcalf v. Prescott, 10 Mont. 283, 25 Pac. 1037; Book v. Justice M. Co., 58 Fed. 106; Southern Cross M. Co. v.

mining claim there is a presumption that such claim exists,[1] and that it is well known.[2] A tree is a fixed natural object, and when marked artificially or naturally there is less room to question its sufficiency than in the case of a shaft.[3] A cañon, or any other prominent feature of the landscape, is a natural object.[4] The natural objects or permanent monuments referred to are not required to be on the ground located, although they may be.[5]

§ 384. Effect of failure to comply with the law as to contents of certificate.—It follows from what we have heretofore said that any notice or certificate of location which is used as the basis of the record which fails to reasonably comply with the requirements of the federal law as to the contents of such record is ineffectual and void.[6] As to the omission of any of the other elements

Europa M. Co., 15 Nev. 383; Gamer v. Glenn, 8 Mont. 451, 20 Pac. 658; Live Yankee Co. v. Oregon Co., 7 Cal. 41; Duncan v. Fulton (Colo. App.), 61 Pac. 244; Riste v. Morton, 20 Mont. 139, 49 Pac. 656; Smith v. Newell, 86 Fed. 56; Wilson v. Triumph Cons. M. Co., 19 Utah, 66, 75 Am. St. Rep. 718, 56 Pac. 300; Kinney v. Fleming (Ariz.), 56 Pac. 723; Morrison v. Regan (Idaho), 67 Pac. 955; McCann v. McMillan, 129 Cal. 350, 62 Pac. 33. Contra: Baxter Mt. G. M. Co. v. Patterson, 3 N. Mex. 179, 3 Pac. 741. See Gilpin etc. Co. v. Drake, 8 Colo. 586, 9 Pac. 787, (overruled by Duncan v. Fulton (Colo. App.), 61 Pac. 244). And see Brown v. Levan (Idaho), 46 Pac. 661, (explained in Morrison v. Regan (Idaho), 67 Pac. 955).

[1] Kinney v. Fleming (Ariz.), 56 Pac. 723.

[2] Bramlett v. Flick, 23 Mont. 95, 57 Pac. 869; Credo M. Co. v. Highland M. and M. Co., 95 Fed. 911.

[3] Quinby v. Boyd, 8 Colo. 194, 6 Pac. 462.

[4] Flavin v. Mattingly, 8 Mont. 242, 19 Pac. 284; Duncan v. Fulton (Colo. App.), 61 Pac. 244; McKinley Creek M. Co. v. Alaska United M. Co., 183 U. S. 563, 22 Sup. Ct. Rep. 84.

[5] North Noonday M. Co. v. Orient M. Co., 6 Saw. 299, 1 Fed. 522; Talmadge v. St. John, 129 Cal. 430, 62 Pac. 79; Credo M. Co. v. Highland M. and M. Co., 95 Fed. 911.

[6] Deeney v. Mineral Creek M. Co. (N. Mex.), 67 Pac. 724; Purdum v. Laddin, 23 Mont. 387, 59 Pac. 153. See Brown v. Levan (Idaho), 46 Pac. 61, and Clearwater Ry. Co. v. San Garde (Idaho), 61 Pac. 137, as explained in Morrison v. Regan (Idaho), 67 Pac. 955.

required by state legislation, in some of the states the
law itself prescribes the penalty by providing that
the failure to insert any of the requirements renders the
location void. This is the rule in Colorado, Nevada,
North and South Dakota. The laws of the other states
and territories are silent upon the subject.

If the California-Arizona rule applicable to local
regulations and customs [1] may be properly invoked in
the case of statutory enactments,—that is, that a forfeiture is not worked unless the custom or local rule in terms
so declares,[2]—the provisions of the statutes in the latter
class of states, exacting requirements in excess of those
made essential by the federal law, are merely directory,
and their omission is accompanied with no serious consequences. We do not see why such rule should not be
applicable alike to local and statutory regulations. As
to the other states, where legislation of the character
noted is found, it may be said that forfeitures are not
favored by the courts, and where a location is made in
good faith and all the essential requirements are complied with, instances are not frequent where the miner
is deprived of substantial rights for failure to strictly
comply with the letter of the law.

§ 385.   **Verification of certificates.**—Two of the states,
Idaho and Montana, require the certificate of location,
or declaratory statement, to be verified by the oath of a
locator.[3] In a preceding section [4] we have suggested
that these provisions may be repugnant to the federal
law, as imposing unnecessary and onerous burdens upon

[1] *Ante*, § 274.

[2] This rule does not obtain in Montana and Nevada. *Ante*, § 274;
Purdum *v.* Laddin, 23 Mont. 387, 59 Pac. 153; Sissons *v.* Sommers, 24
Nev. 379, 77 Am. St. Rep. 815, 55 Pac. 829.

[3] The term ''locator'' has been construed to include the agent who
locates the claim. Dunlap *v.* Pattison (Idaho), 42 Pac. 504.

[4] *Ante*, § 251.

locators. We have there shown that the supreme court of Montana at first doubted the validity of the provision, but afterwards upheld it. The supreme court of Idaho has reached the same conclusion.[1] Where the law makes notices of this character *prima facie* evidence of the facts therein recited, it would seem that the formality of an oath is not an unreasonable requirement. In many states instruments affecting title to real property are required to be verified before they are entitled to record, and all states require some form of acknowledgment to such class of documents. We do not see, upon principle, why the law, as found in Montana and Idaho, should not be upheld.

ARTICLE IX.   THE RECORD.

§ 389. Time and place of record.
§ 390. Effect of failure to record within the time limited.
§ 391. Proof of record.
§ 392. The record as evidence.

§ 389.   **Time and place of record.**—As heretofore frequently indicated,[2] in the absence of a state law or local rule requiring it, there is no necessity for recording any notice or certificate in connection with the acquisition of title to public mineral lands by location.

But as observed in a preceding section,[3] the popular notion is, that notices of location should be recorded somewhere, and although in the absence of a law or rule so declaring, a failure to record is not accompanied with any loss of right,[4] yet the universal rule is to file the notice of location with the county officer charged by the state or territorial laws with the duty of registering instruments affecting title to real estate. In the absence

---

[1] Van Buren *v.* McKinley (Idaho), 66 Pac. 936.
[2] *Ante,* §§ 273, 328.
[3] *Ante,* § 273.
[4] Bramlett *v.* Flick, 23 Mont. 95, 57 Pac. 869.

of a statute a county recorder cannot be compelled to record. But if he chooses to do so, he does it not as county recorder elected by the people, but as a person selected by the miners to do an act not provided for by the recordation laws of the state.[1]

Where the law or regulation requires a record to be made, but does not specify the time within which it is to be effected, we think a reasonable time should be allowed, following the rule heretofore announced as to the time of performance of other acts of location.[2] What constitutes a reasonable time depends upon the circumstances surrounding each particular case, such as the distance from the discovered mine to the place of record, and the means of communication between the two points. For the most part, the states and territories wherein laws exist requiring a record to be made provide for the time within which the notice or certificate is to be lodged with the recording officer. Colorado,[3] allows three months; North Dakota,[4] South Dakota,[5] and Wyoming,[6] sixty days; Washington,[7] ninety days, computed from date of discovery; Idaho,[8] and Arizona,[9] ninety days from date of *location;* Montana[10] and Oregon,[11] sixty days; Nevada,[12] ninety days; New Mex-

---

[1] San Bernardino Co. *v.* Davidson, 112 Cal. 503, 44 Pac. 659. See Kern County *v.* Lee, 129 Cal. 361, 61 Pac. 1124.

[2] *Ante,* § 339.

[3] Mills' Annot. Stats., § 3150.

[4] Rev. Code of 1895, § 1428; *Id.* 1899, § 1428.

[5] Comp. Laws of Dak. 1887, §§ 1999, 2000. Adopted by S. Dak.— Laws of 1890, § 1; Grantham's Annot. Stats. S. Dak. (1899), § 2658, as amended—Laws of 1899, p. 146.

[6] Rev. Stats. (1899), § 2546.

[7] Laws of 1899, p. 69, § 1.

[8] Laws of 1895, p. 25, § 4; Civil Code (1901), § 2559.

[9] Rev. Stats. (1901), § 3234; Jordan *v.* Duke (Ariz.), 53 Pac. 197.

[10] Rev. Code of 1895, § 3612, as amended—Laws of 1901, p. 141, § 2.

[11] Laws of 1898, p. 16, as amended—Laws of 1901, p. 140.

[12] Comp. Laws (1900), § 210.

ico,[1] three months, and Utah,[2] thirty days, from posting the preliminary notice referred to in a preceding article.[3]

Nevada provides for recording with the district recorder and the county recorder.[4]

In Utah, if there is a mining district recorder, the original and a duplicate must be filed with him, and it is made his duty to transmit the duplicate to the county recorder for record. If there is no mining district recorder, the record must be made directly with the county recorder.[5]

In California, it was customary, before the passage of the act of March, 1897, to record in the county recorder's office, as well as with the district recorder, if there was one. In the absence of a written district rule, a custom as to place of record might be shown. But such custom, to be binding, ought to be so well known, understood, and recognized in the district, that locators should have no reasonable ground for doubt as to what was required as to place of record.[6]

In 1897 an act was passed, however, regulating the subject of recording and prohibiting district records. The act has now been repealed,[7] and there is consequently no inhibition of a return to the custom.

Arkansas,[8] authorizes recording with the *ex-officio* recorder of the county, but does not make recording imperative or fix any limit of time in which the record shall be made.

---

[1] Comp. Laws of 1884, § 1566; *Id.* 1897, § 2286.

[2] Laws of 1899, p. 26, § 4.

[3] *Ante,* §§ 350-353.

[4] Comp. Laws (1900), § 210.

[5] Laws of 1899, p. 26, §§ 4, 9.

[6] *Ante,* § 273.

[7] Stats. 1899, p. 148; County of Kern *v.* Lee, 129 Cal. 361, 61 Pac. 1124; Stats. 1900, p. 9.

[8] Act of 1899, p. 113, §§ 1, 2, 3.

§ 390. Effect of failure to record within the time limited.— The mere failure to record a notice, certificate, or declaratory statement within the statutory time does not render the location of the claim invalid, where there are no intervening rights before the record is properly made, if there has been full compliance with the law in all other respects.[1]

This is but the reiteration of a principle announced in a previous section,[2] that the failure to comply with any of the requirements of the law within the time limited *may* subject the ground to relocation;[3] that the locator delays the performance of these acts at his peril; but if he complies with the law prior to the acquisition of any right by a subsequent locator, no one has a right to complain. The claim may not be relocated until after the time to record has expired;[4] and if the first locator does all the other acts with intent to locate, but fails to record within the time limited, he gets a good title, notwithstanding a subsequent locator performs all the acts of location, including recording, prior to the time in which the first locator should have recorded.[5] The acts when completed will relate back to the inception of the right. If the certificate is deposited with the recorder to be recorded, that is sufficient. His failure to record will not injure the locator.[6]

Where the requirement as to recording is fixed by

---

[1] Preston *v.* Hunter, 67 Fed. 996, 999; Faxon *v.* Barnard, 4 Fed. 702, 703; Strepey *v.* Stark, 7 Colo. 614, 5 Pac. 111; Craig *v.* Thompson, 10 Colo. 517, 16 Pac. 24. See, also, Lockhart *v.* Leeds (N. Mex.), 63 Pac. 51.

[2] *Ante,* § 330.

[3] Lockhart *v.* Wills, 9 N. Mex. 344, 54 Pac. 336.

[4] Lockhart *v.* Leeds (N. Mex.), 63 Pac. 51, S. C. *sub nom.* Lockhart *v.* Johnson, 181 U. S. 518, 21 Sup. Ct. Rep. 665. See, also, Belk *v.* Meagher, 104 U. S. 279.

[5] Bramlett *v.* Flick, 23 Mont. 95, 57 Pac. 869. See, also, Shepard *v.* Murphy, 26 Colo. 350, 58 Pac. 588.

[6] Shepard *v.* Murphy, 26 Colo. 350, 58 Pac. 588.

local rule, the failure to record, in our opinion, will not work forfeiture unless the rule itself so provides.

This is the view adopted by the supreme courts of California and Arizona. The contrary rule is applied by the courts in Montana and Nevada.[1]

§ 391. **Proof of record.**—Where a state law or local rule requires the certificate to be recorded with a county officer whose duties are defined by statute, such as recorder, clerk, or register of deeds, the record will prove itself, and, as a rule, certified copies thereof are admissible in evidence with like effect as the original. But in case of records in the mining district, the rule is different. Such records do not prove themselves. They must be produced by the proper officer, whose official character must be shown, and the authenticity of such records must be established.[2] Certified copies of such records cannot be admitted in evidence, unless it be first shown that their custodian was empowered under the local rules to give and authenticate such copies.[3]

§ 392. **The record as evidence.**—Constructive notice by recording is wholly a creature of the statute. A record not provided for by statute or recognized by law gives no notice. Therefore, before a record of a mining location can be introduced in evidence for any purpose, it must appear that it is authorized by law; otherwise, it is irrelevant and inadmissible.[4]

Where such record is authorized, it is *prima facie* evidence only of such facts as are required by law to be

[1] *Ante,* § 274.

[2] Roberts *v.* Wilson, 1 Utah, 292.

[3] Harvey *v.* Ryan, 42 Cal. 626; Roberts *v.* Wilson, 1 Utah, 292; *ante,* § 272. See, also, Attwood *v.* Fricot, 17 Cal. 37, 76 Am. Dec. 567.

[4] Moxon *v.* Wilkinson, 2 Mont. 421; Golden Fleece M. Co. *v.* Cable Cons. M. Co., 12 Nev. 312; Chamberlain *v.* Bell, 7 Cal. 292, 68 Am. Dec. 260; Mesick *v.* Sunderland, 6 Cal. 298, 315; 1 Wharton on Evidence, 3d ed., § 643.

stated therein,[1] provided they are sufficiently stated.[2] A record of a certificate of a location which recites the citizenship of locators, the fact of discovery, and the fact that the location had been marked upon the ground so that the boundaries could be readily traced, is not evidence of any of these facts [3] in any of the states or territories, for the simple reason that no such facts are required to be stated in any of the statutory notices.[4]

Where the right of possession is founded upon an alleged compliance with the law relating to a valid location, all the necessary steps, aside from the making and recording of the location certificate, must, when contested, be established by proof outside of such certificate. The record of the certificate is proof itself of its own performance as one of such steps, and in regular order, generally speaking, the last step in perfecting the location.[5]

While many of the states require the date of the discovery to be stated in the recorded certificate, this would not be evidence of the *fact* of discovery.[6] A discovery once proved, such a record would, *prima facie,* fix the date. Discovery is the most important of all the acts required in the proceedings culminating in a perfected location. It is the foundation of the right without which all other acts are idle and superfluous. With the exception of two states (Idaho and Montana), the certificate is executed with no solemnity. It is

---

[1] 2 Jones on Evidence, § 521.

[2] Strepey v. Stark, 7 Colo. 614, 5 Pac. 111; Jantzen v. Arizona C. Co. (Ariz.), 20 Pac. 93.

[3] Flick v. Gold Hill & L. M. Co., 8 Mont. 298, 20 Pac. 807.

[4] Magruder v. Oregon and California R. R. Co., 28 L. D. 174.

[5] Strepey v. Stark, 7 Colo. 614, 619, 5 Pac. 111; Magruder v. Oregon and California R. R. Co., 28 L. D. 174; Farmington G. M. Co. v. Rhymney G. and C. Co., 20 Utah, 363, 77 Am. St. Rep. 913, 58 Pac. 832, 833.

[6] Smith v. Newell, 86 Fed. 56; Magruder v. Oregon and California R. R. Co., 28 L. D. 174; McQuiddy v. State of California, 29 L. D. 181; Elda M. Co., 29 L. D. 279; Harkrader v. Goldstein, 31 L. D. 87.

neither acknowledged nor sworn to. It is a mere *ex parte* declaration on his own behalf of the party most interested.[1] The same may be said of marking the boundaries.

It is quite true that when a certificate contains a description of the claim with reference to a natural object or permanent monument, the recorded notice to this extent may be *prima facie* evidence of its own sufficiency, for the reason that the statute requires such description to be inserted in the certificate.[2]

The real purpose of the record is to operate as constructive notice of the fact of an asserted *claim* and its extent.[3] When the locator's right is challenged, he should be compelled to establish by proof outside of the certificate all the essential facts, without the existence of which the certificate possesses no potential validity. These facts once proved, the recorded certificate may be considered as *prima facie* evidence of such other facts as are required to be stated therein.

ARTICLE X. CHANGE OF BOUNDARIES AND AMENDED OR ADDITIONAL LOCATION CERTIFICATES.

§ 396. Circumstances justifying change of boundaries.

§ 397. Privilege of changing boundaries exists in the absence of intervening rights, independent of state legislation.

§ 398. Objects and functions of amended certificates.

---

[1] Judge Phillips, in his charge to the jury in Cheesman *v.* Shreeve, 40 Fed. 787, said that certificates of location are presumptive evidence of discovery. But in this case, many years elapsed between the original location and the litigation, and the fact of discovery was supported by the testimony of the parties. Under these circumstances the judge held that every reasonable presumption should be indulged in favor of the integrity of the location. The reasoning, while persuasive so far as this case is concerned, does not militate against the views announced in the text.

[2] See Kinney *v.* Fleming (Ariz.), 56 Pac. 723; Providence G. M. Co. *v.* Burke (Ariz.), 57 Pac. 641.

[3] Meydenbauer *v.* Stevens, 78 Fed. 787.

§ 396. Circumstances justifying change of boundaries.—The difficulties surrounding the locator in determining the precise position of his discovered vein in the earth, the probable course of its apex, and in many instances its width, frequently render it impossible for him to so mark his boundaries within the time allowed by law for that purpose as to entitle him to the full measure of property rights which the law permits him to acquire as the reward for his discovery. It frequently happens that the limited extent of surface exploration possible within the periods allowed him does not develop the true conditions. His markings, therefore, are frequently based on erroneous suppositions and wrong theories. While the government is not concerned with the particular individual who is the recipient of its bounty, and it makes but little difference to it who discovers and develops its mineral resources, its policy is to encourage the search for, and the opening of, mines, and this policy is best subserved by permitting the discoverer to rectify and readjust his lines whenever he may do so without impairing the intervening rights of others.

While the locator marks his boundaries in every instance at his peril, there is no reason why he should be compelled to abide by first impressions, if no one is injured by a subsequent rectification of such boundaries.

It also frequently happens, that at the time a discovery is made, the existence of contiguous prior locations prevents him from giving to his surface that symmetrical form which the law contemplates; or if he makes it in the ideal form, a surface conflict arises, rendering the extent of his rights vague and uncertain. These prior locations are frequently abandoned, and the ground embraced therein becomes subject to reappropriation. As heretofore suggested, when such abandonment or forfeiture becomes effectual, the conflict area does not inure to the advantage of the junior locator.[1] But the courts uphold the right of the junior under such circumstances to re-form his lines and amend his location so as to include the overlapping surface.[2]

There is no statute, law, rule, or regulation which prevents a locator of a mining claim from relocating his own claim, and including additional vacant ground unclaimed by other parties, or even giving to the new location a different name.[3]

Where an application for patent is made, and a survey for that purpose is ordered, the deputy mineral surveyor is controlled by the record of the certificate of location, where one is required,[4] and the markings on the ground, the latter controlling where there is a variation between the descriptive calls of the record and the monuments.[5] While, for the purpose of obtaining parallelism,[6] or casting off excess,[7] the lines may be drawn in, so that, as finally surveyed, the boundaries are approximately within the limits of the surface area as originally claimed, yet no authority is given to extend the surveyed boundaries so as to include area which at the time of the survey is not within the ground actually claimed, or found to be, at least, approximately within the lines connecting the monuments as marked, prior to the order for survey.

It is therefore frequently found necessary to change boundaries before applying for an order for survey;

[1] *Ante*, § 363.

[2] *Id.*

[3] Shoshone M. Co. *v.* Rutter, 87 Fed. 801, 806.

[4] Lincoln Placer, 7 L. D. 81; Rose Lode Claims, 22 L. D. 83; Commissioner's Letter, 1 Copp's L. O. 12.

[5] *Ante*, § 382.

[6] Doe *v.* Sanger, 83 Cal. 203, 214, 23 Pac. 365; Doe *v.* Waterloo M. Co., 54 Fed. 935, 940; Tyler *v.* Sweeney, *Id.* 284; Last Chance M. Co. *v.* Tyler, 61 Fed. 557; Philadelphia M. Claim *v.* Pride of the West, 3 Copp's L. O. 82.

[7] Credo M. and M. Co. *v.* Highland M. and M. Co., 95 Fed. 911.

and when so changed, an amended location is made, and an amended certificate is prepared and recorded, which, if free from conflicts with those whose rights have supervened since the perfection of the original location, is just as valid as if made in the original instance.[1]

Those locating subsequently to the perfection of the amended location are not injured, and have no right to complain.[2]

§ 397. **Privilege of changing boundaries exists, in the absence of intervening rights, independent of state legislation.**—In some of the states and territories, amended locations and certificates are the subject of statutory regulation. This is the case in Colorado,[3] Idaho,[4] Arizona,[5] Montana,[6] Nevada,[7] New Mexico,[8] North Dakota,[9] South Dakota,[10] Washington,[11] and Wyoming.[12]

The provisions in all these states, with the exception of those in Arizona, are on parallel lines with those of Colorado, which are as follows:—

"If, at any time, the locator of any mining claim
" heretofore or hereafter located, or his assigns, shall
" apprehend that his original certificate was erroneous,
" defective, or that the requirements of the law had not
" been complied with before filing, or shall be desirous
" of changing his surface boundaries, or taking in any

[1] Tipton G. M. Co., 29 L. D. 718.
[2] Gleeson v. Martin White M. Co., 13 Nev. 442.
[3] Mills' Annot. Stats., § 3160.
[4] Laws of 1895, p. 27, § 5; Civil Code (1901), § 2566.
[5] Rev. Stats. (1901), § 3238.
[6] Laws of 1901, p. 56, §§ 1, 2.
[7] Comp. Laws (1900), § 213.
[8] Comp. Laws (1897), § 2301.
[9] Rev. Code of 1895, § 1437; Id. 1899, § 1437.
[10] Comp. Laws of Dak. 1887, § 2008. Adopted by South Dak.—Laws of 1890, ch. cv; Grantham's Annot. Stats. S. D. (1899), § 2667.
[11] Laws of 1899, p. 70, § 5.
[12] Rev. Stats. (1899), § 2538.

" part of an overlapping claim which has been aban-
" doned, or in case the original certificate was made prior
" to the passage of this law, and he shall be desirous of
" securing the benefits of this act, such locator, or his
" assigns, may file an additional certificate, subject to
" the provisions of this act; *provided,* that such reloca-
" tion does not interfere with existing rights of others
" at the time of such relocation, and no such relocation,
" or other record thereof, shall preclude the claimant,
" or claimants, from proving any such title, or titles, as
" he, or they, may have held under previous location."

In Arizona the section on this subject is as follows:—

"Location notices may be amended at any time and
" the monuments changed to correspond to the amended
" location; *provided,* that no change shall be made that
" will interfere with the rights of others."

But, in the nature of things, this right exists throughout the mining regions, independently of statutory regulations. The supreme court of California, a state which
has no legislation on the subject, has held that if locators have any apprehension as to the sufficiency of their
original location, there is no reason why they should
not be permitted to modify or amend it.[1]

Of course, the alteration of boundaries, by taking in
new territory and filing amended certificates *where the
antecedent one is absolutely void,* cannot be permitted to
the prejudice of intervening rights.[2] But with this
qualification, the right to change boundaries and rectify
lines exists throughout the mining regions.[3]

In dealing with this subject in the future, we shall

---

[1] Thompson *v.* Spray, 72 Cal. 528, 529, 14 Pac. 182.

[2] Seymour *v.* Fisher, 16 Colo. 188, 27 Pac. 240; Fisher *v.* Seymour,
23 Colo. 542, 49 Pac. 30; Omar *v.* Soper, 11 Colo. 380, 7 Am. St. Rep. 246,
18 Pac. 443; Hall *v.* Arnott, 80 Cal. 348, 22 Pac. 200; Tombstone Townsite Cases (Ariz.), 15 Pac. 26; Wight *v.* Tabor, 2 L. D. 738.

[3] Frisholm *v.* Fitzgerald, 25 Colo. 290, 53 Pac. 1109; Duncan *v.* Fulton
(Colo. App.), 61 Pac. 244; Morrison *v.* Regan (Idaho), 67 Pac. 956;
Sanders *v.* Noble, 22 Mont. 110, 55 Pac. 1037.

assume the correctness of this theory, and, therefore, that the decisions of the courts in states where laws of this character exist, so far as underlying principles are discussed therein, may be resorted to as precedents in states where legislation on the subject is wanting. We think the circumstances set forth in the preceding section justify this assumption.

§ 398. **Objects and functions of amended certificates.** —Where a change of boundaries is sought, the acts necessary to accomplish the desired result are specified by statute in the states enumerated in the preceding section. Where there is no statute, in re-marking the boundaries and preparing and recording the certificate the same formalities should be observed as in the case of an original location.

In speaking of the objects and functions of additional or amended certificates of location, the supreme court of Colorado thus states its views:—

"The evident intent of the statute is, that the addi-
" tional certificate shall operate to cure defects in the
" original, and thereby to put the locator, where no
" other rights have intervened, in the same position that
" he would have occupied if no such defect had oc-
" curred. Such intent is in accord with the principle
" of all curative provisions of law." [1]

And in a later case the same court says:—

"It is to the end that the prospector may cure any
" defects in his location and conserve and protect the
" results of his industry that the authority is given." [2]

Such a certificate may be used as evidence, although the original may be incomplete or imperfect, upon the theory that the amended certificate relates back to a *right* of location accruing by virtue of the prerequisite

---

[1] Strepey v. Stark, 7 Colo. 614, 620, 5 Pac. 111.
[2] Duncan v. Fulton (Colo. App.), 61 Pac. 244.

discovery and an attempted compliance with the law.[1] When the original certificate of location may be deemed void, an additional one may be filed to correct its defects, and both may be put in evidence.[2]

A distinction is drawn between cases where the original certificate is absolutely void, or where the amended certificate seeks to appropriate new and additional ground, and one where the original is simply defective. If in making the amended location it included land not in the original location, and interfered with existing rights as to such land, the amended location would not relate back to the date of the original location, so far as the recently included land is concerned.[3] Where the object is simply to cure imperfections and obvious defects, and there is no attempt to include new ground, the amended certificate will relate back to the original in spite of intervening locations.[4]

"Every one who is at all familiar with mining locations knows that in practice the first record must usually, if not always, be imperfect. Recognizing these difficulties, it has never been the policy of the law to avoid a location for defects in the record, but rather to give the locator an opportunity to correct his record, whenever defects may be found in it. . . . This is the function and proper office of amendments: To put the original in as perfect condition as if it had been complete in the first instance."[5]

---

[1] McGinnis v. Egbert, 8 Colo. 41, 45, 5 Pac. 652; Moyle v. Bullene, 7 Colo. App. 308, 44 Pac. 69; Becker v. Pugh, 9 Colo. 589, 13 Pac. 906; Duncan v. Fulton (Colo. App.), 61 Pac. 244; Strepey v. Stark, 7 Colo. 614, 5 Pac. 111. Dissenting opinion, Frisholm v. Fitzgerald, 25 Colo. 290, 53 Pac. 1109.

[2] Duncan v. Fulton (Colo. App.), 61 Pac. 244.

[3] Morrison v. Regan (Idaho), 67 Pac. 955, 961.

[4] McEvoy v. Hyman, 25 Fed. 596; Tombstone Townsite Cases (Ariz.), 15 Pac. 26; Hall v. Arnott, 80 Cal. 348, 22 Pac. 200; Frisholm v. Fitzgerald, 25 Colo. 290, 53 Pac. 1109, (dissenting opinion); Duncan v. Fulton (Colo. App.), 61 Pac. 244; Morrison v. Regan (Idaho), 67 Pac. 955.

[5] McEvoy v. Hyman, 25 Fed. 596, 600. See, also, Craig v. Thompson, 10 Colo. 517, 16 Pac. 24.

In other words, a reasonable latitude of amendment is allowed, of which the locator cannot be deprived because some one has attempted to relocate his ground.

There is a distinction between amending an original location by re-forming lines and rectifying errors based upon a prior discovery and location, and the relocation of abandoned ground. The former, if properly made, and no other rights have intervened, takes effect, subject to the qualification heretofore stated, by relation, as of the date of the original; whereas, relocation of abandoned ground becomes operative only from the date of its perfection;[1] and whether a given certificate is a mere amendment or a relocation of abandoned ground, will depend upon the facts as they exist, and not upon the recitals of the certificate.[2] The second or amended notice is not an abandonment of the original.[3] An amended notice cannot, by the mere omission to insert names of the original locators, divest the title acquired by the original location,[4] unless done with their knowledge and consent.[5]

Additional territory embraced within an amended location made by one co-tenant will inure to the benefit of all, on the principle that the right to change the boundaries arises out of, and relates back to, the original location.[6]

[1] Cheesman v. Shreeve, 40 Fed. 787, 789.

[2] Id.

[3] Thompson v. Spray, 72 Cal. 528; Weill v. Lucerne M. Co., 11 Nev. 200, 213; Temescal Oil M. and D. Co. v. Salcido, 137 Cal. 211, 69 Pac. 1010.

[4] Thompson v. Spray, 72 Cal. 528, 14 Pac. 182; Hallack v. Traber, 23 Colo. 14, 46 Pac. 110; Mono M. Co. v. Magnolia E. and W. Co., 2 Copp's L. O. 68; In re Teller, 26 L. D. 484, 486; In re Auerbach, 29 L. D. 208.

[5] Morton v. Solambo C. M. Co., 26 Cal. 527; Gore v. McBrayer, 18 Cal. 583; Moore v. Hamerstag, 109 Cal. 122, 125, 41 Pac. 805.

[6] Hallack v. Traber, 23 Colo. 14, 46 Pac. 110. See Reagan v. McKibben, 11 S. Dak. 270, 76 N. W. 943, 945; Van Wagenen v. Carpenter, 27 Colo. 444, 61 Pac. 698.

Where the second, or amended, notice contains names other than those set forth in the original, in an action against strangers this fact cannot be taken advantage of. It may be treated as an original notice as to the persons whose names do not appear on the first, and as a supplemental or amended notice as to those whose names appear on both.[1]

Any radical change of the name of a claim might be construed as an attempt to hide its identity, and mislead adverse claimants in patent proceedings;[2] but the mere dropping of a descriptive prefix—as, for instance, naming a claim the "Tiger" instead of the "Little Tiger," "Shields" in place of "General Shields," or "Flag" instead of "American Flag,"—where the other descriptive portions of the notice are regular, is of no importance.[3]

It is not necessary that the purposes for which a certificate is amended should be specified. The filing of such certificate, if made under proper conditions, is effectual for all the purposes enumerated in the statute, whether such purposes are mentioned in the certificate or not.[4]

ARTICLE XI. RELOCATION OF FORFEITED OR ABANDONED CLAIMS.

§ 402. Circumstances under which relocation may be made.

§ 403. New discovery not essential as basis of relocation.

§ 404. Relocation admits the validity of the original.

§ 405. Relocation by original locator.

§ 406. Relocation by one of several original locators in hostility to the others.

§ 407. Relocation by agent or others occupying contractual or fiduciary relations with original locator.

[1] Thompson v. Spray, 72 Cal. 528, 529, 14 Pac. 182.

[2] Morr. Min. Rights, 10th ed., pp. 112-113.

[3] Seymour v. Fisher, 16 Colo. 188, 199, 27 Pac. 240. See Fisher v. Seymour, 23 Colo. 542, 49 Pac. 30.

[4] Johnson v. Young, 18 Colo. 625, 629, 34 Pac. 173.

§ 408. Manner of perfecting relocations—Statutory reg-
ulations.

§ 409. Right of second locator to
improvements made by
the first.

§ 402.   Circumstances under which relocation may
be made.—In dealing with the subject of relocation, it is
not our purpose at this time to enter into a critical discussion of the subject of abandonment, forfeiture, or the
preservation of the estate from relocation by a resumption of work. The scope of this article is limited to the
manner in which claims may be relocated after the
rights based upon the original location are, by reason
of the default of the owner in fulfilling the requirements
of the law, subject to extinguishment by a new entry
and a new location.

The circumstances under which the estate created by
the perfection of a valid location may be extinguished
by hostile relocation, and the manner in which such
estate may be preserved from such relocation by the
delinquent original locator, will be fully explained in a
succeeding title.[1]

For a failure to perform labor or make improvements
to the value of one hundred dollars annually, computing
the periods from the first day of January next succeeding the date of location, the federal law provides that
" The claim or mine upon which such failure occurs
" shall be open to relocation in the same manner as if
" no location of the same had ever been made, *provided*
" that the original locators or their heirs, assigns, or
" legal representatives, have not resumed work upon
" the claim after failure before such location." [2]

It is one of the essentials upon which the right to
relocate exists that the contingency sanctioned by the
statute must have actually happened,—that is, there
must have been a failure on the part of the original

---

[1] *Post,* tit. VI, ch. v, §§ 623-638; ch. vi, §§ 642-654.
[2] Rev. Stats., § 324.

locator to perform the annual work. No relocation may be made to take effect in the future.[1]

The right of an original locator to amend his location for the purpose of correcting defects or embracing additional ground has been fully considered elsewhere.[2]

It is our present purpose to discuss the manner in which such relocations as are sanctioned by the federal law may be made and to whom the privilege of such relocation is extended.

§ 403. **New discovery not essential as basis of relocation.**—It is a well-established rule that there can be no valid location of a mining claim without a discovery;[3] but it has been held that it is not necessary that the locator should be the first discoverer of a vein, but it must not only be known to him, but must be adopted and claimed by him, in order to give validity to the location.[4]

So, if the original location was based upon a valid discovery, and the relocator finds the vein exposed within the limits of the claim, this is sufficient upon which to base a relocation.[5]

The theory of the law upon which the relocation is permitted is, undoubtedly, that if the original locator who made the discovery manifests his unwillingness to proceed with the development of the ground, and his location becomes subject to forfeiture for failure to perform the necessary work, any one may succeed to the right based upon the original discovery by relocating the ground, so that successive relocations based upon

[1] Belk *v.* Meagher, 104 U. S. 279.
[2] *Ante,* §§ 396-398.
[3] *Ante,* § 335.
[4] Nevada Sierra Oil Co. *v.* Home Oil Co., 98 Fed. 673; Hayes *v.* Lavignino, 17 Utah, 185, 53 Pac. 1029; Jupiter M. Co. *v.* Bodie Cons. M. Co.. 7 Saw. 96, 108, 14 Fed. 354.
[5] Armstrong *v.* Lower, 6 Colo. 393, 395.

successive forfeitures may all be founded upon the one discovery. A new discovery is not requisite for each relocation.

§ 404. **Relocation admits the validity of the original.** —A relocation impliedly admits the validity of the prior location. There can be no relocation unless there has been a prior valid location, or something equivalent, of the same property.[1]

The courts draw a distinction between a locator and relocator, classing the former. as an original discoverer of mineral before unknown, and the latter as the mere appropriator of mineral discovered by another who had failed to exercise the privilege conferred upon him by law. The relocation is equivalent to an admission that the relocator claims a forfeiture by reason of a failure on the part of the first locator to comply with the law. Such being the case, the only inquiry is, as to whether or not the original locator performed the requisite labor.[2]

§ 405. **Relocation by original locators.**—In speaking of relocation by an original locator, we have no reference to locations made for the purpose of curing defects, or readjusting boundaries. We have called these *amended* locations, and, as such, have dealt with them in the preceding article.[3] What we now refer to are cases wherein the original locator seeks to evade the requirements of the law as to development and annual expenditure, and endeavors to perpetuate his estate by periodical relocations.

The question was presented to the supreme court of Utah in the following form: "Can the locator of a " quartz mining claim who has allowed his location to

---

[1] Belk *v.* Meagher, 104 U. S. 279, 289.

[2] Wills *v.* Blain, 4 N. Mex. 378, 20 Pac. 798; Providence G. M. Co. *v.* Burke (Ariz.), 57 Pac. 641.

[3] *Ante,* §§ 396-398.

" lapse by a failure to perform the necessary work
" make a relocation or new location covering the same
" ground?" [1]

The court failed to see any reason why such right
should be denied. It based its ruling upon the following
grounds:—

(1) That right is recognized /by the circuit court of
the ninth circuit [2] and by the land department; [3]

(2) The fact that a prior locator, after his right has
lapsed, may renew it by resuming work, would appear
to be a favor or right granted to such prior locator, but
to deny him the right to relocate is to deny him a
privilege which is given to *strangers.*

The conclusion of the court is, that the prior locator, in addition to the right to resume work, and thus
relieve himself from the danger of incurring forfeiture,
should also have the same rights as strangers to relocate.

We are fully aware of the weight to be given to the
decisions of the supreme court of a state or territory,
and for that reason it is with a great deal of hesitancy
that we intrude our individual views in opposition to
such a decision, in the absence of some authoritative
ruling emanating from a court of equal dignity to support our theories. But the rule announced by the supreme court of Utah is so opposed to what we consider
the true intent and spirit of the mining laws, that we
feel justified in criticising it, and in doing so to deferentially present our reasons for upholding a contrary
doctrine.

---

[1] Warnock *v.* DeWitt, 11 Utah, 324, 40 Pac. 205. This case was appealed to the supreme court of the United States. The appeal was
dismissed for failure to comply with rule 10. Mem. Dec., 18 Sup. Ct.
Rep. 949.

[2] Hunt *v.* Patchin, 35 Fed. 816.

[3] Acting Commissioner Holcomb, Copp's Min. Lands, p. 300.

In the first place, we think the fallacy of the rule is exposed upon the face of the decision, *ex visceribus suis,* considering the cases cited in it as a part of the decision:—

The doctrine asserted by the supreme court of Utah, we respectfully urge, is *not* recognized by the circuit court of the ninth circuit in the case of Hunt *v.* Patchin.[1] That case involved a question between original co-locators, one of whom, by common consent of all, had relocated the claim in his own name, and afterwards undertook to claim the entire title as against his original co-tenants. This the court would not permit him to do. Under these circumstances, the relocating co-tenant could not, with any advantage to himself, deny the validity of the relocation, nor could he exclude his co-tenants from participating in such title as he acquired. In this case, a certificate of purchase was issued to the relocating claimant alone. The validity of the relocation was never questioned by the land department, which tribunal was probably never advised that the basis of the relocation was the dereliction of the relocator and his co-tenants. All that Hunt *v.* Patchin attempts to determine is, that whatever right accrues to one of several original locators under a relocation which is made in his name, by common consent, inures to the benefit of all. But that any such right accrues, the circuit court did not attempt to decide.

The ruling of the land department referred to [2] appears in the form of a letter addressed by Acting Commissioner Holcomb to a man in Leadville. It was not a litigated case. The acting commissioner was of the opinion, that one of several co-locators, all of whom are in default, may relocate in his own name and hold it adversely to his former co-tenants.

---

[1] 35 Fed. 816.   [2] Copp's Min. Lands, p. 300.

As to the conclusion reached by the supreme court of Utah, there is every reason why the right to relocate should be given to strangers and should be denied to the original locator. Under the mining laws, discovery and appropriation are recognized as the sources of title to mining claims, and *development* by *working* as the condition of continued ownership until patent is obtained.[1]

After his discovery, the locator is allowed certain periods to perfect his location, and the period of one year from the first day of January next succeeding the date of his location in which to perform one hundred dollars' worth of labor.

Let us illustrate: A vein is discovered June 1, 1900. The locator has until January 1, 1902, in which to perform his work. He fails to do so; but on January 2, 1902, relocates the claim, basing his right to do so upon his own previous neglect to comply with the law. If he has the same right as a stranger to relocate under these circumstances, he has the same length of time allowed to a stranger to perform the first year's labor after the date of the relocation; that is, until January 1, 1904. On January 2, 1904, he may repeat this proceeding, and obtain an additional two years, and so on indefinitely. It seems to us that this is a manifest fraud upon the government. It is a perversion of the law, and in direct violation of its spirit and intent, to say that the original locator may take advantage of his own dereliction, and use his own neglect and wrong as a foundation to either perpetuate an estate or create a new one. The law under which he obtained his first privilege provides the only method by which his neglect can be condoned, and that is by resuming work prior to relocation. It is illogical to say that he may accomplish this result in any other

[1] Erhardt *v.* Boaro, 113 U. S. 527, 535, 5 Sup. Ct. Rep. 560.

way than by strictly pursuing the methods provided for by the statute.

There is another principle which seems to us to be decisive of the question: The forfeiture is not complete until a relocation has been made. It is the entry of a new claimant with intent to relocate the property, and not mere lapse of time, that determines the right of the original claimant.[1]

The right to enter and resume work prior to the relocation by another is evidence that the original estate is not wholly lost by the failure to do the work.[2]

The supreme court of Colorado thus forcibly states the rule:—

" As between the locator and the general government " the failure to do the annual assessment work does not " result in a forfeiture. In other words, it is not neces- " sary to perform the annual labor except to protect the " rights of the locator against parties seeking to initiate " a title to the same premises. . . . To otherwise ex- " press our views, it might be said that after a valid " location the title thus acquired remains so, whether " the annual assessment work is performed or not, until " forfeited or abandoned." [3]

" Forfeiture is not complete until *some one else* has " appropriated the property." [4]

This is in accord with the views of the land department.[5]

If this doctrine be true, that the estate of the original locator, as between himself and the government, remains unimpaired by the failure to perform the work, how is it

---

[1] Little Gunnell M. Co. *v.* Kimber, 1 Morr. Min. Rep. 536, 539, Fed. Cas. No. 8402.

[2] Lakin *v.* Sierra Buttes G. M. Co., 25 Fed. 337, 343.

[3] Beals *v.* Cone (on rehearing), 27 Colo. 473, 83 Am. St. Rep. 92, 62 Pac. 948, 958.

[4] McCarthy *v.* Speed, 11 S. Dak. 362, 77 N. W. 590, 593.

[5] Wilson *v.* Champagne M. Co., 29 L. D. 491; Coleman *v.* McKenzie, 29 L. D. 359.

possible for such locator to terminate such estate and create a new one. He ought not to be permitted to re-enter and oust himself, predicating such re-entry and ouster on his own delinquency, and permitting him to re-enter and re-oust himself periodically to save the necessity of developing his claim.

To say that the original locator has the power within himself to make effectual a forfeiture arising from his own delinquency by perfecting a relocation, is to place in his hands the extraordinary privilege of holding mineral lands perpetually, without doing any work whatever, at least in those states where the relocator is not required to do preliminary work.[1] Where he is required to perform such work, such performance might be treated as resumption, and no relocation is necessary. In any event, the rule upon this subject should be uniform, because it is based upon the federal statute.

As was said by the supreme court of California, the work prescribed in the act must be done, or the claim is open to relocation, unless work is resumed before the second location is made. The conditions imposed by the act of congress are wise and salutary, and are by no means onerous. "It is the duty of the courts " to hold the locators of mining claims bound by " them."[2]

The right to relocate is given to others as a *penalty* imposed on the original locator for failure on his part to perform the conditions required of him. It is not conceded to him as a reward for his neglect, or as an inducement held out to him to evade the law.

There are several cases which may be said to support, inferentially at least, the doctrine of the Utah case, under discussion. These cases deserve consideration.

---

[1] McCann v. McMillan, 129 Cal. 350, 62 Pac. 31.

[2] Russell v. Brosseau, 65 Cal. 605, 608, 4 Pac. 643; Du Prat v. James, 65 Cal. 555, 4 Pac. 562; Wright v. Killian, 132 Cal. 56, 64 Pac. 98.

Saunders *v.* Mackey[1] was an action to quiet title to a mining claim, where one co-tenant, after having agreed with his co-owners to represent the claim, failed to do so, and relocated in his own name, to the exclusion of his associates. The court suggested that the excluded co-tenant had mistaken his remedy, which was either an action for damages, or to erect a trust, but held that the relocation was valid. The decision of the court seems to have been based upon the theory that the failure to perform the annual work *ipso facto* restored the lands to the public domain, a theory which is not supported by the weight of authority.

Lockhart *v.* Wills[2] and Lockhart *v.* Johnson[3] arose out of facts analogous to those of Saunders *v.* Mackey, with one important distinction. The location in the latter cases was never perfected in the original instance. The preliminary notices were posted by one in the name of all the co-owners, but there was a failure to perform the acts required by the laws of New Mexico as a condition precedent to the creation of a valid location. After the lapse of the statutory period, within which the necessary acts were required to be performed, the co-tenant who initiated the location conspired with other parties to make a location excluding his original co-tenants. This location was made and perfected, and the excluded original associates brought ejectment. The courts held the later location valid. In fact, it was the only location which had ever been perfected. They further held that, under the circumstances, ejectment was not the proper remedy.

In the case of Conway *v.* Hart[4] a claim had been abandoned for several years, when the original owners returned, relocated, and resumed work. The court held the second location to be valid as against one made later

---

[1] 5 Mont. 527, 6 Pac. 361.
[2] 9 N. Mex. 344, 54 Pac. 336.
[3] 181 U. S. 516, 21 Sup. Ct. Rep. 665.
[4] 129 Cal. 480, 62 Pac. 44.

by third parties. The case does not discuss any of the basic principles involved in the ultimate analysis of the subject under discussion.

The foregoing cases are all which have come under our observation which lend any aid to the solution of the problem. It may be that the doctrine of Warnock *v.* DeWitt is the correct one. But we are not able to reconcile it with the principles announced by other courts of equal dignity, which principles are necessarily involved in the determination of the question here discussed. The views of the author coincide with those of Mr. Morrison upon this point.[1]

§ 406. **Relocation by one of several original locators in hostility to the others.**—If we are right in the conclusions reached in the preceding section, that the original locator cannot treat his failure to perform or resume work as the basis of a valid relocation, it must necessarily follow, that one of several locators seeking to obtain the entire title by reason of the failure of any of them to fulfill the requirement of the law, is likewise prohibited from making such relocation. If we are wrong in the deductions previously stated, it follows that a delinquent co-locator may relocate the claim, subject to such redress as the courts will afford the excluded co-owner.

The supreme court of Montana has held that mining claims owned by several in common must be "repre-" sented"—that is, the work must be performed—as if owned by one person; that "representation" is a unity; that co-owners may cause representative work to be done on the claim according to their respective interests, but when completed it must amount to one whole representation; otherwise, the claim is not protected from relocation, and that under such circumstances one of the

[1] Morr. Min. Rights, 10th ed., p. 103.

co-owners might relocate.[1] If this be a correct statement
of the rule, it is manifestly subject to the limitations
pointed out by the decision of the supreme court of the
United States announced in Turner v. Sawyer,[2] wherein
it is said that the general rule, that the purchase of an
outstanding title, or encumbrance, upon the joint estate
for the benefit of one tenant in common inures to the
benefit of all, because there is an obligation between
them arising from their joint claim and community of
interest, and that one of them shall not affect the claim
to the prejudice of others,[3] should apply to a case where
one co-tenant of a mining claim secures the entire title
in his individual name.[4]

The courts generally concede the rule to be, that where
one of several co-owners in a mining claim applies for a
patent in his own name, the excluded co-tenants are not
adverse claimants within the meaning of the law requiring them to intervene in patent proceedings, as they
claim equities which are based upon the legal title thus
conveyed.[5]

The land department rulings are now in harmony with
this doctrine.[6]

Be that as it may, although the views announced by
the supreme court of Montana seem to give support to
the doctrine of the supreme court of Utah, cited in the

---

[1] Saunders v. Mackey, 5 Mont. 523, 6 Pac. 361.

[2] 150 U. S. 578, 586, 14 Sup. Ct. Rep. 192.

[3] For a general discussion of rights and remedies between co-tenants
or co-owners, see, post, §§ 788-793.

[4] Followed in McCarthy v. Speed, 11 S. Dak. 362, 77 N. W. 590, 593,
S. C. (2d appeal), 12 S. Dak. 7, 80 N. W. 135; Van Wagenen v. Carpenter, 27 Colo. 444, 61 Pac. 698. See, also, Freeman on Co-tenancy,
§ 151.

[5] Sussenbach v. First National Bank, 5 Dak. 477, 41 N. W. 662; Brundy
v. Mayfield, 15 Mont. 201, 38 Pac. 1067; Doherty v. Morris, 11 Colo. 12,
16 Pac. 911.

[6] Thomas v. Elling, 25 L. D. 495, S. C., on review, 26 L. D. 220; Coleman v. Homestake M. Co., 30 L. D. 364; post, § 728.

preceding section, we cannot see why the reasoning applied by us in that section to the case of an individual locator should not apply with equal force to one of several locators. In the latter case the obligation rests upon all alike to perform the required work. One of the co-tenants might save the entire estate by himself performing the labor. In such event, he would have a right of contribution against his co-tenants for their proportion of expenditures made to save the common estate,[1] which he might assert, either in an action for partition,[2] or, perhaps, by "advertising out" under the provisions of the Revised Statutes.[3] But to say that one co-owner can make his own delinquency, as well as that of his co-tenants, the basis for acquiring a new title, seems to us repugnant to the intent and spirit of the law.[4]

§ 407. **Relocation by agent or others occupying contractual or fiduciary relations with original locator.**—An agent, trustee, or other person holding confidential relations with the original locator, will not be permitted to relocate mining claims, and secure to themselves advantages flowing from a breach of trust obligations.[5] Neither will one in possession of an unpatented mining claim entering under a lease from the owner be permitted to relocate for non-performance of assessment

[1] See Beck v. O'Connor (Mont.), 53 Pac. 94; Oliver v. Lassing, 57 Neb. 352, 77 N. W. 802.

[2] Holbrooke v. Harrington (Cal.), 36 Pac. 365.

[3] § 2324.

[4] Consult Royston v. Miller, 76 Fed. 50.

[5] Lockhart v. Rollins, 2 Idaho, 503, 514, 21 Pac. 413; Utah M. and M. Co. v. Dickert and M. S. Co., 6 Utah, 183, 21 Pac. 1002; Largey v. Bartlett, 18 Mont. 265, 44 Pac. 962; Fisher v. Seymour, 23 Colo. 542, 49 Pac. 30; Argentine M. Co. v. Benedict, 18 Utah, 183, 55 Pac. 559; Haws v. Victoria Copper Co., 160 U. S. 303, 16 Sup. Ct. Rep. 282; Van Wagenen v. Carpenter, 27 Colo. 444, 61 Pac. 698. See, also, Bunker Hill Co. v. Pascoe (Utah), 66 Pac. 574.

work on the part of the owner.[1] Where, however, a contractual or fiduciary relationship is terminated, the rule no longer applies, and a subsequent relocation by the former agent or trustee has been upheld.[2] An original locator cannot suffer forfeiture and relocate, or cause the ground to be relocated by others in collusion with him, so as to cut off the rights of a mortgagee under a mortgage executed by such original locator.[3]

It has been suggested by the supreme court of Arizona, that an original locator, after sale by quitclaim deed to a third person who fails to perform the annual labor, may relocate and hold the claim.[4] But in such case the obligation to perform the labor rested upon his grantee, and not upon the original locator, and by relocating, he does not profit by his own failure to perform the work. His grantee occupies the position of the original locator, and the latter, in relocating, that of a mere stranger to the title.

§ 408. **Manner of perfecting relocations—Statutory regulations.**—With the exception of the necessity for making a new discovery, the relocation of an abandoned mining claim is made in substantially the same manner as the original.[5]

The ground is "open to relocation in the same manner " as if no location of the same had ever been made."[6] By this is meant, that all the requirements of the law as to marking of boundaries, posting notices, recording certificates, performance of development work, and such other acts as are required by the federal or state laws,

---

[1] Justice M. Co. v. Barclay, 82 Fed. 554, 559; Yarwood v. Johnson (Wash.), 70 Pac. 123.

[2] Page v. Summers, 70 Cal. 121, 12 Pac. 120.

[3] Alexander v. Sherman (Ariz.), 16 Pac. 45.

[4] Blake v. Thorne (Ariz.), 16 Pac. 270.

[5] Armstrong v. Lower, 6 Colo. 393.

[6] Rev. Stats., § 2324.

except the discovery, must be complied with in cases of relocation to the same extent as in original locations. The original locator and the relocator, in this respect, are on the same footing.[1]

But a relocator may adopt stakes and monuments of a former location if they are still on the ground.[2]

Most of the precious-metal-bearing states have legislated upon the subject of relocating abandoned claims.

Colorado has enacted a law which provides that the relocation of abandoned lode claims shall be by sinking a new discovery shaft and fixing new boundaries, in the same manner as if it were the location of a new claim; or the relocator may sink the original shaft ten feet deeper than it was at the time of the abandonment, and erect new, or adopt old, boundaries, renewing the posts, if removed or destroyed. In either case, a new location stake shall be erected. In any case, whether the whole or part of an abandoned claim is taken, the location certificate may state that the whole, or any part, of the new location is located as abandoned property.[3] Arizona,[4] Idaho,[5] Montana,[6] Nevada,[7] New Mexico,[8] North Dakota,[9] South Dakota,[10] Washington,[11] and Wyoming,[12] have statutes of the same general character. The statute of Oregon provides that "abandoned claims " shall be deemed unappropriated mineral lands, and

---

[1] Pelican and Dives M. Co. v. Snodgrass, 9 Colo. 339, 342, 12 Pac. 206.

[2] Conway v. Hart, 129 Cal. 480, 62 Pac. 44.

[3] Mills' Annot. Stats., § 3162.

[4] Rev. Stats. (1901), § 3241.

[5] Laws of 1895, p. 25, § vii; Civil Code (1901), § 2560.

[6] Rev. Code of 1895, § 3615.

[7] Comp. Laws (1900), § 214.

[8] Laws of 1889, p. 42, § iii; Comp. Laws (1897), § 2300.

[9] Rev. Code of 1895, §·1439; Id. (1899), § 1439.

[10] Comp. Laws of Dakota, 1887, § 2010. Adopted by South Dakota— Laws of 1890, ch. cv; Grantham's Annot. Stats. S. Dak. (1899), 2669.

[11] Laws of 1899, p. 69, § 8.

[12] Laws of 1888, p. 89, § 21; Rev. Stats. (1899), § 2552.

" titles thereto shall be obtained as in this act specified,
" without reference to any work previously done there-
" on." [1]   There is no legislation upon the subject in
either California or Utah.

The supreme court of Montana has held that if an
original locator resumes work before the relocator remarks the boundaries, and performs *all* the acts required
to perfect a valid relocation, the forfeiture is not
worked, and the right to relocate is lost.[2] A like doctrine
is supported in California,[3] in which state, however, no
appreciable time is allowed a locator in which to mark
his boundaries.[4] Where, however, under statutes which
either contemplate or provide.for a series of acts, the
performance of which necessarily requires time, such as
the sinking of a new discovery shaft ten feet deep, or an
old one ten feet deeper, the performance of any one of
these acts in the series ought to give the relocator the
necessary time to complete the others. Otherwise, it is
difficult to see how a valid relocation could ever be made,
without the consent of the original locator. He could
" resume work " at any time before the relocator had
completed his development. Unless the relocator can be
protected in his possession, for the purpose of complet-
ing his relocation, there is but little use in his attempting it. Each attempt at relocation would, at some stage,
find the original locator in a state of "resumption."
While forfeitures are odious, we think the courts are
sometimes altogether too lenient in dealing with a class
of people frequently found in mining camps, who will
neither work themselves nor permit others to do so.

---

[1] Laws of 1898, p. 17, § 4.

[2] Gonu *v.* Russell, 3 Mont. 358; doctrine reaffirmed, McKay *v.* Mc-
Dougall, 25 Mont. 258, 87 Am. St. Rep. 395, 64 Pac. 669.

[3] Holland *v.* Mt. Auburn G. Q. M. Co., 53 Cal. 149; Belcher Cons. G. M.
Co. *v.* Deferrari, 62 Cal. 160; Pharis *v.* Muldoon, 75 Cal. 284, 17 Pac. 70.
And see Klopenstine *v.* Hays, 20 Utah, 45, 57 Pac. 712.

[4] *Ante,* § 339.

Judge Hallett is of the opinion that the right of the original locator to resume work and prevent forfeiture lapses, unless the right is exercised before another has taken possession of the property with intent to relocate it,[1] and Mr. Morrison shares these views,[2] which, in our judgment, are sound.[3]

A discussion of what constitutes "resumption" is deferred for treatment in another chapter. Successive relocations may, of course, be made as often as the relocators fail on their part to comply with the law. Where one has made a relocation and permits the time to elapse without performing the requisite work, he should be debarred the same as an original locator from again relocating. Whether or not such is the law depends upon the correctness of our theories advanced in a preceding section.[4]

§ 409. **Right of second locator to improvements made by the first.** — When the estate of the first locator becomes extinguished by his failure to comply with the law, and the second enters and perfects his relocation, the dominion and control over the property passes to the latter. If the former thereafter remains in possession, unless at the time of the relocation he had resumed work, he is a mere occupant without color of title, and the completion of the second location, if effected peaceably and in good faith, operates in law as an ouster of the prior occupant.[5] Thereafter, the relocator is clothed with "the exclusive

---

[1] Little Gunnell M. Co. *v.* Kimber, 1 Morr. Min. Rep. 536, Fed. Cas. No. 8402.

[2] Morr. Min. Rights, 10th ed., p. 91.

[3] The supreme court of Montana discusses this section and disagrees with the conclusions reached. McKay *v.* McDougall, 25 Mont. 258, 87 Am. St. Rep. 395, 64 Pac. 669, 672. See Klopenstine *v.* Hays, 20 Utah, 45, 57 Pac. 712; Justice M. Co. *v.* Barclay, 82 Fed. 554.

[4] *Ante,* § 405.

[5] Belk *v.* Meagher, 3 Mont. 65, 80, S. C., on appeal, 104 U. S. 279, 284; *ante,* §§ 218, 219.

" right of possession and enjoyment of all the surface
" included within the lines of the location."[1]

Such improvements or betterments as have been
placed upon the property by the original locator, if they
fall within the class designated as fixtures, become a
part of the realty, and the subsequent appropriation of
the land carries with it, necessarily, whatever may be
affixed to it. Prior to the determination of his estate by
the perfection of a relocation, it cannot be doubted that
the prior locator may sever and remove all machinery,
buildings, and other improvements which, by the manner
of their attachment to the soil, have become a part of
the freehold. But his right of entry for that purpose
ceases when his estate is terminated.

It is a general rule of law that all improvements of
this character upon public lands of the United States
pass to the purchaser from the government,[2] and the
relocator of a mining claim holds his estate by purchase.[3] One cannot set up equities in improvements
against the government, or a purchaser from it,[4] and
state statutes which permit their removal after the land
has passed into private ownership are void, as interfer-
ing with the primary right of disposal of the soil reserved to the United States upon the admission of the
several states.[5]

It is unnecessary to enter into a detailed discussion of
what constitutes fixtures. It has been frequently held,
that machinery, such as engines, boilers, hoisting-works,
mills, pumps, and things of a like character annexed to

[1] Rev. Stats., § 2322.

[2] Collins v. Bartlett, 44 Cal. 371; Pennybecker v. McDougal, 48 Cal.
163; McKiernan v. Hesse, 51 Cal. 594; Treadway v. Sharon, 7 Nev. 37;
Winans v. Beidler, 6 Okl. 603, 52 Pac. 405.

[3] Meyerdorf v. Frohner, 3 Mont. 282, 320; ante, § 233.

[4] Deffeback v. Hawke, 115 U. S. 392, 6 Sup. Ct. Rep. 95; Sparks v.
Pierce, 115 U. S. 408, 6 Sup. Ct. Rep. 102.

[5] Collins v. Bartlett, 44 Cal. 371.

the soil for mining, become part of the freehold.[1] As such, they will pass to the relocator.

While this is undoubtedly true, upon application for a patent the relocator will not be permitted to include in his estimate of the value of improvements required by law to be made as a condition precedent to patent any of the labor done or improvements made by the original locator.[2]

A grant from the original locator to one who has effected a valid relocation is ineffective for this purpose.[3]

Expenditures for such purpose must have been made by the *relocator* or his *grantees*.[4]

ARTICLE XII. LODES WITHIN PLACERS.

§ 413. Right to appropriate lodes within placers.

§ 414. Manner of locating lodes within placers.

§ 415. Width of lode locations within placers.

§ 413. **Right to appropriate lodes within placers.**— That the two classes of mineral deposits, those falling within the designation of lodes, or veins, and those usually called placers, frequently exist in the same superficial area is a matter of common experience.

That when so found they may be held by the same or different persons, is well settled by both judicial and departmental decisions.[5]

[1] Merritt v. Judd, 14 Cal. 60; Treadway v. Sharon, 7 Nev. 37; Roseville Alta M. Co. v. Iowa G. M. Co., 15 Colo. 29, 22 Am. St. Rep. 373, 24 Pac. 920.

[2] Acting Commissioner Holcomb, Copp's Min. Lands, p. 300; Commissioner Burdett, 1 Copp's L. O. 179; Russell v. Wilson Creek Cons. M. Co., 30 L. D. 321; Yankee Lode, 30 L. D. 289.

[3] Yankee Lode, 30 L. D. 289.

[4] Rev. Stats., § 2322.

[5] Reynolds v. Iron S. M. Co., 116 U. S. 687, 695, 6 Sup. Ct. Rep. 601; Aurora Lode v. Bulger Hill Placer, 23 L. D. 95.

While it is undoubtedly true that a mining location, whether lode or placer, is property in the highest sense of the term, and when perfected is equivalent to a grant from the government,[1] yet it does not follow that the thing granted is the same in both classes of locations, nor that things reserved from the operation of one grant are likewise excepted from the operation of the other.

There is a marked distinction between the surface rights acquired by a lode location and those flowing from a placer location. In the former, there is a grant of the exclusive right of enjoyment of the surface and everything within vertical planes drawn downward through the surface boundaries, subject only to the extralateral right of outside apex proprietors to pursue their veins underneath such surface. No subsequent locator, either lode or placer, can invade such surface, though he may openly and peaceably enter for the purpose of laying his lines in such a manner as to properly define his extralateral right.[2] On the other hand, lodes found within the placer surface, or underneath it, if their existence is known prior to the application for placer patent, are not the subject of a placer grant.[3] Therefore, the placer claimant may not own everything upon the surface or found within vertical planes drawn downward through the surface boundaries. The policy of the government with reference to lodes is to sever them from the body of the public lands, and to deal with them and the land

---

[1] Belk v. Meagher, 104 U. S. 284; Gwillim v. Donnellan, 115 U. S. 45, 5 Sup. Ct. Rep. 1110; Mt. Rosa M. M. and L. Co. v. Palmer, 26 Colo. 56, 77 Am. St. Rep. 245, 56 Pac. 156.

[2] *Ante,* §§ 363, 363a.

[3] Reynolds v. Iron S. M. Co., 116 U. S. 687, 6 Sup. Ct. Rep. 601; Iron S. M. Co. v. Mike & Starr M. Co., 143 U. S. 394, 12 Sup. Ct. Rep. 543; Dahl v. Raunheim, 132 U. S. 260, 10 Sup. Ct. Rep. 74; Clary v. Hazlitt, 67 Cal. 286, 7 Pac. 701; Mt. Rosa M. M. and L. Co. v. Palmer, 26 Colo. 56, 77 Am. St. Rep. 245, 56 Pac. 176.

immediately inclosing them as separate and distinct entities.[1]

The location of mining ground for placer purposes does not effect such severance. The placer claimant *may,* in the absence of a discovery and location by others, obtain the title to the lode, but he has not such right by virtue of his prior placer appropriation, unless the existence of the lode remains unknown until the application for a placer patent is filed.[2] This right to appropriate the lode must flow from the discovery of the *lode.* Whosoever first discovers the lode may appropriate it by complying with the laws conferring privileges upon such discoverers. If he fails to do so, it is open to the next comer; and this rule applies to the placer claimant as well as to strangers. If, having discovered it, he fails to manifest his intention to *claim* it by appropriating it under the lode laws, it may be the subject of appropriation by others, the same as if it were upon the public domain; *provided,* always, that such appropriation is made and perfected peaceably and in good faith.[3] In this respect, the same rules of law which govern the location of mineral land occupied or claimed by others under inchoate agricultural holdings are to be applied. We have fully discussed this subject in preceding articles. It is unnecessary to here repeat what is there said.[4]

There is no reason why a placer claimant may not locate a lode claim within his unpatented placer claim, or consent that others may do so.[5]

The issuance of a placer patent containing within its

---

[1] McCarthy v. Speed, 11 S. Dak. 362, 77 N. W. 590; Waterloo M. Co. v. Doe, 82 Fed. 45, 50.

[2] Aurora Lode v. Bulger Hill Placer, 23 L. D. 95.

[3] McCarthy v. Speed, 11 S. Dak. 362, 77 N. W. 590; Mt. Rosa M. M. and L. Co. v. Palmer, 26 Colo. 56, 77 Am. St. Rep. 245, 56 Pac. 176.

[4] *Ante,* §§ 206, 216, 219.

[5] McCarthy v. Speed, 11 S. Dak. 362, 77 N. W. 590, 592.

limits a lode known to exist prior to the patent application, which lode is not claimed and applied for by the placer claimant as a *lode*, does not cut off the right to appropriate it in hostility to the patentee. His failure to include it in his placer application is a conclusive declaration that he has no right to it.[1]

The courts seem to make a distinction between the right to enter openly and peaceably within the limits of a prior placer claim for the purpose of perfecting the location of a previously discovered lode and the privilege of entering upon the placer surface for the purpose of prospecting or searching for undiscovered lodes. The supreme court of Colorado, while conceding that a stranger may so enter within the placer boundaries to locate a lode previously known to exist therein, holds that he may not make such entry for the purpose of searching for lodes whose existence may be suspected but not demonstrated.[2]

In this respect the court follows the doctrine applied by the courts to locations made under the act of July 26, 1866, under which only one lode could be claimed. Before a stranger to the original location could enter for the purpose of locating a second lode, the fact that two lodes existed within the boundaries was required to be first established.[3]

If a placer claimant has abandoned his claim, or waived the trespass, or by his conduct is estopped from

---

[1] Rev. Stats., § 2333; Sullivan *v.* Iron S. M. Co., 143 U. S. 431, 434, 12 Sup. Ct. Rep. 555; Reynolds *v.* Iron S. M. Co., 116 U. S. 687, 6 Sup. Ct. Rep. 601; Iron S. M. Co. *v.* Mike & Starr G. and S. M. Co., 143 U. S. 394, 402, 12 Sup. Ct. Rep. 543; Iron S. M. Co. *v.* Reynolds, 124 U. S. 374, 8 Sup. Ct. Rep. 598; United States *v.* Iron S. M. Co., 128 U. S. 673, 9 Sup. Ct. Rep. 195; Noyes *v.* Mantle. 127 U. S. 348, 353, 8 Sup. Ct. Rep. 1132.

[2] Clipper M. Co. *v.* Eli M. Co. (Colo.), 68 Pac. 289.

[3] Atkins *v.* Hendry, 1 Idaho, 107.

complaining of it, the subsequent lode location will be considered valid.[1]

The principles discussed in previous sections,[2] concerning the right to enter upon prior claims for the purpose of laying lines or establishing monuments with a view to acquiring something not claimed by or embraced within the prior location, can be aptly applied to the case of lodes "known to exist" within placer claims.

While the land department at one time held that with the issuance of the placer patent its jurisdiction terminated, and thereafter it had no right to entertain a subsequent application for a patent to a lode claim within the patented placer limits,[3] it subsequently changed its ruling to conform to the legal results necessarily flowing from the exposition of the law by the supreme court of the United States.[4]

The same rule is now applied to known lodes within townsites.[5] A finding by a court in an adverse suit brought by a lode claimant against the placer applicant, that there was no known lode, will be treated by the department as an adjudication of the matter.[6] The land department is reluctant to reopen the question of placer character of land at the instigation of a lode claimant where years have elapsed since entry for patent as a placer claim.[7]

[1] Clipper M. Co. v. Eli M. Co. (Colo.), 68 Pac. 289.

[2] §§ 363, 363a.

[3] Rebel Lode, 12 L. D. 683; Pike's Peak Lode, 14 L. D. 47; South Star Lode, 17 L. D. 280.

[4] South Star Lode, on review, 20 L. D. 204; Butte and Boston M. Co., 21 L. D. 125; Cripple Creek G. M. Co. v. Mt. Rosa M. M. and L. Co., 26 L. D. 622; Alice M. Co., 27 L. D. 661; Cape May M. and L. Co. v. Wallace, Id. 676; Ryan v. Granite Hill M. Co., 29 L. D. 522.

[5] Ante, §§ 173, 177; Pacific Slope Lode v. Butte Townsite, 25 L. D. 518; Gregory Lode Claim, 26 L. D. 544.

[6] Alice M. Co., 27 L. D. 661. Post, § 720.

[7] Meaderville M. and M. Co. v. Raunheim, 29 L. D. 465.

It is not our purpose to here define what is meant by a "lode known to exist within the boundaries of a placer " claim," as that phrase occurs in section twenty-three hundred and thirty-three of the Revised Statutes. This will be fully discussed when dealing with the subject of placer patents and the nature and extent of title conferred by placer locations. We are now concerned simply with the manner of locating lodes within placers, their existence being confessedly known prior to the application for the placer patent.

We are justified in deducing from the foregoing the following conclusions:—

(1) A perfected placer location does not confer the right to the possession of veins, or lodes, which may be found to exist within the placer limits at any time prior to filing an application for a placer patent;

(2) Such lodes may be appropriated (a) by the placer claimant, or (b) by others, provided the appropriation is effected by peaceable methods and in good faith;

(3) Where a lode is known to exist within the limits of a placer location at any time prior to the placer application for patent, and is not claimed in the application as a *lode,* the title to such lode does not pass by the patent, but it may be located by any one having the requisite qualifications, provided the location is made peaceably and in good faith.[1]

It frequently happens that after the issuance of a placer or an agricultural patent a valuable lode is discovered within the patented limits. By reason of the nature of the grant, this lode cannot be followed on its downward course beyond the vertical bounding planes. Under such circumstances attempts have been made to surrender or reconvey to the government the title

[1] Mt. Rosa M. M. and L. Co. *v.* Palmer (Colo.), 56 Pac. 176.

deraigned through the patent so as to render a lode location with the accessory extralateral right possible. This
phase of the subject will be discussed in a subsequent
section.[1]

§ 414. **Manner of locating lodes within placers.**—
With the exception of determining the quantity of surface which may be taken in conjunction with a lode
found within a placer claim, a question to be presented
in the next section, there is no difference between the
manner of locating such a lode and any other found
within the public domain. It must be discovered and
developed, the location must be marked upon the surface,
and all other formalities required by federal or state
legislation must be complied with to the same extent
as in case of lodes situated elsewhere. As the right
necessarily flows from discovery, to perpetuate such
right the subsequent acts resulting in a perfected location must be complied with.

As to the surface lines inclosing the lode, while the
inclosed area may possibly be limited, yet their general
direction with reference to the discovered vein must conform to the general rule governing lode locations.[2] In
placer locations, except upon unsurveyed lands, and
under certain specified conditions to be hereafter noted,[3]
the boundaries must conform to the public surveys,
without regard to the course or direction of veins which
may be found therein. Such boundaries perform a
different function from those required in the case of
lode claims.

Whatever may be the dimensions of a placer location
which, when participated in by an association of persons,
may cover an area of one hundred and sixty acres,[4] a

[1] *Post,* § 786.
[2] Reynolds *v.* Iron S. M. Co., 116 U. S. 687, 694, 6 Sup. Ct. Rep. 601.
[3] See next chapter.
[4] Rev. Stats., § 2330.

lode location within a placer cannot exceed the statutory limit as to length—that is, fifteen hundred feet. End-lines must be established within this limit, and, in order to acquire extralateral rights, should cross the located lode and be parallel to each other, or non-divergent in the direction of the dip.[1] A placer boundary may be coincident with a lode boundary if so claimed and marked. But the rights upon the discovered lode will be defined only by the lode boundaries, established and marked as such. In this respect, the statute makes no distinction between lodes within placers and other lodes. In considering this class of lode location, the only debatable question is the quantity of surface which the locator may appropriate for the purpose of inclosing his lode. In all other respects the general rules apply.

§ 415. **Width of lode locations within placers.**—As to the amount of surface which may be appropriated in connection with a lode discovered within a previously located placer claim, the statute seems to be somewhat ambiguous, and its proper construction has been a matter of serious embarrassment to the land department as well as to the courts.

The limit of the superficies of a lode location on the public domain under the federal law is fifteen hundred feet along the lode and three hundred feet on each side of the middle of the vein.

The section providing for the acquisition of title to lodes within a placer location is as follows:—

"Where the same person, association, or corporation " is in possession of a placer claim and also a vein or " lode included within the boundaries thereof, applica- " tion shall be made for a patent for the placer claim " with the statement that it includes such vein or lode, " and in such case a patent shall issue for the placer

[1] *Post,* § 582.

" claim subject to the provisions of this chapter, includ-
" ing such vein or lode claim and twenty-five feet of
" surface on each side thereof. The remainder of the
" placer claim, or any placer claim not embracing any
" vein or lode claim, shall be paid for at the rate of two
" dollars and fifty cents per acre, together with all costs
" of proceedings; and where a vein or lode such as is
" described in section twenty-three hundred and twenty,
" is known to exist within the boundaries of a placer
" claim, an application for a patent for such placer claim
" which does not include an application for the vein or
" lode claim shall be construed as a conclusive declara-
" tion that the claimant of a placer claim has no right of
" possession of the vein or lode claim; but where the
" existence of a vein or lode in a placer claim is not
" known, a patent for the placer claim shall convey all
" valuable mineral and other deposits within the bound-
" aries thereof." [1]

The question presents itself in two aspects.—

(1) Where the lode is located and claimed by the placer claimant;

(2) Where it is located and claimed by strangers to the placer title.

As to the placer claimant, there is no reason why he should not be permitted to select as much of the surface inclosing the lode as the law will permit in case of other lode locations; that is, within the limit of fifteen hundred by six hundred feet, in the absence of state laws or local regulations restricting the right to less. There is no requirement that land contiguous to the lode, and appro-priated with it, should be non-mineral in character. As he owns the surface of the placer, except as against a lode locator, no one can complain if the placer claimant takes any quantity within the prescribed limit. His taking more than the twenty-five feet would simply operate as an abandonment *pro tanto* of the placer claim.

[1] Rev. Stats., § 2333.

But he is required to take at least twenty-five feet on each side of the center of the vein, and pay therefor at the rate of five dollars per acre. The remainder he may enter as placer ground at half that rate.

But let us assume a case of a lode discovered within a prior placer claim by a stranger to the placer title, such discovery antedating the application for a placer patent. That such lode may be located and claimed by the discoverer seems to be well settled. But the extent of surface to which such locator may be entitled, with due regard to the rights of the prior placer claimant, is the subject of debate. The question assumes this form: What is in contemplation of law reserved out of a placer location? or, to what extent is the surface of a prior placer location subject to invasion and diminution by a subsequent discoverer of a lode within the placer boundaries?

The question may be answered in one of four ways:—

(1) Either the lode locator is entitled to the full width allowed to other lode locations, or

(2) He is allowed twenty-five feet on each side of the lode, or

(3) He is allowed no surface, or

(4) He may take only such surface as may be reasonably necessary for the enjoyment of the lode.

The supreme court of the United States held, in Noyes v. Mantle,[1] that a placer patent reserves a lode claim, located prior to the application for patent, to its full extent; but in that case, although the decision as reported is silent as to the date of the placer location, it is quite manifest that the lode was discovered and located prior to the location of the placer.[2] Such prior

---

[1] 127 U. S. 348, 8 Sup. Ct. Rep. 1132.

[2] The record in this case, as filed, discloses the fact that the lode was located in April, and the placer the following October.

location withdraws the area covered, and the subsequent placer locator could, of course, obtain no rights as against the lode locator. This is not the case we have assumed. If, in the Noyes-Mantle case, the lode location in controversy had been the junior in date, we might infer from the decision that the subsequent lode locator was authorized to select, within the boundaries of the placer, a full surface claim. But as heretofore indicated, the lode location in that case antedated not only the application for placer patent, but the *location* of the placer.

When we examine the rulings of the land department, we find that they are not uniform.

Originally that department held that the claimant of a lode within placer limits could only assert the right, as against a placer patentee, to twenty-five feet on each side of the center of the vein. If he sought to claim more, he could only protect his right to the increased area by adversing the placer applicant. Failing to do so, he was limited to a width of fifty feet.[1]

This was before the decision in Noyes *v.* Mantle (*supra*). Subsequent to this decision, the department reached the following conclusions, after quoting from the cases of Noyes *v.* Mantle, and Reynolds *v.* Iron S. M. Co.:—[2]

" It thus appears that the limitation of the width of " the claim in section twenty-three hundred and thirty- " three, Revised Statutes, is only applicable where the " same claimant seeks a patent for a vein, or lode, in- " cluded within the boundaries of his placer claim, and " has no application to a lode claim properly perfected " by another, prior to the date of the application for " patent for placer claim, whose boundaries include the " lode claim. If, therefore, it shall appear from the

---

[1] Shonbar Lode, 1 L. D. 551; *Id.,* 3 L. D. 388.

[2] 116 U. S. 687, 6 Sup. Ct. Rep. 601; second appeal, 124 U. S. 374, 8 Sup-Ct. Rep. 598.

" record that there is a lode claim within the bounda-
" ries of a placer claim, then that lode claim in its full
" extent should be excepted from the placer patent." [1]

But in this case the department declined to patent the
lode claim at all, for the reason that its jurisdiction had
been exhausted by the issuance of the placer patent—a
ruling which, as heretofore noted,[2] was subsequently
changed. A later expression of opinion by the land
department upon the subject under consideration is
found in a decision by Secretary Smith in the case of
the Aurora Lode v. The Bulger Hill and Nuggett Gulch
Placer.[3]

In this case, the placer claims were first located, the
Bulger Hill on March 19th, and the Nuggett Gulch on
April 6, 1881. The Aurora lode was located April 9th
of the same year. The properties had been in litigation,
arising out of patent proceedings, the Aurora lode
claimant having applied for a patent, which was adversed by the placer claimant, the judgment being in
favor of the latter.[4]

Notwithstanding this, the land department entertained the protest of the lode claimant against the issuance of a patent to the placer claimant, and after
discussing the effect of the judgment of the court, and
the relative rights of the two classes of claimants, the
secretary of the interior thus expresses his views:—

"The only question which presents any serious diffi-
" culty to my mind relates to the extent of surface area
" the lode claimant will be entitled to in the event he
" sustains, by proof in the regular way, the allegations
" of his protest. His claim as originally located ap-
" pears to be something over five hundred feet in width
" at the points of conflict with the placer locations. The

---

[1] Pike's Peak Lode, 10 L. D. 200, 203.
[2] § 413.
[3] 23 L. D. 95, 348.
[4] Bennett v. Harkrader, 158 U. S. 441, 15 Sup. Ct. Rep. 863.

" extensive and valuable improvements erected upon
" the claim are alleged to be upon that part within the
" overlap. The surface ground being, however, only
" an incident to the lode, and not a part of it, I am of
" the opinion, that under the judgment of the court,
" the placer claimant is entitled to the surface area
" within the overlap, except so much thereof as is neces-
" sary to the occupation, use, operation, and enjoyment
" of the lode claim by its owners. This may be more or
" less, according to the extent and location of the pres-
" ent improvement, if any, and other conditions pecul-
" iar to this particular claim. I know of no established
" precedent controlling in such a case as this, but in
" view of the superior right of the placer claimant to
" the surface area as established by prior location and
" by the judgment of the court in the adverse proceed-
" ings, I do not think that the superior right of the lode
" claimant to the possession of his lode, if its discovery,
" location, and known existence be true, as alleged,
" should be allowed to carry with it more surface
" ground within the overlap than is necessary for the
" occupation, use, operation, and full enjoyment
" thereof. Having been defeated in the adverse pro-
" ceedings in the court, it would appear to be but just
" and right that the lode claimant should be thus re-
" stricted as touching the surface area of his claim, and,
" indeed, such seems to be necessary in order to give
" effect to the court's judgment."

Without stopping to consider the binding effect of the
judgment in the adverse proceedings as an estoppel upon
the lode claimant, we think that the ruling of the secretary proceeds upon considerations of an equitable
nature, rather than upon anything deducible from the
mining laws. If we assume that nothing is reserved out
of the placer location but the lode itself, we practically
concede that the reservation is of no substantial benefit
to any one, as the right to enjoy it would be practically
denied. The placer locator would hold everything, except the ledge bounded by its inclosing walls, and no
right of entry over or through the placer ground would

be permitted.[1]   Or, at the utmost, the lode claimant
would only be entitled to an *easement* over the placer
ground, upon the principle that a reservation of a thing
out of a grant is a reservation of whatever may be necessary to its enjoyment.

But the mining laws contemplate no such conditions.
The only method by which the lode may be located is
by defining a surface inclosing it.[2]

Since the Department rendered its decision in the
case of the Aurora Lode *v.* The Bulger Hill and Nuggett Gulch Placer (*supra*), the question has been referred to in several cases.[3]

In the case of the North Star lode,[4] Acting Secretary
Ryan said:—

" The difficulties in reaching a correct solution of
" this question are such that the department believes it
" better to withhold a decision thereof until a case is
" reached wherein the opposing views and arguments
" are fully presented, so that the decision may be based
" upon full consideration thereof." [5]

The last expression of opinion by the secretary will be
noted after stating the conclusions reached by the
courts.

So far as the decisions of the courts are concerned,
we have noted but one reported case which analyzes the
statute and announces a definite solution of the question.
We refer to a decision participated in by a majority of
the supreme court of Colorado in the case of Mt. Rosa
Mining and Milling and Land Co. *v.* Palmer.[6]   We

[1] Dower *v.* Richards, 73 Cal. 477, 480, 15 Pac. 105.

[2] *Ante,* §§ 71, 361.

[3] Elda M. and M. Co. *v.* Mayflower G. M. Co., 26 L. D. 573; Cape May
M. and L. Co. *v.* Wallace, 27 L. D. 676.

[4] 28 L. D. 41, 44.

[5] The last expression of opinion by the secretary will be noted after
stating the conclusions reached by the courts.

[6] 26 Colo. 56, 77 Am. St. Rep. 245, 56 Pac. 178.

quote so much thereof as is necessary to show the conclusion reached and the reasoning on which it was based:—

" The question was also involved upon the trial of
" the case of Campbell v. Iron S. M. Co., in the circuit
" court of the United States, for this district, Judge
" Riner presiding. He entertained the view, and in-
" structed the jury to the effect, that a lode claimant,
" in case of a recovery, was entitled to no more than the
" vein or lode, and fifty feet of ground, extending fifteen
" hundred feet in length.

" We think this instruction correctly defines the
" amount of surface ground to which a lode located
" within the boundaries of a placer is entitled, under
" the provisions of section twenty-three hundred and
" thirty-three. As was said in Reynolds v. Iron S. M.
" Co., (supra): 'This section made provision for three
" 'distinct classes of cases: (1.) When the applicant
" 'for a placer patent is at the time in possession of a
" 'vein or lode included within the boundaries of his
" 'placer claim he shall state that fact, and, on payment
" 'of the sum required for a vein claim and twenty-five
" 'feet on each side of it, at five dollars per acre, and two
" 'dollars and fifty cents for the remainder of the placer
" 'claim, his patent shall cover both. (2.) It enacted
" 'that, where no such vein or lode is known to exist at
" 'the time the patent is applied for, the patent for a
" 'placer claim shall carry all valuable mineral and
" 'other deposits which may be found within the bound-
" 'aries thereof. (3.) But, in case where the applicant
" 'for the placer is not in possession of such lode or vein
" 'within the boundaries of his claim, but such vein is
" 'known to exist, and it is not referred to or mentioned
" 'in the claim or patent, then the application shall be
" 'construed as a conclusive declaration that the claim-
" 'ant of the placer mine has no right to the possession
" 'of the vein or lode claim.'

" We think it is manifest that the lode or vein
" referred to in the first and third provisions is
" the same thing, and that whatever a placer claim-
" ant would acquire by availing himself of the

" privilege accorded him by the first provision of
" the section, is reserved by virtue of the third pro-
" vision; in other words, that the same extent of surface
" ground that is incident to such lode or vein, if located
" and patented by the placer claimant, is reserved from
" the placer patent in case of his failure to claim and
" patent the same. If he elects to patent the lode, he is
" required to take twenty-five feet on each side of the
" center of the vein, and pay therefor at the rate of five
" dollars per acre. This is a privilege accorded to him,
" which he may avail himself of, or not, as he sees fit.
" If he elects to waive this privilege, he may do so in
" one of two ways—either by expressly excepting the
" lode from his placer location and application for
" patent, or remaining silent in regard to it. If silent,
" then by implication he declares that he makes no
" claim to such lode and by such silence is bound to the
" same extent, and in the same manner, but no further,
" than he would have been by an express declaration.
" By electing to make no claim to a known lode, or ex-
" press declaration in regard to it, he must be under-
" stood as claiming, for placer purposes, the greatest
" possible area within the boundaries of his placer claim
" and should be held to have relinquished only that
" which he might have taken, which is the lode, with
" the amount of surface ground provided. Why should
" there be any difference between the rights of claim-
" ants of known lodes within the boundaries of a placer?
" We know of none. The object of excepting known
" lodes from placer locations was to prevent titles to
" such lodes being obtained under the guise of a placer;
" at the same time, in order to protect claimants to each
" character of mineral locations to the greatest extent,
" and preserve to each that which was most valuable
" for particular purposes in connection with each class
" of claims. The lode, for convenient working, could
" not be limited to less than twenty-five feet on each side
" of the center of the vein; and the placer, which would
" be valueless without such surface rights, is permitted
" to take title to the remaining area accordingly. Those
" who controvert this view base their contention upon
" the provisions of section twenty-three hundred and

" twenty, which it is said governs the length and width
" of all lode claims, whether made within the bounda-
" ries of a placer claim or not.

" An act on a particular subject must be con-
" strued as a whole. Section twenty-three hundred
" and twenty refers to the location of lodes not
" conflicting with any other class of mineral loca-
" tions; while by section twenty-three hundred and
" thirty-three special conditions with reference to con-
" flicts between the two classes of mineral claims are
" specially provided for; and, to that extent, construing
" the act as a whole, is a limitation or qualification of
" the provisions of section twenty-three hundred and
" twenty, which relates, as stated, to the width of lode
" claims generally, and regulates the width of lode
" claims when made upon lodes within the boundaries
" of a placer, whether such lodes are located by the
" owner of the placer or strangers to that title. By
" this construction full force and effect is given to both
" of these sections, and the purpose of the statute is
" carried out. The government receives for its mineral
" lands the price fixed for lodes and placers, respective-
" ly, and the superior right to the surface area of the
" placer claimant, acquired by his prior location or
" patent, is protected. It is the conclusion of a majority
" of the court that the limitation of the width of a lode
" claim in section twenty-three hundred and thirty-
" three is not only applicable to the placer claimant,
" but applies as well to others who locate a lode within
" the boundaries of his previously located placer.

" Chief Justice Campbell declines to express an
" opinion upon this question, because, in his judgment,
" the stipulation entered into by counsel eliminates it
" from the case.

" It follows that the court below erred in adjudging
" to appellee surface ground in excess of twenty-five
" feet on each side of the lodes in question. For this
" reason, the judgment is reversed, and the case re-
" manded, with directions to enter judgment in accord-
" ance with the views we have expressed." [1]

---

[1] Mt. Rosa M., M., and L. Co. *v.* Palmer, 26 Colo. 56, 63, 56 Pac. 176.

The views thus entertained by the supreme court of Colorado have recently received the approval of the secretary of the interior in a communication addressed by him to the attorney-general.[1] This communication requested that proceedings be instituted in behalf of the United States to cancel a patent issued for a lode claim within a prior located placer, upon the ground, among others, that a surface covering a width of three hundred feet had been patented, whereas the surface width should have been limited to twenty-five feet on each side of the center of the vein. The secretary calls the attorney-general's attention to the views of the department as previously expressed in the cases heretofore commented on, and then gives his unqualified sanction to the doctrine announced by the supreme court of Colorado, in the following language:—

" This decision, coming from the court of last resort " of one of the principal mining states, is entitled to " grave weight, and upon careful consideration of the " reasons assigned for the conclusions reached, the " department is of the opinion that the interpretation " given the statute in said decision is correct."

With this consensus of opinion of the courts and the land department the rule may be considered as practically settled.

[1] April 1, 1902, not reported.

CHAPTER III.

LACERS AND OTHER FORMS OF DEPOSIT NOT "IN PLACE."

ARTICLE I. CHARACTER OF DEPOSITS SUBJECT TO APPROPRIATION UNDER LAWS APPLICABLE TO PLACERS.

II. THE LOCATION AND ITS REQUIREMENTS.

III. THE DISCOVERY.

IV. STATE LEGISLATION AS TO POSTING NOTICES AND PRELIMINARY DEVELOPMENT WORK.

V. THE SURFACE COVERED BY THE LOCATION — ITS FORM AND EXTENT.

VI. THE MARKING OF THE LOCATION ON THE GROUND.

VII. THE LOCATION CERTIFICATE AND ITS RECORD.

VIII. CONCLUSION.

ARTICLE I. CHARACTER OF DEPOSITS SUBJECT TO APPROPRIATION UNDER LAWS APPLICABLE TO PLACERS.

§ 419. The general rule.

§ 420. Specific substances classified as subject to entry under the placer laws.

§ 421. Building-stone and stone of special commercial value.

§ 422. Petroleum.

§ 423. Natural gas.

§ 424. Brick clay.

§ 425. Phosphatic deposits.

§ 426. Tailings.

§ 427. Subterranean gravel deposits in ancient river-beds.

§ 428. Beds of streams.

§ 429. Lands under tide-waters.

§ 419. **The general rule.**—In a preceding chapter,[1] in determining what constitutes "mineral land," which as such is susceptible of appropriation under the mining laws, we have to some extent anticipated much that might be properly said in defining the character of deposits which are subject to appropriation under the laws applicable to placers, and we have there endeavored [2]

---

[1] *Ante,* §§ 85-98.   [2] *Ante,* § 98.

to formulate general rules by which the mineral character of substances is to be established. In conformity with these rules, land of the public domain may be entered under the laws applicable to placers when it is shown to have upon or within it such a substance as falls within the classification named in section ninety-eight, if such substance is found in the form of superficial or other deposits not *in place*. If a discovered deposit satisfies the law as to its mineral character, and it is not found in veins of quartz, or other rock in place, it may be appropriated under the laws applicable to placers. What constitutes "rock in place" has been fully discussed.[1]

We say that all forms of deposit, other than those occurring in veins of rock in place, must be appropriated under the laws applicable to *placers,* for the reason that *placers* present, in popular estimation, the highest type of deposits which do not occur in veins of rock in place, and are the only class of such deposits as are individualized and specially named in the statute.[2]

The right to acquire title to "claims usually called " placers" was granted for the first time by the mining act of July 9, 1870.[3]

This has always been familiarly called the "placer " law," in contradistinction to the "lode law" of July 26, 1866. The subsequent legislation preserved the distinction, so that, colloquially speaking, mineral deposits are to be treated either as lodes or placers. In time, *placer,* which was the name given by the Spaniards to the auriferous gravels of America,[4] has become a generic term, in which all forms of deposit, other than those occurring in veins, are popularly included.

Dr. Raymond, in his "Glossary of Mining and Metal-

[1] *Ante,* §§ 299-301.　　　　　[3] 16 Stats. at Large, p. 217.
[2] Rev. Stats., § 2329.　　　　　[4] Moxon *v.* Wilkinson, 2 Mont. 421

"lurgical Terms,"[1] defines the word *placer* as a deposit of valuable mineral found in particles in *alluvium,* or *diluvium,* or beds of streams, and enumerates gold, tin ore, chromic iron, iron ore, and precious stones, as being found in placers. He adds to the definition the statement that, by the United States statutes, all deposits not classed as veins of rock in place are considered *placers.*

As was said by the supreme court of the United States, in distinguishing the two classes of deposits: " Placer mines, though said by the statute to include all " other deposits of mineral matter, are those in which " this mineral is generally found in the softer material " which covers the earth's surface, and not among the " rocks beneath."[2]

Assuming that our definition of "mineral," outlined in a previous chapter,[3] is based upon a correct interpretation of the law, there should be but little difficulty in determining whether land containing a given substance not in place is subject to entry under the placer laws or not. The element of commercial value, its susceptibility of being extracted and marketed at a profit, and not its metallic or chemical character, are the controlling factors in determining the question.[4]

This is clearly shown, not only by the evolution of denotation, illustrated in the history of English jurisprudence and the decisions of the American courts, but by a long line of departmental rulings, uniform, except as to certain specific substances. As was said by the supreme court of the United States: " The construction " given to a statute by those charged with the duty of

[1] Trans. Am. Inst. M. E., vol. ix, p. 164.
[2] Reynolds v. Iron S. M. Co., 116 U. S. 687, 695, 6 Sup. Ct. Rep. 601.
[3] *Ante,* §§ 85-98.
[4] Pacific Coast Marble Co. v. N. P. R. R. Co., 25 L. D. 233; Aldritt v. Northern Pac. R. R. Co., 25 L. D. 349; Phifer v. Heaton, 27 L. D. 57; McQuiddy v. State of California, 29 L. D. 181.

" executing it, is always entitled to the most respectful
" consideration, and ought not to be overruled without
" cogent reasons." [1]

While this element of profit, or commercial value, has
generally pervaded the rulings of the land department,
we find that in dealing with certain specific substances,
either by reason of their commonplace character, or the
other extreme, their unique and peculiar properties, the
department has lost sight of this controlling factor, and
leaned toward strict and frequently, we think, strained
rules of construction. Owing to the infinite variety in
nature, the application to individual instances of general laws framed and construed on broad theories may
seem to produce absurd results. But this in no sense
proves that the law or the general rule of construction
is absurd. We cannot conceive of any class of deposits
of the general character under consideration which may
not fairly be tested by the general rules announced in
section ninety-eight.

That the true position of the land department upon
this subject may be fairly presented, it is necessary to
consider its rulings as to specific substances.

§ 420. Specific substances classified as subject to entry
under the placer laws.—Among the substances, other
than those of a metallic character, which have been
classified as mineral, and when occurring in the form
of deposits not in place, lands containing which have

[1] *Post*, § 666; United States *v.* Moore, 95 U. S. 760; Hastings and
Dakota R. R. *v.* Whitney, 132 U. S. 357, 10 Sup. Ct. Rep. 112; Hahn *v.*
United States, 107 U. S. 402, 2 Sup. Ct. Rep. 494; Brown *v.* United
States, 113 U. S. 568, 5 Sup. Ct. Rep. 648; Doe *v.* Waterloo M. Co.,
70 Fed. 455; 82 Fed. 45, 50; Calhoun G. M. Co. *v.* Ajax G. M. Co.,
27 Colo. 1, 83 Am. St. Rep. 17, 59 Pac. 607; McFadden *v.* Mountain
View M. and M. Co., 97 Fed. 670; Hawley *v.* Diller, 178 U. S. 476,
20 Sup. Ct. Rep. 986; Hewitt *v.* Schultz, 180 U. S. 139, 21 Sup. Ct.
Rep. 309; United States *v.* Southern Pac. R. R., 184 U. S. 49, 22 Sup. Ct.
Rep. 285; Fairbank *v.* United States, 181 U. S. 283, 21 Sup. Ct. Rep. 648.

been held to be subject to appropriation under the placer laws, we note the following:—

Alum;[1] asphaltum;[2] borax;[3] diamonds;[4] gypsum;[5] kaolin, or china clay;[6] marble;[7] mica;[8] soda, carbonate and nitrate;[9] slate, for roofing purposes;[10] umber;[11] building-stone.[12]

As to these substances, we understand the rule is uniform, the elements of quantity and quality being present, by which the value of the land, for the purpose of removing and marketing the product, is determined. Other substances require specific mention.

§ 421. **Building-stone, and stone of special commercial value.**—As heretofore observed,[13] congress, on August 4, 1892, enacted a law, wherein it provided that any person authorized to enter lands under the mining laws of the United States may enter lands that are chiefly valuable for building-stone under the provisions of the law in relation to placer mineral claims.[14] The previous rulings by the land department, as to whether land containing stone of this character was subject to entry under the placer laws, were not uniform.

---

[1] Copp's Min. Lands, 50; 2 L. D. 707.

[2] Copp's Min. Lands, 50.

[3] *Id.* 50, 100; 2 L. D. 707; Copp's Min. Dec. 194; 1 Copp's L. O. 11.

[4] Copp's Min. Lands, 88.

[5] *Id.* 309; Phifer v. Heaton, 27 L. D. 57; McQuiddy v. State of California, 29 L. D. 181.

[6] Copp's Min. Lands, 121, 176, 209; 1 L. D. 565; Montague v. Dobbs, 9 Copp's L. O. 165; Aldritt v. Northern Pac. R. R. Co., 25 L. D. 349.

[7] Copp's Min. Lands, 176; Pacific Coast Marble Co. v. N. P. R. R. Co., 25 L. D. 233; Schrimpf v. Northern Pac. R. R. Co., 29 L. D. 327.

[8] Copp's Min. Lands, 182.

[9] *Id.* 50; 2 L. D. 707.

[10] Copp's Min. Lands, 143; 1 Copp's L. O. 132.

[11] Copp's Min. Lands, 161.

[12] Forsythe v. Weingart, 27 L. D. 680.

[13] *Ante,* § 139.

[14] 27 Stats. at Large, p. 348.

In the case of Bennett,[1] Commissioner McFarland expressed the opinion that lands of such character were subject to such entry.

Some years later, Assistant Secretary Chandler declined to accept the views of the commissioner, and established the contrary doctrine.[2] The following year, the same assistant secretary "explained" and "distinguished" his previous ruling, and practically adopted the views of Commissioner McFarland in a case involving the interpretation of the law as it existed prior to the passage of the act of August 4, 1892.[3]

Secretary Noble held that this class of land was not "mineral land" so as to preclude its entry under the agricultural land laws, although the proof showed that the tract in question was more valuable for the building-stone it contained than for agricultural purposes, following the first ruling of Assistant Secretary Chandler.[4]

A few months later Secretary Smith held that under the law as it existed prior to the passage of the act of August 4, 1892, land containing a deposit of sandstone of a superior quality for building and ornamental purposes, and valuable only as a stone quarry, might be entered as a placer claim under the general mining laws,[5] which ruling was practically ignored by Assistant Secretary Sims in a later case.[6]

Secretary Bliss originally expressed the opinion that prior to 1892 lands chiefly valuable for building-stone could not be purchased under the placer laws;[7] but on

---

[1] 1884, 3 L. D. 116.

[2] Conlin v. Kelly (1891), 12 L. D. 1.

[3] McGlenn v. Wienbroeer, 15 L. D. 370.

[4] Clark v. Ervin (Feb., 1893), 16 L. D. 122.

[5] Van Doren v. Plested, 16 L. D. 508.

[6] *In re* Delaney, 17 L. D. 120. See, also, *In re* Simon Randolph, 23 L. D. 329.

[7] Hayden v. Jamison, 24 L. D. 403.

review of the same case he vacated his first decision and reached an opposite conclusion.[1] The land department has finally settled the rule that building-stone is a mineral.[2]

The passage of the act of congress referred to, occurring as it did subsequent to Assistant Secretary Chandler's first ruling, was a legislative affirmance of the theory of interpretation applied to other classes of non-metallic substances, and a recognition of the rule which has for its foundation the element of commercial value. More than once congress has intervened when the department has undertaken to disregard this element, by applying arbitrary rules to individual cases. A notable instance will be found when we reach the subject of petroleum.

The supreme court of Montana followed the ruling of Commissioner McFarland in the Bennett case.[3] The supreme court of Washington declined to accept the reasoning of the supreme court of Montana, and held, that the term "mineral" was intended to embrace only deposits of *ore*, and the idea of a non-mineralized deposit was excluded.[4]

As the law now stands, lands containing deposits of building-stone in such quantities as to render them more valuable for quarrying purposes than any other, may be entered as placers under the mining laws, or purchased under the stone and timber act of June 3, 1878.[5]

Lands containing limestone used for fluxing in metallurgical operations, or for the purpose of manufactur-

[1] Hayden v. Jamison, 26 L. D. 373.

[2] Pacific Coast Marble Co. v. N. P. R. R. Co., 25 L. D. 233; Hayden v. Jamison, on review, 26 L. D. 373; Forsythe v. Weingart, 27 L. D. 680; Schrimpf v. N. P. R. R. Co., 29 L. D. 327.

[3] Freezer v. Sweeney, 8 Mont. 508, 21 Pac. 20.

[4] Wheeler v. Smith, 5 Wash. 704, 32 Pac. 784.

[5] 20 Stats. at Large, p. 89; Forsythe v. Weingart, 27 L. D. 680. *Ante,* § 210.

ing the lime of commerce, have been held to be subject to entry under the placer laws.[1]

Sandstone is held to be a mineral,[2] as well as slate, marble,[3] and granite.[4]

§ 422.   Petroleum.—Petroleum has always been recognized as a mineral.[5]   As was said by the supreme court of Pennsylvania: "It is a mineral substance " obtained from the earth by the process of mining, and " lands from which it is obtained may, with propriety, " be called mining lands;"[6] although that court had previously held that while admitting petroleum to be mineral, it was not included in a reservation of " mineral " in a deed.[7]

Judge Ross, sitting as circuit judge in the ninth circuit, held that public land containing petroleum could only be acquired pursuant to the provisions of the mining laws relating to placer claims.[8]   It would seem that

[1] Commissioner Burdett (1875), Copp's Min. Lands, 176; Maxwell v. Brierly (1883), 10 Copp's L. O. 50; Shepherd v. Bird (1893), 17 L. D. 82; Morrill v. Northern Pac. R. R. Co., 30 L. D. 421; Johnston v. Harrington, 5 Wash. 93, 31 Pac. 316.

[2] Beaudette v. N. P. R. R. Co., 29 L. D. 248.

[3] Schrimpf v. N. P. R. R. Co., 29 L. D. 327; Pacific Coast Marble Co. v. N. P. R. R. Co., 25 L. D. 233; Beaudette v. N. P. R. R. Co., 29 L. D. 327; Phelps v. Church of Our Lady, 115 Fed. 883; Armstrong v. Lake Champlain Granite Co., 147 N. Y. 495, 49 Am. St. Rep. 683, 42 N. E. 186; Brady v. Brady, 31 Misc. Rep. 411, 65 N. Y. Supp. 621.

[4] Armstrong v. Lake Champlain Granite Co., 147 N. Y. 495, 49 Am. St. Rep. 683, 42 N. E. 186; Northern Pac. R. R. Co. v. Soderberg, 99 Fed. 506, S. C. on appeal, 104 Fed. 425.

[5] Ante, § 93.

[6] Gill v. Weston, 110 Pa. St. 316, 1 Atl. 921. See, also, Stoughton's Appeal, 88 Pa. St. 198; Thompson v. Noble, 3 Pittsb. 201; Murray v. Allred, 100 Tenn. 100, 66 Am. St. Rep. 740, 43 S. W. 355; Williamson v. Jones, 39 W. Va. 231, 19 S. E. 436.

[7] Dunham v. Kirkpatrick, 101 Pa. St. 36, 47 Am. Rep. 696. See, also, Detlor v. Holland, 57 Ohio St. 492, 49 N. E. 690.

[8] Gird v. California Oil Co., 60 Fed. 531, 532. See, also, Olive L. and D. Co. v. Olmstead, 103 Fed. 588.

this view was entertained by the land department,[1] until Secretary Hoke Smith, in August, 1896, ruled that petroleum lands were not mineral lands, could not be entered under the mining laws,[2] and might be selected by the states in lieu of lost sixteenth and thirty-sixth sections.[3]

Congress promptly intervened, as it had on a previous occasion in reference to building-stone,[4] and by act approved February 11, 1897, ordained:—

"That any person authorized to enter lands under " the mining laws of the United States may enter and " obtain patent to lands containing petroleum, or other " mineral oils, and chiefly valuable therefor, under the " provisions of the laws relating to placer mineral " claims: *Provided,* That lands containing such petro- " leum, or other mineral oils, which have heretofore " been filed upon, claimed, or improved as mineral, but " not yet patented, may be held and patented under the " provisions of this act the same as if such filing, claim, " or improvement were subsequent to the date of the " passage hereof."

The land department subsequently overruled the decision of Secretary Smith.[5]

This, of course, settles the question for the future. We think the act of congress was but a legislative recognition of the law as it previously existed. As was said by Secretary Bliss,—

"This legislative action so promptly taken after the " departure from the earlier rulings and the long estab- " lished practice thereunder is significant and can

[1] *In re* A. A. Dewey, 9 Copp's L. O. 51; Downey *v.* Rogers, 2 L. D. 707; *In re* Samuel Rogers, 4 L. D. 284; Roberts *v.* Jepson, 4 L. D. 60; Peru Oil Co., 16 L. D. 117.

[2] *Ex parte* Union Oil Co., 23 L. D. 222.

[3] Chandler *v.* State of California, Oct 27, 1896.

[4] *Ante,* § 421.

[5] Union Oil Co., on review, 25 L. D. 351; McQuiddy *v.* State of California, 29 L. D. 181.

" hardly be considered as less than a disapproval by
" congress of the changed ruling." [1]

§ 423.   **Natural gas.** —Natural gas is as much an article of commerce as iron ore, oil, coal, petroleum, or any
other of the like products of the earth. [2]

"It is true," said the supreme court of Pennsylvania,
" that gas is a mineral, but it is a mineral with peculiar
" attributes, which require the application of precedents
" arising out of ordinary mineral rights, with much
" more careful consideration of the principles involved
" than the mere decision." [3]

It was held by the court of appeals of Ontario that
natural gas is a mineral within the meaning of a statute
which gives corporations power to sell or lease mineral
rights under highways; [4] and the supreme court of the
United States has decided that this commodity, when
brought into this country from Canada through pipes,
was exempt from duty as "crude mineral." [5]

While, owing to its "fugitive and wandering exist-
" ence within the limits of a particular tract," [6] the
appropriation of it under the mining laws applicable to
placers suggests an apparent absurdity, yet, as it is a
mineral, is an article of commerce, and of great utility
in an economic sense, we do not see why lands shown
to contain it in quantities sufficient to make them more
valuable for that purpose than any other should not be

[1] Union Oil Co., on review, 25 L. D. 351.

[2] State v. Indiana and Ohio O. G. and M. Co., 2 Interstate Com. Rep. 758.
See interesting note in 25 L. R. A. 222.

[3] Westmoreland and Cambria Nat. Gas Co. v. De Witt, 130 Pa. St. 235,
18 Atl. 724, (cited in Murray v. Allred, 100 Tenn. 100, 66 Am. St. Rep.
740, 43 S. W. 355, 359).

[4] Ontario Nat. Gas Co. v. Gosfield, 18 Ont. App. 626.

[5] United States v. Buffalo Nat. Gas Fuel Co., 172 U. S. 339, 19 Sup. Ct.
Rep. 200, affirming 78 Fed. 110, 45 U. S. App. 345, and 73 Fed. 191.
See, also, vol. 62 Eng. and Min. Journal, p. 602.

[6] Brown v. Vandergrift, 80 Pa. St. 147. See, also, Murray v. Allred,
100 Tenn. 100, 66 Am. St. Rep. 740, 43 S. W. 355.

entered under the placer laws. The difference between asphaltum, mineral tar, petroleum, and natural gas, is only one of degree.

§ 424. **Brick clay.**—If lands containing kaolin, or china clay, are subject to entry under the placer laws, it is difficult to see upon what principle lands chiefly valuable for deposits of brick clay should be excepted from such entry. But Secretary Vilas held that, although a given tract was undoubtedly more valuable as a "clay placer" than for any other purpose, it was not mineral land, and could not be appropriated under the mining laws.[1]

The manufactured product from a bed of brick clay is more commonplace than the porcelain obtained from kaolin, or china clay, but we cannot understand why this should make any difference. The element of value in both cases rests upon the marketability of the manufactured product. Under the English decisions, brick clay is classified as a mineral under the "railway clauses " act,"[2] and we can conceive of no logical reason why, in the administration of the federal mining laws, any discrimination should be made as between the finer and coarser grades of a substance, if it can be extracted, removed, and marketed at a profit.

The last expression of the land department, however, is opposed to the classification of deposits of ordinary brick clay as "mineral" within the meaning of the laws applicable to placer locations. Lands containing this substance fall within the definition of agricultural lands.[3]

We deferentially suggest that while it is true that this last analysis is in accordance with previous depart-

---

[1] Dunluce Placer Mine, 6 L. D. 761. See, also, Jordan v. Idaho Aluminum M. and M. Co., 20 L. D. 500.

[2] *Ante,* § 92, p. 100, notes 3 and 4.

[3] King v. Bradford, 31 L. D. 108.

mental rulings as to brick clay, the result reached is not altogether consistent with the principle repeatedly announced by the department with reference to numerous other non-metallic substances,—that marketability at a profit is the test of the mineral character of a given tract of public land.

§ 425. Phosphatic deposits.—The only public land state in the union where the phosphatic deposits occur in appreciable quantities is Florida. They have been extensively mined in South Carolina since 1868, but their existence in Florida was not known until 1887, since which time they have come into prominence, and have assumed considerable economic importance. They are, in general, most abundant in ancient river bottoms, where they have been washed together from their original beds.[1] Since 1890 mining of these deposits has been conducted upon a large scale, the shipments constituting a heavy item in the freights of the several railroads of the state. The raw material is consumed in large quantities in the United States, and it is exported to the various parts of Europe.[2]

Secretary Smith held that land chiefly valuable for phosphatic deposits is mineral in character,[3] although, under a special act of congress, a homestead claimant who had initiated a right in ignorance of the existence of such deposits within the tract might perfect his entry, notwithstanding their discovery prior to the final entry,[4] thus changing the rule governing ordinary mineral lands within inchoate homestead claims, announced in a previous section.[5]

The same secretary also held that under the acts

[1] Dana's "System of Mineralogy," 6th ed., p. 769.
[2] "Preliminary Sketch of the Phosphates of Florida," by George H. Eldridge—Trans. Am. Inst. M. E., vol. xxi, p. 196.
[3] Gary v. Todd, 18 L. D. 58.
[4] Id., on review, 19 L. D. 475.
[5] Ante, § 208.

granting land to the Florida Railway and Navigation Company, passed respectively in 1856 and 1874, lands containing this class of deposits might be selected in satisfaction of the grants.[1] The reasons assigned were:—

(1) That the act of 1856 did not in terms reserve mineral lands;

(2) That in the act of 1874, where mineral lands are reserved, the word "mineral" is used in a limited sense, and cannot be construed to include phosphates.

This decision was subsequently overruled.[2]

We have fully explained the law as we understand it in the article on railroad grants.[3]

As a matter of *present* classification, Secretary Smith concedes that lands of this class are subject to entry under the mining laws. The department treats guano islands found within the public domain as mineral land.[4]

§ 426. **Tailings.**—To suffer tailings to flow where they may, without obstructions to confine them, is equivalent to their abandonment.[5] If they lodge on the lands of another they are considered as an accretion, and belong to him.[6] If they accumulate on vacant and unappropriated public land, it has been the custom in the mining regions of the west to recognize the right of the first comer to appropriate them by proceedings analogous to the location of placer claims.[7] As was said by the supreme court of Nevada,—

---

[1] Tucker *v.* Florida Ry. and Nav. Co., 19 L. D. 414.

[2] Pacific Coast Marble Co. *v.* Northern Pac. R. R. Co., 25 L. D. 233; Florida Cent. and Penin. R. R. Co., 26 L. D. 600.

[3] *Ante,* §§ 158, 159.

[4] Richter *v.* State of Utah, 27 L. D. 95.

[5] Jones *v.* Jackson, 9 Cal. 238, 245.

[6] *Id.*

[7] Dougherty *v.* Creary, 30 Cal. 291, 89 Am. Dec. 116.

Lindley on M.—49

" Although not a mining claim within the strict
" meaning of the expression as generally used in this
" country, a 'tailings claim' is so closely analogous
" to it that the propriety of subjecting the acquisition
" and maintenance of the possession of it to the rules
" governing the acquisition of the right to a strictly
" mining claim at once suggests itself." [1]

The land department has recognized this possessory
right and permitted entries to be made of lands containing beds of tailings, under the laws applicable to
placers.   There are no adjudicated cases in the reports
of department decisions upon this subject which have
come under our observation, but we have knowledge
of several instances where patents for this class of
claims have been issued under the mining laws.

§ 427.   Subterranean gravel deposits in ancient river-
beds.—Subterranean channels of ancient streams into
which beds of auriferous gravels have been deposited
are sometimes called deep, or ancient, placers.   The
most noted of these are found in California.[2]

These gravel-beds lie upon a "bed-rock" which, at
some period of geological history, formed the bed of an
ancient river.   They are usually immediately overlain
by a formation of clay gouge, and on this clay covering
is a capping of lava, sometimes hundreds of feet in
thickness.   These subterranean deposits are reached by
means of tunnels to the bed-rock, and thence following
the meanderings of the channel.   These deposits certainly occupy a fixed position in the mass of the mountain, although they do not fall within the popular
definition of lodes, or veins.   The land department, at

[1] Rogers v. Cooney, 7 Nev. 213.

[2] For interesting and valuable discussion on the subjects of these deep
gravels, see monographs of Mr. Ross E. Browne, "The Ancient River
"Beds of the Forest Hill Divide," California State Mineralogist's report (1890), p. 435, and of Mr. John Hays Hammond, the "Auriferous
"Gravels of California," in the report of 1889, p. 105.

an early period, classified them as "placers," and
patents have uniformly been issued upon locations of
this class of deposits made under the placer laws.[1]

The supreme court of California has upheld this
classification.[2]

The inconvenience of this rule will be shown when we
come to consider the requirements as to a discovery
within the limits of each placer location. But this is
an argument which should be addressed to congress
in order that this class of deposits may receive separate
consideration and be relieved from conditions which are
not unreasonable when applied to superficial placers,
but which become exceedingly onerous and burdensome
when applied to these subterranean deposits.

§ 428. **Beds of streams.**—As to whether gravel deposits lying on the beds of watercourses may be appropriated under the placer laws will depend on circumstances.
If the stream is navigable, certainly no right to appropriate its bed for mining purposes under the federal
mining laws can be sanctioned.

The beds of such rivers and their banks as far as high-
water mark belong to the state, and not to the federal
government. They were not granted by the constitution
to the United States, but were reserved to the states
respectively, and the new states have the same rights of
sovereignty and jurisdiction with regard to this class of
lands as the original states.[3]

The right of the United States to the public lands, and
the power of congress to make all needful rules and
regulations for the sale and disposition thereof, conferred no power to grant the beds of navigable streams.[4]

---

[1] Commissioner's Letter, Copp's Min. Dec. 78.
[2] Gregory v. Pershbaker, 73 Cal. 109, 115, 14 Pac. 401.
[3] Pollard v. Hagan, 3 How. 212; Pollard's Heirs v. Kibbe, 9 How. 471.
[4] Pollard v. Hagan, 3 How. 212.

A grant from the government for land bordering on a navigable stream (*i. e.* one that is navigable in fact) can extend no farther than the edge of the stream.[1]

The state may, if it choose, resign to a riparian proprietor rights which properly belong to it in its sovereign capacity,[2] but this does not sanction a conveyance from the general government which would operate to divest the rights of the state.

A mining claim located upon public lands traversed by a watercourse which is navigable in fact could only extend to the edge of the stream at its high-water stage. The beds of such streams are not public lands.[3]

While congress exercises legislative control over the territories and other political subdivisions not organized as states, it holds lands under the navigable streams in the public domain in trust for the future state, and it has always been the policy of the general government not to impair the right of the ultimate beneficiary by any permanent encumbrance or transfer of this class of lands. The rule on this subject is the same as that applied to lands below ordinary high tide in the case of tidal waters, a subject discussed in the next section.

The state may grant temporary privileges, or perhaps permanent rights, of dredging or carrying on other mining operations in the beds of navigable waters; *provided*, that such operations do not interfere with the public rights of navigation or the private rights of riparian owners. But this is a subject which is not necessary to be here discussed.[4]

---

[1] Packer *v.* Bird, 137 U. S. 661, 669, 11 Sup. Ct. Rep. 212.

[2] *Id.*

[3] Argillite Ornamental Stone Co., 29 L. D. 585; *In re* Fitten, 29 L. D. 451, 453.

[4] Consult Coosaw M. Co. *v.* South Carolina, 144 U. S. 550, 12 Sup. Ct. Rep. 689; State *v.* Black River Phosphate Co., 32 Fla. 82, 13 S. 640. See article by Dr. Rossiter W. Raymond in Engineering and Mining Journal, vol. 65, p. 276.

As to the beds of non-navigable streams, there is no reason why the gravel deposits lying on them may not be appropriated,[1] as the banks may (for it is there that placers are usually found), if the title to the bed resides in the general government and is clear of prior appropriations. No subsequent appropriation of the bed of a non-navigable stream can interfere with the rights of a prior riparian proprietor. In other words, the question to be considered is whether the bed sought to be appropriated is a part of the public domain or not.

As to what rights accrue to a placer locator to the water of a non-navigable stream found within the limits of the location, no definite rule can be stated. It will depend upon the locality in which the claim is situated. If in a state where the *ultra* doctrine of the common law prevails, his rights to the water would be limited to those of a riparian proprietor. If in a state where the riparian doctrines are abrogated or declared never to have been adopted, his right to use the water would depend upon its proper appropriation for that purpose, and the mere location of the placer claim would not of itself confer any right to the water.

Judge Hallett has said, with regard to a case arising in Colorado, that "a placer location *ex vi termini* " imports an appropriation of all waters covered by it " in so far as such waters are necessary for working " the mine. This is true, especially when the location " covers both banks of the stream, because there is a " reasonable presumption that the locator intends to " work the channel and the banks wherever he may " find pay dirt. A placer claim cannot be worked with- " out water. . . . The title to the water is the same as " the title to the land."[2] And the land department has said that the rights of the placer locator to the water

---

[1] Rablin's Placer, 2 L. D. 764.

[2] Schwab *v.* Bean (Colo.), U. S. Cir. Ct. 1898, 1 Leg. Adv. 489.

in such case is simply "usufructuary."[1] This question, however, is hardly germane to the subject presently under consideration. Its solution can only be arrived at from a careful investigation of the water laws of the various states. For this purpose treatises on the law of water should be consulted.

§ 429. Lands under tide-waters.—There is no principle involved in the consideration of the public land system better settled or more clearly enunciated than that lands under tidal waters, and below the line of ordinary high tide, are not "public lands." When a state bordering upon these waters is admitted into the union it becomes, by virtue of its sovereignty, the owner of all lands extending seaward so far as its municipal dominion extends,—*i. e.* in landlocked bays from headland to headland and from the line of ordinary high tide on the shore of the open ocean seaward to the distance of three miles, or a marine league. This same rule applies to islands off the coast which are within the municipal control of the state. This ownership, however, is subject to the public right of navigation.

As to lands of this character forming a part of the territory acquired by the federal government under treaties of cession and purchase which for the time being are not included within the boundaries of any state, but are either within territories (such as Hawaii and Porto Rico), districts (as Alaska), or insular dependencies with a temporary form of government specially devised to meet the exigencies of the occasion (such as the Philippine islands), the United States holds them in trust for the benefit of such states as may be ultimately carved out of them. With reference to

---

[1] Rablin's Placer, 2 L. D. 764.

this class of lands occupying this *status,* the supreme court of the United States has expressed itself as follows:—

" The United States, while they hold the country as a
" territory, having all the powers both of national and
" of municipal government, may grant for appropriate
" purposes titles or rights in the soil below high-water
" mark of tide-waters. But they have never done so by
" general laws; and, unless in some case of international
" duty or public exigency, have acted upon the policy,
" as most in accordance with the interest of the people
" and with the object for which the territories were
" acquired, of leaving the administration and disposi-
" tion of the sovereign rights in navigable waters and
" in the soil under them, to the control of the states,
" respectively, when organized and admitted into the
" union." [1]

It follows from this doctrine that tide-lands bordering a territory cannot be acquired in private ownership under any of the general laws providing for the disposal of public lands, in which category are the federal mining laws. A mining claim cannot be so located as to extend below the line of ordinary high tide.[2]

The discovery in 1898 of the auriferous sands on the southern shore of the Seward peninsula in Alaska, washed by the Bering Sea, attracted an army of fortune-hunters, and the beach in the immediate vicinity of Cape Nome was the scene of great mining activity. The federal mining laws had been extended to Alaska, but as the gold-bearing sands were found to exist below the line of ordinary high tide, there was practically no law which permitted their appropriation or exploitation below that line. As in the case of the discovery of gold in California at a time when there was no federal law whatever on the subject of acquiring public mineral

---

[1] Shively *v.* Bowlby, 152 U. S. 1, 58; 14 Sup. Ct. Rep. 548.
[2] *In re* Logan, 29 L. D. 395.

lands, the miners adopted rules and regulations defining the manner of acquiring, possessing, and enjoying mining privileges on beach claims. As it was conceived that a license could be obtained from the secretary of war, whose permit was necessary as a prerequisite to the maintenance of structures in the navigable waters of the United States, such license was asked and in many instances obtained. These licenses, of course, conferred no rights save immunity from prosecution for carrying on mining operations in navigable waters. The roadstead was an open one, there were no harbor lines, and the permit was granted whenever applied for. These conditions were recognized by congress, and provisions were inserted in the Alaska code[1] governing the exploration and mining of these beach deposits between low and mean high tide on the shores, bays, and inlets of Bering Sea, and authorizing mining below the line of low tide under such regulations as might be prescribed by the secretary of war. This statute is, of course, local in its application. The code specifically sanctioned the adoption of local rules governing the size of the claims, and other details not necessary to be here noted. The act does not contemplate that these beach claims below the line of ordinary high tide shall be patented, the privilege being limited to exploration and mining for gold.

Off the coast of California, at Summerland, in Santa Barbara county, petroleum wells are bored in the ocean below the line of ordinary high tide, and large quantities of crude oil are produced. The secretary of war has granted the same class of permits as noted in the case of Cape Nome, which are, as heretofore observed, ineffectual as conferring any rights. The title to the soil is in the state of California. There is no permission granted by the state, but it has not interfered, and the

[1] § 26. See Appendix.

occupants have not been molested by the only authority which possesses any power in the premises—the state of California. Some conflicts have arisen with the littoral owners, but that is not a matter which presently concerns us.

ARTICLE II. THE LOCATION AND ITS REQUIREMENTS.

§ 432. Acts necessary to constitute a valid placer location under the Revised Statutes, in the absence of supplemental state legislation and local district rules.

§ 433. Requisites of a valid placer location where supplemental state legislation exists.

§ 432. Acts necessary to constitute a valid placer location under the Revised Statutes, in the absence of supplemental state legislation and local district rules.— Generally speaking, the acts required to be performed in order to complete a valid location under the federal laws applicable to placers are the same as are required in cases of lode locations.[1] Section twenty-three hundred and twenty-nine of the Revised Statutes provides:—

" Claims usually called placers, including all forms " of deposit, excepting veins of quartz, or other rock in " place, shall be subject to entry and patent under like " circumstances and conditions as are provided for " vein or lode claims."

This has been construed to mean:—

(1) That there must be a discovery upon which to base the location;[2]

---

[1] McCann v. McMillan, 129 Cal. 350, 62 Pac. 31.

[2] McDonald v. Montana Wood Co., 14 Mont. 88, 43 Am. St. Rep. 616, 35 Pac. 668; Lincoln Placer, 7 L. D. 81; Ferrell v. Hoge, 18 L. D. 81; 19 L. D. 568; Louise M. Co., 22 L. D. 409; Rhodes v. Treaz, 21 L. D. 503; S. P. R. R. v. Griffin, 20 L. D. 663; Reins v. Murray, 22 L. D. 409; Union Oil Co., 23 L. D. 222.

(2) The location must be marked upon the ground so that its boundaries can be readily traced.[1]

As was said in a previous section, referring to lode claims, no notice need be posted, no particular kind of marking is required, nor is any record made necessary. No preliminary development work is prescribed. In the absence of supplemental state or local regulation the discovery and marking the boundaries perfect the location.[2]

§ 433. **Requisites of a valid placer location where supplemental state legislation exists.**—As in the case of lodes,[3] most of the states within the purview of this treatise have enacted laws prescribing that certain acts be performed in order to perfect a placer location, in addition to the requirements of the federal law. These supplemental provisions vary in the different states. Taking the Colorado statutes as a type (although the laws of some of the states are more elaborate), the following acts are required to complete a location of this class:—

(1) Discovery;

(2) Posting a notice of location;

(3) Marking the boundaries in a specified manner;

(4) Recording a certificate of location.

As these features are common to both lode and placer claims, what we have heretofore said with reference to the necessity of complying with these conditions,[4] the

---

[1] White v. Lee, 78 Cal. 593, 12 Am. St. Rep. 115, 21 Pac. 363; Sweet v. Webber, 7 Colo. 443, 4 Pac. 752; Anthony v. Jillson, 83 Cal. 296, 23 Pac. 419; McDonald v. Montana Wood Co., 14 Mont. 88, 43 Am. St. Rep. 616, 35 Pac. 668.

[2] *Ante*, § 328.

[3] *Ante*, § 329.

[4] *Ante*, § 329.

order in which the acts may be performed,[1] and the
effect of locations made by agents,[2] need not be here
repeated.

ARTICLE III. THE DISCOVERY.

§ 437. Rules governing discovery the same as in lode locations.	§ 438. Unit of placer locations— Discovery in each twenty-acre tract.

§ 437. **Rules governing discovery the same as in lode
locations.**—The subject of discovery has been fully
considered when dealing with lode locations in a previous article.[3] The principles there announced apply
with equal force to placers, so far as the character of
the deposits will admit. Discovery is just as essential
in case of placers as it is in lode locations.[4] The supreme court of California at one time expressed the
view that neither the federal laws nor the local rules
and customs of miners required that a discovery should
be made as a prerequisite to a placer location,[5] but this
is obviously a mere *dictum;* it is also opposed to the
current of judicial authority. The land department
has uniformly held that discovery is essential in the
case of placers, going so far at one time as to hold that
such discovery was essential in each twenty-acre tract
within a location of one hundred and sixty acres located
by an association of persons.

In the case of petroleum deposits the courts in California have in recent years been confronted with some
serious problems upon the subject of what constitutes
a sufficient discovery which will sanction a location of

[1] *Ante,* § 330.

[2] *Ante,* § 331.

[3] *Ante,* §§ 335-339.

[4] Nevada Sierra Oil Co. *v.* Miller, 97 Fed. 681, 688; Nevada Sierra Oil
Co. *v.* Home Oil Co., 98 Fed. 673; Olive L. and D. Co. *v.* Olmstead, 103
Fed. 568, 573; Cosmos Exploration Co. *v.* Gray Eagle Co., 112 Fed. 4, 14.

[5] Gregory *v.* Pershbaker, 73 Cal. 109, 117, 14 Pac. 401.

a claim to oil lands under the laws applicable to placers. It is well known that the natural habitat of this class of mineral hydrocarbons is in stratified rocks some distance below the surface, and except for the occasional appearance at the surface in the form of oil seepages, springs, or other indications of the subterranean existence of petroleum, there is nothing to guide the miner in making his location. It requires more or less extensive development in the nature of well-boring and prospecting to determine the nature, extent, and permanency of the deposit.

With reference to these surface indications, Judge Ross, United States circuit judge for the southern district of California, expressed the view that—

" Mere indications, however strong, are not, in my " opinion, sufficient to answer the requirements of the " statute, which requires, as one of the essential condi- " tions to the making of a valid location of unappropri- " ated public land of the United States under the " mining laws, of mineral within the limits of the claim. " . . . Indications of the existence of a thing is not " the thing itself." [1]

This was said, however, not of indications existing within the boundaries of the claim in controversy, but in adjoining lands.

" So, in respect to placer claims," Judge Ross says, " if a competent locator actually finds upon " unappropriated public land petroleum or other min- " eral in or upon the ground, and so situated as to con- " stitute a part of it, it is a sufficient discovery within " the meaning of the statute, to justify a location under " the law, without waiting to ascertain by exploration " whether the ground contains the mineral in sufficient " quantities to pay." [2]

[1] Nevada Sierra Oil Co. v. Home Oil Co., 98 Fed. 673, 676. See, also, Tulare Oil and M. Co. v. S. P. R. R., 29 L. D. 269.

[2] Nevada Sierra Oil Co. v. Home Oil Co., 98 Fed. 673, 676.

This is in consonance with the rule announced by the courts in the case of lodes, that neither the size nor richness of the vein is material, so long as there is a genuine discovery.[1] A discovery of such indications as would in a given district lead a miner to the more valuable deposit, according to the experience in that district would sanction a mining location.[2]

Of course, exploitation on adjacent lands might raise a strong presumption that a given tract contained petroleum. An oil-producing well within each of four sections of land surrounding a fifth would produce a conviction that the oil deposit was underneath the fifth section. This fact might justify the land department in classifying the section in the category of mineral lands, or the government surveyor in returning it as such,[3] but it would not dispense with the necessity of making a discovery.[4]

It is impossible to lay down any arbitrary rule to govern all cases as to what may be a sufficient discovery upon which to predicate a location. It is a question of fact, to be determined from a consideration of all the circumstances and surroundings.[5]

§ 438. **Unit of placer locations—Discovery in each twenty acre tract.**—We have heretofore observed that the unit of lode locations is a surface area aggregating a fraction over twenty acres, and that it is immaterial how many or how few locators participate in that class of locations.[6]

We shall see in a succeeding article that the rule in regard to placers is somewhat different. In placers, the

---

[1] *Ante,* § 336.
[2] Shoshone M. Co. *v.* Rutter, 87 Fed. 801.
[3] State of Washington *v.* McBride, 25 L. D. 169, 181.
[4] Reins *v.* Murray, 22 L. D. 409.
[5] *Ante,* § 336.
[6] *Ante,* § 361.

unit of the location is twenty acres to each individual, with a maximum of one hundred and sixty acres to an association of persons. In other words, unless limited by local rules, and assuming that local regulations may prescribe such a limitation,[1] a single individual may locate a twenty-acre tract, but no more. Where more than one person (not exceeding eight) participate, an area equivalent to twenty acres to each is permitted; but they locate the whole area jointly, becoming tenants in common thereof, and are not, according to the practice, required to each locate a particular specified twenty-acre tract. Such being the case, the question has arisen as to whether one discovery within the limits of the entire area appropriated by an association of persons would be sufficient upon which to base a location as to such area, or whether a discovery is necessary upon each twenty-acre tract or unit of location. In case of lode locations, where an appropriation in excess of the statutory limit of a single location is desired, a separate discovery and separate location are necessary.[2]

In applying the law to this class of cases, the land department now follows the rule that only one discovery is required where a location is made by an association of persons;[3] this, however, has not always been the ruling of the department in such cases,[4] but it is now the settled law, so far as the department is concerned, and there is little reason to apprehend any change.

The supreme court of Montana was committed to this

[1] Copp's Min. Dec. 164.

[2] *Ante,* § 361.

[3] Union Oil Co., on review, 25 L. D. 351, 358; Ferrell *v.* Hoge, 27 L. D. 129; Reins *v.* Raunheim, 28 L. D. 526; Ferrell *v.* Hoge, 29 L. D. 12. See Lincoln Placer, 7 L. D. 81.

[4] Ferrell *v.* Hoge, 18 L. D. 81; S. P. R. R. Co. *v.* Griffin, 20 L. D. 485; Rhodes *v.* Treaz, 21 L. D. 502; Louise M. Co., 22 L. D. 663; Union Oil Co., 23 L. D. 222. See Ferrell *v.* Hoge, on review, 19 L. D. 568.

view even before the land department reversed its older rulings.[1]

However erroneous the earlier view taken by the land department may have been,—*i. e.* that a discovery must be made on each twenty acres,—the requirement was effective in the way of satisfying the department of the mineral character of the entire tract. There is no legal inference because a given twenty-acre tract within an area of one hundred and sixty acres is mineral in character that the adjoining tracts or others are of the same character.[2]

In regard to this point, the department holds that one discovery is a sufficient *prima facie* showing of the character of the entire tract, but it is not conclusive, and the character of the remainder of the tract may be investigated.[3] The wisdom of this rule is peculiarly manifest when we consider the difficulties which would otherwise be found in the locating of deep placers and petroleum lands.[4]

While the land department must be satisfied of the mineral character of the entire tract, it must be noted in this connection that the character of the deposit if not in place may be different in different parts of the claimed area, provided that the several deposits fall within the definition of those valuable and " not in " place." [5]

It has been claimed where there is a valid discovery within a one-hundred-and-sixty-acre tract taken by an

[1] McDonald *v.* Montana Wood Co., 14 Mont. 88, 43 Am. St. Rep. 616, 35 Pac. 668.

[2] Dughi *v.* Harkins, 2 L. D. 721, quoted in Davis *v.* Weibbold, 139 U. S. 507, 11 Sup. Ct. Rep. 628, and in United States *v.* Cent. Pac. R. R. Co., 93 Fed. 871.

[3] Ferrell *v.* Hoge, 29 L. D. 12, S. C. 27 L. D. 129. And see State of Washington *v.* McBride, 25 L. D. 167, 182.

[4] See Louise M. Co., 22 L. D. 663, and Tulare Oil and M. Co. *v.* S. P. R. R. Co., 29 L. D. 269.

[5] Ferrell *v.* Hoge, 29 L. D. 12.

association of persons, that this discovery would be sufficient to hold the entire area irrespective of the character of the land elsewhere therein, upon the theory applied in cases of lode claims, that surface ground is given for the convenient working of the claim. The department held this not to be the correct rule. Ground selected as placer must be mineral land, non-mineral surface not being permitted as an incident to a placer claim.[1]

ARTICLE IV. STATE LEGISLATION AS TO POSTING NOTICES AND PRELIMINARY DEVELOPMENT WORK.

§ 442. State statutes requiring posting of notices on placers.

§ 443. Preliminary development work required by state laws upon placer locations.

§ 442. State statutes requiring posting of notices on placers.—The general observations upon the subject of posting notices following lode discoveries, found in a preceding section,[2] apply with equal force to all classes of locations upon the public mineral lands. With the exception of the common custom generally observed, as there indicated, the posting of a notice is the subject of state or local regulation, in the absence of which none is required.

Some of the states have enacted laws upon the subject with regard to placers, a brief epitome of which will not be out of place:—

Arizona.—Same as lode claims, except that the notice must contain the number of acres claimed instead of the requirements of subdivisions four and five of the section concerning contents of notice on lode claims.[3]

---

[1] Ferrell *v.* Hoge, 29 L. D. 12.
[2] *Ante,* § 350.
[3] Rev. Stats. (1901), §§ 3232, 3242. *Ante,* § 353.

Colorado.—Before recording (thirty days from discovery) the discoverer must post upon the claim a notice containing: (1) The name of the claim; (2) The name of the locator; (3) Date of discovery; and (4) Number of feet or acres claimed.[1]

Idaho.—Requirements are practically the same as in lode claims.[2]

Montana.—The same as in lode claims, except that the number of feet or acres claimed, instead of the length of the lode, must be designated in the notice.[3]

Nevada.—Same as Colorado.[4]

New Mexico, South Dakota, Oregon, and North Dakota.—If any notice is required to be posted, it is the same as in the case of lode claims.[5] Placers are not specially named in their laws upon the subject of posting notices, and it is doubtful if they were intended to apply to placer locations.

Utah.—Same as lode claims, except that the notice should state the number of acres or superficial feet claimed, instead of the length and course of the vein, and the width on either side thereof.[6]

Washington.—The notice must contain (*a*) the name of the claim; (*b*) name of location; (*c*) date of discovery and posting of notice, which shall be considered as the date of the location; (*d*) a description of the claim by reference to legal subdivisions of sections, if the location is made in conformity with the public surveys; otherwise, a description with reference to some natural

---

[1] Mills' Annot. Stats., § 3136.

[2] Laws of 1895, p. 25, §§ 2, 12, as amended—Laws of 1897, p. 12; Civ. Code (1901), § 2563. *Ante,* § 354.

[3] Rev. Code of 1895, § 3610. *Ante,* § 352.

[4] Comp. Laws (1900), § 220.

[5] *Ante,* § 353.

[6] Laws of 1899, p. 69, § 2. *Ante,* § 380.

object or permanent monument as will identify the claim.[1]

Wyoming.—Provisions are the same as in Colorado.[2]

§ 443. **Preliminary development work required by state laws upon placer locations.**—When speaking of the requirement of preliminary development work with respect to lode locations, we expressed the view that the object was twofold:—

(1) To determine the lode character of the deposit;

(2) To compel the discoverer to manifest his intention to claim the ground in good faith under the mining laws.[3]

It is quite obvious that both of these reasons cannot be offered in support of similar requirements in cases of placers, although the latter applies with equal force to them. Only four of the states, however, have attempted any legislation on this subject with respect to placers.

In Idaho [4] it is provided that within fifteen days after making the location, the locator must make an excavation on the claim of not less than one hundred cubic feet, for the purpose of prospecting the same.

In Montana [5] the equivalent of the work done upon lode claims must be done upon placers.

Nevada [6] requires that within ninety days after posting the notice of location the locator shall perform not less than twenty dollars' worth of labor upon the claim for the development thereof.

[1] Laws of 1899, p. 71, as amended—Laws of 1901, p. 292.

[2] Laws of 1888, pp. 89-90, § 22; Rev. Stats. (1899), § 2553, as amended—Laws of 1901, p. 104.

[3] *Ante,* § 344.

[4] Laws of 1895, p. 25, § xii, as amended—Laws of 1897, p. 12; Civil Code (1901), § 2563.

[5] Rev. Code, 1895, § 3611. See Purdum *v.* Laddin, 59 Pac. 153.

[6] Comp. Laws (1900), § 221.

In Washington [1] it is provided that within sixty days from the date of discovery, the discoverer shall perform labor upon the location or claim in developing the same to an amount equivalent in the aggregate to at least ten dollars' worth of such labor for each twenty acres or fractional part thereof contained in such location or claim. To which is added this language: *"Provided,* " however, that nothing in this subdivision shall be held " to apply to lands located under the laws of the United " States as placer claims for the purpose of the develop- " ment of petroleum and natural gas and other natural " oil products."

The remaining states and territories have either passed no laws upon the subject or have repealed such as heretofore existed.

It must be remembered that these requirements are not necessarily connected with the annual labor prescribed by the acts of congress. While this preliminary development work might possibly under certain circumstances be considered in estimating the value of the annual labor for the first year next succeeding the date of location, its requirement is one of the acts of location, and we think such legislation is clearly within the power of the states.[2]

ARTICLE V.   THE SURFACE COVERED BY THE LOCATION — ITS FORM AND EXTENT.

§ 447. Form and extent of placer locations prior to Revised Statutes.

§ 448. Form and extent under Revised Statutes.

§ 448a. Limitation as to size of claims under district rules.

§ 448b. Surface conflicts with prior locations.

§ 449. Placer locations by corporations.

§ 450. Locations by several persons in the interest of one — Number of locations by an individual.

[1] Laws of 1899, p. 71, § 10, as amended—Laws of 1901, p. 292.
[2] *Ante,* § 344.

§ 447. **Form and extent of placer locations prior to Revised Statutes.**—Previous to the act of July 9, 1870, commonly known as the "placer law," congress imposed no limitation to the area which might be included in the location of a placer claim. This, as well as every other thing relating to the acquisition and continued possession of mining claims, was determined by rules and regulations established by miners themselves.[1] The size and shape varied according to the nature of the deposit, for in those days this class of claims embraced hydraulic " diggings," gulch or ravine claims, creek claims, and claims on bars and flats.[2] Locations of these claims were made without regard to the lines of public surveys, as there were none.

The placer law of 1870 [3] provided for the patenting of placer claims under like circumstances and conditions as were provided by the lode law of 1866 for vein or lode claims. It was required, however, that where locations were made upon surveyed lands, the entry in its exterior limits was required to conform to the legal subdivisions of the public lands. For this purpose, it was provided that forty-acre tracts might be subdivided into areas of ten acres, but no location thereafter to be made was permitted to exceed one hundred and sixty acres for any one person or association of persons.

Locations made prior to this act might, if located in conformity with local rules, be patented, whatever their form or area,[4] and any number of contiguous claims, of any size, might be purchased, consolidated, and applied for as one entry.[5]

Under this act, any one person might, unless inhibited

---

[1] St. Louis Smelting Co. *v.* Kemp, 104 U. S. 636, 649.
[2] Yale on Mining Claims and Water Rights, pp. 76, 77.
[3] 16 Stats. at Large, p. 217. See Appendix.
[4] Copp's Min. Dec. 40.
[5] St. Louis Smelting Co. *v.* Kemp, 104 U. S. 636, 651.

by local rules, locate one hundred and sixty acres. An association of persons was limited to a like area.

The general mining act of May 10, 1872,[1] modified the original placer law by fixing the limit of twenty acres for each individual claimant. The limit which might be taken by an association of persons remained the same, as in this respect the act of 1870 was unrepealed.[2]

As to the form of the location, the later act provided that it should conform *as near as practicable* with the United States system of public land surveys and the rectangular subdivisions of such surveys; where it could not be conformed to legal subdivisions, it might be made the same as on unsurveyed lands. This was the state of the law when the federal statutes were revised.

§ 448. **Form and extent under Revised Statutes.**— The Revised Statutes, which embrace the laws of the United States general and permanent in their nature, in force on December 1, 1873, contain the following provisions as to form and extent of surface area:—

"§ 2329.   Claims usually called 'placers,' including " all forms of deposit, excepting veins of quartz, or " other rock in place, shall be subject to entry and " patent, under like circumstances and conditions, and " upon similar proceedings, as are provided for vein or " lode claims; but where the lands have been previously " surveyed by the United States, the entry in its exte- " rior limits shall conform to the legal subdivisions of " the public lands.

"§ 2330.   Legal subdivisions of forty acres may be " subdivided into ten-acre tracts; and two or more per- " sons, or associations of persons, having contiguous " claims of any size, although such claims may be less " than ten acres each, may make joint entry thereof; " but no location of a placer claim, made after the

---

[1] 17 Stats. at Large, p. 91, § 10.

[2] *Ante,* § 72; St. Louis Smelting Co. *v.* Kemp, Fed. Cas. No. 12,239a, 21 Fed. Cas. 205.

" ninth day of July, eighteen hundred and seventy,
" shall exceed one hundred and sixty acres for any
" one person, or association of persons, which location
" shall conform to the United States surveys.

"§ 2331. Where placer claims are upon surveyed
" lands, and conform to legal subdivisions, no further
" survey or plat shall be required, and all placer mining
" claims located after the tenth day of May, eighteen
" hundred and seventy-two, shall conform as near as
" practicable with the United States system of public-
" land surveys, and the rectangular subdivisions of
" such surveys, and no such location shall include more
" than twenty acres for each individual claimant; but
" where placer claims cannot be conformed to legal
" subdivisions, survey and plat shall be made as on
" unsurveyed lands; and where by the segregation of
" mineral lands in any legal subdivision a quantity of
" agricultural land less than forty acres remains, such
" fractional portions of agricultural land may be
" entered by any party qualified by law, for homestead
" or pre-emption purposes."

It will thus be observed :—

(1) That the unit or individual location is twenty
acres;

(2) That not more than one hundred and sixty acres
may be embraced within one location by an association
of persons, of which there must be at least eight; [1]

(3) That the location, if upon surveyed lands, must
conform as near as practicable to the lines of the public
surveys.

The land department was called upon to consider an
entry of a location described as the "W. ½ of lot 1." It
was held :—

"In this case it is clear that as to the designated por-
" tions of lot 1 claimed under said entry, the same do
" not conform to the rectangular or legal subdivisions
" of the public land survey of the section or township in
" which said lot is situated. While said lot 1 is in itself

---

[1] Kirk v. Meldrum, 28 Colo. 453, 65 Pac. 633.

" a legal subdivision of said survey the department is
" not aware of any rule or provision of law whereby
" the subdivision of said lot into smaller legal subdi-
" visions under the system of public land surveys may
" be recognized. It is therefore not only necessary that
" an official survey of the land located and claimed
" should be made as required for the purpose of proper
" description and identification in the patent, but such
" survey appears to be plainly demanded by the statute
" itself." [1]

As to whether it is practicable to make a location or
survey conform to legal subdivisions is a matter which
rests entirely with the land department.

Commissioner McFarland held that the only construction of the language of the act, "as near as practicable,"
which is consistent with the context of the act and the
general intention of congress is, that placer locations
upon surveyed lands must conform to the public surveys in all cases, except where this is rendered impossible by the previous appropriation or reservation of a
portion of the legal subdivision of ten acres upon which
the claim is situated. The location in this case was
made in 1880, and covered the bed of Bear river, in
California, for twelve thousand feet, following the
meanderings of the river, and embraced a small quantity of surface ground along its banks. The entry was
held for cancellation.[2]

This ruling of the commissioner, however, was reversed by Secretary Teller,[3] who held that the placer
law of 1870, which expressly required placer locations
to conform to the lines of the public surveys, was unreasonable, a hardship, and in contravention of the
established custom of the mining regions; therefore, it
was modified by the act of May 10, 1872, so as to pro-

---

[1] Holmes Placer, 29 L. D. 368. See, also, Miller Placer, 30 L. D. 225;
In re Knight, 30 L. D. 227; Mary Darling Placer, 31 L. D. 64.

[2] 10 Copp's L. O. 3. See, also, Copp's Min. Lands, 115.

[3] Rablin's Placer, 2 L. D. 764; Esperance M. Co., 10 Copp's L. O. 338.

vide for exceptional cases where reason and common sense required a different regulation.

The case of the Bear river claim was of this exceptional character. The placer deposit was in a cañon on the banks of a very crooked stream, and where the adjoining lands were totally unfit for mining or agricultural purposes. The placer applicant was permitted to proceed to patent.

There can be no question but that this ruling is in harmony with the custom of miners in California. This particular river was, from 1852 to 1867, the scene of great mining activity, and for miles up and down the stream, during the season when the stage of the water would permit, miners claimed, occupied, and worked its bed, bars, and banks, under regulations defining the extent of their claims by a certain number of feet along the stream, and a width extending to the sides of the gulch.

The ruling of Secretary Teller was followed in a later case by Acting Secretary Muldrow.[1]

While it is true that congress is not bound to shape its legislation so as to conform to the previously existing local customs, yet the history of federal mining legislation shows that great consideration has been paid to such customs. Evidently, there was some reason for the modification of the original placer act in this respect, and there can be no doubt that Secretary Teller states the "old law, the mischief, and the remedy" correctly.

These gulch or river claims, as well as deep placers found in ancient river-beds where the deposits follow the meanderings of the channel, certainly present instances where it would be unreasonable in all cases to insist that a mining claimant should take and pay for, at an increased rate, any considerable amount of land that is useless for mining purposes, for the sake of

---

[1] *In re* Pearsall and Freeman, 6 L. D. 227. But see Miller Placer, 30 L. D. 225.

obtaining title to the small quantity which is useful.[1]
The inconvenience to the government in administering
its land system is no greater in this respect than that
caused by the segregation of lode claims.[2]

A patent for a placer claim should describe with
mathematical accuracy the land intended to be conveyed thereby, and where such a degree of accuracy
cannot be obtained under an application that embraces
land theretofore surveyed and returned in irregular
subdivisions as "lots," an additional survey will be
required.[3]

Lands must be treated as unsurveyed until the plat is
finally approved.[4]

The land department has said that a placer location
must conform to the system of public land surveys and
the rectangular subdivisions of such surveys, whether
the locations are upon surveyed or unsurveyed lands.[5]
This is somewhat ambiguous. The secretary was criticising, in the case cited, an entry of a tract three miles
long by from thirty to fifty feet wide, connecting two
large tracts. The obvious intention was to point out
the necessity for making placer locations in the rectangular form and in subdivisions of surveys conform-
able to the system of public land surveying. Locations
cannot conform to lines of the public surveys until the
lands have been surveyed.

Sometimes part of a township has been surveyed so
that as a matter of calculation it is not difficult to determine the precise or proximate position of adjoining
unsurveyed lands and the section number which would

---

[1] Esperance Mining Claim, 10 Copp's L. O. 338.

[2] For illustration of manner of describing minor subdivisions located
as placers, see Mining Circular, July 26, 1901, pars. 23, 24. See Appendix.

[3] Holmes Placer, 26 L. D. 650.

[4] Copp's Min. Dec. 41. *Ante,* §§ 104, 105, 142; Bullock *v.* Rouse, 81
Cal. 590, 595, 22 Pac. 919; Medley *v.* Robertson, 55 Cal. 396.

[5] Miller Placer, 30 L. D. 225.

be given them when surveyed. The proximity of the unsurveyed to the surveyed lands has led to an error quite common of treating these unsurveyed lands as if the lines of the public surveys had been extended over them, and locating placer claims thereon by the government subdivision which the locator determines would be created when the system of surveys is extended over them. But such a description would not identify anything and would not satisfy the law.[1]

It may be practicable where discoveries are made in a region over which the public surveys have been partially extended to perfect by unofficial and private surveys the township and section lines, and in addition to a description by metes and bounds, which would certainly be necessary, there might be added a statement that the subdivision so located would, if the government surveys were extended, embrace such and such a tract, describing the probable result of the extension of such surveys. But this would be impracticable in most cases, and would entail an expense upon a placer locator not contemplated by the law and the results of which would in no sense be binding upon the government. In new regions over which the government has as yet established neither base nor meridian lines, as in Alaska, or in the unsurveyed public domain far removed from surveyed public lands, the method is not only impracticable but impossible. We incline to the view that, as a general rule, locations upon unsurveyed lands may be made in any form so long as the statutory area is not exceeded.

§ 448a. **Limitation as to size and form of claims under district rules.**—During the period when placer mining claims were governed entirely by the local district

---

[1] Terry v. Megerle, 24 Cal. 610, 85 Am. Dec. 84; Barnado's Heirs v. Ashley's Heirs, 18 How. 43; Grogan v. Knight, 27 Cal. 516; Robinson v. Forrest, 29 Cal. 318; Middleton v. Low, 30 Cal. 596; State v. Central Pac. R. R., 21 Nev. 94, 25 Pac. 442; Bullock v. Rouse, 81 Cal. 590, 22 Pac. 919.

regulations, the size and shape of the claims varied in different localities, based somewhat on the manner of occurrence of the deposits. Since the passage of the congressional laws on the subject there has been no attempt by state or territorial legislation to limit the size of claims to less than the unit of location sanctioned by the United States mining laws,—*i. e.* twenty acres.

As to the power of the local mining districts to provide for such limitation, there has been but little discussion by the courts.

The supreme court of Idaho expressed the view that such a rule or custom was reasonable and entirely in harmony with the spirit of the laws.[1]

The regulations of the land department for many years contained the following:—

"The foregoing provisions of the law are construed to " mean that after the ninth day of July, 1870, no loca- " tion of a placer claim can be made to exceed one hun- " dred and sixty acres whatever may be the number of " locators associated together, or whatever the local " regulations of the district may allow; and that from " and after May 10th, 1872, no location made by an indi- " vidual can exceed twenty acres, and no location made " by an association of individuals can exceed one hun- " dred and sixty acres, which location of one hundred " and sixty acres cannot be made by a less number than " eight *bona fide* locators; *and no local laws or mining* " *regulations can restrict a placer location to less than* " *twenty acres, although the locator is not compelled to* " *take so much.*"[2]

This was changed, however, by the adoption of later rules, which eliminated the last clause quoted above in italics.[3]

Whether this indicates a change of opinion on the part of the department as to the power of the local dis-

---

[1] Rosenthal *v.* Ives, 2 Idaho, 244, 12 Pac. 904.

[2] Circular, Dec. 10, 1891, par. 61.

[3] Circular, Dec. 15, 1897, par. 35, 25 L. D. 573; Circular, June 24, 1899, par. 35, 28 L. D. 599; Circular, July 26, 1901, par. 29. See Appendix.

tricts to place a limitation on the size of claims, or suggests that, in the judgment of the secretary, the subject was one not strictly within the scope of departmental regulations, or that the interpretation of the statute should not be prejudged by him until his jurisdiction in a contested case should be invoked, is difficult to determine.

The regulations of the Cape Nome mining district, Alaska, adopted October 15, 1898, provided that placer claims should be located thirteen hundred and twenty feet long by six hundred and sixty feet, making an area of twenty acres.

The validity of this regulation, so far as it prescribed the form of the location, was involved in a suit tried in the United States district court for the district of Alaska, second division.[1]

The court held that "No miner's rule, regulation, or " custom can limit him in the area or form of his claim, " nor in its width or length; that any such rule, regula- " tion, or custom is void for conflict with both the spirit " and the letter of the placer mining law." [2]

§ 448b. Surface conflicts with prior locations.—The reasons assigned by the courts for permitting junior lode claimants to place the lines of their locations upon or across lands which have been previously appropriated, a matter fully discussed in preceding sections,[1] do not apply with equal force to placers. Yet the doctrine as to lode claims having been extended by the department so as to authorize the junior lode locator to

---

[1] Price v. McIntosh, unreported, pending on writ of error to circuit court of appeals, ninth circuit.

[2] Quoted from transcript in the circuit court of appeals. The property involved in the case was a bench claim in Glacier creek. It was not therefore within the purview of law providing for the exploration and mining for gold on the shore of Bering Sea, below the line of ordinary high tide, discussed in section 429.

[3] §§ 363, 363a.

so locate his claim across prior locations and patented surfaces as to divide the lode claim into non-contiguous tracts, the application of a similar doctrine in a modified form to placer claims was not unexpected. The practice now sanctioned by the department may be briefly summarized: A placer locator may locate a given subdivision of the public surveys not exceeding the statutory limit of twenty acres, and an association may locate not exceeding one hundred and sixty acres, and the location may properly describe the land located by the proper legal subdivision, although the tract so located may embrace within its exterior limits prior segregated and patented lode claims, thus dividing the placer claim into non-contiguous tracts. The patent when issued will describe the land by proper legal subdivisions, excepting, however, the tracts which have been previously segregated. In other words, the government may grant to the placer claimant the particular subdivision less what it has heretofore conveyed to others.[1]

A contrary rule had previously been announced in the case of the Grassey Gulch placer.[2]

The decision in this case was, however, recalled by the secretary, and is no longer a precedent.

It had also at one time been held that the segregation of lode claims within a given subdivision of the public surveys would result in leaving certain fractional areas, which were subsequently designated by lot numbers, and that the placer claimant was compelled to have these irregular fractions surveyed for the purpose of ascertaining the quantity, and enter them as separate tracts,[3] but this ruling subsequently was abrogated, and the practice heretofore noted of applying for the original

---

[1] *In re* Mary Darling, 31 L. D. 64.   [3] *In re* Knight, 30 L. D. 227.
[2] 30 L. D. 191.

government subdivision less the area covered by prior segregated areas was sanctioned.

So far as the courts are concerned, the question has not been definitely determined, but the application of the principles applied by them to lode claims is not accompanied with any serious difficulty.[1]

§ 449. Placer locations by corporations.—As heretofore noted,[2] the supreme court of the United States has determined that a domestic corporation formed under the laws of a state may locate public mineral lands, but intimates that there may be some question raised as to the extent of a claim which a corporation may be permitted to locate as an original discoverer, suggesting that it might perhaps be treated as one person and entitled to locate only to the extent permitted a single individual.[3]

The placer law quoted in a preceding section[4] permits an "association of persons" to locate not to exceed one hundred and sixty acres. A corporation is an association of persons; at the same time we must admit that it is but an artificial individual. We have intimated in a previous section that if such a corporation had a constituency of eight stockholders it might be permitted to appropriate one hundred and sixty acres of land by location. We are not aware that the question has ever been judicially determined. Looking at the object of the statute in permitting consolidation of interests for purposes of development and operation, so clearly outlined by the supreme court of the United States in St. Louis Smelting Company v. Kemp,[5] we cannot say that

---

[1] See Crown Point M. Co. v. Buck, 97 Fed. 463, 465, and the discussion in sections 363, 363a.

[2] Ante, § 226.

[3] McKinley v. Wheeler, 130 U. S. 630, 636, 9 Sup. Ct. Rep. 638.

[4] Ante, § 448.

[5] 104 U. S. 636.

by the use of the term "association of persons" congress meant to exclude corporations from the designation. As eight individuals might locate and unite their interests in an incorporated company without violating the spirit of the law, it is not unreasonable to suggest, that a corporation composed of the eight may accomplish the same purpose by locating one hundred and sixty acres. Our suggestion is based upon the language of the statute. In the absence of any such provision granting privileges to an association of persons, undoubtedly a corporation would simply occupy the *status* of an individual. The question is not by any means easy of solution. It has not been judicially answered.

§ 450. **Locations by several persons in the interest of one—Number of locations by an individual.**—It is a matter of frequent occurrence that an individual locator, desiring to obtain more ground than he is permitted under the law to appropriate in his individual capacity by a single location, resorts to the use of "dummies," and perfects locations in their names, subsequently obtaining conveyances thereof. The courts have held that this is a fraud upon the government.[1]

"The policy of the government in disposing of the
" mineral lands as well as other portions of the public
" domain is to make a general distribution among as
" large a number as possible of those who wish to ac-
" quire such land for their own use rather than to favor
" a few individuals who might wish to acquire princely
" fortunes by securing large tracts of such lands, and
" it is contrary to this policy and to the provisions of
" sections twenty-three hundred and thirty and twenty-
" three hundred and thirty-one of the Revised Statutes
" for one person to cover more than twenty acres of
" placer ground by one location by the device of us-

---

[1] Mitchell v. Cline, 84 Cal. 409, 24 Pac. 164; Gird v. California Oil Co., 60 Fed. 535.

" ing the name of his employees and friends as lo-
" cators." [1]

But the same object can be accomplished without violating the law. There is nothing to prevent a miner from locating, by separate location, as many twenty-acre tracts as he pleases, either contiguous or non-contiguous.[2] The right to locate and develop mining ground is not exhausted by a single location, as in the case of pre-emption and homestead entries.[3] If he can discover mineral within the eight twenty-acre subdivisions of a quarter-section of land, and is willing to develop them to the extent required by law as a condition precedent to the acquisition of title by patent, or to annually perform labor to the extent required by law upon or for the benefit of each, he is clearly entitled to do so. The statute simply inhibits the acquisition by an individual of more than twenty acres by a single location. The question of good faith, however, may be the subject of inquiry by the government, who alone may complain. During the period when rights were governed exclusively by local rules, in certain districts the number of claims which one might locate and hold at one time within that particular district were defined. But there is no trace of this found in the legislation of congress. An attempt was made to incorporate into the Alaska

[1] Durant v. Corbin, 94 Fed. 382.

[2] Lands containing salt deposits are an exception to this rule. The statute authorizing the location of this class of claims prevents the location of more than one claim by the same person. *Post*, § 514a.

[3] We quote the following letter from Hon. Binger Hermann, commissioner of the general land office, under date March 16, 1901, appearing in the "Mining and Scientific Press," vol. 83, p. 157:—

"Relative to the legality of eight persons giving power of attorney "to locate placer claims without number, thereby enabling a few persons "to hold large areas of the public domain, it is well recognized that "under existing mining laws claims may be located by agent; that one "person may locate a claim not exceeding twenty acres, or eight persons "may associate themselves in the location of one claim not to exceed one "hundred and sixty acres. There is no limit to the number of claims "that any person or association of persons may locate."

codes a limitation upon the number of claims an individual or an association might locate in a given district in Alaska, but the attempt was unsuccessful. As heretofore observed with reference to the Philippines,[1] there is a limitation with regard to lode or vein claims.[2]

The amended rules and regulations adopted by the miners at Cape Nome, in June, 1901, provide that "Not " more than one placer claim can be located in said " district in the name of the same person on the same " stream, creek, or gulch."

Regulations of this character are of doubtful validity. It may also be suggested that, even if valid and binding on the government, no one but the United States could complain, following the analogy of locations made by aliens.

ARTICLE VI. THE MARKING OF THE LOCATION ON THE GROUND.

§ 454. Rule as to marking boundaries of placer claims in absence of state legislation.

§ 455. State legislation as to marking boundaries of placer claims.

§ 454. **Rule as to marking boundaries of placer claims in absence of state legislation.**—We have explained in a previous section the necessity for, and object of, marking lode locations upon the ground.[3] While the surface boundaries of a placer claim do not perform all the functions of end- and side-lines of lode locations, nevertheless the marking of a placer location on the ground is just as essential as in the case of lodes.

---

[1] *Ante,* § 361.

[2] The state of Oregon has enacted a law limiting the discoverer of a vein to two claims, all others to one claim, on the same vein, (Hill's Annot. Laws of Oregon (1892), § 3829,) which provision is amenable to the same criticism.

[3] *Ante,* § 371.

Lindley on M.—51

Where the location is upon unsurveyed land, or if upon
surveyed land is of such a character that it is not required to conform to the public surveys,[1] it has never
been doubted that this all-important act of location
should be performed, and that such locations should be
marked in the same manner as lode locations.

The supreme court of the United States, in considering the sufficiency of the marking of a placer location,
held that a notice written upon a stump in the middle of
a creek to the effect that the locator claimed fifteen hundred feet running with the creek and three hundred feet
on each side from the center of the creek, and that the
claim was an extension of another claim, constituted a
sufficient marking. The court said: "The creek was
" identified and between it and the stump there was a
" definite relation, which, combined with the measure-
" ments, enabled the boundaries of the claim to be read-
" ily traced."[2]

Where placer ground is located according to subdivisions of the public surveys, it has been contended that
such marking is not necessary, and that a description in
the posted or recorded notice by fractional subdivisions
of the section, designating the township and range,
serves the purpose of the law, and dispenses with this
requirement as to marking on the ground.

This view has found support in a decision by Assistant Secretary Reynolds, wherein he holds, referring to
the language of section twenty-three hundred and
twenty-nine of the Revised Statutes, that the "like cir-
" cumstances and conditions" apply to discovery, location, and *where the location is made on unsurveyed
lands,* marking the boundaries of the same, as of a lode
claim. He says:—

[1] *Ante,* § 448.
[2] McKinley Creek M. Co. *v.* Alaska United M. Co., 183 U. S. 563, 576,
22 Sup. Ct. Rep. 84. See comments upon this case, *ante,* § 373.

"It does not, in my judgment, mean that when the
" placer is located on surveyed lands it is necessary to
" mark the boundaries. There is no purpose that can
" be subserved by so doing. The public surveys are as
" permanent and fixed as anything can be in that line,
" and any fractional part of a section can be readily
" found, and its boundaries ascertained, by that method,
" for all time to come, and is necessarily more stable
" and enduring than marking it by perishable or de-
" structible stakes or monuments."[1]

The supreme court of Montana inclines to the same
view.[2]

But it seems to us that these decisions overlook several
important matters:—

(1) In the absence of any state legislation or local
rule, no notice need be either posted[3] or recorded.[4]
What evidence is there on the ground, or elsewhere, of
any appropriation which will warn off subsequent intending locators, if there are no marks to indicate it?

(2) Minor subdivisions are not surveyed in the field,
but are protracted in the surveyor-general's office on the
township plats, and the lines are wholly imaginary.[5]

It seems to us that the supreme court of California
presents the logical view of the law. Said that court:—

"The construction contended for does not seem to us
" to be in harmony with the general purpose of the act.
" The purpose of the requirement, that the claimant
" shall mark the boundaries of his claim, is to inform
" other miners as to what portion of the ground is
" already occupied. The men for whose information
" the boundaries are required to be marked, wander
" over the mountains with a very small outfit. They
" do not take surveyors with them to ascertain where
" the section lines run, and ordinarily it would do them

---

[1] Reins v. Murray, 22 L. D. 409.   [4] *Ante,* § 273.
[2] Freezer v. Sweeney, 8 Mont. 508, 21 Pac. 20.   [5] *Ante,* § 106.
[3] *Ante,* § 350.

" no good to be informed that a quarter-section of a par-
" ticular number had been taken up. They would derive
" no more information from it than they would from
" a description by metes and bounds, such as would be
" sufficient in a deed. For the information of these
" men, it is required that the boundaries shall be 'dis-
" 'tinctly marked upon the ground.' The section lines
" may not have been 'distinctly' marked upon the
" ground, or the marks may have become obliterated by
" time or accident. And to say, that the mere reference
" to the legal subdivision is of itself sufficient, would,
" in our opinion, defeat the purpose of the require-
" ment." [1]

The views of the supreme court of Colorado are in
harmony with those of the California courts.[2]

The supreme court of Montana has held that a separate marking of the boundaries as to each twenty-acre
tract within a larger area, located by an association of
persons, is not necessary. It is sufficient if the exterior
boundaries of the larger area be marked.[3]

We think we are justified in the conclusion, that placer
locations must be marked on the ground with the same
care, and for the same object and purpose, as in case of
lode locations.

§ 455. State legislation as to marking boundaries of
placer claims.—There is no legislation on the subject of
marking placer locations in California or Oregon. As
to New Mexico, South Dakota, and North Dakota, it is
difficult to determine whether their laws were intended
to apply to placers or not. Of course, the necessity for
marking arises from the terms of the federal law. State

[1] White v. Lee, 78 Cal. 593, 596, 12 Am. St. Rep. 115, 21 Pac. 363,
(followed in Anthony v. Jillson, 83 Cal. 296, 23 Pac. 419; Temescal
O. and M. Co. v. Salcido, 137 Cal. 211, 69 Pac. 1010).

[2] Sweet v. Webber, 7 Colo. 443, 4 Pac. 752.

[3] McDonald v. Montana Wood Co., 14 Mont. 88, 43 Am. St. Rep. 616,
35 Pac. 668.

or territorial legislation may determine the character of marking within reasonable limits, but cannot dispense with the requirement of the federal laws.

Colorado requires the boundaries to be marked prior to recording the certificate of location (thirty days from discovery) by placing a substantial post at each angle of the claim.[1]

Arizona requires the marking of boundaries by a post or monument of stones at each angle of the claim located. When a post is used, it must be at least four inches square by four feet six inches in length, set one foot in the ground, and surrounded by a mound of stone or earth. If, on account of a bed of rock or precipitous ground, it is impracticable to sink such posts, they may be placed in piles of stones. When a mound of stones is used, it must be at least three feet in height and four feet in diameter at the base. If for any reason it is impossible to erect and maintain either a post or monument of stone at any angle of the claim, a witness post or monument may be used, and must be placed as near the true corner as the nature of the ground will permit.[2]

Idaho,[3] Montana,[4] and Utah[5] require the same marking as in case of lode claims.

Nevada[6] requires the same marking as in lode claims, except that where the location is on public surveyed lands it may be taken by legal subdivisions, and no markings are required other than those of the survey.[7]

Washington[8] requires that the locator shall within

[1] Mills' Annot. Stats., § 3136.
[2] Rev. Stats. (1901), §§ 3242-3243.
[3] Laws of 1895, p. 25, § xii, as amended—Laws of 1897, p. 12; Civ. Code (1901), § 2563; Lode claims, *ante*, § 374.
[4] Rev. Code of 1895, § 3611; Lode claims, *ante*, § 374.
[5] Laws of 1899, p. 26, § 3; Lode claims, *ante*, § 374.
[6] Comp. Laws (1900), § 220; Lode claims, *ante*, § 374.
[7] If the federal statute, properly interpreted, requires a marking on the ground, the Nevada law is repugnant to it and void.
[8] Laws of 1899, p. 71, as amended—Laws of 1901, p. 292.

thirty days from the date of the discovery so distinctly mark his location on the ground that its boundaries may be readily traced, and this whether the claim is located by legal subdivisions of the public surveys or not.

Wyoming requires surface boundaries to be designated before recording the location certificate (ninety days from discovery), by substantial posts or stone monuments at each corner of the claim.[1]

ARTICLE VII. THE LOCATION CERTIFICATE AND ITS RECORD.

§ 459. State legislation concerning location certificates and their record.

§ 459. **State legislation concerning location certificates and their record.**—As in the case of lodes, certificates of location [2] and their record [3] are the subject of state or local regulation. Where such certificates are required, and their record is provided for, the same general rules apply as in the case of lodes. Where a record is made necessary, the requirements of the federal law as to contents of such record are mandatory.[4] There are no specific provisions on the subject in either Washington, Utah, South Dakota, North Dakota, Oregon, or New Mexico. It is possible that in New Mexico, North Dakota, and South Dakota the laws governing lode claims may be construed to cover placers, but it is extremely doubtful if such is the case. Other states make special provision for this class of cases.

Arizona.—Within sixty days after the date of location, the locator must record a copy of the location notice as posted.[5]

---

[1] Laws of 1888, pp. 88-90, § 22; Rev. Stats. (1899), § 2553, as amended —Laws of 1901, p. 104.

[2] *Ante*, § 379.

[3] *Ante*, §§ 273, 328.

[4] *Ante*, § 273.

[5] Rev. Stats. 1901, § 3244; contents of location notice, *ante*, § 442.

California.—Recording in the office of the county recorder seems to be authorized, but is not imperative.[1]

Colorado.—Within thirty days from the discovery a certificate of location must be recorded in the county recorder's office, which must contain: (1) the name of the claim, designating it as a placer; (2) name of locator; (3) date of location; (4) number of acres or feet claimed; (5) description of claim by reference to natural objects or permanent monuments.[2]

Idaho.—Within thirty days from the time of location the locator must file for record, in the district in which the same is situated, or in the office of the county recorder, a substantial copy of his notice of location, which must contain: (1) date of location; (2) name of locator; (3) name and dimensions of the claim; (4) the mining district (if any) and county in which the same is situated; (5) the distance and direction of the post on which the notice is posted from such natural object or permanent monument, if any such there be, as will fix and describe in the notice itself the location of the claim. An affidavit of one of the locators must be attached.[3]

Montana.—The requirements in Montana are substantially the same as in case of lode locations,[4] substituting the number of superficial feet or acres claimed in place of the number of linear feet and surface area embracing the lode.[5]

Nevada.—The contents of the certificate of location are the same as those required in Colorado, with the

---

[1] Civ. Code, § 1159.

[2] Mills' Annot. Stats., § 3136.

[3] Laws of 1895, p. 25, §§ xii, xiii, as amended—Laws of 1897, p. 12; Civ. Code (1901), § 2563.

[4] *Ante,* § 380, p. 493.

[5] Rev. Code, 1895, § 3612.

addition of (6) the kind and amount of work done by him, and the place on the claim where said work was done.[1]

Utah.—Within thirty days from the date of posting the notice of location a substantial copy thereof must be filed for record in the office of the county recorder, or of the mining district recorder, if there be one.[2]

Washington.—Within thirty days from date of discovery, the notice of location must be recorded in the office of the auditor of the county in which the discovery was made.[3]

Wyoming.—Within ninety days after the date of discovery the location certificate must be recorded with the county clerk and *ex officio* register of deeds. The certificate must contain: (1) the name of the claim, designating it as a placer; (2) the name of the locator; (3) date of location; (4) number of feet or acres claimed; (5) a description of the claim by designation of such natural or fixed objects as shall identify the claim beyond question.[4]

ARTICLE VIII. CONCLUSION.

§ 463. General principles announced in previous chapter on lode locations apply with equal force to placers.

§ **463. General principles announced in previous chapter on lode locations apply with equal force to placers.**— The architecture of existing mining legislation is a composite of incongruous elements—an aggregation of

---

[1] Comp. Laws (1900), § 221.

[2] Laws of 1899, p. 26, § 4; contents of location notice, *ante*, § 442.

[3] Laws of 1899, p. 71, as amended—Laws of 1901, p. 292; contents of location notice, *ante*, § 442.

[4] Laws of 1888, pp. 89-90, § 22; Rev. Stats. (1899), § 2553, as amended —Laws of 1901, p. 104.

piecework, which does not present, in outline, that symmetrical form or structure which commends itself to the professional eye. There is a total lack of harmonious blending, and it is often difficult to determine what provisions of the law apply distinctively to lode locations, and what to placers; or what, in contemplation of law, is to be applied to both.

The laws governing both classes had a common origin, and during the period when local rules and customs held sway the only differences between them were as to the extent of property rights enjoyed, and such as were made necessary by the difference in the form in which the deposits occurred. But discovery and appropriation were the sources of the miner's title, and continuous development the condition of its perpetuation in the case of both lodes and placers. Congress manifestly recognized these as the basis of its mining legislation, and as a rule the courts have applied the general underlying principles applicable to one class of locations to the other, so far as the nature of the deposits would permit.

The previous chapter on the subject of lode locations, dealing with the location and its requirements, the discovery, the manner of locating, the marking of the boundaries, the changing of these boundaries, and amendment of location certificates, the relocation of forfeited or abandoned claims, applies in the main to placers, except so far as the nature of placer deposits obviously demand a discrimination. There is no extralateral right attached to a placer claim pure and simple. Therefore, the laws as they are construed by the courts, with reference to end- and side-lines and the pursuit of veins beyond vertical planes drawn through surface boundaries, have no reference to placers.

For the purpose of systematic treatment, owing to certain peculiar attributes pertaining to lode locations, it was necessary to consider the two classes and their mode of appropriation separately. But there are many things in common between them, as we think will be readily observed by a consideration of this and the two preceding chapters.

CHAPTER IV.

TUNNEL CLAIMS.

ARTICLE I. INTRODUCTORY.

II. MANNER OF PERFECTING TUNNEL LOCATIONS.

III. RIGHTS ACCRUING TO THE TUNNEL PROPRIETOR BY VIRTUE OF HIS TUNNEL LOCATION.

ARTICLE I. INTRODUCTORY.

§ 467. Tunnel locations prior to the enactment of federal laws.

§ 468. The provisions of the federal law.

§ **467. Tunnel locations prior to the enactment of federal laws.**—Tunnel locations, or, as they are sometimes called, "tunnel-sites," occupy a unique position in practical mining upon the public domain. They were not unknown during the period antedating the enactment of congressional mining laws. The discovery of a new mineral belt frequently gave birth to local rules upon the subject of tunnels, and it was by no means an uncommon occurrence for tunnel locations to be made on the four slopes of a mountain, their projected lines running into the hill from every conceivable point of the compass, and at different elevations above the mountain's base, from one hundred to several thousand feet. The practical development of the mines was, as a rule, from surface discoveries on the crest of the mountain, or its benches and sloping ridges. Strife or litigation between surface locators and tunnel proprietors rarely, if ever, arose, for the simple reason that, according to the popular view, priority of discovery, whether from the surface or in the tunnel, established a priority right. In many localities, the life of the camp was short, and most of the tunnel projects began and ended with the staking of a line, the incorporation of a company with a fabulous capital, and the tunnel bore barely entering under cover.

We think it may be fairly stated that prior to any legislation upon the subject by congress, in popular estimation, the purpose of a tunnel location was that of discovery of blind veins, or deposits, whose existence it might be difficult, if not impossible, to establish by surface exploration, and that such discovery, by means of the tunnel, should be treated as the equivalent of one made from the surface. As to questions of priority, it was a mere race of diligence. Rights upon the discovered lode dated from the discovery in the tunnel, and not from the date of the tunnel location. Surface prospecting within the vicinity of the projected tunnel line was not inhibited. It is possible that the chances of a successful discovery in some formations were in favor of the tunnel method and this may have been the inducement for projecting it, but the tunnel locator's privilege was not understood to be an exclusive one within any defined surface area. We do not assert that this was the universal rule, or that it was of such general observance as to lead to the inference that congress had it in mind when it legislated upon the subject. We do not know that to have been the fact. We have strong convictions upon the subject, but it would be difficult to assert that in construing congressional legislation, as we are about to do, these antecedent conditions, popular theories, and local experiences should, or could, legally be resorted to as an aid to interpretation.

Dr. R. W. Raymond, while acting as the government's special commissioner for the collection of mining statistics in the states and territories west of the Rocky

Mountains, refers to the "tunnel fever" which flourished in Clear Creek county, Colorado, and other outlying districts in that state, and presented some views on the subject which in the light of subsequent experiences are quite prophetic.[1]

In an able article contributed to the "Mineral Industry,"[2] the same gentleman reviews the history of tunnel legislation and comments in an interesting and logical way upon some of the vices and inherent defects in the legislation, as well as upon some of the embarrassments surrounding the practical application of the law in the light of its more modern interpretation by the courts.

In construing the first mining laws of congress, which were but the crystallization of the miners' rules and customs theretofore in force, the courts had for their guide many adjudications made during the earlier history of mining in the west, enabling them to catch the spirit of these local regulations and interpret the federal law in the light of such precedents. But as to rights flowing from tunnel locations, there were practically no judicial precedents. The "tunnel fever" broke out after the passage of the act of 1866, but too near the passage of the act of 1872 to give opportunity for judicial interpretation. The tunnel laws now under consideration were incorporated in the act of May 10, 1872, and in construing them the courts have been compelled practically to break new ground. The net results thus far reached will be explained and illustrated in the succeeding sections.

§ 468. **The provisions of the federal law.**—We are not at present concerned with the act of congress of February 11, 1875,[3] providing that development work per-

---

[1] "Mineral Resources West of the Rocky Mountains" (1871), p. 322.

[2] Vol. vi, p. 681, (1897).

[3] 18 Stats. at Large, p. 315.

formed in running a tunnel shall be estimated as work done upon the lodes with like effect as if done from the surface. This act has no particular bearing upon the subject now under consideration. We are now called upon to construe section four of the act of May 10, 1872, which is embodied in the Revised Statutes, and is as follows:—

"§ 2323. Where a tunnel is run for the development " of a vein or lode, or for the discovery of mines, the " owners of such tunnel shall have the right of pos- " session of all veins or lodes, within three thousand " feet from the face of such tunnel on the line thereof, " not previously known to exist, discovered in such " tunnel, to the same extent as if discovered from the " surface; and locations on the line of such tunnel of " veins or lodes, not appearing on the surface, made " by other parties after the commencement of the tun- " nel, and while the same is being prosecuted with rea- " sonable diligence, shall be invalid; but failure to " prosecute the work on the tunnel for six months shall " be considered as an abandonment of the right to all " undiscovered veins on the line of such tunnel."

Concerning this legislation, Dr. Raymond very appro- priately remarks:—

"This is the only provision of the Revised Statutes " concerning tunnel rights. Perhaps it is fortunate that " there are no more. Certainly this one is ambiguous " and perplexing enough, and additional ones of the " same character would have made confusion worse con- " founded. . . .

"As an amendment to the act of 1866, it is, taken by " itself, simple and clear enough, though perhaps not " wise. As a part of the act of 1872, it is inconsistent, " incomplete, and mischievous." [1]

These caustic epigrams express the situation, but af- ford no substantial aid in the interpretation of the law.

[1] Monograph, "Tunnel Rights under the United States Mining Law," Mineral Industry, vol. vi, p. 680.

They suggest difficulties almost insurmountable, but give no light upon the rule of construction.

ARTICLE II. MANNER OF PERFECTING TUNNEL LOCATION.

§ 472. Acts to be performed in acquiring tunnel rights.

§ 473. "Line" of tunnel defined.

§ 474. "Face" of tunnel defined.

§ 475. The marking of the tunnel location on the ground.

§ 472. **Acts to be performed in acquiring tunnel rights.**—The statute is silent as to the manner in which a tunnel location is to be perfected. The subject is regulated entirely by rules prescribed by the commissioner of the general land office, under the direction of the secretary of the interior, the authority for such regulation being found in the provisions of the Revised Statutes.[1] These rules, prescribed in pursuance of such authority, become a mass of that body of public records, of which the courts take judicial notice,[2] and when not repugnant to the acts of congress have the force and effect of laws.[3]

By these rules [4] the tunnel locator is required, as soon as his projected tunnel enters cover, to give notice by erecting a substantial board or monument at the "face," or point of commencement thereof, upon which must be posted a good and sufficient notice, containing:—

(1) The names of the parties or company claiming the tunnel right;

[1] § 2478.

[2] Caha v. United States, 152 U. S. 211, 14 Sup. Ct. Rep. 513; Whitney v. Spratt, 64 Pac. 919.

[3] Poppe v. Athearn, 42 Cal. 607; Rose v. Nevada and G. V. Wood and Lumber Co., 73 Cal. 385, 15 Pac. 19; Chapman v. Quinn, 56 Cal. 266; United States v. Mackintosh, 85 Fed. 333, 337; Cosmos Exploration Co. v. Gray Eagle Oil Co., 112 Fed. 4. And see Orchard v. Alexander, 157 U. S. 383, 15 Sup. Ct. Rep. 635; Germania Iron Co. v. James, 89 Fed. 811; James v. Germania Iron Co., 107 Fed. 597.

[4] See Circ. Instructions, July 26, 1901, pars. 16-18. See Appendix.

(2) The actual or proposed course or direction of the tunnel;

(3) The height and width thereof;

(4) The course and distance from such face or point of commencement to some permanent well-known objects in the vicinity, by which to fix and determine the *locus*, as in case of lode claims.[1]

The "boundary *lines*" thereof are to be established by stakes and monuments along such lines, at proper intervals, to the terminus of the three thousand feet from the " face," or point of commencement.[2]

At the time of posting the notice and marking out the lines,[3] a full and correct copy of such notice, defining the tunnel claim, must be filed for record with the mining recorder of the district, to which notice must be attached the sworn statement or declaration of the owners, claimants, or projectors of such tunnel, setting forth the facts in the case, stating the amount expended by themselves and their predecessors in interest in prosecuting work thereon, the extent of work performed, and that it is their *bona fide* intention to prosecute work on the tunnel so located and described, with reasonable diligence. As to what *lines* are to be marked, we shall consider in a subsequent section.

§ 473. "Line" of tunnel defined.—The tunnel proprietor is accorded by the statute the right of possession of all veins or lodes within three thousand feet from the face of the tunnel on the *line* thereof, not previously known to exist, discovered in such tunnel; and locations

---

[1] Nevada has embodied these provisions in a state statute, adding as a requisite the name of the locator. Comp. Laws of 1900, § 226.

[2] Nevada laws provide for the size of stakes and the distance apart. Comp. Laws of 1900, § 227.

[3] Nevada has passed a law allowing sixty days from date of location to record. Comp. Laws of 1900, § 228.

on the *line* of such tunnel of veins or lodes not appearing at the surface, made by other parties after the commencement of the tunnel and while the same is being prosecuted with reasonable diligence, shall be invalid. The word "line" appears in no other connection in the statute. As we shall hereafter note, the statute is silent as to the manner of marking the tunnel location on the ground. The character of this marking is defined in the regulations adopted by the secretary of the interior. These regulations require that the *boundary lines* of the tunnel shall be marked by stakes or monuments placed along such lines at proper intervals to the terminus of the three thousand feet from the face or point of commencement of the tunnel, "and the *lines* so marked will " define and govern as to specific boundaries within " which prospecting for lodes not previously known to " exist is prohibited." [1]

We have therefore to consider the phrase "*line of the* " *tunnel*" in two aspects,—the *line* that is to be marked on the surface, and the *lines* which define boundaries within which prospecting at the surface by third parties is practically inhibited. The natural assumption would be that stated in the regulations,—the *lines* to be marked on the surface means the *lines* within which prospecting is prohibited. But on this subject there seems to be some confusion of thought observable in the decisions.

So far as the land department is concerned, we find the following views to have been expressed:—

In the case of Corning Tunnel M. and R. Co. *v.* Pell,[2] the commissioner of the general land office held that the line of the tunnel named in the statute was the width of the tunnel bore (six feet) and three thousand feet long, not a rectangular parallelogram, three thousand feet

[1] Regulations Land Department, par. 18. See Appendix.
[2] 3 Copp's L. O. 130, 131.
Lindley on M.—52

square or three thousand feet by fifteen hundred feet. All of its rulings on this point have been to the same effect. According to the interpretation by the department, prospecting at the surface was only inhibited within these narrow limits.[1]

This view was fully approved by the supreme courts of Colorado [2] and Montana,[3] and inferentially upheld by the supreme court of Idaho.[4]

The circuit court of appeals for the eighth circuit, while, as we shall hereafter note, determining that the area within which prospecting is inhibited is the rectangular parallelogram three thousand feet square, refers to the discovery on the *line* of the tunnel as necessarily indicating the width and course of the bore.[5]

But there was no attempt to judicially define what was meant by the lines of the tunnel which are required to be marked by departmental regulations. Our deductions as to the required marking will be found in a subsequent section.[6]

§ 474.   "Face" of tunnel defined.—The land department construes the term "face of such tunnel," as used in the Revised Statutes, to mean the first working face formed in the tunnel, and to signify the point at which the tunnel actually enters cover; it being from this point that the three thousand feet are to be measured. There is no room for dispute as to this.[7] While it is true that in the conduct of active mining operations, as work

[1] *In re* David Hunter, 5 Copp's L. O. 130; *In re* John Hunter, Copp's Min. Lands, 222; *In re* J. B. Chaffee, Copp's U. S. Min. Dec. 144.

[2] Corning Tunnel Co. *v.* Pell, 4 Colo. 508, 511.

[3] Hope M. Co. *v.* Brown, 7 Mont. 550, 557, 19 Pac. 218; *Id.*, 11 Mont. 370, 379, 28 Pac. 732.

[4] Back *v.* Sierra Nev. Cons. M. Co., 2 Idaho, 386, 17 Pac. 83.

[5] Enterprise M. Co. *v.* Rico-Aspen Cons. M. Co., 66 Fed. 200.

[6] *Post,* § 475.

[7] See monograph by Dr. Raymond entitled "Tunnel Rights under the "United States Mining Laws," Min. Ind., vol. vi, pp. 681, 686.

advances the face of the drift or tunnel recedes farther
into the hill, and its *locus* is constantly changed, yet
the word as used in the tunnel law can mean but the one
thing, and that is, the first full exposure of height and
width after entering under cover. It was manifestly
intended that the length of the open surface approach to
where the tunnel enters cover was not to be considered
in estimating the three thousand feet, and for that
reason the term "face" was used.

§ 475. **The marking of the tunnel location on the
ground.**—In marking the tunnel location on the surface
it has been the custom to mark it by two parallel lines of
stakes defining the width of the tunnel bore and following the course of the projected tunnel to the length of
three thousand feet. This was the construction placed
by the land department upon the phrase "line of the
" tunnel" employed in the statute, and was the marking
contemplated by the departmental regulations.[1]

Strictly speaking, for the purpose of marking, this
is the line of the tunnel. At the same time it is now
well settled that such marking does not define the area
within which prospecting at the surface is inhibited.[2]

Logically, the marking of the tunnel location should
be effected by marking the exterior boundaries of the
parallelogram, within the area of which prospecting is
not permitted, or, rather, permitted at the peril of the
prospector. As a matter of caution, the line and width
of the projected tunnel bore, as well as the exterior
boundaries of the parallelogram, should be marked at
the surface.

[1] *Ante,* § 473.　　　　　[2] *Post,* § 489.

ARTICLE III.   RIGHTS ACCRUING TO THE TUNNEL PRO-
PRIETOR BY VIRTUE OF HIS TUNNEL LOCATION.

§ 479. Important questions suggested by the tunnel law.

§ 480. Rule of interpretation applied.

§ 481. Length upon the discovered
lode awarded to the tun-
nel discoverer.

§ 482. Necessity for appropriation
of discovered lode by surface location.

§ 483. To what extent does the inception of a tunnel right
and its perpetuation by
prosecuting work with
reasonable diligence op-
erate as a withdrawal of
the surface from explora-
tion by others?

§ 484. The Colorado rule.

§ 485. The Montana rule.

§ 486. The Idaho rule.

§ 487. Judge Hallett's views.

§ 488. The doctrine announced by
the circuit court of ap-
peals, eighth circuit.

§ 489. Tunnel locations before the
supreme court of the
United States.

§ 490. Opinions of the land department.

§ 490a. Rights of junior tunnel locator as against senior
mining claims on the line
of the tunnel.

§ 491. Inquiries suggested in the
light of rules thus far
enunciated by the su-
preme court of the United
States as to the extent of
the rights of a tunnel
locator on a vein discov-
ered in the tunnel.

§ 479. **Important questions suggested by the tunnel
law.**—The provisions of the law upon the subject of tunnel locations present for consideration several important questions, the solution of which has engaged the
attention of the courts, both state and federal. The
inquiries suggested may be thus formulated:—

(1) What are the rights accruing to the tunnel proprietor by virtue of a discovery made in the tunnel,
in the absence of conflicting rights acquired by surface
discovery?

(2) To what extent does the inception of a tunnel
right and its perpetuation by prosecuting work with
diligence operate as a withdrawal of the surface from
exploration by others?

(3) What rights, if any, are secured by a junior tunnel locator as against senior mining locations which are covered by the line of the tunnel bore?

Some incidental questions necessarily arise, the correct solution of which depends upon reaching a satisfactory conclusion, by way of answers, to one or the other of the foregoing inquiries.

§ 480. **Rule of interpretation applied.**—It is an elementary rule in the interpretation of laws that a given statute should be construed in connection with all other statutes which are essentially *in pari materia.*[1]

In applying this doctrine to the tunnel laws, and attempting a construction which would be in harmony with the entire body of the mining law, the courts, state and federal, have encountered serious difficulties, and have reached results which practically place locations on lodes discovered in a tunnel located under the tunnel laws in a distinct category by themselves, leaving still open for discussion many important questions which will have to be adjusted without regard to the main body of the mining laws. This will be made manifest as we outline the state of the law as announced by the courts.

§ 481. **Length upon the discovered lode awarded to the tunnel discoverer.**—Section twenty-three hundred and twenty of the Revised Statutes provides that a mining location based upon a surface discovery may equal, but shall not exceed, fifteen hundred feet in length.

As to the length on the discovered lode to which the tunnel discoverer is entitled, Judge Hallett was of the opinion that it was not fixed by the act of congress, but

[1] Pennington *v.* Coxe, 2 Cranch, 33; Washington Market Co. *v.* Hoffman, 101 U. S. 112; Platt *v.* Union Pac. R. R., 99 U. S. 48; Kohlsaat *v.* Murphy, 96 U. S. 153; Heydenfeldt *v.* Daney G. and S. M. Co., 93 U. S. 634; Neal *v.* Clark, 95 U. S. 704.

was left to local regulation, and that, in the absence of such regulation, nothing would pass but the line of the tunnel.[1]

Prior to the passage of the congressional law, a state statute was in existence in Colorado,[2] fixing the length at two hundred and fifty feet each way from the tunnel, and Judge Hallett held this statute to be controlling after the enactment of the federal law. The supreme court of the United States has incidentally stated that such was the rule, but the case then under consideration arose out of a location made in 1865, at a time when the statute was undoubtedly controlling.[3]

The supreme court of Colorado has determined that this state law was not in force after the passage of the congressional law,[4] and that a discovery in the tunnel entitled the discoverer to fifteen hundred feet in length on the lode, under the provisions of section twenty-three hundred and twenty of the Revised Statutes,[5] which ruling was followed by the circuit court of appeals for the eighth circuit, overruling the decision of Judge Hallett above referred to.[6]

The supreme court of Montana has stated that when veins or lodes are discovered in the tunnel, the claimant will be entitled, as a matter of right, to the vein or lode for fifteen hundred feet in length,[7] and this was

---

[1] Rico-Aspen Cons. M. Co. v. Enterprise M. Co., 53 Fed. 321.

[2] Mills' Annot. Stats., § 3141.

[3] Glacier Mt. S. M. Co. v. Willis, 127 U. S. 471, 481, 8 Sup. Ct. Rep. 1214.

[4] Followed in Enterprise M. Co. v. Rico-Aspen M. Co., 167 U. S. 108, 17 Sup. Ct. Rep. 762; Calhoun G. M. Co. v. Ajax G. M. Co., 27 Colo. 1, 83 Am. St. Rep. 17, 59 Pac. 607, S. C. 182 U. S. 499, 21 Sup. Ct. Rep. 885.

[5] Ellet v. Campbell, 18 Colo. 510, 33 Pac. 521.

[6] Enterprise M. Co. v. Rico-Aspen Cons. M. Co., 66 Fed. 200.

[7] Hope M. Co. v. Brown, 7 Mont. 550, 555, 19 Pac. 218. At one time a state law existed in Montana limiting the extent to three hundred feet on each side of the discovery, but this has since been repealed by implication. Civ. Code of 1895, § 4672; Pol. Code of 1895, § 5186.

the understanding of the law expressed by the commissioner of the general land office.[1]

The supreme court of the United States has definitely settled the question by announcing the rule that the right of a tunnel locator to locate a claim to the vein arises upon its discovery in the tunnel, and may be exercised by locating that claim the full length of fifteen hundred feet on either side of the tunnel, or in such proportion thereof on either side as the locator may desire.[2]

§ 482. **Necessity for appropriation of discovered lode by surface location.**—It being well established that the tunnel discoverer is entitled to fifteen hundred feet in length on his discovered lode, the inquiry naturally suggests itself: How is he to disclose his intention as to the extent and direction in which he shall take it, so as to inform others where his rights end and theirs may begin? How are other prospectors to find out where to search for or locate lodes, with due regard to the rights of the tunnel discoverer?

Judge Hallett, in the case of Rico-Aspen Cons. M. Co. v. Enterprise M. Co.,[3] ruled that in case of a location based upon discovery made in a tunnel, it is as necessary to mark the boundaries on the surface and file a certificate for record as in any other case. This would seem to be in accord with the views of Commissioner Williamson, who instructed the surveyor-general of Colorado, that "no patent can issue for a vein or lode " without surface ground, and as the surface which " overlies the apex of a vein or lode, discovered in a " tunnel can only be ascertained by sinking a shaft, or " by following a lode up on its dip from the point of " discovery, no survey of such lode will be made until

---

[1] Commissioner Drummond, Copp's Min. Dec. 144.

[2] Enterprise M. Co. v. Rico-Aspen M. Co., 167 U. S. 108, 113, 17 Sup. Ct. Rep. 762.

[3] 53 Fed. 321.

" the exact surface ground is first ascertained;"[1] and this ruling has been uniformly adhered to by the land department.

The supreme court of Colorado, however, took a different view. It announced the rule that location on the surface by defining surface boundaries is not necessary.

Its argument is based upon the following reasoning:—

"Section twenty-three hundred and twenty-three was
" obviously designed to encourage the running of tun-
" nels for the discovery and development of veins or
" lodes of the precious metals not appearing upon the
" surface and not previously known to exist. Little
" encouragement would the act give if the discoverer
" of the lode in a tunnel were bound also to find the apex
" and course of such vein, uncover the same from the
" surface, sink his location shaft thereon, mark the
" boundaries thereof, and record his certificate of such
" surface location, the same as if he had made the ori-
" ginal discovery from the surface.

"The location of a lode from the surface is always
" attended with more or less difficulty and uncertainty.
" Mistakes occur in the location of boundary lines, even
" where the apex and course of the vein lie compara-
" tively near the surface. These difficulties and uncer-
" tainties are liable to be greatly increased where a lode
" is discovered by means of a tunnel driven hundreds
" and thousands of feet into the heart of the great
" mountain. To require the discoverer of a lode in a
" tunnel to prospect for the vein upon the surface, and
" uncover and mark its boundaries so as to include the
" apex and course within the lines of the surface loca-
" tion, would be to require a work of supererogation,
" for no surface location is necessary for the convenient
" working of the lode discovered in a tunnel location
" already made. Such requirement would unnecessa-
" rily burden the tunnel locator and discoverer; to the

[1] 4 Copp's L. O. 102. See, also, *In re* David Hunter, Copp's Min. Lands, 231.

" great labor and expense of tunneling as a means of a
" location and discovery, it would add the labor and
" expense devolving upon the ordinary surface discov-
" erer and locator. Besides, such a requirement would
" subject the discoverer of a lode in a tunnel to the
" hazard of a race for its surface location; and thus the
" discoverer might have the fruits of his labor wrested
" from him by a surface locator who had done nothing
" and expended nothing in the original discovery." [1]

The location of the lode discovered in the tunnel in
this case was by posting a notice at the mouth of the
tunnel, claiming seven hundred and fifty feet on each
side of the discovery-point in the tunnel, five hundred
and ninety-four feet from its face. A notice was also
recorded in the county recorder's office, corresponding
with the posted notice.

The supreme court of the United States, in affirming
the decision of the state court, thus expresses itself: —

"It will be noticed that the tunnel company posted at
" the mouth of the tunnel a notice of its discovery of
" this lode and the extent of its claim thereon, and also
" that it caused to be filed in the office of the recorder
" of the county a location certificate, as required by the
" local statute. Mills' Ann. Stats., secs. 3150, 3151. It
" will also be perceived that sec. 2323, Rev. Stats., gives
" to the tunnel discoverer the right of possession of the
" veins. It in terms prescribes no conditions other than
" discovery. The words 'to the same extent' obviously
" refer to the length along the line of the lode or vein.
" Such is the natural and ordinary meaning of the
" words, and there is nothing in the context or in the
" circumstances to justify a broader and different
" meaning. Indeed, the conditions surrounding a
" vein or lode discovered in a tunnel are such as to
" make against the idea or necessity of a surface loca-
" tion. We do not mean to say that there is any impro-
" priety in such a location, the locator marking the
" point of discovery on the surface at the summit of a

[1] Ellet *v.* Campbell, 18 Colo. 510, 519, 520, 33 Pac. 521.

" line drawn perpendicularly from the place of dis-
" covery in the tunnel, and about that point locating
" the lines of his claim, in accordance with other pro-
" visions of the statute. It may be true, as suggested in
" Morrison's Mining Rights, 8th edition, page 182, that
" before a patent can be secured there must be a surface
" location. Rev. Stats., sec. 2325. But the patent is
" not simply a grant of the vein, for, as stated in the
" section 'a patent for any land claimed and located for
" 'valuable deposits may be obtained in the following
" 'manner.' It must also be noticed that sec. 2322, in
" respect to locators, gives them the exclusive right of
" possession and enjoyment of all the surface within
" the lines of their locations, and all veins, lodes, and
" ledges, the tops, or apexes, of which are inside such
" lines. So that a location gives to the locator some-
" thing more than the right to the vein which is the
" occasion of the location. But without determining
" what would be the rights acquired under a surface
" location based upon a discovery in a tunnel, it is
" enough to hold, following the plain language of the
" statute, that the discovery of the vein in the tunnel,
" worked according to the provisions of the statute,
" gives a right to the possession of the vein to the same
" length as if discovered from the surface, and that a
" location on the surface is not essential to a continu-
" ance of that right. We do not mean to hold that such
" right of possession can be maintained without com-
" pliance with the provisions of the local statutes in
" reference to the record of the claim, or without post-
" ing in some suitable place, conveniently near to the
" place of discovery, a proper notice of the extent of the
" claim—in other words, without any practical loca-
" tion. For in this case notice was posted at the mouth
" of the tunnel and no more suitable place can be sug-
" gested, and a proper notice was put on record in the
" office named in the statute." [1]

With this *ex cathedra* statement of the law there are
suggested several important inquiries which remain to
vex the courts and harass the miner. We will present

---

[1] Campbell *v.* Ellet, 167 U. S. 118, 119, 17 Sup. Ct. Rep. 765.

some of these for consideration in a subsequent section.[1]

A discovery may be made in any ordinary tunnel not located under the tunnel laws. To complete his initiatory rights, however, the locator must in such case make a surface location the same as in cases of ordinary surface discovery.[2] It is only when the tunnel-site has been properly located and claimed under the tunnel laws that the vein discovered in the tunnel need not be located at the surface.

§ 483. **To what extent does the inception of a tunnel right and its perpetuation by prosecuting work with reasonable diligence operate as a withdrawal of the surface from exploration by others?**—It seems to be assumed by many, if not all, of the courts that a tunnel location once perfected in accordance with the departmental regulations has the effect of withdrawing from the body of the public domain a certain superficial area, within which, so long as work in the tunnel is prosecuted with reasonable diligence, surface exploration is practically inhibited, or at least the prospector within that area locates at his peril.

We find that this question, with others incidentally involved, has been before the courts of Colorado, Montana, and Idaho, the federal courts in the eighth circuit,

---

[1] *Post,* § 491.

The state of Nevada has endeavored to avoid the dangers flowing from the lack of surface-marking, and has passed an act which provides that claims upon blind veins or lodes discovered in the tunnel shall be located upon the surface and held in like manner as other lode claims (Comp. Laws of Nevada, 1900, § 229). The criticism on this class of legislation is apparent. If under the federal law a location of such veins may be made by simply posting a notice at the mouth of the tunnel, it is beyond the province of the state legislature to impose any other conditions. If any relief is to be obtained, or if it is desired, congress alone can afford it.

[2] Brewster *v.* Shoemaker, 28 Colo. 176, 63 Pac. 308.

and the supreme court of the United States. Ordinarily, a decision by the latter tribunal so forecloses the question decided that further discussion is both unnecessary and unwise. However, there are still so many questions undecided arising out of tunnel locations and the location of blind veins based on discoveries in the tunnel, that we are impressed with the expediency of taking up the subject outlined in the title to this section and dealing with it from an historical or evolutionary point of view.

§ 484.   **The Colorado rule.**—The case of Corning Tunnel Co. *v.* Pell [1] involved a controversy between the tunnel company locating a tunnel in September, 1872, and the locators of the Slide lode, located August 17, 1875.

The Slide lode was fifteen hundred feet in length, and crossed the center line of the tunnel-site nearly at right angles. The discovery shaft was near, but not on, the center line, being about fifty-five feet therefrom. The lode had not been reached or cut by the tunnel.

The tunnel-site as claimed described a parallelogram, three thousand by fifteen hundred feet. The tunnel had been worked with reasonable diligence, and had not been abandoned. The owners of the Slide lode applied for a patent, and the tunnel company adversed. The action was in support of the adverse claim and to try the title to the Slide lode.

It was contended by the tunnel claimant that the "line of the tunnel" meant the entire width and length of the surveyed tunnel-site,—that is, fifteen hundred by three thousand feet; that within these limits, after the commencement of the tunnel and while it is being prosecuted with diligence, no valid location could be made of a vein or lode not appearing upon the surface.

[1] 4 Colo. 507.

The supreme court of Colorado held:—

(1) That there was no law authorizing a tunnel location of any such dimensions; that the line of tunnel was the width marked by the exterior lines or sides of the tunnel;

(2) That the result contended for by the tunnel claimant forbids its adoption, unless the language clearly indicates such to have been the legislative intent. In this case, the tunnel-site location would withdraw from the exploration of prospectors over one hundred acres of mineral lands. A very limited number of tunnel locations would cover and monopolize, in most cases, an entire mining district, giving to a few tunnel-owners all its mines, not upon the condition of discovery and development, but upon the easy condition of a *commencement* of the work on the tunnel and its prosecution with reasonable diligence. The policy of the general government has been to prevent monopoly of its mineral lands, or its ownership in large tracts. But for the existence of this policy, there was but little or no reason for an abandonment of its system of surveys and preemptions applicable to agricultural lands, and the adoption as to its mineral lands of a system that, as to surface claims at least, limits mining locations to an inconsiderable acreage appendant to a discovered lode. The construction claimed is in contravention of this policy; nor can it be justified by the language of the section;

(3) No right of possession of a lode inures to the tunnel claimant until it is *discovered* in the tunnel;

(4) The Slide lode, not having been discovered in the tunnel by the tunnel proprietor, and the "location,"— *i. e. discovery,*—not being on the line thereof, the tunnel proprietor had no right to the lode.

This is a clear enunciation of the rule, that the mere location of the tunnel-site does not withdraw the surface adjacent to the tunnel *line* from exploration and location; that the tunnel is only a means of discovery, and that priority of discovery establishes a priority of right.

Fifteen years later the same tunnel-site was again brought to the attention of the same court, in the case of Ellet *v.* Campbell,[1] upon the following state of facts:—

The tunnel claimant, on February 3, 1875, discovered in the tunnel, on the line thereof, five hundred and ninety-four feet from the face, the Bonanza lode, and located it by posting a notice at the mouth of the tunnel and recording a similar notice as described in a preceding section.[2]

The Bonanza lode did not appear upon the surface of the ground, and was not known to exist prior to discovery in the tunnel. It was not staked on the surface. No discovery shaft was sunk, or work done upon the surface. The annual work on the lode was regularly performed. On July 10, 1886, Campbell, the defendant, and another made a location of the J. L. Sanderson lode, which was identical with the Bonanza lode. Their location was based upon a discovery made in a "cut," two hundred feet to the east of the east line of the bore of the tunnel. At the time of marking the Sanderson location, the locators knew of the discovery theretofore made in the tunnel. The locators of the Sanderson lode applied for a patent, the tunnel claimant adversed, and hence the suit.

Upon this state of facts, the supreme court of Colorado held that having made a discovery in the tunnel, the discoverer is not bound to make another discovery and location of the lode from the surface, in order to be protected against a subsequent surface locator of the same lode.

Having determined that it was not necessary to mark

[1] 18 Colo. 510, 33 Pac. 521.   [2] *Ante,* § 482.

the location on the surface, and that the manner of location heretofore described was sufficient, the appropriation of the lode having been perpetuated by continued performance of the annual work, no other conclusion could possibly have been reached by the court than the one announced.

§ 485.   **The Montana rule.** — At the time the cases considered by the supreme court of Montana arose, there was a state statute, which had been enacted in 1872, and which contained among others the following provisions: —

"Any person or persons pre-empting any tunnel have
" the exclusive right to three hundred feet on each side
" from the center of said tunnel, on any and all lodes
" that he or they may discover in the course of said tun-
" nel."

In June, 1887, the Hope mining company located the Jubilee tunnel in Deer Lodge county, Montana.   In the following December, Brown located a quartz claim within three hundred feet of the line of the tunnel, basing his location upon a *discovery in a tunnel,* and was engaged in extracting ore therefrom when the Hope mining company sought an injunction preventing further mining operations by the quartz claimant.   The ledge in controversy had not been discovered in the Jubilee tunnel, although the complaint alleged that it appeared to cross it.

The supreme court of Montana held: —

(1) That a tunnel claimant upon discovering a vein or lode in his tunnel will be entitled as a matter of right to the vein or lode for fifteen hundred feet in length along its course, and to the extent of three hundred feet on each side thereof from the middle of the vein;

(2) Brown's location is valid, though liable to be divested by the subsequent discovery of the same vein

in the Hope tunnel, if such location is found to be within
three hundred feet from the middle, and fifteen hundred feet from the point of, the tunnel discovery, measured along the vein. That third parties have the right
to locate any veins within three hundred feet of the line
of the tunnel, which is held to be the width of the sides
thereof, but such locations so made are at the risk
of the locators; for upon the discovery of the vein or
lode in the tunnel all locations made subsequent to its
commencement become invalid if they are within the
distances above specified.

The court also adds the following:—

" As a matter of course, veins or lodes *discovered*
" *from the surface,* or previously known to exist, are not
" affected by the right of the tunnel claimant, *which we*
" *may here remark to be most ample and sweeping.*"

The injunction was denied.[1]

It is extremely difficult to ascertain precisely what
the court meant by the language used in the quoted paragraph. If a discovery from the surface made prior to
discovery in the tunnel, but after the perfection of the
tunnel location, would take precedence over the subsequent tunnel discovery, it is difficult to understand the
closing remark, that the tunnel proprietor's rights are
most ample and sweeping.

Another case between the same parties, involving the
same relative rights, came before the same court a few
years later, wherein it appeared that Brown had applied
for a patent for his location made as indicated in the
previous case. The tunnel company adversed, and the
action was to determine the adverse claim.

The court held, upon the showing made, that the
applicant for patent ought to be restrained from prosecuting his proceedings while the tunnel proprietor is
prosecuting his tunnel as required by law, and until it

---

[1] Hope M. Co. *v.* Brown, 7 Mont. 550, 19 Pac. 218.

is demonstrated that such vein, or lode, will not be discovered in the tunnel, or until such tunnel rights are
abandoned by failure to prosecute the tunnel as provided by law.[1]

It must be conceded that the views of the supreme
court of Montana tend to support the doctrine that a
perfected tunnel-site practically withdraws the surface
to the extent of fifteen hundred feet on each side of the
line of the tunnel, and that the withdrawal remains in
force until it is either demonstrated that a given lode
will not be cut in the tunnel or the tunnel-site is abandoned.

§ 486.　The Idaho rule.—In the case of Back *v*. Sierra
Nevada Cons. M. Co.[2] the following state of facts appeared:—

The complaint alleged in substance that Back owned
the Pilgrim tunnel, located April 5, 1886.　On April 6,
1886, defendant's grantors entered *upon the line* of the
tunnel at a point where post number nine on said line
was planted.　They had full knowledge of the existence
of the post and the location of the tunnel.　They commenced to prospect for minerals, and at a depth of
twelve feet discovered a ledge.

This ledge was blind, and would have been intersected
by the tunnel continued on the location line thereof.
Defendant's grantors located and recorded a mining
claim called the Sierra Nevada, and afterwards made
application for patent.　Back filed an adverse claim,
and the suit was brought to determine the rights of the
parties.　A demurrer to the complaint was sustained.
Judgment passed for defendant on failure to answer.
The appeal was prosecuted from the judgment.

[1] Hope M. Co. *v*. Brown, 11 Mont. 370, 28 Pac. 732.
[2] 2 Idaho, 386, 17 Pac. 83.

Lindley on M.—53

It was held by the supreme court of Idaho, reversing the judgment:—

(1) That a tunnel location is a "mining claim," and may protect its rights by adversing application for patent to ledges asserted to have been located on the line of said tunnel subsequent to the tunnel location;

(2) It is evident that, in enacting section twenty-three hundred and twenty-three of the Revised Statutes, congress intended to withdraw from exploration for lodes not appearing upon the surface so much of the public domain as lay upon the *line* of the tunnel;

(3) The tunnel claimant has a right to the possession, for prospecting purposes, of the area in dispute, and to show that the respondent's location was upon the line of his tunnel.

No attempt is made to define what is meant by the *line* of the tunnel.

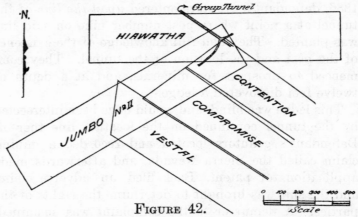

FIGURE 42.

§ 487. **Judge Hallett's views.**—The tunnel law came before Judge Hallett in the case of Rico-Aspen Cons. M. Co. *v.* Enterprise M. Co.[1] His decision is accompanied by a diagram, which we herewith reproduce.

[1] 53 Fed. 321.

The facts were substantially as follows:—

The Rico-Aspen company asserted title to three mining claims,—the Vestal, located in 1879; Contention, January 1, 1888; and Compromise, November 18, 1889. The Hiawatha was not necessarily involved in the litigation, although it may be noted that its location was junior in point of time to the inception of the tunnel right.

The Enterprise mining company perfected its location of the Group tunnel in July, 1887; and in June, 1892, discovered and located the Jumbo II claim, delineating it upon the surface as indicated on the diagram.

Said Judge Hallett, after quoting the language of section twenty-three hundred and twenty-three of the Revised Statutes:—

"Clearly enough, this is a grant of lodes and veins on
" the line of the tunnel, and the only difficulty is in
" ascertaining the extent of the grant. The supreme
" court of this state (referring to Corning Tunnel Co.
" v. Pell) interprets the act as giving only so much of
" such veins and lodes as may be in the tunnel itself.
" But this seems to reduce the grant to a point of insig-
" nificance which deprives the act of all force and
" meaning. Certainly, no one would be at the trouble
" and expense of driving a tunnel through a mountain
" for such small segments of lodes or veins as may be
" in the bore of the tunnel. On the other hand, respond-
" ents contend that the grant is of the length of a sur-
" face location in any direction from the line of the
" tunnel, and as stated, almost the entire length of the
" Jumbo II is in a southwesterly direction from that
" line. Under this construction, the location of a tun-
" nel, followed by some lazy perfunctory work twice in
" the year, will have the effect to withdraw from the
" public domain a tract three thousand feet square, or
" something more than a half section of land; and this
" in the face of the earlier declaration of the statute,
" that 'no location of a mining claim shall be made
" 'until the discovery of the vein, or lode, within the

" 'limits of the claim located.' This view is so far
" inconsistent with the general policy of the law which
" forbids the granting of large areas of valuable min-
" eral lands to one person or company that it seems
" impossible to accept it."

The conclusions reached by Judge Hallett may be
thus summed up:—

(1) The length of a location made upon a lode discovered in a tunnel is not fixed by the act of congress,
but is left to local regulations;

(2) Without local regulation as to length of a claim
founded on a discovery in a tunnel, nothing would pass
but the line of the tunnel itself;

(3) The Colorado statute of 1861 [1] is in force in Colorado, and secures to the tunnel locator two hundred and
fifty feet each way from the tunnel, on all lodes discovered within the tunnel. As to the two hundred and fifty
feet, the tunnel proprietor becomes the owner of the
ledge, its location dating back to the inception of the
tunnel right;

(4) As to the Vestal, owing to the priority of its location, decree passed for complainant. As to the Compromise and Contention, their location should, to the
extent sanctioned by the state law, yield to the rights of
the Jumbo II, which related back to the inception of
the tunnel right.

§ 488. The doctrine announced by the circuit court
of appeals, eighth circuit.—An appeal was taken from
Judge Hallett's decree in the Rico-Aspen-Enterprise
case, and the appellate court declined to adopt his
views.[2] When the case was before Judge Hallett, the
facts as they are recited in the opinion fixed 1879 as the
date of the Vestal location, prior in point of time to the

---

[1] Mills' Annot. Stats., § 3141.
[2] Enterprise M. Co. v. Rico-Aspen Cons. M. Co., 66 Fed. 201.

location of the Group tunnel. For this reason it received but little attention, the reasoning of the judge being particularly addressed to the Contention and Compromise, which were junior in point of time to the tunnel location, although senior with reference to the tunnel discovery.

The case as presented to the appellate court seems to be somewhat different, the controversy apparently centering within the conflict area between the Vestal and Jumbo II, and the record seems to give to the former a date of location, *junior*, in point of time, to the inception of the tunnel right.

The principles involved, however, are, of course, the same.

The questions involved are presented by the appellate court in the following form:—

(1) Are the owners of a valid tunnel mining claim under section twenty-three hundred and twenty-three of the Revised Statutes, who have discovered a blind vein in their tunnel and have duly located and claimed it, entitled, as against the owners of a lode mining claim located from the surface after the location of the tunnel-site, but before the discovery of the vein in the tunnel, to the possession of the vein or lode thus discovered, when such vein was not known to exist prior to the location of the tunnel, but was first discovered in another lode mining claim before its discovery in the tunnel?

(2) If the owners of a tunnel mining claim are entitled to the possession of any portion of such a vein, to what extent are they entitled to it?

Another question was also presented and decided which refers to the effect of a patent issued upon the junior surface location where the tunnel claimant failed to adverse. The discussion of this branch of the case will be deferred until we reach, in another portion of the work, the subject of patent proceedings and the legal effect of a patent when issued.

As preliminary to a discussion of the principles involved, the court announced as follows:—

"There is no tenable middle ground under this sec-" tion between a holding that the diligent owner of a " tunnel is entitled to the possession of all blind veins " he discovers in his tunnel to the same extent along " the veins as if he had discovered them at the surface, " and a holding that by the discoveries and locations " of others, subsequent to the commencement of his " tunnel and before it reaches the veins at all, he " may be deprived of every portion of them, except " possibly the small segments within the bore of the " tunnel."

The conclusions reached by the court may be thus stated:—

(1) The location of a tunnel-site, followed by the prosecution of work thereon with reasonable diligence, gives to the tunnel locator an inchoate right to all hitherto unknown or undiscovered veins which cross the line of the tunnel and are discoverable therein;

(2) That upon discovery in the tunnel, the tunnel locator will be entitled to fifteen hundred feet along the length of the vein, computed in either direction from his tunnel discovery, and that this right cannot be impaired by a discovery and location from the surface, junior in point of time, to the inception of the tunnel right;

(3) The state statute of Colorado, fixing the limit in length at two hundred and fifty feet on each side of the tunnel line, is superseded by the act of congress;

(4) In determining what length on the vein is allowed to the tunnel discoverer, the court resorts to section twenty-three hundred and twenty of the Revised Statutes, but decides that such section performs no other

function in determining the rights of the tunnel discoverers.

The court also holds that the inchoate right given to
the tunnel locator only extends to veins that strike the
line of the tunnel and are discovered in the tunnel.
Others may discover and hold all veins within fifteen
hundred feet of the line of the tunnel that do not strike
or cross its lines, and all that do strike it that are not
discovered in it.

The reasoning applied by the court which, in its
judgment, justified the results reached may be thus
epitomized:—

(A) Section twenty-three hundred and twenty-three
construes itself, and it is unnecessary to resort to public
policy in aid of its interpretation;

(B) If the question of public policy is to be resorted
to, the rights guaranteed to the tunnel locators are in
accord with such policy, which is to encourage the discovery and development of the mineral resources of the
country;

(c) The work of driving tunnels thousands of feet
into the side of a mountain for the purpose of discovering a vein or lode that is not known to exist at all is
an extremely hazardous and expensive undertaking;
that this is common knowledge, and congress must be
taken to have had this knowledge when they enacted the
law. They must have known that such a hazardous
enterprise was not likely to be undertaken unless
rewards commensurate with the risk and expense were
offered.

It is to be added, by way of a side-light on this decision, that the discovery on which the Vestal location
was based was not upon the vein which was discovered
in the tunnel. The right of the tunnel locator to the
vein discovered in the tunnel, in so far as it was found

within the Vestal location, was also defended on the
ground that it was a cross-lode, and that under the rule
then recognized by the state courts of last resort in Colorado, which we will discuss fully in a subsequent
chapter, owners of cross-lodes might follow their vein
into, and underneath, even a prior location.

§ 489. **Tunnel locations before the supreme court of
the United States.**—The case of Glacier Mountain
Silver Mining Company *v.* Willis [1] was an action of
ejectment, wherein the plaintiff sought to recover possession of the Silver Gate tunnel claim, located in 1865,
alleged to be five thousand feet long and five hundred'
feet wide, described by metes and bounds, which was
alleged to embrace many valuable lodes or veins which
had been discovered, worked, and mined by the plaintiff and his grantors. Possession and payment of taxes
for a period in excess of the statute of limitations prescribed by the laws of Colorado were averred, together
with a general allegation of ownership of the tunnel
claim described. The ouster alleged was (1) an entry by
defendants upon the premises and *into the tunnel,*
claiming said tunnel as the War Eagle, and (2) the location by defendants of the Tempest lode claim across
the tunnel, claiming a discovery *in the tunnel* of such
lode.

A special demurrer was interposed upon the ground,
among others, that the claim of plaintiff to a strip of
ground five thousand feet in length by five hundred feet
in width as a tunnel-site is unwarranted and unprece-
dented, and was not, at the date of said pretended location, nor at any subsequent time, authorized by any
local, state, or congressional law.

The court below sustained the demurrer. The su-

[1] 127 U. S. 471, 8 Sup. Ct. Rep. 1214.

preme court of the United States, in reversing the judgment, held:—

(1) That the claim for five thousand feet in length
was void only as to the excess over three thousand feet;

(2) The tunnel location having been made prior to
the passage of the act of May 10, 1872, the rights flowing
therefrom are to be determined under the local rules and
customs in force at the time the location was made.

It is manifest that this decision sheds no light upon
the subject. We refer to it for the reason that in several
of the decisions heretofore cited it was stated that the
conclusions there reached were not opposed to the doctrine of the Glacier Mountain-Willis case. This is quite
true, for the simple reason that the questions which we
are now considering were not there involved, discussed,
or decided. But they were subsequently involved and
decided by the supreme court of the United States in the
case of Enterprise M. Co. *v.* Rico-Aspen M. Co.,[1] and
the doctrine finally settled to the following effect, as
stated in the *syllabus* to the opinion:—

"The clear import of the language of Rev. Stats., sec.
" 2320, is to give to a tunnel-owner discovering a vein
" in the tunnel a right to appropriate fifteen hundred
" feet in length on that vein; which right arises upon
" the discovery of the vein in the tunnel; dates by rela-
" tion back to the time of the location of the tunnel-site;
" may be exercised by locating the claim the full length
" of fifteen hundred feet on either side of the tunnel or
" in such proportion thereof on either side as the locator
" may desire; and is not destroyed or impaired by the
" failure of the owner of the tunnel to adverse a pre-
" vious application for a surface patent before the dis-
" covery of the vein."

§ 490. **Opinions of the land department.**—We note
the following views expressed by the land department:—

[1] 167 U. S. 108, 17 Sup. Ct. Rep. 762.

(1) A claim under a tunnel location is a mining claim, and the locator should adverse a junior application for patent for a lode within its claimed limits;[1]

(2) Prospecting for lodes not previously known to exist is prohibited on the line of the tunnel (*i. e.* the width of the tunnel bore) while work on the tunnel is being prosecuted with reasonable diligence;[2]

(3) In no case can a tunnel proprietor record a claim so as to absorb the actual or constructive possession of other parties, on a lode which had been discovered and claimed outside the *line* of the tunnel before the discovery thereof in the tunnel.[3]

Necessarily, these views are now obsolete, in the light of the rulings of the supreme court of the United States heretofore noted.

§ 490a. **Rights of junior tunnel locator as against senior mining claims on the line of the tunnel.**—There should be little room for the discussion of this question. No subsequent mining location of any kind can impair rights vested under prior locations. And yet it has been contended that one who locates a tunnel claim has the right to drive through property covered by a senior location. In other words, it has been claimed that the grant of a mining claim is accompanied by the implied right of way through it in the interest of a junior tunnel locator, or that state statutes may impose such a burden on prior claims.

As to these contentions, Judge Lunt, in deciding the

[1] Secretary Kirkwood, Bodie Tunnel and M. Co. *v.* Bechtel Cons., 1 L. D. 584.

[2] Commissioner Williamson, *In re* David Hunter, Copp's Min. Lands, 231.

[3] Commissioner Drummond's letter to Chaffee, Copp's Min. Dec. 144. See, also, Corning Tunnel Co. *v.* Pell, 3 Copp's L. O. 130. We have heretofore noted the decisions of this department defining the *line* of the tunnel to be the width of the bore. *Ante,* § 473.

leading cross-lode case of Ajax Gold Mining Company
v. Calhoun Gold Mining Company, thus expressed his
views:—

" The Revised Statutes of the United States do not
" give the tunnel locator any such right, but negative
" any such assumption. A patent to a lode claim grants
" all veins whose tops, or apexes, are within the side-
" lines of the claim, etc., to the lode claim, whether they
" are known or not; hence no discovery of them on sub-
" sequently located ground can be made. There may be a
" vague notion that the right to penetrate a lode claim
" by a tunnel may have existed, and it may have been
" done many times heretofore with or without the
" permission of the owner, but it is idle to pretend that
" any such custom has ripened into law. . . . I do not
" think the tunnel can penetrate the plaintiff's
" claims." [1]

The supreme court of Colorado, in affirming Judge
Lunt's decision, held that under the statutes the subsequent locator has no right to penetrate a senior valid
subsisting location underneath its surface boundaries
extended downwardly, except for the purposes specified
in the mining laws, and that these exceptions do not
include a right to drive a tunnel through such a location
for the purposes of discovery.[2] This rule received the
approval of the supreme court of the United States.[3]

The owner of a location holding the apex of a vein
may enter the land adjoining in the exercise of the extralateral right, but in doing so he must follow the vein on
its downward course. He has no right to approach and
work the vein through crosscut tunnels run underneath
such adjoining lands.[4]

As to the validity of state statutes purporting to grant

[1] 1 Leg. Adv., 426, 429.

[2] Calhoun G. M. Co. v. Ajax G. M. Co., 27 Colo. 1, 83 Am. St. Rep. 17,
59 Pac. 607, 618.

[3] Id., 182 U. S. 499, 21 Sup. Ct. Rep. 885.

[4] St. Louis M. and M. Co. v. Montana M. Co. Ltd., 113 Fed. 900.

a right of way to junior tunnel locators, Judge Lunt, in the opinion above referred to, observed, in speaking of a Colorado statute which had been held not to be in force, that even if it were in force a grave question arises whether a lode claim granted by the United States could be burdened with such an inchoate easement by a state legislature.

There is a law now upon the statute-books of Colorado which attempts to confer the right upon a tunnel-owner to drive his tunnel through and across any located or patented claim in front of the mouth of such tunnel.[1] Idaho has a similar statute.[2]

This class of legislation is unquestionably unconstitutional. It is the taking of private property for a private use, and that without purporting to provide any compensation therefor.

The Colorado statute has been declared unconstitutional by Judge Hallett.[3]

We think it quite well settled that easements and rights of way may be acquired over the public domain, but after it passes into private ownership no such rights can be asserted, except for public purposes, or possibly for limited private uses, if provided for by the state constitution. In such cases, unless consent is obtained, condemnation proceedings are necessary.[4]

So far as the question under consideration involves the exercise of the right of eminent domain, we have heretofore fully presented it.[5] Some reference to it

---

[1] Act of April 17, 1897, Laws of Colo. 1897, pp. 181, 182.

[2] Civ. Code (1901), §§ 2575, 2578; Laws of 1899, pp. 653, 654.

[3] Cone v. Roxana G. M. and T. Co., 2 Leg. Adv. 350; Stratton v. Gold Sovereign M. Co., 1 Leg. Adv. 350; Portland G. M. Co. v. Uinta Tunnel M. and T. Co., 1 Leg. Adv. 494; Matoa G. M. Co. v. Chicago and Cripple Creek G. M. Co., vol. 78, Mining and Scientific Press, p. 379.

[4] See Judge Lunt's opinion in Ajax G. M. Co. v. Calhoun G. M. Co., 1 Leg. Adv. 426, 429; St. Louis M. and M. Co. v. Montana Limited, 113 Fed. 900.

[5] *Ante*, §§ 252-264.

will again be made in presenting the cross-lode questions.[1]

§ 491. Inquiries suggested in the light of rules thus far enunciated by the supreme court of the United States as to the extent of the rights of a tunnel locator on a vein discovered in the tunnel.—It is, as we have seen, now settled that the tunnel locator is entitled to fifteen hundred linear feet on the vein discovered in the tunnel, measured from the discovery in such direction as the locator may designate by a notice posted at the mouth of the tunnel. That he may drift along the vein from the tunnel level to the linear extent and in the direction claimed is now unquestioned. What are his rights in depth? Is he to be confined within rectangular planes, as, it is asserted, was the rule under the act of 1866,[2] or within planes parallel to the tunnel bore? May he fix end-lines arbitrarily, or has he the right to follow the vein downward at all?

If the tunnel law stands alone, there is no express grant of the extralateral right. This right, so far as lodes located at the surface are concerned, is granted by section twenty-three hundred and twenty-two of the Revised Statutes, which is neither adopted by nor referred to in the tunnel laws. Moreover, the right as defined in section twenty-three hundred and twenty-two is limited to locations having the tops, or apexes, of discovered veins within a surface location, and is confined within end-line planes marked at the surface. The only section of the mining laws to which the tunnel sections refer is twenty-three hundred and twenty, and this last-named section is held by the courts to apply only with regard to the length on the lode.[3] If any right to follow the vein downward is

[1] *Post,* §§ 557-561.
[2] *Post,* § 576.
[3] Enterprise M. Co. *v.* Rico-Aspen M. Co., 66 Fed. 201.

to be exercised by the tunnel claimant, the courts will be compelled to define the limitations without any reference to the remaining sections of the Revised Statutes, and without resort to any previous miners' rules and customs, as none such ever existed. From what source will they seek light? Will not an effort to either recognize or define this right to follow the vein in its downward course be amenable to the criticism of judicial legislation? As no surface-marking of the claim on the lode discovered in the tunnel is required, the entire body of the mining law touching the apex and the extralateral right predicated upon end-lines crossing the apex of the lode at the surface is eliminated from consideration, and it would seem that the courts are practically left without guide or compass.

It is conceded that no patent can issue for a claim on a lode without inclosing such claim on the surface within surface boundaries. Herein we have confirmation of the suggestion that blind lodes discovered in a tunnel must be relegated to a category by themselves. The general body of the mining laws does not apply to them. What, then, becomes of the extralateral right?

The suggestion offered by the supreme court of the United States, in its opinion in the Ellet-Campbell case,[1] that there would be no impropriety in marking a location on the surface perpendicularly overlying the underground discovery, might be of practical advantage in the solution of some of the problems here discussed, if the surface location as marked fortuitously included the apex of the vein, which, for obvious reasons, in nine cases out of ten it would not. A surface location on the dip of the vein, although having priority, would not confer extralateral rights. If the rights under such a location are to be defined with reference to the general body of the mining law, they would be subordinated to

[1] 167 U. S. 116, 119, 17 Sup. Ct. Rep. 765.

the rights of a junior location properly covering the apex.

There is still another suggestion which presents increased difficulties. Could the tunnel locator, with his linear claim on the lode discovered in the tunnel, follow that vein upward? If so, how far and within what planes? There is no law which sanctions the following of a vein on its upward course. Let us illustrate some of these inquiries by the use of a diagram.

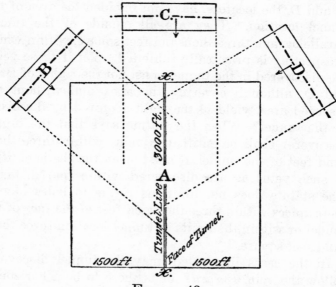

FIGURE 43.

A locates a tunnel-site on the line $x-x$, starting at the base of the mountain, and perfects his location prior to the surface discoveries and locations indicated by B, C, and D on the crest of the mountain. The veins of these surface locations—any one of them may be singled out for illustrative purposes—dip in the direction of the tunnel, as indicated by the arrows and extended endline planes. It is probable, perhaps inevitable, that each one of these veins will, on its downward course, intersect the plane of the tunnel bore, and it requires no stretch of the imagination to assume that at some point, as the tunnel is driven into the hill, it may cut one or all of these veins. What will be the rights of the parties? The angle at which the tunnel must intersect these veins is not specified in the law. Nor does the law specify in terms that the apex of the vein must cross the line of the tunnel. In discovering and locating the claims B, C, and D, the locators, have not invaded the area of the tunnel location. They are all outside of the tunnel parallelogram, three thousand feet square, within which prospecting is practically inhibited. Yet if these veins are discovered in the tunnel, must not the rights of B, C, and D, although covering the apex and without the reserved area, yield to the right acquired by discovery in the tunnel? When the statute says that the tunnel discoverer shall be entitled to veins within three thousand feet of the tunnel, it must mean that he is entitled to such veins as are discovered within that distance. The statute does not limit his rights to lodes having their apices within three thousand feet of the face of the tunnel or within the limits of tunnel location three thousand feet square.

In the cases illustrated, may the tunnel discoverer follow the vein *upward?* or is there to be a horizontal partition between the tunnel locator and the mining claimants of B, C, and D?

CHAPTER V.

COAL LANDS.

ARTICLE I. INTRODUCTORY.
II. MANNER OF ACQUIRING TITLE TO COAL LANDS.

ARTICLE I. INTRODUCTORY.

§ 495. Classification of coal as a mineral—History of legislation—Characteristics of the system.

§ 496. Rules for determining character of land.

§ 497. Geographical scope of the coal-land laws.

§ 495. Classification of coal as a mineral—History of legislation—Characteristics of the system.—As observed in a previous section,[1] prior to the passage of the coal land act of July 1, 1864, the land department did not regard coal as a mineral within the meaning of the prior legislation of congress, yet this substance, although essentially of vegetable origin, has, generally speaking, been classified as mineral, as it came within the etymological signification of the term, being obtained from underground excavations or "mines."[2]

The act above referred to[3] was the first legislation by congress providing a method for the disposal of coal lands. It was followed in the succeeding year by a supplemental act,[4] and in 1873 congress passed a law which is the basis of the existing system.[5]

Whatever may have been the rule as to the classification of coal lands prior to the passage of the act of 1864,

[1] *Ante*, § 140.
[2] *Ante*, § 88.
[3] 13 Stats. at Large, p. 343.

[4] March 3, 1865, 13 Stats. at Large, p. 529.
[5] Rev. Stats., §§ 2347, 2352.

Lindley on M.—54

since that date they are classified as mineral by legislative construction.[1]

As heretofore noted,[2] lands containing coal are not, as a rule, excepted from the operation of the railroad grants,[3] nor are they considered by the department as lands subject to "mineral entry" within the meaning of the act of June 3, 1878,[4] granting the privilege of cutting timber upon so much of the public domain in certain states as is subject to mineral entry.[5]

Coal lands are mineral lands within the meaning, generally, of the laws relating to the public lands.[6] They may not be selected in lieu of lands in forest reserves.[7] But when found within forest reserves they are subject to appropriation the same as other mineral lands.[8]

It will serve no useful purpose to retrace the history of congressional legislation on this subject. The coalland laws form a system peculiar to themselves, having nothing in common with the general mining laws, and strictly speaking, are not *in pari materia*. The ownership and possession of this class of public lands were never subject to regulation by local rules and customs, and from the passage of the first act in relation to them to the present time the method of acquiring title to them has been simple, and unaccompanied by the perplexities that have arisen in the administration of the laws relative to lands containing lodes and placers. Such questions as have arisen in reference to coal have been adjudicated entirely within the land department. No

---

[1] United States *v.* Mullan, 7 Saw. 466, 10 Fed. 785, S. C. on appeal, 118 U. S. 271, 6 Sup. Ct. Rep. 1041; *In re* Crowder, 30 L. D. 92, 95; Brown *v.* Northern Pac. R. R. Co., 31 L. D. 29.

[2] *Ante,* § 152.

[3] See Rocky Mountain C. and I. Co., 1 Copp's L. O. 1.

[4] 20 Stats. at Large, p. 88.

[5] Instructions to Timber Agents, 2 L. D. 827.

[6] Brown *v.* Northern Pac. R. R. Co., 31 L. D. 29.

[7] *Id.*

[8] *In re* Crowder, 30 L. D. 92, 95.

controversies arising out of the proper construction of these laws are, in the process of obtaining title, relegated to the courts for determination. The coal-land system, like that applicable to homestead, pre-emption, and other agricultural entries, is administered by the executive department of the government. For this reason we note the almost total absence of judicial decisions upon the subject, and must look exclusively to the land department for the rules of interpretation.

§ 496. **Rules for determining character of land.**— While the system prescribing the method for obtaining title to lands containing coal is different from that applicable to other mineral lands, the rules for determining whether or not a given tract is subject to entry under the coal-land laws are analogous to those applicable to other classes of mineral deposits.[1]

They may be thus formulated with special reference to coal:—

(1) All classes of coal deposits, whether anthracite, bituminous, lignite, or cannel, are embraced within the coal-land laws;[2]

(2) It must be shown that as a present fact the land is more valuable for the purpose of its coal product than for any other purpose;[3] that the substance exists therein in paying quantities,[4] or that it is sufficiently valuable to be worked as a mine.[5]

These facts must be shown by the actual production of coal,[6] or by satisfactory evidence that, taking the

---

[1] *Ante,* § 98.

[2] Sickle's Min. Dec., 397.

[3] Hamilton *v.* Anderson, 19 L. D. 168; Commrs. of Kings County *v.* Alexander, 5 L. D. 126.

[4] Smith *v.* Buckley, 15 L. D. 321.

[5] Jones *v.* Driver, 15 L. D. 514.

[6] Hamilton *v.* Anderson, 19 L. D. 168; Commrs. of Kings County *v.* Alexander, 5 L. D. 126.

tract as a whole, coal exists therein in sufficient quantities to make the same more valuable for mining than for agricultural purposes.[1]

The extent of the deposit may be shown by the testimony of geological experts and practical miners, taken in connection with the actual production of coal from some portion of the tract.[2]

In determining these facts, means of transportation cannot be taken into consideration as affecting the value of the coal shown to exist.[3]

That lands in the near vicinity,[4] or even those directly adjoining, are shown to contain coal,[5] is insufficient to establish the character of a tract upon which no coal has been developed.[6]

Mere outcroppings[7] or other surface indications will not, in the absence of proof of commercial value of the deposit, prevent the entry of such lands under the preemption or homestead laws.[8]

But it is not necessary to show actual development on each forty-acre subdivision,[9] nor upon all parts of a forty-acre tract.[10]

When, however, a conflict arises between an agricultural and coal claimant, the character of the land to the extent of the entire conflict area is involved, and, necessarily, proofs of a more specific character would be required than in the case of an *ex parte* application to enter under the coal laws.

[1] Mitchell *v.* Brown, 3 L. D. 65; Savage *v.* Boynton, 12 L. D. 612.

[2] Rucker *v.* Knisley, 14 L. D. 113.

[3] Smith *v.* Buckley, 15 L. D. 321.

[4] *In re* Williams, 11 L. D. 462; Scott *v.* Sheldon, 15 L. D. 361.

[5] Commrs. of Kings County *v.* Alexander, 5 L. D. 126; *In re* Archuleta, 15 Copp's L. O. 256.

[6] See, also, Dughi *v.* Harkins, 2 L. D. 721.

[7] Frees *v.* State of Colorado, 22 L. D. 510.

[8] Colorado Coal and Iron Co. *v.* United States, 123 U. S. 307.

[9] Hamilton *v.* Anderson, 19 L. D. 168; McWilliams *v.* Green River Coal Assn., 23 L. D. 127; Reed *v.* Nelson, 29 L. D. 615.

[10] State of Montana *v.* Buley, 23 L. D. 116.

The rules governing hearings to establish the character of lands are found in "General Land Office Regula-
" tions," issued October 31, 1881.[1]

The discovery of coal in paying quantities on land embraced within a homestead claim precludes the completion of the entry;[2] but discovery after purchase, under commuted homestead entry, will not defeat the issuance of the patent.[3]

§ 497. **Geographical scope of the coal-land laws.**—
The system regulating the pre-emption and sale of coal lands has substantially the same geographical scope as the general mining laws. It is in practical operation wherever coal is found in the precious-metal-bearing states and territories,[4] and in Arkansas, Mississippi, Louisiana, Florida, and in certain parts of Oklahoma.[5] As heretofore noted, Alabama,[6] Michigan, Minnesota, Wisconsin, Kansas, and Missouri[7] are excepted from the operation of the federal mining laws,[8] except as to the location of salines.[9]

The coal-land laws were extended to the district of Alaska by act of congress approved June 6, 1900.[10]

---

[1] 1 L. D. 688. See Appendix.

[2] Harnish v. Wallace, 13 L. D. 427; Dickinson v. Capen, 14 L. D. 426.

[3] Arthur v. Earle, 21 L. D. 92.

[4] Ante, § 81.

[5] Ante, § 81, note 1, pp. 96, 113.

[6] For method of acquiring coal lands in Alabama, see Circ. Instructions, 10 Copp's L. O. 54; In re Robert Lalley, Id. 55; In re Harris, 28 L. D. 90.

[7] Ante, § 20.

[8] Ante, § 81.

[9] Post, § 514a.

[10] 31 Stats. at Large, p. 658. See Circular, 30 L. D. 368, Appendix.

ARTICLE II.   MANNER OF ACQUIRING TITLE TO COAL
LANDS.

§ 501. Who may enter coal lands.

§ 502. Different classes of entries.

§ 503. Private entry under Revised
Statutes, section twenty-
three hundred and forty-
seven.

§ 504. Preferential right of purchase under Revised Stat-

utes, section twenty-three
hundred and forty-eight.

§ 505. The declaratory statement.

§ 506. Assignability of inchoate
rights.

§ 507. The purchase price.

§ 508. The final entry.

§ 509. Conclusions.

§ **501. Who may enter coal lands.**—Entries of coal
lands may be made by individuals or associations of
persons. In the case of an individual, he must be above
the age of twenty-one years and a citizen of the United
States, or he must have declared his intention to become
such.[1]

At one time, the department held that married women
could not make entry of this class of lands,[2] but this
construction of the law, which was manifestly erroneous,[3] is no longer followed.

An association of persons, as the term is used in the
coal-land laws, is uniformly construed by the department to include corporations; but each individual of
such association, whether incorporated or not, must
possess the requisite qualifications. The law expressly
so provides. The ownership, by one member of an association seeking to enter coal lands, of interests in other
lands claimed under the coal-land laws, disqualifies
the entire association.[4] The right to purchase coal
lands can be exercised but once.[5]

[1] Rev. Stats., § 2347.
[2] *In re* Nichol, 15 Copp's L. O. 255.
[3] *Ante*, § 224.
[4] *In re* Hawes, 5 L. D. 224; Kerr v. Utah-Wyoming I. Co., 2 L. D. 727.
[5] *In re* Kimball, 3 Copp's L. O. 50; *In re* Eiseman, 10 L. D. 539; *In re*
Dearden, 11 L. D. 351; *In re* Smith, 16 Copp's L. O. 112; *In re* Negus,
11 L. D. 32.

If an association of persons makes a coal entry embracing a less area than it might have applied for, such entry is a bar to a second one.[1] Where a valid reason therefor exists, such as may be instanced by a case where the applicant was unable to complete an asserted right by reason of successful adverse claims to the land sought to be entered,[2] or where the first filing was abandoned on account of the worthless character of the claim, the good faith of the entryman being apparent,[3] the cancellation of his declaratory statement would be without prejudice to a second application for other lands.

The rule applies, generally speaking, to those who have perfected their entries, or when the failure to complete the entry is the result of their own neglect.[4] The rule has no application to a case where one buys, and, prior to entry, sells a preferential right.[5]

A coal entry may be made by one qualified person for the benefit of another,[6] provided the latter is himself qualified and has not exhausted his privilege. An entry sought to be made by one for the benefit of a disqualified person,[7] or for one who, being originally qualified, has previous exhausted his rights,[8] or when made in the interest of a corporation or association of persons, some of whom are either disqualified or have once availed themselves of the privilege,[9] is a fraud upon the govern-

---

[1] *In re* Kimball, 3 Copp's L. O. 50.

[2] *In re* Eiseman, 10 L. D. 539; *In re* Dearden, 11 L. D. 351; Conner *v.* Terry, 15 L. D. 310.

[3] *In re* Burrell, 29 L. D. 328.

[4] *In re* Hutchings, 4 Copp's L. O. 142; *In re* John McMillan, 7 L. D. 181; *In re* Smith, 16 Copp's L. O. 112.

[5] *In re* McConnell, 18 L. D. 414.

[6] Lipscomb *v.* Nichols, 6 Colo. 290. See, also, Union Coal Co., 17 L. D. 351; *In re* Durango L. and C. Co., 18 L. D. 382; *In re* Allen, 8 L. D. 140.

[7] *In re* Adolph Peterson, 6 L. D. 371; Conner *v.* Terry, 15 L. D. 310.

[8] McGillicuddy *v.* Tompkins, 14 L. D. 633.

[9] United States *v.* Trinidad Coal and C. Co., 137 U. S. 160, 11 Sup. Ct. Rep. 57.

ment, and may be annulled upon proper proceedings in that behalf. Contracts whereby such a result is sought to be accomplished are contrary to public policy, and therefore void.[1]

However, an entry by an association of persons, all of whom are qualified at the date of entry, is not vitiated by the fact that at some point of time previously thereto one or more of them was disqualified.[2]

§ 502. **Different classes of entries.**—Coal lands are disposed of:—

(1) By ordinary private entry, under the provisions of section twenty-three hundred and forty-seven of the Revised Statutes;

(2) By pre-emption or preference right of purchase, under section twenty-three hundred and forty-eight.

The two classes of entries have the following features in common:—

(A) The persons or associations must possess the same qualifications;

(B) The purchase price to be paid upon final entry is the same;

(C) Final entries may only be made upon surveyed lands. There can be no segregation of fractional parts;[3]

(D) The tracts applied for must be contiguous.[4]

§ 503. **Private entry under Revised Statutes, section twenty-three hundred and forty-seven.**—The right to enter coal lands under section twenty-three hundred and

[1] Johnson v. Leonard, 1 Wash. 564, 20 Pac. 591.

[2] Kerr v. Utah-Wyoming Imp. Co., 2 L. D. 727; Kerr v. Carlton, 10 Copp's L. O. 255.

[3] Mitchell v. Brown, 3 L. D. 65; In re Cameron, 10 L. D. 195; In re Lyon, 20 L. D. 556.

[4] In re Masterson, 7 L. D. 172, S. C. on review, Id. 577; Kendall v. Hall, 12 L. D. 419.

forty-seven of the Revised Statutes may be exercised upon surveyed lands without previous occupation or improvement. Necessarily, the lands sought to be entered must be vacant, and otherwise unreserved and unappropriated. In other words, they must be public lands.[1] They may only be applied for by government subdivisions and in limited quantities; that is, an individual may not acquire to exceed one hundred and sixty acres, and an association of persons not to exceed three hundred and twenty acres.

To obtain title to lands under this section, the applicant is required to file with the register of the proper land office a verified application,[2] describing the lands sought to be purchased, his qualification under the law to make the entry, and such other facts as to the character and *status* of the land as will establish in the applicant a *prima facie* right of purchase.

If the land is clear on the tract-books, the register certifies the fact to the receiver, and the price is determined according to the rule announced in a subsequent section.[3] Payment must then be made, whereupon the final certificate is issued, and in due time the patent follows.

Private entry will not be allowed so as to embrace one tract in the capacity of an assignee, and another under the individual right of the purchaser.[4]

Until application is made to enter and purchase under this section, the claimant has no right which is worthy of recognition. His possession, if he has any, must yield to one who complies with the law and files upon the land.[5]

[1] *Ante*, § 112.
[2] See form in Circ. Instructions, 1 L. D. 688. See Appendix.
[3] *Post*, § 507.
[4] *In re* Ludlam, 17 L. D. 22.
[5] Leheart *v.* Dunker, 4 L. D. 522.

§ 504. **Preferential right of purchase under Revised Statutes, section twenty-three hundred and forty-eight.** —In order to exercise the preferential right of purchase granted by section twenty-three hundred and forty-eight, there are two essential prerequisites:—

(1) The applicant must be in the actual possession of the lands applied for;[1]

(2) He must, prior to final entry, have opened and improved the mines situated thereon.[2]

The improvements made must be such as to clearly indicate good faith.[3]

In determining what constitutes good faith, the applicant's degree and condition in life may be considered.[4]

Priority of possession and improvement, followed by proper filing and development of the mine in good faith, are the foundation of the preferential right.[5]

" The right to purchase coal lands is initiated by the " actual discovery of coal on the land and the perform- " ance of some act of improvement sufficient to give " notice to the world of an intent to purchase such lands " as coal lands. The right to purchase such lands can- " not be initiated by the filing of a declaratory statement " therefor.

" In case of conflicting claims to coal lands, the " preference right is determined not by the date of the " filing of the declaratory statement . . . but by prior- " ity of possession and improvement."[6]

This right may be exercised by an individual or an association of persons. When exercised by an individual, it is limited to one hundred and sixty acres, and

---

[1] *In re* Negus, 11 L. D. 32; Walker *v.* Taylor, 23 L. D. 110; McDaniel *v.* Bell, 9 L. D. 15.

[2] Walker *v.* Taylor, 23 L. D. 10; Ouimette *v.* O'Connor, 22 L. D. 538.

[3] *In re* Negus, 11 L. D. 32.

[4] Watkins *v.* Garner, 13 L. D. 414.

[5] Bullard *v.* Flanagan, 11 L. D. 515.

[6] Reed *v.* Nelson, 29 L. D. 615, 619.

when by an association of persons, ordinarily to three hundred and twenty acres. Entries by associations consisting of not less than four persons may, however, be extended to six hundred and forty acres, after they shall have expended not less than five thousand dollars in working and improving such mines.

The preferential right may be initiated by entering into possession and improving unsurveyed lands.[1] The right, however, may only be perfected after the lands shall have been surveyed and the township plat filed in the local land office.

§ 505. The declaratory statement.—If the preferential right is initiated upon surveyed lands, the claimant must present to the register of the proper land office, within sixty days after the date of actual possession, and the commencement of improvements upon the land, his declaratory statement of the facts upon which he bases his right. Where the lands upon which the right is initiated by occupation and development are unsurveyed, the time within which the declaratory statement is to be filed commences to run from the date the approved township plat is received at the local land office.[2] Failure to file this instrument within the time specified renders the land subject to entry by another, if he has complied with the law;[3] but in the absence of an adverse claimant, the right to complete the entry is not forfeited.[4]

A second filing for the same tract will not be allowed to one who has failed to comply with the law in the first instance.[5]

The statement must be verified by the oath of the ap-

[1] Holladay Coal Co. v. Kirker, 20 Utah, 192, 57 Pac. 882.
[2] Rev. Stats., § .2349.
[3] Brennan v. Hume, 10 L. D. 160; O'Gorman v. Mayfield, 19 L. D. 508.
[4] In re Grunsfeld, 10 L. D. 508.
[5] Id.

plicant. This duty cannot be delegated to others;[1] but after the same is filed, the subsequent acts required to complete the entry may be performed by a duly authorized agent, acting under a power of attorney.[2]

§ 506. **Assignability of inchoate rights.**—An inchoate right or privilege flowing from an accepted application or declaratory statement may be assigned to one who possesses the necessary legal qualifications;[3] but such assignment, if the assignee perfects the entry, would extinguish the right of both parties to purchase lands under the coal-land laws, and both would thereafter be disqualified from making further entries. However, the sale of an option to purchase which is not taken advantage of, does not disqualify a claimant to enter coal land.[4]

Where such assignments are made, the purchaser may avail himself of the improvement and development of his assignor.

§ 507. **The purchase price.**—The price fixed by law to be paid for coal lands depends upon the situation of the lands with respect to completed railroads.[5] If within fifteen miles of such road, the entryman must pay at the rate of twenty dollars per acre. If more than fifteen miles, ten dollars per acre. The distance from the road

---

[1] White Oaks Imp. Co., 13 Copp's L. O. 159; *In re* Hallowell, 2 L. D. 735.

[2] Rose *v.* Dineen, 26 L. D. 107; par. 34, Circ. Instructions (Coal Lands). See Appendix.

For forms of declaratory statements, and the manner of procedure generally, see the Coal Land Circular Instructions, which appear in full in the Appendix.

[3] Kerr *v.* Carlton, 10 Copp's L. O. 255; Guillet *v.* Durango Land and Coal Co., 26 L. D. 413; par 37, Circ. Instructions (Coal Lands). See Appendix.

[4] Reed *v.* Nelson, 29 L. D. 615.

[5] *In re* Foster, 2 L. D. 730.

(not the distance from the nearest shipping-point), is the test.[1]

The *status* of the land at the date of final proof and payment, with respect to this distance, determines the price thereof, irrespective of the *status* when the preference right is initiated or acquired.[2]

Where the land lies partly within fifteen miles and in part outside such limit, the maximum price must be paid for all legal subdivisions, the greater part of which lie within fifteen miles of such road.[3]

The term "completed railroad" is construed by the department to mean one which is actually constructed on the face of the earth.[4]

Final proofs must be made, and the lands must be paid for, within one year from the time prescribed for filing the respective claims. Upon failure to do so, the lands are subject to entry by any other qualified applicant.[5]

§ 508. **The final entry.**—Within the time fixed by the law, *i. e.* one year from filing the declaratory statement, the claimant must make his application to purchase, and submit proof showing compliance with the law. If there is no opposition, he is permitted to make entry and payment. If there are protests or adverse claims, a hearing is had, and the rights determined within the department.

§ 509. **Conclusions.**—It will be observed that the nature of the inchoate estate created by compliance with the coal laws bears a striking analogy to that conferred by the former agricultural pre-emption act. The same analogy exists as to proceedings to acquire the title.

[1] *In re* Conant, 29 L. D. 637.

[2] *In re* Colton, 10 L. D. 422; *In re* Largent, 13 L. D. 397; *In re* Burgess, 24 L. D. 11.

[3] Par. 14, Circ. Instructions (Coal Lands). See Appendix.

[4] Par. 15, *Id.*

[5] Rev. Stats., § 2350.

One essential difference, however, may be noted: A pre-emption claimant under the agricultural land laws could not assign his rights prior to final entry; a coal claimant may so assign at any stage of the proceedings.

The only feature in common between the coal-land system and the general mining laws is, that in both discovery is required as a condition precedent to the acquisition of title.

The extralateral right has no place in the coal laws. Although many coal veins occupy a more or less inclined position, the only class of entries allowed is by government subdivisions, and the entryman obtains title only to whatever lies within vertical planes drawn through his surface boundaries.

In the case of mining claims, certain prescribed work must be performed annually in order to perpetuate the estate acquired by location. A locator need never apply for a patent. Under the coal laws, no particular amount of expenditure is required, except where an association of not less than four persons seeks to enter six hundred and forty acres, when it is required that they must produce proof of improvements to the extent of five thousand dollars. A patent must be applied for within a year from the filing of the declaratory statement, in case of preferential rights, under section twenty-three hundred and forty-eight of the Revised Statutes. In the case of private entries under section twenty-three hundred and forty-seven, the first step is the application for patent.

As the regulations of the department on the subject of coal are clear and specific, it is not deemed necessary to enter further into the details. We think this and the preceding article present the salient features of the system, and are sufficiently comprehensive for all practical purposes.

CHAPTER VI.

SALINES.

§ 513. Governmental policy with reference to salines.

§ 514. The act of January 12, 1877—Territorial limit of its operation.

§ 514a. The act of January 31, 1901.

§ 515. What embraced within the term "salines."

§ 513. Governmental policy with reference to salines.
—Salt is essentially a mineral,[1] and salt lakes and salt springs legitimately fall within the designation of mineral substances.[2]

Prior to the passage of the act of January 31, 1901, to be hereafter referred to, lands of this character were classed by themselves, and were not subject to entry under any law operative throughout the public land states. The policy of the government since the acquisition of the Northwest territory and the inauguration of the federal land system, and until the passage of the act referred to, had been to reserve salines and salt springs from sale.[3] The object of this reservation was to preserve them for future states. A brief reference to the legislation in this behalf may be of historical value.

§ 514. The act of January 12, 1877—Territorial limit of its operation.—Some of the states, upon their admission to the union, received grants of a certain

[1] Garrard v. Silver Peak Mines, 82 Fed. 578, 589, S. C. on appeal, 94 Fed. 983; Eagle Salt Works, Copp's Min. Lands, 336.

[2] State v. Parker, 61 Tex. 265.

[3] Morton v. State of Nebraska, 21 Wall. 660; Salt Bluff Placer, 7 L. D. 549; Cole v. Markley, 2 L. D. 847; Southwestern M. Co., 14 L. D. 597; Garrard v. Silver Peak Mines, 82 Fed. 578, S. C. on appeal, 94 Fed. 983; In re Geissler, 27 L. D. 515; Oklahoma Territory v. Brooks, 29 L. D. 533; In re Territory of New Mexico, 31 L. D. 389; Hall v. Litchfield, Copp's Min. Lands, 333; Utah Salt Lands, 13 Copp's L. O. 53.

quantity of saline lands, to be selected usually within a stipulated time. Among these we note Oregon,[1] Colorado,[2] and Utah.[3]

Prior to the act of 1901, there was no authority for the disposal of lands chiefly valuable for their salt deposits or salt springs belonging to the United States, except the act of January 12, 1877.[4]

This act[5] provided for their sale at public auction at not less than one dollar and twenty-five cents per acre, or at private sale at the same minimum rate, in the event sales were not effected at public auction; but the operation of the act was confined to states which have had grants of salines which have been fully satisfied, or under which the right of selection might expire by efflux of time. The act, therefore, did not apply to the territories;[6] nor did it apply to Mississippi, Louisiana, California, Nevada,[7] North and South Dakota, Montana, Washington, Idaho, Utah,[8] or Wyoming, none of which received a grant of such lands.

This legislation, however, has been superseded by the act of January 31, 1901, which inaugurates a distinct change of policy.

§ 514a. The act of January 31, 1901.—On January 31, 1901, congress enacted the following law:—

[1] State of Oregon v. Jones, 24 L. D. 116.

[2] State of Colorado, 10 L. D. 222.

For list of the states admitted prior to 1877, see Hall v. Litchfield, 2 Copp's L. O. 179.

[3] 28 Stats. at Large, p. 107, § 8.

[4] Hall v. Litchfield, Copp's Min. Lands, 333; Salt Bluff Placer, 7 L. D. 549; Southwestern M. Co., 14 L. D. 597; In re Geissler, 27 L. D. 515.

[5] 19 Stats. at Large, p. 221.

[6] Utah Salt Lands, 13 Copp's L. O. 53; Circ. Instructions, Apr. 10, 1877, 4 Copp's L. O. 21; In re Geissler, 27 L. D. 515; Oklahoma Territory v. Brooks, 29 L. D. 533.

[7] Southwestern M. Co., 14 L. D. 597; Public Domain, 696.

[8] On Utah's admission as a state she received a donation of all saline lands within the state. 28 Stats. at Large, p. 107, § 8.

"That all unoccupied lands of the United States con-
" taining salt springs, or deposits of salt in any form,
" and chiefly valuable therefor, are hereby declared to
" be subject to location and purchase under the pro-
" visions of the law relating to placer mining claims;
" *provided,* that the same person shall not locate or
" enter more than one claim hereunder." [1]

Upon the passage of this act, the secretary of the interior promulgated the following circular instructions:—

"1. Under this act the provisions of the law relating
" to placer-mining claims are extended to all states and
" territories and the district of Alaska, so as to permit
" the location and purchase thereunder of all unoccu-
" pied public lands containing salt springs, or deposits
" of salt in any form, and chiefly valuable therefor, with
" the proviso, 'That the same person shall not locate or
" 'enter more than one claim hereunder.'

"2. Rights obtained by location under the placer min-
" ing laws are assignable and the assignee may make
" the entry in his own name; so, under this act, a person
" holding as assignee may make entry in his own name,
" *—provided,* he has not held under this act, at any
" time, either as locator, assignee or entryman, any
" other lands; his right is exhausted by having held
" under this act any particular tract, either as locator,
" assignee, or entryman, either as an individual or as a
" member of an association. It follows, therefore, that
" no application for patent or entry, made under this
" act, shall embrace more than one single location.

"3. In order that the conditions imposed by the pro-
" viso, as set forth in the above paragraph, may duly
" appear, the notice of location presented for record,
" the application for patent, and the application to pur-
" chase must each contain a specific statement under
" oath by each person whose name appears therein that
" he never has, either as an individual or as a member

<hr>

[1] 31 Stats. at Large, p. 745.

" of an association, located, applied for, entered, or held
" any other lands under the provisions of this act. As-
" signments made by persons who are not severally
" qualified as herein stated will not be recognized." [1]

Henceforward, except in such states as Utah, to which
all salt lands therein have been previously ceded, the
general mining laws applicable to the discovery and
location of placers apply, with one marked exception,
that the same person may not locate nor enter more than
one claim, thus placing the location of salt lands in this
behalf on the same plane with coal and homestead entries. The right to locate is exhausted by the entry of an
individual claim. The rules in this regard with reference to coal land apply by analogy to some extent at least.

This act would from its phraseology seem to be operative in the states which have heretofore been excepted
from the operation of the general mining laws,—viz.,
Michigan, Minnesota, Wisconsin, Missouri, Kansas, and
Alabama.[2] In other words, the general mining laws, so
far as they are applicable to the appropriation of saline
lands, are in force in all the public land states and the
continental territories enumerated in a previous section,[3] wherein there are unoccupied public lands of the
United States containing salt springs or deposits of salt
in any form.

§ 515. **What embraced within term " salines."**—Deposits of rock salt fall within the designation of salines,
as do salt springs and salt beds,[4] although Commissioner McFarland entertained the view that a *ledge* of
rock salt might be located under the lode laws.[5]

[1] 31 L. D. 131.
[2] *Ante*, § 75.
[3] *Ante*, § 20. Circulars, Nov. 14, 1901, 31 L. D. 130, 131.
[4] Southwestern M. Co., 14 L. D. 597.
[5] In re Megarrigle, 9 Copp's L. O. 113.

This we think would now be the rule [1] were it not for the express language of the statute which provides for the location of salt deposits under the provisions of the law applicable to placers.[2]

As to other so-called mineral springs, Secretary Noble expressed an opinion, which is probably a mere *dictum*, that they also should be classified as salines; [3] but Secretary Teller ruled that lands containing mineral springs not of a saline character are subject to sale under the agricultural land laws.[4]

Sulphur springs are not regarded as saline.[5]

Tracts of land returned by the surveyor-general as saline may be shown to be agricultural in character, and will then be subject to entry under the agricultural land laws.[6] In other words, the return of the surveyor-general concludes no one.[7]

The act of January 31, 1901, provides that salt springs, or *deposits of salt in any form,* and chiefly valuable therefor, are subject to appropriation as placers.[8]

[1] *Ante,* § 323.

[2] *Ante,* § 514a.

[3] Southwestern M. Co., 14 L. D. 597.

[4] Pagosa Springs, 1 L. D. 562. See, also, Morrill *v.* Margaret M. Co., 11 L. D. 563.

[5] Commissioners' Letter, Copp's Min. Dec. 22.

[6] Cole *v.* Markley, 2 L. D. 847.

[7] *Ante,* § 106.

[8] 31 Stats. at Large, p. 745.

CHAPTER VII.

MILLSITES.

§ 519. The law relating to millsites.

§ 520. Different classes of mill-sites.

§ 521. Right to millsite—How initiated.

§ 522. Location of millsite with reference to lode.

§ 523. Nature of use required in case of location by lode proprietor.

§ 524. Millsites used for quartz-mill or reduction-works disconnected with lode ownership.

§ 525. Location of junior lode claims conflicting with senior millsites.

§ 519. **The law relating to millsites.** —Millsites, while they are frequently important accessions to mining rights, occupy a relatively subordinate position in the federal mining system. Prior to the passage of the mining laws, they, in common with many other privileges asserted on the public domain, were regulated exclusively by neighborhood customs and local rules, not necessarily under the name of millsites, but as surface adjuncts to located lodes.

Until the act of May 10, 1872, was passed, there was no law by which title to them could be obtained. Section fifteen of that act provided a method, which is perpetuated in section twenty-three hundred and thirty-seven of the Revised Statutes. This section is as follows:—

" Where non-mineral land not contiguous to the vein " or lode is used or occupied by the proprietor of such " vein or lode for mining or milling purposes, such " non-adjacent surface-ground may be embraced and " included in an application for a patent for such vein

" or lode, and the same may be patented therewith, sub-
" ject to the same preliminary requirements as to sur-
" vey and notice as are applicable to veins or lodes;
" but no location hereafter made of such non-adjacent
" land shall exceed five acres, and payment for the same
" must be made at the same rate as fixed by this chapter
" for the superficies of the lode. The owner of a quartz-
" mill or reduction works not owning a mine in con-
" nection therewith may also receive a patent for his
" millsite, as provided in this section."

§ 520. **Different classes of millsites.**—It will thus be
observed that the law divides patentable millsites into
two classes:—

(1) Such as are used and occupied by the proprietor
of a vein or lode for mining or milling purposes;

(2) Such as have thereon quartz-mills or reduction
works, the ownership of which is disconnected with the
ownership of a lode or vein.[1]

The limit as to area and price per acre is the same in
both classes, and the requirement that the lands embraced therein shall be non-mineral, applies equally to
each class.

There is nothing to prevent one owning several lode
claims from selecting a millsite for each one, provided
that each is actually occupied and used for mining or
milling purposes in connection with the lode to which
it is appurtenant.

It has been held that a lode proprietor may select
more than one tract, if the aggregate does not exceed
five acres,[2] provided, of course, that each tract is used
for mining and milling purposes in connection with the
lode.

[1] Rico Townsite, 1 L. D. 556; Hartman *v.* Smith, 7 Mont. 19, 14 Pac.
648; Hamburg M. Co. *v.* Stephenson, 17 Nev. 449, 30 Pac. 1088.

[2] *In re* J. B. Haggin, 2 L. D. 755.

There is no provision of law by which a millsite can be acquired as additional to, or in connection with, an existing millsite.[1]

§ 521. Right to millsite—How initiated.—The statute is silent as to the manner of locating millsites, but it is not unreasonable to suppose that a location thereof must be made substantially as that of a mining claim.[2] This is the universal practice throughout the mining regions, and this practice is recognized by the land department [3] and the courts.[4]

Some of the states have enacted laws prescribing the manner of locating millsites. Montana,[5] Nevada,[6] and Utah [7] have passed laws providing for the posting and recording of notices; Nevada and Utah also requiring the boundaries to be marked, the former with the same formality as in the case of placer claims, and the latter so that the boundaries thereof can be readily traced.

The mere location of a millsite does not of itself segregate the land from the body of the public domain. A right to be recognized must be based upon possession and use.[8]

Where the land is not in actual use, the claimant must show such an occupation, by improvements or otherwise, as evidences an intended use of the tract in good faith for mining and milling purposes.[9]

Mere intention or purpose on a certain contingency of

---

[1] Hecla Consolidated M. Co., 12 L. D. 75.

[2] Rico Townsite, 1 L. D. 556.

[3] Hargrove v. Robertson, 15 L. D. 499; In re George, 2 Copp's L. O. 114.

[4] Hartman v. Smith, 7 Mont. 19, 14 Pac. 648.

[5] Rev. Pol. Code, 1895, §§ 3610, 3612.

[6] Comp. Laws of 1900, §§ 222-225.

[7] Laws of 1899, p. 26, §§ 2, 3, 4, 10.

[8] Rico Townsite, 1 L. D. 556.

[9] Two Sisters Lode and Millsite, 7 L. D. 557; In re Lenning, 5 L. D. 190.

performing acts of use, or occupation thereon, will not satisfy the law.[1]

It is unnecessary to remark that the tract sought to be obtained for millsite purposes must not only be non-mineral,[2] but it must also be upon the unoccupied, unreserved, and unappropriated domain. As lands not mineral in character may be selected under various laws, the right to appropriate them for millsite purposes cannot be exercised if any lawful possession is held by others. Therefore, millsites may not be selected on lands within the limits of railroad grants after the line of the road has been definitely fixed,[3] nor within the limits of any valid, subsisting agricultural or other holding. As between millsite and agricultural claimants, the rights of the parties are determined by priority of possession.[4]

§ 522. Location of millsite with reference to lode.— As to the requirement that the land selected for millsite purposes should be non-contiguous to the *lode,* it has uniformly been held by the land department that land contiguous to the surface ground of a lode claim was not within the prohibition named. Millsites may abut against the side-lines of a lode claim if the land is non-mineral.[5] Ordinarily, they cannot adjoin the end-lines,[6] upon the theory that the lode will be presumed to cross these lines, and must, to some extent at least, exist in

[1] Ontario S. M. Co., 13 Copp's L. O. 159.

[2] Rico Townsite, 1 L. D. 556; Alta Millsite, 8 L. D. 195; Patterson Quartz Mine, 4 Copp's L. O. 3; Copp's Min. Dec. 129; Cleary *v.* Skiffich, 28 Colo. 362, 65 Pac. 60.

[3] Mongrain *v.* N. P. R. R., 18 L. D. 105; Copp's Min. Dec., 147.

[4] Sierra Grande M. Co. *v.* Crawford, 11 L. D. 338; Adams *v.* Simmons, 16 L. D. 181; *In re* Moore, 11 Copp's L. O. 326.

[5] In re Freeman, 7 Copp's L. O. 4.

[6] *Id.; In re* Long, 9 Copp's L. O. 188.

the adjacent ground beyond them.[1] But as the character of the land is always a question of fact, if it should be determined that the tract contiguous to the end-lines is in fact non-mineral, there is no objection to appropriating it for millsite purposes.[2]

§ 523. **Nature of use required in case of location by lode proprietor.**—The statute does not mention any particular mining purpose for which a millsite, selected by a lode proprietor, shall be used. If used in good faith for any mining purpose at all in connection with a quartz lode, such use would be within the meaning of the statute.[3]

The erection on the tract of a cabin, using the same for storage of tools and supplies, and ores in small quantities, has been held to be within the intent of the law.[4]

It has been said that using land for deposit of tailings, or storing ores, or for shops or houses for workmen;[5] for collecting water to supply motive power for a quartz-mill,[6] or for pumping works,[7] or for obtaining water for use in developing the mine,[8] might be considered proper uses in connection with a located lode.

But land cannot be entered as a millsite simply be-

[1] See Mabel Lode, 26 L. D. 675; Paul Jones Lode (on review), 31 L. D. 359.

[2] National Mining and Exploring Co., 7 Copp's L. O. 179; *In re* Long, 9 Copp's L. O. 188.

[3] Hartman v. Smith, 7 Mont. 19, 14 Pac. 648; Silver Peak Mines v. Valcalda, 79 Fed. 886, S. C. on appeal, 86 Fed. 90.

[4] *Id.* See, also, Eclipse Millsite, 22 L. D. 496.

[5] Satisfaction Extension Millsite, 14 L. D. 173; *In re* Lenning, 5 L. D. 190.

[6] *Id.* But see, *contra,* Peru Lode and Millsite, 10 L. D. 196.

[7] Sierra Grande M. Co. v. Crawford, 11 L. D. 338.

[8] Gold Springs and Denver City Millsite, 13 L. D. 175. See Silver Star Millsite, 25 L. D. 165; Valcalda v. Silver Peak Mines, 86 Fed. 90.

cause it has timber growing thereon, which is valuable
for use on a located lode claim,[1] although the millsite
locator may cut the timber growing on the millsite for
the purpose of constructing his mill thereon.[2]

The department has permitted the entry of ground
for dumpage purposes in tracts of greater area than
five acres,[3] on the theory that it was necessary for use
in connection with mining, the land being more valuable
for that purpose than any other; but this seems to us
an unwarranted interpretation of the law. If ground
on which tailings are deposited may be entered as a
millsite, dumpage grounds may also be entered for like
reasons. It is quite clear that unless they may be entered under the millsite laws for this purpose, they cannot be entered at all.[4]

The fact that the lode claim in connection with which
the millsite is used is patented is immaterial. A millsite may be appurtenant to a patented as well as an
unpatented claim, and patent for the millsite may subsequently be applied for separately.[5]

§ 524. **Millsites used for quartz-mill or reduction
works disconnected with lode ownership.** —The right to
patent a millsite under the last clause of section twenty-
three hundred and thirty-seven of the Revised Statutes
depends upon the existence on the land of a quartz-mill
or reduction works.[6]

While the nature of the use required in case of the

[1] Two Sisters Lode and Millsite, 7 L. D. 557.
[2] *In re* Page, 1 L. D. 614.
[3] 4 Copp's L. O. 102.
[4] See *In re* Burton, 29 L. D. 235.
[5] Eclipse Millsite, 22 L. D. 496.
[6] *In re* Lenning, 5 L. D. 190; *In re* Cyprus Millsite, 6 L. D. 706; Two
Sisters Lode and Millsite, 7 L. D. 557; Le Neve Millsite, 9 L. D. 460;
Brodie Gold Reduction Co., 29 L. D. 143; Cleary *v.* Skiffich, 28 Colo. 362,
65 Pac. 59.

appropriation of a millsite as an adjunct to a located lode is not specified, and the law is satisfied so long as the purposes are reasonably associated with the lode to which it is appurtenant, in the case of sites selected under the last clause of section twenty-three hundred and thirty-seven, the character of the use is distinctly specified. The right to a patent for a millsite under this clause depends upon the presence *on the land sought to be patented* of a quartz-mill or reduction works.[1]

Land not improved or occupied for mining or milling purposes may not be appropriated as a millsite for the purpose of securing the use of water thereon.[2]

Water rights upon the public domain may not be acquired under the millsite laws.

Reservoirs, dams, and plants for generating power do not fall within the designation of quartz-mills and reduction works.[3]

§ 525.   **Location of junior lode claims conflicting with senior millsites.**—We have heretofore observed that junior lode locators enjoy the privilege of placing the lines of their locations upon or across lands which have previously been appropriated by others whether mineral or non-mineral.[4]

The enunciation of this principle, however, has been accompanied by another,—that is, that the junior locator cannot by this method of placing his boundaries infringe upon or impair the rights acquired by the prior appropriator. This last principle is of undoubted application to patented millsites, as the issuance of a patent con-

---

[1] Brodie Gold Reduction Co., 29 L. D. 143.

[2] *In re* Cyprus Millsite, 6 L. D. 706; Mint Lode and Millsite, 12 L. D. 624.

[3] Le Neve Millsite, 9 L. D. 460; *In re* Lenning, 5 L. D. 190; Two Sisters Lode and Millsite, 7 L. D. 557.

[4] *Ante,* §§ 363, 363a.

clusively presumes that the land covered by it is non-mineral.[1] But suppose it is discovered at any time after the location of the millsite and prior to the issuance of a patent therefor that the land embraced within it contains the apex of a discovered vein,—may a junior lode locator place his lines within the millsite boundary so as to deprive the millsite owner of that part of the tract embraced within the junior lode location? Under the placer laws a lode discovered within the limits of the prior placer claim might, by a peaceable entry in good faith on the surface of the placer, be located by a junior lode claimant, with surface ground of the width of fifty feet,[2] and to this extent the rights of the prior placer claimant must yield. But there is no such provision with reference to millsites or other class of non-mineral land. It is quite well settled, we think, that if at any time prior to the issuance of the patent for a millsite, the land is shown to be mineral in character, no patent therefor can issue, and the jurisdiction of the land department continues for the purpose of investigating the character of the land until a patent is issued. Under this state of facts, the question arises, as between a prior millsite claimant and a conflicting junior lode locator who attempts to embrace within a lode location the apex of a previously discovered vein,—would the inquiry as to the character of the land be addressed to its known quality at the date of the millsite location, and thus preclude the junior lode locator from acquiring any rights against the millsite claimant, or would the discovery of the vein within the millsite at any time prior to its passing to patent, render the vein subject to location by one entering peaceably and in good faith for that purpose?

[1] *Post*, § 779.   [2] *Ante*, § 415.

The supreme court of Colorado is of the opinion that the inquiry as to the character of the land must be addressed to its known condition at the time the millsite locator's rights attached,—that is, the date upon which he took the first step in the series which culminated in the perfection of the location. Unless at that date the millsite area contained deposits which were then known to be valuable, and which could be worked at a profit, the junior lode claimant could not acquire any rights as against the millsite claimant.[1]

There is much to be said in favor of this rule, but it seems to us that it is not in harmony with the rule applied in cases of railroad grants,[2] homestead and pre-emption filings,[3] as well as townsite and placer claims. If lands within a millsite location could not be patented when they are discovered to be mineral, why should the millsite claimant be permitted to hold them under a law which interdicts the acquisition by millsite title of mineral lands? There is no presumption arising from a mere location that lands embraced within it are of a given character. If the return of the surveyor-general shows the land to be non-mineral, the presumption that it is of this character is only *prima facie,* and it is subject to contestation.[4]

Perhaps it would be the safer rule, and more in harmony with equitable considerations, to hold that when any claimant initiated an inchoate right to a tract of the public non-mineral land no discovery of mineral subsequent to the taking of the first step in the series of acts which might ultimately culminate in a final entry or patent should defeat the right of the non-mineral appropriator. But clearly this is not the rule followed by the executive department, as we have heretofore noted.

---

[1] Cleary *v.* Skiffich, 28 Colo. 362, 65 Pac. 59.
[2] *Ante,* §§ 154, 156.
[3] *Ante,* §§ 205-206.
[4] *Ante,* § 106.

CHAPTER VIII.

EASEMENTS.

§ 529. Scope of the chapter.

§ 530. Rights of way for ditches and canals—Highways.

§ 531. Location subject only to pre-existing easements.

§ **529. Scope of the chapter.**—It is not our present purpose to deal with that class of easements and privileges which are created by the acts of individuals, nor with those which are necessarily appurtenant to all land acquired and held in private ownership. The scope of this chapter is limited to a consideration of those burdens which the government permits to be imposed upon its public lands, and subject to which it subsequently conveys its title.

§ **530. Rights of way for ditches and canals—Highways.**—During the early period of mining in the west, a system was established by common consent, enabling the miner, in connection with his located mining claim, to exercise certain privileges with respect to the means of working it. Water was essential; therefore, the right to appropriate it, divert it from its natural channel, and conduct it over the public lands by means of flumes and ditches to the place of intended use, became fully recognized and established.

The government was not consulted in this matter, but it passively recognized these rights, as it did the larger privilege of extracting gold from the public mineral lands,[1] and by section nine of the act of July 26, 1866,

---

[1] *Ante,* § 45.

gave legislative sanction to the exercise of these asserted rights. The section is as follows:—

"That whenever, by priority of possession, rights to " the use of water for mining, agricultural, or manu- " facturing, or other purposes, have vested and accrued, " and the same are recognized and acknowledged by the " local customs, laws, and the decisions of courts, the " possessors and owners of such vested rights shall be " maintained and protected in the same, and the right " of way for the construction of ditches and canals for " the purposes aforesaid is hereby acknowledged and " confirmed; *provided, however,* that whenever, after " the passage of this act, any person or persons shall, " in the construction of any ditch or canal, injure or " damage the possession of any settler on the public " domain, the party committing such injury or damage " shall be liable to the party injured for such injury " or damage." [1]

This section was substantially re-enacted in the Revised Statutes. There are some verbal changes, but none affecting its substance or meaning.[2]

It has been contended, that this act only undertook to confirm and protect rights vested prior to its passage, and that it did not necessarily sanction the future acquisition of such privileges. The opinion of the supreme court of the United States in Broder *v.* Natoma Water Company [3] would appear to support this contention, but as was said by the supreme court of California,[4] in construing this opinion, the question was not before the court. The ditch there involved was completed in 1853, and therefore was clearly within the confirmatory clauses of the act.

---

[1] For acts of congress providing for rights of way for canals, ditches, oil pipe-lines, and reservoirs, and regulations thereunder, see 27 L. D. 200.

[2] Jennison *v.* Kirk, 98 U. S. 453, 456.

[3] 101 U. S. 274.

[4] Jacob *v.* Lorenz, 98 Cal. 332, 336, 33 Pac. 119.

The supreme court of Nevada in construing the section in question, after referring to its *"turbid* style," and "grammatical solecisms," says:—

"In its adoption there appear to have been three dis-
" tinct objects in view:—

" *First*—The confirmation of all existing water
" rights;

" *Second*—To grant the right of way over the public
" land to persons desiring to construct flumes or canals
" for mining or manufacturing purposes;

" *Third*—To authorize the recovery of damages by
" settlers on such land, against persons constructing
" such ditches or canals, for injuries occasioned
" thereby." [1]

The court adds:—

"That this section, granting rights of way over the
" public land to all who may desire to construct ditches
" or canals for mining or agricultural purposes, is
" about as clear and certain as the objects and purposes
" of the acts of congress usually are."

The supreme court of California coincides with the views of the supreme court of Nevada as to the scope and intent of the act under consideration.[2]

We have no intention of entering into a discussion of water rights generally, the manner of appropriating them, the purposes for which they may be acquired, or relative rights between such appropriators and riparian proprietors. As water may be the subject of appropriation under certain conditions for many useful purposes, other than as an adjunct to mining operations, and as there is nothing in the manner of perfecting such appropriation peculiar to this particular class of

---

[1] Hobart *v.* Ford, 6 Nev. 77. See, also, Barnes *v.* Sabron, 10 Nev. 217.
[2] Jacob *v.* Lorenz, 98 Cal. 332, 336, 33 Pac. 119; Lorenz *v.* Waldron, 96 Cal. 243, 31 Pac. 54; Jacob *v.* Day, 111 Cal. 571, 44 Pac. 243.

ventures, we shall not undertake to deal with it to any serious extent in this treatise.[1] The law of waters is too broad in its scope to permit its treatment in a collateral way. All that we expect to demonstrate in reference to it is, that mining locations made upon the public lands must be made subject to any easements theretofore lawfully acquired and subsisting, and held for the purposes of conducting water over them. That this is the settled law there can be no doubt.[2]

This is but the reannouncement of the early doctrine, that the miner who selects a piece of ground to work must take it as he finds it, subject to prior rights which have an equal equity, on account of an equal recognition from the sovereign power.[3]

As to highways, section twenty-four hundred and seventy-seven of the Revised Statutes grants the right of way for the construction of highways over public lands not reserved for public uses. A mining location made subsequent to the laying out of a public road crossing it would be subject to the public easement.[4] This is a general principle applicable to all lands acquired from the government.[5]

§ 531. Location subject only to pre-existing easements.—The right of the United States to grant easements and other limited rights on any portion of its public domain cannot be gainsaid, and subsequent pur-

---

[1] *Post,* § 838.

[2] Jacob *v.* Day, 111 Cal. 571, 44 Pac. 243; Rockwell *v.* Graham, 9 Colo. 36, 10 Pac. 284; Welch *v.* Garrett (Idaho), 51 Pac. 405.

[3] Irwin *v.* Phillips, 5 Cal. 140, 63 Am. Dec. 113; Logan *v.* Driscoll, 19 Cal. 623, 81 Am. Dec. 90; Stone *v.* Bumpus, 46 Cal. 218; Maffet *v.* Quine, 93 Fed. 347.

[4] Murray *v.* City of Butte, 7 Mont. 61, 14 Pac. 656.

[5] McRose *v.* Bottyer, 81 Cal. 122, 22 Pac. 393; Bequette *v.* Patterson, 104 Cal. 284, 37 Pac. 917; Schwerdtle *v.* Placer County, 108 Cal. 591, 41 Pac. 448; Smith *v.* Hawkins, 110 Cal. 125, 42 Pac. 453.

chasers must take it burdened with such easements or
other rights.[1]

"But when it has once disposed of its entire estate in
" the lands to one party, it can afterwards no more
" burden it with other rights than any other proprietor
" of lands."[2]

The same doctrine applies to perfected mining locations. After such location has once been completed, the
estate of its owner cannot be subjected to burdens, except for some public use;[3] or if sanctioned by the state
constitution, perhaps, for a private use, upon condemnation proceedings.[4]

This phase of the subject has been discussed by us in
a preceding portion of this work,[5] and it is unnecessary
to here repeat what was there said.

As to other privileges which may be said to be incident to the ownership of mines and mining claims, we
shall consider them when discussing the nature of the
title acquired and rights conferred by location. This
will include the cross-lode question and the privileges
granted, if any, to a junior cross-lode locator.[6]

[1] Amador-Medean G. M. Co. v. S. Spring Hill M. Co., 13 Saw. 523, 36
Fed. 668; Welch v. Garret (Idaho), 51 Pac. 405.

[2] Woodruff v. North Bloomfield Gravel M. Co., 9 Saw. 441, 18 Fed. 753.
See, also, Dower v. Richards, 73 Cal. 477, 15 Pac. 105; Amador Queen M.
Co. v. Dewitt, 73 Cal. 482, 15 Pac. 74.

[3] St. Louis M. and M. Co. v. Montana M. Co., 113 Fed. 900.

[4] People v. Dist. Court, 11 Colo. 147, 17 Pac. 298; Robertson v. Smith,
1 Mont. 410; Noteware v. Sterns, Id. 311.

[5] Ante, §§ 252-264.

[6] Post, §§ 557-561.

TITLE VI.

THE TITLE ACQUIRED AND RIGHTS CONFERRED BY LOCATION.

CHAPTER

  I. THE CHARACTER OF THE TENURE.

 II. THE NATURE AND EXTENT OF PROPERTY RIGHTS CONFERRED BY LODE LOCATIONS.

III. THE EXTRALATERAL RIGHT.

 IV. THE NATURE AND EXTENT OF PROPERTY RIGHTS CONFERRED BY PLACER LOCATIONS.

  V. PERPETUATION OF THE ESTATE BY ANNUAL DEVELOPMENT AND IMPROVEMENT.

 VI. FORFEITURE OF THE ESTATE, AND ITS PREVENTION BY RESUMPTION OF WORK.

CHAPTER I.

THE CHARACTER OF THE TENURE.

§ 535. Nature of the estate as defined by the early decisions.

§ 536. Origin of the doctrine.

§ 537. Actual and constructive possession under miners' rules.

§ 538. Federal recognition of the doctrine.

§ 539. Nature of the estate as defined by the courts since the enactment of general mining laws.

§ 540. Nature of the estate compared with copyholds at common law.

§ 541. Nature of the estate compared with the *dominium utile* of the civil law.

§ 542. Nature of the estate compared with inchoate preemption and homestead claims.

§ 543. Dower within the states.

§ 544. Dower within the territories.

§ **535. Nature of the estate as defined by the early decisions.**—It is somewhat difficult to comprehensively classify the nature of the estate acquired and held by the possessor of a valid mining location by the use of any definitive term recognized by the common law or employed in the United States to designate a particular tenure.[1]

In the early history of mining jurisprudence, the estate or interest acquired by the miner in his claim, held and worked under the local rules and customs, was treated as an interest in real property. It was liable to sale on execution,[2] and was subject to taxation.[3]

---

[1] Judge Knowles in Black v. Elkhorn M. Co., 49 Fed. 549.

[2] McKeon v. Bisbee, 9 Cal. 137, 70 Am. Dec. 642.

[3] State of Cal. v. Moore, 12 Cal. 56; People v. Shearer, 30 Cal. 645; Hale & Norcross M. Co. v. Storey County, 1 Nev. 82; People v. Taylor, 1 Nev. 88; Forbes v. Gracey, 94 U. S. 762.

The supreme court of California thus announced its views:—

"From an early period of our state jurisprudence we
" have regarded these claims to public mineral lands as
" titles. They are so practically. . . . Our courts have
" given them the recognition of legal estates of free-
" hold; and so for all practical purposes, if we except
" some doctrine of abandonment not perhaps applicable
" to such estates, unquestionably they are, and we think
" it would not be in harmony with the general judicial
" system to deny to them the incidents of freehold es-
" tates in respect to this matter."[1]

And in a later case the same tribunal stated the rule to be:—

"That although the ultimate fee in our public miner-
" al lands is vested in the United States, yet, as between
" individuals, all transactions and all rights, interests,
" and estates in the mines are treated as being an estate
" in fee and as a distinct vested right of property in
" the claimant or claimants thereof, founded upon their
" possession or appropriation of the land containing
" the mine. They are treated, as between themselves
" and all persons but the United States, as the owners
" of the land and mines therein."[2]

As was said by the supreme court of Nevada, the
courts and the laws adapting themselves to the necessity
of the case, and governed by rules of common sense,
reason, and necessity, have universally treated the possessory rights of the miner as an estate in fee. Actions
for possession, similar to the action of ejectment,[3] actions to quiet title,[4] actions of trespass, bills for parti-

[1] Merritt v. Judd, 14 Cal. 60, cited and approved in Roseville Alta Co.
v. Iowa Gulch, 15 Colo. 29, 22 Am. St. Rep. 373, 24 Pac. 920; Spencer v.
Winselman, 42 Cal. 479.

[2] Hughes v. Devlin, 23 Cal. 502, 507; Watts v. White, 13 Cal. 321.

[3] Davidson v. Calkins, 92 Fed. 230.

[4] Mt. Rosa M. M. and L. Co. v. Palmer, 26 Colo. 56, 77 Am. St. Rep. 245,
56 Pac. 176.

tion,[1] are constantly maintained. Such interests are held to descend to the heir,[2] to be subject to sale on execution,[3] and to be assets in the hands of executors and administrators for the payment of debts.[4]

§ 536. **Origin of the doctrine.**—The dignity thus attaching to the miner's title had its genesis in the early history of mining in the west, and was founded upon the law of possession. It was the natural result of the recognition by local legislatures of mining rights in the public domain, and the exercise of such rights by appropriation under the local rules and customs. As no intruder upon the possession of a prior appropriator could successfully defend an action involving possessory rights by asserting that the paramount title was in the general government, this antecedent possession was in itself sufficient evidence of title. This was nothing more than the application of a familiar rule of the common law that, as against a mere trespasser, title may be inferred from possession. The actual possessor of real property was so far regarded by law as the owner thereof that no one could lawfully dispossess him of the same without showing some well-founded title of a higher or better character than such possession itself furnishes.[5]

The early announcement of the doctrine by the courts in the mining states that controversies between occu-

---

[1] Dall v. Confidence S. M. Co., 3 Nev. 531, 93 Am. Dec. 419; Aspen M. etc. Co. v. Rucker, 28 Fed. 220, (disapproving Strettell v. Ballou, 3 McCrary, 46, 9 Fed. 256).

But it is seldom that a division of mines may be made. Generally, partition suits must result in sale. Aspen M. and S. Co. v. Rucker, 28 Fed. 220; Lenfers v. Henke, 73 Ill. 405, 24 Am. Rep. 263. See, also, Coleman v. Coleman, 19 Pa. St. 100, 57 Am. Dec. 641.

[2] Lohman v. Helmer, 104 Fed. 178.

[3] Phœnix M. and M. Co. v. Scott, 20 Wash. 48, 54 Pac. 777; Butte Hardware Co. v. Frank, 25 Mont. 344, 65 Pac. 1.

[4] Hale & Norcross G. and S. M. Co. v. Storey County, 1 Nev. 83.

[5] 3 Washburn on Real Property, 3d ed., p. 114; 5th ed., p. 134.

pants of the public mineral lands were to be determined
by the law of possession, and that persons claiming and
in the possession of mining claims on these lands were,
as between themselves and all other persons, except the
United States, owners of the same, having a vested right
of property founded on their possession and appropriation,[1] was the declaration of no new canon of jurisprudence.

The enunciation of the rule that the naked possessor
of land was deemed in law the owner until the general
government or a person showing title under it makes
an entry upon the same, and that when this was done
the right or claim of the possessor must yield to the
paramount authority of the United States or its
grantee,[2] was but a restatement of a well-established
rule of law.

It is also a familiar doctrine of the common law that
where one, under a title deed describing a parcel of land
by metes and bounds, enters upon the premises, claiming
to hold the same under his deed, he is constructively in
possession of all that is included in his deed, though he
actually occupies but a part;[3] and, by the same rule,
any instrument having a grantor and a grantee, and
containing an adequate description of the lands to be
conveyed and apt words for their conveyance, gives
color of title to the lands described.[4]

The application of these elementary rules to the novel
and peculiar conditions surrounding the early history of
the mining industry in the west, evolved a new *color of
title* by which the extent of a miner's right of possession
was determined.

---

[1] Hughes *v*. Devlin, 23 Cal. 502.

[2] Doran *v*. C. P. R. R., 24 Cal. 245.

[3] 3 Washburn on Real Property, 3d ed., p. 118; 5th ed., p. 138.

[4] *Id.*, 3d ed., p. 139; 5th ed., p. 167; Brooks *v*. Bruyn, 35 Ill. 392.

§ 537. **Actual and constructive possession, under
miners' rules.**—It was early announced as a rule of
property that mining claims were held by compliance
with local rules, and *pedis possessio* was not required
to give a right of action. When the claim was defined,
and a party entered into possession of a *part,* that possession was possession of the entire claim as against any
one but the true owner or prior occupant,[1] and priority
of occupation established a priority of right.[2]

This doctrine of constructive possession was even
extended to instances where the right asserted was not
referable to local rules. Thus it was held that mining
ground acquired by an entry under a claim for mining
purposes upon a tract the bounds of which were distinctly marked by physical marks, accompanied with
actual occupancy of a part of the tract, was sufficient
to enable the possessor to maintain ejectment for the
entire claim, although such acts of appropriation were
not done in accordance with any local mining rule.[3]

In such case, however, the extent of such location was
not without limit. The quantity taken must have been
reasonable, and whether it was so or not was to be determined in such cases by the general usages and customs
prevailing upon the general subject. If an unreasonable
quantity was included within the boundaries, the location was ineffectual for any purpose, and possession
under it only extended to the ground actually occupied.[4]

But, as a rule, mere entry and possession gave no

[1] Attwood *v.* Fricot, 17 Cal. 37, 76 Am. Dec. 567; English *v.* Johnson,
17 Cal. 107, 76 Am. Dec. 574; Roberts *v.* Wilson, 1 Utah, 292.

[2] Gibson *v.* Puchta, 33 Cal. 310.

[3] Table Mountain T. Co. *v.* Stranahan, 20 Cal. 199; Hess *v.* Winder, 30
Cal. 349. See Valcalda *v.* Silver Peak Mines, 86 Fed. 90.

[4] Table Mountain T. Co. *v.* Stranahan, 20 Cal. 199. See Mallett *v.*
Uncle Sam M. Co., 1 Nev. 156.

right to the exclusive enjoyment of any given quantity of the public mineral lands.[1]

Where an occupant relied upon constructive possession, it devolved upon him to establish three essential facts:—

(1) That there were local mining customs, rules, and regulations in force in the district embracing the claims;

(2) That particular acts were required to be performed in the location and working of the claims;

(3) That he had substantially complied with the requirements.[2]

This rule was somewhat relaxed in favor of a purchaser who entered under a deed which contained definite and certain boundaries which could be marked out and made known from the deed alone,[3] which was nothing more than a reiteration of the doctrine of the common law relative to entries under color of title, heretofore mentioned. The miner's title extended to such mining lands as were reduced to his actual possession, or to such as were constructively in his possession, according to the rules above enumerated.

§ 538. Federal recognition of the doctrine.—While the government passively encouraged and fostered the system of development of the mineral resources as practiced in the mining states and territories, it gave no legislative expression of its encouragement, or any recognition that the occupants of the public mineral lands were other than mere trespassers, until February 27, 1865, when congress passed an act providing for a district and circuit court for the state of Nevada, the ninth section of which provided as follows:—

[1] Smith v. Doe, 15 Cal. 101; Gillan v. Hutchinson, 16 Cal. 154.
[2] Pralus v. Jefferson G. and S. M. Co., 34 Cal. 558.
[3] Hess v. Winder, 30 Cal. 349.

" That no possessory action between individuals in
" any of the courts of the United States for the recovery
" of any mining title, or for damages to such title, shall
" be affected by the fact that the paramount title to the
" land on which such mines are is in the United States;
" but each case shall be adjudged by the law of posses-
" sion."[1]

This was re-enacted in the Revised Statutes,[2] and
forms a part of the general legislation of congress on
the subject of mineral lands.

The supreme court of the United States, in the case
of Forbes v. Gracey,[3] approved and confirmed the doctrine of the early decisions as to the nature of a locator's
estate.   \

" Those claims," said that court, " are the subject of
" bargain and sale, and constitute very largely the
" wealth of the Pacific Coast states. They are property
" in the fullest sense of the word, and their ownership,
" transfer, and use are governed by a well-defined code
" or codes of law, and are recognized by the states and
" the federal government. These claims may be sold,
" transferred, mortgaged, and inherited, without in-
" fringing the title of the United States."[4]

§ 539. **Nature of the estate as defined by the courts
since the enactment of general mining laws.**—With reference to the character of the estate held by a mining
locator since the passage of the act of July 26, 1866,
the decisions of the courts, both state and federal, are
quite harmonious. They in no way antagonize the theories of the earlier decisions, but adopt them. Naturally,
the definition is enlarged and perfected. A mere occu-

---

[1] 13 Stats. at Large, 441.
[2] § 910.
[3] 94 U. S. 762.
[4] See, also, Del Monte M. and M. Co. v. Last Chance M. Co., 171 U. S.
55, 62, 18 Sup. Ct. Rep. 895.

pant of lands, who is technically a trespasser, has rights of less dignity than one who enters with the consent of the paramount proprietor under rules defining the terms of his occupancy and the extent and limit of his rights.

Prior to the issuance of a patent the locator cannot be said to own the fee-simple title. The fee resides in the general government, whose tribunals, specially charged with the ultimate conveyance of the title, must pass upon the qualifications of the locator and his compliance with the law. Yet, as between the locator and every one else save the paramount proprietor, the estate acquired by a perfected mining location possesses all the attributes of a title in fee, and so long as the requirements of the law with reference to continued development are satisfied, the character of the tenure remains that of a fee. As between the locator and the government, the former is the owner of the beneficial estate, and the latter holds the fee in trust, to be conveyed to such beneficial owner upon his application in that behalf and in compliance with the terms prescribed by the paramount proprietor.[1]

Until patent issues the locator's muniments of title consist of the laws under the sanction of which his rights accrue, the series of acts culminating in a completed valid location, and those necessary to be continuously performed to perpetuate it.

A mining claim perfected under the law is property in the highest sense of that term, which may be bought, sold, and conveyed, and will pass by descent. It has the effect of a grant by the United States of the right of present and exclusive possession of the lands lo-

---

[1] Noyes v. Mantle, 127 U. S. 348, 351, 8 Sup. Ct. Rep. 1132; Dahl v. Raunheim, 132 U. S. 262, 10 Sup. Ct. Rep. 74; Gillis v. Downey, 85 Fed. 483.

cated.[1] Actual possession is not more necessary for the protection of the title acquired to such a claim by a valid location than it is for any other grant.[2]

Although the locator may obtain a patent, this patent adds but little to his security.[3]

The owner of such a location is entitled to the exclusive possession and enjoyment, against every one, including the United States itself.[4]

" Where there is a valid location of a mining claim
" the area becomes segregated from the public domain
" and the property of the locator. . . . He may sell it,
" mortgage it, or part with the whole or any portion of
" it as he may see fit."[5]

He is entitled to the most plenary and summary remedies for quieting his claim cognizable in equity.[6]

As was said by the supreme court of Oregon,[7] the general government itself cannot abridge the rights of the miner. There are equitable circumstances binding upon the conscience of the governmental proprietor that must never be disregarded. Rights have become vested that cannot be divested without the violation of all the principles of justice and reason.[8] The same funda-

[1] Forbes v. Gracey, 94 U. S. 762; Gillis v. Downey, 85 Fed. 483, 487; Stratton v. Gold Sovereign M. and T. Co., 1 Leg. Adv. 350; Phœnix M. and M. Co. v. Scott, 20 Wash. 48, 54 Pac. 777; McCarthy v. Speed, 11 S. Dak. 362, 77 N. W. 590. See, ante, § 322, note 1, p. 581.

[2] Harris v. Kellogg, 117 Cal. 484, 49 Pac. 708; McCarthy v. Speed, 11 S. Dak. 362, 77 N. W. 590; Bramlett v. Flick, 23 Mont. 95; 57 Pac. 869; Belk v. Meagher, 104 U. S. 279; Gwillim v. Donnellan, 115 U. S. 45, 5 Sup. Ct. Rep. 1110.

[3] Chambers v. Harrington, 111 U. S. 350, 4 Sup. Ct. Rep. 428.

[4] McFeters v. Pierson, 15 Colo. 201, 22 Am. St. Rep. 388, 24 Pac. 1076; Gold Hill Q. M. Co. v. Ish, 5 Or. 104; Seymour v. Fisher, 16 Colo. 188, 27 Pac. 240.

[5] St. Louis M. and M. Co. v. Montana Limited, 171 U. S. 650, 655, 19 Sup. Ct. Rep. 61.

[6] Gillis v. Downey, 85 Fed. 483.

[7] Gold Hill Q. M. Co. v. Ish, 5 Or. 104.

[8] To the same effect, see Merced M. Co. v. Fremont, 7 Cal. 317, 327, 68 Am. Dec. 262; Conger v. Weaver, 6 Cal. 548, 65 Am. Dec. 528.

mental rules of right and justice govern nations, municipalities, corporations, and individuals.[1] The government may not destroy the locator's rights by withdrawing the land from entry or placing it in a state of reservation.[2]

The doctrine hereinbefore enunciated has never been seriously questioned. It has been reiterated in many cases in both the state and federal courts.[3]

The supreme court of Oregon has said that the nature of title or rights acquired or held by a locator in possession of a mining claim prior to his compliance with the provisions of the statutes of the United States entitling him to a patent is difficult to determine from authorities; that prior to such compliance it is agreed he has an absolute right of possession; that in many states this possessory right is by statute declared to be an interest in real estate and subject to seizure and sale as such, and the decisions of the courts holding it to be real estate are most, if not all, based upon some statutory provision.[4]

This may be quite true; but it is to be remembered

---

[1] United States v. Northern Pac. R. R., 95 Fed. 864.

[2] Military and National Park Reservations. Opinion Assistant Attorney-General, 25 L. D. 48.

[3] Manuel v. Wulff, 152 U. S. 505, 14 Sup. Ct. Rep. 651; Black v. Elkhorn M. Co., 163 U. S. 445, 16 Sup. Ct. Rep. 1101, S. C. before Judge Knowles, 49 Fed. 549; McFeters v. Pierson, 15 Colo. 201, 22 Am. St. Rep. 388, 24 Pac. 1076; Seymour v. Fisher, 16 Colo. 188, 27 Pac. 240; Wills v. Blain, 4 N. Mex. 378, 20 Pac. 798; Harris v. Equator M. and S. Co., 3 McCrary, 14, 8 Fed. 863; Keeler v. Trueman, 15 Colo. 143, 25 Pac. 311; Houtz v. Gisborn, 1 Utah, 173; Talbott v. King, 6 Mont. 76, 9 Pac. 434; Silver Bow M. and M. Co. v. Clark, 5 Mont. 378, 5 Pac. 570; McKinley Creek M. Co. v. Alaska United M. Co., 183 U. S. 563, 571, 22 Sup. Ct. Rep. 84; McCarthy v. Speed, 11 S. Dak. 362, 77 N. W. 590; Phoenix M. and M. Co. v. Scott, 20 Wash. 48, 54 Pac. 777; Mt. Rosa M. M. and L. Co. v. Palmer, 26 Colo. 56, 77 Am. St. Rep. 245, 56 Pac. 176; Davidson v. Calkins, 92 Fed. 230.

[4] Herron v. Eagle M. Co., 37 Or. 155, 61 Pac. 417.

that the statutory enunciation of the principle was in the beginning but an expression in a higher form of a rule which had its origin in local customs,—the "Ameri-" can common law of mines,"—and the acceptance of the doctrine by the federal tribunals arose out of a consideration of these equitable circumstances. It cannot be doubted that each state may determine for itself the nature or character of actions which may be maintained in its courts for the redress of private wrongs, and may in this behalf, and perhaps others, classify interests in real property as chattels or chattels real, or declare that a given privilege exercised with reference to land shall not be classified as an interest in real estate, for the purpose of either litigation or taxation. But this does not, as we understand it, militate against the dignity of the estate in an unpatented mining claim accorded by the decisions of all the courts, state and federal, from the beginning.

The principles here discussed will again be the subject of consideration when we deal with the nature of the remedies which are available to the owner of a mining claim and the forum in which actions are to be brought to redress injuries thereto.

§ 540. **Nature of the estate compared with copyholds at common law.**—It has been said that the interest of a locator of a mining claim is, in some respects, not unlike that of a copyholder at common law; that both had their origin in local customs, and in each the custom crystallized into law; that the copyholder held his land by the custom of the manor, and while the fee remained in the lord the right to the possession and enjoyment of the premises was in him. He might alienate his lands at will, and on his death they descended to his heirs; the copyholder was a feeholder, yet the fee was in the lord.[1]

The same authority states that the estate of the copyholder might be taken in execution for the payment of his debts. We are not sure that this is a correct statement of the rule of the common law. Blackstone says, speaking of this class of estates, that no creditor could take possession of lands, but could only levy upon the growing profits, so that if the defendant aliened his lands the plaintiff was ousted of his remedy. Therefore, copyhold lands were not liable to be taken in execution upon a judgment.[2] The American authorities seem to support this view.[3]

Be that as it may, there is one essential difference between the two estates with reference, at least, to the extent of the thing possessed and enjoyed.

In copyhold, or customary lands, the lord of the manor is owner of the minerals, but the tenant is in possession of them, and consequently, in the absence of prescription or a special custom to the contrary, the one cannot explore mines without the consent of the other, although the tenant may continue the working of mines and quarries already opened.[4]

§ 541. Nature of the estate compared with the dominium utile of the civil law.—The nature of the estate held by a locator in a mining claim bears some resemblance to the *emphyteusis* or *dominium utile* of the Roman or civil law. Although the *emphyteuta* did not become owner of the thing, yet he had nearly all the

[1] Black *v.* Elkhorn, 52 Fed. 859.
[2] 3 Blackstone, 418-419.
[3] Watson on Sheriffs, 208; Wildey *v.* Bonny, 26 Miss. 35; Colvin *v.* Johnson, 2 Barb. 206; Bigelow *v.* Finch, 11 Barb. 498; 17 Barb. 394.
[4] Rogers on Mines, 270; MacSwinney on Mines, 72; Arundell on Mines, 4; Bainbridge on Mines, 4th ed., p. 37.

rights of an owner. It was *jus in re aliena,* which in its extent and effects nearly resembled ownership. He had the full right of enjoyment, consequently the right of possessing the thing and of reaping all the fruits thereof. He might dispose of the substance of the thing, transfer the exercise of his right to another, and alienate it, *inter vivos* or *causa mortis.* He might mortgage it and burden it with servitudes, without requiring the consent of the *dominus* thereto.

His right to absolutely dispose of his estate was subject only to a preferred right of purchase in the *dominus* at the price offered. At the death of the *emphyteuta,* the *emphyteusis* descended to his heirs. The *emphyteutical* right was usually acquired by grant, although it might be acquired by prescription.[1]

" *Dominium utile* is a right which the vassal hath in " the land, or some immovable thing of his lord, to use " the same and take the profit thereof, hereditarily or " *in perpetuum.*"[2]

§ **542. Nature of the estate compared with inchoate pre-emption and homestead claims.**—Judge Ross, in the case of Black *v.* Elkhorn,[3] makes a comparison between the estate held by a mining locator and a pre-emption claimant prior to final entry and payment. While for the purposes of the case then under consideration, where dower was asserted in an unpatented mining claim, the comparison was not wholly inapt, yet we think the inference which may be drawn, that the estate of a mining locator is of no greater dignity than that of an inchoate pre-emption right, should not pass unchallenged. What are the essential differences between the two estates?

[1] Kaufman's Mackeldey, vol. i, §§ 324-325.
[2] 1 Spence Eq. Jur., 31, 33; Bowers *v.* Keesecker, 14 Iowa, 301.
[3] 52 Fed. 859.

(1) By their pre-emption laws, the United States did not enter into any contract with the settler, nor incur any obligation that the land occupied by him shall ever be offered for sale. They simply declared that *in case any of their lands are thrown open for sale* the privilege to purchase should be first given to parties who had settled upon and improved them.[1]

No estate in the land was acquired or right thereto vested in the claimant of an inchoate pre-emption right, unless and until the amount of purchase money was paid.[2] The same doctrine applies to homestead claims.[3]

With reference to its mineral lands, the government has declared that they are free and open to exploration and *purchase*,[4] and a positive compact is made between the government and the discoverer and locator, whereby the latter, upon compliance with the law, is clothed with the *exclusive* right of possession and enjoyment.[5]

If the government, after a valid mining location has been made, could deprive the locator of his rights, his right of possession certainly would not be *exclusive*.

(2) The pre-emptor is required to apply for patent within a fixed period of time. There is nothing in the mining law requiring a locator to proceed to patent at all. He may never do so, yet his estate is fully maintained in its integrity so long as the law which is a muniment of his title is complied with. An application for a patent is not essential to the acquisition or mainte-

---

[1] Hutchings *v.* Low, 15 Wall. 77; Campbell *v.* Wade, 132 U. S. 34, 10 Sup. Ct. Rep. 9; Black *v.* Elkhorn M. Co., 49 Fed. 549.

[2] Wittenbrock *v.* Wheadon, 128 Cal. 150, 79 Am. St. Rep. 32, 60 Pac. 664, and cases cited.

[3] Wagstaff *v.* Collins, 97 Fed. 3, and cases cited.

[4] Rev. Stats., § 2319.

[5] Rev. Stats., § 2322; Erhardt *v.* Boaro, 113 U. S. 527, 5 Sup. Ct. Rep. 560; Black *v.* Elkhorn M. Co., 59 Fed. 549.

nance of a mining claim.[1] The patent adds but little to the security of the locator.[2]

That the general government itself cannot deprive the locator of rights accrued under the mining laws has, we think, been fully demonstrated.

(3) Prior to entry and payment, the pre-emptor cannot convey or assign his interest to others.[3]

Such a conveyance or assignment would extinguish the pre-emption right.[4]

The right to transfer a mining claim has never been questioned.[5]

(4) It is not until entry and payment under a pre-emption claim that the land becomes subject to taxation by the state.[6]

As we have heretofore shown,[7] mining claims are so subject.

(5) Inchoate pre-emption claims are not subject to execution so as to enable the purchaser at the sale to obtain title from the government.[8]

The contrary has always been the rule as to mining claims.

[1] Coleman v. McKenzie, 29 L. D. 359.

[2] Chambers v. Harrington, 111 U. S. 350, 4 Sup. Ct. Rep. 428; Gold Hill Q. M. Co. v. Ish, 5 Or. 104; Chapman v. Toy Long, 4 Saw. 28, Fed. Cas. No. 2610; Shafer v. Constans, 3 Mont. 369.

[3] Dillingham v. Fisher, 5 Wis. 475; McLane v. Bovee, 35 Wis. 27; Trulock v. Taylor, 26 Ark. 54; Busch v. Donohue, 31 Mich. 482; Frisbie v. Whitney, 9 Wall. 187; Aiken v. Ferry, 6 Saw. 79; Fed. Cas. No. 112; Lamb v. Davenport, 18 Wall. 307; Schoolfield v. Houle, 13 Colo. 394, 22 Pac. 781.

[4] Quinn v. Kenyon, 38 Cal. 499.

[5] St. Louis M. and M. Co. v. Montana M. Co., 171 U. S. 650, 655, 19 Sup. Ct. Rep. 61.

[6] Carroll v. Safford, 3 How. 441; Witherspoon v. Duncan, 4 Wall. 210.

[7] Ante, § 539.

[8] Moore v. Besse, 43 Cal. 511; Bray v. Ragsdale, 53 Mo. 170; Cravens v. Moore, 61 Mo. 178; 1 Freeman on Ex., § 176; Dougherty v. Marcuse, 3 Head, 323; Crutsinger v. Catron, 10 Humph. 24; Rhea v. Hughes, 1 Ala. 219, 34 Am. Dec. 772; Hatfield v. Wallace, 7 Mo. 112; Brown v. Massey, 3 Humph. 470.

(6) An inchoate pre-emption could not be disposed of by will.[1] Heirs alone would have the right to complete the entry. In such cases the heirs do not take title by descent from their ancestor, but the land is conveyed to them directly from the United States by virtue of the privilege of purchase given to them expressly by the provisions of section twenty-two hundred and sixty-nine of the Revised Statutes.[2]

In the case of the death of a homestead claimant who has earned title to the land the right to submit final proof and obtain patent is in the widow under the terms of the statute.[3]

Heirs would only be entitled (under the statute), in the event there was no widow.[4]

In the absence of any statute upon the subject, the privilege given by the government would lapse with the death of the pre-emptor.[5]

Devisees, as such, would not be recognized by the government.[6]

Even an administrator could not perfect the right, unless it was established that there was in existence some person for whose benefit the right might be perfected.[7]

Unpatented mining claims descend to the heir, or may be devised the same as patented claims or other classes of real property.

[1] Wittenbrock v. Wheadon, 128 Cal. 150, 79 Am. St. Rep. 32, 60 Pac. 664, citing Rogers v. Clemans, 26 Kan. 522.

[2] Id.

[3] Rev. Stats., § 2291; Boyle v. Wolfe, 27 L. D. 572.

[4] Currans v. Williams' Heirs, 20 L. D. 109; Runey v. Bourke's Heirs, 27 L. D. 596.

[5] Wittenbrock v. Wheadon, 128 Cal. 150, 79 Am. St. Rep. 32, 60 Pac. 664.

[6] Rev. Stats., § 2269.

[7] Elliott v. Figg, 59 Cal. 117.

We have heretofore shown [1] the analogy between the mine locator's estate and the *dominium utile* of the civil law. No such analogy exists with reference to pre-emption claims. [2]

What has heretofore been said in reference to inchoate pre-emption claims applies with equal force to federal homestead claims prior to final entry. It seems to us that the distinction between the character of the estate held by a pre-emptioner or homestead claimant, prior to final entry, and the owner of a perfected mining location is decidedly marked.

It has been said that the mining laws provide for three classes of titles:—

(1) Possessory: a location prior to entry and payment;

(2) Complete equitable: a location after entry and payment and before patent;

(3) Fee simple: after patent. [3]

While this may be true in one sense, yet a patent cannot confer any greater rights than those flowing from a valid perfected mining location. Pre-emption and homestead claims pass through the same gradations of title, but the nature and extent of the possessory right conferred are essentially different.

§ 543. Dower within the states.—Each state regulates for itself the laws of descent, the domestic relation, and property rights between husband and wife. The subject of dower is one upon which congress may legislate so far as the territories are concerned, but within the states it is powerless to grant the right, or deny its

---

[1] *Ante*, § 541.

[2] Bowers *v.* Keesecker, 14 Iowa, 301.

[3] America Hill Quartz Mine, 3 Sickle's Min. Dec. 377, 385; Benson M. etc. Co. *v.* Alta M. etc. Co., 144 U. S. 428, 12 Sup. Ct. Rep. 877.

existence where the state creates it. Therefore, in determining what rights, if any, the wife has in the lands or possessions of the husband, in any given state, we must, as a rule, look to state legislation and the decisions of state courts. Of the precious-metal-bearing states, no dower right whatever exists in California, Colorado, Idaho, Nevada, North Dakota, South Dakota, Washington, or Wyoming. In Montana a widow is entitled to the third part of all lands whereof her husband was seised of an estate of inheritance, and equitable estates are subject to such dower right.[1]

There can be no doubt that as to a patented mining claim, or one that has passed to entry and for which a certificate of purchase has been issued, the dower right would attach, the same as it would to any other class of lands; but as to whether such right could be asserted in a perfected mining location prior to entry and payment has been the cause of serious controversy.

In the case of Black v. Elkhorn Mining Co.,[2] Judge Knowles held that such an estate was subject to the wife's dower, but where the husband had conveyed the property to a purchaser who subsequently applied for and received a patent, the wife having failed to assert her rights by adverse claim, the dower right was lost.

The case was taken to the United States circuit court of appeals,[3] which court held that a mere locator of a mining claim, owning only a possessory right conferred by the statute, has no such estate in the property as against the United States or its grantee as will permit rights of dower to be predicated thereon by virtue of any state legislation. In other words, Judge Knowles gave

---

[1] Civ. Code, § 228; Chadwick v. Tatem, 9 Mont. 354, 23 Pac. 729; Black v. Elkhorn M. Co., 47 Fed. 600.

[2] 47 Fed. 600.

[3] 52 Fed. 859.

the right judgment but the wrong reason for it. The
supreme court of the United States affirmed the ruling
of the circuit court of appeals [1] on parallel lines of reasoning.

To what extent the doctrine of the supreme court of
the United States might be deemed binding on the conscience of the state courts is a question not necessary for
us to determine.[2] The result reached is manifestly in
consonance with the preconceived notions of practition-
ers in the mining regions. A contrary rule would have
disturbed many mining titles, and opened the door to
vexatious litigation. If in the process of reasoning
by which the ultimate conclusion has been reached the
dignity of the mining locator's estate has suffered to a
slight extent, it has suffered in a good cause. We are
fully justified from the foregoing authorities in accepting as a settled doctrine, that in states where the dower
right exists by virtue of state legislation, such right will
not attach to a mining claim held simply by location.

The states of Oregon and Utah have dower laws similar to those of Montana. Nebraska and Florida, both of
which states are nominally subject to the general mining
laws of congress, but which are not classified as metal-
bearing states, likewise make provision for dower rights
in the wife.[3]

§ 544. **Dower within the territories.**—The same rule
as to the dower right existing in the states by virtue of
state legislation applies with equal force in the territories, where that right is established by act of congress.
Under the Edmunds-Tucker amendment to the anti-

[1] Black v. Elkhorn M. Co., 163 U. S. 445, 16 Sup. Ct. Rep. 1101.

[2] Held to be binding as applying the principle to community property.
Phœnix M. and M. Co. v. Scott, 20 Wash. 48, 54 Pac. 777.

[3] For interesting note on the subject of "Dower in Mines," see
3 C. C. A. 316.

polygamy act,[1] congress provided that a widow should be endowed of a third part of all the lands whereof her husband was seised of an estate of inheritance. The act was, of course, applicable to the then territory of Utah. Whether or not it applied to the other territories was a mooted question until recently. The question arose in Wyoming, which, while still a territory, passed a law abolishing dower.[2]

A widow asserted a right to dower under section eighteen of the Edmunds-Tucker act, claiming that the passage by congress of that act superseded the territorial law and restored the dower right. The supreme court of Wyoming [3] held that the act applied only to Utah, and was not operative in any other territory.

This ruling was affirmed by the supreme court of the United States on writ of error.[4]

Dower has been abolished by action of the territorial legislature in Arizona. In New Mexico there is no specific mention of dower in any of its legislation. In this territory the law of community property prevails, which had its origin in the system of the civil law, and was adopted in California and most of the Pacific states and territories.[5]

The dower laws of Oregon have been adopted for Alaska.[6]

It may be conceded that with the exception of those states heretofore enumerated, and the district of Alaska, the dower right does not exist in any of the states or territories within the purview of this treatise.

---

[1] Act of March 3, 1887, § 18, 24 U. S. Stats. at Large, p. 638.
[2] Act of Dec. 10, 1869; Rev. Stats. Wyo., 1887, § 2221.
[3] France v. Connor, 3 Wyo. 445, 27 Pac. 569.
[4] 161 U. S. 65, 16 Sup. Ct. Rep. 497.
[5] France v. Connor, 27 Pac. 569, S. C. 3 Wyo. 445.
[6] Carter's Annot. Code of Alaska, p. 363.

Whether or not it is necessary in any of the states or territories for a wife to join with the husband in a conveyance of real property, by which term we include mining locations, depends, of course, upon the laws of the several state and territorial jurisdictions.[1] It is beyond the scope of this treatise to enter into a detailed statement of the rules of law regulating conveyancing in these different states. They are general laws, affecting all classes of real property without distinction.

[1] It has been held in Idaho that a mining claim located in that state by a husband is community property. Jacobsen v. Bunker Hill and Sullivan M. and C. Co., 2 Idaho, 863, 28 Pac. 396. A contrary doctrine seems to have been reached by the supreme court of Washington. Phœnix M. and M. Co. v. Scott, 20 Wash. 48, 54 Pac. 777.

CHAPTER II.

THE NATURE AND EXTENT OF PROPERTY RIGHTS CONFERRED BY LODE LOCATIONS.

ARTICLE I. INTRODUCTORY—INTRALIMITAL RIGHTS.
II. CROSS-LODES.

ARTICLE I. INTRODUCTORY—INTRALIMITAL RIGHTS.

§ 548. General observations.

§ 549. Classification of rights with reference to boundaries.

§ 550. Extent of the grant as defined by the statute.

§ 551. The right to the surface and presumptions flowing therefrom.

§ 552. Intralimital rights not affected by the form of surface location.

§ 553. Pursuit of the vein on its course beyond bounding planes of the location not permitted.

§ 548. General observations.—It has been satisfactorily established that the estate created by a valid perfected mining location, as between the locator and every one else save the government, is in the nature of a fee simple. Under ordinary circumstances this would be a sufficient characterization of the estate. The attributes of a fee-simple estate are well understood, and no explanation is required. But the peculiarities of the mining law render it necessary to elaborate and define with greater particularity than is possible by the use of a single descriptive term the nature and extent of property rights conferred by perfected mining locations.

There are certain rights which may be said to be common to all classes of locations. There are others

which are peculiar to one or the other. In order to treat
the subject analytically, we are compelled to deal with
the two classes separately, first considering the subject
of lodes, or veins.

§ 549. **Classification of rights with reference to
boundaries.**—Property rights conferred by lode locations may be subdivided for the purpose of convenience
into two classes:—

(1) Those which are confined to things embraced
within the boundaries of the location. By the term
" boundaries," as we here employ it, we include not only
the surface lines, but the vertical planes drawn downward through them. If we may be excused for introducing into the mining vocabulary coined and eccentric
words, we would classify these rights as *intralimital;*

(2) Those which, while depending for their existence
upon the ownership of things within the boundaries,
may be exercised under certain conditions and restrictions out of, and beyond, those boundaries. These rights
may be classified as *extralimital.*

Whether these terms will ever come into general use
or not, they will at least enable the author to formulate
his views, express them according to his conception of
the law, and group the different elements under distinctive and homogeneous titles. For the purpose of
classification, therefore, we may say that property
rights flowing from a valid lode location are either
intralimital or extralimital. We will examine the
nature and extent of these rights in the order named.

§ 550. **Extent of the grant as defined by the statute.**
—Section twenty-three hundred and twenty-two of the
Revised Statutes provides, that,—

" Locators shall have the exclusive right of posses-
" sion and enjoyment of all the surface included within
" the lines of their locations, and of all veins, lodes, or
" ledges, throughout their entire depth, the top, or
" apex, of which lies inside of such surface lines ex-
" tended downward vertically, although such veins,
" lodes, or ledges may so far depart from a perpendicu-
" lar in their course downward as to extend outside the
" vertical side-lines of such surface locations."

This section is replete with what Judge Lewis, in
considering another portion of mining law, character-
izes as "grammatical solecisms."[1]

In the language of Dr. Raymond,—

" This phraseology has the merit of clearly convey-
" ing the meaning intended, though descriptive geom-
" etry and the English language suffer somewhat in the
" operation. . . . But the goal is reached, though the
" vehicle is damaged."[2]

The section clearly grants the following intralimital
rights:—

(1) Exclusive dominion over the surface;[3]

(2) The right to certain parts of all veins whose tops,
or apices, are found within vertical planes drawn downward through the surface boundaries.[4] The extent to

---

[1] Hobart v. Ford, 6 Nev. 77.

[2] Law of the Apex, Trans. Am. Inst. M. E., vol. xii, pp. 387, 392.

[3] Mullins v. Butte Hardware Co., 25 Mont. 525, 65 Pac. 1004, 1007.
There is one limitation upon the locator's right to the surface which
should be noted,—i. e. his right to timber growing thereon. The owner
of a mining claim prior to patent may fell and use so much of the
timber as may be necessary in the development and working of the
claim, but he has no right to cut the timber on such claim with intent to
export or remove the same. Such cutting with intent to remove would
render the mineral claimant or his licensee amenable to the provisions of
§ 2461 of the Revised Statutes. Teller v. United States, 113 Fed. 273.

[4] Del Monte M. and M. Co. v. Last Chance M. etc. Co., 171 U. S. 55, 88,
18 Sup. Ct. Rep. 895; Calhoun Gold M. Co. v. Ajax Gold M. Co., 182 U. S.
499, 508, 21 Sup. Ct. Rep. 885; S. C. 27 Colo. 1, 83 Am. St. Rep. 17,

which the locator is entitled to such veins within his surface boundaries will depend upon a number of circumstances, to be fully considered in connection with the subject of extralateral right.

It is quite manifest from a reading of the section that no title passes *by virtue of the location* to any part of any vein which has its top, or apex, wholly outside of the boundaries of such location.

§ 551. **The right to the surface and presumptions flowing therefrom.** — Whatever may be reserved out of the grant created by the perfection of a valid lode location, one thing is quite manifest. The right of a senior locator to the exclusive possession of the surface cannot be invaded, assuming, of course, that at the time to which the location relates no rights of way or servitudes were imposed upon the land.[1] While, as we shall hereafter see, outside apex proprietors may penetrate underneath the surface in the lawful pursuit of their veins, the law expressly preserves the surface from invasion.

The only qualification to this rule is the privilege accorded under certain circumstances to junior locators to place the lines of their locations upon or across the senior claim, discussed in previous sections.[2] The use of such privilege is not to be considered an invasion, as no rights can be asserted thereby in hostility to the senior title.

What are the presumptions, if any, flowing from the ownership of the surface?

59 Pac. 607; Campbell *v.* Ellet, 167 U. S. 116, 119, 17 Sup. Ct. Rep. 765; Crown Point M. Co. *v.* Buck, 97 Fed. 462, 465; Mt. Rosa M. and M. Co. *v.* Palmer, 26 Colo. 56, 77 Am. St. Rep. 245, 56 Pac. 176; Judge Hallet's charge in Matoa G. M. Co. *v.* Chicago-Cripple Creek G. M. Co., Mining and Scientific Press, vol. 78, p. 374.

[1] *Ante*, § 531.

[2] *Ante*, §§ 363, 363a.

Prima facie, everything within the vertical bounding planes belongs to the locator.

In the language of Judge Hallett,—

" We may say, that there is a presumption of owner-
" ship in every locator as to the territory covered by his
" location, and within his own boundaries he is regard-
" ed as the owner of all valuable deposits until some one
" shall show a higher right."

While the courts do not altogether agree as to the weight of testimony necessary to overthrow this presumption, there is an undoubted consensus of opinion in support of the above rule.[1]

We may safely base our discussion of the more important elements of the law applicable to lode locations upon this presumption, and, as we progress, endeavor to show the circumstances under which, and extent to which, it may be overcome, reaching ultimate conclusions by such gradations as the nature of the subject will permit.

§ 552.   **Intralimital rights not affected by the form of surface location.** — We have heretofore suggested that the ideal location, the one which confers the greatest property rights susceptible of being conveyed under the mining laws, contemplates a surface regular in form along the course of the vein, with end-lines crossing it, substantially presenting the form of a parallelogram.[2]

[1] St. Louis M. and M. Co. *v.* Montana M. Co., 113 Fed. 900, 902; Parrot Silver and Copper Co. *v.* Heinze, 25 Mont. 139, 87 Am. St. Rep. 386, 64 Pac. 329; Maloney *v.* King, 25 Mont. 188, 64 Pac. 351; Leadville M. Co. *v.* Fitzgerald, 4 Morr. Min. Rep. 380, 385, Fed. Cas. No. 8158; Doe *v.* Waterloo M. Co., 54 Fed. 935; Cons. Wyoming M. Co. *v.* Champion M. Co., 63 Fed. 540; Duggan *v.* Davey, 4 Dak. 110, 26 N. W. 887; Iron S. M. Co. *v.* Campbell, 17 Colo. 267, 29 Pac. 513; Cheesman *v.* Shreve, 37 Fed. 36; Montana Co., Limited, *v.* Clark, 42 Fed. 626; Cheesman *v.* Hart, 42 Fed. 98; Bell *v.* Skillicorn, 6 N. Mex. 399, 28 Pac. 768; Jones *v.* Prospect Mt. T. Co., 21 Nev. 339, 31 Pac. 642. See, also, *post,* § 866.

[2] *Ante,* § 360.

A departure from the ideal, however, if the statutory limit is not exceeded as to area, does not destroy or impair the intralimital rights of a locator. The requirement as to non-parallelism of end-lines affects only the extralimital or, strictly speaking, the extralateral rights.[1]

It frequently happens that locations originally made to approximate the ideal are reduced to irregularly shaped surfaces by reason of conflicts with prior appropriators. In such cases the right to pursue the vein on its downward course outside of the locator's vertical bounding planes may not exist; but in other respects the locator's right to whatever may be found within such planes is the same as in the case of a location of the highest type. It is unquestionably true that neither the form of the surface location nor the position of the vein as to its course controls or restricts the intralimital rights.

According to Judge Ross,[2] this is the logical deduction flowing from the decision of the supreme court of the United States in the Elgin case.[3]

§ 553. **Pursuit of the vein on its course beyond bounding planes of the location not permitted.**—Subject to the extralateral right of outside apex proprietors, a locator may be said to own all those parts of such veins having their tops, or apices, within the boundaries as are found within such boundaries. Wherever a vein on its course, or strike, passes out of and beyond any one of these boundaries, the right of the locator to it ceases. Whatever may be his privilege with reference to the pursuit of his vein in depth, longitudinally it cannot be followed beyond any of the boundaries. We have fully

[1] *Ante*, § 365.
[2] Doe *v.* Waterloo M. Co., 54 Fed. 935, 938.
[3] Iron S. M. Co. *v.* Elgin M. etc. Co., 118 U. S. 196, 6 Sup. Ct. Rep. 1177.

explained the rights upon located veins as they were asserted under, and prior to, the passage of the act of 1866.[1] It having been definitely settled by the supreme court of the United States in the Flagstaff-Tarbet case,[2] that under the act of 1866 a locator could not pursue his vein on its strike beyond the lines of his location, the application of the doctrine of that case to locations made under the act of 1872 was natural and logical. The rule may be said to be elementary.[3]

This being true, it follows that no other locator can, in the pursuit of his vein *on its strike*, pass through the bounding plane of a senior location, with the possible exception of the owner of a cross-lode.[4] An entry underneath the surface of a prior location is only permitted in the exercise of a right to pursue a vein on its *downward course*. This suggests the subject of cross-lodes.

ARTICLE II.   CROSS-LODES.

§ 557. Section twenty-three hundred and thirty-six of the Revised Statutes and its interpretation.

§ 558. The Colorado rule.

§ 559. Cross-lodes before the supreme court of Montana.

§ 560. The Arizona-California rule.

§ 561. The views of the supreme court of the United States.

§ 562. General deductions.

§ 557. Section twenty-three hundred and thirty-six of the Revised Statutes and its interpretation. — As we have observed in a previous chapter,[5] under local rules

---

[1] *Ante*, § 58.

[2] *Ante*, § 60; fig. 3, p. 92, and illustrations with § 586, *post*.

[3] Argentine M. Co. *v.* Terrible M. Co., 122 U. S. 478, 7 Sup. Ct. Rep. 1356; Terrible M. Co. v. Argentine M. Co., 5 McCrary, 639, 89 Fed. 583; Wolfley *v.* Lebanon M. Co., 4 Colo. 112; Patterson *v.* Hitchcock, 3 Colo. 533; Hall *v.* Equator M. and S. Co., Morr. Min. Rights, 3d ed., p. 282, Fed. Cas. No. 5931; New Dunderberg *v.* Old, 79 Fed. 598.

[4] *Post*, § 562.

[5] *Ante*, § 58.

existing prior to the passage of the act of 1866, as well as under the act itself, the lode was the principal thing granted, and the adjacent surface, if any was actually appropriated, was a mere incident; that only one lode could be held by a single location, and that this could be followed on its course, or strike, wheresoever it might lead, to the lawfully claimed limit, without the necessity of inclosing it within surface boundaries.

Where surface boundaries had been established by the prior locator for the convenient working of his lode, a subsequent locator appropriating a separate vein might pursue it into and through the surface ground of the senior locator, but no one was permitted to invade such surface for the purpose of searching for undiscovered veins.[1]

Such being the recognized rules, it is not difficult to imagine instances of two lodes held in different ownership intersecting or crossing each other on their strike, or onward course, without creating any conflict of title, except at the place of lode intersection or within the space of actual lode crossing.

The act of 1866 made no provision in terms for the determination of rights growing out of such crossings or intersections.

Such were the conditions existing when the act of 1872 was passed, which contained the following provision, now preserved in section twenty-three hundred and thirty-six of the Revised Statutes:—

"Where two or more veins intersect or cross each " other, priority of title shall govern, and such prior " location shall be entitled to all ore or mineral con- " tained within the space of intersection; but the subse- " quent location shall have the right of way through the

---

[1] Atkins v. Hendree, 1 Idaho, 95.

Lindley on M.—58

" space of intersection for the purposes of the conve-
" nient working of the mine. . . ."[1]

This is the enunciation of a rule of law, the usefulness of which when applied to the conditions existing at
the time of its passage cannot be denied. It established
a rule of decision based upon the equitable maxim that
" priority in time establishes a priority of right." The
application of this provision to locations made prior to
its enactment is not involved in any serious embarrassment. It is only where attempts are made to apply the
rule to locations made and rights asserted under the act
of 1872 that apparent difficulties have been encountered, giving rise to a conflict of opinion and diversity of
decision.

Whatever may have been the relationship existing
between the lode, which was the subject of location, and
the adjacent surface ground under the act of 1866,
under the existing law the right to any portion of any
lode is, as a general rule, dependent upon its having its
top, or apex, within the surface boundaries of the location. Of course, there may be exceptions to this rule,
as heretofore pointed out. A location overlying the dip
of a vein may hold everything within the vertical
boundaries, in the absence of an outside apex proprietor with a location which conferred an extralateral
right.[2] A regular valid location, once perfected under
the law, vests in the proprietor the ownership of not
only the lode upon the discovery of which the location
is predicated, but of all other lodes the tops, or apices,
of which may be found within such surface boundaries or within vertical planes drawn through them. The
ownership of such other lodes so found is not made to
depend upon their general direction or the position they

[1] Act of May 10, 1872, § 14.   [2] *Ante*, § 364.

may occupy with reference to the originally discovered lode.

The only limitation upon the grant authorized by section twenty-three hundred and twenty-two of the Revised Statutes is the extralateral right reserved to other locators to follow lodes having apices within their boundaries, on their downward course, outside of and beyond such boundaries, and underneath adjoining surfaces.

Instances may be conceived where two veins might intersect or cross on their strike outside of vertical planes drawn through the surface lines of the several locations. In other words, lodes may intersect on their strike without the existence of any surface conflict or the invasion of the territory included within vertical planes drawn through surface boundaries.[1]

To cases of this character the application of the rule under consideration is accompanied with no more difficulty than its application to cross-lodes located under or prior to the act of 1866.

But some difficulty has been encountered by the courts in different jurisdictions in construing section twenty-three hundred and twenty-six of the Revised Statutes and endeavoring to harmonize it with other sections of the mining laws, resulting in a radical conflict of opinion. While time and the progressive interpretation of the general body of the mining laws have induced some of the courts to recede from their original doctrines, closing the breach to some degree, yet there is still a radical difference of opinion upon one of the most important questions arising out of the "cross- " lode" conditions which still awaits final adjustment by the supreme court of the United States.

---

[1] See concurring opinion of Chief Justice Beatty in Wilhelm *v.* Silvester, 101 Cal. 358, 364, 35 Pac. 997.

In order to ascertain to what extent the courts are in harmony, and to point out wherein there is still a wide divergence of views, it will be necessary to state the rule in the different jurisdictions, the reasoning upon which such rule is predicated, and the extent to which the supreme court of the United States has given its sanction to one view or the other—or has declined to pass upon either. We may then state the net results in the form of general deductions.[1]

§ **558.** **The Colorado rule.**—The inception of what may be termed the earlier Colorado rule is found in an opinion given by Judge Hallett, sitting as circuit judge in the United States circuit court, district of Colorado, upon a motion to dissolve an injunction in the case of Hall *v.* Equator Mining and Smelting Co.[2]

The controversy arose between the Colorado Central lode, owned by the plaintiff, and the Equator lode, owned by the defendant. The Equator was located in 1866. The date of the location of the Central is not

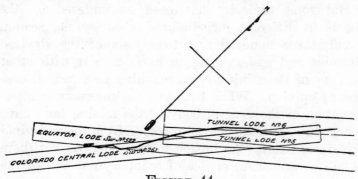

FIGURE 44.

disclosed by the reported decisions; but the court records establish the fact that it was discovered November 30, 1872.

---

[1] *Post,* § 562.　[2] Fed. Cas. No. 5931; Morr. Min. Rights, 3d ed., p. 282.

Both parties claimed under United States patents issued after the passage of the act of 1872. Plaintiff held the senior patent, based on a junior location. The relative position of the two claims is shown in the diagram (figure 44) on the preceding page.

The controversy related to a body of ore found in or under the east end of the Central location, and extending thence westward to and across the intersection with the Equator location.

The motion to dissolve the injunction was heard upon affidavits. There was a sharp conflict as to the facts. The learned judge, with respect to the showing made, uses this language:—

"As was anticipated when the bill was removed into
" this court, there is no agreement between the parties
" as to the structure of the lode or lodes and their out-
" crop. The affidavits suggest several theories without
" giving certainty to any of them. There may be two
" veins uniting in their onward course at some point
" east of the Central location, and thence going west-
" ward as one vein, with an outcrop in that location or
" south of it. And the vein may be so wide at the top
" as to enter both locations at the point where this con-
" troversy arose. And there may be two veins uniting
" on the strike or on the dip at the very place in dis-
" pute. But as to this, it is only necessary to say, that
" the facts are not satisfactorily stated to lead to a just
" conclusion. . . . It is enough that there is a strong
" controversy in which the right of neither party clearly
" appears. On that alone we interfere to preserve the
" property for him who may at law prove his right
" to it."

The motion to dissolve the injunction was denied, and the parties were relegated to the action of eject-ment, then pending, for a trial of the questions of fact.

The court thereupon proceeds as follows:—

"What has been said relates mainly to a question of
" fact, which it is the opinion of the court should be

" tried by a jury. Some general remarks in addition,
" as to the proper construction of the act of congress,
" may assist the parties in that investigation."

And after "assuming that these are lodes crossing
" each other in the manner indicated by the locations,"
the judge enunciates the following doctrine:—

"The general language of section twenty-three hun-
" dred and twenty-two seems to comprehend all lodes
" having their tops, or apices, in the territory described
" in the patent, whether the same lie transversely or
" collaterally to the principal lode on which the loca-
" tion was made.

"Considered by itself, such would be the meaning
" and effect of that section. But there is another sec-
" tion relating to cross-lodes, which is of different im-
" port. It was numbered fourteen in the original act
" of 1872, section twenty-three hundred and thirty-six,
" Revised Statutes, second edition, and is as follows:
" . . . [Then follows quotation of section twenty-
" three hundred and thirty-six.] It will be observed,
" that by this section the first locator and patentee of a
" lode gets only such part of cross and intersecting
" veins as lie within the space of intersection, to the
" exclusion of the remainder of such lodes and veins
" lying within his own territory. So far, this section
" is in conflict with section twenty-three hundred and
" twenty-two, before mentioned, and the matter of pre-
" cedence between them is settled by an arbitrary rule
" established long ago. As between conflicting stat-
" utes, the latest in date will prevail, so between con-
" flicting sections of the same statute, the last in the
" order of arrangement will control.[1]

"The presumption that one section of a statute was
" adopted before another, seems to be very slight, and
" perhaps this rule has no other merit than to afford
" the means of solving a difficult question. But the
" rule appears to be well established, and to be appli-

---

[1] Citing Bacon's Abr. Stat. D. Dwarris, 156; Brown v. County Commrs.,
21 Pa. St. 37; Smith v. Moore, 26 Ill. 392.

" cable to the present case. It gives to section twenty-
" three hundred and thirty-six, Revised Statutes, or
" section fourteen, as it stood in the original act, a con-
" trolling effect over the prior section, and limits the
" right of the first locator of a mine in and to cross and
" intersecting veins to the ore which may be found in
" the space of intersection. If there are in fact two
" lodes crossing each other in these locations, the plain-
" tiffs, having the elder title by patent, have the better
" right, but it is limited as last stated. So much as to
" the theory that there are two lodes intersecting in
" their onward course."

There can be no question but that Judge Hallett, in
rendering the foregoing decision, based only upon a
hypothetical state of facts and presented in the form of
a few "general remarks," exceeded the necessities of
the case under consideration.

Upon the trial of the case on the merits, a state of
facts was developed entirely different from the hypothesis above assumed. Instead of two lodes intersecting
each other in the manner indicated by the locations,
there was but *one* lode, with part of its width in one
location and part in the other.[1]

Yet a precedent had been established by these "few
" general remarks" which was for many years recognized in Colorado as controlling, without even a criticism of the logic of its reasoning or a consideration of
the circumstances under which the decision was rendered.

In Branagan *v.* Dulaney,[2] the question arose upon the
sufficiency of the answer filed by the defendant, a junior
locator, justifying a trespass within the lines of the
plaintiff, a senior locator, on the ground that the de-

---

[1] Carpenter's Mining Code, 3d ed., p. 65. See note to 11 Fed. Cas.
No. 5931.

[2] 8 Colo. 408, 8 Pac. 669.

fendant was the owner of a cross-lode and had a right under Revised Statutes, section twenty-three hundred and thirty-six, to drift through the territory covered by the senior location.

The court below having sustained the demurrer to the answer, judgment passed for plaintiff.

On appeal, the supreme court reversed the judgment, basing its decision upon Hall v. Equator (*supra*), and the "arbitrary rule of construction suggested by the " court" in that case, and holding, in effect, that the answer stated a complete defense.

This doctrine has been followed or sanctioned by the supreme court of Colorado until a recent period.[1]

The circuit court of appeals, eighth circuit, in Oscamp v. Crystal River Mining Company,[2] gave its apparent sanction to the doctrine thus enunciated by declining to controvert it, and in a later case invoked it as an aid to the interpretation of the tunnel laws.[3]

It thus appears that a "few general remarks" made by a judge upon a motion for a preliminary injunction, upon a hypothetical state of facts which was subsequently determined to have had no potential existence, ripened into a rule of property, which, when applied to certain localities and conditions found in that state, is productive of unique results. An illustration of the practical application of the rule so long accepted by the supreme court of Colorado is shown by an inspection of the official map of the mining region of Cripple Creek in that state.

---

[1] Lee v. Stahl, 9 Colo. 208, 11 Pac. 77, 13 Colo. 174, 22 Pac. 436; Morgenson v. Middlesex M. and M. Co., 11 Colo. 176, 17 Pac. 513; Omar v. Soper, 11 Colo. 380, 7 Am. St. Rep. 246, 18 Pac. 443; Coffee v. Emigh, 15 Colo. 184, 25 Pac. 83.

[2] 58 Fed. 293.

[3] Enterprise M. Co. v. Rico-Aspen Cons. M. Co., 66 Fed. 200, 210.

In figure 45 we reproduce from that map a quarter section of land, upon the surface of which mining claims have been officially surveyed, many of which have been patented, overlapping in the manner indicated.[1]

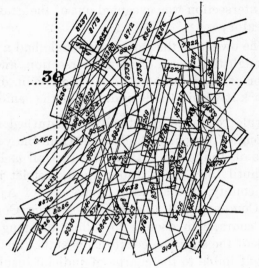

FIGURE 45.

The rule thus enunciated established two principles:—

(1) The owner of the junior cross-lode was the owner of so much of his cross-vein as was found within the vertical boundaries of the senior location, except the

---

[1] While the rule, the practical operation of which is intended to be illustrated in figure 45, has been in some degree modified by the cases hereafter referred to, yet the illustration is still applicable to the modified rule, which denies to the junior cross-locator the ownership of the cross-vein within the boundaries of the prior location, but permits him to drift through the senior claim. Besides this, the complexities shown in the figure are certain to arise to a greater or less degree from the practical application of the rule permitting junior locators to place the lines of their claims upon or across those of a senior claim, fully discussed in previous sections (ante, §§ 363, 363a). The contrast between the situation disclosed in figure 45 and that flowing from a different interpretation of the law in other jurisdictions will be observed by comparing figure 45 with figure 50 (post, § 560).

ore within the space of actual *vein* intersection. The ore within this space belonged to the senior locator. In other words, that portion of the cross-vein within the senior locator's boundaries on each side of this space of vein intersection was excepted out of the grant to the prior locator;

(2) The owner of the junior cross-lode had a right of way through this space of vein intersection, and, being the owner of the remainder of the cross-vein, of course could work it within the boundaries of the senior claim.

This rule remained practically undisturbed in Colorado, though frequently challenged, from the year 1879 (the date of Judge Hallett's ruling in Hall *v.* Equator, *supra*,) until 1898, when Judge Lunt, district judge of El Paso county, in that state, in the case of Ajax Gold Mining Company *v.* Calhoun Gold Mining Company,[1] had the courage to decline to follow the long line of decisions of the supreme court of his state, thus rendering himself liable to the charge of judicial insubordination. As to this Judge Lunt thus expressed himself:—

"A very strenuous effort was made by the counsel
" for the plaintiff to induce the court to deny this right
" upon the ground that Hall *v.* Equator Mining etc.
" Co., 11 Fed. Cas., p. 222, No. 5931, Morr. Min. Rights,
" 282, 3d ed., 1879; Branagan *v.* Dulaney, 8 Colo. 408
" (1885), 8 Pac. 669, and the Colorado cases based
" thereon, were not, at the time they were rendered,
" carefully considered, do not express the true and
" just interpretation of the United States act, and
" should be disregarded. I am frank to say that
" an extensive attempt on my part to obtain a
" consensus of the opinion of the legal profession,
" especially those who are prominent in mining
" law, has convinced me that a very general desire
" exists in the profession to have this question again

---

[1] Reported in full in 1 Leg. Adv., p. 426.

" presented to the supreme court, based upon the belief
" that after a more careful consideration and examina-
" tion of this all-important question of title, the
" supreme court may reconsider its former opinion and
" fall in line with the apparently more just rule of the
" courts of California and Arizona. By reason of this
" opinion of the bar, and it must be expressly under-
" stood that without any intention whatever of presum-
" ing to lightly disregard and overrule a decision of
" the supreme court, I shall decide against what is
" known as the 'Colorado rule' of cross-veins, with the
" hope and expectation that the question will be final-
" ly determined and the very general feeling of doubt
" as to the rule within the profession set at rest. I feel
" fortified in my opinion by the language of the chief
" justice on page 405, in the case of Argonaut etc. Co.
" v. Turner, 23 Colo. 400,[1] where the significant use of
" the word 'perhaps' is apparent, and also by the opin-
" ion of Mr. Morrison, given in his work on cross-veins,
" and again from the information given me as to the
" consideration given to the case of Branagan v. Du-
" laney, and also by the comments on Hall v. Equator
" etc. Co. in first Lindley,[2] section 558, and the Cali-
" fornia and Arizona cases."[3]

The facts of the case which called forth the opinion
may be illustrated by reference to a diagram (figure
46) which accompanies the opinions of the supreme
court of Colorado and the supreme court of the United
States, to be hereafter referred to.

The Ajax company owned the Monarch, Mammoth
Pearl, and Ajax lode claims, and the Calhoun company
owned the Ithaca tunnel-site and the Victor Consolidated lode. All the claims of the Ajax company were
prior to the tunnel-site and lode claim of the Calhoun
company. The outcrop of the vein in the Victor Consolidated, it was assumed, followed practically the
course of the Victor side-lines and passed through the

[1] 58 Am. St. Rep. 245, 48 Pac. 685. [2] 1st edition. [3] 1 Legal Adv., p. 432.

north and south end-lines of the claim, necessarily crossing the Monarch and Mammoth Pearl claims of the Ajax company and the veins therein. As to these two last-named claims, the Victor vein was therefore essentially a cross-vein.

The questions considered by the court, so far as the subject now under discussion is concerned, were as follows:—

(1) Whether or not the Ithaca tunnel is entitled to a right of way through the Mammoth Pearl and Monarch claims;

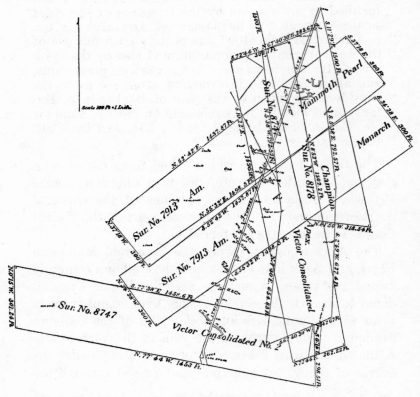

FIGURE 46.

(2) Whether or not the Calhoun company has acquired by virtue of said tunnel and tunnel-site location the ownership of the blind veins cut therein,—to wit, veins or lodes not appearing on the surface and not known to exist prior to the date of location of said tunnel-site;

(3) Whether or not the Calhoun company is the owner of and entitled to the ore contained in the vein of its Victor Consolidated claim within the surface boundaries and across the Monarch and Mammoth Pearl.

Judge Lunt held:—

(1) That the Calhoun company had no right to drive the Ithaca tunnel underneath the surface of the Monarch and Mammoth Pearl claims, and its further prosecution must be enjoined;

(2) The Calhoun company could not acquire by virtue of the tunnel and tunnel-site location the ownership of any blind veins within the Monarch or Mammoth Pearl locations. All such veins passed to the owners of these claims by virtue of the priority of their location;

(3) As a corollary to this, the Calhoun company is not the owner of any of the ore found in the Victor Consolidated claim underneath the surface of the Mammoth Pearl and Monarch claims, and must pay the value of such ore extracted to the Ajax company.

The judge adds (italics are ours) :—

"If the defendant *desires to follow* its alleged Victor
" Consolidated cross-vein as a cross-vein to the veins
" of the Mammoth Pearl and Monarch claims, it will
" not be entitled to any ore within these claims from
" the point where its cross-vein enters the Mammoth
" Pearl claim (on the south) until it leaves the north

" side-line of the Mammoth Pearl and again enters " its own territory of the Victor Consolidated lode " claim."

From this we infer that in Judge Lunt's opinion the cross-lode locator has a right to follow the vein through the senior location,—yielding the ore therein encountered to the owner of the latter,—but he could not, as we have already shown, reach the cross-vein by means of a crosscut tunnel (such as the Ithaca tunnel).

The supreme court of Colorado sustained Judge Lunt in all of these rulings, accepting gracefully his apology for reversing the former decisions of that court.[1]

As to the right of way to which the junior cross-lode locator might be entitled, the court was clearly of the opinion that this was reserved to him, to be exercised within or on the vein, the "space of intersection" being held to mean the intersection of the *claims* and not *vein* intersection.

The case was taken to the supreme court of the United States on writ of error, and the decision of the supreme court of Colorado was affirmed, with the exception of that part of it which dealt with the right of way reserved to the junior cross-lode locator. As to this question the court declined to express an opinion, as it was not necessarily involved.[2] We will have occasion to again recur to this decision.[3]

§ 559. Cross-lodes before the supreme court of Montana.

—The subject of cross-lodes came before the supreme court of Montana in the case of Pardee v. Murray.[4] This case involved a controversy between the

---

[1] Calhoun G. M. Co. *v.* Ajax G. M. Co., 27 Colo. 1, 83 Am. St. Rep. 17, 59 Pac. 607.

[2] Calhoun G. M. Co. *v.* Ajax G. M. Co., 182 U. S. 499, 21 Sup Ct. Rep. 885.

[3] *Post,* § 561.

[4] 4 Mont. 234, 2 Pac. 16.

Salmon, located in 1866, and the Cliff Extension, No. 2, located in 1867, on the one hand, and the Shark Town and Scratch All lodes, discovered and located in 1875. The relative position of the claims of the contending parties is shown in figure 47.

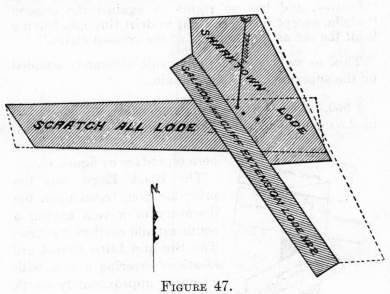

FIGURE 47.

The court thus expressed its views as to the meaning of the section of the Revised Statutes under consideration:—

"If a vein with a prior location crossed another, such
" vein would not disturb the possession of the subse-
" quent location, except as to the extent of the cross-
" vein, and would entitle the prior location to the ore
" and mineral contained in the space of intersection.
" If with a subsequent location, the locator would be
" entitled only to a right of way to the extent of his
" cross-vein, for the purpose of working his mine, and
" to no other right; and if he should take the ore con-
" tained in the space of intersection, he would be a tres-
" passer against whom the prior locator in possession

" of the surface ground might maintain an action of
" trespass."

This suggests the view adopted by Mr. Morrison in
his " Mining Rights," [1]—

"That a cross-lode takes no estate in the claim it
" crosses, and has no rights as against the crossed
" claim, except the mere right to drift through, leaving
" all the ore as the property of the crossed claim."

This, as we have seen, is the rule ultimately adopted
by the supreme court of Colorado.

§ 560.　**The Arizona-California rule.**—A case arose
in Arizona out of the following facts, which are illustrated by a diagram, which we
here reproduce as figure 48.

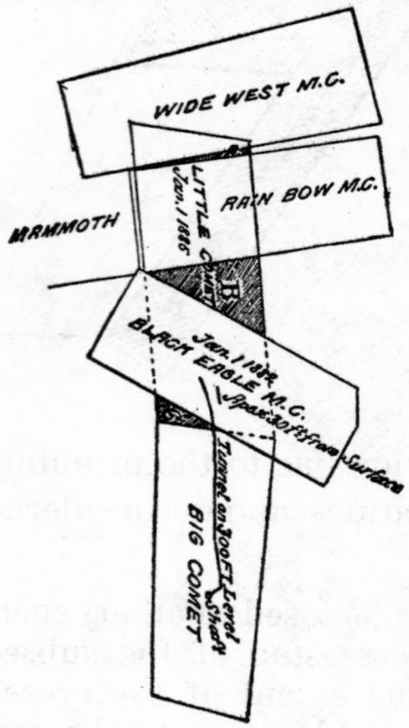

FIGURE 48.

The Black Eagle was the
prior location, based upon the
discovery of a vein having a
southeast and northwest course.
The Big and Little Comet are
locations covering a vein with
a course approximately north
and south, the owners of which,
through means of a tunnel
originating in the Big Comet,
had penetrated underneath the
Black Eagle surface, justifying their right to do so under
section twenty-three hundred
and thirty-six of the Revised
Statutes, claiming the Comet vein to be a cross-vein. The
surface conflict area is shown on the diagram. The
earlier Colorado rule was urged in support of their contention.

[1] 10th ed., p. 127.

The supreme court of Arizona declined to follow the original doctrine of the Colorado courts, and in a well-considered opinion [1] asserts that,—

"The construction urged and supported by the " Equator and subsequent Colorado decisions violates " the language of the statute, injects into it things not " there, results in conflict in the statute among its parts, " and makes infinitely more complex the old system of " lode claims."

With reference to cases arising under the act of 1872, the rule announced in Arizona recognizes the controlling force of surface boundaries, and denies the right to the junior locator of a so-called cross-lode to invade the domain of the senior claimant for any purpose. Says the court:—.

"Section twenty-three hundred and twenty-two gives, " not the lode alone, but all lodes, veins, and ledges, " throughout their entire depth, the top, or apex, of " which lies inside of the surface lines of the claim ex- " tended downward vertically; and as lodes may dip, " so that, when followed, they may be found to extend " beyond the boundaries of the claim, congress further " provides that they may nevertheless be followed. In " other words, congress has said to the miners, 'Com- " 'ply with the requirements that we impose, and the " 'government of the United States will grant abso- " 'lutely to you a piece of the earth bounded at the sur- " 'face by straight lines, distinctly marked, and by " 'planes extending through those lines to the center of " 'the earth; and you shall have all lodes of mineral- " 'bearing rock whose apex is within these boundaries.' " This is simple, plain, and the miners' rights are there- " under easy of ascertainment."

The opinion of the court is elaborate, and a clear exposition of the law from its standpoint. The court fails to see any conflict between the different sections of the

[1] Watervale M. Co. v. Leach (Ariz.), 33 Pac. 418.
Lindley on M.—59

law, and thus denies the necessity for invoking the rule of statutory construction applied by Judge Hallett.

The position assumed in this decision compels the owners of lodes located under the act of 1866 to adverse the application for patent filed by one asserting rights to an overlapping surface location. The right of the first locator to pursue his so-called cross-lode into the overlapping claim is lost by failure to adverse. This is in harmony with the rule in Colorado[1] only so far as it affected the right to the ore at the space of intersection.

In California it has been held that, as to ledges, rights to which accrued prior to the act of May 10, 1872, the act itself reserves them without the necessity of adversing,[2] and the supreme court of Utah, by a divided court, coincides with the views announced in California;[3] but as to locations made subsequent to 1866, the supreme court of California agrees with the supreme court of Arizona.

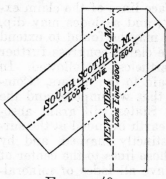

FIGURE 49.

The question presented to the California court[4] arose out of an attempt to locate a so-called cross-lode over the surface of a prior location. The conflict between the two is illustrated in figure 49, the New Idea being prior in point of time.

In an elaborate opinion, written before the Arizona decision was published, the California court reached

[1] Lee v. Stahl, 13 Colo. 174, 22 Pac. 436, 9 Colo. 208, 11 Pac. 77.
[2] Eclipse G. and S. M. Co. v. Spring, 59 Cal. 304.
[3] Blake v. Butte Silver M. Co., 2 Utah, 54.
[4] Wilhelm v. Silvester, 101 Cal. 358, 35 Pac. 997.

the same conclusion as that enunciated by the supreme court of Arizona.

Commenting on the Colorado rule, the supreme court of California asserts,—

"That it would leave the rights of prior locators in " the greatest confusion; their property interests in " their claims would be undefined, and the result would " be ruinous litigation and perhaps personal conflicts."

Chief Justice Beatty, whose wide judicial experience in mining litigation in Nevada and California, in both trial and appellate courts, is a matter of current history, writes a concurring opinion, embodying forcible reasons for the rule announced by the court.

He says:—

"There is no proposition in geometry plainer or more " easily demonstrable than this: that surface locations " on cross-veins may be so made as not to conflict, while " at the same time the portions of the veins included in " or covered by the respective locations will intersect in " depth—in some cases within the surface lines of one " or the other location extended downward vertically, " and in other cases altogether without the surface lines " of both locations. This results from the fact that " veins generally, if not universally, descend into the " earth not vertically, but at a greater or less inclina- " tion or dip."

Chief Justice Beatty's view is, that the law under consideration was intended to meet the conditions assumed by him, an underground crossing or intersection of two veins on the strike or dip, without any surface conflict between the two locations.

We have endeavored to present the case assumed by him on figure 49A an isometrical projection exhibiting two veins intersecting on their strike, or partly on the strike and partly on the dip, the plane of intersection being to some extent within the extralateral right of both claims, but without any conflict at the surface. While the illustration is necessarily imperfect, owing to the difficulty of presenting such conditions by the method of perspective, yet it serves to demonstrate the persuasive force of the chief justice's views. This construction of the law disposes of the necessity of harmonizing supposed conflicts between different sections of the statute, giving operation and effect to all its provisions.

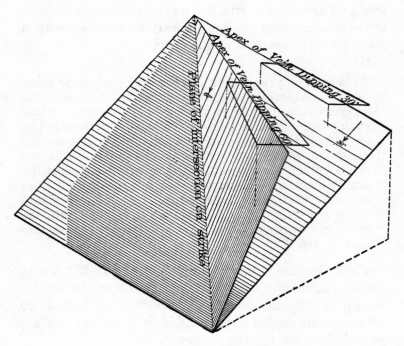

FIGURE 49A.

The practical application of the Arizona-California rule is shown in the accompanying figure 50, which represents a quarter section of land covered by official mining surveys in the Grass Valley region of the latter state, in which locality the California case arose.

A comparison of this figure with the one illustrative of the Colorado rule, shown on page 921, illustrates the radical difference between the two doctrines. The irregularly shaped surfaces shown in the California illustration are accounted for by patenting a number of claims in one group, showing only the exterior lines of the composite, a practice at one time followed by the land department. Under the existing rules, group surveys preserve the interior lines of all individual locations embraced therein.

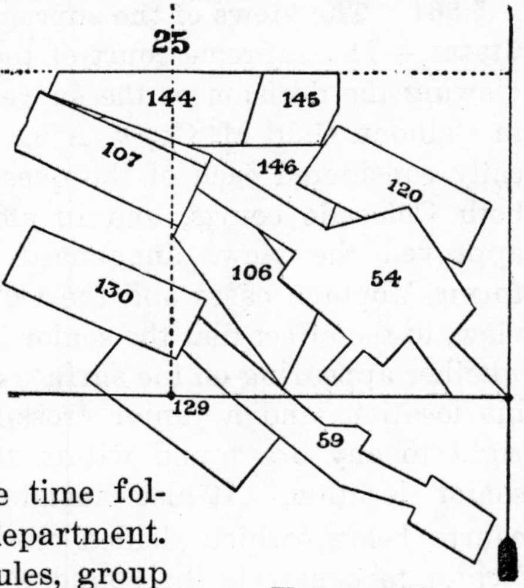

FIGURE 50.

The Arizona-California rule denies to the junior cross-lode locator the ownership of any part of the cross-vein within the boundaries of the senior location. The later Colorado decisions accept this as a correct exposition of the law.

As to any right of way reserved to the junior cross-lode locator through the senior crossed claim, there was no discussion in the California case, but it is quite manifest that the analysis by the court of the federal mining laws and its expressed views therein negative the idea that a junior locator has any such right of way.

In the Arizona case this question was necessarily involved, as the entry by the junior cross-lode claimant (the Little Comet, on figure 48, *ante*) was by means of a tunnel or drift along the so-called cross-vein. The decision denies the right of the junior cross-lode locator to enter within the limits of the prior location.

§ 561. The views of the supreme court of the United States.—The supreme court of the United States in reviewing the decision of the supreme court of Colorado in Calhoun Gold M. Co. *v.* Ajax Gold M. Co.,[1] specifically considered each of the questions passed upon by both Colorado courts, and in affirming the judgment approved the views announced in the Arizona-California-Montana cases and the Colorado case under review, to the effect that the senior locator owns all veins, whether appearing on the surface or blind, found within his location, and a junior cross-lode claimant has no right to any ore found within the boundaries of the senior location. It also sustained the view of the courts below, which denied the right of the tunnel locator to penetrate the bounding planes of the senior location.

As to the right of way problem, it said:—

"Section 2336 imposes a servitude upon the senior
" location but does not otherwise affect the exclusive
" rights given the senior location. It gives a right of
" way to the junior location. To what extent there may
" be some ambiguity; whether only through the space
" of the intersection of the veins, as held by the supreme
" courts of California, Arizona, and Montana, or
" through the space of intersection of the claims, as held
" by the supreme court of Colorado in the case at bar.
" It is not necessary to determine between these views.
" One of them is certainly correct, and therefore the
" contention of the plaintiff in error is not correct, and,
" more than that, it is not necessary to decide on this
" record. A complete interpretation of the sections
" would, of course, determine between these views, but

[1] 182 U. S. 499, 21 Sup. Ct. Rep. 885.

" on that determination other rights than those sub-
" mitted for judgment may be passed upon, and we
" prefer therefore to reserve our opinion."

§ 562. General deductions.—We may here recapitu-
late the net result obtained from a consideration of all
the adjudicated cases on the subject of cross-lodes.

All courts now agree upon the following propositions :—

(1) The grant to the senior locator is of *all* veins
found within his location regardless of their course, and
whether they were previously known to exist or were
blind and undiscovered. There is no limitation implied,
and the grant is exclusive. A junior cross-lode locator
has no right to any ore found upon the cross-vein within
the boundaries of a senior claim;

(2) The owner of a junior tunnel-site cannot by
means of a crosscut tunnel penetrate within the boundaries of a senior claim for any purpose.

As to what rights of way the owners of junior located
veins may have as against senior claimants where the
veins intersect or cross, it may be said that all courts
agree that where two veins cross on their dips, the
senior takes all the ore within the space of vein intersection and the junior has a right of way through
the space. The same may be said of veins crossing on
their strike or course where there is no surface conflict between the locations, as illustrated in figure
49A.

But where there is a surface conflict, and there are
cross-lodes and cross-locations such as were considered
in the various cases heretofore illustrated, there is a disagreement.

In Colorado and Montana the junior cross-lode claimant has a right to drift through the senior claim, follow-

ing the cross-vein, yielding the ore encountered to the senior locator.

In California and Arizona he has no such right. Until the supreme court of the United States finally approves one or the other of these views, each state and territory will be left to determine which of the two conflicting rules is best supported by logic and reason.

Use and Abuse
of
America's Natural Resources

An Arno Press Collection

Ayres, Quincy Claude. **Soil Erosion and Its Control.** 1936

Barger, Harold and Sam H. Schurr. **The Mining Industries, 1899-1939.** 1944

Carman, Harry J., editor. **Jesse Buel: Agricultural Reformer.** 1947

Circular from the General Land Office Showing the Manner of Proceeding to Obtain Title to Public Lands. 1899

Fernow, Bernhard E. **Economics of Forestry.** 1902

Gannett, Henry, editor. **Report of the National Conservation Commission, February 1909. Three volumes.** 1909

Giddens, Paul H. **The Birth of the Oil Industry.** 1938

Greeley, William B. **Forests and Men.** 1951

Hornaday, William T. **Wild Life Conservation in Theory and Practice.** 1914

Ise, John. **The United States Forest Policy.** 1920

Ise, John. **The United States Oil Policy.** 1928

James, Harlean. **Romance of the National Parks.** 1939

Kemper, J. P. **Rebellious River.** 1949

Kinney, J. P **The Development of Forest Law in America.** *Including,* Forest Legislation in America Prior to March 4, 1789. 1917

Larson, Agnes M. **History of the White Pine Industry in Minnesota.** 1949

Liebig, Justus, von. **The Natural Lawss of Husbandry.** 1863

Lindley, Curtis H. **A Treatise on the American Law Relating to Mines and Mineral Lands.** Two volumes. 2nd edition. 1903

Lokken, Roscoe L. **Iowa—Public Land Disposal.** 1942

McGee, W. J., editor. **Proceedings of a Conference of Governors in the White House, May 13–15, 1908.** 1909

Mead, Elwood. **Irrigation Institutions.** 1903

Moreell, Ben. **Our Nation's Water Resources—Policies and Politics.** 1956

Murphy, Blakely M., editor. **Conservation of Oil & Gas: A Legal History, 1948.** 1949

Newell, Frederick Haynes. **Water Resources: Present and Future Uses.** 1920.

Nimmo, Joseph, Jr. **Report in Regard to the Range and Ranch Cattle Business of the United States.** 1885

Nixon, Edgar B., editor. **Franklin D. Roosevelt & Conservation, 1911–1945.** Two volumes. 1957

Peffer, E. Louise. **The Closing of the Public Domain.** 1951

Preliminary Report of the Inland Waterways Commission. 60th Congress, 1st Session, Senate Document No. 325. 1908

Puter, S. A. D. & Horace Stevens. **Looters of the Public Domain.** 1908

Record, Samuel J. & Robert W. Hess. **Timbers of the New World.** 1943

Report of the Public Lands Commission, with Appendix. 58th Congress, 3d Session, Senate Document No. 189. 1905

Report of the Public Lands Commission, Created by the Act of March 3, 1879. 46th Congress, 2d Session, House of Representatives Ex. Doc. No. 46. 1880